JavaFX™ Developer's Guide

Developer's Library Series

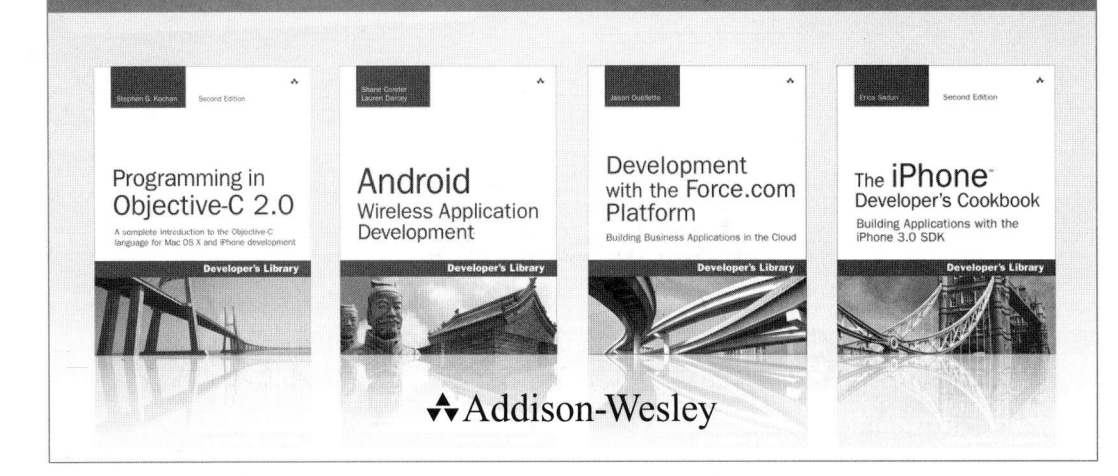

Visit **developers-library.com** for a complete list of available products

The **Developer's Library Series** from Addison-Wesley provides practicing programmers with unique, high-quality references and tutorials on the latest programming languages and technologies they use in their daily work. All books in the Developer's Library are written by expert technology practitioners who are exceptionally skilled at organizing and presenting information in a way that's useful for other programmers.

Developer's Library books cover a wide range of topics, from open-source programming languages and databases, Linux programming, Microsoft, and Java, to Web development, social networking platforms, Mac/iPhone programming, and Android programming.

JavaFX™ Developer's Guide

Kim Topley

✦Addison-Wesley

Upper Saddle River, NJ • Boston • Indianapolis • San Francisco
New York • Toronto • Montreal • London • Munich • Paris • Madrid
Capetown • Sydney • Tokyo • Singapore • Mexico City

JavaFX™ Developer's Guide
Copyright © 2011 by Pearson Education, Inc.

All rights reserved. No part of this book shall be reproduced, stored in a retrieval system, or transmitted by any means, electronic, mechanical, photocopying, recording, or otherwise, without written permission from the publisher. No patent liability is assumed with respect to the use of the information contained herein. Although every precaution has been taken in the preparation of this book, the publisher and author assume no responsibility for errors or omissions. Nor is any liability assumed for damages resulting from the use of the information contained herein.

Library of Congress Cataloging-in-Publication Data

Topley, Kim.
   JavaFX developer's guide / Kim Topley.
      p.   cm.
   Includes bibliographical references and index.
   ISBN 978-0-321-60165-0 (pbk. : alk. paper) 1. Java (Computer program language) 2. JavaFX (Electronic resource) 3. Graphical user interfaces (Computer systems) 4. Application software—Development. 5. Internet programming. I. Title.
   QA76.73.J38T693 2010
   005.13'3—dc22

                                                                                                       2010010696

Text printed in the United States on recycled paper at Edwards Brothers in Ann Arbor, Michigan.
First Printing, October 2010

ISBN 13: 978-0-321-60165-0
ISBN 10:   0-321-60165-3

Trademarks
All terms mentioned in this book that are known to be trademarks or service marks have been appropriately capitalized. Pearson cannot attest to the accuracy of this information. Use of a term in this book should not be regarded as affecting the validity of any trademark or service mark.

Warning and Disclaimer
Every effort has been made to make this book as complete and as accurate as possible, but no warranty or fitness is implied. The information provided is on an "as is" basis. The author and the publisher shall have neither liability nor responsibility to any person or entity with respect to any loss or damages arising from the information contained in this book.

Bulk Sales
Pearson offers excellent discounts on this book when ordered in quantity for bulk purchases or special sales. For more information, please contact U.S. Corporate and Government Sales, 1-800-382-3419, corpsales@pearsontechgroup.com.

For sales outside of the United States, please contact: International Sales, international@pearsoned.com.

Visit us on the web: informit.com/aw

For information regarding permissions, write to: Pearson Education, Inc., Rights and Contracts Department, 501 Boylston Street, Suite 900, Boston, MA, 02116;
Fax: (617) 671-3447.

Acquisitions Editor
Greg Doench

Development Editor
Michael Thurston

Managing Editor
John Fuller

Full-Service Production Manager
Julie B. Nahil

Copy Editor
Keith Cline

Indexer
Rebecca Salerno

Proofreader
Apostrophe Editing Services

Publishing Coordinator
Michelle Housley

Book Designer
Gary Adair

Composition
Jake McFarland

For the D in KADMAS,

the center of my universe.

Contents at a Glance

About the Author xxv

Preface xxvi

I: Introduction to JavaFX

1 An Overview of JavaFX 3

2 JavaFX Script Basics 17

3 JavaFX Script Development 33

4 A Simple JavaFX Application 45

II: The JavaFX Script Language

5 Variables and Data Types 89

6 Expressions, Functions, and Object Literals 121

7 Sequences 153

8 Controlling Program Flow 179

9 Binding 195

10 Triggers 221

11 JavaFX Script Classes 239

12 Platform APIs 285

13 Reflection 309

III: User Interfaces with JavaFX

14 User Interface Basics 341

15 Node Variables and Events 375

16 Shapes, Text, and Images 433

17 Coordinates, Transforms, and Layout 503

18 Animation 591

19 Video and Audio 627

- **20** Effects and Blending **651**
- **21** Importing Graphics **703**
- **22** Cross-Platform Controls **737**
- **23** Style Sheets **811**
- **24** Using Swing Controls **829**
- **25** Building Custom Controls **865**
- **26** Charts **911**

IV: Miscellaneous

- **27** Using External Data Sources **949**
- **28** Packaging and Deployment **1025**
- **A** Using JavaFX Command-Line Tools **1049**
- **B** CSS Properties **1061**

  Index **1071**

Table of Contents

About the Author xxv

Preface xxvi

I: Introduction to JavaFX

1 An Overview of JavaFX 3
   The JavaFX Platform 3
   The JavaFX Script Language 5
      Variable Declarations 6
      Access to Java APIs 6
      Object Literals 7
      Binding 8
      Scripts and Compilation 8
   The JavaFX Runtime 9
      User Interface Classes 9
      Video and Audio 10
      Animation 10
      Network Access 12
   JavaFX Development Tools 13
   Deployment 14
      Java Platform Dependencies and Installation 14
      The Java Plug-In 15
      Converting an Applet to an Installed Application 15

2 JavaFX Script Basics 17
   Source File Structure 17
   Comments 18
      Single-Line Comments 18
      Multiline Comments 18
      Documentation Comments 19
   The package Statement 20
   The import Statement 20
      Import by Name 20
      Wildcard Imports 21
      Static Imports 21
      Automatic Imports 22

      Direct Class References   23
  Other JavaFX Statements   23
      Variable Declarations   23
      Value Assignment and Data Manipulation   23
      Using Java Methods   24
      Binding Expressions   24
      Functions   25
      Flow-of-Control Statements   26
      Class Definitions   26
      Triggers   26
  JavaFX Keywords and Reserved Words   27
  Script Execution and Arguments   28
  Predefined Variables   31

3 JavaFX Script Development   33
  Compiling and Running JavaFX Code   33
      Development Using the NetBeans IDE   34
      Development with the Eclipse IDE   39
  Documentation in JavaFX Source Code   43
      Viewing JavaFX Documentation in NetBeans   43
      Viewing JavaFX Documentation in Eclipse   44

4 A Simple JavaFX Application   45
  Building the SnowStorm Application   46
      Creating the SnowStorm Project   46
      Building the User Interface   47
      Adding the Animation   58
      Counting the Snowflakes   64
  SnowStorm on the Web, a Phone, and TV   65
      Running SnowStorm Using Java Web Start   65
      Running SnowStorm as an Applet   67
      Running SnowStorm on the Mobile Emulator   70
      Running SnowStorm on the JavaFX TV Emulator   72
  Debugging the SnowStorm Application   72
      Setting Breakpoints   72
      The Call Stack View   73
      Inspecting Variables   73

Contents

        Changing Variable Values   74
        Stepping Through Code   75
        Disabling and Removing Breakpoints and Resuming Execution   76
    Profiling the SnowStorm Application   77
        Using the NetBeans Profiler   77
    Source Code for the SnowStorm Application   82

II: The JavaFX Script Language

5 Variables and Data Types   89
    Variable Declarations   89
        Declaring Variables with var   89
        Declaring Variables with def   92
        Variable Scopes   93
    Object Types   94
        Creating a JavaFX Object Instance   95
        Invoking JavaFX Functions   95
        Accessing Variables   96
        Using Java Classes in JavaFX Code   97
    Basic Data Types   97
        Numeric Types   97
        The Boolean Type   102
        The String Type   103
        String Localization   108
    Type Inference   117
    Visibility of Variables   119

6 Expressions, Functions, and Object Literals   121
    Expressions and Operations   121
        Numeric Operations   123
        Boolean Operations   129
        Object and Class Operations   130
    JavaFX Functions   134
        Declaring Functions   134
        Functions and Variables   137
        Functions Within Functions   138

Invoking JavaFX Functions   138
Invoking Java Methods   138
Function Variables   139
Anonymous Functions   145
Visibility of Functions   147
Object Literals   147
Initializing a JavaFX Object   148
Variables in Object Literals   149
Functions in Object Literals   150

7 Sequences   153

Sequence Creation   153
The String Form of a Sequence   155
Range Notation   156
Sequence Equality and Copying   157
Querying Sequences   158
Obtaining the Size of a Sequence   158
Obtaining an Element of a Sequence   159
Obtaining Part of a Sequence   160
Querying a Sequence by Condition   160
Modifying Sequences   162
Replacing Elements   162
Inserting Elements   163
Removing Elements   165
Replacing a Range of Elements   166
Operations on Sequences   167
Comparing Sequences   167
Searching for Elements   168
Finding the Largest and Smallest Elements   169
Sorting a Sequence   171
Searching and Updating a Sorted Sequence   172
Shuffling a Sequence   174
Java Arrays   174
Array Variable Declaration   174
Array Variable Initialization   175
Array Operations   176
Array Size   177

8 Controlling Program Flow   179
The if Statement   179
The while Statement   181
    The break Statement   182
    The continue statement   184
The for Statement   184
    Iterating over a Sequence   184
    The for Statement as an Expression   186
    Iterating over a Subset of a Sequence   187
    Iterating over Multiple Sequences   188
    Iterating over an Iterable   190
    Iterating over an Array   193
Exception Handling   193

9 Binding   195
Binding to Variables and Expressions   195
    Binding to a Script Variable   195
    Binding in an Object Literal   196
    Binding to an Expression   199
    Binding and the def Statement   201
    Binding to an Instance Variable   201
    Binding with a Conditional Expression   202
    Bidirectional Binding   203
    Eager and Lazy Binding   206
Binding and Functions   207
    Binding and Unbound Functions   207
    Binding and Bound Functions   209
    Optimization of Bound Function Evaluation   212
    Content of a Bound Function   213
Binding and Sequences   217
    Binding to a Sequence   217
    Binding to a Transformed Sequence   218
    Binding to the Size of a Sequence   219
    Binding to a Range of Sequence Elements   219

10 Triggers 221

Triggers on Simple Variables 221
  Declaring a Trigger 221
  Getting the Previous Value 223
  Triggers and Binding 223
  Using a Trigger to Enforce Constraints 224
Triggers and Sequences 229
  Replacing Elements in a Sequence 230
  Removing Elements from a Sequence 231
  Inserting Elements into a Sequence 233
  Example Use of a Sequence Trigger 234
Triggers and Instance Variables 236

11 JavaFX Script Classes 239

JavaFX Class Declaration 240
  An Example JavaFX Class 241
  Class Visibility 242
  Instance Variables 243
  Instance Functions 246
Subclassing and Abstract Classes 249
  An Abstract Base Class 249
  Extending the Base Class 251
  Function Overloading 253
  Function Overriding 254
  Function Selection by Classname 258
Using Bound Functions 258
Variable Overrides 259
Class Initialization 261
  Initialization Order 261
  Using the init and postinit Blocks 263
Classes and Script Files 265
Mixins 266
  Implementing Logging with a Mixin 267
  Mixin Characteristics 272
  Mixins and Inheritance 273
  Mixins and Triggers 280
  Initialization and Mixins 281

12 Platform APIs 285

Built-In Functions 285
    Writing to the System Output Stream 286
    Object Comparison 286
Arguments and System Properties 287
    Application Arguments 287
    Named Arguments 288
    System Properties 290
Application Shutdown 292
Deferring Operations 294
Functions for Internationalization 295
    Changing String Localization Defaults 296
Local Storage 298
    Reading and Writing Data 299
    Storage Metadata 301
    Removing Data 303
    Resource Names and Access Control 305
Conditional Features 307

13 Reflection 309

Context and Classes 309
    The Reflection Context 309
    Reflective Access to Classes 310
Types and Values 314
    Representation of Types 314
    Values 317
Variables and Functions 320
    Reflecting on Variables 322
    Reflecting on Functions 323
    Filtered Searches 326
    Reflecting on Variables and Functions 327
Using Reflection 328
    Creating Class Instances: Part 1 328
    Reading and Setting Variable Values 328
    Invoking Functions 330
    Creating and Accessing Sequences 333
    Creating Class Instances: Part 2 336

III: User Interfaces with JavaFX

14 User Interface Basics   341
   The Stage Class   342
      Stage Appearance and State   342
      Stage Position and Size   348
      Style and Opacity   354
      Extensions   357
   The Scene Class   358
   Nodes   360
      Node Organization   361
      Events   367
      Colors   367
      Effects   368
   Alerts   369
      Information Alert   369
      Confirm Alert   370
      Question Alert   371
   3D Features   372
      Cameras and the Z-Axis of the Scene Graph   372

15 Node Variables and Events   375
   Cursors   375
   Colors   378
      Solid Colors   379
      Linear Gradients   383
      Radial Gradients   392
   Events   401
      Mouse Events   401
      The Mouse and the MouseEvent Class   403
      Keyboard Events   425

16 Shapes, Text, and Images   433
   Shapes   433
      Basic Shapes   434
      Paths   451
      SVGPath   456
   Stroking and Filling Shapes   456

Stroking Shapes 456
Shape Filling 463
The Text Class 466
Text Content and Positioning 466
Text Fill and Stroke 470
Text Decoration 471
Fonts 472
Font Characteristics 473
Physical and Logical Fonts 476
The Font Class 477
Listing Fonts and Font Families 479
Selecting Fonts 479
Groups and Custom Nodes 482
Images 486
Loading an Image 486
Displaying an Image 497

17 Coordinates, Transforms, and Layout 503

Transforms 503
Translation 506
Rotation 508
Scaling 511
Shearing 515
Combining Transforms 517
Transform Order 517
Combining Transforms and Node Variable Settings 521
Clipping 523
Coordinates and Bounds 527
Getting Node Bounds 527
Coordinate System Conversions 537
Node Layout 538
Node Sizes and Layout 539
The Flow Container 547
The Stack Container 555
The HBox and VBox Containers 559

The Tile Container   563
  The Panel Container   572
  The ClipView Node   574
  Centering Nodes   577
SnowStorm Revisited   579
  Placing the Background Image   581
  Placing and Animating the Snow   582
Coordinates and Screens   585
  Discovering Screens   585
  Using Two Screens   588
  Changing Screen Arrangement   589

18 Animation   591

Timelines   591
  Time Literals and the Duration Class   595
  Key Frames   596
  Interpolation and Interpolators   600
Controlling a Timeline   605
  Repeating an Animation   605
  Automatically Reversing an Animation   607
  Pausing, Stopping, and Restarting an Animation   608
  Changing the Speed and Direction of an Animation   609
  Starting a Timeline from the End   610
  Using a Timeline as a Timer   611
  Animation Length   613
Transitions   613
  The Transition Class   613
  TranslateTransition   614
  RotateTransition   616
  ScaleTransition   617
  FadeTransition   618
  PathTransition   619
  PauseTransition   622
  Sequential and Parallel Transitions   622

19 Video and Audio 627

The Media Class 628
The MediaPlayer Class 630
    Controlling Media Playback 630
    Restricting and Repeating Playback 632
    Volume Control 633
    Monitoring Playback 634
    Synchronizing External Events with Playback 637
The MediaView Class 639
    Size and Position of the Video Frame 640
    The Viewport 644
    Transforms and Effects 646

20 Effects and Blending 651

Effects Overview 651
    Effects Chains 651
    Effects and Nodes 652
    Effects and Groups 655
The JavaFX Effects Classes 656
    GaussianBlur 656
    BoxBlur 657
    MotionBlur 659
    DropShadow 660
    InnerShadow 663
    Shadow 664
    Bloom 665
    Glow 666
    Identity 667
    Flood 669
    ColorAdjust 669
    InvertMask 671
    Reflection 671
    SepiaTone 673
    PerspectiveTransform 673
    DisplacementMap 679

Contents   xix

    Blending   686
        The Blend Effect   686
        The Group Blend Mode   688
    Lighting   690
        The surfaceScale Variable   692
        The Bump Map   693
        DistantLight   694
        PointLight   697
        SpotLight   698

21 Importing Graphics   703
    The JavaFX Production Suite   703
    Using Adobe Illustrator and Photoshop Graphics   705
        Exporting Graphics from Adobe Illustrator   705
        Previewing the JavaFX Format Files   708
        Loading Graphics into a JavaFX Application   710
        Specifying Animation Paths with Illustrator   717
        Embedding Fonts   720
        Embedding Images   724
        Using a Stub Node   725
        Creating Multiple Copies of a Graphics Element   731
    Importing SVG Graphics   733

22 Cross-Platform Controls   737
    Controls Overview   737
    The Label Control   738
        Label and the Labeled Class   739
        Basic Labels   741
        Positioning of Text and Graphics   742
        Multiline Text   746
        Text Overruns and Wrapping   747
    Button Controls   749
        The Button Class   749
        The Hyperlink Class   752
        The ToggleButton, RadioButton, and CheckBox Classes   756

Contents

The TextBox Control   761
  TextBox Width   764
  TextBox Height   764
  Editability   764
  Setting and Getting the Content of the TextBox   766
  Selection   769
  Copy and Paste   771
The PasswordBox Control   771
The ListView Control   773
  Creating a ListView   773
  ListView Selection   778
  ListView Cell Rendering   782
The ChoiceBox Control   786
The ScrollBar Control   787
  ScrollBar Value and Range   789
  User Gestures   789
  Using the ScrollBar Control   790
The ScrollView Control   794
  Scrollbar Display and Values   797
  Scrollable Node Size   797
The Slider Control   797
  Basic Slider Operation   798
  Tick Marks   800
The ProgressIndicator and ProgressBar Controls   804
  Using the ProgressBar and ProgressIndicator Controls   804
The Separator Control   807
Tooltips   808

23 Style Sheets   811

Style Sheet Basics   811
  Using a Style Sheet   812
  Style Sheet Structure   813
  Selection by ID   814
Style Sheet Property Specifications   824
  Fonts   824

Paints   826
Effects   828

24   Using Swing Controls   829

Swing Component Wrappers   829
   SwingComponent Variables   830
   SwingComponent as a Node   830
   Accessing the Wrapped Swing Component   832
Labels   833
   Text and Icon   834
   Positioning the Content of SwingLabel   836
Text Input   839
   Configuring the SwingTextField Control   840
   Handling Input   842
Buttons   843
   The SwingAbstractButton and SwingButton Classes   843
   Toggle Buttons   846
   Radio Buttons and Check Boxes   848
The SwingList Class   849
   Creating a SwingList Control   850
   Handling the Selection   852
The SwingScrollPane Class   852
The SwingComboBox Class   854
   Using a Noneditable SwingComboBox   855
   Using an Editable SwingComboBox   856
The SwingSlider Class   857
Using Other Swing Components   860
   Using a Generic JavaFX Wrapper   860
   Creating a JavaFX Wrapper Class   862

25   Building Custom Controls   865

Custom Nodes   865
The CoordinateGrid Node   866
Custom Containers   869
   A Border Container   869
   Using the Panel Class   884

Custom Controls   887
  Custom Control Architecture   887
  Control Appearance and Styling   890
  A Skeleton Custom Control   890
  A Media Player Control Bar   895

26 Charts   911
Chart Basics   911
  Chart Components   912
  Chart Data   914
  Chart Interaction   914
Pie Charts   914
  Creating a Pie Chart   914
  A 3D Pie Chart   916
  Customizing a Pie Chart   917
Bar Charts   919
  Creating a Bar Chart   919
  A 3D Bar Chart   922
  Bar Chart Customization   922
Line Charts   926
  Creating a Line Chart   926
  Line Chart Customization   928
Area Charts   930
Scatter Charts   932
Bubble Charts   934
Chart Interaction   936
Common Customizations   937
  Chart Customization   937
  XY Chart Customization   939
  Axis Customization   941

IV: Miscellaneous

27 Using External Data Sources   949
The HttpRequest Class   950
  Basic Use of the HttpRequest Class   950
  Lifecycle of an HTTP Request   952
  GET Requests   955

PUT Requests   965
POST Requests   971
DELETE Requests   973
Using RESTful Web Services   974
    Parsing XML   975
    A Twitter Web Service Client   983
    A JSON Web Service Client   988
RSS and Atom Feeds   995
    Feeds Overview   996
    RSS Feeds   997
    Atom Feeds   1004
Tasks and Progress Monitoring   1008
    Task State Variables   1009
    Progress Monitoring   1010
    A State Monitoring Example   1011
Asynchronous Operations and Database Access   1014
    A Database Access Task   1015
    Implementing the Database Access Task   1018

28 Packaging and Deployment   1025

Packaging and Deployment for the Desktop   1026
    Creating a Packaged Application and Applet with javafxpackager   1026
    Application Deployment   1029
    Applet Deployment   1033
    Setting and Reading Parameters   1037
    Incorporating Libraries   1039
    Compressing the JAR Files   1042
    Signing Applications and Applets   1043
Packaging and Deployment for Mobile Devices   1045
    Creating a Packaged Mobile Application   1046
    Deployment   1047

A Using JavaFX Command-Line Tools   1049

Development Using Command-Line Tools   1049
    Compiling a JavaFX Application   1050
    Running a JavaFX Application   1051
    Development Using an Ant Script   1052
Generating Documentation from JavaFX Source   1055

B CSS Properties   1061

Properties Applicable to Nodes   1061
    Group Properties   1062
    ImageView Properties   1062
    Text Properties   1062

Properties Applicable to Shapes   1063
    ClipView Properties   1064
    Rectangle Properties   1064

Properties Applicable to Containers   1064
    Flow Properties   1065
    HBox Properties   1065
    Stack Properties   1065
    Tile Properties   1066
    VBox Properties   1066

Properties Applicable to Controls   1067
    Properties Applicable to Labeled Nodes   1067
    ListView Properties   1068
    ScrollBar Properties   1068
    ScrollView Properties   1069
    Separator Properties   1069
    Slider Properties   1069
    TextBox and PasswordBox Properties   1070

Index   1071

About the Author

Kim Topley is a freelance computer consultant, based in England. He has worked in the computer industry for 30 years, writing microcode for mainframe computers, device drivers, file systems, and security features for the UNIX operating system, communications protocol stacks for Cray supercomputers, and C and Java applications for financial institutions. He learned Java as a result of a chance encounter with the book *Core Java* in a bookshop in 1995 and has written four Java books—*Core JFC* and *Core Swing: Advanced Programming*, both published by Prentice Hall, and *J2ME in a Nutshell* and *Java Web Services in a Nutshell* for O'Reilly Media. Kim has a keen interest in space flight and aviation and has a private pilot's license, which he would make more frequent use of if the weather in England allowed it.

Preface

The official launch of the Java programming language coincided with huge public interest in the World Wide Web. Home computers were becoming affordable, and large numbers of homes were connected to the Internet, mostly using slow, dial-up lines (remember those?), and Netscape Navigator was by far the most popular web browser. In 1994, a version of this browser was shipped with a plug-in that allowed Java applets to be embedded in HTML web pages. Applets brought motion and dynamic content to what had formerly been a mainly static World Wide Web. So great was the impact that a bouncing-head animation, which was actually a Java applet, was shown on an evening news broadcast in the United Kingdom. It seemed that applets and the Java programming language were set for a bright future.

The 1.0 release of the Java Development Kit (JDK) included the compiler together with a relatively small set of class libraries that provided mainly I/O and networking facilities and a primitive user interface toolkit called AWT (Abstract Window Toolkit). One of the most novel things about Java and AWT was that they allowed the programmer to write an application that would run unchanged on both Microsoft Windows and UNIX. The platform became more robust with the release of JDK 1.1, which for a long time was the standard Java platform and was used to write both applets and free-standing applications, deployed on corporate intranets.

Although Java was born as a desktop technology, it didn't stay that way for very long. Novel though it was, there were problems with the applet programming model as implemented in JDK 1.1. The most obvious was speed—both of delivery and of execution. Before the arrival of Java Archive (JAR) files, an applet's class files were hosted on a website and downloaded individually, on demand. This meant that anything other than a very simple applet was slow to start and would be prone to freezing during execution if a new class file had to be fetched. Furthermore, the early versions of the Java Virtual Machine (JVM) were not well optimized, especially when it came to garbage collection, which would often cause execution to appear to be suspended for a noticeable time.

Neither was AWT a comprehensive toolkit—there were very few components, meaning that an applet or application either had to be very basic or its author had to invest considerable time and effort to write and debug custom components. Unfavorable comparisons were being made with native applications and this continued even with the release of Swing, a more comprehensive user interface toolkit that was an add-on to JDK 1.1. Swing was (and is) very powerful, but it is complex, and it gained a reputation, at least partially justified, for being slow and unwieldy.

Swing was integrated into the next major release of the Java platform, which was given the name Java 2 Standard Edition, to distinguish it from the Enterprise Edition, which was focused on the application programming interfaces (APIs) need to build web applications. The other major desktop feature in the Java 2 SE, or JDK 1.2 as it was also known, was Java2D. Java2D greatly improved the graphical capabilities of the platform, with improved font support, the ability to treat text as a shape, the ability to rotate, shear, and scale shapes, and a host of other features. All of this was implemented by a new *graphics pipeline*, which was powerful but also slow. Swing applications originally implemented on JDK 1.1 ran more slowly on the Java 2 platform. In addition to this, the Java2D APIs were seen as hard to learn and difficult to use. Interest in Java as a desktop platform began to wane as more and more companies turned to web applications to satisfy their needs. The performance problems in Java2D and Swing were addressed with subsequent releases so that by the time JDK 1.4 appeared, desktop applications written with Swing could outperform those running on the now obsolete JDK 1.1, but this was not enough to prompt a serious revival in the fortunes of desktop Java.

Fortunately for Java desktop developers, at the JavaOne conference in May 2007, Sun Microsystems made several announcements that were aimed at reclaiming the desktop from other vendors that had moved in to satisfy the need for a rich client-side platform—specifically Adobe with Flash and Flex and Microsoft with its newly announced Silverlight product. Sun announced a major overhaul of its client-side technologies, beginning with J2SE itself and culminating with a new technology called JavaFX.

What Is JavaFX?

Sun's marketing organization describes JavaFX as a new platform for writing *rich Internet applications* (RIAs), or to those of us who would prefer to skip the marketing hype, it is a new language and runtime environment that lets you write rich client applications and then deploy them to users' desktops, mobile devices, Blu-ray players, and TVs (provided that they have the appropriate supporting environment). For a high-level description of the language and its runtime, see the introduction in Chapter 1, "An Overview of JavaFX."

JavaFX runs on the Java platform. The early releases were exclusively targeted at the Microsoft Windows and Apple Mac OS X platforms, but there are now fully supported versions for Linux and OpenSolaris, and a developer release that runs on mobile devices based on Windows Mobile is also available. By the time you read this book, it is likely that you can buy mobile handsets that include a fully supported JavaFX software stack.

From a developer's point of view, writing JavaFX applications couldn't be easier. If you are familiar with Java or a similar language such as C++, you will find the transition to the syntax of the JavaFX Script language easy to make. Much of what you already know remains true in JavaFX, and there are some new features that, once you use them, you will wonder how you ever managed to work without them. The most obvious of these is *binding*, which enables you to link one piece of application state to another.

There is a whole chapter on binding in this book, but there is a simple introduction to the concept in Chapter 1.

The JavaFX user interface libraries offer a clean and very easy-to-use API. If you are a Swing developer, you will recognize many of the concepts, but you may be disappointed at first because the feature set is smaller than that provided by Swing. This is, of course, only a temporary state of affairs. Over time, the API will be expanded, and it should eventually be possible to do in JavaFX almost anything that Swing allows today.[1] On the plus side, the concepts of the *scene graph* and *nodes* make it easy to build impressive user interfaces. As you'll see in the first few chapters of this book, the features built in to the scene graph APIs let you accomplish in a few lines of JavaFX code things that would have taken many more lines of Java code and also an intimate knowledge of the Java2D APIs. Even better, the resulting code will run (with a few exceptions) on both your desktop and on your mobile phone, so you don't need to work with two different APIs and two different development environments to create a truly portable application.[2]

For those of us who are developers first and artists second (or, like me, not an artist at all), JavaFX makes it easy to work with professional graphic designers to create a user interface that doesn't look like it was designed by a programmer, to be used by another programmer. You can import graphic elements or an entire user interface that was originally created in Adobe Illustrator or Adobe Photoshop and then animate it in response to user actions or the passage of time. This capability is provided by the JavaFX Production Suite, a separate download that contains plug-ins that export graphics from the Adobe development tools in a format that can be read by the JavaFX runtime.

If you are reading this book because you expect to use JavaFX at your place of work, you probably already have an audience of users waiting for your application, but if you are intending to develop an application as a private enterprise and you would like to make some money from it, you could try posting it in the *Java Warehouse*. JavaFX applications in the Java Warehouse appear in and can be sold from the *Java Store*. The Java Warehouse and Java Store were announced at JavaOne in 2009 and should represent a revenue opportunity for talented Java and JavaFX programmers. You can find the Java Warehouse at http://java.sun.com/warehouse and the Java Store at http://www.java.sun.com/store.

---

[1] In the meanwhile, you can always use Java APIs to do almost anything that you can't do directly in JavaFX.

[2] Of course, there are limitations to this. It is easily possible to write a JavaFX application that works well on the desktop but is completely unusable on a mobile device, primarily because mobile devices have smaller screens and less powerful processors. However, if you are careful, it is certainly possible to write a JavaFX application that works on more than one type of device.

How This Book Is Organized

This book is a complete guide to the JavaFX platform—the language, the user interface libraries, and the tools that you can use to develop JavaFX applications. It is divided into three parts. The first part contains an introduction to the platform and a detailed description of the JavaFX script programming language, the second discusses the user interface libraries, and the third covers the APIs that let you access external systems and the tools provided to let you package and deploy your JavaFX applications. Here is an overview of what you'll find in each chapter.

- Chapter 1, "An Overview of JavaFX," contains an overview of the JavaFX platform, the JavaFX script language, and the tools for development and deployment of JavaFX applications.

- Chapter 2, "JavaFX Script Basics," introduces the JavaFX script language by looking at the structure of a JavaFX script file, how scripts are compiled, and how they are executed.

- Chapter 3, "JavaFX Development," shows you how to create a new JavaFX project in both the NetBeans and Eclipse integrated development environments (IDEs) and walks you through the coding, compilation, and execution of a simple JavaFX application. You also see how to compile and run JavaFX applications from the command line and how to extract documentation from JavaFX source files.

- Chapter 4, "A Simple JavaFX Application," builds a more complex JavaFX application and then shows you how to run it as a desktop application, an applet, and on an emulated mobile device. The second half of this chapter shows you how to debug and profile JavaFX code.

- Chapter 5, "Variables and Data Types," is the first of nine chapters that describe the JavaFX script language in detail, beginning with what you need to know about variables and the data types that the language supports. We also discuss the support that the JavaFX runtime provides for the internationalization of applications that need to support more than one native language.

- Chapter 6, "Expressions, Functions, and Object Literals," discusses the arithmetic, Boolean, and other operators that the language provides and introduces the two types of functions that exist in JavaFX. JavaFX functions are first-class citizens of the language, which means, among other things, that you can have a variable that refers to a function, and you can pass a function reference as an argument to another function. This chapter also discusses object literals, which are the nearest thing that JavaFX has to a Java constructor.

- Chapter 7, "Sequences," introduces one of the more powerful features of JavaFX—sequences. Although they are superficially like Java arrays, the ability of sequences to report changes to their content, when used together with either binding or triggers, makes it easy to create user interfaces that display or let the user manipulate lists of objects.

- Chapter 8, "Controlling Program Flow," covers the JavaFX keywords that enable you to change the flow of control in an application. The `if`, `while`, and `for` statements are, as you might expect, similar to their Java equivalents, but there are some important differences. For example, `if` is an expression, which means it can return a value, and `for` operates on a sequence of values and may return a sequence of derived values.

- Chapter 9, "Binding," discusses what is probably the single most important feature of JavaFX. The `bind` keyword enables you to create an association between an expression and a variable so that whenever the value of the expression changes, its new value is written to the variable without programmer intervention. As you'll see in this chapter and throughout the book, this makes it much easier to create user interfaces in JavaFX than it is in Java.

- Chapter 10, "Triggers," introduces the trigger mechanism, which allows arbitrary code to be run when the value of a variable changes.

- Chapter 11, "JavaFX Script Classes," shows you how to write your own JavaFX classes. Unlike Java, code in JavaFX does not have to be coded inside an explicit class definition. As a result, it is possible to write complete applications without knowing how to define a JavaFX class. However, if you want to create a library of reusable code, you need to create your own JavaFX classes.

- Chapter 12, "Platform APIs," covers a subset of the JavaFX runtime that is not part of the user interface libraries, including APIs that allow you to access application parameters and system properties and a couple of classes that allow even untrusted applications to store information on a user's computer.

- Chapter 13, "Reflection," discusses the reflective capabilities of the JavaFX platform. Reflection is a feature that can be of great use to developers who write frameworks or software tools where the data types of the objects being manipulated are not always known in advance. This chapter covers all the JavaFX reflection APIs.

- Chapter 14, "User Interface Basics," is the opening chapter of the part of the book that covers the user interface classes. It introduces the `Stage` and `Scene` classes, which represent the top-level container of an application, and provides a high-level view of the scene graph and the nodes from which it is composed.

- Chapter 15, "Node Variables and Events," takes a detailed look at the variables that are common to all nodes and the node events that your application registers for to track mouse and keyboard activity. It also discusses colors and color gradients.

- Chapter 16, "Shapes, Text, and Images," opens with a discussion of the basic node types that are provided by the JavaFX runtime (such as rectangles, circles, ellipses, and so on) and covers font handling and the rendering of text in JavaFX. Finally, you'll see how to load, display, and, if necessary, resize an image.

- Chapter 17, "Coordinates, Transformations, and Layout," describes the coordinate system used to place and describe the size of a node and the transformations, such as rotation, translation, and scaling, that can be applied to a node. The second half of the chapter introduces the `Container` class and a variety of its subclasses that have an embedded node layout policy.

- Chapter 18, "Animation," describes the animation features of JavaFX. Using just constructs, you can change the position or appearance of a node or group of nodes over a period of time to give the impression of an animation. This chapter covers both the `Timeline` class, which is the basis for JavaFX animation, and a set of higher-level classes called transitions that let you specify an animation in a more abstract fashion.

- Chapter 19, "Video and Audio," covers the JavaFX classes that let you play video and audio clips. As you'll see, JavaFX supports several platform-specific media formats (including MP3, WMV, and AVI) and a cross-platform format that can be played on any platform that supports JavaFX.

- Chapter 20, "Effects and Blending," shows you how to apply a range of graphical effects to a node. The effects supported include shadowing, blurring, and various different lighting effects. Effects are currently supported only on the desktop platform.

- Chapter 21, "Importing Graphics," describes how you, as a JavaFX developer, can work with a designer to create graphics that you can then import into your application. The JavaFX Production Suite, which is downloaded separately from the JavaFX SDK, provides plug-ins that enable a graphic designer to prepare a graphic in Adobe Photoshop or Adobe Illustrator and export it in a form that is suitable for import into a JavaFX application. You'll see a couple of examples that illustrate the overall workflow, and another that shows you how to capture graphics created in a graphics tool that creates output in SVG (Scalable Vector Graphics) format.

- Chapter 22, "Cross-Platform Controls," discusses the node-based controls that allow user input and display lists of data and other information to the user. These controls work on the desktop, on mobile devices, and with Java TV.

- Chapter 23, "Style Sheets," shows you how to change the appearance of your application without changing a line of code by using a style sheet. The style sheets supported by the JavaFX runtime are similar to the Cascading Style Sheets (CSS) documents used with HTML and provide many of the same features. Style sheets work with the basic node classes, controls, and custom controls.

- Chapter 24, "Using Swing Controls," shows you how to embed Swing components into your JavaFX application. An embedded Swing component is a node, which means that you can rotate it, scale it, shear it, change its opacity, and so on. The JavaFX runtime contains equivalents for many of the standard Swing components, and those that are not directly supported, including third-party components, can be made available to a JavaFX application through a wrapper class.

- Chapter 25, "Building Custom Nodes," describes how to create your own custom nodes, controls, and layouts and how to use style sheets to change their appearance or behavior.

- Chapter 26, "Charts," covers the JavaFX classes that let you render data in the form of a chart. Support is provided for various different types of charts, including pie charts, line charts, area charts, and scatter charts. All these classes are highly customizable, either in code or from a style sheet.

- Chapter 27, "Using External Data Sources," discusses the support in the JavaFX runtime for retrieving data from a web server or a web service and presenting it to the user. At the lowest level, you can use the `HttpRequest` class to make an asynchronous call to a web server. If the data is returned in Extensible Markup Language (XML) or JavaScript Object Notation (JSON) format, you can use the `PullParser` class to parse it and then display the results in your user interface. At a higher level, JavaFX provides a couple of classes that read an RSS or Atom feed and convert the content to JavaFX objects, thus saving you the trouble of parsing it yourself.

- Chapter 28, "Packaging and Deployment," covers the `javafxpackager` command, which allows you to package your JavaFX application and shows you how to deploy it for delivery as a desktop application, an applet, or to a mobile device.

This book is *not* intended to be read from front to back. Most chapters have a mixture of basic and advanced material, so you definitely do not need to read everything in a chapter before you can progress to the next. I recommend that you install the software that you need, get the example source code, and then read the first four chapters. At this point, you should have a good grasp of the fundamentals of the language and how to compile and run JavaFX application.

Given that this book is aimed mainly at developers who have experience with Java, the odds are good that you will be able to get a grip on the JavaFX Script language very quickly, and you should only need to skim over the language chapters before diving into the in-depth coverage of the graphical user interface (GUI) libraries in Part III, " User Interfaces with JavaFX." You'll find that each of the GUI chapters contains detailed information on the topic that it covers, so feel free to skip from chapter to chapter picking out the information that you need from each. When you need more detail on a language feature, you can return to the relevant chapter in Part II, "The JavaFX Script Language," and read about it.

Getting the Software

This book includes more than 400 example JavaFX applications. Most of them are small and are focused on a single aspect of the language or the runtime libraries. To get the best from this book, you need to download and install both the example source code and the JavaFX runtime and documentation, as described in the paragraphs that follow. In addition to the software listed here, you need to have a Java Development Kit installed. The minimum requirement for running JavaFX applications is Java 5, but I recommend that you get the latest release of the platform that is currently available. To use all the features of the JavaFX platform, you need at least Java 6 update 10. You can download the JDK from http://java.sun.com/javase/downloads/index.jsp.

The JavaFX SDK

There are two ways to install a JavaFX runtime on your computer: You can get the JavaFX SDK, which allows you to develop applications using an editor of your choice and a set of command line tools; or you can get the JavaFX plug-in for either the NetBeans or Eclipse IDEs. In fact, it is a good idea to get both the SDK and an IDE plug-in, because the API documentation in the SDK is, at least in my opinion, easier to use than the help facility in an IDE, while the IDEs allow you to find your way around the APIs more easily because they provide code completion, automatic management of imports, and an easy way to execute your applications either on the desktop or on a mobile device emulator.

To download the SDK, go to http://javafx.com. There, you will find a link to the downloads page where you will find most of the additional software that you need. The `bin` directory of the SDK contains command-line tools that let you run the compiler, package an application for deployment, extract and format JavaFX documentation, and run a compiled application. You'll find documentation for the command-lines tools in the `docs` directory and the API documentation for the platform in the directory `docs/api`. It is worth bookmarking the API documentation in your browser because you will probably refer to it frequently.

The text and examples in this book refer to and have been tested with JavaFX version 1.3, which was released in April 2010.

The NetBeans IDE

If you'd like to use the NetBeans IDE to compile and run the example source code for this book, you can get it from the download page at http://javafx.com. Alternatively, you can download it from the NetBeans site at http://www.netbeans.org/features/javafx. Be sure to choose a package that contains the JavaFX plug-in.

If you already have the IDE (version 6.9 or higher supports JavaFX 1.3), you can add the JavaFX plug-in by going to Tools, Plugins, opening the Available Plugins tab, and installing the JavaFX Kit and JavaFX SDK plug-ins. If these plug-ins do not appear, click the Reload Catalog button to update the list.

Having installed the IDE, you need to install the plug-ins for web application development, which are required for the examples in Chapter 27, "Using External Data Sources." See the "GlassFish" section, below, for further information.

As new releases of the JavaFX SDK appear, you can update the IDE plug-in from the Installed tab of the Plugins window. This is the recommended approach because it is simple and ensures that you have the latest IDE features for JavaFX. Alternatively, you can download and install a new SDK and then make it available in the IDE as follows:

1. Go to Tools, Java Platforms, and click Add Platform.
2. Select JavaFX Platform and click Next.
3. Assign a name for the SDK and navigate to its install directory, and then click Finish.

You can assign your new SDK version to a JavaFX project by right-clicking the project node in the Projects window, selecting Properties and the Libraries, and choosing the SDK to be used from the JavaFX Platform combo box.

The Eclipse Plug-In for JavaFX

There are two Eclipse plug-ins for JavaFX, one provided by Sun Microsystems, the other by Exadel (http://www.exadel.com). In this book, we use the Sun Microsystems plug-in, which requires Eclipse version 3.4 or later.

Plug-In Installation and Update for Eclipse 3.4

To install the Sun Microsystems plug-in, do the following:

1. On the Eclipse main menu bar, choose Help, Software Updates, and then open the Available Software tab.
2. Click the Add Site button and enter the following URL into the Add Site dialog: **http://javafx.com/downloads/eclipse-plugin/**.
3. The site will be added to the available software list. Open the site node to show the JavaFX Features node and select it.
4. Click the Install button to install the plug-in.

You can update the plug-in to a later release, or check whether there is an update, as follows:

1. Select Help, Software Updates, and then open the Installed Software tab.
2. Select the row for JavaFX Feature.
3. Click Update.

If an update is available, you will be prompted to accept the license, and then the update will be installed.

Plug-In Installation and Update for Eclipse 3.5

The steps required to install the plug-in for Eclipse 3.5 are as follows:

1. On the main menu bar, select Help, Install New Software.
2. In the Work With field on the Available Software dialog, enter the URL **http://javafx.com/downloads/eclipse-plugin/**, and then click Add.
3. In the Add Site dialog that appears, give the site a name (for example, JavaFX Plugin) and click OK.

4. After a short pause, an entry for JavaFX Features appears in the Available Software dialog. Select the check box for this entry, and then click Next.
5. The plug-in details will be obtained and displayed. Click Next, and on the next page, review the license. If it is acceptable, select I Accept the Terms of the License Agreement, and then click Finish to install the plug-in.

To update the plug-in to a later release, or to check whether an update is available, select Help. Check for Updates and follow the instructions to install a new version of the plug-in.

GlassFish

You need a web server, such as the one that comes with the GlassFish application server, to run the examples for Chapter 27. You also need to install plug-ins for NetBeans or Eclipse that let you work with GlassFish from within the IDE. In this section, we describe how to work with GlassFish from within NetBeans.

Installing GlassFish

You can get GlassFish from the GlassFish community downloads page at https://glassfish.dev.java.net/public/downloadsindex.html. I used GlassFish version 2 when writing this book, but the examples should also work with version 3. During the installation process, you will be asked for the username and password to be used for server administration. You must supply these values again when registering the application server with the NetBeans or Eclipse IDE plug-in.

Installing the NetBeans Plug-Ins

To install the plug-ins required to work with the GlassFish application server from within the NetBeans IDE, do the following:

1. From the main menu, select Tools, Plugins, and open the Available Plugins tab.
2. Select Java Web Applications and click Install. Follow the prompts until the plug-in, and a few other plug-ins that it requires, is installed.
3. You now need to register you GlassFish server with the plug-in, which you can do as follows:
    a. On the main menu, select Window, Services. This opens the Service view.
    b. Right-click the Servers node and select Add Server.
    c. In the Add Server Instance dialog, select the version of GlassFish that you installed and click Next.
    d. In the Server Location field, enter the installation directory of your GlassFish server and click Next.
    e. Enter the administrator username and password that you assigned when installing GlassFish and click Finish.

Your GlassFish server should now appear under the Servers node in the Services view. If you expand the Databases node, you should see a JavaDB entry with URL jdbc:derby://localhost:1527/sample. Start the database server by right-clicking the sample node and selecting Connect. When the database starts, expand the APP node and then the Tables node, and you should see the CUSTOMER table from the sample database. This table will be used in Chapter 27.

The JavaFX Production Suite

The JavaFX Production Suite provides plug-ins for Adobe Photoshop and Adobe Illustrator that let you export artwork in a form that can be easily imported into a JavaFX application. You'll find a full description of the Production Suite, together with installation instructions, in Chapter 21, "Importing Graphics."

JavaDB

One of the examples in Chapter 27 uses the JavaDB database. If you use Windows and you have the Java 6 JDK installed, you already have JavaDB on your computer—you'll find it at C:\Program Files\Sun\JavaDB. Otherwise, you should download JavaDB from http://developers.sun.com/javadb/downloads/index.jsp and install it.

The Example Source Code

A Zip file containing the example source code for this book can be found at http://www.informit.com/title/9780321601650. (Click on the Downloads tab.) Extract the content of the file into a directory and then set the value of the javafxsdk.dir property in the build.properties file so that it points to the directory in which you installed the JavaFX SDK. You can then import the source code into the NetBeans or Eclipse IDE.

> **Note**
>
> You need to set this property only if you plan to build and run the examples from the command line, which requires that you also download the JavaFX SDK. If you plan to use an IDE to build and run the examples, you do not need to edit this file. You will find instructions for building and running the examples from the command line in Appendix A, "Using JavaFX Command-Line Tools."

Importing the Example Source Code into the NetBeans IDE

Assuming that you have installed all the relevant plug-ins, you can import the example source code into NetBeans as follows:

1. On the main menu, select File, Open Project.
2. In the Open Project dialog, navigate to the directory in which you installed the example source code and then into the desktop subdirectory.

3. Select the project file in that directory (it's called JavaFX Book Desktop NetBeans Project) and click Open Project.

You may get a message about a missing reference, which we will resolve shortly. Close the message dialog and the project will be imported.

Repeat this process for the projects in the subdirectories `gui`, `moregui`, `intro`, `language`, and `server/ExternalData`.

To fix the missing reference problem, do the following:

1. Right-click the node for the JavaFX Book Desktop NetBeans Project and select Resolve Reference Problems.
2. In the Resolve Reference Problems dialog, click Resolve to open the Library Manager dialog, and then click New Library.
3. In the New Library dialog, enter the name **JavaDBJavaFXBook** and click OK.
4. In the Library Manager dialog, click Add JAR/Folder and navigate to the directory in which JavaDB is installed. If you run the Java 6 JDK on Windows, you will find JavaDB in the folder `C:\Program Files\Sun\JavaDB`. Otherwise, you should install JavaDB as described in the section "JavaDB," earlier in this Preface. Navigate to the `lib` directory and select the file `derbyclient.jar`. Click OK, and then click OK to close the Library Manager.

To run any of the examples, right-click the source file and select Run File. You'll find more information on how to run the examples in Chapter 3, "JavaFX Script Development," and Chapter 4, "A Simple JavaFX Application."

Importing the Example Source Code into the Eclipse IDE

If you have the JavaFX plug-in installed, you can build and run the example source code in Eclipse.

Warning

Compiling all the example source code requires a lot of Java heap space. To make sure that you don't run out of memory, specify a larger heap when running Eclipse, like this:
`eclipse.exe -vmargs -Xmx1024M`

To import the example source code, do the following:

1. On the main menu, select File, Import.
2. In the Import dialog, select General, Existing Projects into Workspace, and then click Next.
3. Enter the directory in which you installed the example source code as the root directory.
4. Select all the projects that appear in the Projects list, and then click Finish.

To run an example, right-click the JavaFX file and select Run As, JavaFX Application. When the Edit Configuration dialog appears, click Run. You'll find more information on how to run the examples in Chapters 3 and 4.

Conventions

`Courier` font is used to indicate JavaFX and Java code, both in code listings and in the code extracts embedded in the text. Lines of code that are of particular interest are highlighted in bold.

Throughout this book, you will find tables that list the accessible variables of JavaFX classes. Each row corresponds to one variable, and the columns contain the variable's name, its type, the permitted modes of access, its default value, and a description. Here's an example:

Variable	Type	Access	Default	Description
focused	Boolean	R	(None)	Whether the Stage is focused
icons	Image[]	RW	Empty	The icons used in the title bar of the top-level container
title	String	RW	Empty string	The title used in the title bar of the top-level container
visible	Boolean	RW	true	The visibility of the Stage

The value in the Access column contains the permitted access modes for application code (more specifically, for code that is not related to the owning class—that is, code that is not in the same package as the class or in a subclass). The possible access modes are as follows.

R   The value can be read.
W   The value can be written at any time.
I   The value can be set, but only when an instance of the class is being created (that is, at initialization time).

Further Information

Even though JavaFX is a recent innovation, there are already many sources that you can refer to for up-to-date information. The most obvious of these is the JavaFX website at http://javafx.com, where you can download the latest release, find hints and tips, and browse through a gallery of examples. There is also a set of forums dedicated to JavaFX at http://forums.sun.com/category.jspa?categoryID=132 and a JavaFX blog at http://blogs.sun.com/javafx/.

JavaFX is still a young technology and currently lacks some of the features that you'll find in Swing or in comparable toolkits. If you can't find what you need in the JavaFX runtime, you might find it instead at http://jfxtras.org/, a site dedicated to the development, discussion, and extension of the JavaFX platform. Here you will find third-party controls, shapes, layout containers, and lots of sample code to help you get the most out of the platform.

Feedback

Although this book has been reviewed for technical accuracy, it is inevitable that some errors remain. If you find something that you think needs to be corrected or that could be improved, or if there is something that you think could usefully be added in future editions of this book, please contact the author by e-mail at kimtopley@gmail.com.

Acknowledgments

This is the eighth time that I have been through the process of writing a book. Two of those books didn't see the light of day, but the six that did (one of them being a second edition) have been interesting, character-building experiences. There is no doubt that writing a book involves a major commitment of time and effort. This book was conceived when the first version of JavaFX was officially announced at JavaOne in 2007. By the time I finished the first draft, I had been working on it in my spare time for more than two years. Naturally, I blame the time overrun on Sun Microsystems, who caused me to discard at least 300 pages of text by throwing away virtually all the language and libraries between the announcement in 2007 and the next JavaOne in May 2008, but in so doing creating a much better product.

I am, once more, indebted to my editor, Greg Doench, who accepted my proposal for this book based on a very sketchy outline and shepherded the whole project to completion despite my attempts to frustrate the process by repeatedly adding "just one more" section to an ever-growing table of contents. Thanks also to Michael Thurston, Keith Cline, Julie Nahil, and the rest of the Addison-Wesley team who converted this book from a raw manuscript to the final result that you now hold in your hands. Along the way, reviewers Peter Pilgrim and Joe Bowbeer provided insightful technical feedback for which I'm very grateful.

I was lucky enough to receive help from members of the JavaFX team at Sun Microsystems while writing this book. My thanks go, in no particular order, to Brian Goetz, Amy Fowler, Richard Bair, Robert Field, and Per Bothner, who took the time to answer my questions even when they were busy trying to meet deadlines of their own.

Introduction to JavaFX

1

An Overview of JavaFX

This chapter provides a high-level overview of JavaFX, from the core JavaFX platform to the tools that you can use to build and deploy JavaFX applications. Built on top of Java, JavaFX is designed to simplify the process of creating applications that can be deployed across devices ranging from cell phones to desktops, with little or no additional work being required to move your code between these different device types. JavaFX applications are written using JavaFX Script, a new and easy-to-use language that is introduced in the second part of this chapter. The core of the platform is the JavaFX runtime library, which applications can use to build user interfaces, create animations, read data from RSS and Atom feeds, and to play video and audio files, among other things. After a brief discussion of the features of the runtime library, we look at the development tools that you can use to build JavaFX applications, and then we examine the options available for packing and deploying your application.

The JavaFX Platform

The JavaFX platform consists of a compiler, a set of runtime libraries, and some developer tools, including plug-ins for the NetBeans and Eclipse integrated development environments (IDEs) that enable you to develop JavaFX applications in a highly productive environment. One strength of JavaFX is that it runs on the Java platform, which means that an application written with JavaFX can make use of all the security and deployment features of Java and also has access to all the Java application programming interfaces (APIs) in addition to those provided by the JavaFX runtime itself. Figure 1-1 shows the overall architecture of the JavaFX platform.

JavaFX applications are written in the JavaFX Script language, which is the subject of Part II of this book. JavaFX Script has a syntax that is close enough to that of Java to make it easy for Java developers to learn, yet different enough to make learning it an interesting and worthwhile experience. You'll find an overview of JavaFX Script later in this chapter.

Chapter 1 An Overview of JavaFX

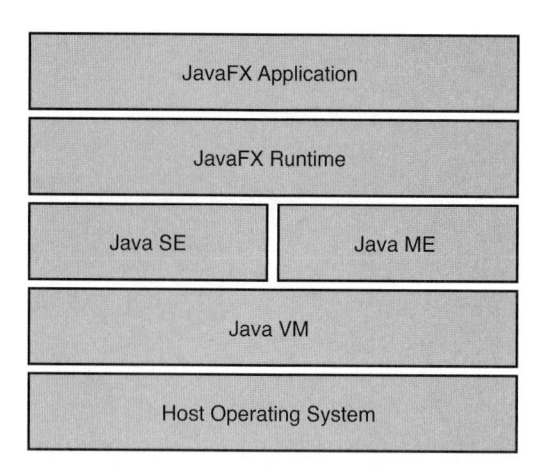

```
┌─────────────────────────────────────┐
│        JavaFX Application           │
└─────────────────────────────────────┘
┌─────────────────────────────────────┐
│         JavaFX Runtime              │
└─────────────────────────────────────┘
┌─────────────────┬───────────────────┐
│     Java SE     │     Java ME       │
└─────────────────┴───────────────────┘
┌─────────────────────────────────────┐
│             Java VM                 │
└─────────────────────────────────────┘
┌─────────────────────────────────────┐
│        Host Operating System        │
└─────────────────────────────────────┘
```

Figure 1-1   JavaFX platform architecture

JavaFX applications run under the control of the JavaFX runtime. At the time of this writing, there are three versions of the runtime: one for desktop environments, which runs on top of Java SE; another for mobile devices, which runs on Java ME; and a third version that runs on JavaTV. When you download JavaFX, all three versions are installed, and the correct version is automatically selected when you compile and test your applications in the NetBeans or Eclipse IDE.

The JavaFX runtime insulates the application from the details of the underlying Java platform, which means that it is possible, for the first time, to write a single application that can be deployed in multiple environments with little or no change. In other words, with proper use of the JavaFX APIs, you can write an application that will run on a desktop, in a browser (as an applet), on a cell phone (as a MIDlet), or on suitably equipped TVs. To do this, you do not need to understand the details of writing applets, MIDlets, or Xlets.

To make this possible, the JavaFX APIs are grouped into *profiles*. A profile is defined by the subset of the complete set of JavaFX APIs that it provides. At the time of this writing, there are two profiles:

- **The common profile**, which contains those parts of the API that are available and work in the same way on all supported platforms. This includes the bulk of the user interface classes.
- **The desktop profile**, which contains extensions that rely on the presence of the Java SE platform. One such feature is reflection, which is a part of Java SE but not of Java ME.

A JavaFX application that uses only features from the common profile can be deployed and executed on any device that supports JavaFX, but one that takes advantage of features of the desktop profile can be run only on platforms that support that specific profile. Some features can be used by *any* application but which do nothing on some platforms. An example of this is the Effects API, which is discussed in Chapter 20, "Effects and Blending." It is possible to use the `javafx.runtime.Platform` class, which we discuss in Chapter 12, "Platform APIs," to determine at runtime whether features that fall in this category are available to your application.

The API documentation that accompanies the JavaFX software development kit (SDK) indicates which packages and classes are provided with each profile. This book covers both the common and desktop profiles, and clearly indicates those features that are not part of the common profile.

The JavaFX Script Language

The JavaFX Script language was designed to make it easier for developers to write JavaFX applications and, specifically, graphical user interface (GUI) applications. As you'll see as you read through Part II of this book, JavaFX Script has several features geared to the needs of the GUI developer. You will also discover that JavaFX is a much more "relaxed" language than Java. For example, here is the canonical "Hello, World" example as it would be written in JavaFX Script:

```
// "Hello, World" in JavaFX
println("Hello, World")
```

As you can see, only a single line of executable code is required.[1] Compare this to its Java equivalent:

```
public class HelloWorld {
    public static void main(String[] args) {
        System.out.println("Hello, World");
    }
}
```

In Java, you have to create a class, define a `main()` method with a specific signature, and then write the code that you want to execute. In JavaFX, you can skip the first two parts and just write the code. JavaFX does have classes, of course, but you will find that

---

[1] You might have noticed that there is no semicolon at the end of this line of code. A semicolon is needed only to separate two JavaFX statements, so in this case we can get away without one. You also don't need a semicolon after the last statement of a function or, more generally, after the final statement of a block. Of course, if your Java instincts were to cause you to add a semicolon here as a reflex action, that's okay, too—you won't get a warning or an error from the compiler. This is an example of the more relaxed syntax rules that make JavaFX easier to work with than Java.

they don't feature nearly as prominently as they do in Java. In fact, this book hardly mentions user-defined classes until Chapter 11, "JavaFX Script Classes."

Variable Declarations

Variable declarations are more relaxed in JavaFX than they are in Java. Here's how you declare and initialize a string variable in JavaFX:

```
var hello = "Hello, World";
```

Variable declaration requires the keyword `var` (or `def`, as you'll see in Chapter 5, "Variables and Data Types"), but you don't have to specify the type of the variable—in this case, the compiler can deduce that its type must be `String` because of the way in which it is initialized. This feature of the language is called *type inference* and is discussed more fully in Chapter 5. In some circumstances, type inference does not work, but in the most common cases, this feature relieves you of the need to explicitly state the types of your variables.

Although a variable's type need not always be explicitly given, it is fixed once it has been determined. This means that, like Java, JavaFX is a *statically typed* language, by comparison with JavaScript, which supports dynamically typed variables and is consequently less type-safe. In JavaFX, the following code is not legal:

```
var hello = "Hello, World";
hello = 123;   // Error!
```

As a result of its declaration, the variable `hello` is of type `String`, even though this is not explicitly stated in the code. The type is permanently associated with the variable, so it is not legal to assign to it any non-`String` value, such as the numeric value `123` used in this example. In JavaScript and other dynamically typed languages, this reassignment of type would be legal.

Access to Java APIs

Although JavaFX has its own runtime libraries, JavaFX Script applications can also access the APIs provided by the underlying Java platform. For example, the following code uses the `java.lang.System` and `java.util.Random` classes to seed and print a random integer:

```
package javafxintro;

import java.lang.System;
import java.util.Random;

var random = new Random(System.currentTimeMillis());
println(random.nextInt(10));
```

The ability to access Java classes in this way makes it possible for JavaFX to leverage the existing capabilities of the underlying platform, such as networking or database access, where these features exist. However, relying on Java APIs might cause your application to become platform-dependent. For example, the following code is valid JavaFX, but it is not fully portable:

```
package javafxintro;

import java.lang.Math;

println(10 * Math.random());
```

The problem with this code is that the `java.lang.Math` class is only partially implemented on mobile devices—on Mobile Information Device Profile (MIDP)-based cell phones, of which many millions are currently in use, the `random()` method is not implemented. Consequently, this code will not compile if you attempt to build it for the JavaFX mobile profile. By contrast, the `Random` class that was used in the previous example *is* available in the MIDP profile of Java ME, so it is safe to use it in a JavaFX application that might run on a cell phone.[2]

Object Literals

A special syntax for object initialization in JavaFX, called an *object literal*, replaces the `new` keyword in Java. Here's an example of an object literal:

```
Text {
    x: 20
    y: 20
    font: Font { size: 24 }
    content: "Hello, World"
}
```

This code creates an instance of the `javafx.scene.text.Text` class and initializes its `x`, `y`, `font`, and `content` variables. The compiler ensures that the value to be assigned to each variable is compatible with its declared type. Object literals can be nested—in this example, a nested object literal is used to initialize the `font` variable with an instance of the `javafx.scene.text.Font` class in which the value of the `size` variable has been set to `24`. Object literals are discussed in Chapter 5 "Variables and Data Types," and Chapter 6, "Expressions, Functions, and Object Literals."

---

[2] In this case, there is another alternative—the JavaFX runtime includes the class `javafx.util.Math`, which also includes a `random()` function. This function is part of the common profile and therefore is available on all JavaFX platforms.

Binding

Writing GUI applications often involves keeping different pieces of application state in sync with each other. For example, you might build a form containing an input field and an OK button and want the button to be enabled only when the input field is not empty. In Java, you do this by writing a listener that is called whenever the content of the input field is changed and either enables or disables the button depending on the field's content. In JavaFX, you can dispense with the listener and directly bind the state of the button to the input field's content, like this:

```
Button {
    text: "OK"
    disable: bind textBox.rawText.trim() == ""
}
```

Assuming that the `textBox` variable refers to an instance of the platform-independent text input control `TextBox` (discussed in Chapter 22, "Cross-Platform Controls"), the expression `textBox.rawText` gets the text that has been typed into the control, uses the `trim()` method to remove leading and trailing whitespace, and compares the result to the empty string.[3] The result of this code is that the `disable` variable of the button will be set to `true` (thus disabling it, so that attempts to press it are ignored) if there is no text in the `TextBox` and `false` if there is. The `bind` keyword ensures that this linkage is maintained, so that as the content of the `TextBox` changes, the result will be recomputed and the value of the `disable` variable will be updated automatically. Binding is probably the single most useful feature of JavaFX, and you will see it used very frequently in the examples in this book.

Scripts and Compilation

JavaFX Script is compiled to class files by the JavaFX compiler and is then executed on the Java Virtual Machine (JVM). After a script has been compiled, it is indistinguishable from a compiled Java source file. The compiler is responsible for mapping each JavaFX Script source file to one or more class files. Most of the time, you do not need to be concerned with how this is achieved, because the tools that are shipped with the JavaFX SDK hide the details, as discussed in Chapter 3, "JavaFX Script Development," and Chapter 4, "A Simple JavaFX Application." One of the rare occasions on which you will see the mapping is when you need to analyze the stack trace of an uncaught exception.

---

[3] Notice that we use the `==` operator to compare the value of the `rawText` variable to the empty string. In Java, we have to use the `equals()` method to make this comparison, but JavaFX allows us to use `==` instead, because `==` is translated by the compiler to an invocation of `equals()`, as you'll see later in this book. This is another of the many ways in which JavaFX is more programmer-friendly than Java.

Fortunately, it is usually easy to map from the stack frames in the stack trace to your original JavaFX code.

JavaFX Script can also be compiled and executed on-the-fly by using the Java Scripting API, which is built in to Java SE 6 (and also available as a separate download for Java 5). This can prove useful if you need to download a script from a remote server and execute it on the user's platform. You can only do this if you have both the JavaFX compiler and the classes for the Java Scripting API available to the Java VM that is executing your application, which means that it is not possible to do this on platforms that provide only the common profile.

The JavaFX Runtime

The JavaFX runtime can be divided into two parts—the part of the runtime that is profile-independent and is used by both applications and the JavaFX compiler itself, and the part that is profile-dependent and on which the compiler has no dependencies. Some of the profile-independent runtime is directly used only by the compiler and the runtime libraries, but there are many public APIs that your JavaFX application can use, including the `println()` function that writes to the standard output stream, functions that let you read command-line arguments, applet parameters and system properties, and an API that lets you store information in a device-independent way. Many of these useful functions are covered in Chapter 12, "Platform APIs."

The APIs that are part of the common profile appear in all implementations of the runtime libraries. The code that implements these APIs in the three existing runtimes may not be the same, but the API itself is, and they are functionally equivalent. The runtime for JavaFX Desktop also contains implementations of the APIs that are unique to the desktop profile.

The runtime libraries are the subject of Parts III and IV of this book. Here, we briefly look at some of the most important features that they provide.

User Interface Classes

The majority of the runtime library consists of classes that are concerned with creating user interfaces. In JavaFX, a user interface is a collection of *nodes*. A node may represent a shape of some kind, such as a circle or a rectangle, some text, or something more complex such as a player for video or audio content. Nodes can be placed within a *scene*, which represents a complete user interface, or in a *group*, which is then placed in a scene or in another group. Operations are provided that enable you to move, rotate, scale, or shear individual nodes. Nodes in a group can be treated as a separate unit to which any of these operations can be applied. Applying a rotation to a group, for example, causes the whole group to be rotated.

Figure 1-2 shows a simple JavaFX application that consists of a number of nodes, running on a Windows PC. The background image is a node, as are each of the white circles that represent snowflakes. The text at the bottom of the application that counts the number of visible snowflakes is also a node.

Figure 1-2 A simple JavaFX application

This application uses APIs from the common profile only, so it can be run unchanged on any cell phone that is enabled for JavaFX. Figure 1-3 shows the same application running on a mobile device emulator. You'll see how this example is implemented in Chapter 4.

Video and Audio

JavaFX provides support for playback of video and audio streams on both desktop and mobile devices. Playing audio or video is just a matter of creating a specific type of node called a `MediaView`, placing it in a scene, and letting the JavaFX runtime do the rest for you.

Figure 1-4 shows an example of video playback on a PC running the JavaFX Desktop platform.

As a general rule, you can play any type of audio or video for which the host platform has support. This means, for example, that JavaFX on the Windows platform can play anything that Windows Media Player can play. In addition, a couple of cross-platform formats can be played on any device that can run JavaFX. For further information, refer to the detailed discussion of the video and audio features of JavaFX in Chapter 19, "Video and Audio."

Animation

JavaFX has built-in support for *animation*, both in the language and in the runtime. Animation refers to the ability to vary the value of one or more variables over a specified period of time. If these variables represent the position of an object, the result will be that

Figure 1-3 A JavaFX application running on a mobile device emulator

Figure 1-4 Video playback in JavaFX

the object will appear to move. If, on the other hand, you were to vary the opacity of an object, that object would appear to fade in or fade out over time.

The following code uses both the compiler and the runtime support to create and play an animation that lasts for 10 seconds.

```
1    var t = Timeline {
2        keyFrames: [
3            at (0s) { node.translateX => 0 }
4            at (10s) { node.translateX => 200 }
5        ]
6    }
7    t.play();
```

The `Timeline` class, used on line 1, is part of the common profile in the JavaFX runtime. The code on line 3 says that at an elapsed time of 0 seconds, the `translateX` variable of the node referred to by the `node` variable (which is not shown in this code snippet) should be set to 0. The code on line 4 says that when 10 seconds has passed, the `translateX` variable of that same node should have the value `200`. In between these two times, the variable will have intermediate values computed by the platform so that, for example, after 2 seconds the value might be (approximately) `40`, after 4 seconds it might be `80`, and so on.[4] The `translateX` variable controls the horizontal position of a node, so the effect of this code will be that the node will appear to move horizontally across the screen at a uniform speed, covering 200 pixels in 10 seconds.

The syntax `at (10s)` and the symbol `=>` are translated by the compiler into some more complex code that creates a `KeyFrame` object and initializes some of its variables. You will find all the details and many more examples of animation in Chapter 4, "A Simple JavaFX Application," and in Chapter 18, "Animation."

Network Access

Because JavaFX is intended to be used to write rich Internet applications, some support for retrieving data over the Internet would be expected. It is possible to use the networking support provided by the underlying Java platform, but there are two problems with this:

- The networking APIs in Java SE and Java ME are very different from each other, which makes it impossible to write a platform-independent application that is also network-aware without also writing a platform-dependent glue layer to encapsulate the different networking APIs.

---

[4] The process of computing the intermediate values in an animation is called *interpolation* and is performed by an *interpolator*. The JavaFX runtime includes some standard interpolators, and you can also write your own. Refer to Chapter 18 for more information on this subject.

- Accessing data over the Internet is a slow process that must not be performed in the thread that is used to manage the user interface. Unlike Java, JavaFX does not have language-level support for concurrency—there is no equivalent of the `synchronized` keyword. In fact, in JavaFX, application code is discouraged from managing threads.

To solve both of these problems, the JavaFX runtime provides classes that wrap common network operations and handle them in internally managed background threads. The intent is that an application should specify what needs to be done and then allow the runtime to take care of the details of handling it asynchronously. When the task is completed, application code is notified via a callback in the main thread. In this way, all the concurrency concerns can be managed by the JavaFX runtime in a manner appropriate to the host platform. For example, the runtime provides support for invoking an HTTP-based service, such as a RESTful Web Service, with asynchronous notification of the completion of the operation, together with progress reports as data is received. You'll find the details of these APIs in Chapter 27, "Using External Data Sources."

JavaFX Development Tools

The JavaFX SDK provides a set of tools that can be used to build and package a JavaFX application. It contains the following:

- A command-line compiler that is based on the Java compiler and has the same command-line arguments. You can use this compiler to manually compile your application or as part of a batch script to build a whole project. A JavaFX-specific option allows you to specify whether to compile for the desktop, mobile, or TV version of JavaFX.
- An Ant task that you can use to compile JavaFX source files using an Ant build file. The task simply runs the command-line compiler, passing it arguments obtained from the build file.
- An application launcher that runs a JavaFX application. There is an option that determines whether the application should be launched in desktop, mobile, or TV mode.
- A command-line utility called `javafxpackager` that builds a complete JavaFX application and packages it for delivery to either a desktop, mobile, or TV platform.
- A command-line utility called `javafxdoc` that extracts documentation comments from a set of JavaFX source files and converts them to a set of HTML documents, in a similar way to the `javadoc` utility.

In addition to the command-line tools, there are plug-ins for both the NetBeans and Eclipse IDEs that enable you to compile, package, run, and debug your JavaFX application without leaving the comfort of your development environment. This book assumes that you will be using one of these plug-ins to run the example code, and you'll see how to use both of them when we create a simple but complete JavaFX application in Chapter 4.

It is possible to create graphical assets using commercial tools such as Adobe Photoshop and Adobe Illustrator that can then be imported into a JavaFX application. The JavaFX Production Suite, which is a separate download from the JavaFX SDK, provides plug-ins that export graphics from Photoshop and Illustrator in a format that is understood by the JavaFX runtime. You can also prepare artwork using an SVG (Scalable Vector Graphics) editor such as Inkscape. The JavaFX Production Suite provides a utility that enables you to view SVG files and convert them so that they can be read and used by your JavaFX application. These tools are discussed in Chapter 21, "Importing Graphics."

Deployment

A JavaFX application can currently be packaged and deployed for execution in four different ways:

- As a desktop application delivered and installed using Java Web Start
- As an applet delivered by a web browser and executed in the Java plug-in
- As a TV application for a device that supports the JavaFX TV profile
- As a mobile application delivered to a cell phone or other mobile device

The details of the packaging for each of these cases are handled by the `javafxpackager` utility, which we will discuss in Chapter 27, or by your IDE. However, some general points are worth noting here.

Java Platform Dependencies and Installation

Each version of the JavaFX platform has dependencies on the type of JRE (Java Runtime Environment) on which it is designed to run. For JavaFX Desktop, the minimum requirement is Java SE 5, although some features (for example, transparency) are not enabled unless Java SE 6 update 10 or higher is installed. For JavaFX Mobile, the minimum requirement is a device that supports Connected Limited Device Configuration (CLDC) 1.1, Mobile Information Device Profile (MIDP) 2.0, and the Mobile Services Architecture (MSA) specification, together with a suitable JavaFX runtime. For full details, refer to the Release Notes for the version of the JavaFX platform that you intend to use.

A long-standing issue with the use of Java as a desktop technology has been the need for the user to download and install an appropriate version of the Java platform. Even though most PCs and laptops now ship with a version of Java SE installed, it may be still necessary for the user to upgrade to a newer JRE in order to run a JavaFX application. Prior to Java SE 6 update 10, installing or upgrading the JRE meant waiting for a very large download to complete. By contrast, an application written using Adobe Flash, Flex, or Microsoft Silverlight requires a much smaller download and therefore would start much more quickly. Beginning with update 10, Java SE 6 includes a feature referred to as the *Consumer JRE*. The Consumer JRE splits the Java runtime into a small kernel that is initially downloaded, and various optional parts are fetched and installed only if they are required. The result of this is that Java applications, applets, and JavaFX applications that require a fresh or upgrade installation of the JRE will now start much more quickly than with earlier versions of the JRE.

The Java Plug-In

The original Java plug-in, which is responsible for hosting applets within the execution environment of a web browser, was the cause of many of the problems that resulted in Java applets being less popular than they should have been and contributed to the subsequent rise of alternative technologies like Flash, Flex, and Silverlight, including the following:

- The initial phase of loading an applet is performed in the main thread of the browser, which causes the browser to freeze for a time whenever a web page containing a Java applet is visited, whether or not the user actually wants to use that applet.
- Only one instance of the plug-in can execute within a browser instance, and that plug-in instance runs every applet within a single Java VM. This causes problems when it is necessary to run applets that require different versions of the JRE at the same time.
- It is not possible for applets to change certain Java VM settings, such as the maximum heap size. This can make it impossible for an applet author to have sufficient control over the applet's execution environment to guarantee correct operation.

These problems were all fixed with the introduction of a new Java plug-in as part of the Java SE 6 update 10 release. Users who have this version of the JRE installed will have a much better experience with both JavaFX and Java applets than those using earlier versions, and further improvements are likely as a result of additional work being done to modularize the Java platform in Java SE 7.

Converting an Applet to an Installed Application

An interesting feature of the new Java plug-in that can be exploited by JavaFX applications is the ability to convert an applet to an installed application. The idea is to allow the user to see and experiment with your application by running it first as an applet within the web browser. In this mode, future use of the application requires the user to return to the hosting web page so that the applet is reloaded.

The new Java plug-in allows the user to immediately install the applet as an application by just dragging it from the web page and dropping it onto the desktop. After this has been done, the application becomes independent of the web browser and can be launched directly from the user's desktop. You'll learn how to use this neat little feature in Chapter 4.

2

JavaFX Script Basics

This chapter begins our discussion of the JavaFX Script programming language by looking at the structure of a JavaFX source file. All JavaFX code is placed in source files, which, by convention, use the naming suffix `.fx` and are converted by the JavaFX compiler into a set of equivalent class files for execution on the Java Virtual Machine. In this chapter, you see how to structure a JavaFX source file, how to import and use code in existing Java and JavaFX classes, and how a JavaFX script is executed.

Source File Structure

A JavaFX source file is structured like this:

- Optional `package` statement
- Optional `import` statements
- Optional JavaFX statements

Here is a simple JavaFX application that prints a random number:

```
1    package javafxintro;
2
3    import java.lang.System;
4    import java.util.Random;
5
6    var random = new Random(System.currentTimeMillis());
7    println(random.nextInt(10));
```

As you can see, this application is in a package called `javafxintro`, it imports two classes (both of which are incidentally Java classes), and it has two executable statements (on lines 6 and 7).

The source file can contain any number of statements, which are, loosely speaking, executed in the order in which they appear. However, some statements, such as those that declare classes (see Chapter 11, "JavaFX Script Classes"), logically take effect before any statements are executed, independently of their position within the source.

Comments

Comments can appear anywhere in a source file. JavaFX supports three different comment styles: single-line comments; multiline comments; and documentation comments, which are a variant of multiline comments that are intended to be extracted from the source by the `javafxdoc` command and converted into documentation, typically in HTML.

Single-Line Comments

Any sequence of characters that begins with // is assumed to be a comment, and everything up to the end of the line on which it appears is disregarded by the compiler. The comment may appear on a line on its own or at the end of any JavaFX statement, as shown here:

```
// Standalone single-line comment. The whole line is ignored.
var hello = "Hello"; // This is an end-of-line comment.
```

Multiline Comments

Comments that require more than one line can be typed as multiple single-line comments, like this:

```
// This is a comment that spans
// two lines.
```

Alternatively, you can use the syntax for a multiline comment, which looks like this:

```
/* This is another comment that spans
   two lines. */
```

Everything from the opening /*, up to and including the closing */, is ignored. The same syntax can also be to add a comment within a line of source code:

```
/* This is a single line comment */
var area = /* Formula for area of a circle */ Math.PI * radius * radius;
```

There are several different ways to write a multiline comment. The style that you use is irrelevant to the compiler, but it is common practice to put the opening and closing delimiters on separate lines:

```
/*
   A multiline comment written in a
   different style.
*/
```

Code editors in some integrated development environments (IDEs) will format a comment for you as you type and will typically supply a leading * character at the start of each line, giving something that looks like this:

```
/*
 * A multiline comment written in a
 * different style.
 */
```

Multiline comments cannot be nested, and so it is not possible to comment out code that contains such a comment by enclosing it in another one:

```
1      /* Commenting out code using a comment does not work.
2         /*
3          * A comment that the programmer wants to comment out.
4          */
5         var name:String;
6      */ // <- This is a syntax error
```

Here, the intent is to comment out both the code on line 5 and the comment that precedes it. However, the preceding source is invalid because the comment that begins on line 1 actually ends with the first end-of-comment-delimiter on line 4. The variable declaration on line 5 is then processed by the compiler, and the close comment delimiter on line 6 is seen as a syntax error because it is not within a comment.

The simplest way to comment out code that has embedded comments is to turn each line into a single-line comment:

```
// /*
//   * This comment and the following code are commented out.
//   */
// var name:String;
```

> **Tip**
>
> It is possible to include the characters that represent an end-comment delimiter inside a comment by escaping the closing / like this:
>
> ```
> /* Start of comment *\/, comment ends here -> */
> ```
>
> However, this is not easy to read and should be avoided.

Documentation Comments

JavaFX source files can have documentation embedded within comment blocks. Documentation comments are like multiline comments but begin with the characters /** instead of /*:

```
/**
 * This is a documentation comment.
 */
```

These comments can be extracted and built in to HTML documentation. The tools that you can use to do this are described in Appendix A, "Using JavaFX Command-Line Tools."

The `package` Statement

The `package` statement, if present, must be the first line in a JavaFX source file that is neither blank nor a comment. No more than one `package` statement is allowed, and it must look like this:

```
package javafx.scene.shape;
```

The package name qualifies the names of all the JavaFX classes declared in the file, in the same way as a Java package name qualifies the name of a Java class. You'll learn more about this when we discuss JavaFX classes in Chapter 11.

The `import` Statement

Following the optional `package` statement and before the executable content of a JavaFX source file, you can place any number of `import` statements.[1] In JavaFX, `import` statements are used to introduce compiled Java or JavaFX classes defined elsewhere (such as in a JAR file) so that they can be more easily referenced by using just the class name, rather than the more verbose package name plus class name that would otherwise be required.

Import by Name

The following code extract imports the `Date` class from the Java package `java.util` and uses it to print the current date and time on the standard output stream:

```
import java.util.Date;    // import one class, by name

println(new Date());
```

You can use the same technique to import a JavaFX class. Here's how you would import and use the JavaFX `Stage`, `Scene`, and `Text` classes to display a window on the user's desktop:

```
import javafx.scene.Scene;         // Imports the JavaFX Scene class
                                   // from the javafx.scene package
import javafx.scene.text.Text;
import javafx.stage.Stage;

Stage {
    title: "Hello, world"
    scene: Scene {
            content: [
                Text {
```

---

[1] In fact, `import` statements can appear *anywhere* after the `package` statement, and they are not required to precede the first use of the class or classes that they introduce. For the sake of clarity, it is better to group them together at the top of the source file.

```
                    x: 20
                    y: 20
                    content: "Hello, World"
                }
            ]
        }
    }
}
```

Wildcard Imports

As in Java, you can import either a single class per line, as shown in the preceding examples, or a whole package. The following code extract imports all the classes in the `java.util` package:

```
import java.util.*;  // "Wildcard" syntax - imports all classes
                     // in the java.util package

println(new Date());
```

Although not supported at the time of this writing, it is planned in a future release to allow the use of the symbol ** to import all the classes that are in a package and its subpackages in a single `package` statement. For example, the following imports all the classes in the package `javafx.scene` along with those in the subpackages `javafx.scene.effect`, `javafx.scene.text`, and so on (or at least it will when this feature is supported):

```
import javafx.scene.**;
```

Although it is entirely a matter of personal preference (or, in some cases, approved coding style), single-class imports are often preferred over wildcard imports because they make it easier to see at a glance exactly which classes are being used in a source file. IDEs will typically create and maintain the import list for you. In NetBeans, pressing Ctrl-Shift-I adds `import` statements for all the classes that are actually used in a JavaFX source file and remove any `imports` that have been added but that are not actually required. You can do the same thing in Eclipse with Ctrl-Shift-O.

Static Imports

You can import variables and functions defined in JavaFX or Java classes by using a syntax that is equivalent to the static import feature in Java.[2] For example, the class `javafx.animation.Interpolator` declares constants that refer to different strategies for

---

[2] As you'll see later, in JavaFX you can declare variables and functions *outside* of a class definition, so both variables and functions can be statically imported in JavaFX.

interpolating between two values during an animation.[3] One way to refer to these constants is to import the `Interpolator` class and then use the class and constant names together:

```
import javafx.animation.Interpolator;
```

```
// Print the value of the constant
DISCRETE println(Interpolator.DISCRETE);
// Print the value of the constant EASEIN
println(Interpolator.EASEIN);
```

If you prefer (and again this is a matter of style), you can use a static import and omit the class name when referring to the constants:

```
// Equivalent to a Java static import:
import javafx.animation.Interpolator.*; // Note the ".*"
```

```
// Print the value of the constant DISCRETE
println(DISCRETE);
```

```
// Print the value of the constant EASEIN
println(EASEIN);
```

If you only need to refer to one constant, you can explicitly import just that constant, like this:

```
import javafx.animation.Interpolator.EASEIN;
```

```
println(EASEIN);
```

Automatic Imports

A small number of classes and functions are automatically imported into every JavaFX source file. You do not need to add `import` statements to use any of the following:

- The class `java.lang.Object`. Note, however, that no other classes in the `java.lang` package are automatically imported.
- The basic type `javafx.lang.Duration`, which is used in conjunction with the animation features, described in Chapter 18, "Animation."
- The class `javafx.lang.FX`.
- All the public functions in the class `javafx.lang.Builtins`.

Among the public functions imported from `javafx.lang.Builtins` are `print()` and `println()`, which are similar to the methods of the same name in the Java class

---

[3] Animation is discussed in Chapter 18.

`java.lang.System`. The automatic import of these functions allows you to write information to the standard output stream more easily than you can in Java:

```
print("Hello, World");     // No trailing newline
println("Hello, World");   // Trailing newline added
```

Functions with the same names can also be found in the `javafx.lang.FX` class, but they are simply delegates for the actual implementations in `javafx.lang.Builtins`. The API provided by these two classes is discussed in Chapter 12, "Platform APIs."

Direct Class References

You are not obliged to import every Java or JavaFX class that your code uses—instead, you can refer to any class by using its fully qualified name, which must include the package designator. This can be convenient if you want to quickly add a few lines into a file for testing or prototyping purposes. The following example shows another way to print the current date and time, without requiring an import of the `java.util.Date` class:

```
println(new java.util.Date());
```

Other JavaFX Statements

Following the `package` and `import` lines is the body of the script, written using JavaFX statements. The following paragraphs give an overview of the statement types that JavaFX provides. Further details can be found in Part II of this book.

Variable Declarations

Like Java, JavaFX requires you to declare any variables that you intend to use. A variable is declared and given a name using either the `var` or `def` keywords, which are discussed in detail, along with the JavaFX type system, in Chapter 5, "Variables and Data Types." Variables can be declared in the body of the script or within a class definition. The former are referred to as *script variables*, the latter as *instance variables*.

Value Assignment and Data Manipulation

Value assignment in JavaFX uses the same syntax as in Java and many other programming languages. For example, the following assigns the value 3 to a variable called `value` that has already been defined and is of the appropriate type:

```
value = 3;
```

The right side of this statement can be an expression of arbitrary complexity. JavaFX also supports a variable type called a *sequence* that is, in many ways, like a Java array.[4] There

---

[4] Java arrays are also supported to allow JavaFX to invoke Java methods that have array-valued arguments or return an array.

are data-manipulation statements that allow you to add and remove elements from a sequence and to change the value of an existing element. For example, the following statement inserts a new value into a sequence variable called names:

```
insert "John" into names;
```

Chapter 7, "Sequences," covers sequences in detail.

Using Java Methods

You can invoke the methods of a Java class using a syntax that is identical to that used by Java itself. Static methods are referenced by name:

```
import java.lang.System;
System.out.println("Hello, JavaFX World"); // println is a static method
```

Instance methods are invoked in the usual way:

```
var textArea:javax.swing.JTextArea = new javax.swing.JTextArea();
textArea.setText("JavaFXWorld");
textArea.<<insert>>("Hello, ", 0);
```

Note the syntax used in the last line of this code. The name of the insert() method of the Java JTextArea class has been quoted in this way (using *French quotes*) because it clashes with the JavaFX keyword insert. You can use the same syntax to surround and make legal *any* identifier name that would otherwise be illegal. See Chapter 5 for further details.

Binding Expressions

One of the most useful features of JavaFX is the ability to *bind* the value of one data element to that of another, or to the value of an expression. When you create a binding in this way, changes in the value of the expression cause the value of the bound element to be updated. For example, the following code binds the value of the variable a to an expression that depends on the value of the variable b:

```
var a = bind b + 3;
```

If the variable b initially has the value 0, this statement will initially cause a to be assigned the value 3. However, it does more than that. If the value of b is subsequently changed to 1, the value of a will *automatically* be changed to 4. In this example, the binding is *unidirectional*, which means that a change in the value of b will cause the value of a to be adjusted accordingly, but it is not possible to programmatically change the value of a, because that would break the invariant that a is always 3 greater than b.

The following statement creates a *bidirectional* binding:

```
var a = bind b with inverse
```

The difference between a unidirectional binding and a bidirectional binding is that the latter allows the values on *both* sides of the binding to be modified. In this example, if the value of a were to be changed to 4, b would automatically be set to 4, too. Binding, which is covered in Chapter 9, "Binding," is useful when creating user interfaces, as you'll see later in this book.

Functions

JavaFX functions allow you to encapsulate a set of JavaFX statements in the same way as a Java method does. Functions can be defined as part of a JavaFX class (*instance functions*), but may also appear outside of a class definition, in the body of a script (*script functions*).

When a function is used in conjunction with binding, the value that it returns may be reevaluated when the inputs upon which it depends are modified. This is a powerful feature because it makes it possible to assign the result of the function to a variable and for that variable to be automatically updated as the values from which the result was calculated are changed. For example, consider the following JavaFX script:

```
1    function average(a, b) {   // Definition of a function
2        return (a + b) / 2;
3    }
4
5    var x = 2;
6    var y = 4;
7    var avg = bind average(x, y); // Binds "avg" to the return value
8    println("Average is {avg}");
9
10   y = 8;  // Causes the value of "avg" to be changed
11   println("Average is {avg}");
```

The `function` statement on the first three lines of this code defines a JavaFX function that accepts two values and returns their average. The key to this example is the following line of code:

```
var avg = bind average(x, y);
```

This binds the value of the variable `avg` to the result of applying the `average()` function to the variables x and y. It also invokes the function and assigns the returned value, in this case 3, to `avg`. Thus, the first line of the output from this script would be the following:

```
Average is 3
```

> **Note**
> The syntax `"string {value}"` used on line 11 represents a string with an embedded expression that is evaluated at runtime. For more details, see Chapter 4, "A Simple JavaFX Application."

When the value of the variable y is changed from 4 to 8, it might not appear that anything else should be affected, and you might expect that the last line of the script would print the same average value, but it actually prints the following:

```
Average is 5
```

The value of the variable `avg` has been changed even though there is no explicit code to update it. The change happens because `avg` was bound to the return value of the function and one of the inputs to that operation, the value of the variable `y`, which was used as one of its arguments, has changed. This causes the result of the function to be reevaluated and the new value assigned to `avg`. We discuss this in more detail in Chapter 9.

> **Note**
> Binding does not work with expressions that involve the invocation of Java methods.

Flow-of-Control Statements

Statements in a JavaFX script are normally executed in order, from the first line to the last line, but several statements allow you to modify the flow of control:

- `if/else`: Allows code to be executed based on the result of evaluating a `Boolean` expression.
- `try/catch/finally`: Surrounds a block of code that may throw an exception and allows action to be taken should the exception occur.
- `throw`: Throws an exception that may or may not be caught and handled in a surrounding `try/catch` block.
- `while` and `for`: Executes a block of statements zero or more times. The `while` statement continues to execute the block until a `Boolean` expression evaluates to `false`. The `for` statement executes the block once for each element in a given sequence or `Iterable` (such as a `java.util.List`). Each element is made available to the code within the block as the value of a named variable. An interesting feature of the `for` statement is that it can return a value. You'll see why this is useful in Chapter 8, "Controlling Program Flow."
- `return`: Terminates execution of a function, and may return a value to its caller.

These statements are all discussed in Chapter 8, with the exception of `return`, which is covered in Chapter 6, "Expressions, Functions, and Object Literals."

Class Definitions

JavaFX allows you to encapsulate data and its associated behavior in a class. Class data is held as instance variables, while the behavior is implemented by instance functions. JavaFX classes support polymorphism and can be subclassed. A JavaFX class can inherit behavior from a single base class and from one or more of a special type of class called a *mixin*. A JavaFX class can be abstract and can implement Java interfaces, but there is no such thing as a JavaFX interface. Classes and mixins are discussed in detail in Chapter 11.

Triggers

A trigger is a block of JavaFX code that is executed when an event occurs. For example, you can attach a trigger to a JavaFX variable and execute arbitrary code whenever its value changes, like this:

```
var name = "JavaFX Developer's Guide" on replace {
    println(name)
};
```

This code attaches a trigger to a variable called name. The code in the trigger block is called when the initial value is assigned to the variable and on every subsequent assignment. As result, the value of this variable will be printed whenever it changes. Triggers are very much like Java event listeners (or observers), except that the JavaFX runtime takes care of the details of managing triggers, whereas in Java you would have to handle the registration and removal of the listener code yourself. In many cases where you would need to register a listener in Java, such as updating part of a user interface when the underlying data changes, you can use the JavaFX binding feature instead. When something more complex is required, however, you would implement it in a trigger. Triggers are discussed in Chapter 10, "Triggers."

JavaFX Keywords and Reserved Words

Keywords in JavaFX are of two types: those that are reserved, and those that are not reserved. Table 2-1 lists the keywords that are reserved in JavaFX 1.3. Reserved words may be used only where the grammar allows—you cannot use them for the names of classes, functions, or variables.[5] The remaining keywords, listed in Table 2-2 are not reserved, but have special meaning in specific contexts. Outside of these contexts, they can be used as variable, function, or class names.

Table 2-1   **JavaFX Reserved Words**

abstract	after	and	as	*assert*	at
attribute	before	bind	bound	break	catch
class	continue	def	delete	else	*exclusive*
extends	false	finally	for	from	function
If	import	indexof	insert	instanceof	lazy
mixin	mod	nativearray	new	not	null
or	override	package	*private*	protected	public
public-init	public-read	return	reverse	sizeof	*static*
super	then	this	throw	true	try
typeof	var	while			

---

[5] It is possible to use a reserved word as a class, variable, or function name if you surround it with French quotes—for example, <<insert>>—but this is not recommended.

Table 2-2 **JavaFX Keywords That Are Not Reserved Words**

first	in	init	into	invalidate	*inverse*
last	on	postinit	replace	step	*trigger*
tween	where	*with*			

Not all the keywords in Table 2-1 and Table 2-2 are actually used at the time of this writing. Those that are not currently in use are shown in italic font. These words are either holdovers from earlier versions of the language or are reserved for possible future use.

Script Execution and Arguments

The entry point for a Java application is a class with `main()` method. The JavaFX equivalent of the `main()` method is the `run()` function, which has the following signature:

```
public function run(args:String[]):Object
```

This syntax, which is explained more fully in Chapter 6, declares a function with a single argument called `args`, which is a sequence of strings[6] and which returns a result of type `Object`. The `args` argument is initialized by the JavaFX runtime with the values of any command-line arguments, so the declaration of `run()` is very much like that of the Java `main()` method:

```
public static void main(String[] args)
```

The overwhelming majority of the scripts that you'll see in this book (and, probably, almost all the scripts that you will write) do not contain a `run()` function, because in most cases there is no need to supply one. If your script does not explicitly declare a `run()` function, the compiler generates one that contains all the executable code in the script. In some cases, however, you are required to supply this function. Here are the rules:

- If your script does not contain any function, variable, or class declarations that are visible outside the script, a `run()` function is not required. This covers the vast majority of JavaFX scripts that implement application code, as opposed to code intended for reuse, such as custom graphical user interface (GUI) components and library functions, where most of the script's content will be public.

- If your script contains any function, variable, or class declarations that *are* visible outside the script *and* it has executable code, the executable code must be placed in the `run()` function.

- If your script contains a `run()` function, no executable code may appear outside of it.

---

[6] You are not obliged to use any particular name for the argument of the `run()` function. The use of the name `args`, as shown here, is just a convention.

We'll examine these rules in the context of an example that you saw earlier, which we repeat here for ease of reference:

```
1    function average(a, b) {   // Definition of a function
2        return (a + b) / 2;
3    }
4
5    var x = 2;
6    var y = 4;
7    var avg = bind average(x, y); // Binds "avg" to the return value
8    println("Average is {avg}");
9
10   y = 8;  // Causes the value of "avg" to be changed
11   println("Average is {avg}");[7]
```

The code on lines 1 to 3 is a function declaration, lines 5 to 7 are variable declarations, and the rest is executable code. Because none of the declarations has an access modifier that makes the corresponding function or variable visible outside the script (such as `public`; see Chapter 5, "Variables and Data Types"), there is no need to wrap any of this in a `run()` function, so the preceding code is legal.

If we were to make the function public, the compiler would not allow the code on lines 8 to 11 to appear in the body of the script. Instead, it would need to be moved into the `run()` function, like this:

```
1    public function average(a, b) {   // Visible outside the script
2        return (a + b) / 2;
3    }
4
5    var x = 2;
6    var y = 4;
7    var avg = bind average(x, y); // Binds "avg" to the return value
8
9    public function run(args:String[]) {
10       println("Average is {avg}");
11
12       y = 8; // Causes the value of "avg" to be changed
13       println("Average is {avg}");
14   }
```

Notice that the variable declarations on lines 5 to 7 do not *have* to be moved into the `run()` function, although it would make perfect sense to do so. These declarations are valid because they are not considered to be executable code, even though they have initializers that will cause code to be executed. In reality, no real difference exists between this code and the version that follows, which is more readily understandable:

---

[7] The syntax `"string {value}"` represents a string with an embedded expression that is evaluated at runtime. For more details, see Chapter 4, "A Simple JavaFX Application."

Chapter 2 JavaFX Script Basics

```
public function average(a, b) {   // Visible outside the script
    return (a + b) / 2;
}

public function run(args:String[]) {
    var x = 2;
    var y = 4;
    var avg = bind average(x, y); // Binds "avg" to the return value
    println("Average is {avg}");

    y = 8;  // Causes the value of "avg" to be changed
    println("Average is {avg}");
}
```

Library code and components are typically implemented in scripts that do not have any executable code at all. Scripts with no executable code do not need a `run()` function, although it is legal to include one if you want to. A typical use for a `run()` function in a library script is to provide some basic tests for the features that the script exports, like this:

```
public function average(a, b) {   // Definition of a function
    return (a + b) / 2;
}

public function run(args:String[]) {
    var x = 2;
    var y = 4;
    var avg = bind average(x, y); // Binds "avg" to the return value
    if (avg != 3) {
        println("Test 1: ERROR: avg is {avg}, not 3");
    }

    y = 8;  // Causes the value of "avg" to be changed
    if (avg != 5) {
        println("Test 2: ERROR: avg is {avg}, not 5");
    }
}
```

Here, the `run()` function contains two simple tests for the `average()` function, which is the useful content of this script. If, as in this case, your `run()` function does not need access to the command line arguments or doesn't need to return anything, you can omit the corresponding parts of its declaration. The keyword `public` is also optional, so the simplest possible way to declare this function is as follows:

```
function run() {
}
```

A script that does not have a `run()` function does not have direct access to its command-line arguments, but you can still get them by using the `getArgument()` function of the `javafx.lang.FX` class, which is described in Chapter 12.

Predefined Variables

Four variables, listed in Table 2-3, are automatically defined in every script. Appropriate values are assigned to these variables by the JavaFX runtime when a script that references them is executed.[8]

Table 2-3 **Predefined Script Variables**

Name	Value
__FILE__	The string form of a URL that refers to the class file generated from the JavaFX script in which it appears.
__SOURCE_FILE__	The string form of a URL that refers to the JavaFX script source file.
__DIR__	The string form of a URL that refers to the directory that contains the class file generated from the JavaFX script in which it appears, including a trailing /.
__PROFILE__	A string that indicates the environment in which the JavaFX script is being executed. The values that are currently defined are `"desktop"`, `"mobile"`, `"tv"`, and `"browser"`.

The following script prints the values of three of these variables:

```
println("__FILE__ is {__FILE__}");
println("__DIR__ is {__DIR__}");
println("__PROFILE__ is {__PROFILE__}");
```

Here's a typical result of running this code from the command line:

```
__FILE__ is file:/E:/JavaFX/EXAMPLES/classes/javafxbasics/PredefinedVariables.class
__DIR__ is file:/E:/JavaFX/EXAMPLES/classes/javafxbasics/
__PROFILE__ is desktop
```

In this case, the compiled classes are in a directory structure, so the __DIR__ variable points to the directory to which the class file for the script has been written, while __FILE__ refers to the class file within that directory. Note the trailing / in the value of the __DIR__ variable.

If this example were to be run from the NetBeans IDE, the class files would be packaged into a JAR file before execution and the output would be different:

```
__FILE__ is
```

---

[8] The compiler only generates these variables and the code to initialize them for those scripts that actually reference them.

```
jar:file:/E:/JavaFX/EXAMPLES/NetBeans/JavaFX%20Book%20Intro/dist/
JavaFX_Book_Intro.jar!/javafxbasics/PredefinedVariables.class
__DIR__ is
jar:file:/E:/JavaFX/EXAMPLES/NetBeans/JavaFX%20Book%20Intro/dist/
JavaFX_Book_Intro.jar!/javafxbasics/
__PROFILE__ is desktop
```

Without any modification to the script, the variables now refer to the class in the JAR file and the directory in the JAR file in which it resides. As a result of this, you can use the __FILE__ and __DIR__ variables to locate resources, such as image files or media files, that are packaged with your application in a way that is independent of where the application is installed or how it is executed. You'll see examples of this later in this book.

The __SOURCE_FILE__ variable refers to the location of the source file from which the class file was compiled. It is a constant and therefore does not depend on the way in which the class files are packaged or executed. This variable is intended to be used when JavaFX is used in "scripting mode"; that is, a source file is compiled and executed immediately via the `eval()` function in the `javafx.lang.FX` class or through the Scripting APIs defined in JSR-233.

3

JavaFX Script Development

You can develop and debug a JavaFX application in several different ways:

- Using an integrated development environment such as NetBeans or Eclipse
- Using command-line tools
- Using an Ant build script

Which of these you choose to use is, of course, a matter of personal preference. In some cases, you might need to use more than one of them—for example, it is common to use an integrated development environment (IDE) for initial development and then to submit the code to a source code control system, from which the application is then built using an Ant build script. This chapter shows you how to use the NetBeans and Eclipse IDEs to build and run a simple JavaFX application. You can find information on using command-line tools and Ant build scripts in Appendix A, "Using JavaFX Command-Line Tools."

You can use JavaFX to write freestanding desktop applications, cell phone applications, TV applications, or browser-based applets. In this chapter, we confine ourselves to an overview of JavaFX development for the desktop, but in Chapter 4, "A Simple JavaFX Application," you'll see how to use the NetBeans and Eclipse IDEs to run a single application on the desktop, in a browser, and in the cell phone and TV emulators.

Compiling and Running JavaFX Code

To illustrate how to compile and run JavaFX code, we build a simple application consisting of a single JavaFX source file that displays the value of a counter and increments it once per second, for a period of 10 seconds. We make the following assumptions:

- You have downloaded and installed the example source code for this book in a folder that we refer to using the symbolic name EXAMPLESDIR. If you have not yet done this, refer to the Preface for download and installation instructions.
- You have installed the necessary plug-in for JavaFX for the IDE that you are going to use. The instructions in this section assume that you use the NetBeans or Eclipse IDEs and their respective JavaFX plug-ins.

Development Using the NetBeans IDE

To compile and run JavaFX code in NetBeans, you first need to create a JavaFX project. To do this, start the NetBeans IDE and select File, New Project. In the New Project Wizard, select the category JavaFX and the project type JavaFX Script Application, as shown in Figure 3-1.

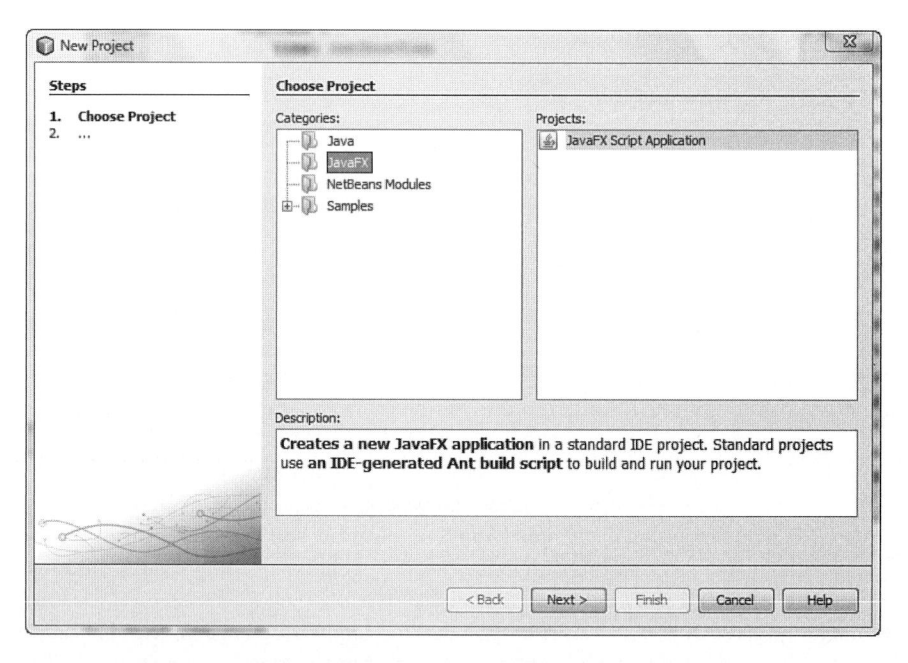

Figure 3-1   Selecting a JavaFX project in the NetBeans New Project Wizard

Now click the Next button to open the New JavaFX Project Wizard, shown in Figure 3-2. In the Project Name field, enter **ExampleAnimationProject** and make sure that the option Create Main File at the bottom of the wizard is *not* selected.

When you click the Finish button, the wizard creates an empty project in a platform-dependent location, which is shown beneath the Project Name field, and then opens it in the IDE.

Right-click the node for ExampleAnimationProject in the Project view of the IDE, and then choose New, Empty JavaFX File from the pop-up menu that appears. In the New Empty JavaFX File Wizard, enter **ExampleAnimation** as the filename and **javafxbasics** for the package name, as shown in Figure 3-3.

Clicking the Finish button creates a JavaFX source file called ExampleAnimation.fx and opens it in the editor. As you can see in Figure 3-4, the file contains an appropriate package statement and some comments identifying its author and indicating where code should be added.

Compiling and Running JavaFX Code | 35

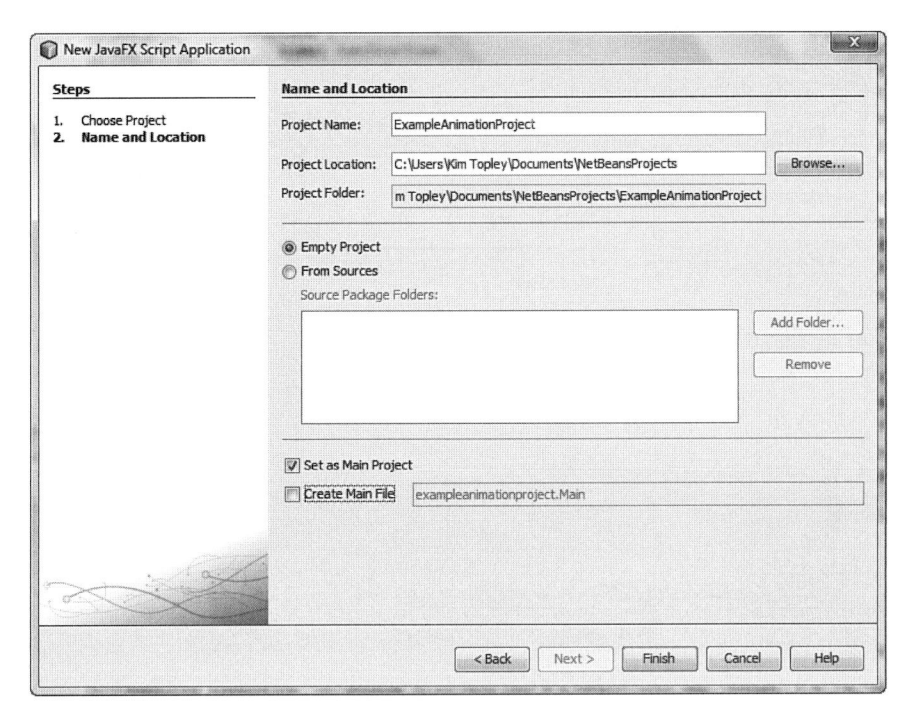

Figure 3-2   The New JavaFX Project Wizard

Figure 3-3   Creating a new JavaFX source file

Chapter 3 JavaFX Script Development

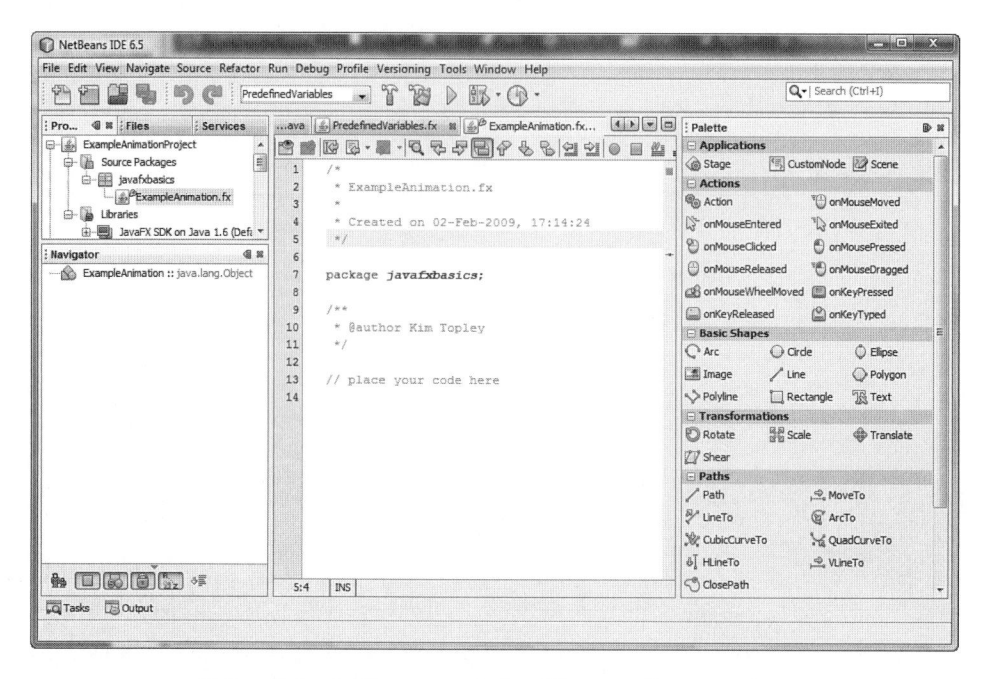

Figure 3-4   Adding an empty JavaFX source file to a project

In terms of the file system, you can see from Figure 3-5 that the location of the source file reflects the package in which the code has been placed. The package `javafxbasics` is represented by a folder of the same name placed directly inside the project's source folder, and the source file, `ExampleAnimation.fx`, has been created in that folder. This is the same structure as that used for Java source code.

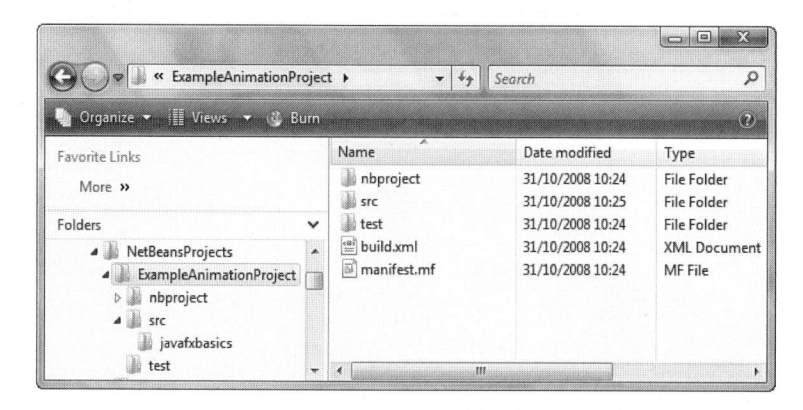

Figure 3-5   File system view of a JavaFX project

Compiling and Running JavaFX Code

At this point, you can either type the example source code directly into the editor, or you can copy and paste it from a file in the book's example source code. If you want to type the code yourself, you'll find it in Listing 3-1. To save time, you can open the JavaFX script file called `ExampleAnimation.fx` in the folder `EXAMPLESDIR\intro\src\javafxbasics` in a text editor, copy it to the Clipboard, and then paste it into the NetBeans IDE editor. Either way, you should end up with the result shown in Figure 3-6.

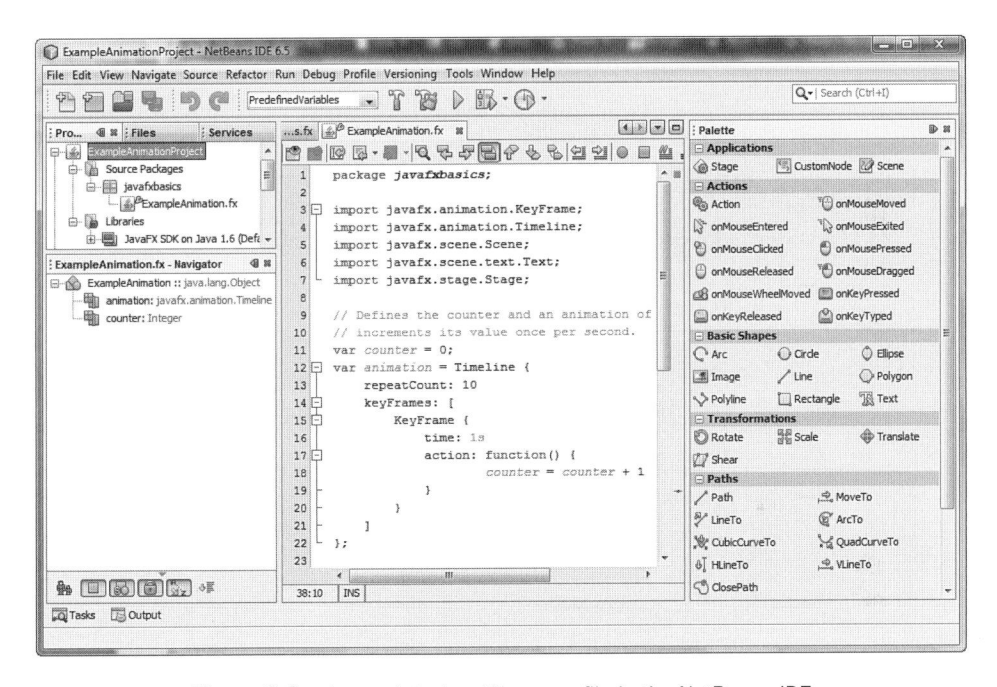

Figure 3-6 A complete JavaFX source file in the NetBeans IDE

Listing 3-1 **A JavaFX Script That Displays an Animated Counter**

```
package javafxbasics;

import javafx.animation.KeyFrame;
import javafx.animation.Timeline;
import javafx.scene.Scene;
import javafx.scene.text.Text;
import javafx.stage.Stage;

// Defines the counter and an animation of that counter that
// increments its value once per second.
var counter = 0;
```

```
var animation = Timeline {
    repeatCount: 10
    keyFrames: [
        KeyFrame {
            time: 1s
            action: function() {
                        counter = counter + 1
                }
        }
    ]
};

// Displays the counter on the screen
Stage {
    title: "Animated Counter"
    visible: true
    resizable: false
    width: 250
    height: 100
    scene: Scene {
        content: [
            Text {
                content: bind "Counter value is {counter}"
                x: 70
                y: 40
            }
        ]
    }
}

// Starts the animation of the counter.
animation.play();
```

In a more complex application, you would have several JavaFX files spread over more than one package. You can use the NetBeans IDE to create and manage both the JavaFX source files and the associated packages by repeating the steps listed earlier for each file.

It is worth mentioning again that, as shown in Listing 3-1, JavaFX does *not* require you to place all of your code and variables inside a class definition. Although you can create classes if you want to, it is perfectly normal (and very common) to put code, variable definitions, and function definitions directly in the JavaFX source file, subject to the restrictions discussed in the section "Script Execution and Arguments" in Chapter 2, "JavaFX Script Basics."

Here, we are interested only in how to compile and run this code, so for now don't be too concerned about how the code works. To compile the application without running it, do one of the following:

- Select Run, Build Main Project from the main menu. This compiles all the files in the project. In this simple case, there is only one file.
- Right-click ExampleAnimationProject in the Projects view and select either Build Project or Clean and Build Project from the pop-up menu. This builds all the files in the project.
- Right-click `ExampleAnimation.fx` in the Projects view and select Compile File from the pop-up menu. Despite its name, this menu item actually compiles all the files in the project.

There are several ways to run the application:

- Right-click the `ExampleAnimationProject` node in the Projects view and select Run Project. The first time you do this, a dialog opens to allow you to select which JavaFX file in the project is to be run. Select the class `javafxbasics.ExampleAnimation`, and then click OK.
- Right-click the `ExampleAnimation.fx` file in the Projects view and select Run File from the context menu.
- Select Run, Run Main Project from the main menu. This also presents a dialog that allows you to choose the class to run when this option is used for the first time.

All of these options compile your source code before running it, so in most cases you can skip the separate compilation step. If you have done everything correctly, you should now see a window containing a counter that counts up from 1 to 10, as shown in Figure 3-7.

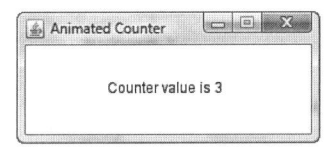

Figure 3-7 Running the example JavaFX application

Development with the Eclipse IDE

Eclipse also has a JavaFX plug-in, and in this section you see how to use it to run the animation example from Listing 3-1. These instructions assume that you have already installed the plug-in. If you have not yet done so, follow the installation instructions in the Preface.[1]

---

[1] As noted in the Preface, there are currently two JavaFX plug-ins for Eclipse. The instructions in this chapter are specific to the Sun Microsystems plug-in.

Chapter 3 JavaFX Script Development

To create a JavaFX project, select File, New, JavaFX, JavaFX Project, and in the New Project Wizard, enter **ExampleAnimationProject** as the project name. Make sure that you have a suitable JRE selected in the JRE section and select Desktop as the JavaFX profile, as shown in Figure 3-8. Click the Next button on this page of the wizard and the following one. You should now be looking at a Template Projects page, on which you can choose a starting point for your project. Here, we need a project with no initial content, so select Empty Project and click the Finish button to create the project.

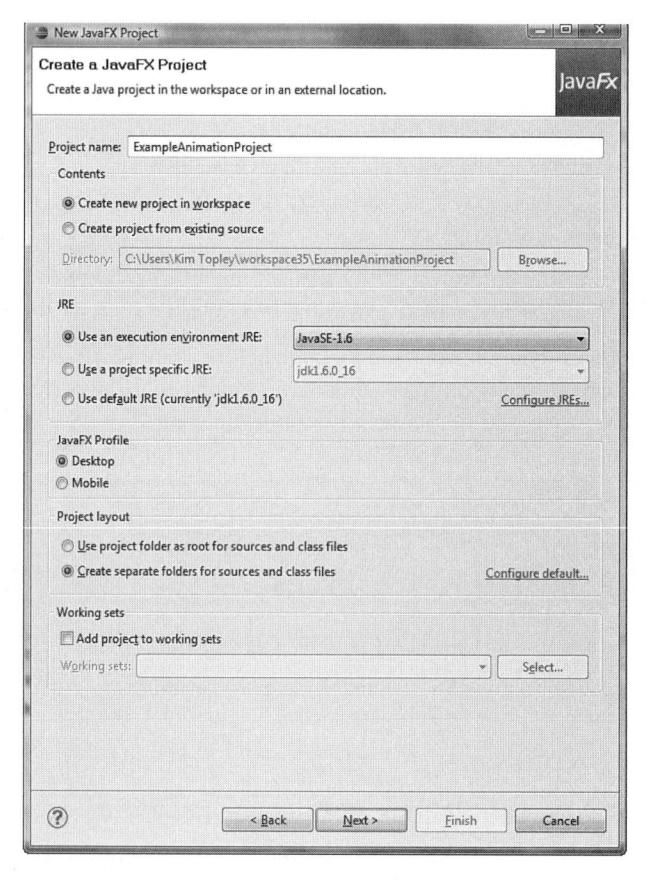

Figure 3-8   Creating a project for JavaFX development in Eclipse

After you create the project, the plug-in opens it in the JavaFX perspective, which is shown in Figure 3-9. On the right side of this perspective, notice the Snippets view, which is similar to the Palette window in NetBeans (which you can see on the right of Figure 3-6). You can use the Snippets view to accelerate development by dragging pre-written code into a JavaFX source file, as discussed in the next chapter.

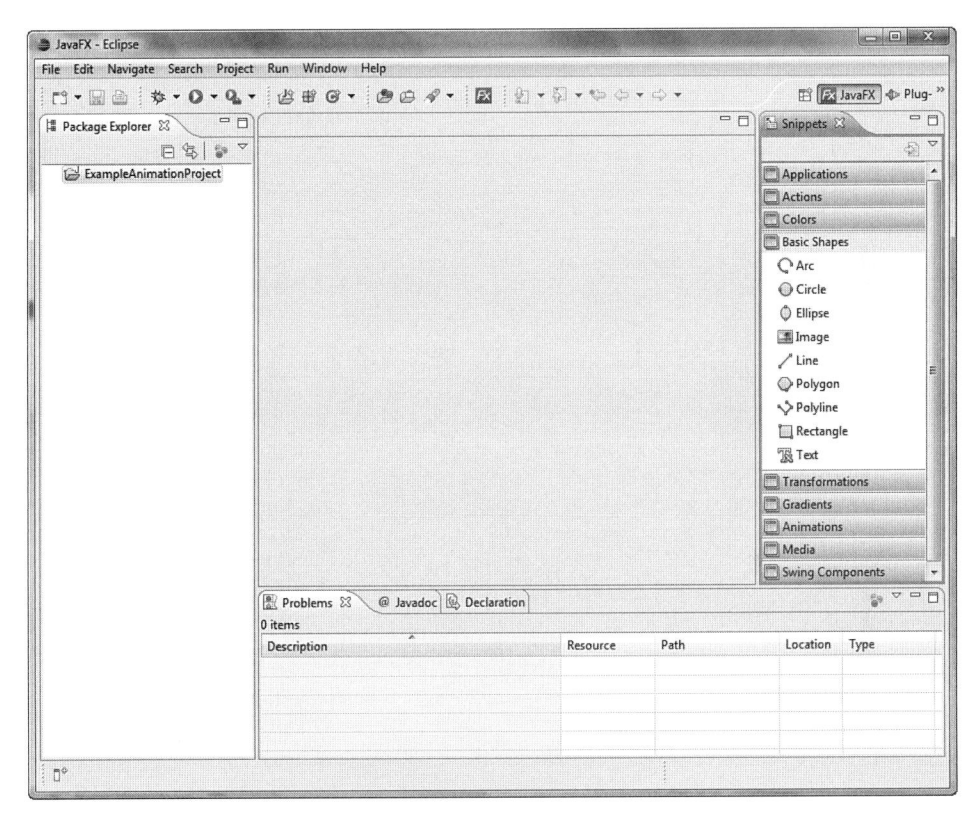

Figure 3-9   The Eclipse JavaFX perspective

Next, you need to create a new package and an empty JavaFX script file. To create the package, select File, New, Package, enter **javafxbasics** as the package name in the New Java Package Wizard, and click Finish. To create the script file, select File, New, Empty JavaFX Script to open the JavaFX Script Wizard, enter **javafxbasics** as the package name and **ExampleAnimation** as the script filename, and then click Finish. The script file is added to the ExampleAnimationProject node in the Package Explorer view and is opened in the editor.

Chapter 3 JavaFX Script Development

Now you can either type in the code shown in Listing 3-1, or copy and paste it from the file `EXAMPLESDIR\intro\src\javafxbasics\ExampleAnimation.fx`. At this point, your IDE should look like Figure 3-10.

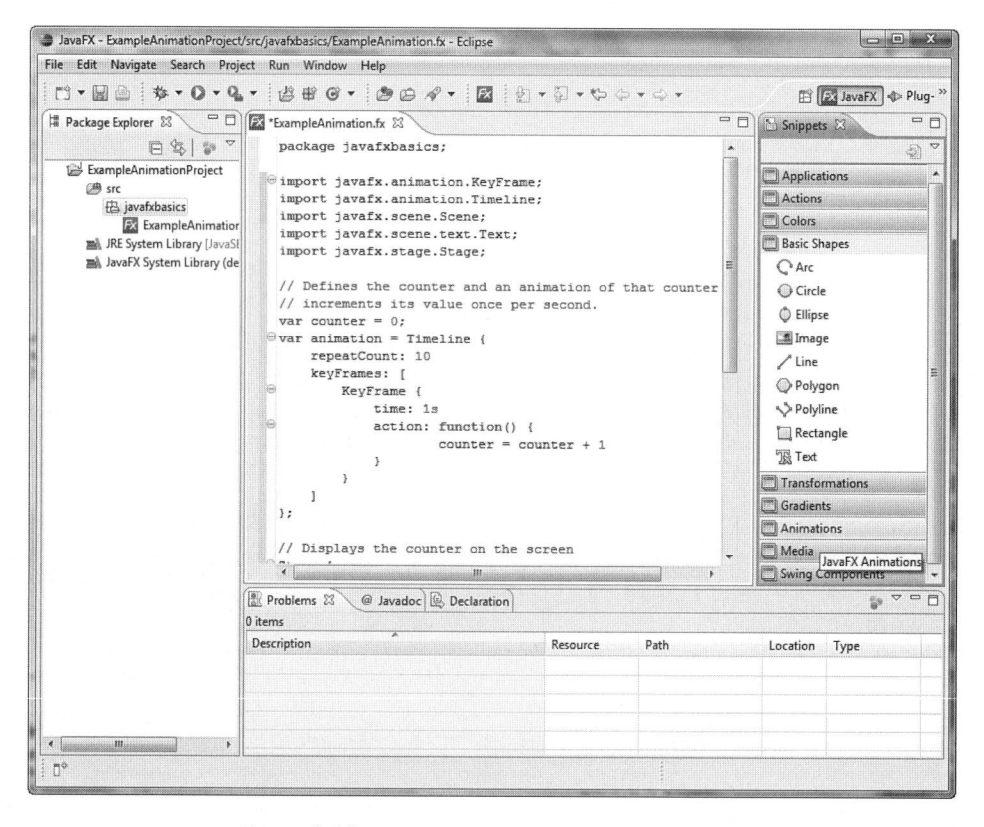

Figure 3-10   A JavaFX script file in the Eclipse IDE

If you have automatic build enabled in Eclipse (Project, Build Automatically), the script will already have been compiled. If not, you can compile it by selecting Project, Build Project or simply by running it. To run the script, select Run, Run As, JavaFX Application, which opens a dialog in which you can configure the launch configuration that will be used. In Chapter 4, you'll see how to use this to run a JavaFX script in different execution environments, but for now, just accept the defaults and run the script by clicking Run. You should see a window with a counter incrementing from 1 to 10, as shown in Figure 3-7.

> **Note**
> If the Run as JavaFX Application menu item does not appear, either click in the JavaFX source file in the editor or select the node for the file `ExampleAnimation.fx` in the Package Explorer view and try again.

Documentation in JavaFX Source Code

You can embed documentation comments in JavaFX source code just as you can in Java. You can use the same tags for documenting your classes, variables, and functions as you do in Java. You can use the `javafxdoc` command, which we discuss in Appendix A, to extract your documentation and convert it to HTML files, or you can view it directly in the IDE.

Viewing JavaFX Documentation in NetBeans

NetBeans has a pane that displays the JavaFX documentation for any documented element of a JavaFX script. To see how this works, make sure you have the JavaFX Book Intro project open in the IDE (refer to the Preface for details on how to import the example source code into NetBeans), and then open the file `JavaFXDocExample.fx` in the editor. To open the documentation pane, select Window, Other, Javafxdoc View. The pane opens, by default, at the bottom of the IDE window. To view the documentation for a class, variable, or function, just select its name in the editor. In Figure3-11 the class name has been selected, and you can see the documentation in the Javafxdoc view, which is below the editor pane.

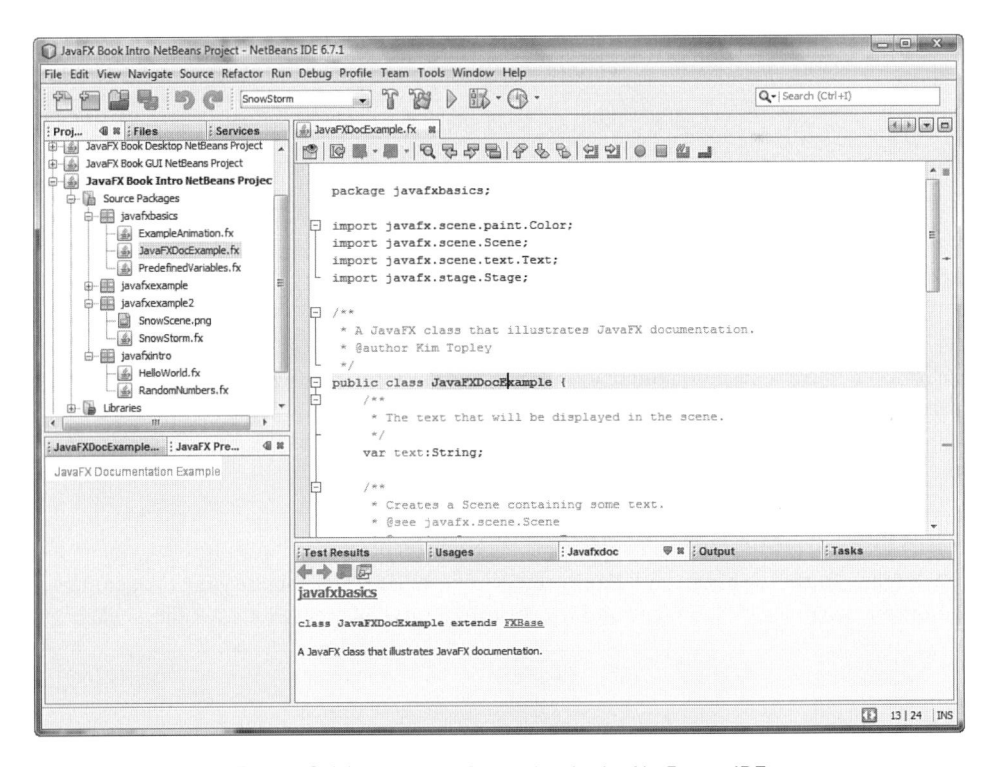

Figure 3-11   The Javafxdoc view in the NetBeans IDE

44 Chapter 3 JavaFX Script Development

You can also view the documentation for any of the classes, functions, and variables that are referred to in your code by selecting the reference in your source file. In Figure 3-12, the documentation for the `javafx.scene.paint.Color` class appears in the Javafxdoc view because a reference to that class has been selected in the editor.

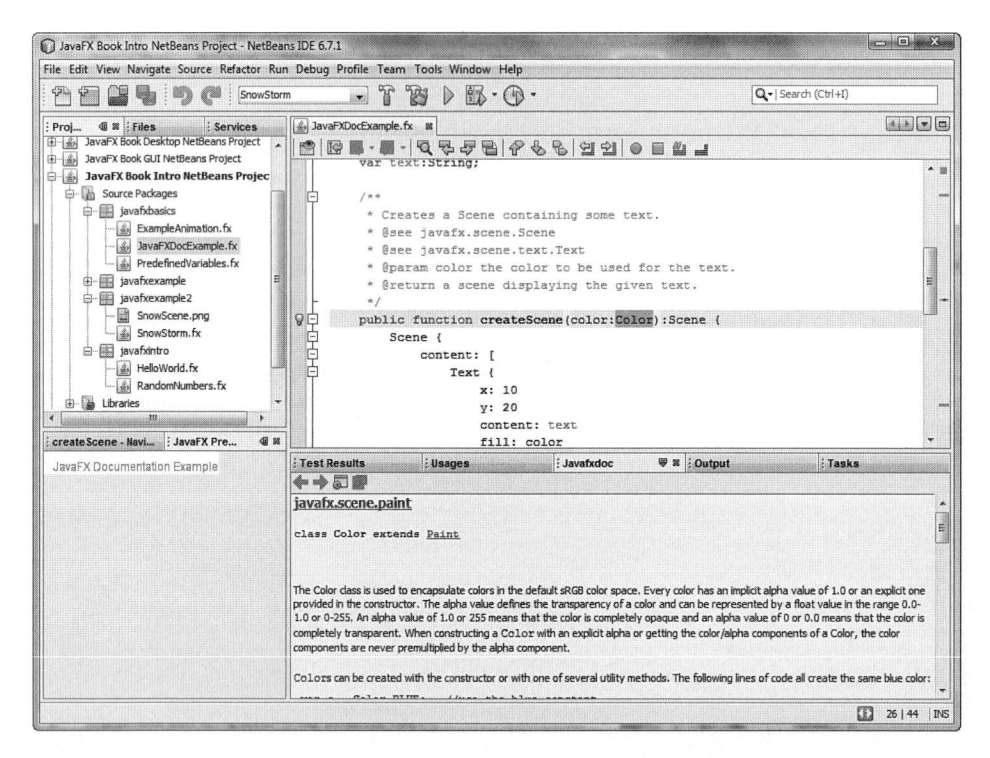

Figure 3-12 Displaying the Javafxdoc for a referenced class

You can generate the documentation for all the JavaFX scripts in a project by selecting that project in the Projects view and then selecting Run, Generate Javadoc. The documentation is placed in a directory called `dist\javadoc` relative to the base directory of the JavaFX project.

Viewing JavaFX Documentation in Eclipse

At the time of this writing, the Eclipse JavaFX plug-in does not format JavaFX documentation, and there is no equivalent of the NetBeans Javafxdoc view. However, this is likely to change.

4

A Simple JavaFX Application

Now that you have been introduced to the basics of JavaFX Script and seen how to compile and run some code, it's time to look at a slightly less-trivial example. The Snow-Storm application that we build in this chapter displays an image of a snow-covered building and animates a number of snowflakes falling in front of it to create the impression of a chilly winter scene, as shown in Figure 4-1.

Figure 4-1 The SnowStorm application

In the second part of this chapter, you see how to use the NetBeans IDE to debug and profile this application.

Building the SnowStorm Application

You can find the source code for the SnowStorm application in the folder `intro\src\javafxexample` relative to the location at which you have installed the examples for this book and, for reference purposes, at the end of this chapter. You can run it from the command line by opening a command window, making the `examples` folder your working directory, and typing the following command:

```
ant build run -Dexample.class=javafxexample.SnowStorm
```

Alternatively, and more conveniently, you can run the application from within your IDE. The source code consists of a single file in the `javafxexample` package of the JavaFX Book Intro project, which you should have imported into the IDE while installing the examples. If you have not yet done this, refer to the installation procedure for the example source code in the Preface of this book. To run the application from NetBeans, right-click the file `SnowStorm.fx` and select Run File.

The point of this example is to show you some of the features of the JavaFX Script language and its runtime libraries that make it well suited for building graphical applications, such as the built-in animation, the binding features, and the scene graph library, which we use to draw the graphical elements such as the background image and the snowflakes. Although we haven't yet formally covered the language syntax or the scene graph library itself, it should not be too difficult to understand how this application works. Everything that you see here is covered in much more detail in the chapters that follow.

Creating the SnowStorm Project

Although you can run the application directly from the source code in the JavaFX Book Intro project, it is more instructive to build it from scratch, so as a first step, we create a new IDE project for it[1]:

1. Open NetBeans and select File, New Project.

2. On the New Project page, select JavaFX, JavaFX Script Application, and then click Next.

3. On the New JavaFX Script Application page, use **SnowStorm** as the project name and select a suitable project location. Make sure that Empty Project and Set as Main Project are selected and Create Main File is *deselected*. Click Finish to create the project.

4. In the Projects view, right-click the SnowStorm project and select New, Empty JavaFX File. On the New Empty JavaFX File page, type **SnowStorm** for the filename and **javafxexample** as the package name, and then click Finish.

---

[1] In this chapter, you learn how to build the SnowStorm application with NetBeans. Eclipse developers should find it easy to adapt the instructions here for use with the Eclipse JavaFX plug-in.

5. In the Projects view, expand the node for the SnowStorm package to show the
   `SnowStorm.fx` file, and then copy the image file from
   `intro\src\javafxexample\SnowScene.png` relative to the installation directory of
   the example source code for this book to the same folder as `SnowStorm.fx`. You can
   do this by copying the image file to the Clipboard and pasting it into the
   `javafxexample` package node in the IDE, or by copying the file manually between
   the two locations.

If you use Eclipse, the sequence of steps required is similar. Refer to the discussion of the Eclipse plug-in in Chapter 3, "JavaFX Script Development," for an example of project creation.

At this point, your SnowStorm project should look like Figure 4-2.

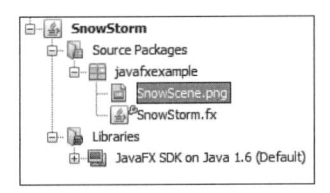

Figure 4-2   The SnowStorm project in the NetBeans IDE

There are two aspects of the SnowStorm application that we implement separately. The first is the static part, consisting of the background image, the text that shows the number of snowflakes, and the window in which the application appears on the desktop. The second is the dynamic part—the animation of the snowflakes and the continuous updating of the number of snowflakes.

Building the User Interface

If you are used to building Swing applications, you would probably start with a JFrame and place the controls that make up your user interface in its content pane. By using a JFrame, you are basically committing yourself to running your application on the user's desktop. To allow your application to run in a browser, you would need to change it to use an applet as its top-level container, whereas to move it to a mobile phone you would need to modify it again to host it in a MIDlet. By choosing the top-level container, as you have to in Java, you restrict yourself to a single execution environment. To make it possible to run JavaFX applications in any of these environments, the user interface is not based on a specific top-level container—instead, it is built as a *scene* within a *stage*, both of which are platform-independent.

Constructing the Stage and Scene

The stage, represented by the `javafx.stage.Stage` class, acts as a stand-in for the top-level container, while the scene, an instance of the `javafx.scene.Scene` class, is the actual container in which you place the elements of your user interface. At runtime, the stage is linked to an appropriate top-level container that depends on the environment in which your application is actually running. The selection and management of that container is the responsibility of the JavaFX runtime. As you'll see in Chapter 14, "User Interface Basics," the `Stage` class has instance variables that you can use to customize the appearance and behavior of the top-level container, such as its title, if it has one.

To start building the user interface, you need to add the code to create a stage and a scene to the `SnowStorm.fx` file. You could type this code yourself, but there is a quicker way to do it:

1. In NetBeans, make sure that the Palette view is showing; if it is not, open it by selecting Window, Palette. Eclipse users should open the Snippets view, which can be found in the JavaFX perspective.

2. Open the Applications section of the Palette view, click the Stage icon, and drag it into the editor.

When you drop the Stage icon, the code required to create a stage and an embedded scene is added, together with the necessary import lines, as shown in Figure 4-3.

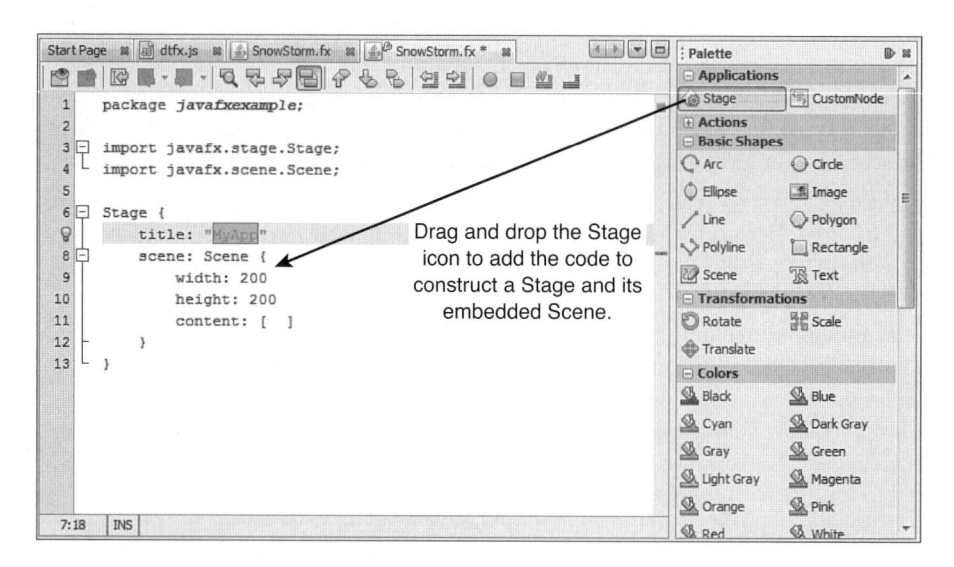

Figure 4-3 Adding a stage and a scene to the SnowStorm application

Now change the value of the `title` variable of the stage from MyApp to **JavaFX Snow Storm** and delete the lines that set the `width` and `height` properties of the scene. Your code should now look like this:

```
1     package javafxexample;
2
3     import javafx.stage.Stage;
4     import javafx.scene.Scene;
5
6     Stage {
7         title: "JavaFX Snow Storm"
8         scene: Scene {
9             content: [ ]
10        }
11    }
```

The code on lines 6 to 11 consisting of the name of the stage class followed by curly braces is an *object literal*. It constructs an instance of the `Stage` class in which the variables listed inside the braces are set to the given values. Here, the `title` variable of the stage is set to `"JavaFX Snow Storm"`, and the `scene` variable is set to an instance of the `Scene` class that is created by the nested object literal on lines 8 to 10. Object literals are discussed in detail in Chapter 6, "Expressions, Functions, and Object Literals."

You may be wondering why we deleted the lines that set the width and height of the scene. If you set explicit values for those variables, the scene will size itself accordingly, and so will the stage. For this application, we actually want the scene to be just large enough to hold the background image, so we don't want to hard code the `height` and `width` values, because the scene can figure out for itself how large it needs to be if it isn't explicitly told.

Adding the Image to the Scene

We need the scene to display the snowy background image and the text shown at the bottom left of Figure 4-1. In JavaFX, the components of the user interface that appear inside a scene are called *nodes* because they are all instances of the `javafx.scene.Node` class. A node typically represents a shape of some kind, such as a rectangle, a circle, an image, or some text.[2] Each shape type has its own `Node` subclass, with variables that allow you to specify the parameters of the shape. For example, the `Rectangle` subclass has variables that let you set the position of its top-left corner, its width, and its height. The

---

[2] There are also more complex nodes, such as text input controls, sliders, and lists, and a media player that can play audio and video. It is also possible to write your own custom nodes. Nodes are discussed in Part III of this book, beginning in Chapter 14.

Palette view in NetBeans has icons that represent the various simple shapes that the JavaFX GUI library provides.

The nodes that make up a scene are listed in its `content` variable, which, in our application, is currently empty:

```
scene: Scene {
    content: [ ]
}
```

The notation [ ] is an initializer for a sequence variable. As you saw in Chapter 2, "JavaFX Script Basics," a sequence is similar to a Java array in that it may have multiple values. In this case, the initializer is empty, so the `content` variable currently has no nodes, and the scene will have no visible content. We need to add to the scene a node that can display an image, which we can do as follows:

1. Open the Basic Shapes section of the Palette view.

2. Select Image and drag it onto the editor.

3. Drop the Image between the initializer brackets of the `content` variable.

With a little bit of reformatting, your code should now look like this:

```
1     package javafxexample;
2
3     import javafx.stage.Stage;
4     import javafx.scene.Scene;
5     import javafx.scene.image.ImageView;
6     import javafx.scene.image.Image;
7
8     Stage {
9         title: "JavaFX Snow Storm"
10        scene: Scene {
11            content: [
12                ImageView {
13                    image: Image {
14                        url: "{__DIR__}/myPicture.png"
15                    }
16                }
17            ]
18        }
19    }
```

The newly added code is shown on lines 12 to 16. `ImageView` is a node that displays the image referred to by its `image` variable, which is of type `Image`. `Image` is a JavaFX class that represents an encoded image, loaded from the source referred to by its `url` variable. At this point, this variable is set to an arbitrary value; we actually need it to refer to the file `SnowScene.png` that is in the same folder as the `SnowStorm.fx` file. To do this, edit line 14 as shown here:

```
url: "{__DIR__}SnowScene.png"
```

The value that will be assigned to the `url` variable is a string formed by taking the value of the predefined variable `__DIR__` and appending to it the literal value `SnowScene.png`.[3] As you saw in Chapter 2, the variable `__DIR__` is set, at runtime, to the URL of the folder that contains the script class, including a trailing `/`. Because the image that we need is in the same folder as the script file, the value `{__DIR__}SnowScene.png` will resolve to a URL that refers to the image file.

If you now run the code by right-clicking the `SnowStorm.fx` file in the Projects view and selecting Run File, the image will be loaded and displayed, as shown in Figure 4-4.

Figure 4-4   The SnowStorm application with the background image loaded

As you can see, the stage is exactly the right size for the image that it is displaying. If the stage is not given an explicit size, it uses the preferred size of its nested scene. The scene, in turn, uses its preset width and height if they are set. If they are not set (as in this case because we deleted the lines that initialized its `width` and `height` variables), it gets its preferred size from the space requirements of the nodes in its `content` variable. Here, there is only one node, so the scene reports to the stage that it wants to be the same size as the `ImageView`, and the stage sets its own size so that the `Scene` has the size that it requires.

The initial size of the stage is correct, but, by default, if the application is running on the desktop, the user can resize the stage by making the hosting window larger or smaller.

---

[3] For more information on the syntax used in the construction of the value for the `url` variable, refer to "Embedded Expressions" in the section on string values in Chapter 5, "Variables and Data Types."

This has the effect of leaving whitespace around the edge of the image, as shown in Figure 4-5.

Figure 4-5   The result of resizing the window of the SnowStorm application

We don't really want to allow the user to do this, and it's easy to disable this behavior. The Stage class has a variable called `resizable` that controls whether the user can resize it. By default, this is `true`, but if you change its value to `false`, the stage will be locked to its initial size, and the user will not be able to resize it.[4] To set the value of this variable, add the line of code shown in bold here to the object literal for the stage:

```
Stage {
    title: "JavaFX Snow Storm"
    resizable: false
    scene: Scene {
```

Using the Preview Pane

Instead of compiling and running a JavaFX application every time you make changes to it, you can use the Preview button that you'll find at the left side of the toolbar above the code editor, as shown in Figure 4-6.

---

[4] Note that this setting does not prevent application code resizing the stage by changing its `height` and `width` values.

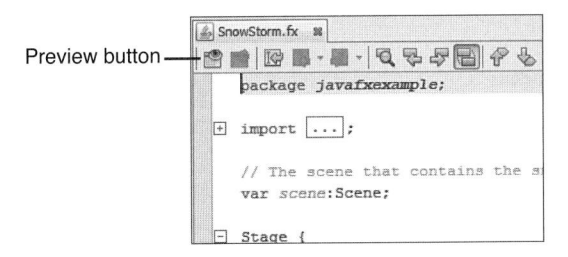

Figure 4-6   The Preview button in the NetBeans IDE

While this button is pressed, NetBeans will compile your code after every change. If there are no compilation errors, it will open a view to display the result of running the application, provided that the code actually creates a user interface. In this case, the view will be too small for the whole user interface to be visible, so it would be a good idea to drag it out into a separate window on the desktop and resize it.[5] You may find that using this feature makes it easier to experiment with different nodes and variable values, or you might find that it slows you down. To switch this feature off, click the Preview button again.

Adding the Text

The next step in the development of the SnowStorm application is to place the text that will show the number of snowflakes. The number of snowflakes varies over time, so we need to arrange for this text to change as snowflakes appear and disappear. You'll see how this is done in the "Counting the Snowflakes" section later in this chapter. For now, we'll just arrange for the fixed string `"Snowflakes"` to be displayed.

You display text by adding a `Text` node to the scene, so start by dragging a `Text` item from the Basic Shapes section of the Palette window and dropping it below the `ImageView` initializer in the editor. With a little reformatting, your code will now look like this:

```
1     package javafxexample;
2
3     import javafx.stage.Stage;
4     import javafx.scene.Scene;
5     import javafx.scene.image.ImageView;
6     import javafx.scene.image.Image;
7     import javafx.scene.text.Text;
8     import javafx.scene.text.Font;
9
10    Stage {
```

---

[5] The `resizable` variable of the `Stage` has no effect on the container into which NetBeans places the `Scene` when it is dragged out of the preview pane.

54 Chapter 4 A Simple JavaFX Application

```
11          title: "JavaFX Snow Storm"
12          resizable: false
13          scene: Scene {
14              content: [
15                  ImageView {
16                      image: Image {
17                          url: "{__DIR__}SnowScene.png"
18                      }
19                  }
20                  Text {
21                      font : Font {
22                          size: 24
23                      }
24                      x: 10, y: 30
25                      content: "HelloWorld"
26                  }
27              ]
28          }
29      }
```

The code that has been added on lines 20 to 26 will cause the text `HelloWorld` to display 10 pixels from the left side and 30 pixels from the top of the scene, using a 24-point font (which means that the text characters will be up to 24 pixels high), as shown in Figure 4-7.

Figure 4-7   Adding text to the SnowStorm application

This isn't really what we want, so we need to change the values of the text object's variables so that the correct string is shown and so that it appears where we want it to. To

change the string that is displayed and to make the text a little smaller, modify the
content variable of the text object and the size variable of the embedded font object,
like this[6]:

```
Text {
    font : Font {
        size: 20              // New font size
    }
    x: 10, y: 30
    content: "Snowflakes: 0"  // New (temporary) text
}
```

> **Note**
> The elements in a sequence are usually separated by commas, like this: [1, 2]. Note, however, that the initializers for the ImageView and Text objects are separated only by whitespace, because this is how the code is written by the IDE when you drop a value into a sequence initializer. The compiler will, in fact, accept sequence elements that are separated by whitespace rather than commas (as long as the elements are object literals), but we will often include the comma separators in the code examples in this book.

Next, we need to arrange for the text to appear near the bottom of the image instead of near the top. The position of the text is given by its x and y variables. These are given relative to the upper-left corner of the scene, which has coordinates x = 0 and y = 0. The x and y values increase as you move from left to right and from top to bottom, respectively, as shown in Figure 4-8.

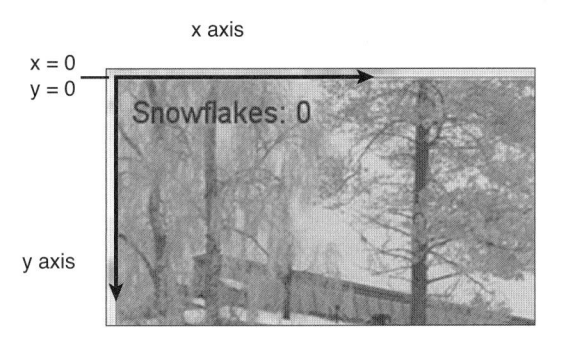

Figure 4-8   The coordinate system

To get the text to appear where we want it to, we need to set the y coordinate of the text object to be 10 pixels less than the height of the scene. To do this, we need to get the height of the scene, which is available from its height variable. To get access to the value of this variable, we need another variable that refers to the scene object itself. Here's how

---

[6] You'll find a full discussion of text and fonts in Chapter 16, "Shapes, Text, and Images."

the code looks when the lines that correctly position the `Text` node has been added, with the changes highlighted in bold:

```
1      package javafxexample;
2
3      import javafx.stage.Stage;
4      import javafx.scene.Scene;
5      import javafx.scene.image.ImageView;
6      import javafx.scene.image.Image;
7      import javafx.scene.text.Text;
8      import javafx.scene.text.Font;
9
10     // The scene that contains the snow.
11     var scene:Scene;
12
13     Stage {
14         title: "JavaFX Snow Storm"
15         resizable: false
16         scene: scene = Scene {
17             content: [
18                 ImageView {
19                     image: Image {
20                         url: "{__DIR__}SnowScene.png"
21                     }
22                 }
23                 Text {
24                     font : Font {
25                         size: 20
26                     }
27                     x: 25
28                     y: bind scene.height - 10
29                     content: "Snowflakes: 0"
30                 }
31             ]
32         }
33     }
```

Line 11 declares a variable called `scene` that we use to hold a reference to the scene; we set its value on line 16 when the `scene` property of the stage object is being initialized:

```
Stage {
    title: "JavaFX Snow Storm"
    resizable: false
    scene: scene = Scene {
```

The expression `scene = Scene { ... }` first assigns the `Scene` reference to the `scene` variable declared on line 11 and then returns the value of that variable. This return value is then assigned to the `scene` property of the stage. By using this syntax, we can keep the declaration of the scene object nested inside the object literal for the stage. This makes the code slightly more readable than the alternative, which would be to declare and initialize the scene object in the same place as the `scene` variable, like this:

```
var scene:Scene = Scene { // Initializers as shown in the code above };
```

```
Stage {
    title: "JavaFX Snow Storm"
    resizable: false
    scene: scene
}
```

The code that positions the text object is shown on lines 27 and 28. Notice that we moved the text slightly to the right by changing its x coordinate from `10` to `25`. The code that sets the y value is worthy of a little more discussion:

```
y: bind scene.height - 10
```

The aim was to place the text 10 pixels above the bottom of the scene, so you might have expected this line to have read as follows:

```
y: scene.height - 10
```

Unfortunately, this code does not work. The reason for this is that when the text object is initialized, the enclosing scene hasn't yet been given its final size. In fact, its `height` and `width` variables would both be zero. As a result, the text object's y coordinate would be set to `-10`, with the result that it would be placed 10 pixels above the top of the scene! We need to ensure that the y coordinate is set *after* the scene has been properly sized. The simplest way to do that is to arrange for the value of y to be adjusted whenever the value of the scene's height is changed. That is exactly what a binding does:

```
y: bind scene.height - 10
```

What actually happens as a result of adding this line of code is the following:

1. When the text object is initialized, its y variable is set to `-10` because the scene's height at that time is 0 pixels.

2. The scene is given its proper height, based on the height of the image, say 375 pixels, so the value of `scene.height` changes to `375`.

3. Because the value of `scene.height` has changed and because y is bound to an expression that depends on it, y will be assigned the correct value, which is (375 − 10) = `365`.

Binding is a powerful tool. To achieve the same effect as this in a Swing application, you would need to register a `ComponentListener` with the equivalent of the scene and implement its `componentResized()` method to adjust the position of the `Text` component. That would take considerably more than the single word of code that it takes to declare a binding!

58   Chapter 4   A Simple JavaFX Application

With these code changes, the initial construction of the application is complete. If you run it now, you'll get the result shown in Figure 4-9. The next step is to add the animation.

Figure 4-9   The completed user interface of the SnowStorm application

Adding the Animation

To implement the animated part of this example, we need to do two things:

- Periodically add a number of new snowflakes at the top of the scene
- Periodically move all the existing snowflakes downward and remove those that reach the bottom of the scene

In a Swing application, you would translate the requirement for a periodic action into a method that is invoked on the expiry of a timer. JavaFX has a much more flexible feature that can be used to implement periodic actions, called a *timeline*. In its most general form, a timeline consists of a series of *key frames* that occur at specified times. For a full discussion of timelines and key frames, see Chapter 18, "Animation." In this chapter, we use a timeline as a means of executing some code at regular intervals.

Adding New Snowflakes

Because the snowflakes appear within a scene, they have to be nodes. The easiest way to represent a snowflake in node form is to use a small, white circle, so each snowflake will be an instance of the `javafx.scene.shape.Circle` class. We need to keep a reference to each snowflake that we create so that we always know how many there are and so that we

can move them down the screen. To do this, we create a sequence variable called
snowflakes to which every snowflake will be added:

```
// The snowflakes
var snowflakes:Circle[];
```

How often should we create new snowflakes? There is no easy answer to this question. If we create snowflakes too frequently, or if we create too many of them, we may find that the application spends too much time animating them, and it may appear to the user to be sluggish. If we don't create enough snowflakes, the snowstorm effect may be lost. We also need to keep in mind that this application could be used on a mobile device that has limited computing power. For this example, we adopt a compromise and create 5 new snowflakes every 500 milliseconds, so we need to set up a timeline that executes the code to create the snowflakes twice every second.

Here's the code that defines the number of snowflakes to be created, declares the timeline, and starts its timer. Add this code to the end of the SnowStorm.fx file:

```
1     // Time interval for new snow.
2     def newSnowTime = 500ms;
3
4     // Number of snowflakes per row
5     def snowflakesPerLine = 5;
6
7     // Random number generator
8     def rand = new Random(System.currentTimeMillis());
9
10    // Periodically add snow
11    def addSnowTimeline = Timeline {
12        repeatCount: Timeline.INDEFINITE
13        keyFrames: [
14            KeyFrame {
15                time: newSnowTime
16                action: addNewSnow
17            }
18        ]
19    };
20    addSnowTimeline.play();
```

The variable declaration on line 2 includes the literal value 500ms. This is an example of a *time literal,* and it evaluates to an instance of the javafx.lang.Duration class representing a time interval of 500 milliseconds. The compiler recognizes the time literal syntax, generates the code to create the corresponding Duration object, and infers that this is the type of the newSnowTime variable. As you'll see in Chapter 18, you can use this syntax to specify a duration in hours, minutes, seconds, and milliseconds, and you can also perform arithmetic operations on Duration objects.

The code on line 8 creates and initializes a random number generator that we use when adding and moving the snowflakes. Random is a Java class in the java.util package. We could also have used the random() function in the javafx.util.Math package (see

Chapter 12, "Platform APIs") but not the method of the same name in the `java.lang.Math` class because it is not available on mobile devices.

The code on lines 11 through 19 creates the timeline, which is an instance of the `javafx.animation.Timeline` class. In general, a timeline will have multiple key frames, each of them indicating an intermediate state of an animation/action that should be performed at a specified time offset from the point at which the animation starts. In this case, we need to do only one thing, so we need just one key frame.

The `keyFrames` variable contains an instance of the `javafx.animation.KeyFrame` class for each key frame in the timeline. Here, there is only one key frame, which will be executed after 500 milliseconds. This time interval is given as the value of the `time` variable on line 15, and the code to be executed is contained in a function called `addNewSnow()`, which is assigned to the `action` variable of the `KeyFrame` object on line 16. Note that because we haven't yet declared a function called `addNewSnow()`, the preceding code will not yet compile.

It might seem strange that you can assign the name of a function to a variable in this way, because there is no similar concept in Java. It is possible to do this in other languages, including C and C++, where pointers to functions can be stored in variables or passed as function call arguments. Unlike Java, JavaFX supports functions as *first-class types*, which means that you can declare a variable whose type is a function, you can read and assign such a variable, you can invoke the function through a function variable, you can pass a function as an argument to another function, and you can return a function from a function. You can find the details in Chapter 6, "Expressions, Functions, and Object Literals."

The value `Timeline.INDEFINITE` assigned to the `repeatCount` variable on line 12 causes the single key frame in this timeline to be repeated indefinitely, until it is explicitly stopped or the application exits. As a result, the application regularly creates new snowflakes.

A timeline does not start until it is asked to, so on line 20 of the preceding code, we start it by invoking its `play()` function.

Now let's take a look at the implementation of the `addNewSnow()` function. Add the following code to end of the `SnowStorm.fx` file and click Ctrl-Shift-I (in NetBeans) or Ctrl-Shift-O (in Eclipse) to automatically add the import lines for the classes that the animation code uses:

```
1     // Adds new snow to the scene.
2     function addNewSnow() {
3         var sectionWidth =
4             (scene.width + snowflakesPerLine - 1) / snowflakesPerLine;
5         for (i in [0..<snowflakesPerLine]) {
6             var x = sectionWidth * i + rand.nextInt(sectionWidth);
7             var snowflake = Circle {
8                 centerX: x
9                 centerY: 0
10                radius: 2
11                cache: true
```

```
12                  fill: Color.WHITE
13              }
14              insert snowflake into scene.content;
15              insert snowflake into snowflakes;
16          }
17      }
```

The aim of this code is to add `snowFlakesPerLine` new snowflakes to the top of the scene. We would like these snowflakes to be fairly randomly placed and not grouped together too closely. To achieve this, we divide the width of the scene into approximately `snowFlakesPerLine` sections and then place one snowflake in each. The variable `sectionWidth` declared on lines 3 and 4 is initialized to the width of each of these sections, based on the actual width of the scene and the number of snowflakes required. For example, if the scene is 500 pixels wide and `snowFlakesPerLine` has the value `5`, `sectionWidth` will be `100`, and there will be one new snowflake approximately every 100 pixels across the scene.

The snowflakes are created by the `for` loop on lines 5 to 16. As you can see, the JavaFX `for` statement is a little different from its Java counterpart (for the details, refer to Chapter 8, "Controlling Program Flow"). The syntax `[0..<snowflakesPerLine]` creates a sequence of integers starting with 0 and ending at `snowflakesPerLine - 1`, and the `for` statement then iterates over the values in this sequence, so the code on line 5 is equivalent to the following `for` statement in Java:

```
for (i = 0; i < snowflakesPerLine; i++)
```

Within the body of the loop, we calculate the x coordinate of one of the snowflakes, using the loop variable `i` to represent the number of the section that contains that snowflake. The x coordinate of the start of the section is (`i * sectionWidth`). You can easily see that this is correct because if `sectionWidth` has the value `100`, the x coordinate of the leftmost section should be `0`, that of the next section should be `100`, the next will be `200`, and so on. Within a section, we want the snowflake to be randomly placed, so we add to the x coordinate an offset obtained from the random number generator, in the range 0 to `sectionWidth`, exclusive.

Lines 7 to 13 create the circle node that represents the snowflake. To draw a circle, you need to specify the position of its center, its radius, and its color. Here, the x coordinate of the center is the value just calculated, the y coordinate is always zero, so that the snowflake appears at the top of the scene, the radius is fixed at 2 pixels, and its color is white (as befits a snowflake!) The `cache` variable, set on line 11, is a performance optimization that allows the runtime to keep and reuse a copy of the pixels that represent the circle so that it doesn't have to redraw the circle from scratch every time. For such a simple and small shape, this probably won't make much difference, but for a larger shape, using this setting could save a significant amount of rendering time.

Having created the snowflake and determined where it should appear, we add it to the scene by inserting it in the `content` sequence, as shown on line 14. The JavaFX `insert` statement adds an object (in this case, the snowflake) at the end of a sequence (here, the content variable of the scene). The scene draws its content nodes starting with the first element of the sequence and ending with the last. The result is that the nodes that appear later in the sequence are drawn in front of earlier ones. Because the background image is the first node in the scene, the snowflakes will all be drawn in front of it, which is the effect that we need. For the same reason, the snowflakes will also be drawn in front of the text, which is the second element in the sequence. This is acceptable, but with a little more coding, you could arrange for the snowflakes to be drawn behind the text. We leave that as an exercise for you, which you should attempt after reading Chapter 7, "Sequences."

Finally, on line 14, we also add each circle node to the `snowflakes` sequence. We do this so that the code that moves the snowflakes, which is shown in the next section, can find them easily. We also use this sequence in the "Counting the Snowflakes" section, later in this chapter.

If you run the example at this point, you should see new snowflakes accumulating at the top of background image, and, over time, the whole of the top line should be filled. Our next task is to arrange for those snowflakes to fall to earth.

Making the Snowflakes Move

Making the snowflakes fall to the ground is another animation, which we implement using another timeline. What we want to do is periodically add a small value to the y coordinate of each snowflake so that it gradually moves toward the bottom of the scene. On its own, this would make all the snowflakes fall vertically down, which is not very interesting. To give the scene a more realistic appearance, we want to make the snowflakes appear to be moving in the wind by adding a small, random value to their x coordinates to create the impression of sideways motion. As before, the question of how frequently we should move the snowflakes and how far they should move is not clear-cut.

The values that are used in the example source code, which are the result of experimentation, are shown here, together with the timeline used to invoke the code that implements the movement. You should add this code to the end of your `SnowStorm.fx` file. Note that it won't compile at this point because it references a function that is not yet implemented.

```
1     // Animating the snowflakes
2
3     // Time interval for moving the snow.
4     def moveSnowTime = 100ms;
5
6     // How far the snow falls in each frame
7     def snowFallDistance = 4;
8
9     // Drift distance
10    def snowDriftDistance = 4;
11
12    // Periodically move snow
13    def moveSnowTimeline = Timeline {
```

```
14          repeatCount: Timeline.INDEFINITE
15          keyFrames: [
16              KeyFrame {
17                  time: moveSnowTime
18                  action: moveSnow
19              }
20          ]
21      }
22      moveSnowTimeline.play();
```

The intent of this code is that the snowflakes should move downward by 4 pixels (the value of the `snowFallDistance` variable) every 100 milliseconds (given by `moveSnowTime`) and, at the same time, it may also move either left or right by 4 pixels (the value of the `snowDriftDistance` variable). The timeline repeats indefinitely, and on each cycle it invokes a function called `moveSnow()`, the implementation of which is shown here:

```
1       // Animates the snow.
2       function moveSnow() {
3           for (snowflake in snowflakes) {
4               // Move the snowflake down the screen
5               snowflake.centerY += snowFallDistance;
6               var random = rand.nextDouble();
7
8               // Add some random sideways movement
9               if (random > 0.7) {
10                  snowflake.centerX += snowDriftDistance;
11              } else if (random < 0.3) {
12                  snowflake.centerX -= snowDriftDistance;
13              }
14
15              // If the snowflake is off the screen, remove it
16              if (snowflake.centerY >= scene.height) {
17                  delete snowflake from scene.content;
18                  delete snowflake from snowflakes;
19              }
20          }
21      }
```

Line 3 of this code is a `for` loop that iterates over all the elements in the `snowflakes` sequence. Each time the loop is executed, a reference to the next snowflake from the sequence is assigned to the `snowflake` variable. The compiler infers that this variable is of type `Circle` because `snowflakes` is a sequence of `Circle` objects.

On line 5, the snowflake's y coordinate is increased by `snowFallDistance`, so that it appears to move down the screen. To determine whether the snowflake should also move sideways and in which direction, the code on line 6 gets a random number between 0 and 1. If this number happens to be greater than 0.7, the x coordinate of the snowflake is increased by `snowDriftDistance`, making it move to the right. If the random number is less than 0.3, the x coordinate is decreased by the same amount, making it move to the left. For values between 0.3 and 0.7, the x coordinate is unchanged, and the snowflake will move vertically downward.

Lines 16 to 19 detect whether the snowflake has reached the bottom of the scene, by comparing its y coordinate with the height of the scene. If it has, it removes the snowflake's node from the `content` sequence of the scene, which causes it to disappear, and also from the `snowflakes` sequence, which means it won't be moved again when this function is next called.[7]

If you add the preceding code to the end of the `SnowStorm.fx` file and fix up the import lines using your IDE's shortcut, you can run it to see the snowflakes falling.

Counting the Snowflakes

Finally, we would like the text at the bottom of the scene to show how many snowflakes are currently falling. We already know how many snowflakes there are—this is given by the number of elements in the `snowflakes` sequence. You can get the number of elements in a sequence by using the `sizeof` operator, like this:

```
sizeof snowflakes
```

To display this in the `Text` node, we change the code that initializes it to the following:

```
1   Text {
2       x: 25
3       y: bind scene.height - 10
4       font: Font {
5           size: 20
6       }
7       content: bind "Snowflakes: {sizeof snowflakes}"
8   }
```

The part of the text string on line 7 that is surrounded by braces is an *embedded expression*. The expression is evaluated, and its value is included in the string itself, before it is assigned to the `content` variable of the text node. Because we use the `bind` keyword in the object literal, whenever the size of the sequence changes, the expression is reevaluated and the new string is automatically written to the `content` variable. This means that the

---

[7] You might have noticed that this code removes the snowflake from the `snowflakes` sequence while the `for` loop is iterating over it. This might seem to be a dangerous thing to do. In Java, removing an element from a collection that is being iterated causes a `ConcurrentModificationException`, unless the element is removed by using the iterator's `remove()` method. In JavaFX, this is actually a safe operation because the removal causes a new sequence to be (logically) created in place of the old one. As a result, the iteration operation is unaffected because it is using the original copy of the sequence and does not see the modification. For more on this, see Chapter 7.

number of snowflakes displayed on the screen will always be updated whenever a snowflake is added to or removed from the `snowflakes` sequence. Binding, which is one of the most powerful features of JavaFX, is covered in Chapter 9, "Binding."

This completes the SnowStorm application. If you now run the code, you should see the snow falling and the number of snowflakes being continuously updated.

SnowStorm on the Web, a Phone, and TV

So far in this chapter, you have run the SnowStorm example as a desktop application from within the IDE. In the real world, an application has to be packaged, delivered, and possibly installed before it can be used. The JavaFX SDK provides a tool called `javafxpackager` that enables you to package an application so that it can be run on the desktop, from a web browser, on a cell phone, or on a TV enabled for JavaFX TV. We discuss `javafxpackager` in Chapter 28, "Packaging and Deployment," but you don't need to wait until then to run the example application in all of these host environments, because both the NetBeans and Eclipse plug-ins let you choose a target environment and then package and execute the application accordingly.

To run a packaged JavaFX application as an applet or through Java Web Start, you *must* be connected to the Internet, because in both cases an online copy of the JavaFX runtime is used rather than the one that is installed on your computer. If you are connected to the Internet but your computer fails to fetch the JavaFX runtime, you might need to adjust your proxy settings. On Windows, you can do this as follows:

1. Open the Windows Control Panel and start the Java Control Panel by double clicking the Java icon.

2. Click Network Settings.

3. In the window that appears, configure the IP address and port of your network proxy.

Running SnowStorm Using Java Web Start

Java Web Start is a useful tool that enables you to deliver and install desktop applications over the Internet or via a corporate intranet. Users navigate to your application through a link on a web page that points to a Java Network Launching Protocol (JNLP) file, which is a descriptor that contains information about the application, including, among other things, its name, an image to use while the application is being fetched from the web server, the version or versions of the Java platform on which the application can be run, references to the JAR files that make up the application, and any parameters used to configure the application's behavior. When the user's browser receives a JNLP file from a web server, it hands control to Java Web Start, which uses the information in the file to download the application code and launch it. Java Web Start is already installed on any machine that has a Java Runtime Environment.

When the application has been launched for the first time, Java Web Start creates a cached copy (in the file store local to the user) that it can use for future launches, thus avoiding the overhead of repeated downloads of JAR files. Java Web Start also checks whether it has the most up-to-date copy of the application and automatically replaces its cached copy when a new version is released.

Although the application is initially accessed through a web browser, it executes entirely outside of it (unlike an applet) and, after installation, may be launched directly from shortcuts installed on the user's desktop, without any intervention by the browser. If you'd like to read more about Java Web Start, go to the Java Web Start product page at http://java.sun.com/javase/technologies/desktop/javawebstart/index.jsp.

The NetBeans and Eclipse IDE plug-ins can create a JNLP file and then launch it using Java Web Start. All you have to do is change a setting in the application's run configuration.

Running with Java Web Start from NetBeans

To run SnowStorm using Java Web Start, make sure that its project is the main project in the IDE. If it is not the main project (the name of the main project is shown in boldface), right-click its owning project's node in the Projects view and select Set as Main Project. Now right-click the project node and select Properties to open the Project Properties window. Under Categories, select Run, which opens the page shown in Figure 4-10.

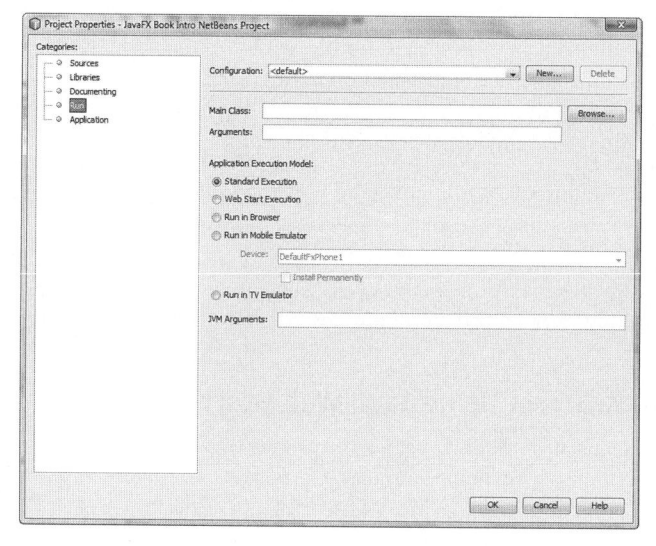

Figure 4-10   Configuring the Run properties of a JavaFX application in NetBeans

Click the New button and, in the window that appears, type the name **SnowStorm** and click OK. This name will be used to identify the run configuration that you are creating. Click the Browse button next to the Main Class field, choose `javafxexample.SnowStorm`, and click Select Main Class. Finally, under Application Execution Model, select Web Start Execution and click OK. This will close the Project Properties dialog.

You are now ready to launch the application using Java Web Start. To do so, you can do either of the following:

- Right-click the file `SnowStorm.fx` in the Projects view and select Run File.
- Make sure that the SnowStorm project is selected in the Projects view. Now choose SnowStorm from the drop-down on the Run toolbar and click the Run button, as shown in Figure 4-11.

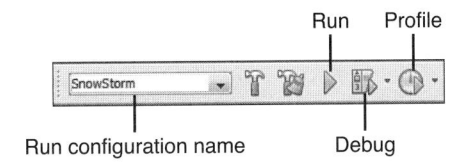

Figure 4-11 Selecting a run configuration from the Run toolbar in NetBeans

NetBeans creates a JNLP file, packages your application in a JAR file, and then launches it using Java Web Start.

Running with Java Web Start from Eclipse

To run SnowStorm using Java Web Start under Eclipse, you need to create a suitable run configuration. Select Run, Run Configurations to open the Run Configurations dialog, and then right-click JavaFX Application and select New. This opens a page that lets you tailor the parameters used to launch a JavaFX application, as shown in Figure 4-12.

Change the configuration name to **SnowStorm**, select SnowStorm as the project, set the Profile Target to Desktop Profile – Run with Web Start, and supply `javafxexample.SnowStorm` as the main class. Now when you click Run, Eclipse will save the configuration and launch the application using Java Web Start.

Running SnowStorm as an Applet

Applets were the original delivery mechanism for Java applications. Applets are started and downloaded automatically by a plug-in installed in the user's web browser, which means that they do not require manual installation. For this reason, applets are easy to run, but their limitations became clear soon after they first appeared. Because of shortcomings in the plug-in implementation, users complained that applets were slow to start and often caused the browser to hang while the code was being downloaded. The perception of applets as an inadequate delivery mechanism may change as a result of a complete rewrite of the browser plug-in that was delivered with Java SE 6 update 10 in the second half of 2008. The most significant feature of this rewrite is that applets are no longer loaded and executed within the browser process—instead, they run in one or more Java Virtual Machines (JVMs) hosted in separate processes. Among other things, this ensures that the browser does not appear to freeze while an applet is loading. It also makes it possible for

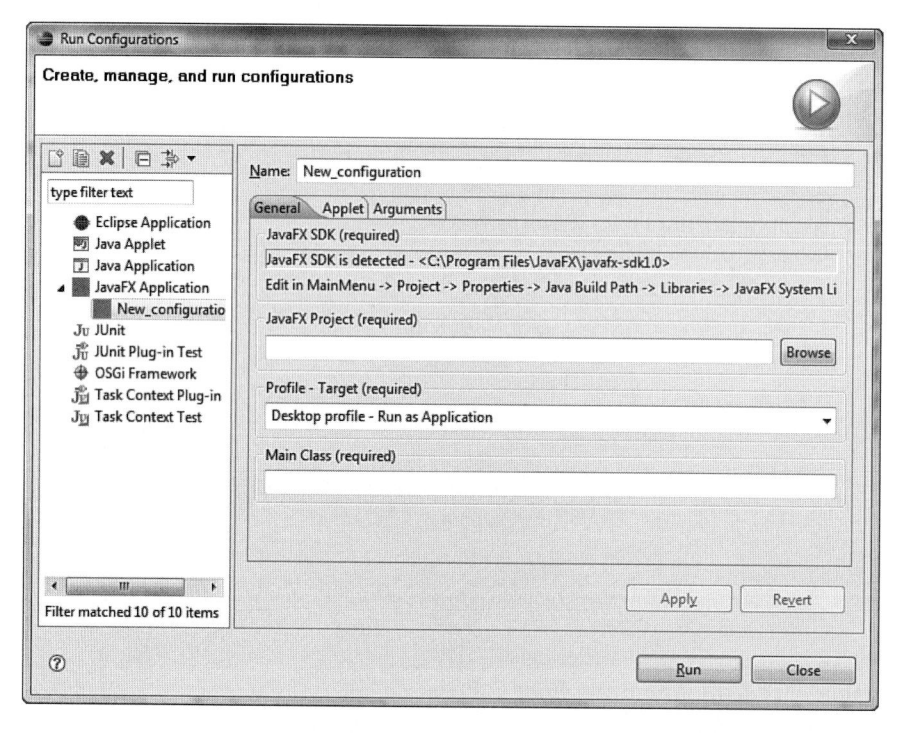

Figure 4-12   Creating a JavaFX run configuration for Eclipse

each applet to use its preferred version of the Java platform, whereas previously all applets had to share the same JVM instance.

Running as an Applet from NetBeans

To run SnowStorm as an applet from NetBeans, you need to modify the run configuration that you created in the previous section and also add some applet-specific details.

First, ensure that SnowStorm is the main project in the Projects view and then select Customize from the drop-down on the Run toolbar. This opens the Project Properties page and shows the Run information page. Choose the SnowStorm configuration and select Run in Browser. Next, under Categories, select Application. This opens the page shown in Figure 4-13.

On this page, you specify the width and height of the area in which the applet will run in the browser. This needs to be large enough to accommodate the Stage, because if it is too small, the user will see only part of the image. The image itself is 500 pixels wide and 375 pixels high, so these values should be used to set the applet's size, as shown in Figure 4-13. For reasons that we'll discuss shortly, make sure that Draggable Applet is selected. Click OK to close the Project Properties dialog, and then click the Run button

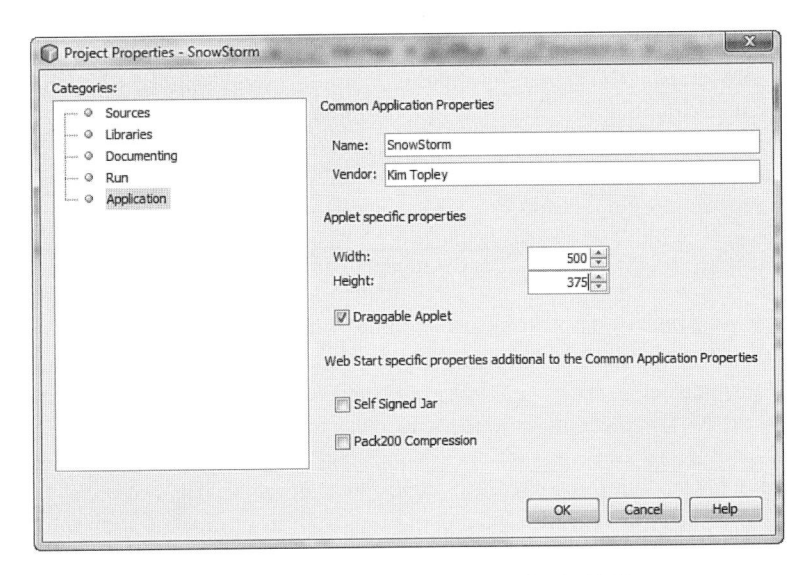

Figure 4-13 Specifying applet properties in NetBeans

on the Run toolbar. NetBeans creates a skeleton HTML page and launches it in your browser. Figure 4-14 shows a typical result.

Figure 4-14 SnowStorm as an applet

Running as an Applet from Eclipse

Running SnowStorm as an applet from within Eclipse requires a similar small change to the run configuration that you created in the "Running with Java Web Start from Eclipse," earlier in this chapter. First, select Run, Run Configurations. When the Run Configurations dialog opens, select the configuration for SnowStorm. On the General tab, change the Profile Target to Desktop Profile – Run as Applet, and then on the Applet tab, set the applet width to 500 and its height to 375. Now click Run to launch the applet in your browser.

Converting an Applet into a Desktop Application

Provided that you have selected Draggable Applet in the run configuration, you can drag the SnowStorm applet out of the browser page and drop it onto your desktop. To do this, hold down the Alt key, click and hold the left mouse button inside the SnowStorm applet, and drag the mouse across the screen. The stage will follow the mouse and, when you release the mouse button, a small cross will appear at the top right of the applet's window. If you click this cross, the applet will go back to its original position in the browser window.

If, instead, you leave the applet dragged out on the desktop and close the browser window, you will be prompted to create shortcuts. If you agree to this, a desktop shortcut will be created that will launch SnowStorm as a desktop application without involving the browser. This feature lets you allow users to initially try your application in applet form and then to install it by just dragging it out of the browser.

Running SnowStorm on the Mobile Emulator

Many millions of cell phones in use today have an embedded JVM. The Java platform on a cell phone is a slimmed-down version of Java SE that does not include Swing, AWT, Java2D, and many of the other APIs that desktop developers have become used to. Shortage of memory space means that even those packages and classes that *are* included are not necessarily complete. Programming a Java application for a cell phone—or writing a MIDlet, as they are called—is very different to writing a Swing application for the desktop. However, provided you are careful, it is possible to write a JavaFX application that will run *without changes* both on the desktop and in a cell phone. The JavaFX SDK includes an emulator that lets you compile your application and then run it as if it were executing on a mobile device.[8]

Using the Mobile Emulator from NetBeans

You probably won't be surprised to discover that you can run SnowStorm in the mobile emulator simply by changing a single setting in your NetBeans Run configuration.

---

[8] The mobile emulator is not a perfect simulation of any real handset, but it is a useful tool that can shorten the development cycle. In practice, it is advisable to test your application on a representative set of real devices before releasing it to customers.

Ensure that SnowStorm is the main project in the Projects view, and then select Customize in the drop-down in the Run toolbar. When the Project Properties dialog opens, select Run under Categories and change the Application Execution Model to Run in Mobile Emulator. Click OK to close the dialog, and then click the Run button on the Run toolbar.

NetBeans will compile the application for the mobile platform, open the mobile emulator, which is a separate program, and start the SnowStorm application in the simulated mobile device. You can see how this typically looks in Figure 4-15.

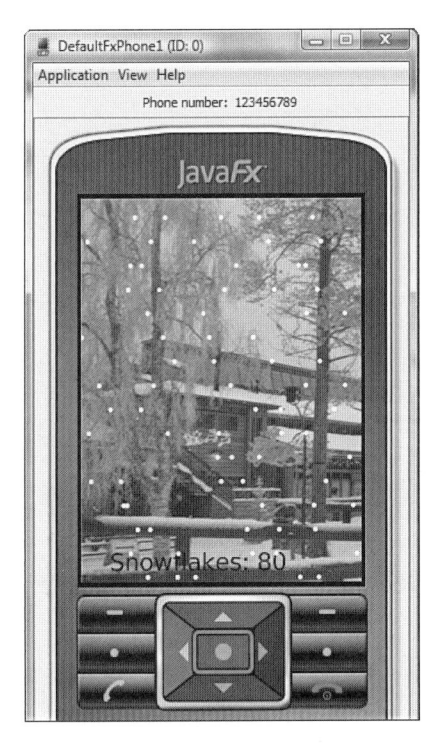

Figure 4-15   Running SnowStorm in the mobile emulator

Using the Mobile Emulator from Eclipse

To run SnowStorm in the mobile emulator from Eclipse, select the SnowStorm project in the Package Explorer view and select Run, Run Configurations. When the Run Configurations dialog opens, select the configuration for SnowStorm. On the General tab, change the Profile Target to Mobile Profile – Run in Emulator, and then click Run. The mobile emulator will start, and the SnowStorm application will be run as a MIDlet.

Running SnowStorm on the JavaFX TV Emulator

To run the SnowStorm example on the JavaFX TV emulator, simply select the TV emulator in the Project properties page in the NetBeans IDE or the Run configuration in Eclipse and run the application in the normal way.

Debugging the SnowStorm Application

Both NetBeans and Eclipse provide comprehensive debugging support for Java applications, and the same features can be used to debug JavaFX code. In this section, we briefly look at how to use NetBeans to place breakpoints in JavaFX code, step through the code, and inspect and change the values of variables. It is a simple matter to adapt the instructions in this section so that they work with Eclipse. You'll find more information about how to debug Java and JavaFX applications in the help documentation for both IDEs.

Setting Breakpoints

To set a breakpoint in JavaFX code, all you have to do is locate the line of code at which you want execution to be suspended and then either click in the left margin of the editor or place the cursor on the line and click Ctrl-F8. To suspend the execution of the SnowStorm application whenever it is time to move the snowflakes down the screen, locate the `moveSnow()` function and set a breakpoint on the first executable line of code after the `for` statement, as shown in Figure 4-16. As you can see, a square appears in the editor margin on the left, and the line is highlighted.

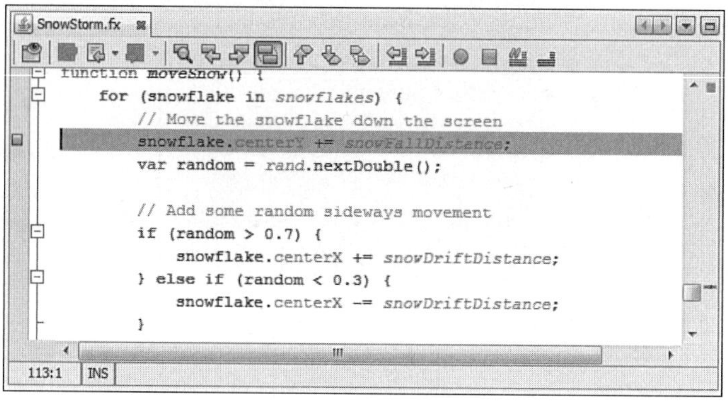

Figure 4-16   Inserting a breakpoint in JavaFX code

If you haven't already done so, create a run configuration for the SnowStorm application as described in the "Running SnowStorm using Java Web Start" section, earlier in this chapter. Make sure that you have selected Standard Execution as the execution model, as shown in Figure 4-10, and then select the run configuration in the drop-down on the Run toolbar. Now, instead of clicking the green Run button to start the application, click the Debug button to its right. (Refer to Figure 4-11 if you are unsure of the location of these buttons.) The application will run until it encounters the breakpoint in the `moveSnow()` function. When the breakpoint is reached, it will be brought into view and highlighted in the editor, and various debugging panes will be automatically opened, as shown in Figure 4-17.

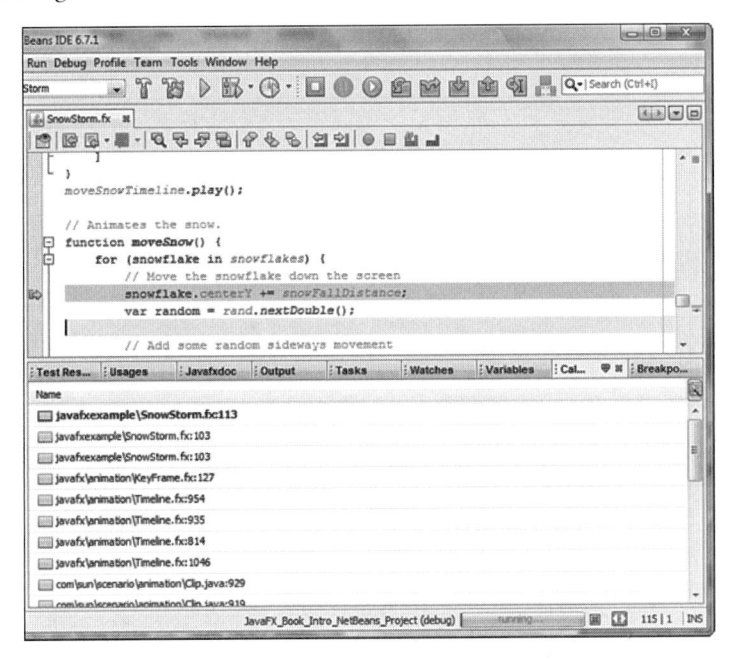

Figure 4-17   Execution suspended at a breakpoint

The Call Stack View

The Call Stack view, which is visible in Figure 4-17, can be used to find out how the application's flow of control reached your breakpoint. The most recent entries are at the top, starting with the line at which the breakpoint was encountered. Looking one line further down, you can see that the `moveSnow()` function was called from line 103 of the `SnowStorm.fx` file, which is in the `action` function of the snow movement timeline, as you would expect. (See Listing 4-1 at the end of the chapter to see how the line numbers map to the code.) The rest of the call stack shows the code path that the JavaFX runtime takes to schedule the activity within a timeline.

Inspecting Variables

With the application stopped at a breakpoint, you can use the Local Variables view to inspect the values of any variables that are in scope, as shown in Figure 4-18.

You can see, for example, that the variable `snowFallDistance` has the value 4, which is the actual value assigned to it on line 92 of the code. In the case of variables that refer to objects or sequences, you can expand the entry to show further detail. For example, in

74   Chapter 4 A Simple JavaFX Application

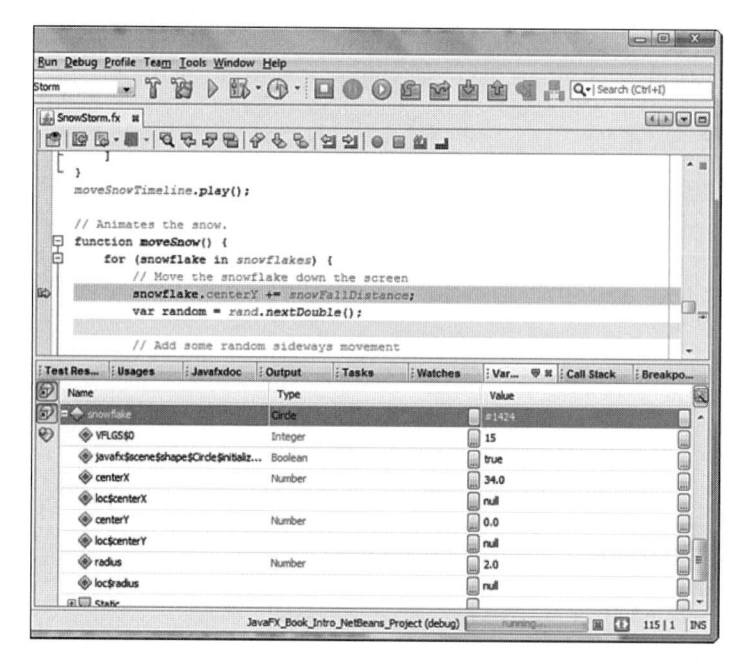

Figure 4-18   The Local Variables pane

Figure 4-18 the entry for the `snowflake` variable, which is an instance of the `javafx.scene.shape.Circle` class, has been expanded so that you can see its instance variables. As you can see, its center is currently at the coordinates x = 34 and y = 0. The content of this view varies as you step through the application's code—variables that come into scope are added, those that go out of scope are removed, and any changes in the values of the variables are reflected immediately.

Changing Variable Values

The Local Variables view allows you to modify a variable by simply typing the new value in place of the old. This means that you can change the value of `snowFallDistance` from 4 to a new value of 8 by typing that value into the Value column and pressing Enter. Figure 4-19 shows what the Local Variables view looks like after this change has been made.

Figure 4-19   Modifying a variable value

The application is currently stopped on the following line of code:

`snowflake.centerY += snowFallDistance;`

As you can see, the change made to the `snowFallDistance` variable will affect the value of the y coordinate of the snowflake as soon as this line of code is executed. The result should be that every snowflake moves twice as quickly as it otherwise would have. You can see whether this is the case by removing the breakpoint and then allowing the application to resume, or you can simply step over this line of code, allowing it to execute, and then inspect the result.

Stepping Through Code

Next to the Run toolbar in the main window of the IDE is the Debug toolbar, shown in Figure 4-20, which contains buttons that you can use to stop or resume execution and step through the application's code.

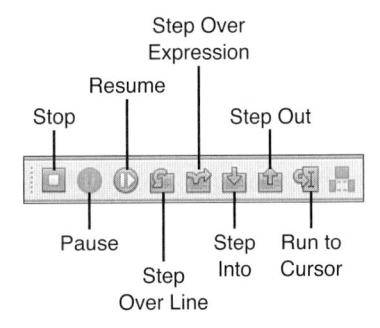

Figure 4-20   The Debug toolbar

Five buttons enable you to progressively execute lines of code:

- Step over Line: Executes the current line of code and stops before running the following line
- Step over Expression: Executes a method call within a line of code and remains within that line unless the whole line has now been executed, at which point it steps to the next line
- Step Into: Behaves like Step over Line unless the current expression is a function call, in which case it steps into the function and stops on its first executable line
- Step Out: Executes the rest of the current function and steps out, stopping at a point immediately after that at which the function was invoked
- Run to Cursor: Resumes the application and runs until the flow of control reaches the current location of the cursor or until another breakpoint is reached

If you now click the Step over Line button, NetBeans allows the code on line 113 of Listing 4-1 to be executed and then pause the application again. Line 113 adds the value of the variable `snowFallDistance`, which was just changed from 4 to 8, to the y coordinate of the snowflake. You can see the result in Figure 4-21. As you can see, the y coordinate of the snowflake changed from 0 to 8, indicating that the change that was made to the variable in the "Changing Variable Values" section, earlier in this chapter, was effective.

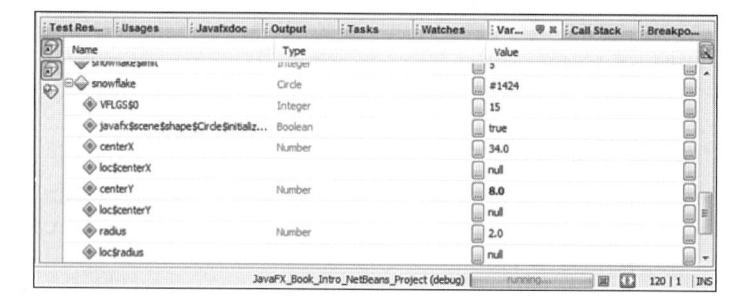

Figure 4-21   Stepping over one line of code

Disabling and Removing Breakpoints and Resuming Execution

After you have inspected and possibly corrected the state of an application, you usually want to resume execution. You do this by clicking the Resume button on the Debug toolbar, which is the green one to the left of center in Figure 4-20. The application then runs until it terminates or hits another breakpoint. If you don't want it to stop at a breakpoint any more, you can either disable or remove that breakpoint.

To disable a breakpoint, move the cursor to the margin of the line on which the breakpoint has been set and right-click to open the context menu shown in Figure 4-22.

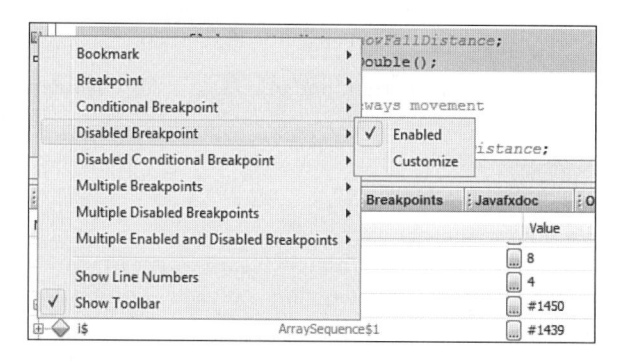

Figure 4-22   Breakpoint context menu

Open the Disabled Breakpoint submenu and click the Enabled item to toggle its state to Disabled. The highlight color on the breakpointed line will change to indicate that the breakpoint is disabled. A disabled breakpoint does not cause execution to stop, but it can be reenabled later by following the same sequence of steps. By contrast, if you remove the breakpoint, which you can do by simply clicking in the margin of the breakpointed line, NetBeans loses track of it. It is better to disable a breakpoint than to remove it if you think you might need to use it again later.

Profiling the SnowStorm Application

After you've completed, debugged, and deployed your application, you can sit back and wait for the compliments to flood in from your users, or at least that's what you hope. Sometimes, however, they complain. Even an application that appears to be functionally correct can have problems, and among these, perhaps the hardest to deal with is a performance problem. Performance problems come in two different flavors: either the application runs too slowly (or hogs too much resource and causes the user's PC to run slowly) or it chews up more and more memory, which can make everything slow down. The easiest way (and sometimes the only practical way) to solve a performance problem is to use a profiler. Profiling should be a routine part of the development process, because it can help to find bottlenecks and memory leaks before they become a problem in your production environment.

The NetBeans IDE includes a powerful and easy-to-use profiler that can monitor the CPU usage of your application and its memory consumption. In this section, we'll use it to examine the runtime performance characteristics of the SnowStorm application. There is also a freestanding profiler called `jvisualvm` that is based on the one in NetBeans. If you have Java 6 update 7 or later installed, you'll find it in the same folder as the rest of the JDK tools. Once you have seen how to use the NetBeans profiler, you will find it easy to use `jvisualvm`. You can find more information at http://visualvm.dev.java.net.

Using the NetBeans Profiler

To profile the SnowStorm application with the NetBeans profiler, select SnowStorm in the Run toolbar and then click the Profile button. (See Figure 4-11 for the location of this button.) The first time you do this, you will be prompted for permission to link the profiler to the project. Approve this, and then the Profile dialog, shown in Figure 4-23, will open.

Profiling always makes an application run more slowly because the process involves adding extra code to the functions and classes being monitored, which is executed as functions are called and as they return. The profiler allows you to choose which parts of your application to profile. The less you profile, the lower the overhead will be. The Filter field in the Profiler window lets you choose which classes should be profiled. By default, this will be only the classes in your project, and this is usually the best initial choice. If necessary, you can rerun the profiling session with additional classes selected. If you need even more profiling, you can define a filter that selects exactly the packages or the individual classes that are to be profiled. The Overhead indicator at the bottom of the Profile dialog indicates approximately how intrusive the selected level of profiling will be. For the purposes of this example, accept the default—that is, profile only your own project's classes and do not add any additional filtering.

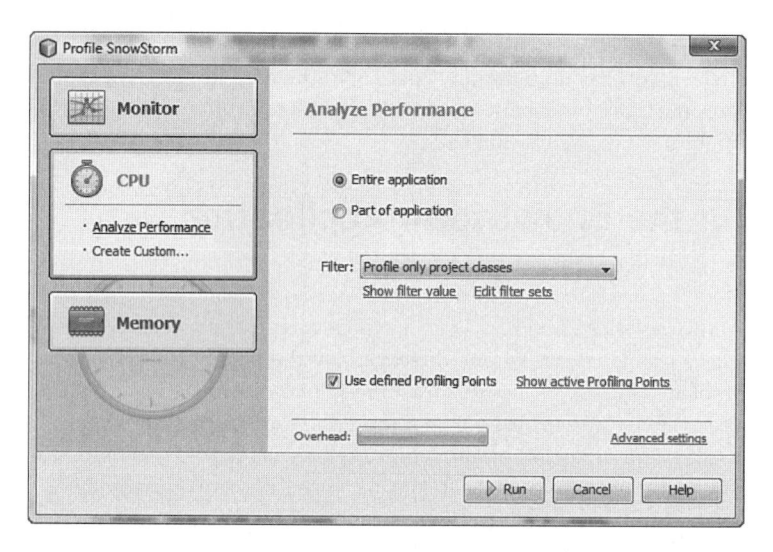

Figure 4-23 The NetBeans Profile dialog

Having decided how much to profile, you next need to choose whether to examine your application's CPU utilization or its memory consumption. This choice is made in the panel on the left side of the Profile dialog. We'll cover these two options separately. The sections that follow cover only a small part of what can be done with the profiler. I recommend that you read the documentation included with the IDE to find out more about this extremely powerful tool.

CPU Profiling

To select CPU profiling, click anywhere in the CPU block in the Profile dialog, and then click Run. Before NetBeans starts your application, it may need to perform a calibration operation. When this is complete, your application will be run under the control of the profiler. You can interact with the profiler through the Profiler view, which is opened automatically and is shown in Figure 4-24.

You can get a real-time view of the profiler's results by clicking the Live Results button. This shows which functions are consuming the greatest amount of CPU time. You can see a snapshot of the results for the SnowStorm application in Figure 4-25.

As you can see, the application is spending almost all of its time (97% of it) in the `moveSnow()` and `addNewSnow()` functions. This is not really surprising, because the application is all about animating snowflakes. The percentages shown are the amount of time spent in each method, *as a proportion of the time for which the application is running*. This does *not* mean that these functions are consuming 97% of your computer's available CPU time! To get a feel for exactly how much time it might be using, click the Thread button in the Profiler view. You will be prompted to enable thread monitoring and then the thread-

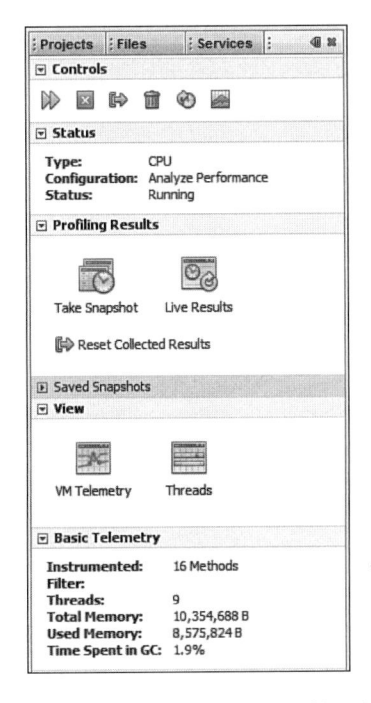

Figure 4-24   The NetBeans Profiler view

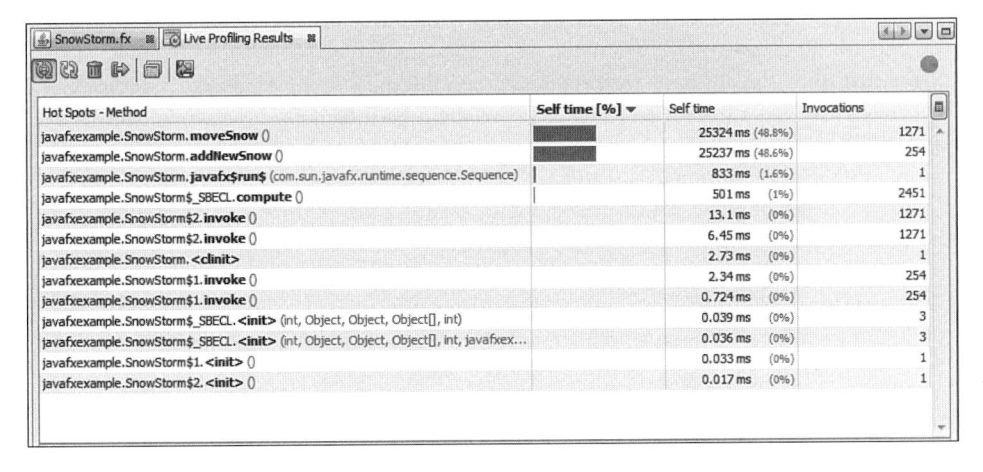

Figure 4-25   Live CPU profiling results

monitoring pane, shown in Figure 4-26, will open. Allow the application to run for a while so that enough profiling points are collected.

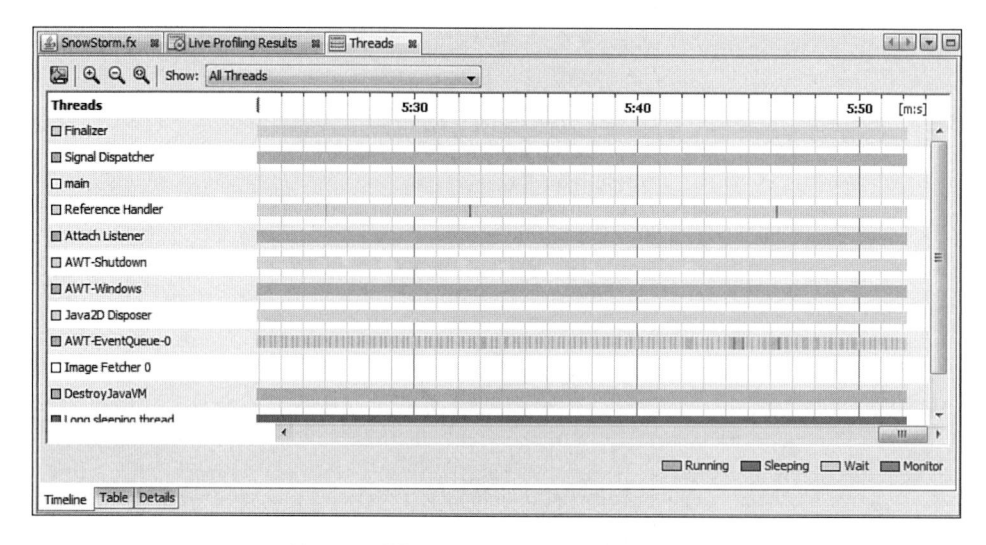

Figure 4-26   The thread-monitoring pane

JavaFX code runs entirely in the thread labeled `AWT-EventQueue-0`. The background color (yellow onscreen) indicates the period of time for which this thread has been monitored. The times at which the thread is actually running application code are indicated by green and red lines. As Figure 4-26 shows, there are comparatively few of these, because the code in the profiled functions runs so quickly that it hardly registers. This tells us that this application does not have a problem with CPU resource consumption. You will notice that some threads have a continuous green line, which would appear to indicate that they are always running. In fact, this is not the case. It happens because the thread is executing native code (for example, blocked while reading a socket) and therefore appears to the profiler to be running.

As well as viewing live results, you can take a snapshot of performance data by clicking the Take Snapshot button. Each snapshot appears as a tab in the editor area of the main window. You can flick between tabs to compare snapshots or you can save a snapshot to a file so that it can be loaded back and analyzed later, using the Save buttons shown at the top left of Figure 4-27.

Memory Profiling

You can use the memory-profiling feature of the NetBeans profiler to investigate memory leaks. The SnowStorm application doesn't have any memory leaks, but it would if we had forgotten to remove a snowflake from the `snowflakes` sequence after it had reached the bottom of the scene. To give ourselves a memory leak to look it, comment out line 126 of the file `SnowStorm.fx`, like this:

```
124         if (snowflake.centerY >= scene.height) {
125             delete snowflake from scene.content;
```

```
126    //            delete snowflake from snowflakes;
127    }
```

Now start the profiler by clicking the Profile button as before, but this time choose Memory Profiling in the Profile dialog. The Profile dialog offers you the option of increasing or decreasing the amount of profiling information to be gathered. As before, collecting more information causes more overhead, so the usual approach is to accept the default for the first run and add more later, if you need to. To start gathering information, click the Run button. When the application starts running, the profiling pane appears, and you can click the Live Results button to see the objects that are being created, as shown in Figure 4-28.

When looking for memory leaks, it is important to realize that a lot of garbage may remain uncollected until the JVM needs to reclaim space. Just because there is apparently a large number of a particular type of object shown in the memory profile does not necessarily mean that those objects are not being collected when they should. If you suspect a leak, the first thing to do is to force a full garbage collection. You can do this by clicking the button that looks like a dustbin on the profiling pane. If you do this, you'll find that there is clearly a memory leak. For one thing, the total amount of used memory is increasing and does not fall very far after garbage collection. This value can be seen in the Basic Telemetry section at the bottom of the profiling pane and also in Figure 4-29.

If you look at the objects that are taking up most space, you'll see that they all belong to the JavaFX runtime. None of them is obviously anything to do with code in the SnowStorm application. Just to make sure, let's see what is happening to objects that we might have created. To do this, type the value **javafx.scene.shape** in the Filter field below the memory profiling results and press Enter. This narrows down the results only to

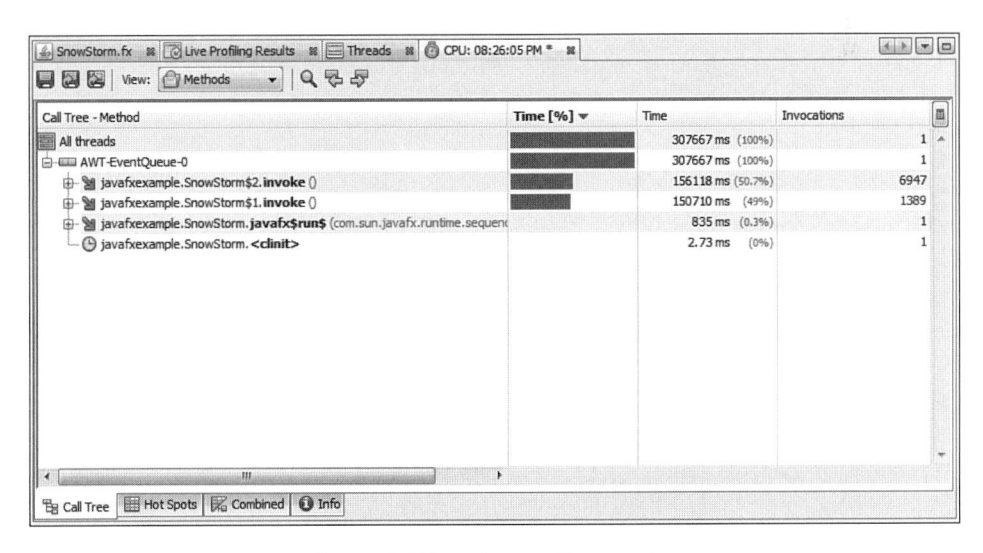

Figure 4-27   A CPU profile snapshot

82   Chapter 4 A Simple JavaFX Application

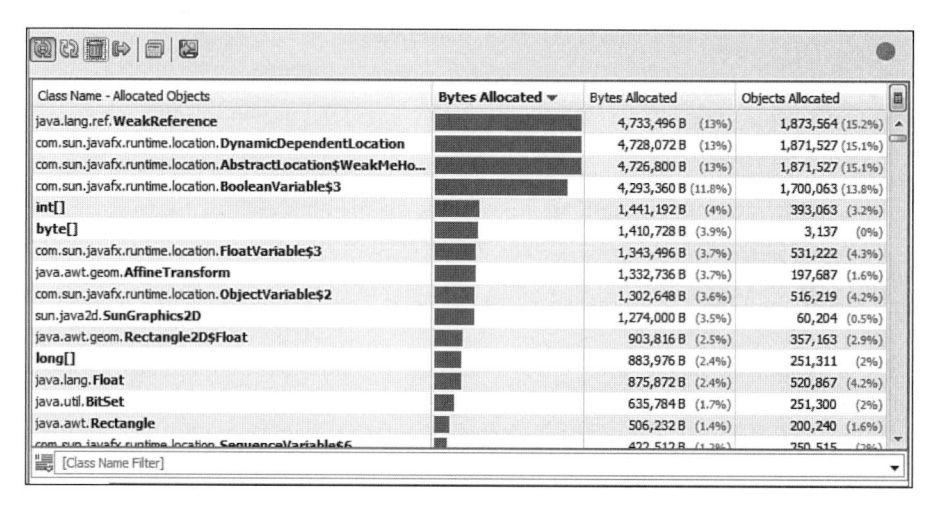

Figure 4-28   Using the memory profiler

Figure 4-29   Basic Telemetry in the NetBeans profiler

objects whose classnames match the filter string. You will immediately see that lots of circle objects have been allocated and, most significantly, if you force a garbage collection, none of them are released—the count of active instances continues to rise. This points pretty directly to the bug that we deliberately introduced. If you fix the bug and rerun the profiler, you'll see that the memory leak is gone.

As with the CPU profiler, the memory profiler enables you to take and save snapshots for comparison or later analysis.

Source Code for the SnowStorm Application

For reference, here is the complete source code for the SnowStorm application.

Listing 4-1   The SnowStorm Application

```
1    package javafxexample;
2
3    import java.lang.System;
4    import java.util.Random;
5    import javafx.animation.KeyFrame;
6    import javafx.animation.Timeline;
```

Source Code for the SnowStorm Application

```
7       import javafx.scene.image.Image;
8       import javafx.scene.image.ImageView;
9       import javafx.scene.paint.Color;
10      import javafx.scene.Scene;
11      import javafx.scene.shape.Circle;
12      import javafx.scene.text.Font;
13      import javafx.scene.text.Text;
14      import javafx.stage.Stage;
15
16      // Static user interface setup
17
18      // The scene that contains the snow.
19      var scene:Scene;
20
21      Stage {
22          title: "JavaFX Snow Storm"
23          resizable: false
24          scene: scene = Scene {
25              content: [
26                  ImageView {
27                      image: Image {
28                          url: "{__DIR__}SnowScene.png"
29                      };
30                  },
31                  Text {
32                      x: 25
33                      y: bind scene.height - 10
34                      font: Font {
35                          size: 20
36                      }
37                      content: bind "Snowflakes: {sizeof snowflakes}"
38                  }
39              ]
40          }
41      }
42
43      // Animation
44
45      // The snowflakes
46      var snowflakes:Circle[];
47
48      // Time interval for new snow.
49      def newSnowTime = 500ms;
50
51      // Number of snowflakes per row
52      def snowflakesPerLine = 5;
53
54      // Random number generator
```

Chapter 4 A Simple JavaFX Application

```
55    def rand = new Random(System.currentTimeMillis());
56
57    // Periodically add snow
58    def addSnowTimeline = Timeline {
59        repeatCount: Timeline.INDEFINITE
60        keyFrames: [
61            KeyFrame {
62                time: newSnowTime
63                action: addNewSnow
64            }
65        ]
66    };
67    addSnowTimeline.play();
68
69    // Adds new snow to the scene.
70    function addNewSnow() {
71        var sectionWidth =
72            (scene.width + snowflakesPerLine - 1) / snowflakesPerLine;
73        for (i in [0..<snowflakesPerLine]) {
74            var x = sectionWidth * i + rand.nextInt(sectionWidth);
75            var snowflake = Circle {
76                centerX: x
77                centerY: 0
78                radius: 2
79                cache: true
80                fill: Color.WHITE
81            }
82            insert snowflake into scene.content;
83            insert snowflake into snowflakes;
84        }
85    }
86    // Animating the snowflakes
87
88    // Time interval for moving the snow.
89    def moveSnowTime = 100ms;
90
91    // How far the snow falls in each frame
92    def snowFallDistance = 4;
93
94    // Drift distance
95    def snowDriftDistance = 4;
96
97    // Periodically move snow
98    def moveSnowTimeline = Timeline {
99        repeatCount: Timeline.INDEFINITE
100       keyFrames: [
101           KeyFrame {
```

```
102                    time: moveSnowTime
103                    action: moveSnow
104                }
105            ]
106        }
107        moveSnowTimeline.play();
108
109        // Animates the snow.
110        function moveSnow() {
111            for (snowflake in snowflakes) {
112                // Move the snowflake down the screen
113                snowflake.centerY += snowFallDistance;
114                var random = rand.nextDouble();
115
116                // Add some random sideways movement
117                if (random > 0.7) {
118                    snowflake.centerX += snowDriftDistance;
119                } else if (random < 0.3) {
120                    snowflake.centerX -= snowDriftDistance;
121                }
122
123                // If the snowflake is off the screen, remove it
124                if (snowflake.centerY >= scene.height) {
125                    delete snowflake from scene.content;
126                    delete snowflake from snowflakes;
127                }
128            }
129        }
```

II

The JavaFX Script Language

5

Variables and Data Types

JavaFX applications manipulate data held either in script variables or as instance variables of JavaFX classes.[1] Every item of data has a specific type, such as `String` or `Number`, which determines the values that it accepts and the operations that may be performed on it. Like Java, JavaFX has a small set of basic data types that are intrinsic to the language. It also has a runtime library of class types that are not part of the language itself, and which you can use to build user interfaces, retrieve information from a web server, and so on. In this chapter, you learn about the basic data types, how to declare and initialize script variables, and how to make use of both JavaFX and Java classes in your application.

The example code for this chapter can be found in the `javafxdatatypes` package in the JavaFX Book Language project, unless otherwise specified.

Variable Declarations

A JavaFX variable is declared using either a `var` or a `def` statement. Syntactically, these statements are identical, so we'll use only the `var` statement in most of the examples that follow.

Declaring Variables with `var`

The syntax of the `var` statement is as follows:

```
[modifiers] var identifier[:type][ = expression] [trigger clause];
```

A variable declaration consists of several parts, most of which are optional:

- The optional *modifiers* determine the visibility of the variable to code outside of the script and the access granted to that code. We discuss this in the "Visibility of Variables" section, later in this chapter.

---

[1] JavaFX code can also access data in Java classes, but that is not really relevant to the discussion in this chapter.

- The *identifier* is the name by which the variable is known.
- The *type* is the JavaFX data type of the variable, which is almost always optional. If you don't specify the type, the compiler attempts to work out what it should be. This is a very useful feature that we discuss more fully in the "Type Inference" section, later in this chapter. In this chapter, for the sake of clarity, some of the examples include an explicit type, but in reality, when writing code it is much easier and more natural to omit the type whenever possible.
- The optional *expression* supplies an initial value for the variable.
- The optional *trigger clause* allows you to execute one or more statements when the value of the variable is initially set or when it changes. It is discussed in Chapter 10, "Triggers."

The identifier name is subject to the same constraints as those applied to identifiers in Java, as follows:

- The first character must be an uppercase or lowercase letter, a dollar sign ($), or an underscore (_).[2]
- The other characters must be uppercase or lowercase letters, a dollar sign, an underscore, or a numeric digit.
- The name may not be a JavaFX reserved word.

It is possible to break these rules by enclosing the identifier in French quotes. The following example creates a variable called var, which would otherwise clash with the JavaFX keyword:

```
var <<var>>:String = "A variable called var";
var anotherString:String = <<var>>;
```

The quotes must be used both when the variable is declared and wherever it is used. It is also possible to create variables whose names are numeric:

```
var <<1234>>:Number;
```

The motivation for this feature is to simplify the automatic generation of JavaFX source code from sources that do not have the same rules for identifiers (such as Scalable Vector Graphics [SVG] files), but the use of this technique in hand-written code is not recommended.

---

[2] Strictly speaking, the first character of an identifier must be one for which the method isJavaIdentifierStart() in the class java.lang.Character returns true, whereas subsequent characters must be chosen from the set for which isJavaIdentifierPart() is true. This includes the set of characters in the simpler preceding description.

The following declaration creates a variable called `value` whose type is `Number` (a JavaFX type that will be introduced later in this chapter) and assigns the value 3 to it:

```
var value:Number = 3;
```

The initializer may be an expression of arbitrary complexity that resolves to a value of type `Number` or to a value of a type that can be converted to `Number`. As a simple example, the following declarations create two variables called `value1` and `value2` with given initial values and a third called `sum` that is initialized to the sum of the first two:

```
var value1:Number = 3;
var value2:Number = 4;
var sum:Number = value1 + value2;
```

JavaFX expressions are covered in detail in Chapter 6, "Expressions, Functions, and Object Literals."

Like Java, it isn't necessary to assign a value to a variable when you declare it, so the following code is valid and prints `Value is 3`:

```
var value:Number;
value = 3;
println("Value is {value}");
```

The expression within the curly braces in the preceding example is an *embedded expression*. The expression is evaluated at runtime, and the result is inserted in its place. See "Embedded Expressions" later in this chapter for more details.

Unlike Java, there is also no absolute requirement to initialize a variable before you use it, so the following code is legal in JavaFX even though it would not be if it appeared in a method definition in Java:

```
var value:Number;
println("Value is {value}");
```

This is allowed because a variable that has no explicit assignment at the point of declaration is given a default value, which depends on its type. The default values for the basic types are listed in Table 5-1, later in the chapter, from which you can see that the initial

Table 5-1 **The Basic JavaFX Data Types**

Type Name	Description	Closest Java Type	Default Value
Number	A floating-point value	java.lang.Float	0.0
Integer	An integer value	java.lang.Integer	0
Byte	A small, signed value	java.lang.Byte	0
Short	A small, signed value	java.lang.Short	0
Long	A long value	java.lang.Long	0
Float	A floating-point value	java.lang.Float	0
Double	A double-precision floating-point value	java.lang.Double	0

Table 5-1 The Basic JavaFX Data Types (*Continued*)

Type Name	Description	Closest Java Type	Default Value
`Character`	A single Unicode character	`java.lang.Character`	`\u0000`
`Boolean`	The value `true` or `false`	`java.lang.Boolean`	`false`
`String`	An immutable string	`java.lang.String`	Empty string
`Duration`	A length of time	None	0

value of the variable `value` in the preceding code would be `0.0`. Uninitialized string variables are assigned the empty string:

```
var emptyString:String;
println("String is [{emptyString}]");
```

The preceding code prints the following:

```
String is []
```

JavaFX does not have the separate concepts of "primitive" and "boxed" types like the `int` and `Integer` types in Java. All variables act like reference (boxed) types.

Declaring Variables with `def`

The syntax of the `def` statement is the same as `var`. Here's an example of a variable declared using `def`:

```
def PI:Number = Math.PI;
```

You should use `def` when you want to declare a variable whose value will not change,[3] like the value of `PI` previously shown.

A `def` statement *must* include an initializer, so the following code is not valid:

```
def PI:Number;     // Not valid - must be initialized.
```

Following declaration, assignment to or modification of the variable is not allowed:

```
def value:Number = 10; // OK
value++;              // Invalid - modification not allowed.
value = 11;           // Invalid - modification not allowed.
```

---

[3] Actually, the value of a variable declared using a `def` statement *can* change if it were initialized with a binding—for details, see Chapter 8, "Controlling Program Flow." For this reason, using `def` is not quite the same as applying the Java `final` keyword to a variable declaration.

Variable Scopes

Variables can be declared in the body of a script, within a code block (such as an `if` statement or a `for` loop) or within a class definition. The location of the declaration determines the variable's scope. The following applies equally to both `var` and `def` declarations.

Variables declared in the body of a script (script variables) are visible from anywhere inside the script:

```
def n:Number = Math.PI;        // A script variable
println("Value is {n}");       // A reference to the script variable
```

Script variables can be made visible to code executing in other scripts; see "Visibility of Variables," later in this chapter. By default, a script variable can be used only within the script in which it is declared.

A variable declared within a code block, such as a function, (see Chapter 6) is referred to as a *local variable*. It is visible only with that block (and any nested blocks):

```
function computeArea(radius:Number, debug:Boolean):Number {
    var area:Number = Math.PI * radius * radius; // A local variable
    if (debug) {
        println("Area is {area}"); // A reference to the local variable
    }
}   // The local variable is now out of scope

println("{area}");    // Compilation error - area not known here
```

A JavaFX class holds its state in instance variables, which are declared in the same way as other variables. Each instance of the class has a separate copy of its instance variables (hence the name):

```
public class Position {
    public-init var x:Number;
    public-init var y:Number;
}
```

The preceding code declares a class called `Position` that has two instance variables called `x` and `y`, both of type `Number`. Access to these variables requires an instance of the class:

```
var pos:Position = Position {
                x: 10      // Initialize x to 10
                y: 20      // Initialize y to 20
            };
println("x is {pos.x}, x is {pos.y}");
```

The `public-init` modifier indicates that these variables can be initialized and read by any code, but after initialization may only be modified by code in the script in which the declaration appears. For information on how to create your own JavaFX classes, see Chapter 11, "JavaFX Script Classes."

Object Types

You can declare a variable that refers to any instance of any object by using that object's classname as the type. For example, the following code declares a variable that references an instance of the `javafx.stage.Stage` class:

```
import javafx.stage.Stage;
var stage:Stage = Stage { title: "Stage Title" };
```

The declared type of the variable may be a JavaFX class, a Java class, or a Java interface[4]:

```
import java.lang.Comparable;
import java.text.DateFormat;
import java.util.GregorianCalendar;
import javafx.stage.Stage;

var stage:Stage = Stage { title: "Stage Title" };      // A JavaFX class
var df:DateFormat = DateFormat.getDateInstance();       // A Java class
var comp:Comparable = new GregorianCalendar();          // A Java interface
```

If the type is a JavaFX or Java class, any value that is subsequently assigned to it must be either an instance of that specific class or of a subclass. For example, the following code is valid because `Text` is a subclass of `Node`, both being classes in the GUI library:

```
import javafx.scene.Node;
import javafx.scene.text.Text;
var node:Node = Text {};    // Text is a subclass of Node.
```

If the type is an interface, its value must be an instance of a JavaFX or Java class that implements that interface:

```
// GegorianCalendar implements Comparable
var comp:Comparable = new GregorianCalendar();
```

The compiler checks that the type of a variable is compatible with any value assigned to it and will reject any attempt to perform an incompatible assignment.

As a special case, any object variable may be assigned the distinguished value `null`, which is typically used to mean "no object." Unlike Java, dereferencing an object reference that has the value `null` does *not* throw a `NullPointerException`. Instead, the result is the default value of the data type being referenced. For example, the `visible` instance variable of the `Stage` class is a `Boolean`, for which the default value is `false`, so the following code prints `false`:

```
import javafx.stage.Stage;

var stage:Stage = null;
```

---

[4] This list does not contain JavaFX interface because there is no such thing!

```
println(stage.visible);    // Dereferencing null yields the default
                           // value of the type - here, Boolean
```

JavaFX classes may have state (represented by its instance variables) and functions that can be invoked to have the class perform an operation and possibly return a value. The public functions and instance variables of a class make up its application programming interface (API). The API for the classes in the JavaFX runtime can be found in the reference documentation that is delivered with the JavaFX SDK. JavaFX classes can also have instance variables and functions that are not part of its public interface and which are therefore not available to application code. Whether a function or an instance variable is part of the API is determined by its visibility and access modifiers. See the section "Visibility of Variables," later in this chapter, the section "Visibility of Functions" in Chapter 6, and the discussion of JavaFX classes in Chapter 11 for details.

Creating a JavaFX Object Instance

To create a JavaFX object with the default values for all of its instance variables, use the following syntax:

```
import javafx.stage.Stage
var stage:Stage = Stage {};
```

The curly brackets after the classname form an object literal, which, in this case, is empty. An object literal is used to initialize an object's instance variables while it is being instantiated. The following code creates a Stage and specifies initial values for its title and visible instance variables:

```
var stage:Stage = Stage {
            title: "Stage Title"
            visible: true
        };
```

An instance variable is initialized by quoting its name followed by a colon and then an expression that supplies the required value. Instance variables for which there is no initializer are given their default value, which is taken from the class definition. Object literals can also contain local variable declarations and bindings and are discussed further in Chapter 6.

Invoking JavaFX Functions

As in Java, to invoke a function defined within a JavaFX class, you need an instance of that class. The following code creates a Stage and then invokes its close() function:

```
var stage:Stage = Stage {
            title: "Stage Title"
            visible: true
        };
stage.close()
```

Functions may have arguments and may return a value:

```
var duration:Duration = 1s;
var half:Duration = duration.div(2);
```

The first line uses a special syntax provided by the compiler to create an instance of the `Duration` class that represents a time interval of 1 second. The second line invokes the `div()` function of that class with argument 2, which returns a new `Duration` object. In this case, the new value is assigned to a variable called `half`.

As noted in Chapter 4, "A Simple JavaFX Application," in JavaFX functions do not need to be declared inside a class. You can invoke a function that is declared outside a class, but in the same script, (a script function) by simply quoting its name and supplying appropriate argument values—no class instance is required:

```
public function computeArea(radius:Number, debug:Boolean):Number {
    var area:Number = Math.PI * radius * radius;
    if (debug) {
        println("Area is {area}");
    }
}
var area:Number = computeArea(2.0);
```

A script function that has modifiers that make it visible outside the script can be referenced by qualifying it with the name of the script.[5] For example, if the `computeArea()` function previously shown were declared in a script file called `Circles.fx` that is in a package called `geometry`, it could be invoked from outside the script like this:

```
var area:Number = geometry.Circles.computeArea(1.0);
```

As another example, the `javafx.scene.paint.Color` class declares a number of public script functions that let you create `Color` instances. The following code invokes one of the overloaded `color()` functions in that class, which returns a `Color` instance initialized with the `red`, `green`, and `blue` values passed as arguments:

```
import javafx.scene.paint.Color;
var aColor:Color = Color.color(0.5, 0.4, 0.3);
```

Accessing Variables

To access an *instance* variable, you need an instance of its owning class, whereas a *script* variable can be referenced by qualifying it with the script name. The following code sets and then reads the `visible` instance variable of a `Stage` object:

```
var stage:Stage = Stage { title: "Stage Title" };
stage.visible = true;    // Sets the "visible" instance variable
```

---

[5] Think of a script function as being like a static function in Java.

```
                           // of the stage
var isVisible:Boolean = stage.visible;    // Gets the value of "visible"
println("Stage visible: {isVisible}");
```

By contrast, the script variable BLACK of the Color class can be read simply by using its name, qualified by that of the class, as if it were a static variable in a Java class:

```
var color:Color = Color.BLACK;
```

Using Java Classes in JavaFX Code

A JavaFX application can use a Java class just as easily as a JavaFX class, and in almost all cases, the syntax is the same. The only difference is that the creation of a Java object instance usually requires the use of the new keyword, which operates in the same way as it does in Java, instead of an object literal[6]:

```
import java.util.Date;
var date:Date = new Date(99, 10, 20);
```

This code creates an instance of the Java Date class that is initialized to refer to November 20, 1999. When a Java method or constructor is invoked, the JavaFX types of the arguments that are supplied are converted as necessary to their corresponding Java types. In the previous example, the three arguments are all JavaFX Integer types, which are automatically converted to the Java primitive type int before the Date constructor is called.

An object literal can be used instead of new to construct an instance of a Java class when that class has a constructor that does not require any arguments, so the following lines of code are equivalent:

```
var d1:Date = Date {};
var d2:Date = new Date();
```

Basic Data Types

JavaFX has 11 basic data types, as listed in Table 5-1 (along with the Java types to which they most closely relate).

This section discusses the first ten of these data types; the Duration type is mainly used in conjunction with the language features that make it possible to create animations and is covered in Chapter 18, "Animation."

Numeric Types

JavaFX has two principal numeric types—Integer and Number—and six others that are more or less the same as the Java types of the same name. The JavaFX Integer type is

---

[6] You can also use the new keyword to create a JavaFX object, but the preferred style is to use an object literal.

essentially the same as the Java class `java.lang.Integer`, while `Number` corresponds to `java.lang.Float`. The JavaFX `Number` and `Float` types are actually the same—`Float` was included in the language for the sake of uniformity with the rest of the Java-derived numeric types. Wherever possible, `Number` should be used in place of `Float`.

> **Note**
>
> In JavaFX 1.0, `Integer` and `Number` were the only numeric types available. The additional six types were added in the JavaFX 1.1 release to make it easier for the compiler to choose between overloaded Java methods that have one or more numeric arguments. In some cases, with only two possible numeric types, it is not obvious which overloaded method should be used. By providing numeric types that map directly to their Java counterparts, the compiler makes it possible for the programmer to indicate exactly which variant of an overloaded method is required. For more information on this, see Chapter 6.

The ranges of values that these types can hold are shown in Table 5-2. Arithmetic operations that generate values that are outside these ranges do not report an error—instead, the value is either silently truncated to one that is inside the allowed range or converted to one of three special, fixed values that indicate an error condition. See the section "Range Errors in Arithmetic Operations" in Chapter 6 for details.

Table 5-2   **Value Ranges for JavaFX Numeric Types**

Type	Maximum Value	Minimum Value
Integer	+2147483647	-2147483648
Number	+3.4028235E38	-3.4028235E38
Byte	+127	-128
Short	+32767	-32768
Long	+ 9223372036854775807	-9223372036854775808
Float	+3.4028235E38	-3.4028235E38
Double	+1.7976931348623157E308	-1.7976931348623157E308
Character	\u0000	\uFFFF

Integer Types

The values of the integer-valued types (`Integer`, `Byte`, `Short`, and `Long`) can be represented in decimal, octal, or hexadecimal notation:

```
var decimalNumber:Integer = 255;
var octalNumber:Integer = 0377;      // Octal 377 = decimal 255
var hexNumber:Integer = -0xFF;
println("Values: {decimalNumber}/{octalNumber}/{hexNumber}");
```

Hexadecimal numbers begin with `0x` or `0X` followed by at least one further character from the range `0` to `9` and `A` to `F`, in either uppercase or lowercase. Octal numbers begin with `0` followed by at least one digit in the range `0` to `7`.

The result of running the preceding code is the following:

```
Values: 255/255/-255
```

When a literal value to be assigned is too large, the compiler flags an error:

```
var b:Byte = 255;          // Max value is +127: error
var s:Short = 32768;       // Max value is +32767: error
var i:Integer = 2147483648; // Max value is 2147483647: error
```

Number Types

`Number`, `Float`, and `Double` are the JavaFX types that hold floating-point values. Normally, number literals are written in decimal, but octal and hexadecimal notation can also be used, provided that there is no fractional part:

```
var number1:Number = 377.123; // Decimal number
var number2:Number = 0377;    // Octal number
var number3:Number = 0xFF;    // Hex number

// Octal fractional number not allowed: compilation error
var number4:Number = 0377.123;

// Hex fractional number not allowed: compilation error
var number5:Number = 0xFF.123;
```

Floating-point values can also be written in exponential form:

```
var bigNumber:Number = 1.234E+6;
var smallNumber:Number = 1.234E-3;
println("bigNumber: {bigNumber}, smallNumber: {smallNumber}");
```

This code prints the following:

```
bigNumber: 1234000.0, smallNumber: 0.001234
```

The exponent is introduced by the letter `E` or `e`, followed optionally by a sign and the exponent value itself in decimal. Embedded whitespace is not allowed, so `1.234 E-6` is not valid.

Conversion of Numeric Values

The compiler will automatically convert an `Integer` (or `Byte`, `Short`, `Character` or `Long`) value to a `Number` (or a `Float` or `Double`) on assignment:

```
var intValue:Integer = 1234;
var numberValue:Number = intValue; // Conversion from Integer to Number
println("intValue: {intValue}, numberValue: {numberValue}");
```

The code above prints the following:

```
intValue: 1234, numberValue: 1234.0
```

The same is true of expressions that evaluate to an `Integer` value:

```
var numberValue:Number = 1 + 2 + 3 + 4;
```

These conversion are valid and risk-free because a `Number` can hold any value that an `Integer` can, without loss of precision. The reverse is not true, however—a `Number` can hold a fractional value or one that is too large to be represented by an `Integer`. For that reason, an implicit conversion from `Number` to `Integer` is allowed but is flagged with a warning at compile time:

```
// Gives a warning: 1234.00 is a Number, not an Integer
var intValue1:Integer = 1234.00;

var numberValue1:Number = 1234.12;

// Gives a warning: assignment of Number to Integer
var intValue2:Integer = numberValue1;
```

The same rules apply for assignments involving the other numeric types.

In some cases, you know that assignment of a `Number` value to an `Integer` (for example) is what you want, even if some precision might be lost. In that case, you can suppress the warning by converting the `Number` value to an `Integer` using the `as` operator:

```
// Assigns 1234 to intValue1, no warning
var intValue1:Integer = 1234.00 as Integer;
```

When the exact value of a `Number` variable cannot be represented by an `Integer`, information is lost:

```
var intValue1:Integer = 1234.55 as Integer;
println("{intValue1}");
```

Because `intValue1` cannot hold a number with a fractional part, it is simply truncated, and the result is the value `1234`. Note the result is truncated, *not* rounded to the nearest whole number. Similarly, the result of the following code is the value `-1234`, not `-1235`, although the latter is mathematically more accurate:

```
var intValue1:Integer = -1234.55 as Integer;
println("{intValue1}");
```

If a `Number` whose value is larger than the largest representable `Integer` is assigned to an `Integer` variable, the result of the assignment is the largest possible `Integer` value with the same sign as the `Number`:

```
// This is larger than the largest positive Integer
var intValue1:Integer = 9000000000.00 as Integer;
```

```
// This is larger in magnitude than the largest negative Integer
var intValue2:Integer = -9000000000.00 as Integer;

println("intValue1: {intValue1}, intValue2: {intValue2}");
```

The output of this code is as follows:

```
intValue1: 2147483647, intValue2: -2147483648
```

Character Types

The `Character` type represents a single Unicode character and holds an unsigned integer value in the range `0` to `65535`, inclusive. A `Character` variable can be initialized by using an integer literal, in the normal way:

```
var c:Character = 0x41; // The letter 'A'
```

Java char values are automatically converted to the `Character` type on assignment:

```
var c:Character = "Hello".charAt(0); // Assigns 'H'
```

> **Note**
>
> At the time of this writing, there is no JavaFX equivalent of the following Java statement:
>
> ```
> char c = 'a';
> ```
>
> In JavaFX, `'a'` is a `String` literal, not a character literal, so this assignment fails because the types are incompatible. There is an issue filed against the compiler that might result in this being fixed at some point, so that any of the following would assign the Unicode character value for the letter `'h'` to the variable `c`:
>
> ```
> var c:Character = "h";
> var c:Character = 'h;
> var c:Character = "Hello, World";
> ```

An attempt to assign a literal value that is outside the permitted range causes a compilation error:

```
var c:Character = -1;    // Invalid - compilation error
var d:Character = 65536; // Invalid - compilation error
```

As with the other numeric types, this error can be suppressed by using the as operator:

```
var c:Character = -1 as Character; // Actually assigns the value 65535
```

It is legal to directly assign a `Character` value to a `Character` variable, but the assignment of other types requires an explicit conversion:

```
var b:Byte = 0x41;
var c:Character = 0x41;
var i:Integer = 0x41;
```

```
var l:Long = 0x41;

var c1:Character = b as Character;    // Conversion required
var c2:Character = c;                 // No conversion required
var c3:Character = i as Character;    // Conversion required
var c4:Character = l as Character;    // Conversion required
```

Arithmetic operations involving a `Character` value require an explicit conversion if the result is to be assigned to a `Character` variable:

```
var c:Character = 0x41;
c = c + 1 as Character; // Conversion required.
```

However, no conversion is required when the pre- and post-increment and decrement operators are used:

```
var c:Character = 0x41;
c++;    // No conversion required.
```

Numeric Types and `null`

An attempt to assign the value `null` to a numeric type results in a compilation error:

```
var value1:Integer = null;   // Compilation error - cannot be null
var value2:Number = null;    // Compilation error - cannot be null
```

An assignment of `null` from another variable or as the result of a more complex expression actually results in the assignment of the default value of the assigned variable's type:

```
var o:java.lang.Object = null;
var value1:Integer = o as Integer;      // value1 is set to 0
var value2:Number = o as Number;        // value2 is set to 0.0
var value3:Character = o as Character;  // value3 is set to 0
```

The `Boolean` Type

`Boolean` values in JavaFX are identical to their Java counterparts. To declare a `boolean` variable, use the type name `Boolean`. This code prints the default value of a `boolean` variable, which is `false`:

```
var b:Boolean;
println("Default boolean value: {b}");
```

A `boolean` variable can only take the value `true` or `false`:

```
var b:Boolean = true;
b = false;
```

Like the numeric types, `boolean` variables cannot be assigned an initial value of `null`. Assignment of a `null` value at runtime causes the variable to be set to `false`:

Basic Data Types   103

```
var b1:Boolean = null;        // Compilation error
var o:Object = null;
var b2:Boolean = o as Boolean;  // Assignment of null gives false
```

You can obtain a `boolean` value from a string by using the `java.lang.Boolean.valueOf()` method, which returns `false` if the input value is not recognized:

```
boolean = java.lang.Boolean.valueOf("true");  // yields true
boolean = java.lang.Boolean.valueOf("false"); // yields false
boolean = java.lang.Boolean.valueOf("XXXX");  // yields false
```

The `String` Type

A string is an immutable, ordered collection of zero or more Unicode characters. A JavaFX string is similar to a Java `String`—anything you can do with the latter, you can also do with the former.

String Literals

String literals are denoted as they are in Java—as a sequence of characters surrounded by double quotes:

```
var string:String = "Hello, World";
```

Certain special characters can be represented using escape sequences. Table 5-3 lists the valid escape sequences.

A Unicode escape sequence can be used to represent any character but is typically used when the character that you want is not available on the keyboard or in the file encoding that you are using. For example, the Unicode value for the French character é (e-acute) is

Table 5-3   **String Literal Escape Sequences**

Escape Sequence	Meaning
\b	Backspace
\f	Form feed
\n	Newline
\r	Carriage return
\t	Horizontal tab
\"	A double quote
\'	A single quote
\\	A backslash
\unnnn	The Unicode character whose value is nnnn (hex)
\012	The Unicode character whose value is 012 (octal)

0x00E9. If you don't have a French keyboard, you can still include this character in a string by specifying its Unicode value:

```
println("e-acute is \u00E9");
```

If you want to include a double quote (") in a string, you can use either the Unicode value or the escape sequence shown in Table 5-3:

```
println("This is a double quote: \u0022, and so is this: \".");
```

The preceding code prints the following:

```
This is a double quote ", and so is this: ".
```

The other way to include a double quote is to use *single* quotes to denote the string literal. When you do this, you can simply type a double quote wherever you need one:

```
println('This is a double quote - " - in a single-quoted string.');
```

This code prints the following:

```
This is a double quote - " - in a single-quoted string.
```

Naturally, if you want a single quote inside a single-quoted string, you have to use an escape sequence:

```
println('"That\'s one small step for man..."');
```

This code prints the following:

```
"That's one small step for man..."
```

The default value of a `String` variable is the empty string. Assigning `null` to a `String` actually assigns the empty string:

```
var s:String;
s = null;
println("s is the empty string? {s == ''}");
```

The preceding code prints this:

```
s is the empty string? true
```

String Concatenation

You can split long strings into pieces and have the compiler concatenate them, by placing them next to each other, like this:

```
var s:String =
    "That's one " "small step for man, " "one giant leap for mankind";
```

Single quotes and double quotes produce the same result, provided you escape nested quotes properly:

```
var s:String =
    'That\'s one ' 'small step for man, ' 'one giant leap for mankind';
```

Basic Data Types   105

You can also spread the parts over several lines:

```
var s:String = "That's one "
               "small step for man, "
               "one giant leap for mankind";
```

All the preceding examples produce the following string, at compile time:

```
"That's one small step for man, one giant leap for mankind"
```

Note that the newlines in the source file do *not* appear in the string. If you need newline characters, you can embed them by using the escape sequence \n, like this:

```
var s:String = "That's one\n"
               "small step for man,\n"
               "one giant leap for mankind";
```

Another way to create the same string is like this:

```
var s:String =
    "That's one\nsmall step for man,\none giant leap for mankind";
```

Both of these create a string that looks like this when printed:

```
That's one
small step for man,
one giant leap for mankind
```

> **Note**
> The + operator cannot be used to combine String variables in JavaFX.

Embedded Expressions

Text between matched curly braces within a JavaFX string is extracted at compile time and treated as an expression (see Chapter 6). The expression is evaluated at *runtime*, and the result is converted to a string and inserted in place of the expression itself. Here's an example:

```
var string:String = "Hello";
println("Value is {string}, length: {string.length()}");
```

This produces the following output:

```
Value is Hello, length: 5
```

In this example, the expressions are simple, but they need not be. Here's another, slightly more interesting example:

```
var odd:Boolean = (java.lang.System.currentTimeMillis() mod 2) != 0;
println("Current time is {if (odd) "odd" else "even"}.");
```

The first line gets the current system time from the Java System.currentTimeMillis() method and sets the value of the variable odd to true if the time has an odd value (that is, the remainder on division by 2 is not 0) and `false` if it does not. The expression in the string on the second line is a JavaFX `if` statement, which is covered in Chapter 8, "Controlling Program Flow":

```
if (odd) "odd" else "even"
```

Unlike the Java `if` statement, the JavaFX version always returns a value. Here, it returns the string value `odd` if the value of the variable `odd` is `true` and `even` if it is `false`. The output of this example will vary depending on exactly when the current time is read, but will be one of the following:

```
Current time is even.
Current time is odd.
```

Because the characters `{` and `}` are used to indicate the presence of an expression, if you want them to appear within a string, you must use the Unicode value or escape them in the usual way:

```
println("Open curly bracket: \{, close curly bracket: \}.");
```

This prints the following:

```
Open curly bracket: {, close curly bracket: }.
```

Note that both the open and closing braces must be escaped.

Embedded Formatting

The second expression example previously shown compiles to code that is roughly equivalent to the following Java statements:

```
boolean odd = (System.currentTimeMillis() % 2) != 0;
println(String.format("Current time is %s.", odd ? "odd" : "even"));
```

Note that the embedded expression is replaced by the string `%s`, and then the `String.format()` method is used to interpolate the result of the expression into the string before it is printed. If you are not familiar with the enhanced formatting facilities added in J2SE 5, consult the Javadoc documentation for the `java.util.Formatter` class before reading further.

The `%s` in the string to be formatted is an example of a *format specifier*. Whenever you include an expression in a JavaFX string, that expression will, by default, be replaced by `%s`, and code similar to that previously shown will be generated. At runtime, the `%s` format specifier converts the result of the expression to a string as follows:

- If the expression result is `null`, the string `null` is used.
- Otherwise, if the expression returns an object that implements the `java.util.Formattable` interface, it is converted to string form by invoking its `formatTo()` method. This allows custom formatting to be performed.
- Otherwise, and this is most common case, the `toString()` method of the expression value is used to convert it to string form.

Basic Data Types   107

In many cases, this default behavior is adequate. However, JavaFX allows you to include an explicit format specifier with any embedded expression, which gives you more control over how the result of the expression is formatted. The general form of an embedded expression is as follows:

{[*format specifier*] *expression*}

The format specifier, if it is present, must start with the character %, must precede the expression, and must be separated from it by whitespace. If no format specifier is given, %s is assumed, so that

{*expression*}

is equivalent to

{%s *expression*}

The valid format specifiers are defined by the `java.util.Formatter` class. Table 5-4 shows some examples.

With reference to the last example, note that the `java.util.Formatter` class only provides useful format specifiers that produce *one element* of a date or time value. Although a few format specifiers output more complete dates, they are not locale-sensitive, and therefore the resulting date or time might look strange to some users. For example, the following code uses the %tF specifier to format the date:

```
println("Date: {%tF time}");
```

Table 5-4   **Examples of Embedded Formatting**

Formatting	Result
`var value:Number = 1.23456789;` `"Value: {%f value} "`	Value: `1.234568` By default, `%f` formats a `Number` with 6 digits of precision.
`var value:Number = 1.23456789;` `"Value: {%.3f value} "`	Value: `1.235` `%.3f` specifies 3 digits of precision.
`var value:Number = 1.23456789;` `"Value: {%-10.3f value} padded"`	Value: `1.235` padded `%-10.3f` requires at least 10 characters of output; a - sign forces left alignment, so whitespace padding is added on the right.
`var value:Number = 12.3456789;` `"Value: {%.3E value}"`	Value: `1.235E+01` `%.3E` converts number to floating-point notation.

`var time:java.util.Date =`
`        new java.util.Date();`
`"Date: {%ta time} {%td time}`
`{%th time} {%tY time} "`
	Date: Thu 29 May 2008
	Format specifiers beginning with `%t` or `%T` can be used to format parts of the date and time.

And this produces the following result:

```
Date: 2008-05-29
```

This is accurate, but it may or may not be the form in which you would usually expect to see a date written, depending on where you live. Fortunately, as you'll see in the next section, it is easy to write JavaFX applications so that they can be translated into other languages.

String Slicing

Strings can be sliced using the `substring()` function.[7] The following code obtains two substrings from the string `"Hello, World"`:

```
var string:String = "Hello, World";
var part1:String = string.substring(0, 5);
var part2:String = string.substring(7);
println("part1: {part1}, part2: {part2}");
```

The output from this code is as follows:

```
part1: Hello, part2: World
```

There are two variants of the `substring()` function:

```
public String substring(int startIndex, int endIndex);
public String substring(int startIndex);
```

The first form returns the characters in positions `startIndex` through `endIndex - 1` of the original string, while the second returns everything from position `startIndex` to the end of the string.

It is important to remember that, as in Java, a `String` operation does not affect the string on which it is performed—instead, it creates a new string that is returned from the function call, leaving the original unmodified.

String Localization

A few years ago, the odds were that an application would be written by a single developer or by a team of developers for the benefit of users who were often in the same building and usually in the same country, or who at least spoke the same language. In those days, things like language and the conventions for writing dates and numbers were not an issue—programmers simply hard-coded messages and formatting into their programs.

---

[7] There is no formal definition of the set of supported functions provided by the `String` type. Because it is mapped directly to `java.lang.String`, it is currently possible to use all the functions of that class on a `String` object.

Nowadays, applications are downloaded from the Internet and reach audiences all over the world. Such applications cannot simply be written in English or use fixed date and number formats. Internet applications have to be *internationalized*, which means that all the messages that users will see have to be identified so that they can be translated, while numbers and dates have to be accepted and output in the form that the users understands, wherever they reside.

The Java platform provides classes that allow the programmer to create an internationalized application, which can then be *localized*—customized for specific languages and locations—by a translator. Before looking at how JavaFX supports the creation of language-neutral applications, a brief review of how this is done in Java would be useful. Having done that, we'll then take a look at how much easier it is to do the same thing in JavaFX.

> **Note**
>
> You can safely skip this section, which is somewhat advanced, on first reading and continue with the section "Type Inference."

Internationalization and Localization in Java

Let's suppose your application needs to tell the user the day and date. You need it to output a message like this:

```
Today is Saturday and the date is 5/31/08
```

There are two problems to be solved here:

- The date shown above is formatted for the United States. In the United Kingdom, the reader would be surprised to see that it is month 31 and would be much happier to be told that the date is 31/05/08.
- The text is all in English. It needs to be in the user's native language.

Let's deal with the first of these issues. Here is some Java code that would print the message that we require and that works in any locale supported by the Java platform on which it is running:

```
1    GregorianCalendar cal = new GregorianCalendar();
2    int dayNumber = cal.get(GregorianCalendar.DAY_OF_WEEK);
3    DateFormatSymbols symbols = new DateFormatSymbols();
4    String day = symbols.getWeekdays()[dayNumber];
5
6    DateFormat df = DateFormat.getDateInstance(DateFormat.SHORT);
7
8    println("Today is " + day + " and the date is "
9            + df.format(cal.getTime()));
```

The approach taken here is to break the problem into two parts: getting the day name and getting the formatted date. Line 1 creates a `GregorianCalendar` object, initialized with the current date and time. Line 2 uses the logic in the `GregorianCalendar` to get the number of today's day of the week, which is a value in the range 1 through 7. To get the name of the day, we use this value in conjunction with the `getWeekdays()` method of the `DateFormatSymbols` class, which returns the day names as an array. The returned day names are translated according to the default locale, which is set automatically from the user's desktop settings when the application starts. Therefore, in the United Kingdom and the United States, the last entry in this array would be `Saturday`, whereas in France it would be `samedi`.

Line 6 gets a date formatter that can convert a date (in the form of a `java.util.Date` object) to string form according to the convention's of the user's locale. The following expression causes the date to be returned in string form:

```
df.format(cal.getTime())
```

Running this code in three different locales gives the following results:

- United States: Today is Saturday and the date is 5/31/08
- United Kingdom: Today is Saturday and the date is 31/05/08
- France: Today is samedi and the date is 31/05/08

This all seems correct, apart from the fact that the last line really should be entirely in French! This leads us to the second part of the problem: how to arrange for a translated message to be used instead of the hard-coded English text. In Java, this is done by extracting all of an application's messages to one or more text files, replacing each of them in the code by a key that references the corresponding translated message, and then preparing copies of the files in which the messages have been translated into the various languages that the application supports. Having done this, adding support for a new language is just a matter of adding new translation files—no further code changes are required.

In the preceding example, the message was constructed by concatenating four different strings, two of which are fixed text and two generated values:

```
println("Today is " + day + " and the date is "
        + df.format(cal.getTime()));
```

The first step is to convert this to one string, which is necessary for two reasons:

- We need to use one key to look up the translated version of the text.
- The order of elements in a sentence may vary from language to language, whereas in the preceding code, the order is fixed.

To combine the four elements into a single string, we use the `format()` method of the `String` class:

```
String text = String.format("Today is %s and the date is %s", day,
                    df.format(cal.getTime())); 
println(text);
```

Next, we move the string to a file and replace it with a key. The key can be any value; by convention, it is chosen based on the purpose of the message. In this case, we'll choose to use the key `date.text`. The text is stored in a resource bundle and loaded using the methods of the `java.util.ResourceBundle` class. You can put the files in the resource bundle anywhere you like as long as they are accessible at runtime. One convention that is often used is to place the strings in a file that is named after the class in which they are used. Here, we'll assume that the code is in a class called `pkg.LocalizedDate`, so the strings to be translated would go in a file called `pkg/LocalizedDate.properties`, which must be packaged with the application at build time.[8] Here's how the `pkg/LocalizedDate.properties` file should look:

```
date.text = Today is %s and the date is %s
```

The code to look up this text and format it is as follows:

```
ResourceBundle bundle = ResourceBundle.getBundle("pkg.LocalizedDate");
String localizedText = bundle.getString("date.text");
String text = String.format(localizedText, day,
                            df.format(cal.getTime()));
```

As you can see, the `ResourceBundle getBundle()` method is used to find the file and convert it into a `ResourceBundle` object, and then the `getString()` method of that object is used to look up the text given its assigned key. Finally, that text is passed to the `format()` method.

So far, so good, but we haven't yet translated the message. Obviously, we can't store the translation in the the file `pkg/LocalizedDate.properties`, because that would overwrite the English language message. Instead, we exploit the fact that the `getBundle()` method looks not only for a file with the given name (for a Java class with that name, too—a fact that we ignore here for simplicity), but also for other files whose names depend on the current locale.

The application's locale is an instance of the `java.util.Locale` class. It is made up of a language code, a country code, and a variant. Because the variant component is hardly used, we ignore it here. If you are in the United States, your locale is likely to be `en_US`, which indicates that your language is English and your country is the United States. In the United Kingdom, the locale is most likely to be `en_GB`—English language and country Great Britain. The `Locale` class defines constants called `Locale.US` and `Locale.UK` that correspond to these two cases. In general, you can construct a `Locale` object for any combination of language and country, like this:

```
Locale locale = new Locale("fr", "CH"); // Swiss French
```

---

[8] The easiest way to achieve this is to put the `LocalizedDate.properties` file in the same folder as the `LocalizedDate.java` file and have your IDE simply copy it to the `classes` subdirectory of your project. If you use an Ant build script, you can use a `<copy>` task to achieve the same effect. You can see an example of this in the `build.xml` file in this book's example source code.

Although it is useful for testing to be able to create arbitrary locales, it is usually not necessary to do this in production code because the correct default locale is preset from the user's desktop settings.

Assuming that you are in the United States, the `getBundle()` method with the preceding parameters looks for files with the following names, in the order shown:

- pkg/LocalizedDate_en_US.properties
- pkg/LocalizedDate_en.properties
- pkg/LocalizedDate.properties

Any key/value pairs from whichever of these files exist will be loaded into the `ResourceBundle`, with those found first in the preceding list taking precedence. So, for example, if all three of these files were to exist and a value for the key `date.text` were to be found in all of them, only the one in the file `pkg/LocalizedDate_en_US.properties` would be used. Therefore

- Any translations that are specific to English in the United Sates should be in the file pkg/LocalizedDate_en_US.properties.
- Any translations that are common to all English-speaking countries should be in the file pkg/LocalizedDate_en.properties.
- Fallback translations, which are used when there is no translation for a key in either the `language` or `language_country` file (or when these files do not exist), should be in the file pkg/LocalizedDate.properties.

Given this, you should be able to see that, to make our example work in any French-speaking country, we should add a file called `pkg/LocalizedDate_fr.properties` with the following content:

date.text = Aujourd'hui est %s et la date est %s

If you want to specialize this message for French speakers in Switzerland, you create a file called `pkg/LocalizedDate_fr_CH.properties`, as well. Listing 5-1 shows the complete source code for this example.

Listing 5-1   **Internationalization in Java**

```
package javafxdatatypes;

import java.text.DateFormat;
import java.text.DateFormatSymbols;
import java.util.GregorianCalendar;
import java.util.Locale;
import java.util.ResourceBundle;

public class LocalizedDate {
    public static void main(String[] args) {
        DateFormatSymbols symbols = new DateFormatSymbols();
        GregorianCalendar cal = new GregorianCalendar();
```

```
            int dayNumber = cal.get(GregorianCalendar.DAY_OF_WEEK);
            String day = symbols.getWeekdays()[dayNumber];
            DateFormat df = DateFormat.getDateInstance(DateFormat.SHORT);

            ResourceBundle bundle =
                    ResourceBundle.getBundle("pkg.LocalizedDate");
            String localizedText = bundle.getString("date.text");
            String text = String.format(localizedText, day,
                                        df.format(cal.getTime()));

            System.out.println(text);
    }
}
```

The results of running this code with the locale set for the United States, the United Kingdom, and France are shown here:

- United States: Today is Saturday and the date is 5/31/08
- United Kingdom: Today is Saturday and the date is 31/05/08
- France: Aujourd'hui est samedi et la date est 31/05/08

Internationalization and Localization in JavaFX

As you can see, creating an internationalized Java application that has only a single text message requires several lines of nontrivial code. Fortunately, it is much easier to do the same thing in JavaFX. The first step is to convert the application from Java into JavaFX, which gives us this:

```
import java.util.Date;
import java.text.DateFormat;

var date:Date = new Date();
var fmt:DateFormat = DateFormat.getDateInstance(DateFormat.SHORT);
println("Today is {%tA date} and the date is {fmt.format(date)}");
```

You will notice that in JavaFX, there is no need to use the `GregorianCalendar` and `DateFormatSymbols` classes to get the day name because the `%tA` format specifier does all the work required to extract the name of the day, in localized form, from the value of the associated expression, as long as the type of that expression is `Date` or `Calendar`. We still need to use the `DateFormat` class to get the date because there is no format specifier that returns the date in a locale-independent format.[9] Internationalizing this code is simple—all you need to do is prefix the string with the tokens ##, giving the result shown in Listing 5-2.

---

[9] The closest approximation is `%tD`, which returns the date in form month/day/year. This is correct in the United States but incorrect in most other locales.

Listing 5-2 Internationalization in JavaFX

```
package javafxdatatypes;

import java.util.Date;
import java.text.DateFormat;

var date:Date = new Date();
var fmt:DateFormat = DateFormat.getDateInstance(DateFormat.SHORT);
println(##"Today is {%tA date} and the date is {fmt.format(date)}");
```

Prefixing a string with ## is an instruction to the compiler to generate code that causes the string's value to be replaced, at runtime, with a localized version for the user's locale. Having seen the Java version of this application, you would probably expect that the translations would be kept in a resource bundle, and you would be correct, but the details are slightly different in JavaFX than they are in Java. There are two main differences:

- In the Java version, we replaced the text to be translated by a key and then made an entry mapping the key to the translated text in a separate file. In JavaFX, a modified version of the text itself is used as the key, so there is no need to invent a key of your own.
- In the Java example, the resource bundle contained a version of the message that was used as a fallback for those locales for which no translation is provided in a file called `LocalizedDate.properties`. If this file were missing or did not have an entry for the key being used, the string would be translated to nothing. In JavaFX, *there is no fallback file*—the fallback text is the text that is supplied in the application itself.

In JavaFX, the translated strings are, by default, held in files in the same directory as the JavaFX file that references them. The names of these files are (again, by default) derived from the name of the JavaFX file. In this case, given that the code is in a file called `javafxdatatypes/LocalizedDate.fx`, the translated strings would be held in the following files[10]:

- `javafxdatatypes/LocalizedDate_fr_FR.fxproperties`
- `javafxdatatypes/LocalizedDate_fr.fxproperties`

As in Java, translated strings in the first file, if present, take precedence over those in the second. Notice two things about this list of files:

---

[10] The source files for this example are in the JavaFX Book Desktop project because the `DateFormat` class is not available on MIDP-based mobile devices, and therefore this example cannot be run with the JavaFX Mobile version. Localization is, however, fully supported in JavaFX Mobile.

- The filename suffix is .fxproperies, not .properties.
- As noted earlier, there is no need to create a file called javafxdatatypes/LocalizedDate.fxproperties containing the fallback translations. In fact, if this file were to exist, it would be ignored.

It is possible to change these defaults so that you could, for example, keep all the translated strings for every class in a package in a single file instead of in a per-class file. You'll see how to do this in Chapter 12 "Platform APIs."

The key in a translation file is the same as the text being localized, except that each embedded expression is replaced by its format specifier, or by %s if it does not have one. In the case of the string in Listing 5-2, the key would be as follows:

```
"Today is %tA and the date is %s"
```

The translation file for the French language would therefore contain this:

```
"Today is %tA and the date is %s" = "Aujourd'hui est %tA et la date est %s"
```

Note that both the key and the message have surrounding quotes. This is necessary because the key could contain whitespace (as it does here) or the character =, which would otherwise cause problems for the code that parses the file's content. The type of quotes used in the translation key do *not* need to match those in the JavaFX source file—one can use double quotes and the other single quotes.

The translated message appears to have an implicit dependency on the order in which the expressions appeared in the original message, but this is not really the case. Suppose we want to reverse the order of the day and the date for French-speaking users in Canada. We would need the translated text to be like this:

```
La date est 31/5/2008 et est aujourd'hui samedi
```

To specialize for users in Canada, we would create a file called javafxdatatypes/LocalizedDate_fr_CA.fxproperties containing the following text:

```
"Today is %tA and the date is %s" = "La date est %s et est aujourd'hui %tA"
```

Unfortunately, this doesn't work because the values used to substitute for the format specifiers are always passed in the order in which they appear in the original text, so in this case the %s would be applied to the Date object and the %tA to the localized date value. We can, however, explicitly specify the ordinal of the value to which a format specifier should be applied by placing it after the % character and following it with a $, like this:

```
"Today is %tA and the date is %s" = "La date est %2$s et est aujourd'hui %1$tA"
```

This specifies that %s should be applied to the second value and %tA to the first. With this change, running the example in various locales gives the following results:

- United States: Today is Saturday and the date is 5/31/08
- United Kingdom: Today is Saturday and the date is 31/05/08
- France: Aujourd'hui est samedi et la date est 01/06/08
- French Canada: La date est 08-05-31 et est aujourd'hui samedi

In cases where the text to be localized is constructed from concatenated strings, the lookup key is still the complete string. For example, you could choose to print the date and time like this:

```
println(##"Today is " "{%tA date}" " and the date is "
        "{fmt.format(date)}");
```

The fact that the string has been broken down into smaller pieces has no effect on the localization because the compiler recombines them, so that the translation key is the same as if a single string had been used.

Translation Ambiguities

Using the original language text as the key to look up a translation is a simplification that is worthwhile in most cases, but sometimes it can cause problems. For example, the word *File* in English can be either a noun or a verb. In other languages (for example, French), there may be different words for the noun and the verb. If the text were the only key that could be used to find a translation, it would be impossible to arrange for the following code to give the correct results in French:

```
println(##"File");  // Here, we want the noun
println(##"File");  // Here, we want the verb
```

To solve this problem, you can provide an override key (also referred as a context key) that is used to look up the translated string instead of the message text. Here's how you could rewrite the code above so that the override key is used to look up the translation:

```
println(##[NOUN_FILE]"File");
println(##[VERB_FILE]"File");
```

Now the keys `NOUN_FILE` and `VERB_FILE` must be used in the translation files instead of the original text, like this:

```
"NOUN_FILE"="Fichier"
"VERB_FILE"="Ranger"
```

Running this code in the U.S. locale (or in any locale for which there are no translations provided) produces the following result:

```
File
File
```

In the French locale, you would see the following:

```
Fichier
Ranger
```

It is worth pointing out that the ## syntax works for any string in a JavaFX file, even if your code doesn't explicitly use the embedded expression syntax. For example, consider the following line from Listing 4-2:

```
println(##"Today is {%tA date} and the date is {fmt.format(date)}");
```

Replacing this line with the following would produce the same result, and the same translation file content would apply to it[11]:

```
var s:String = String.format(##"Today is %tA and the date is %s", date,
                        fmt.format(date));
println(s);
```

Internationalization and Numeric Values

Proper internationalization of numeric values requires that you use the numeric format specifiers like `%d` and `%f`, which are locale-sensitive, rather than `%s`, which might seem to work but is, in fact, wrong. Here's an example[12]:

```
var value:Number = 12345.67890;
println("Using %%s: {value}");
```

The embedded expression is of type `Number`, but because there is no format specifier, it is defaulted to `%s`. The results of running this code in the United States, the United Kingdom, and in France are as follows:

- United States: Using %s: 12345.6789
- United Kingdom: Using %s: 12345.6789
- France: Using %s: 12345.6789

The results are all the same, because `%s` is locale-insensitive for numeric values. To get the correct result, use `%f` instead:

```
var value:Number = 12345.67890;
println("Using %%f: {%f value}");
```

This gives the results shown here. Notice that the decimal separator in the French version is now a comma, which is correct.

- United States: Using %f: 12345.678900
- United Kingdom: Using %f: 12345.678900
- France: Using %f: 12345,678900

Type Inference

In all the examples you have seen so far, the type of a variable has been explicitly specified at declaration time. In Java, this is mandatory, but in JavaFX it is not. In some circumstances, the compiler will allow you to omit the type declaration. When you do

---

[11] The code shown is, in fact, more or less what the compiler would generate when it encounters the original code.

[12] The string `"Using %%s"` is translated literally to `"Using %s"`—the two percent signs are needed to indicate that the characters `%s` are not intended to be interpreted as a format specifier.

this, the compiler attempts to infer the correct type for the variable from its context and the way in which it is used. For example, consider the following two declarations:

```
var value1 = 1;
var value2 = 1.0;
```

In neither case is the variable type explicitly stated, but the values used as initializers give the compiler enough of a clue as to what the type should be. In this case, the compiler will deduce that `value1` should be of type `Integer` and `value2` of type `Number`.

You don't always need to provide an initializer for the compiler to determine the type of the variable. The following declaration will correctly cause `value3` to be assigned the type `Number`:

```
var value3;
value3 = 23.567;
```

The compiler can even cope with this:

```
var value4;
if (Math.random() > 0.5) {
    value4 = 1;
} else {
    value4 = 1.234;
}
```

In this case, it decides that `value4` should be an `Integer` and then produces a warning when an attempt is made to assign the value `1.234` to it, because of the implicit conversion from `Number` to `Integer`. To remove the warning, you must explicitly declare the type of the variable to be `Number`.

If an integer value is too large for an `Integer` variable, the compiler infers `Long` instead, and similarly a floating-point value that is too large for a `Float` causes the compiler to infer `Double`:

```
var a = 2147483648;   // Inferred type is Long
var b = 3E39;         // Inferred type is Double
```

The fact that the type of a variable is not explicitly specified does not mean that it does not have a type or that its type is not fixed. In some languages (for example, Ruby), the effective type of a variable is determined by the value that it contains and therefore may vary over time. In JavaFX, this is not the case—the compiler determines the type once and for all and thereafter treats the variable as being of that type. That means that the following is valid:

```
import javafx.stage.Stage;
var stage = Stage {};
stage.close();
```

This code is valid because the compiler will infer that the variable `stage` must be of type `Stage`, and therefore the object that it refers to has a `close()` function. It is not valid to attempt to reassign this variable to point to a `Text` object because a `Text` object is not a `Stage`:

```
// Not valid - stage is of type javafx.stage.Stage
stage = javafx.scene.text.Text {};
```

The compiler can infer the type of a variable when the initializer contains a function invocation, even if the function is a Java method or constructor invocation. For example, the compiler will correctly deduce that the type of the `date` variable in the following code is `java.util.Date`:

```
var date = new java.util.Date();
```

Although JavaFX does not have any syntax that corresponds to Java generics, the compiler can deduce the correct type for a variable that is assigned a value returned from a Java method that has been genericized. For example, consider the following Java class:

```
public class Names {
    public List<String> getNames() {
        List<String> names = new ArrayList<String>();
        names.add("Armstrong");
        names.add("Aldrin");
        names.add("Collins");
        return names;
    }
}
```

The `getNames()` method of this class returns a `List` that is declared to contain `Strings`. Now let's write some JavaFX code that uses this method:

```
1    var nameSource = new Names();       // Inferred type: "Names"
2    var names = nameSource.getNames(); // Inferred type: List<String>
3    var length = names.get(0).length();
4    println("Length of first name: {length}");
```

On line 2, we declare a variable called `names` that invokes the `getNames()` function of our Java class, and the compiler correctly infers that this variable should be of type `List<String>`. You can see that this is the case because the code on line 3 uses the `length()` method of whatever is the first item in the list. For this to compile, the compiler must know that the list contains `Strings`.

Visibility of Variables

The visibility of a script variable to code outside the script in which it is defined is determined by modifiers that may be placed before the `var` or `def` keyword in the variable declaration. The modifiers and the types of access that they allow are listed in Table 5-5. When reading this table, keep in mind that write access is actually permitted only for variables declared using `var` because `def` variables are always read-only.

Table 5-5 **Visibility and Access Modifiers for Script Variables**

Modifiers	Access from Script	Access from Package	Access from Subclass	Access from Outside Package
(None)	Read, write	None	None	None
`public`	Read, write	Read, write	Read, write	Read, write
`protected`	Read, write	Read, write	Read, write	None
`package`	Read, write	Read, write	None	None
`public-read`	Read, write	Read	Read	Read
`public-read package`	Read, write	Read, write	Read	Read
`public-read protected`	Read, write	Read, write	Read, write	Read

As you have already seen, a variable declared without any modifiers is visible only within the same script. At the other end of the spectrum, `public` script variables are visible to any code. In between these two extremes, there are two narrower scopes with associated keywords:

- `package`: Grants access to code in the same package as the script that declares the variable. This mode is typically used when you want to make a variable available to other parts of your own code, but not to the users of your code, or to unit tests, kept in the same package, that need greater access to a class than should be granted to other code.
- `protected`: Grants the same access as `package` but also allows code in subclasses to read and write the variable. Subclass access is discussed in Chapter 11.

Only one of `public`, `package`, and `protected` may be used. These visibility modifiers permit both read and write access, but sometimes you want users of your code to able to read a variable but not to write to it, while at the same time making it possible for your own code to modify its value. In this case, you should use the `public-read` modifier:

```
public-read var count = 0;
```

As a result of this declaration, any code can read the variable, but only code in the same script can modify it. You can also use the `package` and `protected` modifiers to additionally grant write access to code in scripts that are in the same package or in subclasses:

```
// Code in the same script or in the same package can modify
public-read package var count = 0;

// Code in the same script or in subclasses or in the same
// package can modify
public-read protected var count  = 0;
```

6

Expressions, Functions, and Object Literals

Almost everything in JavaFX is an expression, even things that you would ordinarily not think of as an expression, such as an `if` statement or a `for` statement. In fact, we probably shouldn't even call them "statements" because they can both return a value and be used as part of another expression. The first part of this chapter discusses JavaFX expressions with the more limited meaning of expressions in other languages like Java. You'll see all the operators that are available in JavaFX and the data types to which they can be applied. The second part of this chapter takes a closer look at JavaFX functions, which are more powerful than Java methods in the sense that they can appear outside class definitions, can be manipulated like other data types, and can even be passed as arguments to other functions. Finally, we discuss object literals, which provide a convenient and easy-to-read means of creating and initializing JavaFX objects.

Expressions and Operations

The operators that are supported by JavaFX are listed in Table 6-1, together with the data types that can appear as their operands. Operators shown with a lower priority value in this table are more tightly binding than those with a higher priority value. That means that given any pair of operators, the one that is higher up in the table is evaluated first. For example, in the following expression, the multiplication operator has lower numerical priority than the addition operator and so is evaluated first, and the result of the expression is 23:

3 + 4 * 5

Table 6-1 **JavaFX Operators**

Priority	Operator	Description	Category
1	`function()`	A JavaFX function or Java method call	Object/class
	`()`	An expression in parentheses	N/A
	`new`	Instantiates a new object	Object/class
	`{ object literal }`	Instantiates and initializes a new object	Object/class
2	`++` (postfix)	Post-increment	Numeric
	`--` (postfix)	Post-decrement	Numeric
3	`++` (prefix)	Pre-increment	Numeric
	`--` (prefix)	Pre-decrement	Numeric
	`-`	Unary minus (as in `-1`)	Numeric
	`not`	Logical negation	Boolean
	`sizeof`	Size of a sequence	Sequence
	`reverse`	Reverse of a sequence	Sequence
	`indexof`	Index of a sequence element	Sequence
4	`*`	Multiplication	Numeric
	`/`	Division	Numeric
	`mod`	Remainder on division	Numeric
5	`+`	Addition	Numeric
	`-`	Subtraction	Numeric
6	`==`	Equality	All
	`!=`	Inequality	All
	`<`	Less than	Numeric
	`<=`	Less than or equal to	Numeric
	`>`	Greater than	Numeric
	`>=`	Greater than or equal to	Numeric
7	`instanceof`	Type checking	Object/class
	`as`	Casting	Object/class
8	`and`	Logical AND	Boolean
9	`or`	Logical OR	Boolean
10	`+=`	Add and assign	Numeric
	`-=`	Subtract and assign	Numeric
	`*=`	Multiply and assign	Numeric
	`/=`	Divide and assign	Numeric
11	`=`	Assignment	All

The default evaluation order can be changed by enclosing part of the expression in parentheses, like this:

```
(3 + 4) * 5
```

Parentheses are more tightly binding than arithmetic operations, so in this case, the addition is performed first and the result would be `35`.

In general, JavaFX operators behave in the same way as their Java counterparts. The following sections briefly look at each of them, grouped by the category of data on which they operate, with the exception of the sequence operators, which are covered in Chapter 7, "Sequences."

Numeric Operations

Each operand of a numeric operation must be one of the numeric types and the result will be either another numeric value or a `Boolean`, as described in the following sections. For the sake of brevity, we refer to `Byte`, `Short`, `Character`, `Integer`, and `Long` as integer types and to `Float`, `Number`, and `Double` as floating-point types.

Arithmetic Operations

JavaFX provides the same arithmetic operations as Java, with the same semantics. The result of an arithmetic operation is always an integer type or a floating-point type, depending on the types of the operands:

- If both operands are integer types, the result is an integer type.
- If both operands are floating-point types, the result is a floating-point type.
- If one operand is a floating-point type and the other is an integer type, the integer value is first converted to a floating-point value, the operation is performed, and the result will be a floating-point type.

The following examples illustrate these rules:

```
var a = 1 + 2;
```

Because both operands are `integers`, the result type inferred for the variable `a` is `Integer`, and the value assigned to it is `3`.

```
var b = 1.0 + 2.0;
```

In this case, both operands are `Number` types, so the type of `b` is `Number`, and the result is `3.0`.

```
var c = 1.0 + 2;
```

Here, the operands are of mixed types. The integer value 2 is converted to the floating-point 2.0, and the inferred type of c is Number. The result is 3.0.

The +, -, *, and / operators do what you would expect them to do, unless the resulting value is too large or too small to be represented as an integer or floating-point type, an issue that is covered in the "Range Errors in Arithmetic Operations" section, later in this chapter.

The mod operator is the same as the Java % operator, returning the remainder of an integer division of the left operand by the right operand.

Here are some examples of these operators applied to operands that are Integer types:

```
var a = 123 + 456;     // Result = 579
var b = 456 - 123;     // Result = 333
var c = 5 * 40;        // Result = 200
var d = 40 / 5;        // Result = 8
var e = 32 / 5;        // Result = 6
var f = 32 mod 5;      // Result = 2 (remainder on division by 5)
```

The value assigned to the preceding variable e is 6 rather than 6.4 because the result of an integer division is also an integer. The exact answer is truncated to produce 6. The result of dividing −32 by 5 would be −6 because the result is always rounded toward 0.

When one or both of the operands is a floating-point type, numeric operations are not always mathematically accurate, as the following examples illustrate:

```
var a = 1.234 + 2.345;         // Result = 3.579
var b = 1.234 - 2.345;         // Result = -1.1110001
var c = 0.0001 * Math.PI;      // Result = 3.1415925742264873E-4
var d = 1.0/41.0;              // Result = 0.024390243
var e = d * 41;                // Result = 0.99999994
var f = 3E10 + 1E-10;          // Result = 3.0000001E10
```

As you can see, the subtraction on the second line results in a slightly inaccurate value being assigned to the variable b. Errors like these occur because not all decimal fractional numbers can be accurately represented in the binary floating-point form used to represent the values of the Number type.

The value PI (defined by the class javafx.util.Math) used in the expression 0.0001 * Math.PI is of type Double. As a result, the whole expression evaluates to a Double, and the variable c will also be of type Double. This is why this particular result has more decimal places than the results of the other expressions, which are all of type Number.

The result shown for the operation 1.0/41.0 is 0.024390243. This is not the true mathemetical result—in fact, it is accurate to only eight decimal places. When this result is multiplied by 41 on the next line of code, the small error in the division causes the result to be not quite 1.0, which would be the correct answer. Small errors like this are common in floating-point arithmetic, and they accumulate, so that the more operations you perform, the less accurate your final result will be. If you need complete accuracy, you can use the Java `BigDecimal` type, albeit with the possibility of worse performance.[1]

The last example illustrates another floating-point error. Here, a small value (`1.0E-10`) is added to a large value (`3.0E10`). The correct result is `30000000000.0000000001`, a number that has 21 digits of precision, which is beyond the capability of the JavaFX `Number` type. As a result, the least significant digits of the result are lost, and the value `3.0000001E10` is assigned to the variable `f`.

The operators `+=`, `--=`, `*=`, and `/=` combine an arithmetic operation and an assignment. For example `a += 3` is just a syntactic shorthand for `a = a + 3` as it is in Java.

The `++` and `--` operators work exactly as they do in Java. They both increment or decrement the associated variable, but prefix increment and decrement return the modified value, whereas the postfix operation returns the original value:

```
var a = 3;
var b = ++a;    // Prefix increment--Assigns 4 to a and to b
a = 3;
var c = a++;    // Postfix increment--Assigns 4 to a, but 3 to c.
```

Range Errors in Arithmetic Operations

Like Java, JavaFX does not always throw exceptions when an arithmetic operation produces a result that cannot be represented using the possible values of the numeric type to which the result is assigned (with one exception, described next). This section illustrates some of the errors that can occur.

Integer Overflow

Integer overflow in an operation involving `integer` types occurs when a number larger than 2147483647 or smaller than −2147483648 is produced, like this:

```
var result1:Integer = 2147483647 + 1;    // Overflow: result too large
println("Result #1 is {result1}");

var result2:Integer = -2147483647 - 2;   // Overflow: result too large
println("Result #2 is {result2}");
```

The result of running this code is as follows:

```
Result #1 is -2147483648
Result #2 is 2147483647
```

Clearly, these are not the results that might be expected, although they are perfectly logical to anybody who understands how two's complement binary arithmetic works.

---

[1] However, this option is available only with the desktop profile because neither the Java ME CLDC configuration nor the MIDP profile includes the `BigDecimal` class.

Chapter 6 Expressions, Functions, and Object Literals

Operations involving the other integer types are similarly subject to overflow when a value is produced that is outside the ranges listed in Table 5-2 in Chapter 5, "Variables and Data Types." No error is reported when an overflow occurs, but an error *is* reported if an attempt is made to divide an `integer` by zero:

```
var result:Integer = 1 / 0;
```

This code throws a `java.lang.ArithmeticException`, which can be caught and handled as described in Chapter 9, "Binding."

Number Overflow

As is the case with integer values, an overflow occurs when the result of a floating-point operation is a value that is too big to be represented in a variable of type `Number` or `Double`. Because the largest representable value of type `Number` is $+3.4028235E38$, any result with an exponent larger than 38 will produce an overflow condition, as the following code illustrates:

```
var number:Number = 1.0E20;

// Result should be 1.0E+40, which is too big
var product1:Number = number * number;

// Result should be -1.0E+40, which is too big
var product2:Number = -number * number;

println("Result1: {product1}, infinite? {product1.isInfinite()}");
println("Result2: {product2}, infinite? {product2.isInfinite()}");
```

The output from this code is as follows:

```
Result1: Infinity, infinite? true
Result2: -Infinity, infinite? true
```

When a floating-point operation produces an overflow, the result of the operation is converted to a special value that represents either positive or negative infinity. You can programmatically detect this by calling the `isInfinite()` method of the resulting `Number`. See the section "Infinity and `NaN`," later in this chapter, for more on this special value.

Number Underflow

Underflow is the reverse of overflow. It occurs when a calculation would produce a result that is too *small* to be represented by a `Number` or a `Double`, depending on the operand types. An operation that underflows actually produces the result `0.0`. The smallest number that can be stored in a `Number` is approximately `1.4e-45`, so an operation that would produce a value with an exponent numerically less than `-45` will cause an underflow[2]:

---

[2] For a `Double` variable, the smallest representable value is approximately `4.9e-324`.

```
var number:Number = 1.0E-23;
var product:Number = number * number;
println("Result: {product}");
```

The accurate result would be `1.0E-46`, but the underflow condition causes the variable `product` to be set to `0.0`. No error is reported.

Division of a Nonzero Value by Zero

Mathematically, the result of dividing a nonzero value by zero is infinity, and so it is in JavaFX, as shown by the following code:

```
var result1:Number = 1.0 / 0.0;
var result2:Number = -1.0 / 0.0;
println("Result1: {result1}, infinite? {result1.isInfinite()}");
println("Result2: {result2}, infinite? {result2.isInfinite()}");
```

This code produces the following result:

```
Result1: Infinity, infinite? true
Result2: -Infinity, infinite? true
```

Division of Zero by Zero

Division of a `Number` by zero produces an infinite result, *unless* the dividend is also zero. Mathematically, the result of this operation could be any value at all, so there is no single correct result. Any operation that does not have a single correct result produces the value `NaN`, which stands for *Not a Number*. Division by zero is one example of an operation that produces `NaN`; taking the square root of a negative value is another. The following code shows how to determine whether an operation has produced the value `NaN`:

```
var result1:Number = 0.0 / 0.0;
var result2:Number = -0.0 / 0.0;
println("Result1: {result1}, NaN? {result1.isNaN()}");
println("Result2: {result2}, NaN? {result2.isNaN()}");
```

The output is as follows:

```
Result1: NaN, NaN? true
Result2: NaN, NaN? true
```

Notice that, unlike infinity, `NaN` is *not* a signed quantity.

Comparison Operations

The comparison operators compare two numeric values and produce a `boolean` result. In the case of a comparison involving integer types, the results are clear-cut and accurate:

```
var a = 3;
var b = 3;
println("a == b? {a == b}"); // Prints "a == b? true"
println("a != b? {a != b}"); // Prints "a != b? false"
var c = 4;
```

Chapter 6 Expressions, Functions, and Object Literals

```
println("a < c? {a < c}");   // Prints "a < c? true"
println("a > c? {a > c}");   // Prints "a > c? false"
println("a <= b? {a <= b}"); // Prints "a <= b? true"
```

The inexact nature of floating-point arithmetic may produce results that are surprising when one or both of the operands is a `Number`. For example, let's revisit an example shown earlier:

```
var d = 1.0/41.0;              // Result = 0.024390243
println("(1.0/41.0) * 41.0 == 1? {d * 41 == 1}");
                   // Prints " (1.0/41.0) * 41.0 == 1? false"
```

If the result of the division in the first line of this code were accurately represented, the comparison in the second line would return `true`. However, it is not, so the result is actually `false`. When comparing the results of arithmetic operations involving floating-point types, it is best to check whether one value is very close to the other. For example, the following code takes the absolute value of the difference between the actual result and the expected result and checks that they differ by no more than 0.000001:

```
println("Math.abs((1.0/41.0) * 41.0 - 1) < 1E-6? "
     "{Math.abs((1.0/41.0) * 41.0 - 1) < 1E-6}");
// Prints "Math.abs((1.0/41.0) * 41.0 - 1) < 1E-6? true"
```

Infinity and `NaN`

Infinity and `NaN` have special properties when they are involved in arithmetic and comparison operations.

NaN

The result of performing any arithmetic operation involving `NaN` is always `NaN`, as the following code illustrates:

```
var NaN:Number = 0.0 / 0.0;
println("NaN + 1: {NaN + 1}, NaN + Nan: {NaN + NaN}, "
      "NaN - NaN: {NaN - NaN}, NaN / NaN: {NaN / NaN}");
println("NaN / 2: {NaN / 2}, NaN mod NaN: {NaN mod NaN},"
      "NaN mod 1000: {NaN mod 1000}");
```

Each of these operations results in the value `NaN`:

```
NaN + 1: NaN, NaN + Nan: NaN, NaN - NaN: NaN, NaN / NaN: NaN
NaN / 2: NaN, NaN mod NaN: NaN, NaN mod 1000: NaN
```

`NaN` is not equal to anything, including itself. It is also neither greater nor less than any other value, as demonstrated by the following code:

```
var NaN:Number = 0.0/0.0;
println("NaN == NaN? {NaN == NaN}, NaN != NaN? {NaN != NaN},"
      "NaN  > NaN? {NaN > NaN}, NaN < NaN? {NaN < NaN}");
println("NaN > 1000? {NaN > 1000}, NaN < 1000? {NaN < 1000}");
```

This gives the following result:

```
NaN == NaN? false, NaN != NaN? true, NaN > NaN? false, NaN < NaN? false
NaN > 1000? false, NaN < 1000? false
```

Because `NaN` cannot even be compared to itself, the only way to determine whether the variable v holds the value `NaN` is to call `v.isNan()`.

Infinity

The result of performing arithmetic operations on infinity is either infinity or `NaN`. The following code shows examples of operations that return each of these results:

```
var inf:Number = 1.0/0.0;
println("inf + 1: {inf + 1}, inf + inf: {inf + inf},"
        "inf - inf: {inf - inf}, inf / inf: {inf / inf}");
println("inf / 2: {inf / 2}, inf mod inf: {inf mod inf},"
        "inf mod 1000: {inf mod 1000}");
```

The result of running this code is as follows:

```
inf + 1: Infinity, inf + inf: Infinity, inf - inf: NaN, inf / inf: NaN
inf / 2: Infinity, inf mod inf: NaN, inf mod 1000: NaN
```

Unlike `NaN`, it *is* possible to compare infinity to other values:

```
var posInf:Number = 1.0 / 0.0;
var negInf:Number = -1.0 / 0.0;
println("posInf > negInf? {posInf > negInf},"
        "posInf > 1000? {posInf > 1000},"
        "negInf < 1000? {negInf < 1000}");
println("posInf == negInf? {posInf == negInf},"
        "posInf == posInf? {posInf == posInf},"
        "negInf == negInf? {negInf == negInf}");
```

The results are as you might expect:

```
posInf > negInf? true, posInf > 1000? true, negInf < 1000? true
posInf == negInf? false, posInf == posInf? true, negInf == negInf? true
```

`Boolean` Operations

The operators `and` and `or` require two `Boolean` operands and produce a `Boolean` result:

- The `and` operator evaluates to `true` if *both* of its operands are `true`, otherwise to `false`.
- The `or` operator evaluates to `true` if *either* of its operands is `true` and to `false` if they are both `false`.

The `and` operator is equivalent to `&&` in Java, whereas `or` is the same as `||`. JavaFX does not have any equivalent of Java's bitwise logical operators `&` and `|` and neither does it have an exclusive `or` operator.

Both operators evaluate their operands only if it is absolutely necessary to do so. For example, consider the following two functions, both of which return a fixed `Boolean` value (functions are discussed later in this chapter):

```
function one() { return true }
function two() { return false }
```

The following expression evaluates to `false` because the second operand has value `false`:

```
one() and two()
```

To determine this, both functions need to be invoked. However, if the expression were written in the following way, only the function `two()` would be called, because it returns `false`, and if either operand of the `and` operator returns `false`, the overall result is `false`:

```
two() and one()
```

There is, therefore, no need to invoke function `one()` in this case. Similarly, in this case, it is only necessary to invoke function `one()` to determine that the result should be `true`, and function `two()` will not be called at all.

```
one() or two()
```

If function `one()` had returned `false`, however, it would have been necessarry to invoke function `two()` to determine the result of the operation.

The unary `not` operator evaluates to `true` if its operand is `false` and to `false` if its operand is `true`:

```
var value = true;
value = not value;   // value is now false
value = not value;   // value is now true
```

The `not` operator is more tightly binding than `and`, which is itself more tightly binding than `or`.

The `==` and `!=` operators when applied to `Boolean` operands produce the obvious results:

```
false == false
true == true
false != true
true != false
```

Object and Class Operations

Various operators can be applied to a Java or JavaFX class or to an object instance.

Object Creation

The new operator creates and initializes a Java or JavaFX object given its classname. When you are creating a Java object, parameters may be passed to its constructor[3]:

```
// A JavaFX Stage
var stage = new javafx.stage.Stage();

// A Java label. Note the constructor parameter
var javaLabel = new javax.swing.JLabel("Label");
```

As you have already seen, the preferred way to create and initialize a JavaFX object is to use an object literal, supplying initial values for its properties:

```
import javafx.stage.Stage;
var stage = Stage {
            title: "Stage Title"
            visible: true
         };
```

Object literals are discussed further in the "Object Literals" section at the end of this chapter.

Function Invocation

As you saw in the "Invoking Java Functions" section in Chapter 5, the . operator can be used to invoke a function member of a JavaFX object or a method of a Java object. The function may require arguments and may return a value:

```
var stage = javafx.stage.Stage {};

// Invoke the close() function of the JavaFX Stage object
stage.close();
```

Functions are discussed later in this chapter.

The as Operator

The as operator is the equivalent of a cast in Java:

```
import javafx.scene.Node;
import javafx.scene.text.Text;

var node:Node = Text {};
var text:Text = node as Text;
```

---

[3] As noted in Chapter 4, "A Simple JavaFX Application," although you can use new to create a JavaFX object, it is more usual to use an object literal. Unlike a Java class, a JavaFX class does not have a constructor, and therefore you cannot supply arguments if you choose to create a JavaFX object using the new keyword.

Here, a cast is necessary because the variable `node` is typed as `Node` not `Text`, but the assignment on the last line requires a `Text` object. `Text` is a subclass of `Node`.

If the object being cast is not an instance of the specified type, a `ClassCastException` will be thrown[4]:

```
import javafx.scene.Node;
import javafx.scene.shape.Circle;
import javafx.scene.text.Text;
var node:Node = Circle {};
var text:Text = node as Text;
```

In this example, the variable `node` refers to a `Circle`, which is another subclass of `Node`. The cast on the last line fails because a `Circle` is not a `Text` object.

The value `null` can be cast to *any* class or interface type:

```
import javafx.stage.Stage;
var stage:Stage = null as Stage; // null can be cast to any type
```

The `as` operator can also be used to assign the value of a floating-point type to an integer type without generating a compiler warning:

```
var number:Number = 3.14159265;
var integer:Integer = number as Integer;
```

Note that conversions of this type may cause information may be lost, and in this case it will be, because the fractional part of the value assigned to the `number` variable is not zero. The possibility of information loss is the reason for the compiler warning, which the as operator suppresses.

The `instanceof` Operator

The `instanceof` operator is used to determine whether an object is of a given type:

```
import javafx.scene.Node;
import javafx.scene.shape.Circle;
import javafx.scene.text.Text;

var node:Node = Circle {};
println("is node a Circle? {node instanceof Circle}");   // true
println("is node a Text? {node instanceof Text}");       // false
```

The `instanceof` operator returns `true` if the object to its left satisfies any of the following criteria:

- It is an instance of the exact specified type.
- The specified type is a class, and the object is an instance of a subclass of that class.

---

[4] The `as` operator differs in this respect from the similar operator in C#, which returns `null` instead of throwing an exception if its first operand is not of the type specified by its second operand.

- The specified type is an interface, and the object's class implements that interface.
- The specified type is a mixin class, and the object incorporates that mixin. (See Chapter 11, "JavaFX Script Classes," for a discussion of mixin classes.)

The following code illustrates the first three of these cases:

```
import javafx.scene.Node;
import javafx.scene.text.Text;
import java.lang.Comparable;
import java.util.Date;

var text:Text = Text{};

// Exact match - text IS a Text
println("text instanceof Text? {text instanceof Text}");  // true

// Text is a subclass of Node, so text is also a Node
println("text instanceof Node? {text instanceof Node}"); // true

// Date implements the Comparable interface, so date is a Comparable
var date:Date = new Date();
println("date instanceof Comparable? {date instanceof Comparable}");
                                                            // true
```

The value `null` is not an instance of any type:

```
import javafx.scene.Node;
import javafx.scene.text.Text;
import java.lang.Comparable;
import java.util.Date;

var text:Text = null;
println("text instanceof Text? {text instanceof Text}");     // false
println("text instanceof Node? {text instanceof Node}");     // false

var date:Date =null;
println("date instanceof Comparable? {date instanceof Comparable}");
                                                            // false
```

Contrast this with the fact that, as in Java, `null` can be cast (using the `as` operator) to an instance of any type.

Object Comparison

The `==` and `!=` operators can be used to determine whether two object instances are equal. In Java, these operators determine whether their operands refer to the same *instance* of an object. In JavaFX, however, the comparison performed by the `==` operator is the same as that performed by the `equals()` function, as follows:

```
var date1 = new Date(1970, 6, 4);
```

```
var date2 = new Date(1970, 6, 4);
var date3 = new Date(1971, 6, 5);
println(date1 == date2);    // Prints true
println(date1 == date3);    // Prints false
println(date1 != date2);    // Prints false
```

Notice that in JavaFX, the objects referred to by the variables `date1` and `date2` are considered to be equal by the `==` operator, whereas in Java they would not be, because they are different `Date` instances.

JavaFX Functions

A JavaFX function is a group of statements and expressions that apply some logic that may be based on supplied parameters or other state. A function may return a value and/or modify some state within the application. The logic in the body of the function is invoked by quoting the function's name together with the values of any required arguments. Placing code in a function makes it reusable without having to replicate it in multiple places, which would cause problems should that code ever need to be changed.

JavaFX has two types of function: *bound* and *unbound*. The motivation for two different types of function is that they behave differently in a *binding context*—that is, when some application state is bound to the value returned by the function. In this chapter, we restrict ourselves to discussing unbound functions and leave bound functions until we cover binding in Chapter 9.

Declaring Functions

A function can be declared within a JavaFX class or anywhere that a statement can appear within a JavaFX source file. The syntax is the same in both cases. Because we don't discuss the topic of writing JavaFX classes until Chapter 11, the examples in this chapter all show functions declared at the level of the script file,[5] which are referred as *script functions* (by contrast to functions declared in the body of a class, which are *instance functions*).

The syntax of a function declaration is as follows:

```
[modifiers] function name([arguments]) [:return type] { body }
```

Here's a simple example that contains all the possible components of a function declaration:

```
public function square(x:Number):Number { return x * x }
```

---

[5] In fact, functions that are coded directly inside the source file *are* within the scope of a JavaFX class, even though they may not appear to be. For the most part, you don't need to know that this is the case. If you want to know more, you'll find the details in Chapter 11.

The *modifiers* that may be applied to a function determine the visibility of the function to other code. See the section "Visibility of Functions," later in this chapter, for the details.

The *function name* is mandatory and must follow the rules for JavaFX identifiers listed in "Variable Declarations" in Chapter 5. The name should be meaningful and descriptive of what the function is supposed to do.

The *arguments*, if present, must be separated by commas. For each argument, both the type and a name must be given. The name is used in the body of the function to refer to the argument.

The *return type* specifies the type of the value that the function returns. If this is not specified, it will be inferred at compile time from the type of the expression in the function body that generates the return value. A function that does not need to return a value should be declared with a return type of `Void`.

> **Note**
>
> You may have noticed that a JavaFX function does not have a `throws` clause, but this does not mean that it will not throw an exception. Although JavaFX code can throw and catch exceptions, you are not forced to handle checked exceptions as you would in Java, and therefore functions do not declare the exceptions that they might throw. JavaFX exception handling is covered in Chapter 8, "Controlling Program Flow."

The following simple function prints the current date and time to the standard output stream. It is an example of a function that requires no arguments and returns no value:

```
import java.util.Date;

function printDateAndTime():Void {
    println(new Date());
}
```

Notice that the return type, in this case `Void`, is separated from the argument list by a colon.

The following function, called `average`, returns the average of two values passed as arguments:

```
function average(value1:Number, value2:Number):Number {
    return (value1 + value2) / 2;
}
```

The function arguments are called `value1` and `value2`; both are of type `Number`. Argument names are subject to the same rules as all JavaFX identifiers, and each argument must have a unique name. Within the body of the function, wherever the argument names are used, the corresponding value passed by the caller of the function will be substituted.

The return value in this example is declared to be of type `Number`. The value that will be returned is given by the expression attached to the `return` statement, which must be consistent with the declared return type. You do not actually need to use the `return` keyword at all, so the following code is equivalent to that previously shown:

```
function average(value1:Number, value2:Number):Number {
    (value1 + value2) / 2;
}
```

This works because JavaFX treats a set of statements or expressions enclosed in braces, such as the body of a function, as a *block expression*. The value of a block expression is defined to be the value of its last expression, so in the case of the preceding code, the value of the block expression, and therefore that of the function, is the result of evaluating the expression

```
(value1 + value2) / 2;
```

Note also that the final semicolon in a block expression is optional, so this code is also valid:

```
function average(value1:Number, value2:Number):Number {
    (value1 + value2) / 2    // Note - no semicolon
}
```

Finally, you can allow the compiler to infer the return type of your function, so the definition of the `average()` function can be simplified even further, to this:

```
function average(value1:Number, value2:Number) {
    (value1 + value2) / 2    // Note - no semicolon
}
```

> **Note**
>
> In the case of a function that is visible outside the script in which it is defined (such as a public function), it is good practice to define the exact return type so that callers know which type to expect. Leaving the return type unspecified risks breaking calling code if you change the implementation of the function in such a way as to cause its inferred return type to change.

In JavaFX as in Java, arguments are passed by value, not by reference. Unlike Java, it is not legal to assign a value to a function argument from within the body of the function. Consider the following code:

```
function getTopmostNode(node:Node):Node {
    while (node != null and node.parent != null) {
        node = node.parent;    // Compilation error
    }
    node;
}
```

As you have already seen, `Node` is a class in the GUI library that represents part of a scene graph—essentially, it is an element of a user interface. There are various types of basic node (such as lines, rectangles, and ellipses) that can be used to draw shapes, and there is a node type called `Group` that groups together and acts as a parent to other nodes. The link from a basic node to its owning parent can be found by reading its `parent` variable, which is another object of type `Node`. The code shown above finds the topmost parent of a node by first getting its immediate parent, then the parent of that parent, and so on, until it reaches a node that does not have a parent. In a function like this, it is necessary to have a variable of type `Node` that can be used to reference the current node as the code traverses the parent hierarchy, but it is not legal in JavaFX to use the `node` argument for this purpose. (And some consider it to be bad style, which is why the compiler enforces this restriction.) Instead, you need to define a new variable, like this:

```
function getTopmostNode(node:Node):Node {
    var nextNode = node;         // Use a local variable
    while (nextNode != null and nextNode.parent != null) {
        nextNode = nextNode.parent;
    }
    nextNode;
}
```

The following code uses the preceding function. It constructs a `Group`, places a `Rectangle` in that group, and gets the topmost node of the `Rectangle`, which should be the `Group`:

```
var rectangle = Rectangle { x: 0 y: 0 width: 100 height: 100 };
var group = Group {
    content: rectangle
}

var topMost = getTopmostNode(group);
println("topmost: {topMost}, node: {rectangle}");
```

Functions and Variables

Script functions have access to script variables that are in scope at the point of declaration of the function. This means that functions can read and manipulate values that are not passed as arguments. Here is an example:

```
var s = "Original Text";

function printVariableS() {
    println("Text is {s}");
}

printVariableS();

s = "Changed Text";
printVariableS();
```

The function `printVariables()` reads and prints the value of the variable `s`, which is defined outside of the function body. When it is first called, it prints `Original Text`, after which the value of `s` is changed, and the function is called again. The output from the second call is `Changed Text`, which demonstrates that the function is reading the live value of the variable.[6]

Functions Within Functions

It is legal to declare a function within another function. The inner function has access to any local variables declared within the outer function as well as any script variables that are in scope. You'll see an example of this in the "Anonymous Functions," section later in this chapter.

Invoking JavaFX Functions

A JavaFX script function (that is, one defined directly in the source file) can be invoked simply by quoting its name and supplying any necessary arguments, as shown in the previous example:

```
var topMost = getTopmostNode(group);
```

Functions defined in classes need an instance of the defining class or a subclass of the defining class. For example, as you have already seen, the `Stage` class in the `javafx.stage` package has a function called `close()` that can be used to close the stage when it is no longer required:

```
var stage = Stage { title: "Stage Title" };
stage.close()
```

As you can see, the function is invoked by applying the `.` operator to the variable `stage`, which refers to an instance of the `Stage` class.

Invoking Java Methods

Calling a Java method from JavaFX code is syntactically the same as invoking a JavaFX function. Static methods are called in the usual way, by quoting the classname and method name together with arguments, if there are any:

---

[6] Java has no equivalent of script-level functions. The closest approximation is a method in an anonymous inner class. Such a method would also have access to variables that are in scope at the time of its declaration, but they would have to be declared `final`, so their value would never be seen to change. Access to script-level variables from a function is an example of a *closure;* see http://en.wikipedia.org/wiki/Closure_(computer_science). Proposals are being considered to add a similar feature to Java.

```
import java.text.DateFormat;

// Calls the static method getDateInstance() of DateFormat
var dateFormat = DateFormat.getDateInstance();
```

Instance methods of Java classes are invoked in the same way as JavaFX functions:

```
// Calls instance method format() of DateFormat
var str = dateFormat.format(new java.util.Date());
```

The JavaFX compiler converts the types of the arguments that it is given to those of the arguments required by the Java method, where possible. For example, the `java.lang.Math` class has four static methods that return the absolute value of the supplied argument:

```
public static double abs(double a);
public static float abs(float a);
public static int abs(int a);
public static long abs(long a);
```

Each method has a different numeric argument type. Suppose we write the following JavaFX code:

```
var a:Number = -3.14159265;
var absValue = java.lang.Math.abs(a);
```

The parameter `a` has the JavaFX type `Number`, which is not any of the Java types `double`, `float`, `int`, or `long`. The JavaFX compiler chooses the variant of the `abs()` method that has an argument type that most closely matches the type of the parameter that has been supplied. In this case, it will choose the variant that accepts an argument of type `float` because it is the closest available match to `Number`. At runtime, the `Number` value will be converted to a `float` and passed to the `abs()` method. If instead you were to supply an `Integer` value, like this, the compiler would choose the variant that accepts an argument of type `int`:

```
var n:Integer = -32;
var absValue = java.lang.Math.abs(n);
```

In some cases, a widening conversion is required, as in the following example:

```
var a:Short = -32;
var absValue = java.lang.Math.abs(a);
```

In this case, the argument is of type `Short`, but there is no variant of the `abs()` method that accepts an argument of the Java primitive type `short`, so the compiler converts the `Short` to an `Integer` and chooses the method `Math.abs(int)`.

Function Variables

JavaFX functions are much more flexible than Java methods—not only can you declare a function outside a class definition, but you can also assign a function to a variable, pass a function as an argument to another function, and even return a function from a function call. These features make JavaFX functions *first-class citizens* of the language.[7] It is cumbersome to do any of these things with Java methods because it requires that you invent an interface and pass around references to it. As you'll see, first-class functions are much easier to use than artificially created Java interfaces.

The syntax for a function variable declaration is as follows:

```
[modifiers] var|def name:function([args])[:return type] [= initializer];
```

For example, the following code declares a variable called `fn` that can be assigned a reference to *any* function that accepts an argument of type `Number` and returns a `Number` value:

```
var fn:function(arg:Number):Number;
```

Notice that the part of the declaration that follows the variable name has the same syntax as a function declaration except that, as you are not actually declaring a function here, the name of the function is replaced by the placeholder keyword `function`.

The declaration above specifies that functions that are to be assigned to the variable `fn` must accept a single argument of type `Number`, which has been arbitrarily named `arg`. As there is no function body, this name is not actually used anywhere (and additionally, any functions that may be assigned to this variable are not required to name their argument `arg`). For this reason, it is not mandatory to give the argument a name at all, so the preceding declaration could also have been written like this:

```
var fn:function(:Number):Number;
```

Although this is shorter, it is also less clear, because there is no hint as to what the argument might be used for. Note that the `:` before the argument type is still required. The return type is also optional and, if you omit it, `:Void` is assumed.[8]

Using a Function Variable

Let's look at an example that makes use of a function variable. Suppose you were writing an application that needed to get a random number in the range 0 to N for some value N. There are various ways to generate random numbers, so you might like to try out some different approaches before making a final choice of algorithm. To do this, you could write several different functions, each of which uses a different random number

---

[7] See http://en.wikipedia.org/wiki/First-class_function for a discussion of what is meant by the term *first-class function*—essentially, it means that a function can be used anywhere that a value of any other kind can be used.

[8] The return type is taken as `Void` rather than being inferred because there is no function body available to make type inference possible.

generation algorithm. To switch between algorithms, you must modify all the places in your code that need a random number so that they call the function that uses the algorithm that you want to test. This would be both tedious and error-prone. A better way is to use a function variable.

The first step is to define the common signature for the random number functions. That's easy—you have already seen it:

```
function xxx(max:Number):Number
```

We will implement two versions of this function that use the two different random number generators to return a number in the range 0 (inclusive) to the value of the max argument (exclusive). Here's the first one, called random1(), which uses the random() function of the javafx.util.Math class:

```
function random1(max:Number):Number {
    print("random1: ");
    return Math.random() * max;
}
```

As you can see, this function prints a message so that we can see that it has been called. The second version uses the nextDouble() method of the java.util.Random class. This is not a static method, so we need to create an instance of Random first:

```
var seededRandom = new Random();
function random2(max:Number):Number {
    print("random2: ");
    return seededRandom.nextDouble() * max;
}
```

To write code that does not depend on which of these two methods is to be used, we declare a function variable called getRandom, and then invoke the function using that variable:

```
// Variable definition
var getRandom:function(:Number):Number;

// Assign the first function to the variable and invoke it
getRandom = random1;
println("{getRandom(10)}");

// Assign the second function to the variable and invoke it
getRandom = random2;
println("{getRandom(10)}");
```

Choosing which function should be invoked is simply a matter of assigning it, by name, to the variable:

```
getRandom = random1;
```

Then we use the variable name to invoke the function:

```
println("{getRandom(10)}");
```

It is important to note that the invocation code is the same in both cases—only the referenced function has changed. The output from this code shows that both functions were called:

```
random1: 7.955331635323349
random2: 3.0557449745743446
```

Obviously, you should get a different pair of random numbers between `0` and `10` every time you run this code, subject, of course, to the limitations of the random number algorithm.

Passing a Function to Another Function

Building on the previous example, suppose we want to not only call either of the random number generation functions but also to print out how long each of them took to generate a number. One way to do this is to add the necessary code to both of the random number functions. This technique only works if you can modify the source of the function whose execution time you want to measure. In this section, you learn another way that does not make this assumption. The idea is to create another function that includes the timing code, which will invoke either of the random number functions previously shown, recording the system time before and after the call. It will know which function to call because we will pass that function to it as a parameter. Here's the function that does the work:

```
1      function timing(f:function(:Number):Number, arg:Number,
2                      name:String):Number {
3          print("Calling {name}...");
4          var start:Number = System.nanoTime();
5          var result = f(arg);
6          var time:Number = System.nanoTime() - start;
7          println("Result is {result}, time {time} nanoseconds");
8          result
9      }
```

As you can see, this function has three arguments. The first is the function that it should time, the second is the argument to pass to that function, and the third is the name of the function that is being timed, which will be printed along with the timing information.

The function argument, shown on line 1, is the one that is of interest here. It is declared in the same way as if it had been a variable declaration, except that the `var` and `def` keywords are not used. The argument name, here `f`, is used within the body to refer to the function. Line 5 shows how to invoke the function:

```
var result = f(arg);
```

This looks exactly like a normal function call, except that the function name in this case is actually a reference to the argument f rather than a function whose name is actually f. Here's how the timing() function is called:

```
timing(random1, 4, "random1");
timing(random2, 4, "random2");
```

As with variable assignment, the functions to be executed are passed by name. Here is the resulting output:

```
Calling random1...random1: Result is 3.9868746713812024, time 61251.0 nanoseconds
Calling random2...random2: Result is 3.4120310769010644, time 78641.0 nanoseconds
```

Of course, these timings are not very meaningful, because both random1() and random2() print to the standard output stream.[9]

Functions can return functions as well as accept function arguments. To demonstrate this, we are going to write a function that randomly selects and returns one of the random number generating functions. This is isn't very useful in reality, but it does allow us to show the syntax of the function declaration and how you would write the code.

Here is how you declare a function that returns a function:

```
function choose():function(:Number):Number {
    if (Math.random() >= 0.5) random1 else random2
}
```

The most complicated thing about this is the actual declaration on the first line. The code itself is simple—get a random number between 0 and 1 and return either the function random1() or the function random2(), depending on whether the number is less than or greater than or equal to 0.5. The function declaration breaks into two pieces, which are shown together with what they represent, in Figure 6-1.

function choose():function(:Number):Number

Declares a function called "choose"

...returning a function that accepts a Number and returns a Number

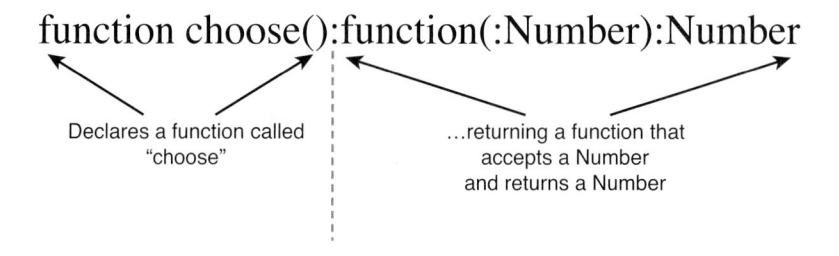

Figure 6-1 Declaration of a function that returns another function

---

[9] In any case, no conclusions about performance should be based on only one measurement!

This declaration is actually the same as all the other function declarations that you have seen so far, except that more words are required to specify the return type, which makes it look more complicated than it actually is.[10]

You invoke this function like any other. Here's a loop that calls it ten times[11]:

```
1    for (i in [1..10]) {
2        def f:function(:Number):Number = choose();
3        println(f(4));
4    }
```

The code on line 2 invokes `choose()` and assigns the returned function to the variable `f`.[12] Line 3 invokes the function and prints the result. Here's the result of running this once, which demonstrates that both functions are being called:

```
random1: 3.733331854719099
random2: 2.633386473641948
random2: 1.5361280165149975
random1: 2.152131354957821
random2: 1.5555729899300328
random1: 3.783056254059573
random1: 1.8344515105724022
random1: 0.8343740967334363
random2: 3.570944412453987
random1: 3.222864647265261
```

Assigning the function reference to a variable and then using that variable is one way to invoke the returned function. There is another, more terse, syntax that avoids the use of an intermediate variable:

```
for (i in [1..10]) {
    println(choose()(4));
}
```

The expression `choose()(4)` invokes the function `choose()` and then invokes the function that it returns with argument 4. It is slightly easier to see this if you read it like this:

```
( choose() ) (4)
```

---

[10] It can get more complex. Suppose the function being returned itself returns a function. C programmers might be reminded of the syntax needed to declare function pointers, which is quite esoteric until you understand it. What exactly *does* `char *(*ptr)(char *, int)` mean?
[11] The `for` statement, like the `if` statement used in the function itself, is covered in Chapter 7.
[12] Notice that the variable `f` is declared using `def` rather than `var`. This is a stylistic choice that emphasizes the fact that the value will not change after it has been assigned.

Anonymous Functions

Function variables are not the only things that can hold a reference to a function—a JavaFX class can have an instance variable for which the value is a function. This is typically used to allow the class to invoke an application-defined method when a specific event occurs. For example, the `javafx.stage.Stage` class has an instance variable called `onClose` that is effectively defined like this:

```
public var onClose:function():Void = close;
```

This function is called when the your application's stage is being closed. Here's an example that uses the `onClose` variable:

```
1    function stageClose() {
2        println("'{stage1.title}' closing");
3    }
4
5    def stage1:Stage = Stage {
6        title: "Close Action #1"
7        width: 400 height: 400 x: 100 y: 10 visible: true
8        onClose: stageClose
9    }
```

On lines 1 through 3, we declare the function that we want to have called when the stage is closing. In this case, we just print a message that contains the stage's title. Notice, though, that in this function we need a reference to the stage to get the value of its `title` variable, but at this point, we haven't even created the stage. To make this possible, we declare a variable called `stage1` that we initialize with a reference to the actual `Stage` object. We couldn't declare the stage first because we want to install the `onClose` handler in the object literal that creates the stage, as previously shown. Although this code works, it is clumsy because we have had to create the function `stageClose()` and the script variable `stage1` that we aren't going to use anywhere else. In Java, you would use an anonymous inner class in this situation, and JavaFX provides a similar concept—an *anonymous function*—which is just what we need here.

As its name suggests, an anonymous function is a function that does not have a name. The following code creates an anonymous function that returns a random number:

```
function():Number {
    return Math.random();
};
```

As you can see, the function declaration consists of the word `function` followed by the arguments in parentheses (in this case, there are none) followed by the return type and the function body. Of course, because this function is anonymous, there is no way to reference it, so typically you would assign it to a variable, as shown next. You can use an anonymous function in several places. The following sections contain some examples.

Anonymous Functions and Function Variables

It is possible to define a function variable and directly assign an anonymous function to it, as this example demonstrates:

```
var fn1 = function():Number {
           return Math.random();
        };
println("A random number: {fn1()}");
```

As with all uses of anonymous functions, the prime benefit of this is that there is no need to invent a name for the function being assigned to the variable.

Returning an Anonymous Function from Another Function

Functions that return a function can return an anonymous function:

```
function getRandomSource():function(:Number):Number {
    return function (max:Number):Number {
        return Math.random() * max;
    }
}
```

This (rather artificial) example shows a function that, when you call it, returns to you another function from which you can obtain a random number. Here's how you would use it:

```
println("Random from anonymous function: {getRandomSource()(4)}");
```

An Anonymous Function as an Initializer in an Object Literal

One of the most common uses of an anonymous function is to initialize an instance variable, such as the `onClose` instance variable of the `Stage` class that you saw earlier in this section. Recall that using a named function to initialize this instance variable resulted in some clumsy code. Here's how you could do the same thing with an anonymous function:

```
def stage2:Stage = Stage {
    title: "Close Action #2"
    width: 400 height: 400 x: 500 y: 10 visible:true
    onClose: function() {
             println("'{stage2.title}' closing");
          }
}
```

As you can see, all the code is now contained within the initialization of the stage. It is clear that the code in the anonymous function is intended only to be called in response to the closing of the stage, which makes understanding easier and maintenance simpler. This is a pattern that you will use a lot when writing JavaFX applications.

When an instance variable requires a function that has one or more arguments, it is not necessary to restate the argument types when initializing that instance variable in an object literal. For example, the `Rectangle` class in the `javafx.scene.shape` package has several function-valued instance variables (inherited from its parent class, `javafx.scene.Node`) that allow application code to be called in response to various events, such as those generated when the mouse is over the part of the screen occupied by the `Rectangle`. The `onMouseMoved` instance variable, which is a typical example, is defined like this:

```
public var onMouseMoved: function(e:MouseEvent):Void
```

Here's one way to assign a handler to this instance variable:

```
// Restates "MouseEvent " as the argument type onMouseMoved: onMouseMoved: function(evt:MouseEvent) {
    println("Mouse at {evt.x}, {evt.y}");
}
```

Because the declaration of the instance variable `onMouseMoved` includes the information that the function argument is of type `MouseEvent`, it is not necessary to respecify this when assigning a handler to it. As a result, the preceding code could also be written more succinctly like this:

```
// No need to restate the argument type - it is implicit
onMouseMoved: function(evt) {
    println("Mouse at {evt.x}, {evt.y}");
}
```

Visibility of Functions

Like variables, a function declaration can have an associated visibility modifier. The following modifiers can be applied to function declarations:

- No modifier: The function is visible only in the script in which it is declared.
- `public`: The function is visible everywhere.
- `package`: The function is visible in all scripts that are in the same package as the declaring script.
- `protected`: The function is visible in all scripts that are in the same package as the declaring script and in any subclasses of the class that owns it. See Chapter 11 for more about this.

Object Literals

As you have already seen, object literals are used to create and initialize an instance of a JavaFX class. In this section, we look more closely at the syntax of an object literal.

Initializing a JavaFX Object

Initializing a JavaFX object is the most common use for an object literal. The syntax requires that you specify the name of the class followed by the instance variables of the class that you want to provide initial values for, enclosed in braces. Each instance variable is initialized by providing its name and an expression that resolves to the required initial value, separated by a colon. For example, the following code creates two `Stage` objects with the same width and height, places them next to each other on the user's desktop, and makes them visible:

```
1      var s1:Stage = Stage {
2                      title: "Stage 1"
3                      x: 20
4                      y: 20
5                      width: 200
6                      height: 300
7                  }
8
9      var s2:Stage = Stage {
10                     title: "Stage 2"
11                     x: s1.x + s1.width
12                     y: s1.y
13                     width: s1.width
14                     height: s1.height
15                 }
```

Lines 1 through 7 initialize the first stage, supplying values for the instance variables that determine its position (x and y), its size (`width` and `height`), and the text in its title bar (`title`). All the initializers in this case are constant values.

Lines 9 through 15 initialize the second stage. As you can see, some of the initial values in this case are expressions that depend on values assigned to the instance variables of the first stage:

- The x value is the x value of the first stage plus its width, which has the effect of placing the second stage to the immediate right of the first.
- The y value is the same as that of the first stage, which causes their title bars to be vertically aligned.
- The `width` and `height` are set from those of the first stage, which causes the stages to have the same size.

There is no need, as shown in this example, to have an explicit separator between the initializers, nor is it necessary to place them on separate lines but, if you want, you can use either a comma or a semicolon as a separator:

```
var s3:Stage = Stage {
              title: "Stage 3"        // No separator
```

```
            x: 10,              // Comma
            y: 10;              // Semicolon
            width: 100 height: 200  // More than one per line
    }
```

Object literals can be nested, allowing the creation of object trees. The following example constructs a stage with a nested `Text` object displaying `Hello, JavaFX World`:

```
1   var s4:Stage = Stage {
2               title: "Stage 4"
3               x: 200
4               y: 200
5               width: 300 height: 200
6               scene: Scene {
7                   content: [
8                       Text {
9                           content: "Hello, JavaFX World"
10                          x: 20
11                          y: 80
12                      }
13                  ]
14              }
15  }
```

The nested object literal on lines 8 through 12 initializes the `Text` object, installing the message and positioning it relative to the scene, which represents the useful area of the stage, and is itself created by the nested object literal on lines 6 to 14.

An object initializer can supply values for the any of the instance variables of a class to which the script has write access and includes instance variables that the class inherits from its superclasses, if any. An arbitrary script has write access to an instance variable for which the access modifier is `public` or `public-init`, the latter of which is a modifier that can be only be used inside a class definition. See Chapter 11 for more details

Variables in Object Literals

It is possible to declare variables inside an object literal. A variable defined in this way would typically be used to simplify what would otherwise be a complex initializer expression and is scoped to the object literal in which it is defined, plus any nested object literals. Here is an example:

```
1   var s5:Stage = Stage {
2       var area:Integer =  bind s5.height * s5.width as   Integer
3       title: bind "Stage area is {area} square pixels"
4       height: 200
5       width: 300
6       x: 100
7       y: 10
8   }
```

The intent here is to display the area of the stage in square pixels in its title bar. To do so, we need to multiply its width by its height. The variable `area` declared on line 2 is bound to the product of the stage's width and height, which means that as they change, its value will be updated so that it always represents the current area of the stage. This variable can be referenced anywhere within the object literal, but not outside of it. Here, the value is used in the initializer for the instance variable `title` on line 3. Again, the `bind` operator is used, so that when either the width or height change, so will the value of `area` and consequently so will the stage title.

There are a couple of important points to note in this code. First, on line 2, the values of the stage's instance variables are referenced using the variable `s5` to which the stage is assigned. This might look strange at first, because it may seem that the value of `s5` is being used before it is actually set. However, JavaFX guarantees that this will not be the case—it is safe to reference this value from within the object literal. As a Java programmer, you may have been hoping to do one of the following:

```
var s5: Stage = Stage {    // This code does not compile!
    var area:Integer = bind height * width

var s5: Stage = Stage {    // This code does not compile!
    var area:Integer = bind this.height * this.width
```

However, neither of these works because *the object literal is not evaluated in the context of the instance of the object being created*, and therefore there is no `this` reference, either implicit or explicit.

The second point to note is that the variable `area` is referenced on line 3 without any qualifier. This works because the variable declaration and its use *are* in the same context (that of the object literal), and therefore no qualifier is required.

Functions in Object Literals

You can use object literal functions to create an anonymous JavaFX class that implements a Java interface. For example, the following code adds a `PropertyChangeListener` to a JavaBean:

```
1    var bean = ....;
2    bean.addPropertyChangeListener(PropertyChangeListener {
3        public override function      propertyChange(evt:PropertyChangeEvent) {
4            println("Event {evt.getPropertyName()}");
5        }
6    });
```

Compare this JavaFX code with the corresponding Java code, where the differences are highlighted:

```
1    bean.addPropertyChangeListener(new PropertyChangeListener() {
2        public void propertyChange(PropertyChangeEvent evt) {
```

```
3                println("Event " + evt.getPropertyName());
4            }
5        });
```

Note the following points:

- The definition on lines 1 and 2 of the JavaFX code looks very much like the anonymous inner class construction on the same lines of the Java code, but it is actually an object literal declaration, which is why the `new` keyword is not needed.
- The JavaFX version of the `propertyChange()` function requires the keyword `function` before the name and the return type is placed before the function body. In this case, the return type is `Void`, so it doesn't need to be explicitly stated. The JavaFX version also requires the keyword `override`, which indicates that the `propertyChange()` function is an implementation of a function declared in the `PropertyChangeListener` interface, as opposed to a completely new function. You can consider the override keyword to be the JavaFX equivalent of the `@Override` annotation in Java. For more on this, see Chapter 11.
- The syntax for the argument definition is different—in JavaFX, the parameter name precedes the type.

7
Sequences

JavaFX has an extremely useful data type called a *sequence* that is the subject of this chapter. A sequence is a one-dimensional, ordered collection of zero or more elements that share a common base type. In some ways, a sequence is like a Java array, but it also has some of the characteristics of a Java collection. In the first part this chapter, you see how to create sequences, how to modify them, and how to query them.

Although sequences are the primary multivalue data type in JavaFX, there is also basic support for Java arrays, which are supported only to make it possible to efficiently work with Java methods that require array arguments or return array values. The JavaFX support for Java arrays is discussed in the second part of this chapter.

Sequence Creation

The syntax for declaring a sequence makes it look a little like a Java array declaration. The following code creates four sequences containing, respectively, `Integers`, `Numbers`, `Strings`, and `Objects`:

```
var integers:Integer[] = [1, 2, 3, 4, 5];
var numbers:Number[] = [1.1, 2.2, 3.3, 4.4, 5.5];
var strings:String[] = ["The", "cat", "sat", "on", "the", "mat"];
var objects:Object[] = ["String", 1, 2.4, new Date()];
```

Notice that the initial value of a sequence is specified by listing the required elements in order, separated by commas and surrounded by square brackets. The same syntax is used wherever a literal sequence value is required, such as this assignment to an existing sequence variable:

```
integers = [3, 2, 1];
```

The JavaFX compiler can infer the type of a sequence based on its initial value, so the preceding sequence definitions can be written more succinctly like this:

```
var integers = [1, 2, 3, 4, 5];
var numbers = [1.1, 2.2, 3.3, 4.4, 5.5];
var strings = ["The", "cat", "sat", "on", "the", "mat"];
var objects = ["String", 1, 2.4, new Date()];
```

The compiler infers a type of `Object[]` for the last of these because it is the only common base class shared by the initial values in the initializer.

Sequences can be of any size, including zero. Here is how you would create a sequence of `Integer`s that is initially empty:

```
var emptySequence1:Integer[] = [];
```

You can achieve the same thing by assigning the value `null` to a sequence variable, because `null` is treated as an empty sequence in this context:

```
var emptySequence2:Integer[] = null;
```

A sequence that consists of only one element can be constructed without the need for the square brackets. So

```
// Singleton sequence.
var singleton:Integer[] = 1;
```

The preceding code is the same as

```
var singleton:Integer[] = [1];
```

The language syntax also allows you to use a sequence as an element of another sequence, like this:

```
var flattened:Integer[] = [1, [2, 3], [4, 5, 6]];
println("Flattened sequence: {flattened.toString()}");
```

It is important to note, though, that nested sequences are not supported, so this code does *not* create some kind of two-dimensional array. Instead, the elements of the apparently nested sequences are flattened into the outer sequence, giving the following result:

```
Flattened sequence: [ 1, 2, 3, 4, 5, 6 ]
```

Sequences are, therefore, one-dimensional.

You can create an immutable sequence by using `def` rather than `var`:

```
def fixed = [1, 2, 3, 4, 5];
```

An attempted assignment to an immutable sequence generates a compilation error:

```
fixed = [3, 4, 5, 6];  // Compilation error
fixed[1] = 23;         // Compilation error
```

You can get the elements of a sequence in reverse order by using the `reverse` operator. For example

```
var range:Integer[] = [1, 2, 3, 4, 5, 6, 7, 8, 9, 10];
var reverseRange:Integer[] = reverse range;
println("Range: {range.toString()}");
println("Reverse of range: {reverseRange.toString()}");
```

This code produces the following output:

```
Range: [ 1, 2, 3, 4, 5, 6, 7, 8, 9, 10 ]
Reverse of range: [ 10, 9, 8, 7, 6, 5, 4, 3, 2, 1 ]
```

The String Form of a Sequence

The `reverse` operator does *not* modify the sequence to which it is applied—it just returns a new sequence with the elements in reverse order. This is, in fact, a general rule—every operation that would result in a sequence being modified actually returns a modified copy, leaving the original sequence unchanged.

The String Form of a Sequence

You can convert the content of a sequence into a readable string form by using the sequence name in an expression embedded within a string, like this:

```
println("Integers: {integers}");
println("Numbers: {numbers}");
println("Strings: {strings}");
println("Objects: {objects}");
println("Empty 1: {emptySequence1}");
println("Empty 2: {emptySequence2}");
```

However, this produces a representation that is not particularly useful for debugging:

```
Integers: 12345
Numbers: 1.12.23.34.45.5
Strings: Thecatsatonthemat
Objects: String12.4Sat Jun 07 14:59:03 BST 2008
Empty 1:
Empty 2:
```

As you can see, the result is constructed by appending the string representations of the individual elements in order, but with no separators, so it is difficult to see where the boundaries are. For debugging purposes, it is better to use the `toString()` function, which is implemented by every sequence:

```
println("toString() integers: {integers.toString()}");
println("toString() numbers: {numbers.toString()}");
println("toString() strings: {strings.toString()}");
println("toString() objects: {objects.toString()}");
println("toString() Empty 1: {emptySequence1.toString()}");
println("toString() Empty 2: {emptySequence2.toString()}");
```

The `toString()` function surrounds the sequence content with square brackets and adds a comma and a space between the elements, making is possible to distinguish them and to see more easily when a sequence is empty:

```
toString() integers: [ 1, 2, 3, 4, 5 ]
toString() numbers: [ 1.1, 2.2, 3.3, 4.4, 5.5 ]
toString() strings: [ The, cat, sat, on, the, mat ]
toString() objects: [ String, 1, 2.4, Sat Jun 07 14:59:03 BST 2008 ]
toString() Empty 1: [ ]
toString() Empty 2: [ ]
```

Range Notation

Sequences that consist of consecutive numeric values can be created using a shorthand *range* notation, as the examples in Table 7-1 show. A range consists of a pair of numbers (or numeric expressions, or one of each) that represents the bounds of the range, separated by two periods, and an optional step value.

Table 7-1   **Constructing Sequences Using Range Expressions**

Range Expression	Result	Comment
`var range1:Integer[] = [1..5];`	`[ 1, 2, 3, 4, 5 ]`	This range consists of the integer values from `1` to `5` inclusive, with an implicit step of `1`.
`var range2:Integer[] = [1..5 step 2];`	`[ 1, 3, 5 ]`	The numbers `1` through `5`, with an explicit step of `2`.
`var range3:Integer[] = [5..1 step -1];`	`[ 5, 4, 3, 2, 1 ]`	The numbers `5` through `1` with a step value of `-1`, which produces a sequence of decreasing values.
`var range4:Number[] = [1..5 step 0.5];`	`[ 1.0, 1.5, 2.0, 2.5, 3.0, 3.5, 4.0, 4.5, 5.0 ]`	A sequence of values from `1` through `5`, with a step value of `0.5`. Fractional step values are not allowed in the definition of `Integer` sequences, for obvious reasons.
`var range5:Integer[] = [1..<5];`	`[ 1, 2, 3, 4 ]`	A sequence of values from `1` to `5` *exclusive*, with an implied step of 1. Note that this notation allows the end value of the range to be excluded, but there is no way to specify that the first value should not be included.
`var range6:Integer[] = [5..<1 step -1];`	`[ 5, 4, 3, 2 ]`	A descending sequence of integers from `5` down to `1`, exclusive.

> **Note**
>
> A positive step (even an implicit one) should be used only when the second bound is larger than the first, and a negative step when the second bound is smaller. The following code, which breaks this rule, may not do what you would expect it to:
>
> `var seq:Integer[] = [5..1];`
>
> This looks like it might produce `[5, 4, 3, 2, 1]`, but in fact it creates an empty sequence because the step value is implicitly `1` and the second bound is less than the first. Because this is unlikely to be what you intended, the compiler will issue a warning if it determines that the sequence would be empty for this reason.

While the preceding examples create sequences of determinate size, the upper and lower bound and the step value can all be expressions, with the result that the size of the sequence would depend on runtime values. For example

```
var bound1:Integer = (Math.random() * 10) as Integer;
var bound2:Integer = (Math.random() * 10) as Integer;
var range:Integer[] = [Math.min(bound1, bound2)..Math.max(bound1, bound2)];
```

This code assigns two random numbers in the range 0 to 10 (exclusive) to the variables bound1 and bound2 and then creates a sequence containing all the integers including and between those two values, in ascending order.

Sequence Equality and Copying

Sequences can be compared for equality using the == operator.

```
var seq1:Integer[] = [1..5];
var seq2:Integer[] = [1..5];
println("seq1 == seq2? {seq1 == seq2}");
```

In the preceding code, seq1 and seq2 refer to two sequences that are created using the same range expression. The result of running this code is the following:

```
seq1 == seq2? true
```

Two sequences are equal if

- They are both null (that is, empty) *or*
- They have the same number of elements *and* each element in one sequence is equal to the corresponding element in the same position in the other sequence.

It is important to note that assigning the value of one sequence variable to another does *not* have the same effect as it would in Java:

```
var seq1:Integer[] = [1..5];
var seq2:Integer[] = seq1;
```

This code creates a five-element sequence, assigns it to the variable seq1, and then assigns the value of seq1 to the variable seq2. In Java, seq1 and seq2 would now be pointing to the same sequence (or they would if Java had sequences—to make sense of this statement, think of a sequence as an array for the moment), and changes made to either seq1 or seq2 would be visible in the other. In JavaFX, this is *not* the case—the assignment actually makes a (logical) copy of the sequence and assigns that to seq2.[1]

---

[1] The copy is logical because nothing need actually be copied at the point of assignment. As an optimization, the two sequence variables can be made to refer to the same storage until one of them is modified, at which point a copy is made, and the update is made to the copied sequence content.

To demonstrate this, we'll add an element to the original sequence using the `insert` keyword (which you'll see later in this chapter) and compare them:

```
insert 6 into seq1;
println("After insert, seq1: {seq1.toString()},"
        "seq2: {seq2.toString()}");
```

The output shows that the sequence referred to by `seq1` has been changed, but the one that `seq2` points to has not:

```
After insert, seq1: [ 1, 2, 3, 4, 5, 6 ], seq2: [ 1, 2, 3, 4, 5 ]
```

A sequence of a given type can be assigned to any sequence variable whose type is the same as that of the original sequence, or a base class or mixin of that type, or an interface implemented by the original type. If that sounds like a mouthful, it is easy to explain what is meant by example. The following code is legal because `Rectangle` is a subclass of `Node`:

```
var rectangles:Rectangle[] = [Rectangle{}, Rectangle{}];
var nodes:Node[] = rectangles;
```

The assignment succeeds because a sequence of rectangles is also a sequence of nodes. Similarly, the following code is valid because `String` implements the `Comparable` interface:

```
var comparables:Comparable[] = ["A", "B"];
```

A sequence value can only be assigned to a sequence variable. Although this might sound obvious, it is different from the way in which Java arrays are treated. A Java array is a type of `Object` and therefore can be assigned to a variable of type `Object`, but in JavaFX this is not the case—sequences are *not* `Object`s, so the following code does not compile:

```
var rectangles:Rectangle[] = [Rectangle{}, Rectangle{}];
var o:Object = rectangles;   // Error: cannot assign to Object
```

Querying Sequences

After you have created a sequence, there are various ways to get information from it. In addition to the constructions shown in this section, sequences are frequently used in conjunction with the `for` statement, which is described in Chapter 8, "Controlling Program Flow."

Obtaining the Size of a Sequence

The number of elements in a sequence can be obtained by using the `sizeof` operator:

```
var tenInts:Integer[] = [1..10];
var noInts:Integer[] = [];
println("Size of tenInts: {sizeof tenInts}, "
        "size of noInts: {sizeof noInts}");
```

This code produces the following output:

```
Size of tenInts: 10, size of noInts: 0
```

Obtaining an Element of a Sequence

The value of an individual element of a sequence can be obtained by placing its index in square brackets after the sequence name. If the index is a floating-point value, it is truncated to an `Integer` before use (and a warning is generated in case you didn't intend to use a nonintegral index). The index of the first element in a sequence is 0:

```
var tenInts:Integer[] = [1..10];
var int0 = tenInts[0];      // Result is 1
var int9 = tenInts[9];      // Result is 10
var int9a = tenInts[9.2];   // Result is also 10
```

The index can also be an expression that returns a numeric value. The following expression returns the value of the last element of the sequence `tenInts`:

```
tenInts[sizeof tenInts - 1]
```

If the index is negative or greater than or equal to the size of the sequence, the result is the default value of the sequence type. In other words, *it is not an error to attempt to access an element that it is outside the bounds of the sequence*. For example

```
var integers:Integer[] = [1, 2, 3, 4, 5];
var numbers:Number[] = [1.1, 2.2, 3.3, 4.4, 5.5];
var strings:String[] = ["The", "cat", "sat", "on", "the", "mat"];
var objects:Object[] = ["String", 1, 2.4, new Date()];
println("integers[-1] = {integers[-1]}, integers[10] = {integers[10]}");
println("numbers[-1] = {numbers[-1]}, numbers[10] = {numbers[10]}");
println("strings[-1] = {strings[-1]}, strings[10] = {strings[10]}");
println("objects[-1] = {objects[-1]}, objects[10] = {objects[10]}");
```

This code would print the following:

```
integers[-1] = 0, integers[10] = 0
numbers[-1] = 0.0, numbers[10] = 0.0
strings[-1] = , strings[10] =
objects[-1] = null, objects[10] = null
```

Because the compiler converts a single element to a sequence when assigning to a sequence variable, you can use the indexing syntax to create a single-element sequence from an existing sequence, like this:

```
var seqOfOne:Integer[] = tenInts[4];
println("seqOfOne: {seqOfOne.toString()}");
```

This code prints the following:

```
seqOfOne: [ 5 ]
```

It is more succinct than the following equivalent line of code:

```
var seqOfOne:Integer[] = [tenInts[4]];
```

Obtaining Part of a Sequence

You can use the range syntax that you saw earlier in this chapter to extract a contiguous range of elements from a sequence. The bounds of the expression may be constants or numeric expressions:

```
var tenInts:Integer[] = [1..10];

// Elements 0 through 2 - produces [1, 2, 3]
var subseq1:Integer[] = tenInts[0..2];

// Produces [8, 9, 10]
var subseq2:Integer[] = tenInts[sizeof tenInts - 3..sizeof tenInts - 1];
```

As before, if the upper bound is preceded by the symbol <, it is treated as an exclusive bound. This is commonly used when you want everything from a certain index up to but not including the last element in the sequence. For example, the syntax [n..<] yields the set of elements from index n up to, but *excluding*, the last element of the sequence:

```
println("{tenInts[0..<].toString()}");
```

The preceding code produces the result

```
[ 1, 2, 3, 4, 5, 6, 7, 8, 9 ]
```

This includes everything but the last element sequence. If you omit the upper bound, it defaults to the last element:

```
println("{tenInts[0..].toString()}");
```

This code prints the following

```
[ 1, 2, 3, 4, 5, 6, 7, 8, 9, 10 ]
```

A negative bound is replaced by index 0, while a bound that exceeds the number of elements in the sequence is replaced by the maximum valid index. For example

```
var subseq4:Integer[] = tenInts[7..120];   // Produces [8, 9, 10]
var subseq5:Integer[] = tenInts[-7..1];    // Produces [1, 2]
```

If the upper and lower bound have the same value, the result is a single-element sequence containing the element at the specified index:

```
var subseq6:Integer[] = tenInts[7..7];   // Produces [8]
```

If the upper bound is smaller than the lower bound, the result is an empty sequence:

```
var subseq7:Integer[] = tenInts[7..6];   // Produces []
```

Querying a Sequence by Condition

Another way to extract a subset of the elements of a collection is to use a query.
The simplest way to explain this is by example. The following code creates a new sequence that contains all the elements of the sequence tenInts that have values greater than 5:

```
var tenInts:Integer[] = [1..10];
var greater5:Integer[] = tenInts[n | n > 5];
```

The symbol | indicates a query. The identifier to the left is used to represent an element from the sequence in the query expression that appears on the right, so the way to read the expression on the right of the second line of code is "those values in the sequence `tenInts` whose value is greater than 5."

The type of the element identifier is taken from that of the sequence, so in this case n is implicitly defined to be of type `Integer`. Logically speaking, the value of each element of the sequence is assigned in turn to n, and then the query expression is evaluated. If the query expression evaluates to `true`, the element appears in the resulting sequence. Because the expression n > 5 is `true` only for values greater than 5, the sequence that results from the preceding code is as follows:

```
[6, 7, 8, 9, 10]
```

The name n used in this example is arbitrary—any valid identifier name that is not already in use could have been used.

The query expression can be of arbitrary complexity. As a further example, this code bounds the elements in the preceding returned sequence as well as next:

```
tenInts[n | n > 5 and n < 9]
```

The result of executing this code is the following sequence:

```
[6, 7, 8]
```

The unary operator `indexof` can be used in a sequence query to return the index of the current element of the sequence as the condition is evaluated. For example, consider the following code:

```
var tenStrings:String[] = ["a", "b", "c", "d", "e", "f",
                           "g", "h", "i", "j"];
println("{tenStrings[n | indexof n > 1].toString()}");
```

This code constructs a sequence from the content of `tenStrings` containing those elements for which the index of the element in the original sequence is greater than 1 and then prints the result. The evaluation works like this:

- Assign "a" to n; indexof n is 0, indexof n > 1 is `false`, element not included.
- Assign "b" to n; indexof n is 1, indexof n > 1 is `false`, element not included.
- Assign "c" to n; indexof n is 2, indexof n > 1 is `true`, element included.

And so on. The result is the following:

```
[ c, d, e, f, g, h, i, j ]
```

Modifying Sequences

You can modify a sequence in any of the following ways:

- Replacing an element with a new value
- Inserting a new element
- Removing an element
- Replacing a range of elements with new values

The last of these is the most general operation and, as you'll see, it can be used to implement any of the others.

You can attach a trigger to a sequence that will be notified when its content is changed. For details, see Chapter 10, "Triggers." Modifications to a sequence variable declared using the `def` keyword are not allowed, and a compilation error will result.

Replacing Elements

To replace an element, simply refer to it by index and assign the required new value:

```
tenInts[4] = 24;
println("tenInts after replacing index 4: {tenInts.toString()}");
```

The preceding code replaces the element at index 4 of the sequence `tenInts` with the value 24, with the following result:

```
tenInts after replacing index 4: [ 1, 2, 3, 4, 24, 6, 7, 8, 9, 10 ]
```

The value to be inserted must be compatible with the type of the sequence variable—in this case, it would need to be an `Integer`. The following code would be rejected by the compiler because a `String` is not an `Integer`:

```
tenInts[4] = "Hello";
```

The following code is accepted but produces a warning because of the possible loss of precision implied in the conversion from `Number` to `Integer`:

```
tenInts[4] = 24.0;
```

Consider the following example, which we saw earlier in this section:

```
var rectangles:Rectangle[] = [Rectangle{}, Rectangle{}];
var nodes:Node[] = rectangles;
```

This code create a sequence of rectangles and then assigns it to a sequence variable of type `Node[]`. This is legal because a rectangle *is* a kind of node. Now suppose we replace the first element of the `nodes` sequence with a node that is not a rectangle, such as a circle:

```
nodes[0] = Circle {};
```

The sequence `nodes` now contains a circle and two rectangles. It is therefore no longer a sequence of rectangles. Does this mean that the sequence pointed to by the `rectangles` variable, which was assigned to the `nodes` variable, is no longer a sequence of rectangles?

If it did, we would have subverted the type safety of the language. In fact, it does not because, as you saw earlier, when the `rectangles` sequence was assigned to the `nodes` variable, a (logical) copy of the sequence was made. Therefore, the replacement of any elements of the `nodes` sequence does not affect the original sequence of rectangles and type safety is preserved.

Assigning `null` to an element of a sequence of numeric or `Boolean` types is illegal and results in a compilation error:

```
tenInts[4] = null;  // Compilation error
```

Assigning `null` to an element of sequence of `String` or `Duration` objects is the same as assigning the default value of the sequence type—an empty string or a `Duration` of 0 seconds:

```
var strings = ["First", "Second"];
strings[0] = null;
println(strings.toString());
```

The preceding code prints the following:

```
[ , Second ]
```

Assigning `null` to an element of a sequence of object types has the effect of removing that element, so the following code results in a sequence containing just the second rectangle:

```
var rectangles:Rectangle[] = [Rectangle{}, Rectangle{}];
rectangles[0] = null;
```

Inserting Elements

You can add a new element to a sequence by using the `insert` statement. The simplest form of this statement inserts the value of an expression at the end of an existing sequence:

```
var tenInts:Integer[] = [1..10];
insert 32 into tenInts;
println("tenInts after insert 32: {tenInts.toString()}");
```

This produces the following result:

```
tenInts after insert 32: [ 1, 2, 3, 4, 5, 6, 7, 8, 9, 10, 32 ]
```

It is possible to append multiple values to a sequence by supplying them in sequence form:

```
var tenInts:Integer[] = [1..10];
insert [21, 22] into tenInts;
println("tenInts after insert [21, 22]: {tenInts.toString()}");
```

Because sequences are flattened on insertion, the result is that the values 21 and 22 are added to the end of the sequence `tenInts`:

```
tenInts after insert [21, 22]: [ 1, 2, 3, 4, 5, 6, 7, 8, 9, 10, 21, 22 ]
```

Inserting `null` is the same as inserting an empty sequence, so both of the following lines of code leave the sequence unchanged[2]:

```
insert null into tenInts;   // Leaves tenInts unchanged
insert [] into tenInts;     // Leaves tenInts unchanged
```

> **Note**
>
> Because `null` is the same as an empty sequence, you cannot create a sequence that contains an element whose value is `null`. This is not the same as Java arrays and most Java collections, which allow `null` entries.

The values to be inserted can be the result of an arbitrary expression, provided that the type is correct—in this case, the expression would have to evaluate to either an `Integer` or a sequence of `Integers`:

```
var tenInts:Integer[] = [1..10];
insert tenInts[n | n > 7] into tenInts;
println("tenInts after query insert: {tenInts.toString()}");
```

The expression in this code creates a sequence of those elements in `tenInts` that are greater than 7—that is, [8, 9, 10]—and then inserts it at the end of that same sequence, producing the following result:

```
tenInts after query insert: [ 1, 2, 3, 4, 5, 6, 7, 8, 9, 10, 8, 9, 10 ]
```

Two other forms of the `insert` statement allow you to place an element before or after another element. These two forms use the keywords `before` and `after` in place of `into` and require you to specify the position of the element relative to which the insertion should be performed. For example, the following code inserts the value 6 before the second element of the sequence:

```
var tenInts:Integer[] = [1..10];
insert 6 before tenInts[1];
println("tenInts after insert before second: {tenInts.toString()}");
```

This code prints the following:

```
tenInts after insert before second: [ 1, 6, 2, 3, 4, 5, 6, 7, 8, 9, 10 ]
```

Similarly, the following code inserts 6 *after* the second element:

---

[2] It is legal to insert `null` into a sequence of *any* type (including numerics), but as you saw in the previous section, it is not legal to attempt to replace an element of a numeric or `Boolean` sequence with the value `null`.

```
var tenInts:Integer[] = [1..10];
insert 6 after tenInts[1];
println("tenInts after insert after second: {tenInts.toString()}");
```

The result of this code is this:

```
tenInts after insert after second: [ 1, 2, 6, 3, 4, 5, 6, 7, 8, 9, 10 ]
```

If the expression that yields the value to be inserted produces a sequence, more than one insertion could be performed at the given location. For example

```
var tenInts:Integer[] = [1..10];
insert [100, 101] after tenInts[1];
println("tenInts after insert [100, 101] after second: {tenInts.toString()}");
```

The output from this is the following, which is the result of flattening the sequence [100, 101] and inserting it after the element at index 1:

```
tenInts after insert [100, 101] after second: [ 1, 2, 100, 101, 3, 4, 5, 6, 7, 8, 9, 10 ]
```

Removing Elements

You can remove elements from a sequence by using the `delete` keyword, which has several different forms. The simplest form identifies the element to be deleted using the sequence name and the element's index:

```
var tenInts:Integer[] = [1..10];
delete tenInts[2];
println("tenInts after delete of index 2: {tenInts.toString()}");
```

This code deletes the third element of the sequence, giving this result:

```
tenInts after delete of index 2: [ 1, 2, 4, 5, 6, 7, 8, 9, 10 ]
```

You can delete more then one element at a time by using a range expression. The following code deletes all the elements from index 5 through to the one before the last:

```
var tenInts:Integer[] = [1..10];
delete tenInts[5..<];
println("tenInts after delete of [5..<]: {tenInts.toString()}");
```

The result of this operation is as follows:

```
tenInts after delete of [5..<]: [ 1, 2, 3, 4, 5, 10 ]
```

The element to be deleted can also be specified by value instead of by index, like this:

```
var moreInts:Integer[] = [[1..5], [1..5]];
println("moreInts: {moreInts.toString()}");
delete 3 from moreInts;
println("moreInts after delete 3: {moreInts.toString()}");
```

This code creates a sequence containing the numbers 1 through 5 twice:

```
moreInts: [ 1, 2, 3, 4, 5, 1, 2, 3, 4, 5 ]
```

The `delete` operation removes the value 3 from this sequence. As there are two elements with this value, both are removed, leaving a sequence containing only eight elements:

```
moreInts after delete 3: [ 1, 2, 4, 5, 1, 2, 4, 5 ]
```

Finally, you can delete every element in the sequence like this:

```
delete moreInts;
```

Replacing a Range of Elements

You can use a range expression to remove or replace a contiguous run of elements of a sequence or to insert new elements. In most cases, insertion or removal should be performed using the `insert` or `delete` keyword, as shown earlier, because they make the intent clearer, and the range expression syntax is reserved for replacement.

The following code replaces two adjacent values in a sequence with two new values:

```
var tenInts:Integer[] = [1..10];
tenInts[0..1] = [20, 21];
println("tenInts after replace of [0..1]: {tenInts.toString()}");
```

Here's the output from the preceding code:

```
tenInts after replace of [0..1]: [ 20, 21, 3, 4, 5, 6, 7, 8, 9, 10 ]
```

There is no requirement for the replacement sequence to contain the same number of values as the range being replaced. Here's an example that replaces the first two elements of the sequence with three values:

```
var tenInts:Integer[] = [1..10];
tenInts[0..1] = [20, 21, 22];
println("tenInts after replace of [0..1]: {tenInts.toString()}");
```

The result of this is as follows:

```
tenInts after replace of [0..1]: [ 20, 21, 22, 3, 4, 5, 6, 7, 8, 9, 10 ]
```

You can replace several elements with one new value in the same way:

```
var tenInts:Integer[] = [1..10];
tenInts[0..1] = 20;      // Shorthand - 20 is the same as [20]
println("tenInts after replace of [0..1]: {tenInts.toString()}");
```

This reduces the sequence to only nine elements:

```
tenInts after replace of [0..1]: [ 20, 3, 4, 5, 6, 7, 8, 9, 10 ]
```

You can use the range syntax to remove a run of elements by replacing them with `null` or an empty sequence, like this:

```
var tenInts:Integer[] = [1..10];
tenInts[0..1] = [];
println("tenInts after replace of [0..1]: {tenInts.toString()}");
```

The result is the same as if you had written `"delete tenInts[0..1]"`:

```
tenInts after replace of [0..1]: [ 3, 4, 5, 6, 7, 8, 9, 10 ]
```

Insertion using a range expression is also possible, but far more obscure. Here's an example:

```
var tenInts:Integer[] = [1..10];
tenInts[5..4] = [21, 22, 23];
println("tenInts after replace of [5..4]: {tenInts.toString()}");
```

The result of this operation is the following:

```
tenInts after replace of [5..4]: [ 1, 2, 3, 4, 5, 21, 22, 23, 6, 7, 8, 9, 10 ]
```

As you can see, the sequence `[21, 22, 23]` has been inserted *before* the element with index 5, which is the first index in the given range. Note that the second index of the range is actually less than the first—this is what indicates that an insertion is required. If the range had been `[5..5]`, the element with index 5 would have been replaced.

By convention, when an insertion is required, the second index is given the value one less than the first, but this is not mandatory—the range `[5..3]` would have given the same result. To insert at the start of a sequence, use the range `[0..-1]`. To insert at the end, use `[sizeof tenInts..sizeof tenInts - 1]` or `[sizeof tenInts..<]`. As noted earlier, using a range expression to perform an insertion is much less clear than using the `insert` keyword.

Operations on Sequences

The `insert` and `delete` keywords and the slicing syntax let you perform a limited range of operations on a sequence, but there are some things that are not easy to achieve without writing a small amount of code. For example, there is no easy way to look for an element in a sequence and return its index. The `javafx.util.Sequences` class contains a set of functions that reduce this task and others like it to a single line of code. In this section, we take a look at what this class provides.

Comparing Sequences

Consider the following code:

```
var date1A:GregorianCalendar = new GregorianCalendar(2009, 10, 20);
var date1B:GregorianCalendar = new GregorianCalendar(2009, 10, 20);
var date2A:GregorianCalendar = new GregorianCalendar(2009, 10, 21);
var date2B:GregorianCalendar = new GregorianCalendar(2009, 10, 21);

var datesA = [date1A, date2A];
var datesB = [date1B, date2B];
println("datesA == datesB? {datesA == datesB}");
```

Two sequences of `GregorianCalendar` objects are created and compared for equality. As noted earlier, two sequences are equal if they are of the same length and each element of the first sequence is equal to the corresponding element in the other sequence, where equality is determined by using the `equals()` method of the object concerned. In this case, the sequences are equal because they have the same number of elements, `date1A` is equal to `date1B`, and `date2A` is equal to `date2B`. Not surprisingly, therefore, this code prints the following:

```
datesA == datesB? true
```

Although this is normally the behavior you would want, it is sometimes useful to know whether two sequences contain exactly the same object *instances*—not just paired objects that are equal. You can do this using the `isEqualByContentIdentity()` function:

```
public function isEqualByContentIdentity(seq1: Object[],
                                         seq2: Object[]): Boolean
```

This function compares the sequence elements using *reference equality*, so the two sequences will be considered to be different if any element in one sequence is not the same object instance as its counterpart in the other. Here's some code that illustrates this:

```
println("datesA/datesB same? "
    "{Sequences.isEqualByContentIdentity(datesA, datesB)}");
```

We know that `datesA` and `datesB` are equal, but the elements in these sequences are different instances of objects that happen to be equal to each other. Hence, this code prints the following:

```
datesA/datesB same? false
```

However, if we create another sequence containing the same elements as those in `datesA` and compare that with `datesA` using `isEqualByContentIdentity()`, we get a different result:

```
var datesC = [date1A, date2A];
println("datesA/datesC same? "
    "{Sequences.isEqualByContentIdentity(datesA, datesC)}");
```

This prints the following:

```
datesA/datesC same? true
```

Incidentally, this trivial case also returns `true`, as you might expect:

```
Sequences.isEqualByContentIdentity(datesA, datesA)
```

Searching for Elements

There is no easy way to find the index of a given element of a sequence. One way to do so is to loop over each element of the sequence using the `for` statement described in Chapter 8 until you find the one you are looking for. Fortunately, the `Sequences` class provides four functions that do this work for you:

```
public function indexOf(seq: Object[], key: Object): Integer
public function nextIndexOf(seq: Object[], key: Object,
                            pos: Integer): Integer
```

```
public function indexByIdentity(seq: Object[], key: Object): Integer
public function nextIndexByIdentity(seq: Object[], key: Object,
                                    pos: Integer): Integer
```

There are two groups of functions. The functions in the first group look for an element that is *equal* to the one passed as the `key` argument. Those in the other look for the exact *instance* that is passed to them. Because the equality check is the only difference between these groups, we'll look only at the functions in the first group.

The following code illustrates both the `indexOf()` and `nextIndexOf()` functions:

```
1    var strings = ["A", "B", "C", "A", "B"];
2
3    // Look for the first "A".
4    var index = Sequences.indexOf(strings, "A");
5    println('Index of "A": {index}');
6
7    // Look for the second "A".
8    index = Sequences.nextIndexOf(strings, "A", index + 1);
9    println('Second index of "A": {index}');
10
11   // Look for another "A", which will not succeed.
12   index = Sequences.nextIndexOf(strings, "A", index + 1);
13   println('Third index of "A": {index}');
```

The sequence `strings` contains two elements with value `"A"`. The `indexOf()` call on line 4 returns the index of the first `"A"`, which is at index 0:

```
Index of "A": 0
```

The `nextIndexOf()` function requires a sequence, a value to look for, and an index. It searches the sequence starting at the given index, rather than at the fixed index of 0 used by `indexOf()`. To search for the second `"A"`, we ask it to start at an index one greater than the location at which the first `"A"` was found, as shown on line 8. This results in the following:

```
Second index of "A": 3
```

Because there isn't another `"A"`, when we call `nextIndexOf()` for the second time on line 12, we get back the value `-1`, which is how both `indexOf()` and `nextIndexOf()` indicate that no match was found:

```
Third index of "A": -1
```

Finding the Largest and Smallest Elements

The `max()` and `min()` functions in the `Sequences` class return, respectively, the largest and smallest element in a sequence. There are two variants of each of these functions. Let's look first at the simpler variants:

```
public function max(seq: Comparable[]): Comparable;
public function min(seq: Comparable[]): Comparable
```

These functions can be used when the sequence consists of elements that implement the `Comparable` interface. Many types implement this interface, including `String` and the numeric types. The value returned is the element in the sequence that has the greatest or least value. For example

```
var ints = [99, 88, 1, 23, 44];
var maxInt:Integer = Sequences.max(ints) as Integer;
var minInt:Integer = Sequences.min(ints) as Integer;
println("ints: max is {maxInt}, min is {minInt}");
```

This code prints the following:

```
ints: max is 99, min is 1
```

Compare the preceding output with this code, which involves a sequence of strings:

```
var strs = ["Abcd", "A", "AA", "ZZ", "Z"];
var maxStr:String = Sequences.max(strs) as String;
var minStr:String = Sequences.min(strs) as String;
println("strings: max is {maxStr}, min is {minStr}");
```

The output from this code is this:

```
strings: max is ZZ, min is A
```

It is important to note that the `max()` and `min()` functions return a value of type `Comparable`. If you want to assign the result to a variable of a more specific type, you need to use a cast, as previously shown:

```
var maxStr:String = Sequences.max(strs) as String;
```

If the elements in a sequence do not implement `Comparable`, or if you want to compare the elements in a different way, you can use the variants of these functions that accept a Comparator:

```
public function max(seq: Object[], c: Comparator): Object
public function min(seq: Object[], c: Comparator): Object
```

For example, the following code finds the strings from the preceding sequence that have the maximum and minimum number of characters. Strings that have the same number of characters are compared using their `compareTo()` function, which provides the normal alphabetic ordering among strings of equal length.[3]

```
var comp:Comparator = Comparator {
    override function compare(o1: Object, o2:Object): Integer {
        var s1 = o1 as String;
        var s2 = o2 as String;
```

---

[3] The syntax used in the implementation of the `Comparator` in this example should look somewhat familiar to you. It is the JavaFX equivalent of an anonymous inner class that implements the `Comparator` interface. You'll see more of this in Chapter 10.

```
        var l1 = s1.length();
        var l2 = s2.length();
        if (l1 == l2) {
            return s1.compareTo(s2);
        } else if (l1 < l2) {
            return -1;
        } else {
            return 1;
        }
    }

    override function equals(o:Object): Boolean {
        return o == comp;
    }
};

println("strings with comparator: max is {Sequences.max(strs, comp)}");
println("strings with comparator: min is {Sequences.min(strs, comp)}");
```

The result of running this code is the following:

```
strings with comparator: max is Abcd
strings with comparator: min is A
```

As noted in Chapter 6, "Expressions, Functions, and Object Literals," the `override` keyword in the preceding code indicates that the associated function definitions are overrides of those in a base class or, in this case, implementations of interface methods. For more details, see Chapter 11, "JavaFX Script Classes."

Sorting a Sequence

The `Sequences` class has two functions that return a sorted copy of a sequence. As with the `max()` and `min()` functions, the difference is the way in which the elements of the sequence are compared:

```
public function sort(seq: Comparable[]): Comparable[]
public function sort(seq: Object[], c: Comparator): Object[]
```

In both cases, a new sequence is returned, leaving the original unmodified. The returned sequence is arranged in ascending order with respect either to the `Comparator` supplied or to the elements' natural sort order if a `Comparator` is not used. If the source sequence contains adjacent elements that are equal, their relative order will not be changed when the sort is performed. This is an important characteristic of a sorting algorithm (referred to as *stability*), which makes it possible to re-sort a sequence that is already partially sorted without any unnecessary rearrangement of its content.

The following example sorts a sequence of `Integers` and prints both the sorted sequence and the original to demonstrate that it is not modified:

```
var ints = [99, 88, 1, 23, 44];
```

```
var sortedInts:Integer[] = Sequences.sort(ints) as Integer[];
println("Sorted ints: {sortedInts.toString()}");
println("ints after sort: {ints.toString()}");
```

The result is as follows:

```
Sorted ints: [ 1, 23, 44, 88, 99 ]
ints after sort: [ 99, 88, 1, 23, 44 ]
```

Notice the cast on the line of code that performs the sort:

```
var sortedInts:Integer[] = Sequences.sort(ints) as Integer[];
```

The variant of the `sort()` function used here accepts and returns a sequence of `Comparable` objects. To assign this to an `Integer` sequence variable, an explicit cast is necessary.

The same thing can be done with a sequence of strings:

```
var strs = ["Abcd", "A", "AA", "ZZ", "Z"];
var sortedStrs:String[] = Sequences.sort(strs) as String[];
println("Sorted strings: {sortedStrs.toString()}");
println("strings after sort: {strs.toString()}");
```

This code produces the following output:

```
Sorted strings: [ A, AA, Abcd, Z, ZZ ]
strings after sort: [ Abcd, A, AA, ZZ, Z ]
```

To demonstrate the second variant of this function, we'll use the string length `Comparator` shown in the previous section to sort the same sequence of strings by length:

```
var strs = ["Abcd", "A", "AA", "ZZ", "Z"];
var sortedStrs:String[] = Sequences.sort(strs, comp) as String[];
println("Sorted strings: {sortedStrs.toString()}");
```

Because the `Comparator` used here orders the strings by length, the resulting sequence has the shortest string first and the longest last.

```
Sorted strings: [ A, Z, AA, ZZ, Abcd ]
```

Searching and Updating a Sorted Sequence

If you know that a sequence is sorted in ascending order, you can use the `binarySearch()` functions to look for a given element. These functions have two advantages over the `indexOf()` function that you saw earlier:

- They are much faster at searching a large sequence because they use a binary chop algorithm to locate the required element, exploiting the fact that the sequence is known to be in ascending order.

- If the element is not in the sequence, they return a value that indicates where the element should be inserted to preserve the ordering.

Here is how the `binarySearch()` functions are defined:

```
public function binarySearch(seq: Comparable[],
                             key: Comparable): Integer
public function binarySearch(seq: Object[], key: Object,
                             c: Comparator): Integer
```

The first variant assumes that the sequence is sorted according to the natural ordering of its elements, while the second requires that it be sorted according to the rules applied by the given `Comparator`. If this is not the case, then the results are undefined (which is almost certainly not what you wanted). Here is an example that looks for the value 44 in a sorted sequence of `Integers`:

```
var sortedInts = [ 1, 23, 44, 88, 99 ];
var intIndex = Sequences.binarySearch(sortedInts, 44);
println("Sorted ints: {sortedInts.toString()}, 44 is at index {intIndex}");
```

This gives the following:

```
Sorted ints: [ 1, 23, 44, 88, 99 ], 44 is at index 2
```

What happens if the required element is not present? This example looks for the value 55 in the same sequence:

```
intIndex = Sequences.binarySearch(sortedInts, 55);
println("Sorted ints: {sortedInts.toString()}, 55 is at index {intIndex}");
```

The result is a negative value:

```
Sorted ints: [ 1, 23, 44, 88, 99 ], 55 is at index -4
```

A negative value indicates that the element was not already in the sequence. More than that, though, it tells us where the element should be inserted. If the return value is x, the element should be inserted at the index (-x - 1). The reason for the -1 is so that an index of zero becomes -1 instead of -0, which is indistinguishable from zero. With this knowledge, we can insert the 55 in the correct location in the sequence to preserve the ordering:

```
var insertIndex = -intIndex - 1;
insert 55 before sortedInts[insertIndex];
println("Sorted ints after insert: {sortedInts.toString()}");
```

The result of running this code is as follows:

```
Sorted ints after insert: [ 1, 23, 44, 55, 88, 99 ]
```

As you can see, the sequence is still properly ordered.

Shuffling a Sequence

In some circumstances, you need to randomly reorder the elements of a sequence. You might do this, for example, if you are writing a card game and you want to shuffle the virtual deck. The `Sequences` class provides the following function that enables you to do this in one line of code:

```
public function shuffle(seq: Object[]):Object[]
```

Here's an example that shuffles a sequence of `Integers` three times. Note that, as with all the other functions in this class, the result of the `shuffle()` function is a new sequence—the original is unchanged:

```
var ints = [99, 88, 1, 23, 44];
var shuffledInts:Integer[] = Sequences.shuffle(ints) as Integer[];
println("First shuffle: {shuffledInts.toString()}");

shuffledInts = Sequences.shuffle(ints) as Integer[];
println("Second shuffle: {shuffledInts.toString()}");

shuffledInts = Sequences.shuffle(ints) as Integer[];
println("Third shuffle: {shuffledInts.toString()}");
```

The results that you get will, of course, vary over time. Here's the output that I got when I ran this code:

```
First shuffle: [ 44, 88, 99, 1, 23 ]
Second shuffle: [ 23, 99, 1, 44, 88 ]
Third shuffle: [ 23, 88, 99, 44, 1 ]
```

Java Arrays

JavaFX allows you to declare a variable that refers to a Java array. This feature is intended to be used to allow Java methods that require array-valued arguments or return arrays to be called from JavaFX code without incurring the expense of converting between a JavaFX sequence and a Java array. Because of this limited scope, the set of operations that you can perform on an array variable is smaller than that provided by sequences.

Array Variable Declaration

The normal array syntax in Java is used for sequences in JavaFX, so an additional keyword is used to declare an array variable:

```
var arrayVar:nativearray of Integer;
```

The type part of the declaration can be any JavaFX or Java type, so the following are also valid:

```
var arrayVar1:nativearray of String;
var arrayVar2:nativearray of Object;
```

You can declare a multidimensional array variable by adding one `nativearray of` clause for each dimension. The following code is the JavaFX equivalent of the Java declaration `int[][] arrayVar3;`:

```
var arrayVar3:nativearray of nativearray of Integer;
```

Array Variable Initialization

The default value of an array variable is `null`. No specific JavaFX syntax allows you to create a Java array (that is, there is no equivalent to the Java expression `new int[10]`) because the expectation is that, in most cases, an array variable will be set to the value returned by a Java method, like this:

```
var text = "Hello, world";
var chars:nativearray of Character = text.toCharArray();
```

The `toCharArray()` method of the `java.lang.String` class returns a value of type `char[]`. The declaration of the `chars` variable in this example is translated by the compiler to `char[]`, so it is compatible with the return value of the `toCharArray()` method.

Another way to initialize an array variable is from the value of a sequence:

```
var integers = [1, 2, 3, 4, 5] as nativearray of Integer;
```

In this case, the compiler first creates the sequence and then converts it to an integer array. A more obscure way to populate an array variable, which is available only in the desktop profile, is to use Java reflection. Here is an example that illustrates the technique:

```
var integers1 = java.lang.reflect.Array.newInstance(Integer.TYPE, 10)
                as nativearray of Integer;
```

Because the `newInstance()` method of the `java.lang.reflect.Array` class returns a value of type `Object`, an explicit cast to `nativearray of Integer` is required to force the compiler to correctly infer the type of variable. In the absence of this cast, `integers1` would be of type `Object` rather than `int[]`.

This code creates an array of ten integers, with each element set to zero. It is, therefore, the equivalent of the following Java code:

```
int[] integers1 = new int[10];
```

Note that we specified the type of the array element as `Integer.TYPE` (which corresponds to the Java primitive `int`) rather than `Integer.class` (which is the type of the boxed integer class `java.lang.Integer`). The following code would compile but would result in a `ClassCastException` at runtime because the `newInstance()` method would return an array of type `java.lang.Integer[]`, which cannot be assigned to a variable of type `int[]`:

```
var integers2 = java.lang.reflect.Array.newInstance(Integer.class, 10)
                as nativearray of Integer;   // ClassCastException
```

You can use a similar technique to create a multidimensional array in which each element is set to its default value. The following code creates a two-dimensional array of `Integers` with each element initially set to `0`:

```
var integers3 = java.lang.reflect.Array.newInstance(Integer.TYPE, 10, 5)
                    as nativearray of nativearray of Integer;
```

> **Note**
>
> Although the preceding code is correct, it does not compile in JavaFX 1.3 because of a compiler bug that should be fixed in a later release.

Array Operations

You can access and modify the elements of an array using the same syntax as you would in Java:

```
1    var text = "Hello, world";
2    var chars:nativearray of Character = text.toCharArray();
3    println("Character 7 is {chars[7]}");
4    chars[7] = 'W'.charAt(0);
5    var textCopy = new String(chars);
6    println("Modified text is ");
```

The output from this code is the following:

```
Character 7 is w
Modified text is [Hello, World]
```

Lines 1 and 2 declare a native array of characters and initialize it from the content of a string. On line 3, we use the normal array access operator `[]` to get and print the element at index 7, which in this case is a lowercase `'w'`. On line 4, we again use the array access operator to replace this element with an uppercase `'W'`. Note that because there is (currently) no syntax for a character literal in JavaFX, we use the `charAt()` method of `java.lang.String` to convert the string `'W'` to the character that we need.

On lines 5 and 6, we convert the character array back to a string by using the following constructor of the `java.lang.String` class:

```
public String(char[] chars);
```

This demonstrates that it is possible to pass array values to Java constructors and functions that require them.

It is not possible to use the JavaFX sequence operators `insert` and `delete` with a native array, nor is it possible to use the range syntax (for example, `chars[3..4]`) to extract or modify a slice of a native array.

Array Size

You can get the size of an array at runtime in one of two ways, both of which are illustrated in the following code extract:

```
println("Number of characters is {chars.length}");
println("Number of characters is {sizeof chars}");
```

The first line uses the `length` variable of the array to gets its size. This syntax is supported for compatibility with Java. The second line uses the JavaFX `sizeof` operator to get the same information. Which of these you choose to use is a matter of personal taste. Both possibilities also work with multidimensional arrays:

```
var integers3 = java.lang.reflect.Array.newInstance(Integer.TYPE, 10, 5)
                        as nativearray of nativearray of Integer;
println("Array length: {integers3.length}, "
        "element 0 length: {sizeof integers3[0]}");
```

This code prints the length of the array—that is, the number of elements in its first dimension, which is 10, and the number of elements in the nested array at element 0, which is 5:

```
Array length: 10, element 0 length: 5
```

8

Controlling Program Flow

This chapter looks at the JavaFX statements that control the flow of execution within a JavaFX script—`if`, `while`, `for`, and `throw`. As you'll see, the `while` statement is almost identical to its Java equivalent, whereas the JavaFX `if` and `for` statements are significantly more powerful because they can also be embedded in expressions. The second part of this chapter covers exception handling in JavaFX, which is less intrusive than it is in Java and is likely to be of relevance more to library implementers than to application developers.

The `if` Statement

The syntax of the JavaFX `if` statement looks like this:

```
if (boolean expression) [then] statement [else statement]
```

In its simplest form, the `if` statement lets you execute one or more other statements if, and only if, a given boolean expression, enclosed in mandatory parentheses, evaluates to `true`. If more than one statement is to be executed, they must be enclosed in braces to form a block expression. If there is only one statement, the braces are optional but still recommended. The following two examples are equivalent:

```
// The compiler does not require braces when there is only
// one conditional statement:
if (Math.random() > 0.5)
    println("Random number > 0.5");

// Nevertheless, always using braces is recommended:
if (Math.random() > 0.5) {
    println("Random number > 0.5");
}
```

In both cases, the `println()` function will be called if the value of a random number is greater than `0.5` and will be skipped if it is not.

You can, if you want, include the word `then` after the expression, but this is decorative only:

```
// Optional use of 'then'
if (Math.random() > 0.5) then println("Random number > 0.5");

// 'then' is also allowed with braces
if (Math.random() > 0.5) then {
    println("Random number > 0.5");
}
```

You probably noticed that in the first example, the conditional statement is not surrounded by braces. Despite earlier advice to the contrary, it is common practice to omit the braces when the whole statement fits on a single line.

If you want to do execute different code depending on whether the conditional expression evaluates to `true` or `false`, you can include an `else` clause. The body of this clause must be enclosed in braces if it contains more than one statement:

```
if (Math.random() > 0.5) then {
    // Executed if the condition evaluates to true
    println("Random number >  0.5");
} else {
    // Executed if the condition evaluates to false.
    println("Random number <= 0.5");
}
```

In JavaFX, the `if` statement is actually an expression because it returns the value that is returned by the last executed statement in the `then` or `else` clause, depending on which is executed. This is a powerful feature. To see how useful this can be, look back at the previous example. This code prints one message if a condition is `true` and another if it is `false`, but the invocation of the `println()` method is duplicated. Using the fact that `if` is an expression, we can simplify this code as follows:

```
var text = if (Math.random() > 0.5) "Random number > 0.5"
           else "Random number <= 0.5";
println(text);
```

The value that is assigned to the variable `text` is either the first or the second string, depending on which clause of the `if` expression is executed. When used in this way, an `if` expression is the JavaFX equivalent of the `?:` operator pair in Java:

```
// Java code
String text = Math.random() > 0.5 ? "Random number > 0.5"
                                  : "Random number <= 0.5";
```

The code can be simplified further by removing the variable `text` and embedding the `if` statement directly in the argument list of the `println()` function:

```
println(if (Math.random() > 0.5) "Random number > 0.5"
        else "Random number <= 0.5");
```

The same syntax also works when there are multiple statements to be executed in either block of the `if` expression. For example, if we want to count the number of times the random number has been greater than or not greater than `0.5`, we could do this[1]:

```
var greater = 0;
var notGreater = 0;
var text = if (Math.random() > 0.5) {
              greater++;
              "Random number > 0.5 ({greater})";
          } else {
              notGreater++;
              "Random number <= to 0.5 ({notGreater})";
          };
println(text);
```

As you saw earlier in this book, the value of a block expression is the value of its last executed statement, which, in this case, is one of the string-valued expressions. The value returned by the `if` expression is, therefore, the value returned either by the block expression that makes up the main clause, or the one that is in the `else` clause.

Going slightly further, the previous example does not actually need a block expression because we can make use of the pre-increment operator to write it even more succinctly, like this:

```
var greater = 0;
var notGreater = 0;
var text = if (Math.random() > 0.5) {
               "Random number > 0.5 ({++greater})";
           } else {
               "Random number <= 0.5 ({++notGreater})";
           };
println(text);
```

The `while` Statement

The `while` statement lets you repeatedly execute a block of statements until a given boolean expression evaluates to `false`. The syntax is the same as it is in Java:

```
while (boolean expression) {
    statement
}
```

The body of the loop could be a single statement, or a block of several statements enclosed in braces. Unlike `if`, the `while` statement does *not* return a value and cannot be used as part of an expression.

---

[1] Of course, this `if` statement should really be in a loop. Loops are discussed next.

At the start of each iteration of the loop, the boolean expression is evaluated. If its value is `false`, the loop ends. If it is `true`, the body of the loop is executed, and then the boolean expression is evaluated again, and so on. Here is an example that prints the integers from 1 to 10, inclusive[2]:

```
var i = 1;
while (i <= 10) {
    println(i);
    i++;
}
```

A `while` loop would never terminate unless the body of the loop or the boolean expression had a side effect that caused the condition being tested to eventually return `false`. In this case, the value `i` used in the expression is incremented, causing the loop to end when it reaches the value `11`.

The `break` Statement

In some cases, it is necessary to terminate a `while` loop before the condition expressed by the boolean expression is satisfied. You can use the `break` statement to do this. When this statement is encountered, it causes the immediately enclosing `while` statement to be terminated.[3] It is not uncommon to find `while` statements that do not really use the boolean expression at all, like this one:

```
// In this example, the "while" expression always evaluates to "true"
while (true) {
    // Do some work (not shown)
    if (some condition) {
        break;
    }
    // Do some more work (not shown)
}
```

As another example of the use of the `break` statement, consider the following object literal:

```
var nodes = Group {
    content: [
        Rectangle { x: 10 y: 10 width: 100 height: 10
                    fill: Color.RED },
        Text { x: 10 y: 30 content: "Hello, World" },
        Rectangle { x: 10 y: 50 width: 100 height: 10
                    fill: Color.RED },
```

---

[2] This code is not particularly elegant. A neater way to do this would be to use the `for` statement, discussed in the next section.

[3] The `break` and `continue` statements can also be used in the body of a `for` statement.

```
        Text { x: 10 y: 70 content: "Hello Again, World" },
    ]
}
```

Group is a JavaFX object from the GUI scene graph library (covered later in this book) that groups together scene graph nodes. This code creates and places two rectangles and two text objects, one above the other. If displayed, the result would look something like that shown in Figure 8-1.

Figure 8-1 A group containing four scene graph nodes

Now suppose we want to write some code to scan the nodes in a group, looking for the first text node, and then print its content. Obviously, we need to get hold of the sequence containing the child nodes and loop over each of them, looking for children of type Text. We need to terminate the loop as soon as we have found the first text node. This will happen before we reach the end of the sequence, unless the group does not actually contain a text node, in which case we need to stop when all the nodes in the group have been checked. The fact that the loop may need to end early is the trigger for the use of a break statement:

```
1    var index = 0;
2    var firstText:Text = null;
3    while (index < sizeof nodes.content) {
4        var node = nodes.content[index++];
5        if (node instanceof Text) {
6            firstText = node as Text;
7            break;
8        }
9    }
10   println('{if (firstText != null) "Text is {firstText.content}"
11           else "No Text"}')
```

The boolean expression on line 3 of this code will cause the loop to terminate only when all the nodes in the group have been processed. However, the break statement on line 7 causes control to pass to line 10 when the first text node is found, thus terminating the loop early, having set the firstText variable to indicate that a text node was found. The code on line 10 uses an if expression to print either the content of the text node or a message indicating that there was no text node in the group.

Note that JavaFX has no equivalent of the labeled break statement in Java.

The `continue` statement

Like `break`, the `continue` statement causes the current iteration of a `while` loop to end, but instead of terminating the loop, execution continues at the first statement of the next loop iteration. Suppose we want to change the code in the previous example so that it returns a sequence containing the content of all the text nodes. To do this, we need to contribute an entry to the sequence for every text node but do nothing for the other nodes in the group. Here is an implementation of this that makes use of the `continue` statement:

```
1    var texts:String[] = null;
2    var index = 0;
3    while (index < sizeof nodes.content) {
4        var node = nodes.content[index++];    // Get the next Node
5        // If not a Text node, return to the top of the loop (line 4)
6        if (not (node instanceof Text)) {
7            continue;
8        }
9        insert "'{(node as Text).content}'" into texts;
10   }
11   println(texts.toString());
```

Line 4 of this code gets the next node from the group. Line 6 checks whether it is a text node and, if it is not, the `continue` statement on line 7 causes control to pass back to line 4, with the result that the loop reaches line 9 and contributes an entry to the sequence only in the case of a text node.

Like `break`, there is no labeled variant of `continue`.

The `for` Statement

Whereas the JavaFX `if` and `while` statements are very much like their Java equivalent, the `for` statement is not. In JavaFX, the `for` statement is used to iterate over one or more sequences or Java collections.

Iterating over a Sequence

The simplest form of the `for` statement looks like this:

```
for (variable in sequence) {
    statement;
}
```

Here's an example that iterates over all the nodes in a group and prints the classname of each node that it encounters:

```
1    var group = Group {
2        content: [
3            Rectangle { x: 10 y: 10 width: 100 height: 10
4                        fill: Color.RED },
```

```
5                       Text { x: 10 y: 30 content: "Hello, World" },
6                       Rectangle { x: 10 y: 50 width: 100 height: 10
7                                    fill: Color.RED },
8                       Text { x: 10 y: 70 content: "Hello Again, World" },
9               ]
10      }
11      for (node in group.content) {
12              println(node.getClass().getName());
13      }
```

The output looks like this:

```
javafx.scene.shape.Rectangle
javafx.scene.text.Text
javafx.scene.shape.Rectangle
javafx.scene.text.Text
```

The `for` statement on lines 11 to 13 iterates over the sequence of nodes in the `content` variable of the group. Because the type of the `content` variable is `Node[]`, the compiler infers that the type of the `node` variable in the `for` statement is `Node` and assigns each member of the sequence to it in successive iterations of the loop, starting with the element at index 0 and ending with the last. The `node` variable is valid only within the body of the loop, which, in this case, just prints the classname of each node.

The `for` statement can also imitate its Java counterpart by iterating over a sequence of numbers. For example

```
for (i in [0..9]) {
    println(i);
}
```

This is equivalent to the following Java code:

```
for (int i = 0; i <= 9; i++) {
    System.out.println(i);
}
```

Here, the value of the loop variable is incremented by one each time, but other values are possible, using the sequence syntax that was described in Chapter 7, "Sequences":

```
for (i in [0..9 step 2]) { }    // Values 0, 2, 4, 6, 8
for (i in [9..0 step -1]) { }   // Value 9, 8, 7, 6, 5, 4, 3, 2, 1, 0
```

Of course, you can also iterate over arbitrary numbers:

```
for (i in [0, 4, 9, 32, 64]) { }
```

The iterated values are not limited to numbers:

```
for (s in ["A", "B", "C"] {
    println(s);
}
```

You can use the `break` and `continue` statements in the body of a `for` loop, just as you can in a `while` statement. The following code iterates over the nodes in the group shown in an earlier example and prints the content of every text node:

```
for (node in nodes.content) {
    if (node instanceof Text) {
        println((node as Text).content);
    }
}
```

The following code finds only the first text node and then prints the associated text, using a `break` statement to terminate the loop once this has been done:

```
for (node in nodes.content) {
    if (node instanceof Text) {
        println((node as Text).content);
        break;
    }
}
```

The `for` Statement as an Expression

Like `if`, the `for` statement is actually an expression that returns a sequence value. The value is constructed by logically creating an empty sequence and then adding the result of each completed iteration of the loop to that sequence. The type of the sequence is the same as the compile-time type of the value produced within the loop. Here's an example:

```
var strings = for (node in nodes.content) {
                  node.getClass().getName()
              }
println(strings.toString());
```

Here, the `for` loop iterates over the nodes in the group. Each pass of the loop returns a value that is the name of the node's class. Therefore, the type of the `strings` variable to which the result is assigned is `String[]`. Although in this example there is only one statement in the body of the loop, there can be arbitrarily many—only the value returned by the last statement is used. Here is the result of executing this code:

```
[ javafx.scene.shape.Rectangle, javafx.scene.text.Text,
 javafx.scene.shape.Rectangle, javafx.scene.text.Text ]
```

Using a `for` loop to transform a sequence of objects into a sequence of different objects is a common idiom in GUI programming. There is an example of this in the section "Binding to a Transformed Sequence" in Chapter 9, "Binding."

It is possible to use a `for` expression to create a sequence that contains elements that correspond to only a subset of the sequence on which it operates. Suppose that we want to create a sequence containing only the text nodes from the child nodes of a group. We could try to do it like this:

```
var textNodes = for (node in nodes.content) { // This is illegal
```

```
                    if (node instanceof Text) node as Text
            }
println(textNodes.toString());
```

The idea is that the body of the `for` loop should return a value for a text node and nothing for other types. However, the compiler doesn't allow it. Here's the error message:

```
'void' type not allowed here
var textNodes = for (node in nodes.content) {
1 error
```

The reason is that every iteration of the loop returns a value, even if it doesn't seem to. In the case of a node that is not of type `Text`, the value returned is `Void`, which cannot be assigned to a sequence. We can easily fix this, as follows:

```
var textNodes = for (node in nodes.content) {
                    if (node instanceof Text) node as Text else null
            }
println(textNodes.toString());
```

This modified version returns the value `null` for a non-`Text` node. As you saw in Chapter 7, `null` is equivalent to an empty sequence, so adding `null` to a sequence leaves it unchanged.

Iterating over a Subset of a Sequence

The previous example used a `for` statement, an `if` statement, and a `break` statement together to produce a new sequence based on a subset of an existing sequence. There is actually a more elegant way to achieve the same effect, by using the `where` clause of the `for` statement:

```
for (variable in sequence where boolean-expression) {
    statements;
}
```

The `where` clause provides a Boolean-valued expression in which the current element of the sequence is available via the loop variable. The body of the loop is executed only for those elements for which this expression returns the value `true`. This allows us to rewrite the previous example so that only the text nodes are actually passed to the body of the loop:

```
var textNodes = for (node in nodes.content where node instanceof Text) {
                    // Body executed only for Text nodes
                    node as Text
            }
println(textNodes.toString());
```

As another example, the following code returns a subsequence of the nodes in the group that contains only those nodes whose index position is greater than `1`:

```
var subset = for (node in nodes.content where indexof node > 1) {
                 // Body executed only for nodes in positions > 1
```

```
                node
        }
println(subset.toString());
```

Iterating over Multiple Sequences

So far, we have used the `for` statement to iterate over all or part of a single sequence. In fact, `for` is more general than that—you can iterate over as many sequences as you like. Here is the full syntax:

```
for (variable1 in sequence [where boolean-expression]
        [, variable2 in sequence [where boolean-expression] ]*) {
    statements;
}
```

The following code iterates over two numeric ranges:

```
for (i in [0, 1], j in [0, 1, 2]) {
    println("i = {i}, j = {j}");
}
```

When there is more than one sequence, the sequence farthest to the right is iterated most quickly, followed by the one to its left, and so on. To illustrate this point, here's the output from the preceding code:

```
i = 0, j = 0
i = 0, j = 1
i = 0, j = 2
i = 1, j = 0
i = 1, j = 1
i = 1, j = 2
```

As you can see, `i` is assigned its first value, namely 0; then the loop is executed three times with each of the possible values for `j`. The process is repeated with `i` taking the value 1. This `for` statement is therefore equivalent to the following nested `for` loops in Java:

```
for (int i = 0; i <= 1; i++) {
    for (int j = 0; j <= 2; j++) {
        System.out.println("i = " + i + ", j = " + j);
    }
}
```

You can add a `where` clause to any of the iterated sequences. The following code iterates over all the values in the first sequence but only the elements in the second sequence that are in even-numbered positions:

```
for (i in ["a", "b", "c"], j in ["W", "X", "Y", "Z"]
        where (indexof j mod 2) == 0) {
    println("i = {i}, j = {j}");
}
```

The result of running this code is as follows:

```
i = a, j = W
i = a, j = Y
i = b, j = W
i = b, j = Y
i = c, j = W
i = c, j = Y
```

It is possible for one iterated sequence to be derived from another. For example, suppose we create two groups of nodes and place the groups in their own sequence, like this:

```
var group1 = Group {
    content: [
        Rectangle { x: 10 y: 10 width: 100 height: 10
                    fill: Color.RED },
        Text { x: 10 y: 30 content: "Hello, World" },
        Rectangle { x: 10 y: 50 width: 100 height: 10
                    fill: Color.RED },
        Text { x: 10 y: 70 content: "Hello Again, World" },
    ]
}
var group2 = Group {
    content: [
        Text { x: 10 y: 10 content: "Hello, Another World" },
        Rectangle { x: 10 y: 30 width: 100 height: 10
                    fill: Color.RED },
        Text { x: 10 y: 50 content: "Hello Again, Another World" },
    ]
}

var groups = [group1, group2];
```

The following code iterates over the `groups` sequence and, for each group in this sequence, it also iterates over the content of that group and prints the content of any nested text nodes:

```
for (group in groups,
        node in group.content where node instanceof Text) {
    println("Group #{indexof group}, node text is "
            "{(node as Text).content}");
}
```

This code works as follows:

1. The value `group1` is assigned to the variable `group`, which is inferred to be of type `Group`.

2. The value of `group1.content` is used as the second sequence, and then the variable `node` is assigned successively to refer to the text nodes in that group, by virtue of the `where` clause.

3. The value `group2` is assigned to the variable `group`.

4. The value of `group2.content` is used as the second sequence, and then the variable `node` is assigned successively to refer the text nodes in the second group.

Here is the result:

```
Group #0, node text is Hello, World
Group #0, node text is Hello Again, World
Group #1, node text is Hello, Another World
Group #1, node text is Hello Again, Another World
```

As you can see, the text nodes in both groups have been processed, and the other nodes have been ignored. Notice also the use of the `indexof` operator to display the index of each group node rather than the group object itself.

Iterating over an Iterable

You can use the `for` statement to iterate over any object that implements the `java.lang.Iterable` interface, which includes all the standard Java collection classes like `List` and `Map`.

Iterating over a List

Here's an example that iterates over the entries in a Java `List`:

```
1    var names = new ArrayList();
2    names.add("Armstrong");
3    names.add("Aldrin");
4    names.add("Collins");
5
6    // Iterate over a list of strings
7    for (name in names) {
8        println(name);
9    }
```

As you can see on line 7, the syntax used to iterate over a `List` is the same as that used for a sequence. This code visits each name in the list, in order, as you can see here:

```
Armstrong
Aldrin
Collins
```

It is also possible to iterate over a subset of the content of an `Iterable` using the `where` clause, as shown in the following code that uses the same list of names:

```
for (name in names where (name as String).startsWith("A")) {
    println(name);
}
```

In this case, the body of the loop is executed only for those names in the list that start with the letter *A*. Note that we need to use the `as` operator to cast the name to a `String` because the declaration of the `List` does not include any information that would allow the compiler to deduce the type of its content, which cause the inferred type of this variable to be `Object`. It is impossible to provide the type information, because JavaFX does not support the generics syntax that is available in Java. Here's the output from the preceding code:

```
Armstrong
Aldrin
```

By contrast, if the list is obtained from a genericized Java method, the compiler *can* infer the type of the elements in the list and the cast shown in the preceding example is not required. For example, in the following Java code, the `getNames()` method is declared to return a `List` of `String` objects:

```java
import java.util.ArrayList;
import java.util.List;

public class NameSource {
    public List<String> getNames() {
        List<String> names = new ArrayList<String>();
        names.add("Armstrong");
        names.add("Aldrin");
        names.add("Collins");
        return names;
    }
}
```

Line 2 of the following code assigns the result of invoking the `getNames()` method to a variable called `javaNames`. From the information stored in the Java class file, the compiler infers that the type of this variable should be `List<String>`, from which it follows that the type of the variable name in the for loop on line 3 must be `String`, and therefore no cast is required when invoking its `startsWith()` method:

```
1     var nameSource = new NameSource();
2     var javaNames = nameSource.getNames();
3     for (name in javaNames where name.startsWith("A")) {
4         println(name);
5     }
```

Iterating over a Map

A `java.util.Map` is not an `Iterable`, but it has three associated collections that can be iterated in the same way as a `List`:

- A `Set` containing all the keys
- A `Set` containing all the values
- A `Set` containing all the (key, value) pairs

The following code creates a Map with three entries and then iterates over its keys, values, and (key, value) pairs:

```
1    var map = new HashMap();
2    map.put("KeyA", "ValueA");
3    map.put("KeyB", "ValueB");
4    map.put("KeyC", "ValueC");
5
6    // Iterate over the keys of a Map
7    for (key in map.keySet()) {
8        println("Key: {key}");
9    }
10   println("----------------");
11
12   // Iterate over the values in a Map
13   for (value in map.values()) {
14       println("Value: {value}");
15   }
16   println("----------------");
17
18   // Iterate over the entries in a Map
19   for (e in map.entrySet()) {
20       var entry = e as Map.Entry;
21       println("Key: {entry.getKey()}, value {entry.getValue()}");
22   }
23   println("----------------");
```

Lines 7 to 9 obtain the set of keys in the map and iterate over it, printing one line for each key:

```
Key: KeyA
Key: KeyB
Key: KeyC
```

Lines 13 to 15 do the same for the values in the map:

```
Value: ValueA
Value: ValueB
Value: ValueC
```

Finally, lines 19 through 22 iterate over all the (key, value) pairs in the map, producing the following output:

```
Key: KeyA, value ValueA
Key: KeyB, value ValueB
Key: KeyC, value ValueC
```

Iterating over an Array

You can use the `for` statement to iterate over the values in a Java array, as the following example shows:

```
var chars = "Hello, World".toCharArray();
for (c in chars) {
    print("{c}:");
}
println("");
```

The type of the variable chars is inferred to be `nativearray of Character`. The `for` statement is executed once for each element of the array, giving the following result:

```
H:e:l:l:o:,: :W:o:r:l:d:
```

Exception Handling

Exception handling in Java has been the subject of much debate from the very beginning, largely because of checked exceptions. Checked exceptions must be declared by Java methods that throw them and must either be caught by any code that calls that method or be propagated to the caller of that code (and so on). Although this is fine in theory, it is unpopular with some developers because it can lead to the creation of lots of boilerplate code that is almost never executed and often clutters application logic.

JavaFX exception handling is almost identical to that in Java, apart from the fact that checked exceptions are handled in the same way as unchecked exceptions. This is good news for most Java programmers moving to JavaFX because you are no longer obliged to catch and handle exceptions.

The easiest way to describe exception handling in JavaFX is to look at an example. Suppose you want to write a JavaFX function to append some text to a file. To do this, you need to use various classes in the `java.io` package, which are notorious for their use of exceptions derived from the checked exception `java.io.IOException`. Here's how you might implement the function:

```
1   function appendToFile(filePath:String, text:String) {
2       var writer:BufferedWriter = null;
3       try {
4           writer = new BufferedWriter(new FileWriter(filePath, true));
5           writer.write(text);
6           writer.flush();
7       } catch (ex:IOException) {
8           Logger.getLogger("").log(Level.SEVERE,
9                   "Failed to write to {filePath}", ex);
```

```
10                throw ex;
11            } finally {
12                if (writer != null) {
13                    writer.close();
14                }
15            }
16    }
```

Superficially, this looks very much like its Java equivalent, but there are some significant differences, which you'll see as we look at the code in more detail.

The basic structure of exception handling is the same as it is in Java—the code is introduced by a `try` statement, which may be followed by one or more optional `catch` blocks and an optional `finally` block. As in Java, there must be either at least one `catch` block or a `finally` block. The semantics of these blocks are the same as they are in Java, as follows:

- If an exception is thrown, it is passed to the `catch` block that specifies the same exception or the nearest superclass of that exception. If there is no such block, the exception is thrown out of the enclosing method.

- The code in the `finally` block is executed when control leaves the `try` block, whether an exception was thrown. This code is guaranteed to be executed, making it the ideal place to put cleanup operations.

In the preceding example, the `BufferedWriter` declared on line 2 is a resource that must be closed when it is no longer needed. This is done in the `finally` block on lines 12 through 14. Notice that this code is protected by a `null` check in case the variable `writer` does not get assigned. This would be the case if the constructors of the `FileWriter` or `BufferedWriter` classes were to throw an exception, as would happen if the file already existed but were read-only to the user, for example. As noted earlier, placing this code in the `finally` block ensures that the `BufferedWriter` will always be closed (which, as a side effect, also causes the `FileWriter` to be closed).

If an `IOException` is thrown from the code on lines 4 through 6, it will be caught in the `catch` block on line 8, written to the log and then rethrown to the caller of this function by the JavaFX `throw` statement on line 10, which is the same as its Java equivalent. If the `catch` block had been omitted, the exception would have thrown to the caller anyway.

Notice that the `catch` statement uses JavaFX variable declaration syntax:

```
} catch (ex:IOException) {
```

In the spirit of JavaFX, you don't actually need to specify `IOException` here; you can simplify it to this:

```
} catch (ex) {
```

This will catch any exceptions, so it is equivalent to specifying `Throwable` as the exception type.

If you don't catch an exception, it will be propagated to the calling code. If the exception is not caught at any level, it will be caught by the JavaFX runtime and printed to the standard error stream.

9
Binding

Binding enables you to link one value in a JavaFX application to another so that if the second value changes, the first is automatically updated and stays in step with it. You can bind a value to a script variable, an instance variable of a JavaFX class, an expression (including a block expression), the return value of a function, a sequence, or a part of a sequence. The most common uses for binding in JavaFX involve linking GUI components or the properties of a graphical node to some kind of state in an underlying model, and this is also the easiest and most direct way to demonstrate what can be done with binding. For that reason, many of the examples in this section use GUI components that we have not yet discussed in any detail. Fortunately, the JavaFX user interface components are easy to use, so it should not be difficult for you to understand what is happening, even if you choose not to skim some of the GUI chapters before reading the rest of this section.

The examples for this chapter can be found in the `javafxbinding` package in the JavaFX Book Language project.

Binding to Variables and Expressions

A binding, which can be either unidirectional or bidirectional, can be created in two ways:

- When declaring and initializing a script variable or an instance variable of a JavaFX class (see Chapter 11, "JavaFX Script Classes")
- When supplying the initial value for an instance variable in an object initializer

Binding to a Script Variable

The following example declares two script variables a and b and binds the value of b to that of a so that an assignment to a causes the same value to be written to b:

```
var a = "Hello, world";
var b = bind a;
```

The preceding code causes the value `"Hello, World"` to be assigned to `a` and then, by virtue of the binding, to `b`. Subsequent changes to the value of `a` are automatically propagated to `b`:

```
a = "Goodbye, world";
println("a is '{a}', b is '{b}'");
```

This code prints the following:

```
a is 'Goodbye, world', b is 'Goodbye, world'
```

This binding is *unidirectional*—that is, changes propagate in only one direction, from `a` to `b`, but not the other way around. The binding asserts that the value of `b` will always be the same as that of `a`. To ensure that this is always the case, direct assignments to `b` are not allowed, so if you try to do this, you get a runtime exception:

```
b = "Not allowed to change the value of a bound variable";
```

You can use the `isReadOnly()` function to determine whether a script or instance variable is read-only because it is the target of a binding:

```
println("{isReadOnly(b)}");
```

This code prints `true`, because the variable `b` in the preceding code is bound to the value of the variable `a`.

Binding in an Object Literal

An initializer in an object literal can bind the value of an instance variable of a JavaFX class to another value or to an expression. As you might expect, the effect of this is that the value of the instance variable will always be the same as the value to which it is bound. The following code, which you'll find in the file `javafxbinding/BindingCreation.fx` in the JavaFX Book Language project, defines a new JavaFX class called `ValueHolder` with a single instance variable called `value` of type `Integer` (creating JavaFX classes is covered in detail in Chapter 11):

```
class ValueHolder {
    var value:Integer;
}
```

Now let's declare a script variable called `targetValue`, initially set to the value 1:

```
var targetValue = 1;
```

Having done this, we can create an instance of the `ValueHolder` class in which the value variable is bound to the value of `targetValue`, by using a binding expression in the object initializer:

```
var holder = ValueHolder {
            value: bind targetValue;
        };
```

As a result of this code, the `value` variable of the `ValueHolder` instance will initially be set to 1. If we now change the value of `targetValue`, the `value` variable will change accordingly:

```
println(holder.value);   // Prints "1"
targetValue = 2;
println(holder.value);   // Prints "2"
```

It is important to note this binding just causes the value of the `value` variable of the instance of the `ValueHolder` class that we created on line 1 to be changed. In some cases, you need to create a new instance of the class whenever the value of an initialized variable changes. You'll see several examples of this when we discuss the GUI libraries later in this book. In terms of this example, if you need to create a new `ValueHolder` each time the value of the `targetValue` variable is changed, you can do so like this:

```
var holder = bind ValueHolder {
    value: targetHolder
};
```

Note the difference between this code and that shown previously: Here, the **bind** keyword appears outside the object initializer, not as part of the initializer itself. When the binding is created in this way, changing the value of `targetHolder` will cause a new `ValueHolder` instance to be created and assigned to the `holder` variable:

```
println(holder.value);   // Prints "1"

// Causes a new ValueHolder to be created and assigned to holder
targetValue = 2;

// Prints "2", but refers to a different ValueHolder instance.
println(holder.value);
```

It is possible to mix both modes of binding. For example, suppose we have a class called `ValueHolder2` with two instance variables called `holder1` and `holder2` and that we then create an instance of it like this:

```
var holder = bind ValueHolder2 {
                    holder1: target1
                    holder2: bind target2
}
```

Now, if the value of the variable `target1` changes, a new instance of `ValueHolder2` will be created with the `holder1` variable set to the modified value of `target1` and with `holder2` still set to the current value of `target2`. On the other hand, if the value of `target2` changes, all that will happen is that the `holder2` variable of the existing `ValueHolder2` instance will be updated with the new value of `target2`.

Chapter 9 Binding

Here's a more complex example that demonstrates how to bind an instance variable of one object to the value of an instance variable of another. The source code for this example is in the file `javafxbinding/BindLabelToText.fx` in the JavaFX Book GUI project.

```
1    Stage {
2        var scene:Scene;
3        title: "Simple Binding"
4        visible: true width: 250 height: 120
5        scene: scene = Scene {
6            content: [
7                VBox {
8                    var textBox:TextBox;
9                    width: bind scene.width height: bind scene.height
10                   nodeHPos: HPos.CENTER vpos: VPos.CENTER
11                   content: [
12                       textBox = TextBox {
13                           text: "Please type here"
14                           selectOnFocus: true
15                       }
16                       Label {
17                           text: bind textBox.rawText
18                           vpos: VPos.CENTER
19                       }
20                   ]
21               }
22           ]
23       }
24   }
```

A `TextBox` is a user input control that lets you enter a value, which is stored in an instance variable called `rawText`. A `Label` is a component that displays the value that is assigned to its `text` variable but does not allow user input. As you type, the value of the `rawText` variable of the `TextBox` changes to reflect the content of the input field. On line 17 of the preceding code, the `Label`'s object initializer binds the value of its `text` variable to that of the `rawText` variable of the `TextBox`, so whatever you enter in the `TextBox` is also displayed by the label, as shown in Figure 9-1.

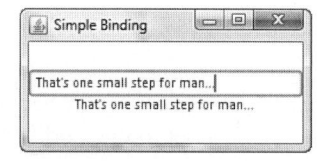

Figure 9-1   A simple binding

If you have ever built a form to display the properties of an object, you will be familiar with the need to attach listeners to the object so that changes to its properties can be reflected on the screen. JavaFX binding takes away the pain of writing most of this code by arranging for changes in the value on the right side of the binding, which in this case would be an instance variable of the object displayed to be reflected in the property of the GUI component that is displaying the value of that property.

> **Note**
>
> You can initialize a variable with a binding only if you have permission to write to that variable. As you'll see later in this book, it is possible to declare a variable so that it is either read-only or initialize-only. It is not legal to try to use a binding expression to initialize such a variable.

Binding to an Expression

The examples that you have seen so far have bound one variable directly to the value of another, but binding is more general than that. The right side of a binding operation can be any expression (even a block expression) that evaluates to a value that is compatible with the type of the bound variable. Here's a variant of the previous example that surrounds the text from the input field with quotes before displaying it in the label[1]:

```
1    Stage {
2        var scene:Scene;
3        title: "Expression Binding #1"
4        visible: true width: 250 height: 120
5        scene: scene = Scene {
6            content: [
7                VBox {
8                    var textBox:TextBox;
9                    width: bind scene.width height: bind scene.height
10                   nodeHPos: HPos.CENTER vpos: VPos.CENTER
11                   content: [
12                       textBox = TextBox {
13                           text: "Please type here"
14                           selectOnFocus: true
15                       }
16                       Label {
17                           text: "You typed: {textBox.rawText}"
18                           vpos: VPos.CENTER
19                       }
20                   ]
21               }
```

---

[1] The source code for this example is in the file `javafxbinding/BindLabelToExpression.fx` in the JavaFX Book Desktop project.

```
22            ]
23         }
24     }
```

Figure 9-2 shows a typical result of running this code.

The only significant change in this example is the following code, on line 15:

```
text: bind "You typed: {textBox.rawText}"
```

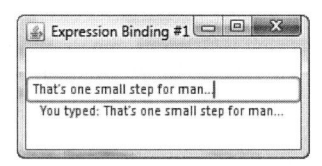

Figure 9-2 Binding to the value of an expression

Here, the bound value is a string with a nested expression that depends on the value of the `rawText` variable of the `TextBox`. Whenever that value changes, the nested expression is reevaluated and substituted into the string, and the result is assigned to the `text` variable of the `Label`.

You can embed more than one expression in the string, and the bound variable will be updated when the value of either expression changes. The following code, which is taken from the file `javafxbinding/BindLabelToExpression2.fx` in the JavaFX Book GUI project, causes the label to display the length of the string that you type as well as the string itself, as you can see in Figure 9-3:

```
text: bind "You typed: {textBox.rawText}"
"\n({textBox.rawText.length()} characters)"
```

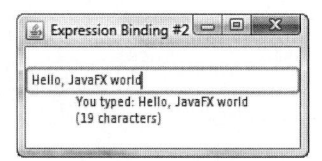

Figure 9-3 Binding with two embedded expressions

Binding also works with arithmetic operations:

```
var a = 23;
var b = bind a + 10;
```

This code initializes `b` with the value `33` and ensures that it is always `10` greater than the value assigned to a.

Binding and the `def` Statement

As you saw in Chapter 5, "Variables and Data Types," the `def` statement creates a variable that is initialized when declared and which cannot subsequently be changed. More correctly, the variable cannot be changed *by assignment*, but its value *can* change if it is bound to an expression whose value can change. For example

```
var value = 10;
def twiceTheValue = bind 2 * value;
```

The variable `twiceTheValue` is initially assigned the value `20`, as a result of the binding. Even though its value cannot be directly changed, the binding ensures that it tracks the variable `value` so that the following code prints `30`:

```
value = 15;
println("{twiceTheValue}");
```

Binding to an Instance Variable

You have already seen an example that bound the value of the `text` variable of a `Label` to that of the `rawText` variable of a `TextBox` in an object initializer. You can also bind a script variable to the value of an instance variable, as the following example shows:

```
1    class ValueHolder {
2        var value:Integer;
3    }
4
5    var holder1 = ValueHolder { value: 1234 };
6    var holder2 = ValueHolder { value: 3456 };
7    var holder = holder1;
8
9    var v = bind holder.value;
10   println("Value #1: {v}");
11   holder1.value = 9876;
12   println("Value #2: {v}");
```

The code on lines 1 through 3 are a repeat of the definition of a JavaFX class called `ValueHolder` that we used in an earlier example in this chapter. Lines 5 through 7 create two instances of this class and then assign a reference to one of them to the script variable `holder`. On line 9, we create a binding between the variable `v` and the `value` variable of the `ValueHolder` referred to by `holder`, which currently refers to the instance created on line 5. It should be no surprise that the result of the `println()` call on line 10 is the following:

```
Value #1: 1234
```

This is the expected result because `1234` is the value of the `value` variable of the first `ValueHolder` object. It should also be clear that because line 11 assigns `9876` to the `value` variable of the first `ValueHolder` and `v` is bound to this variable, the output from line 12 will be the following:

```
Value #2: 9876
```

Now suppose that we do this:

```
holder = holder2;
println("Value #3: {v}");
```

This code makes the script variable `holder` refer to the *other* `ValueHolder` instance. Given that `v` is bound to `holder.value`, what effect should this assignment have? The answer is that after this assignment, `v` will have the value `3456`:

```
Value #3: 3456
```

This is quite logical, because we bound `v` to the `value` variable of whatever the variable `holder` refers to, not to the `value` variable of the `ValueHolder` that `holder` initially referred to. As a result, changing the value of either the variable `holder` or the `value` variable of the `ValueHolder` to which it refers will cause `v` to be updated. Another way of thinking about this is that if a variable is bound to `a.b.c.d`, it is effectively also bound to all of `a.b.c`, `a.b`, and `a`.

Binding with a Conditional Expression

The ability to bind to an expression includes binding to the result of an `if` expression (or to an expression that includes one or more `if` expressions). As an example of why this is useful, suppose you are implementing a user interface that shows the progress of a long operation, such as a download, and you want to show how much time remains. If the time remaining is in a variable called `timeLeft`, which is updated as the download progresses, you can display a suitable message like this:

```
Label {
    text: bind "{timeLeft} seconds remaining"
}
```

This works, but there is a grammatical issue with the text that appears 1 second before the operation completes, as shown in Figure 9-4.

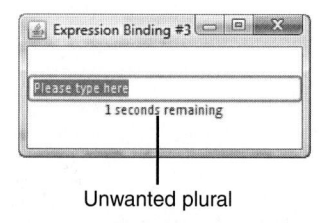

Figure 9-4   An incorrect progress message

What you need to do to fix this is to use a slightly different message when only 1 second remains. This is easily achieved by binding the `Label`'s `text` variable to the result of an `if` expression, like this[2]:

```
Label {
    text: bind if (timeLeft == 1) "{timeLeft} second remaining"
                else "{timeLeft} seconds remaining"
}
```

This gives the result shown in Figure 9-5. As you can see, the code is quite readable and conveys the intent clearly.

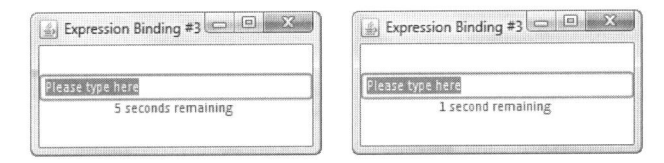

Figure 9-5   Using a bind to a conditional expression

Bidirectional Binding

The bindings you have seen so far have all been unidirectional. Sometimes it is useful to make a binding bidirectional. A bidirectional binding is established through the use of the keywords `with inverse`:

```
var a = 23;
var b = bind a with inverse;
```

Now, as with a unidirectional binding, changes to the value of `a` cause `b` to be updated. However, a bidirectional binding also allows the bound variable, in this case `b`, to be modified and ensures that the value of `a` stays in step with it. As a consequence, this assignment, which would not be allowed in the case of a unidirectional binding, is legal:

```
b = 100;
```

This causes the value of `a` to also be changed to `100` so that the invariant expressed by the binding is maintained. Note that at the time of this writing, the only form of bidirectional binding allowed is to a script variable or to instance variable. It is not possible to bind to the value of a more general expression, such as this:

```
var b = bind a + 23 with inverse; // Not allowed
```

---

[2] You'll find this code in the file `javafxbinding/BindLabelToExpression3.fx` in the JavaFX Book Desktop project.

The following is an example of a bidirectional binding to an instance variable, using the `ValueHolder` class that we created in an earlier example:

```
1    class ValueHolder {
2        var value:Integer;
3    }
4
5    var holder = ValueHolder { value: 1234 };
6    var boundValue = bind holder.value with inverse;
7
8    println("boundValue is {boundValue}");
9    boundValue = 4567;
10   println("Value is holder is now {holder.value}");
11   holder.value = 7890;
12   println("boundValue changed to {boundValue}");
```

The code on line 6 creates a bidirectional binding between the variable `boundValue` and the value variable of an instance of the `ValueHolder` class. The output from this script illustrates how the bidirectional binding works:

```
boundValue is 1234
Value is holder is now 4567
boundValue changed to 7890
```

Bidirectional bindings are often needed when building user interfaces. It is common to use a GUI component to map an instance variable of a model class that represents part of the state of an application. If you use a unidirectional binding, you can arrange for the content of the model to be reflected in the state of the GUI component, or vice versa, depending on which way you define the binding. However, if you want to allow both the user and the application to change the state of the model and to keep those states synchronized, you need to bind them bidirectionally.

We illustrate this by using a variation on the example shown in Figure 9-3, which bound the `text` variable of a `Label` to the `rawText` variable of a `TextBox`. First, we move the bound text to a script variable, and then we bind the `text` variables of the `Label` and the `rawText` variable of the `TextBox` to that script variable, instead of creating a binding between the two GUI components[3]:

```
TextBox {
    text: bind modelText
    selectOnFocus: true
}

Label {
    text: bind "You typed: {modelText}"
```

---

[3] The code for this example is in the file `javafxbinding/BidirectionalBinding.fx` in the JavaFX Book GUI project.

```
            "\n({modelText.length()} characters)"
    vpos: VPos.CENTER
}
```

On its own, this code change makes no real difference, but now we add another `TextBox` that is bound to the same script variable and make the bindings of both `TextBox` controlss bidirectional. Listing 9-1 shows the code for this example, with the most important lines highlighted.

Listing 9-1   **A Bidirectional Binding**

```
var model Text: String = "Please type here";
Stage {
    var scene:Scene;
    title: "Bidirectional Binding"
    visible: true width: 250 height: 120
    scene: scene = Scene {
        content: [
            VBox {
                width: bind scene.width height: bind scene.height
                nodeHPos: HPos.CENTER vpos: VPos.CENTER
                content: [
                    TextBox {
                        text: bind modelText with inverse
                        selectOnFocus: true
                    }
                    Label {
                        text: bind "You typed: {modelText}"
                            "\n({modelText.length()} characters)"
                        vpos: VPos.CENTER
                    }
                    TextBox {
                        text: bind modelText with inverse
                        selectOnFocus: true
                    }
                ]
            }
        ]
    }
}
```

Figure 9-6 shows the result of running this code.

Because both `TextBoxes` have a bidirectional binding to the `modelText` variable, they can both update its value, and they will both be updated by any changes made to it. So, if you type into the upper text field, the binding from that component's `text` property causes the value to be written to the `modelText` variable when the focus leaves the field, from where it will be propagated both to the `Label` and to the lower `TextBox`. Similarly, whatever is typed in the lower `TextBox` is copied to `modelText` and also to the `Label` and

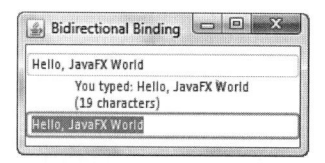

Figure 9-6 Linking application state using a bidirectional binding

to the upper `TextBox`. Notice that the `Label` only needs a unidirectional binding to `modelText` because it does not accept any input and therefore cannot cause the variable's content to change. The linkages established by the two bidirectional bindings and the single unidirectional binding are shown graphically in Figure 9-7.

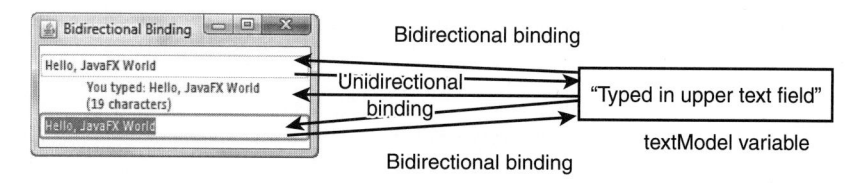

Figure 9-7 Unidirectional and bidirectional bindings

Eager and Lazy Binding

By default, when the value of the expression on the right side of a binding changes, the bound variable is updated immediately. In most cases, particularly if the value of the bound variable affects the user interface, this is the desired effect. However, a performance penalty is associated with this. If you don't need the bound variable to be updated immediately, you can create a *lazy* binding instead, by using the `lazy` keyword (the default binding style is referred to as *eager* binding), like this:

```
1    var a = "Hello, world";
2    var b = bind lazy a on replace {
3        println("Variable b changed to '{b}'");
4    }
5    a = "Changed";
6    println("After change of value of a");
7    var c = b;
```

We create the lazy binding on line 2, where we also attach a trigger that will print a message when the value of the bound variable `b` is actually updated. (Triggers are discussed in detail in the next chapter.) Here's the result of running this code:

```
After change of value of a
Variable b changed to 'Changed'
```

As you can see, the value of variable `a` is changed on line 5 of the code, but the value of `b` is not updated immediately—this is obvious because the message printed by the trigger does not appear before the result of the `println()` statement on line 6. In fact, the value of a lazily bound variable is not updated until it is read, in this case on line 7. Deferring the update of a bound variable in this way, especially if the binding expression is complex, can improve the performance of your application if the bound value is read less frequently than it would be updated.

Binding and Functions

You can create a binding to the return value of a function by simply invoking the function (alone or as part of an expression) on the right side of a binding assignment. JavaFX has two types of function, called *unbound* and *bound* functions. The functions that you have seen so far in this book have all been unbound, and the example in this section also uses an unbound function. You'll be introduced to bound functions in the section "Binding and Bound Functions," later in this chapter.

Binding and Unbound Functions

Suppose we want to write a function that calculates the area of a circle, rounded to the nearest integer, given its radius. That's simple enough—it takes only three lines of code:

```
function computeArea(radius:Integer):Integer {
    Math.round(Math.PI * radius * radius) as Integer
}
```

Now suppose we want to write an application that displays a circle and a slider that controls the circle's radius, as shown in Figure 9-8.[4] As the user drags the slider, the circle's radius should change to match the slider's value, and both the radius and the area should be updated.

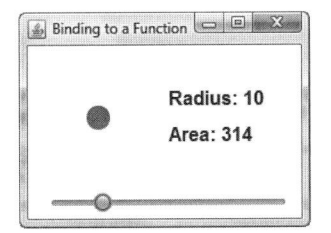

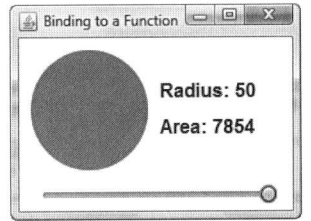

Figure 9-8 Binding to a function that calculates the area of a circle of varying radius

---

[4] The source code for this example is in the file `javafxbinding/FunctionBinding.fx` in the JavaFX Book GUI project.

You should by now recognize that there is an obvious case here for binding—the `radius` variable should be bound to the value of the slider, and the strings that display the radius and the area should be bound to the `radius` variable and to the result of the function that calculates the area, respectively. We haven't yet covered the GUI classes that you need to create this application, so we'll skip those details and show you only those parts of the code that involve bindings.

First, the radius is defined and set to a reasonable initial value:

```
var radius = 10.0;
```

The linkage from the slider value to the `radius` variable is a binding in the object literal that initializes the slider when it is created:

```
Slider {
    min: 1
    max: 50
    vertical: false
    value: bind radius with inverse
    translateX: 20
    translateY: 120
}
```

The slider value is allowed to range from `1` up to `50` and, because of the binding, it starts with the initial value of the variable `radius`, which is `10`. As the user drags the slider, its `value` variable changes, and this is propagated to the `radius` variable because of the binding. We set up a bidirectional binding because we need to copy the value of the slider to the `radius` variable, not the other way around. Another way to do this is to create a unidirectional binding from the `radius` variable to the `value` variable of the slider:

```
var slider = Slider {
    min: 1
    max: 50
    vertical: false
    value: 10
    translateX: 20
    translateY: 120
}
var radius = bind slider.value;
```

This works, but it is not good practice to have application state, which is what the `radius` variable represents, depend directly on a GUI component in this way. As a rule, dependencies should be from the GUI components to values in the application model. This makes it possible to change the components that are used in the user interface without requiring any modification of the application logic.

The text that represents the radius is displayed using a `Text` object:

```
Text {
    content: bind "Radius: {radius}"
    x: 120
```

```
    y: 50
}
```

The `content` variable is bound to a string containing the value of the `radius` variable. As a result, it will be updated whenever the radius changes, and the `Text` object will display the new value on the screen.

The `content` variable of the second `Text` object is bound to an expression that includes the result of invoking the `computeArea()` function with the current radius as its parameter:

```
Text {
    content: bind "Area: {computeArea(radius)}"
    x: 120
    y: 80
}
```

The highlighted code is an example of a binding to a function. Although in this case only the function result is required, it is possible to create a bound expression that involves more than one function invocation, as follows:

```
var v = bind fn1(arg1) + fn2(arg2);
```

In this example, `fn1()` and `fn2()` are assumed to be functions that each require a single argument.

When a binding involves a function invocation, it is necessary to assign a new value to the target of the binding whenever the result of the function would change. In the case of an unbound function, the function is invoked automatically, and its value substituted in its surrounding expression *whenever the value of any of its arguments changes*. In the case of the `computeArea()` function, a change in the value of the `radius` variable, which is the function's sole argument, will cause the function to be invoked again and its new value substituted into the bind expression, which is then assigned to the `text` variable of the `Text` node. Hence, as the user moves the slider on the screen, the corresponding change in the `radius` variable causes the displayed area to be updated.

Binding and Bound Functions

Now let's make a small change to the example shown in Figure 9-8 that will illustrate the difference between an unbound and a bound function—we'll add the ability for the user to track *either* the area of the circle *or* its circumference as the radius varies. To make this possible, we add two radio buttons that allow the user to select which of these values should be displayed, as shown in Figure 9-9.[5]

---

[5] This modified example can be found in `javafxbinding/BoundFunction.fx` in the JavaFX Book Desktop project.

Chapter 9 Binding

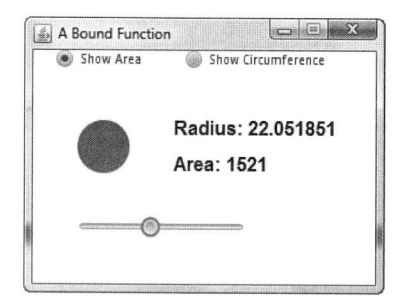

Figure 9-9 Allowing selection of the display of area or circumference

To implement this, we first add a function that computes the circumference given the radius:

```
function computeCircumference(radius:Integer):Integer {
    Math.round(2 * Math.PI * radius) as Integer;
}
```

To reflect the user's selection of area or circumference, we add a Boolean-valued script variable that indicates whether the user wants to see the area:

```
var showArea = true;
```

The state of this variable is bound to the selection state of the radio buttons shown at the top of Figure 9-9 but, because we haven't yet covered radio buttons, we won't show that code here. We also add a function that returns a string containing either the area or the circumference of the circle, depending on the state of the `showArea` variable:

```
function getAreaOrCircumference(radius:Integer) {
    if (showArea) "Area: {computeArea(radius)}"
            else "Circumference: {computeCircumference(radius)}"
}
```

Finally, the value returned by this function is displayed in a `Text` object:

```
Text {
    content: bind getAreaOrCircumference(radius)
    x: 120
    y: 80
}
```

If you were to run the example with the code shown so far, you would see the user interface shown in Figure 9-10. If you were to move the slider to change the radius of the circle, the displayed area would be updated as it was in the previous example. So far, so good. If you were now to select the Circumference radio button, you would expect the circumference to appear in place of the area. But, as you can see in Figure 9-10, that does not happen; the area is still displayed.

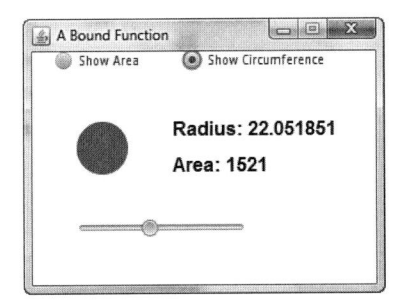

Figure 9-10   A case for using a bound function

Selecting one of the radio buttons changes the value of the `showArea` variable, which is used in the body of the `getAreaOrCircumference()` function:

```
function getAreaOrCircumference(radius:Integer) {
    if (showArea) "Area: {computeArea(radius)}"
             else "Circumference: {computeCircumference(radius)}"
}
```

This isn't enough to cause this function result to be reevaluated because the value of an unbound function *depends only on its arguments*—in this case, only a change in the circle's radius will cause the function to be invoked again. There are two ways to fix this. The first is to make the value of `showArea` one of the function arguments. This would work, but in general this is not a good solution because in a more complex application you may end up having to pass arguments like `showArea` through multiple levels of function calls. A better solution is to make `getAreaOrCircumference()` a *bound* function, which just requires the addition of the keyword `bound`:

```
bound function getAreaOrCircumference(radius:Integer) {
    if (showArea) "Area: {computeArea(radius)}"
             else "Circumference: {computeCircumference(radius)}"
}
```

The value returned by a bound function is reevaluated when *any* of its dependencies changes—that is, when its arguments *or* any of the values used in the function body, such as `showArea` in this example, are modified. With this change, toggling the selected radio button causes the displayed value to switch between area and circumference, as shown in Figure 9-11.

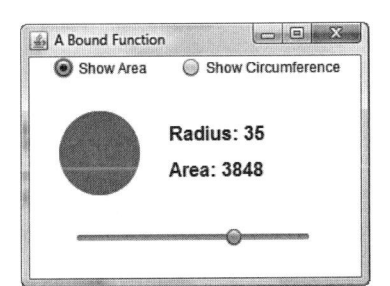

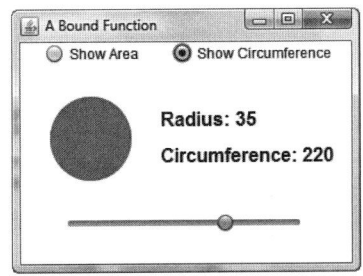

Figure 9-11   Using a bound function

Optimization of Bound Function Evaluation

In the preceding section, we said that the value returned by a bound function is reevaluated when its inputs change—we did *not* say that the function is invoked again to compute the return value. The compiler is permitted to optimize the evaluation of an expression involving a bound function by arranging for only those parts of the function that directly depend on the dependency that has changed to be reevaluated. In fact, it is frequently not necessary for the compiler to rerun the whole function. For example, suppose we were to write a bound function called `complex()` that derives its result from the results of two other functions called `slowFunction1()` and `slowFunction2()`:

```
1    function slowFunction1(arg:Number):Number {
2        println("slowFunction1");
3        Math.atan(arg)
4    }
5    function slowFunction2(arg:String):String {
6        println("slowFunction2");
7        arg.toUpperCase()
8    }
9
10   var inputString = "Input Value";
11   bound function complex(arg:Number):String {
12       "The results are {slowFunction1(arg)}"
13       " and {slowFunction2(inputString)}"
14   }
```

In this artificial example, the bound function `complex()` depends both on its numeric argument and on the value of the variable `inputString`, binding it to a variable called `result`, like this:

```
var arg = 1.0;
var result = bind complex(arg);

println(result);
```

This produces the following output:

```
slowFunction1
slowFunction2
The results are 0.7853981633974483 and INPUT VALUE
```

As you can see, and as you would expect, both `slowFunction1()` and `slowFunction2()` were called during the assignment to the variable `result`. Now let's modify the value of the variable `arg` and print the new value of `result`:

```
arg = 0.0;
println(result);
```

This produces the following:

```
slowFunction1
The results are 0.0 and INPUT VALUE
```

As expected, the value of `result` has changed, as if the function `complex()` had been reinvoked because of the change to the value of its argument. However, as you can see from the output, `slowFunction1()` was called, but `slowFunction2()` was not. It is clear from the definition of the function `complex()` that changing the value of `arg` will only affect the result of `slowFunction1()`, so there is no need to call `slowFunction2()` as a result of this change. Instead, the value returned on its last invocation is reused and combined with the new value from `slowFunction1()` to produce the new return value for `complex()`.

Now let's change the value of the variable `inputString` and print the result:

```
inputString = "New Value";
println(result);
```

A change in the value of `inputString` affects only the result of `slowFunction2()`, so the output this time looks like this:

```
slowFunction2
The results are 0.0 and NEW VALUE
```

Again, only the function whose result will be affected by the change is reevaluated.

Content of a Bound Function

This optimization that you have just seen is very useful, but it is not free. Although it is not obvious from these examples, limitations apply to what can appear in the body of a bound function that do not apply to an unbound function. The rules boil down to this:

- Every statement of a bound function, with the exception of the last, must be a `var` or `def` statement that includes a value assignment.
- The final statement of the function must be an expression that provides the function's return value (optionally preceded by the keyword `return`).
- The function must not have any side effects—that is, it cannot modify any state outside of the function itself, such as variables declared elsewhere.

Here's a modified version of the `getAreaOrCircumference()` function that shows the general form of a bound function, for illustrative purposes only:

```
1    var showArea:Boolean = true;
2
3    bound function getAreaOrCircumference(radius:Integer) {
4        def circumference = Math.round(2 * Math.PI * radius) as Integer;
5        def area = Math.round(Math.PI * radius * radius) as Integer;
6        if (showArea) "Area: {area}"
7            else "Circumference: {circumference}"
8    }
```

This doesn't look efficient because it always appears to calculate both the area and the circumference when only one is needed. However, as it's a bound function, if only the value of `showArea` changes, neither of the calculations on lines 4 and 5 will be repeated when a new return value is required. When the radius changes, however, everything will be recalculated.

Debugging a Bound Function

The first rule in the preceding list implies that there cannot be any void expressions in a bound function, which is inconvenient because it makes it difficult to debug the logic by including `println()` statements. As a result, the following code will not compile:

```
bound function getAreaOrCircumference(radius:Integer) {
    def circumference = Math.round(2 * Math.PI * radius) as Integer;
    def area = Math.round(Math.PI * radius * radius) as Integer;

    // The next line does not compile - void expression not allowed
    println("Area is {area}, circumference is {circumference}.");
    if (showArea) "Area: {area}" else "Circumference: {circumference}"
}
```

Fortunately, there is a workaround—as you saw earlier in this section, a bound function can invoke an unbound function,[6] and that unbound function can be used to print debug information. The only requirement is that the called function must be part of an expression and therefore must return a value. To meet this requirement, we can create a function that accepts a value that you want to print and some text to be printed with it and returns the value that it is given, like this:

```
var debug = true;
function debugNumber(text:String, value:Number) {
    if (debug) {
        println("{text}: {value}");
    }
    value
}
```

Given this function, we can rewrite `getAreaOrCircumference()` with debugging included, as follows:

```
bound function getAreaOrCircumference(radius:Integer) {
    def circumference = debugNumber("Circumference",
                    Math.round(2 * Math.PI * radius) as Integer);
    def area = debugNumber("Area",
                    Math.round(Math.PI * radius * radius) as Integer);
    if (showArea) "Area: {area}" else "Circumference: {circumference}"
}
```

---

[6] A bound function can, of course, also call another bound function.

This change is not very intrusive into the logic of the function, and the debugging can easily be disabled by assigning the value `false` to the variable `debug`. Running the example shown in Figure 9-11 with debugging enabled produces output like this:

```
Circumference: 63.0
Area: 314.0
Circumference: 69.0
Area: 380.0
```

As it is an unbound function, `debugNumber()` will be called whenever either of its arguments changes value. In the preceding code, this will happen whenever the radius changes because in both cases the arguments include an expression that depends on the radius. Therefore, when the radius changes, you will see two lines of debug output. However, when the `showArea` variable changes, only the last line of the function needs to be reevaluated, and in this case, you would not see any debug output because neither the area nor the circumference will have been recalculated.

Variables and Bound Functions

Another consequence of the requirement for a bound function not to have any side effects is that you can't assign a value to a variable that's not defined inside the function. Assignment includes the use of the increment and decrement operators, so the following code, which attempts to count the number of times that a bound function is called, is illegal:

```
var count = 0;
bound function getAreaOrCircumference(radius:Integer) {
    count++;   // Compilation error - side effects not allowed.
    def circumference = debugNumber("Circumference",
                    Math.round(2 * Math.PI * radius) as Integer);
    def area = debugNumber("Area",
                    Math.round(Math.PI * radius * radius) as Integer);
    if (showArea) "Area: {area}" else "Circumference: {circumference}"
}
```

If you really need to do something like this, the solution is again to use an unbound function:

```
var count = 0;
function bumpCount() {
    count++;
}

bound function getAreaOrCircumference(radius:Integer) {
    var x = bumpCount();
    def circumference = debugNumber("Circumference",
                    Math.round(2 * Math.PI * radius) as Integer);
    def area = debugNumber("Area",
                    Math.round(Math.PI * radius * radius) as Integer);
    if (showArea) "Area: {area}" else "Circumference: {circumference}"
}
```

Because it is used in a bound function, `bumpCount()` has to return a value and that value *must* be assigned to a variable even though it is not going to be used, or that first rule requiring all but the last statement in a bound function to be an assignment would be broken.

Loops in Bound Functions

The examples that you have seen so far illustrate that a bound function may contain conditional expressions, but what about loops? It is not legal to write a bound function that contains a `while` statement, because a `while` statement cannot return a value, but it is possible to use a `for` statement, as long it returns a value. Here's an example that illustrates this:

```
1    var threshold:Number;
2
3    bound function subset(args:Number[]):Number[] {
4        var results = for (arg in args) {
5                    Math.sin(Math.toRadians(arg)) as Number
6                };
7        return results[n | n > threshold];
8    }
```

The `subset()` function accepts a sequence of `Number`s, which are taken to be angles measured in degrees, converts each of them to radians, calculates the sine of each angle, and returns a sequence containing the sine values that are larger than a threshold given by a variable that is declared outside the function. The calculation is performed on each angle individually by the `for` loop on lines 4 through 6, resulting in a new sequence of `Number`s that is then trimmed to those that exceed the threshold by the sequence expression on line 7. The following code sets the threshold to 0 and binds the variable `results` to the result of invoking `subset()` on a set of angles:

```
// Return the positive sine values.
threshold = 0.0;
var values:Number[] = [0, 45, 90, 135, 180, 225, 270, 315, 360];
var results = bind subset(values);
println(results.toString());
```

This code prints the following:

```
[0.70710677, 1.0, 0.70710677, 1.2246469E-16 ]
```

Now if we change the value of the `threshold` variable, the value of the `results` variable will be reevaluated because it is bound to the result of the function, and the function is bound and depends on `threshold`:

```
// Requests the sine values that are greater than 0.5.
// Causes subset() to be re-evaluated.
threshold = 0.5;
println(results.toString());
```

This gives the following results:

```
[0.70710677, 1.0, 0.70710677 ]
```

Binding and Sequences

The ability to bind to a sequence is one of the most useful features of JavaFX. You can bind to a whole sequence, the size of a sequence, a range of elements from a sequence, or, most powerfully, to the result of applying a filter/transformation to a sequence. Applications that display the results of database queries are the most obvious application of sequence binding, because the binding allows the user interface to update automatically as modifications are made to the data being displayed.

Binding to a Sequence

Binding one sequence to another simply causes the second sequence to become a read-only copy of the sequence to which it is bound. The following code, from the file `javafxbinding/BindToSequence1.fx` in the JavaFX Book Language project, creates a sequence of names, binds the variable `namesCopy` to it, and prints the value of that variable:

```
var names = ["Armstrong", "Aldrin", "Collins"];
var namesCopy = bind names;
println("Names copy original: {namesCopy.toString()}");
```

The result is the original set of names:

```
Names copy original: [ Armstrong, Aldrin, Collins ]
```

Modifications made to the original sequence are reflected in `namesCopy`:

```
insert ["Conrad", "Bean", "Gordon"] into names;
println("Names copy modified: {namesCopy.toString()}");
```

The result of running this code is the following:

```
Names copy modified: [ Armstrong, Aldrin, Collins, Conrad, Bean, Gordon ]
```

However, as with other unidirectional bindings, you can't modify the bound copy of the sequence—the following code results in a runtime exception:

```
insert ["Lovell", "Haise", "Swigert"] into namesCopy; // Not valid
```

You can use this technique when you have a sequence that you need to both update and to expose to other code, without allowing that code to make any changes to it. In this example, to expose the sequence to external code, you would return a reference to the `namesCopy` variable.

Binding to a Transformed Sequence

Binding to a sequence is simple enough. Sometimes you need to create a second sequence whose content is the same as that of the first, but with a transformation of some kind applied. For example, given a list of names, you might want to maintain a list of those same names but in uppercase. The following code, from the file `javafxbinding/BindToSequence2.fx`, illustrates this:

```
var names = ["Armstrong", "Aldrin", "Collins"];
var upperCaseNames = bind for (name in names) name.toUpperCase();
println(upperCaseNames);
insert ["Conrad", "Gordon", "Bean" ] into names;
println(upperCaseNames);
```

To create the second sequence, we simply bind to the result of applying a `for` loop to the original set of names. Each iteration of the `for` loop applies a transformation, in this case conversion to uppercase, to an element of the input sequence to produce the corresponding element of the output sequence. The statement on line 3 of this code prints the content of the transformed sequence from the `upperCaseNames` variable:

[ARMSTRONG, ALDRIN, COLLINS]

On line 4, we insert three more names into the source list. Because the `upperCaseNames` variable is bound to the value of an expression that depends on the source list, it is updated with new elements that correspond to the names added, but with the transformation to uppercase applied. As a result, the `upperCaseNames` variable finishes with all six names in uppercase:

[ARMSTRONG, ALDRIN, COLLINS, CONRAD, GORDON, BEAN]

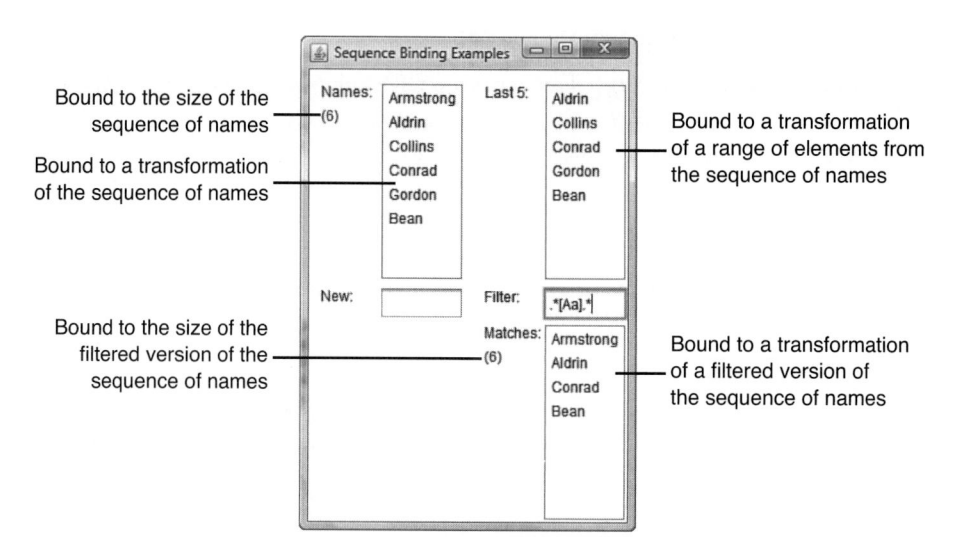

Figure 9-12   A user interface built around bound sequences

Binding to the Size of a Sequence

You can arrange for a variable to track the size of a sequence by binding it to an expression containing the `sizeof` keyword. This code, from the file `javafxbinding/BindToSequence3.fx`, reports the size of a sequence before and after new elements have been inserted:

```
var names = ["Armstrong", "Aldrin", "Collins"];
var count = bind sizeof names;
println("Original length: {count}");
insert ["Conrad", "Gordon", "Bean" ] into names;
println("After insert: {count}");
```

Here's the output from this example:

```
Original length: 3
After insert: 6
```

The code on line 2 binds the variable `count` to the number of elements in the sequence, which is initially 3, hence the first line of output. The insertion of three more names on line 4 causes the expression to be reevaluated, with the result that the value of `count` is changed to 6, as reported by the second `println` statement.

Binding to a Range of Sequence Elements

You can track a subset of a sequence by binding to a range of its elements. The following code, from `javafxbinding/BindToSequence4.fx`, binds the variable `result` to the last two elements of the `names` sequence:

```
var names = ["Armstrong", "Aldrin", "Collins"];
var result = bind names[sizeof names - 2 ..];
println(result);
insert ["Conrad", "Gordon", "Bean" ] into names;
println(result);
```

The `result` variable initially contains the last two of the three entries in the `names` sequence:

```
[ Aldrin, Collins ]
```

Adding three more names causes the binding expression to be reevaluated, with the result that the `result` variable still contains the last two entries, but this time of the enlarged sequence:

```
[ Gordon, Bean ]
```

10
Triggers

As you saw in the preceding chapter, binding enables you to link the state of one variable to another, relieving you of the responsibility of writing the largely boilerplate code that would be required to achieve the same effect in a Java application. Sometimes when the value of variable changes you need to do something more than a mechanical update of all the state in the application that directly depends on that variable. Triggers give you the ability to execute arbitrary code whenever the value of a script variable or an instance variable is changed. In this chapter, you see how to declare a trigger and what can be done when a trigger is executed.

The source code for this chapter is in the `javafxtriggers` package in the JavaFX Book Language project.

Triggers on Simple Variables

You can attach a trigger to either a script variable or an instance variable. The syntax is the same in either case. Initially, we discuss only how to declare a trigger for a simple variable, leaving the slightly more complex syntax that is used when attaching a trigger to a sequence variable until later in this chapter.

A trigger is attached to a variable when it is declared. This is fine for variables that you declare yourself, such as the script variables that you see in the examples that follow. It is not so convenient if you want to attach a trigger to an instance variable of a class that you did not write, or if you want to attach a trigger to a variable in some instances of a class and not in others. Fortunately, there are ways to solve this problem, which we cover in the "Triggers and Instance Variables" section, later in this chapter.

Declaring a Trigger

A trigger is created by adding an `on replace` clause to the declaration of a variable. The following code creates a trigger that prints the value of the associated script variable whenever it is changed:

```
var value:Integer on replace {
    println("value changed to {value}");
};
```

The trigger block may contain any valid JavaFX statements. Within the block, the value of the variable can be obtained by referencing its name, in the usual way. When the variable's value is changed, the trigger block will be executed, as shown by the following code:

```
var value:Integer on replace {
    println("value changed to {value}");
};
value = 1;
value = 2;
```

The output from this code is the following:

```
value changed to 0
value changed to 1
value changed to 2
```

As you can see, even though there are only two assignments to the variable, the trigger is fired three times—twice for the explicit assignments and once, represented by the first line of output, for the assignment of the variable's default value, which in this case is 0. The trigger does *not* fire if the value of the variable is not actually changed:

```
var value:Integer on replace {
    println("value changed to {value}");
};

value = 1;
value = 1;    // This does not fire the trigger.
```

Here, there are two assignments after initialization, but the second does not change the variable's value, so the trigger only fires twice:

```
value changed to 0
value changed to 1
```

The trigger declaration can be combined with an initializer, in which case the trigger fires first for the assignment of the given initial value:

```
var value:Integer = 32 on replace {
    println("value changed to {value}");
};
value = 1;
value = 2;
```

The preceding code prints the following:

```
value changed to 32
value changed to 1
value changed to 2
```

Getting the Previous Value

Sometimes it is useful to know what the value of a variable was before the change that caused a trigger to fire. You can get the previous value by adding a variable name to the trigger declaration:

```
var value:Integer = 32 on replace oldValue {
    println("value changed from {oldValue} to {value}");
};
value = 1;
```

On seeing the identifier `oldValue` (which could be any legal identifier name), the compiler creates a variable of that name, with the same type as the trigger variable and that is scoped to the trigger block. The preceding code, which initializes the variable to 32 and then changes its value to 1, prints the following:

```
value changed from 0 to 32
value changed from 32 to 1
```

You'll see an application of this feature in the "Using a Trigger to Enforce Constraints" section, later in this chapter.

A third variant of the trigger syntax lets you create another variable that receives the new value of the trigger variable:

```
var value:Integer = 32 on replace oldValue = newValue {
    println("value changed from {oldValue} to {newValue}");
};
value = 1;
```

In this case, the identifier after the equals sign is used to implicitly declare a variable that will be assigned the new value of the trigger variable. This syntax is not especially useful in a trigger attached to a simple variable—it is intended to be used in conjuction with sequence triggers, as you'll see in the "Triggers and Sequences" section.

Triggers and Binding

You can attach a trigger to a variable that is bound in the same way as you would to any other variable. This applies both to `var` and `def` statements. The following code binds the variable `boundValue` to the value of another variable called `targetValue` and reports whenever the value of `boundValue` is changed, which can only occur as a result of a new value being assigned to `targetValue`:

```
var targetValue = 1;
// NOTE: using "def" to create a bound variable. "def" variables
// can change value as the result of a binding.

def boundValue = bind targetValue on replace {
    println("boundValue changed to {boundValue}");
```

```
}
targetValue = 2;
```

The output from this code is as follows:

```
boundValue changed to 1
boundValue changed to 2
```

Using a Trigger to Enforce Constraints

Triggers are commonly used to enforce constraints on the state of a class's instance variables. In Java, you typically protect the state of an instance variable by making it private and providing a public setter method that ensures that only valid values are accepted and makes any changes to related state in the class that might be required. In JavaFX, instance variables are commonly public, which means that code outside the class can change their values. If your class needs to restrict the values that may be assigned to such a variable or adjust related state, it can do so with a trigger.

For example, look at the following JavaFX class declaration, which you can find in the file `javafxtriggers/ConstraintTriggers1.fx`. Although we haven't formally covered JavaFX classes yet, it is similar enough to Java that the syntax should be clear:

```
class RandomNumbers {
    var random = new Random(System.currentTimeMillis());
    public var min:Number = 1 on replace { range = max - min; };
    public var max:Number = 10 on replace { range = max - min; };
    var range:Number = max - min;

    public function getRandom():Number {
        min + range * random.nextFloat();
    }
}
```

The idea is that every time the `getRandom()` function is called, it returns a random number that is no smaller than the value of the `min` variable and no bigger than `max`. The variables `max` and `min` are public, so they can be changed by code outside the class at any time.

As an optimization, an additional variable called `range` is initially set to the difference between `max` and `min` and is used in the `getRandom()` function. Whenever either `max` or `min` is changed, the value of `range` needs to be adjusted, and as you can see, we achieve this in a pair of triggers attached to the `max` and `min` variables. We need to code the triggers so that they enforce the following constraints:

- The value of `max` must always be strictly greater than that of `min`.
- The value of `min` must always be greater than or equal to 1. (This is for illustrative purposes only.)

We need to decide what to do if the constraints are violated. There are two obvious choices:

- Reject the change by throwing an exception.
- Ignore the change by restoring the variable to its previous value.

In the following sections, we examine both of these possibilities.

Rejecting an Invalid Value

Let's first look at how to reject an illegal value for either max or min by throwing an `IllegalArgumentException`.[1] We apply the check by adding an `if` statement to each of the triggers and throwing the exception if the constraints are violated. You'll find this code in the file `javafxtriggers/TriggerConstraints2.fx`:

```
class RandomNumbers {
    var random = new Random(System.currentTimeMillis());
    public var min:Number = 1 on replace {
                    if (min < 1 or min >= max) {
                            throw new IllegalArgumentException(
                                    "Invalid min value: {min}");
                    }
                    range = max - min;
                };
    public var max:Number = 10 on replace {
                    if (max <= min) {
                            throw new IllegalArgumentException(
                                    "Invalid max value: {max}");
                    }
                    range = max - min;
                };
    var range:Number = max - min;

    public function getRandom():Number {
        min + range * random.nextFloat();
    }
}
```

Although this code looks correct, it isn't. If you were to initialize an instance of this class with valid bounds, like this, you would see an exception:

```
RandomNumbers { min: 5 max: 20 };
```

---

[1] Strictly speaking, we're not dealing with arguments, so we should create and use a more specific exception. For the sake of simplicity, the example uses an existing exception that approximates what we are trying to indicate to the class user.

Here is the result of running this code:

```
Exception in trigger:
java.lang.IllegalArgumentException: Invalid min value: 5.0
```

Why has this happened? The minimum value, in this case `5`, is not less than `1` and is smaller than the maximum value of `20`, so the constraints have not actually been violated. The problem is that the `min` and `max` variables are initialized one after the other, not both together. This is what actually happens:

1. The class is instantiated, and `min` and `max` both have the value `0`, the default for variables of type `Number`.

2. The initial value for the variable `min` is set. There are two possible initial values for this variable—`1` as specified in the variable declaration or `5` from the object initializer. As you'll see in Chapter 11, "JavaFX Script Classes," the value in the object initializer takes precedence, so `min` is now set to `5`.

3. Because the value of `min` has changed from `0` to `5`, its trigger is fired, and the test `if (min < 1 or min >= max)` is executed. At this stage, `max` is still `0`, so `min` is greater than `max` and the test fails, resulting in the exception previously shown.

So how do we fix this? The problem is that until `max` is initialized, we shouldn't be applying any checks that depend on its value. Because `0` is not actually a valid value for `max`, we could skip the second part of the check if `max` is `0`, which is its initial state:

```
if (min < 1 or (max != 0 and min >= max)) {
    throw new IllegalArgumentException(
                    "Invalid min value: {min}");
}
```

This works, but it's not a good solution in the general case—it would not be appropriate if `0` *were* a valid value for `max`. Fortunately, there is a simple answer. We can just test whether `max` has been initialized yet by using the `isInitialized()` function (discussed in Chapter 11), like this[2]:

```
public var min:Number = 1 on replace {
                    if (min < 1 or
                           (isInitialized(max) and min >= max)) {
                        throw new IllegalArgumentException(
                                    "Invalid min value: {min}");
                    }
                    range = max - min;
                };
public var max:Number = 10 on replace {
                    if (isInitialized(min) and max <= min) {
```

---

[2] This code is in the file `javafxtriggers/ConstraintTriggers3.fx`.

```
                throw new IllegalArgumentException(
                        "Invalid max value: {max}");
        }
        range = max - min;
    };
```

The preceding code correctly applies the constraints. Here's an example that uses valid bounds:

```
var r1 = RandomNumbers { min: 5 max: 20 };
println("Random number between {r1.min} and {r1.max}: "
        "{r1.getRandom()}");
```

This example prints the following, although, of course, the actual value printed will be different (almost) every time it is executed:

```
Random number between 5 and 20: 7.2363137984007766
```

If invalid bounds are used, the result may not be quite what you would expect:

```
var r2 = RandomNumbers { min: -1 max: 20 };
println("Random number between {r2.min} and {r2.max}: "
        "{r2.getRandom()}");
```

The output is as follows:

```
Exception in trigger:
java.lang.IllegalArgumentException: Invalid min value: -1.0
        (Stack trace - not shown)
Random number between -1 and 20: 3.4428346919715347
```

The exception is expected, of course, because the initial value for `min` is negative. However, despite this, the second line of code is still executed even though the `RandomNumbers` object is in an invalid state. This is because although the exception aborts execution of the trigger, it is simply caught by the JavaFX runtime and written to the standard error stream—it does not propagate back to the script, which continues execution as if nothing were wrong. Clearly, then, just throwing an exception from a trigger is not sufficient to prevent an object getting into an invalid state.

Reverting to the Previous Value

The other option we have when an invalid value is written to a variable is to simply write back the previous value. We could combine this approach with the one in the preceding section by also throwing an exception so that at least there is a record that something went wrong. Here's a version of the `RandomNumbers` class with triggers that restore the previous value in the event of an error and also throws an exception, which you'll find in the file `javafxtriggers/ConstraintTriggers4.fx`:

```
class RandomNumbers {
    var random = new Random(System.currentTimeMillis());
    public var min:Number = 1 on replace oldValue {
```

```
                        if (min < 1 or
                            (isInitialized(max) and min >= max)) {
                            min = oldValue;
                            throw new IllegalArgumentException(
                                "Invalid min value: {oldValue}");
                        }
                    };
    public var max:Number = 10 on replace oldValue {
                        if (isInitialized(min) and max <= min) {
                            max = oldValue;
                            throw new IllegalArgumentException(
                                "Invalid max value: {oldValue}");
                        }
                    };
    var range:Number = bind max - min;

    public function getRandom():Number {
        min + range * random.nextFloat();
    }
}
```

You can see that both triggers declare a variable called `oldValue` that the runtime will set to the previous value when the trigger is called, and assign it to either `min` or `max` as appropriate if a constraint is violated. You'll also note that we now use a binding to maintain the value of the `range` variable. This removes the need to explicitly reassign the value to `max - min` in both triggers and separately for the success and failure cases. Now if we were to rerun the error case from the previous section, we would get a slightly different result.

```
var r2 = RandomNumbers { min: -1 max: 20 };
println("Random number between {r2.min} and {r2.max}: "
        "{r2.getRandom()}");
```

This time, we don't get any output; instead, we get a stack overflow. Here's what happens:

1. The `RandomNumbers` object is created. The `min` and `max` variables temporarily both have the value `0`.

2. The value `-1` (from the object literal) is assigned to the `min` variable.

3. Because `min` has changed, its trigger fires. As the new value is less than `1`, it is considered to be invalid, so `min` is reverted to its old value, in this case `0`.

4. Because the value of `min` has changed again, the trigger fires from within the first trigger execution. It sees that the value of `min` is `0`, which is still invalid, so it changes back to what it sees as the previous value—namely `-1`. This returns us to step 2, and the process continues until the JVM's call stack overflows.

The problem is caused by the fact that in step 3, we reverted `min` to its old value, which is itself invalid. This can happen only during initialization because any other value that is stored will have been validated by the trigger. The fix is to revert `min` to its previous value if initialization has been completed, or to a known valid value if it has not. Here is the final version of the triggers for the `RandomNumbers` class, which can be found in the file `javafxtriggers/ConstraintTriggers5.fx`:

```
public var min:Number = 1 on replace oldValue {
                    if (min < 1 or
                            (isInitialized(max) and min >= max)) {
                        min = if (min >= 1) oldValue
                              else 1;
                        throw new IllegalArgumentException(
                                "Invalid min value: {oldValue}");
                    }
                };
public var max:Number = 10 on replace oldValue {
                    if (isInitialized(min) and max <= min) {
                        max = if (min >= 10) oldValue
                              else 10;
                        throw new IllegalArgumentException(
                                "Invalid max value: {oldValue}");
                    }
                };
```

Unfortunately, we have to detect that `min` has not been initialized by testing for a valid value. We can't use the `isInitialized()` function to do this—it will return `true` in this case because the trigger is firing as a result of the initialization of the variable. This is the best that we can do in the current release of JavaFX.

Triggers and Sequences

The syntax used to attach a trigger to a sequence variable is shown in the following example:

```
var numbers = [0..10] on replace oldVals[low..high] = newVals {
    println("oldVals: {oldVals.toString()}");
    println("low = {low}, high = {high}");
    println("newVals = {newVals.toString()}");
    println("Result = {numbers.toString()}");
    println("-------------------------");
}
```

The identifiers used in the `on replace` clause are arbitrary, so you are not required to use the names shown here. Their meanings are as follows:

- `oldVals`: The sequence as it was before a change was made.

- `low`: An integer variable initialized to the index of the first element in the original sequence (in `oldVals`) that is affected by the change.
- `high`: An integer variable initialized to the index of the last element in the original sequence (in `oldVals`) that is affected by the change.
- `newVals`: A sequence containing the elements that were added to or modified by the change. The type of this sequence is the same as that of the sequence to which the trigger is attached. In the previous code, the type would be `Integer[]`.

We'll examine how to interpret the information provided by these variables using a series of examples based on the integer sequence and the trigger shown above, which prints all the values supplied to the trigger and the state of the sequence after each operation has been performed. You'll find the code in the file `javafx/SequenceTriggers.fx`.

Notice that the trigger syntax does not provide anything that directly indicates whether an insertion, deletion, or replacement has been performed, but this can be inferred from the values passed to the trigger, as follows:

- if `high` < `low`, the operation was an insertion. You'll learn more about this in the "Inserting Elements into a Sequence" section, later in this chapter.
- if `high` >= `low` and `newVals` is empty, the operation was a removal. See the section "Removing Elements from a Sequence," later in this chapter.
- Otherwise, the operation was a replacement of one contiguous range of elements with another. We look at this case first.

Replacing Elements in a Sequence

Initially, the sequence `numbers` contains the integers from `0` through `10` in ascending order:

```
numbers = [0, 1, 2, 3, 4, 5, 6, 7, 8, 9, 10];
```

We start by replacing the second element in the sequence with a new value:

```
numbers[1] = 100;
```

The trigger for this operation produces the following output:

```
Replace element at index 1 with a new value
oldVals: [ 0, 1, 2, 3, 4, 5, 6, 7, 8, 9, 10 ]
low = 1, high = 1
newVals = [ 100 ]
Result = [ 0, 100, 2, 3, 4, 5, 6, 7, 8, 9, 10 ]
```

As you can see, the variable `oldVals` contains the value of the sequence before the operation was performed. The variables `low` and `high` indicate which element of the sequence was affected by the operation. Because `low` and `high` both have the value `1`, we can tell that only one element was affected and that its value before the operation was `1`, because this is value of the element at index `1` in the variable `oldVals`. The variable `newVals` holds the new values—in this case, there is only one new value, the element `100` from the right side of the assignment statement.

Typically in a sequence trigger, you use the values provided to work out what has changed and act accordingly. The easiest way to do this is to view every trigger as if it were reporting a replacement operation. As you'll see later, this works for insertions and removals as well as for element replacements like the one in this example. In this case, it's easy to see what happened if you read the information printed by the trigger like this:

```
"Elements 1 through 1 (i.e., low through high) of the sequence for which
the value before this change was [0, 1, 2, 3, 4, 5, 6, 7, 8, 9, 10] (i.e.
the value of the variable oldVals) were replaced by the single value 100
(i.e., the value of the variable newVals)."
```

Now let's see what happens if we replace one element by a sequence containing more than one value:

```
numbers[1..1] = [200..204];
```

This time, the trigger prints the following:

```
oldVals: [ 0, 100, 2, 3, 4, 5, 6, 7, 8, 9, 10 ]
low = 1, high = 1
newVals = [ 200, 201, 202, 203, 204 ]
Result = [ 0, 200, 201, 202, 203, 204, 2, 3, 4, 5, 6, 7, 8, 9, 10 ]
```

As before, `low` and `high` have the same value, so you can see that only element 1 of the original sequence was affected. Now, however, `newVals` contains five elements, which are the values that replace element number 1, in the order in which they appear in the modified sequence.

Removing Elements from a Sequence

A removal is characterized by the `newVals` sequence having no elements. The `high` and `low` values indicate how many elements were removed and where those elements were in the sequence (which is always a contiguous range). Our first example removes a single element from the `numbers` sequence:

```
delete numbers[1];
```

This gives the following result:

```
oldVals: [ 0, 200, 201, 202, 203, 204, 2, 3, 4, 5, 6, 7, 8, 9, 10 ]
low = 1, high = 1
newVals = [ ]
Result = [ 0, 201, 202, 203, 204, 2, 3, 4, 5, 6, 7, 8, 9, 10 ]
```

As you can see, `newVals` is empty, which indicates a removal. The `low` and `high` variables show that only the single element formerly at index 1 was removed, and you can use these bounds together with `oldVals` to see that the element removed had the value 200 (the value of `oldVals[1]`).

Removing a range of elements gives a similar result:

```
delete numbers[8..];
```

This code removes all elements starting with the one at index 8:

```
oldVals: [ 0, 201, 202, 203, 204, 2, 3, 4, 5, 6, 7, 8, 9, 10 ]
low = 8, high = 13
newVals = [ ]
Result = [ 0, 201, 202, 203, 204, 2, 3, 4 ]
```

The fact that more than one element has been removed is evident from the values of the variables `low` and `high`, which show that six elements have been deleted from the sequence, starting at index 8.

Sometimes, what appears to be a single operation can result in more than one invocation of the trigger. For example, consider the following code:

```
insert 0 into numbers;
delete 0 from numbers;
```

The first line adds a 0 at the end of the sequence. This causes the trigger to fire to report an insertion, which we ignore for now. After this insertion, the sequence looks like this:

```
[ 0, 201, 202, 203, 204, 2, 3, 4, 0 ]
```

The second line of code removes *any* element in the sequence that has the value 0. Because there are two such elements, the trigger fires twice. The first trigger reports the following values:

```
oldVals: [ 0, 201, 202, 203, 204, 2, 3, 4, 0 ]
low = 8, high = 8
newVals = [ ]
Result = [ 0, 201, 202, 203, 204, 2, 3, 4 ]
```

This indicates that the element at index 8 has been removed. Note that when the trigger is invoked, only this element has been removed—the 0 at element 0 is still in place. The second trigger invocation reports the subsequent removal of this second 0 element:

```
oldVals: [ 0, 201, 202, 203, 204, 2, 3, 4 ]
low = 0, high = 0
newVals = [ ]
Result = [ 201, 202, 203, 204, 2, 3, 4 ]
```

Finally, let's delete the whole sequence:

```
delete numbers;
```

This gives the following result:

```
oldVals: [ 201, 202, 203, 204, 2, 3, 4 ]
low = 0, high = 6
newVals = [ ]
Result = [ ]
```

Inserting Elements into a Sequence

In the case of replacement or removal, the `low` and `high` variables refer to the elements in the sequence that are replaced or removed. In the case of an insertion, there is no existing element that is affected, so it is not obvious what the values of these variables should be in this case. Bear in mind that it must be possible to unambiguously deduce from these values and from that of the sequence containing the new elements that an insertion has occurred. The values that are actually assigned for an insertion where the first new element appears at index n in the sequence are as follows:

```
low = n
high = n - 1
```

This probably looks a little strange, because the `high` value is smaller than the `low` value. Only one value is needed to indicate where the insertion occurred, so this index is assigned to the variable `low`. If `high` were then to be set to the same value as `low`, it would look as if a replacement of a single element had been made. If `high` were set to a larger value than `low`, it would indicate the replacement of (`high` - `low` + 1) elements. Setting `high` to the value (`low` - 1) (or any other value that is less than `low`) makes it easy for the trigger code to determine that an insertion has occurred.

Let's start again with the numbers sequence initialized to [0..10] and then insert an element at the start:

```
numbers = [0..10];
insert 0 before numbers[0];
```

The insertion on the second line results in the following output from the trigger:

```
oldVals: [ 0, 1, 2, 3, 4, 5, 6, 7, 8, 9 ]
low = 0, high = -1
newVals = [ 0 ]
Result = [ 0, 0, 1, 2, 3, 4, 5, 6, 7, 8, 9 ]
```

The fact that `high` is less than `low` indicates an insertion, and the value of `low` shows that the first element was inserted at index 0. The `newVals` variable indicates that only one element was inserted. Insertion at the end produces a similar result, but with a different value for `low`:

```
insert 10 into numbers;
```

The result is as follows:

```
oldVals: [ 0, 0, 1, 2, 3, 4, 5, 6, 7, 8, 9 ]
low = 11, high = 10
newVals = [ 10 ]
Result = [ 0, 0, 1, 2, 3, 4, 5, 6, 7, 8, 9, 10 ]
```

Here, `low` has the value 11, but the sequence only had 11 elements before the insertion, so the maximum valid index would have been 10. The fact that the insert index is greater than this shows that the element was added at the end.

Not all insertions involve one new element. Here's one that does not:

```
insert [100..105] into numbers;
```

The resulting output shows that six elements have been added to the end of the sequence:

```
oldVals: [ 0, 0, 1, 2, 3, 4, 5, 6, 7, 8, 9, 10 ]
low = 12, high = 11
newVals = [ 100, 101, 102, 103, 104, 105 ]
Result = [ 0, 0, 1, 2, 3, 4, 5, 6, 7, 8, 9, 10, 100, 101, 102, 103, 104, 105 ]
```

Finally, when a sequence is assigned its initial value, an insert trigger is fired. This statement

```
var numbers = [0..10];
```

produces the following output from the trigger:

```
oldVals: [ ]
low = 0, high = -1
newVals = [ 0, 1, 2, 3, 4, 5, 6, 7, 8, 9 ]
Result = [ 0, 1, 2, 3, 4, 5, 6, 7, 8, 9 ]
```

Example Use of a Sequence Trigger

You've seen how triggers work, so let's look at how you might use one. Triggers are typically used to protect the state of a class or to keep otherwise unrelated application state synchronized in circumstances in which it would not be possible to use a binding. You have already seen an example of the former, so here we take a look at an example of the latter.

Suppose we have a sequence of numbers and we want to maintain a separate variable whose value is the sum of the numbers in the sequence:

```
var numbers:Integer[];
var total:Integer;
```

One way to do this is to declare a function that returns the sum of the values in a sequence and use binding to assign its value to the variable `total`:

```
function sum(values:Integer[]):Integer {
    var sum = 0;
    for (i in [0..<sizeof values]) {
        sum += values[i];
    }
    return sum;
}
var total = bind sum(numbers);
```

This works, but a possible performance problem exists because whenever a change is made to the sequence, the total has to be recomputed from scratch. If the sequence has a large number of elements, that could take a long time. Fortunately, this isn't necessary because we can use the previous value of the total to minimize the amount of work that needs to be done.

For example, suppose the initial sequence contains the value 0 through 10. The total would then be 55. If we now add the value 11, we don't need to recalculate the sum from the beginning. Instead, we add 11 to the total, making 66. If more than one element is added, we add them all to the total. Similarly, if an element is removed, we subtract its value from the total. If an element is replaced, we treat the operation as a removal followed by an addition. This is clearly a task for a trigger. Here's the code that implements that idea:

```
1    var total = 0;
2    var numbers:Integer[] on replace oldVals[low..high] = newVals {
3        var totalAdded = 0;
4        for (i in [0..<sizeof newVals]) {
5            totalAdded += newVals[i];
6        }
7        var totalRemoved = 0;
8        for (i in [low..high]) {
9            totalRemoved += oldVals[i];
10       }
11        total += totalAdded - totalRemoved;
12   }
```

When the trigger is executed, the `newVals` variable contains those elements that were added to the sequence, if any. The code on lines 3 through 6 calculates the sum of those elements. In the case of a removal, `newVals` will be empty, the loop starting on line 4 will not be executed, and the total to be added will remain 0, which is correct.

Similarly, the values removed can be obtained from the `oldVals` sequence, using the indices stored in the variables `low` and `high`. The code on lines 7 through 10 sums the values of the removed elements. In the case of an insertion, there are no elements being removed, and `high` will be less than `low`, so the loop starting on line 8 will not be executed, which again gives us the correct result.

After we have the total added and the total removed, we use them to adjust the overall total, as shown on line 11.

Note the following about this code:

- We don't need special code to initialize the `totalAdded` variable when the initial value is assigned to the sequence, other than to set its value to 0, because the sequence assignment will fire the trigger and report the addition of the initial set of elements, and this will cause the initial total to be correctly set.
- The trigger doesn't need explicit code for insert, remove, or replace operations—because of the way in which the variables passed to it are set, we can use the same code no matter which operation is performed.

Using the preceding code, we can demonstrate that the trigger works as expected by first assigning a value to the sequence variable, removing an element, adding another one, and finally replacing an element:

```
// Assign the initial sequence content
numbers = [0..10];
println("After initial assignment, total is {total}");

// Remove a value
delete 10 from numbers;
println("After remove 10 from numbers, total is {total}");

// Insert a value
insert 45 into numbers;
println("After inserting 45 into numbers, total is {total}");

// Replace a value
numbers[0] = 30;
println("After replacing element 0 with 30, total is {total}");
```

The output from this code is as follows:

```
After initial assignment, total is 55
After remove 10 from numbers, total is 45
After inserting 45 into numbers, total is 90
After replacing element 0 with 30, total is 120
```

Triggers and Instance Variables

The trigger syntax you have seen so far allows you to attach a trigger to a variable at the point of its declaration. Sometimes it is useful to attach a trigger to a variable that was declared in somebody else's code. You can attach a trigger to an instance variable of any object that your code instantiates by adding an override declaration in the object initialize, but only if you have write access to that variable, which means that the variable must have been declared as a var and it must have the modifier public. For example, the Stage class in the GUI library has an instance variable called visible that reflects whether it should be on the screen. You obviously can't attach a trigger to the declaration of this variable, but you can do this:

```
Stage {
    title: "Test Stage"
    width: 200
    height: 100
    override var visible = true on replace {
        println("Visible changed to {visible}");
    }
}
```

This code sets the value of the `visible` variable to `true` and adds a trigger that is called whenever the variable's value changes. The `override` keyword indicates that we are referring to the existing variable called `visible` in the class definition—if you omit it, it will look like you are trying to declare a local variable of that name in the object literal.

Note that it is not possible to add a trigger to a variable in an object that has already been instantiated. You cannot, therefore, directly attach a triggers to an instance variable of an object that your code does not create.

If you want to add a trigger to a variable in an arbitrary class, or one to which you do not have write access, you have to do so indirectly by creating a new variable that is bound to the variable's value and then attaching the trigger to your new variable. This works because the binding will keep your variable synchronized with the original, so changes to the original will fire the trigger on your variable.

For example, the `Node` class in the GUI libraries, which represents a user interface element, has a variable called `hover` that is `true` when the cursor is over the screen space occupied by the node. This variable is read-only, so you cannot override it in an object literal to attach a trigger to it. The following code, which you'll find in the file `javafxtriggers/InstanceVariableTrigger.fx`, shows how you can track the state of this variable:

```
1    Stage {
2        title: "Instance Trigger"
3        scene: Scene {
4            var rect: Rectangle;
5            width: 200 height: 200
6            content: [
7                rect = Rectangle {
8                    x: 10 y: 10 width: 100 height: 100
9                    fill: Color.YELLOW
10                   def hover = bind rect.hover on replace {
11                       println("Hover is {hover}");
12                   }
13               }
14           ]
15       }
16   }
```

Line 4 declares a variable that we use to refer to the node whose `hover` variable is to be tracked, which in this case is a rectangle. Lines 10 to 12 declare a local variable that is bound to the `hover` variable of the rectangle and attach a trigger to it. Here, the trigger just prints the value of the variable whenever it changes, which is when the mouse enters and leaves the bounds of the rectangle.

Adding a trigger to a variable in an object literal does not replace any trigger that may have been added to it by the author of that class—both triggers are registered and both fire when the variable is initialized or changed. The JavaFX runtime does not guarantee the order in which these triggers will be executed.

11

JavaFX Script Classes

In Java, classes are everywhere, but JavaFX is a much more informal language—you can write whole applications without having to create a single class of your own. Most of the examples in the first half of this book do not include a class declaration.[1] However, if you are going to be creating reusable functionality, such as new controls to be used in your own or your company's applications, you need to have a good understanding of JavaFX classes, which are the subject of this chapter.

As in Java, a JavaFX class may have state, represented by its instance variables, and operations that use/modify that state, in the form of instance functions. Although Java and JavaFX classes have much in common, there are various differences:

- JavaFX classes do not have constructors. Instead, initialization is performed using an object literal. A JavaFX class can, however, contain code that performs a similar function to a constructor, which will be executed while it is being initialized. See the "Class Initialization" section, later in this chapter.
- JavaFX classes allow function overloading and overriding. In JavaFX, function overriding must be explicitly indicated using the `override` keyword. See the "Function Overloading" and "Function Overriding" section, later in this chapter.
- JavaFX does not have a `static` keyword to declare class members and functions, but it does have script variables and script functions. See the "Script Functions and Variables" section, later in this chapter.
- There is no concept of a JavaFX interface, but a JavaFX class can implement a Java interface.
- Both Java and JavaFX have abstract classes. A JavaFX class in which all functions are declared to be abstract is a good approximation to a Java interface.

---

[1] This is not the same as saying that there aren't any classes. As you'll see in this chapter, all JavaFX scripts are compiled to at least one Java class even if there is no explicit class declaration.

- Like Java, JavaFX has inner classes, although the syntax is different, as you'll see in the "Classes and Script Files" section, later in this chapter.
- Java classes can extend only one base class, whereas JavaFX supports a form of multiple inheritance called *mixins* that allows you to write classes containing functionality that is designed to be incorporated into other classes. A JavaFX class can inherit behavior from any number of mixin classes. Mixins are discussed at the end of this chapter.

The example source code for this chapter can be found in the package `javafxclasses` in the JavaFX Book Language and JavaFX Book Desktop projects.

JavaFX Class Declaration

The syntax of a JavaFX class declaration is as follows:

```
[modifiers] class identifier [extends extends-list] { Class body }
```

The optional *modifiers* determine the visibility of this class to other scripts and specify whether the class is abstract or concrete—see "Class Visibility" and "Abstract Classes," later in this chapter, for details.

The *classname* is subject to the same rules as any other identifier in a JavaFX application. It must be unique within its containing package and must not be the same as any of the reserved words listed in Chapter 2, "JavaFX Script Basics." In most cases, the classname will be the same as that of the file in which it is declared.

The optional *extends* clause lists the Java/JavaFX class or classes from which this class is derived and any Java interfaces that it implements. As with Java classes, every JavaFX class is ultimately derived from `java.lang.Object` and, if there is no `extends` clause or if the extends clause lists only interfaces, the base class *is* `java.lang.Object`. There are rules that limit the combinations of classes and interfaces that may appear in this list, as covered in the "Subclassing and Abstract Classes" section, later in this chapter.

A class could represent a real-world object or an object that has meaning within the context of an application or a library. An object modeled by a class has *state* and *operations*. The state of the object is represented by instance variables and the operations by instance functions, both of which are declared within the class body. There is no restriction on the order in which these may appear. Each instance of a JavaFX class has its own unique copy of its instance variables.

As noted earlier, unlike a Java class, a JavaFX class does not have a special function that acts as a constructor. Instead, instance initialization is performed by the assignment of default or application-specified values to its instance variables, which may cause triggers to be invoked, and by the optional use of the `init` and `postinit` blocks. See the "Class Initialization" section, later in this chapter, for details.

A JavaFX class cannot be declared final. As a result, any JavaFX class can be subclassed.

An Example JavaFX Class

Listing 11-1 shows a simple JavaFX class.

Listing 11-1 **A Simple JavaFX Class**

```
1    package javafxclasses;
2
3    import javafx.geometry.Rectangle2D;
4
5    public class ExampleRectangle1 {
6        public var x:Number;
7        public var y:Number;
8        public var width:Number;
9        public var height:Number;
10
11       public function getArea():Number {
12           width * height;
13       }
14
15       public function getBounds():Rectangle2D {
16           Rectangle2D {
17               minX: x
18               minY: y
19               width: width
20               height: height
21           }
22       }
23
24       public override function toString():String {
25           "Rectangle at ({x}, {y}), width: {width}, height:    {height}"
26       }
27   }
```

This class represents a rectangular shape. Its name, `ExampleRectangle1`, has been chosen to avoid confusion with the `Rectangle` class in the JavaFX GUI library; a numeric suffix was added because we are going to show you a different version of this class later in this chapter. Because there is no `extends` clause in the class declaration on line 5, this class extends `java.lang.Object`.

The rectangle is described by the coordinates of its top-left corner together with its width and height. These are represented by the instance variables declared on lines 6 through 9. Because these variables are all public, they can be directly read or modified by code outside the class at any time. In Java, allowing direct access to class state in this way is generally not considered to be a good idea. Instead, you would typically make these variables private and allow access to them through public getter and setter methods. The primary reason for this is to ensure that all changes to them are made by code provided by the class itself so that the new values can be checked for validity and any dependent state can be updated, thus ensuring that the state of the class is always internally consistent. As you have already seen, in JavaFX, bounds checking and the maintenance of state can be performed by using a trigger/binding, so public variables are much more common than they are in Java. Other access modifiers can be used to make instance variables read-only or initialize-only to code outside the class. These are described in the section "Instance Variables," later in this chapter.

The class has three instance functions that return information that is derived from its state: The `getArea()` function returns the area of the rectangle; `getBounds()` returns its bounds (that is, its position and size); and `toString()` gets a string representation of its state, which is useful for debugging. These functions are all invoked via an instance of the class, like this:

```
1    var rect = ExampleRectangle1 { x: 0 y: 0 width: 10 height: 20 };
2    var area = rect.getArea();
3    println("Area of {rect} is {area}");
```

Line 1 creates an instance of the class with the specified coordinates, width, and height and assigns it to the variable `rect`. Line 2 invokes the `getArea()` function of the newly created instance and assigns the result to `area`. Finally, line 3 prints the result, which looks like this:

```
Area of Rectangle at (0.0, 0.0), width: 10.0, height: 20.0 is 200.0
```

The nested expression `{rect}` in the string literal on line 3 causes the `toString()` function of `ExampleRectangle1` to be invoked. Because every JavaFX class is derived from `java.lang.Object`, this function is bound to exist, but the value returned by the `toString()` implementation provided by `java.lang.Object` is not very useful, so the `ExampleRectangle1` class provides its own implementation of this function that prints the coordinates and size of the rectangle. Because the `toString()` function in `ExampleRectangle1` overrides the one in `java.lang.Object`, we need to explicitly indicate this by including the `override` keyword in its declaration, like this:

```
public override function toString():String {
```

See the section "Function Overriding," later in this chapter, for more on the use of this keyword.

Class Visibility

You can use the modifiers listed in Table 11-1 to define the scope within which a class is visible. At most one modifier is allowed, and it must appear before the `class` keyword in the class declaration.

The class `ExampleRectangle1` is declared with the `public` modifier, so it can be used by code in any package. This is the normal way to declare a library class that is intended

Table 11-1 **Class Visibility Modifiers**

Modifier	Effect
(none)	The class is visible only within the script in which it is declared.
`public`	The class is visible everywhere.
`package`	The class is visible to all code in the same package.
`protected`	The class is visible to all code in the same package *and* in subclasses of its top-level class. This modifier can only be used when declaring a class that is not the script class. See the "Classes and Script Files" section, later in this chapter, for the meaning of the term *script class*.

to be of general use. A class that is only to be used in the script in which it is declared should have no access modifier:

```
class OnlyInThisScript {
}
```

Classes that need to be used by more than one script but which are not intended for general use should be declared with the `package` modifier, and all code that references them should be in the same package:

```
package myPackage;

package class OnlyInSamePackage {
    // Only visible to classes in "myPackage", but not to classes
    // in "myPackage.mySubackage" or any other package.
}
```

If this is not possible, typically because access is required from a script that is in a sub-package of the declaring package, the access modifier will have to be `public`, even though this is not ideal.

Instance Variables

An instance variable is declared with exactly the same syntax as a script variable (see Chapter 5, "Variables and Data Types"), as follows:

```
[modifiers] var identifier[:type] [ = expression] [trigger clause];
[modifiers] def identifier[:type] [ = expression] [trigger clause];
```

Choosing between `var` and `def`

Use a `var` statement if the value of the variable can be changed, or `def` if either the variable represents a constant or is the target of a unidirectional binding:

```
1    public class VariablesExample {
2        public var radius = 0;            // value is expected to change
```

```
3          def PI = 3.1415;                    // A constant
4          public def circumference = bind 2 * PI * radius;  // Bound
5      }
```

The preceding class provides a read-only variable that holds the value of the circumference of a circle whose radius is given by the `radius` variable. The intent is that application code should set a radius and then read back the corresponding circumference:

```
var e = VariablesExample { radius: 1 };
println("Radius: {e.radius}, circumference: {e.circumference}");

e.radius = 2;
println("Radius: {e.radius}, circumference: {e.circumference}");
```

The variable `radius` is public, so that it can be written and read by application code and is declared using a `var` statement to allow its value to be changed. By contrast, because the `circumference` variable is bound, it is appropriate to declare it using a `def` statement, as shown on line 4.[2] Finally, the variable `PI` declared on line 3 holds a fixed value that approximates the value of pi. Because its value will never change, it is declared using a `def` statement.

Variable Access Modifiers

The access modifiers are almost identical to those that apply to script variables, with the exception of an additional modifier called `public-init` that can be used to control whether application code can set the initial value of a variable from an object literal. The legal combinations of these modifiers and the access that they grant are listed in Table 11-2. Note that a variable declared using `def` cannot be written or assigned a value from an object literal no matter what visibility modifiers are applied to it.

Notice that `public-init` implies `public-read`. The intent of `public-init` is to allow code anywhere to set the initial value of a variable, without permitting later modification. Consider the following (artificial) class:

```
public class ShowInit {
    public var canChange:Integer;
    public-init var canInit:Integer;
}
```

Code in the same script can read, initialize, or write both variables, but this is not true for code in a different script:

```
var s = ShowInit { canChange: 1 canInit: 2 };
```

---

[2] The `circumference` variable *could* have been declared using `var`, but that would not change the fact that a unidirectional binding makes it read-only. In cases like this, a `def` statement should be used to make it clear that the variable cannot be modified.

JavaFX Class Declaration   245

Table 11-2   **Access Modifiers for Instance Variables**

Modifier(s)	Code Access	Object Literal Initialization
(none)	Code in the same script can read and write. Other code has no access.	Can be initialized by an object literal in the same script only.
`public`	Can be read and written by any code.	Can be initialized by an object literal in any script.
`package`	Can be read and written only by code in the same package.	Can be initialized by an object literal in any script in the same package
`protected`	Can be read and written by code in the same package or in a subclass.	Can be initialized by an object literal in any script in the same package or in a subclass.
`public-read`	Can be read by code anywhere but written only by code in the same script.	Can be initialized by an object literal in the same script.
`public-read package`	Can be read by code anywhere but written only by code in the same package.	Can be initialized by an object literal in the same package.
`public-read protected`	Can be read by code anywhere but written only by code in the same package or in a subclass.	Can be initialized by an object literal in the same package or a subclass.
`public-init`	Can be read by code anywhere but written only by code in the same script.	Can be initialized by code anywhere.
`public-init package`	Can be read by code anywhere but written only by code in the same package.	Can be initialized by code anywhere.
`public-init protected`	Can be read by code anywhere but written only by code in the same package or in a subclass.	Can be initialized by code anywhere.

This code is legal, because the `public` and `public-init` modifiers allow any code to set the initial value of the instance variables. However, only the `public` variable can be modified later by code in a different script:

```
// This code is assumed to be in a different script to the one that
// defines the ShowInit class.
s.onChange = 4;     // Legal - modifier is "public"
s.canInit = 4;      // Compilation error - modifier is "public-init"
```

It is not legal to attempt to bind the value of a `public-init` variable in an object literal from code outside the defining script:

```
var value = 1;
var s = ShowInit { canInit: bind value }    // Compilation error
```

This is not permitted because it would allow arbitrary code to cause the value of the instance variable `canInit` to change by modifying the script variable `value`.

`public-init` is the nearest JavaFX equivalent to a final variable of a Java class for which the value is set from its constructor. Because JavaFX classes do not have parameterized constructors, the only way to express this restriction in JavaFX is to use the `public-init` modifier.

Initialization and Triggers

Instance variables can be assigned a default value at declaration time in the same way as script variables can. Note, however, that the initial value assignment in the class declaration can be overridden by an object literal or by a subclass. For more details, see the "Class Initialization" and "Subclassing and Abstract Classes" sections, later in this chapter.

Similarly, an instance variable can have a trigger. The use of instance variable triggers is discussed in the "Class Initialization" section.

Instance Functions

A class can have any number of instance functions. An instance function is declared within the body of the class and uses the same syntax as a script function, as follows:

```
[modifiers] function name([arguments]) [:return type] { body }
```

The modifiers determine whether the function is abstract (see "Abstract Classes") or bound (as discussed in Chapter 6, "Expressions, Functions, and Object Literals") and its accessibility, by which is meant the scope within which code can invoke or override the function. The possible accessibility modifiers and their meanings, which are the same as those discussed in connection with script functions in Chapter 6, are listed in Table 11-3. Only one of these modifiers can be used. Overriding of functions is discussed in the "Function Overriding" section, later in this chapter.

Table 11-3 **Instance Function Accessibility Modifiers**

Modifier	Meaning
(none)	Can be invoked or overridden by code in the same script
`public`	Can be invoked or overridden by any code
`package`	Can be invoked or overridden by code in the same package
`protected`	Can be invoked or overridden by code in the same package or in a subclass

Function Name and Overloading

The function name must be a valid JavaFX identifier.[3] It is *not* required to be unique within the scope of the class declaration, which means that you can have more than one function with the same name, provided that no two of these functions have the same *signature*. As in Java, the signature of a function consists of the function name and the types of its arguments in the order in which they appear. The type of the function's return value is not considered to be part of the signature. Declaring more than one function with a given name is called *function overloading*.

The usual reason for function overloading is to provide similar functionality given one or more different sets of arguments. For example, the class `javafx.geometry.Rectangle2D` has four functions named `contains()` that determine whether a given point or a given rectangular area lie within the bounds of the rectangle:

```
public contains(p:Point2D) : Boolean
public contains(x: Number, y: Number) : Boolean
public contains(r: Rectangle2D) : Boolean
public contains(x: Number, y: Number, w: Number, h: Number) : Boolean
```

Although these functions have the same name, the argument lists are different, and this is what allows the compiler to distinguish between them. The return types of these four functions are the same, and this will normally be the case, but it is not a requirement.

Access to Instance Variables

An instance function has access to all the instance variables in its declaring class. A function can read or write the value of a variable by using its name in an expression or as the target of an assignment statement. The following extract from the class `ExampleRectangle1` illustrates this:

```
1      public class ExampleRectangle1 {
2          public var x:Number;
3          public var y:Number;
4          public var width:Number;
5          public var height:Number;
6
7          public function getArea():Number {
8              width * height;
9          }
```

On line 8 of this code, the instance function `getArea()` reads the instance variables `width` and `height` by quoting their names. The value of the variable is read from the

---

[3] You can use an invalid identifier as a function name provided that you surround it with French quotes: `function <<1234>>() {}`. This is, of course, not recommended.

instance of the `ExampleRectangle1` object on which the function has been invoked. It is also possible to use the keyword `this` to indicate that the variables should be read from the current instance of the class:

```
public function getArea():Number {
    this.width * this.height;
}
```

A function can read variables from another instance of the same class given a reference to that class. For example, the following function determines whether the width of the current instance of the `ExampleRectangle1` class is the same as that of another instance:

```
public class ExampleRectangle1 {
    public function hasSameWidth(ExampleRectangle1 r):Boolean {
        // "width" gets the width from this instance.
        // "r.width" gets the width from another instance.
        width == r.width;
    }
```

Function Arguments and Variable Shadowing

If one of the arguments of an instance function has the same name as an instance variable of the same class, then when that name is used in the body of the function, it refers to the argument and not to the instance variable. The argument is said to *shadow* the instance variable:

```
1   public class ExampleRectangle1 {
2       public var x:Number;
3       public var y:Number;
4       public var width:Number;
5       public var height:Number;
6
7       public function setWidth(width:Number):Void {
8           this.width = width;
9           println("Width has been set to {this.width}");
10      }
```

The preceding example adds to our example class a function called `setWidth()` that changes the value of the instance variable `width` and prints the result. As you can see, the name of the function argument is the same as that of the instance variable whose value it sets and therefore shadows it. Within this function, references to the name `width` would yield the value of the argument and not that of the instance variable. To refer to the instance variable, its name must be qualified with the keyword `this`, as shown on line 8, where the value of the argument is assigned to the instance variable and on line 9 where the value of the instance variable is read.

Subclassing and Abstract Classes

In JavaFX as in Java, you can extend or modify the functionality of an existing class by subclassing. Subclassing allows you to do some or all the following:

- Add additional state by introducing new instance variables.
- Change the default value of an existing instance variable.
- Add a trigger to an existing instance variable.
- Add new functionality by introducing new functions.
- Modify or replace the behavior of an existing function by overriding it.

You'll see examples of this in the sections that follow.

An Abstract Base Class

To illustrate subclassing, we first create a suitable JavaFX base class by taking as our starting point the `ExampleRectangle1` class shown in Listing 11-1. Clearly, a rectangle is one of various different shapes that you could want to represent, such as circles, ellipses, lines, and so on. If we were to create an `ExampleCircle` class following the pattern from Listing 11-1, there would be no obvious relationship between rectangles and circles. To express the relationship, we create a base class called `ExampleShape` and assign to it the state and operations that we want all our shapes to have. Listing 11-2 shows the implementation of this class.

Listing 11-2   **An Abstract JavaFX Base Class**

```
1    package javafxclasses;
2
3    import javafx.geometry.Point2D;
4    import javafx.geometry.Rectangle2D;
5    import javafx.scene.paint.Color;
6    import javafx.scene.paint.Paint;
7
8    /**
9     * A base class for geometric shapes.
10    */
11   public abstract class ExampleShape {
12       /**
13        * The stroke paint for this shape.
14        */
15       public var strokePaint:Paint = Color.BLACK;
16
17       /**
```

```
18          * The fill paint for this shape, if it has one
19          */
20         public var fillPaint:Paint;
21
22         /**
23          * Returns whether this shape should be filled.
24          * @return true to fill the shape.
25          */
26         public function shouldFill():Boolean {
27             return fillPaint != null;
28         }
29
30         /**
31          * Gets the area of the shape.
32          * @return the area of the shape.
33          */
34         public abstract bound function getArea():Number;
35
36         /**
37          * Gets the bounds of the shape.
38          * @return the bounds of the shape.
39          */
40         public abstract bound function getBounds():Rectangle2D;
41
42         /**
43          * Returns whether this shape contains a given point.
44          * @param point a point
45          * @return true if the given point lies within the shape.
46          */
47         public abstract bound function con   tains(point:Point2D):Boolean;
48
49         public override function toString():String {
50             "Stroke: {strokePaint}, fill: {fillPaint}"
51         }
52     }
```

ExampleShape is an abstract class, which is indicated by the abstract modifier on line 11. It is logical for this class to be abstract because you would never expect to instantiate something that is just a shape—instead, you would create instances of concrete shapes such as rectangles, circles, lines, and so on. In this case, we are also required to make the class abstract because it declares three abstract functions on lines 34, 40, and 47. An abstract class is, however, not absolutely required to contain any abstract functions.

As in Java, an abstract function declaration defines the signature of a function that all concrete subclasses must implement. The getArea(), getBounds(), and contains() functions will be implemented in different ways by the various shape-specific subclasses, as you'll see in the next section. The important point is that the abstract function declaration guarantees to application code that these functions will be provided, with the given signature, by any shape.

All three of the abstract functions in this class are bound, for a reason that we'll discuss later.

This class also declares two instance variables, both of type `javafx.scene.paint.Paint`. As you'll see later in this book, a `Paint` defines the color or colors used to draw or fill a shape or some text. In the simplest case, a `Paint` is a solid color, such as `Color.BLACK`, that causes all the pixels it affects to have the same color. A `Paint` can also be a gradient or any other distribution of colors. In this case, the variable `strokePaint` is intended to be the color used to draw the outline of the shape, defaulted to black on line 15, while `fillPaint` is the color used to optionally fill its interior. By default, `fillPaint` is `null`, which is meant to indicate that the shape should not be filled. The concrete function `shouldFill()` declared on lines 26 to 28 can be used to determine whether filling is required.

Extending the Base Class

With the base class in place, we can now create subclasses that represent concrete shapes. Each different shape will have its own instance variables that define its outline and will also implement the three abstract methods required by the base class definition. Listing 11-3 shows the implementation of a subclass that represents a rectangle with its sides parallel to the coordinate axes.

Listing 11-3 **A JavaFX Implementation of a Rectangular Shape**

```
1    package javafxclasses;
2
3    import javafx.geometry.Point2D;
4    import javafx.geometry.Rectangle2D;
5
6    public class ExampleRectangle extends ExampleShape, Cloneable {
7        public var x:Number;
8        public var y:Number;
9        public var width:Number;
10       public var height:Number;
11
12       public override bound function getArea():Number {
13           width * height;
14       }
15
16       public override bound function getBounds():Rectangle2D {
17           Rectangle2D {
18               minX: x minY: y width: width height: height
19           }
20       }
21
```

```
22          public override bound function contains(point:Point2D):Boolean   {
23              return point.x >= x and point.x < x + width
24                  and point.y >= y and point.y < y + height;
25          }
26
27          public bound function contains(rect:ExampleRectangle):Boolean    {
28              var topLeft = Point2D { x: rect.x y: rect.y };
29              var bottomRight = Point2D {
30                              x: rect.x + rect.width - 1
31                              y: rect.y + rect.height - 1
32                          };
33              return contains(topLeft) and contains(bottomRight);
34          }
35
36          public override function toString():String {
37              "Rectangle at ({x}, {y}), width: {width}, height:    {height}"
38              ", {super.toString()}"
39          }
40
41          public override function clone():ExampleRectangle {
42              return ExampleRectangle {
43                  x: x
44                  y: y
45                  width: width
46                  height: height
47              };
48          }
49      }
```

A subclass is declared by including an `extends` clause in the `class` statement. In this case, the `ExampleRectangle` class extends the JavaFX class `ExampleShape`:

`public class ExampleRectangle` **`extends`** `ExampleShape {`

The `extends` clause may contain any or all the following:

- The name of one Java class *or* of one JavaFX class *or* of one Java-derived JavaFX class
- The names of any number of Java interfaces
- The names of any number of mixin classes

A Java-derived JavaFX class is one that either directly extends a Java class (other than `java.lang.Object`) or a class that is derived from such a class. For example, if a JavaFX class called `JavaFXDate` extends the Java class `java.util.Date`, `JavaFXDate` is a Java-derived class. If you define another class called (say) `MyJavaFXDate` that extends `JavaFXDate`, `MyJavaFXDate` would also be a Java-derived class.

A mixin is a special type of class that is explicitly designed to be incorporated into other classes. You would use a mixin to package reusable functionality and then add it to another class by including it in the `extends` list of that class. Mixins are discussed at the end of this chapter.

Although no special declaration is required to extend a Java class, one requirement must be met: The Java class must have a no-argument constructor that is accessible to the subclass. That is, it must be public or protected, or be package private, and the Java class must in the same package as the JavaFX class. This is required because JavaFX classes do not have a constructor and therefore cannot provide arguments to the constructor of the Java class

A JavaFX class with no `extends` clause or with an `extends` clause that does not contain a Java-derived class is implicitly derived from `java.lang.Object`. It follows, therefore, that all JavaFX classes inherit the behavior and methods of `java.lang.Object`.

Note that unlike Java, JavaFX does not have the keyword `implements` to indicate the implementation of an interface—in JavaFX, the names of implemented interfaces are listed in the `extends` clause:

```
// This class implements the java.lang.Comparable interface
class MyJavaFXClass extends MyOtherClass, Comparable {
}
```

A subclass inherits all the behavior and the visible instance variables and functions of its base class. Whether a variable or function is visible to the subclass depends on the modifiers used in its declaration and where the subclass is defined:

- All public and protected functions and variables are available to the subclass.
- All script-private functions and variables are available if the subclass is declared in the same script as the base class.
- All package functions and variables are available if the subclass is in the same package as the base class.

Subclasses may add state in the form of new instance variables or new functions. The `ExampleRectangle` class shown in Listing 11-3 adds the state necessary to define a rectangle (the instance variables `x`, `y`, `width`, and `height`) together with an overload of the `contains()` function. A subclass may also override functions and variables declared in the base class.

Function Overloading

You have already seen that it is legal for a class to have more than one function with the same name provided that no two of them have the same set of arguments. It is also possible for a subclass to add an *overload* of a function defined in a base class. In Listing 11-3, the `ExampleRectangle` class adds an overload of the `contains()` function declared in `ExampleShape`:

```
public bound function contains(rect:ExampleRectangle):Boolean {
    var topLeft = Point2D { x: rect.x y: rect.y };
    var bottomRight = Point2D {
                x: rect.x + rect.width - 1
```

```
                       y: rect.y + rect.height - 1
                  };
    return contains(topLeft) and contains(bottomRight);
}
```

This overload is legal because it requires an argument of type `ExampleRectangle`, whereas the function of the same name in `ExampleShape` requires a `Point2D`. It returns `true` if the rectangle supplied as the argument is wholly contained within the `ExampleRectangle` on which the function is invoked.

Function Overriding

A subclass can override any function in its base classes to which it has access, as defined by the modifiers applied to the base class function, listed in Table 11-3.

A concrete subclass is *required* to override any abstract functions declared in its base class, unless there is more than one class in the hierarchy between itself and the base class and all abstract functions have been implemented in a different class. For example, if the base class A declares an abstract function called `doIt()` and if there is a subclass of B that implements `doit()`, a subclass C of B could, but does not need to, override `doIt()` itself because an implementation already exists in class B.

Overriding a Function

There are three possible reasons for overriding a function:

- To provide the implementation of an abstract function defined in a base class
- To completely replace the implementation of the overridden function
- To perform additional steps before and/or after the overridden function

In Listing 11-3, the code on lines 12 to 25 provides implementations of the abstract functions defined in the class `ExampleShape`. Here, for example, is the concrete implementation of the `getArea()` function:

```
public override bound function getArea():Number {
    width * height;
}
```

Note the following points about this declaration:

- The name and argument list of the implementation are the same as those of the abstract function declaration.
- The `override` keyword is used to indicate that this is an override of an existing function. This is required even if the function is the implementation of an abstract function. If you omit this keyword when it is required, you will get a warning from the compiler.

If the function being overridden is bound, the overriding function must also be bound, and vice versa. The `getArea()` function shown here is declared to be bound to match the declaration in the base class.

The `ExampleRectangle` class also overrides the `toString()` function. Here is the implementation of this function from `ExampleShape`:

```
// ExampleShape implementation
public override function toString():String {
    "Stroke: {strokePaint}, fill: {fillPaint}"
}
```

This code returns a string that contains the stroke and fill paints. The `override` keyword is required because `toString()` is actually defined by `java.lang.Object`, so this version of the function is itself an override. The implementation in the `ExampleRectangle` class looks like this:

```
// ExampleRectangle implementation
public override function toString():String {
    "Rectangle at ({x}, {y}), width: {width}, height: {height}"
    ", {super.toString()}"
}
```

In this case, the new implementation does not completely replace the one in the `ExampleShape` class—instead, it invokes it to get the stroke and fill colors. As in Java, you invoke a function in a superclass by using the keyword `super`:

```
{super.toString()}
```

If `super` were omitted here, the `toString()` function would, of course, be invoking itself, which would result in a stack overflow. Here's some code that calls the `toString()` function of the `ExampleRectangle` class:

```
var r1 = ExampleRectangle { x: 0 y: 0 width: 100 height: 200 };
println(r1);
```

Here's the output, which clearly shows the contribution made by the overridden base class version of this function:

```
Rectangle at (0.0, 0.0), width: 100.0, height: 200.0, Stroke:
javafx.scene.paint.Color[red=0,green=0,blue=0,opacity=1.0], fill: null
```

Overrides and Visibility

As in Java, you cannot reduce the visibility of a function when you override it. Therefore, if you override a public function, the override must also be public. If you override a protected function, the override must be protected or public, and so on. It is permissible to omit the modifier, in which case the function implicitly inherits the visibility of the function that it is overriding:

```
// This function is public, not script-private
override function toString():String {
```

Because the `toString()` function in the base class is public, so is the overriding function.

Overrides and Return Type

In most cases, the return type of an overriding function will be the same as that of the function that it overrides. For example, the `contains()` functions in the `ExampleRectangle` class and the `ExampleShape` class both explicitly state that a `Boolean` is returned:

```
public override bound function contains(point:Point2D):Boolean {
```

As a shorthand, it is permissible to omit the return type when overriding a function, so the override in the `ExampleRectangle` class could also be written like this:

```
// Both the visibility (public) and the return type (Boolean) are
// inferred from the base class declaration.
override bound function contains(point:Point2D) {
```

The return type is *not* required to be the same as that of the overridden function—it can instead by a subtype of the overridden function's return type. (This is referred to as *covariance*.) For example, the `clone()` method of `java.lang.Object` is declared like this:

```
protected Object clone() throws CloneNotSupportedException
```

On lines 41 through 48 of Listing 11-3, there is an implementation of `clone()` for the `ExampleRectangle` class. We could have declared the overriding `clone()` function like this:

```
public override function clone() {
```

The compiler would infer a return type of `Object` for this function when the class is compiled. This would be fine, but it doesn't help with type inference when this function is used by code outside the class. With the preceding declaration, the compiler would infer a type of `Object` for the variable `newRect` in the following code:

```
var rect = ExampleRectangle { x: 0 y: 0 width: 100 height: 200 };
var newRect = rect.clone(); // newRect is of type Object
```

We can, instead, change the return type to `ExampleRectangle`, because this is a subclass of the return type of the overridden function:

```
public override function clone():ExampleRectangle {
```

With this change, the compiler can infer the correct type for the variable `newRect`:

```
var rect = ExampleRectangle { x: 0 y: 0 width: 100 height: 200 };
var newRect = rect.clone(); // newRect is of type ExampleRectangle
```

Function Dispatch

When a function is overridden, the selection of which version to implement is made at run-time based on the *actual type* of the object on which the function is called. Consider the following class hierarchy, in which the `toString()` function is overridden in all three classes:

```
class A {
    public override function toString():String {
        "A"
    }
}

class B extends A {
    public override function toString():String {
        "B"
    }
}

class C extends B {
    public override function toString():String {
        "C"
    }
}
```

Now suppose we create three instances of class C, but assign each of them to a variable of a different type and then invoke the `toString()` function of all three instances:

```
var a:A = C {};
println(a);
var b:B = C {};
println(b);
var c:C = C {};
println(c);
```

The output from this code is the following:

```
C
C
C
```

This happens because all three objects are actually instances of class C, and the variant of `toString()` provided by that class is executed, even though in the first two cases the variable type is not declared to be C. Using an instance of class B, on the other hand, causes B's implementation of `toString()` to be called:

```
var a:A = B {};
println(a);      // Prints "B"
var b:B = B {};
println(b);      // Prints "B"
```

Function Selection by Classname

You have seen that it is possible to invoke a superclass function by using the keyword super. For example, we could rewrite the `toString()` function of the preceding class C like this:

```
public override function toString():String {
    "C + {super.toString()}"
}
```

And the result of calling this function is as follows:

```
C + B
```

It is also possible to explicitly state the name of the superclass whose implementation of `toString()` is required, like this:

```
public override function toString():String { // In class C
    "C + {B.toString()}"
}
```

This feature proves useful when a class inherits a function with the same name and signature from more than one base class (such as might be the case if the class includes a mixin). For a class with only a single base class, it is safer and clearer to use super instead. Note that you cannot use this syntax to invoke a function that has been overridden in an intermediate class:

```
public override function toString():String { // In class C
    "C + {A.toString()}"     // Compilation error
}
```

This is not permitted because it would cause the execution of the override of `toString()` in class B to be skipped, which might be a problem for some classes.[4]

Using Bound Functions

The `getArea()`, `getBounds()`, and `contains()` functions of ExampleShape were declared to be bound. You may be wondering why. Recall that when you bind to the result of a nonbound function its result is reevaluated only when the values of its arguments change. However, the results of these three functions depend only on the state of the object itself. For example

```
1    var rect = ExampleRectangle { x: 0 y: 0 width: 100 height: 200 };
2    def area = bind rect.getArea();
```

---

[4] In JavaFX 1.1, this erroneous reference to the hidden version of the `toString()` function is actually allowed. This is a fault that has been reported to the compiler time and which will eventually be fixed.

```
3        println("Area: {area}");
4
5        rect.width = 200;
6        println("Area after change: {area}");
```

Line 2 binds the variable area to the result of calling the getArea() function and, as a result, assigns the value 20,000 to it. On line 5, the width of the rectangle is changed, which obviously affects its area. However, because the changed value is *not* an argument of the getArea() function, the area will not be recomputed *unless* getArea() is declared to be a bound function. The same applies to both the getBounds() and contains() functions. Whenever you create a function whose result depends at least in part on object state that can be changed, you need to consider whether to make the function be bound. If you want the result of the function to change when the state that it depends on is changed, you must make it a bound function.[5]

Variable Overrides

A subclass can override the definition of a variable declared in any of its superclasses. This does *not* result in the creation of a new variable—instead, it allows you to change the variable's default value or add an additional trigger to it, as the following code illustrates:

```
1     package javafxclasses;
2
3     class Base {
4         public var value = 32 on replace {
5                 println("Base: value set to {value}");
6             };
7     }
8
9     class Derived extends Base {
10        override var value = 64 on replace {
11                println("Derived: value set to {value}");
12            };
13    }
14
15    var b = Base {};
16    var d = Derived {};
```

---

[5] Technically, you could argue that the toString() function of this class should also be bound. However, you can't achieve this because its original declaration is not as a bound function and you cannot change that in a subclass. All functions declared in Java classes are implicitly not bound.

Line 4 declares a variable called `value` in the class `Base` that has an initial value of 32 and a trigger that reports when the value of the variable is set. Creating an instance of this class produces the following output:

```
Base: value set to 32
```

The class `Derived` declared on line 9 extends `Base` and therefore inherits the variable `value`. The declaration on line 10 overrides the definition of this variable and assigns a new default value and a new trigger. When an instance of `Derived` is created, the following output appears:

```
Base: value set to 64
Derived: value set to 64
```

Variable overrides have the following characteristics:

- An override is effective only if the keyword `override` is used in the declaration. If this keyword is omitted, you get a compilation error.
- An override cannot change the visibility of the overridden variable. Because of this, you can omit the visibility modifier when overriding a variable, as shown on line 10 of the code. The variable is declared as public in the class `Base` and remains so despite the override on line 10.
- If an override sets a new default value, the original default value is ignored. In the previous example, the initial value of the overridden variable is 64, not 32 as specified in the original definition.
- A trigger added by an override is *additional to* any existing trigger—it is not possible to remove a trigger added by a superclass. This restriction is necessary because the superclass may be using the trigger to correctly set additional state that depends on the value of the variable. The order in which multiple triggers attached to the same variable are fired is implementation-dependent and therefore should not be relied upon.

An override can also be specified in an object literal. The same syntax and all the same rules apply. For example

```
Derived {
    override var value = 96 on replace {
            println("Object literal: value set to {value}");
        }
}
```

The output from the preceding code is this:

```
Base: value set to 96
Derived: value set to 96
Object literal: value set to 96
```

As you can see, the initial value is now the one assigned in the object literal, and all three triggers have been executed. Initial values specified in an object literal always take precedence over the default values in the class definition.

> **Note**
>
> It is not possible to override a variable declared using a `def` statement or one that has the `public-read` access modifier, because if this were allowed, it would be possible to change the value of a variable that should be read-only either to all code or to code outside its defining class.

Class Initialization

As you have already seen, JavaFX classes do not have constructors. A JavaFX class can set its initial state using a combination of the following:

- Variable initializers, which provide default initial values for instance variables
- Triggers, which can set associated state when the initial value of an instance variable is set
- One or more `init` blocks, which are executed during object initialization, in the order in which they appear in the class definition
- One or more `postinit` blocks, which are executed once an object instance has been initialized, in the order in which they appear in the class definition

Initialization Order

The simplest way to explain the initialization of a JavaFX object is by example. Let's first create a simple class that has all four of the features listed above:

```
1     class InitBase {
2         public-init var baseValue = 32 on replace {
3                     println("Base: baseValue set to {baseValue}");
4                 }
5
6         init {
7             println("Base init called, baseValue = {baseValue}");
8         }
9
10        postinit {
11            println("Base postinit called, baseValue = {baseValue}");
12        }
13    }
```

Lines 2 through 4 define an instance variable called `baseValue` with a default initial value of 32 and a trigger that reports when its value is set. Lines 6 through 8 define an `init` block. As you can see, the syntax is just the keyword `init` followed by a block of code. Similarly, lines 10 through 12 define the `postinit` block using the same syntax. In this case, the `init` and `postinit` blocks just report that they have been called and print the value of the instance variable. In a real class, these blocks would either be omitted or perform a more useful function. Now suppose we were to create an instance of this class, like this:

```
InitBase { baseValue: 40 }
```

This results in the following output (to which line numbers have been added for reference):

```
1    Base: baseValue set to 40
2    Base init called, baseValue = 40
3    Base postinit called, baseValue = 40
```

Line 1 is printed by the trigger attached to the variable `baseValue`. As you can see, the value from the object literal has been assigned in place of the default in the class definition. Line 2 is printed when the `init` block is executed, and line 3 comes from the `postinit` block. The order of initialization, therefore, is as follows:

1. Initial values are assigned to the instance variables. As you have seen in earlier sections of this chapter, the initial value is either the default value for the variable type, the default value given in the initializer, a value assigned in an override declared in a subclass, or the value that appears in the object literal, with the value that appears latest in this list taking precedence. As the initial value is assigned to the instance variables of a class, the associated triggers, if any, are fired.

2. The `init` block is executed. Any changes to variable values made in this block will cause the associated triggers to fire again. See the "Use of the `init` and `postinit` Blocks" sections, later in this chapter, for a discussion of what should and should not be done in an `init` block.

3. The `postinit` block is executed. Again, changes to variable values will cause triggers to fire.

From this simple example, it might not be obvious why there are separate `init` and `postinit` blocks, because it appears that one is executed immediately after the other. The distinction is clearer if we create a derived class and look at how it is initialized:

```
1    class InitDerived extends InitBase {
2        public-init var derivedValue = 64 on replace {
3            println("Derived: derivedValue set to {derivedValue}");
4        }
5
6        init {
7            println("Derived init called, derivedValue = {derivedValue}");
8        }
9
10       postinit {
11           println("Derived postinit called, derivedValue= "
12               "{derivedValue}");
13       }
14   }
```

This class adds an additional instance variable with its own default initial value and trigger and an `init` and `postinit` block, which we can create an instance of like this:

```
InitDerived { baseValue: 40 derivedValue: 64 }
```

This code produces the following output:

```
Base: baseValue set to 40
Derived: derivedValue set to 64
Base init called, baseValue = 40
Derived init called, derivedValue = 64
Base postinit called, baseValue = 40
Derived postinit called, derivedValue = 64
```

As you can see, the initialization steps of the base class and the derived class are interleaved, unlike Java where the base class constructor is invoked first and completes before a subclass constructor executes. The full order of initialization is as follows:

1. Initial values are assigned to the instance variables, starting with those in the base class, followed by those in each subclass, in the order of the class hierarchy. As each value is assigned, the associated triggers, if any, are fired.

2. The `init` blocks are executed, starting with the one in the base class, followed by those in each subclass, in the order of the class hierarchy.

3. The `postinit` blocks are then executed, starting with the one in the base class, followed by those in each subclass, in the order of the class hierarchy.

The distinction between the `init` and `postinit` blocks is that the `init` blocks are executed while the state of the object is being set, while the `postinit` blocks are run after the whole object has been initialized. All the `init` blocks are executed before any of the `postinit` blocks.

Using the `init` and `postinit` Blocks

The `init` block is executed while its owning object is being initialized and after all the initial values for the variables in that class (and subclasses) have been set. Typical tasks for this block include the following:

- Checking that the initial values of the instance variables are valid, if this has not already been done by their associated triggers
- Checking that the initial values are consistent with each other
- Setting the values of any variables that cannot be initialized from an object initializer and which depend on values that could be assigned by the object initializer

As an example of the last bullet point, suppose you want to create a JavaFX class with an embedded `HashMap` and you want to allow application code to configure the initial capacity of the `HashMap`. You can do this by allocating the map in the `init` block of your JavaFX class[6]:

```
class MapBasedClass {
    public-init var capacity = 32;
    var map:Map;

    init {
        map = new HashMap(capacity);
    }
}
```

The `init` block should *not* set the value of a variable that could be set from an object initializer, unless it is known that a value has not already been set. The reason for this restriction is that object initializer values are installed before the `init` block is run, so any value set from this block will overwrite the value set by application code. If you need to assign a value to a variable that *could* be set from an object initializer, either make it the default value in the variable declaration, which allows application code to override it by using the object initialize, or use the `isInitialized()` function to check whether a value has already been supplied:

```
1    class InitializeTest {
2        public-init var value;
3
4        init {
5            if (not isInitialized(value)) {
6                value = 32;
7            }
8        }
9    }
```

In the preceding code, no default value is assigned to the variable value on line 2. In the `init` block, a test is made to determine whether the variable has been initialized and, if not, the value 32 is assigned. In a more realistic example, the value assigned would probably be computed from other state in the same object or in related objects.

The `isInitialized()` function returns `true` in the following circumstances:

- If a value has been assigned by an object initializer
- If this class is subclassed and the variable is overridden to assign a default value

Instantiating the class without assigning a value causes the value 32 to be assigned:

```
var i = InitializeTest {};
println(i.value);    // Prints 32
```

---

[6] Thanks to Brian Goetz for this example, which appeared as part of a discussion in the JavaFX compiler development forums.

However, a value set in an object initializer is not changed by the `init` block:

```
i = InitializeTest { value: 64 };
println(i.value);    // Prints 64
```

The `postinit` block can be used to perform actions that can take place only once the object is fully initialized, one example of which is publishing the object externally. If your object needs to attach itself as a listener to some state in another class, for example, it should do this in the `postinit` block rather than in `init` if there is the possibility that an event might be delivered to it before it has fully initialized.

Classes and Script Files

A JavaFX source file can contain any number of class definitions, some or all of which may be public classes. None of the classnames need to match that of the source file. This is different to Java, where only one class in a source file can be public and the name of that class must match that of the source file.

The code in Listing 11-4 shows two classes, a script function and a script variable, all defined in the same script file.

Listing 11-4 **Classes and Script Files**

```
1    package javafxclasses;
2    // A script variable
3    var mainClassCount:Integer;
4
5    // A script function
6    public function getMainClassCount():Integer {
7        mainClassCount
8    }
9
10   // The script class
11   public class MainClass {
12       // An instance variable
13       var index:Integer = mainClassCount++;
14
15       // An instance function
16       public function getIndex():Integer {
17           index;
18       }
19   }
20
21   // A non-script class
22   public class AnotherClass {
23       public function anotherFunction() {
24           println("anotherFunction called");
25       }
26   }
```

Assuming that this script file is called `javafxclasses/MainClass.fx`, which is consistent with the package declaration on line 1, the JavaFX compiler will automatically create a JavaFX class called `javafxclasses.MainClass`, whether or not there is a declaration of a class with that name in the file. If there is no such class declaration, the compiler generates one that is public and extends `java.lang.Object`. In this case, there *is* an explicit declaration of a class with this name on line 11, which is also public and also implicitly extends `java.lang.Object`. We'll refer to the class with the same name as the script file (be it explicitly declared or created by the compiler) as the *script class*.

The instance variable declared on line 13 and the instance function on line 16 are related to the JavaFX script class in the same way as methods and fields are to their containing Java class.

The script variable on line 3 and the script function on line 6 behave as if they were static members of the script class, `javafxclasses.MainClass`. This applies to *any* variable or function declared outside a class definition—they are all treated as being in the naming scope of the script class. You can reference the script function on line 6 from outside the script using the same syntax as you would use for static members in Java—namely `MainClass.getMainClassCount()`.

The script variable on line 3 is not visible outside the script, but it if were, it would be referenced by the name `MainClass.mainClassCount`.

JavaFX does not have any syntax that allows you to declare a class within a class (a nested class), but any class that is not the script class is actually treated as if it were a static nested class of the script class. That means, for example, that `AnotherClass`, declared on line 22, effectively has the full name `javafxclasses.MainClass.AnotherClass`. Within the script file, you can just refer to it using the name `AnotherClass`. From outside of the script, however, you can do any of the following:

```
// Use the full classname
var a1 = javafxclasses.MainClass.AnotherClass {};

// Import MainClass and use a relative name
import javafxclasses.MainClass;
var a2 = MainClass.AnotherClass {};

// Import everything in MainClass and use the simple name
import javafxclasses.MainClass.*;
var a3 = AnotherClass {};
```

Mixins

It is common to have functionality that could be used in more than one place. One way to provide reusable functionality is to put it into a class and then allow other classes to inherit it by extending that class. The problem with this approach in a single-inheritance language like Java is that a class can be derived only from one other class. If you need to write a Java class that incorporates functionality from more than one other class, you can't do it by inheritance. The `Observable` class in the `java.util` package is an example of a class that is better implemented as a mixin, because many objects could usefully be `Observable` while also inheriting from some other base class.

Another way to arrange for one class to reuse the functionality of a class without reimplementing that functionality is to use the composite pattern. To use this pattern, your class provides the API of the other class by defining all the functions from the interface of that class that you want to make available to your users and implementing those functions by delegating them to an instance of that other class that is private to your class. You can create a class that incorporates (or wraps) the behavior of the `Observable` class by using this technique. Here's a snippet of a partial implementation of this idea:

```
1   public class MyClass extends SomeOtherClass {
2       var delegate:Observable = Observable {};
3
4       public function addObserver(o:Observer):Void {
5           delegate.addObserver(o);
6       }
7
8       public function deleteObserver(o:Observer):Void {
9           delegate.deleteObserver(o);
10      }
11  }
```

The API of this class provides two of the methods that are part of the `Observable` class and delegates their implementation to a hidden instance of `Observable`. In reality, to make this useful you must add the whole `Observable` API to your class. This technique works for small delegate classes that have a stable API (such as `Observable`), but it is not ideal, because changes in the API of the delegate class are not available through the wrapper class unless you add new delegating methods to its implementation. Mixins avoid this problem because their API becomes part of the API of the class of which they are a part, in the same way as the API of a base class is part of that of a subclass.

Implementing Logging with a Mixin

An example of a feature that could usefully be incorporated in many different classes is logging. Logging is commonly performed by creating an instance of the `java.util.logging.Logger` class and invoking one of its `log()` methods when something needs to be recorded. Here, for example, is an example of a class that uses this technique to log the fact that its `init` block has been called:

```
1   package javafxclasses;
2
3   import java.util.logging.Level;
4   import java.util.logging.Logger;
5
6   public class LoggedClass {
7       var level = Level.WARNING;
```

```
8          var logger = Logger.getLogger("javafxclasses");
9          init {
10             logger.log(level, "In init");
11         }
12     }
```

The logger that the class will use is created on line 8. The Logging API allows you to create multiple named loggers that can be individually configured to write output to different locations. It is common practice for every class in a package to share the same logger. We use that pattern here by supplying the name of the owning package as the name of the logger when it is created on line 8. The logger itself is used on line 10 to record the fact that the `init` block has been invoked. Here is the result of running this example:

```
26-May-2010 20:22:40 javafxclasses.LoggedClass userInit$
WARNING: In init
```

There is nothing especially complicated about this pattern, but there is a downside to it—every class that wants to log something has to create a `Logger` instance and needs to adhere to the rule that the logger should be named after the package that owns that class. It would be better if this functionality could be encapsulated so that the class itself could rely on the presence of a logger variable that refers to a correctly configured logger. This is an ideal case for using a mixin because

- It is a well-defined task that can be completely implemented in a separate class.
- The functionality can usefully be used in many classes that are otherwise unrelated (and, in particular, do not have a common base class where this code could otherwise be placed).

The implementation of this functionality as a mixin is shown in Listing 11-5.

Listing 11-5 Implementing Logging in a Mixin Class

```
1      package javafxclasses;
2
3      import java.lang.Throwable;
4      import java.util.logging.Level;
5      import java.util.logging.Logger;
6
7      public mixin class Logging {
8          protected var loggerName = getPackageName();
9          protected var logger = Logger.getLogger(loggerName);
10         public var level = Level.INFO;
11
12         public function isLogging():Boolean {
13             level != Level.OFF;
14         }
15         protected function log(level:Level, text:String) {
16             logger.log(level, text);
```

```
17          }
18
19          protected function log(level:Level, text:String, t:Throwable) {
20              logger.log(level, text, t);
21          }
22
23          protected function log(text:String) {
24              logger.log(level, text);
25          }
26
27          protected function log(text:String, t:Throwable) {
28              logger.log(level, text, t);
29          }
30
31          public override function toString():String {
32              "Logging mixin, log level is {level}"
33          }
34
35          function getPackageName():String {
36              var className = getClass().getName();
37              var index = className.lastIndexOf(".");
38              return if (index == -1) "default"
39                  else className.substring(0, index);
40          }
41      }
```

Apart from the word `mixin` in the class declaration on line 7, this is just like any other class definition. This class declares three variables and a set of functions that use them:

- The `loggerName` variable is the name of the `Logger` that will be used. It is set to the name of the package of the hosting class. In a mixin, as in any other class, the `getClass()` method returns the `Class` object for the actual class of which the mixin is a part, not that of the mixin class itself. In the `getPackageName()` method, we strip off the trailing part of the classname to leave only the name of the package.[7]
- The `logger` variable is the actual `Logger` that the mixin functions will use.
- The `level` variable is the default level at which log entries will be written by those functions that do not have an explicit level parameter. This variable has a default value of `Level.INFO`, but is public and can be changed by application code at any time.

---

[7] The expression `getClass().getPackage().getName()` returns the same value, but under some circumstances, the `getPackage()` method returns `null`, so we get the package name by string manipulation instead.

The `log()` functions form the bulk of the API of the mixin. They allow subclasses to write log entries to the `Logger` given by the `logger` variable. Encapsulating the creation of the logger in the mixin class frees the class that uses it (the "mixee" class) from the responsibility of managing the logger.

Within the implementation of the mixin class, the keyword `this` is typed to the mixin class itself and can be used explicitly or implicitly to access variables and functions defined in the mixin. On line 13, for example, the reference to `level` is a shorthand for `this.level` and returns the value of the `level` variable in the same mixin instance.

Listing 11-6 shows a class that uses the `Logging` mixin.

Listing 11-6   Using a Mixin Class

```
1      package javafxclasses;
2
3      import java.util.logging.Level;
4
5      public class LoggedClassWithMixin1 extends Logging {
6          override var level = Level.WARNING;
7          init {
8              log("In init");
9          }
10     }
11
12     function run() {   // Test code
13         var c = LoggedClassWithMixin1 {};
14         println(c.level);
15         println(c.isLogging());
16     }
```

The mixin class is incorporated into `LoggedClassWithMixin1` by using the `extends` keyword. The effect of this is to make the API and variables of the mixin available to the mixee class in the same way as if the mixin class had been an ordinary base class of the mixee. In this case, most of the mixin functions are protected and are therefore visible only to the mixee class, but the `isLogging()` function and the `level` variable of the mixin are public and therefore become part of the public API of the `LoggedClassWithMixin1` class. This is illustrated in the `run()` function on lines 13 to 15 of Listing 11-6, which instantiates an instance of this class and then accesses the `level` variable and the `isLogging()` function by using the variable `c`, which refers to the mixee class instance. In this case, access is possible because the test code and the test class are in the same package, but this same code would work even if it were in a script in a different package.

Line 6 of Listing 11-6 shows that the initial value of a mixin variable, in this case the `level` variable, can be overridden in the mixee class, in the same way as the initial value of a subclass variable can be changed, subject to the normal access rules. The result of running this example is as follows (the output may not appear in the order shown here):

```
1      26-May-2010 20:24:14 javafxclasses.Logging log$impl
2      WARNING: In init
3      WARNING
4      true
```

The first two lines are the result of the `log()` call in the `init` block of the mixee class on line 8 of Listing 11-6. The standard preamble on line 1 indicates where the call came from (the `log()` function of the `Logging` class), and this is followed on line 2 by the actual logged message. The WARNING text at the start of this line is the logging level used when the entry was made, which shows that the variable override on line 6 of Listing 11-6 was effective. Lines 3 and 4 of the output show the value of the `level` variable and the result of calling the `isLogging()` function, on lines 14 and 15 of Listing 11-6.

Mixin variables can be assigned values in an object initializer in the same way as variables of the mixee class. Listing 11-7 illustrates this.

Listing 11-7   Initializing a Variable of a Mixin Class

```
1      package javafxclasses;
2
3      import java.util.logging.Level;
4
5      public class LoggedClassWithMixin2 extends Logging {
6          init {
7              log("In init");
8          }
9      }
10
11     function run() {
12         var c = LoggedClassWithMixin2 {
13             level: Level.FINE
14         };
15         println("Level is {c.level}");
16     }
```

In this example, the class `LoggeClassWithMixin2` is another mixee that incorporates the `Logging` mixin. In this case, the `level` variable is not overridden in the class definition. Instead, its value is set from the object literal on lines 12 to 14. The output from this example confirms that this assignment is effective:

```
Level is FINE
```

At this point, you may be wondering in what way incorporating a mixin class differs from the normal process of extending a base class, because everything that you have seen so far is consistent with normal inheritance. You'll see the differences in the next section.

Mixin Characteristics

Now that you have seen an example of a mixin class, let's take a closer look at the characteristics of a mixin.

As we have already said, a mixin is a JavaFX class that is intended to be included as part of the implementation of other classes. A mixin is declared in the same way as an ordinary JavaFX class, except that its declaration *must* include the word `mixin`, as shown in Listing 11-5. A mixin class can implement Java interfaces and may extend one or more other mixin classes, but it cannot be derived from either a Java or a non-mixin JavaFX class. A mixin class is abstract by definition, so it is not possible to create an instance of a mixin.[8]

You can think of a mixin class as being similar to a Java interface, in the sense that it may define abstract methods that concrete subclasses or mixee classes are required to implement. However, mixins can do three things that Java interfaces cannot:

- They can declare variables. Variables that are declared in a mixin class become part of the mixee class. The level variable in the `Logging` mixin in Listing 11-5 is an example of this.

- They can provide implementations of the functions that they declare. The `Logging` mixin in Listing 11-5 provides concrete implementations for all of its declared functions.

- They can define script functions (that is, static functions in Java terms) that appear to be script functions of the mixee class.

As a (not very useful) example of the last point, the following code, which is assumed to be in a file called `HelloMixin.fx`, declares a mixin class with a script function called `sayHello()`:

```
1    public function sayHello() { println("Hello") };
2
3    public mixin class HelloMixin {
4    }
5
6    public class HelloMixinTest extends HelloMixin {
7    }
8
9    public function run() {
10       HelloMixinTest.sayHello();
11   }
```

The class `HelloMixinTest` on line 6 incorporates `HelloMixin` and in so doing acquires the script function `sayHello()`, which can then be referred to on line 10 as if it were actually part of the `HelloMixinTest` class.

---

[8] A mixin is automatically abstract—you don't need to add the `abstract` keyword to its declaration and, in fact, it is an error to do so.

An instance of a class that incorporates a mixin can be assigned to a variable that has the type of the mixin, as shown in the following example:

```
1    class LoggedClassWithMixin3 extends Logging {
2    }
3
4    var c = LoggedClassWithMixin3 {};
5    var logging:Logging = c;
6    println(c instanceof Logging);    // prints "true"
```

One line 4, we create an instance of the class `LoggedClassWithMixin3`, which incorporates the `Logging` mixin from Listing 11-5. On line 5, we assign a reference to this instance to a variable of type `Logging`, demonstrating that a class that incorporates a mixin is an instance of that mixin. For the same reason, the `instanceof` test on line 6 succeeds and prints `true`.

Mixins and Inheritance

Using a mixin is similar to extending an ordinary class, but there are some subtle differences when the mixin and the mixee classes declare the same functions/variables. The easiest way to explain the rules is by example. In this section, we look at several different inheritance scenarios and explain how the compiler determines which function/variable will be the one used by the mixee class.

Inheritance from One Mixin Class

Inheritance from a single mixin is the simplest case. Listing 11-8 shows an example of this.

Listing 11-8   Inheritance from a Single Mixin Class

```
1    package javafxclasses;
2
3    mixin class Mixin1 {
4        var name = "Mixin1";
5
6        function doSomething() {
7            println("Mixin1 doSomething()");
8        }
9    }
10
11   class Mixee1 extends Mixin1 {
12       override var name = "Mixee1";
13
14       override function doSomething() {
15           println("Mixee1 doSomething()");
16       }
17   }
18
19   var m = Mixee1 {};
```

```
20          println("Variable: {m.name}");
21          m.doSomething();
```

In this example, the mixin and the mixee class both declare a variable called `name` and a function called `doSomething()`. The code on lines 19 to 21 prints the value of name and calls the function, with the following result:

```
Variable: Mixee1
Mixee1 doSomething()
```

This result should not surprise you—the initial value of the variable and the declaration of the function in the mixee class are used in preference to those in the mixin. Notice, however, that both of the declarations in the mixee class (on lines 12 and 14) require the use of the `override` keyword.

> **Note**
>
> It is important to realize that, as with ordinary inheritance, the fact that there are two declarations of the variable `name` does not mean that there are two distinct variables. The mixee class contains only one variable called `name`. The precedence rules determine only which of the possible initial values is assigned to that variable.

Within a mixee class, functions declared within a mixin are not considered to be "superclass" functions, even though the mixee extends from the mixin class. This means that the following modification of the code from lines 14 to 16 of Listing 11-8 would be illegal:

```
11      class Mixee1 extends Mixin1 {
12          override var name = "Mixee1";
13
14          override function doSomething() {
15              super.doSomething();   // Compilation error.
16          }
17      }
```

This does not work because the `super` keyword refers to the immediate non-mixin superclass of `Mixee1`, which is `java.lang.Object`, *not* the mixin class. However, you *can* access the mixin's implementation of `doSomething()` by referencing it by name:

```
11      class Mixee1 extends Mixin1 {
12          override var name = "Mixee1";
13
14          override function doSomething() {
15              Mixin1.doSomething();   // OK: calls doSomething() in Mixin1.
16          }
17      }
```

Inheritance from a Mixin That Extends Another Mixin

It is perfectly legal for one mixin class to be derived from another. When a mixin of this type is incorporated into a mixee class, the rules that determine which members of the mixins become part of the mixee class are slightly more complicated than they are in the example that you have just seen. Listing 11-9 illustrates this case.

Listing 11-9 **Incorporating a Mixin That Is Derived from Another Mixin**

```
1       package javafxclasses;
2
3       mixin class Mixin1 {
4           var name = "Mixin1";
5
6           function doSomething() {
7               println("Mixin1 doSomething()");
8           }
9       }
10
11      mixin class Mixin2 extends Mixin1 {
12          override var name = "Mixin2";
13
14          override function doSomething() {
15              println("Mixin2 doSomething()");
16          }
17      }
18
19      class Mixee1 extends Mixin2 {
20      }
21
22      class Mixee2 extends Mixin2 {
23          override var name = "Mixee2";
24      }
25
26      var m1 = Mixee1 {};
27      println("Variable: {m1.name}");
28      m1.doSomething();
29
30      var m2 = Mixee2 {};
31      println("Variable: {m2.name}");
32      m2.doSomething();
```

Here, the mixin class `Mixin2` is derived from another mixin called `Mixin1`. These classes both have a declaration for a variable called `name` and a function called `doSomething()`. As you might expect, the declarations of these members on lines 12 and 14 require the `override` keyword because they are overriding the original declarations in the `Mixin1` class. The class `Mixee1` declared on lines 19 and 20 incorporates `Mixin2`, but does not declare any variables or functions of its own. The code on lines 26 to 28 creates an instance of `Mixee1`, prints the value of its `name` variable, and invokes it `doSomething()` function. Here are the results:

```
Variable: Mixin1
Mixin2 doSomething()
```

This may not be what you expected to see. The second line shows that the `doSomething()` function from the `Mixin2` class has been called in preference to the one in the base mixin, which is what you probably expected, but the first line is a little surprising—it indicates that the default value of the `name` variable from the *base* mixin takes precedence over the default value assigned in the *derived* mixin! This is the reverse of what would happen if these were ordinary classes—the default value of a variable in a derived mixin *does not* take precedence over the default value in the base mixin, despite the fact that the compiler requires you to use the `override` on the variable in the derived mixin. You might wonder whether there is any point in overriding a variable in a derived mixin. The answer is that there is, because you can use the override to add a trigger to the variable, as you'll see in the "Mixins and Triggers" section, later in this chapter.

The class `Mixee2` on lines 22 to 24 also incorporates the derived mixin, but in this case it also overrides the variable `name` and supplies a different default value. The code on lines 30 to 32 produces the following output:

```
Variable: Mixee2
Mixin2 doSomething()
```

This result is not surprising—it demonstrates again that a default value assigned to the variable by the mixee class overrides the one declared by the mixin, as you saw in the previous section.

Inheritance from Two or More Mixins

Mixin classes are intended to provide functionality that is likely to be useful in more than one context, so incorporating two or more mixins into a class is likely to be common. The result of deriving a class from two or more mixins is to include the public API of all of those mixins in the public API of the class itself. In the simplest case, an example of which is shown in Listing 11-10, the mixins do not declare functions/variables with conflicting names.

Listing 11-10   A Class Incorporating Two Mixins

```
1       package javafxclasses;
2
3       mixin class Mixin1 {
4           var name1 = "Mixin1:name1";
5
6           function doSomething1() {
7               println("Mixin1:doSomething1()");
```

```
8          }
9     }
10
11    mixin class Mixin2 {
12         var name2 = "Mixin2:name2";
13
14         function doSomething2() {
15             println("Mixin2:doSomething2()");
16         }
17    }
18
19    class Mixee extends Mixin1, Mixin2 {
20    }
21
22    var m = Mixee {};
23    println("name1: {m.name1}");
24    println("name2: {m.name2}");
25    m.doSomething1();
26    m.doSomething2();
```

The class `Mixee` inherits both of the functions and variables declared by the two mixin classes `Mixin1` and `Mixin2`. It should be no surprise that the result of running this code is the following:

```
name1: Mixin1:name1
name2: Mixin2:name2
Mixin1:doSomething1()
Mixin2:doSomething2()
```

Now let's add another function to the `Mixin2` class:

```
mixin class Mixin2 {
    var name2 = "Mixin2:name2";

    function doSomething1() {
        println("Mixin2:doSomething1()");
    }
    function doSomething2() {
        println("Mixin2:doSomething2()");
    }
}
```

Adding a function called `doSomething1()` is not, of itself, a problem, even though both the `Mixin1` and `Mixin2` classes now have a function with the same name and signature. A problem only arises when an attempt is made to use this function through a class, such as `Mixee1`, that incorporates both of these mixin classes:

```
var m = Mixee {};
println("name1: {m.name1}");
println("name2: {m.name2}");
m.doSomething1();   // Compilation error
m.doSomething2();
```

This code, which is the same as that on lines 22 to 26 of Listing 11-10, no longer compiles because the reference to the doSomething1() function is ambiguous—does it refer to the version in the Mixin1 class or the one in the Mixin2 class? There is no way for the compiler to decide. The only way to resolve this is to introduce functions in the Mixee class that provide access to the doSomething1() functions, as shown in Listing 11-11:

Listing 11-11 Resolving Ambiguous Function References in Mixin Classes

```
1    class Mixee extends Mixin1, Mixin2 {
2        public function doSomething1Mixin1() {
3            Mixin1.doSomething1();
4        }
5        public function doSomething1Mixin2() {
6            Mixin2.doSomething1();
7        }
8    }
9
10   var m = Mixee {};
11   println("name1: {m.name1}");
12   println("name2: {m.name2}");
13   m.doSomething1Mixin1();
14   m.doSomething1Mixin2();
15   m.doSomething2();
```

Lines 2 to 7 add cover functions to the mixee class that delegate to the otherwise ambiguous functions in the two mixin classes. With these functions in place, either of the mixin methods can be called through the appropriate cover method, as shown on lines 13 and 14. Note that the syntax used to specify which of the doSomething1() functions is to be used is the same as that described in the section "Function Selection by Classname," earlier in this chapter:

```
public function doSomething1Mixin1() {
    Mixin1.doSomething1();
}
```

Now let's create two mixin classes that have variables of the same name, as shown in Listing 11-12.

Listing 11-12   **Mixins with Clashing Variables**

```
1     package javafxclasses;
2
3     mixin class Mixin1 {
4         var name = "Mixin1:name";
5     }
6
7     mixin class Mixin2 {
8         var name = "Mixin2:name";
9     }
10
11    class Mixee extends Mixin1, Mixin2 {
12    }
13
14    var m = Mixee {};
15    println("name1: {m.name}");
```

The mixin classes `Mixin1` and `Mixin2` both declare a string variable called `name`. This is not an issue until the class `Mixee` incorporates both mixins and an attempt is made to reference a variable called `name` through a reference to that class, as shown on line 15. Which version of the variable should be used? The compiler actually chooses the one declared by `Mixin1` because `Mixin1` appears first in the `extends` list of the mixee class, so this code prints the following:

`name1: Mixin1:name`

Had `Mixin2` appeared first in the `extends` list, its declaration of the variable would have been used instead.

Inheritance from a Mixin and a Base Class

So far, you have seen examples of a JavaFX class that incorporates one or more mixins but is otherwise derived from `Object`. It is also possible to create a class that inherits from another base class and from one or more mixins. The result of this will be a mixee class that includes the public API of both its base class and its mixins. As is often the case with mixins, we need to look at what happens when the same function or variable is declared in both the base class and a mixin that is incorporated into the same mixee class, as shown in Listing 11-13.

Listing 11-13   **Inheriting from a Base Class and a Mixin**

```
1     package javafxclasses;
2
3     mixin class Mixin {
4         var name = "Mixin name";
5
```

```
6           public function doSomething() {
7               println("mixin doSomething");
8           }
9       }
10
11      class Base {
12          var name = "Base name";
13
14          public function doSomething() {
15              println("Base doSomething");
16          }
17      }
18
19      class Mixee extends Mixin, Base {
20      }
21
22      var m = Mixee {};
23      println(m.name);
24      m.doSomething();    // Compilation error
```

Here, the class `Mixee` is derived from `Base` and incorporates the mixin class `Mixin`. Both `Base` and `Mixin` declare a variable called `name` and a function called `doSomething()`. The reference on line 23 to the `name` variable is resolved to the declaration in the `Base` class on line 12, in preference to the variable of the same name in the mixin. However, the code on line 24 causes a compilation error—the compiler does not choose to prefer the declaration of this function in the base class over that in the mixin.

Mixins and Triggers

When a variable declaration in a mixin includes a trigger, that trigger applies even if the variable declaration is apparently overridden by one in another mixin, in the mixee, or in the mixee's base class. The same applies to the triggers in the mixee class and its base class, if any. This is no different from the situation that exists with normal inheritance, as the example in Listing 11-14 shows.

Listing 11-14 Using Triggers with Mixins

```
1       package javafxclasses;
2
3       mixin class Mixin {
4           var name = "Mixin" on replace {
5               println("Mixin trigger, value is {name}");
6           }
7       }
8
```

```
9      class Mixee extends Mixin {
10         override var name = "Mixee" on replace {
11             println("Mixee trigger, value is {name}");
12         }
13     }
14
15     var m = Mixee {};
```

In this example, both the mixin and mixee class attach a trigger to the name variable (on lines 4 and 10). As you have already seen, the precedence rules dictate that the initial value assigned to this variable is the one set in the mixee class, but both triggers are attached and both fire, as the output from this example shows:

```
Mixin trigger, value is Mixee
Mixee trigger, value is Mixee
```

Initialization and Mixins

Like ordinary classes, mixins can have both init and postinit blocks, which are called during the initialization of any class of which the mixin is a part. The order of invocation of the init and postinit blocks in the mixee class is as follows:

1. The init block of the mixee's superclass is called.
2. The init blocks of the mixin classes are called, in the order in which they appear in the extends clause of the mixee class declaration.
3. The init block of the mixee class is called.
4. The postinit block of the mixee's superclass is called.
5. The postinit blocks of the mixin classes are called, in the order in which they appear in the extends clause of the mixee class declaration.
6. The postinit block of the mixee class is called.

The code in Listing 11-15 illustrates the initialization order.

Listing 11-15   **Order of Initialization in Classes with Mixins**

```
1      package javafxclasses;
2
3      mixin class Mixin1 {
4          init { println("Mixin1 init") }
5          postinit { println("Mixin1 postinit") }
6      }
7
8      mixin class Mixin2 extends Mixin1 {
```

```
9       init { println("Mixin2 init") }
10      postinit { println("Mixin2 postinit") }
11  }
12
13  mixin class Mixin3 {
14      init { println("Mixin3 init") }
15      postinit { println("Mixin3 postinit") }
16  }
17
18  class Base {
19      init { println("Base init") }
20      postinit { println("Base postinit") }
21  }
22
23  class Mixee1 extends Mixin1, Mixin2, Mixin3, Base {
24      init { println("Mixee init") }
25      postinit { println("Mixee postinit") }
26  }
27
28  println("Create instance of Mixee1");
29  var m1 = Mixee1 {};
30
31  class Mixee2 extends Mixin3, Mixin1, Mixin2, Base {
32      init { println("Mixee init") }
33      postinit { println("Mixee postinit") }
34  }
35
36  println("\nCreate instance of Mixee2");
37  var m2 = Mixee2 {};
```

This code contains the following:

- Three mixin classes called `Mixin1`, `Mixin2`, and `Mixin3`. Note that the class `Mixin2` is derived from `Mixin1`.
- A class called `Base`.
- Two mixee classes, `Mixee1` and `Mixee2`, that are both derived from `Base` and incorporate all three of the mixins. The only difference between these two classes is the order of mixins in their `extends` clauses.

Each of these classes declares `init` and `postinit` blocks that write a message to indicate that they have been executed. When an instance of `Mixee1` is created on line 29 of the code, execution of these blocks results in the following output:

```
Create instance of Mixee1
Base init
Mixin1 init
Mixin2 init
```

```
Mixin3 init
Mixee init
Base postinit
Mixin1 postinit
Mixin2 postinit
Mixin3 postinit
Mixee postinit
```

As you can see, this is consistent with the rules set out earlier in this section. The only point of interest here arises because `Mixin2` is derived from `Mixin1` and therefore the initialization of the `Mixin2` instance might be expected to cause the `init` and `postinit` blocks of `Mixin1` to be called, in addition to their invocations as a result of `Mixin1` itself also appearing in the `extends` clause. Because `Mixin1` appears before `Mixin2`, this would indicate the following order of `init` (and `postinit`) blocks:

```
Base
Mixin1 (as a result of its appearance in the extends clause)
Mixin1 (as the base mixin of Mixin2)
Mixin2
Mixee1
```

In fact, each `init` or `postinit` block is called only once, and later invocations are suppressed. This results in the suppression of the second invocation of the `init` and `postinit` blocks of `Mixin1`, giving the order shown in the preceding output.

The order of mixin classes in the declaration of `Mixee2` on lines 31 to 34 of Listing 11-15 is different from that in `Mixee1` and the order of execution of its initialization blocks reflects this:

```
Create instance of Mixee2
Base init
Mixin3 init
Mixin1 init
Mixin2 init
Mixee init
Base postinit
Mixin3 postinit
Mixin1 postinit
Mixin2 postinit
Mixee postinit
```

12

Platform APIs

In this chapter, we look at a number of classes and functions in the JavaFX runtime that don't fit elsewhere in this book. Almost all of these classes and functions are part of the common profile, which means that they are available on any platform that supports JavaFX.

We start by looking at some commonly used functions that are immediately available to all applications because the compiler automatically imports them for you. The most useful of these is `println()`, which we have already used many times in the example source code for this book. We then look at how JavaFX applications can access program arguments and system properties, and you see which of these properties are available on the various platforms on which JavaFX is available. Next, you learn how to defer code for later execution, how to run cleanup code when the Java Virtual Machine (JVM) is closed down, and how to do more with JavaFX internationalization.

For security reasons, Java applets and Java Web Start applications are not allowed direct access to the persistent storage of the devices on which they run, unless they have been signed by their author and the user explicitly permits access. Java Web Start includes an API that allows *unsigned* applications to save information on the user's PC, without compromising security, but there is no such facility for applets. The JavaFX runtime provides a feature that allows both applications and applets to read from and write to a secured area of the user's file system, whether they have been cryptographically signed. Even better, the same API, which we cover in the section "Local Storage," can be used to save data on a mobile device.

Most of the examples for this chapter can be found in the `platformapi` package in the JavaFX Book Language project.

Built-In Functions

All the functions in the `javafx.lang.Builtins` class are automatically imported by the compiler, so you can refer to them simply by name, with no qualifying class or package name. In this section, we look at the functions in this class that are provided for writing output and for comparing two Java or JavaFX objects. We do not discuss the `isInitialized()` and `isReadOnly()` functions, which are also built in, because they were discussed in Chapter 11, "JavaFX Script Classes," and Chapter 9, "Binding," respectively.

Writing to the System Output Stream

The `print()` and `println()` functions write a string representation of their single argument to the system output stream. The only difference between these two functions is that `println()` appends a newline to the value that is written. Here's an example that prints the current date and time followed by a newline character:

```
import java.util.Date;
var date = new java.util.Date();
println(date);
```

The argument is converted to string form by calling its `toString()` method, which means that you get a readable result when printing the content of a sequence:

```
var numbers = [1..5];
println(numbers);
```

This code produces the following output:

```
[ 1, 2, 3, 4, 5 ]
```

As noted earlier in this book, sequences are not well formatted for readability when they appear as an embedded expression. For more on this, see the "The String Form of a Sequence" section in Chapter 7, "Sequences."

Object Comparison

In Chapter 6, "Expressions, Functions, and Object Literals," you saw that the `==` operator in JavaFX is different from its Java equivalent because the comparison is performed using the `equals()` method of the object on the left of the operator, with the object on its right as the argument. In Java, the `==` operator evaluates to `true` if, and only if, its operands are exactly the same object instance (this is commonly referred to as *reference equality*) or, for primitives such as `int`, have the same value, whereas in JavaFX, it evaluates to `true` if the operands are "equal" in a more abstract sense. In some cases, it is important to distinguish whether you have two equal instances or the same instance twice. There is no way to do this with the JavaFX `==` operator, but the built-in function `isSameObject()` can be used to make this distinction, as the following code illustrates.[1]

```
import java.util.Date;
var date1 = new Date();
var date2 = date1;
var date3 = new Date(date1.getTime());
```

---

[1] You'll find this code in the file `platformapi/SameObject.fx` in the JavaFX Book Language project.

```
println("date1 same as date2? {isSameObject(date1, date2)}"); // true
println("date1 same as date3? {isSameObject(date1, date3)}"); // false
```

The variables `date1` and `date2` refer to the same instance of the `java.util.Date` class, so in both Java and JavaFX, the expression `date1 == date2` would evaluate to `true`. However, the variable `date3` refers to a different `Date` instance. In Java, `date1 == date3` would be `false`, but in JavaFX it returns `true`, because `date3` refers to the same time as `date1`, which means that they are equal according to the `equals()` method of the `Date` class. The last two lines of code use the built-in `isSameObject()` function to compare first `date1` with `date2` and then `date1` with `date3`. The first comparison returns `true` because `date1` and `date2` refer to the same `Date` instance, but the second returns `false` because `date1` and `date3` are different instances. The `isSameObject()` function always returns the same result as the Java `==` operator would.

Arguments and System Properties

A JavaFX application that declares a `run()` function in its entry point class can access its command-line arguments directly using the argument that is passed to that function, as described in the section "The `run()` Function" in Chapter 2, "JavaFX Script Basics." There are at least two cases in which it is either not possible or at least not convenient to get the command-line arguments in this way:

- Application code that is not in the `run()` function might need access to the application's line arguments. In some cases, it may be possible to arrange to pass the arguments as function call parameters from the `run()` function, but this is at best inconvenient.
- An applet has neither a `run()` function nor command-line arguments. It may, however, have applet parameters. Similarly, an application running on a mobile device has no command-line arguments, but it could have MIDlet parameters that are stored in its JAD (Java Application Descriptor) file.

Application Arguments

Application code that needs access to its arguments can use the `getArguments()` function in the `javafx.lang.FX` class. This function returns a sequence of strings that contains the command-line arguments in the order in which they were supplied to the application launcher. Here's an example that shows how to use this function:

```
1    var arguments:String[] = FX.getArguments();
2    println("Number of arguments: {sizeof arguments}");
3    for (i in [0..<sizeof arguments]) {
4        println("Arg #{i}: {arguments[i]}");
5    }
```

The code on line 1 retrieves the command-line arguments. If there are none, this will retrieve an empty sequence. Line 2 uses the `sizeof` operator to get the number of arguments present, while line 3 uses the `for` statement to loop over the sequence, printing each argument together with its index in the sequence.

You can run this code by making the `src` directory of the example source code for this book your working directory, compiling the example using the following command:

```
javafxc -d ..\classes platformapi\*.fx
```

To run the example, do this:

```
javafx -cp ../classes platformapi.AppArguments1 One small step for man
```

Alternatively, there is a run configuration for this example that you can use if you are using the NetBeans IDE, which includes these arguments. To use it, make JavaFX Book Language project the main project in the IDE and select AppArguments1 from the Run drop-down in the toolbar. (Refer to Figure 4-11 in Chapter 4, "A Simple JavaFX Application," if you are not sure where to find this drop-down.) In either case, the output includes the following:

```
Number of arguments: 5
Arg #0: One
Arg #1: small
Arg #2: step
Arg #3: for
Arg #4: man
```

Named Arguments

Applets have named parameters declared within the `<applet>` tag, such as the URL parameter in the HTML snippet shown here:

```
<applet codebase="..." code="...">
    <param name="URL" value="javafx.com">
</applet>
```

Similarly, a MIDlet (which is the equivalent of an applet in cell phones and other devices that run the MIDP profile of Java ME) may have named parameters that are configured in its JAD file. Named parameters can be obtained by using the `getArgument()` function of the `javafx.lang.FX` class. This function requires the parameter name as its argument and returns the corresponding parameter value as a `java.lang.Object`, which, on all current platforms, will actually be a `String`.

The following code illustrates the use of this method to retrieve the value of a parameter with the name URL. Note the use of `as` to cast the `Object` returned by `getArgument()` to a string.

```
var param:String = FX.getArgument("URL") as String;
println('argument "URL" is: {param}');
```

If no value has been supplied in the applet or MIDlet configuration for the named parameter, this method returns `null`, which would be converted to the empty string by the `as` operator. Therefore, to determine whether a value has actually been supplied for a named parameter, do one of the following:

```
// 1: Assign to an Object variable and check for null.
var param = FX.getArgument("URL");
if (param != null) {
   // Value was supplied
}

// 2: Assign to a String variable and check for the empty string.
var strParam:String = FX.getArgument("URL") as String;
if (strParam != "") {
    // Value was supplied
}
```

There is a reserved argument called `javafx.applet` that is defined during execution of a JavaFX script in an applet container. The value of this argument is a reference to the hosting `JApplet`:

```
var applet:JApplet = FX.getArgument("javafx.applet") as JApplet;
```

You can also use the `getArgument()` function to retrieve the command-line arguments of a JavaFX application. In this case, the name of each argument is its index on the command line in string form. The first command-line argument is named 0, the second 1, and so on. The code shown here retrieves the first two arguments on the command line of an application:

```
println('Named arg "0" is {FX.getArgument("0")}');
println('Named arg "1" is {FX.getArgument("1")}');
```

If *all* of an application's command-line arguments are of the form `name=value`, they are converted so that they can be retrieved by name in the same way as applet and MIDlet arguments. To illustrate this, run the following example:

```
javafx -cp ../classes -platformapi.AppArguments2 url=http://javafx.com
proxyHost=myProxy proxyPort=180
```

Alternatively, use the NetBeans run configuration called `AppArguments2`. The code for this example looks like this:

```
println("Argument 'url' is {FX.getArgument('url')}");
println("Argument 'proxyHost' is {FX.getArgument('proxyHost')}");
println("Argument 'proxyPort' is {FX.getArgument('proxyPort')}");
```

As you can see, the argument values are requested by name. The output from this example is as follows. Note only the part of each argument that follows the equals sign on the command line is returned:

```
Argument 'url' is http://javafx.com
Argument 'proxyHost' is myProxy
Argument 'proxyPort' is 180
```

These two methods of retrieving command-line arguments are mutually exclusive—
you must use either one or the other. Here are the rules:

- If your application requires *any* arguments of the form name=value and you want to retrieve them by name, *all the* arguments must be of that form, and then you can *only* request them by name.

- If *any* argument is not of the form name=value, you cannot request any argument by name.

To clarify this, suppose your application has an argument list like this:

```
url=http://javafx.com proxyHost=myProxy proxyPort=180
```

Because every argument is of the form name=value, you *must* use code like FX.getArgument("url") to retrieve each argument, or use the FX.getArguments() function and retrieve them by index. Attempting to fetch arguments by position will not work—FX.getArgument("0") will return null. If, instead, the arguments look like the following example, you can *only* fetch the arguments by position—FX.getProperty("0") would work, but FX.getProperty("url") would return null:

```
url=http://javafx.com -noproxy
```

System Properties

The FX.getProperty() function returns the value of a named JavaFX property:

```
public function getProperty(name:String):String
```

JavaFX property names all have the javafx. prefix. These properties are logically distinct from the Java properties that are returned by the System.getProperty() method, although many of them have similar names and the same values as Java system properties. JavaFX properties are set by the host platform and are read-only. No API allows you to determine at runtime which properties are defined. A request for a property that does not exist returns null. (Although it probably should return an empty string, to be consistent with the simplified style of programming used by JavaFX.)

Table 12-1 lists the properties that are available on the desktop platform.

Table 12-2 lists the properties that are available on the mobile platform.

The code in the file platformapi/SystemProperties.fx in the JavaFX Language project prints the values of all the system properties listed in the preceding tables. By running this example as a Java Web Start application, in a browser and on the mobile emulator, you can see which properties are available in each of these environments and what their values are.

Table 12-1 **Desktop JavaFX Properties**

Property Name	Description
javafx.version	The JavaFX release number
javafx.runtime.version	The version number of the JavaFX runtime
javafx.java.version	The host Java Runtime Environment version
javafx.java.vendor	The host Java Runtime Environment vendor
javafx.java.vendor.url	The host Java vendor URL
javafx.java.io.tmpdir	The default path for temporary files
javafx.java.ext.dirs	The location of platform extensions
javafx.os.name	The host operating system name
javafx.os.arch	The host operating system architecture
javafx.os.version	The host operating system version
javafx.file.separator	File separator
javafx.path.separator	Path separator
javafx.line.separator	Line separator
javafx.user.home	The user's home directory
javafx.user.dir	The user's current working directory
javafx.timezone	The user's time zone
javafx.language	The user's language
javafx.region	The user's region (for example, en_US)
javafx.encoding	The user's native file encoding
javafx.applet.codebase	The codebase from which the applet was downloaded, or the empty string if the code is not executing in an applet
javafx.application.codebase	The codebase from which an application was downloaded by Java Webstart, or the empty string if the code is not running in an application that was downloaded by Java Webstart

Table 12-2 **Mobile JavaFX Properties**

Property Name	Description
`javafx.version`	The JavaFX release number.
`javafx.runtime.version`	The version number of the JavaFX runtime.
`javafx.me.profiles`	The J2ME profiles that the host device supports, separated by spaces (for example, `"MIDP-2.1 JAVAFX-1.1"`).
`javafx.me.msa.version`	The version of the Mobile Service Architecture that the device supports, such as 1.1. See JSR 248.
`javafx.me.m3g.version`	The version of the Mobile 3D Graphics specification that the device supports, such as 1.1. See JSR 184.
`javafx.me.m2g.version`	The version of the Scalable 2D Vector Graphics API for J2ME that the device supports, such as 1.1. See JSR 226.
`javafx.me.io.file.File Connection.version`	The version of the J2ME FileConnection specification that the device supports, such as 1.0. See JSR 75.
`javafx.me.commports`	A comma-separated list of available serial ports, such as COM1. See JSR 118.
`javafx.me.jtwi.version`	The version of the Java Technology for the Wireless Industry specification that the device supports, such as 1.0. See JSR 185.
`javafx.supports.mixing`	Whether the device support audio mixing (`true` or `false`). See JSR 135.
`javafx.supports.audio.capture`	Whether audio capture is supported (`true` or `false`). See JSR 135.
`javafx.supports.video.capture`	Whether video capture is supported (`true` or `false`). See JSR 135
`javafx.supports.recording`	Whether recording is supported (`true` or `false`). See JSR 135.
`javafx.audio.encodings`	The supported audio capture formats (for example, `encoding=pcm&rate=22050&bits=16&channels=1`). See JSR 135.
`javafx.video.encodings`	The supported video capture formats (for example, `encoding=rgb565`). See JSR 135.

Application Shutdown

A JavaFX application can terminate itself by calling the `FX.exit()` function. Unlike the method of the same name in the `java.lang.System` class, there is no argument that represents an exit status. So why use this function in preference to `System.exit()`? One reason is to allow the JavaFX runtime to perform any necessary cleanup, which won't happen if you call `System.exit()`. The other reason is that the JavaFX `FX.exit()` function runs any shutdown actions (described in the next section) that have been registered, whereas `System.exit()` does not.

A *shutdown action* is a function that is executed when a JavaFX application is terminating. It is the JavaFX equivalent of a shutdown hook in Java SE. (See the API documentation for the Java SE `java.lang.Runtime` class if you are not familiar with shutdown hooks.) JavaFX shutdown actions are implemented entirely in the JavaFX runtime and are therefore available on all platforms, unlike shutdown hooks, which are not available on mobile devices running MIDP.

The following code demonstrates how to write and install a shutdown action:

```
1    function shutdownAction1():Void {
2        println("In shutdown action #1");
3    }
4
5    function shutdownAction2():Void {
6        println("In shutdown action #2");
7    }
8
9    FX.addShutdownAction(shutdownAction1);
10   FX.addShutdownAction(shutdownAction2);
11
12   FX.exit();
```

Lines 1 through 5 declare two functions to be used as shutdown actions. As you can see, no argument is passed to a shutdown action, and it does not return anything. Typically, you would use a shutdown action to release resources that your application allocated (such as network connections) or write saved state to persistent storage. In this example, we simply write a message so that we can see that the function has been invoked.

To register a shutdown action, call the following function in the `javafx.lang.FX` class[2]:

```
public function addShutdownAction(action:function():Void):Integer;
```

The value returned by this function is a "handle" that can be used to remove the action using the `removeShutdownAction()` function:

```
var handle = FX.addShutdownAction(shutdownAction1);
var success = FX.removeShutdownAction(handle);
```

The value returned by the `removeShutdownAction()` function is `true` if the action were removed and `false` if not, which would imply that the supplied handle is invalid.

---

[2] `addShutdownHook()` is actually a Java method. The declaration shown here uses the JavaFX syntax that produces the same signature as the Java method.

When more than one shutdown action is registered, as is the case on lines 9 and 10 of the first example above, they are executed in reverse order of registration (that is, last-in, first-out), as the result of running the preceding code[3]:

```
In shutdown action #2
In shutdown action #1
```

If the same function is registered twice, it will be called twice (although this is not likely to be very useful!):

```
FX.addShutdownAction(shutdownAction1);
FX.addShutdownAction(shutdownAction2);
FX.addShutdownAction(shutdownAction2);
FX.exit();
```

The preceding code produces the following output, which shows that the second shutdown action is executed twice:

```
In shutdown action #2
In shutdown action #2
In shutdown action #1
```

An uncaught exception thrown during the execution of a shutdown action causes the rest of that action to be aborted, but has no other effect—any remaining shutdown actions will still be executed. Similarly, if `FX.exit()` is called from within a shutdown action, a `java.lang.IllegalStateException` will be thrown, which will abort that handler, but have no further effect.

Deferring Operations

Sometimes it is useful to able to postpone an operation so that it is not performed inline with the currently executing function. You can do this by using `FX.deferAction()`, which arranges for the function passed to it to be called at some time in the near future. Here is how the `deferAction()` function is declared, expressed in JavaFX syntax. (It is actually a Java method, so the actual declaration is equivalent but not exactly the same.)

```
public function deferAction(fn:function():Void):Void;
```

In a GUI application running on the desktop, the deferred function is called on the AWT event thread, so the effect is the same as you would achieve by calling the `SwingUtilities.invokeLater()` method. If you are writing a JavaFX application that is intended to be portable across different GUI platforms (for example, desktop, MIDP mobile phone), `deferAction()` gives you a platform-independent mechanism for scheduling later execution of code. It does *not* allow you to write a multithreaded JavaFX program.

---

[3] You'll find this code in the file `platformapi/ShutdownActions1.fx`.

> **Note**
>
> As you saw in Chapter 2, the JavaFX runtime assumes that your code runs only in a single thread, and there is no synchronization mechanism in JavaFX that could protect against race conditions caused by conflicting reads from and writes to variables or to guarantee the apparent ordering of operations as seen across different threads. One consequence of a lack of proper synchronization is that it is possible that the effect of an operation B that is performed after an operation A in the same thread may be observed from a different thread before the effect of operation A is seen in that other thread. It is, therefore, not safe to try to write concurrent code in JavaFX. See the book *Java Concurrency in Practice* by Brian Goetz et al., published by Addison-Wesley (http://www.informit.com/store/product.aspx?isbn=0321349601) for a full discussion of the problems of concurrent programming.

The following example, which you'll find in the file `platformapi/OperationDeferral.fx`, demonstrates the use of `deferAction()`:

```
1   function calledLater() {
2       println("In deferred action");
3   }
4
5   println("Deferring an action");
6   FX.deferAction(calledLater);
7   println("Scheduled deferred action");
```

The code to be deferred is contained in the function defined on lines 1 through 3, and the call on line 6 arranges for it to be invoked at some future time. When the deferred function executed, it simply prints a message. The output from this code is this:

```
Deferring an action
Scheduled deferred action
In deferred action
```

This shows that the deferred action was called after the main code in the script was executed.

Functions for Internationalization

In Chapter 5, "Variables and Data Types," you saw how easy it is to write desktop JavaFX applications that can be localized for use in different parts of the world.[4] As a reminder and for the purposes of illustration, one of the examples that we used in that chapter is reproduced here, with only its package name changed:

```
1   package platformapi;
2
3   import java.util.Date;
```

---

[4] The localization features of JavaFX are not available on the mobile platform.

```
4        import java.text.DateFormat;
5        import javafx.util.StringLocalizer;
6
7        var date:Date = new Date();
8        var fmt:DateFormat = DateFormat.getDateInstance(DateFormat.SHORT);
9        println(##"Today is {%tA date} and the date is "
10               "{fmt.format(date)}");
```

This code prints the date and time in a format that is suitable for the user's locale. The characters ## before the string literal on lines 9 and 10 cause the JavaFX runtime to look for a translated version of the string that is suitable for the native language and country of the user running the application. By default, the runtime locates the translated string by looking for resource files in the same package as the JavaFX class file and then uses the text in the code as a key to locate the translation. In the example shown here, we'll assume that the user is a French speaker in Canada, so the JVM's locale will be fr_CA.

The location of the resource file is based on that of the class file. In the example above, the class is called platformapi.LocalizedDate, so the runtime uses platformapi/LocalizedDate as the base name for the resource file (relative to the class path) and looks for resource files called platformapi/LocalizedData_fr_CA.fxproperties and platformapi/LocalizedDate_fr.fxproperties. If either of these is found, the text shown on line 9 is used as the key for the translation. Here's some typical content for a JavaFX resource file:

```
"Today is %tA and the date is %s" = "La date est %2$s et est aujourd'hui %1$tA"
```

The process of locating the resource file, looking up the translation and substituting it in the println() statement happens automatically because when the compiler sees a string literal preceded by ##, it translates it into code that uses the runtime's support for localization. The code generated by the compiler results in the behavior described earlier, but this is just the default. The java.util.StringLocalizer class, which we discuss in the next section, allows you to change this behavior slightly.

Changing String Localization Defaults

By default, the base name of the resource file for a class called pkg.cls is pkg/cls. This simple mapping makes it easy to understand where you should put translated strings for every class in your application that needs them. However, with this default policy, if you have lots of classes, you will also have lots of resource files, one per class. If you prefer to reduce the number of resource files, you can do one (or both) of the following:

- Create a mapping that causes the runtime to look for all translations for the classes in a single package (or in multiple packages) in one resource file.
- Create a mapping that places all the translations for an arbitrary set of classes in a single resource file.

Mappings are established using the `associate()` function of the `StringLocalizer` class, which has two variants, the first of which establishes a package-level mapping and the second a class-level mapping:

```
public function associate(properties: String, packageName: String):Void
public function associate(properties: String, packageName: String,
                          scriptFileName: String):Void
```

Creating a Package Mapping

The first variant of the `associate()` function causes translation lookups from any class in the named package to be resolved from the specified properties file. In terms of our example, we can use this function to change the location of translated messages for all classes in the `platformapi` package as follows:

```
StringLocalizer.associate("platformapi/PackageStrings", "platformapi");
```

The second argument is the name of the package for which a mapping is to be established. The components of the package name must be separated by periods in the normal way. The first argument is the base name of the file that contains the translated strings. In this case, the file is in the same package as the class file, but this is not required—you could decide to put all of your translated strings in a separate location. For example, the following code arranges for the translations to be retrieved from a file in the `resources` package:

```
StringLocalizer.associate("resources/PackageStrings", "platformapi");
```

By making multiple calls to this function, you can arrange for more than one package to be mapped to the same base name. Taken to the extreme, you could arrange for all of your application's translations to be held in a single file.

You can use either / or . as the component separator in the properties file base name, so the first example above is equivalent to this:

```
StringLocalizer.associate("platformapi.PackageStrings", "platformapi");
```

During the lookup, the suffix `.fxproperties` is added. So for a user whose locale is `fr_CA`, the search path that will be used for all classes in the `platformapi` package would now be

1. `platformapi/PackageStrings_fr_CA.fxproperties`
2. `platformapi/PackageStrings_fr.fxproperties`

Creating a Class Mapping

The second variant of the `associate()` function creates a mapping between a single class and a translation file base name. Because there is a one-to-one mapping by default, there are only two possible reasons for using this function:

- To use a nondefault name for the translation file.

- If you have a package mapping in place, you can associate specific classes that would otherwise be covered by the package mapping with a different file.

The following code causes the base name for lookups for translated messages from the class `Test` in the package `platformapi` to be `resources/TestMessages`:

```
StringLocalizer.associate("resources/TestMessages ", "platformapi",
                    "Test");
```

When there is both a class-level and a package-level mapping that would affect the same class, the class-level mapping is used.

Removing Mappings

Mappings created by the `associate()` function can be removed by using the `disassociate()` function, which also has two variants:

```
public function dissociate(packageName: String) : Void
public function dissociate(packageName: String,
                    scriptFileName: String) : Void
```

The first form removes a package-level mapping together with any class-level mappings that might exist for classes in that package. The second form removes a single class-level mapping.

Local Storage

Most applications require persistent storage. If you are writing a game, you probably want to save a list of high scores, or if you are writing a business application, you might want to save the user's preferences. Access to local storage on the user's device is problematic for a couple of reasons:

- The storage mechanism is platform-dependent and so are the APIs used to access it. On a desktop system, persistent data is stored in files, but on a mobile device, nonvolatile memory is used instead.

- Access to local storage is usually restricted, for security reasons. For example, unsigned applications and applets are not allowed access to the user's file system, to prevent unauthorized reading or modification of data.

The JavaFX runtime provides a simple local storage facility that addresses both of these issues. The public API consists of only two classes, which delegate to platform-dependent implementations that work with whatever storage mechanism exists on the host device, thus addressing the issue of platform-independence. Security concerns are addressed by not allowing the application free access to whatever local storage is present. Instead, data is stored in an area of the file system or nonvolatile memory that is entirely managed by the JavaFX runtime. It is impossible for an untrusted JavaFX application to read or write data outside of this dedicated area, so there is no possibility that it could violate the security of the user's device. Because the local storage mechanism is completely under the control of the JavaFX runtime, you do not need to sign your application to make use of it.

Reading and Writing Data

To write some data to local storage, you first need to create an instance of the `javafx.io.Storage` class, giving the name of the resource[5] to which you want to write. As you'll see in the section "Resource Names and Access Control," later in this chapter, the resource name can either be relative or absolute. For simplicity, we'll confine ourselves to the use of relative resource names for now. Once you have a `Storage` object, you can get a `Resource` object that lets you read and write the content of the underlying storage. Here's a simple example that illustrates the API[6]:

```
1     package platformapi;
2
3     import javafx.io.Storage;
4     import java.io.DataOutputStream;
5     import java.lang.System;
6
7     var s = Storage {
8         source: "Hello";
9     }
10
11    var r = s.resource;
12    var os = new DataOutputStream(r.openOutputStream(true));
13    os.writeLong(System.currentTimeMillis());
14    os.writeUTF("Hello, World");
15    os.close();
16    println("Entry written");
```

The `Storage` object is created on lines 7 to 9. The `source` variable is initialized with the name of the resource, which in this case is called `"Hello"`. A relative resource name must not contain a / character because these are used to separate the elements of an absolute name, examples of which you will see later in this chapter. During initialization, the `Storage` object creates a `javafx.io.Resource` object that refers to the storage resource named by the `source` variable and stores it in its `resource` variable.

One lines 11 and 12, we get the `Resource` instance and use its `openOutputStream()` function to get an `OutputStream` that can be used to write to the resource:

```
public function openOutputStream(overwrite:boolean):OutputStream;
```

---

[5] Throughout this section, we use the term *resource* rather than *file* to emphasize the fact that the actual representation of the resource may not be a file.

[6] You'll find this example in the file `LocalStorage1.fx` in the `platformapi` package of the JavaFX Book Language project.

Chapter 12 Platform APIs

If the resource does not yet exist, it is created automatically. If it *does* exist, its content may or may not be overwritten, depending on the value of the `overwrite` argument. If this argument is `true`, any existing content will be lost; if it is `false`, the existing content will be preserved and new data is appended to it.

Any data written to the `OutputStream` is stored in the resource and flushed when the `OutputStream` is closed Writing directly to an `OutputStream` is not very convenient because its methods deal only with bytes and byte arrays. There are various ways to write a `String` to an `OutputStream`, one of which is to wrap the `OutputStream` in an `OutputStreamWriter`, like this:

```
var r = s.resource;
var w = new OutputStreamWriter(os, "UTF-8");
w.write("Hello again, world");
w.close();
```

Although this approach looks convenient, it works only for `Strings`. To write a numeric value, you would need to convert it to an array of bytes in some way and then write the array to the `OutputStream`. You would also need to implement the reverse conversion to read the value back. Such a conversion is already implemented in the `DataOutputStream` and `DataInputStream` classes, along with a pair of methods—`readUTF()` and `writeUTF()`—that allow you to read and write `Strings`. These classes are easy to use and are available on both desktop and mobile devices. In the previous example, we use them to write a `Long`, representing the current time, and a `String` to the resource:

```
var r = s.resource;
var os = new DataOutputStream(r.openOutputStream(true));
os.writeLong(System.currentTimeMillis());
os.writeUTF("Hello, World");
os.close();
```

> **Note**
>
> If you need your JavaFX application to be portable across various different platforms, you need to make sure that you only use subclasses of `OutputStream` or `Writer` that are available on all of those platforms. The `DataOutputStream` and `OutputStreamWriter` classes used here are implemented on both the mobile and desktop platforms, so this example will work in both environments.

Reading the content of a resource is very similar, as the following code, from the file `platformapi/LocalStorage2.fx`, shows:

```
1    package platformapi;
2
3    import javafx.io.Storage;
4    import java.io.DataInputStream;
5    import java.util.Date;
6
7    var s = Storage {
```

```
 8            source: "Hello";
 9        }
10
11        var r = s.resource;
12        var is = new DataInputStream(r.openInputStream());
13        var instant = is.readLong();
14        var str = is.readUTF();
15        is.close();
16
17        var d = new Date(instant);
18        println("Entry written at: {d}");
19        println("Content is '{str}'");
```

As before, we create a `Storage` object with the same resource name and get the corresponding `Resource` object. We then use the `openInputStream()` function to get an `InputStream` that we can use to read the content of the resource and wrap it in a `DataInputStream`, and then use its `readLong()` and `readUTF()` methods to recover the data that we wrote earlier. The output from this code shows that the correct data was returned:

```
Entry written at: Sat Nov 14 18:15:08 GMT 2009
Content is 'Hello, World'
```

Storage Metadata

The `Storage` and `Resource` classes have variables and functions that provide metadata that describes the local storage available to your application.

Listing Resources

The `Storage` class has a script function that lets you get the names of the resources that have been created by your application (and by other applications that share its local storage) in the location that is used when a relative resource name is supplied:

```
public function list():String[]
```

As you'll see in the "Resource Names and Access Control" section, later in this chapter, it is possible to get access to resources that your application did not create, but these resources, if they exist, are not returned by this method. The following code, which you will find in the file `platformapi/LocalStorage3.fx`, lists the resources that exist in the local storage space that is used by the application:

```
var names:String[] = Storage.list();
for (name in names) {
    println("Resource name: '{name}'");
}
```

The output from this code shows the resource that was created by our earlier example:

```
Resource name: 'Hello'
```

Although this resource was created by a different JavaFX script, it is still visible to *this* script. In general, resources created by one application are visible to another only if they share the same *codebase* or, under some circumstances, if they have the same *domain*. In this case, the resource is visible because the application that created it and the application that called the `list()` function have the same codebase—namely, the same JAR file into which they have been bundled by the IDE. We discuss this further in the "Resource Names and Access Control" section, later in this chapter.

Available and Used Space

The `Storage` class has two script variables that track the amount of allocated and available space in the local storage area. Here's an example of the use of these variables:

```
println("Total bytes: {Storage.totalBytes}");
println("Available bytes: {Storage.availableBytes}");
```

Here's the result of running this code on my laptop:

```
Total bytes: 1048576
Available bytes: 1048554
```

Running the same code on the mobile emulator gives this result:

```
Total bytes: 524288
Available bytes: 524262
```

The `totalBytes` variable represents the maximum amount of space that the application is allowed to use on the device, while the `availableBytes` variable records how much of this space is currently available for allocation. As you would probably expect, less space is available on the mobile device than on my laptop. However, it is important to note that the maximum advertised space does not necessarily reflect any physical characteristic of the device—in the desktop implementation, it is a property obtained from a property file that is part of the JavaFX runtime. It represents the total space available to all applications that share the same domain. In other words, if one application from a domain uses half this space, the combined space available to the other applications is limited to only half of the maximum available.

Resource Metadata

The `Resource` object has five variables that represent its metadata, as listed in Table 12-3.

Table 12-3 Variables of the `Resource` Class

Variable	Type	Access	Description
`name`	`String`	R	The name of the resource
`length`	`Long`	R	The current size of the content associated with this resource
`maxLength`	`Long`	R	The maximum content size for this resource
`readable`	`Boolean`	R	Whether the resource can be read
`writable`	`Boolean`	R	Whether the resource can be written

The following code, which you can find in the file `platformapi/LocalStorage5.fx`, illustrates the use of these variables:

```
1    package platformapi;
2
3    import javafx.io.Storage;
4
5    var s = Storage {
6        source: "Hello";
7    }
8
9    var r = s.resource;
10   println("Name: {r.name}");
11   println("Length: {r.length}");
12   println("MaxLength: {r.maxLength}");
13   println("Readable: {r.readable}");
14   println("Writable: {r.writable}");
```

The `Storage` and `Resource` objects in this code refer to the resource that was created in our earlier examples. Here is the output from this code:

```
Name: Hello
Length: 0
MaxLength: 8192
Readable: true
Writable: true
```

The `name` variable is the name of the resource as supplied to the `source` variable of the `Storage` object, except that when an absolute path is used, the `name` variable will contain only the last component of the full resource path. The `length` variable reflects the space currently occupied by the resource, while `maxLength` is the maximum permissible allocation for this resource. The `readable` and `writable` variables indicate whether the resource can be read or written to, respectively. It is not clear under what circumstances a resource might not be readable or writable and, at the time of this writing, these variables seem to always have the value `true`.

> **Note**
>
> In the previous output, the `length` variable has the value 0. This is a bug, which has been reported and should be fixed in a future version of the JavaFX platform.

Removing Data

You can remove either a single resource or all resources within the area to which your application has access. To remove a specific resource, use the `clear()` function of its `Storage` object; to remove all resources in the application's private storage area, use the `clearAll()` script function of the `Storage` class, as shown in the following code:

```
1    package platformapi;
2
3    import javafx.io.Storage;
```

```
4
5      // Create two resource.
6      var s = Storage {
7          source: "Hello"
8      }
9      Storage {
10         source: "Goodbye"
11     }
12
13     println("------------- RESOURCES BEFORE ---------------");
14     for (name in Storage.list()) {
15         println("Resource: {name}");
16     }
17     println("----------- END RESOURCES BEFORE -------------");
18
19     // Remove the first resource
20     s.clear();
21
22     println("------------- RESOURCES AFTER ---------------");
23     for (name in Storage.list()) {
24         println("Resource: {name}");
25     }
26     println("----------- END RESOURCES AFTER -------------");
27
28     // Remove the remaining resource
29     Storage.clearAll();
30     println("------------- RESOURCES AT END ---------------");
31     for (name in Storage.list()) {
32         println("Resource: {name}");
33     println("----------- END RESOURCES AT END -------------");
```

Lines 6 to 11 create two resources called Hello and Goodbye in the application's private area. Note that the resource is created even if no content is written. Lines 13 to 16 list the resources that exist, to demonstrate that they have been created:

```
------------- RESOURCES BEFORE ---------------
Resource: Goodbye
Resource: Hello
----------- END RESOURCES BEFORE -------------
```

On line 20, we call the clear() function of the Storage object that refers to the Hello resource, which removes it, and then lists the resources again:

```
------------- RESOURCES AFTER ---------------
Resource: Goodbye
----------- END RESOURCES AFTER -------------
```

Finally, on line 29, we use the `clearAll()` function to remove the remaining resource, with the following result:

```
------------- RESOURCES AT END ---------------
----------- END RESOURCES AT END -------------
```

Resource Names and Access Control

So far, we have only used relative resource names like `Hello` and `Goodbye`, without saying what these names are relative to. The namespace used for resources is not a real one, so you won't actually find a file called `Hello` in the file system when you create a resource of that name. Instead, the JavaFX runtime creates a file in a private area that will contain the actual data for the resource and maintains a mapping from the logical name of a resource to that file.

Resource Names

The full name of a resource is based on the codebase of the JavaFX application that creates it. The codebase is the value of the `javafx.application.codebase` property and reflects the location from which the code was loaded. For a Java Web Start application, the codebase is obtained from the `<jnlp>` element of the JNLP file and refers to the directory on the web server that contains the JNLP file and, usually, the JAR files for the application. For a JavaFX applet, the codebase is typically specified in the `<applet>` tag and, again, it refers to the directory that contains the JAR files for the applet.

For example, suppose that your company has three JavaFX applications, two belonging to the accounts department and one to human resources. Each application has its own JNLP file, and the JNLP files (and the JAR files, which we don't show here) are held in a directory structure that represents the company's internal organization, like this:

```
http://myorg.com/accounts/AccountsApp1.jnlp
http://myorg.com/accounts/AccountsApp2.jnlp
http://myorg.com/hr/HRApp1.jnlp
```

The codebase for both of the accounting applications would be `http://myorg.com/accounts`, while that of the HR application would be `http://myorg.com/hr`.

Now let's suppose the `AccountsApp1` application creates a resource with a relative name of `Hello`. The JavaFX runtime appends this name to the codebase to form the complete (internal) name of the resource, which would then be `http://myorg.com/accounts/Hello`. If the same application created another resource called `Goodbye`, the runtime would actually create a resource with the internal name `http://myorg.com/accounts/Goodbye`.

If this application were now to use the `list()` function to discover the set of resources available to it, the runtime would look for and return the relative names of all the resources whose internal names start with the application's codebase so, as you can now see, this would return `Hello` and `Goodbye`. Similarly, the `clearAll()` function removes all the resources whose names would be returned by the `list()` function.

Now suppose that `AccountsApp2` were to attempt to create a resource called `Hello`. The codebase for this application is `http://myorg.com/accounts`, the same as that of `AccountsApp1`, so the internal name of this resource would be `http://myorg.com/accounts/Hello`, which means that it is actually referencing the same resource as the one created by `AccountsApp1`. In fact, *all applications with the same codebase share the same logical local storage.* In our example, this means that all the accounting applications use the same local storage area and can access each other's resources.

Access Control

If the HR application were now to create a resource called `Hello`, its internal name would be `http://myorg.com/hr/Hello`. Because the HR application does not have the same codebase as the accounts applications, they do *not* share the same local storage. As a result, the internal names for the resources of the HR application are different from those of the accounting applications, so the HR application cannot access the local storage of the accounts applications and vice versa.

It should also be clear that applications on different servers cannot access each other's local storage, even if the rest of the codebase for these applications is the same. This is just as well, because otherwise you might find another company's applications on a user's computer reading and writing data belonging to your company's applications!

Absolute Resource Names

Although applications that have different codebases cannot access each other's private resource area, it is possible for them to share resources if they are resident on the same host. As a result, the HR and accounting applications *can* share data. To do so, they must use absolute resource names. The absolute name of a resource is the part of the name that follows the name's *domain*. In the case of an HTTP URL, the domain is the part that includes the server name (and port if specified). In terms of our examples, the domain name is `http://myorg.com/`, so the absolute names of the resource `Hello` in the accounting application and of the resource with the same relative name in the HR application are as follows:

- /accounts/Hello
- /hr/Hello

As a consequence of this, the following `Storage` objects, if created in either of the accounting applications, actually refer to the same resource:

```
Storage {
    source: "Hello"
}
```

```
Storage {
    source: "/accounts/Hello"
}
```

An application can access a resource that is in its own private area *or* in any logical directory that contains that private area. What this means is that the accounting applications can access resources in `/accounts` and in the parent directory `/`. Similarly, the HR application can access resources in `/hr` and in its parent directory, `/`. As you can see, both applications can access resources in the directory `/`, so resources that need to be shared between them should be created there. For example, the resource referred to by the following `Storage` object can be accessed by either of the accounting applications and the HR application:

```
Storage {
    source: "/shared"
}
```

Conditional Features

Some features of the JavaFX runtime are not available on all platforms. In some cases, the classes that implement these features are not included in the runtime, and you can't compile an application that uses one of these features for a platform that does not support it. An example of this is the `AppletStageExtension` class, which exists only in the desktop profile. There is another set of features that are part of the common API but that are not functional on some platforms or devices. The classes that contain the API for these features are present in all versions of the runtime, so you can always compile code that uses them, but they do nothing at runtime if the target platform does not support them.

It is sometimes useful to be able to detect whether the device that you are running on implements one of these conditional features. You can do this by calling the `isSupported()` method of the `javafx.runtime.Platform` class, passing it an argument that specifies the feature that you are interested in. The following code, from the file `platformapi/ConditionalFeatureExample.fx` in the JavaFX Book Language project, prints the availability of all the conditional features in the JavaFX 1.3 platform.

```
println("Effects? "
        "{Platform.isSupported(ConditionalFeature.EFFECT)}");
println("Input methods? "
        "{Platform.isSupported(ConditionalFeature.INPUT_METHOD)}");
println("Shape clipping? "
        "{Platform.isSupported(ConditionalFeature.SHAPE_CLIP)}");
println("Scene3D? "
"{Platform.isSupported(ConditionalFeature.SCENE3D)}");
```

The permitted argument values, defined by the `ConditionalFeature` package, are as follows:

- `EFFECT`—Refers to the effects API described in Chapter 20, "Effects and Blending."
- `INPUT_METHOD`–Indicates whether the platform supports the ability to enter characters that are not available on the keyboard, such as characters from the Chinese or Japanese character sets.
- `SHAPE_CLIP`–Refers to the ability to clip a node using an arbitrary shape. Clipping is discussed in Chapter 17, "Coordinates, Transforms, and Layout."
- `SCENE3D`–Corresponds to the basic 3D features that are part of the JavaFX 1.3 API.

13
Reflection

In this chapter, we look at the JavaFX Reflection application programming interface (API). Reflection is primarily of use to tools such as integrated development environments (IDEs) and code generators that need to work, at runtime, with classes that they have no prior knowledge of. Using reflection, you can load any class given its name, create an instance of that class, discover its variables and functions, read and set the values of those variable, and invoke its functions.

The classes that implement the JavaFX Reflection API can be found in the `javafx.reflect` package. It is possible to use the Java Reflection APIs in the `java.lang.reflect` package to inspect a JavaFX class, but Java reflection gives a Java view of a JavaFX class, which is not quite the same as the JavaFX view of that class. We don't discuss Java reflection in this book, and you don't need to have any knowledge of it to understand the material presented here. The Reflection API is part of the JavaFX desktop profile. It is not available in runtimes that provide only the common profile.

You can find the source code for the examples in this chapter in the `javafxreflection` package in the JavaFX Book Desktop project.

Context and Classes

The starting point for the JavaFX Reflection API is the *reflection context*. You can use the reflection context to get reflective information for any class to which your application has access.

The Reflection Context

The reflection context is implemented by the class `javafx.reflect.FXContext`, which, like all the classes that make up the Reflection API, is actually an immutable Java class. It provides a static method that returns a reflection context instance:

```
var ctx = FXContext.getInstance();
```

Note that this is *not* a singleton, so multiple calls to this method will return different `FXContext` instances. You can use an `FXContext` object to do any of the following:

- Get an `FXClassType` object for any JavaFX class that provides reflective access to that class (like the Java `Class` object). This is covered in the next section.
- Retrieve objects that represent the JavaFX primitive types—see the section "Types and Value," later in this chapter, for more information.
- Construct a sequence consisting of types that were not known to the application at compile time, as described in the "Using Reflection" section, later in this chapter.
- Create and initialize an instance of a JavaFX class.

Reflective Access to Classes

The reflective information for a class is contained in an instance of the `FXClassType` class. `FXClassType` is one of several classes that represent JavaFX types, the rest of which are discussed in the "Types and Values" section.

Getting Class Information

You can get the `FXClassType` object for a class from the `findClass()` method of `FXContext`. The following code gets the `FXClassType` object for the `javafx.scene.control.Control` class (which is part of the GUI runtime) and then prints its name:

```
var ctx = FXContext.getInstance();
var textBoxClass = ctx.findClass("javafx.scene.control.TextBox");
println(textBoxClass.getName());
```

The output from this code is the full name of the class:

```
javafx.scene.control.TextBox
```

The `findClass()` method locates a named class by using the context class loader for the thread from which it is invoked and returns the corresponding `FXClassType` object. This means that you can get the class information for any class that your JavaFX application could load. If the named class cannot be located, a `java.lang.ClassNotFoundException` is thrown.

The `getName()` method of `FXClassType` returns the full name of the class that it describes.

Getting Superclass Information

You can discover the classes from which a given class is derived and the Java interfaces that it implements by calling the `getSuperClasses()` method, which has the following signature[1]:

```
public List<FXClassType> getSuperClasses(boolean all)
```

---

[1] JavaFX reflection is actually implemented in Java, so the API that you'll see in this chapter uses Java syntax.

Context and Classes

For example, we'll use this method to get the superclasses of the `TextBox` class, the actual class hierarchy of which is shown in Figure 13-1.

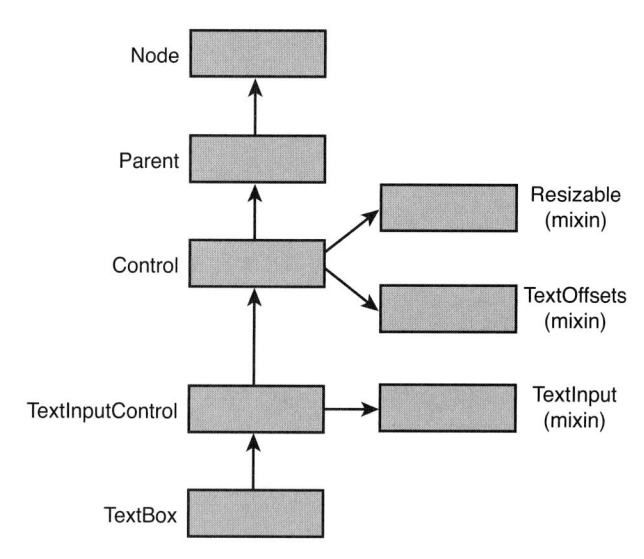

Figure 13-1 Class hierarchy for `javafx.scene.control.TextBox`

If called with argument `false`, the `getSuperClasses()` method returns a list containing a single `FXClassType` object that represents the immediate superclass of the target class:

```
var supers = textBoxClass.getSuperClasses(false); //Immediate superclass
println("Superclasses: ");
for (s in supers) {
    println(s.getName());
}
```

The preceding code prints the name of the immediate superclass of `TextBox`:

`javafx.scene.control.TextInputControl`

Calling this method with argument `true` causes all the superclasses of the `TextBox` class to be returned:

```
var supers = textBoxClass.getSuperClasses(true); // All superclasses
println("Superclasses: ");
for (s in supers) {
    println(s.getName());
}
```

Chapter 13 Reflection

Here's the result of running the preceding modified code:

```
com.sun.javafx.runtime.FXBase
java.lang.Object
javafx.scene.Node
javafx.scene.Parent
javafx.scene.control.Control
javafx.scene.control.TextBox
javafx.scene.control.TextInputControl
javafx.scene.input.TextInput
javafx.scene.layout.Resizable
javafx.scene.text.TextOffsets
```

If you compare this list with Figure 13-1, you'll see that the list is not ordered according to the class hierarchy—it is, in fact, alphabetical by package and then by class within package. Notice also that, perhaps surprisingly, the `TextBox` class itself appears in this list.

When a class implements Java interfaces, an `FXClassType` object for each of those interfaces is included in the superclass information. The following code declares a JavaFX class called `MyDate` that is a (trivial) subclass of the Java class `java.util.Date` and then gets and prints its superclass information:

```
class MyDate extends java.util.Date {
}

var myDateClass = ctx.findClass("javafxreflection.ReflectClass.MyDate");
supers = myDateClass.getSuperClasses(true);
println("MyDate superclasses: ");
for (s in supers) {
    println(s.getName());
}
```

This class definition appears in the file `javafxreflection/ReflectClass.fx` in the JavaFX Book Desktop project, which means that `MyDate` is not the script class for that file. As you saw in Chapter 11, "JavaFX Script Classes," the fully qualified name of this class is actually `javafxreflection.ReflectClass.MyDate`, so this is the name that must be passed to `findClass()` to get its `FXClassType` object. The output from this code is as follows:

```
MyDate superclasses:
java.io.Serializable
java.lang.Cloneable
java.lang.Comparable
java.lang.Object
java.util.Date
javafxreflection.ReflectClass.MyDate
```

As you can see, this list includes the complete class hierarchy from `java.lang.Object` through `java.util.Date` to `MyDate` itself. It also contains the interfaces that are implemented by `MyDate`, which are inherited from `java.util.Date`—namely `Serializable`, `Cloneable`, and `Comparable`. Because JavaFX does not have the separate concept of an interface, the `FXClassType` object does not have a property that distinguishes between classes and interfaces.

Other Class Information

In addition to a list of superclasses, you can use the `FXClassType` object for a class to get the following information:

- Reflective information for a named function or variable
- A list of all class members—that is, the functions and variables that it declares
- A list of all member variables (script and instance)
- A list of all member functions (script and instance)
- A subset of the member variables, selected using an application-supplied filter
- A subset of the member functions, selected using an application-supplied filter

You'll see in later sections how to get and use this information. The `FXClassType` class also has a number of other methods that we briefly discuss here.

`isJfxType()`

The `isJfxType()` method returns `true` if the `FXClassType` object represents a JavaFX class and `false` if it represents a Java class or interface:

```
var textBoxClass = ctx.findClass("javafx.scene.control.TextBox");
println("TextBox isJfxType(): {textBoxClass.isJfxType()}"); // true
var dateClass = ctx.findClass("java.util.Date");
println("Date is isJfxType(): {dateClass.isJfxType()}");    // false
```

`isMixin()`

The `isMixin()` method returns `true` if the class represented by the `FXClassType` object is a mixin (see Chapter 12, "Platform APIs").

`isAssignableFrom()`

The `isAssignableFrom()` method accepts an argument of type `FXClassType` and returns `true` if an instance of the class passed to it could be assigned to the class on which the method is invoked. For example

```
1    var controlClass = ctx.findClass("javafx.scene.control.Control");
2    var textBoxClass = ctx.findClass("javafx.scene.control.TextBox");
3    var myDateClass =
4            ctx.findClass("javafxreflection.ReflectClass.MyDate");
5
6    // Next line prints "true"
7    println("{controlClass.isAssignableFrom(textBoxClass)}");
8
9    // Next line prints "false"
10   println("{controlClass.isAssignableFrom(myDateClass)}");
```

Because `TextBox` is a subclass of `Control`, an instance of `TextBox` could be assigned to a variable of type `Control`, like this:

```
var c:Control = TextBox {}; // Legal assignment
```

Therefore, the call to `isAssignableFrom()` on line 7 returns `true`. By contrast, `MyDate` is not a subclass of `Control`, so the assignment in the following line of code is not legal, and as a result the code on line 10 returns `false`:

```
var c:Control = MyDate {};   // Illegal assignment.
```

Types and Values

Once you have an `FXClassType` object, you can use it to discover the variables and functions that the class declares. You'll see how to do that in the section "Variables and Functions," later in this chapter, but before we get to that, we need to take a look at how the Reflection API represents types and values.

Representation of Types

Types are represented by a set of classes that are derived from `javafx.reflect.FXType`. The class hierarchy for these classes, which are discussed in the sections that follow, is shown in Figure 13-2.

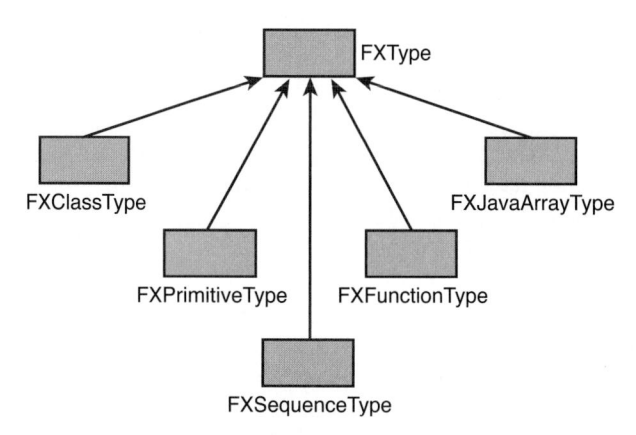

Figure 13-2   The representation of types in the JavaFX Reflection API

FXType

`FXType` is the abstract base class for all the other type classes. It has a `name` variable, which is used by some, but not all, of its subclasses—as you'll see in the sections that follow, in the case of types that do not have a meaningful name, such as function types, this variable has the value `null`.

FXPrimitiveType

The `FXPrimitiveType` class represents the built-in JavaFX types and the pseudo-type `Void`. There is a different instance of this class for each of the different types, which can be retrieved by calling the corresponding methods of the `FXContext` class, as listed in Table 13-1. The table also shows the value of the `name` property for each of these objects.

Table 13-1 **FXContext** Methods Used to Retrieve FXPrimitiveType Instances

JavaFX Type	Method	Name Property
Boolean	getBooleanType()	Boolean
Byte	getByteType()	Byte
Character	getCharacterType()	Character
Double	getDoubleType()	Double
Float	getFloatType()	Float
Integer	getIntegerType();	Integer
Long	getLongType()	Long
Number	getNumberType()	Float
Short	getShortType()	Short
Void	getVoidType()	Void

Note that the `FXPrimitiveType` instance for the `Number` type is the same as the one for `Float`.

Here's how you would get the `FXPrimitiveType` object for a JavaFX `Integer`:

`var intType:FXPrimitiveType = FXContext.getInstance().getIntegerType();`

Note that the `String` and `Duration` types do not have `FXPrimitiveType` instances. Instead, they are treated as classes and are represented by an instance of the `FXClassType` class, which you can get by using the `findClass()` method of `FXContext`:

`var stringType = ctx.findClass("java.lang.String");`
`var durationType = ctx.findClass("javafx.lang.Duration");`

The `FXClassType` object for `String` can also be obtained by invoking the `getStringType()` method of `FXContext`:

`var stringType = ctx.getStringType();`

FXClassType

An `FXClassType` object represents a JavaFX class. You have already seen some of the API provided by this class. The remaining functions, which allow you to retrieve information on the variables and functions that the class declares, are discussed in the "Variables and Functions" section, later in this chapter.

FXSequenceType

The `FXSequenceType` class represents a JavaFX sequence, like this one:

```
var seq:Number[] = [1.0, 2.0, 3.0];
```

The `FXSequenceType` object for this sequence provides the information that corresponds to the part of the code that is shown in bold. The fact that the variable `seq` is a sequence is revealed by the fact that its type object is an `FXSequenceType`, and the fact that it is a sequence of numbers can be found by calling the `getComponentType()` function of the `FXSequenceType` object:

```
public FXType getComponentType();
```

The return value is the type of the sequence's elements, in this case an `FXPrimitiveType` object that is equal to the one returned by the `getNumberType()` function of `FXContext`.

The `name` property of an `FXSequenceType` object is `null`. This property is *not* the name of the variable shown in the preceding code because an `FXType` object represents an abstract type, *not* an instance of a variable of that type. An actual variable is represented by an instance of the `FXVarMember` class, which is discussed in the "Reflecting on Variables" section. It is the `FXVarMember` object that holds the variable's name.

FXJavaArrayType

`FXJavaArrayType` is the same as `FXSequenceType`, except that it corresponds to a Java array (that is, a `nativearray` type). Like `FXSequenceType`, it has a `componentType` property that holds the type of the array members.

FXFunctionType

An `FXFunctionType` represents a family of functions with a particular signature, like the portion of the following code that is in bold font:

```
var fn:function(:Number, :String):Number;
```

A function type holds the number and types of the arguments and the type of the return value, all of which are represented by `FXType` objects. Given an `FXFunctionType` instance, you can get the return type by calling the `getReturnType()` method:

```
public FXType getReturnType()
```

A void function has as its return type the `FXPrimitiveType` object returned by the `getVoidType()` method of `FXContext`.

To get the types of a function's arguments from its `FXFunctionType` object, you first have to get the number of arguments and then invoke the `getArgumentType()` method with the index of each argument:

```
var count = functionType.minArgs();
```

```
for (i in [0..<count]) {
    println("Arg {i} type is {functionType.getArgumentType(i)}");
}
```

The method that returns the actual number of arguments has the slightly surprising name `minArgs()` because the API design allows for future support of the *varargs* feature introduced to Java in J2SE 5.0. For a variable argument function, the `minArgs()` method would return the number of arguments that appear before the optional arguments—in other words, the minimum number of arguments that could be used in an invocation of the function. Variable argument functions are not currently implemented.

Values

As you'll see in the "Variables and Functions" section, you can use reflection to get an `FXVarMember` object that refers to a script or instance variable. After you have an `FXVarMember` object, you can use its `getValue()` method to get the variable's actual value or its `setValue()` method to change it. Here are the declarations of these methods:

```
public FXValue getValue(FXObjectValue obj)
public void setValue(FXObjectValue obj, FXValue value);
```

The value read or being set is not supplied directly—instead, it is wrapped in an `FXValue` object. There are several `FXValue` subclasses that represent values of different types, as shown in Figure 13-3.

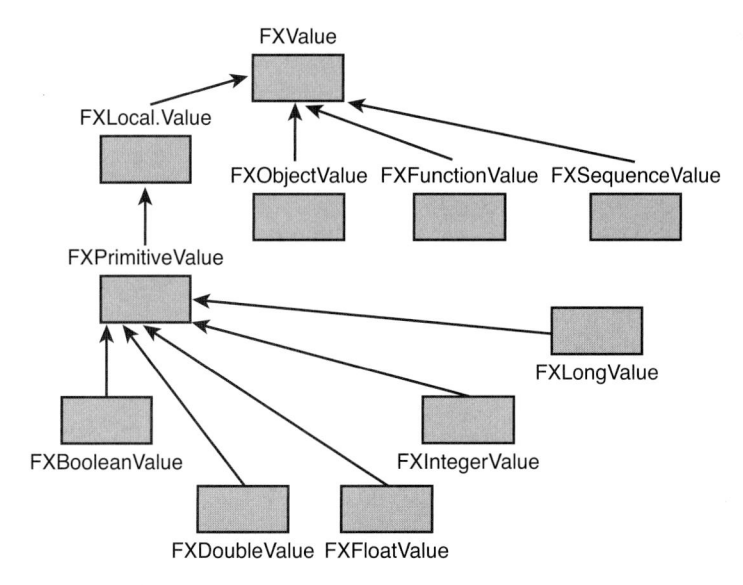

Figure 13-3 The representation of values in the JavaFX Reflection API

FXValue

The `FXValue` class itself does not hold a value. Instead, it provides methods that provide generic information about the value, which are overridden by subclasses. The actual method to be called to get the associated value is subclass-dependent, which means that you need to check the class type of an `FXValue` object and then cast it appropriately to get the value. No method allows the value to be changed—all `FXValue` objects are immutable, so the value is set only at construction time.

Table 13-2 describes the methods of the `FXValue` class.

Table 13-2   **The Methods of the `FXValue` Class**

Method	Description
`public FXType getType()`	Gets the `FXType` object for this value.
`public boolean isNull();`	Returns whether the value is `null`. What this actually means depends on the concrete value type. In the case of the `FXPrimitiveValue` subclasses and `FXFunctionValue`, always returns `false`. For `FXObjectValue`, returns whether the associated object reference is `null`. For `FXSequenceValue`, returns `true` if the sequence is empty.
`public int getItemCount()`	Gets the number of items in the associated value. If `isNull()` returns `true`, this returns `0`. Otherwise, for a sequence, it returns the number of elements in the sequence, and for the other types, it returns `1` because there is only one associated value.
`public FXValue getItem(int index)`	Gets the associated value with the given index. The index must be in the range `0` to `getItemCount() - 1`. This is typically used to access the elements of a sequence.
`public String getValueString()`	Returns a string representation of the value, which is subclass-dependent.

`FXPrimitiveValue` and Subclasses

As the name suggests, the subclasses of `FXPrimitiveValue` hold JavaFX primitive values. There are no subclasses corresponding to `Byte`, `Character`, and `Short` values—these values are always mapped to `FXIntegerValue` instead, while a `Number` value is represented by `FXFloatValue`. The actual wrapped value can be obtained from the methods listed in Table 13-3.

Table 13-3   **Obtaining the Value from an `FXPrimitiveValue` Object**

Class	Methods
`FXBooleanValue`	`public boolean booleanValue()`
	`public Object asObject()` (returns a `java.lang.Boolean`)
`FXDoubleValue`	`public double doubleValue()`
	`public Object asObject()` (returns a `java.lang.Double`)

Table 13-3 Obtaining the Value from an `FXPrimitiveValue` Object (*Continued*)

Class	Methods
FXFloatValue	`public float floatValue()`
	`public Object asObject()` (returns a `java.lang.Float`)
FXIntegerValue	`public int intValue()`
	`public Object asObject()` (returns a `java.lang.Integer`, a `java.lang.Byte`, or a `java.lang.Short`)
FXLongValue	`public long longValue()`
	`public Object asObject()` (returns a `java.lang.Long`)

`FXPrimitiveValue` is itself derived from `FXLocal.Value`, which represents a value held in the local Java Virtual Machine (JVM). The distinction between local and nonlocal values is relevant only when reflecting on objects in a remote JVM, which is not currently supported.

`FXObjectValue`

`FXObjectValue` is the wrapper for all object references, including the JavaFX types `String` and `Duration`. This class has methods that allow you to invoke the functions of the wrapped object, which we cover in the "Using Reflection" section, later in this chapter. It does *not* have a method that allows you to retrieve the wrapped value. Although this might seem strange (and inconvenient), there is a good reason for it.

The JavaFX Reflection APIs are designed to allow you to write code that can manipulate objects either in the same JVM as your code or in a remote JVM. To retrieve the value represented by an `FXObjectValue` instance, it would be necessary to load and initialize an instance of that object's class. If that object is in the same JVM as your code, the class file is available, so it is possible to create an instance. If the object were in a remote JVM (which, as noted earlier, is not currently supported), there would be no guarantee that the required class file is available to your code, so the default assumption is that the class could not be loaded. You would still be able to get the values of a remote object's variables or invoke its functions by using the Reflection API, as described in the "Variables and Functions."

In the case that your code is running in the same JVM as the object for which you have an `FXObjectValue`, it *is* possible to get the wrapped object, because in this case, the `FXObjectValue` objects that you get are actually instances of a subclass called `FXLocal.ObjectValue`, and this class has a method called `asObject()` that will return the wrapped value:

```
var objectValue:FXObjectValue = ..... // Get an FXObjectValue
var object = (objectValue as FXLocal.ObjectValue).asObject();
```

You'll see some examples that use this method later in this chapter.

FXFunctionValue

The `FXFunctionValue` class represents an executable function, which could be a script function, an instance function, or an anonymous function. In the example shown here, the code that is highlighted in bold is the part that would be represented by an `FXFunctionValue`.

```
var fn = function(arg1:Integer, arg2:Integer):Integer {
         arg1 + arg2;
       };
println(fn(1, 2));
```

Once you have an `FXFunctionValue` object for a function, you can use its `apply()` method to invoke the function with given argument values and retrieve the return value, as described in the "Invoking Functions" section, later in this chapter.

FXSequenceValue

`FXSequenceValue` is a wrapper for a JavaFX sequence. The `getItemCount()` method returns the number of items in the sequence. To retrieve individual elements, call the `getItem()` method with the index of the element that you want. See the "Creating and Accessing Sequences" section, later in this chapter, for the details.

Variables and Functions

As you have just seen, the `FXType` and `FXValue` classes represent, respectively, the types and values of variables and functions in the JavaFX Reflection API. To make use of them, you need to get a reference to a real variable or function.

Variables and functions are members of JavaFX classes. This applies even to those variables and functions that appear outside of a class definition, which are actually members of the script class (that is, the class whose name is the same as that of the script). A class member is represented by the class `FXMember`, which has subclasses `FXVarMember`, which represents a member variable, and `FXFunctionMember`, which represents a member function, as shown in Figure 13-4.

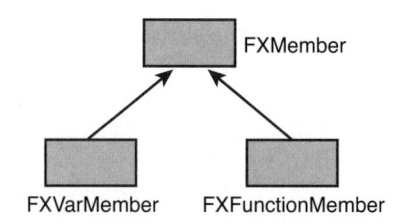

Figure 13-4 **FXMember** and its subclasses

The `FXMember` class has three methods, listed in Table 13-4, that return information common to both variable and function members.

Table 13-4 **Methods of the `FXMember` Class**

Method	Description
`public FXClassType getDeclaringClass()`	Returns the `FXClassType` object for the class that owns this member
`public String getName()`	Returns the variable or function name
`public Boolean isStatic()`	Returns `true` for a script variable (which is implemented as a static member of a Java class), `false` for a script variable

In the sections that follow, we'll use the code in Listing 13-1 to illustrate how to discover the variables and functions of a class.

Listing 13-1 **Reflection Example**

```
1      package javafxreflection;
2
3      public var scriptVar = "A script variable";
4      public function add(arg1:Integer, arg2:Integer):Integer {
5          arg1 + arg2
6      }
7      public var aFunction = add;
8
9      public class FunctionsAndVariables {
10         public var instanceVar = 0;
11
12         public function multiply(arg1:Number, arg2:Number):Number {
13             arg1 * arg2
14         }
15
16         public function multiply(arg1:Integer, arg2:Integer):Integer {
17             arg1 * arg2;
18         }
19
20         public function sayHello():Void {
21             println("Hello");
22         }
23
24         public function say(what:String):Void {
25             println(what);
26         }
27     }
```

This code is in a file called `javafxreflection/FunctionsAndVariables.fx` in the JavaFX Book Desktop project. Notice that it contains a script variable called `scriptVar`, a declaration of a function called `add()`, a function variable called `aFunction`, and a declaration of a class called `FunctionsAndVariables`. We'll make use of all these elements in the sections that follow.

Reflecting on Variables

Reflective access to a variable is provided by the `FXVarMember` class. To discover the variables of a class, you first need to get its `FXClassType` object, which, as you have already seen, is obtained from the `FXContext`:

```
var ctx = FXContext.getInstance();
var classType = ctx.findClass("javafxreflection.FunctionsAndVariables");
```

After you have the `FXClassType` object for a class, you can use it to get reflective information for a specific variable of that class or for all of its variables.

Getting a Named Variable

The `getVariable()` method of `FXClassType` returns the `FXVarMember` object for a named variable of that class. The following code gets the `FXVarMember` object for the script variable called `scriptVar`, declared on line 3 of Listing 13-1:

```
var scriptVarMember = classType.getVariable("scriptVar");
println("scriptVar name: {scriptVarMember.getName()}");
println("   script variable? {scriptVarMember.isStatic()}");
```

The output from this code is as follows:

```
scriptVar name: scriptVar
   script variable? True
```

You can get the `FXVarMember` object for the instance variable `instanceVar` declared on line of Listing 13-1 in exactly the same way:

```
var instanceVarMember = classType.getVariable("instanceVar");
println("instanceVar name: {instanceVarMember.getName()}");
println("   script variable? {instanceVarMember.isStatic()}");
```

This code produces the following result:

```
instanceVar name: instanceVar
   script variable? false
```

In both of these examples, the variable is declared by the actual class whose `FXClassType` object is being used. The `getVariable()` method will also return information for variables that are declared in any of the superclasses of that class. If the `getVariable()` function is invoked with the name of a variable that is not declared in the target class or any of its subclasses, it returns `null`.

The `FXVarMember` class provides functions that allow you get and set the value of the variable (see the section "Reading and Setting Variable Values"), and the method `getType()` that returns the type of the variable as an `FXType` object. Here's how you get and print the declared type of the variable `instanceVar`:

```
println("instanceVar type: {instanceVarMember.getType().getName()}");
```

This code prints the following:

```
instanceVar type: Integer
```

Getting All Variables of a Class

The `getVariables()` function returns a list containing one `FXVarMember` object for each of the variables of a class:

```
public java.util.List getVariables(boolean all)
```

If called with argument `false`, only those variables declared by the class itself are returned. To get a list of the variables declared by the class *and* all of its superclasses, call the function with argument `true`. The following code retrieves the `FXVarMember` objects for all the variables of the `FunctionsAndVariables` class declared on lines 9 to 27 of Listing 13-1 and prints the results:

```
var variables = classType.getVariables(false);
for (varMember in variables) {
    println("Variable name: {varMember.getName()}");
    println("   script variable? {varMember.isStatic()}");
    println("   variable type: {varMember.getType().getName()}");
}
```

Here's the output:

```
Variable name: instanceVar
   script variable? false
   variable type: Integer
Variable name: scriptVar
   script variable? true
   variable type: java.lang.String
```

Reflecting on Functions

As is the case with variables, `FXClassType` has methods that let you get information either for a single member function or for all the member functions of a JavaFX class. A function member is described by an `FXFunctionMember` object, which provides methods that allow you to call the function with specific arguments (see "Invoking Functions" later in this chapter) and the `getType()` method, which returns the function's type. Although the return value of the `getType()` method is formally declared as `FXType`, it is actually of type `FXFunctionType`.

Getting a Specific Member Function

The `getFunction()` method of `FXClassType` returns information about a specific instance or script function in the target class or in any of its superclasses:

```
public FXFunctionMember getFunction(String name, FXType[] argTypes)
```

The `argTypes` argument specifies the types of the function's arguments, in the order in which they appear. If the function does not have any arguments, the `argTypes` argument can be omitted. The following code gets the `FXFunctionMember` object for the `sayHello()` function declared on line 20 of Listing 13-1. Because this function has no arguments, we do not supply any argument types to the `getFunction()` method:

```
var helloFnMember = classType.getFunction("sayHello");
println("Function name: {helloFnMember.getName()}");
println("   script function? {helloFnMember.isStatic()}");
println("   function type: {helloFnMember.getType()}");
```

The output is as follows:

```
Function name: sayHello
   script function? false
   function type: function():Void
```

When the target function has arguments, a sequence containing the corresponding `FXType` objects, in the correct order, is required. The following code gets the reflective information for the variant of the `multiply()` function declared on line 16 of Listing 13-1 that accepts a pair of `Integer` types:

```
var integerType = ctx.getIntegerType();
var intMultMember = classType.getFunction("multiply",
                                          [integerType, integerType]);
println("Function name: {intMultMember.getName()}");
println("   script function? {intMultMember.isStatic()}");
println("   function type: {intMultMember.getType()}");
```

Note that we use the `getIntegerType()` method of `FXContext` to get the `FXType` object for an `Integer` (recall that this is actually an instance of `FXPrimitiveType`), which is required for the argument list passed to the `getFunction()` method. To get an `FXFunctionMember` object for the version of the `multiply()` function that has arguments of type `Number`, you just need to change the `FXType` values in the argument list:

```
var numberType = ctx.getNumberType();
var numberMultMember = classType.getFunction("multiply",
                                             [numberType, numberType]);
println("Function name: {numberMultMember.getName()}");
println("   script function? {numberMultMember.isStatic()}");
println("   function type: {numberMultMember.getType()}");
```

Here's the output from these two blocks of code, showing that information for the correct functions has been returned in each case:

```
Function name: multiply
    script function? false
    function type: function(Integer,Integer):Integer
Function name: multiply
    script function? false
    function type: function(Float,Float):Float
```

Note that the `Float` type appears in place of `Number` in the last line of output, because this is the internal representation of the `Number` type.

As another example, this code gets the `FXFunctionMember` object for the `say()` function declared on line 24 of Listing 13-1, which requires a single argument of type `String`:

```
var stringType = ctx.getStringType()
var whatMember = classType.getFunction("say", stringType);
println("Function name: {whatMember.getName()}");
println("   script function? {whatMember.isStatic()}");
println("   function type: {whatMember.getType()}");
```

Getting All Member Functions

The `getFunctions()` method of `FXClassType` returns an `FXFunctionMember` object for each function in that class:

```
public java.util.List getFunctions(boolean all);
```

As with the `getVariables()` method, this method either returns only the functions declared in the class itself (argument `false`) or those of the class and its superclasses (argument `true`). Here's an example that prints the functions declared by the `FunctionsAndVariables` class shown in Listing 13-1:

```
var functions = classType.getFunctions(false);
for (funcMember in functions) {
    println("Function name: {funcMember.getName()}");
    println("   script function? {funcMember.isStatic()}");
    println("   function type: {funcMember.getType()}");
}
```

The output looks like this:

```
Function name: add
    script function? true
    function type: function(Integer,Integer):Integer
Function name: multiply
    script function? false
    function type: function(Float,Float):Float
Function name: multiply
    script function? false
```

```
        function type: function(Integer,Integer):Integer
Function name: say
   script function? false
   function type: function(java.lang.String):Void
Function name: sayHello
   script function? false
   function type: function():Void
```

Filtered Searches

Sometimes, it is useful to be able to get a subset of the variables and functions in a class. It is possible to do this by creating an `FXMemberFilter` that selects only those items that you are interested in. The key to the `FXMemberFilter` class is the following method:

`public boolean accept(FXMember member)`

This method must be implemented to return `true` if the variable or function passed as its argument should be included in the filtered set of objects and `false` if it should not. The default implementation of this method allows the `FXMemberFilter` object to be configured so that it can be used to provide the same functionality as the search methods that you have already seen. To implement a custom search, you need to create your own filter (as either a Java or JavaFX class) that overrides this method.

Suppose, for example, that you want to write a filter that returns all methods in a class whose name starts with `mult`. This is exactly what an IDE would need to do to provide code completion in a JavaFX code editor. The code in Listing 13-2 is a JavaFX implementation of a filter that accepts only those functions passed to it for which the name begins with the value in its `match` variable.[2]

Listing 13-2   **A Filter That Accepts Functions Based on the Function Name**

```
1      class FunctionNameFilter extends FXMemberFilter {
2          public-init var match:String;
3
4          public override function accept(member:FXMember):Boolean {
5              if (not (member instanceof FXFunctionMember)) {
6                  return false;
7              }
8              return match == ""
9                      or member.getName().startsWith(match);
10         }
11     }
```

---

[2] You could make this example more interesting by accepting a regular expression instead of just the leading part of the name.

The interesting code in this example is in lines 4 through 10 of the `accept()` function. This function is called with every candidate member (variable or function) from a specific class. It immediately excludes variable members by testing the type of its `member` argument, and then checks whether the name of the function is acceptable and returns `true` if it is. As implemented here, setting the match property of this filter to the empty string has the effect of accepting all functions.

You use a filter by passing it to either of the following `FXClassType` functions:

```
public java.util.List getFunctions(FXMemberFilter filter, boolean all)
public java.util.List getVariables(FXMemberFilter filter, boolean all)
```

The argument `all` should be `false` if only the functions or variables of the class itself should be considered for a match, or `true` to allow the functions or variables of both the class and its superclasses to be included. Here's an example that shows how to use this filter to find all the functions in the class shown in Listing 13-1 whose names begin with `mult`.

```
var ctx = FXContext.getInstance();
var classType = ctx.findClass("javafxreflection.FunctionsAndVariables");
var filter = FunctionNameFilter { match: "mult" };
var matches = classType.getFunctions(filter, true);
for (matched in matches) {
    println("Matched: {matched.getName()}");
    println("   signature: {matched.getType()}");
}
```

The output from this code shows that the `FunctionsAndVariables` class has two such functions:

```
Matched: multiply
   signature: function(Integer,Integer):Integer
Matched: multiply
   signature: function(Number,Number):Number
```

Although this example filtered only on the function name, it is also possible to consider the number and types of the function's arguments. This information can be obtained from the `FXMember` object passed to the filter's `accept()` function.

Reflecting on Variables and Functions

In the previous two sections, you have seen how to get information on the variables and functions in a class. The APIs you have seen so far return *either* variable *or* function information. Sometimes, it is useful to be able to process all members of a class, both variables and functions. You can do this by using the `getMembers()` functions of `FXClassType`, which both return a list of `FXMember` objects:

```
public java.util.List getMembers(boolean all)
public java.util.List getMembers(FXMemberFilter filter, boolean all);
```

These methods are similar to the `getVariables()` and `getFunctions()` methods that you have already seen, so we won't discuss them any further here.

Using Reflection

Up to this point, you have seen how to get objects that represent JavaFX classes, variables, and functions and how to interpret the content of those objects. In this section, you'll see how to use them to create and manipulate instances of JavaFX classes at runtime.

Creating Class Instances: Part 1

The simplest way to reflectively create an instance of a JavaFX object is to use the `newInstance()` method of its `FXClassType` object:

```
public FXObjectValue newInstance()
```

The following code uses this technique to create a `TextBox` control:

```
1    var ctx = FXContext.getInstance();
2    var controlClassType =    ctx.findClass("javafx.scene.control.TextBox");
3    var objectValue = controlClassType.newInstance();
4    var localObjectValue = objectValue as FXLocal.ObjectValue;
5    var textBox = localObjectValue.asObject();
6    println("Control is {textBox}");
```

The `TextBox` is actually created on line 3. However, what is returned is not a `TextBox` but an `FXObjectValue` object that wraps the newly created `TextBox`. As you saw earlier in this chapter, `FXObjectValue` does not have a method that allows you to retrieve the `TextBox`, so we need to cast the `FXObjectValue` to `FXLocal.ObjectValue` and use its `asObject()` method instead.

The `newInstance()` method creates an object instance in which all the variables are set to the default values as defined in the class declaration. You can change the values of these variables by using functions that are covered in the next section. However, this is not quite the same as creating an object instance with an object literal, because values set in an object literal override the defaults, whereas creating an object and then changing the values of its variables causes the default values to be set first, followed by the new values. In the section "Creating Class Instances: Part 2," later in this chapter, you'll see how to create an instance of an object exactly as if it had been initialized from an object literal.

Reading and Setting Variable Values

To read or set the value of a variable, you need to get its `FXVarMember` object. Once you have this, you can then invoke one of these methods:

```
public FXValue getValue(FXObjectValue obj);
public void setValue(FXObjectValue obj, FXValue newValue);
```

The `FXVarMember` class describes either a script or instance variable of a class, but it is not linked to a specific instance of that class. To operate on an instance, you need to wrap it in an `FXObjectValue` and pass it to the `getValue()` or `setValue()` functions. Because a script variable is not linked to a particular instance of its owning class, you can use `null` for the object reference when reading or setting its value. In the sections that follow, we use the `FunctionsAndVariables` class in Listing 13-1 as the basis for the code examples that illustrate these methods.

Reading and Writing the Value of a Script Variable

We'll start by showing how to read the value of the script variable `scriptVar`. Here's some code that accomplishes this:

```
1       var classType =
2               ctx.findClass("javafxreflection.FunctionsAndVariables");
3       var scriptVarMember = classType.getVariable("scriptVar");
4       var value = scriptVarMember.getValue(null);
5       var actualValue = getActualValue(value);
6       println("Value of scriptVar is '{actualValue}'");
```

Lines 1 to 3 use the `getVariable()` method of `FXClassType` to get the `FXVarMember` object for the variable that we want to read. Line 4 actually reads the value. Because this is a script variable, we use `null` as the object reference when calling the `getValue()` method. The value is returned as an instance of `FXValue`. As you saw earlier, getting the wrapped value from the `FXValue` object is not a simple matter. Because this is a common operation, the required code can usefully be wrapped into a script function, which is called on line 5 of the preceding code. Here is the implementation of that function:

```
function getActualValue(value:FXValue):Object {
    var actualValue = null;
    if (value instanceof FXLocal.Value) {
        actualValue = (value as FXLocal.Value).asObject();
    }
    return actualValue;
}
```

This code works only if the value returned by `getValue()` is an instance of `FXLocal.Value`, which is true when local reflection is being used. Because local reflection is the only form of reflection currently implemented, this is a safe assumption for now.

Here's the code that writes a new value to the same script variable:

```
1       var newValue = "New Value";
2       var newObjectValue = (ctx as FXLocal.Context).mirrorOf(newValue);
3       scriptVarMember.setValue(null, newObjectValue);
```

The intent of this code is to assign the string `"New Value"` to the variable, but it is not possible to just pass the string itself—the `setValue()` method requires an `FXObjectValue`. There is no direct way to get an `FXObjectValue` from a string. Instead,

you have to assume that local reflection is in use and cast the `FXContext` reference to
`FXLocal.Context`, which is the subclass of `FXContext` that implements local reflection.
This class has a method called `mirrorOf()`, which can be used to convert an arbitrary
object to an `FXObjectValue`. With that done, you can use the `setValue()` method to
change the variable's value.

Reading and Writing the Value of an Instance Variable

The only difference between reading and writing the value of a script variable and that of
an instance variable is that the latter requires an `FXObjectValue` that wraps the target
object instance. The following code creates an instance of the `FunctionsAndVariables`
class and reads the value of the instance variable `instanceVar`:

```
1    var instance = FunctionsAndVariables {};
2    var instanceObjectValue =
3            (ctx as FXLocal.Context).mirrorOf(instance);
4    var instanceVarMember = classType.getVariable("instanceVar");
5    value = instanceVarMember.getValue(instanceObjectValue);
6    actualValue = getActualValue(value);
7    println("Value of instanceVar is '{actualValue}'");
```

Lines 2 and 3 use the `mirrorOf()` method of `FXLocal.Context` to convert the class
instance to an `FXObjectValue` so that it can be passed to the `getValue()` method of the
`FXVarMember` object for the target instance variable on line 4. The remainder of the code
converts the returned `FXType` object to the corresponding result value and prints it.

Setting the value of an instance variable follows the same pattern:

```
1    var newIntValue = ctx.mirrorOf(32);
2    instanceVarMember.setValue(instanceObjectValue, newIntValue);
```

In this case, we are setting the value of the `instanceVar` variable, which is an
`Integer`. We use the `mirrorOf()` method of `FXContext` to convert an integer to a suitable `FXValue`, and then supply that, together with the `FXObjectValue` object for the class
instance, to the `setValue()` method of the variable's `FXVarMember` object.

Invoking Functions

There are three ways to reflectively invoke either a script function or an instance function, and this section presents examples of all three.

Invoking a Function through a Function Variable

The class `FunctionsAndVariables` in Listing 13-1 includes a declaration of a function
variable called `aFunction`:

```
public function add(arg1:Integer, arg2:Integer):Integer {
    arg1 + arg2
}
public var aFunction = add;
```

If you were to get the `FXFunctionMember` for `aFunction` and then read its value, it would be an `FXFunctionValue` object referring to the `add()` function defined in the same class[3]:

```
var aFunctionMember = classType.getVariable("aFunction");
value = aFunctionMember.getValue(null);
println(value);
```

This code prints the following:

```
javafx.reflect.FXLocal$FunctionValue@edf389
```

The class `FXLocal.FunctionValue` is a subclass of `FXFunctionValue` that represents a function value when local reflection is in use. The `FXFunctionValue` class declares a method called `apply()` that lets you invoke the function with a given set of arguments:

```
public FXValue apply(FXValue[] args)
```

This method does not allow you to specify the object instance on which the function is to be invoked. That is because an `FXFunctionValue` has a built-in association with a particular instance. In this case, because the target function is a script function, it is not associated with any particular instance of its owning class.

We already know that this function requires two integer arguments and returns an integer value. If we didn't know that, we could get its `FXFunctionType` from the `FXFunctionValue` object and then examine the types of each of its arguments by calling the `getArgumentType()` method of `FXFunctionType`. To invoke the function, you need to create `FXValue` objects for its two integer arguments and then call the `apply()` method of `FXFunctionValue`:

```
1    var functionValue = value as FXFunctionValue;
2    var arg1 = ctx.mirrorOf(1);
3    var arg2 = ctx.mirrorOf(2);
4    value = functionValue.apply([arg1, arg2]);
5    actualValue = getActualValue(value);
6    println(
7        "Result of invoking add() via FXFunctionValue is {actual
     Value}");
```

On line 1, we cast the value obtained earlier from the `FXFunctionMember` object to `FXFunctionValue`. This is required because the declared return type of the `getValue()` method, and therefore the inferred type of the `value` variable is `FXValue`. The target function is invoked on line 4, and the `FXValue` that it returns is converted back to a usable value and printed on lines 5 to 7. The output from this code is as follows:

```
Result of invoking add() via FXFunctionValue is 3
```

---

[3] The `FXObjectValue` argument passed to the `getValue()` method in this code is `null` because `aFunction` is a script variable.

Invoking a Member Function

To invoke a member function, you first need to get its `FXFunctionMember` object. `FXFunctionMember` has a method that returns an `FXFunctionValue` that you can then use to invoke the method on a given instance of its owning class:

```
public FXFunctionValue asFunction(FXObjectValue targetInstance);
```

The following code demonstrates the process:

```
1    var integerType = ctx.getIntegerType();
2    var intMultMember =
3            classType.getFunction("multiply",
4                                  [integerType, integerType]);
5    objectValue = (ctx as FXLocal.Context).mirrorOf(instance);
6    functionValue = intMultMember.asFunction(objectValue);
7
8    arg1 = ctx.mirrorOf(2);
9    arg2 = ctx.mirrorOf(3);
10   value = functionValue.apply([arg1, arg2]);
11   actualValue = getActualValue(value);
12   println(
13       "Result of multiply() via FXFunctionMember is {actualValue}");
```

Lines 1 and 2 get the `FXFunctionMember` object for the instance function `multiply()` of the `FunctionsAndVariables` class shown in Listing 13-1. In this case, we want the variant that accepts two parameters of type `Integer`. Line 5 gets an `FXObjectValue` wrapping the instance of the `FunctionsAndVariables` class on which the function is to be invoked. Line 6 uses the `asFunction()` method of `FXFunctionMember` to get an `FXFunctionValue` object that can be used to call the `multiply()` function on the specified instance of the `FunctionsAndVariables` class. Note that in this step, if the `FXFunctionMember` represented a script function, you would pass a `null` instance reference to the `asFunction()` method.

The rest of the code is the same as that shown in the previous section to invoke a function represented by an `FXFunctionValue` object. The result of running this code is as follows:

```
Result of multiply() via FXFunctionMember is 6
```

Invoking a Function Given an `FXObjectValue`

In the code shown in the previous section, we obtained an `FXFunctionMember` for an instance function and applied it to a specific instance of its owning class to get an `FXFunctionValue` object, which was then used to invoke the function. To make this possible, the instance on which the function was to be called was converted to an `FXObjectValue`. `FXObjectValue` has two methods that simplify the task of reflectively invoking an instance function of the object that it refers to. The first of these is declared as follows:

```
public FXValue invoke(FXFunctionMember method, FXValue[] args);
```

Using Reflection

Using this method, we can rewrite the example shown in the last section like this:

```
1    var integerType = ctx.getIntegerType();
2    var intMultMember =
3        classType.getFunction("multiply", [integerType, integer    Type]);
4    objectValue = (ctx as FXLocal.Context).mirrorOf(instance);
5    value = objectValue.invoke(intMultMember,
6                               [ctx.mirrorOf(4), ctx.mirrorOf(5)]);
7    actualValue = getActualValue(value);
8    println("Result of multiply() via FXObjectValue         #1:{actualValue}");
```

Lines 1 through 4 are the same as the earlier example—they get the `FXFunctionMember` for the required function and create an `FXObjectValue` for the target object instance. The difference is on line 5. Instead of getting an `FXFunctionValue` from the `FXFunctionMember`, we just call the `invoke()` method of `FXObjectValue`, passing it the function to be called in the form of the `FXFunctionMember` object, together with the arguments to be passed to the function.

`FXObjectValue` has another variant of `invoke()` that makes it even easier to call an instance function:

```
public FXValue invoke(String name, FXValue[] args);
```

In this case, we supply only the name of the target function and the required arguments—the steps needed to get the `FXFunctionValue` are performed internally. Using this method, the preceding code can be rewritten like this:

```
1    objectValue = (ctx as FXLocal.Context).mirrorOf(instance);
2    value = objectValue.invoke("multiply",
3                               [ctx.mirrorOf(4), ctx.mirrorOf(5)]);
4    actualValue = getActualValue(value);
5    println("Result of multiply() via FXObjectValue #2: {actual
     Value}");
```

As you can see, this is much simpler than all the previous examples, because most of the work is done by the `invoke()` method itself. Note that the actual types of the arguments passed to the `invoke()` method, in this case two `Integers`, are used to choose between the two variants of the `multiply()` function in the `FunctionsAndVariables` class.

Creating and Accessing Sequences

This section describes how to use the Reflection APIs to retrieve values from a sequence and to create a new sequence with a given element type.

Accessing a Sequence

If you use the Reflection APIs to read a sequence variable or to invoke a function that returns a sequence, you will get a value of type `FXSequenceValue`. The following example declares a script variable that is a sequence of `Strings` in a class called

Chapter 13 Reflection

`SequenceReflection` and then gets an `FXSequenceValue` that refers to the content of that variable.

```
// Declare a sequence
var sequence = ["A", "B", "C", "D"];

// Get the value of the sequence.
var ctx = FXContext.getInstance();
var classType = ctx.findClass("javafxreflection.SequenceReflection");
var sequenceMember = classType.getVariable("sequence");
var value = sequenceMember.getValue(null);
var seqValue = value as FXSequenceValue;
```

You can get the type of the sequence from the `getType()` method of `FXSequenceValue`. The actual type returned by this method is `FXSequenceType`, which provides a method called `getComponentType()` that returns the type of the elements in the sequence:

```
// Get the sequence type
var seqType = seqValue.getType() as FXSequenceType;
var elementType = seqType.getComponentType();
println("Sequence type is {seqType}");
println("Element type is {elementType}");
```

The result is the following:

```
Sequence type is java.lang.String[]
Element type is class java.lang.String
```

To get the individual elements, you first call the `getItemCount()` method of the `FXSequenceValue` object and then call `getItem()` to retrieve each element as an `FXValue`.:

```
// Get and print the elements
println("Number of elements: {seqValue.getItemCount()}");
for (i in [0..<seqValue.getItemCount()]) {
    var elementValue = seqValue.getItem(i);
    var actualValue = getActualValue(elementValue);
    println("   Element {i}: {actualValue}");
}
```

The preceding code retrieves all the elements in the order in which they appear in the sequence:

```
Number of elements: 4
   Element 0: A
   Element 1: B
   Element 2: C
   Element 3: D
```

Creating a Sequence

The `FXContext` class provides two methods that enable you to dynamically construct sequences. One of these constructs the sequence in a single step, while the other returns a class that has methods that allow you to construct a sequence piece by piece.[4]

The `makeSequence()` method constructs a sequence from a set of values and an element type:

```
public FXValue makeSequence(FXType elementType, FXValue[] values)
```

Here's an example that creates and initializes a sequence of `Integer` types:

```
var intType = ctx.getIntegerType();
var values:FXValue[] =
                [ctx.mirrorOf(1), ctx.mirrorOf(2), ctx.mirrorOf(3)];
value = ctx.makeSequence(intType, values);
```

This code is equivalent to the following explicit declaration:

```
var seq:Integer[] = [1, 2, 3];
```

The elements provided can themselves be `FXSequenceValues`, in which case the elements of the nested sequence are flattened into the one being created, or `null`. A `null` entry is effectively ignored (or, if you prefer, treated as an empty nested sequence), so the following code creates the same sequence as that shown previously:

```
var intType = ctx.getIntegerType();
var values:FXValue[] =
    [ctx.mirrorOf(1), ctx.mirrorOf(2), null as FXType, ctx.mirrorOf(3)];
value = ctx.makeSequence(intType, values);
```

It does not make much sense to use the `makeSequence()` method in a JavaFX application because it requires a sequence as its input simply returns a copy of that sequence. This method *is* useful if you want to construct a JavaFX sequence from Java code, because in that case you would supply a Java array containing the values that will make up the sequence.

An alternative approach that does not involve the use of an existing sequence is provided by the `makeSequenceBuilder()` method:

```
public FXSequenceBuilder makeSequenceBuilder(FXType elementType)
```

`FXSequenceBuilder` is a class in the `javafx.reflect` package that lets you build a sequence by adding individual values. At the end, you use its `getSequence()` method to

---

[4] There is also a third method, `makeSequenceValue()`, which is not covered here because it doesn't add anything useful to the functionality provide by `makeSequence()`.

get the completed sequence. Here's an example that illustrates the use of this class to construct the same sequence of three integer values as in the preceding one:

```
var builder = ctx.makeSequenceBuilder(intType);
builder.append(ctx.mirrorOf(1));
builder.append(ctx.mirrorOf(2));
builder.append(ctx.mirrorOf(3));
value = builder.getSequence();
```

All the values passed to the `append()` method must be assignable to the element type of the sequence. If any of them is not, a `ClassCastException` is thrown. It is legal to call the `append()` method with an argument that is an `FXSequenceValue`, provided that its element type is compatible with that of the sequence being constructed. The effect is to flatten the supplied sequence into the new one. It is not legal to call the `append()` method with a `null` argument.

The `getSequence()` method returns an `FXValue`, which is actually an `FXSequenceValue`. Its component type is the one supplied to the `makeSequenceBuilder()` method, and its elements are the ones supplied by the `append()` calls, in the order in which they were added. After the `getSequence()` method has been called, attempts to add more elements will result in an `IllegalStateException`. Only the first call to `getSequence()` will return a useful value; subsequent calls return `null`.

Creating Class Instances: Part 2

In "Creating Class Instances: Part 1," you saw that you can use the `newInstance()` method of an `FXClassType` object to create an instance of that object in which all the instance variables are set to their defaults. If you want to use this method to create an object in which the instance variables have different values, you have to do it in two steps. For example, consider the following class:

```
public class TestObject {
    public-init var value = 10 on replace {
                        println("Trigger: value set to {value}");
                      };
}
```

To reflectively create an instance of this class using the `newInstance()` method but with the variable `value` set to 20, you must do this:

```
var objectValue = classType.newInstance();
var valueVarMember = classType.getVariable("value");
valueVarMember.setValue(objectValue, ctx.mirrorOf(20));
```

Although this works, it is not the same as using the following object literal:

```
TestObject {
    value: 20
}
```

The difference is that the object literal would just assign the value 20 instead of the default, whereas the code shown above assigns first the default value (10), and then the required value (20), as the output from the trigger associated with the `value` variable shows:

```
Trigger: value set to 10
Trigger: value set to 20
```

Although this makes no real difference in this case, for some objects it may be important to assign the correct default value. Fortunately, there is a way to do this. You have to first allocate the object, then set the values of variables, and then complete object initialization. The following code illustrates how to do this:

```
objectValue = classType.allocate();
objectValue.initVar("value", ctx.mirrorOf(20));
objectValue.initialize();
```

The `allocate()` method of `FXClassType` creates an uninitialized instance of the object and returns it as an `FXObjectValue`. The `initVar()` method of `FXObjectValue` sets the *initial* value of the named variable, and finally, the `initialize()` method completes the object initialization process, causing the `init` and `postinit` blocks of the class to be run, as usual. The trigger output shows that the default value of 10 was never assigned to the `value` variable:

```
Trigger: value set to 20
```

Note that `initVar()` can be invoked only before the `initialize()` method is called.

III

User Interfaces with JavaFX

14

User Interface Basics

As you saw in Chapter 4, "A Simple JavaFX Application," the starting point for building user interfaces in JavaFX is the `javafx.stage.Stage` class, which acts as a link between your application and the component that is used as the top-level container of the application when it is executed. The nature of the top-level container depends on the environment in which the application is running: On the desktop, it is a frame; in a browser, it is an applet; on a cell phone, it is a MIDlet; and on a TV device, it is an Xlet. These four containers have different application programming interfaces (APIs), so if you were writing a graphical user interface (GUI) application in Java, your code would be at least partly dependent on the container being used. By contrast, in JavaFX, your application only needs to know about the variables and functions provided by the `Stage` class, because the JavaFX runtime is responsible for creating and managing the top-level container that is appropriate for your actual execution environment.

The user interface itself is built using *nodes*—instances of the `javafx.scene.Node` class—arranged within a *scene*, implemented by the class `javafx.scene.Scene`. The `Scene` and `Stage` classes are discussed in the first part of this chapter.

There are several different types of node, ranging from simple shapes like rectangles and circles, to more complex controls that include Swing components (which are only available on the desktop) and a media viewer that lets you play music and video. You'll find an overview of the `Node` class in the second part of this chapter, but the details are deferred to the next chapter and the three that follow it. You can also create custom nodes that provide functionality that is not available in the JavaFX software development kit (SDK). You'll see some examples of this in Chapter 25, "Building Custom Controls."

Unlike the JavaFX language, which is the same on all platforms, some parts of the GUI libraries are only available in the desktop profile. Where this is the case, the text makes this clear.

You'll find the source code for the examples in this chapter in the package `javafxuibasics` in the JavaFX Book GUI project.

The `Stage` Class

The stage is the top-level object in a JavaFX application. Many applications require only a single stage, although it is possible, at least on the desktop, to have more than one. Not all the features of the stage are meaningful in every possible execution environment. For example, the icon that appears in the title bar of the window that hosts the application on the desktop has no equivalent on a cell phone.

Stage Appearance and State

The stage has four variables that either affect its appearance or reflect its active state, as listed in Table 14-1.[1]

The code in Listing 14-1 illustrates the use of these variables. We discuss each of them in the sections that follow. You find this code in the file `javafxuibasics/StageAppearance.fx`.

Table 14-1 Variables That Determine the Appearance of the Stage

Variable	Type	Access	Default	Description
contains-Focus	Boolean	R	(None)	Whether the stage is focused
icons	Image[]	RW	Empty	The icons used in the title bar of the top-level container
title	String	RW	Empty string	The title used in the title bar of the top-level container
visible	Boolean	RW	true	The visibility of the stage

Listing 14-1 Illustrating Stage Appearance and State

```
1    package javafxuibasics;
2
3    import javafx.scene.image.Image;
4    import javafx.stage.Stage;
5
6    var stage:Stage = Stage {
7        title: bind "Stage: ({stage.x}, {stage.y})"
8        icons: [
9            Image { url: "{__DIR__}frame_icon_16.png" },
10           Image { url: "{__DIR__}frame_icon_24.png" },
```

---

[1] For the meanings of the abbreviations in the Access column of this table and the others like it in this book, refer to the Preface.

```
11              Image { url: "{__DIR__}frame_icon_32.png" },
12          ]
13          width: 250
14          height: 100
15      }
16      var containsFocus = bind stage.containsFocus on replace {
17          println("Stage contains focus? {containsFocus}");
18      }
19      var visible = bind stage.visible on replace {
20          println("Stage visible? {visible}");
21      }
```

Title

The title variable is a string that appears in the window decorations of the top-level container created from the stage. This variable is usually set when the stage is created and then left unchanged, but it is possible to modify it later, if required. In Listing 14-1, the text assigned to this variable on line 7 is bound to the x and y coordinates of the stage. If you run this example as a desktop application and then drag the window around the screen, you notice that the window title changes as it moves, as shown in Figure 14-1.

Icons

The value of this variable is a sequence of Image objects from which the JavaFX GUI runtime will select a suitable element to use as the icon in the application's top-level container, which we refer to here as the *window icon*. The optimum size for the window icon varies from platform to platform. On Windows, for example, it is best to provide an image that is 16 pixels square. Where more than one image is given, the one that most closely matches the best size for the host platform will be selected. If none of the images is the correct size, one will be chosen and scaled to the best size. You will usually get a better result if you supply an image of the correct size and do not allow the window icon to be created by scaling.

The code on lines 8 to 12 of Listing 14-1 supplies three images, loaded from the same location as the script file itself by the Image class, which is discussed in Chapter 16, "Shapes, Text, and Images." These images are respectively 16×16, 24×24, and 32×32 pixels in size.

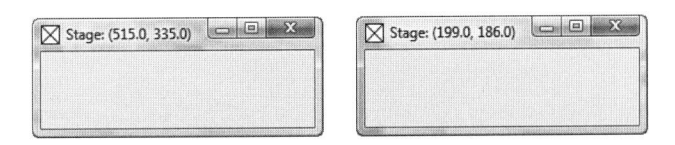

Figure 14-1   The title and icons variables of the **Stage** class

The window icon is also used in the iconified representation of the stage on the taskbar, and it appears in the Windows task switcher, which you can open by clicking Alt-Tab. On the left of Figure 14-2, you can see that the window icon used in the Windows taskbar is 16×16 pixels, while the one that appears in the Windows task switcher, shown on the right of the figure, is 32×32 pixels.

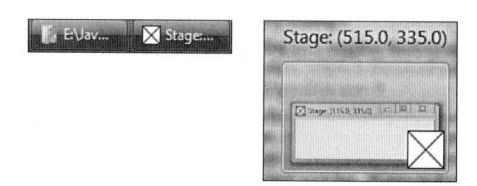

Figure 14-2   Icons on the Windows platform

If you don't set the `icons` variable, a default image is used.

Visibility

When read, the `visible` variable reflects whether the stage is currently visible; when set, it changes the visible state, causing the stage to appear or disappear. The default value is `true`, so the stage will be made visible after initialization unless the object literal explicitly assigns the value `false`.

In Listing 14-1, the code on lines 19 to 21 attaches a trigger to a variable that is bound to the `visible` state of the stage and prints its value whenever it changes. Running this example and then immediately closing the window results in the following output from the trigger, reflecting the fact that the stage is initially visible and then becomes invisible when it is closed:

```
Stage contains focus? false
Stage visible? true
Stage contains focus? true
Stage visible? false
```

It does not follow that a visible stage can actually be seen by the user. On the desktop, for example, the stage's top-level window may be partly or completely obscured by other windows or it may be iconified. Moving another window to obscure the stage's window has no effect on this variable. In fact, there is no way to know whether the user can actually see the stage.

`containsFocus`

The `containsFocus` variable reflects whether the stage's top-level container is the active one on the user's screen. On the desktop, this means that the stage is in the window that the user is currently working with and to which keyboard presses will be directed. The active window is usually rendered differently from other windows so that the user can easily identify it. This is typically done by changing the color of its title bar.

The `containsFocus` variable is read-only to application code. Its value changes as users change the focus of their work. On lines 16 to 18 of Listing 14-1, a trigger is attached to a variable that is bound to its value, to allow state changes to be tracked. When this example is run, the stage becomes the active window, and the focused variable is set to `true`. Activating a different window by clicking it causes the stage to be deactivated, and the value of this variable changes to `false`.

Z-Order Control

The stage has two functions that let you raise or lower its top-level window on the desktop:

```
public function toFront():Void
public function toBack():Void
```

What these functions actually do depends on the host platform. All that you can rely on is that `toFront()` moves the stage on which it is invoked so that it is in front of any other stages belonging to the same application. Similarly, `toBack()` moves the stage so that it is behind all the other stages in the application and possibly behind windows belonging to other applications. The relative positioning of stages is referred to as the *Z-order*, which makes sense if you imagine a coordinate system in which the X and Y axes lie respectively along the top and the left side of screen and the Z extends vertically outward from the screen's surface.

The code in Listing 14-2, which you'll find in the file `javafxuibasics/StageZOrder.fx`, demonstrates the use of these functions.

Listing 14-2   The `toFront()` and `toBack()` Functions

```
1     package javafxuibasics;
2
3     import javafx.animation.KeyFrame;
4     import javafx.animation.Timeline;
5     import javafx.scene.Scene;
6     import javafx.scene.text.Text;
7     import javafx.stage.Stage;
8
9     var stage1 = Stage {
10        title: "Stage 1"
11        x: 100 y: 200
12        scene: Scene {
13            content: Text {
14                content: "Stage 1"
15                y: 20
16            }
17        }
```

```
18      }
19
20      Stage {
21          title: "Stage 2"
22          x: 150 y: 250
23          scene: Scene {
24              content: Text {
25                  content: "Stage 2"
26                  y:20
27              }
28          }
29      }
30
31      var timeline = Timeline {
32          repeatCount: Timeline.INDEFINITE
33          autoReverse: true
34          keyFrames: [
35              KeyFrame {
36                  time: 0s
37                  action: function() { stage1.toFront() }
38              },
39              KeyFrame {
40                  time: 5s
41                  action: function() { stage1.toBack(); }
42              }
43          ]
44      }
45      timeline.play();
```

This code creates two stages with nested Text objects that indicate which stage is which. The code on lines 31 to 45 creates an animation that first moves Stage 1 to the front (on line 37) and then moves it to the back (line 41). If you run this code, you should see the two stages changing their relative positions every 5 seconds. Animation is discussed in detail in Chapter 18, "Animation."

On some platforms, moving the stage to the front will also move the application into the foreground so that the stage appears in front of any windows belonging to other applications. This can be annoying for the user because he may be entering data into a spreadsheet and suddenly find that another application has taken control and is unexpectedly processing his keyboard input. Some versions of the Windows platform do not allow an application to move itself into the foreground in this way, except under specific circumstances.[2] Because the behavior is not the same across all platforms, it is best not to use the toFront() function to activate a stage unless it is in direct response to a user action

---

[2] You can read more about this at http://msdn.microsoft.com/en-us/library/ms633539(VS.85).aspx.

Closing the Stage

The stage can be closed either programmatically or by user request. Application code can initiate the process by calling the `close()` function. A user closes the stage by clicking the Close button in the title bar of its desktop window, which also causes the `close()` function to be called. You can register a function that will be called while the stage is being closed by assigning a reference to it to the stage's `onClose` variable.

The code in Listing 14-3 (which you'll find in the file `javafxuibasics/StageClose.fx`) illustrates both the `close()` function and the `onClose` variable. Lines 20 to 22 install an anonymous function that will be called when the stage is closed. Lines 25 to 36 create and start a 10-second countdown, at the end of which the `close()` function is called.

Listing 14-3   The `close()` Function and the `onClose` Variable of the Stage

```
1     package javafxuibasics;
2
3     import javafx.animation.Interpolator;
4     import javafx.animation.KeyFrame;
5     import javafx.animation.Timeline;
6     import javafx.scene.Scene;
7     import javafx.scene.text.Text;
8     import javafx.stage.Stage;
9
10    var count = 10;
11    var stage = Stage {
12        title: bind "Close Example: {count}"
13        width: 300 height: 100
14        scene: Scene {
15            content: Text {
16                content: bind "Close Example: {count}"
17                y: 20
18            }
19        }
20        onClose: function() {
21            println("onClose() called");
22        }
23    }
24
25    var timeline = Timeline {
26        keyFrames: [
27            KeyFrame {
28                time: 10s
29                values: count => 0 tween Interpolator.LINEAR
30                action: function() {
```

```
31                          stage.close()
32                      }
33                  }
34              ]
35          }
36      timeline.play();
```

If you run this example and wait until the countdown timer expires, you will see that the stage closes and the onClose function on lines 20 to 22 is called. If you run it again and close the top-level window yourself, you'll see that this also causes the onClose function to be called. The onClose function is typically used to save any application state that would need to be recovered when the application is next started. It is important to note the following:

- There is no way for the application to stop the stage being closed. This is different from a Swing application, where it is possible to post a dialog that enables the user to confirm the close operation and abort it if the user chooses not to proceed.
- When the onClose function returns, the stage is closed and, if there are no more active stages, the application exits.

Stage Position and Size

The Stage class has a set of variables that allow application code to read and change its position and size. These variables are listed in Table 14-2 and are discussed in the sections that follow. In an applet or on a mobile device, the stage is always set to the size of the area allocated to the applet or to the available space on the mobile device's screen, so these variables are effectively read-only. With the exception of the "Stage Size on Mobile Devices" subsection, much of the discussion in the rest of this section is, therefore, relevant only to the desktop environment.

Stage Bounds

The position and size of the top-level window that represents the stage can be read from its x, y, width, and height variables.

Table 14-2 **Stage Variables That Determine Its Position and Size**

Variable	Type	Access	Default	Description
x	Number	RW	See text	x coordinate, relative to the screen
y	Number	RW	See text	y coordinate relative to the screen
width	Number	RW	0	Width in pixels
height	Number	RW	0	Height in pixels
resizable	Boolean	RW	true	Whether the user can resize the stage
iconified	Boolean	RW	false	Whether the stage is iconified
fullScreen	Boolean	RW	false	Sets or clears full-screen mode

The Stage Class 349

The x and y coordinates are relative to the screen. If initial values are not provided for both x and y, the stage is centered on the user's screen. If an initial value is provided for one but not the other, the uninitialized variable is assigned the value 0. Changing the values of these variables causes the stage window to move to the corresponding position on the user's screen. Similarly, if the user moves the window, the x and y variables are updated to reflect the new position of the top-left corner of the window.

By default, the stage sizes itself based on the requirements of its nested scene. You can override this by providing initial values for its width/height variables. Changing these values programmatically causes the stage to adopt the specified size and, conversely, if the user resizes the window, the width and height variables change accordingly.

The code in Listing 14-4 (from the file javafxuibasics/StageBounds.fx) creates a scene containing a rectangle and a circle and wraps it in a stage. The x, y, width, and height variables of the stage are not initialized, but triggers are attached to each of them so that their values can be printed whenever they change.

Listing 14-4   **Stage Size and Position**

```
1     package javafxuibasics;
2
3     import javafx.scene.paint.Color;
4     import javafx.scene.Scene;
5     import javafx.scene.shape.Circle;
6     import javafx.scene.shape.Rectangle;
7     import javafx.stage.Stage;
8
9     Stage {
10        title: "Stage Bounds Example"
11        scene: Scene {
12            content: [
13                Rectangle {
14                    x: 10 y: 10
15                    width: 200 height: 200
16                    fill: Color.YELLOW
17                    stroke: Color.BLACK
18                },
19                Circle {
20                    centerX: 150 centerY: 150
21                    radius: 80
22                    fill: Color.GREEN
23                    stroke: Color.BLACK
24                }
25            ]
26        }
27        override var x on replace { println("x -> {x}") };
28        override var y on replace { println("y -> {y}") };
29        override var width on replace { println("width -> {width}") };
```

```
30            override var height on replace { println("height -> {height}")   };
31       }
```

When this example is run, the stage is placed in the center of the screen (the default position when the values of both the x and y variables are defaulted) and is exactly the right size to contain the content of its scene, as shown in Figure 14-3.

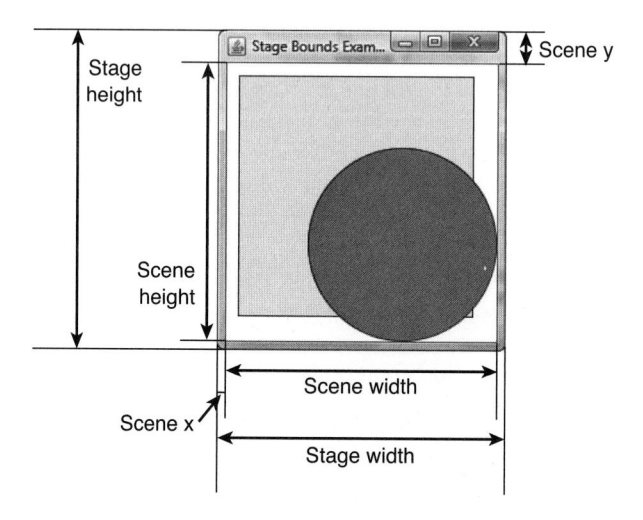

Figure 14-3   Stage width and height variables

As you can see, the stage is slightly wider and taller than the scene because of the extra space required by its window decorations. If you were to assign explicit values to the width and height variables of the stage, those values would have to take this difference into account. However, the size of the decorations is platform-dependent, so it is better to explicitly set the size of the scene instead. (See the discussion of the Scene class later in this chapter.)

If you move or resize the window, you'll see trigger output that shows that the x, y, width, and height variables are updated accordingly:

```
width -> 263.0
width -> 273.0
height -> 283.0
x -> 539.0
y -> 269.0
```

Stage Size on Mobile Devices

As noted earlier, on a mobile device, the stage always occupies the whole of the user's screen. However, this doesn't mean that this size is fixed, because some devices are sensitive to their orientation and rotate the screen content when the user rotates the physical handset. When this happens, the `width` and `height` variables of the stage are changed to match. The code in Listing 14-5 (which is in the file `javafxuibasics/StageBounds2.fx`) displays the width and height of the stage in two text nodes.

Listing 14-5 **Tracking Stage Width and Height Changes**

```
package javafxuibasics;

import javafx.scene.Scene;
import javafx.scene.text.Font;
import javafx.scene.text.Text;
import javafx.stage.Stage;

var stage:Stage = Stage {
    title: "Stage Bounds 2"
    scene: Scene {
        content: [
            Text {
                y: 20 font: Font { size: 20 }
                content: bind "Stage width: {stage.width}"
            },
            Text {
                y: 60 font: Font { size: 20 }
                content: bind "Stage height: {stage.height}"
            }
        ]
    }
}
```

If you run this example using the mobile emulator, you get the result shown at the top of Figure 14-4. As you can see, the stage is initially 240 pixels wide and 320 pixels high.

Now select View, Orientation, Rotate Counterclockwise to simulate the user changing the orientation of the device. As you can see at the bottom of Figure 14-4, this causes the `width` and `height` variables of the stage to be updated to match the new aspect of the screen.

Resizability

In some cases, it is not appropriate to allow the user to resize the stage. You saw an example of this in Chapter 4, where we wanted the size of the stage to always exactly match that of its background image. By default, resizing is allowed, but you can prevent it by setting the `resizable` variable to `false`. This stops the user resizing or maximizing the stage, but it will still change size if the values of its `width` and `height` variables are modified by application code.

352   Chapter 14 User Interface Basics

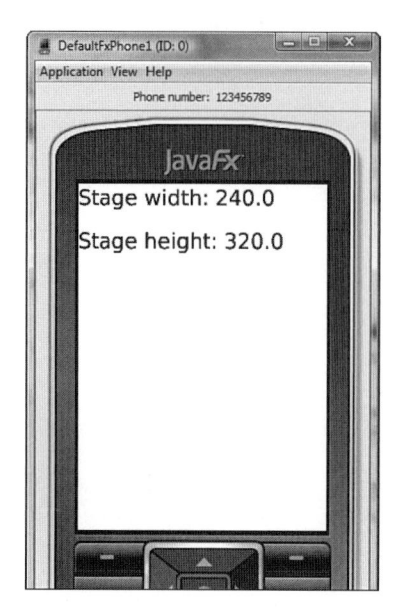

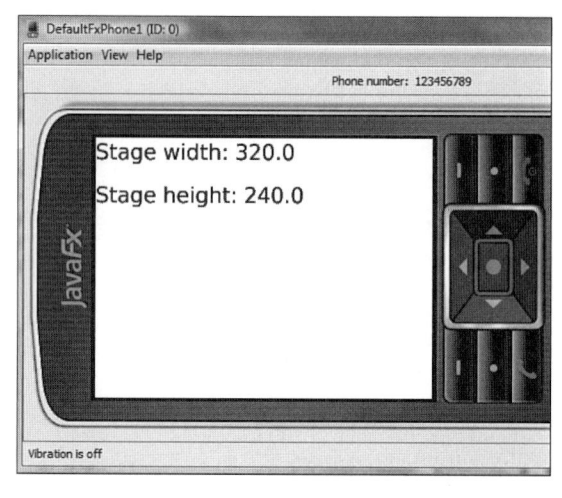

Figure 14-4   The effect of rotating a mobile device handset

Iconified State

The iconified state of the stage is tracked by its `iconified` variable. If you set this variable to `false`, the stage will become iconified. If you set it to `true`, it will restore itself to its previous size and position. Similarly, the state of this variable will change when the user iconifies or restores the window.

Full-Screen Mode

If you are using JavaFX to write a game, you might want to run your application in full-screen mode. You can switch into full-screen mode, as shown in Listing 14-6, by setting the `fullScreen` variable of the stage to `true`, which you will find in the file `javafxuibasics/FullScreen.fx`.

Listing 14-6   Using the Full-Screen Mode of the Stage

```
1     package javafxuibasics;
2
3     import javafx.animation.Interpolator;
4     import javafx.animation.KeyFrame;
5     import javafx.animation.Timeline;
6     import javafx.scene.paint.Color;
7     import javafx.scene.Scene;
8     import javafx.scene.shape.Rectangle;
9     import javafx.scene.text.Font;
10    import javafx.scene.text.Text;
11    import javafx.stage.Stage;
```

```
12
13      var time = 10;
14      var scene: Scene;
15      var stage: Stage = Stage {
16          title: "Fullscreen Example"
17          fullScreen: true
18          scene:
19          scene = Scene {
20              content: [
21                  Rectangle {
22                      x: 0
23                      y: 0
24                      fill: Color.WHITE
25                      width: bind scene.width
26                      height: bind scene.height
27                      onMousePressed: function(evt) {
28                          stage.fullScreen = not stage.fullScreen;
29                      }
30                  }
31
32                  Text {
33                      x: 100
34                      y: 100
35                      font: Font {
36                          size: 32
37                      }
38                      content: bind "Fullscreen - time to close: {time}"
39                  }
40              ]
41          }
42      }
43
44      var timeline = Timeline {
45          keyFrames: [
46              KeyFrame {
47                  time: 10s
48                  values: time => 0 tween Interpolator.LINEAR
49                  action: function() {
50                      stage.close()
51                  }
52              }
53          ]
54      };
55      timeline.play();
```

The initialization of the `fullScreen` variable on line 17 causes the stage to open in full-screen mode. Clicking anywhere within the stage with the mouse toggles the value of this variable between `true` and `false`, which causes the stage to switch into and out of full-screen mode. You can find the code that performs the mode switch in the mouse event handler on lines 27 to 29. Mouse handling is discussed in Chapter 15, "Node Variables and Events."

In full-screen mode, there are no window decorations and therefore no way for the user to close your application, unless you provide one. The code in Listing 14-6 uses a `Timeline` to create a countdown that is shown on the screen and closes the `Stage` when it reaches `0`.

> **Note**
>
> There are actually two different full-screen modes. In *full-screen exclusive* mode, the application actually switches its windowing mode so that it occupies the whole screen. In *simulated full-screen* mode, this is emulated by wrapping the stage in a top-level window that happens to fill the whole screen. There is no programmatic way to choose between these two. Full-screen exclusive mode is used when the application has the `fullScreenExclusive` permission. An application that is run from the command line will have this permission by default, but an applet or an application run by Java Web Start must be cryptographically signed to get it.

Style and Opacity

The `style` and `opacity` variables, the details of which are shown in Table 14-3, control some aspects of the visual appearance of the stage. On platforms that support it, you can use these variables to create a completely or partially transparent stage.

Table 14-3   **The `style` and `opacity` Variables**

Variable	Type	Access	Default	Description
style	StageStyle	RI	StageStyle.DECORATED	The style of the stage
opacity	Number	RW	1.0	The opacity of the stage

Stage Styles

The `style` variable has three possible values, defined in the `javafx.stage.StageStyle` class:

- DECORATED: The stage has window decorations, such as the title bar and buttons that allow the user to close, iconify, or maximize the stage window.
- UNDECORATED: The stage has no window decorations.
- TRANSPARENT: The stage is transparent, potentially allowing the user's desktop to be seen through it.

The style can be set only when the stage is initialized and the default value is `StageStyle.DECORATED`. When the style is set to `StageStyle.UNDECORATED`, the stage loses its window decorations, so it does not provide any way for the user to resize it or to close it. You can see the effect on the left side of Figure 14-5.[3] When the stage style is `StageStyle.TRANSPARENT`, its window decorations are removed, and it is made completely transparent. On its own, this is not enough to allow the user's desktop to be seen through the area occupied by the stage, because the scene, which appears in front of it, is filled with a solid color. To achieve a completely transparent stage, you also need to set the background fill of the scene to a transparent color, like this (which is taken from the code in the file `javafxuibasics/TransparentStage.fx`):

```
var stage:Stage = Stage {
    width: 300
    height: 100
    style: StageStyle.TRANSPARENT   // Makes the Stage transparent
    scene: Scene {
        fill: Color.TRANSPARENT     // Makes the Scene transparent
        content: [
            Text {
                x: 10
                y: 32
                font: Font { size: 24 }
                content: bind "TRANSPARENT\nClosing in {count}"
            }
        ]
    }
}
```

You can see the result of this code on the right side of Figure 14-5. The `TRANSPARENT` style works only if you have a version of the Java Runtime Environment (JRE) that supports transparent windows. On Windows, for example, you need to have Java SE 6 update 10 or higher, whereas on the Apple Mac, transparency is supported for Java 5. If your platform does not support this feature, `StageStyle.TRANSPARENT` is the same as `StageStyle.UNDECORATED`.

Stage Opacity

The `opacity` variable of the stage class allows you to create a partially transparent window, assuming that you are using a version of Java that supports transparency. The opacity applies equally to the stage window, its window decorations, and its content. If this variable has value `1.0`, the stage will be completely opaque. This is the default state. If `opacity` is set to `0`, the stage and its content are made transparent and will therefore be completely invisible. Any value in between causes the stage to be partly transparent, with smaller values allowing more of the desktop to be seen through the stage.

The code in Listing 14-7 creates a stage that is initially opaque and then starts an animation that cycles the value of the `opacity` variable from `1.0` to `0.0` and back again until

---

[3] The code that creates this `Stage` is in the file `javafxuibasics/UndecoratedStage.fx`.

356 Chapter 14 User Interface Basics

Figure 14-5   Undecorated and transparent stages

the stage is closed. You'll find this code in the file
`javafxuibasics/TranslucentStage.fx`.

Listing 14-7   **Using the Stage Opacity Variable**

```
package javafxuibasics;

import javafx.animation.Interpolator;
import javafx.animation.KeyFrame;
import javafx.animation.Timeline;
import javafx.scene.paint.Color;
import javafx.scene.Scene;
import javafx.scene.text.Font;
import javafx.scene.text.Text;
import javafx.stage.Stage;
import javafx.stage.StageStyle;

var opacity = 1.0;
var stage:Stage = Stage {
    title: "Translucent Frame"
    width: 300
    height: 100
    opacity: bind opacity
    scene: Scene {
        content: [
            Text {
                x: 10
                y: 32
                font: Font { size: 24 }
                content: bind "Opacity: {opacity}"
            }
        ]
    }
}

var timeline = Timeline {
    repeatCount: Timeline.INDEFINITE
```

```
        autoReverse: true
        keyFrames: [
            KeyFrame {
                time: 0s
                values: opacity => 1.0;
            },
            KeyFrame {
                time: 5s
                values: opacity => 0.0 tween Interpolator.LINEAR;
            }
        ]
    };
    timeline.play();
```

Figure 14-6 shows the translucent effect.

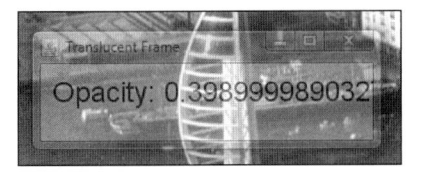

Figure 14-6 A translucent stage

It is possible to use the `opacity` variable and the `TRANSPARENT` style at the same time. The effect of the `TRANSPARENT` style is to remove the window decorations and to make the stage background transparent, with the result that the `opacity` value applies only to the content of the stage.

Extensions

The `extensions` variable, which is described in Table 14-4, holds a list of `javafx.stage.StageExtension` objects that allow additional state to be defined and used by different JavaFX GUI profiles.

Table 14-4 The `extensions` Variable

Variable	Type	Access	Default	Description
extensions	StageExtension[]	RW	Empty	Extensions that provide additional information for specific GUI profiles

The desktop profile defines an extension called `AppletStageExtension` that can be used to control the process of dragging a JavaFX applet out of its hosting browser window and dropped onto the user's desktop, which you saw in Chapter 4, among other things.

The `Scene` Class

The scene is the part of the stage that hosts the user interface of a JavaFX application. Every stage has a single scene that is installed by assigning it to the `scene` variable. It is possible to change the scene that is displayed by reassigning this variable, which can be a useful technique.

The `Scene` class defines a small number of public variables, as listed in Table 14-5.

The meaning of many of these variables is obvious, whereas others are discussed in the next chapter. Here, we discuss only the variables that relate to the scene's position and size.

Table 14-5 **Variables Defined by the `Scene` Class**

Variable	Type	Access	Default	Description
`stage`	`Stage`	R	N/A	Points to the stage hosting this scene. Set automatically when the scene is installed in the stage.
`x`	`Number`	R	N/A	The `x` coordinate of the scene relative to the stage.
`y`	`Number`	R	N/A	The `y` coordinate of the scene _relative to the stage.
`width`	`Number`	RI	See text	The width of the scene.
`height`	`Number`	RI	See text	The height of the scene.
`fill`	`Paint`	RW	`Color.WHITE`	The `Paint` used to fill the background of the scene. This may be a solid color or a gradient. `Paint` and `Color` are discussed in the next chapter.
`cursor`	`Cursor`	RW	`null`	The default cursor to be shown when the cursor is over this scene. Cursors are discussed in the next chapter.
`stylesheets`	`String[]`	RW	Empty	An ordered list of references to style sheets that are used to configure the nodes in this scene.

Table 14-5   Variables Defined by the `Scene` Class (*Continued*)

				A style sheet can be used to install a consistent set of colors and fonts across all nodes in the scene without requiring them to be specified separately for each node. Style sheets are discussed in Chapter 23, "Style Sheets."
camera	Camera	RW	null	The camera used to view the scene. This is used only in an environment that supports the 3D scene graph. See "3D Features" later in this chapter for more information.
content	Node[]	RW	Empty	The nodes that make up the user interface. See the "Nodes" section, later in this chapter.

The x and y variables represent the position of the top-left corner of the scene relative to the stage. These variables are read-only because this position is fixed and depends on the execution environment and on the style of the stage. In the case of an application running in a desktop environment that uses a decorated stage, the relationship between the stage and the scene is as shown in Figure 14-3. Notice that the x and y variables of the scene represent respectively the width of the window decoration at the left of the stage window and the height of the caption bar. In the case of an undecorated stage, both x and y would be 0, and the scene would completely cover the stage.

You can also see in Figure 14-3 that the width and height variables of the scene differ from those of the stage by the size of the window decorations. For an undecorated stage, the width and height of the scene are the same as those of the stage.

The width and height variables are read-only after the scene has been created, but you can set initial values for them. Here is how they are used:

- If no value is set for the width variable, the scene calculates its required width based on the nodes that it contains; otherwise, the specified width is used.
- Similarly, if no value is set for the height variable, it is calculated from the space requirements of its nodes; otherwise, the specified height is used.

If the width and height variables of the stage are not set, it uses the values provided by the scene to compute how large it needs to be given the size of its decorations, if it needs any. If the width/height variables of the stage *have* been set, the value requested by the scene is ignored.

In some cases, the stage cannot meet the scene's requirements. This may happen because it has explicitly set `width` and `height` values, which cause it to ignore the scene's preference, or because it is constrained by the screen space (in the case of a mobile device) or browser space (in the case of an applet) that is available to it. If this happens, the stage uses whatever space is available and sets the size of the scene accordingly.

A couple of examples should make this clearer. Consider the following code:

```
Stage {
    style: StageStyle.DECORATED
    scene: Scene {
        Width: 300
        Height: 100
    }
}
```

Assume first that this code is running on the desktop and that the window decorations require a title bar that is 28 pixels high and side and bottom decorations that are each 8 pixels wide. Referring to Figure 14-3, you can see that the stage would need to be (100 + 28 + 8) = 136 pixels high and (300 + 8 + 8) = 316 pixels wide. Assuming that is allowed, the stage will adopt this size, so the scene's `width` and `height` variables will be unchanged, and its `x` and `y` variables will be set to `8` and `28`, respectively.

Now let's consider the case in which the same code is executing on a mobile device that has a screen that is 240 pixels wide and 320 pixels high. There are no window decorations on a mobile device, so in this case the stage needs to be the same size as the scene—300 pixels wide and 100 pixels high. Unfortunately, the screen is too narrow to accommodate a 300-pixel-wide stage, so the stage actually sets its `width` variable to that of the screen—240 pixels.

On a mobile device, the stage always exactly fills the available screen space, so it will also set its height to that of the screen—320 pixels—which is larger than that required by the scene. Because there is no overhead for window decorations, the scene will also be sized to 240 pixels wide and 320 pixels high. As you can see, the initial `width` and `height` values of both the stage and scene are not actually used on a mobile device, but they *are* correctly set once the user interface has been made visible.

If the stage is resized, the `width` and `height` values of the scene will be changed so that the relationship shown in Figure 14-3 is preserved.

Nodes

Nodes are the basic building blocks of the user interface of a JavaFX application. The JavaFX runtime provides a number of node types that you can use to build a scene, including simple geometric shapes, platform-independent controls, a media player, and wrappers for some of the Swing components, all of which will be covered in some detail in the next few chapters. In this section, we look at how nodes are organized within a scene and briefly discuss the features common to all types of node.

Node Organization

The nodes in a scene are organized as a *directed acyclic graph,* which is a fancy way of describing a tree structure in which there are no links that point back up the tree. The graph (commonly referred to as the *scene graph*) is rooted in the content variable of the scene, which is a sequence of nodes. Nodes that represent shapes are *leaves* in the scene graph—that is, they do not have child nodes of their own. There are also *branch* nodes. A branch node is one that can contain other nodes, one example of which is the class javafx.scene.Group. Nodes that can contain other nodes are all derived from javafx.scene.Parent, which is a direct subclass of Node.

In this chapter, we use the Group class as an example when we need to construct a tree of nodes. Chapter 17, "Coordinates, Transforms, and Layout," introduces the Container class, which is similar to Group but which is typically subclassed to add the ability to lay out its child nodes in the same way as a layout manager would lay out the contents of an Abstract Window Toolkit (AWT) container. Most of what we say in this chapter about the Group class also applies to Container.

Figure 14-7 shows a simple scene graph consisting of four leaf nodes and a group node. Note that this diagram shows only the hierarchical relationship between the nodes, not their relative positions on the screen, which are determined by state held within the individual nodes.

In this example, the content variable of the scene has two elements: one referring to a group consisting of a text node, a rectangle node, and a circle node; the other to a single text node. Like scene, the Group class and the Container class both have a content variable of type Node[] that contains references to their children. A node nested inside another node has a reference to that node in its parent variable (which is of type Parent). In the case of a node that is a direct child of the scene (and therefore is not nested within a node), the parent reference is null. Every node also has a reference to the scene to which it belongs, in its scene variable.

Whether it is embedded directly in the scene or in a Parent node, a node instance can appear only once within a scene.

Identification

The id variable can be used to assign a string identifier to a node. The lookup() function can be used to search the descendents of the node on which it is invoked for a node with a given identifier. The identifier is intended mainly for application use, so there are no restrictions on the characters that may be used, but if you want to use the id in conjunction with a style sheet, you should avoid special characters (for example, # and .). Style sheets are discussed in Chapter 23.

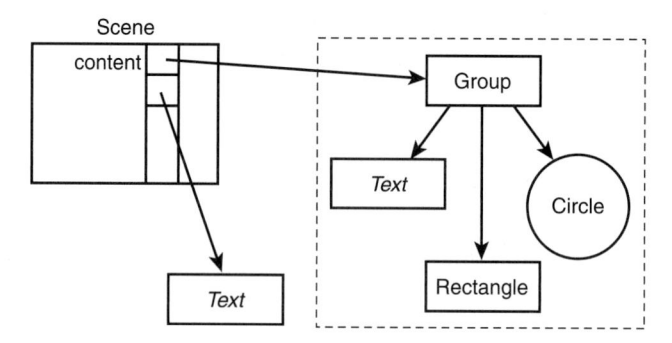

Figure 14-7   A scene graph containing one group and four leaf nodes

Coordinates

The position of a node is specified relative to the coordinate system of its parent if it has one, or of the scene if it does not. The x-axis of the scene's coordinate system runs parallel to the top of the scene, and the y-axis runs from its top to its bottom. The top-left corner of the scene is the origin and has coordinates (0, 0). The x coordinate increases from left to right, and the y coordinate from top to bottom. The coordinate system of a group is the same, except that its origin is at the top-left corner of the group. It is possible to move, rotate, or skew the coordinate system of any node (but not the coordinate system of the scene) by applying a transformation, as you'll see in Chapter 17. For now, we'll confine ourselves to the standard coordinate system.

The code in Listing 14-8 creates a scene containing a text node and a group, which itself contains a circle and another text node. You'll find the code for this example in the file javafxuibasics/SceneAndGroup.fx.

Listing 14-8   **Creating a Scene with a Nested Group**

```
1    package javafxuibasics;
2
3    import javafx.scene.Group;
4    import javafx.scene.paint.Color;
5    import javafx.scene.Scene;
6    import javafx.scene.shape.Circle;
7    import javafx.scene.text.Text;
8    import javafx.stage.Stage;
9
10   Stage {
11       title: "A Scene and a Group"
12       scene: Scene {
13           content: [
14               Text {
```

```
15                    x: 10 y: 30
16                    content: "Text in the Scene"
17                },
18                Group {
19                    translateX: 120
20                    translateY: 20
21                    content: [
22                        Circle {
23                            centerX: 50 centerY: 50
24                            radius: 40 fill: Color.GREEN
25                        },
26                        Text {
27                            x: 20 y: 110
28                            content: "Text in the Group"
29                        }
30                    ]
31                }
32            ]
33        }
34    }
```

Figure 14-8 shows the result of running this code.

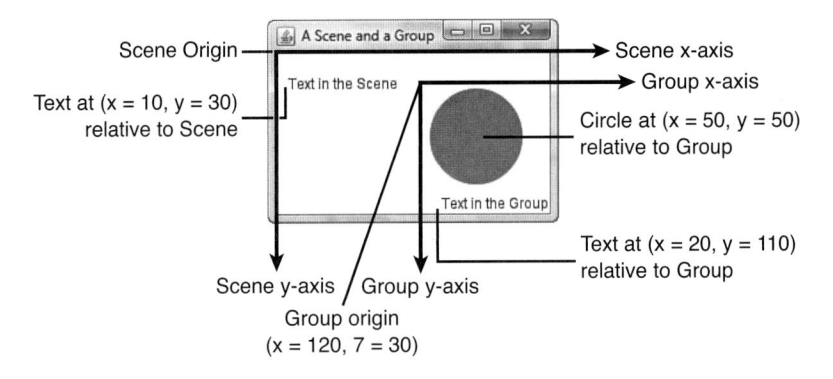

Figure 14-8 Scene and group coordinates

The text node created on lines 14 to 17 of Listing 14-8 appears at the top left of the scene because its coordinate origin is at (0, 0), relative to the scene itself (because it is a direct child of the scene), and the text that it contains is drawn at (10, 30) relative to that node's origin.[4] The group declared on lines 18 to 31 has its origin at (120, 20) relative to the scene; these coordinates are given by the `translateX` and `translateY` variables, which literally cause the coordinate origin for the group to be translated by the specified amounts, as shown in Figure 14-8.[5]

The nodes within the group itself are positioned relative to the group's origin, so the circle declared on lines 22 to 25 has its center at (50, 50) relative to the group, but (170, 70) relative to the scene. Similarly, the text node in the group has its origin at (0, 0) relative to the group, and the text itself appears at (20, 110) relative to the group, which is (140, 130) relative to the scene.

Managing nodes in groups is useful because any transform or effect that is applied to the group will also affect the nodes that it contains. If we were to rotate the group by 90 degrees, for example, the result would be to rotate all the nodes in that group, too. Rotating the group requires only one extra line of code:

```
Group {
    translateX: 120
    translateY: 20
    rotate: 90
    content: [
```

The effect of this change (which you'll find in the file `javafxuibasics/RotatedGroup.fx`) is shown in Figure 14-9. For more on node transformations, see Chapter 17.

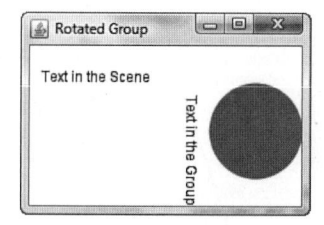

Figure 14-9 The effect of rotating a group

Groups can be nested within groups, to any depth.

Visibility

The visibility of a node is determined by its `visible` variable. To be visible, a node must satisfy all the following criteria:

- Its `visible` attribute must be `true`.

---

[4] If you are used to coordinates in AWT and Swing, some of what you read here might surprise you. We return to the topic of coordinate systems in Chapter 17.

[5] We'll take a much closer look at these variables and coordinate systems in Chapter 17.

- The group within which it is contained, if any, must also have its `visible` attribute set to `true`. If that group is nested within another group, that group must also be visible, and so on.
- The stage that contains the node must be visible.

You can change the visibility of a node by changing the value of its `visible` variable. A node that is not visible is not taken into account when calculating the size of scene or of the group, if any, that it is part of. If the `visible` variable of a group is set to `false`, the group and all the nodes that it contains will disappear from the scene.

Z-Order

The order in which nodes appear in the content sequence of the scene or of a group is significant if some of them overlap others because the sequence order also determines the Z-order. The rule is that the nodes that appear earlier in the sequence are drawn *before* and therefore appear *behind* those that appear later in the sequence. The code shown in Listing 14-9, which you'll find in the file `javafxuibasics/SceneZOrder.fx`, illustrates this by placing an overlapping rectangle and circle in a group.

Listing 14-9 **Node Z-Order**

```
1    package javafxuibasics;
2
3    import javafx.scene.Group;
4    import javafx.scene.paint.Color;
5    import javafx.scene.Scene;
6    import javafx.scene.shape.Circle;
7    import javafx.scene.shape.Rectangle;
8    import javafx.stage.Stage;
9
10   Stage {
11       title: "Scene Z-Order"
12       scene: Scene {
13           content: [
14               Group {
15                   var circle:Circle;
16                   var rect:Rectangle;
17                   content: [
18                       circle = Circle {
19                           centerX: 100 centerY: 100
20                           radius: 40    fill: Color.YELLOW
21                           onMousePressed: function(evt) {
22                               circle.toFront();
23                           }
24                       },
25                       rect = Rectangle {
26                           x: 10 y: 10
27                           width: 140 height: 90
```

```
28                         fill: Color.RED
29                         onMousePressed: function(evt) {
30                             rect.toFront();
31                         }
32                     }
33                 ]
34             }
35         ]
36     }
37 }
```

Because the circle appears before the rectangle in the group's `content` sequence (see lines 17 to 33), it is drawn first and is therefore partly obscured by the rectangle, as shown on the left of Figure 14-10.[6]

The Z-order can be changed by rearranging the order of elements in the group's `content` variable. The node class provides two convenience functions that move the target node either to the front or back of the Z-order by changing its location in its parent group's `content` sequence:

```
public function toFront():Void
public function toBack():Void
```

On lines 21 to 23 and 29 to 31 of Listing 14-9, calls to the `toFront()` function will be invoked when either the circle or the rectangle is clicked with the mouse. (Mouse handling is covered in Chapter 15.) Clicking the circle moves it in front of the rectangle, as shown on the right of Figure 14-10.

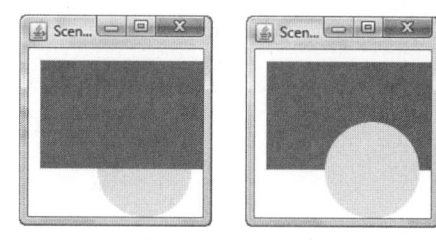

Figure 14-10   How the order of nodes in the `content` sequence of a group affects Z-order

---

[6] In this example, the part of the rectangle that overlaps the circle completely obscures what is underneath it. However, this is just the default. The group class has a variable called `blendMode` that lets you choose from 19 different ways to combine the pixels of overlapping nodes in a group. Blending and the `blendMode` variable are discussed in Chapter 20, "Effects and Blending."

Events

Nodes can receive notification of mouse and keyboard events. You can use these events to trigger an action within your application or, if you are writing a custom node, a state change within the node that may itself result in the notification of an event to the application. As an example of event handling, the code on lines 21 to 23 of Listing 14-9 registers a function that is called whenever a mouse button is pressed while the cursor is over the rectangle. Event handling is discussed in Chapter 15.

Colors

Some node subclasses have variables that determine the color or colors that will be used in the node's visual representation.[7] For example, both the `Rectangle` and `Circle` classes have variables called `fill` and `stroke` that represent, respectively, the color used to fill the interior of the shape and the color used to draw its outline. The following code, from the file `javafxuibasics/NodeColors.fx`, creates a circle that has a yellow interior and a black outline, as shown on the left side of Figure 14-11.

```
Circle {
    centerX: 50,
    centerY: 50
    radius: 40
    fill: Color.YELLOW
    stroke: Color.BLACK
}
```

In this case, the circle is filled with a solid color defined by the `javafx.scene.paint.Color` class, but color handling in JavaFX is more general than that. It is also possible to fill a shape with a color gradient, as you'll see in Chapter 15, and it is possible to control the opacity of the shape by setting its `opacity` variable to a value between `0` and `1`. The following code creates a circle with an `opacity` of `0.3`, which causes it to be semitransparent, as shown on the right side of Figure 14-11.

```
Circle {
    centerX: 150,
    centerY: 50
    radius: 40
    fill: Color.YELLOW
    stroke: Color.BLACK
    opacity: 0.3
}
```

---

[7] Colors are not meaningful for all nodes, so these variables are not part of the `Node` class. For example, `Group` does not have any visual representation and therefore does not require any colors.

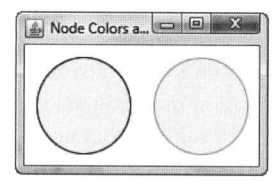

Figure 14-11   Stroke and Fill colors and the use of opacity

Effects

One of the most impressive features of JavaFX is the ease with which it is possible to apply attractive graphical effects to a node or a group of nodes. The `javafx.scene.effect` and `javafx.scene.effect.light` packages contain a set of predefined effects that you can use by just assigning one to the effect variable of a node. It is also possible to apply more than one effect to a node by chaining them together. The following code creates a scene that contains some text, to which the reflection effect has been applied, giving the result shown in Figure 14-12.[8] Effects are discussed in Chapter 20, "Effects and Blending."

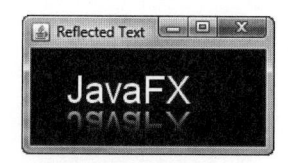

```
Text {
    font: Font { size: 32 }
    fill: Color.WHITE
    x: 30
    y: 45
    content: "JavaFX"
    effect: Reflection {
              topOpacity: 0.9
              bottomOpacity: 0.0
              topOffset: 1
              fraction: 0.7
            }
}
```

Figure 14-12   A text node with a reflection effect applied

---

[8] You'll find this code in the file `javafxuibasics/ReflectedText.fx` in the JavaFX Book GUI project.

It is important to note that effects are not part of the common profile and do not work on mobile devices.

Alerts

At the time of this writing, JavaFX does not have any equivalent of a modal or nonmodal dialog. The closest equivalent is the `Alert` class, which lets you display a modal message box containing some text and one or more predefined buttons. As you'll see in the examples that follow, the appearance of the message box is platform-dependent, and you have minimal control over its content.

Information Alert

The information alert allows you to display a message, to which the user must respond by clicking the OK button. You can open an information alert using either of the following script functions of the `javafx.stage.Alert` class:

```
public function inform(message:String):Void
public function inform(title:String, message:String):Void
```

The values of the `title` and `message` arguments are displayed in a platform-dependent way in the message box. The following code displays a stage containing some text that invites you to click to see an information alert. If you click in the stage, the code on lines 11 to 13 opens a message box containing some text that includes the position of the cursor when the mouse was clicked:

```
1    var scene:Scene;
2    Stage {
3        title : "Alerts 1"
4        scene: scene = Scene {
5            content: [
6                Rectangle {
7                    x: 0 y: 0
8                    width: bind scene.width height: bind scene.height
9                    fill: Color.TRANSPARENT
10                   onMouseClicked: function(evt) {
11                       Alert.inform("Mouse Clicked",
12                       "Mouse was clicked at ({evt.x}, {evt.y}).\n"
13                       "Click OK to close.");
14                   }
15               }
16               Text {
17                   textOrigin: TextOrigin.TOP
18                   content: "Click to show an information alert"
19               }
20           ]
21       }
22   }
```

The appearance of the message box when this example is run on the desktop is shown on the left of Figure 14-13, and on a mobile device on the right.

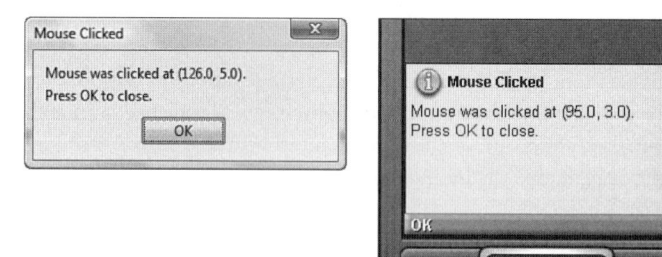

Figure 14-13   An information alert, incorporating both title and message

Notice that in both cases the message is accompanied by an icon that indicates that the text is for information only and an OK button that will close the alert when it is clicked. The title string appears in the title bar of the alert in the desktop version but is placed next to the icon on the mobile platform. If you don't supply a title, a platform-dependent default is used.

In this example, the text to be displayed includes a newline character and, as you can see, this results in a line break in the message box. On the mobile platform, there is a limit on the width of the area available for the text, and if this is exceeded, the text will wrap onto the next line. On the desktop platform, there is no in-built limit, so if you supply a long text string without line breaks, the result will be a very wide message box.

Confirm Alert

If you need to get the user's permission to perform an action, you can do so by using either a confirm or a question alert. The difference between these two is largely how you frame the question to be asked. You can display a confirm alert with either of the following functions:

```
public function confirm(message:String):Boolean
public function confirm(title:String, message:String):Boolean
```

For example, the following code asks permission to delete a file and prints the user's response. You can see the result of running this code on the desktop on the left of Figure 14-14 and on a mobile device on the right.

```
var response = Alert.confirm("Confirm Delete",
            "Click 'OK' to delete the file,\n'Cancel' to abort.");
println("Response was {response}");
```

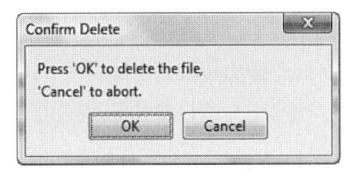

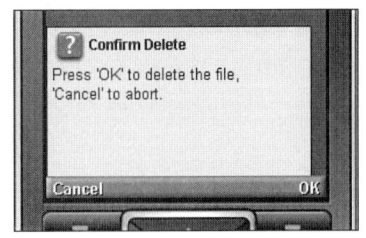

Figure 14-14   A confirm alert

These functions block until the user clicks either the OK or Cancel button and then returns true if OK was pressed or false for Cancel. As with the information alert, you can break the message up into multiple lines separated by newline characters if you need to and optionally include a title string.

Question Alert

A question alert is similar to the confirm alert, the difference being that a question alert expects the message to be a question to which the user can answer either yes or no. Here are the functions that you use to display a question alert:

```
public function question(message:String):Boolean
public function question(title:String, message:String):Boolean
```

The following code is a variant of the preceding example and uses a question alert rather than a confirm alert to get the user's permission to delete a file. Figure 14-15 shows the result of running this code:

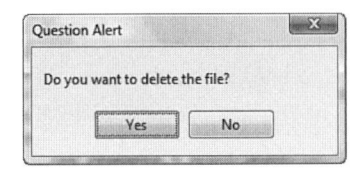

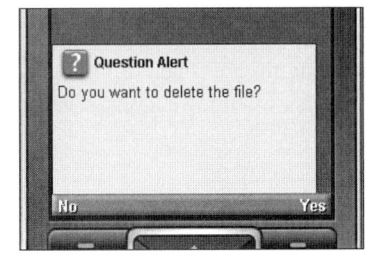

```
var response = Alert.question("Question Alert",
                              "Do you want to delete the file?");
println("Response was {response}");
```

Figure 14-15   A question alert

3D Features

In JavaFX 1.3, some new features were added that are the beginnings of support for a 3-D scene graph. The 3D support that exists in this release is basic and amounts to the following:

- The ability to translate nodes along the z-axis and the x- and y-axes provided by the 2D scene graph
- The ability to view a scene using either a parallel or a perspective camera
- The ability to rotate nodes about any of the three axes
- The ability to scale nodes along all three axes

In this section, you see a simple example that illustrates the use of a perspective camera and translation of a node along the z-axis of a scene. We discuss rotation and scaling along all three axes in Chapter 17, "Coordinates, Transforms, and Layout." You should expect to see much more support for a 3D scene graph in future releases.

The 3D features are all dependent on a new graphical infrastructure called the *Prism toolkit*. As of JavaFX 1.3, this is supported only by the Java TV runtime, so you cannot use any of these features on the desktop or on a mobile device.

Cameras and the Z-Axis of the Scene Graph

In the examples that you have seen so far, there are only two axes—the x-axis, which runs from left to right and the y-axis, which runs from top to bottom. Although we haven't mentioned it so far, there is also a z-axis, which is logically perpendicular to the scene. The coordinates on the z-axis start at 0 on the scene itself; positive z values are used for the space behind the scene and negative values for the space in front of the scene.

You can position a node along the z-axis by setting the value of its `translateZ` variable. Increasing the value of this variable makes the node move further away from the user, whereas decreasing it moves it closer. The following example, which you can find in the file `javafxuibasics/JavaFX3D.fx` in the JavaFX Book GUI project, varies the `translateZ` variable of a rectangle from 0 to −300 over a period of 5 seconds, which has the effect of lifting the rectangle off the scene and moving it toward the user. The operation is then reversed, causing the shape to appear to move back onto the surface of the scene.

```
1    var z:Number;
2    Stage {
3        title : "JavaFX 3D Features"
4        scene: Scene {
5            width: 300
6            height: 300
7            camera: bind PerspectiveCamera {
8                fieldOfView: 30
9            }
```

```
10              content: [
11                  Rectangle {
12                      x: 0
13                      y: 0
14                      width: 100
15                      height: 100
16                      translateX: 100
17                      translateY: 100
18                      translateZ: bind z;
19                      fill: Color.GREEN
20                      effect: DropShadow {
21                          radius: 10
22                      }
23                  }
24              ]
25          }
26      }
27
28      Timeline {
29          repeatCount: Timeline.INDEFINITE
30          autoReverse: true
31          keyFrames: [
32              at(0s) {
33                  z => 0
34              }
35              at (5s) {
36                  z => -300
37              }
38          ]
39      }.play();
```

The position of the rectangle along the z-axis is controlled by its `translateZ` variable, which is bound to the value of the script variable z on line 18. The movement of the rectangle along that axis is caused by the timeline on lines 28 to 39. Timelines are discussed in Chapter 18, "Animation."

If you run this example using the TV emulator, you see the rectangle slowly grow in size as its z coordinate decreases, thereby moving it closer to your eye, and then shrink back to its original size as its z coordinate returns to 0. You can see two stages in this process in Figure 14-16.

The rectangle's size changes as it moves toward or away from your eye because the scene is viewed using the `PerspectiveCamera` installed on lines 7 to 9. A `PerspectiveCamera` enhances the impression of a three-dimensional scene by making things further away look smaller than things that are closer.[9] You can also install a `Parallel`

---

[9] The `fieldOfView` variable of the `PerspectiveCamera` class is meant to limit the part of the scene that the viewer can see, but in JavaFX 1.3 it does not work.

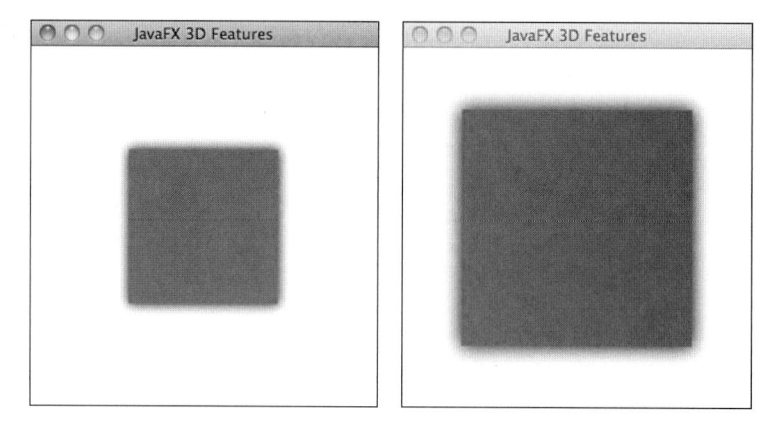

Figure 14-16   Animating a rectangle along the z-axis

`Camera`, which does not provide the perspective effect. If you were to change lines 7 to 9 of this example to install a `ParallelCamera` and run the example again, you would see that the rectangle's size does not change as it moves along the z-axis—because of this, it is impossible to tell that there is any movement at all, until the rectangle gets too close to the viewer, at which point it disappears. `ParallelCamera` is intended to be used when you don't need 3D effects and is effectively the default if you don't install a `PerspectiveCamera`. Whichever camera you use, it is positioned a fixed distance above the center of the scene and looks directly down at it. This limits the usefulness of the 3D features for this release, because it is not possible to produce different views of the scene by moving the camera.

> **Note**
> The JavaFX TV emulator is supported only on Windows. If you are not using Windows, you can still run this example by forcing the use of the Prism toolkit. To do this in NetBeans, right-click the node for the JavaFX Book GUI project and select Properties; then select Run. This opens the form shown in Figure 4-10 in Chapter 4, "A Simple JavaFX Application." In the JVM Arguments field, enter "`-Xtoolkit prism`" (without the quotes) and then run the example. Unfortunately, the Prism toolkit does not work with older graphics cards that do not have graphics acceleration features built in. You can do the same thing in Eclipse by adding these JVM arguments to the Run Configuration for this example.

15

Node Variables and Events

Nodes are the core of the user interface in a JavaFX application. In the first part of this chapter, following on from the introduction in Chapter 14, "User Interface Basics," we look at cursors and colors, which are features that are common to almost all node types. In the second part of this chapter, you see how to handle the events that are generated when the user interacts with the nodes in your application using either the keyboard or the mouse.

Unless otherwise specified, the example source code for this chapter can be found in the `javafxnodes` package of the JavaFX Book GUI project.

Cursors

When the mouse is over your application, its position is indicated by the mouse cursor. The shape of the default mouse cursor is determined by the platform on which the application is running, but JavaFX allows you to change the cursor shape for any node by setting its `cursor` variable, which causes the cursor to adopt the specified shape while the mouse is over that node. If the node is a group, the specified cursor will be shown whenever the mouse is over that group, unless it moves over a nested node that has its own `cursor` variable set to request a different one for that particular node.

There are 16 standard cursors, each of which is represented by a constant defined in the `javafx.scene.Cursor` class. These cursors, together with graphics showing their appearance on the Windows platform, are shown in Table 15-1.

Setting the cursor for a node is just a matter of assigning the required value to its `cursor` variable. To install the TEXT cursor on a rectangle, for example, you do this:

```
Rectangle {
    cursor: Cursor.TEXT
}
```

The code in the file `javafxnodes/NodeCursors.fx` creates a scene containing 20 groups, each of which consists of a text node inside a rectangle, as shown in Figure 15-1. It is also possible to create a custom cursor from an image.

Table 15-1 **Standard Cursors on the Microsoft Windows Platform**

Cursor Name	Appearance
CROSSHAIR	✜
DEFAULT	▷
E_RESIZE	⇔
H_RESIZE	⇔
HAND	☝
MOVE	✥
N_RESIZE	↕
NE_RESIZE	⤢
NW_RESIZE	⤡
S_RESIZE	↕
SE_RESIZE	⤡
SW_RESIZE	⤢
TEXT	I
V_RESIZE	↕
W_RESIZE	⇔
WAIT	◯

> **Note**
> Although the `cursor` variable and the `Cursor` class both exist on the mobile platform, they do not necessarily work. On Mobile Information Device Profile (MIDP)-based devices, setting the `cursor` variable has no effect.

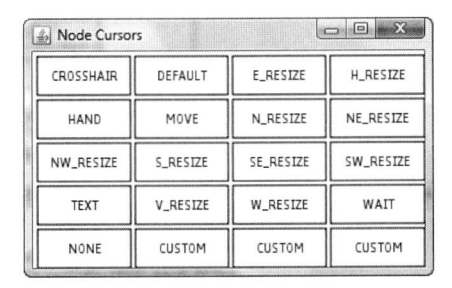

Figure 15-1   Node cursors

The cursor variable of each of the groups in the top four rows is set to the standard cursor whose name is on the text node. If you move the mouse over any of these areas, you see the cursor change to the shape shown in the Appearance column of Table 15-1. The cursor takes on the shape assigned to the group even though it is actually over the text or rectangle node because the cursor variable of these nested nodes has the value null. The cursor for a node that does not specify its own cursor is determined by its nearest node ancestor that has a non-null value in its cursor variable, which in this case is the enclosing group.

When the mouse is outside the bounds of any of the groups, it is over the scene. The scene also has a cursor variable, which, in this example, is set to Cursor.WAIT, so you see a WAIT cursor when the mouse is not over any of the rectangular cells in Figure 15-1.

The cursor variables of the leftmost of the four groups in the bottom row of Figure 15-1 are all set to the special value Cursor.NONE, which means that no cursor at all should be displayed when the mouse cursor is over any of these groups. Removing the cursor completely in this way is not recommended because its disappearance may confuse the user. The other three groups in this row are assigned a custom cursor. You create a custom cursor from an image by using the ImageCursor class (which is a subclass of Cursor). Here's the code that creates the custom cursor used in this example:

```
var crossHair = ImageCursor {
    image: Image { url: "{__DIR__}Crosshair.png" }
    hotspotX: 16 hotspotY: 16
}
```

The Image class, which we cover in the next chapter, loads an image from the location given by its url variable. This image is assigned to the image variable of the CursorImage object. The hotspotX and hotspotY variables refer to the position within the image of the actual cursor point, which is reported in the events that are delivered when the mouse is moved or clicked, as discussed in "Mouse Events" later in this chapter.

The optimal image size for a cursor image is platform-dependent. You can use the getBestSize() method of the ImageCursor class to determine this size, or if you have candidate cursor images of various sizes, you can have the JavaFX runtime choose the best one to use by calling the `chooseBestCursor()` method.

Colors

Every node that has a visual representation has variables that allow you to control its use of color. The basic nodes provided in the JavaFX SDK are derived from a `Node` subclass called `javafx.scene.shape.Shape`, which defines the variables `fill` and `stroke` for this purpose. The `stroke` color is used for the outline of the shape and the `fill` color is used to paint its interior. The following code, from the file `javafxnodes/StrokeFillCircle.fx`, creates a circle that has a black outline and is filled with yellow, as shown in Figure 15-2.

```
Circle {
    centerX: 100
    centerY: 100
    radius: 80
    stroke: Color.BLACK
    fill: Color.YELLOW
}
```

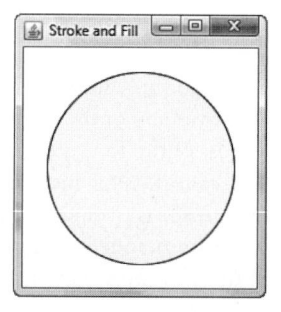

Figure 15-2   Stroke and fill colors applied to a `Circle` node

The `stroke` and `fill` variables are both of type `javafx.scene.paint.Paint`, which is an abstract class that is defined to provide a color value for every pixel of the area to which it is applied. The most commonly used `Paint` subclass is `javafx.scene.paint.Color`, which provides the same color for every pixel—in other words, it is a solid color. There are two other `Paint` types in the JavaFX software development kit (SDK)—`LinearGradient` and `RadialGradient`—that fill an area with a smooth transition from a start color to an end color.

If you set the `fill` variable to `null`, the shape will not be filled and will appear to be transparent. Similarly, if you set the `stroke` variable to `null`, the shape's outline will not be drawn. Setting both variables to `null` produces an invisible shape. Using the color `Color.TRANSPARENT` as the fill or stroke has the same effect as using the value `null`.

Solid Colors

You can use a solid color by assigning a value of type `javafx.scene.paint.Color` to either the `stroke` or `fill` variables of a node. The easiest way to specify a color is to use one of the predefined values in the `Color` class, which has definitions for more than 140 standard colors, the names of which you can find in the documentation for that class. Using them is simply a matter of quoting the name, because they are all script variables:

```
Rectangle {
    fill: Color.YELLOW
    stroke: Color.BLACK
```

Note that the names of the predefined colors are all in uppercase.

If you need a color that is not one of the standard set, you can create a `Color` object that represents it. There are various different ways to specify color. In JavaFX, as in Java, the most common way to do so is to supply the combination of red, green, and blue (RGB) values that make up the color. A color may also have a fourth element, the alpha value (or A value), that specifies its opacity. Using a color that is not fully opaque as the `fill` or `stroke` color of a node allows some portion of the color of whatever is behind the node to be seen through it. An example of this is shown in Figure 15-3,[1] where the circle is filled with a semi-opaque green color that allows the yellow rectangle to be seen through it.

Figure 15-3 The effect of a semi-opaque color

`Color` objects are immutable, so you can safely reuse the same instance without the risk that the represented color will be changed by modifying its RGBA components.

The individual R, G, B, and A values of a color are sometimes referred to as *channel values*. Depending on context, the channel values may be specified as an `Integer` value in the range 0 to 255 inclusive, or as a `Number` from 0.0 to 1.0. Specifying 0 causes none of that channel to be included, while the value 255 (or 1.0) causes the maximum possible amount to be used. Choosing 0 for each of the RGB channels gives black, while using the value 255 (or 1.0) for all channels produces the color white. Here are some more examples:

---

[1] You can find this code in the file `javafxnodes/SemiOpaqueColor.fx`.

- R = 0, G = 0, B = 255 - blue
- R = 255, G = 0, B = 0 - red
- R = 123, G = 0, B = 0 - a darker red
- R = 128, G = 128, B = 128 - gray
- R = 32, G = 32, B = 32 - a darker gray
- R = 255, G = 255, B = 0 - yellow
- R = 200, G = 200, B = 0 - a darker yellow

One way to create a `Color` from the corresponding RGB values is to use an object literal:

```
var red = Color { red: 1.0 };
var yellow = Color { red: 1.0 green: 1.0 blue: 0 }
```

In an object literal, you specify the RGBA components using the variable names `red`, `green`, `blue`, and `opacity` and supply a value in the range `0` to `1.0`. The default value for `red`, `green`, and `blue` is `0`, but for `opacity` it is `1.0`, which produces an opaque color.

Alternatively, you can use either of the following functions defined in the `Color` class:

```
public function color(r:Number, g:Number, b:Number, a:Number):Color
public function color(r:Number, g:Number, b:Number):Color
```

Again, each component value must be in the range `0` to `1.0`. The first variant lets you supply an opacity value, while the second creates a fully opaque color (with the opacity set to `1.0`). Here are some examples:

```
var c1 = Color.color(1.0, 1.0, 0.0);        // Opaque yellow
var c2 = Color.color(1.0, 1.0, 0.0, 0.5);   // Semi-opaque yellow
```

If you prefer to specify the RGBA components as integers, you can use the `rgb()` functions instead:

```
public function rgb(r:Integer, g:Integer, b:Integer, a:Integer):Color
public function rgb(r:Integer, g:Integer, b:Integer):Color
```

In this case, the components must be in the range `0` to `255`, as shown in the following examples:

```
var c1 = Color.rgb(255, 255, 0);        // Opaque yellow
var c2 = Color.rgb(255, 255, 255, 128); // Semi-opaque yellow
```

Yet another way to create a `Color` is provided by the overloaded `web()` function, which is declared as follows:

```
public function web(colorName:String, opacity:Number):Color
public function web(colorName:String):Color
```

The format of the `colorName` argument is similar to that used in the CSS (Cascading Style Sheets) specification, hence the name of the function. You can encode the color in several ways:

- As a six-digit hexadecimal number, preceded by # or 0x. Either upper- or lowercase letters may be used. For example, #FF0000 represents red and is equivalent to red = 255, green = 0, blue = 0. Similarly, 0xFFEE00 produces a yellowish color with red = 255, green = 238, blue = 0.
- As a three-digit hexadecimal number, preceded by # or 0x. In this encoding, each digit represents one of the RGB channels, but in the range 0 to 15 instead of 0 to 255. Each of the three digits is converted to two identical digits, so that #def is equivalent to #ddeeff in the six-digit form. This encoding allows much fewer colors than the six-digit variant. Under this form, #fff is white, and 0xff0 is yellow.
- As a color name. The names that are accepted are the same as those of the colors defined by the Color class, independently of case. For example, you could specify yellow, green, or chartreuse (or even YELLOW, GREEN, or ChaRTreuSE).

If the color string is not recognized, it is taken as black.

The opacity value is in the range 0 to 1.0 and defaults to 1.0. Here are some examples:

```
var c1 = Color.web("#ffff00");      // Fully opaque yellow
var c2 = Color.web("#ff0");         // Also fully opaque yellow
var c3 = Color.web("#ff0000", 0,5); // Semi-opaque red
var c4 = Color.web("chartreuse");   // A sort of green color
```

If you prefer to think in terms of the hue, saturation, and brightness (HSB) color model,[2] you can use the hsb() function to get a Color:

```
public function hsb(h:Number, s:Number, b:Number, a:Number):Color
public function hsb(h:Number, s:Number, b:Number):Color
```

Here are some examples:

```
var c1 = Color.hsb(0, 1.0, 1.0, 0.5);  // Semi-opaque red
var c2 = Color.hsb(0, 1.0, 1.0);       // Fully opaque red
```

Finally, it is possible to create a JavaFX Color from an Abstract Window Toolkit (AWT) Color instance by using the rgb() function, passing the red, green, and blue components of the AWT color as its arguments:

```
var awtColor:java.awt.Color = java.awt.Color.WHITE;
var javafxColor = Color.rgb(awtColor.getRed(), awtColor.getGreen(),
                            awtColor.getBlue())
```

It's not likely that you will need to do this often, although this technique is useful if you want to use the Swing JColorChooser component, because that component deals entirely in AWT colors. The code in Listing 15-1 shows how to open the JColorChooser and then convert the color that the user selects to a JavaFX color. You'll find this code in the file javafxnodes/UseJColorChooser.fx, which is in the JavaFX Book Desktop project

---

[2] For an explanation of the HSB model, see http://en.wikipedia.org/wiki/HSL_color_space.

because AWT colors and the `JColorChooser` component exist only on the desktop platform.

Listing 15-1 Using the Swing `JColorChooser` Component

```
1     package javafxnodes;
2
3     import javafx.scene.Group;
4     import javafx.scene.paint.Color;
5     import javafx.scene.Scene;
6     import javafx.scene.shape.Rectangle;
7     import javafx.scene.text.Text;
8     import javafx.stage.Stage;
9     import javax.swing.JColorChooser;
10
11    var fill:Color = Color.WHITESMOKE;
12    var scene:Scene;
13
14    Stage {
15        title: "Use JColorChooser"
16        resizable: false
17        scene:
18        scene = Scene {
19            width: 200
20            height: 200
21            fill: bind fill
22            content: [
23                Group {
24                    content: [
25                        Rectangle {
26                            x: 0
27                            y:0
28                            width: bind scene.width
29                            height: bind scene.height
30                            fill: Color.TRANSPARENT
31                        }
32                        Text {
33                            x: 35
34                            y: 20
35                            content: "Click to change color"
36                        }
37                    ]
38                    onMousePressed: function(evt) {
39                        var c:java.awt.Color;
40                        c = JColorChooser.showDialog(null,
41                                    "Select a color",     null);
42                        if (c != null) {
43                            fill = Color.rgb(c.getRed(), c.getGreen(),
44                                    c.getBlue());
45                        }
```

```
46              }
47          }
48      ]
49  }
50 }
```

This application creates a scene that is entirely covered by a group consisting of a transparent rectangle and some text, as shown on the left of Figure 15-4.

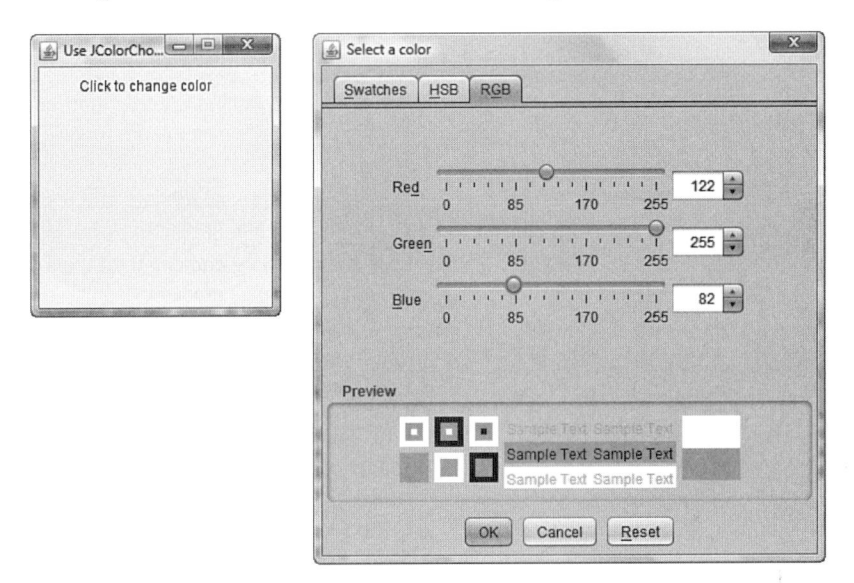

Figure 15-4 Using the Swing `JFileChooser` to get a JavaFX `Color`

When the user clicks with the mouse anywhere in the scene, the function on lines 38 to 46 is called. This function opens the `JFileChooser`, shown on the right of Figure 15-4, and waits until the user has selected a color, converts it to a `javafx.scene.paint.Color`, and stores the result in the script variable called `fill`, to which the `fill` variable of the scene is bound. As a result, the scene's background changes to the selected color.

Linear Gradients

A *color gradient* fills each pixel of an area with a color that depends on that pixel's position. JavaFX supports two types of gradients: *linear*, which we discuss in this section; and *radial*, which is covered in the section that follows.

The colors in a linear gradient vary along a straight line called the *axis* of the gradient. The axis is specified by its start and end points, which may be given either relative to the bounds of the host shape (the default) or as absolute pixel locations. A gradient requires at least two colors, but may have more. The positions on the axis at which the gradient has one of these colors are referred to as *stops*.

A linear gradient is represented by the `javafx.scene.paint.LinearGradient` class, which is a subclass of `Paint`. The variables that can be used to specify the gradient are listed in Table 15-2. The parameters of a `LinearGradient` cannot be changed after it has been initialized.

Table 15-2   Variables of the `LinearGradient` Class

Variable	Type	Access	Default	Description
proportional	Boolean	RI	true	Specifies whether start and end positions are relative (`true`) or absolute (`false`)
startX	Number	RI	0.0	The x coordinate of the start of the gradient
startY	Number	RI	0.0	The y coordinate of the start of the gradient
endX	Number	RI	1.0	The x coordinate of the end of the gradient
endY	Number	RI	1.0	The y coordinate of the end of the gradient
stops	Stop[]	RI	Empty	The positions at which specific colors must be used
cycleMethod	Cycle Method	RI	NO_CYCLE	Specifies the method used to determine colors outside of the area covered by the start and end points

Simple Linear Gradients

The easiest way to illustrate this class is by example. The code in Listing 15-2, from the file `javafxnodes/LinearGradient1.fx`, creates a linear gradient that runs from the left to the right of the scene. In this case, the gradient is used as the fill for the scene, but it could be equally well used with any node that has a `fill` variable.

Listing 15-2   A Horizontal `LinearGradient`

```
1       Stage {
2           title: "Linear Color Gradient"
3           x: 0 y: 0
4           scene: Scene {
5               width: 200 height: 200
6               fill: LinearGradient {
7                   proportional: true
```

```
8                  startX: 0.0 startY: 0.5
9                  endX: 1.0 endY: 0.5
10                 stops: [
11                     Stop { offset: 0.0 color: Color.WHITE }
12                     Stop { offset: 1.0 color: Color.BLACK }
13                 ]
14             }
15         }
16  }
```

The direction of the gradient is determined by its axis, which is defined by the values of the startX, startY, endX, and endY variables. In this example, they are set on lines 8 and 9. The axis and the resulting fill are shown in Figure 15-5.

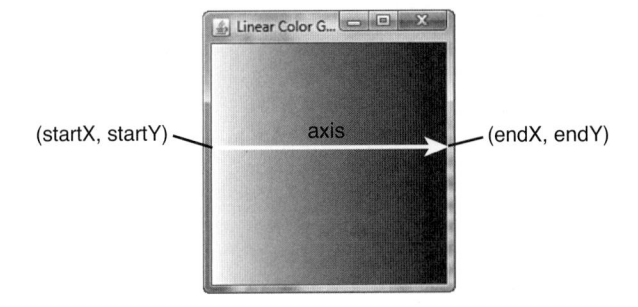

Figure 15-5   A horizontal **LinearGradient** fill

The axis runs from (0, 0.5) to (1, 0.5), where the values are in proportion to the width and height of the filled area, because the proportional variable of the LinearGradient is true. This is usually the most convenient way to describe the gradient because it is independent of the size of the area to be filled. Because the start and end x positions are 0 and 1, the gradient axis covers the whole width of the scene. It is possible to define a gradient axis that extends over only part of an area, as you'll see later.

The stops variable contains a sequence of Stop objects that defines points along the axis at which the value of the gradient will be specified colors. The variables of this object are listed in Table 15-3.

Table 15-3   The **Stop** Object

Variable	Type	Access	Default	Description
offset	Number	RI	0.0	An offset along the gradient axis, in the range 0.0 to 1.0 inclusive
color	Color	RI	null	The Color that should be used at the specified offset

On lines 10 to 13 of Listing 15-2, the `Stop` objects create a gradient that transitions smoothly from white at the start of the axis to black at the end. The `offset` value in a `Stop` object is always in the range `0.0` to `1.0` and is not affected by the value of the `proportional` variable of the gradient.

The colors used along the axis of a proportional gradient are adjusted if the length of the axis changes. In this case, if the scene is resized, the gradient will still transition from white to black over its whole width, as shown in Figure 15-6, which should be compared with Figure 15-5.

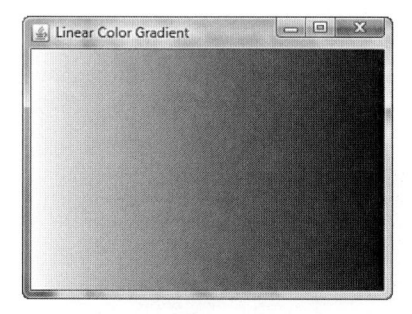

Figure 15-6 The effect of resizing an area filled with a proportional `LinearGradient`

Changing the start and end points of the axis may result in a change in the direction of the gradient. The following code (also from the file `javafxnodes/LinearGradient1.fx`) creates a vertical gradient from white at the top to black at the bottom, as shown in Figure 15-7.

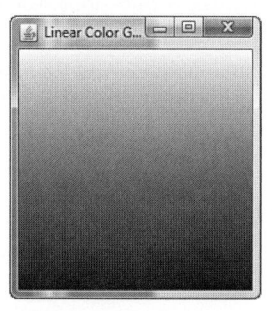

Figure 15-7 A vertical `LinearGradient` fill

```
LinearGradient {
    proportional: true
    startX: 0.5 startY: 0.0
    endX: 0.5 endY: 1.0
```

```
    stops: [
        Stop { offset: 0.0 color: Color.WHITE }
        Stop { offset: 1.0 color: Color.BLACK }
    ]
}
```

Multicolor Linear Gradients

At least two stops are required to define a gradient, but more are possible. Here's an example of a diagonal gradient that starts as green in the top-left corner of the scene, transitions to white halfway across, and then to black in the bottom-right corner, which gives the result shown in Figure 15-8. You'll find this code in the file `javafxnodes/LinearGradient2.fx`.

```
LinearGradient {
    proportional: true
    startX: 0.0 startY: 0.0
    endX: 1.0 endY: 1.0
    stops: [
        Stop { offset: 0.0 color: Color.GREEN }
        Stop { offset: 0.5 color: Color.WHITE }
        Stop { offset: 1.0 color: Color.BLACK }
    ]
}
```

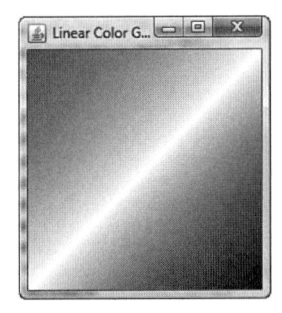

Figure 15-8   A diagonal gradient with three stops

Incomplete Specification of Stops

In the examples you have seen so far, the Stop objects cover the whole axis from 0.0 to 1.0. If the first Stop does not have offset 0.0, one is created with the same color as the first actual Stop, and similarly for the last Stop, so that the whole axis is covered. The following set of Stop objects neither starts nor ends at the endpoints of the gradient axis:

```
stops: [
    Stop { offset: 0.2 color: Color.WHITE }
    Stop { offset: 0.6 color: Color.BLACK }
]
```

Because the first offset is not 0, an additional `Stop` with offset 0 and color white is added. A final `Stop` with offset 1.0 and color black is also added at the end, resulting in the gradient shown in Figure 15-9.[3]

```
stops: [
    Stop { offset: 0.0 color: Color.WHITE } // Automatically added
    Stop { offset: 0.2 color: Color.WHITE }
    Stop { offset: 0.6 color: Color.BLACK }
    Stop { offset: 1.0 color: Color.BLACK } // Automatically added
]
```

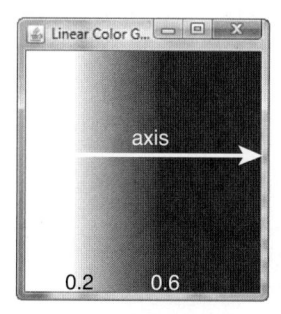

Figure 15-9 A gradient with `Stop` objects that do not cover the whole axis

Cycle Methods

If the axis does not cover the whole area to be filled, there are three possible ways for the area outside the axis to be painted. You specify which you want to use by setting the `cycleMethod` variable of the `LinearGradient` object. The first method simply extends the end colors over the area for which there is no definition. It is used when `cycleMethod` is `CycleMethod.NO_CYCLE`, which is also the default:

```
LinearGradient {
    proportional: true
    startX: 0.2 startY: 0.0    // Axis does not cover the whole
    endX: 0.6 endY: 0.0        // width of the area to paint
    stops: [
        Stop { offset: 0.0 color: Color.WHITE }
        Stop {offset: 1.0 color: Color.BLACK }
    ]
    cycleMethod: CycleMethod.NO_CYCLE
}
```

---

[3] This code is from the file `javafxnodes/LinearGradient3.fx`.

This gradient, which you'll find in the file `javafxnodes/LinearGradient4.fx`, is shown in Figure 15-10. As you can see, it happens to be the same as the one shown in Figure 15-9.

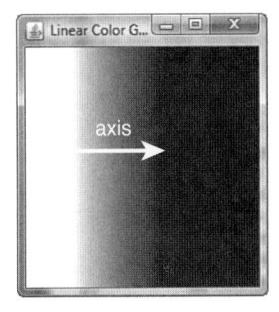

Figure 15-10 A gradient with cycle method = **NO_CYCLE**

The second possibility repeats the gradient over the areas for which there is no definition. This approach is taken when `cycleMethod` has value `CycleMethod.REPEAT`:

```
LinearGradient {
    proportional: true
    startX: 0.2 startY: 0.0    // Axis does not cover the whole
    endX: 0.6 endY: 0.0        // width of the area to paint
    stops: [
        Stop { offset: 0.0 color: Color.WHITE }
        Stop {offset: 1.0 color: Color.BLACK }
    ]
    cycleMethod: CycleMethod.REPEAT
}
```

This gives the result shown in Figure 15-11.[4]

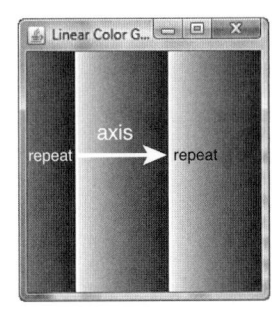

Figure 15-11 A gradient with cycle method = **REPEAT**

---

[4] The source code is in the file `javafxnodes/LinearGradient5.fx`.

The colors used in the areas outside the axis are a repeat of those used along the axis itself. The axis pattern is repeated as many times as is necessary to fill the whole area.

The final possibility is similar to `REPEAT` but uses a *reflection* of the colors used on the axis. This algorithm is used when `cycleMethod` has the value `CycleMethod.REFLECT`, as it does in the following example, which is taken from the file `javafxnodes/LinearGradient6.fx`. Figure 15-12 shows the result:

```
LinearGradient {
    proportional: true
    startX: 0.2 startY: 0.0    // Axis does not cover the whole
    endX: 0.6 endY: 0.0        // width of the area to paint
    stops: [
        Stop { offset: 0.0 color: Color.WHITE }
        Stop {offset: 1.0 color: Color.BLACK }
    ]
    cycleMethod: CycleMethod.REFLECT
}
```

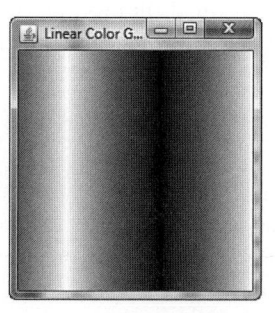

Figure 15-12 A gradient with cycle method = **REFLECT**

When the axis does not cover the whole area to be painted *and* the `Stop` objects do not cover the whole axis, two things happen:

- Stops are added so that the whole axis is covered. This causes the start/end colors to be used at the extremities of the axis.
- The `cycleMethod` is used to determine how to fill the areas outside the axes.

Nonproportional Gradients

In the examples that you have seen so far, the axis has been specified using proportional coordinates. If the `proportional` variable of the `LinearGradient` is `false`, the `startX`, `startY`, `endX`, and `endY` variables are all taken as absolute positions in the same coordinates used to specify the position of the shape being filled. The following example, from the file `javafxnodes/LinearGradient8.fx`, uses absolute coordinates to define a three-color horizontal gradient:

```
Stage {
    title: "Linear Color Gradient"
    x: 0 y: 0
    scene: Scene {
        width: 200 height: 200
        fill: LinearGradient {
            proportional: false
            startX: 0 startY: 100
            endX: 200 endY: 100
            stops: [
                Stop { offset: 0.0 color: Color.PINK }
                Stop { offset: 0.5 color: Color.WHITE }
                Stop { offset: 1.0 color: Color.BLACK }
            ]
        }
    }
}
```

Notice that the axis is now defined in absolute coordinates and stretches across the whole scene, by virtue of the fact that both the end position on the x-axis and the scene width are 200. Notice also that the offsets in the `Stop` objects are still fractions in the range `0.0` to `1.0`. This gradient is shown on the left of Figure 15-13.

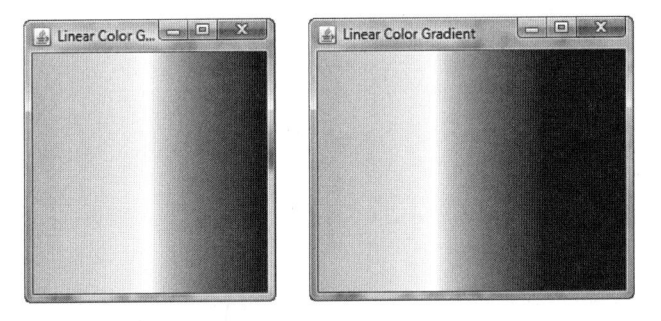

Figure 15-13   A nonproportional `LinearGradient`

If the scene grows in size, the gradient is *not* rescaled to match, because the ends of its axes are specified with absolute coordinates. Instead, the additional space is filled as dictated by the value of the `cycleMethod` variable. In this example, `cycleMethod` is defaulted to `NO_CYCLE`, so the terminal color, in this case black, is used to fill the space to the right of the axis, as shown on the right side of Figure 15-13. Compare this with the behavior of a proportional gradient, as shown later in Figure 15-15 and Figure 15-16.

Using a LinearGradient as a Stroke

You have seen several examples in which the gradient has been used as the fill for a shape. It is also possible to use a gradient to stroke the outline of a shape. The following code from the file `javafxnodes/LinearGradient9.fx`, uses a white-to-black linear gradient to draw the outline of a circle. Figure 15-14 shows the result:

```
Stage {
    title: "Linear Gradient Stroke"
    scene: Scene {
        width: 200
        height: 200
        content: [
            Circle {
                centerX: 100
                centerY: 100
                radius: 90
                fill: Color.YELLOW
                strokeWidth: 4
                stroke: LinearGradient {
                    startX: 0.0 startY: 0.5
                    endX: 1.0 endY: 0.5
                    stops: [
                        Stop { offset: 0 color: Color.WHITE }
                        Stop { offset: 1.0 color: Color.BLACK }
                    ]
                }
            }
        ]
    }
}
```

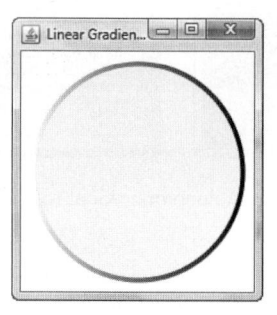

Figure 15-14   Using a `LinearGradient` as a stroke

Radial Gradients

A radial gradient, implemented by the class `javafx.scene.paint.RadialGradient`, produces circular bands of color surrounding a focus point, where the colors are interpolated between two or more stops. In the simplest case, the focus point is the same as the center point of the gradient, which results in concentric circles of color. Table 15-4 lists the variables that determine the characteristics of a radial gradient.

Table 15-4 **Variables of the `RadialGradient` Class**

Variable	Type	Access	Default	Description
`proportional`	Boolean	RI	`true`	Specifies whether the center, radius, and focus variables are relative (`true`) or absolute (`false`)
`centerX`	Number	RI	0	The `x` coordinate of the center of the circle used to define the gradient
`centerY`	Number	RI	0	The `y` coordinate of the center of the circle used to defined the gradient
`radius`	Number	RI	1.0	The radius of the circle that defines the gradient
`focusX`	Number	RI	`centerX`	The `x` coordinate of the gradient's focus point
`focusY`	Number	RI	`centerY`	The `y` coordinate of the gradient's focus point
`stops`	Stop[]	RI	Empty	The positions at which specific colors must be used
`cycleMethod`	CycleMethod	RI	`NO_CYCLE`	Specifies the method used to determine the colors used outside of the circle defined the by center and radius values

A Simple Radial Gradient

The code in Listing 15-3, taken from the file `javafxnodes/RadialGradient1.fx`, fills a `Rectangle` with a radial gradient using the colors pink, white, and green.

Listing 15-3 A Radial Gradient

```
1    package javafxnodes;
2
3    import javafx.scene.paint.Color;
4    import javafx.scene.paint.RadialGradient;
5    import javafx.scene.paint.Stop;
6    import javafx.scene.Scene;
7    import javafx.scene.shape.Rectangle;
8    import javafx.stage.Stage;
9
10   Stage {
11       title: "Radial Gradient"
12       scene: Scene {
13           width: 200 height: 200
14           content: [
15               Rectangle {
16                   x: 10 y: 10
17                   width: 180 height: 180
18                   stroke: Color.BLACK
19                   fill: RadialGradient {
20                       proportional: true
21                       centerX: 0.5 centerY: 0.5
22                       radius: 0.75
23                       stops: [
24                           Stop { offset: 0.0 color: Color.PINK }
25                           Stop { offset: 0.5 color: Color.WHITE }
26                           Stop { offset: 1.0 color: Color.GREEN }
27                       ]
28                   }
29               }
30           ]
31       }
32   }
```

Figure 15-15 shows the results of the preceding code.

The centerX and centerY values determine where the center of the radial gradient is placed. When proportional is true, these value must be in the range 0 to 1 and give the position relative to the bounds of the shape that it is being used to fill. In this example, the values are both 0.5, so the center of the gradient coincides with the center of the rectangle. The radius variable determines the size of the area over which the colors in the stops variable are to be applied. Here, the radius is 0.75, so the colors will be applied over 0.75 of the size of the rectangle. Outside of this region, the cycleMethod will be used to determine the colors to be used. Because no cycleMethod has been specified, the default of

NO_CYCLE is implied, so the last color in the stops sequence, namely green, will be used to fill the area outside the gradient circle.

Figure 15-15   A square filled with a radial gradient

Changing the Bounds of the Filled Shape

The shape shown in Figure 15-15 is a square and the radial gradient consists of concentric circles of color, where the bounding radius is 0.75 of the size of the square. When the filled shape is a rectangle that is not square, the concentric circles of color become concentric ellipses, as shown in Figure 15-16. This is the same RadialGradient as the one used in Figure 15-15—only the width of the filled shape and that of the enclosing stage have been changed.[5]

```
Rectangle {
    x: 10 y: 10
    width: 280 height: 180
    stroke: Color.BLACK
    fill: RadialGradient {
        proportional: true
        centerX: 0.5 centerY: 0.5
        radius: 0.75
        stops: [
            Stop { offset: 0.0 color: Color.PINK }
            Stop { offset: 0.5 color: Color.WHITE }
            Stop { offset: 1.0 color: Color.GREEN }
        ]
    }
}
```

---

[5] You can find this code in the file javafxnodes/RadialGradient2.fx.

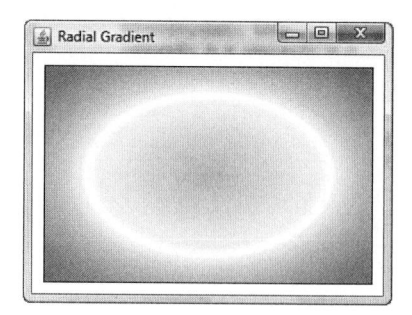

Figure 15-16 A nonsquare rectangle filled with a radial gradient

The scaling of the `radius`, which determines the actual shape of the gradient, is actually based on the bounding box of the shape being filled (or stroked). Listing 15-4, from the source code in `javafxnodes/RadialGradient3.fx`, shows an example that uses the same `RadialGradient` to fill a triangle, constructed using the `javafx.scene.shape.Polygon` class that is discussed in the next chapter.

Listing 15-4 **A `RadialGradient` in a Triangle**

```
package javafxnodes;

import javafx.scene.paint.Color;
import javafx.scene.paint.RadialGradient;
import javafx.scene.paint.Stop;
import javafx.scene.Scene;
import javafx.stage.Stage;
import javafx.scene.shape.Polygon;

// RadialGradient in a triangle
Stage {
    title: "Radial Gradient"
    scene: Scene {
        width: 200 height: 200
        content: [
            Polygon {
                points: [ 100,10, 140,180, 60,180 ]
                stroke: Color.BLACK
                fill: RadialGradient {
                    proportional: true
                    centerX: 0.5
                    centerY: 0.5
                    radius: 0.75
                    stops: [
```

```
                    Stop {offset: 0.0 color: Color.WHITE }
                    Stop {offset: 0.5 color: Color.YELLOW }
                    Stop { offset: 1.0 color: Color.GREEN }
                ]
            }
        }
    ]
  }
}
```

Figure 15-17 shows the gradient produced by this code.

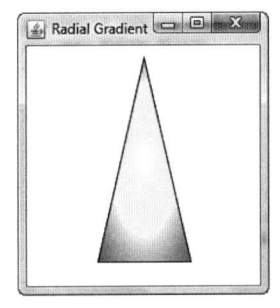

Figure 15-17   Using a radial gradient to fill a triangle

This particular triangle is taller than it is wide, so the bounding box is a tall rectangle, which causes the color circles of the gradient to be transformed into ellipses with their major axes aligned along the y-axis.

Moving the Center of the Gradient

If the center of the radial gradient is moved by changing the centerX/centerY values, the gradient effect shifts away from the center of the filled shape. The code in Listing 15-5, which you'll find in the file javafxnodes/RadialGradient4.fx, uses the RadialGradient from the earlier examples, but with the centerX and centerY values changed to 0.25 and 0.75, respectively.

Listing 15-5   Moving the Center of a `RadialGradient`

```
Stage {
    title: "Radial Gradient"
    scene: Scene {
        width: 200 height: 200
        content: [
```

```
Rectangle {
    x: 10 y: 10
    width: 180 height: 180
    stroke: Color.BLACK
    fill: RadialGradient {
        proportional: true
        centerX: 0.25 centerY: 0.75
        radius: 0.75
        stops: [
            Stop { offset: 0.0 color: Color.WHITE }
            Stop { offset: 0.5 color: Color.YELLOW }
            Stop { offset: 1.0 color: Color.GREEN }
        ]
    }
}
    ]
  }
}
```

Figure 15-18 shows the effect of this.

Figure 15-18 Moving the center of a `RadialGradient`

Notice that although the color circles are no longer centered at the middle of the square, they are still concentric. Contrast this with the effect of moving the focus, an example of which you'll see in the upcoming "Changing the Focus" section.

Effect of Cycle Methods

As with linear gradients, the `cycleMethod` variable determines how the pixels outside the defining circle or ellipse of the `RadialGradient` are colored. The default, `NO_CYCLE`, has the effect of coloring those pixels with the color used in the last `Stop`, as you have seen in the examples so far in this section. If the first `Stop` in the definition of the gradient is not at offset 0.0, the innermost pixels are filled with the color in the first Stop. Here's a gradient that demonstrates this, taken from the file javafxnodes/RadialGradient5.fx:

```
RadialGradient {
    proportional: true
    centerX: 0.5 centerY: 0.5
    radius: 0.75
    stops: [
        Stop { offset: 0.3 color: Color.PINK }
        Stop { offset: 0.6 color: Color.WHITE }
        Stop { offset: 1.0 color: Color.GREEN }
    ]
}
```

Because there is no explicit Stop at offset 0, the center of the gradient will be filled with the color used in the first actual Stop—in this case, pink. Points that are outside the defining circle will be colored with the color of the last Stop, which, in this case, is green. See Figure 15-19.

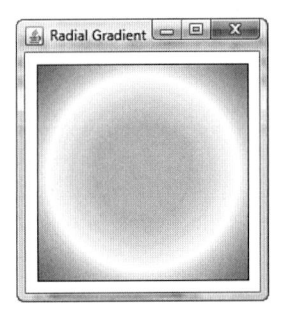

Figure 15-19   A **RadialGradient** with cycle method **NO_CYCLE**

The other cycle methods, REPEAT and REFLECT, have the same effect as they do with a LinearGradient. The result of using REPEAT with the gradient above but with a slightly smaller radius is shown on the left of Figure 15-20, and REFLECT is shown on the right.[6]

Changing the Focus

In all the examples you have seen so far, the color rings have been centered on the center point of the RadialGradient. In general, the color rings are centered on a point called the *focus*, whose position is defined by the variables focusX and focusY. By default, the values of focusX and focusY are the same as those of centerX and centerY, respectively,

---

[6] These examples come from the files javafxnodes/RadialGradient6.fx and javafxnodes/RadialGradient7.fx, respectively.

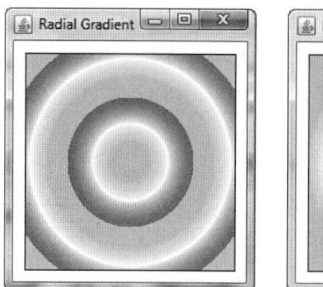

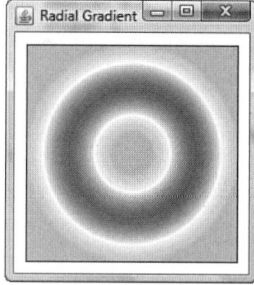

Figure 15-20   The **REPEAT** and **REFLECT** cycle methods

but you can move the focus elsewhere. The effect will be that the first color ring is placed at the focus and the last on the perimeter of the defining circle. The rings in between will be placed at interpolated positions between the focus and the perimeter. The code in Listing 15-6, which you will find in the file `javafxnodes/RadialGradient8.fx`, creates a `RadialGradient` in which the focus is moved toward the top left of the defining circle by setting both the `focusX` and `focusY` variables to `0.25`.

Listing 15-6   **Moving the Focus of a `RadialGradient`**

```
Stage {
    title: "Radial Gradient"
    scene: Scene {
        width: 200 height: 200
        content: [
            Rectangle {
                x: 10 y: 10
                width: 180 height: 180
                stroke: Color.BLACK
                fill: RadialGradient {
                    proportional: true
                    centerX: 0.5 centerY: 0.5
                    focusX: 0.25 focusY: 0.25
                    radius: 0.75
                    stops: [
                        Stop { offset: 0.0 color: Color.GREEN }
                        Stop { offset: 0.5 color: Color.WHITE }
                        Stop { offset: 1.0 color: Color.BLACK }
                    ]
                }
            }
        ]
    }
}
```

As shown in Figure 15-21, the inner rings of color, which are green, appear around the focal point, but the centers of the rings that are farther out move progressively back toward the center of the defining circle.

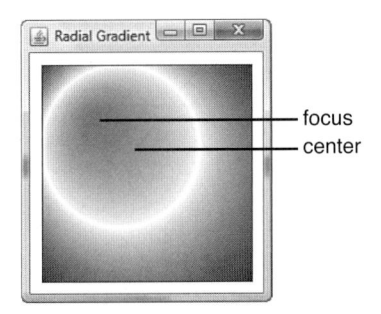

Figure 15-21   Effect of moving the focus of a
`RadialGradient`

If the `focusX` and `focusY` variables refer to a point that is outside the perimeter of the defining circle, the focus will be implicitly moved to the closest point on the circle's perimeter.

Events

The variables discussed so far in this chapter and in the previous chapter have been mainly concerned with changing the appearance of the node on which they are set. This section describes a set of variables that let you detect user interaction with a node. A user can interact with a node using either the mouse or the keyboard, causing events to be delivered to that node.

Some nodes intercept these events and report them to application code in a slightly different way. For example, if you click a button (described in Chapter 22, "Cross-Platform Controls") with the mouse, several mouse events will be generated, which the button itself will handle. When the mouse is pressed, the button will draw itself so that it looks as if it has been pushed in. When the mouse is released, the button will redraw itself in it normal state and will also call the JavaFX function installed as the value of its `action` attribute, if there is one:

```
Button {
    text: "Click Me"
    action: function() { println("Button clicked") }
}
```

The same thing happens if the user gives the button the input focus and then presses the Spacebar key, except that in this case the button is responding to keyboard events

402 Chapter 15 Node Variables and Events

rather than mouse events. This behavior is specific to the `Button` class—other nodes handle keyboard and mouse events in different ways.

Because nodes like `button` convert these low-level events into the more useful invocation of a function like that shown above, you don't always need to deal with mouse and keyboard events yourself. However, you *do* need to know how to handle these events if you want to add behavior of your own, such as allowing the user to move nodes around the screen or moving a node to the front of the Z-order when it is clicked.

Mouse Events

The JavaFX runtime reports mouse events by calling functions that you can assign to any of the eight node variables listed in Table 15-5.

Table 15-5 Node Function Variables for Mouse Event Reporting

Variable	Function Argument	When Called
`onMouseEntered`	`MouseEvent`	As the mouse enters the area occupied by the node
`onMouseExited`	`MouseEvent`	As the mouse leaves the area occupied by the node
`onMousePressed`	`MouseEvent`	When the mouse is pressed while it is over the node
`onMouseReleased`	`MouseEvent`	When the mouse is released while it is over the node, or after a mouse drag operation
`onMouseClicked`	`MouseEvent`	When the mouse is clicked one or more times while over the node
`onMouseMoved`	`MouseEvent`	As the mouse is moved while it is over the node with no buttons pressed
`onMouseDragged`	`MouseEvent`	When the mouse is moved over the node with one or more buttons pressed
`onMouseWheelMoved`	`MouseEvent`	When the user moves the mouse wheel, if there is one

Each of these variables is public and requires a function that is of `Void` type and which accepts a `java.scene.input.MouseEvent` as its argument. Here are the actual definitions:

```
public var onMouseEntered: function(:MouseEvent):Void
public var onMouseExited: function(:MouseEvent):Void
public var onMousePressed: function(:MouseEvent):Void
```

```
public var onMouseReleased: function(:MouseEvent):Void
public var onMouseClicked: function(:MouseEvent):Void
public var onMouseMoved: function(:MouseEvent):Void
public var onMouseDragged: function(:MouseEvent):Void
public var onMouseWheelMoved: function(:MouseEvent):Void
```

With one exception,[7] mouse events are delivered to a node only while the mouse is within its boundaries. Before we look at when these events are delivered, we need to discuss the way in which JavaFX models the mouse and how this is reflected in the `MouseEvent` class.

The Mouse and the `MouseEvent` Class

The JavaFX GUI library models the mouse as a device that enables the user to move the cursor around the screen, with three buttons that may be in either a pressed or released state at any given time. These characteristics of the mouse are reflected in the variables of the `MouseEvent` object that is passed to all the mouse-related callback methods. Some mice also have (or can simulate) a wheel that can be rotated either toward or away from the user. This aspect of the mouse is covered in "The Mouse Wheel" section, later in this chapter. On a mobile device, the mouse might actually be a stylus that is used to tap the screen, or even the user's finger.

The `MouseEvent` object has a large number of variables, all of which we discuss in this section. `MouseEvent` objects are created only by the JavaFX GUI runtime, so all its variables are read-only to application code. Table 15-6 lists the more commonly used of these variables.

Table 15-6   Some Common Variables of the `MouseEvent` Class

Variable	Type	Access	Description
node	Node	R	The node to which this event is delivered. This is one of the nodes that the mouse is currently over, except in the case of a mouse drag event. See the section "Mouse Dragging," later in this chapter, for further information.
source	Node	R	The node that is immediately under the mouse (except in the case of a mouse drag event). See the section "Mouse Event Propagation," later in this chapter, for the difference between this variable and the node variable.

---

[7] The exception is the mouse dragged event, as described in the "Mouse Dragging" section, later in this chapter.

x	Number	R	The x coordinate of the mouse when the event was created, relative to the origin of the node given by the `node` variable.
y	Number	R	The y coordinate of the mouse when the event was created, relative to the origin of the node given by the `node` variable.
sceneX	Number	R	The x coordinate of the mouse when the event was created, relative to the scene containing the source node.
sceneY	Number	R	The y coordinate of the mouse when the event was created, relative to the scene containing the source node.
screenX	Number	R	The x coordinate of the mouse when the event was created, relative to the user's screen.
screenY	Number	R	The y coordinate of the mouse when the event was created, relative to the user's screen.

Tracking Mouse Motion

The functions assigned to the node variables `onMouseEntered`, `onMouseExited`, and `onMouseMoved` are called as the mouse enters, moves over, and leaves the area occupied by a node. The code in Listing 15-7, taken from the file `javafxnodes/MouseEvents1.fx`, creates a yellow rectangle and assigns functions to these variables that print the details of the events that they receive. Figure 15-22 shows the scene created by this code.

Figure 15-22   Tracking the movement of the mouse

Listing 15-7   Mouse Movement Events

```
Stage {
    title: "Mouse Events 1"
    scene: Scene {
        width: 200
        height: 150
        content: [
```

```
            Rectangle {
                x: 10 y: 10
                width: 180 height: 130
                fill: Color.YELLOW stroke: Color.BLACK
                onMouseEntered: function(evt) {
                    println("Enter {evt}");
                }
                onMouseExited: function(evt) {
                    println("Exit {evt}");
                }
                onMouseMoved: function(evt) {
                    println("Move {evt}");
                }
            }
        ]
    }
}
```

If you move your mouse cursor over the scene from left to right as indicated by the arrow, without pressing any buttons, you see the events that are generated, some of which are reproduced here:

```
Enter MouseEvent [x=10.0, y=29.0, button=NONE ENTERED]
Move MouseEvent [x=10.0, y=29.0, button=NONE MOVED]
Move MouseEvent [x=11.0, y=29.0, button=NONE MOVED]
Move MouseEvent [x=13.0, y=29.0, button=NONE MOVED]
Move MouseEvent [x=14.0, y=29.0, button=NONE MOVED]
Move MouseEvent [x=16.0, y=29.0, button=NONE MOVED]
[ More events not shown ]

Move MouseEvent [x=188.0, y=29.0, button=NONE MOVED]
Move MouseEvent [x=189.0, y=29.0, button=NONE MOVED]
Move MouseEvent [x=190.0, y=29.0, button=NONE MOVED]
Exit MouseEvent [x=191.0, y=29.0, button=NONE EXITED]
```

As you can see, for each event we show the type, the x and y coordinates of the mouse at the time of the event relative to the coordinate system of the source node, and the buttons that were pressed, in this case none.

The first event, which is delivered to the rectangle's onMouseEntered handler, reports the mouse entering the rectangle at coordinates (10, 29), which is on its left edge, 29 pixels down from the top. This is the point labeled A in Figure 15-22. After the mouse enters the rectangle, there is a series of events, which are delivered to the onMouseMoved handler, that report its progress over the rectangle. The last event, delivered to the rectangle's onMouseExited handler, records the mouse leaving the panel at (191, 29), or point B in Figure 15-22. No events are reported before or after these times because the mouse was not over a node that has any registered mouse handlers.

Note

It might seem strange that the x coordinate has value 10 as the mouse enters the rectangle. Remember that these coordinates are relative to the coordinate system used to place the rectangle, *not* relative to the top-left corner of the rectangle itself. Had we instead moved the origin from the top left of the scene by using the translateX and translateY (or layoutX and layoutY) variables rather than x and y, the event would have reported an x coordinate of 0. For more on this, see Chapter 17, "Coordinates, Transforms, and Layout," which discusses coordinate systems and transformations in detail.

You might have noticed that there are events reporting the mouse moving over the points (11, 29) and (13, 29), but no event was generated as it passed over (12, 29). There is no guarantee that an event will be generated for each position that the mouse occupies, and if the mouse is moved more quickly, there will be more gaps like this one.

For each onMouseEntered call to a node, there will always be a corresponding onMouseExited call to the same node.

Mouse Event Propagation

The code in Listing 15-8, from the file javafxnodes/MouseEvents2.fx, adds a green circle to the example that you have just seen. The rectangle and circle overlap, as shown in Figure 15-23.

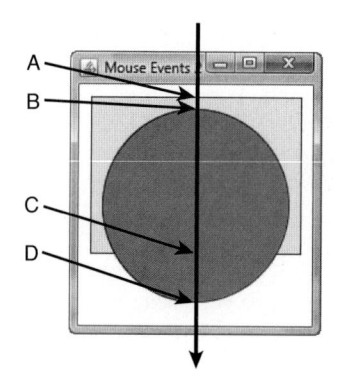

Figure 15-23 Moving the cursor from top to bottom

Listing 15-8   **Mouse Event Propagation**

```
Stage {
    title: "Mouse Events 2"
    scene: Scene {
        width: 200
        height: 200
        content: [
```

```
Rectangle {
    x: 10 y: 10
    width: 180 height: 130
    fill: Color.YELLOW stroke: Color.BLACK
    onMouseEntered: function(evt) {
        println("Enter Rectangle ({evt.x}, {evt.y})");
    }
    onMouseExited: function(evt) {
        println("Exit Rectangle ({evt.x}, {evt.y})");
    }
    onMouseMoved: function(evt) {
        println("Move Rectangle ({evt.x}, {evt.y})");
    }
}
Circle {
    centerX: 100 centerY: 100
    radius: 80
    fill: Color.GREEN stroke: Color.BLACK
    onMouseEntered: function(evt) {
        println("Enter Circle ({evt.x}, {evt.y})");
    }
    onMouseExited: function(evt) {
        println("Exit Circle ({evt.x}, {evt.y})");
    }
    onMouseMoved: function(evt) {
        println("Move Circle ({evt.x}, {evt.y})");
    }
}
            ]
        }
}
```

If you run the preceding code and move the mouse cursor from top to bottom, as indicated in Figure 15-23, you'll see output that looks like this (where some events have been removed for the sake of clarity):

```
1       Enter Rectangle (95.0, 11.0)
2       Move Rectangle (95.0, 11.0)
3       Move Rectangle (95.0, 15.0)
4       Enter Circle (95.0, 21.0)
5       Move Circle (95.0, 21.0)
6       Move Rectangle (95.0, 21.0)
7       Move Circle (95.0, 29.0)
8       Move Rectangle (95.0, 29.0)

        [More events not shown ]
```

Chapter 15 Node Variables and Events

```
9       Move Circle (95.0, 114.0)
10      Move Rectangle (95.0, 114.0)
11      Move Circle (95.0, 128.0)
12      Move Rectangle (95.0, 128.0)
13      Exit Rectangle (95.0, 143.0)
14      Move Circle (95.0, 143.0)
15      Move Circle (95.0, 156.0)
16      Move Circle (95.0, 170.0)
17      Exit Circle (95.0, 183.0)
```

On lines 1 to 4, you see the events that are generated as the mouse enters the rectangle, moves downward, and enters the area covered by the circle. As the cursor continues to move, you can see from the events on lines 5 through 12 that its motion is reported to the `onMouseMoved` handlers of both the circle and the rectangle. This is because the mouse is now traveling over both nodes, even though the circle hides the rectangle. This is the default behavior for *all* mouse events—they are delivered first to the node under the mouse that is topmost, and then to any other nodes that occupy the same position, in front-to-back order.

On line 13, the mouse leaves the rectangle, and its subsequent movement is reported only to the circle's `onMouseMoved` handler, until it leaves the circle at line 17.

If you don't want mouse events to be propagated in this way, you can set the node's `blockMouse` variable to `true`. This stops any mouse events being delivered to nodes that are underneath the node on which it is set. The following code change, which you'll find in the file `javafxnodes/MouseEvents3.fx`, prevents the propagation of events from the circle to the rectangle:

```
Circle {
    centerX: 100 centerY: 100
    radius: 80
    fill: Color.GREEN stroke: Color.BLACK
    blocksMouse: true
```

With this change, we get the following result:

```
1       Enter Rectangle (95.0, 11.0)
2       Move Rectangle (95.0, 11.0)
3       Move Rectangle (95.0, 15.0)
4       Move Rectangle (95.0, 18.0)
5       Exit Rectangle (95.0, 21.0)
6       Enter Circle (95.0, 22.0)
7       Move Circle (95.0, 22.0)
8       Move Circle (95.0, 26.0)

        [More events not shown ]

9       Move Circle (95.0, 176.0)
10      Move Circle (95.0, 179.0)
11      Exit Circle (95.0, 183.0)
```

This time, you can see that when the mouse enters the circle, an event is also delivered to the rectangle to indicate that the mouse is no longer over it. Subsequent movements are reported only to the circle.

When mouse events are generated for nodes that are part of a group, those events will also be propagated to the group, unless blocked by one of the nodes. However, mouse events *cannot* be delivered to the scene because scene is not a subclass of Node. If you want to be able to handle mouse events that happen anywhere within the scene, you need to cover the scene with a rectangle and assign mouse event handlers to the rectangle itself. Listing 15-9, which is taken from the file javafxnodes/MouseEvents4.fx, illustrates how to do this.

Listing 15-9 Using a Rectangle to Receive Events on the Scene

```
1    var scene:Scene;
2    Stage {
3        title: "Mouse Events 4"
4        scene: scene = Scene {
5            width: 200
6            height: 200
7            content: [
8                Rectangle {
9                    x: 0 y: 0
10                   width: bind scene.width height: bind scene.height
11                   fill: Color.TRANSPARENT
12                   onMouseEntered: function(evt) {
13                       println("Enter Rectangle ({evt.x}, {evt.y})");
14                   }
15                   onMouseExited: function(evt) {
16                       println("Exit Rectangle ({evt.x}, {evt.y})");
17                   }
18                   onMouseMoved: function(evt) {
19                       println("Move Rectangle ({evt.x}, {evt.y})");
20                   }
21               }
22               Circle {
23                   centerX: 100 centerY: 100
24                   radius: 80
25                   fill: Color.GREEN stroke: Color.BLACK
26                   blocksMouse: true
27                   onMouseEntered: function(evt) {
28                       println("Enter Circle ({evt.x}, {evt.y})");
29                   }
30                   onMouseExited: function(evt) {
31                       println("Exit Circle ({evt.x}, {evt.y})");
32                   }
33                   onMouseMoved: function(evt) {
```

```
34                              println("Move Circle ({evt.x}, {evt.y})");
35                          }
36                      }
37                  ]
38              }
39          }
```

In this example, the rectangle has been expanded to cover the whole scene by placing it at coordinates (0, 0) and binding its width and height to those of the scene. Notice also that its `fill` has been set to `Color.TRANSPARENT` so that it does not hide the scene itself.[8] Because the circle has its `blocksMouse` variable set to `true`, any mouse events generated inside the boundary of the circle will be delivered only to the handler's registered for the circle, whereas those generated outside will go only to the handlers of the rectangle.

If you want to be able process *all* mouse events from a central location, you can do so by moving the rectangle so that it follows the circle in the `content` sequence of the scene. This causes the transparent rectangle to be in front of the circle, as a result of which every mouse event is delivered to it first. The handlers attached to the circle will not be affected because events generated while the mouse is over it will be propagated to them in the normal way, as long as the `blocksMouse` variable of the rectangle is `false`. You'll learn more about the propagation of mouse events in the "Delivery of Mouse Events" section, later in this chapter.

Mouse Buttons

The functions assigned to the `onMousePressed`, `onMouseReleased`, and `onMouseClicked` variables of a node are called when the user presses and releases any of the mouse buttons. The events delivered to these functions report the mouse position using the variables listed in Table 15-6 together with the additional information shown in Table 15-7.

Table 15-7   MouseEvent Variables Relating to Mouse Buttons

Variable	Type	Access	Description
button	Mouse Button	R	The mouse button whose state has changed
clickCount	Integer	R	The number of mouse clicks
middleButtonDown	Boolean	R	Whether the middle button of the mouse is pressed

---

[8] Setting the `fill` to `null` would also make the rectangle transparent, but it would not serve our purpose here because mouse events are not delivered to a node for which the `fill` is `null`, unless the mouse is over a part of the node that is colored using the stroke. See the "Delivery of Mouse Events" section, later in this chapter, for more on this.

Table 15-7   MouseEvent Variables Relating to Mouse Buttons *(Continued)*

Variable	Type	Access	Description
primaryButtonDown	Boolean	R	Whether the primary button is pressed
secondaryButtonDown	Boolean	R	Whether the secondary button is pressed
popupTrigger	Boolean	R	Whether this event represents a pop-up gesture

The code in Listing 15-10, which you'll find in the file `javafxnodes/MouseEvents5.fx`, assigns functions to the `onMousePressed`, `onMouseReleased`, and `onMouseClicked` variables of a rectangle and prints the events that are delivered.

Listing 15-10   **Mouse Button Events**

```
function displayMouseEvent(type:String, evt:MouseEvent):Void {
    println("{type}. Clicks: {evt.clickCount},"
            " button: {evt.button},"
            " primary: {evt.primaryButtonDown},"
            " middle: {evt.middleButtonDown},"
            " secondary: {evt.secondaryButtonDown}");
}

Stage {
    title: "Mouse Events 5"
    scene: Scene {
        width: 200
        height: 150
        content: [
            Rectangle {
                x: 10 y: 10
                width: 180 height: 130
                fill: Color.YELLOW stroke: Color.BLACK
                onMousePressed: function(evt) {
                    displayMouseEvent("Pressed", evt);
                }
                onMouseReleased: function(evt) {
                    displayMouseEvent("Released", evt);
                }
                onMouseClicked: function(evt) {
                    displayMouseEvent("Clicked", evt);
                }
            }
        ]
    }
}
```

If you were to move the mouse over the rectangle, and then press and release the left mouse button, the following events would be reported:

```
Pressed. Clicks: 1, button: PRIMARY, primary: true, middle: false,
secondary: false
Released. Clicks: 1, button: PRIMARY, primary: false, middle: false,
secondary: false
Clicked. Clicks: 1, button: PRIMARY, primary: false, middle: false,
secondary: false
```

The first event is delivered to the rectangle's `onMousePressed` handler as you press the button, the second is passed to its `onMouseReleased` handler when the button is released, and the last to the `onMouseClicked` handler immediately afterward. Whenever you press and then release a mouse button, a set of three events like this will be generated. The first and second events allow you to take specific action when the mouse is either pressed or released—for example, a button might repaint itself as if it were pressed in response to the first event and paint itself again in its unpressed state when the second event occurs, whereas the mouse clicked event allows you to treat the press/release gesture as a single operation.

The `button` attribute of the event indicates which button has been pressed, released, or clicked. Table 15-8 lists the possible values.

Table 15-8 **Possible Values of the `Button` Attribute**

`MouseButton.NONE`	No button has been pressed or released.
`MouseButton.PRIMARY`	The primary mouse button has been pressed or released.
`MouseButton.MIDDLE`	The middle mouse button has been pressed or released.
`MouseButton.SECONDARY`	The secondary mouse button has been pressed or released.

Which button is reported as primary and which as secondary depends on how your mouse is configured. For a right-handed person, the primary button is usually the left one, and the secondary button is on the right. If you are left-handed and you have reconfigured your mouse accordingly, these will be reversed.

Not all mice have three buttons, so not all these values may be possible on any given system. Mice used with Windows PCs generally have two buttons, those on UNIX systems often have three, and Apple Mac users sometimes have only one, which appears as the primary button in JavaFX. It may be possible to simulate additional mouse buttons by using keys in conjunction with the mouse. For example, on the Apple Mac, holding down the Ctrl key while pressing the single mouse button simulates pressing the secondary button. On a mobile device that has a touch screen, tapping the screen will result in events that report the use of the primary button.

The `clickCount` attribute counts the number of mouse clicks that have been made. If you press and release the mouse slowly, this count will always be 1. However, if you click more rapidly, you can get larger values, as the following output shows:

```
Pressed. Clicks: 1, button: PRIMARY, primary: true, middle: false,
secondary: false
Released. Clicks: 1, button: PRIMARY, primary: false, middle: false,
secondary: false
Clicked. Clicks: 1, button: PRIMARY, primary: false, middle: false,
secondary: false
Pressed. Clicks: 2, button: PRIMARY, primary: true, middle: false,
secondary: false
Released. Clicks: 2, button: PRIMARY, primary: false, middle: false,
secondary: false
Clicked. Clicks: 2, button: PRIMARY, primary: false, middle: false,
secondary: false
Pressed. Clicks: 3, button: PRIMARY, primary: true, middle: false,
secondary: false
Released. Clicks: 3, button: PRIMARY, primary: false, middle: false,
secondary: false
Clicked. Clicks: 3, button: PRIMARY, primary: false, middle: false,
secondary: false
Pressed. Clicks: 4, button: PRIMARY, primary: true, middle: false,
secondary: false
Released. Clicks: 4, button: PRIMARY, primary: false, middle: false,
secondary: false
Clicked. Clicks: 4, button: PRIMARY, primary: false, middle: false,
secondary: false
Pressed. Clicks: 5, button: PRIMARY, primary: true, middle: false,
secondary: false
Released. Clicks: 5, button: PRIMARY, primary: false, middle: false,
secondary: false
```

It is normal to interpret a single mouse click as a selection operation and a double-click (that is, a mouse click with a `clickCount` of 2) as an activation operation, which may cause some additional action to occur. For example, in a list of photographs, single-clicking might select a photograph, while double-clicking would open the photograph for viewing. Note before an event with a `clickCount` value of 2 is delivered, an event with `clickCount` set to 1 will be seen, so every activation gesture will have been preceded by one that would appear to be a selection. It is unusual to give any specific meaning to a click count greater than 2.

The `popupTrigger` variable does not correspond to a fixed mouse button. Instead, it returns `true` if the `MouseEvent` should be interpreted as a request to open a context menu. The precise gesture that opens a context menu is platform-dependent—on Windows, it would be the release of mouse button three, while on the Apple Mac it would result from holding down the mouse button with the Ctrl key on the keyboard pressed.

Chapter 15 Node Variables and Events

By using the `popupTrigger` variable, you can avoid hard-coding the platform specifics in your JavaFX application.

Modifier Keys

The `MouseEvent` class has four variables, listed in Table 15-9, that record the state of certain keys on the keyboard at the time that the event is generated.

Table 15-9 **Modifier Key Variables in the `MouseEvent` Class**

Variable	Type	Access	Description
altDown	Boolean	R	The Alt key is pressed.
controlDown	Boolean	R	The Ctrl key is pressed.
metaDown	Boolean	R	The Meta key is pressed.
shiftDown	Boolean	R	The Shift key is pressed.

By modifying the `displayMouseEvent()` function used in the last example, you can see the values of these variables. You'll find the modified code in the file `javafxnodes/MouseEvents6.fx`:

```
function displayMouseEvent(type:String, evt:MouseEvent):Void {
    print("{type}. Clicks: {evt.clickCount},"
          " button: {evt.button},"
          " primary: {evt.primaryButtonDown},"
          " middle: {evt.middleButtonDown},"
          " secondary: {evt.secondaryButtonDown}. Keys: ");
    if (evt.altDown) {
        print("ALT ");
    }
    if (evt.controlDown) {
        println("CTRL ");
    }
    if (evt.metaDown) {
        println("META ");
    }
    if (evt.shiftDown) {
        print("SHIFT ")
    }
    println("");
}
```

The Ctrl and Shift keys are present on all keyboards, but the Alt and Meta keys are not. On the Apple Mac, the Alt key is actually the Option key and the Meta key is the Command (or Apple) key. On a Windows PC, there is no Meta key. You can see how the key modifier variables are set by clicking the yellow Rectangle while holding down one or more of these keys.[9] The following events are typical examples:

```
Clicked. Clicks: 1, button: PRIMARY, primary: false, middle: false,
secondary: false. Keys: ALT
Clicked. Clicks: 1, button: PRIMARY, primary: false, middle: false,
secondary: false. Keys: CTRL
Clicked. Clicks: 1, button: PRIMARY, primary: false, middle: false,
secondary: false. Keys: SHIFT
Clicked. Clicks: 1, button: PRIMARY, primary: false, middle: false,
secondary: false. Keys: ALT CTRL
```

The last event was actually generated by pressing the Alt Gr key on my keyboard, but could equally well result from holding down both the Alt and Ctrl keys.

Mouse Dragging

In the "Tracking Mouse Motion" section, earlier in this chapter, you saw the events that are generated as the mouse moves over a node when none of its buttons are pressed. If the cursor is moved over a node while there *is* a button pressed, a different event is generated. Moving the mouse with a button pressed (or dragging the stylus over the screen of a mobile device) is interpreted as a *drag* gesture. A drag has three parts:

1. A mouse button is pressed, resulting in an event being delivered to the onMousePressed handler of the node over which the mouse is placed.

2. The mouse is moved with the button still pressed. This causes events to be delivered to the onMouseDragged handler instead of the onMouseMoved handler of the node on which the drag began.

3. The mouse is released and an event is delivered to the onMouseReleased handler of the node on which the drag began.

The code in Listing 15-11, from the file javafxnodes/MouseEvents7.fx, registers mouse handling functions that print these events.

Listing 15-11   **Mouse Drag Events**

```
1      Stage {
2          title: "Mouse Events 7"
3          scene: Scene {
4              width: 500
5              height: 500
6              content: [
7                  Rectangle {
8                      x: 10 y: 10
```

---

[9] Although mouse clicks are used in this example, this is not necessary—these variables are valid for every mouse event.

Chapter 15 Node Variables and Events

```
9                       width: 50 height: 50
10                      fill: Color.YELLOW stroke: Color.BLACK
11                      onMousePressed: function(evt) {
12                          println("Pressed: {evt}");
13                      }
14                      onMouseDragged: function(evt) {
15                          println("dragAnchorX: {evt.dragAnchorX}, "
16                                  "dragAnchorY: {evt.dragAnchorY}, "
17                                  "dragX: {evt.dragX}, "
18                                  "dragY: {evt.dragY}");
19                      }
20                      onMouseReleased: function(evt) {
21                          println("Released: {evt}");
22                      }
23                  }
24              ]
25          }
26      }
```

The event delivered to the `onMouseDragged` handler provides drag-related information in the four variables in the `MouseEvent` class listed in Table 15-10.

Table 15-10 **Drag-Related Variables of the `MouseEvent` Class**

Variable	Type	Access	Description
dragAnchorX	Number	R	The x coordinate of the mouse when the current drag gesture was started
dragAnchorY	Number	R	The y coordinate of the mouse when the current drag gesture was started
dragX	Number	R	The x offset of the mouse from its position when the current drag gesture was started
dragY	Number	R	The y offset of the mouse from its position when the current drag gesture was started

Moving the mouse into the yellow rectangle, pressing the left mouse button, and holding it down while moving the mouse outside the rectangle and then releasing it results in output like this:

```
Pressed: MouseEvent [x=56.0,y=55.0,sceneX=56.0,sceneY=55.0,
button=PRIMARY]
dragAnchorX: 56.0, dragAnchorY: 55.0, dragX: 1.0, dragY: 0.0
dragAnchorX: 56.0, dragAnchorY: 55.0, dragX: 2.0, dragY: 1.0
dragAnchorX: 56.0, dragAnchorY: 55.0, dragX: 2.0, dragY: 2.0
dragAnchorX: 56.0, dragAnchorY: 55.0, dragX: 3.0, dragY: 3.0
dragAnchorX: 56.0, dragAnchorY: 55.0, dragX: 3.0, dragY: 4.0
dragAnchorX: 56.0, dragAnchorY: 55.0, dragX: 4.0, dragY: 4.0
```

```
dragAnchorX: 56.0, dragAnchorY: 55.0, dragX: 4.0, dragY: 5.0
dragAnchorX: 56.0, dragAnchorY: 55.0, dragX: 5.0, dragY: 6.0
Released: MouseEvent [x=61.0, y=61.0, sceneX=61.0, sceneY=61.0,
button=PRIMARY]
```

As you can see, the `dragAnchorX` and `dragAnchorY` variables are fixed throughout—they refer to the point at which the drag began, as you can see by comparing them to the x and y coordinates of the event delivered to the `onMousePressed` handler at the start of the drag process. As the mouse is moved, the `dragX` and `dragY` values indicate how far the mouse pointer is from where it was when the mouse was pressed. The actual x coordinate of the mouse can, therefore, be obtained by adding `dragAnchorX` to `dragX`, and similarly for the y coordinate.

During this drag operation, the mouse was moved outside the bounds of the `Rectangle` in which it was started. Nevertheless, events continued to be delivered to the `onMouseDragged` handler of the rectangle until the drag terminated as a result of the mouse button being released. This is the only case in which a mouse event is reported to a node when the mouse is outside of that node. Although it is not shown here, the `onMouseExited` handler would have been called when the mouse moved outside the rectangle. If it were to move back into the rectangle again during the course of the drag, an event would then be delivered to the `onMouseEntered` handler.

As an example of the use of the `onMouseDragged` handler, the class shown in Listing 15-12, which you'll find in the file `javafxnodes/MouseEvents8.fx`, can be linked to any node to allow it to be dragged around its hosting scene by using the mouse.

Listing 15-12 **A Class That Implements Node Dragging**

```
1    class NodeDragger {
2        public-init var node:Node;
3        var startX:Number;
4        var startY:Number;
5
6        function onMousePressed(evt:MouseEvent):Void {
7            startX = evt.node.translateX;
8            startY = evt.node.translateY;
9        }
10       function onMouseDragged(evt:MouseEvent):Void {
11           evt.node.translateX = startX + evt.dragX;
12           evt.node.translateY = startY + evt.dragY;
13       }
14
15       postinit {
16           node.onMousePressed = onMousePressed;
17           node.onMouseDragged = onMouseDragged;
18       }
19   }
```

The algorithm used here is a simple one:

- When the mouse is clicked over the node that an instance of the `NodeDragger` class is associated with, record the node's location by reading its `translateX` and `translateY` values (which are discussed in Chapter 17) and save them in the instance variables `startX` and `startY`. This is done on lines 7 and 8 of Listing 15-12.
- While the mouse is being dragged, the `dragX` and `dragY` variables of each `MouseEvent` indicate how far the mouse cursor has moved from the point at which it was pressed. This is exactly the distance by which the node should be moved, so to give effect to the drag, on lines 11 and 12, these values are just added to the saved copies of `translateX` and `translateY`, and the results are the new values for `translateX` and `translateY`.

To associate a `NodeDragger` with a node, it is only necessary to create an instance and initialize its `node` variable to point to the node. The code on lines 16 and 17, in the `postinit` block of the `NodeDragger`, installs the functions of the `NodeDragger` class as the `onMousePressed` and `onMouseDragged` handlers of the target node. Here's an example, from the same source file as the `NodeDragger` class, that creates this linkage:

```
var rect:Rectangle;

Stage {
    title: "Mouse Events 8"
    scene: Scene {
        width: 500
        height: 500
        content: [
            rect = Rectangle {
                x: 10 y: 10
                width: 50 height: 50
                fill: Color.YELLOW stroke: Color.BLACK
            }
        ]
    }
}

NodeDragger { node: rect }    // Link the NodeDragger to the Rectangle
```

The Mouse Wheel

Support for the mouse wheel is limited to one variable in the `MouseEvent` object and a `Node` function that is called when the mouse wheel is moved. The `MouseEvent` variable is described in Table 15-11.

Table 15-11 Mouse Wheel Support in the `MouseEvent` Class

Variable	Type	Access	Description
wheelRotation	Number	R	The distance by which the mouse wheel has been moved

Whenever the mouse wheel is moved, a `MouseEvent` in which the `wheelRotation` is set to indicate how far it has moved is delivered to the `onMouseWheelMoved` function of the node that contains the mouse pointer. The value is positive if the mouse wheel has been moved toward the user and negative if it has been moved away. The magnitude of the value increases if the user moves the wheel more quickly. There is no support for block movement, which is a mode that the user can select to request that the application that receives mouse wheel events should interpret the rotation value as the number of blocks (typically pages of text) by which to scroll rather than a number of units (typically lines). It is also not possible to configure the mouse wheel to scroll by more than one unit for each turn of the wheel.

Delivery of Mouse Events

It is generally true, as stated earlier, that mouse events are delivered to a node when it is inside the boundary of that node. However, that is not the whole story. The code in Listing 15-13, which you will find in the file `javafxnodes/MouseEvents9.fx`, places two rectangles and a text node into a group and registers handlers that report mouse entry, mouse exit, and mouse movement or all four nodes. Figure 15-24 shows the result of running this code.

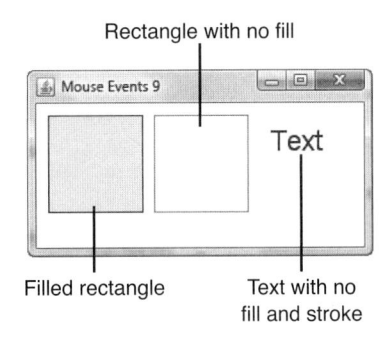

Figure 15-24 Mouse event delivery on various nodes

Listing 15-13 Mouse Event Delivery on Various Nodes

```
1    Stage {
2        title: "Mouse Events 9"
3        scene: Scene {
4            width: 280
```

```
5              height: 120
6              content: [
7                  Group {
8                      onMouseEntered: function(evt) {
9                          print("Group enter");
10                         println("  node: {evt.node}, "
11                                 "source: {evt.source}");
12                     }
13                     onMouseExited: function(evt) {
14                         print("Group exit");
15                         println("  node: {evt.node}, "
16                                 "source: {evt.source}");
17                     }
18                     onMouseMoved: function(evt) {
19                         print("Group move");
20                         println("  node: {evt.node}, "
21                                 "source: {evt.source}");
22                     }
23                     content: [
24                         Rectangle {
25                             x: 10 y: 10
26                             width: 80 height: 80
27                             fill: Color.YELLOW stroke: Color.BLACK
28                             onMouseEntered: function(evt) {
29                                 print("Yellow rectangle enter");
30                                 println("  node: {evt.node}, "
31                                         "source: {evt.source}");
32                             }
33                             onMouseExited: function(evt) {
34                                 print("Yellow rectangle exit");
35                                 println("  node: {evt.node}, "
36                                         "source: {evt.source}");
37                             }
38                             onMouseMoved: function(evt) {
39                                 print("Yellow rectangle move");
40                                 println("  node: {evt.node}, "
41                                         "source: {evt.source}");
42                             }
43                         }
44                         Rectangle {
45                             x: 100 y: 10
46                             width: 80 height: 80
47                             fill: null stroke: Color.RED
48                             onMouseEntered: function(evt) {
49                                 println("No-fill rectangle enter "
50                                         "({evt.x}, {evt.y})");
51                             }
52                             onMouseExited: function(evt) {
```

```
53                              println("No-fill rectangle exit "
54                                      "({evt.x}, {evt.y})");
55                          }
56                          onMouseMoved: function(evt) {
57                              println("No-fill rectangle move "
58                                      "({evt.x}, {evt.y})");
59                          }
60                      }
61                      Text {
62                          font: Font { size: 24 }
63                          x: 200 y: 40
64                          content: "Text"
65                          onMouseEntered: function(evt) {
66                              println("Text enter ({evt.x},      {evt.y})");
67                          }
68                          onMouseExited: function(evt) {
69                              println("Text exit ({evt.x},       {evt.y})");
70                          }
71                          onMouseMoved: function(evt) {
72                              println("Text move ({evt.x},       {evt.y})");
73                          }
74                          pickOnBounds: false
75                      }
76                  ]
77              }
78          ]
79      }
80  }
```

The rectangle on the left is filled with a solid color, and if you move the mouse over it, you will find that events are delivered, as described earlier in this chapter. Here is a typical sequence of events generated as the mouse moves into this rectangle from the left of the window:

```
Yellow rectangle enter   node: Rectangle, source: Rectangle
Group enter   node: Group, source: Rectangle
Yellow rectangle move   node: Rectangle, source: Rectangle
Group move   node: Group, source: Rectangle
Yellow rectangle move   node: Rectangle, source: Rectangle
Group move   node: Group, source: Rectangle
Yellow rectangle move   node: Rectangle, source: Rectangle
Group move   node: Group, source: Rectangle
```

As you would expect, events are delivered to the rectangle as the mouse enters and moves over it. You will also notice that these same events are delivered to the group. This happens because the rectangle is a child of the group node; mouse events are always propagated to the parent of a node unless that node prevents it by setting its `blocksMouse` variable to `true`. This is not the same as the propagation that you saw earlier in this chapter, which was the result of the mouse moving over overlapping nodes that have the same parent.

The `node` variable of the event is always set to the node to which the event is actually *delivered*—in the case of events delivered to the rectangle, this variable refers to the rectangle, whereas for the propagated events delivered to the group, it refers to the `Group`. However, the `source` variable *always* refers to the rectangle. This variable always refers to the leaf node that is directly under the mouse and which is the original source of the event.

Propagation of mouse events to the group node makes it possible for you to handle all such events by just registering handlers with the group rather than with each individual leaf node. The setting of the `source` variable ensures that the handlers at the group level can always determine which leaf node originated the event. It is important to note, however, that events are delivered to the group *only* while the mouse is over a leaf node in that group and not while it is between nodes. Therefore, if you move the mouse outside of the yellow rectangle and into the space between it and the other nodes, events are not delivered to the group until the mouse reenters one of the other nodes.

The rectangle in the middle of Figure 15-24 is a little different from the one in Figure 15-22—its `fill` is explicitly set to `null` on line 47 of Listing 15-13. Here is a typical stream of events resulting from moving the mouse from left to right over the left side of this rectangle:

```
No-fill rectangle enter (100.0, 56.0)
Group enter   node: Group, source: Rectangle
No-fill rectangle move (100.0, 56.0)
Group move   node: Group, source: Rectangle
No-fill rectangle exit (101.0, 56.0)
Group exit   node: Group, source: Rectangle
```

As you can see, the mouse enters and apparently exits the rectangle immediately after crossing the boundary. That's because when a node has a `null` fill, the area that appears to be its interior is considered to be *outside* of its boundary, and *no* mouse events will be delivered to it while the mouse is over that area. Note that this only happens if the `fill` is `null`—if the rectangle (or any other shape) were to be filled with a transparent color, or even if the rectangle were made transparent by setting its opacity value to 0 or using the color `Color.TRANSPARENT`, the interior would still be considered to be filled and mouse events will be delivered. However, if the rectangle is hidden by setting its `visible` variable to `false`, no mouse events at all will be delivered to it.

Mouse Events and the `pickOnBounds` Variable

By default, the boundary used to determine when the mouse is inside a node is its visual boundary. In the case of a circle, for example, the mouse is considered to be inside the shape when it is over its edge or inside the drawn area of the circle. You can change this behavior by setting the `pickOnBounds` variable of the node to `true`. The effect of this is to make the rectangular area enclosing the shape, the boundary for reporting mouse entry and exit events. In the case of a circle, this would mean that the mouse would be considered to be over the shape whenever it is inside the rectangular area defined by the circle's left, right, top, and bottom edges. This is usually not what you want, but it *is* useful for `Text` nodes. In the case of a `Text` node, unlike other shapes, the `pickOnBounds` variable is `true` by default, with the result that mouse events are delivered to it whenever the mouse is over the rectangular area occupied by the text. You can see why this is useful if you set the `pickOnBounds` variable for a `Text` node to `false`, as has been done on line 74 of Listing 15-13. Here's a stream of events generated by moving the mouse over part of the `Text` node. (For clarity, the events delivered to the group have been omitted.)

```
Text enter  (207.0, 31.0)
Group enter  node: Group, source: Text
Text move  (207.0, 31.0)
Group move  node: Group, source: Text
Text move  (208.0, 31.0)
Group move  node: Group, source: Text
Text exit  (209.0, 31.0)
Group exit  node: Group, source: Text
Text enter  (216.0, 31.0)
Group enter  node: Group, source: Text
Text move  (216.0, 31.0)
Group move  node: Group, source: Text
Text move  (217.0, 31.0)
Group move  node: Group, source: Text
Text exit  (218.0, 31.0)
Group exit  node: Group, source: Text
```

As you can see, the mouse appears to be entering and leaving the node as it moves across it. In fact, when `PickOnBounds` is `false`, only the pixels occupied by the text are considered to be part of the shape, so as the mouse moves between the individual letters, and even over gaps in the glyphs that represent the letters, it alternates between being inside and outside of the shape. The magnified screen shot in Figure 15-25 explains this more clearly.

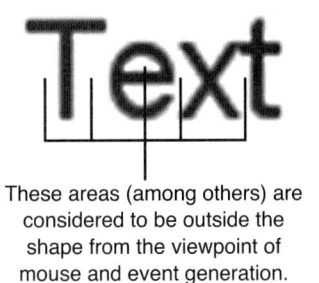

These areas (among others) are considered to be outside the shape from the viewpoint of mouse and event generation.

Figure 15-25   Mouse events and the `Text` node

This behavior makes it difficult for the user to actually click on the text because the whitespace around the glyphs do not respond to the mouse. For this reason, it is usually a good idea to leave the `pickOnBounds` variable set to its default value, which enables the user to click anywhere in the area occupied by the `Text` node.

Mouse-Related Node State

As you have already seen, you can detect whether the mouse is over a node by monitoring the events generated as the mouse enters and leaves it. However, if you only want to know whether the mouse is over the node, you can do this much more easily by using the `hover` variable of the `Node` class. This variable is automatically `true` when the mouse is over the node and `false` when it is not. To illustrate this, the code in Listing 15-14, which is taken from the file `javafxnodes/Hover.fx`, creates a scene that looks the same as that shown in Figure 15-24, but uses the `hover` variable to set the `fill` or `stroke` colors of the three shapes depending on whether the mouse is inside or outside the shape.

Listing 15-14 **The `hover` Variable**

```
1     var rect1:Rectangle;
2     var rect2:Rectangle;
3     var text:Text;
4
5     Stage {
6         title: "Mouse Hover"
7         scene: Scene {
8             width: 280 height: 120
9             content: [
10                rect1 = Rectangle {
11                    x: 10 y: 10
12                    width: 80 height: 80
13                    fill: bind if (rect1.hover) {
14                             Color.RED
15                         } else {
16                             Color.YELLOW
17                         }
18                    stroke: Color.BLACK
19                }
20                rect2 = Rectangle {
21                    x: 100 y: 10
22                    width: 80 height: 80
23                    stroke: bind if (rect2.hover) {
24                             Color.RED
25                         } else {
26                             Color.ORANGE
27                         }
28                    fill: null
29                }
```

```
30                  text = Text {
31                      font: Font { size: 24 }
32                      x: 200 y: 40
33                      content: "Text"
34                      fill: bind if (text.hover) {
35                              Color.RED
36                          } else {
37                              Color.BLACK
38                          }
39                      stroke: bind text.fill
40                  }
41              ]
42          }
43      }
```

Lines 13 to 17 bind the `fill` color of the leftmost rectangle according to the state of its `hover` variable so that it is red when the mouse is over it and yellow when it is not. The second rectangle has a `null` fill, so, as you saw in the previous section, the mouse is only considered to be over it when it is over the stroked outline. Therefore, the code on lines 23 to 27 causes the outline of the rectangle to be red when the mouse is over the outline itself and orange when it is anywhere else. Finally, the text will be red when the mouse is over its stroked part and black when it is not, which causes it to flash as you move the mouse from left to right over the individual letters.

When the mouse is over the intersection of two or more nodes, each of those nodes will have their `hover` variable set to `true`. Similarly, the `hover` variable of a group is `true` when the mouse is over *any* of the nodes in that group.

Keyboard Events

The user's key presses generate key events that can be captured by your application. Whereas mouse events go to the node underneath the mouse (and may also be propagated), key events always go to the node that has the *input focus* and to no other node. *Key events are not propagated.* If there isn't a node with the input focus, these events are simply discarded.[10] Nodes such as `TextBox` and `SwingTextField` that are provided to make it easy for you to handle the user's text input automatically grab the input focus when the user clicks them.

---

[10] AWT and Swing have more powerful application programming interfaces (APIs) that let you handle key events from outside the focused component. Hopefully, JavaFX will eventually have a similar facility.

Nodes and the Input Focus

The `Node` class has four variables and a function that are focus-related. The variables are described in Table 15-12.

Table 15-12 **Focus-Related Node Variables**

Variable	Type	Access	Default	Description
`disable`	Boolean	RW	`false`	Controls the disabled state of the node.
`disabled`	Boolean	R	`false`	`true` if the node is currently disabled, `false` if it is not.
`focusTraversable`	Boolean	RW	`true` `false`	Indicates whether the node participates in tab traversal using the Tab key.
`focused`	Boolean	R	`false`	`true` if the node currently has the input focus, `false` if it does not.

A node gets the input focus only when its `requestFocus()` method is called. If you need a node in your scene graph to receive keyboard input, you must call this function first. Some nodes, such as the `TextBox` and `Button` controls that are discussed in Chapter 22, "Cross-Platform Controls," do this automatically when the user clicks them with the mouse, whereas other nodes do not.

In general, focus is not automatically moved between nodes when the user presses the `Tab` or `Shift-Tab` keys. However, this feature *is* implemented for nodes derived from the `Control` class. The tab traversal mechanism implemented for these classes moves the focus between nodes for which the `focusTraversable` variable has the value true. If you need focus traversal for other node types, you need to implement it yourself by acting on the delivery of key events to your nodes.

To receive the input focus, a node must be visible and not be disabled—that is, its `disabled` variable must be `false`. A node may be disabled either because it has been made so explicitly by setting its `disable` variable to `false`, or because one if its ancestor nodes is disabled. Disabling a group will, therefore, disable all nodes in the group, and the `disabled` variable of each of those nodes will be `false`, even though the value of the `disable` variable for that same node could be `true` (because it has not been individually disabled).

> **Note**
>
> Notice that there are two variables here: `disable` represents the required state of the node; while `disabled` represents its actual state, which is influenced by its own `disable` variable and the `disable` variables of the nodes within which it is nested.

Events   427

When a scene first displays, the focus is assigned to the first node in its content sequence that is not disabled and for which the `focusTraversable` variable is `true`.

The code in Listing 15-15, which you'll find in the file `javafxnodes/KeyEvents.fx`, creates a user interface that demonstrates the input focus and also allows us to examine keyboard events.

Listing 15-15 The Input Focus and Keyboard Events

```
1    package javafxnodes;
2
3    import javafx.scene.control.TextBox;
4    import javafx.scene.input.KeyEvent;
5    import javafx.scene.Scene;
6    import javafx.stage.Stage;
7    import javafx.scene.control.Button;
8
9    function displayKeyEvent(type:String, evt:KeyEvent) {
10       print("{type}: char - '{evt.char}', code - '{evt.code}' ");
11       println("    text - '{evt.text}'");
12       print("   Modifiers:");
13       print("{if (evt.altDown) 'ALT ' else ''}");
14       print("{if (evt.controlDown) 'CTRL ' else ''}");
15       print("{if (evt.metaDown) 'META ' else ''}");
16       println("{if (evt.shiftDown) 'SHIFT ' else ''}");
17   }
18
19   Stage {
20       title: "Key Events"
21       resizable: false
22       scene: Scene {
23           var textBox:TextBox
24           width: 200
25           height: 100
26           content: [
27               textBox = TextBox {
28                   translateX: 10
29                   translateY: 20
30                   columns: 24
31                   onKeyPressed: function(evt) {
32                       displayKeyEvent("Pressed", evt);
33                   }
34                   onKeyReleased: function(evt) {
35                       displayKeyEvent("Released", evt);
36                   }
37                   onKeyTyped: function(evt) {
38                       displayKeyEvent("Typed", evt);
39                   }
40               }
```

```
41                      Button {
42                          translateX: 40
43                          translateY: 60
44                          text: bind if (textBox.disabled) {
45                                          "Enable text input"
46                                      } else {
47                                          "Disable text input"
48                                      }
49                          action: function() {
50                              textBox.disable = not textBox.disable;
51                              if (not textBox.disabled) {
52                                  textBox.requestFocus();
53                              }
54                          }
55                      }
56                  ]
57              }
58      }
```

This code creates a scene consisting of a text box and a button, as shown in Figure 15-26.

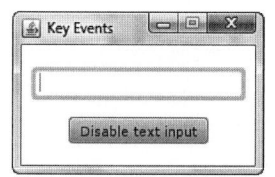

Figure 15-26   Illustrating the input focus and keyboard events

Initially, the text box has the input focus. To indicate this, it draws a highlighted area around itself. If you press a few keys, you see that the text box accepts and displays them. Pressing the Tab key moves the focus to the button, causing the text box to remove its highlight and the button to add one of its own, as shown in Figure 15-27. This automatic movement of the focus occurs because TextBox is a subclass of Control.

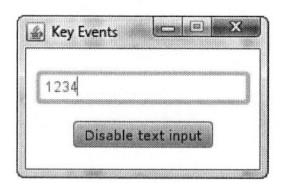

Figure 15-27   Moving the input focus to the button

Pressing the button by clicking with the mouse or pressing the Spacebar key on the keyboard will set the `disable` variable of the text box to `true`, causing it to redraw itself to indicate that it can no longer accept input, as shown in Figure 15-28.

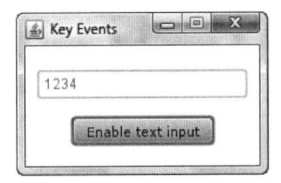

Figure 15-28   A disabled `TextBox`

Now if you press the Tab key or click in the text box, you will find that it is no longer possible to give it the input focus. Click the button again, and the text box will be re-enabled and again able to be focused.

Receiving Key Events

To process key events, you assign a function to one or more of the following variables of a node:

```
public var onKeyPressed:function(:KeyEvent):Void
public var onKeyTyped:function(:KeyEvent):Void
public var onKeyReleased:function(:KeyEvent):Void
```

Each of these functions is passed an argument of type `javafx.scene.input.KeyEvent` that describes a change in the state of the keyboard. On lines 31 to 39 of Listing 15-15, we assign to each of these variables a function that prints information about the events that it receives. Some of the variables of the `KeyEvent` class are listed in Table 15-13. We discuss these variables in some detail in this section and the sections that follow.

Table 15-13   **Variables of the `KeyEvent` Class**

Variable	Type	Access	Description
char	String	R	The character associated with this event
code	KeyCode	R	The key code for the key that has been pressed or released
code	Node	R	The node that is the source of the event
text	String	R	A string that describes the `KeyCode` value

If you click in the text box and then press and release the A key on your keyboard, you see three keyboard events:

```
Pressed: char - '', code - 'VK_A'      text - 'A'
    Modifiers:
Typed: char - 'a', code - 'VK_UNDEFINED'      text - ''
```

```
    Modifiers:
Released: char - '', code - 'VK_A'      text - 'A'
    Modifiers:
```

The first and last events seem natural—one is reported when the key is pressed, the other when it is released. So why is there a third event? There are actually two different categories of key events—low-level ones, delivered to the `onKeyPressed` and `onKeyReleased` functions, that report what actually happened, and a higher-level event that is usually more meaningful to application code, delivered to the `onKeyTyped` function.

Types of Key Events

The key-pressed event reports the pressing of the A key. You can tell that it's the A key because of the value of the `code` attribute, which is of type `javafx.scene.input.KeyCode`. This class defines a large number of constant instances that correspond to keys on a keyboard. The one that corresponds to the A key is called `KeyCode.VK_A`. If you look at the documentation for this class, you see that there is no instance called `KeyCode.VK_a`—that is because, like the keyboard itself, the `KeyCode` class does not distinguish between upper- and lowercase letters. It is important to realize that the key-pressed and key-released events report the operation of a *key*, not the typing of a letter or other symbol, and at this level there is no concept of upper- or lowercase letters. This concept is, however, recognized by the higher-level key-typed event, which is concerned with *characters*, not keys.

You can see that the `char` attribute of the key-typed event is `a`, whereas that of the key-pressed and key-released events is an empty string. Note also that the `code` attribute of the key-typed event does not convey any useful information. These differences reflect the character-oriented nature of the key-typed event and the key-oriented nature of the other two.

The `KeyCode` class itself represents a key on the keyboard. It does not have any public instance variables, but it does provide two public class functions:

```
public function values():KeyCode[]
public function valueOf(name:String):KeyCode
```

The `values()` function returns a sequence containing all the possible `KeyCode` instances. The `valueOf()` function returns the `KeyCode` instance for a given key given by its name. For example, this code gets and prints the `KeyCode` for the A key:

```
var keyCode = KeyCode.valueOf("VK_A");
println("keyCode for VK_A is {keyCode}");
```

To test whether a particular key on the keyboard has been pressed, compare the value of the `code` variable from a `KeyEvent` delivered to the key-pressed or key-released handler with the `KeyCode` instance for that key:

```
var code = evt.code;
if (code == KeyCode.VK_A) {
    // The 'A' key has been pressed
}
```

This does not work in the key-typed handler because the `code` variable is not set in the event delivered to that handler.

Modifier Keys

If you type an uppercase A into the text box in Figure 15-26, you see a stream of events like this:

```
Pressed: char - '', code - 'VK_SHIFT'     text - 'Shift'
    Modifiers:SHIFT
Pressed: char - '', code - 'VK_A'         text - 'A'
    Modifiers:SHIFT
Typed: char - 'A', code - 'VK_UNDEFINED'  text - ''
    Modifiers:SHIFT
Released: char - '', code - 'VK_A'        text - 'A'
    Modifiers:SHIFT
Released: char - '', code - 'VK_SHIFT'    text - 'Shift'
    Modifiers:
```

This set of events clearly shows the difference between the high-level and low-level events. The first event is generated as a result of the Shift key being pressed. This is indicated in two ways: first because the code variable of the event has the value `KeyCode.VK_SHIFT`, and second because the variable `shiftDown` in the same event has the value `true`. This is one of four variables in the `KeyEvent` class that represent the state of special keys on the keyboard. Table 15-14 lists these variables. There is no key-typed event for this key because Shift does not map to any valid Unicode character.

Table 15-14   Key Modifier Variables in the `KeyEvent` Class

Variable	Type	Access	Description
altDown	Boolean	R	`true` when the Alt key is pressed
controlDown	Boolean	R	`true` when the Ctrl key is pressed
metaDown	Boolean	R	`true` when the Meta key is pressed
shiftDown	Boolean	R	`true` when the Shift key is pressed

The second event is generated in response to the pressing of the A key. Note that this is the same as the one shown earlier for lowercase A, apart from the fact that now the `shiftDown` variable is `true`, which indicates that the A key and the Shift key are now both pressed.

The third event is the key-typed event for the combination of the Shift key and the A key, which has an uppercase `A` in its char field. If you were building a string based on keys typed on the keyboard, you would register to receive this event and append the value of its char variable.[11]

The last two events are generated as first the A key and then the Shift key are released.

Repeated Keys

The examples that you have seen so far show the same number of key-pressed events as key-released events, but this is not always the case. If you press and hold down the A key, you'll see this sequence of events:

```
Pressed: char - '', code - 'VK_A'      text - 'A'
    Modifiers:
Typed: char - 'a', code - 'VK_UNDEFINED'     text - ''
    Modifiers:
Pressed: char - '', code - 'VK_A'      text - 'A'
    Modifiers:
Typed: char - 'a', code - 'VK_UNDEFINED'     text - ''
    Modifiers:
Pressed: char - '', code - 'VK_A'      text - 'A'
    Modifiers:
Typed: char - 'a', code - 'VK_UNDEFINED'     text - ''
    Modifiers:
Pressed: char - '', code - 'VK_A'      text - 'A'
    Modifiers:
Typed: char - 'a', code - 'VK_UNDEFINED'     text - ''
    Modifiers:
Released: char - '', code - 'VK_A'      text - 'A'
    Modifiers:
```

The first two events happen immediately. After the key has been held down for a short period, you'll see further identical pairs of key-pressed and key-typed events until the key is released.

Noncharacter Keys

Not all keys on the keyboard have a character representation. For example, press the F1 key. Here are the events that you will see:

```
Pressed: char - '', code - 'VK_F1'      text - 'F1'
    Modifiers:
Released: char - '', code - 'VK_F1'      text - 'F1'
    Modifiers:
```

Because no character in any character set corresponds to the F1 key, only key-pressed and key-released events are generated.

---

[11] You would also want to handle the Backspace and Delete keys, which would require you to receive key-pressed events and act on those for which the value of the code variable is either KeyCode.VK_BACK_SPACE or KeyCode.VK_DELETE.

16

Shapes, Text, and Images

The last two chapters introduced the concept of a node-based scene graph and demonstrated some of the ways in which you can control the appearance of a node and detect user interaction with nodes. This chapter opens by looking at a specific set of node subclasses called *shapes*. We have already made use of two of the shape classes in our examples so far—`Circle` and `Rectangle`. Here, we take a look at both of these classes, and the other shapes that the JavaFX runtime supports, in much more detail.

The second part of this chapter is concerned with two specific node subclasses that are worthy of greater attention. The first is the `Text` class, which is used to render text. Along with this discussion, this chapter introduces the support that JavaFX provides for fonts. The second is `ImageView`, which allows you to embed an image in your scene graph. This section also covers the `Image` class, which is responsible for loading and decoding image files.

Unless otherwise noted, you will find the example source code for this chapter in the package `javafxshapes` in the JavaFX Book GUI project.

Shapes

Formally speaking, a shape is an instance of a subclass of the `javafx.scene.shape.Shape` class, which is itself derived from `javafx.scene.Node`. All the shape classes discussed in this section can be found in the `javafx.scene.shape` package. Every shape has variables that, in some way, specify its location and overall size. The variables used to fix points within the shape are coordinates that are, by default, relative to the owning scene if the shape is an element of the `content` sequence of a scene, or to the shape's parent node (typically a group) if it is not, as shown in Figure 14-8 in the "Coordinates" section in Chapter 14, "User Interface Basics." As you'll see in Chapter 17, "Coordinates, Transforms, and Layout," after you have defined the position and size of a shape, you can use the features of the `Node` class to move it somewhere else, resize it, rotate it, or skew it. In this chapter, we keep things simple and deal only with the default forms produced by each shape subclass.

The `Shape` class itself adds to `Node` the ability to specify how the outline of the shape is to be drawn and how it should be filled with color. In the last two chapters, you have seen examples that use the `stroke` and `fill` variables of the `Shape` class to change the colors used to draw a shape. All these examples used a simple, single-pixel solid line as the outline. In fact, it is possible to emphasize the outline more by using a wider stroke line, or to use a dashed outline pattern, as you'll see in the "Stroking Shapes" section, later in this chapter. By default, all shapes are filled with solid black. If you want to create a shape that is not filled, set the value of the `fill` variable to `Color.TRANSPARENT` and `stroke` to the required outline color. The default stroke is `null`, except for `Line`, `Polyline`, and `Path`, which are stroked in black.

There is one shape subclass that we do not discuss in this chapter: `DelegateShape`. As its name suggests, it is a proxy that stands in for and gets its outline from another shape. It is primarily intended to be used for shape animation and is therefore covered in Chapter 18, "Animation."

Basic Shapes

The JavaFX runtime has nine classes that can be used to draw basic shapes. More advanced shapes can be constructed by building a *path* from variants of these shapes called *path elements*. Paths and path elements are discussed in the section "Paths," later in this chapter.

Lines

To draw a straight line, use the `Line` class. A line is defined by two points, one of which is arbitrarily called the starting point, the other the ending point. If the starting points and ending points are the same, only a single point is drawn.[1] The variables of the `Line` class that define these two points are listed in Table 16-1.

Table 16-1 **Variables of the Line Class**

Variable	Type	Access	Default	Description
startX	Number	RW	0.0	The x coordinate of the starting point of the line
startY	Number	RWs	0.0	The y coordinate of the starting point of the line
endX	Number	RW	0.0	The x coordinate of the ending point of the line
endY	Number	RW	0.0	The y coordinate of the ending point of the line

---

[1] The reason that there is no separate shape class that draws a point is that a point is a special case of a line.

The code in Listing 16-1, which you will find in the file `javafxshapes/Lines.fx`, draws four straight lines: one horizontal, one vertical, and two diagonals. Figure 16-1 shows the result.

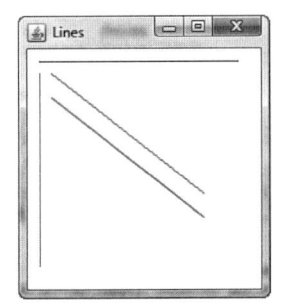

Figure 16-1   Drawing straight lines with the `Line` class

Listing 16-1   **Using the `Line` Class**

```
1    package javafxshapes;
2
3    import javafx.stage.Stage;
4    import javafx.scene.Scene;
5    import javafx.scene.shape.Line;
6    import javafx.scene.paint.Color;
7
8    Stage {
9        title: "Lines"
10       scene: Scene {
11           width: 200
12           height: 200
13           content: [
14               Line {
15                   startX: 10 startY: 10
16                   endX: 180 endY: 10
17                   stroke: Color.BLACK
18               }
19               Line {
20                   startX: 10 startY: 20
21                   endX: 10 endY: 180
22                   stroke: Color.RED
23               }
24               Line {
25                   startX: 20 startY: 20
26                   endX: 150 endY: 120
```

```
27                    smooth: false
28                    stroke: Color.GREEN
29                }
30                Line {
31                    startX: 20 startY: 40
32                    endX: 150 endY: 140
33                    smooth:true
34                    stroke: Color.GREEN
35                }
36            ]
37        }
38    }
```

It should be apparent that there is a marked difference in the quality of the two diagonal lines—the upper one is much more ragged than the lower one. This difference is caused by the value of the `smooth` variable, which is inherited from the `Shape` class. The upper line, which is created by the code on lines 24 to 29 of Listing 16-1, has this variable set to `false`, while the lower line, declared on lines 30 to 35, has it set to `true`. The value `true` causes the JavaFX runtime to apply anti-aliasing to the line, by adding additional pixels with colors that depend both on the color used to draw the line and on its background color, which makes it appear much smoother than it otherwise would. This feature applies to all shape classes, and it is enabled by default; there is a small performance penalty for using it, so in some circumstances you may want to turn it off.

Rectangles

The `Rectangle` class draws a rectangular (or square) shape with its top-left corner at a given position and with its sides parallel to the `x` and `y` coordinate axes. By using the transformations described in Chapter 17, it is possible to create a rectangle whose sides are not parallel to an axis, or to skew the rectangle into a parallelogram. Table 16-2 describes the variables that control the position and size of the shape.

Table 16-2   **Variables of the `Rectangle` Class**

Variable	Type	Access	Default	Description
x	Number	RW	0.0	The `x` coordinate of the top-left corner of the rectangle
y	Number	RW	0.0	The `y` coordinate of the top-left corner of the rectangle
width	Number	RW	0.0	The width of the rectangle
height	Number	RW	0.0	The height of the rectangle
arcWidth	Number	RW	0.0	The horizontal diameter of the corner arcs
arcHeight	Number	RW	0.0	The vertical diameter of the corner arcs

The code in Listing 16-2 creates two rectangles, one of which is a square with rounded corners, as shown in Figure 16-2.[2]

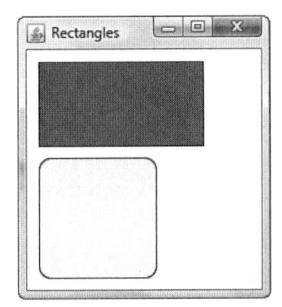

Figure 16-2 Drawing rectangles with the **Rectangle** class

Listing 16-2 **Drawing Rectangles**

```
1     package javafxshapes;
2
3     import javafx.stage.Stage;
4     import javafx.scene.Scene;
5     import javafx.scene.shape.Rectangle;
6     import javafx.scene.paint.Color;
7
8     Stage {
9         title: "Rectangles"
10        scene: Scene {
11            width: 200
12            height: 200
13            content: [
14                Rectangle {
15                    x: 10 y: 10
16                    width: 140 height: 70
17                    stroke: Color.BLACK
18                    fill: Color.GREEN
19                }
20                Rectangle {
21                    x: 10 y: 90
22                    width: 100 height: 100
23                    arcWidth: 20 arcHeight: 20
```

---

[2] You can find this code in the file javafxshapes/Rectangles.fx.

```
24                          stroke: Color.BLACK
25                          fill: Color.YELLOW
26                      }
27                  ]
28              }
29      }
```

The rounded corners are actually quadrants of an ellipse whose dimensions are controlled by the `arcWidth` and `arcHeight` variables. The relationship of the ellipse to rectangle's corners is illustrated in Figure 16-3, which shows the special case in which the ellipse is actually a circle.

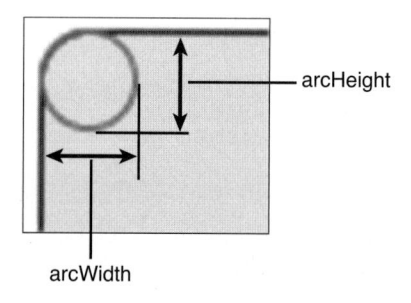

Figure 16-3   The `arcWidth` and `arcHeight` variables of the `Rectangle` class

Note that you actually specify the horizontal and vertical *diameters* of the ellipse, not its radii. This contrasts to the `Ellipse` class, which you'll see shortly, where you specify the radiuses.

Circles

`Circle` is a simple class that draws a circle with a given radius around a specified center point, using the variables listed in Table 16-3.

Table 16-3   Variables of the `Circle` Class

Variable	Type	Access	Default	Description
centerX	Number	RW	0.0	The x coordinate of the center of the circle
centery	Number	RW	0.0	The y coordinate of the center of the circle
radius	Number	RW	0.0	The radius of the circle

You have already seen several examples of the use of this class, including Listing 14-4 and Figure 14-3 in Chapter 14.

Ellipses

The `Ellipse` class draws an ellipse with its major and minor axes parallel to the coordinate axes, as specified by the variables listed in Table 16-4. You can apply a rotation transformation to create a rectangle with its axes at any required angle to those of the coordinate system.

Table 16-4 Variables of the `Ellipse` Class

Variable	Type	Access	Default	Description
centerX	Number	RW	0.0	The x coordinate of the center of the ellipse
centerY	Number	RW	0.0	The y coordinate of the center of the ellipse
radiusX	Number	RW	0.0	The horizontal radius of the ellipse
radiusY	Number	RW	0.0	The vertical radius of the ellipse

The code in Listing 16-3, which you will find in the file `javafxshapes/AnEllipse.fx`, draws an ellipse with a horizontal major axis. The result of running this code is shown in Figure 16-4.

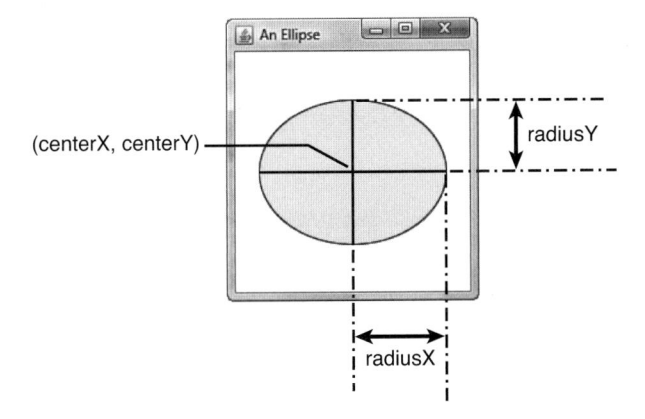

Figure 16-4 The variables that define an ellipse

Listing 16-3 **Drawing an Ellipse**

```
package javafxshapes;

import javafx.scene.paint.Color;
```

440   Chapter 16 Shapes, Text, and Images

```
import javafx.scene.Scene;
import javafx.scene.shape.Ellipse;
import javafx.stage.Stage;


Stage {
    title: "An Ellipse"
    scene: Scene {
        width: 200
        height: 200
        content: [
            Ellipse {
                centerX: 100,
                centerY: 100
                radiusX: 80,
                radiusY: 60
                stroke: Color.BLACK
                fill: Color.YELLOW
            }
        ]
    }
}
```

Polygons and Polylines

Both polygons and polylines are constructed by drawing straight lines linking pairs of an ordered set of points, defined by the `points` variable, as described in Table 16-5. If the first and last point are not the same, a shape drawn using the `Polygon` class will be automatically closed by a line segment drawn between the first and last points, whereas a `Polyline` shape will remain open.

Table 16-5   Variables of the `Polygon` and `Polyline` classes

Variable	Type	Access	Default	Description
points	Number[]	RW	Empty	Sequence of number pairs that represent the coordinates of the line ending points

The code in Listing 16-4, from the file `javafxshapes/APolygon.fx`, creates a hexagon by specifying the locations of its vertices, giving the result shown in Figure 16-5.

Listing 16-4   **Drawing a Polygon**

```
package javafxshapes;

import javafx.stage.Stage;
```

Shapes   441

```
import javafx.scene.Scene;
import javafx.scene.shape.Polygon;
import javafx.scene.paint.Color;

Stage {
    title: "A Polygon"
    scene: Scene {
        width: 200
        height: 200
        content: [
            Polygon {
                points: [ 100,10,   180,60,  180,130,
                          100,180,  20,130,  20,60]
                fill: Color.TRANSPARENT
                stroke: Color.BLACK
            }
        ]
    }
}
```

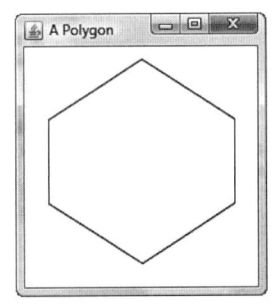

Figure 16-5   A hexagon created using the
Polygon class

The values in the `points` sequence are alternately the x and y coordinates of the vertices of the hexagon. They have been grouped together in Listing 16-4 so as to make it clear where each coordinate pair begins and ends. It is an error, and nothing is drawn, if this sequence has an odd number of elements.

The `Polygon` and `Polyline` classes have the same application programming interface (API), so to create a `Polyline` with the same vertices as the `Polygon` shown in Listing 16-4, it is only necessary to change the classname:

```
Polyline {
    points: [ 100,10,   180,60,  180,130,
              100,180,  20,130,  20,60]
    fill: Color.TRANSPARENT
    stroke: Color.BLACK
}
```

This code, which you will find in the file `javafxshapes/APolyline.fx`, produces the shape shown in Figure 16-6. As you can see, the `Polyline` class does not close the shape by joining its first and last points. By default, all shapes are filled with solid black, which is not likely to be what you want when using the `Polyline` class. To draw only the outline, set the `stroke` to the required outline color and `fill` either to `null` or `Color.TRANSPARENT`.

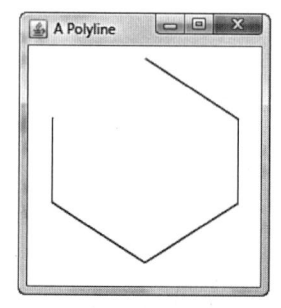

Figure 16-6 An open hexagon created using the `Polyline` class

Arcs

The `Arc` shape draws a portion of the outline of an ellipse. The variables that control the arc are listed in Table 16-6.

Table 16-6 **Variables of the `Arc` Class**

Variable	Type	Access	Default	Description
centerX	Number	RW	0.0	The x coordinate of the center of the ellipse
centerY	Number	RW	0.0	The y coordinate of the center of the ellipse
radiusX	Number	RW	0.0	The horizontal radius of the ellipse
radiusY	Number	RW	0.0	The vertical radius of the ellipse
startAngle	Number	RW	0.0	The starting angle of the arc, in degrees
length	Number	RW	0.0	The length of the arc, in degrees
type	ArcType	RW	ArcType.OPEN	The arc type

The code in Listing 16-5 (which you will find in the file `javafxshapes/Arcs.fx`) draws three arcs that use each of the different arc types, giving the result shown in Figure 16-7.

Shapes 443

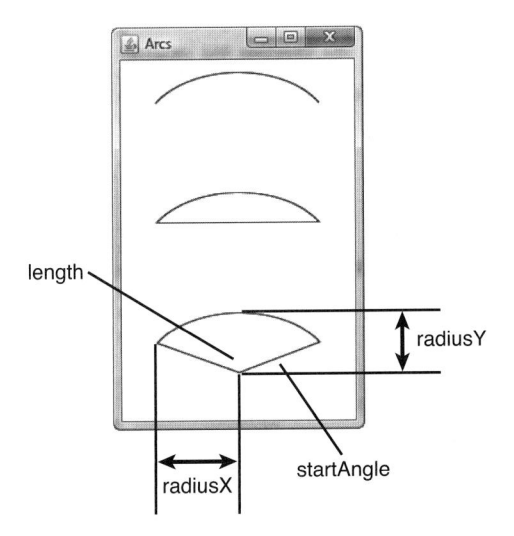

Figure 16-7   Three elliptic arcs

Listing 16-5   Drawing Arcs

```
package javafxshapes;

import javafx.stage.Stage;
import javafx.scene.Scene;
import javafx.scene.shape.Arc;
import javafx.scene.shape.ArcType;
import javafx.scene.paint.Color;

Stage {
    title: "Arcs"
    scene: Scene {
        width: 200
        height: 300
        content: [
            Arc {
                centerX: 100 centerY: 60
                radiusX: 80 radiusY: 50
                startAngle: 30 length: 120
                type: ArcType.OPEN
                fill: Color.TRANSPARENT
                stroke: Color.BLACK
            }
            Arc {
                centerX: 100 centerY: 160
                radiusX: 80 radiusY: 50
                startAngle: 30 length: 120
```

```
                    type: ArcType.CHORD
                    fill: Color.TRANSPARENT
                    stroke: Color.BLACK
                }
                Arc {
                    centerX: 100 centerY: 260
                    radiusX: 80 radiusY: 50
                    startAngle: 30 length: 120
                    type: ArcType.ROUND
                    fill: Color.TRANSPARENT
                    stroke: Color.BLACK
                }
            ]
        }
}
```

The `radiusX` and `radiusY` values determine the horizontal and vertical radiuses of the ellipse of which the arc is part of the outline. If these values are equal, the arc is circular. The `startAngle` variable determines the position on the ellipse at which the arc begins. As shown on the bottom curve in Figure 16-7, this angle is measured from the 3 o'clock position and is measured counterclockwise if the value is positive, as it is in all three cases in Listing 16-5, and clockwise if it is negative. The `length` variable is the number of degrees through which the arc turns. Again, this is counterclockwise if the value is positive and clockwise if it is negative.

The `type` variable specifies how the arc should be closed. An arc with type `ArcType.OPEN`, which is used for the top arc in Figure 16-7, is not closed at all, one with type `ArcType.CLOSED` is closed by drawing a straight line between its starting and ending points, while one with type `ArcType.ROUND` is closed by linking the ending points of the arc to its center to make a pie shape, as shown at the bottom of Figure 16-7.

Quadratic Curves

The `QuadCurve` class draws a quadratic Bezier curve, which is basically a parabolic shape drawn between two points that may or not be symmetrical about a line drawn at right angles to the line connecting those points. If this sounds a little obscure, all will become clear when you see some examples. If you want to read a more mathematical description of what a Bezier curve is, see the Wikipedia article at http://en.wikipedia.org/wiki/Bezier_curves.

A quadratic curve is defined by its starting and ending points and a third point, known as the *control point*, whose position relative to the starting and ending points determines the overall shape of the curve. The variables of this class, which define the locations of these three points, are listed in Table 16-7.

The easiest way to see the effect of the control point is to run the code shown in Listing 16-6, which draws the starting and ending points and the control points as small

Shapes

Table 16-7 **Variables of the `QuadCurve` Class**

Variable	Type	Access	Default	Description
startX	Number	RW	0.0	The x coordinate of the starting point of the curve
startY	Number	RW	0.0	The y coordinate of the starting point of the curve
endX	Number	RW	0.0	The x coordinate of the ending point of the curve
endY	Number	RW	0.0	The y coordinate of the ending point of the curve
controlX	Number	RW	0.0	The x coordinate of the control point
controlY	Number	RW	0.0	The y coordinate of the control point

circles, together with the corresponding quadratic curve (see lines 55 to 64).[3] This code uses a variant of the `NodeDragger` class that you saw in Chapter 15, "Node Variables and Events," to enable you to drag all three points around the scene. As you do so, the coordinates of the starting and ending points are printed, and the shape of the curve is updated to reflect their current positions.

Listing 16-6 **Drawing a `QuadCurve`**

```
1    package javafxshapes;
2
3    import javafx.scene.input.MouseEvent;
4    import javafx.scene.Scene;
5    import javafx.scene.paint.Color;
6    import javafx.scene.shape.Circle;
7    import javafx.scene.shape.QuadCurve;
8    import javafx.stage.Stage;
9
10   var start:Circle;
11   var end:Circle;
12   var control:Circle;
13
14   var startX = 20.0 on replace { printValues() };
15   var startY = 100.0 on replace { printValues() };
16   var endX = 180.0 on replace { printValues() };
17   var endY = 100.0 on replace { printValues() };
18   var controlX = 100.0 on replace { printValues() };
19   var controlY = 50.0 on replace { printValues() };
20
```

---

[3] You can find this code in the file `javafxshapes/AQuadCurve.fx`.

446   Chapter 16 Shapes, Text, and Images

```
21      function printValues() {
22          println("startX: {startX}, startY: {startY}, "
23                  "endX: {endX}, endY: {endY}, "
24                  "controlX: {controlX}, controlY: {controlY}");
25      }
26
27      class CircleDragger {
28          public-init var circle:Circle;
29          var startX:Number;
30          var startY:Number;
31
32          function onMousePressed(evt:MouseEvent):Void {
33              startX = circle.centerX;
34              startY = circle.centerY;
35          }
36
37          function onMouseDragged(evt:MouseEvent):Void {
38              circle.centerX = startX + evt.dragX;
39              circle.centerY = startY + evt.dragY;
40          }
41
42          postinit {
43              circle.onMousePressed = onMousePressed;
44              circle.onMouseDragged = onMouseDragged;
45          }
46      }
47
48      Stage {
49          title: "Quadratic Curve"
50          scene: Scene {
51              width: 200
52              height: 200
53              content: [
54                  QuadCurve {
55                      startX: bind startX
56                      startY: bind startY
57                      endX: bind endX
58                      endY: bind endY
59                      controlX: bind controlX
60                      controlY: bind controlY
61                      fill: null
62                      stroke: Color.RED
63                  }
64                  start = Circle {
65                      centerX: bind startX with inverse
66                      centerY: bind startY with inverse
67                      radius: 3
68                  }
```

```
69                    end = Circle {
70                        centerX: bind endX with inverse
71                        centerY: bind endY with inverse
72                        radius: 3
73                    }
74                    control = Circle {
75                        centerX: bind controlX with inverse
76                        centerY: bind controlY with inverse
77                        radius: 3
78                    }
79                ]
80            }
81    }
82
83    CircleDragger { circle: start }
84    CircleDragger { circle: end }
85    CircleDragger { circle: control }
```

Figure 16-8 shows some typical quadratic curves.

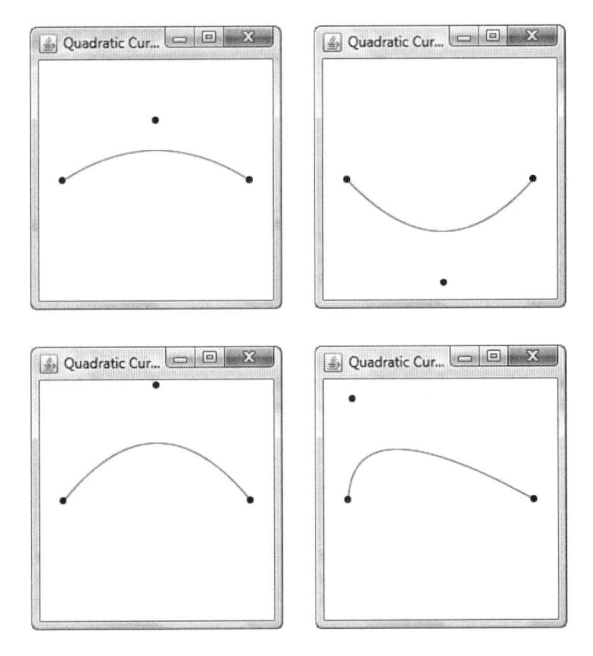

Figure 16-8   Some quadratic curves

The outline of this shape always links the starting and ending points and curves outward toward the control point. The further the control point moves from the other two points, the more pronounced is the inflection (or turn) in the curve, as you can see in the top right of Figure 16-8. When the control point is moved to the other side of the line joining the starting and ending points, the curve also moves to that side, as shown in the bottom left of Figure 16-8. Finally, moving the control point nearer to one of the ending points, as in the bottom right of Figure 16-8, causes the turning point of the curve to move toward that ending point, as well, and produces a result that is no longer symmetrical about the center of the line joining these points.

Cubic Curves

A `CubicCurve` is a Bezier curve that has two control points. The variables of the `CubicCurve` class, listed in Table 16-8, allow you to specify the coordinates of the starting and ending points of the curve and of its two control points.

Table 16-8 Variables of the `CubicCurve` Class

Variable	Type	Access	Default	Description
startX	Number	RW	0.0	The x coordinate of the starting point of the curve
startY	Number	RW	0.0	The y coordinate of the starting point of the curve
endX	Number	RW	0.0	The x coordinate of the ending point of the curve
endY	Number	RW	0.0	The y coordinate of the ending point of the curve
controlX1	Number	RW	0.0	The x coordinate of the first control point
controlY1	Number	RW	0.0	The y coordinate of the first control point
controlX2	Number	RW	0.0	The x coordinate of the second control point
controlY2	Number	RW	0.0	The y coordinate of the second control point

Some examples of cubic curves are shown in Figure 16-9. This figure was created using the code in the file `javafxshapes/ACubicCurve.fx`.

As you can see in the top left of the figure, a cubic curve, like a quadratic curve, stretches out toward its control points. When the control points are moved further away from the starting and ending points, the curvature at the turning point becomes more pronounced, as shown in the top right of Figure 16-9. When the control points are not

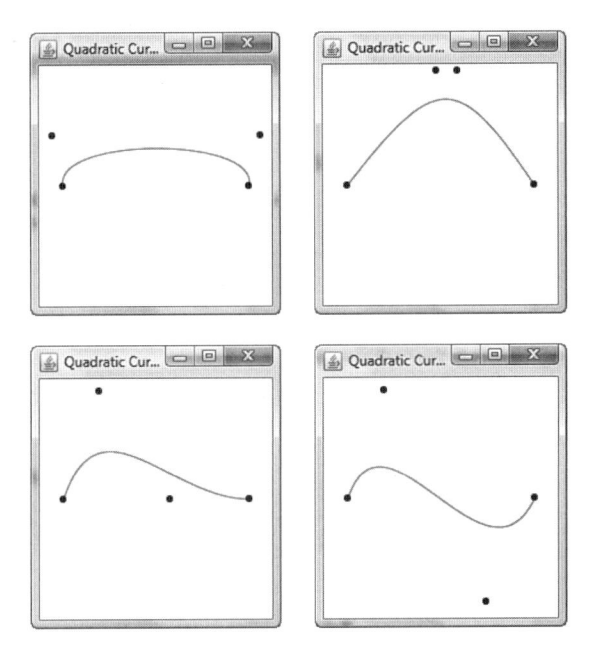

Figure 16-9   Some `CubicCurves`

symmetrically placed relative to the starting and ending points, as shown in the bottom left of the figure, the curve is not symmetrical either. Finally, if the control points are on opposite sides of the line joining the starting and ending points, as is the case in the bottom right of Figure 16-9, there will be two turning points in the curve.

`ShapeIntersect` and `ShapeSubtract`

The `ShapeIntersect` and `ShapeSubtract` classes are shapes that represent, respectively, the intersection and the difference between two given sequences of shapes. Both of these classes have two public variables, called a and b, each of type `Shape[]`. The `ShapeIntersect` class draws a shape that represents the area that is common to the two sets of shapes, while the `ShapeSubtract` class draws the shape that results from subtracting the shapes in variable b from those in variable a.

> **Note**
> `ShapeIntersect` and `ShapeSubtract` are part of the desktop profile and therefore cannot be used on mobile devices.

450   Chapter 16 Shapes, Text, and Images

The following code draws two shapes, a rectangle and a circle, and then creates the result of applying the `ShapeIntersect` and the `ShapeSubtract` classes to these two shapes, as shown in Figure 16-10.[4]

```
Stage {
    title: "Shape Operations"
    scene: Scene {
        width: 200
        height: 150
        content: [
            Rectangle { x: 10 y: 20 width: 140 height: 20
                        fill: Color.YELLOW }
            Circle { centerX: 80 centerY: 30 radius: 20
                     fill: Color.GREEN }
            ShapeIntersect {
                a: Rectangle { x: 10 y: 60 width: 140 height: 20 }
                b: Circle { centerX: 80 centerY: 70 radius: 20 }
                fill: Color.ORANGE
            }
            ShapeSubtract {
                a: Rectangle { x: 10 y: 100 width: 140 height: 20 }
                b: Circle { centerX: 80 centerY: 110 radius: 20 }
                fill: Color.RED
            }
        ]
    }
}
```

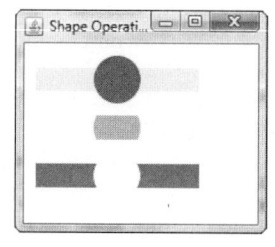

Figure 16-10   Illustrating the `ShapeIntersect` and `ShapeSubtract` classes

The rectangle and circle are shown at the top of Figure 16-10. The intersection of these two shapes, as produced by the `ShapeIntersect` object, is shown in the middle, and

---

[4] You can find this code in the file `javafxshapes/ShapeOperations.fx` in the JavaFX Book Desktop project.

the result of subtracting the circle from the rectangle, using `ShapeSubtract`, at the bottom. Note that `ShapeIntersect` and `ShapeSubtract` rely only on the *geometry* of the shapes that they are given; the `fill` and `stroke` values are ignored, so subtracting a green circle from a yellow rectangle does not leave a yellow rectangle—the resulting shape would be filled with black by default or, as in this example, is explicitly filled with red.

> **Note**
>
> There is no `ShapeAdd` class because there is no need for it—the functionality that would be provided by this class is basically the same as that of the `Group` class.

Paths

All the classes that you have seen so far in this section allow you to draw a single, basic shape. It is possible to construct more complex, connected shapes by using these basic building blocks, but it is slightly cumbersome because each requires its own starting and ending points, so you have to give the positions of the points at which one shape joins to the next twice—once as the ending point of the first shape and again as the starting point of the next. Furthermore, filling such a shape requires you to individually fill its component parts.

There is a much easier way to build complex shapes. The `Path` class lets you specify the components of the shape's outline as a sequence of path elements, each represented by an instance of the `PathElement` class. The starting point of each path element is implicitly defined to be the ending point of the previous one, so there is no need to specify any point twice. In addition, a shape defined by a path can be filled as if it were a single shape (which, in fact, it is).

The variables of the `Path` class are listed in Table 16-9.

Table 16-9   Variables of the `Path` Class

Variable	Type	Access	Default	Description
Elements	PathElement[]	RW	Empty	The `PathElement`s that make up the path
fillRule	FillRule	RW	FillRule.NON_ZERO	Determines how the shape is filled

The `fillRule` variable is used to determine whether a given point is to be regarded as inside or outside the shape when applying the fill color, if there is one. In some cases, it is not obvious what should be properly regarded as the inside or outside of the shape. For more details, see the "Shape Filling" section, later in this chapter.

There are eight different types of path element that can be combined to create a shape. The `PathElement` class itself has only one public variable, as shown in Table 16-10.

Table 16-10 Variables of the `PathElement` Class

Variable	Type	Access	Default	Description
`absolute`	`Boolean`	RW	`true`	Specifies whether coordinates in this element are absolute (`true`) or relative (`false`)

No matter how many elements it has, a path is only a single node and therefore has a single stroke and a single fill. It is not possible to separately color individual elements.

`MoveTo`, Lines, and `ClosePath`

The first element of a path must always be a `MoveTo`. This class has only two public variables, x and y, both of type `Number` that set the starting point for the next element in the path.

There are three path elements that draw straight-line segments: `LineTo`, `HLineTo`, and `VLineTo`. The most general of these is `LineTo`, which joins its implicit starting point to the point given by its x and y variables. The `HLineTo` class draws a horizontal line from its starting point to a point with a given x coordinate, while the `VLineTo` class draws a vertical line to a given y coordinate.

Paths are not automatically closed. You can close a path by explicitly drawing a straight line from the ending point of the last element to the starting point of the first, but a more convenient way to do this is to use the `ClosePath` element, which uses the `Path`'s memory of its first and most recent points to draw the line required to close the path.

The code in Listing 16-7, which is from file `javafxshapes/StraightLinePaths.fx`, uses the `MoveTo`, `HLine`, `LineTo`, and `ClosePath` elements to build a path that looks like a five-pointed star, as shown in Figure 16-11.

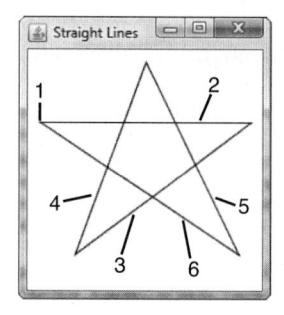

Figure 16-11 Using straight line path elements

Listing 16-7 Using Straight Line Path Elements to Draw a Five-Pointed Star

```
1    package javafxshapes;
2
3    import javafx.scene.paint.Color;
4    import javafx.scene.Scene;
```

```
5        import javafx.scene.shape.ClosePath;
6        import javafx.scene.shape.HLineTo;
7        import javafx.scene.shape.LineTo;
8        import javafx.scene.shape.MoveTo;
9        import javafx.scene.shape.Path;
10       import javafx.stage.Stage;
11
12       Stage {
13           title: "Straight Lines"
14           scene: Scene {
15               width: 200
16               height: 200
17               content: Path {
18                   fill: null
19                   stroke: Color.BLACK
20                   elements: [
21                       MoveTo { x: 10 y: 60 }                       // 1
22                       HLineTo { x: 180 absolute: false }           // 2
23                       LineTo { x: -150 y: 110 absolute: false }    // 3
24                       LineTo { x: 60 y: -160 absolute: false }     // 4
25                       LineTo { x: 80 y: 160 absolute: false }      // 5
26                       ClosePath {}                                 // 6
27                   ]
28               }
29           }
30       }
```

The `Path` node that draws this shape is created on lines 17 to 28. The first element is a `MoveTo` that moves the logical pen that will draw the shape to (10, 60) relative to the scene, which is the point labeled (1) in Figure 16-11. The `HLine` element on line 22 moves the pen 180 pixels to the right, as shown by the horizontal line labeled (2) in the figure. Notice that the `absolute` variable for this element, and all the following elements in this path, is set to `false` so that we can use relative coordinates—this makes it possible to move the whole shape just by changing the x and y variables in the `MoveTo` element. The next three elements, of type `LineTo`, create the diagonal lines labeled (3), (4), and (5). The last diagonal line, number (6) in Figure 16-11, is drawn by the `ClosePath` element on line 26 of Listing 16-7. The starting and ending points of `ClosePath` are implicit, so there is no need to specify the location of point (1) to close the shape.

Arcs and Curves

The `ArcTo`, `QuadCurveTo`, and `CubicCurveTo` elements are similar to the shapes with similar names that we discussed earlier in this chapter. The `QuadCurveTo` and `CubicCurveTo` classes have almost the same variables as their standalone counterparts, apart from the fact that it is only necessary to specify the ending point, so we won't discuss them any further. The `ArcTo` class, however, is slightly more complex. Its variables are listed in Table 16-11.

Chapter 16 Shapes, Text, and Images

Table 16-11 Variables of the `ArcTo` Class

Variable	Type	Access	Default	Description
x	Number	RW	0.0	The x coordinate of the ending point of the arc
y	Number	RW	0.0	The y coordinate of the ending point of the arc
radiusX	Number	RW	0.0	The horizontal radius of the arc
radius	Number	RW	0.0	The vertical radius of the arc
largeArcFlag	Boolean	RW	false	The large arc flag (see text)
sweepFlag	Boolean	RW	false	The sweep flag (see text)
xAxisRotation	Number	RW	0.0	The x-axis rotation in degrees

The first four variables are easy to understand—the arc is a segment of an ellipse with given horizontal and vertical radiuses, which starts at the current position of the `Path` of which it is an element and ends at the given x and y coordinates. However, these four variables are not enough to uniquely define an arc. Assuming for now that the `xAxisRotation` variable has value `0.0`, two possible ellipses could define the shape of the arc to be drawn—namely the ones labeled A and B at the top of Figure 16-12. As you can see, these ellipses provide four possible arcs—two taken from ellipse A and two from ellipse B, which are shown as arcs 1 to 4 in Figure 16-12. The arc that is actually drawn depends on the values of the `largeArcFlag` and `sweepFlag` variables. These variables are used as follows:

1. The `sweepFlag` selects which ellipse is used. If `sweepFlag` is `true`, the ellipse that is drawn counterclockwise through the two points is selected; otherwise, the ellipse that is drawn clockwise is chosen.

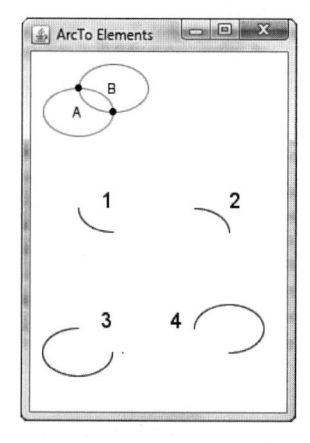

Figure 16-12 Examples of the `ArcTo` element

2. If `largeArcFlag` is `true`, the larger of the two possible arcs in the selected list is used; otherwise, the smaller arc is used.

In the examples that follow, the current position of the path is assumed to be at (0, 0), the ending point of the `ArcTo` element is at (30, 20), the horizontal radius is 30, and the vertical radius is 20. These parameters match the two ellipses shown at the top of Figure 16-12. Let's consider first the following `ArcTo` element:

```
ArcTo {
    x: 30 y: 20 absolute: false
    radiusX: 30 radiusY: 20
    largeArcFlag: false sweepFlag: false
}
```

The `sweepFlag` value selects the ellipse that is drawn clockwise *from* the starting point (0, 0) *to* the ending point (30, 20). Looking at Figure 16-12, you can see that this is ellipse B. The `largeArcFlag` value means that we need the shorter arc of ellipse B. Therefore, this example corresponds to the arc labeled 1 in Figure 16-12.

The following example is the same, but the value of `sweepFlag` has been changed from `false` to `true`:

```
ArcTo {
    x: 30 y: 20 absolute: false
    radiusX: 30 radiusY: 20
    largeArcFlag: false sweepFlag: true
}
```

In this case, we need the smaller arc of the counterclockwise ellipse, which is ellipse A. Therefore, this code corresponds to the arc labeled 2 in the figure. Here's another example:

```
ArcTo {
    x: 30 y: 20 absolute: false
    radiusX: 30 radiusY: 20
    largeArcFlag: true sweepFlag: false
}
```

As you have already seen, the `sweepFlag` value of `false` corresponds to ellipse B, and the `largeArcFlag` value selects its larger arc. This code, therefore, produces the arc labeled 3 in Figure 16-12. The final case, shown here, corresponds to arc number 4:

```
ArcTo {
    x: 30 y: 20 absolute: false
    radiusX: 30 radiusY: 20
    largeArcFlag: true sweepFlag: true
}
```

The `xAxisRotation` variable has the effect of rotating the x-axis (and, of course, the y-axis) of the candidate ellipses from which the arc is obtained through the given angle, so that their axes are no longer parallel to the coordinate axes. A positive value rotates the axes counterclockwise.

SVGPath

The `SVGPath` class creates a shape from path data in the format defined by the Scalable Vector Graphics (SVG) specification, which you can find at http://www.w3.org/TR/SVG/. Discussion of SVG is beyond the scope of this book, so we'll confine ourselves to an example that demonstrates how to use this class.

The following code, which you can find in the file `javafxshapes/AnSVGPath.fx`, draws the same five-pointed star that results from the path object in Listing 16-7:

```
Stage {
    title: "SVGPath"
    scene: Scene {
        width: 200
        height: 200
        content: SVGPath {
            fill: null
            stroke: Color.BLACK
            content: "M 10 60 h 180 l -150 110 60 -160 80 160 z"
        }
    }
}
```

An SVG path definition is a string consisting of single-letter commands followed by parameters. The path definition is the value of the content variable of the `SVGPath` object. Here, the command begins with `M 10 60`, which is equivalent to `MoveTo (10, 60)`, followed by `h 180`, which is the same as `HLineTo` with `x = 180` and relative coordinates, and so on. You can use this class to make any SVG path definition a part of your scene graph.

Stroking and Filling Shapes

So far in this book, we have used a single-pixel, solid line to draw the outline of a shape. In this section, you'll see how to set the width and pattern of the outline, and how to determine which parts of a shape that has intersecting sides are actually filled.

Stroking Shapes

The appearance of the outline of a shape is controlled by the seven variables listed in Table 16-12. You have already seen the `stroke` variable, which determines the color (or color gradient) used to draw the outline. In this section, we discuss the effect of the other six variables.

Table 16-12 **Shape Variables That Control Outline Drawing**

Variable	Type	Access	Default	Description
stroke	Paint	RW	See text	The `Paint` used to stroke the outline of the `Shape`
strokeWidth	Number	RW	1	The width of the outline stroke, in pixels

Table 16-12 Shape Variables That Control Outline Drawing (*Continued*)

Variable	Type	Access	Default	Description
strokeDashArray	Number[]	RW	[1.0]	Determines where there are gaps in the outline
strokeDashOffset	Number	RW	0	Specifies the distance into strokeDashArray that applies to the first point of the outline
strokeLineCap	Stroke LineCap	RW	SQUARE	Determines how the ends of the stroke outline are drawn
strokeLineJoin	Stroke LineJoin	RW	MITER	Specifies how the points at which lines meet are to be drawn
strokeMiterLimit	Number	RW	10	Limits the length of a miter join

Stroke Width and Line Endings

The `strokeWidth` variable sets the width of the shape's outline. By default, this is 1 pixel. The following code, which comes from the file `javafxshapes/WideLines.fx`, draws a vertical line that is 10 pixels wide, as shown on the left of Figure 16-13.

```
Line {
    startX: 20 startY: 20
    endX: 20 endY: 180
    strokeWidth: 10
}
```

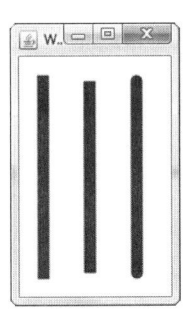

Figure 16-13 Wide lines and line caps

You might expect that this line would be 160 pixels long, but it is, in fact, slightly longer. It is actually extended at both ends by 5 pixels, because the variable `strokeLineCap` has its default value of `StrokeLineCap.SQUARE`, which causes a square "cap" that is half as long as the width of the line to be added at both ends of the line. For thin lines, this makes no real difference, but its effect becomes more pronounced when you make the line wider.

The reason for adding this cap is that if you were to construct a right-angled corner by joining two lines together and the lines were not extended, you would otherwise see a gap at the corner. You can simulate this effect by setting `strokeLineCap` to the value `StrokeLineCap.BUTT`, which draws a line that starts and ends exactly at the specified points, as shown in the middle of Figure 16-13. The result of drawing two lines that have this `strokeLineCap` value and start at the same point is shown in Figure 16-14. The extra pixels added by the default `strokeLineCap` setting would fill this ugly gap.

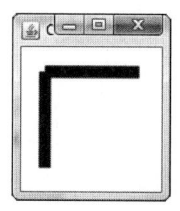

Figure 16-14 Joining two lines with `strokeLineCap` set to `StrokeLineCap.BUTT`

The third possible value for the `strokeLineCap` variable, `StrokeLineCap.ROUND`, also causes extra pixels to be added at both ends of the lines, but in this case they are arranged so as to give the impression of a rounded end, as shown on the right of Figure 16-13.

Although the examples you have seen so far demonstrate the use of `strokeLineCap` with straight lines, this variable actually applies to the ending points of any shape, as demonstrated in Figure 16-15, which shows an arc and an unclosed path that both have this variable set to `StrokeLineCap.ROUND`.

Figure 16-15 Rounded ending points on an arc and a path

Joins

The `strokeLineJoin` variable lets you choose what should happen where two successive elements of a path meet. There are three possibilities, all of which are shown in Figure 16-16.

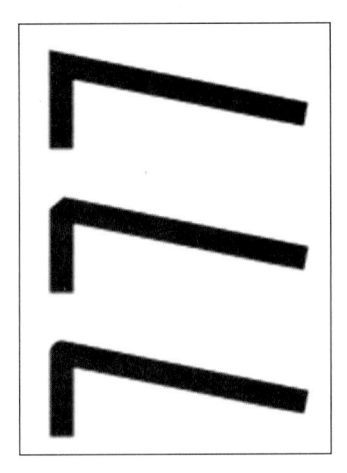

Figure 16-16   Line join styles

The three paths in this figure all consist of two lines. The topmost shape was created using the following code:

```
Path {
    strokeWidth: 10
    strokeLineJoin: StrokeLineJoin.MITER
    elements: [
        MoveTo { x: 20 y: 50 }
        LineTo { x: 0 y: -30 absolute: false}
        LineTo { x: 100 y: 20 absolute: false }
    ]
}
```

The value `StrokeLineJoin.MITER` causes the meeting point between the two path elements to be given a triangular shape, created by extending both lines until they meet. This is the default style. So if you want this effect, you do not need to set an explicit value for the `strokeLineJoin` variable. In the case that the two lines are nearly parallel, this style could create a very long join. It is possible to limit the length of the join by setting the `strokeMiterLimit` variable, which sets a limit on the ratio of the miter length (that is, the length of the triangle created by the join) to the stroke width of the lines themselves. When this ratio exceeds the value of `strokeMiterLimit`, the join is automatically converted to bevel style.

Chapter 16 Shapes, Text, and Images

The value `StrokeLineJoin.BEVEL` creates a flat join by linking together the other edges of the two path segments as shown in the center of Figure 16-16. The third possible value, `StrokeLineJoin.ROUND`, is similar, but links the edges of the path segments with a filled circular arc, as shown at the bottom of Figure 16-16.

Outline Dashing

The `strokeDashArray` variable is a sequence of `Numbers` that can be used to give a shape a dashed outline. The simplest way to explain it is by example. The code shown in Listing 16-8 draws a circle and a square that both have dashed outlines, as shown in Figure 16-17, which you can find in the file `javafxshapes/DashedOutlines.fx`.

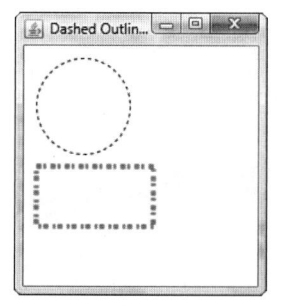

Figure 16-17 A circle and a square with dashed outlines

Listing 16-8 **Dashed Shape Outlines**

```
1    Stage {
2        title: "Dashed Outlines"
3        scene: Scene {
4            width: 200
5            height: 200
6            content: [
7                Circle {
8                    centerX: 50 centerY: 50
9                    radius: 40 fill: null
10                   stroke: Color.BLACK
11                   strokeLineCap: StrokeLineCap.BUTT
12                   strokeDashArray: [ 3, 3 ]
13               }
14               Rectangle {
15                   x: 10 y: 100
16                   width: 100 height: 50
17                   fill: null
18                   stroke: Color.RED
19                   strokeWidth: 4
```

```
20                    strokeLineCap: StrokeLineCap.BUTT
21                    strokeDashArray: [ 4, 2, 2, 4 ]
22                }
23            ]
24        }
25    }
```

The even-numbered entries in the `strokeDashArray` sequence give the lengths of the solid parts of the dashed pattern, and the odd entries are the lengths of the gaps. The entries on line 12 of Listing 16-8 result in a pattern that has dashes that are 3 pixels long, followed by gaps that are of the same length. The `strokeDashArray` on line 21 creates a pattern that has a 4-pixel dash, followed by a 2-pixel gap, a 2-pixel dash, and finally a 4-pixel gap, after which the pattern repeats. You can have as many elements in this sequence as you need to create the pattern that you want. If you supply an odd number, the sequence is effectively concatenated to itself to create one with an even number, so that [4, 2, 3] would be interpreted as [4, 2, 3, 4, 2 ,3].

Notice that both of these examples use `StrokeLineCap.BUTT` as the line ending type. This is necessary because each dashed segment is treated as a line and is given the end style specified by the `strokeLineCap` value of the shape. If you use the default value or specify round ends, you might not get the effect that you expect. If we were to remove lines 11 and 20 from the code in Listing 16-8, the line endings would have the default style, which is `StrokeLineCap.SQUARE`, giving the result shown in Figure 16-18.

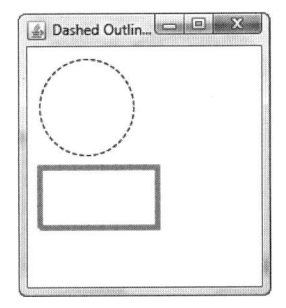

Figure 16-18   Dashed outlines with the default line cap style

As you can see, the rectangle no longer has a dashed outline pattern. The reason for this is that when the line ending style is `StrokeLineCap.SQUARE`, each dash is extended at each end by an amount that is half of its `strokeWidth`. As a result, the dashes are extended from 4 pixels to 8 pixels (2 additional pixels at each end). These additional pixels fill the space where there should be gaps, so give the appearance of a solid rectangle. This does not appear to affect the circle, because its `strokeWidth` is only 1, so the line ending style extends the dashes by 0 pixels on each end. If you want to use SQUARE or ROUND endings, the gap sizes must be greater than the `strokeWidth` of the shape, or you won't actually see any gaps. The following code uses ROUND line endings and increases the gaps to 6 pixels:

```
Rectangle {
    x: 10 y: 100
    width: 100 height: 50
    fill: null
    stroke: Color.RED
    strokeWidth: 4
    strokeLineCap: StrokeLineCap.ROUND
    strokeDashArray: [ 4, 6, 2, 6 ]
}
```

Figure 16-19 shows the result of running this code, magnified so that you can see where the individual pixels are placed. You can clearly see that the pixels added to create the rounding effect intrude into the gaps, reducing them from the 6 pixels that have been requested to only 2 (which is 6 minus the `strokeWidth` value of 4).

Figure 16-19 A dashed outline with round line endings

The `strokeDashOffset` variable determines from where in the dash pattern the first pixel of the outline should be taken. By default, this is 0, so the first pixel is taken from the first entry of the `strokeDashArray` sequence. Suppose we change the code shown above to the following:

```
Rectangle {
    x: 10 y: 100
    width: 100 height: 50
    fill: null
    stroke: Color.RED
    strokeWidth: 4
    strokeLineCap: StrokeLineCap.BUTT
    strokeDashArray: [ 4, 6, 2, 6 ]
    strokeDashOffset: 5
}
```

The effect of this is to start the dashed outline 5 pixels into the pattern, which would cause the first dash and 1 pixel of the gap to be skipped, resulting in a 5-pixel gap, followed by a 2-pixel dash, a 6-pixel gap, a 4-pixel dash, and so on. The important point to note is that `strokeDashOffset` is a length in pixels, *not* an index into the `strokeDashArray` sequence.

Shape Filling

You have already seen that you can use the `fill` variable to fill the interior of a shape with either a solid color or a `Paint`, such as a gradient. In this section, we look more closely at how this applies to shapes that are open or where it is not clear which points are inside the shape's boundary.

Filling Open Shapes

The `Polyline` shape shown in Figure 16-6 is not closed. What happens if we try to fill this shape with a solid color? Should the color spill out onto the `Scene`, or should it stop somewhere? This question is easily answered by setting its `fill` variable:

```
Polyline {
    points: [ 100,10,  180,60, 180,130,
              100,180, 20,130, 20,60]
    fill: Color.YELLOW
    stroke: Color.BLACK
}
```

The result of running this code, which you'll find in the file `javafxshapes/FilledPolyline.fx`, is shown in Figure 16-20. As you can see, the fill color remains inside the boundary of the shape—in fact, it acts as if the shape had been closed.

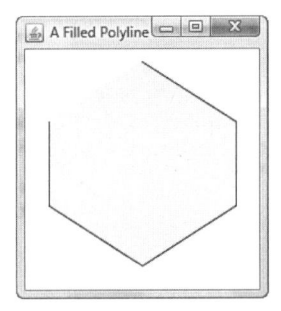

Figure 16-20   Filling an open shape

Filling More Complex Shapes

Now let's turn our attention to the five-pointed star shown in Figure 16-11. If we fill this shape, what should happen to the pentagonal area at the center of the star? Should the points in that area be considered to be inside or outside the shape? The answer is that it depends on the value of the shape's `fillRule` variable, which has two possible values—`FillRule.NON_ZERO`, which is the default and `FillRule.EVEN_ODD`. Figure 16-21 shows the effects of these two rules.

464   Chapter 16 Shapes, Text, and Images

Figure 16-21   Filling complex shapes

The star at the top of the figure uses `FillRule.NON_ZERO`[5]:

```
Path {
    fill: Color.YELLOW
    fillRule: FillRule.NON_ZERO
    stroke: Color.BLACK
    elements: [
        MoveTo { x: 10 y: 60 }
        HLineTo { x: 180 absolute: false }
        LineTo { x: -150 y: 110 absolute: false }
        LineTo { x: 60 y: -160 absolute: false }
        LineTo { x: 80 y: 160 absolute: false }
        ClosePath {}
    ]
}
```

With this rule, the points in the enclosed pentagon are considered to be inside the shape. On the other, in the lower star, which uses `FillRule.EVEN_ODD`, these same points are considered to be *outside* the shape and so are not filled:

```
Path {
    fill: Color.YELLOW
    fillRule: FillRule.EVEN_ODD
    stroke: Color.BLACK
    elements: [
        MoveTo { x: 10 y: 220 }
        HLineTo { x: 180 absolute: false }
```

---

[5] The code for the examples in this section is in the file `javafxshapes/FilledStar.fx`.

```
        LineTo { x: -150 y: 110 absolute: false }
        LineTo { x: 60 y: -160 absolute: false }
        LineTo { x: 80 y: 160 absolute: false }
        ClosePath {}
    ]
}
```

So how do these rules work? For any given point, the first thing to do when determining whether the point is inside or outside the shape is to draw a line through that point, in any direction, but ensuring that it does not pass through a vertex of the shape. What happens next depends on which rule is being used.

The *nonzero winding rule*, which is the default for JavaFX shapes, is illustrated at the top of Figure 16-22.

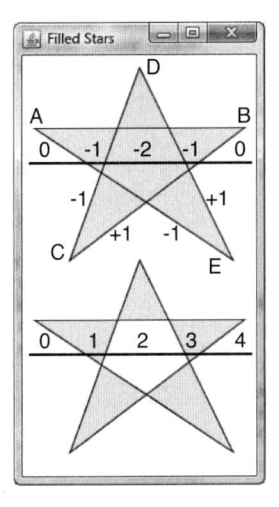

Figure 16-22 Fill rules for shapes

To determine whether a point is inside or outside the shape according to the nonzero winding rule, do the following:

1. Label each segment of the path with `+1` if the pen moves in the positive y direction when drawing it and with `-1` if it moves in the negative y direction. Segments that are parallel to the y-axis should be assigned the value `0`. In Figure 16-22, the figure was drawn in the order A–B–C–D–E–A; so A–B has value `0`, B–C has value `+1` (remembering that y increases as we move down), C–D has value `-1`, D–E has value `+1`, and E–A has value `-1`.

2. Initialize a counter to `0`. Moving along the line from left to right and starting outside, each time you cross a line, add that line's value to the counter. The values for each of the regions in the shape are shown above the line in Figure 16-22.

Regions for which the counter value is 0 are outside the shape, and those that have a nonzero value are inside. You can see that this result tallies with the regions that are actually filled in the star at the top of Figure 16-22. If the shape had been drawn in the opposite direction, the values and accumulated values would have been the same, but with opposite signs. Because all that matters is whether the value in a region is 0, the same areas would be filled.

The *even-odd winding rule*, shown at the bottom of Figure 16-22, is easier to evaluate. To determine whether a point is inside or outside the shape, draw a line through it as before, initialize a counter to 0. Moving along the line from left to right, each time a segment of the path is crossed, increment the counter by 1. Regions in which the counter is odd are inside the shape and should be filled; those for which the counter is even are outside and should not be filled.

The `Text` Class

The `Text` class is a shape that draws a text string onto your scene. The appearance of the text is determined by several variables of the `Text` object, including the font, which we discuss in the next section.

Because `Text` is a shape, you can do everything with it that you can do with any other shape, including setting the `stroke` and `fill` variables to control the text color and changing the stroke style if you don't want the individual letters to have solid outlines. As you'll see in upcoming chapters, you can also apply transformations, such as rotations and scaling, and effects like reflection to your text.

Text Content and Positioning

Table 16-13 describes the variables of the `Text` class that you can use to set the string to be displayed and to control its positioning.

Table 16-13   **Variables of the Text Class That Determine Content and Position**

Variable	Type	Access	Default	Description
`content`	`String`	RW	Empty string	The text to be rendered
`x`	`Number`	RW	0.0	The x coordinate of the text
`y`	`Number`	RW	0.0	The y coordinate of the text
`textOrigin`	`TextOrigin`	RW	`BASELINE`	Determines the position of the text relative to its (x, y) coordinates
`textAlignment`	`TextAlignment`	RW	`LEFT`	Determines the horizontal alignment of the text

Table 16-13 Variables of the Text Class That Determine Content and Position (*Continued*)

Variable	Type	Access	Default	Description
wrappingWidth	Number	RW	0	A wrapping constraint for the text

Displaying Text

The text to be drawn is the value of the `content` variable, and the x and y variables determine where the text appears relative to the scene or to the `Text` object's parent. There are three possible positions within the text to which these coordinates can refer. These three possibilities are illustrated by the code in Listing 16-9, which you'll find in the file `javafxshapes/Text1.fx`, the result of which is shown in Figure 16-23.

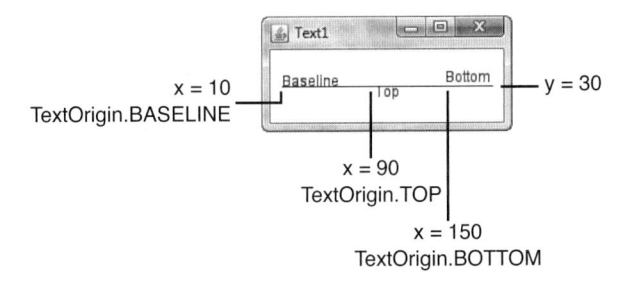

Figure 16-23 Text positioning and the **TextOrigin** class

Listing 16-9 **Text Positioning and the TextOrigin Class**

```
1    package javafxshapes;
2
3    import javafx.scene.Scene;
4    import javafx.scene.text.Text;
5    import javafx.scene.text.TextOrigin;
6    import javafx.stage.Stage;
7    import javafx.scene.shape.Line;
8    import javafx.scene.paint.Color;
9
10   Stage {
11       title: "Text1"
12       scene: Scene {
13           width: 200
14           height: 60
15           content: [
16               Text {
17                   x: 10 y: 30
18                   textOrigin: TextOrigin.BASELINE
```

```
19                  content: "Baseline"
20              }
21              Text {
22                  x: 90 y: 30
23                  textOrigin: TextOrigin.TOP
24                  content: "Top"
25              }
26              Text {
27                  x: 150 y: 30
28                  textOrigin: TextOrigin.BOTTOM
29                  content: "Bottom"
30              }
31              Line {
32                  startX: 10 startY: 30
33                  endX: 190 endY: 30
34                  strokeWidth: 1
35                  stroke: Color.BLACK
36              }
37          ]
38      }
39  }
```

This example uses three `Text` objects with the same y value, but with different values for `textOrigin`. In all cases, the x coordinate gives the starting horizontal position of the text. A horizontal reference line indicates the y coordinate of all three `Text` objects. The leftmost instance, created on lines 16 to 20 of Listing 16-9, has its `textOrigin` set to `TextOrigin.BASELINE`, which is the default, and results in the text being drawn with its baseline at the specified y coordinate, so that it appears to sit neatly on the reference line. The middle instance, resulting from lines 26 to 30, has the top of the text at the given position, while the rightmost example places the bottom of the text at the given y coordinate.

The difference between `TextOrigin.BASELINE` and `TextOrigin.BOTTOM` is that in the latter case, space is left below the text for any possible descenders—that is, letters such as *y* that are drawn partly below the baseline. You can see this additional space, the size of which is based on information in the font used to draw the text, between the bottom of the drawn text and the reference line on the right of Figure 16-23.

The `Text` node is automatically sized so that it exactly fits the text that it contains. It is not possible for application code to change its width or height.

Multiline Text, Alignment, and Wrapping

The `Text` class can render more than one line of text. This happens when either there are newlines in the value of the `content` variable, or the text reaches its *wrapping limit* as specified by the `wrappingWidth` variable.

The following code, from the file `javafxshapes/Text2.fx`, produces three lines of text, as shown on the left of Figure 16-24. Each newline character in the `content` variable causes a new line of text to be drawn, all within the bounds of the same `Text` node.

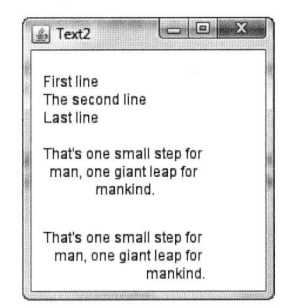

Figure 16-24 Multiline text and alignment examples

```
Text {
    x: 10 y: 30
    content: "First line\nThe second line\nLast line"
}
```

As you can see, the individual lines are left-justified within the area occupied by the Text node. This is the default, but it can be changed, as shown in the next example:

```
Text {
    x: 10 y: 90
    wrappingWidth: 150
    textAlignment: TextAlignment.CENTER
    content: "That's one small step for man, "
            "one giant leap for mankind."
}
```

Here, there are no embedded newlines, but the wrappingWidth variable is set to 150, forcing the content onto more than one line, as you can see in the center of Figure 16-24. The text is automatically word-wrapped so that no line is wider than 150 pixels.[6] In this case, each line is horizontally centered in the space available because the textAlignment variable is set to TextAlignment.CENTER. The value TextAlignment.RIGHT, used in the following code, causes each row of text to be right-aligned instead, as shown at the bottom of Figure 16-24.

```
Text {
    x: 10 y: 160
    wrappingWidth: 150
    textAlignment: TextAlignment.RIGHT
    content: "That's one small step for man, "
            "one giant leap for mankind."
}
```

---

[6] Words that are longer than the wrappingWidth are simply split across multiple lines.

Text Fill and Stroke

By default, a `Text` object has no stroke and is filled with solid black. You can change either of these variables in the same way as you can with any other shape. Some examples of different `stroke` and `fill` settings are shown in Figure 16-25.

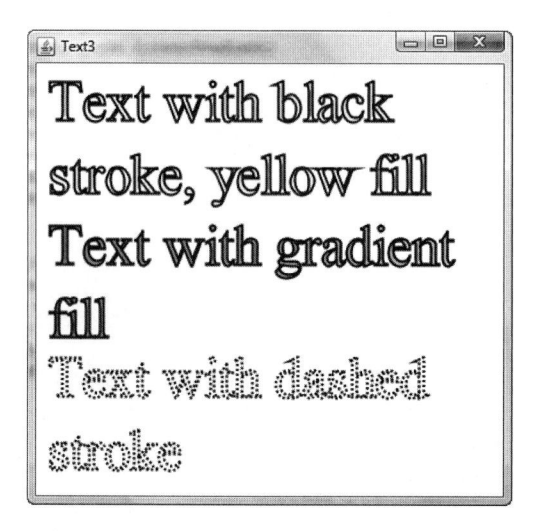

Figure 16-25   Text fill and stroke examples

The text at the top of the figure was created with the following code, from the file `javafxshapes/Text3.fx`:

```
Text {
    x: 10 y: 10 textOrigin: TextOrigin.TOP
    font: Font { name: "Serif" size: 48 }
    fill: Color.YELLOW
    stroke: Color.BLACK
    strokeWidth: 2
    content: "Text with black\nstroke, yellow fill"
}
```

The text is filled with solid yellow and has a 2-pixel outline that is stroked in black. A large font is used to make the effects easier to see. In general, using different stroke and font colors does not work well with small font sizes.

The middle example in Figure 16-25 shows that you don't have to fill text with a solid color:

```
Text {
    x: 10 y: 130 textOrigin: TextOrigin.TOP
    font: Font { name: "Serif" size: 48 }
    fill: LinearGradient {
```

```
            startX: 0.0 startY: 0.0
            endX: 1.0 endY: 0.0
            stops: [
                Stop { offset: 0.0 color: Color.RED }
                Stop { offset: 1.0 color: Color.LIGHTGRAY }
            ]
        }
    stroke: Color.BLACK
    strokeWidth: 2
    content: "Text with gradient\nfill"
}
```

In this case, the text is filled with a linear gradient that starts with red on the left of the `Text` object and progresses to light gray on the right. You can see that the gradient is applied in the same way to both rows of text.

Finally, the text at the bottom of Figure 16-25 has no fill and is stroked with a dashed outline that has 2 solid pixels followed by a 2-pixel gap:

```
Text {
    x: 10 y: 240 textOrigin: TextOrigin.TOP
    font: Font { name: "Serif" size: 48 }
    fill: null
    stroke: Color.BLACK
    strokeWidth: 2
    strokeLineCap: StrokeLineCap.BUTT
    strokeDashArray: [2, 2]
    content: "Text with dashed\nstroke"
}
```

As with earlier examples, the `strokeLineCap` variable has been set to `StrokeLineCap.BUTT` so that the gaps are not overrun by the effects of the stroke line endings.

Text Decoration

The `Text` class has two `Boolean` variables, listed in Table 16-14, that specify whether specific decorations should be added.

Table 16-14   Variables of the `Text` Class That Control Decorations

Variable	Type	Access	Default	Description
strikethrough	Boolean	RW	false	Specifies whether a solid line should be drawn through the text
underline	Boolean	RW	false	Determines whether a solid line should be drawn below the text

These variables are simple toggles that specify whether the corresponding decoration is applied. The following code, which you'll find in the file `javafxshapes/Text4.fx`, enables both decorations and produces the result shown in Figure 16-26.

```
Stage {
    title: "Text4"
    scene: Scene {
        width: 200
        height: 120
        content: [
            Text {
                x: 10 y: 30
                underline: true
                content: "Text with underline"
            }
            Text {
                x: 10 y: 90
                strikethrough: true
                content: "Text with strikethrough"
            }
        ]
    }
}
```

Fonts

The appearance of the text drawn by a `Text` object is determined by the value of its `font` variable, which is of type `javafx.scene.font.Font`. The first part of this section describes the characteristics of a font and how these are represented in JavaFX. The second part describes the API that allows you to discover which fonts are available and to create a `Font` instance that has specific characteristics.

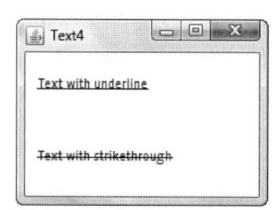

Figure 16-26   The `strikethrough` and `underline` variables of the `Text` class

Font Characteristics

A font provides the character shapes (or *glyphs*) that are used to render text. There are many different *families* of fonts, each of which has its own distinctive set of glyphs. Within a family, there is always a font whose name is the same as that of the family, and there may be other fonts that have the same appearance apart from characteristics called the *font weight*, the *font posture*, and the *font position*, all of which are discussed next. Each family has a unique name, known as the *font family name*, and each font within a family also has a unique name, referred to either as the *font name* or the *font face name*.

Font Family Name and Font Name

Figure 16-27 shows a scene containing eight `Text` objects, each of which is using a different font. This scene is produced by the code in the file `javafxshapes/Fonts1.fx`.

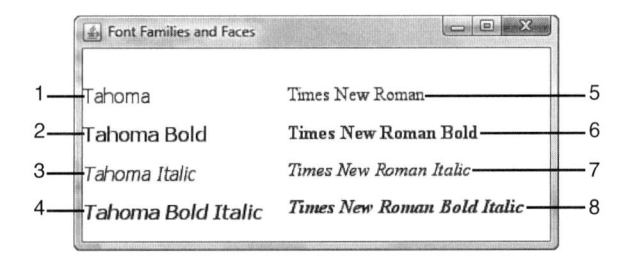

Figure 16-27   Font families and font faces

The `Text` objects in the left column are all using fonts from the *Tahoma* family. As you can see from the screenshot of the set of fonts installed on my Windows laptop in Figure 16-28, the Tahoma family contains two fonts that have the following names:

- *Tahoma*, used by the `Text` object labeled 1
- *Tahoma Bold*, used by the `Text` object labeled 2

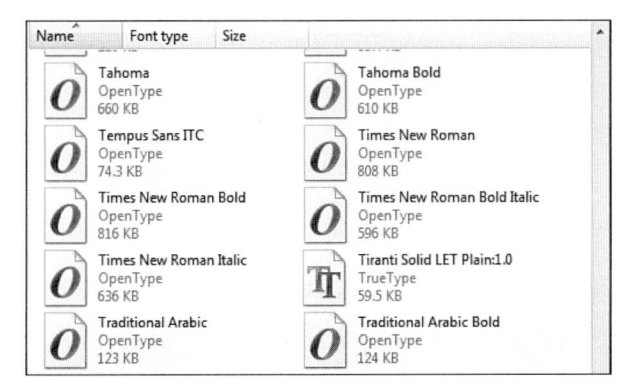

Figure 16-28   Font files

The `Text` objects labeled 3 and 4 claim to use fonts called *Tahoma Italic* and *Tahoma Bold Italic*, but no such fonts exist on my system. Instead, the JavaFX runtime synthesizes them by applying transformations to glyphs taken from the Tahoma and Tahoma Bold fonts to produce the italicized glyphs.

The `Text` objects on the right of Figure 16-27 use fonts from the *Times New Roman* family, which has four fonts:

- *Times New Roman*, used by the `Text` object labeled 5
- *Times New Roman Bold*, used by the `Text` object labeled 6
- *Times New Roman Italic*, used by the `Text` object labeled 7
- *Times New Roman Bold Italic*, used by the `Text` object labeled 8

All four of these fonts are actually installed on my system, as you can see in Figure 16-28.

If you compare the text in the left and right columns of Figure 16-27, you'll see that the glyphs that appear in the left column are noticeably different from those on the right, because fonts from two different font families have been used. However, within a column, the glyphs used are very similar, because the fonts used are in the same family.

Font Weight

Loosely put, a font's weight is a measure of how bold it is. There are various levels of boldness that a font might support. For example, the Rockwell font family has two "bold" fonts called Rockwell Bold and Rockwell Extra Bold. As you have seen, both the Tahoma and Times New Roman families have a single bold font. In JavaFX, the weight of a font is specified by a constant defined by the `FontWeight` class. There are 11 possible weights, not all of which will give distinct results, because the font to which they are applied may not support them:

BOLD	DEMI_BOLD	DEMI_LIGHT	EXTRA_BOLD
EXTRA_LIGHT	HEAVY	LIGHT	MEDIUM
REGULAR	SEMI_BOLD	ULTRA_BOLD	

The value `FontWeight.REGULAR` refers to the normal weight of the font and is used to obtain a font that is neither bold nor light. Any text in Figure 16-27 that does not contain the word *Bold* is rendered using a regular font.

Font Posture

The posture indicates whether or not the font is italicized. It is represented in JavaFX by the `FontPosture` class, which defines two possible values:

- `FontPosture.REGULAR`: a normal, upright font
- `FontPosture.ITALIC`: an italic font

The text in Figure 16-27 that contains the word *Italics* is drawn using an italic font.

Font Position

Font position refers to the position of the font's glyphs relative to the text baseline. The `FontPosition` class defines three possible values for this characteristic:

- `FontPosition.REGULAR`: Glyphs appear in the normal place, as dictated by the `textOrigin` variable of a `Text` object, for example.
- `FontPosition.SUBSCRIPT`: Glyphs appear lower than normal, possibly partially below the text baseline.
- `FontPosition.SUPERSCRIPT`: Glyphs appear higher than usual, like the "degree" symbol in 32°F.

> **Note**
> Although the `FontPosition` class is part of the common profile, the `position` variable of the `Font` class is not, so font positioning is not available on mobile devices.

The following code, which you'll find in the file `javafxshapes/Fonts2.fx` in the JavaFX Book Desktop project, creates three `Text` objects that use regular, superscript, and subscript variants of the Tahoma font. Notice that the two `Text` objects that have the superscript and subscript fonts are placed in the same location, but, as you can see in Figure 16-29, the rendered text does not overlap:

```
Stage {
    title: "Superscript and Subscript Fonts"
    width: 250
    height: 80
    scene: Scene {
        content: [
            Text {
                font: Font { name: "Tahoma" size: 24 }
                x: 10 y: 30
                content: "Normal"
            }
            Text {
                font: Font {
                    name: "Tahoma" size: 24
                    position: FontPosition.SUPERSCRIPT
                }
                x: 100 y: 30
                content: "super"
            }
            Text {
                font: Font {
                    name: "Tahoma" size: 24
                    position: FontPosition.SUBSCRIPT
                }
                x: 100 y: 30
```

```
                content: "sub"
            }
        ]
    }
}
```

Figure 16-29   Regular, subscript, and superscript fonts

Unlike weight and posture, which may be characteristics of the font itself, position is normally something that is implemented by the software that renders the text. JavaFX takes care of this for you.

Font Size

The font size determines the height of the font. It is specified not in pixels, but in *points*, where one point is 1/72nd of an inch. On a screen with a resolution of 72dpi, a pixel would also be 1/72nd of an inch tall, so in this case the font size would be the same as its height in pixels. On a 300dpi printer, however, a point would still be approximately 1/72nd of an inch but would now correspond to just over 4 pixels on the paper surface. The effect of the definition of a point is that a glyph in a 72-point font would be approximately an inch tall on both the screen and on the printed page, despite the fact that these devices have very different resolutions.

Font sizes are usually integers, but JavaFX allows you to specify a nonintegral font size, so 9.5 would be valid.

Physical and Logical Fonts

Fonts such as Tahoma, Tahoma Bold, and Times New Roman are *physical fonts*. Physical fonts are fonts for which the data files that define the shapes of the characters are actually installed on the host computer. The set of fonts that are installed and where they reside are platform-dependent. Third-party software, such as word processing applications, may install additional fonts. On the Windows platform, you can see all the available fonts by opening the Fonts applet in the Control Panel, an example of which was shown in Figure 16-28.

A few physical fonts are always guaranteed to be installed on any computer that has a desktop Java Runtime Environment (JRE), as follows:

- Lucida Bright Regular
- Lucida Bright Demibold
- Lucida Bright Demibold Italic
- Lucida Bright Italic

- Lucida Sans Regular
- Lucida Sans Demibold
- Lucida Sans Typewriter Regular
- Lucida Sans Typewriter Bold

JavaFX provides an additional cross-platform font called "Amble Cn".

If you could only use physical fonts, it would be difficult to write an application that is guaranteed to work properly on all platforms because, beyond the limited set listed above, you would never know for sure which fonts you could rely on. For this reason, JavaFX (like Java) also supports *logical fonts*. There are five logical fonts, which are always available on desktop systems:

- Serif
- SansSerif
- Monospaced
- Dialog
- DialogInput

As you'll see in the next section, from a programming point of view, physical and logical fonts are indistinguishable—you can use logical font names just as if they were the names of physical fonts. In fact, a logical font is simply an alias for a physical font. The mapping between a logical font and its corresponding physical font is both platform- and locale-dependent; that is, the fonts depend on the user's natural language. For example, for an English-speaking user on the Windows platform, the mappings shown in Table 16-15 are defined, among others:

Therefore, if your JavaFX application requests a Serif font on the Windows platform, it is most likely going to wind up using the physical Times New Roman font.

Table 16-15   **Logical Font Mappings on the Windows Platform**

Logical Font Name	Physical Font
Serif	Times New Roman
SansSerif	Arial
Monospaced	Courier New
Dialog	Arial
DialogInput	Courier New

The `Font` Class

An instance of the `Font` class represents a logical or physical font that has the characteristics defined by its variables. `Font` is an immutable class, so you can safely use a single instance to represent the same font anywhere within your application. Alternatively, it is possible (and usually simpler) to create multiple `Font` instances that amount to the same font. The `Font` class has several class functions that let you list the available fonts and search for a font that has given characteristics.

The variables of the `Font` class are listed in Table 16-16. Note that most of these variables are only present in the desktop profile.

Table 16-16   **The Variables of the `Font` Class**

Variable	Type	Access	Default	Description
`name`	`String`	RI	Empty	The font name.
`embolden`	`Boolean`	RI	`false`	Requests a bold or bolder font when `true`. *Desktop profile only.*
`oblique`	`Boolean`	RI	`false`	Requests an italicized or more italicized font when `true`. *Desktop profile only.*
`position`	`FontPosition`	RI	`null`	The required `FontPosition`, where `null` means `REGULAR`. *Desktop profile only.*
`size`	`Number`	RI	12	The required font size, in points.
`autoKern`	`Boolean`	RI	`true`	Requests that automatic kerning be performed. (Requires Java 6. On earlier platforms, kerning is always enabled.) *Desktop profile only.*
`ligatures`	`Boolean`	RI	`true`	Requests that font ligatures be used, if the font supports them. (Requires Java 6. On earlier Java platforms, ligatures will always be used if they are available.) *Desktop profile only.*
`letterSpacing`	`Number`	RI	0	The amount of extra space to be used between letters. (Requires Java 6. On earlier platforms, the standard spacing will always be used.) *Desktop profile only.*
`family`	`String`	R	N/A	The family to which the font belongs. Set based on the chosen font.
`style`	`String`	R	N/A	The style of the chosen font. See text.

With the exception of `family` and `style`, these variables must all be set or defaulted when the `Font` object is created, to specify the characteristics of the font that is required.

During the initialization of the `Font` object, the required font is located, based on the value of the `name` variable. If it does not exist, a default is used instead. The `name` variable is always changed to refer to the font that is actually loaded, so it is possible to determine whether you got the font that you wanted. The `family` and `style` variables are also set to refer to the loaded font's family and its style, which indicates whether the font is a bold/italic variant.

Listing Fonts and Font Families

The `Font` class has functions that let you get a list of all the font and font families that are installed on your system. The following code, from the file `javafxshapes/Fonts3.fx`, gets and prints a list of all the installed font families:

```
println("Font families:");
for (family in Font.getFamilies()) {
    println(family);
}
```

This list would include entries for the logical font families provided by the JRE, such as `Dialog`, `DialogInput`, and so on, as well as all the available physical fonts.

The `getFontNames()` function returns the names of all the available physical and logical fonts:

```
println("\n\nFonts:");
for (name in Font.getFontNames()) {
    println(name);
}
```

Finally, a variant of the `getFontNames()` function accepts a font family name and returns the names of all the installed fonts in that family. This code returns all the available fonts in the Tahoma family:

```
println("\n\nTahoma fonts:");
for (name in Font.getFontNames("Tahoma")) {
    println(name);
}
```

The output from this code on my desktop system is as follows:

```
Tahoma fonts:
Tahoma
Tahoma Bold
```

Selecting Fonts

There are two different ways to create a `Font` object: You can either use an object initializer, or you can use one of the functions of the `Font` class that looks for a font given a family name and specific characteristics. If you want to get a subscript or superscript font, you can only do so by using an object literal.

Using an Object Literal

To create a font using an object literal, you typically supply at least a font name and a size. If you want a bold or italic font and your code is known to be running on a JavaFX runtime that supports the desktop profile, you could also set the `embolden` and `oblique` variables as appropriate. The following code, from the file `javafxshapes/Fonts4.fx`, requests a 24-point Times New Roman Bold font and prints the result:

```
var font = Font { name: "Times New Roman Bold" size: 24 }
println("Name: {font.name}, family: {font.family}, "
        "style: {font.style}");
```

On my system, this prints the following:

```
Name: Times New Roman Bold, family: Times New Roman, style: Bold
```

As you can see, the name is unchanged, which means that the actual font that was requested was found. The family and style variables have been set to the appropriate values for that font. Similarly, the following code loads a bold and italic version of the font:

```
font = Font { name: "Times New Roman Bold Italic" size: 24 }
println("Name: {font.name}, family: {font.family}, "
        "style: {font.style}");
```

Here's the result:

```
Name: Times New Roman Bold Italic, family: Times New Roman, style: Bold Italic
```

In these two examples, we have explicitly requested bold and bold/italic variants of a font by using the full font name. Alternatively, in the desktop profile (but *not* on a mobile device), you can request a plain font and use the `embolden` and `oblique` attributes to change the font characteristics:

```
font = Font { name: "Times New Roman" size: 24 embolden: true
              oblique: true }
println("Name: {font.name}, family: {font.family}, "
        "style: {font.style}");
```

The result is the following:

```
Name: Times New Roman, family: Times New Roman, style:
```

Notice that we got back the exact font that we asked for, not the bold and italic variant of that font. When you create a font by using an object literal, the runtime does not try to locate the most suitable font. Instead, it gets the font that you requested and then algorithmically enhances the text so that it looks bold/oblique, if those characteristics have been requested. This will usually be more expensive at runtime and may give a result that is inferior to that which would be achieved by using a font that has the bold/italic characteristics built in to it.

If you request a bold font and ask for it to be emboldened, any text drawn with that font will be emboldened twice—once because the font glyphs will be bold and twice because the runtime will make those glyphs more bold. Similarly, adding the oblique characteristic to an italic font will make the font even more oblique.

If you request a font that does not exist, you get back a default:

```
font = Font { name: "Tahoma Italic" size: 24 }
println("Name: {font.name}, family: {font.family}, "
       "style: {font.style}");
```

The preceding code requests the Tahoma Italic font, which does not exist. You might hope to get a Tahoma font and that the runtime would enhance it to make it oblique, but that's not what happens:

```
Name: Dialog.plain, family: Dialog, style: plain
```

The runtime always returns a platform-specific defaul font when it doesn't recognize the font that you have requested.[7] Because the Italic was only part of the requested font's name, it is not recognized and an oblique variant is not created.

If you don't supply the font name at all, an empty string is used, and once again you get the default font:

```
font = Font { size: 24 }
println("Name: {font.name}, family: {font.family}, "
       "style: {font.style}");
```

The result of this code is the same as the previous example:

```
Name: Dialog.plain, family: Dialog, style: plain
```

Using a Search Function

Four search functions in the `Font` class locate and return `Font` objects based on a font *family* name and specified characteristics:

```
public function font(family:String, weight:FontWeight,
                    posture:FontPosture, size:Number):Font
public function font(family:String, weight:FontWeight, size:Number):Font
public function font(family:String, posture:FontPosture, size:Number):Font
public function font(family:String, size:Number):Font
```

The last three of these functions are special cases of the first in which the argument values that are not specified take default values of `FontPosture.REGULAR` and `FontWeight.REGULAR`.

The following code, from the file `javafxshapes/Fonts5.fx` in the JavaFX Book Desktop project, requests a 24-point, plain Tahoma font:

---

[7] On a mobile device, you get a font that's simply called "default."

```
font = Font.font("Tahoma", 24);
println("Name: {font.name}, family: {font.family}, "
        "style: {font.style}");
```

The result is what you would expect:

```
Name: Tahoma, family: Tahoma, style:
```

Here's an example that supplies a font family name that does not exist:

```
font = Font.font("", 24);
println("Name: {font.name}, family: {font.family}, "
        "style: {font.style}");
```

Requesting a nonexistent family results in the default font being returned:

```
Name: Dialog.plain, family: Dialog, style: plain
```

To get a bold font, use the `FontWeight.BOLD` argument:

```
font = Font.font("Tahoma", FontWeight.BOLD, 24);
println("Name: {font.name}, family: {font.family}, "
        "style: {font.style}");
```

The result is the following:

```
Name: Tahoma Bold, family: Tahoma, style: Bold
```

Notice that, unlike when you use the `embolden` variable in an object literal, the search function actually returns the Tahoma Bold font, which should give better results than if the runtime were to embolden the plain font. Note that you can't actually specify Tahoma Bold because the name argument is a font *family* name, not a font name.

This final example requests a bold and italic Tahoma font:

```
font = Font.font("Tahoma", FontWeight.BOLD, FontPosture.ITALIC, 24);
println("Name: {font.name}, family: {font.family}, "
        "style: {font.style}");
```

No such font exists, but you don't get the default font—instead, you get something close:

```
Name: Tahoma Bold, family: Tahoma, style: Bold
```

You can use the value of the `style` variable to detect that you didn't get a bold and italic font.

Groups and Custom Nodes

Although individual shapes are useful, they can be even more useful when used as a group. As you saw in Chapter 14, the `Group` class allows you to create a collection of nodes that can be manipulated as if they were a single node, in the following senses:

- The group has its own coordinate system relative to which its nodes are placed. This means that you can construct a group without regard to where it will appear in the scene.

- All the transformations that can be applied to a node, which we discuss in Chapter 17, can also be applied to a group and act on it as if it were a single unit. For example, if you rotate a group by setting its `rotate` variable, the whole group rotates as a unit, rather than each individual node being rotated about its own pivot point.

`Group` inherits these characteristics from its superclass, the `Parent` class. Everything that we say about `Group` in this section applies equally to the other subclasses of `Parent`, including `CustomNode`.

Let's examine how `Parent` nodes work by creating a simple custom node consisting of a circle crossed by two perpendicular lines. The implementation of this node, which we call `Wheel` because the result looks something like a wheel, is shown in Listing 16-10. The resulting node can be seen in Figure 16-30. You can find the code itself in the file `javafxshapes/Wheel.fx`.

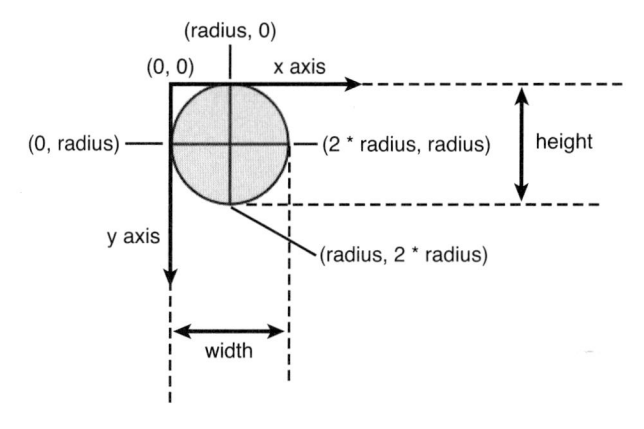

Figure 16-30   An example of a custom node

Listing 16-10   **A Custom Node**

```
1    package javafxshapes;
2
3    import javafx.scene.CustomNode;
4    import javafx.scene.Group;
5    import javafx.scene.Node;
6    import javafx.scene.paint.Color;
7    import javafx.scene.shape.Circle;
8    import javafx.scene.shape.Line;
9
10   public class Wheel extends CustomNode {
11       public var fill: Color = Color.WHITE;
12       public var stroke: Color = Color.BLACK;
13       public var radius: Number = 20;
14
```

```
15          override var children =
16              Group {
17                  content: [
18                      Circle {
19                          centerX: bind radius centerY: bind radius
20                          radius: bind radius
21                          fill: bind fill stroke: bind stroke
22                          strokeWidth: 2
23                      }
24                      Line {
25                          startX: bind radius startY: 0
26                          endX: bind radius   endY: bind 2 * radius
27                          stroke: bind stroke
28                          strokeWidth: 2
29                      }
30                      Line {
31                          startX: 0 startY: bind radius
32                          endX: bind 2 * radius endY: bind radius
33                          stroke: bind stroke
34                          strokeWidth: 2
35                      }
36                  ]
37              }
38          }
```

CustomNode is an abstract class that is derived from Parent and which requires that subclasses either assign a node or nodes to its children variable (the preferred approach) or implement the following function that returns a single node, typically a Group:

```
protected function create():Node
```

The node or nodes returned from this function or assigned to the children variable implement the functionality that the custom node provides. In Listing 16-10, the children variable is assigned a group containing three nodes—a circle and two lines—that provide the custom node's visual representation. The Wheel class is used in the same way as any other node, as the following code, from the file javafxshapes/Wheel1.fx, shows:

```
Stage {
    title: "Wheel #1"
    scene: Scene {
        width: 200
        height: 200
        content: [
            Wheel {
                fill: Color.YELLOW
                stroke: Color.BLACK
```

```
                radius: 50
            }
        ]
    }
}
```

The internal structure of a custom node is not visible to the code that uses it. The variables `fill`, `stroke`, and `radius` specify the size of the wheel and its colors. As you can see in Listing 16-10, these values are used to set the `fill` and `stroke` colors of the shapes that make up the node, and to determine the center point and radius of the circle and the ending points of the two lines. Notice that coordinates used when creating these shapes are relative to the origin of the custom node itself, as you can see in Figure 16-30. Because the values assigned to the variables of the nested shapes are all bound to those of the custom node itself, the application can change the fill, stroke and radius of a `Wheel` instance, and these changes will be propagated to those shapes automatically.

The width and height of a group are determined entirely by its content. As you can see in Figure 16-30, in the case of the `Wheel` class, the width and height are both twice the radius of the circle. If we were to add another shape that was partly or completely outside the bounds of the circle, the dimensions of the group would be adjusted automatically to include the space occupied by this additional shape. The `Group` class does not have `width` and `height` variables that allow you to read its bounds. Instead, you would have to use one of the variables (like `boundsInLocal`) that you'll see in the section "Coordinates and Bounds" in Chapter 17.

The content of a group or a custom node are manipulated as a single unit. The following code, from the file `javafxshapes/Wheel2.fx`, exploits this fact by using its `translateX` and `translateY` variables (inherited from `Node`) to move a `Wheel` object to a position that is 30 pixels to the right of and below the origin of the scene, with the result shown in Figure 16-31. You'll read much more about positioning and applying transformations to nodes in Chapter 17:

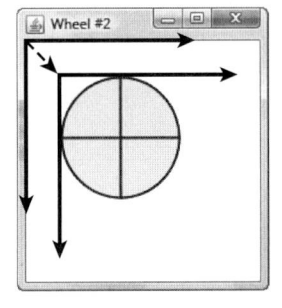

Figure 16-31   Translating a custom node

```
Stage {
    title: "Wheel #2"
    scene: Scene {
        width: 200
        height: 200
        content: [
            Wheel {
                translateX: 30
                translateY: 30
                fill: Color.YELLOW
                stroke: Color.BLACK
                radius: 50
            }
        ]
    }
}
```

Images

Displaying an image in a JavaFX application is a two-step process. First, you need to load the raw data for the image, a task that is performed by the `javafx.scene.image.Image` class. Once you have an `Image` object, you wrap it in instance of `ImageView`, which is a node and therefore can be added to your scene. This section discusses both of these classes.

Loading an Image

JavaFX makes loading an image a straightforward task. The code in Listing 16-11, which you'll find in the file `javafxshapes/Images1.fx`, illustrates how to load an image and display it on the screen.

Listing 16-11   **Loading and Displaying an Image**

```
1    package javafxshapes;
2
3    import javafx.scene.image.Image;
4    import javafx.scene.image.ImageView;
5    import javafx.scene.Scene;
6    import javafx.stage.Stage;
7
8    Stage {
9        title: "Images 1"
10       scene: Scene {
11           width: 500
12           height: 500
13           content: [
14               ImageView {
15                   image: Image {
```

```
16                              backgroundLoading: true
17                              url: "{__DIR__}images/Portsmouth.JPG"
18                         }
19                     }
20                 ]
21             }
22         }
```

Figure 16-32 shows the result of running this code.

Figure 16-32   A large image displayed in a small scene

This image is actually a photograph of the city of Portsmouth, which is on the south coast of England. It is much larger than the space available in the scene, so only its top-left corner is visible. To make it possible to see the whole image, we could either scale it so that it fits in the scene or we could allow the user to scroll the image around with the mouse. You'll see how to do both of these things in this section and the next.

The `Image` Class

The `Image` class is responsible for loading an image, decoding it, and creating an in-memory representation that is suitable for display. The public variables of this class are listed in Table 16-17 and are discussed in more detail in the sections that follow. The supported

488 Chapter 16 Shapes, Text, and Images

image types on the desktop platform include BMP, JPEG, PNG, and GIF, including animated GIFs. Mobile devices support fewer image types.

Table 16-17   **Variables of the `Image` Class**

Variable	Type	Access	Default	Description
`url`	`String`	RI	Empty	The URL of the image to be loaded
`height`	`Number`	RI	0	The image height
`width`	`Number`	RI	0	The image width
`preserveRatio`	`Boolean`	RI	`false`	Whether the aspect ratio of the image should be preserved when it is resized
`smooth`	`Boolean`	RI	`true`	Whether an algorithm that produces a higher quality result should be used when the image is resized
`placeholder`	`Image`	RW	`null`	An image to be used while this image is being loaded, if `backgroundLoading` is true
`backgroundLoading`	`Boolean`	RI	`false`	Whether the image should be loaded in a background thread
`error`	`Boolean`	R	`false`	Set to indicate that an error occurred while the image was being loaded
`progress`	`Number`	R	0	The proportion of the total image data that has been loaded, as a percentage

Specifying the Location of the Image

The location of the image to be loaded is given by the `url` variable, which must be a URL in string form. For an image on the Internet, you would simply give its full URL, like this:

```
Image {
    backgroundLoading: true
    url: http://www.jpl.nasa.gov/images/mer/2004-06-02/05-JR-05-apollo15-380-382.jpg
}
```

You can also load images from the file system or from the codebase of your applet or application. The most common requirement is to load an image that is packaged in the same directory as the class file from which it is referenced, or in a location that is fixed relative to that class file. To do this, you build the image URL by using the `__DIR__` variable as shown on line 17 of Listing 16-11:

```
url: "{__DIR__}images/Portsmouth.JPG"
```

As you have already seen, the `__DIR__` variable is a string URL that refers to the directory containing the executing class. When your application is running in NetBeans or is deployed and installed by the user, it will refer to the location of the class within the application's JAR file. Here's a typical example:

```
jar:file:/C:/EXAMPLES/dist/JavaFX_Book_GUI.jar!/javafxshapes/
```

In this case, the image is in a subdirectory called `images`, so the full URL will be as follows:

```
jar:file:/C:/EXAMPLES/dist/JavaFX_Book_GUI.jar!/javafxshapes/images/Portsmouth.JPG
```

Note that there is no need to add a / after the `__DIR__` reference in the URL because the value of this variable includes the trailing URL.

> **Warning**
> In some cases, supplying an additional / can cause the image to fail to load.

If the image is in a directory that is in a fixed location within the JAR file, you can't use the `__DIR__` variable to give its location. For example, suppose you want to put all your images in a directory called `images` at the top-level of your JAR file. You could attempt to reference the image like this:

```
url: "{__DIR__}../images/Portsmouth.JPG"
```

However, this is not guaranteed to work, because not all class loaders allow the .. syntax in a resource path. On a desktop system, you can instead use the `getResource()` method of the Java class `java.lang.Class` to locate the image, as illustrated by the following code from the file `javafxshapes/Images3.fx` in the JavaFX Book Desktop project:

```
var clazz = java.lang.Class.forName("javafxshapes.Images3");
var url = "{clazz.getResource("/images/PortsmouthSmall.JPG")}";
```

The first line of this code gets the `Class` object for the JavaFX class, given its full name. The second line uses the `getResource()` method of that class to locate the image. Because the resource name passed to `getResource()` starts with /, it is assumed to be an absolute name, and the search is relative to the classpath of the application. On mobile devices based on Mobile Information Device Profile (MIDP), the `Class.getResource()` method does not exist, so the only way to load local images is by using the `{__DIR__}` syntax shown earlier in this section.

Fetching the Image Data

The process of loading the image begins automatically as a result of creating an `Image` object. When the load process is complete, the `width` and `height` variables are set to reflect the image's size.

By default, the loading process is synchronous and will be complete before the next line of code is executed. This is not always a good idea, because it will cause the user interface to be frozen until the whole image has been read, which could be a noticeable amount of time, especially if it is large and is being accessed over the Internet. You can make the loading process asynchronous by setting the `backgroundLoading` variable to `true`, as shown on line 16 of Listing 16-11. When you do this, the image is loaded and decoded in the background, and your application can continue to respond to the user interface.

During an asynchronous load, it is desirable to provide some feedback so that the user knows that the operation is in progress. There are a couple of ways that you can do this. First, you can provide a placeholder image that will be displayed in place of the real image while it is being loaded, as shown here[8]:

```
1       var url = "http://www.jpl.nasa.gov/images"
2                "/mer/2004-06-02/05-JR-05-apollo15-380-382.jpg";
3       Stage {
4           var scene:Scene;
5           var imageView:ImageView;
6           title: "Images 4"
7           scene: scene = Scene {
8               width: 500
9               height: 500
10              content: [
11                  imageView = ImageView {
12                      translateX: bind (scene.width -
13                                      imageView.layoutBounds.width) /     2
14                      translateY: bind (scene.height -
15                                      imageView.layoutBounds.height) /    2
16                      image: Image {
17                          backgroundLoading: true
18                          url: url
19                          placeholder: Image {
20                              url:     "{__DIR__}images/small.gif"
21                          }
22                      }
23                  }
24              ]
25          }
26      }
```

---

[8] This code comes from the file `javafxshapes/Images4.fx`.

The code on lines 19 to 21 installs the placeholder image, which will be shown until the data for the main image has been loaded, as shown in Figure 16-33. Notice that this image is loaded synchronously, to ensure that it is available for display before the process of loading the main image begins. This means that a small delay will still occur before the application's main window opens. To minimize this delay, it is best to use a small placeholder image that is packaged with the application itself. Loading a *small* image should be no more expensive than loading the application's class files.

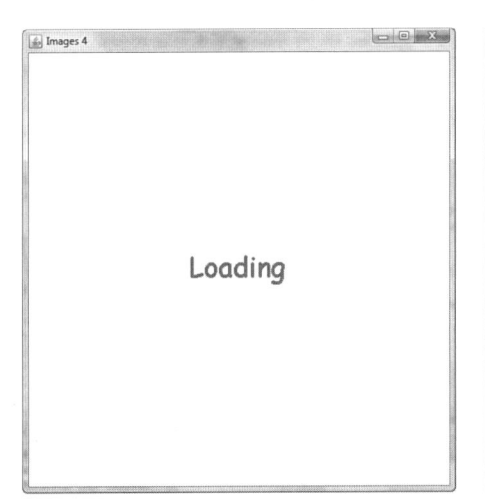

Figure 16-33 Using a placeholder image during an asynchronous load operation

The code on lines 12 to 15 uses the `translateX` and `translateY` variables to center both the placeholder and the loaded image within the scene. You'll see how this code works in the "Node Layout" section in Chapter 17.

Another way to provide the user with feedback while the image is loading is to monitor the `progress` and `error` variables of the `Image` object and display some text or some other indicator of progress until the load has been completed or has failed.[9]

The `progress` variable contains a value that represents the approximate percentage of the image data that has been loaded so far. It starts at 0 and progresses to 100. The `error` variable is set to `true` if the image fails to load and, at the same time, the `progress` variable is set to 100. The following code, from the file `javafxshapes/Images5.fx`, displays

---

[9] Note that these variables are valid even if the image is loaded synchronously, but in that case the value of the `progress` variable will appear to go directly from 0 to 100.

492   Chapter 16 Shapes, Text, and Images

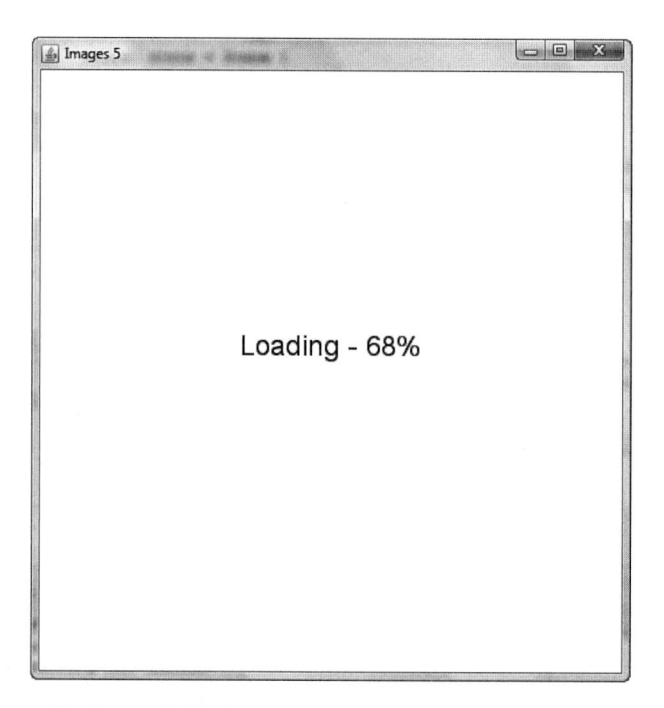

Figure 16-34   Reporting the progress of an image load operation

the percentage of the image that has been loaded, or reports an error if the image fails to load. The result is shown in Figure 16-34.

```
1      var url = "http://www.jpl.nasa.gov/images"
2                "/mer/2004-06-02/05-JR-05-apollo15-380-382.jpg";
3
4      Stage {
5          var scene:Scene;
6          var imageView:ImageView;
7          var text:Text;
8          var image:Image;
9          title: "Images 5"
10         scene: scene = Scene {
11             width: 500
12             height: 500
13             content: [
14                 imageView = ImageView {
15                     translateX: bind (scene.width -
16                                      imageView.layoutBounds.width) /    2
17                     translateY: bind (scene.height -
```

```
18                              imageView.layoutBounds.height) / 2
19                  image: image = Image {
20                              backgroundLoading: true
21                              url: url
22                  }
23              }
24              text = Text {
25                  translateX: bind (scene.width -
26                              text.layoutBounds.width) / 2
27                  translateY: bind (scene.height -
28                              text.layoutBounds.height) / 2
29                  font: Font { size: 24 }
30                  content: bind if (image.error) "Load Failed"
31                              else "Loading - {image.progress}%"
32                  visible: bind image.error
33                              or image.progress != 100
34              }
35          ]
36      }
37  }
```

The Text object created on lines 24 to 34 displays the progress information. It is visible only when an error has occurred or when there is still image data to be loaded. The text either reports that the image has failed to load or shows the percentage of the image that has been loaded so far.

An asynchronous load operation can be canceled by calling the `cancel()` function of the Image class. Cancellation is considered to be an error, so the error variable will be set to true and progress to 100.

Resizing the Image

If you know that the image you are loading is too large to be displayed in the space that you have available, or if you just want to display the image as a thumbnail, you can resize it. Both the Image and ImageView classes have variables that allow you to change the size of the viewed image. The differences between these two approaches are as follows:

- Using the Image class to resize the image makes the change permanent—that is, all views of that image using the same Image object will use the new size. Reducing the image size will result in lower memory utilization.

- Using the ImageView class to resize the image allows you to have several views of the same image that have different sizes. Also, because the variables in the ImageView class that determine the size are writeable, you can vary them to give the effect of zooming in or zooming out on the image.

In this section, we discuss resizing the image using the variables provided by the Image class. To resize an image, you set the width/height variables of the Image object to the required values. If you need to preserve the aspect ratio of the image, which would normally be the case, set `preserveRatio` to `true`. What actually happens depends on the value of this variable. First, let's assume that `preserveRatio` is `false`. In this case

- If `width` is greater than `0`, the image will be scaled to the specified width. If `width` is `0`, the image will have its natural width.[10]

- If `height` is greater than `0`, the image will be scaled to the specified height. If `height` is `0`, the image will have its natural height.

Because `preserveRatio` is `false`, the aspect ratio can be adjusted arbitrarily by changing the relative values of the `width` and `height` variables. The following code, which you'll find in the file `javafxshapes/Images6.fx`, changes the width of an image to 100 pixels, but leaves its height unchanged. This results in the long, thin image shown in Figure 16-35.

```
Stage {
    title: "Images 6"
    scene: Scene {
        width: 200
        height: 450
        content: [
            ImageView {
                image: Image {
                    backgroundLoading: true
                    url: url
                    preserveRatio: false
                    width: 100
                }
            }
        ]
    }
}
```

When `preserveRatio` is `true`, there are four possible cases:

- If `width` and `height` are both `0`, no resize has been requested, and the image will retain its natural size.

- If `width` is greater than zero and `height` is `0`, the image will be scaled to the given width, and the height will be adjusted so that the aspect ratio is preserved.

- If `height` is greater than zero and `width` is `0`, the image will be scaled to the given height, and the width will be adjusted so that the aspect ratio is preserved.

---

[10] Negative values for either `width` or `height` are treated as `0`, so the image will not be resized.

Figure 16-35   Resizing an image without preserving the aspect ratio

- If height and width are both greater than 0, the image will be scaled so that its width and height are not greater than the given values and so that the aspect ratio is still preserved.

Some examples should make this clearer. The following code, from the file javafxshapes/Images7.fx, specifies a width of 200 while preserving the aspect ratio:

```
Stage {
    title: "Images 7"
    scene: Scene {
        width: 200
        height: 220
        content: [
            ImageView {
                image: Image {
                    backgroundLoading: true
                    url: url
                    preserveRatio: true
                    width: 200
                }
            }
        ]
    }
}
```

The actual width of this image is 380 pixels. Scaling it to 200 pixels is a reduction by a factor of 1.9. To preserve the aspect ratio, the height must also be scaled from 382 pixels by the same factor, which results in a final height of 201 pixels and the result shown in Figure 16-36.

Figure 16-36   Resizing an image to a specified width while preserving the aspect ratio

This code, which you'll find in the file `javafxshapes/Images8.fx`, sets values for both the `width` and the `height` variables:

```
Stage {
    title: "Images 8"
    scene: Scene {
        width: 300
        height: 250
        content: [
            ImageView {
                image: Image {
                    backgroundLoading: true
                    url: url
                    preserveRatio: true
                    width: 300
                    height: 250
                }
            }
        ]
    }
}
```

When both values are set, the image must be scaled to meet both limits, while also preserving the aspect ratio. In this case, the image is actually 380 pixels wide but must be reduced to 300 pixels, which is a reduction by a factor of 1.27. Scaling the height by the same factor reduces it from 382 to 300 pixels. This is still greater than the 250 pixels allowed, so the height must be scaled by a further factor of 1.2. This same factor must also be applied to the width, bringing it down from 300 to 250, as well, and thus preserving the aspect ratio. Figure 16-37 shows the result.

Figure 16-37   Resizing an image within specified bounds while preserving the aspect ratio

Resizing an image will either lose information (if the image is made smaller) or require interpolation of pixel data (if the image is enlarged). To produce a high-quality result can be a relatively slow process, so the JavaFX runtime allows you to make a trade-off between quality and speed of execution. If quality is more important than execution speed, set the `smooth` variable of the `Image` object to `true` (which is the default). On the other hand, if execution speed is more important and you can accept a lower quality result, set `smooth` to `false`.

Displaying an Image

As you have already seen, loaded images are displayed using the `ImageView` class. Table 16-18 describes the public variables of this class.

The `image` variable refers to the `Image` to be displayed. The same loaded image can be displayed by more than one `ImageView` a time. It is also possible to change the image being displayed by writing a new value to this variable.

The `x` and `y` variables specify the position of the point at which the top left of the image will be displayed, in the coordinate system of the `ImageView` object. By default, the width and height of the `ImageView` object match those of the image itself. You can change the size of the `ImageView` by using the `fitWidth`, `fitHeight`, and `preserveRatio` variables, which work in the same way as the `width`, `height`, and `preserveRatio` variables of the `Image` class, except that they only affect the way in which the image is rendered and don't change the data in the `Image` object itself. Unlike the corresponding variables of the `Image` class, these variables can be written at any time, so it is possible to move the image or to dynamically resize it by changing their values.

Table 16-18 Variables of the `ImageView` Class

Variable	Type	Access	Default	Description
image	Image	RW	null	The `Image` to be displayed
x	Number	RW	0	The `x` coordinate at which the image is to be displayed
y	Number	RW	0	The `y` coordinate at which the image is to be displayed
fitHeight	Number	RW	0	The height of the area in which the image is to be displayed
fitWidth	Number	RW	0	The width of the area in which the image is to be displayed
preserveRatio	Boolean	RW	false	Specifies whether the image aspect ratio should be preserved when it is resized
smooth	Boolean	RW	See text	Whether a smooth scaling algorithm should be used when resizing the image
viewport	Rectangle 2D	RW	null	The rectangular area of the image that should be displayed

The `viewport` variable allows you to define a rectangular region of the image that is to be displayed. If this is not `null`, only the portion of the image that lies within the specified region is drawn in the space occupied by the `ImageView`. Figure 16-38 shows the relationship of the viewport to the whole image. When the viewport is set, the `ImageView` occupies only the area bounded by the viewport, and its size matches that of the viewport.

If the image is too large to display all at once, like the one shown in Figure 16-32, you can use this feature, in conjunction with the mouse, to allow the user to drag the image around so that parts of it that are not visible can be made visible. The code in Listing 16-12, which you will find in the file `javafxshapes/Images9.fx`, implements a draggable viewport. The `viewport` variable of the `ImageView` is bound to the value of `viewport` variable declared on line 15. This variable is itself bound to a `Rectangle2D` object with its top-left corner at (`viewportX`, `viewportY`) for which the width and height always match those of the `Scene`. To make the viewport appear to move over the image, we need to change the values of the variables `viewportX` and `viewportY` so that the viewport appears to track the mouse cursor as it is dragged around.

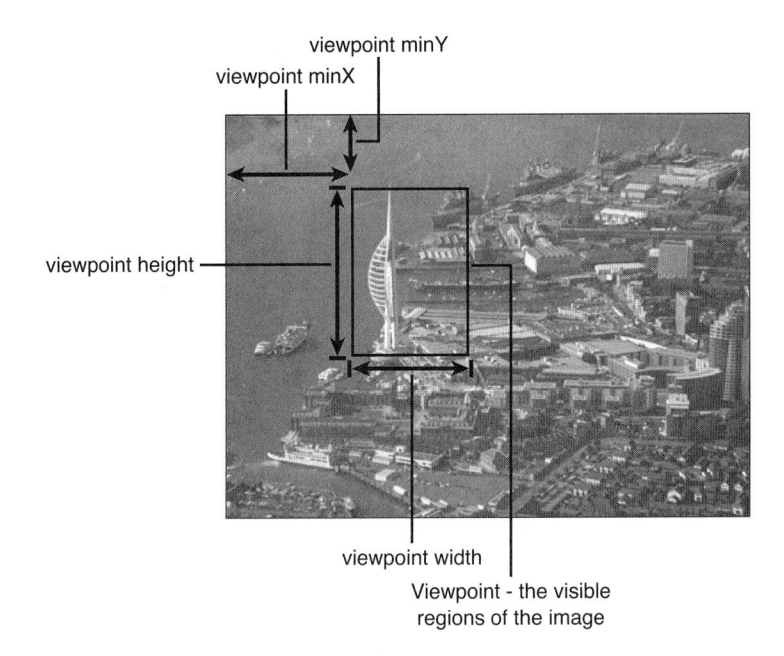

Figure 16-38 The `ImageView` viewport

Listing 16-12 **Using the Mouse to Move the Viewport over an Image**

```
1     package javafxshapes;
2
3     import javafx.geometry.Rectangle2D;
4     import javafx.scene.Cursor;
5     import javafx.scene.image.Image;
6     import javafx.scene.image.ImageView;
7     import javafx.scene.Scene;
8     import javafx.stage.Stage;
9
10    var scene:Scene;
11    var image:Image;
12    var imageView:ImageView;
13    var viewportX:Number;
14    var viewportY:Number;
15    var viewport:Rectangle2D = bind Rectangle2D {
16                                   minX: viewportX
17                                   minY: viewportY
```

Chapter 16 Shapes, Text, and Images

```
18                             width: scene.width
19                             height: scene.height
20                         };
21
22       function updateViewport(deltaX:Number, deltaY:Number):Void {
23           var newX = viewportX + deltaX;
24           var newY = viewportY + deltaY;
25           if (newX + viewport.width > image.width) {
26               newX = image.width - viewport.width;
27           }
28           if (newX < 0) {
29               newX = 0;
30           }
31           if (newY + viewport.height > image.height) {
32               newY = image.height - viewport.height;
33           }
34           if (newY < 0) {
35               newY = 0;
36           }
37           viewportX = newX;
38           viewportY = newY;
39           println("viewportX: {viewportX}, viewportY: {viewportY}");
40       }
41
42       Stage {
43           title: "Images 9"
44           scene: scene = Scene {
45               width: 500
46               height: 500
47               content: [
48                   imageView = ImageView {
49                       image: image = Image {
50                           backgroundLoading: true
51                           url: "{__DIR__}images/Portsmouth.JPG"
52                       }
53                       viewport: bind viewport
54
55                       var lastX:Number;
56                       var lastY:Number;
```

```
57                    onMousePressed: function(evt) {
58                            lastX = evt.x; lastY = evt.y;
59                            imageView.cursor = Cursor.MOVE
60                    }
61                    onMouseDragged: function(evt) {
62                            var deltaX = lastX - evt.x;
63                            var deltaY = lastY - evt.y;
64                            lastX = evt.x; lastY = evt.y;
65                            updateViewport(deltaX, deltaY);
66                    }
67                    onMouseReleased: function(evt) {
68                            imageView.cursor = Cursor.DEFAULT
69                    }
70            }
71        ]
72    }
73 }
```

This process starts in the `onMousePressed` handler of the `ImageView`, on lines 57 to 60. Here, we save the coordinates of the mouse when it is first clicked, and then change the cursor so that it is obvious to the user that the image can be moved.[11] The cursor is restored on line 68, when the mouse is released. As the mouse is moved, the `onMouseDragged` handler on lines 61 to 66 is called. The coordinates in the mouse event, together with the last saved position of the mouse, are used to calculate how far the mouse has moved, and then the current mouse position is saved for use on the next entry to this handler. Finally, the `updateViewport()` function is called, with arguments that reflect the distance moved.

The job of `updateViewport()`, which is shown on lines 22 to 40 of Listing 16-12, is to adjust the values of the `viewportX` and `viewportY` variables by the distance by which the mouse is moved. The crucial point here is that we want the image to move in the direction of the mouse so that it feels to the user like he is moving the image around under the viewport. That means that, if the mouse is moved toward the top left, the viewport must appear to move toward the bottom right of the image, which is achieved by increasing the values of `viewportX` and `viewportY`. Given this, the code in the `updateViewport()` function, most of which is concerned with making sure that the user is not allowed to drag the viewport outside of the image itself, should be easy to understand.

---

[11] Obviously, this will have no effect on a mobile device because the mobile profile does not support changing the cursor.

17

Coordinates, Transforms, and Layout

In the last few chapters, you have been introduced to the concept of a scene graph, and you have seen many of the types of nodes that are provided by the JavaFX runtime. The first part of this chapter is concerned with *transforms*, which enable you to move, resize, and rotate a node. This chapter examines and illustrates all the available transforms, with the exception of the perspective transform, which is discussed in Chapter 20, "Effects and Blending." Transforms cause the bounds (that is, the size/position) of a node to change. In the second half of this chapter, we discuss coordinate systems and the various different bounds that are associated with a node.

The third part of this chapter discusses the support that JavaFX provides for automatic layout of nodes. The core of this support lies in the Container class. Various subclasses of Container implement different node layout algorithms, all of which are covered in this chapter. We defer discussion of custom layouts to Chapter 25, "Building Custom Controls."

This chapter closes with two short sections. The first shows you how to use the knowledge of node layout that you will have acquired to improve the SnowStorm application that you saw in Chapter 4, "A Simple JavaFX Application," so that it works properly with any screen size. The second deals with the application programming interface (API) that JavaFX provides to allow you to find out how many screens there are on the device on which your application is running, how large they are, and where they are logically placed relative to each other.

Transforms

You can apply five different types of transform to a node: translation, rotation, scaling, shearing, and an affine transform, which is a generalization of the other four types. The Node class has several variables that allow you to specify the transforms to be applied. These variables are listed in Table 17-1.

Table 17-1 **Transform-Related Variables of the Node Class**

Variable	Type	Access	Default	Description
`rotate`	`Number`	RW	0	The angle through which the node is to be rotated about its center point. A positive value produces a clockwise rotation.
`rotationAxis`	`Point3D`	RW	`Rotate.Z_AXIS`	The axis about which the rotation takes place.
`scaleX`	`Number`	RW	`1.0`	The amount by which the node is to be scaled along the x-axis.
`scaleY`	`Number`	RW	`1.0`	The amount by which the node is to be scaled along the y-axis.
`scaleZ`	`Number`	RW	`1.0`	The amount by which the node is to be scaled along the z-axis.
`transforms`	`Transform[]`	RW	Empty	A set of transformations.
`translateX` or `layoutX`	`Number`	RW	`0.0`	The distance along the x-axis by which the node's origin is to be moved.
`translateY` or `layoutY`	`Number`	RW	`0.0`	The distance along the y-axis by which the node's origin is to be moved.
`translateZ`	`Number`	RW	`0.0`	The distance along the z-axis by which the node's origin is to be moved.

In some cases, there is more than one way to apply a transform to a node. Rotation, scaling, and translation can be performed either by assigning values to the corresponding variables from Table 17-1 or by adding an element to the `transforms` sequence. Shearing and arbitrary affine transforms are only possible through the `transforms` variable. As you'll see in the sections that follow, the effect of a transform that is applied through the dedicated node variables is not necessarily the same as one that appears in the `transforms` sequence.

Transforms are represented by subclasses of the `javafx.scene.transform.Transform` class. As well as being the base class for transforms, `Transform` has script functions that can be used to obtain instances of concrete `Transform` objects. For example, if you want to apply a rotation via the `transforms` variable of a node, you have the choice of either creating and initializing an instance of the `Rotate` class by using an object literal or getting one by calling the `rotate()` function of the `Transform` class. The choice is largely a matter of taste.

In the sections that follow, we discuss the five available transforms and the effect that each of them has on a node. In most cases, a transform is explained by demonstrating its effect on a rectangle that is initially defined using the following code:

```
Rectangle {
    x: 30
    y: 60
    width: 100
    height: 40
    fill: Color.YELLOW
}
```

This untransformed rectangle is shown in Figure 17-1. So that you can see exactly how each transform affects it, a coordinate grid with the same transform applied has been added to the scene. The grid is drawn by a custom node, the implementation of which is shown in Chapter 25.

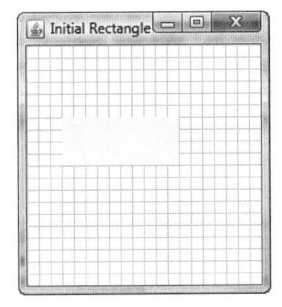

Figure 17-1   An untransformed rectangle

Translation

Translation has the effect of moving a node a specified distance relative to the scene or to its containing parent node (that is, `Group` or `Container`). One way to apply a translation to a node is by using its `translateX`, `translateY`, and `translateZ` variables. Here's an example that moves the rectangle shown in Figure 17-1 by 30 pixels horizontally and 40 pixels vertically, the result of which is shown in Figure 17-2:

```
Rectangle {
    x: 30
    y: 60
    width: 100
    height: 40
    fill: Color.YELLOW
    translateX: 30
    translateY: 40
}
```

> **Note**
> You can also perform a translation by setting a node's `layoutX` and `layoutY` variables. These work in exactly the same way as `translateX` and `translateY`. If you set both pairs of variables, the effect is to translate the node by a distance `translateX` + `layoutX` along the x-axis and by `translateY` + `layoutY` along the y-axis. As you'll see later in this chapter, `layoutX` and `layoutY` are conventionally used by containers to position nodes according to their specific layout policy, whereas `translateX` and `translateY` are used when a node is in a group (which does not perform automatic positioning of nodes) or to move the node relative to its assigned location in a container. The `translateX` and `translateY` variables are also manipulated by the `PathTransition` class, which we'll discuss in Chapter 18, "Animation."

Translating a node doesn't move it relative to the origin of its own coordinate system. Instead, *it creates a new coordinate system for the node that is offset from the original by the amount of the translation.* In Figure 17-2, the original coordinate system—that of the scene—is represented by the lighter grid, and the new coordinate system of the rectangle is indicated

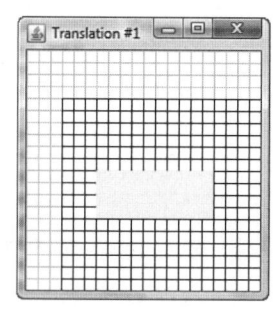

Figure 17-2   Translation using the **translateX** and **translateY** variables

by the darker grid. As you can see, the new coordinate system is offset from the original along each axis by the amount of the translation along that axis.

Translating a rectangle by setting its `translateX` and `translateY` variables is not at all the same as adding the same amount to its x and y variables—changing the x and y variables moves the rectangle to the same location as the translation variables would *but does not move the origin of the coordinate system* for that rectangle. We'll talk more about this in the "Coordinates and Bounds" section, later in this chapter.

The second way to translate a node is to add a `Translate` object to its `transforms` variable. The `Translate` class has public variables called x, y, and z, described in Table 17-2, that hold the distance by which the coordinate origin is to be moved. Like the translation variables of the `Node` class, these variables may hold positive, 0, or negative values.

Table 17-2   Variables of the `Translate` Class

Variable	Type	Access	Default	Description
x	Number	RW	0	The distance to move the coordinate origin in the x direction
y	Number	RW	0	The distance to move the coordinate origin in the y direction
z	Number	RW	0	The distance to move the coordinate origin in the z direction

> **Note**
> As discussed in Chapter 14, "User Interface Basics," movement along the z-axis is possible only on platforms that use the Prism toolkit, which, at the time of this writing, is supported only by the Java TV runtime. The same applies to the other 3D features mentioned in this chapter.

The following code initializes and installs a `Translate` object that moves the coordinate origin of the rectangle 10 pixels left and 20 pixels upward, giving the result shown in Figure 17-3.

```
Rectangle {
    x: 30
    y: 60
    width: 100
    height: 40
    fill: Color.YELLOW
    transforms: Translate { x: -10 y: -20 }
}
```

In this case, the origin of the new coordinate system is above and to the left of the scene's coordinate system and so is not visible in the figure, but you can see that a shift has

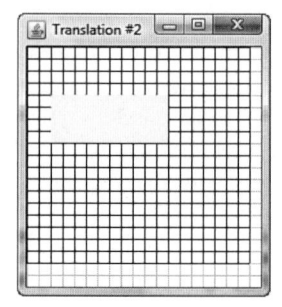

Figure 17-3   Translation using a **Translate** object

taken place because the grid representing the scene's coordinate system is visible on the right and lower sides of the figure.

Another way to create a `Translate` object is to use the following script function of the `Transform` class:

```
public function translate(x:Number, y:Number):Translate
```

> **Note**
> At the time of this writing, there is not a variant of this function that includes an offset along the z axis.

The following code, which uses this function, has the same effect as that shown above:

```
Rectangle {
    x: 30
    y: 60
    width: 100
    height: 40
    fill: Color.YELLOW
    transforms: Transform.translate(-10, -20)
}
```

Rotation

The coordinate system of a node can be rotated either by setting its `rotate` variable or by including a `Rotate` transform in its `transforms` variable. The following code uses the `rotate` variable to make a rectangle appear to rotate clockwise through 45 degrees, giving the result shown in Figure 17-4:

```
Rectangle {
    x: 30
    y: 60
```

```
    width: 100
    height: 40
    fill: Color.YELLOW
    rotate: 45
}
```

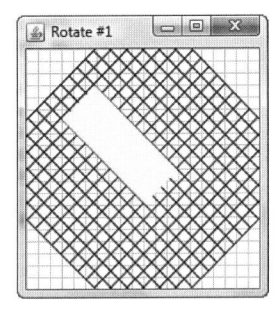

Figure 17-4 Rotation using the **rotate** variable

When you use the `rotate` variable, the coordinate system is rotated about the node's center point, in this case the point at (80, 80). Comparing the rectangle in Figure 17-4 with the untransformed one in Figure 17-1, you can see that it has been rotated about its center. You can arrange for a rotation about a different pivot point by using a `Rotate` object, the variables of which are listed in Table 17-3.

Table 17-3 **Variables of the Rotate Class**

Variable	Type	Access	Default	Description
angle	Number	RW	0	The rotation angle (positive for clockwise, negative for counter-clockwise)
axis	Point3D	RW	Rotate.Z_AXIS	The axis about which the rotation is performed
pivotX	Number	RW	0	The x coordinate of the pivot point
pivotY	Number	RW	0	The y coordinate of the pivot point
pivotZ	Number	RW	0	The z coordinate of the pivot point

If, as in the following code, you don't specify the pivot point, it defaults to the origin of the node's coordinate system, whereas the axis defaults to the z-axis, which means that the rotation takes place in the plane of the computer screen. The object literal in the following code does not initialize any of these variables, so the rectangle's coordinate system is rotated around its origin at (0, 0), giving the result shown in Figure 17-5:

```
Rectangle {
    x: 30
    y: 60
    width: 100
    height: 40
    fill: Color.YELLOW
    transforms: Rotate { angle: 45 }
}
```

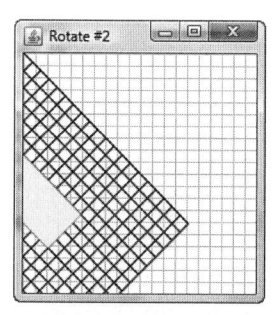

Figure 17-5   Rotation about the origin of coordinates

In the following example, the pivot point is at (30, 60) relative to the node's coordinate system. The screenshot in Figure 17-6 shows that this is indeed the point around which the coordinate system is rotated:

```
Rectangle {
    x: 30
    y: 60
    width: 100
    height: 40
    fill: Color.YELLOW
```

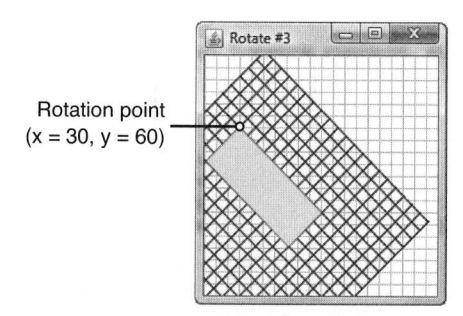

Figure 17-6   Rotation around a specified point

```
    transforms: Transform.rotate(45, 30, 60)
}
```

This code uses the `rotate()` function of the `Transform` class, which has the following definition:

```
public function rotate(angle:Number, pivotX:Number,
                       pivotY:Number):Rotate;
```

If the platform supports a 3D scene graph, it is possible to rotate a node about an arbitrary axis given by the `axis` variable of the `Rotate` transform, or the `rotationAxis` variable of the node itself. The following code extract, from the file `javafxtransforms/Rotate4.fx`, rotates a rectangle through 60 degrees about the y-axis:

```
Rectangle {
    x: 30
    y: 80
    width: 100
    height: 40
    fill: Color.GREEN
    rotationAxis: Rotate.Y_AXIS
    rotate: 60
}
```

You can see the result of running this example in the Java TV emulator in Figure 17-7.

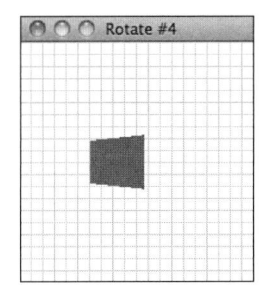

Figure 17-7   A rotation about the y-axis

Scaling

Scaling has the effect of increasing or reducing the apparent width/height of a node. As with the other transforms that you have seen so far, you can apply a scale by setting the values of the `scaleX`, `scaleY`, and `scaleZ` variables, or you can add a `Scale` transform to the `transforms` variable. The following code scales the rectangle by a factor of 1.2 horizontally and 1.5 vertically, giving the result shown in Figure 17-8:

```
Rectangle {
    x: 30
    y: 60
    width: 100
```

```
    height: 40
    fill: Color.YELLOW
    scaleX: 1.2
    scaleY: 1.5
}
```

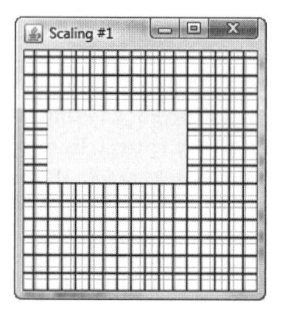

Figure 17-8 Scaling using the **scaleX** and **scaleY** variables

You can see that the rectangle's width has apparently increased from 100 to 120 pixels (a factor of 1.2) and its height from 40 to 60 (a factor of 1.5), but if you compare the result with the original state shown in Figure 17-1, you can see that the rectangle has also moved—instead of its top-left corner being at (30, 60) in the original coordinate space (shown by the lighter colored grid lines), it is now at (20, 50). The reason for this is that when you apply a scale using the node variables, the coordinate system is resized *about the center* of the node. As a result, the center of the node remains where it is (in this case at (80, 80)) and the rest changes size around it. In this case, because there is an increase in size of 20 pixels in both directions, each side of the rectangle has to move 10 pixels away from its center.

As with all the other transforms, what has actually happened is that the coordinate system has been scaled so that the grid squares are now actually rectangles that are larger by a factor of 1.2 horizontally and 1.5 vertically. If you measure the rectangle in its own coordinate system, by counting the darker rectangles in Figure 17-8, you'll see that it is still 100 units wide and 40 units high, but in the original coordinate system, indicated by the lighter grid lines, it is 120 units wide and 60 units high.

Scaling by a negative amount has the effect of *reflecting* the coordinate system of the node in the direction of the negative scale. The following code applies a negative scale in both directions to a Text node, giving the result shown in Figure 17-9:

```
Text {
    x: 50
    y: 60
    content: "HELLO"
    scaleX: -1.0
    scaleY: -1.0
}
```

Figure 17-9   Effects of negative **scaleX** and **scaleY** values

The scene on the right side of the figure shows the Text object with the scale applied. As you can see, the text has been drawn reversed (due to the negative value of scaleX) and upside down (because scaleY is negative). The Text node has not actually moved because the scale operation is relative to its center. Compare this with the result of using negative scale values with the Scale transform, which you'll see shortly.

You can scale the coordinate system around a different point by using a Scale object. The variables of this class are listed in Table 17-4.

Table 17-4   **Variables of the Scale Class**

Variable	Type	Access	Default	Description
x	Number	RW	1.0	The scale factor to be applied along the x-axis
y	Number	RW	1.0	The scale factor to be applied along the y-axis
z	Number	RW	1.0	The scale factor to be applied along the z-axis
pivotX	Number	RW	0.0	The x coordinate of the center of the scale operation
pivotY	Number	RW	0.0	The y coordinate of the center of the scale operation
pivotZ	Number	RW	0.0	The z coordinate of the center of the scale operation

The following code scales the coordinate system of a Text object around the point (20, 20), giving the result shown on the right of Figure 17-10:

```
Text {
    textOrigin: TextOrigin.TOP
    x: 50
```

```
    y: 60
    content: "HELLO"
    transforms: Transform.scale(1.5, 2.0, 20, 20)
}
```

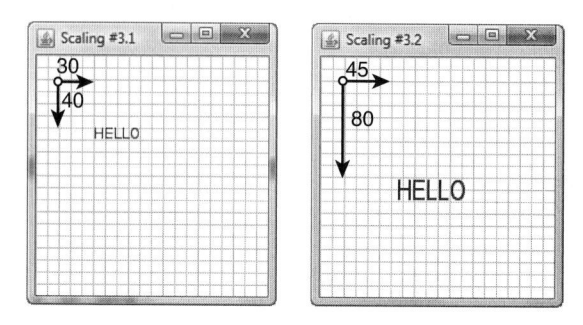

Figure 17-10 Scaling a `Text` object about a specific point

This code uses the `scale()` function of the `Transform` class:

```
public function scale(x:Number, y:Number,
                     pivotX:Number, pivotY:Number):Scale;
```

For the sake of clarity, only the original, unscaled coordinate system is shown in Figure 17-10. As you can see, the effect of this transform is to both scale and move the `Text` object. Because (20, 20) is the pivot point, it is the only point that is not affected by the `Scale` operation. To calculate the effect on any part of the `Text` object, it is necessary to measure the distance of that point from the pivot point along each axis and then apply the scale factors to those distances. The top-left corner of the `Text` object is initially 40 pixels below and 30 pixels to the right of the pivot point, as shown on the left of Figure 17-10. As you can see on the right of the figure, these distances change to (2.0 ★ 40) = 80 pixels below and (1.5 ★ 30) = 45 pixels to right. The width and height of the `Text` object are also increased by the same factors.

When you use a negative scale factor, the sense of the corresponding coordinate axis is reversed. Using a negative y scale, for example, causes `y` coordinates to increase as you move upward rather than downward. The following example applies a y scale of -1 with a pivot point at (0, 40), leaving the x-axis unscaled. The result is shown on the right in Figure 17-11.

```
Text {
    textOrigin: TextOrigin.TOP
    x: 50
    y: 60
    content: "HELLO"
    transforms: Transform.scale(1.0, -1.0, 0, 40)
}
```

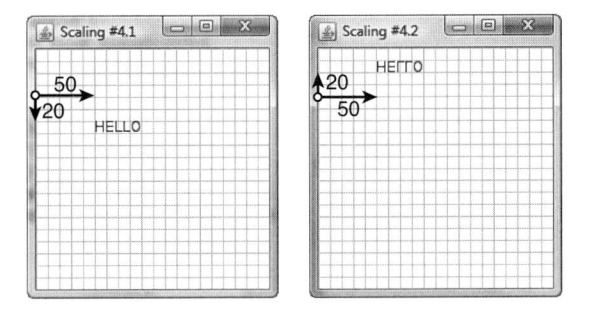

Figure 17-11   Effect of a negative scale factor

You can see that the effect of the negative y scale is to reflect the `Text` object about the pivot point: It starts 20 pixels below the horizontal line drawn through this point, as shown on the left in Figure 17-11 and finishes up 20 pixels above that line.

Shearing

A shear operation, which is also commonly referred to as a skew, is a rotation of one or both of the coordinate axes independently of the other, converting a rectangle into a parallelogram. The amounts by which the axes are rotated are controlled by the x and y variables of the `Shear` class, which are described in Table 17-5. A shear can only be applied by using a `Shear` transform—the node class does not provide any variables that allow you to directly specify a shear.[1] Let's start with a simple shear along one axis. The following code creates a shear in the positive x direction, which causes the y-axis to be rotated in the counterclockwise direction, as shown in Figure 17-12. This code uses the following function of the `Transform` class:

```
public function shear(x:Number, y:Number):Shear;
Rectangle {
    x: 30
    y: 60
    width: 100
    height: 40
    fill: Color.YELLOW
    transforms: [ Transform.shear(0.5, 0.0)]
}
```

A shear of 0.5 along the x-axis means that for every unit moved along the y-axis, move half a unit along the x-axis. That means, for example, that the point (0, 10) in the untransformed coordinate system is moved by the shear operation to (5, 10) in the new coordinate system (move down 10, therefore move across 5). As you can see by comparing the

---

[1] Note that there is no support for shearing along the z-axis in JavaFX 1.3.

Chapter 17 Coordinates, Transforms, and Layout

Table 17-5   **Variables of the `Shear` Class**

Variable	Type	Access	Default	Description
x	Number	RW	1.0	The shear multiplier for the x-axis
y	Number	RW	1.0	The shear multiplier for the y-axis

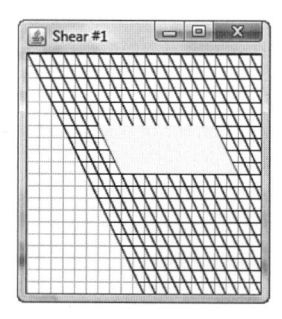

Figure 17-12   A shear along the x-axis

dark and light grids in Figure 17-12, this has the effect or rotating the y-axis toward the x-axis and, consequently, the vertical sides of the rectangle are no longer vertical. Note, however, that all four sides of the rectangle are still parallel to its coordinate axes.

It is possible to skew in both directions at the same time, as this example shows:

```
Rectangle {
    x: 30
    y: 60
    width: 100
    height: 40
    fill: Color.YELLOW
    transforms: [ Shear { x: 0.25 y: 0.25 } ]
}
```

The result of applying this shear, which affects both axes, is shown in Figure 17-13.

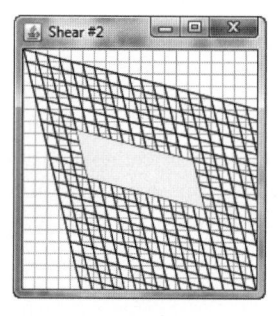

Figure 17-13   A shear along both axes

A shear amount of 1.0 produces a rotation of 45 degrees. A value greater than 1.0 causes a rotation that is greater than 45 degrees. Negative values cause the axes to move in the other direction, as the following example demonstrates:

```
Rectangle {
    x: 30
    y: 60
    width: 100
    height: 40
    fill: Color.YELLOW
    transforms: [ Shear { x: -0.25 } ]
}
```

The shear value of -0.25 causes the y-axis to be rotated clockwise so that for each 4 units moved along the original y-axis, there is a movement of 1 unit along the negative x-axis, as shown in Figure 17-14.

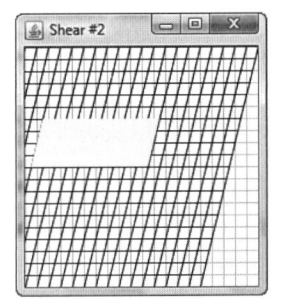

Figure 17-14   A negative shear

Combining Transforms

In the examples that you have seen so far, only one transform has been used at a time, but it is often useful to apply more than one transform to a node. In this section, we look at some examples of multistep transforms.

Transform Order

When you use multiple transforms, you need to know the order in which they will take effect because this affects the result:

1. The translation implied by the `translateX`, `translateY`, `translateZ`, `layoutX`, and `layoutY` variables of the node

2. The rotation implied by the `rotate` variable of the node, which takes place about the center of the node as positioned by the translation in step 1

3. The scale implied by the `scaleX`, `scaleY` and `scaleZ` variables of the node, about the center of the node as positioned by the translation in step 1

4. The transforms in the `transforms` variable, in the order in which they appear in the sequence

Let's first look at what happens when we apply two transforms using a node's transforms variable. Here's an example that translates and then rotates a node's coordinate system:

```
Rectangle {
    x: 30
    y: 60
    width: 100
    height: 40
    fill: Color.YELLOW
    transforms: [
        Transform.translate(40, 40),
        Transform.rotate(45, 0, 0)
    ]
}
```

Given the transformation order described earlier, you would expect the translation to take effect first and then the rotation. The easiest way to see this is to think of it as a two-step process and to imagine what the effect would be after each step. The effect of applying just the translation is shown on the left of Figure 17-15.

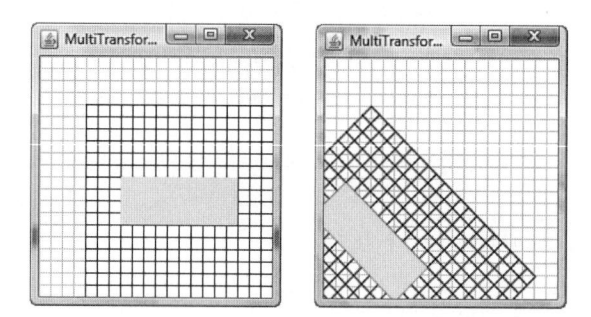

Figure 17-15   A translation followed by a rotation

As you can see, the coordinate system of the rectangle has moved down and to the right by 40 pixels. The result of adding the rotation is shown on the right of Figure 17-15. The important thing to notice about this example is the point about which the rotation occurred. Here's the definition of the rotation:

```
Transform.rotate(45, 0, 0)
```

This specifies that the pivot point of the rotation is the origin of the coordinate system. However, you can see that the rotation was about the point (40, 40) relative to the scene, which is the point to which the node's coordinate system was translated. The point to note here is that as each transform is applied, the changes that are made to the node's coordinate system will affect the next transform. In this case, the first transform moved the coordinate origin, so the rotation in the second transform takes place around the new origin, not the original one. Keep in mind that coordinates in `Transform` objects are relative to the origin *at the time that the transform is applied*, and you won't go too far wrong when trying to work out what a sequence of transforms does.

Now let's see what happens if the same transforms are applied, but in the opposite order, like this:

```
transforms: [
    Transform.rotate(45, 0, 0),
    Transform.translate(40, 40)
]
```

The effect of the rotation is shown on the left of Figure 17-16. As you can see, the rotation takes place around the initial coordinate origin of the node, which in this case is still in the same place as that of the scene.

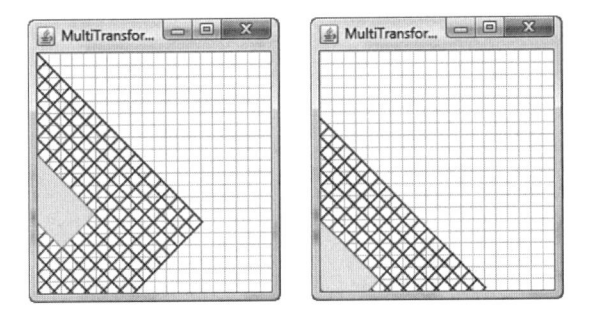

Figure 17-16   A rotation followed by a translation

Now when the translation is applied, the node moves 40 pixels to the right and down. However, the coordinate axes have been rotated, so this movement is *not* parallel to the coordinate axes of the scene, but to the rotated axes, giving the result shown on the right of Figure 17-16. Had the translation been relative to the coordinate axes of the scene, the rectangle would have been placed further to the right and higher up.

Let's look at another example. The following code first translates the rectangle's coordinate system to (20, 20) and then scales it by a factor of 1.5 in each direction. You can see the result of applying first the translation and then the scale in Figure 17-17:

```
Rectangle {
    x: 30
    y: 60
    width: 100
    height: 40
    fill: Color.YELLOW
    transforms: [
        Transform.translate(20, 20),
```

```
            Transform.scale(1.5, 1.5, 0, 0),
    ]
}
```

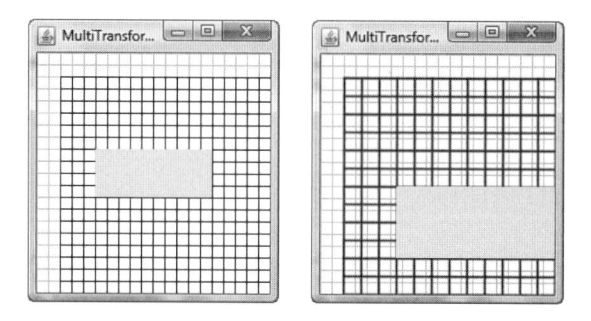

Figure 17-17   A translation followed by a scale

Now let's reverse the order of the transforms:

```
Transform.scale(1.5, 1.5, 0, 0),
Transform.translate(20, 20)
```

Now, the first thing that happens is that the coordinate system of the rectangle is scaled so that each grid square is 1.5 times larger than the squares in the coordinate system of the scene. You can see this effect on the left of Figure 17-18.

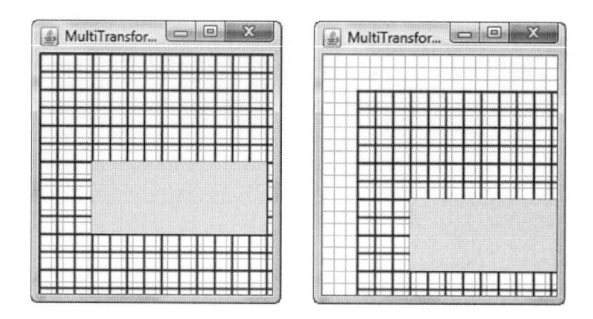

Figure 17-18   A scale followed by a translation

Following the scale, the rectangle's coordinate system is translated by 20 units along both the x-axis and y-axis. This translation is relative to the rectangle's *new*, scaled coordinate system, which means that it will move by 30 units as measured in the scene's coordinates. You can see this very clearly if you compare the result on the right of Figure 17-18 with the result of applying the transforms in the other order in Figure 17-17.

Combining Transforms and Node Variable Settings

Those transforms in the `transforms` variable can be combined with those caused by the `scaleX`, `scaleY`, `scaleZ`, `rotate`, `translateX`, `translateY`, `translateZ`, `layoutX`, and `layoutY` variables of the node class. The order in which these transforms are applied was described in the previous section. Here we take a look at a couple of examples that demonstrate the effect of combining these two ways of specifying transforms.

Translation and a Rotate Transform

For our first example, we'll use the `translateX` variable to apply a horizontal translation together with a `Rotate` transform in the `transforms` variable, like this:

```
Rectangle {
    x: 30
    y: 60
    width: 100
    height: 40
    fill: Color.YELLOW
    translateX: 40
    transforms: [
        Transform.rotate(45, 0, 0)
    ]
}
```

As noted in the "Transform Order" section, earlier in this chapter, the translation specified by the `translateX` variable in the node is applied first, followed by the rotation in the `transforms` variable. Figure 17-19 shows the result.

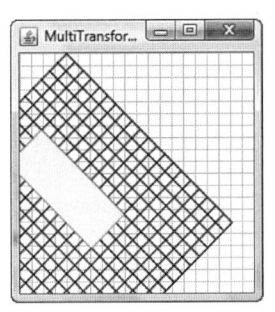

Figure 17-19 Using **translateX** with a **Rotate** transform

Looking at the origin of the transformed coordinate grid, shown with black grid lines, you can see that it has moved 40 pixels to the right, and the rotation has then taken place about this point.

Scaling and a Translate Transform

Our second example uses the `scaleX` variable in the node together with a `Translate` object in the `transforms` variable:

```
Rectangle {
    x: 30
    y: 60
    width: 100
    height: 40
    fill: Color.YELLOW
    scaleX: 1.5
    transforms: [
        Transform.translate(10, 0)
    ]
}
```

Figure 17-20 shows the result.

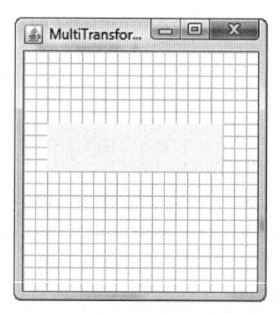

Figure 17-20 Using **scaleX** with a **Translate** transform

Here's how the transformation works. The first step is to apply the `scaleX` value. As mentioned earlier in this chapter, scale operations based on the `scaleX` and `scaleY` variables take place about the *center* of the node and leave the position of the center unchanged. Before the scale, the center was at x = 80, y = 80, and it will remain here after the scale, even though the node's width will increase from 100 to 150. For this to be possible, the x coordinate of the node as measured in the coordinate space of the Scene must be changed to 80 - 75 (half the width), or 5. Because `scaleY` is implicitly 1.0, there is no change in the y coordinate or height of the node. At this point,, the bounds of the rectangle relative to the scene are x = 5, y = 60, width = 150, height = 40.

Now, we apply the translation, which is by 10 pixels in the x direction. However, this is 10 pixels *measured in the coordinate space of the* rectangle, which has been scaled by a factor of 1.5 in the x direction. Therefore, the translation as seen in the scene's coordinate space is 10 * 1.5 = 15 pixels along the x-axis. Adding 15 to current x coordinate of 5 gives 20, so the final bounds of the rectangle in the scene's coordinate space are x = 20, y = 60, width = 150, and height = 40. This is exactly the result shown in Figure 17-20.

Clipping

Normally, when you add a node to a scene, you want the entire node to be rendered, and this is what happens by default. Under some circumstances, however, you might want the user to be able to see only part of a node. An example of this is shown in Figure 17-21.

Figure 17-21   Showing part of a node

At first glance, it might appear that you are looking at an image that is overlaid with a black rectangle with a circular hole in it. The scene does, in fact, contain a rectangle and an image (in an `ImageView` node), but the rectangle is actually *behind* the image, not in front of it. Normally, if you were to place an `ImageView` in front of a rectangle of the same size, the rectangle would be completely covered and therefore obscured by the `ImageView`. In this case, only that portion of the `ImageView` that lies inside a circular area is being rendered, thus allowing the parts of the rectangle that are outside that area to be seen.

The partial rendering of a node is achieved by setting its *clip*. The clip is itself a node. When you associate a clip with a node, only the part of that node that is covered by the interior of the clip node is rendered. The following code, which is the implementation of the example in Figure 17-21, shows how to apply a clip:

```
1       var image:Image = Image {
2           url: "{__DIR__}images/portsmouthSmall.jpg"
```

```
3        };
4        var imageView:ImageView;
5        Stage {
6            title: "Clip #1"
7            scene: Scene {
8                width: image.width
9                height: image.height
10               content: [
11                   Rectangle {
12                       width: bind image.width
13                       height: bind image.height
14                       fill: Color.BLACK
15                   }
16                   imageView = ImageView {
17                       var centerX = image.width / 2
18                       var centerY = image.height / 2
19                       image: image
20                       clip: bind Circle {
21                                   centerX: centerX
22                                   centerY: centerY
23                                   radius: 100
24                       }
25                       onMouseDragged: function(evt) {
26                           centerX = evt.x;
27                           centerY = evt.y;
28                       }
29               }
30               ]
31           }
32       }
```

The circle that defines the clip is created on lines 20 to 24 and is assigned to the clip variable of the `ImageView` node. The clip node exists in the same coordinate space as the `ImageView` node to which it is applied, so the code on lines 17 and 18 that declares and assigns the `centerX` and `centerY` variables, together with the assignment of these values to the same variables of the circle object, cause the clip to be centered over the mid-point of the `ImageView`. Therefore, the clip initially allows only a circular area around the center of the `ImageView` to be seen, as shown in Figure 17-21.

To make this example more interesting, the mouse handler declared on lines 25 to 28 causes the `centerX` and `centerY` variables to be set to the location of the mouse if the mouse is pressed and then dragged while it is over the clipped part of the `ImageView`. Because the value of the `clip` variable is bound to a circle whose center point depends on these variables, the result will be that clicking the mouse inside the clipped area and then dragging it around will cause the circle, and therefore the clipping area, to follow the mouse, giving the impression of a window that can be moved around to show different parts of the image. This works only if the mouse is initially clicked inside the circle, because mouse events that occur outside the clipped area are not delivered to the `ImageView`—they are delivered to the rectangle instead.

If the node that is assigned to the `clip` variable is made invisible, it no longer operates as a clip and the whole of the underlying node, in this case the `ImageView`, will be rendered.

Note that the clipping node is defined like this:

```
clip: bind Circle {
    centerX: centerX
    centerY: centerY
    radius: 100
}
```

This definition causes a new circle object to be created and assigned to the `clip` variable when either of the `centerX` or `centerY` variables is changed. It is important that a new value be assigned because the implementation of this feature in the `Node` class will only adjust the clip when the value of the `clip` variable changes. This alternative code would not work:

```
clip: Circle {
    centerX: bind centerX
    centerY: bind centerY
    radius: 100
}
```

This code only causes the `centerX`/`centerY` variables of the existing circle object to be updated in response to changes in the variables to which they are bound. These changes are not visible to the code in the `Node` class that manages the clip.

The clip is affected by any transforms that are applied to the node that it is linked to—in fact, those transforms are also applied to the clip. The following code creates a yellow rectangle and installs a clip that is a group consisting of two shapes, a `Text` node and a circle:

```
1     Rectangle {
2         x: 50
3         y: 50
4         width: 100
5         height: 100
6         scaleX: bind scale
7         scaleY: bind scale
8         fill: Color.YELLOW
9         clip: Group {
10            content: [
11                Circle {
12                    centerX: 100
13                    centerY: 100
14                    radius: 20
15                }
16                Text {
```

```
17                      textOrigin: TextOrigin.TOP
18                      x: 70
19                      y: 50
20                      content: "JavaFX"
21                      font: Font { size: 20 }
22                  }
23              ]
24          }
25      }
```

When this rectangle is placed in a scene, the only parts of it that can be seen are those areas that are covered by the text and circle nodes, as shown on the left of Figure 17-22.

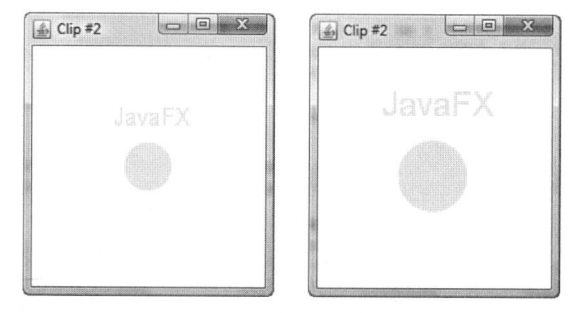

Figure 17-22   The effects of applying a transform to a clipped node

The rectangle's `scaleX` and `scaleY` variables are both bound to a script variable called scale. When the value of this variable is changed, the rectangle will change size, and its clip will be transformed in the same way. Here's an extract from the code that causes the value of the `scale` variable to increase from `1.0` to `1.5` and then back to `1.0` over a total of 4 seconds. This process repeats indefinitely:

```
var t = Timeline {
    repeatCount: Timeline.INDEFINITE
    autoReverse: true
    keyFrames: [
        at (0s) { scale => 1.0 tween Interpolator.EASEBOTH }
        at (2s) { scale => 1.5 tween Interpolator.EASEBOTH }
    ]
};
t.play();
```

The result is that the clipped area, represented by the yellow-filled text and circle nodes, moves outward to match the scale applied to the rectangle, as shown on the right of Figure 17-22.

Coordinates and Bounds

If you are a Swing developer, you will be used to getting the position and size of a component by calling its `getBounds()` method. The bounds that this method returns are relative to the coordinate system of the component's parent container. Swing and AWT have a simple model in which the coordinate systems all use the same measuring units, and there is only one x-axis and one y-axis. It is, therefore, a simple matter to interpret the bounds of a Swing component and to convert the coordinates of a point from the coordinate system of one component to those of another.

In JavaFX, things are not so simple. As you have seen, by applying a scale transformation, you can arrange for the measuring units of one node to be different from those of another node. Worse still, if you apply a rotation or a shear, you change the orientation of the affected node's coordinate axes. In either case, it will not be a simple matter to convert coordinates as seen by a node into those seen by another. In fact, in JavaFX it is not really meaningful to talk about the bounds of a node as if there were only one possible set of bounds. In this section, we look at how to deal with these issues.

Getting Node Bounds

The `Node` class provides three variables that represent the bounds of a node:

```
public-read var boundsInLocal:Bounds
public-read var boundsInParent:Bounds
public-read var layoutBounds:Bounds
```

These variables are all of type `javafx.geometry.Bounds`, which is an immutable object whose variables are listed in Table 17-6.[2] To decide which of these three variables to use as a node's bounds, you need to know what each of the different bounds represents:

- The bounds in the `layoutBounds` variable correspond to the actual geometry of the node as seen in its own coordinate system. By this, we mean the geometry of the node *before* any transformations,[3] clip, or effect have been applied.
- The bounds in the `boundsInLocal` variable are the bounds of the node as seen in its own coordinate system *after* any effects (see Chapter 18) and the clip have been applied, but *before* the application of any transforms.
- The bounds in the `boundsInParent` variable are the bounds as seen in the coordinate system of the node's parent (that is, its owning scene, group, or container), after the application of *all* transforms. Depending on the transformations that have been applied, these bounds could be very different from the node's layout or local bounds.

---

[2] `Bounds` is an abstract class. The bounds that are returned by these methods are actually instances of a concrete subclass called `BoundingBox`.

[3] Here, the term *transform* refers to a `Transform` in the `transforms` sequence or one specified using the transform-related variables of the `Node` (`scaleX`, `scaleY`, and so on).

Table 17-6 **Variables of the Bounds Class**

Variable	Type	Access	Default	Description
minX	Number	RI	0.0	The x coordinate of the upper-left back corner of the bounded region
minY	Number	RI	0.0	The y coordinate of the upper-left back corner of the bounded region
minZ	Number	RI	0.x0	The z coordinate of the upper-right back corner of the bounded region
width	Number	RI	0.0	The width of the bounded region
height	Number	RI	0.0	The height of the bounded region
depth	Number	RI	0.0	The depth of the bounded region
maxX	Number	R	minX + width	The x coordinate of the lower-right front corner of the bounded region
maxY	Number	R	minY + height	The y coordinate of the lower-right front corner of the bounded region
maxZ	Number	R	minZ + depth	The z coordinate of the lower-right front corner of the bounded region

The `layoutBounds` are the bounds used by container classes when placing a node according to its layout policy, as you'll see later in this chapter. When manually placing nodes (in a group, say), you could choose to use either the `layoutBounds` or the `boundsInLocal`, depending on whether you want to take into account the clip and effects, both of which may change the size and shape of the node. The simplest way to explain these different bounds is by reference to examples.

Bounds with No Clip, Effects, or Transforms

When no transforms, clip, or effects are applied, it is easy to understand what the various bounds of a node represent. We'll illustrate this by returning to the rectangle that we used for the examples in the previous section, which is defined like this and shown in Figure 17-23:

```
var node = Rectangle {
    x: 30
    y: 60
    width: 100
    height: 40
    fill: Color.YELLOW
}
```

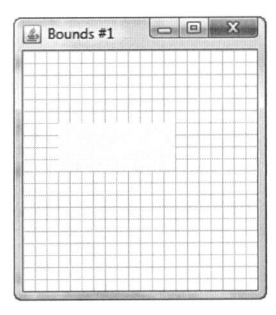

Figure 17-23 Bounds of a rectangle with no clip, effects, or transforms applied

To get the various bounds for this node, we use the following code:[4] `println("Layout bounds: {node.layoutBounds}");`
`println("Local bounds: {node.boundsInLocal}");`
`println("Parent bounds: {node.boundsInParent}");`

This gives the following output:

```
Layout bounds: BoundingBox [minX:30.0, minY:60.0, minZ:0.0, width:100.0, height:40.0, depth:0.0, maxX:130.0, maxY:100.0, maxZ:0.0]
Local bounds: BoundingBox [minX:30.0, minY:60.0, minZ:0.0, width:100.0, height:40.0, depth:0.0, maxX:130.0, maxY:100.0, maxZ:0.0]
Parent bounds: BoundingBox [minX:30.0, minY:60.0, minZ:0.0, width:100.0, height:40.0, depth:0.0, maxX:130.0, maxY:100.0, maxZ:0.0]
```

Not surprisingly, the bounds are all the same—the layout bounds and local bounds are the same because there is no effect or clip, and the local bounds and parent bounds are the same because there are no transforms applied.

---

[4] You'll find this code in the file `javafxtransforms/Bounds1.fx` in the JavaFX Book GUI project.

Bounds with a Clip Applied

When you apply a clip/effect to a node, the `boundsInLocal` and `boundsInParent` values change to reflect their effect. For example, the following code applies a clip that reduces the visible part of the yellow rectangle, as shown in Figure 17-24:

```
Rectangle {
    x: 30
    y: 60
    width: 100
    height: 40
    fill: Color.YELLOW
    clip: Rectangle {
        x: 40 y: 70 width: 20 height: 20
    }
}
```

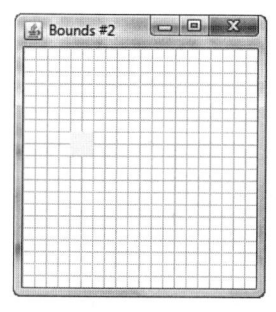

Figure 17-24   Bounds of a rectangle with a clip applied

The result of running this code, which is in the file `javafxtransforms/Bounds2.fx`, is as follows:

```
Layout bounds: BoundingBox [minX:30.0, minY:60.0, minZ:0.0, width:100.0,
height:40.0, depth:0.0, maxX:130.0, maxY:100.0, maxZ:0.0]
Local bounds: BoundingBox [minX:40.0, minY:70.0, minZ:0.0, width:20.0,
height:20.0, depth:0.0, maxX:60.0, maxY:90.0, maxZ:0.0]
Parent bounds: BoundingBox [minX:40.0, minY:70.0, minZ:0.0, width:20.0,
height:20.0, depth:0.0, maxX:60.0, maxY:90.0, maxZ:0.0]
```

As you can see, the layout bounds still reflect the full bounds of the rectangle, even though most of it is not visible. As a result, space for the whole rectangle would be allocated if it were placed into a container subclass. The local bounds, however, refer only to the part of the rectangle that is actually visible, as you can see by reading off the coordinates of that area in Figure 17-24. The parent bounds are the same as the local bounds in this case because there are no transforms.

Bounds with Transforms Applied

When one or more transforms are applied to a node, the `boundsInLocal()` and `boundsInParent()` functions will return different values. To illustrate this, the following code, which you'll find in the file `javafxtransforms/Bounds3.fx`, applies a translation to the rectangle from our earlier examples, the result of which is shown in Figure 17-25. Note that, for simplicity, we have not included a clip in this example:

```
Rectangle {
    x: 30
    y: 60
    width: 100
    height: 40
    fill: Color.YELLOW
    transforms: [
        Translate { x: 60 y: 30 },
    ]
}
```

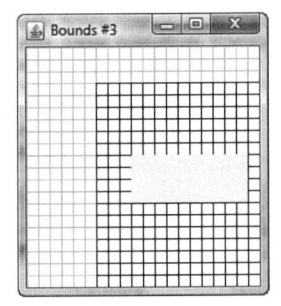

Figure 17-25   Bounds of a rectangle with a translation applied

The bounds of the translated rectangle are as follows:

```
Layout bounds: BoundingBox [minX:30.0, minY:60.0, minZ:0.0, width:100.0,
height:40.0, depth:0.0, maxX:130.0, maxY:100.0, maxZ:0.0]
Local bounds: BoundingBox [minX:30.0, minY:60.0, minZ:0.0, width:100.0,
height:40.0, depth:0.0, maxX:130.0, maxY:100.0, maxZ:0.0]
Parent bounds: BoundingBox [minX:90.0, minY:90.0, minZ:0.0, width:100.0,
height:40.0, depth:0.0, maxX:190.0, maxY:130.0, maxZ:0.0]
```

The layout and local bounds, which can be read from the darker coordinate grid, are the same (and reflect the bounds of the rectangle in its own coordinate system) because, by definition, they are unaffected by any transformations that are applied. However, the parent bounds, which can be read off from the lighter coordinate grid in Figure 17-25, are different—the width and height are the same, but the x and y coordinates have changed by the distance by which the rectangle has been translated along each of these axes.

Now let's add a rotation, giving the result shown in Figure 17-26[5]:

```
transforms: [
  Translate { x: 60 y: 30 },
  Rotate { angle: 45 }
]
```

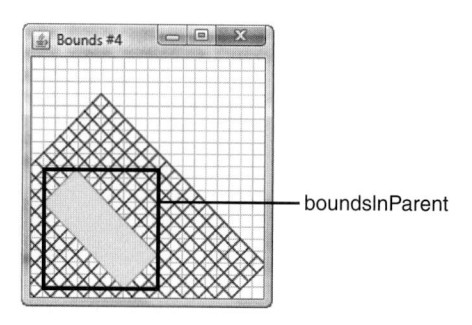

Figure 17-26 Bounds of a rectangle with a translation and a rotation applied

The resulting bounds are as follows:

```
Layout bounds: BoundingBox [minX:30.0, minY:60.0, minZ:0.0, width:100.0,
height:40.0, depth:0.0, maxX:130.0, maxY:100.0, maxZ:0.0]
Local bounds: BoundingBox [minX:30.0, minY:60.0, minZ:0.0, width:100.0,
height:40.0, depth:0.0, maxX:130.0, maxY:100.0, maxZ:0.0]
Parent bounds: BoundingBox [minX:10.502525, minY:93.63961, minZ:0.0,
width:98.99495, height:98.99494, depth:0.0, maxX:109.497475,
maxY:192.63455, maxZ:0.0]
```

Here, you can see that the layout and local bounds are still the same (because there is neither a clip nor an effect present), but according to the parent bounds, both the position *and* the size of the rectangle are very different. This is because the parent bounds correspond to the outlined area in Figure 17-26, the size and top-left corner of which are not the same as that of the rectangle.

As a further example, let's remove the rotation and apply a translation and a scale instead. This code can be found in the file `javafxtransforms/Bounds5.fx`:

---

[5] This example is in the file `javafxtransforms/Bounds4.fx`.

```
Rectangle {
    x: 30
    y: 60
    width: 100
    height: 40
    fill: Color.YELLOW
    transforms: [
        Translate { x: 60 y: 30 },
        Scale { x: 1.2 y: 1.2 }
    ]
}
```

The result of applying these transforms is shown in Figure 17-27.

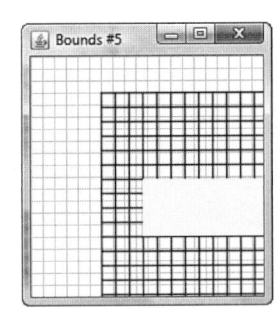

Figure 17-27 Bounds of a rectangle with a translation and a scale applied

Here are the bounds of this transformed rectangle:

```
Layout bounds: BoundingBox [minX:30.0, minY:60.0, minZ:0.0, width:100.0,
height:40.0, depth:0.0, maxX:130.0, maxY:100.0, maxZ:0.0]
Local bounds: BoundingBox [minX:30.0, minY:60.0, minZ:0.0, width:100.0,
height:40.0, depth:0.0, maxX:130.0, maxY:100.0, maxZ:0.0]
Parent bounds: BoundingBox [minX:96.0, minY:102.0, minZ:0.0, width:120.0,
height:48.0, depth:0.0, maxX:216.0, maxY:150.0, maxZ:0.0]
```

Looking at the parent bounds, you can see that the x and y position have changed as a result both of the translation and the scaling and that the width and height as seen in the parent are both 1.2 times what they are in the local bounds, which is consistent with the scaling factor applied.

Finally, let's add the rectangle to a group and apply a translation both to the group and to the rectangle itself:

```
var scene:Scene;
var node:Node;
Stage {
    title: "Bounds #6"
    scene:
```

Chapter 17 Coordinates, Transforms, and Layout

```
scene = Scene {
    width: 200
    height: 200
    content: [
        Group {
            transforms: Translate { x: 30 y: 20 }
            content: [
                node = Rectangle {
                    x: 30
                    y: 60
                    width: 100
                    height: 40
                    fill: Color.YELLOW
                    transforms: [
                        Translate { x: 10 y: 10 },
                    ]
                }
            ]
        }
    ]
}
```

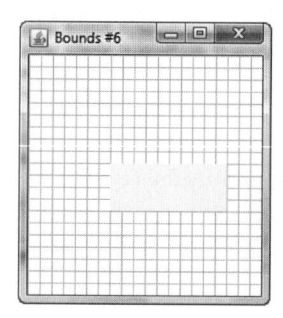

Figure 17-28   A rectangle within a group with translations applied to both

Here, the group is translated 30 pixels to the right and 20 pixels down relative to the scene, while the rectangle is translated 10 pixels to the right and 10 pixels down from the group. Figure 17-28 shows the result.

The bounds that would be reported for the rectangle with these transformations applied are the following:

```
Layout bounds: BoundingBox [minX:30.0, minY:60.0, minZ:0.0, width:100.0,
height:40.0, depth:0.0, maxX:130.0, maxY:100.0, maxZ:0.0]
Local bounds: BoundingBox [minX:30.0, minY:60.0, minZ:0.0, width:100.0,
height:40.0, depth:0.0, maxX:130.0, maxY:100.0, maxZ:0.0]
```

```
Parent bounds: BoundingBox [minX:40.0, minY:70.0, minZ:0.0, width:100.0,
height:40.0, depth:0.0, maxX:140.0, maxY:110.0, maxZ:0.0]
```

You can see that the parent and local bounds differ by the amount of the translation applied to the rectangle relative to the group, which is its parent. The translation of the group relative to the scene is not visible in any of the rectangle's bounds, but you could discover it, if you needed to, by getting the bounds of the group itself.

Positioning and Translation

All the `Shape` subclasses have variables that control the position of the shape within its local coordinate system. In the case of the rectangle class, for example, these are called `x` and `y`. All node subclasses (which includes the `Shape` subclasses) also have variables called `translateX`, `translateY`, `layoutX`, and `layoutY`. At first sight, this could be confusing, because these three pairs of variables appear to be doing the same thing. However, as was pointed out earlier in this chapter, they are not the same—the `translateX`, `translateY`, `layoutX`, and `layoutY` variables move the coordinate origin of the node, whereas the `x` and `y` variables do not.

To illustrate the difference, let's first create a rectangle and use its `x` and `y` variables to place it at (30, 60) relative to the scene. Figure 17-29 shows the result:

```
Rectangle {
    x: 30
    y: 60
    width: 100
    height: 40
    fill: Color.YELLOW
    onMouseMoved: function(evt) {
            println("Mouse at ({evt.x}, {evt.y})")
        }
}
```

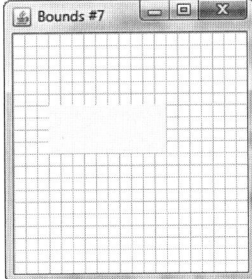

Figure 17-29 Positioning a rectangle by using its **x** and **y** variables

The local and parent-relative bounds of this node are as follows:

```
Local bounds: BoundingBox [minX:30.0, minY:60.0, minZ:0.0, width:100.0,
height:40.0, depth:0.0, maxX:130.0, maxY:100.0, maxZ:0.0]
```

```
Parent bounds: BoundingBox [minX:30.0, minY:60.0, minZ:0.0, width:100.0,
height:40.0, depth:0.0, maxX:130.0, maxY:100.0, maxZ:0.0]
```

The fact that these bounds are the same confirms that the origin of the node's coordinate system is the same as that of its parent—in other words, when you set the x and y variables, you do not affect the node's coordinate system. The node-relative coordinates events delivered to the mouse handler for this node further confirm this fact. Here are some of the events that are received as the mouse crosses the left side of the rectangle:

```
Mouse at (30.0, 80.0)
Mouse at (31.0, 80.0)
Mouse at (32.0, 80.0)
```

Now let's use the `translateX` and `translateY` variables rather than x and y:

```
Rectangle {
    width: 100
    height: 40
    fill: Color.YELLOW
    translateX: 30
    translateY: 60
    onMouseMoved: function(evt) {
                println("Mouse at ({evt.x}, {evt.y})")
    }
}
```

Comparing this rectangle, shown in Figure 17-30, with the one in Figure 17-29, you can see that it occupies the same location in the scene, but the position of the dark colored grid indicates that setting the `translateX` and `translateY` variables has caused the coordinate origin for the rectangle to be moved.

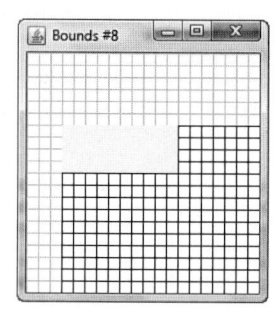

Figure 17-30 Positioning a rectangle by using its **translateX** and **translateY** variables

The local and parent bounds reported for this rectangle are as follows:

```
Local bounds: BoundingBox [minX:0.0, minY:0.0, minZ:0.0, width:100.0,
```

```
height:40.0, depth:0.0, maxX:100.0, maxY:40.0, maxZ:0.0]
Parent bounds: BoundingBox [minX:30.0, minY:60.0, minZ:0.0, width:100.0,
height:40.0, depth:0.0, maxX:130.0, maxY:100.0, maxZ:0.0]
```

You can see that the local bounds of the rectangle are different—in this case, the rectangle is placed at the origin of its coordinate system, because its x and y variables are both defaulted to 0. However, because the `translateX` and `translateY` variables caused the coordinate system of the rectangle to be moved relative to the scene, its parent bounds are the same as they were when the x and y variables were used to place it. The mouse events in this case are also different:

```
Mouse at (0.0, 20.0)
Mouse at (1.0, 20.0)
Mouse at (2.0, 20.0)
```

As you can see, the location of the mouse is reported relative to the new position of the coordinate grid.

Coordinate System Conversions

It is sometimes useful to convert the coordinates of a point as seen in one coordinate system to the corresponding values in another. The node class provides convenience functions that make this easy to do.

You can convert from the coordinate space of a node to that of its parent by calling either of the `localToParent()` functions of the node:

```
public function localToParent(localX:Number, localY:Number):Point2D
public function localToParent(localPoint:Point2D):Point2D
```

The reverse mapping can be performed by using the `parentToLocal()` functions:

```
public function parentToLocal(parentX:Number, parentY:Number):Point2D
public function parentToLocal(parentPoint:Point2D):Point2D
```

There are also functions that map between coordinates of the local node and those of its enclosing scene:

```
public function localToScene(localX:Number, localY:Number):Point2D
public function localToScene(localPoint:Point2D):Point2D
public function sceneToLocal(sceneX:Number, sceneY:Number):Point2D
public function sceneToLocal(scenePoint:Point2D):Point2D
```

To determine whether a point is within the bounds of a node, you can use either of the `contains()` functions of that node instance:

```
public function contains(localX:Number, localY:Number):Boolean
public function contains(localPoint:Point2D):Boolean
```

The `localX`, `localY`, and `localPoint` arguments must be expressed in the local coordinate system of the node on which these functions are called. If you have the coordinates of the point as seen from another coordinate system, you can use the conversion functions above to convert them. One way to convert the location of a point within one `Node` to the local coordinate system of another node is to go through the coordinate system of their common scene. For example, to convert the coordinates (`xForNode1, xForNode2`) in the local coordinate system of `node1` to the coordinate system of `node2`, assuming both nodes are in the same scene, do the following:

```
var scenePos = node1.localToScene(xForNode1, yForNode1);
var node2Point = node2.sceneToLocal(scenePos.x, scenePos.y);
```

There are also variants of the functions listed above that work with `Bounds` objects rather than points:

```
public function localToParent(localBounds:Bounds):Bounds
public function parentToLocal(parentBounds:Bounds):Bounds
public function localToScene(localBounds:Bounds):Bounds
public function sceneToLocal(sceneBounds:Bounds):Bounds
```

The following two node functions allow you to determine whether the shape of a node intersects a given rectangular area:

```
public function intersects(localX:Number, localY:Number,
                           localWidth:Number, localY:Number):Boolean
public function intersects(localRect:Bounds):Boolean
```

Take care to ensure that the bounds of the area in question are given in the coordinate system of the node on which these functions are invoked.

Node Layout

You may have noticed that most of the examples in this book explicitly position and size the nodes that they use. Manually placing and sizing the nodes that make up your user interface can be tedious work, and it is very fragile, too, because changes you make to one part of the scene might require you to manually move or resize the nodes in another part. Manual placement also makes it hard to build user interfaces that work well when the user resizes the scene.

JavaFX supports automatic layout of nodes through the `Container` class, which is part of the `javafx.scene.layout` package. `Container` is an abstract class that is derived from `Group` and which can therefore contain other nodes. There are various subclasses of `Container`, each of which positions and sizes their child nodes according to a specific policy.

We take a look at the `Container` subclasses provided with the JavaFX runtime in the sections that follow, and in Chapter 25 you'll see how to implement a custom layout policy by writing your own `Container` subclass.

> **Note**
>
> A `Container` is not the same as a Swing `JPanel`. In particular, it does not have a `fill` variable that would allow you to set its background color. To create a filled container, you need to use a trick that you'll see in the "Setting the Fill Color for a Container" section, later in this chapter.

Node Sizes and Layout

When a container is positioning and sizing nodes, it may take into account how large each node wants to be. Depending on its layout policy, a container may make use of any or all the following node sizes:

- The *preferred* width or height is the width or height that the node would ideally like to have. A text node, for example, would like to be wide enough and tall enough to be able to display its text content using its assigned font.
- The *minimum* width or height is the smallest width or height that the node would like to have. In many cases, this is the same as the preferred width or height.
- The *maximum* width or height is the largest width or height that the node would like to have. For nodes that don't have a maximum size constraint, the value `Number.MAX_VALUE` is typically used.

The sizes are obtained differently depending on whether or not the node is `Resizable`. `Resizable` is a mixin class that is included by all the JavaFX UI controls that we discuss in Chapter 22, "Cross-Platform Controls," but *not* by the shape nodes that were covered in Chapter 16, "Shapes, Text, and Images." This means that both controls and shape nodes can be position by a container, but shape nodes can never be resized. Here are the rules that determine how the preferred, maximum, and minimum sizes are obtained[6]:

- For a node that is `Resizable`, the preferred/minimum/maximum sizes are obtained from its `getPrefWidth()`, `getPrefHeight()`, `getMinWidth()`, `getMinHeight()`, `getMaxWidth()`, and `getMaxHeight()` functions. Node subclasses that are `Resizable` are required to implement these methods in such a way as to return reasonable values for these sizes.
- For a node that is not `Resizable`, the width and height of the node obtained from its layout bounds are used for all of the preferred, minimum, and maximum values. This implies that such a node will always appear to be able to accept only a single width or height value, which is consistent with the fact that it is not resizable.

In some cases, a container will set the sizes of its child nodes as part of its layout policy. It will do this for nodes that are `Resizable` by assigning values to the `width` and `height` variables. Width and height values are not set for nodes that are not `Resizable` (such as rectangles and circles) because there is no way for a specific width or height to be set for these nodes.

---

[6] These rules can be circumvented for any given `Node` by assigning a value to its `layoutInfo` variable. See the "Overriding the Layout Behavior of a Container" section for details.

> **Note**
>
> Although it is not a `Container`, the `Group` class also has a layout policy, of sorts—it does not position its child nodes but any node that is `Resizable` is given its preferred size. If you don't want this behavior, you can disable it by setting the group's `autoSizeChildren` variable to `false`.

A container lays out its child nodes in a rectangular area that is determined by the values of its `width` and `height` variables. This is true even if the container itself is actually smaller or larger than the area described by these variables. A container allocates space to all of its nodes, including those that are not visible. It is also possible to specify that some nodes are not to be managed by the container, with the result that they will be positioned according to the values of their `translateX`, `translateY`, `layoutX`, and `layoutY` variables. We discuss this in the "Setting the Fill Color for a Container" section, later in this chapter.

Containers place their children when child nodes are added or removed, when they or resized, or when any change is made to a variable that might affect the position/sizes of any of its child nodes. This happens automatically, so there is usually no need to force the container to redo its layout. However, should you find a need to force the layout of a container to be redone, you can use two functions that are inherited from the `Parent` class to do this:

- `public function layout():Void`
- `public function requestLayout():Void`

The first of these functions performs the layout synchronously, with the result that it is complete when the call returns. The second simply requests that the container lays out its children at some time in the near future. The JavaFX runtime performs pending layouts on a regular basis through the use of a timer. In most cases, it is better to use `requestLayout()` than `layout()`, especially if it is likely that multiple requests to lay out the same container might be made within a short period of time.[7]

Containers and Layout

Each different container class has its own layout policy, which determines how its child nodes will be positioned and sized. In the sections that follow, you'll see the layout policies of all the containers in the JavaFX runtime. It is important to note that a container does not apply its layout policy directly to the nodes themselves—rather, for each node it determines a *layout area* and then places the node within that area. The size and position of each layout area is determined partly by the layout policy of the container and partly by properties of the node that will occupy that area. Similarly, the position and size of the node within its layout area are controlled by properties of the node itself, although default behavior can be applied from the properties of the container.

---

[7] These differences between these two functions are similar to those between the `validate()` and `revalidate()` functions provided by the Swing `JComponent` class.

Layout Areas and LayoutInfo

The following code, from the file `javafxtransforms/LayoutAreas1.fx`, shows the relationship between a container's layout areas and the positions and sizes of its child nodes:

```
1    Stage {
2        var scene:Scene;
3        title : "Layout Areas #1"
4        scene: scene = Scene {
5            width: 200
6            height: 100
7            content: VBox {
8                width: bind scene.width
9                height: bind scene.height
10               spacing: 12
11               padding: Insets { top: 4 left: 4
12                                 bottom: 4 right: 4 }
13               content: [
14                   TextBox {
15                       columns: 15
16                   }
17                   TextBox {
18                       columns: 15
19                       layoutInfo: LayoutInfo {
20                           hfill: false
21                       }
22                   }
23               ]
24           }
25       }
26   }
```

This code uses a `VBox` container to place two `TextBox` controls, both of which are configured (on lines 15 and 18) to be 15 columns wide. The layout policy of `VBox` is to arrange its child controls one above the other, in the order in which they appear in its `content` variable. Figure 17-31 shows the result of running this code.

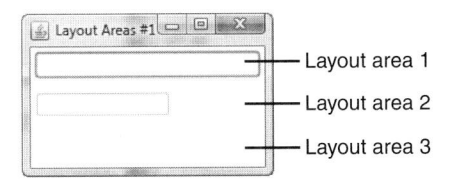

Figure 17-31   Layout areas and node positioning

The black rectangles in this figure indicate the layout areas assigned by the `VBox` for each of the two `TextBox` controls. As you can see, both controls are positioned within their respective layout area, but they are not treated equally—the `TextBox` at the top fills the entire width of the container, whereas the one at the bottom does not. When a `Resizable` node (such as a control) is placed within its layout area, the container may choose to size it so that it fills the entire area, or it may not. This choice is made separately for both the horizontal and vertical dimensions of a node and is determined by the values returned by the following functions of the `Resizable` mixin:

```
public function getHFill():Boolean    // Horizontal fill
public function getVFill():Boolean    // Vertical fill
```

Each `Resizable` has its own implementation of these functions that return an appropriate value, as determined by the implementer of the class. In the case of the `TextBox` class, the `getHFill()` function returns `true` and `getVFill()` returns `false`. Because `getHFill()` returns `true` and the layout areas are wider than the space needed to display 15 columns of text, the `VBox` has expanded the `TextBox` at the top so that it fills all of its layout area. In fact, a `Resizable` node will be resized only up to its maximum width (as returned by its `getMaxWidth()` function), but in the case of `TextBox`, the maximum width is unbounded, so it has been expanded to fit the whole width of the layout area. Nodes that are not `Resizable` (such as `Rectangle`, `Circle`, and so on) are always given their actual widths no matter how large or small their layout areas might be.

The second layout area is the same size as the first, but its `TextBox` has been left at its preferred width. The reason for this is the `LayoutInfo` object installed in its `layoutInfo` variable on lines 19 to 21 of the sample code:

```
layoutInfo: LayoutInfo {
    hfill: false
}
```

The `LayoutInfo` object lets you specify or override layout behavior on a per-node basis. Values in the `LayoutInfo` object take precedence over values obtained from the node or those configured in the container itself. In this case, the value of the `hfill` variable overrides the value returned by the `getHFill()` function of the `TextBox`, so the `VBox` does not expand it to fill the available space, leaving it instead at its preferred size.

The full set of variables of the `LayoutInfo` class is shown in Table 17-7.

When you create a `LayoutInfo` object, you typically assign values to only those variables that override the default behavior of the container, which we'll discuss in the sections that follow. In Figure 17-31, for example, the second `TextBox` is aligned to the left of its layout area, because that is the default behavior of `VBox`. You can override this for all nodes in the `VBox` by assigning a value to its `nodeHPos` variable, or you can override it for a single node by creating a `LayoutInfo` object for that node and setting its `hpos` variable.

Growing and Shrinking Layout Areas

In the example that you have just seen, not all the available space in the `VBox` was allocated to the two layout areas. Each layout area is tall enough to provide the space for the node that it contains and no more. When, as in this case, more vertical space is available than required, the container may expand one or more of its layout areas to occupy that space.

Table 17-7   Variables of the `LayoutInfo` class

Variable	Type	Access	Description
`height`	Number	RW	Overrides the preferred height of a `Resizable` node
`hfill`	Boolean	RW	Specifies whether the width of a `Resizable` node should be adjusted toward that of its layout area, limited by its maximum width
`hgrow`	Priority	RW	Whether the layout area for the node should be expanded horizontally when there is unallocated horizontal space
`hpos`	HPos	RW	The horizontal position of the node within its layout area
`hshrink`	Priority	RW	Whether the layout area for the node should be reduced in width when there is insufficient horizontal space
`margin`	Insets	RW	Specifies an area of empty space that should be left around the outside of the node
`maxHeight`	Number	RW	Overrides the maximum height of a `Resizable` node
`maxWidth`	Number	RW	Overrides the maximum width of a `Resizable` node
`minHeight`	Number	RW	Overrides the minimum height of a `Resizable` node
`minWidth`	Number	RW	Overrides the minimum width of a `Resizable` node
`vfill`	Boolean	RW	Specifies whether the height of a `Resizable` node should be adjusted toward that of its layout area, limited by its maximum height
`vgrow`	Priority	RW	Whether the layout area for the node should be expanded vertically when there is unallocated vertical space
`vpos`	VPos	RW	The vertical position of the node within its layout area
`vshrink`	Priority	RW	Whether the layout area for the node should be reduced in height when there is insufficient vertical space
`width`	Number	RW	Overrides the preferred width of a `Resizable` node

Similarly, when insufficient space is available, the layout areas may be reduced in size. This behavior is controlled by the values returned by the `getVGrow()` and `getVShrink()` functions of the `Resizable` node. As with the `getVFill()` function, these values are hard-coded by the implementer of the node concerned, but you can override them by setting the `vgrow` and `vshrink` values of a `LayoutInfo` object. There are similar functions (`getHGrow()` and `getHShrink()`) that control the behavior in the horizontal direction, and a corresponding pair of `LayoutInfo` variables (`hgrow` and `hshrink`).

The following code uses the `vgrow` variable of `LayoutInfo` to change the way in which the layout areas are allocated:

```
1   Stage {
2       var scene:Scene;
3       title : "Layout Areas #2"
4       scene: scene = Scene {
5           width: 200
6           height: 100
7           content: VBox {
8               width: bind scene.width
9               height: bind scene.height
10              padding: Insets { top: 4 left: 4
11                                bottom: 4 right: 4 }
12              spacing: 12
13              nodeVPos: VPos.CENTER
14              nodeHPos: HPos.TRAILING
15              content: [
16                  TextBox {
17                      columns: 15
18                      layoutInfo: LayoutInfo {
19                          vgrow: Priority.SOMETIMES
20                      }
21                  }
22                  TextBox {
23                      columns: 15
24                      layoutInfo: LayoutInfo {
25                          hfill: false
26                          vgrow: Priority.ALWAYS
27                          maxHeight: 100
28                      }
29                  }
30              ]
31          }
32      }
33  }
```

You can see the result of running this code, which you'll find in the file `javafxtransforms/LayoutAreas2.fx`, in Figure 17-32.

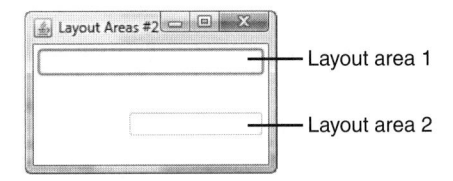

Figure 17-32   Distributing space among layout areas

There are two obvious differences between this example and the previous one, which was shown in Figure 17-31:

- The space occupied by the first layout area is unchanged, but the second layout area has now been allocated all the remaining vertical space in the container.
- The `TextBox` in the second layout area is vertically centered and aligned to the right of that area.

The difference in the allocation of space to layout areas is because of the values assigned to the `vgrow` variables of the `LayoutInfo` objects on lines 19 and 26. There are three possible values for this variable (and for the variables `hgrow`, `vshrink`, and `hshrink`):

- `Priority.NEVER`: The layout area is never grown (or shrunk) when there is too much or too little space available.
- `Priority.SOMETIMES`: The layout area will be grown (or shrunk) only if any additional space cannot all be allocated to layout areas that have the value `Priority.ALWAYS` (and similarly when there is insufficient space).
- `Priority.ALWAYS`: The layout area is always a candidate for distributing additional space (or reclaiming space when there is not enough).

In Figure 17-32, the scene has more vertical space than is required to place both of the `TextBox` controls, and both `LayoutInfo` objects permit space to be allocated to their respective nodes. Because the `vgrow` variable for the second `TextBox` has value `Priority.ALWAYS`, the `VBox` allocates all the extra space to the second layout area. If there were more than one node with this setting, the additional space would have been shared by all of those nodes.

Because the second layout area is larger than the space required for the second `TextBox`, the `VBox` has to decide where to place it within that area. This is determined by the values of the `nodeHPos` and `nodeVPos` variables of the `VBox` class, which are set on lines 13 and 14. As you can see, `nodeHPos` is set to `HPos.TRAILING`, which causes the `TextBox` to placed at the trailing edge of the container, while `nodeVPos` has the value `VPos.CENTER`, which is consistent with the result shown in Figure 17-32.[8] This is not quite the end of the story, however. The `vgrow` variable for the first layout area has value `Priority.SOMETIMES`, which means that it will be allocated extra space only if all the additional vertical space cannot be assigned to areas with value `Priority.ALWAYS`. In the case of this example, the second layout area will receive all the extra space until its height reaches 100 pixels, because of the value of the `maxHeight` variable on line 27. If the scene is resized vertically, you will eventually find that the second layout area will reach this height, at which point any extra vertical space is assigned to the first area, as shown in Figure 17-33.

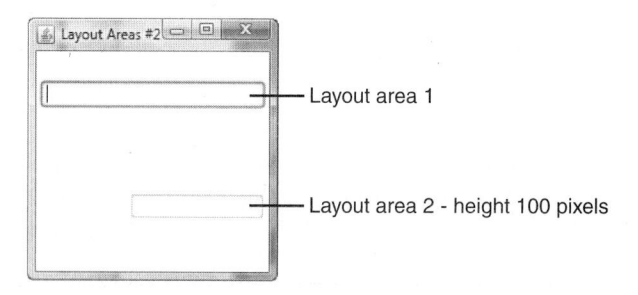

Figure 17-33   Resizing of layout areas

Before we start our discussion of the individual container types, it is worth noting again the difference between the fill and grow/shrink variables:

- The grow/shrink variables determine whether the layout area for a node will be expanded (or contracted) if there is more (or less) space in the container than is needed to place all of its child nodes.
- The fill variables determine whether the node will be expanded or contracted to fit the space allocated to its layout area. These variables have no effect if the node is not `Resizable`. If the node *is* resized, it is always kept within the bounds specified by its minimum and maximum sizes. When the node does not fill its layout area, its

---

[8] As you'll see when we discuss the individual container types in the sections that follow, the `nodeHPos` and `nodeVPos` values are defaults that apply to all the child nodes in the container, but they can be overridden for individual nodes by the `hpos` and `vpos` varaiables of a `LayoutInfo` object.

position within that area is controlled by the `nodeHPos` and `nodeVPos` variables of the container, which may be overridden by the `hpos` and `vpos` variables of a `LayoutInfo` object.

The `Flow` Container

The `Flow` container arranges its child nodes either in rows or columns. If there is insufficient space to place all the nodes into a row or column, those that remain are flowed over into another row or column (hence the name of the container). If you are a Swing developer, you will recognize `Flow` as the JavaFX equivalent of the `FlowLayout` layout manager. The variables that control the behavior of `Flow` are listed in Table 17-8 and are explained in the sections that follow.

Table 17-8 Variables of the `Flow` Class

Variable	Type	Access	Default	Description
vertical	Boolean	RW	false	Determines whether a vertical (`true`) or horizontal (`false`) layout of child `Node`s is required.
padding	Insets	RW	(0, 0, 0, 0)	Empty space to be left around the outside of the container. Use this variable to create an empty border area in which nodes will not be placed.
wrapLength	Number	RW	400	The preferred width for a horizontal `Flow` or preferred height for a vertical `Flow`.
hgap	Number	RW	0	The horizontal gap between `Node`s.
vgap	Number	RW	0	The vertical gap between `Node`s.
hpos	HPos	RW	HPos.LEFT	The overall horizontal alignment of each flow within the width of the container.

548   Chapter 17   Coordinates, Transforms, and Layout

Table 17-8   **Variables of the `Flow` Class** *(Continued)*

Variable	Type	Access	Default	Description
vpos	VPos	RW	VPos.TOP	The overall vertical alignment of each flow within the height of the container.
nodeHPos	HPos	RW	HPos.CENTER	The horizontal alignment of each node within its assigned space. Applies only when `vertical` is `true`.
nodeVPos	VPos	RW	VPos.CENTER	The vertical alignment of each node within its assigned space. Applies only when `vertical` is `false`.

Horizontal and Vertical Flows

A `Flow` container provides either a horizontal or vertical layout depending on the value of the `vertical` variable. By default, it lays out its children in rows, in the order in which they appear in its `content` sequence, giving each node its preferred width and height.[9] The code in Listing 17-1 demonstrates the use of a horizontal `Flow` container to position six `Image` nodes, giving the result shown in Figure 17-34.

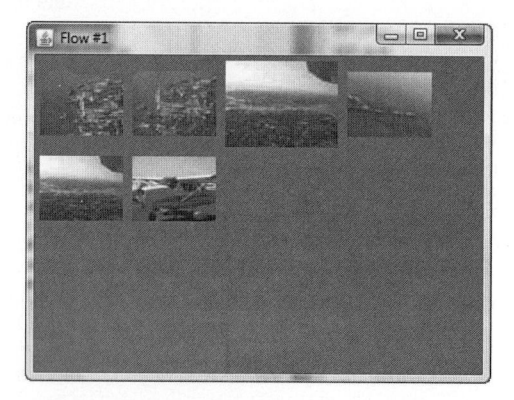

Figure 17-34   A `Flow` container providing a horizontal layout

---

[9] As you'll see later in this section, `Flow` does not grow or shrink layout areas, but it can be instructed to expand `Resizables` horizontally/vertically so that they fill their layout areas.

Listing 17-1   Creating a Horizontal Layout with a `Flow` Container

```
1    var scene:Scene;
2    Stage {
3        title: "Flow #1"
4        width: 400
5        height: 300
6        scene: scene = Scene {
7            fill: Color.GRAY
8            content: [
9                Flow {
10                   width: bind scene.width
11                   height: bind scene.height
12                   padding: Insets { top: 4 left: 4
13                                     bottom: 4 right: 4}
14                   hgap: 8
15                   vgap: 8
16                   content: [
17                       ImageView {
18                        image: Image {url:  "{__DIR__}images/img1.jpg"}
19                       },
20                       ImageView {
21                        image: Image {url:  "{__DIR__}images/img2.jpg"}
22                       },
23                       ImageView {
24                       image: Image {url:  "{__DIR__}images/img3.jpg"}
25                       },
26                       ImageView {
27                       image: Image {url:  "{__DIR__}images/img4.jpg"}
28                       },
29                       ImageView {
30                       image: Image {url:  "{__DIR__}images/img5.jpg"}
31                       },
32                       ImageView {
33                       image: Image {url:  "{__DIR__}images/img6.jpg"}
34                       },
35                   ]
36               }
37           ]
38       }
39   }
```

On lines 10 and 11 of this example, the `width` and `height` variables of the `Flow` are bound to those of its containing scene, which means that it will resize automatically if the stage is resized by the user. As you can see, the nodes are arranged in rows. Because there is not enough room to fit everything into a single row, the last two images are placed on a separate row below the first one. If the width or height of the `Flow` is changed (for example, by resizing the stage), the layout will be recalculated, which may result in nodes being moved between rows or rows being added or removed.

The distance between the nodes in a row is controlled by the `hgap` variable, which, in this case, is set to provide an 8-pixel gap. When more than one row is needed, the distance between rows is determined by the value of the `vgap` variable, which, in this example, is also 8 pixels.

The behavior of the `Flow` container when the `vertical` variable has the value `true` is similar, except that the nodes are arranged in columns rather than rows. The result of making this change to the code in Listing 17-1 is shown in Figure 17-35.

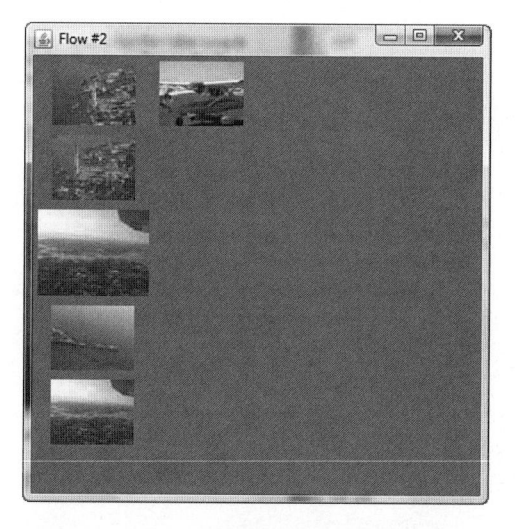

Figure 17-35 A `Flow` container providing a vertical layout

As you can see, there is insufficient space to accommodate all the nodes in one column, so a second one has been created. In the case of a vertical layout, the `vgap` variable controls the vertical distance between nodes in a column, and the `hgap` variable specifies the horizontal distance between successive columns.

Flow Alignment

The `hpos` and `vpos` variables can be used to control how the flows of nodes are aligned relative to the bounds of the `Flow` container. If you look back to Figure 17-34, you'll see that the nodes in the second row, which is not full, are aligned to the left of the container. This is also true of the nodes on the first row, although it is not as obvious because that row is almost full. In a horizontal layout, you can change this alignment by setting the `hpos` variable to one of the values defined by the `javafx.geometry.HPos` class. The default is `HPos.LEFT`, which accounts for the left alignment seen in Figure 17-34. Making

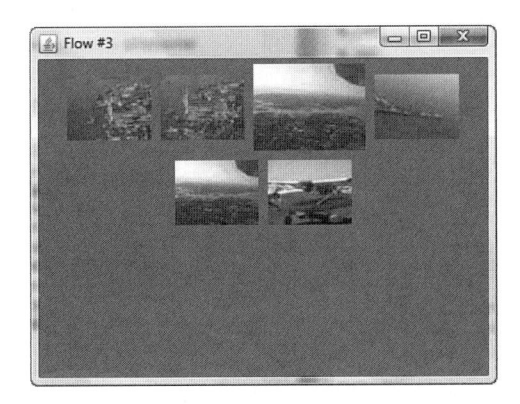

Figure 17-36 Specifying the horizontal flow
alignment for a horizontal flow

the following change to the code in Listing 17-1 causes the content of each row to be center-aligned, as shown in Figure 17-36:

```
Flow {
    width: bind scene.width
    height: bind scene.height
    padding: Insets { top: 4 left: 4
                      bottom: 4 right: 4 }
    hgap: 8
    vgap: 8
    hpos: HPos.CENTER
    content: [
        ImageView {
            image: Image { url: "{__DIR__}images/img1.jpg" }
        },
```

The effect of the values `HPos.LEADING` and `HPos.TRAILING` depend on the reading direction of the user's locale. If the reading direction is left to right, `LEADING` is the same as `LEFT`, and `TRAILING` is the same as `RIGHT`; if it is right to left, `LEADING` equates to `RIGHT`, and `TRAILING` to `LEFT`. Using `LEADING` and `TRAILING` instead of `LEFT` and `RIGHT` makes your application independent of the user's reading direction.

Whereas the `hpos` variable controls the horizontal alignment of the flows in the container, the `vpos` variable determines their vertical position. By default, this variable has the value `VPos.TOP`, which causes the flows to appear at the top of the container, as you can see in Figure 17-36. Changing the value to `VPos.CENTER` or `VPos.BOTTOM` moves the flows to the center or the bottom, respectively. Here, the `vpos` variable is used to move the flows to the bottom of the container:

```
Flow {
    width: bind scene.width
    height: bind scene.height
    padding: Insets { top: 4 left: 4
```

```
                    bottom: 4 right: 4 }
    hgap: 8
    vgap: 8
    hpos: HPos.CENTER
    vpos: VPos.BOTTOM
    content: [
        ImageView {
            image: Image { url: "{__DIR__}images/img1.jpg" }
        },
```

Figure 17-37 shows the result of this change.

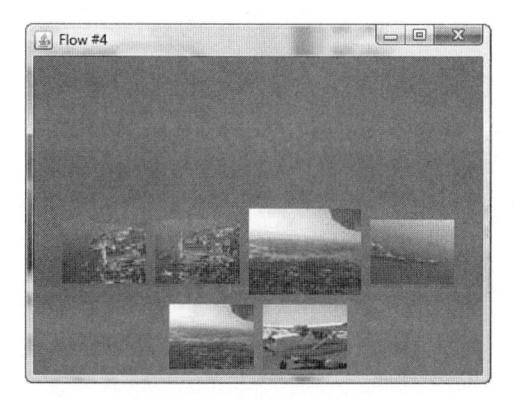

Figure 17-37 Specifying the vertical flow alignment for a horizontal flow

The same variables can be used to control the placement of the flows in a vertical Flow. If you look back at Figure 17-35, you'll see that the default value of the vpos variable, VPos.TOP, causes the images in the partly empty second column to appear at the top of the container, while the default value of hpos results in the two columns of images being placed on its left side. The following code changes vpos to VPos.BOTTOM and hpos to HPos.RIGHT, with the effect shown in Figure 17-38:

```
Flow {
    width: bind scene.width
    height: bind scene.height
    padding: Insets { top: 4 left: 4
                      bottom: 4 right: 4 }
    hgap: 8
    vgap: 8
    vertical: true
    hpos: HPos.RIGHT
    vpos: VPos.BOTTOM
    content: [
```

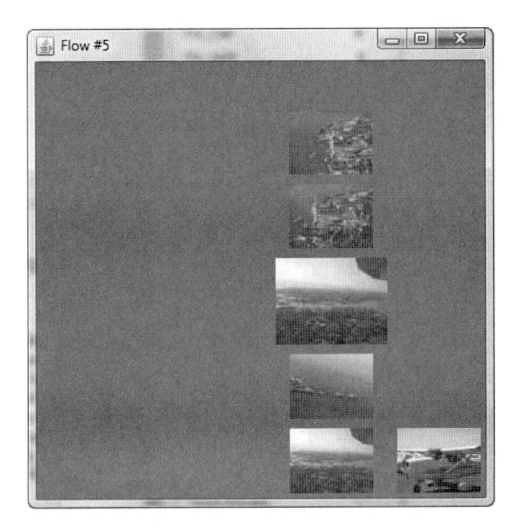

Figure 17-38   Specifying the horizontal and
vertical flow alignment for a vertical flow

Node Alignment

You may have noticed that one of the images that we are using is larger than the others. In Figure 17-36, this is the third image from the left on the top row. As you can see, the images on both rows are placed so that their horizontal centers line up, which has the effect of moving the smaller images on the top row down a little so that they align with the larger one. This behavior is controlled by the `nodeVPos` variable, which has the value `VPos.CENTER` by default. You can force nodes in the same row to instead be top- or bottom-aligned by setting this variable to `VPos.TOP` or `VPos.BOTTOM`, respectively. Here is how one would amend this layout so that the nodes in each row are aligned to the top of the space allocated to the row, with the result shown in Figure 17-39:

```
Flow {
    width: bind scene.width
    height: bind scene.height
    padding: Insets { top: 4 left: 4
                      bottom: 4 right: 4 }
    hgap: 8
    vgap: 8
    hpos: HPos.CENTER
    nodeVPos: VPos.TOP
    content: [
```

Similarly, in a vertical `Flow`, the default behavior is for the vertical centers of the nodes in each column to be aligned, as you can see in the left column of Figure 17-35. You can change this by modifying the value of the `nodeHPos` variable. The following code causes

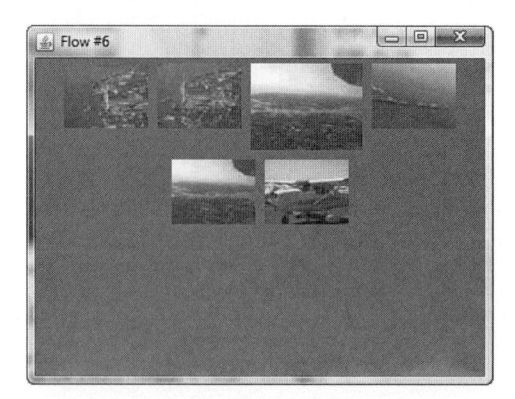

Figure 17-39 Controlling vertical node alignment in a flow

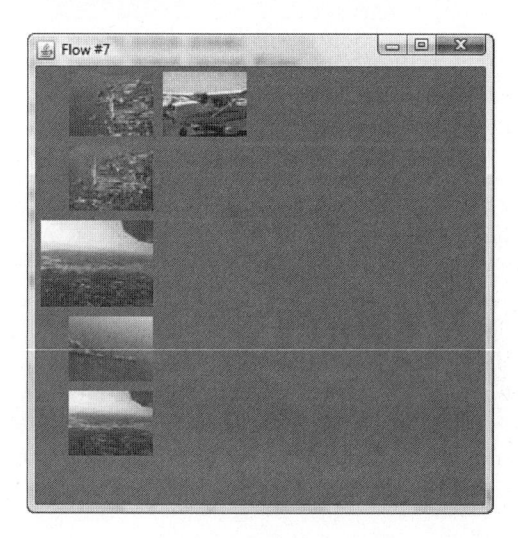

Figure 17-40 Illustrating vertical node alignment in a flow

all the nodes in a column to be right-aligned, as you can see from the result shown in Figure 17-40:

```
Flow {
    width: bind scene.width
    height: bind scene.height
    padding: Insets { top: 4 left: 4
                      bottom: 4 right: 4 }
    hgap: 8
    vgap: 8
    vertical: true
```

```
nodeHPos: HPos.RIGHT
content: [
```

Layout Areas and Node Size

`Flow` does not grow or shrink layout areas, but it can expand a node to fill either the vertical or horizontal space allocated to that node's layout area. In a vertical flow, the height of the layout area for a node is the preferred height of that node, while its width is the width of that node's column (and similarly for a horizontal flow). The node may or may not be expanded horizontally to fit its layout area depending on the value returned by its `getHFill()` function, or the `hfill` variable of its `LayoutInfo` object, if it has one. In all the examples you have seen so far, the node has been an `ImageView`, for which `getHFill()` returns `false`, so the nodes in each vertical flow have been given their preferred widths. The following code replaces the first node in the `Flow`'s content sequence by a `TextBox`, for which the `getHFill()` function returns `true`:

```
Flow {
    width: bind scene.width
    height: bind scene.height
    padding: Insets { top: 4 left: 4
                      bottom: 4 right: 4 }
    hgap: 8
    vgap: 8
    vertical: true
    nodeHPos: HPos.RIGHT
    content: [
        TextBox {
            columns: 2
        }
    },
```

The result of running this code is shown in Figure 17-41.

As you can see, the `TextBox`, which requests space for only two columns of text, has been expanded horizontally to fit the width of its layout column. If this node had been assigned a maximum width that was less than the width of the layout column, it would only have been expanded up to that maximum width, and it would still have been right-aligned within the column. As always, resizing of nodes applies only to `Resizables`—nodes such as `ImageView` are not `Resizable`, and therefore are always given their preferred height and width irrespective of the values of the `hfill` and `vfill` variables.

The `Stack` Container

The `Stack` container attempts to arrange it child nodes so that they have their preferred heights and widths, but, if allowed, will expand a node up to either the size of the container or to its maximum size.. Child nodes are, as with any other container, drawn so that the first child in the `children` sequence is at the back of the stack and the last at the front. This means that children that appear later in the sequence will partly or completely obscure those that appear later.

Figure 17-41 Using the `LayoutInfo hfill` variable in a flow

The layout policy for this container is as follows:

- A node that is not `Resizable` is always given its preferred height and width, even if that would make it larger than the `Stack` itself.
- A node that is `Resizable` and for which either the `getHFill()` function returns `false` or the `hfill` variable of its `LayoutInfo` object (if it has one) is `false` is given its preferred width (and similarly with respect to its height and the `getVFill()` function and `vfill` variable).
- A node that is `Resizable` and for which either the `getHFill()` function returns `true` or the `hfill` variable of its `LayoutInfo` object (if it has one) is `true` is resized up to the smaller of the container width and its own maximum size (and similarly with respect to its height and the `getVFill()` function and `vfill` variable).

If a child node does not cover all the container, then its position within the container will depend on the nodeHPos and nodeVPos values described in Table 17-9.

Table 17-9 Variables of the `Stack` Class

Variable	Type	Access	Default	Description
nodeHPos	HPos	RW	HPos.CENTER	Determines the horizontal position of a `Node` that does not occupy the full width of the container

Node Layout 557

Table 17-9 Variables of the `Stack` Class *(Continued)*

Variable	Type	Access	Default	Description
nodeVPos	VPos	RW	VPos.CENTER	Determines the vertical position of a Node that does not occupy the full height of the container
Padding	Insets	RW	(0, 0, 0, 0)	Empty space around the edges of the container

By default, any child node that doesn't fill the container will be centered within it. Listing 17-2 creates a `Stack` with two children—an image node and a text node. Because neither of these nodes is `Resizable` and both `nodeHPos` and `nodeVPos` have their default values, they are each centered within the container, as shown in Figure 17-42.

Figure 17-42 A stack containing two children with default positioning

Listing 17-2 **A Stack with Default Positioning**

```
var scene:Scene;
Stage {
    title : "Stack #1"
    scene: scene = Scene {
        width: 400
        height: 400
        fill: Color.GRAY
        content: [
```

```
Stack {
    width: bind scene.width
    height: bind scene.height
    content: [
        ImageView {
            image: Image {
                url: "{__DIR__}images/img7.jpg"
            }
        }
        Text {
            font: Font { size: 24 }
            content: "Text overlaid on an Image"
        }
    ]
}
```

This default positioning of child nodes means that `Stack` offers a simple way to arrange for one node to be centered over another. If centering is not what you want, you can change the positioning of all the child nodes by setting the `nodeHPos` and `nodeVPos` variables. The following code causes both the text and the image from the previous example to be right-aligned within the container, as shown in Figure 17-43:

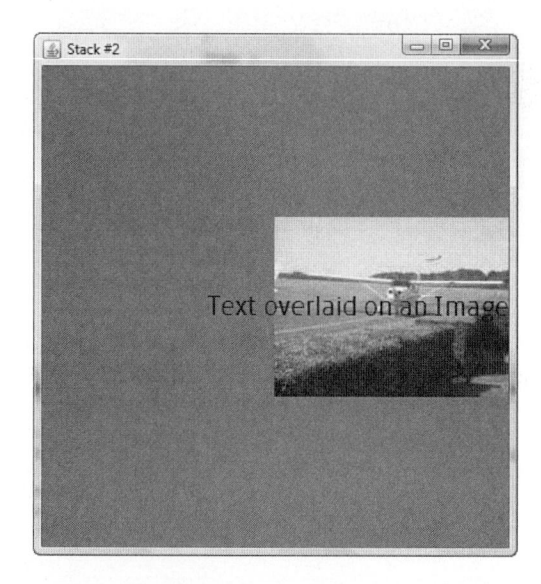

Figure 17-43   A stack containing two children that are right-aligned

```
Stack {
    width: bind scene.width
    height: bind scene.height
    nodeHPos: HPos.RIGHT
    content: [
```

The `nodeHPos` and `nodeVPos` variables apply the same positioning constraints to every child. As with other containers, if you want to left-align some nodes and right-align others, you can do so by using the `hpos` and `vpos` variables of a `LayoutInfo` object.

The `HBox` and `VBox` Containers

The `javafx.scene.layout.HBox` and `javafx.scene.layout.VBox` classes implement a simple layout policy that organizes child nodes in either a horizontal or vertical line. Unlike `Flow`, the nodes in these containers are always arranged in either a single row (for `HBox`) or a single column (for `VBox`)—nodes that do not fit are not wrapped to another row or column.

The `HBox` Container

The `HBox` container arranges its child nodes in a single row. The details of the layout policy can be configured using the variables listed in Table 17-10, most of which should, by now, be familiar to you.

Table 17-10   **Variables of the `HBox` Class**

Variable	Type	Access	Default	Description
fillHeight	Boolean	RW	true	Whether the layout areas should use the whole height of the container
spacing	Number	RW	0	The horizontal gap between adjacent nodes
padding	Insets	RW	(0, 0, 0, 0)	The empty space to be left around the edge of the container
hpos	HPos	RW	HPos.LEFT	The horizontal position of the row within the `HBox`
vpos	VPos	RW	VPos.TOP	The vertical position of the row within the `HBox`

Table 17-10   **Variables of the HBox Class** *(Continued)*

Variable	Type	Access	Default	Description
nodeVPos	VPos	RW	VPos.TOP	The vertical position of the nodes within their layout areas
nodeHPos	HPos	RW	VPos.LEFT	The horizontal position of the nodes within their layout areas

The code in Listing 17-3 creates an HBox containing two images and a ListView, which displays a list of items. All the variables that control the HBox's layout policy have their default values, with the exception of spacing, which is set to provide 4-pixel gaps between nodes. The width and height variables of the HBox are bound to those of the scene so that the HBox resizes with the scene itself.

Listing 17-3   An HBox with Default Positioning

```
var scene:Scene;
Stage {
    title : "HBox #1"
    scene: scene = Scene {
        width: 300
        height: 200
        fill: Color.GRAY
        content: [
            HBox {
                width: bind scene.width
                height: bind scene.height
                spacing: 4
                content: [
                    ImageView {
                        image: Image { url: "{__DIR__}images/img1.jpg" }
                    },
                    ImageView {
                        image: Image { url: "{__DIR__}images/img2.jpg" }
                    },
                    ListView {
                        items: [
                            "First", "Second", "Third"
                        ]
                    }
                ]
            }
        ]
```

                }
            ]
        }
    }
}

You can see the result of running this code on the left of Figure 17-44. As you can see, the nodes are placed in a single row, which is left-justified in and at the top of the HBox. The two images are ImageView objects, which are not Resizable, but the ListView *is* Resizable. As you can see, the HBox has allocated the ImageView objects their preferred sizes and placed them at the top of the container. The rest of the horizontal space has been allocate to the ListView, which has also been sized to match the height of the container. You can see that the ListView expands to occupy any additional space by resizing the scene, as shown on the right of Figure 17-44.

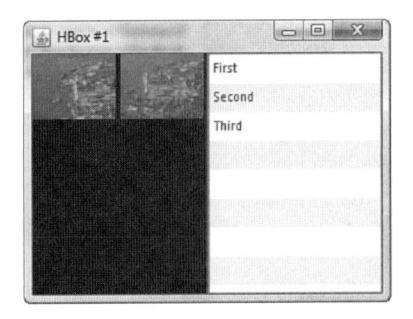

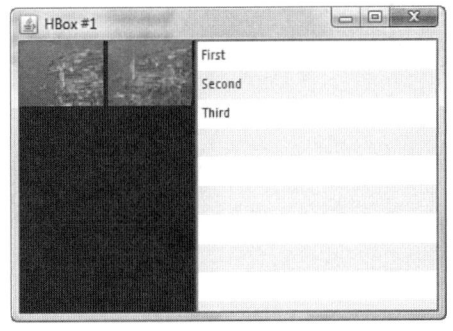

Figure 17-44   An **HBox** container with default settings

The behavior of HBox is similar to that of VBox which we discussed at length earlier in this chapter. For each node, HBox assigns a layout area, which by default matches the node's preferred width and is as tall as the container itself. Any extra horizontal space in the container is then allocated to the layout areas according to the values returned by their getHGrow() and getHShrink() functions or the hgrow and hshrink variables of their LayoutInfo objects. Layout areas occupied by nodes like ImageView that are not Resizable are not adjusted.

The ListView control is Resizable and its getHGrow() function returns true, so its layout area is expanded horizontally to absorb any extra space, as shown on the right of Figure 17-44. The position of a node within its layout area is determined by its nodeHPos and nodeVPos variables or the hpos and vpos variables of its LayoutInfo object.

If the fillHeight variable is set to false, the HBox will not stretch the layout areas to match its own height.

When there is additional vertical space in the container, the vertical position of the row of nodes can be changed by installing a suitable value in the vpos variable. Similarly, if there is unused horizontal space, you can adjust the horizontal alignment of the nodes within the row by using the `hpos` variable. The code shown in Listing 17-4 creates and HBox with three images and aligns the row to the bottom and right of the container.

Listing 17-4   An `HBox` with Custom Node Alignment

```
var scene:Scene;
Stage {
    title : "HBox #2"
    scene: scene = Scene {
        width: 300
        height: 200
        fill: Color.GRAY
        content: [
            HBox {
                width: bind scene.width
                height: bind scene.height
                spacing: 4
                fillHeight: false
                hpos: HPos.RIGHT
                vpos: VPos.BOTTOM
                content: [
                    ImageView {
                        image: Image { url: "{__DIR__}images/img1.jpg" }
                    },
                    ImageView {
                        image: Image { url: "{__DIR__}images/img2.jpg" }
                    },
                    ImageView {
                        image: Image { url: "{__DIR__}images/img3.jpg" }
                    }
                ]
            }
        ]
    }
}
```

The result of running this code is shown in Figure 17-45.

Note that the value of the `vpos` variable is ignored if `fillHeight` is `true` (which is the default), because in that case the height of the row matches the height of the container.

The `VBox` Container

`VBox` is very similar to `HBox`, the difference being that it arranges its child nodes in a single column rather than in a row. The variables that you can use to configure it, which are listed in Table 17-11, are the same as those of `HBox`, apart from the substitution of and `fillWidth` for `fillHeight`.

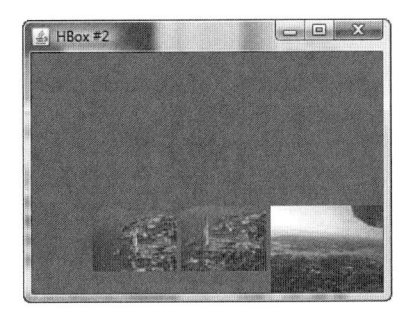

Figure 17-45 Changing the positioning of nodes in an HBox

Table 17-11 Variables of the `VBox` Class

Variable	Type	Access	Default	Description
fillWidth	Boolean	RW	true	Whether the layout areas should use the whole with of the container
spacing	Number	RW	0	The vertical gap between adjacent `Node`s
padding	Insets	RW	(0, 0, 0, 0)	The empty space to be left around the edge of the container
hpos	HPos	RW	HPos.LEFT	The horizontal position of the column within the `HBox`
vpos	VPos	RW	VPos.TOP	The vertical position of the column within the `HBox`
nodeHPos	HPos	RW	HPos.LEFT	The horizontal position of the `Node`s within the column
nodeVPos	VPos	RW	HPos.TOP	The vertical position of the `Node`s withing the column

Because you have already seen several examples of the layout policy of `VBox` in the "Containers and Layout" section, earlier in this chapter, we don't discuss it any further here.

The `Tile` Container

The `Tile` container allocates its available space to *tiles* of equal size and places its child nodes within those tiles. It is superficially similar to the Abstract Window Toolkit (AWT) `GridLayout` but in reality is quite different. The variables that control the behavior of this container are listed in Table 17-12 and are discussed in detail in the sections that follow.

Table 17-12 **Variables of the `Tile` Class**

Variable	Type	Access	Default	Description
autoSizeTiles	Boolean	RW	True	Automatically calculates the size of the tiles based on the preferred sizes of the nodes. If `false`, uses the fixed `tileHeight` and `tileWidth` values instead.
vertical	Boolean	RW	false	Whether tiles should be laid out from top to bottom (`true`) or left to right (`false`).
padding	Insets	RW	(0, 0, 0, 0)	The empty space to be left around the edge of the container.
hgap	Number	RW	0	The horizontal gap between tiles.
vgap	Number	RW	0	The vertical gap between tiles.
tileHeight	Number	RW		The height to use for each tile. Used only if `autoSizeTiles` is `false`.
tileWidth	Number	RW		The width to use for each tile. Used only if `autoSizeTiles` is `false`.
rows	Number	RW		The number of rows to use in the preferred size calculation.
columns	Number	RW		The number of columns to use in the preferred size calculation.
hpos	HPos	RW	HPos.LEFT	The horizontal position of the rows within the container.
vpos	VPos	RW	VPos.TOP	The vertical position of the columns within the container.
nodeHPos	HPos	RW	HPos.CENTER	The horizontal position of each node within its tile.
nodeVPos	VPos	RW	VPos.CENTER	The vertical position of each node within its tile.

In trying to understand how the `Tile` container works, it is important to separate its behavior when computing its preferred size from what happens when it is actually laying out its child nodes. If you don't keep these two phases separate in your mind, the results that you get could be quite confusing. You'll see the calculations that are performed in each of these two phases and how they are controlled by the variables in Table 17-12 in the examples that follow. For the sake of simplicity, we will initially assume that the `hpos`, `vpos`, `nodeHPos`, and `nodeVPos` variables have their default values.

Default Behavior of the `Tile` Container

The simplest way to use `Tile` is to add the nodes that you want to display to its `content` variable and add the `Tile` to the scene. The code in Listing 17-5 demonstrates the default behavior of the `Tile` container with five image children, all the same size.

Listing 17-5 **Using the `Tile` Container**

```
Stage {
    title : "Tile #1"
    scene: Scene {
        fill: Color.GRAY
        content: [
            Tile {
                hgap: 2
                vgap: 2
                content: [
                    ImageView {
                        image: Image {
                            url: "{__DIR__}images/img1.jpg"
                        }
                    }
                    ImageView {
                        image: Image {
                            url: "{__DIR__}images/img2.jpg"
                        }
                    }
                    ImageView {
                        image: Image {
                            url: "{__DIR__}images/img4.jpg"
                        }
                    }
                    ImageView {
                        image: Image {
                            url: "{__DIR__}images/img5.jpg"
                        }
                    }
                    ImageView {
                        image: Image {
                            url: "{__DIR__}images/img6.jpg"
```

```
                    }
                  }
                ]
              }
            ]
          }
        }
}
```

In this example, only the `hgap` and `vgap` variables do not have their default values. Because the `vertical` variable has not been set, the `Tile` container will lay out its children horizontally, as shown at the top of Figure 17-46.

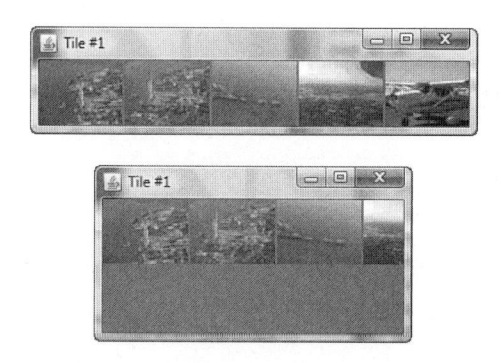

Figure 17-46 A `Tile` container with horizontal layout and one row

As you can see, the image nodes have been placed in a single row, and the stage has been sized so that they are all visible. A single row is used because the layout is horizontal and none of the `rows`, `columns`, `width`, or `height` variables has been set. You'll see the effect of setting some or all these variables in the sections that follow. The space allocated to each node, referred as the *tile size*, is calculated so that it can accommodate all the nodes in the container—the tile width is the largest preferred width of all the child nodes, and its height is the largest preferred height. In this example, the nodes are all images of the same size. As you'll see later, it is possible to override this calculation and set an explicit tile width/height.

Given the tile width and height and the number of nodes to be placed, the `Tile` container calculates its own width and height and installs them in its `width` and `height` variables. These values are used by the scene to determine its own size, which in turn influences the size of the stage.

If you resize the stage, you might expect that the image nodes would be moved around to occupy the space available, but this is not the case, as you can see in the screenshot at the bottom of Figure 17-44. Despite the fact that the stage has been made narrower and taller so that there is now insufficient space to show all the images in a single row, nothing has been moved to the vacant space. This is because there is no relationship between the size of the scene and that of the `Tile` container and, as a result, neither the width nor the height of the container has been changed. If you want to have the container rearrange its content when the size of the stage changes, you have to arrange for its width/height to change at the same time, which you typically do by binding these variables to the `width` and `height` variables of the scene. You'll see the effect of this in a later section.

You get a similar effect if you set the `vertical` variable to `true`, as shown in the following code extract. This causes the images to be laid out in a single column instead of a row, as you can see in Figure 17-47:

```
Tile {
    hgap: 2
    vgap: 2
    vertical: true
    content: [
```

Figure 17-47 A Tile container with vertical layout and one column

In this case, the stage is slightly wider than it needs to be to accommodate the images, because the host operating system (Windows Vista) needs enough space to be able to draw the controls in the title bar of the window. Although it is not possible to see this from the screenshot, the `Tile` container is only wide enough to fit the images themselves, so the space to the right of the `Images` is occupied by the scene, not the `Tile`.

Specifying Rows and Columns

If you specify the number of rows or columns to use, this information is used both to calculate the preferred height/width of the `Tile` container and when laying out its child nodes. You need only specify one of the `row` and `columns` values—the other one will be calculated based on the number of nodes to be laid out. In fact, only one of these values will be used, depending on whether you want horizontal or vertical tiling:

- If `vertical` is `true`, the `rows` value is used, and the `columns` value is calculated and overwritten.
- If `vertical` is `false`, the `columns` value is used, and the `rows` value is calculated and overwritten.

The following code creates a vertical `Tile` and specifies that its children should be organized into two rows. The result of running this code with the same images used in previous examples is shown on the left of Figure 17-48:

```
Tile {
    hgap: 2
    vgap: 2
    rows: 2
    vertical: true
    content: [
```

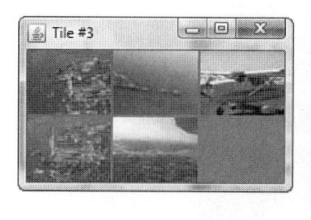

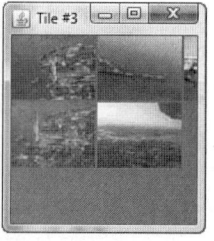

Figure 17-48 A `Tile` with vertical layout and a specified number of rows

Because there are five child nodes and two rows have been requested, the `Tile` organizes them into three columns, working vertically from top to bottom so that the first node in the `content` sequence is at top left, the second immediately below it, the third at the top of the second column, and so on. You can see that the size of the `Tile` has been set to exactly match the space required for this arrangement. Resizing the stage does not cause the `Tile` to change its layout based on the new size because, as before, its width and height are not bound to those of the stage. Therefore, as you can see on the right of Figure 17-48, the layout will be clipped if there is insufficient space to display everything.

Specifying Width and Height

If you specify the `width`/`height` of the `Tile` container, the `rows` and `columns` variables are no longer used to determine the layout. Instead, the container calculates and sets the values of the `rows` and `columns` variables as follows:

- If `vertical` is `false` and the container `width` is specified, the number of columns is calculated based on the tile width, the size of the horizontal gap, and the specified width. The number of rows is calculated from the column count and the number of nodes in the content sequence. In this case, the height value, if it is specified, does not affect the layout.

- If vertical is true and the container height is specified, the number of rows is calculated based on the tile height, the size of the vertical gap, and the specified height. The number of columns is calculated from the row count and the number of nodes in the content sequence. The width value, if it is set, does not affect the layout.

In the following example of a horizontal Tile container, the width, row, and column variables are all assigned values. The width variable is bound to the value of the width variable of the enclosing scene so that the effect of resizing can be seen:

```
Tile {
    hgap: 2
    vgap: 2
    rows: 8
    columns: 1
    width: bind scene.width
    vertical: false
    content: [
```

The result of running this code with the same set of images as we have been using in all the examples in this section is shown on the left of Figure 17-49.

Figure 17-49 The effect of setting the width variable on a horizontal **Tile** container

As you can see, the images have been arranged into two columns and three rows. Because this is a horizontal layout and the value of the width variable has been set, the number of columns is calculated based on the number of tiles that fit into the space available, and then the row count is set accordingly. The rows and columns values in the object literal are ignored, and the computed values are stored instead.

If you resize the stage, you will find that that the Tile recalculates the column count. This can be seen on the right of Figure 17-49, where the stage, and hence the scene, has been made wide enough for three columns instead of the initial two. Notice also that the stage height has been reduced so that it is smaller than the vertical extent of the Tile, with the result that its content is clipped.

Specifying Tile Size

By default, the tile size is calculated based on the sizes of all the `Tile`'s child nodes. You can override this behavior by setting the values of the `tileWidth`/`tileHeight` variables and also setting `autoSizeTiles` to `false`. The following code forces the tiles to be 100 pixels square. You can see the result of this in Figure 17-50:

```
Tile {
    width: bind scene.width
    height: bind scene.height
    hgap: 2
    vgap: 2
    autoSizeTiles: false
    tileWidth: 100
    tileHeight: 100
    content: [
```

Figure 17-50   Changing the tile size of a `Tile` container

Adjusting Horizontal and Vertical Positioning

The `hpos` and `vpos` variables allow you to control how the tiled area is positioned within the `Tile` container itself. By default, it is aligned to the top and left of the container, as the examples that you have seen in this section have shown. The following code moves the tiled area to the bottom right of the container, as you can see in Figure 17-51:

```
Tile {
    width: bind scene.width
    height: bind scene.height
    hgap: 2
    vgap: 2
```

```
   autoSizeTiles: false
   tileWidth: 100
   tileHeight: 100
   hpos: HPos.RIGHT
   vpos: VPos.BOTTOM
   content: [
```

Figure 17-51   Changing the horizontal and vertical positioning of the tiled area

When a Node is smaller than the tile that has been created for it, its position within that Tile is controlled by the nodeHPos and nodeVPos variables. By default, a node is centered within its tile. The following modification to the preceding example causes each node to be placed at the bottom right of its tile:

```
Tile {
   width: bind scene.width
   height: bind scene.height
   hgap: 2
   vgap: 2
   autoSizeTiles: false
   tileWidth: 100
   tileHeight: 100
   hpos: HPos.RIGHT
   vpos: VPos.BOTTOM
   nodeHPos: HPos.RIGHT
   nodeVPos: VPos.BOTTOM
   content: [
```

You can see the result of this modification by comparing the result of running it, shown in Figure 17-52, with the default positioning in Figure 17-51.

Figure 17-52 Changing the positions of node within their tiles

In the case of a `Resizable` node, the container will resize it up to the smaller of its maximum width (height) and the width (height) of its tile if the node's `getHFill()` method (`getVFill()` method) returns `true` or the `hfill` (`vfill`) variable of its `LayoutInfo` object is `true`.

The `Panel` Container

The `Panel` container does not implement a layout policy. Instead, it allows you to implement a layout policy of your own by supplying functions that are called when determining the container's size and when laying out its content. We cover the `Panel` class as part of our discussion of custom layouts in Chapter 25.

Setting the Fill Color for a Container

The `Container` class does not have a `fill` variable, so you can't easily fill its background with a solid color or gradient. However, you can get the same effect by adding a rectangle to its `content` sequence and setting the `fill` variable of that rectangle. For this to work, the rectangle must be the first item in the container's `content` sequence (so that all the other nodes are drawn in front of it), it must be placed at the origin of the container, and its `width` and `height` must be bound to those of the container.

This sounds simple, but there is a problem: By default, the container will move and resize the rectangle according to its layout policy! For example, if the rectangle were the added to a `Tile`, it would simply appear as one of the tiles in the layout. To stop this from happening, you need to exclude the rectangle from the container's layout policy by using the `managed` variable that the `Rectangle` class inherits from `Node`. The code in Listing 17-6 shows how to do this.

Listing 17-6 Filling the Background of a Container

```
1    var scene:Scene;
2    Stage {
3        title : "Tile #9"
4        scene: scene = Scene {
5            width: 400
6            height: 200
7            fill: Color.BLACK
8            var t:Tile;
9            content: [
10                t = Tile {
11                    hgap: 5
12                    vgap: 5
13                    width: bind scene.width
14                    height: bind scene.height
15                    content: [
16                        Rectangle {
17                            fill: LinearGradient {
18                                startX: 0.0 endX: 1.0
19                                startY: 0.0 endY: 0.0
20                                stops: [
21                                    Stop { offset: 0.0
22                                           color: Color.LIGHTGRAY }
23                                    Stop { offset: 1.0
24                                           color: Color.GREY }
25                                ]
26                            }
27                            managed: false
28                            width: bind t.width
29                            height: bind t.height
30                        }
31                        ImageView {
32                            image: Image {
33                                url: "{__DIR__}images/img1.jpg"
34                            }
35                        }
36                        ImageView {
37                            image: Image {
38                                url: "{__DIR__}images/img2.jpg"
39                            }
40                        }
41                        ImageView {
42                            image: Image {
43                                url: "{__DIR__}images/img4.jpg"
44                            }
45                        }
46                        ImageView {
```

```
47                          image: Image {
48                              url: "{__DIR__}images/img5.jpg"
49                          }
50                      }
51                      ImageView {
52                          image: Image {
53                              url: "{__DIR__}images/img6.jpg"
54                          }
55                      }
56                  ]
57              }
58          ]
59      }
60  }
```

In this example, the container whose background we want to fill is a `Tile` containing five images. The size of the `Tile` is bound to that of its enclosing scene so that it grows and shrinks as the stage is resized. The rectangle containing the background fill is added to the `Tile`'s `content` sequence on lines 16 to 32. As you can see, it is the first element in the sequence, and its size is bound to that of the `Tile`. The most important part of this code is line 27, which sets the `managed` variable of this object to `false`, which excludes it from the layout policy of the container, with the result that the `Tile` will not attempt to changes its size or position. You can see the result in Figure 17-53.

Figure 17-53   Using an unmanaged rectangle to provide a background for a `Tile` container

The `ClipView` Node

`ClipView` manages a single child, displaying all or part of it, depending on the relative sizes of the child and the `ClipView`. If the child is larger than the `ClipView`, only a portion of it will be visible at any given time. By varying the values of the `clipX` and `clipY` variables of the `ClipView`, it is possible to make it behave as a moving window through which a part of its child node can be seen. If the `ClipView` is *pannable* (which it is, by default), the user can use the mouse to move the `ClipView` window and therefore bring a different region of the child node into view. Unlike the other classes in this section, `ClipView` is a custom node, not a container.

The variables of the `ClipView` class are listed in Table 17-13.

Table 17-13 **Variables of the `ClipView` Class**

Variable	Type	Access	Default	Description
node	Node	RW		The node to be displayed by the `ClipView`
clipX	Number	RW	0	The x coordinate of the location in the child node that will be placed at the top left of the `ClipView`
clipY	Number	RW	0	The y coordinate of the location in the child node that will be placed at the top left of the `ClipView`
pannable	Boolean	RW	true	Whether the user can move the `ClipView` window over the child node
maxClipX	Number	R		The largest possible value of `clipX`
maxClipY	Number	R		The largest possible value of `clipY`

Listing 17-7 shows a typical example of the use of the `ClipView` class.

Listing 17-7 **Using the `ClipView` Class**

```
1    var scene:Scene;
2    def margin = 10;
3    Stage {
4        title : "ClipView #1"
5        scene: scene = Scene {
6            width: 200
7            height: 200
8            fill: Color.BLACK
9            content: [
10               ClipView {
11                   layoutX: margin
12                   layoutY: margin
13                   width: bind scene.width - 2 * margin
14                   height: bind scene.height - 2 * margin
15                   node: ImageView {
```

```
16                          image: Image {
17                              url: "{__DIR__}images/Portsmouth.JPG"
18                          }
19                      }
20                  }
21              ]
22          }
23      }
```

This code creates a `ClipView` width of a child `ImageView` containing an image that is much larger than the `ClipView` itself. The `ClipView` is placed in the scene with its top corner at coordinates (10, 10) and sized so that there is a 10-pixel margin around it. Notice that the `ClipView` is placed by using the `layoutX` and `layoutY` variables instead of `translateX` and `translateY`. As noted earlier in this chapter, this is the conventional way to apply layout positioning to a node. You can see the result of this code on the left of Figure 17-54.

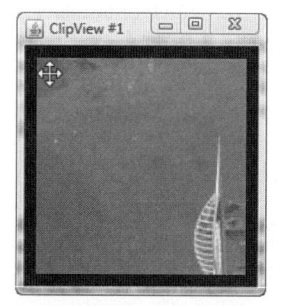

Figure 17-54   Illustrating the `ClipView` class

As you can see the `ClipView` acts as a window on the image. Because panning is enabled by default, when the mouse is moved over the `ClipView`, the cursor is changed to indicate that the user can drag the underlying node so that a different part of it is visible.[10] You can see the result of dragging the image on the right of Figure 17-54. The panning effect is achieved by adjusting the values of the `clipX` and `clipY` variables by the amount by which the mouse is dragged. When the `pannable` variable is `true`, this is done automatically by the `ClipView` class. Application code can also change the position of the `ClipView` window by modifying these variables. This works whatever the value of the `pannable` variable is.

The `maxClipX` and `maxClipY` variables always contain the maximum legal values for `clipX` and `clipY`, respectively. If an attempt is made to set `clipX` to a negative value, it is

---

[10] The cursor might not change on mobile devices; refer to the discussion of cursors in Chapter 15, "Node Variables and Events."

forced to 0, and similarly if the value assigned to `clipX` is greater than `maxClipX`, it is forced to be `maxClipX`. Similar checks are applied to `clipY`. Because this happens automatically, application code does not usually need to be concerned about the actual values of `maxClipX` and `maxClipY` when setting the `clipX` or `clipY` variables.

In the example in Listing 17-7, the width of the `ClipView` is 180 pixels, and the width of the image being displayed is 500 pixels, so the value of `maxClipX` will be (500 − 180) or 320. This value ensures that the user (or application code) can move the image until its right side is at the right edge of the `ClipView`, but no further. If the stage is widened, the width of the `ClipView` will also increase, and `maxClipX` will decrease by the same amount.

Centering Nodes

One of the things you will probably need to do quite frequently is to place one node so that it is centered over another and then remains centered over it even when the other node is moved or resized. You can see a typical example of this in Figure 17-55, which shows a text node object that is centered on a rectangle. Placing the text object properly is a matter of determining the appropriate values for its `layoutX` and `layoutY` values because, as you already know, layout is conventionally performed by setting these variables.

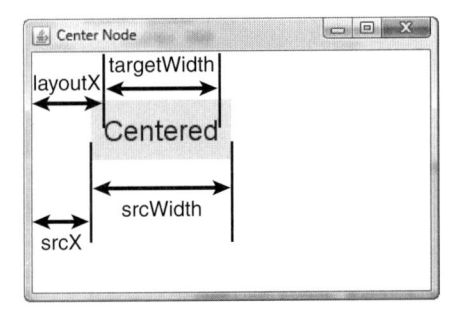

Figure 17-55 Centering a node over another node

With regard to the annotations in Figure 17-55, the problem is to determine the distance shown as `layoutX` value. The problem of calculating the correct value for `layoutY` is similar, so we don't discuss that here.

It should be clear from the diagram that the correct value for `layoutX` can be obtained by adding to the x position of the rectangle (shown as `srcX`) the value of the expression (`srcWidth - targetWidth`)/2. So, how do we get these values? As you have already seen, several functions would return the bounds of the rectangle, from which we can get the values for `srcX` and `srcWidth`. Which of these bounds should we use? It is not appropriate to use the local bounds because that does not take into account any transformation that might be applied to the rectangle. Nor should we use the scene bounds because, in the general case, the nodes in question might be parented by a group nested within the scene, not by the scene itself. The correct bounds to use are the parent bounds because these represent what you see on the screen.

Chapter 17 Coordinates, Transforms, and Layout

What about getting the bounds of the text object, from which we can obtain `targetWidth`? One possible answer is to use the parent bounds again. This approach would work, but convention dictates that we use the node's *layout bounds* instead.

As you have already seen, the layout bounds, which can be obtained from the `layoutBounds` variable, are the bounds that a node has *before* any of the clips, effects, or transforms in its `transforms` variable or those implied by its `scaleX`, `scaleY`, `translateX`, `translateY`, `translateZ`, and `rotate` variables have been applied. If it seems strange to you that we choose to use the bounds before transformations have been applied (as do all the standard container classes), the reason is that if you use the layout bounds to determine where to place the node, you can then apply transforms to scale, rotate, or shear it relative to its default location. One application of this is to make the node expand slightly when the mouse moves over it and return to its original size when the mouse leaves.

Given all of this, the following code creates and positions the rectangle and text nodes:

```
1   var scaleX = 1.0;
2   var scaleY = 1.0;
3   var angle = 0;
4   var timeline:Timeline;
5   Stage {
6       title: "Center Node"
7       scene: Scene {
8           width: 340
9           height: 200
10          var rect:Rectangle;
11          var text:Text;
12          content: [
13              rect = Rectangle {
14                  x: 50 y: 40 width: 120 height: 50
15                  fill: Color.YELLOW
16                  transforms: bind Scale {
17                      x: scaleX y: scaleY
18                      pivotX: 50 pivotY: 50
19                  }
20                  onMousePressed: function(evt) {
21                      timeline.play();
22                  }
23              },
24              text = Text {
25                  content: "Centered"
26                  font: Font { size: 24 }
27                  layoutX: bind centerX(rect, text);
28                  layoutY: bind centerY(rect, text);
29                  rotate: bind angle
30              }
31          ]
32      }
33  }
```

The rectangle is created on lines 13 to 23. As you can see, its `transforms` variable includes a `Scale` transform that is bound to the values of two script variables. We will use these variables later to cause the rectangle to expand, which should cause the text node to move so that it remains centered over it.

The code that places the text object is on lines 27 and 28. As noted earlier, we follow the convention of using the `layoutX` and `layoutY` variables to move the node to its correct position. In this case, the calculation of these values is delegated to two bound functions that take as arguments the rectangle and the text object. You can also see that on line 29 the `rotate` variable of the text object is bound to another script variable. Again, we will use this later to observe the effect of a rotation on the positioning of the text.

The interesting code is in the bound functions, which are almost identical. Here is the function that calculates the `layoutX` value:

```
1    bound function centerX(src:Node, target:Node):Number {
2        var srcX = src.boundsInParent.minX;
3        var srcWidth = src.boundsInParent.width;
4        var targetX = target.layoutBounds.minX;
5        var targetWidth = target.layoutBounds.width;
6        return srcX + (srcWidth - targetWidth) / 2 - targetX;
7    }
```

In this function, the source node is the rectangle, and the target node is the one to be positioned—in this case, the text object. As you can see, the `srcX` and `srcWidth` values shown in Figure 17-54 are obtained from the parent bounds of the rectangle, whereas `targetX` and `targetWidth` come from the layout bounds of the target node. The return value is simply calculated as described earlier. Because this is a bound function, this value will be recalculated when any of its dependencies change, which will be the case whenever the bounds of the rectangle or the text node changes. As a result of this, the `layoutX` and `layoutY` values of the text node will be changed automatically to keep it centered over the rectangle.

To demonstrate that this works, run the example code (which you'll find in the file `javafxtransforms/CenterNode.fx` in the JavaFX Book GUI project) and click the rectangle. This causes the script variables that you saw earlier to be animated so that the rectangle expands in both directions and then contracts to its original size. At the same time, the text node rotates around its center. You should observe that the center of the text node is always over the center of the rectangle, as shown in Figure 17-56.

SnowStorm Revisited

The SnowStorm example that you saw in Chapter 4 works well on the desktop or on a mobile device that has a small screen. However, to keep the code simple, it does not cater for all possibilities. In particular, it does not work very well when on a device that has a screen that is larger in either direction than the background image, as you can see in Figure 17-57.

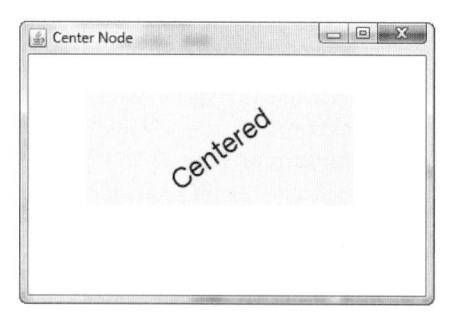

580   Chapter 17 Coordinates, Transforms, and Layout

Figure 17-56   Effect of scaling the target rectangle and rotating the `Text` node

Figure 17-57   Running the SnowStorm example on a mobile device with a high-resolution screen

The high-resolution screen of the device used here (which is actually the first JavaFX developer phone on the market) is taller than the background image, with the result that the image is anchored to the top, leaving an ugly white area below. In addition, although you can't actually see this, the snowflakes float all the way to the bottom of the screen before being removed, so for about half of their lifecycle, they are not visible and simply consume memory resource, and the CPU resource required to move them. With the extra knowledge that you have gained over the past few chapters, you can easily fix both of these problems.

> **Note**
>
> You can find the modified source code for this example in the file
> `javafxexample2/SnowStorm.fx` in the JavaFX Book Intro project.

Placing the Background Image

Fixing the problem of the background image is easy. We could either scale it, preserving its aspect ratio, or center it on the screen and fill the rest of the screen with black. Scaling it might work for some devices, but doubling its size is likely to give a blurred result, so we'll leave it at its original size and center it on the screen instead.

If you refer back to Chapter 4, you'll see that the user interface for this example consists of an `ImageView` node, a text node, and a number of circles that are added and removed from the scene as required. The `ImageView` is placed at the top of the scene and the text object at the bottom. To make this example work on any size of screen, we need to use the `layoutX` and `layoutY` values of the `ImageView` object so that it is centered on the scene. This is quite easy to do. The code changes required are shown in Listing 17-8, which you should compare with Listing 4-1 in Chapter 4.

Listing 17-8 *Modifying SnowStorm to Center the Background Image*

```
1    // The background image
2    def image:Image = Image {
3                url: "{__DIR__}SnowScene.png"
4            };
5
6    // The ImageView that holds the background image
7    var imageView:ImageView;
8
9    Stage {
10       title: "JavaFX Snow Storm 2"
11       resizable: true
12       scene: scene = Scene {
13           width: image.width
14           height: image.height
15           fill: Color.BLACK
16           content: [
17               imageView = ImageView {
18                   layoutX: bind (scene.width - image.width) / 2
19                   layoutY: bind (scene.height - image.height) / 2
20                   image: image
21               },
22               Text {
23                   x: 25
24                   y: bind scene.height - 10
25                   font: Font {
26                       size: 20
```

```
27                        }
28                        fill: Color.YELLOW
29                        content: bind "Snowflakes: {sizeof snowflakes}"
30                    }
31                ]
32            }
33    }
```

Several changes have been made to this code. First, we have extracted the image object and assigned it to variable that we can reference elsewhere, as shown on lines 2 to 4. Second, we have also created a variable that we can use to refer to the `ImageView`. You'll see how this is used in the next section. We also set the initial size of the scene so that it matches that of the image, and we set its fill to black. On the desktop, the scene size will be honored, but on a mobile device, it will not. (As you know, the size of the stage is determined by that of the screen, so the size of the scene will be determined accordingly, independently of the values that we set here for its `width` and `height` variables.) We have also made the stage resizable because we no longer need to constrain it to exactly the size needed to contain the image. Finally, the color of the text has been changed to yellow so that it can be seen against both a black and a white background.

The code that centers the image on the scene is shown on lines 18 and 19. All we need to do is set the `layoutX` and `layoutY` variables so that the center of the `ImageView` is over the center of the scene. It should be obvious how this code works.

Placing and Animating the Snow

The original implementation assumed that the background image covered the whole screen. The code relies on this in several places:

- When adding snow, it works out how many snowflakes to add based on the width of the scene.
- The snowflakes are always placed at the top of the scene, which may no longer coincide with the top of the image.
- As the snowflakes move, a small amount of sideways motion is added at random. This may cause a snowflake to move off the screen for a while. This is not an issue when the background image covers the whole screen, but if it does not, the snowflakes may wander out to the margin area to the left or right of the image.
- The snowflakes are not removed until they reach the bottom of the scene, which could be a long time after they move out of the area occupied by the background image.

To solve all these problems, we need to know the actual bounds of the image relative to the scene. In fact, we need to know the bounds of the part of the scene that is actually occupied by the image. With this knowledge, we can adjust all the logic that implements the placement, movement, and removal of the snowflakes so that it uses only the bounds of this area rather than the bounds of the whole scene.

We can get the bounds of the `ImageView` relative to the scene from its `boundsInParent` variable, because the scene is the parent of the `ImageView`. Once we have this, we can adjust it to get the bounds of the part of this area that is within the scene. Remember that the image may be taller, shorter, wider, or narrower than the scene, so its bounds may be larger are smaller. We can encapsulate the logic that determines the bounds of this area, relative to the scene, in a bound function, like this:

```
1     // Gets the bounds of the area occupied by the snow
2     bound function getSnowBounds():Bounds {
3         var imageBounds = imageView.boundsInParent;
4         var bounds = BoundingBox {
5             width: Math.min(scene.width, imageBounds.width)
6             height: Math.min(scene.height, imageBounds.height)
7             minX: Math.max(0, imageBounds.minX)
8             minY: Math.max(0, imageBounds.minY)
9         }
10    }
```

The code on line 3 gets the bounds of the `ImageView` relative to the scene. The rest of the code adjusts these bounds so that they represent the intersection of this area with the scene itself. As an example of why this is necessary, assume that the scene is 400 pixels wide. The image is 500 pixels across and is centered on the scene, so its x coordinate relative to the scene will be -50. The code on line 7 above corrects this so that the x coordinate of the bounded area is 0 instead of -50. Similarly, line 5 adjusts the width so that the bounded area is no larger than the scene itself, which in this case will be 400 pixels.

> **Note**
> This code uses the `min()` and `max()` functions provided by the `javafx.util.Math` class. There are similar functions in the `java.lang.Math` class, but these are not available on mobile devices. Portability requires that we use the `Math` class in the `javafx.util` package instead.

Now that we have the correct bounds of the area in which we can place the snow, we can fix the other problems. First, we need to remove any snow that we have added if the bounds of the snow area change, which would happen if the user were to resize the top-level window on the desktop. We can do this easily by triggering on changes to the bounds:

```
def imageBounds:Bounds = bind getSnowBounds() on replace {
    removeSnow();
}
```

The `removeSnow()` function simply removes all the nodes that represent the snow from the scene and then clears the snowflakes sequence, which has a copy of these nodes:

```
// Removes all snow.
function removeSnow():Void {
    for (snowflake in snowflakes) {
        delete snowflake from scene.content;
```

```
        }
        snowflakes = [];
}
```

In the following sections, we'll also use the value of the `imageBounds` variable to fix the other problems previously listed.

Initial Placement of Snow

Snow is added to the scene in the `addNewSnow()` function. In the original implementation, the number of snowflakes added depended on the width of the scene, and new snowflakes, which are circles, were always added with their `centerY` values set to `0`, which caused them to appear at the top of the scene. Here's the modified version of this function:

```
1   function addNewSnow() {
2       var sectionWidth =
3           (imageBounds.width + snowflakesPerLine - 1) / snowflakesPerLine;
4       for (i in [0..<snowflakesPerLine]) {
5           var x = sectionWidth * i + rand.nextInt(sectionWidth);
6           var snowflake = Circle {
7               centerX: imageBounds.minX + x
8               centerY: imageBounds.minY
9               radius: snowflakeRadius
10              cache: true
11              fill: Color.WHITE
12          }
13          insert snowflake into scene.content;
14          insert snowflake into snowflakes;
15      }
16  }
```

The code on lines 2 and 3 determine the width of the sections within which the snowflakes are created—one is created in each section. Originally, the section width depended on the scene width, but here it depends on the width of the snow area, which may be less than that of the scene.

The positioning of each new snowflake has also been changed. As you can see on lines 7 and 8, the `centerX` and `centerY` variables of the circle object that represents the snowflake are now offset by the bounds of the snow area. This ensures that we do not create new snowflakes offscreen if the image is wider than the scene, or in the margin area outside the image if it is narrower.

Snow Movement and Removal

Movement of the snow is implemented in the `moveSnow()` function. Here is the modified version of this function, which you should compare with the original in Listing 4-1.

```
1   function moveSnow() {
2       for (snowflake in snowflakes) {
3           // Move the snowflake down the screen
4           snowflake.centerY += snowFallDistance;
```

```
5                  var random = rand.nextDouble();
6
7                  // Add some random sideways movement
8                  var x = snowflake.centerX;
9                  if (random > 0.7) {
10                     x += snowDriftDistance;
11                 } else if (random < 0.3) {
12                     x -= snowDriftDistance;
13                 }
14                 x = Math.max(imageBounds.minX + snowflakeRadius, x);
15                 snowflake.centerX =
16                         Math.min(x, imageBounds.maxX - snowflakeRadius);
17
18                 // If the snowflake is off the screen, remove it
19                 if (snowflake.centerY >= imageBounds.maxY) {
20                     delete snowflake from scene.content;
21                     delete snowflake from snowflakes;
22                 }
23             }
24     }
```

The changes on lines 14 to 16 ensure that the random lateral motion applied to a snowflake does not take it outside the bounds of the snow area. This is necessary because if we were to allow this and the image is narrower than the scene, we would see snowflakes in the margin area to the left and right of the image. The second change, on line 19, ensures that snowflakes are removed as they reach the bottom of the image, not when they reach the bottom of the scene.

With these changes, the application now runs properly on my JavaFX developer phone, as you can see in Figure 17-58.

Coordinates and Screens

So far, we have assumed that your applications are running on a system with only one screen. This is not always the case. It is quite common to have desktop systems with two, four, or even more screens. When this is the case, it is possible for either the user or your application to place a stage on any of the screens. A JavaFX application can discover how many screens are available, their sizes, and how they are positioned relative to other screens, by using the `javafx.stage.Screen` class, which we discuss in this section.

Discovering Screens

You can get information about the screens on your system from the script variables `screens` and `primary` of the `Screen` class. The `screens` variable is of type `Screen[]`, while `primary` is a single `Screen` object that refers to the primary display for your system. Table 17-14 describes the variables of the `Screen` class.

586   Chapter 17 Coordinates, Transforms, and Layout

Figure 17-58   The modified SnowStorm application on a JavaFX phone

Table 17-14   **Variables of the `Screen` Class**

Variable	Type	Access	Default	Description
`dpi`	`Number`	R	N/A	The screen resolution in dots per inch
`bounds`	`Rectangle2D`	R	N/A	The actual bounds of the screen
`visualBounds`	`Rectangle2D`	R	N/A	The visual bounds of the screen, which are always contained by the actual bounds

The code in Listing 17-9 uses the Screen API to get and print the details of all the screens attached to the system on which it is run. It also creates a stage that displays the coordinates of its top-left corner in its title bar. We will use this stage to show how the coordinate system is affected by the presence of more than one screen.[11]

---

[11] You'll find this code in the file `javafxtransforms/Screens1.fx` in the JavaFX Book GUI project.

Listing 17-9 **Using the Screen API**

```
1     var screens = Screen.screens;
2     var primary = Screen.primary;
3     var index = Sequences.indexOf(screens, primary);
4     println("Number of screens: {sizeof screens}");
5     println("Index of primary: {index}");
6
7     for (i in [0..<sizeof screens]) {
8         var screen = screens[i];
9         println("Screen {i}");
10         println("  DPI: {screen.dpi}");
11         println("  Bounds: {screen.bounds}");
12         println("  Visual bounds: {screen.visualBounds}");
13         println("");
14     }
15
16    var stage:Stage = Stage {
17        title: bind "Position: ({stage.x}, {stage.y})"
18        width: 400
19        height: 300
20    }
```

The first part of this code, lines 1 to 14, gets the `Screen` objects that represent all the attached displays and the `Screen` object for the primary display. It then prints the number of displays that it found, the index of the primary display, and the details for each of them. Here's the output when I run this script on my laptop with only its inbuilt display attached:

```
Number of screens: 1
Index of primary: 0
Screen 0
  DPI: 96.0
  Bounds: Rectangle2D [minX = 0.0, minY=0.0, maxX=1280.0, maxY=800.0,
                      width=1280.0, height=800.0]
  Visual bounds: Rectangle2D [minX = 0.0, minY=0.0, maxX=1280.0,
                      maxY=770.0, width=1280.0, height=770.0]
```

The bounds and visual bounds are expressed in terms of a global coordinate system that covers all the attached displays. You'll learn more about this in the next section. You can see that these two bounds are not always the same. The difference between them is that the `bounds` variable refers to the size of the screen itself, while the `visualBounds` variable corresponds to the usable area. In this case, the visual bounds are smaller in height by 30 pixels because of the Windows taskbar, which appears at the bottom of the display area. If I change my display settings so that the taskbar is auto-hidden, the visual bounds and the bounds would be the same.

Using Two Screens

If your system has more than one screen, you can choose whether and how the desktop is extended across them. Windows provides a configuration dialog that lets you drag around a representation of each available monitor to create the logical configuration that you want. Figure 17-59 shows a typical example.

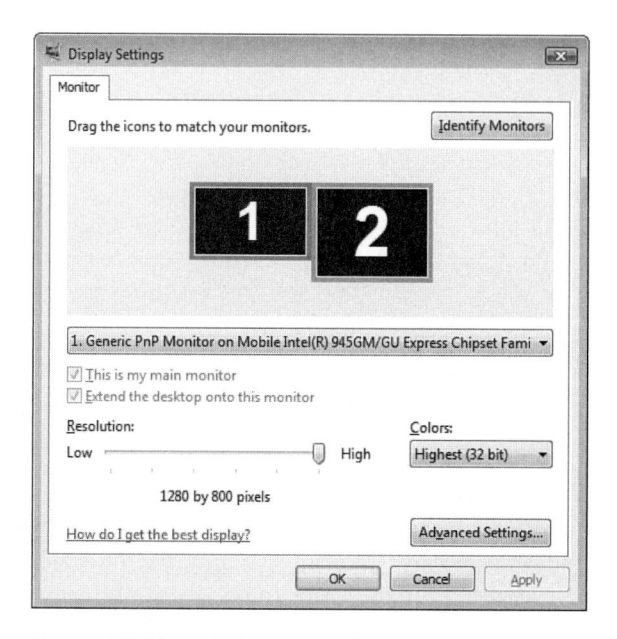

Figure 17-59 Windows setup for a two-screen configuration, with the primary on the left

Here, I have added an external monitor to my laptop, which is shown in the figure as Screen 2. As you can see, it has a greater resolution than my laptop's internal display. Running the code from Listing 17-9 with this configuration gives the following results:

```
Number of screens: 2
Index of primary: 0
Screen 0
  DPI: 96.0
  Bounds: Rectangle2D [minX = 0.0, minY=0.0, maxX=1280.0, maxY=800.0,
                      width=1280.0, height=800.0]
  Visual bounds: Rectangle2D [minX = 0.0, minY=0.0, maxX=1280.0,
                             maxY=770.0, width=1280.0, height=770.0]

Screen 1
  DPI: 96.0
  Bounds: Rectangle2D [minX = 1280.0, minY=0.0, maxX=2560.0,
                      maxY=1024.0, width=1280.0, height=1024.0]
```

```
Visual bounds: Rectangle2D [minX = 1280.0, minY=0.0, maxX=2560.0,
                  maxY=1024.0, width=1280.0, height=1024.0]
```

You can see that both monitors are listed, and that the second monitor has a resolution of 1280×1024 pixels. The important thing to note is that the `minX` value for the second monitor is `1280`, which indicates that the coordinate system has been extended from the first monitor onto the second. If I drag the stage created by this example onto the second monitor, I get the result shown in Figure 17-60.

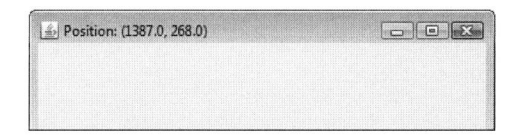

Figure 17-60 A stage on the secondary monitor, with the primary monitor on the left of it

If you look at the title bar, you'll see that the x coordinate of the stage is now `1387`, which indicates that it is on the second screen and 107 pixels from its left edge. With this arrangement of windows, valid x coordinates run from `0` to `2560`, and valid y coordinates from `0` to `1024`, although only the range `0` to `770` is usable on the primary screen.

Changing Screen Arrangement

Now suppose I change the window configuration so that the external monitor is logically on the left of the primary monitor, as shown in Figure 17-61.

If I run the example code again, I get the following output:

```
Number of screens: 2
Index of primary: 0
Screen 0
  DPI: 96.0
  Bounds: Rectangle2D [minX = 0.0, minY=0.0, maxX=1280.0, maxY=800.0,
                  width=1280.0, height=800.0]
  Visual bounds: Rectangle2D [minX = 0.0, minY=0.0, maxX=1280.0,
                  maxY=770.0, width=1280.0, height=770.0]

Screen 1
  DPI: 96.0
  Bounds: Rectangle2D [minX = -1280.0, minY=0.0, maxX=0.0, maxY=1024.0,
                  width=1280.0, height=1024.0]
  Visual bounds: Rectangle2D [minX = -1280.0, minY=0.0, maxX=0.0,
                  maxY=1024.0, width=1280.0, height=1024.0]
```

As you can see, the secondary monitor now occupies the x coordinate range from -1280 to 0. This is because the top-left corner of the primary screen is always given the coordinates (0, 0), and therefore anything to its left must have negative x coordinates. If I had placed the secondary monitor above the primary one, its x coordinates would have

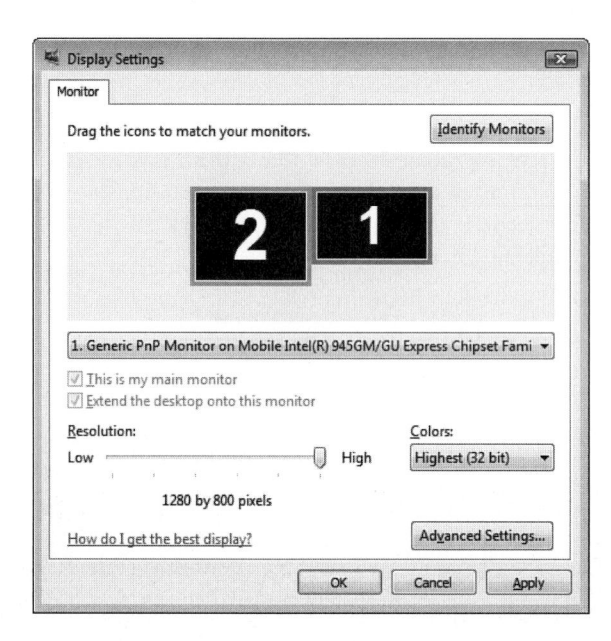

590 Chapter 17 Coordinates, Transforms, and Layout

Figure 17-61 Windows setup for a two-screen configuration, with the primary monitor on the right

been positive, but it would have had negative y coordinates instead. Dragging the stage onto the secondary monitor in this configuration shows that its coordinate is negative, as you can see in Figure 17-62.

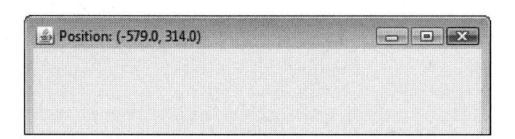

Figure 17-62 A stage on the secondary monitor, with the primary monitor on the right

18

Animation

Animation is one of the most important and exciting features of JavaFX. Although it is possible to create an animation using the Java2D application programming interfaces (APIs) in the Java platform, it is an order of magnitude simpler to do so with JavaFX. The Oxford English Dictionary defines *animation* as "the technique of filming a sequence of drawings or positions of models to create an illusion of movement." Movement is only one facet of animation in JavaFX. As you see in this chapter, the basic animation facility is part of the core JavaFX platform, not the graphical user interface (GUI) libraries. It boils down to the ability to change the value of one or more variables over a defined period of time. Depending on which variables and objects are involved, this could result in motion or it could cause objects to appear or disappear or change color, among other things.

The first part of this chapter discusses the `Timeline`, `Duration`, and `KeyFrame` classes, the cornerstones of animation in JavaFX. You see several examples that demonstrate how to use these classes, in conjunction with the GUI libraries, to create user interfaces that change over time, much like the SnowStorm application that you saw in Chapter 4, "A Simple JavaFX Application." The second part of this chapter looks at transitions, which are prebuilt classes that make it easier for you to include certain types of animation without having to work directly with a timeline.

You can find the example code for this chapter in the `javafxanimation` package in the JavaFX Book More GUI project.

Timelines

As you saw in Chapter 4, animation is controlled by a *timeline*. The timeline uses *key frames* to define the variables whose values are to be set at specific points in the animation. The code in Listing 18-1 creates a timeline that moves a circle from one side of the scene to the other over a period of 3 seconds, using a custom node class (called `Wheel`) that we developed in Chapter 16, "Shapes, Text, and Images."[1]

---

[1] This code is in the file `javafxanimation/Animation1.fx`.

Listing 18-1   A Simple Animation

```
1     package javafxanimation;
2
3     import javafx.animation.Timeline;
4     import javafx.scene.Node;
5     import javafx.scene.Scene;
6     import javafx.scene.paint.Color;
7     import javafx.stage.Stage;
8
9     var node: Node;
10    var scene: Scene;
11    Stage {
12        title: "Animation #1"
13        scene: scene = Scene {
14            width: 500
15            height: 100
16            content: [
17                node = Wheel {
18                        fill: Color.YELLOW
19                        stroke: Color.BLACK
20                        radius: 50
21                }
22            ]
23        }
24    }
25
26    var timeline = Timeline {
27        keyFrames: [
28            at (3s) {
29                node.translateX => scene.width - node.layoutBounds.width;
30                node.rotate => 360;
31            }
32        ]
33    }
34    timeline.play();
```

The code on lines 17 to 21 creates an instance of the `Wheel` class and places it at the origin of the scene, as shown in the top frame of Figure 18-1.[2]

The animation is provided by the `Timeline` object on lines 26 to 33. As you can see, a single key frame specifies what should happen 3 seconds after the animation starts, which happens when its `play()` function is called on line 34. We'll look at the details of the

---

[2] The `Wheel` appears at the origin because its `translateX` and `translateY` variables both have their default value of `0`.

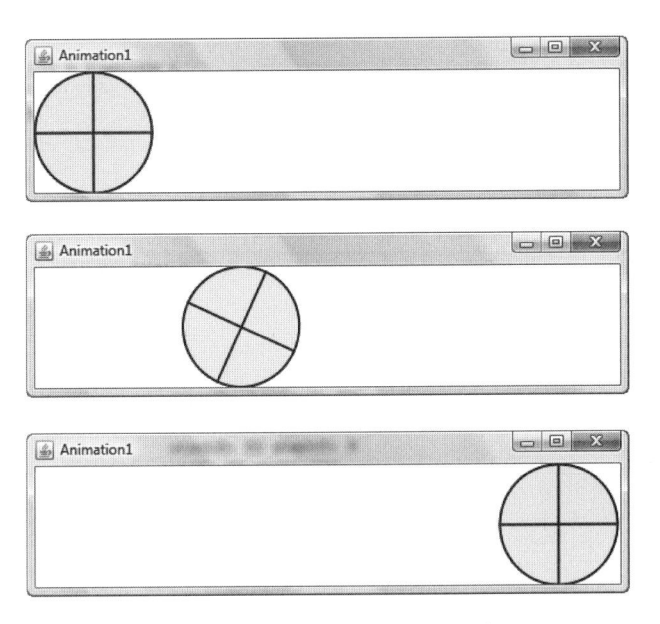

Figure 18-1   Animating a circle across the scene

timeline in the sections that follow. The important point to note here is that to create this animation, it is only necessary to specify where the circle should be when the animation is complete and how long it should take to get there.

Although in this case there is only one defined key frame, a second one will be created automatically when the animation is started. This *implicit* key frame represents the initial state of all the variables that are affected by the animation, and it is associated with an elapsed time of zero. *An implicit starting key frame is only created when, as in this example, one is not actually included in the definition of the timeline.*

The key frames in this simple animation describe only the start and end conditions. In more complex animations, there would be other key frames that specify various intermediate states.

When the animation runs, the wheel moves from left to right across the scene as a result of the change to its `translateX` variable caused by the code on line 29 of Listing 18-1. At the same time, the code on line 30 causes it to rotate through 360 degrees. You can see the effect of this in the middle and bottom frames of Figure 18-1. The position of the wheel and the distance through which it has rotated at any given elapsed time between 0 and 3 seconds are both calculated by the JavaFX runtime. The process of calculating the values of the `translateX` and `rotate` variables at times between 0 and 3 seconds is called *interpolation*. There are various different ways to interpolate the values of these variables, which we'll discuss in the section "Interpolation and Interpolators," later in this chapter. In this case, we use the default, which is *linear interpolation*. As a result, after 1 second, the wheel will be one-third of the way across the scene and will have rotated through 120 degrees, and after 2 seconds it will be two-thirds of the way across and will have turned through 240 degrees.

> **Note**
>
> In this example, we use the `translateX` variable to change the position of the wheel rather than `layoutX`. This is consistent with the convention that `layoutX` is used only for node layout.

The variables of the `Timeline` class, all of which we discuss in detail in the rest of this chapter, are listed in Table 18-1. This class, along with the others that are covered in this chapter (with the exception of `Duration` which is in `javafx.lang`), is in the `javafx.animation` package.

Table 18-1   **Variables of the `Timeline` Class**

Variable	Type	Access	Default	Description
`keyFrames`	`KeyFrame[]`	RW	Empty	The key frames that define the animation
`repeatCount`	`Number`	RW	`1`	The number of times that this animation should be run
`autoReverse`	`Boolean`	RW	`false`	Whether the animation should reverse direction at the end of each cycle
`time`	`Duration`	RW	`0.0`	The current elapsed time within the animation
`rate`	`Number`	RW	`1.0`	Controls the rate and direction of the animation
`framerate`	`Number`	RW	Platform-dependent	The maximum number of frames per second for this animation
`interpolate`	`Boolean`	RW	`true`	Whether interpolation should be performed
`currentRate`	`Number`	R		The current rate and direction of the animation
`cycleDuration`	`Duration`	R		The duration of the current cycle of the animation
`totalDuration`	`Duration`	R		The duration of the whole animation
`paused`	`Boolean`	R		Whether the animation is currently paused

Table 18-1 Variables of the `Timeline` Class (*Continued*)

Variable	Type	Access	Default	Description
running	Boolean	R		Whether the animation is currently running

Time Literals and the `Duration` Class

The times that appear in key frames are all instances of the `javafx.lang.Duration` class. The compiler provides syntax that allows you to conveniently create `Duration` objects by using *time literals*.

Time Literals

A time literal specifies a length of time in hours, minutes, seconds, or milliseconds. The following are valid time literals.

- `10ms`: 10 milliseconds
- `5s`: 5 seconds
- `2m`: 2 minutes
- `3.5m`: 3 minutes, 30 seconds
- `1h`: 1 hour
- `1.5h`: 1 hour, 30 minutes

No whitespace may appear between the number and the time unit, so `3.5 s` is not valid. The following code declares a variable called d of type `Duration`, initialized to 3.5 seconds:

```
var d = 3.5s;
```

You can specify times that are not whole hours, minutes, or seconds by combining time literals, like this:

```
var d = 1h + 2m + 4s + 3.5ms;
```

You can also subtract time literals. The following code initializes the variable d to a time of 40 minutes:

```
var d = 1h - 20m;
```

The usual multiply and divide operators can be used to combine a `Duration` with a numeric value, and you can also divide one `Duration` by another:

```
var d1 = 1h * 2;    // 2 hours
var d2 = 1h / 3;    // 20 minutes
var n = d1 / d2;    // 6
```

You can compare `Durations` by using the `==`, `!`, `<`, `<=`, `>`, and `>=` operators:

```
var d1 = 1h;
var d2 = 59m;
```

```
println(d1 > d2);  // Prints "true"
println("${d1 == d2 + 1m}"); // Prints "true"
```

`Duration` Class Functions

The time literal syntax only works when the actual time value is known in advance. When the time is held in a variable, you can use the `valueOf()` function of the `Duration` class to get a `Duration` object corresponding to a time interval given in milliseconds:

```
var time = 3500; // milliseconds
var d = Duration.valueOf(time);
```

The `Duration` class provides several arithmetic and comparison functions. `Duration` objects are immutable, so the arithmetic operations all return a new `Duration` object initialized with the value of the result. The `add()` and `sub()` functions add or subtract two `Duration` objects and return a new `Duration` object; the `negate()` function returns a `Duration` that has the same value but the opposite sign to the one on which it is invoked:

```
var d1 = 1h;
var d2 = 20m;
var d3 = d1.add(d2);   //1 hour, 20 minutes
var d4 = d1.sub(d2);   // 40 minutes
var d5 = d1.negate();  // -1 hours
```

The `mul()` and `div()` functions allow you to multiply or divide a `Duration` by a numeric value. There is also a variant of `div()` that accepts an argument of type `Duration`:

```
var d1 = 1h;
var d2 = 20m;
var d3 = d1.mul(2);  // 2 hours
var d4 = d2.div(2);  // 10 minutes
var n = d3.div(d4);  // 12
```

The `ge()`, `gt()`, `le()`, and `lt()` functions compare one `Duration` to another, although this is more easily done using the comparison operators, as you saw earlier in this section:

```
var d1 = 1h;
var d2 = 59m;
println(d1.gt(d2));      // Prints "true"
println(d1.le(d2 + 2m)); // Prints "true"
```

Key Frames

The key frames for an animation are listed in the `keyFrames` variable of the `Timeline` object. The key frames may be specified in any order; when the `Timeline` object is started, an internal sequence is created that contains the key frames in ascending order of time. It is possible to add and remove key frames while the animation is in progress.

Table 18-2 describes the variables of the `KeyFrame` class.

Table 18-2   Variables of the KeyFrame Class

Variable	Type	Access	Default	Description
time	Duration	RW	0s	The elapsed time at which the values in this key frame should be set and the action function called, if there is one.
values	KeyValue[]	RW	Empty	The variables and the values that should be assigned to them when this key frame is reached.
action	function() :Void	RW	null	A function that should be called when this key frame is reached.
canSkip	Boolean	RW	false	Specifies whether multiple calls to the action function can be combined if the timeline is getting behind.

In most cases, the variables in a key frame will be set when the object is initialized and left unchanged. Changes to key frames after the animation has started are ignored. If you need to make a change and have it taken into account in the same execution of the animation, you must call the evaluateKeyValues() method of the owning Timeline.

There are two ways to write the key frames for a timeline: the full form that initializes the keyFrames variable in the usual way, and a shorthand form that is converted by the compiler to an equivalent set of KeyFrame objects.

Longhand Initialization of a `KeyFrame` Object

The most obvious way to create a KeyFrame object is to use an object literal. The code in Listing 18-2, which you'll find in the file javafxanimation/Animation2.fx, initializes a KeyFrame object that will be processed one second after the start of its owning timeline.

Listing 18-2   Using an Object Initializer to Create a `KeyFrame` Object

```
var value1 = 0.0 on replace {
    if (timeline != null) {
        println("value1 = {value1} at {timeline.time}")
    }
};
var value2 = 0.0 on replace {
    if (timeline != null) println(
        "value2 = {value2} at {timeline.time}")
    }
};

var timeline = Timeline {
    keyFrames: [
```

598 Chapter 18 Animation

```
            KeyFrame {
                time: 1s
                values: [
                    value1 => 10.0,
                    value2 => 20.0
                ]
            }
        ]
    };
    timeline.play();
```

The `values` variable contains one or more expressions that specify a variable and a value that should be assigned to that variable when the key frame is processed. The operator `=>` is used to separate the variable name from the expression that supplies the target value and the optional interpolator, which is discussed in the "Interpolation and Interpolators" section.

In this example, there is no explicit key frame for the elapsed time of zero, so one is created that assigns the initial values of `0.0` to both `value1` and `value2` when the timeline is started. (These values are assigned because they are the actual values of these variables when the timeline starts.) While the animation is in progress, intermediate values are assigned to these variables at intervals that are determined by the JavaFX runtime, subject to the constraint that after one second has elapsed, `value1` will have the value `10`, and `value2` will be `20`. Here is a typical sequence of value assignments, in which only those near the start and end of the time period are shown:

```
value2 = 0.48000002 at 24ms
value1 = 0.24000001 at 24ms
value2 = 0.74 at 37ms
value1 = 0.37 at 37ms
value2 = 1.04 at 52ms
value1 = 0.52 at 52ms
value2 = 1.38 at 69ms
value1 = 0.69 at 69ms
value2 = 1.68 at 84ms
value1 = 0.84 at 84ms
value2 = 2.0 at 100ms
value1 = 1.0 at 100ms
    (Lines omitted here)
value2 = 19.279999 at 964ms
value1 = 9.639999 at 964ms
value2 = 19.6 at 980ms
value1 = 9.8 at 980ms
value2 = 19.92 at 996ms
value1 = 9.96 at 996ms
value1 = 10.0 at 1000ms
value2 = 20.0 at 1000ms
```

The time between assignments depends on various factors, which include the rate at which the timeline is being played, which is controlled by the `rate` variable, and the maximum number of frames per second, which can be set using the `framerate` variable. For more information on these variables, see the section "Controlling a Timeline," later in this chapter.

If you create a timeline in this way, you can assign an action function to any of its key frames. See "Using a Timeline as a Timer" for a discussion of the action function.

Shorthand Initialization of a `KeyFrame` Object

The shorthand form relieves you of the need to explicitly create `KeyFrame` objects. Instead, you specify the values for the `time` and `values` variables, and the compiler builds the object literals that become the key frames. Listing 18-3 (from the file `javafxanimation/Animation3.fx`) shows how you would rewrite the example shown on Listing 18-2 using the shorthand form.

Listing 18-3   Creating a `KeyFrame` Object Using a Shorthand Notation

```
var value1 = 0.0 on replace {
    if (timeline != null) {
        println("value1 = {value1} at {timeline.time}")
    }
};
var value2 = 0.0 on replace {
    if (timeline != null) println(
        "value2 = {value2} at {timeline.time}")
    }
};

var timeline = Timeline {
    keyFrames: [
        at (1s) {
            value1 => 10.0;
            value2 => 20.0;
        }
    ]
};
timeline.play();
```

When you use this form, the elapsed time for each key frame is given by the `at` clause. The value supplied in parentheses *must* be a time literal—no expressions or even variable names are allowed. This means that you can only use this form when the elapsed times are fixed and known at compile time. The variable list is enclosed in a block expression that follows the `at` clause. The syntax is the same as shown in the earlier example, except that if there is more than one variable involved, as is the case here, the variable/value clauses must be separated by semicolons.

It is not possible to assign an `action` function to a key frame if you are using the shorthand notation.

Interpolation and Interpolators

The intermediate values that are assigned to a variable that appears in a key frame are calculated by an *interpolator* that takes into account the required start and end values and the current position within the part of the animation that affects the variable.

There are six standard interpolators provided by the `Interpolator` class in the `javafx.animation` package, which are listed in Table 18-3. They differ in the way that they calculate the current position within the animation during the processing of a key frame. In the examples that you have seen so far, no interpolator has actually been specified, so the default, which is linear interpolation, has been used.

Table 18-3 **The Standard Interpolators**

Name	Description
`Interpolator.LINEAR`	This is the default interpolation. The change in the value of the associated variable is proportional to the elapsed time.
`Interpolator.DISCRETE`	Discrete interpolation causes the variable to retain its initial value until the end of the key frame, at which point it is given its target value.
`Interpolator.EASIN`	Same as `LINEAR`, except that value changes more slowly at the start of the key frame.
`Interpolator.EASEOUT`	Same as `LINEAR`, except that value changes more slowly at the end of the key frame.
`Interpolator.EASEBOTH`	Same as `LINEAR`, except that value changes more slowly at the start and end of the key frame.
`Interpolator.SPLINE`	The way in which the variable's value changes depends on a spline curve that is associated with the `Interpolator`.

You specify the interpolator that you want by using the `tween` keyword, followed by an instance of an object that extends the `javafx.animation.Interpolator` class, typically one of those listed in Table 18-3. The following code uses the `EASEBOTH` interpolator, which causes the variable value to change more slowly at the beginning and end of the key frame than it does in the middle, and `DISCRETE`, which causes the variable's value to remain constant and then jump to the target value at the end of the key frame[3]:

```
Timeline {
    keyFrames: [
```

---

[3] You can find this code in the file `javafxanimation/Animation4.fx`.

```
        at (1s) {
            value1 => 10.0 tween Interpolator.EASEBOTH;
            value2 => 20.0 tween Interpolator.DISCRETE;
        }
    ]
};
```

In this example, `value2` would remain at its initial value until 1 second has passed and then its value would change to `20`. By contrast, the value of the variable `value1` would increase slowly from `0` for a short time, increase more quickly, and then more slowly again just before 1 second has elapsed. One way to visualize this behavior is to imagine how a car might behave on an empty road. When it starts, there is a period when it covers less distance each second because it has to accelerate, a period of time when it travels at more or less constant speed, and finally a third period when it covers less distance because it has to slow down before stopping. If you use the `EASEIN` interpolator, you get the slow start but not the slow end, whereas the `EASEOUT` interpolator gives you the slow end but not the slow start.

You can use an interpolator with any numeric value and also with a variable of any class that extends `javafx.animation.Interpolatable`. In the JavaFX runtime, all the shape classes that you saw in Chapter 16 are `Interpolatable`, as is the `Color` class. That means that you can change the colors associated with a node over time, and you can also morph between shapes.

Interpolating Colors

Animating the color of a shape is as simple as referencing its `fill` or `stroke` variable in a key frame. The interpolation provided by the `Color` class operates on all four color channels, which means that you can control the alpha channel to make the color appear to fade in or out. You can achieve a similar effect by animating the `opacity` variable of a node, as shown in Listing 18-4, which comes from the file `javafxanimation/Animation5.fx`.

Listing 18-4 **Animating Color and Opacity**

```
1       var circle1:Circle;
2       var circle2:Circle;
3       Stage {
4           title: "Animation #5"
5           scene: Scene {
6               width: 200
7               height: 100
8               content: [
9                   circle1 = Circle {
10                      centerX: 50
11                      centerY: 50
12                      radius: 40
13                  }
14                  circle2 = Circle {
```

```
15                    centerX: 150
16                    centerY: 50
17                    radius: 40
18              }
19          ]
20      }
21  }
22
23  var timeline = Timeline {
24      keyFrames: [
25          at (0s) {
26              circle1.fill => Color.color(1.0, 1.0, 0.0, 0);
27              circle2.fill => Color.color(1.0, 1.0, 0.0);
28              circle2.opacity => 0;
29          }
30          at (5s) {
31              circle1.fill => Color.RED tween Interpolator.EASEBOTH;
33              circle2.opacity => 1.0 tween Interpolator.EASEBOTH;
34          }
35      ]
36  }
37  timeline.play();
```

The code on lines 1 to 21 creates two circles that are placed next to each other, both with the default `fill` color of black. The timeline on lines 23 to 36 animates both the `fill` and the `opacity` variables of these circles.

When the timeline is started, the `fill` of the circle on the left is changed to a fully transparent yellow, while the circle on the right is filled with opaque yellow, but its `opacity` is set to `0`. As a result, neither circle will initially be visible.

Over the next 5 seconds, the `fill` color of the circle on the left is gradually changed to red, and its alpha channel is changed to 1 (see line 31). As a result, it will at first appear to be filled with a partly transparent yellow and will then change through intermediate colors to a fully opaque yellow. You can see two different stages of this animation in Figure 18-2.

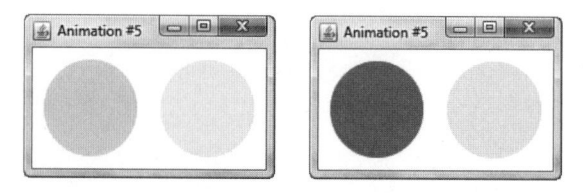

Figure 18-2   Illustrating color and opacity animation

Timelines 603

Line 32 animates the `opacity` variable of the circle on the right, changing it from 0 to 1 over the same 5-second period. As a result, it will appear to fade in until it is completely opaque, as shown on the right of Figure 18-2.

Shape Morphing

You can use the fact that all the shape classes in the JavaFX runtime extend `Interpolatable` to morph one shape into another. To do this, you make use of the `DelegateShape` class, which is in the `javafx.scene.shape` package. `DelegateShape` inherits all the variables of the `Shape` class and adds one more, which is described in Table 18-4.

Table 18-4   **Variables of the `DelegateShape` Class**

Variable	Type	Access	Default	Description
shape	Shape	RW	null	The shape from which this `DelegateShape` gets its geometry

When you add a `DelegateShape` to a scene, it is invisible until its `shape` variable is set, at which point it takes on the geometry of that shape. However, it ignores the `fill`, `stroke`, and other variables of that shape, so you need to set the required values for these variables on the `DelegateShape` itself. To achieve the effect of morphing, you need to animate the `shape` variable of the `DelegateShape`, starting from the initial shape and ending with the target shape. There is an example of this in Listing 18-5, which you'll find in the file `javafxanimation/Animation6.fx`.

Listing 18-5   **Using a `DelegateShape` to Morph One Shape to Another**

```
1      var shape:DelegateShape;
2      Stage {
3          title: "Animation #6"
4          scene: Scene {
5              width: 150
6              height: 150
7              content: [
8                  shape = DelegateShape { }
9              ]
10         }
11     }
12
13     var timeline = Timeline {
14         keyFrames: [
15             at (0s) {
16                 shape.shape => Circle {
```

```
17                              centerX: 75 centerY: 75
18                              radius: 50
19                          };
20              shape.fill => Color.YELLOW;
21          }
22          at (5s) {
23              shape.shape => Rectangle {
24                              x: 20 y: 20
25                              width: 100 height: 100
26                          };
27              shape.fill => Color.GREEN;
28          }
29          at (10s) {
30              shape.shape => Ellipse {
31                              centerX: 75 centerY: 75
32                              radiusX: 60 radiusY: 40
33                          };
34              shape.fill => Color.RED;
35          }
36      ]
37  }
38  timeline.play();
```

The scene in this example contains a `DelegateShape` that initially points at nothing. When the timeline on lines 13 to 37 is started, it assigns a circle and the color yellow to the `DelegateShape`, giving it the appearance shown on the left of Figure 18-3.

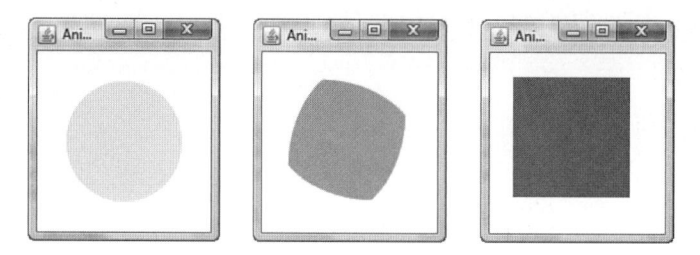

Figure 18-3   Shape morphing—the early stages

Over the course of the next 5 seconds, the shape variable of the `DelegateShape` is morphed to a rectangle. The two steps in this process are shown in the center and right of Figure 18-3. What actually happens is that at each intermediate frame of the animation, a new shape that is part way between the original circle and the target rectangle is created and assigned to the shape variable of the `DelegateShape`, which is the target of animation on line 23 of Listing 18-5. Over the same time period, the `fill` color of the `DelegateShape` gradually changes from yellow to green.

The second part of the animation, on lines 29 to 35 of Listing 18-5, causes the `DelegateShape` to morph again from the green rectangle to a red ellipse, as shown, left to right, in Figure 18-4.

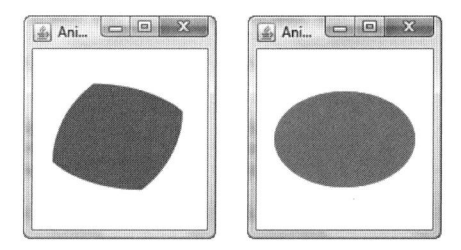

Figure 18-4 Shape morphing—the final stages

Controlling a Timeline

In the examples you have seen so far in this chapter, all the animations have been allowed to start, execute once, and then stop. In this section, you see how to use the variables and functions of the `Timeline` class to cause an animation to be repeated, to make it run in reverse, and to change the rate at which it plays, to stop and restart it and to pause it.

Repeating an Animation

By default, when an animation completes its last key frame, it stops. If you want the animation to run more than once, you can set the `repeatCount` variable. A positive value causes the animation to be executed the specified number of times. A negative value runs the animation indefinitely—by convention, the constant value `Timeline.INDEFINITE` is used in this case. If `repeatCount` has the value 0, the animation will not run at all.[4]

The code in Listing 18-6, from the file `javafxanimation/Animation7.fx`, creates a rectangle with its long side parallel to the x-axis. The `Timeline` object created on lines 15 to 20 causes the rectangle to be rotated clockwise through 90 degrees over a period of 2 seconds so that its long side ends up parallel to the y-axis, as shown on the right of Figure 18-5.

---

[4] The `repeatCount` actually indicates the number of times the animation will run in total, not the number of repeats after the initial run. Therefore, a `repeatCount` of 0 means the animation will run zero times.

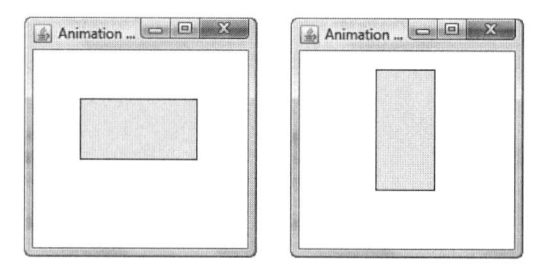

Figure 18-5   Rotating a rectangle through 90 degrees

Listing 18-6   **Rotating a Rectangle**

```
1   var node: Node;
2   Stage {
3       title: "Animation #7"
4       width: 200 height: 200
5       scene: Scene {
6           content: [
7               node = Rectangle {
8                   x: 40 y: 40 width: 100 height: 50
9                   fill: Color.YELLOW stroke: Color.BLACK
10              }
11          ]
12      }
13  }
14
15  var timeline: Timeline = Timeline {
16      repeatCount: Timeline.INDEFINITE
17      keyFrames: [
18          at (2s) { node.rotate => 90 }
19      ]
20  }
21  timeline.play();
```

When a timeline is repeated, the values of all the variables that have been changed are reverted to the values that they had at the start of the first key frame. These could be the values that applied when the timeline was started, or the values set in the key frame for time 0s. In Listing 18-6, there is no explicit key frame with an elapsed time of zero, so the initial value of the rotate variable, which is 0, is stored when the animation starts. At the start of a repeat cycle, the rotate variable is reset to this value, which causes the rectangle to return instantaneously to its original orientation before the animation starts over. If there had been an explicit first key frame that assigned an initial value to this variable, the result would have been different:

```
var timeline: Timeline = Timeline {
    repeatCount: Timeline.INDEFINITE
    keyFrames: [
        at (0s) { node.rotate => 30 },
        at (2s) { node.rotate => 90 }
    ]
}
```

The code above assigns the value 30 to the `rotate` variable at time 0, so when the animation starts, the rectangle will immediately rotate through 30 degrees and then through a further 60 degrees over a period of 2 seconds. At the start of the second and subsequent cycles, the `rotate` variable will be reset to 30 rather than 0, because that is its value after the key frame at time 0 has taken effect.

Automatically Reversing an Animation

By default, when an animation is repeated, it restarts from the beginning. Sometimes, it is useful to have the animation instead run in reverse when it is repeated. You can arrange for this to happen by setting the `autoReverse` variable to `true`, as shown in the following code:

```
var timeline: Timeline = Timeline {
    repeatCount: Timeline.INDEFINITE
    autoReverse: true
    keyFrames: [
        at (2s) { node.rotate => 90 }
    ]
}
timeline.play();
```

Here's what happens when this animation is played:

1. The rectangle rotates clockwise from 0 degrees to 90 degrees over a period of 2 seconds.

2. The animation reverses, and the rectangle rotates counterclockwise from 90 degrees to 0 degrees over a period of 2 seconds.

3. The animation reverses again, and the rectangle rotates clockwise from 0 degrees to 90 degrees over a period of 2 seconds.

4. ...and so on.

In this case, at the end of the animation, the `rotate` variable is not reset to its initial value. Instead, it starts with its final value of 90, and the interpolation is run in reverse so that the variable is assigned decreasing values that will result in it having its initial value at the end of all the even-numbered cycles.

Pausing, Stopping, and Restarting an Animation

Normally, you will start an animation and allow it to run to its conclusion, but you may want to provide the user with the means to suspend it or even to stop it. The `Timeline` class provides functions that let you do this. The example code in the file `javafxanimation/Animation8.fx` creates a scene that contains the animation from Listing 18-1 together with some buttons that let you use these functions to control the timeline, as shown in Figure 18-6. You can use this example to experiment with the functions and variables that we discuss in this section and the next.

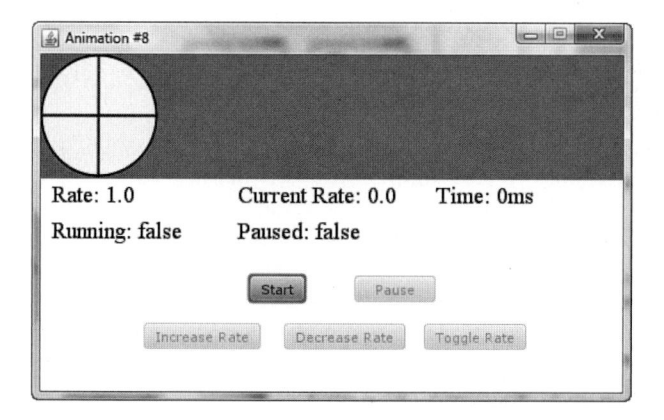

Figure 18-6 Controlling a timeline

The button labeled Start initiates the animation by invoking the timeline's `play()` function. Once the animation is running, the label changes to Stop, and the adjacent Pause button is enabled.

Clicking the Pause button causes the timeline's `pause()` function to be called. This causes the animation to be suspended, and the button's label is changed to Resume. No further changes will be made to the animated variables until the timeline is resumed as a result of clicking the Resume button. To resume a paused timeline, you just call the `play()` function again. This function starts or resumes the timeline from its current position but does nothing if the timeline is already running. If you want to have the timeline restart from the beginning (which you can do at any time, whether it is currently running or paused), use the `playFromStart()` function.

If you click the Stop button, the animation will be stopped by calling the timeline's `stop()` function. Once a timeline has been stopped, both the `play()` and `playFromStart()` functions will restart it from the beginning.

It is possible to move the timeline forward or backward by an arbitrary amount by setting its `time` variable. The following code causes the animation to immediately adopt the state that would exist 1.5 seconds from its start:

```
timeline.time = 1.5s;
```

If the animation is paused when this variable is changed, nothing will happen until the `play()` function is called.

Three read-only variables track the state of the animation. The `running` variable is set to `true` when `play()` or `playFromStart()` is called and becomes `false` when the animation is stopped. It remains `true` if the animation is paused. The `paused` variable reflects whether the animation has been paused. Both `running` and `paused` are reset to `false` when the animation is stopped. The `time` variable represents the current time within the timeline. In this example, the `time` variable will start from `0s` and increment to `3s` and then start counting back down to `0s` when it reverses at the end of each forward cycle. The values of all three variables are shown continuously in the example shown in Figure 18-6.

Changing the Speed and Direction of an Animation

By default, when a timeline is started, it proceeds in the forward direction in real time—that is, the time specified for each key frame is the actual time taken to reach that key frame. You can play the animation faster or slower by changing the value of the `rate` variable, which initially has the value `1`. Assigning the value `2` to this variable causes the animation to run at twice the normal speed, so a key frame with a time of 3 seconds would be reached after 1.5 seconds. On the other hand, the value `0.5` halves the speed of the animation, so this same key frame would take 6 seconds to be reached at that rate.

In the example shown in Figure 18-6, you can use the Increase Rate and Decrease Rate buttons to add 1 to or subtract 1 from the absolute value of the `rate` variable. Setting the `rate` variable to `0` (which you can do by clicking the Decrease Rate button) causes the animation to pause.

The read-only variable `currentRate` tracks the rate that is in effect at any given time, and is also sensitive to the direction of the animation. If you start the animation in Figure 18-6 from the beginning, the circle will roll from left to rate at the standard rate, and `currentRate`, which is shown below the circle, will be set to `1.0`. If you then click the Increase Rate button, both `rate` and `currentRate` will change to `2.0`, and the circle will move faster. When the circle reaches the right side of the scene, the animation will reverse (because `autoReverse` is `true` and `repeatCount` has value `INDEFINITE`), and the circle will start moving from right to left. At this point, you will see that `rate` still has the value `2.0`, but `currentRate` has changed to `-2.0`. The negative sign indicates that the animation is running in reverse. The absolute value of `currentRate` always represents the speed of the animation.

You can cause the animation to immediately play in the reverse direction by flipping the sign of the `rate` variable. The Toggle Rate button effectively does this:

```
timeline.rate = -timeline.rate;
```

If you click this button while the circle is moving from left to right with a `rate` value of `1.0`, you will see that `rate` will change to `-1.0`, the circle will begin to move from its current position back toward it starting point, and `currentRate` will also change to `-1.0`, because the animation is now running backward.

The `framerate` variable represents the maximum number of animation steps that should be performed in a second. The default value of this variable is platform-dependent. Increasing it may or may not produce a better quality animation at the cost of extra CPU cycles. Decreasing it may reduce your CPU load but may also have a negative effect on the animation.

Starting a Timeline from the End

If you want to run a timeline in reverse, you need to do two things:

- Set the `rate` variable to a negative value (usually `-1`).
- Set the `time` variable to the time of the last key frame.

This is illustrated by the following code, from the file `javafxanimation/Animation9.fx`:

```
1    var value = 0.0 on replace {
2        if (timeline != null) {
3            println("value = {value} at {timeline.time}")
4        }
5    };
6    var timeline = Timeline {
7        keyFrames: [
8            at (1s) { value => 10.0 }
9        ]
10   };
11
12   timeline.rate = -1;
13   timeline.time = timeline.keyFrames[0].time;
14   timeline.play();
```

If played in the normal (forward) direction, the timeline would increase the value of the variable `value` from `0` to `10` in 1 second. However, by setting the `rate` and `time` as shown on lines 12 and 13, the variable actually decreases from `10` to `0`, as the following extract from the output of this code demonstrates. Notice also that the value of the `time` variable is decreasing, as you would expect when an animation is played in reverse:

```
value = 10.0 at 857ms
value = 8.57 at 857ms
value = 8.309999 at 831ms
value = 8.16 at 816ms
```

```
    ...
value = 1.13 at 113ms
value = 0.96000004 at 96ms
value = 0.79999995 at 80ms
```

Using a Timeline as a Timer

A `Timeline` is used to change the value of one or more variables over time. This is useful if you know in advance that this is what you need to do. In some cases, though, you need to be more dynamic, especially when writing games. For example, you might model a missile as a shape together with an associated `Timeline` that moves it from left to right across the scene. To do this, you need to create a key frame that specifies the final position of the missile and the amount of time that it should take to reach that point. Although this would work, it takes no account of the fact that the missile might collide with something, at which point you would need to animate an explosion and then remove both the missile and its victim from the scene. This is not a process that can be directly modeled using just a key frame.

In general, a game is most easily implemented as a loop, where you process every moving object on a regular basis, something like this:

```
while (game still in progress) {
    Wait 20 milliseconds
    Process all objects
}
```

In a Swing application, you would probably use the `javax.swing.Timer` class to implement a repeating action. In JavaFX, you can use the `action` variable of the `KeyFrame` class to achieve the same thing much more easily, like this:

```
var count = 0 on replace { println("count = {count}"); }
var timeline = Timeline {
    repeatCount: 10
    keyFrames: [
        KeyFrame {
            time: 20ms
            action: function() {
                    count = count + 1
                }
        }
    ]
}
timeline.play()
```

This code creates a timeline with a single key frame that is repeated ten times, once every 20 milliseconds. In this case, no variables are being animated. Instead, the `action` function of the key frame is called. This function is called when the key frame that declares it is reached. In this case, the `action` function is called once every 20ms and simply increments the value of the variable `count`, but it could equally contain the entire

Chapter 18 Animation

logic of a game. If this looks familiar to you, it is probably because this is essentially the same code as we used for the SnowStorm application, which you saw in the section "Adding New Snowflakes" in Chapter 4.

The point of this example is to show how to invoke a function on a regular, timed basis, but you might be wondering whether it is necessary to use an `action` function to implement a timed counter. If you know the target value of the counter and the time over which it should reach that value, you could use a `Timeline` without an `action` function, in the usual way:

```
var count = 0 on replace { println("count = {count}"); }
var timeline = Timeline {
    keyFrames: [
        at (200ms) { count => 10 }
    ]
}
timeline.play();
```

Here, the trigger is called whenever the value of `count` changes, and you could use it to perform your timed action. However, this doesn't necessarily work because there is no guarantee which values will be assigned to the variable `count` over the 200ms period of this animation. All that can be known for certain is that it will have the value `10` when the animation finishes. Here is the result of running this code on my system:

```
count = 0
count = 7
count = 8
count = 9
count = 10
```

It is worth noting that the following code does *not* work:

```
var count = 0 on replace { println("count = {count}"); }
var timeline = Timeline {
    repeatCount: 10
    keyFrames: [
        at (20ms) { count => count + 1 }
    ]
}
timeline.play();
```

On the face of it, this code increments the value of `count` ten times, because the timeline is repeated that many times, so it appears that this variable should have the value `10` when the timeline finishes. However, this is not what happens, because there is an implicit key frame at time `0` that resets `count` to its initial value of `0` at the start of every cycle. Therefore, the result of this code is to change `count` from `0` to `1`, ten times over!

If an `action` function takes a long time to execute or if there is a lot animation or other work going on, it might not be possible for key frames to be reached exactly when their `time` variable specifies that they should. In these circumstances, the JavaFX runtime will skip the execution of `action` functions if it is permitted to do so. This is controlled by the value of the `canSkip` variable in the `KeyFrame` object. Setting this value to `true` when possible gives the runtime the greatest possible chance of catching up to the timeline.

Animation Length

The `cycleDuration` and `totalDuration` variables of the `Timeline` class are read-only values that contain respectively the length of a single cycle of the timeline and the total length of all cycles. The following code (from the file `javafxanimation/Animation13.fx`) constructs a timeline and prints the values of both of these variables:

```
var count = 0;
var timeline = Timeline {
    repeatCount: 10
    keyFrames: [
        at (20ms) { count => count + 1 }
    ]
}

println("Duration of a cycle: {timeline.cycleDuration}");
println("Total duration: {timeline.totalDuration}");
```

The output from this code is the following:

```
Duration of a cycle: 20ms
Total duration: 200ms
```

The *cycle time* is the time value of the last key frame in the timeline, which is 20ms in this case. The *total duration* is the cycle time multiplied by the repeat count, or 10 ★ 20ms which is 200ms, as shown in the output. When the repeat count is `Timeline.INDEFINITE`, the total duration value will be `Duration.INDEFINITE`.

Transitions

You can animate any of the variables of a node to produce effects such as translation, fade, rotation, and so on. To do so, you need to create a timeline, associate it with the node, and then start it. The JavaFX runtime includes a small number of classes that do most of this work for you. These classes, which are called *transitions*, are all derived from the abstract class `Transition` and can be found in the `javafx.animation.transition` package. There are six predefined transitions and two convenience classes that allow you to run multiple transitions one after the other or in parallel. These classes are discussed in detail in the sections that follow.

The `Transition` Class

A transition is a timeline that is managed by the JavaFX runtime. The `Transition` class derives from `Timeline`, and therefore it can be used in (mostly) the same way as any other timeline. In particular, you can use the `Timeline`-provided functions and variables to start, stop, pause, and vary the rate and direction of a transition. Each `Transition` subclass provides a set of variables and functions that allow the runtime to construct a suitable set of key frames for the `Timeline`. Application code must not attempt to install its own key frames in a `Transition` object.

The variables that are common to all transitions are listed in Table 18-5. Each individual transition has additional variables that are specific to the effect that it provides. These variables are listed in the sections that follow.

Table 18-5 The Variables of the `Transition` Class

Variable	Type	Access	Default	Description
node	Node	RW	null	The node on which this transition operates
interpolator	Interpolator	RW	EASEBOTH	The interpolator to be used to generate the values for the transition
action	function(): Void	RW	null	The function to be called at the end of each cycle of the transition

`TranslateTransition`

The `TranslateTransition` class moves a node from its current position or from a specified position, over a straight line path, either by a specified amount or to a given target position. The `duration` variable gives the time interval over which the transition is performed. For a more general transition that moves a node around a given path, see the "`PathTransition`" section, later in this chapter. The variables that control this transition are listed in Table 18-6.

Table 18-6 Variables of the `TranslateTransition` Class

Variable	Type	Access	Default	Description
duration	Duration	RW	400ms	The time over which the transition should be performed
fromX	Number	RW	See text	The start x coordinate of the translation
fromY	Number	RW	See text	The start y coordinate of the translation
fromZ	Number	RW	See text	The start z coordinate of the translation
toX	Number	RW	See text	The end x coordinate of the translation
toY	Numer	RW	See text	The end y coordinate of the translation
toZ	Numer	RW	See text	The end z coordinate of the translation
byX	Number	RW	See text	The x distance to be moved
byY	Number	RW	See text	The y distance to be moved
byZ	Number	RW	See text	The z distance to be moved

When the transition is started, the node is initially moved to the location given by the `fromX`, `fromY` and `fromZ` variables by setting its `translateX`, `translateY` and `translateZ` variables to these values. If none of `fromX`, `fromY` and `fromZ` has been set, the node starts from its current location. The end position of the transition is determined as follows:

- If the `toX` value is defined, the x coordinate of the end location is `toX`; otherwise it is the starting x coordinate plus the value of the `byX` variable. If `byX` is not specified, the start and end x coordinates are the same—in other words, there will be no motion along the x-axis.

- If the `toY` value is defined, the y coordinate of the end location is `toY`; otherwise it is the starting y coordinate plus the value of the `byY` variable. If `byY` is not specified, the start and end y coordinates are the same—in other words, there will be no motion along the y-axis.

- If the `toZ` value is defined, the z coordinate of the end location is `toZ`; otherwise it is the starting z coordinate plus the value of the `byZ` variable. If `byZ` is not specified, the start and end y coordinates are the same—in other words, there will be no motion along the z-axis.

These rules give the `toX`, `toY` and `toZ` variables precedence over `byX`, `byY` and `byZ`.

The translation is performed by interpolating the `translateX`, `translateY`, and `translateZ` variables of the target node from the start values to the end values over the specified elapsed time. By default, the `EASEBOTH` interpolator is used, but this can be changed by setting the `interpolator` variable inherited from `Transition`.

The code in Listing 18-8, which you will find in the file `javafxanimation/Transitions1.fx`, moves a wheel from the top-left corner of the `Scene` to its bottom-right corner over a period of 2 seconds and then, by virtue of the `autoReverse` setting, back to the left corner. This process repeats forever.

Listing 18-8 Using a `TranslateTransition` to Move a Shape over Time

```
1     package javafxanimation;
2
3     import javafx.animation.Timeline;
4     import javafx.animation.transition.TranslateTransition;
5     import javafx.scene.paint.Color;
6     import javafx.scene.Scene;
7     import javafx.stage.Stage;
8     import javafxanimation.Wheel;
9
10    var wheel = Wheel {
11        radius: 20 fill: Color.YELLOW stroke: Color.BLACK
12    };
13
14    Stage {
15        title: "Transitions #1" resizable: false
```

```
16        scene: Scene {
17            width: 200
18            height: 200
19            content: [
20                wheel
21            ]
22        }
23    }
24
25    var transition = TranslateTransition {
26        duration: 2s
27        node: wheel
28        repeatCount: Timeline.INDEFINITE
29        autoReverse: true
30        fromX: 0 fromY: 0
31        byX: 160 byY: 160
32    };
33    transition.play();
```

`RotateTransition`

The `RotateTransition` class rotates a node about its center point from a given angle to either a target angle or by a specified amount. The variables that control the rotation are listed in Table 18-7.

Table 18-7   Variables of the `RotateTransition` Class

Variable	Type	Access	Default	Description
duration	Duration	RW	400ms	The time over which the transition should be performed
axis	Point3D	RW	See text	The axis about which the rotation takes place
fromAngle	Number	RW	See text	The starting angle for the rotation
toAngle	Number	RW	See text	The ending angle for the rotation
byAngle	Number	RW	See text	The end angle for the rotation

   As usual, the angles are measured in degrees. The value `0` corresponds to the 3 o'clock position, and positive angles represent a rotation in the clockwise direction. The transition is performed by modifying the `rotate` variable of the node. If the `fromAngle` value is not specified, the transition starts from the current value of the node's `rotate` variable. The transition ends either at `toAngle`, if it is specified or after a rotation through `byAngle` degrees if it is not. If neither the `toAngle` variable nor the `byAngle` variable is set, the transition consists only of setting the `rotate` variable of the node to its initial value.

The following code (from the file `javafxanimation/Transitions2.fx`) rotates a wheel object from an initial angle of 30 degrees to a final angle of 120 degrees over a period of 2 seconds, and back again. Because no axis is specified in the transition, the rotation takes place about the axis specified by the `rotationAxis` variable of the node itself, which in this case has been defaulted to the z-axis. This process is repeated indefinitely:

```
RotateTransition {
    duration: 2s
    node: wheel
    repeatCount: Timeline.INDEFINITE
    autoReverse: true
    fromAngle: 30
    toAngle: 120
};
```

ScaleTransition

The `ScaleTransition` class manipulates the `scaleX`/`scaleY`/`scaleZ` variables of a node so that it appears to be resized around its center point over a given period of time. The variables that control the animation are listed in Table 18-8.

Table 18-8 **Variables of the `ScaleTransition` Class**

Variable	Type	Access	Default	Description
duration	Duration	RW	400ms	The time over which the transition should be performed
fromX	Number	RW	See text	The initial value for the `scaleX` variable
fromY	Number	RW	See text	The initial value for the `scaleY` variable
fromZ	Number	RW	See text	The initial value for the `scaleZ` variable
toX	Number	RW	See text	The final value for the `scaleX` variable
toY	Number	RW	See text	The final value for the `scaleZ` variable
toZ	Number	RW	See text	The final value for the `scaleY` variable
byX	Number	RW	See text	The amount by which the `scaleX` variable is to be changed
byY	Number	RW	See text	The amount by which the `scaleY` variable is to be changed
byZ	Number	RW	See text	The amount by which the `scaleZ` variable is to be changed

As with the other transitions, the initial value of the scale along each axis is given by the `fromX`, `fromY`, and `fromZ` values but, if either of these is not set, the value of the node's `scaleX`/`scaleY`/`scaleZ` variable is used instead. The target values are given by `toX`/`toY`/`toZ`. If either of these is not set, the target value is the initial value plus either `byX`, `byY` or `byY` and, as usual, if these values are also not set, the effect is only to set the `scaleX`, `scaleY`, or `scaleZ` variable to the initial value.

The following code, from the file `javafxanimation/Transitions3.fx`, scales a wheel object from 0.5 along both axes to a maximum of 2.5 along the x-axis and 2.0 along the y-axis:

```
ScaleTransition {
    duration: 2s
    node: wheel
    repeatCount: Timeline.INDEFINITE
    autoReverse: true
    fromX: 0.5
    byX: 2.0
    fromY: 0.5
    toY: 1.5
};
```

A scale that operates only along one axis can be created by not specifying any values for the other axes. This code produces no scaling along the y-axis and z-axis:

```
ScaleTransition {
    duration: 2s
    node: wheel
    repeatCount: Timeline.INDEFINITE
    autoReverse: true
    fromX: 0.5
    byX: 2.0
};
```

FadeTransition

The `FadeTransition` class animates the `opacity` variable of a node to create a fade-in or fade-out effect using the parameters listed in Table 18-9.

Table 18-9   Variables of the `FadeTransition` Class

Variable	Type	Access	Default	Description
`duration`	Duration	RW	400ms	The time over which the transition should be performed
`fromValue`	Number	RW	See text	The initial opacity value
`toValue`	Number	RW	See text	The final opacity value
`byValue`	Number	RW	See text	The amount by which the opacity value should be changed

The `opacity` goes from `fromValue` to either `toValue` or to its initial value plus `byValue`, over the specified time period. If `fromValue` is not specified, the node's initial opacity is used. The following code, which you'll find in the file `javafxanimation/Transitions4.fx`, fades a wheel object so that it goes from fully opaque to fully transparent over a period of 2 seconds, back to fully opaque over the next 2 seconds, and so on:

```
FadeTransition {
    duration: 2s
    node: wheel
    repeatCount: Timeline.INDEFINITE
    autoReverse: true
    fromValue: 1.0
    byValue: -1.0
};
```

It is possible for either the start or end opacity values to be outside of the range `0.0` to `1.0`, inclusive. If this is the case, those values *are* used, but they have no effect. For example, if `fromValue` were `0.0` and `toValue` were `10.0`, the `opacity` variable would be animated from `0.0` to `10.0`, but no change would be apparent after the limiting value of `1.0` has been reached.

PathTransition

The `PathTransition` class allows you to animate an object by moving around an arbitrary path. Table 18-10 lists the variables of this class.

Table 18-10 Variables of the `PathTransition` Class

Variable	Type	Access	Default	Description
duration	Duration	RW	400ms	The time over which the transition should be performed
path	Animation-Path	RW	null	The path along which the target node is to be animated
orientation	Orientation-Type	RW	Orientation Type.NONE	Determines whether the target node is rotated as it is moved

The path along which the node is moved is given by the `path` variable, which is of type `AnimationPath`. The `AnimationPath` class, which is also in the `javafx.animation.transitions` package, provides two class functions that let you convert a `Path` or an `SVGPath` to an `AnimationPath`:

```
public function createFromPath(path:Path):AnimationPath
public function createFromPath(path:SVGPath):AnimationPath
```

Chapter 18 Animation

The code in Listing 18-9, which you'll find in the file `javafxanimation/Transitions5.fx`, moves a wheel object around a path that consists of a cubic curve and three line segments, as shown in Figure 18-7.

Figure 18-7 Animating an object along a path

Listing 18-9   Using a `PathTransition` to Animate a Shape

```
1    package javafxanimation;
2
3    import javafx.animation.Timeline;
4    import javafx.animation.transition.AnimationPath;
5    import javafx.animation.transition.OrientationType;
6    import javafx.animation.transition.PathTransition;
7    import javafx.scene.paint.Color;
8    import javafx.scene.Scene;
9    import javafx.scene.shape.ClosePath;
10   import javafx.scene.shape.CubicCurveTo;
11   import javafx.scene.shape.HLineTo;
12   import javafx.scene.shape.MoveTo;
13   import javafx.scene.shape.Path;
14   import javafx.scene.shape.VLineTo;
15   import javafx.stage.Stage;
16   import javafxanimation.Wheel;
17
18   var wheel = Wheel {
19       radius: 20 fill: Color.YELLOW stroke: Color.BLACK
20   };
21
22   var path = Path {
23       elements: [
24           MoveTo { x: 10 y: 100 }
25           CubicCurveTo {
26               x: 190 y: 10
```

```
27                controlX1: 50 controlY1: 10
28                controlX2: 150 controlY2: 200
29            }
30            VLineTo { y: 190}
31            HLineTo { x: 10 }
32            ClosePath { }
33        ]
34        strokeWidth: 2 strokeDashArray: [8, 9]
35        stroke: Color.BLUE
36    };
37
38    Stage {
39        title: "Transitions #5"
40        scene: Scene {
41            width: 200 height: 200
42            content: [
43                wheel, path
44            ]
45        }
46    }
47
48    var transition = PathTransition {
49        duration: 5s
50        node: wheel
51        repeatCount: Timeline.INDEFINITE
52        autoReverse: true
53        orientation: OrientationType.NONE
54        path: AnimationPath.createFromPath(path)
55    };
56    transition.play();
```

The path along which the wheel is to be moved is defined by the `Path` object that is declared on lines 22 to 36, using some of the path elements that were introduced in Chapter 16. Both the wheel and the path are placed in the `content` sequence of the scene so that both are visible. The path itself is the blue dashed shape in Figure 18-7. You are not required to make the path visible and, in most cases, you would not do so.

The `PathTransition` object is created on lines 48 to 55. As you can see, its `path` variable is set to the `AnimationPath` object returned by the `createFromPath()` function. As a result of the values assigned to the `duration`, `repeatCount`, and `autoReverse` variables, the wheel will traverse the entire path in 2 seconds, reverse direction, and return to its starting point (and will continue to do this indefinitely).

The `orientation` variable determines whether the target node should be rotated as it moves. When this variable is set to `OrientationType.NONE`, the node is not rotated, so in this case the spokes of the `Wheel` will remain parallel to the coordinate axes, as you can see in Figure 18-7. If `orientation` is set to `OrientationType.ORTHOGONAL_TO_TANGENT`, the node is rotated so that it appears to always be facing along the path as it moves. You can see the effect of this variable by comparing the alignment of the wheel's spokes in Figure 18-7, where the orientation variable is set to `NONE`, with the alignment in Figure 18-8, which uses the value `ORTHOGONAL_TO_TANGENT`.

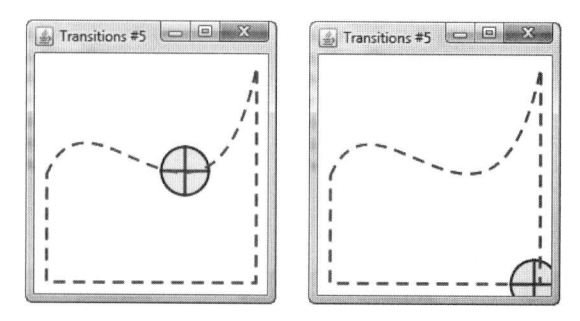

Figure 18-8   Animating an object along a path and rotating its axes at the same time

`PauseTransition`

The `PauseTransition` class adds only a variable called `duration` of type `Duration` to its base class. When it is started, it causes a delay of `duration` milliseconds, which may be repeated by using the `repeatCount` variable. This might not sound very useful, but you will see an example of its use in the next section.

Sequential and Parallel Transitions

The `SequentialTransition` and `ParallelTransition` classes let you execute a set of transitions either one after the other or all at the same time. The single variable that each of these classes adds to the `Transition` base class is described in Table 18-11.

Although this variable is formally defined as a sequence of `Timeline` objects, in most cases its content will actually be `Transitions`.[5] In the case of a `SequentialTransition`,

Table 18-11   Variable of the `SequentialTransition` and `ParallelTransition` Classes

Variable	Type	Access	Default	Description
content	Timeline[]	RW	Empty	The `Timelines` that are to be executed, either in sequence or in parallel

---

[5] Prior to JavaFX version 1.2, the `KeyFrame` class had a `timelines` variable that allowed you to nest one or more timeline inside another, starting the nested timelines at a given point in the master timeline. As of JavaFX 1.2, this feature was superseded by the `SequentialTransition` and `ParallelTransition` classes.

the timelines in the `content` variable are executed one after the other, so that the second one starts when the first one ends, and so on. For a `ParallelTransition`, all the transitions in the `content` variable are started at the same time and run in parallel (hence the name of the class.)

The code in Listing 18-10, which you'll find in the file `javafxanimation/Transitions7.fx`, demonstrates the use of the `SequentialTransition`, `ParallelTransition` and `PauseTransition` classes. It uses these classes, together with some of the other transitions, to do the following:

1. Move a wheel object from the top left of the scene to the top center, over a time period of 2 seconds.

2. Pause for half a second.

3. Move the wheel object from the top to the bottom of the scene over a period of 5 seconds and then back up, five times, while simultaneously (that is, in parallel) rotating it through five complete turns.

Listing 18-10 **Using the `SequentialTransition` and `ParallelTransition` Classes**

```
1     package javafxanimation;
2
3     import javafx.animation.transition.ParallelTransition;
4     import javafx.animation.transition.PauseTransition;
5     import javafx.animation.transition.RotateTransition;
6     import javafx.animation.transition.SequentialTransition;
7     import javafx.animation.transition.TranslateTransition;
8     import javafx.scene.paint.Color;
9     import javafx.scene.paint.LinearGradient;
10    import javafx.scene.paint.Stop;
11    import javafx.scene.Scene;
12    import javafx.stage.Stage;
13    import javafxanimation.Wheel;
14
15    var wheel: Wheel;
16    var scene: Scene;
17    Stage {
18        title: "Transitions #7"
19        resizable: false
20        scene:
21        scene = Scene {
22            width: 200
23            height: 300
24            fill: LinearGradient {
25                startX: 0 startY: 0
26                endX: 1.0 endY: 1.0
```

```
27              stops: [
28                  Stop { offset: 0.0 color: Color.WHITE }
29                  Stop { offset: 0.5 color: Color.LIGHTGREY }
30                  Stop { offset: 1.0 color: Color.BLACK }
31              ]
32          }
33          content: [
34              wheel = Wheel {
35                  fill: Color.YELLOW stroke: Color.BLACK
36                  radius: 20
37              }
38          ]
39      }
40  }
41
42  var transition = SequentialTransition {
43      node: wheel
44      content: [
45          TranslateTransition {
46              duration: 2s
47              toX: (scene.width - wheel.layoutBounds.width)/ 2
48              toY: 0
49          }
50          PauseTransition {
51              duration: 0.5s
52          }
53          ParallelTransition {
54              content: [
55                  TranslateTransition {
56                      duration: 5s repeatCount: 10
57                      autoReverse: true
58                      byX: 0
59                      toY: scene.height - wheel.layoutBounds.height
60                  }
61                  RotateTransition {
62                      duration: 10s repeatCount: 5
63                      toAngle: 360
64                  }
65              ]
66          }
67      ]
68  }
69  transition.play();
```

The transitions are created on lines 42 to 68. The first thing to note is that none of the nested `Transition` objects have their `node` variable explicitly set. This is because both `SequentialTransition` and `ParallelTransition` propagate the value of their own `node` variable to each element of the `content` sequence that does not specify a `node` value. As a result, we only need to set the `node` variable of the `SequentialTransition` on line 43 for the whole transition to be applied to the same node.

The rest of the code should be self-explanatory. The `TranslateTransition` on lines 45 to 49 moves the wheel right by half the width of the scene, and the `PauseTransition` on lines 50 to 52 causes a half-second wait before the `ParallelTransition` on lines 53 to 66 moves the wheel down and then up five times and rotates it five times, both at the same time, over a total period of 50 seconds.

Note that it is not possible to set the total time of either of these transition classes or to make them repeat or automatically reverse because both `SequentialTransition` and `ParallelTransition` ignore the values of their `duration`, `repeatCount`, and `autoReverse` variables.

19

Video and Audio

It has been possible for many years to play both audio and video in Java, but the application programming interfaces (APIs) that are provided to do this are complex. In JavaFX, it is almost trivial to embed a media player that will play some sound or a video clip into your application. The code shown in Listing 19-1 is all that it takes.

Listing 19-1   **Media Playback with JavaFX**

```
var mediaURL = "http://sun.edgeboss.net/download/sun/media/1460825906/"
               "1460825906_2956241001_big-buck-bunny-640x360.flv";

Stage {
    title: "Media #1"
    resizable: false
    scene: Scene {
        width: 640
        height: 360
        content: [
            MediaView {
                mediaPlayer: MediaPlayer {
                    autoPlay: true;
                    media: Media {
                        source: mediaURL
                    }
                }
            }
        ]
    }
}
```

This code opens a short video hosted by Sun Microsystems and streams it onto your screen. As you can see, there are three key classes that cooperate to play the content of a video file:

- `MediaView` is a node that renders video delivered by a `MediaPlayer`.
- `MediaPlayer` is a class that can play either an audio or a movie clip, which it obtains from a `Media` object.
- A `Media` object encapsulates the audio or video file to be played.

After you have created these three objects and linked them together, you can just let them get on with the job of playing your media file. In this chapter, we discuss in detail the `Media`, `MediaPlayer`, and `MediaView` classes (which you'll find in the `javafx.scene.media` package) and show you how to integrate them into your JavaFX application.

You can find the example code for this chapter in the `javafxmedia` package of the JavaFX Book GUI project.

The Media Class

The `Media` class contains a reference to the media to be played. It opens the media file and reads the metadata that describes the tracks that are available, the playback duration, and the picture size if the file contains video. The variables of this class are listed in Table 19-1.

Table 19-1 **Variables of the Media Class**

Variable	Type	Access	Default	Description
`source`	`String`	RW	Empty	The URL of the media file
`duration`	`Duration`	R		The playback duration of the media content
`width`	`Number`	R		The width of the video frame, or 0 if there is no video content
`height`	`Number`	R		The height of the video frame, or 0 if there is no video content
`tracks`	`Track[]`	R		The tracks that make up the media content
`metadata`	`Metadata[]`	R		Metadata held in the media file
`onError`	`function (:MediaError) :Void`	RW	`null`	Function to be called when an error occurs while opening or playing the file content

Setting the `source` variable causes the media file to be read. If the file does not exist, is not accessible, is corrupt, or uses a media format that is not supported on the host platform, the function referred to by the `onError` variable is called with a `MediaError` object that describes the problem. If no error handler has been installed (so that this variable is `null`), an exception is thrown instead. The `onError` function is also called if an error occurs during playback.

Once the media file has been opened, values will be set for the other variables. It is important to note that these variables may not be populated immediately, because it is usually necessary to wait for metadata to be read from the file before the appropriate values are known. It is therefore not a good idea to assume that these values are valid as soon as the `Media` object has been initialized. The best way to deal with this is to bind application state that depends on these values to the values themselves and then use a trigger to handle changes, like this:

```
var media = Media { source: someURL };
var duration = bind media.duration on replace {
                  println("Duration is {duration}"
            }
```

The `duration` variable gives the total media playback time, as a `Duration` object. The `width` and `height` variables contain the size of the video frame in pixels. If there is no video content (as would be the case for an MP3 file, for example), these variables will both have the value `0`. By default, the `MediaView` object, which is a bare-bones video player that we discuss later in this chapter, adjusts its size to match the `width` and `height` values of the media that it is playing.

You can find out what a media file contains by examining the information in the `tracks` variable. This sequence has one element for each of the supported track types that are found in the file. A track is represented by the `Track` class, which is an abstract class that has only a single variable, called `name`, that contains the name assigned to the track. The `Media` class recognizes six different track types, all of which are defined in the `TrackType` class, but there are specific `Track` subclasses only for three of them: audio, video, and subtitles. Each subclass has variables that provide information that is specific to the corresponding track type. For example, both the `AudioTrack` and `SubtitleTrack` classes have a variable called `language` that contains the language in which the track was recorded.

Some media files contain metadata that can be displayed by players to give the user more information. The JavaFX runtime reads the metadata and converts it to objects of type `Metadata` that are then installed in the `metadata` variable. Each `Metadata` object contains a name and the associated value. For example, MP3 files commonly have metadata in ID3 format, as described at http://www.id3.org, that stores such things as the artist name, media title, and so on.

When you set the `source` variable of a `Media` object, at least some part of the file will be read and held in memory. If you no longer need access to the information in the `Media` object, you should release it by setting the `source` variable to `null`.

JavaFX supports two cross-platform formats: FXM and FLV. Media encoded in either of these formats can be played on any device that has a JavaFX runtime, including mobile devices.

FLV is the video and audio format used in Flash applications; FXM is a subset of FLV and is the "official" JavaFX cross-platform media format. It uses the VP6 video encoding developed by On2 Technologies, together with an MP3 sound track. On2 Technologies provides a utility that enables you to convert media in other formats into an FXM file, which you can then use in your JavaFX application. This utility is not free. Visit the On2 Technologies website at http://www.on2.com for more information.

In addition to FXM and FLV, JavaFX can also handle media file encoded in various platform-specific formats, but only on the platforms that support those formats. There is a complete and current list of these formats, by platform, in the Release Notes for the JavaFX software development kit (SDK). On Windows, for example, you can play MP3, WAV, WMV, AVI, and ASF files. Obviously, using a platform-specific format is acceptable only if you know that your application will be used only on that platform.

The `MediaPlayer` Class

The `MediaPlayer` and `MediaView` classes can be combined to form a basic video player. `MediaView` is a node that renders video content in a rectangular area, while the `MediaPlayer` class provides variables and functions that allow you to control and monitor the playback of media data obtained from a `Media` object. To display video, you need both a `MediaPlayer` and a `MediaView` object, whereas audio can be played with just a `MediaPlayer`.

As you can see in Figure 19-1, which shows the result of running the code in Listing 19-1,[1] the `MediaView` class does not provide any visual controls to allow the user to start, stop, or pause playback or to change the volume level—its only function is to display picture frames from a video source. If you need a more complete player, you need to create your own by using the platform-independent controls that we discuss in Chapter 22, "Cross-Platform Controls." Some of the later examples in this chapter add buttons that allow you basic control over media playback.

Controlling Media Playback

The `MediaPlayer` class has a number of variables and functions that relate to media playback. The variables are listed in Table 19-2.

---

[1] You can try this example for yourself by running the code in the file `javafxmedia/Media1.fx` in the JavaFX Book GUI project.

Figure 19-1 Using the `MediaView` and `MediaPlayer` classes to play video and audio

Table 19-2 Playback-Related Variables in the `MediaPlayer` Class

Variable	Type	Access	Default	Description
`autoPlay`	Boolean	RW	`false`	Starts playback as soon as possible if `true`
`media`	Media	RW		The media to be played
`rate`	Number	RW	1.0	The rate and direction at which the media should be played
`repeatCount`	Number	RW	1.0	The number of times that the media should be played
`currentCount`	Number	RW		The number of times that the media has so far been repeated because playback was started
`startTime`	Duration	RW		The time from which playback should begin or be resumed following a pause or repeat
`stopTime`	Duration	RW		The time at which playback should stop (and begin the next cycle when repeating)

Before you can play video or audio, you have to create a `Media` object that refers to the content to be played and then install it in the `media` variable of the `MediaPlayer`. Having done this, you have a choice of two ways to start playback. The first is to set the `autoPlay` variable to `true`, which causes playback to begin as soon as data is available. This setting is used in Listing 19-1 at the start of this chapter. If you don't want immediate playback, you can use the `play()` function instead. Typically, you would provide a button or other control that the user would press to cause this function to be called, as you'll see in some of the later examples in this chapter.

You can pause or stop playback by calling the `pause()` or `stop()` functions, respectively. The difference between these two functions is that after `stop()`, the next call to `play()` will cause playback to begin from the start of the clip, whereas following a `pause()` it resumes from its current position. The `play()` function does nothing if playback is already in progress. You can see the effects of these functions by running the code in the file `javafxmedia/Media2.fx` in the JavaFX Book GUI project, which adds a couple of buttons to the `MediaView` that allow you to exercise the `play()`, `pause()`, and `stop()` functions.

Ordinarily, the media content will play in the forward direction and at its normal rate. If you want faster or slower playback, you can use the `rate` variable to request this. Setting this variable to 2 requests playback at twice normal speed, whereas the value -1 requests reverse playback at normal speed. Some file formats do not support playback at anything other than the normal rate.

Restricting and Repeating Playback

By default, a media file is played once, from start to finish. If you want to play only part of it, you can do so by setting the `startTime`/`stopTime` variables to delimit the part to be played. When one or both of these variables are set, the file content will be played from the start or from `startTime`, if it is set, to the end, or to `stopTime`. Both of these variables are of type `Duration`. Here's an example that plays a 30-second clip of the media content that starts 20 seconds from its beginning:

```
var mediaPlayer = MediaPlayer {
    startTime: 20s
    stopTime: 50s
    media: Media { url: mediaURL }
}
mediaPlayer.play();
```

When the `startTime` variable has been set, the `stop()` function resets the `MediaPlayer` so that the next call to `play()` will begin playback from the specified start time instead of from the start of the media content.

It is also possible to play either the whole file, or the part of it that is bounded by the `startTime` and `endTime` variables, more than once. To do this, set the `repeatCount` variable to the total number of times that you want the media to be played. The following code plays the same extract as that previously selected, a total of ten times:

```
var mediaPlayer = MediaPlayer {
    startTime: 20s
    stopTime: 50s
```

```
    repeatCount: 10
    media: Media { url: mediaURL }
}
mediaPlayer.play();
```

Two distinguished values can be assigned to the `repeatCount` variable, both represented by constants defined by the `MediaPlayer` class, as follows:

- REPEAT_NONE: The clip is not repeated; that is, it is played exactly once. This is the default.
- REPEAT_FOREVER: The clip is played continuously until `stop()` is called or until `repeatCount` is changed to a different value.

While playback is in progress, you can determine how many repeats have taken place by monitoring the `currentCount` variable, which increases from 0 on the first playback cycle to `repeatCount-1` on the last[2]:

```
var count = bind mediaPlayer.currentCount on replace {
    println("Playing cycle number {count}");
}
```

Volume Control

You can control the playback volume and other audio parameters by using the `MediaPlayer` variables listed in Table 19-3.

These variables should be self-explanatory. Usually, you would couple them to controls in your user interface. The following code uses an animation to modify the balance and volume of a `MediaPlayer` over a 10-second period. You can try it by running the code in the file `javafxmedia/Media4.fx` in the JavaFX Book GUI project:

```
var timeline = Timeline {
    repeatCount: Timeline.INDEFINITE
    keyFrames: [
        at (0s) { mediaPlayer.volume => 0;
                  mediaPlayer.balance => -1.0 }
        at (5s) { mediaPlayer.volume => 1.0;
                  mediaPlayer.balance => 1.0 }
        at (10s) { mediaPlayer.volume => 0.0;
                   mediaPlayer.balance => 0.0 }
    ]
}
timeline.play();
```

---

[2] The code snippets shown here are from the file `javafxmedia.Media3.fx` in the JavaFX Book GUI project.

Table 19-3   Audio Control Variables in the `MediaPlayer` Class

Variable	Type	Access	Default	Description
`volume`	`Number`	RW	`1.0`	Controls the audio volume. `0.0` is silent, `1.0` is maximum volume.
`mute`	`Boolean`	RW	`false`	When `true`, audio output is cut off. When `false`, the audio plays at the level specified by the `volume` variable.
`balance`	`Number`	RW	`0.0`	Specifies the sound balance between the left and right speaker. The default value, `0.0`, centers the sound. Value `-1.0` moves the sound entirely to the left speaker, while `1.0` moves it entirely to the right speaker. Intermediate values adjust the sound levels in the left and right speakers so that the center point appears to be at the position given by the value of this variable—between the left speaker and the center for a negative value and between the center and the right speaker in the case of a positive value.
`fader`	`Number`	RW	`0.0`	In a four-speaker sound system, this variable controls the forward/back position of the sound. Value `-1.0` moves the sound to the back, `0.0` places it in the middle (that is, equal sound from front and back), and `1.0` moves it to the front. Intermediate values are handled similarly to the `balance` variable.

Monitoring Playback

The `MediaPlayer` class has several variables and function variables that you can use to monitor its state, both before and during playback. These variables are listed in Table 19-4, and are discussed in the following paragraphs.

The `status` variable reflects the current state of the player. It has four possible values, all of which are defined as constants in the `MediaPlayer` class:

- `BUFFERING`: The player is currently buffering data. This may occur while the player is playing or when it is paused.
- `PAUSED`: The player is paused or stopped.
- `PLAYING`: The player is actually playing the media content.
- `STALLED`: The player is waiting for more media data to become available. This happens when the data was not streamed fast enough to keep up with playback.

Table 19-4 `MediaPlayer` Variables That Can Be Used to Monitor Its State

Variable	Type	Access	Description
`Status`	`Integer`	R	The state of the player
`paused`	`Boolean`	R	Whether playback is currently paused
`currentTime`	`Duration`	RW	The current position of the play head
`bufferProgressTime`	`Duration`	R	The time up to which the media content can be played without stalling the player
`onBuffering`	`function (:Duration): Void`	RW	Called when the player is buffering data
`onEndOfMedia`	`function():Void`	RW	Called when the player reaches the end of the media content
`onError`	`function (:MediaError):Void`	RW	Called when an error occurs while playing the media
`onRepeat`	`function():Void`	RW	Called at the start of a repeat cycle
`onStalled`	`function (:Duration)`	RW	Called when the player is stalled waiting for data

The `paused` variable has the value `true` when the player is either paused or stopped. In most cases, when the player is paused, the `status` variable will have the value `PAUSED`, but if the player is buffering data, which can happen when it is paused, the `status` variable would have the value `BUFFERING`.

The `currentTime` variable represents the point in time that has been reached during playback. This value increases while the player is playing and is constant while it is paused or stalled. This variable is reset to the value of the `startTime` variable (which defaults to 0, or the start of the media content) when playback is stopped and at the start of each repeat cycle. It is also possible to resume playback at an arbitrary point in the media content by writing to this variable.

The `bufferProgressTime` variable indicates how much of the media content has been read and buffered in the player. A player automatically buffers data to avoid being stalled in case at some points during the playback the network cannot deliver it as quickly as it can be played.

Most of these variables have access modifiers that do not allow them to be written to by application code, so it is not legal to use an `override var` statement to attach a trigger to them to react to changes in their values. Instead, you can bind a script or instance variable to any of these values and then attach a trigger to that variable, like this:

Chapter 19 Video and Audio

```
var currentTime = bind mediaPlayer.currentTime on replace {
    println("Current time is {currentTime}");
}
var bufferTime = bind mediaPlayer.bufferProgressTime on replace {
    println("Buffered time is {bufferTime}");
}
var status = bind mediaPlayer.status on replace {
    if (status == MediaPlayer.BUFFERING) {
        println("status == BUFFERING")
    } else if (status == MediaPlayer.PAUSED) {
        println("status == PAUSED");
    } else if (status == MediaPlayer.PLAYING) {
        println("status == PLAYING");
    } else if (status == MediaPlayer.STALLED) {
        println("status == STALLED");
    }
}
var paused = bind mediaPlayer.paused on replace {
    println("Paused = {paused}");
}
```

If you run the code in the file `javafxmedia/Media5.fx` in the JavaFX Book GUI project, which includes the code shown above, you can watch these variables change as the media is played. Here is an extract showing some typical results, where some lines have been removed for clarity:

```
1       Current time is 0ms
2       Buffered time is 0ms
3       status == PAUSED
4       Paused = true
5       Buffered time is 104811ms
6       Paused = false
7       Buffered time is 128993ms
8       status == PLAYING
9       Current time is 1202ms
10      Current time is 1237ms
            ....
11      Current time is 3729ms
12      Current time is 3849ms
13      Paused = true
14      Buffered time is 143968ms
15      status == PAUSED
16      Current time is 3955ms
17      Paused = false
18      status == PLAYING
19      Buffered time is 199522ms
20      Current time is 3915ms
```

In this example, the `Media` object has its `autoPlay` variable set to `false`, so playback does not begin until the `MediaPlayer`'s `start()` function is called. Lines 1 to 5 appear before this happens and, as you can see, it initially reports that it is paused. On line 6, the Start button has been clicked and playback begins. The `status` and `paused` variables change to reflect this fact. Notice that the player is also reporting that it is buffering data. On line 13, the Pause button has been clicked and the `status` and `paused` variables changed again. Finally, on line 17, the Start button is clicked to resume playback.

The five function variables `onBuffering`, `onEndOfMedia`, `onError`, `onRepeat`, and `onStalled` can be used to receive notification of the corresponding events as playback proceeds. You might use these functions to display a message to indicate an error, or that media playback has been suspended because the player is stalled waiting for data. The `onBuffering` function is called with a `Duration` value that indicates approximately how much playback data has been buffered, while `onStalled` is given a `Duration` that is an estimate of how long it will be before enough data will be available to allow playback to continue. The `onError` function receives a value of type `MediaError` that represents the error that has been encountered. `MediaError` has an `Integer` variable called `cause` that gives the cause of the error and a `String` variable called `message` that provides a human-readable reason. The possible `cause` values can be found in the documentation for the `MediaError` class.

Synchronizing External Events with Playback

Sometimes it is useful to be able to synchronize other parts of the user interface with the playback of video and audio. An obvious example is an application that played back a video recording of a presentation and simultaneously displayed the speaker's slides, changing them to track the speaker's progress. The `MediaPlayer` class provides two ways to do this.

The most obvious way is to bind a local variable to the `currentTime` variable and then attach a trigger to that variable. When the trigger fires, the next slide can be shown, if it is time to do so:

```
var currentTime = bind mediaPlayer.currentTime on replace {
    // Switch slides if necessary, based on currentTime
}
```

The code required to switch slides would involve something like searching through a sequence of `Duration`s to work out which slide should be visible at any given time. Although it is not difficult to implement this, `MediaPlayer` has another feature that does this work for you—it is possible to attach a sequence of callbacks to a `MediaPlayer` object, which will be automatically invoked at specified times. The timers are of type `MediaTimer` and are attached to the `MediaPlayer` via its `timers` variable. The variables of this class are listed in Table 19-5.

Table 19-5 Variables of the `MediaTimer` Class

Variable	Type	Access	Default	Description
time	Duration	RW	null	The playback time at which this timer should fire
action	function (:MediaTimer): Void	RW	null	The function to be called when the timer fires

The time variable represents the *playback* time, not the *elapsed* time. This means that the time during playback might be paused and is not counted, which is exactly what you want if you need to stay in synchronization with video playback. The code in Listing 19-2 demonstrates the use of the `MediaTimer` class.[3]

Listing 19-2 Using a `MediaTimer`

```
1    package javafxmedia;
2
3    import javafx.scene.media.Media;
4    import javafx.scene.media.MediaPlayer;
5    import javafx.scene.media.MediaTimer;
6    import javafx.scene.media.MediaView;
7    import javafx.scene.Scene;
8    import javafx.stage.Stage;
9
10   var mediaURL =
11           "http://sun.edgeboss.net/download/sun/media/1460825906/"
12           "1460825906_2956241001_big-buck-bunny-640x360.flv";
13
14   var timers = [
15       MediaTimer { time: 10s action: function(t) {println("10s") }},
16       MediaTimer { time: 20s action: function(t) {println("20s") }},
17       MediaTimer { time: 30s action: function(t) {println("30s") }},
18   ];
19   Stage {
20       title: "Media #7"
21       resizable: false
22       scene: Scene {
23           width: 640
24           height: 400
25           content: [
26               MediaView {
```

---

[3] You can find this code in the file `javafxmedia.Media7.fx` in the JavaFX Book GUI project.

```
27                  mediaPlayer: MediaPlayer {
28                      autoPlay: true
29                      media: Media { source: mediaURL }
30                      timers: timers
31                  }
32              }
33          ]
34      }
35  }
```

The `MediaTimers` created on lines 15 to 17 of this code are intended to fire 10, 20, and 30 seconds into playback. In this case, when a timer fires, it simply prints a message. The timers are linked to the `MediaPlayer` object through its timer variable, which is set on line 30 of Listing 19-2.

> **Note**
> At the time of writing, the `MediaTimer` feature is not supported in the JavaFX runtime. This issue is being tracked as a bug at http://javafx-jira.kenai.com/browse/RT-3415.

The `MediaView` Class

As you have already seen, `MediaView` is a class that renders video content. Because it is a node, it can be placed in a scene graph and have transformations applied to it in the same way as any other node, although these transformations are not guaranteed to be honored by every implementation. The variables of the `MediaView` class that control its size and position and the video content to be played are listed in Table 19-6.

Table 19-6   Some of the Variables of the `MediaView` Class

Variable	Type	Access	Default	Description
mediaPlayer	MediaPlayer	RW		The `MediaPlayer` that is the source of the video data for this viewer
onError	function (:MediaError): Void	RW		Function called when an error occurs during playback.
x	Number	RW	0	The x coordinate of the `MediaView` relative to its coordinate origin
y	Number	RW	0	The y coordinate of the `MediaView` relative to its coordinate origin

Table 19-6   Some of the Variables of the `MediaView` Class (*Continued*)

Variable	Type	Access	Default	Description
`fitWidth`	`Number`	RW	`0`	The width of the bounding box within which the `MediaView` should appear
`fitHeight`	`Number`	RW	`0`	The height of the bounding box within which the `MediaView` should appear
`preserveRatio`	`Boolean`	RW	`true`	Specifies whether the aspect ratio of the `MediaView` should be preserved when it is scaled to fit its bounding box
`smooth`	`Boolean`	RW	`true`	Specifies whether a higher quality but slower algorithm is used to scale the video content when the `MediaView` is sized to fit its bounding box
`viewport`	`Rectangle2D`	RW	`null`	Defines a rectangular area of the video frame that will be displayed. If this is `null`, the whole frame is displayed

The video content is provided by a `MediaPlayer` object. As you have already seen, playback control is exercised by using the methods of the `MediaPlayer`. Some `MediaPlayer`s can be linked to more than one `MediaView` at a time, which allows you to display the same video more than once at different sizes or with different effects applied. This is only possible if the `supportsMultiViews` variable of the `MediaPlayer` has the value `true`.

Size and Position of the Video Frame

By default, the `MediaView` renders video in a rectangular area that is anchored at the origin of its coordinate system and is the same size as the video frame, obtained from the `width` and `height` variables of the `Media` object in its `MediaPlayer`. All the examples that you have seen so far have used this default. You can change the size/position of this area by using the `x`, `y`, `fitWidth`, `fitHeight`, and `viewport` variables.

In many cases, you will have a fixed area in which you want to display a video. If the video is larger than this area, you need to rescale it so that it fits. The `fitWidth` and `fitHeight` variables, in conjunction with the `preserveRatio` variable, allow you to specify the size of the area that is to be used to render the video. These work in the same way as the corresponding variables in the `Image` class, which you saw in Chapter 16, "Shapes, Text, and Images":

- If `fitWidth` and `fitHeight` are both either 0 or negative (which is the default), the `MediaView` is sized to exactly fit the video.[4]

- If `fitWidth` is positive and `preserveRatio` is `false`, the `MediaView` is sized so that its width is `fitWidth`. Similarly, if `fitHeight` is positive and `preserveRatio` is `false`, the `MediaView` is sized so that its height is `fitHeight`.

- If `preserveRatio` is true and either or both of `fitWidth` and `fitHeight` is positive, the `MediaView` is scaled so that its aspect ratio is preserved, but its width and height are both no greater than the bounds set by `fitWidth` and `fitHeight` (or the corresponding dimension of the video frame if either of these variables is 0 or negative).

If you wanted to fit a video into an area that is 700 pixels wide and 500 pixels high and at the same time preserve its access ratio, you set the `fitWidth`, `fitHeight`, and `preserveRatio` variables accordingly:

```
MediaView {
    preserveRatio: true
    fitWidth: 700
    fitHeight: 500
    mediaPlayer: MediaPlayer { .... }
}
```

This will cause the `MediaView` to be 700 pixels wide and 500 pixels high and will scale the video to fit in that area. Although this is fine if you play a video with a frame size that is larger than this, you might not want the frame to be scaled up if it would fit within the available space. What you probably want to do in this case is show the video at its natural size if it fits, but centered in the playing area. You can do this by carefully setting the `fitWidth`, `fitHeight`, `layoutX`, and `layoutY` variables of the `MediaView`. The code in Listing 19-3 is a custom node that handles this for you.

Listing 19-3 A Custom Node That Handles Resizing and Centering of Video

```
1    package javafxmedia;
2
3    import javafx.geometry.Rectangle2D;
4    import javafx.scene.CustomNode;
5    import javafx.scene.Group;
```

---

[4] For now, we'll assume that the viewport variable is `null`. Setting the viewport variable changes the behavior, as you'll see shortly.

```
6     import javafx.scene.media.Media;
7     import javafx.scene.media.MediaPlayer;
8     import javafx.scene.media.MediaView;
9     import javafx.scene.Node;
10    import javafx.scene.paint.Color;
11    import javafx.scene.paint.Paint;
12    import javafx.scene.shape.Rectangle;
13
14    public class ScalingMediaView extends CustomNode {
15        public var width: Number;
16        public var height: Number;
17        public var fill: Paint = Color.TRANSPARENT;
18        public var stretch: Boolean = false;
19        public var mediaPlayer: MediaPlayer;
20        public var viewport:Rectangle2D;
21
22        var media: Media = bind if (mediaPlayer == null) null
23                                 else mediaPlayer.media;
24
25        var mediaView: MediaView = MediaView {
26            mediaPlayer: bind mediaPlayer
27            layoutX: bind (width - mediaView.layoutBounds.width) / 2
28            layoutY: bind (height - mediaView.layoutBounds.height) / 2
29            fitWidth: bind if (stretch or media.width > width) width
30                           else 0
31            fitHeight: bind if (stretch or media.height > height)
32                            height
33                            else 0;
34            preserveRatio: true
35            viewport: bind viewport;
36        }
37
38        protected override function create():Node {
39            return Group {
40                content: [
41                    Rectangle {
42                        x: 0 y: 0
43                        width: bind width height: bind height
44                        fill: bind fill
45                    }
46                    mediaView
47                ]
48            }
49        }
50    }
```

The `width` and `height` variables of the `ScalingMediaView` class specify the size of the area that is available for rendering video. The `fill` variable specifies the `Paint` that will be used to fill the background area of the node, which will only be seen if the video does not fill all the available space. By default, this is set to `Paint.TRANSPARENT`, which allows whatever is behind the node to be seen. The `stretch` variable should be set to `true` if the video should be scaled to fit the available space even if it is smaller. If this is set to `false`, the video will only ever be scaled down, not up.

The `create()` function declared on lines 38 to 49 returns the nodes that will be used to represent the `ScalingMediaView`. The rectangle acts as the background and is filled with the `Paint` specified by the `fill` variable. Its size is given by the `width` and `height` variables. In front of the rectangle is a `MediaView` object, the size of which will be determined based on that of the video to be displayed, but which will never be larger than the area specified by the `width` and `height` variables of `ScalingMediaView`. Because the bounds of a group are the union of the bounds of its nested nodes, the bounds of the `ScalingMediaView` will always be determined by the `width` and `height` variables.

The code that initializes the `MediaView` on lines 25 to 35 is the most interesting part of this custom node. Let's look at how the `fitWidth` variable is set first. We need the following behavior:

- If the width of the video frame is greater than that specified for the `ScalingMediaView`, we need the video to be scaled down so that it is the same width as the `ScalingMediaView`. We do this by setting `fitWidth` to the value of the `width` variable.

- If the width of the video frame is less than that specified for the `ScalingMediaView` but `stretch` is `true`, we *do* want the video to be scaled up to fit the available area. This means we need `fitWidth` to be the same as the width of the available area, so again we need to set `fitWidth` to the value of the `width` variable.

- If the width of the video frame is less than that specified for the `ScalingMediaView` and `stretch` is `false`, we *do not* want the video to be scaled up to fit the available area, so we need `fitWidth` to be 0. This will cause the `MediaView` to have the same width as the video frame.

You should be able see that we can express all the preceding behaviors using the following code and that a similar line provides the same behavior for the height:

```
fitWidth: bind if (stretch or media.width > width) width
          else 0
```

Centering the `MediaView` in the space occupied by the `ScalingMediaView` is simple—we use the same technique that you have seen in earlier chapters:

```
layoutX: bind (width - mediaView.layoutBounds.width) / 2
layoutY: bind (height - mediaView.layoutBounds.height) / 2
```

The script file `javafxmedia/Media8.fx` in the JavaFX Book GUI project uses the `ScalingMediaView` to display a video in a `Scene` that is deliberately sized so that it is larger than the video frame. The `ScalingMediaView` for this example is created as follows:

```
Stage {
    title: "Media #8"
    scene: scene = Scene {
        width: 700
        height: 500
        content: [
            ScalingMediaView {
                width: bind scene.width
                height: bind scene.height
                stretch: false
                fill: Color.BLACK
                mediaPlayer: MediaPlayer {
                    autoPlay: true
                    media: Media { source: mediaURL }
                }
            }
        ]
    }
}
```

As you can see, the size of the `ScalingMediaView` always tracks that of its enclosing `Scene` and the stretch variable is false, which means that the video will not be stretched to occupy an extra space. Figure 19-2 shows the result of running this example.

This particular video is 640 pixels wide and 360 pixels high, so it is smaller than the 700×500-pixel stage. As you can see, it is both horizontally and vertically centered, and the space that is not occupied is filled with black, as specified by the `fill` variable of the `ScalingMediaView`.

If the stage is made smaller than the video frame, the code on lines 28 to 31 of Listing 19-3 will cause the `fitWidth` and `fitHeight` variables of the embedded `MediaView` to be set so that the video is scaled to fit the available space while preserving its aspect ratio, as shown in Figure 19-3.

The Viewport

By default, `MediaView` renders the whole video frame, but you can use the `viewport` variable to choose an arbitrary rectangular area from the frame instead, just as you can with the `Image` class, discussed in Chapter 16. When the `viewport` variable is set, the part of the frame that is at the top-left corner of the specified area is drawn at the top left of the `MediaView`, and the `MediaView` sizes itself based on the `width` and `height` variable of the viewport.

Figure 19-2 Centering a `MediaView`

Figure 19-3 Scaling a `MediaView` to fit the available space

The `ScalingMediaView` class shown in Listing 19-3 has a variable called `viewport` that can be used to set the viewport of its embedded `MediaView`. The following code sets this variable to illustrate how the viewport works:

```
Stage {
    title: "Media #9"
    scene:
    scene = Scene {
        width: 700
        height: 500
        content: [
            ScalingMediaView {
                width: bind scene.width
                height: bind scene.height
                stretch: false
                fill: Color.BLACK
                viewport: Rectangle2D {
                    minX: 40 minY: 40 width: 400 height: 200
                }
                mediaPlayer: MediaPlayer {
                    autoPlay: true
                    media: Media { source: mediaURL }
                }
            }
        ]
    }
}
```

Here, the viewport is 400 pixels wide, 200 pixels high, and starts 40 pixels down and from the left of the video frame, so this is the portion of the frame that will be rendered in the `MediaView`. You can see the result of running this code (which is in the file `javafxmedia/Media9.fx`) in Figure 19-4.

If you apply a viewport and also set the `fitWidth` and `fitHeight` variables, only the part of the video frame that is in the viewport is rescaled to the specified size. If, in the preceding example, you were to set the `stretch` variable of the `ScalingMediaView` class to `true`, you would get the result shown in Figure 19-5.[5]

Transforms and Effects

A `MediaView` is a node, and therefore you should be able to apply transformations and transitions to it. However, the `MediaView` class has a set of `Boolean`-valued variables that indicate whether specific transformations will be honored if set. Table 19-7 describes these variables.

---

[5] The code for this example is in the file `javafxmedia/Media10.fx`.

The MediaView Class   647

Figure 19-4   Using the viewport variable of **MediaView**

Figure 19-5   Using **fitWidth** and **fitHeight** with a viewport

Chapter 19 Video and Audio

Table 19-7   More Variables of the `MediaView` Class

Variable	Type	Access	Description
compositable	Boolean	R	true if the `MediaView` supports opacity
rotatable	Boolean	R	true if the `MediaView` can be rotated using its `rotate` variable
transformable	Boolean	R	true if the `MediaView` can be sheared and can be transformed using its `Transforms` variable

Assuming that the transforms that you want to perform are permitted, applying them is just as simple as it is with any other node. As an example, Listing 19-4 shows how to apply a `ScaleTransition` to a `MediaView`.

Listing 19-4   Applying a Transition to a `MediaView`

```
1     var mediaURL =
2             "http://sun.edgeboss.net/download/sun/media/1460825906/"
3             "1460825906_2956241001_big-buck-bunny-640x360.flv";
4
5     var mediaPlayer: MediaPlayer;
6     var mediaView: MediaView;
7     var done = false;
8     var currentTime = bind mediaPlayer.currentTime on replace {
9         if (currentTime > 0s and not done) {
10            done = true;
11            var s = ScaleTransition {
12                node: mediaView
13                fromX: 0.5 fromY: 0.5
14                toX: 1.0 toY: 1.0
15                interpolator: Interpolator.LINEAR
16                duration: 3s
17            };
18            s.play();
19        }
20    }
21
22    Stage {
23        title: "Media #11"
24        resizable: false
25        scene: Scene {
26            width: 640
27            height: 360
28            fill: Color.BLACK
29            content: [
```

```
30                  mediaView = MediaView {
31                      mediaPlayer: mediaPlayer = MediaPlayer {
32                          autoPlay: true;
33                          media: Media {
34                              source: mediaURL
35                          }
36                      }
37                  }
38              ]
39          }
40      }
```

The code on lines 7 to 19 monitors the `currentTime` variable of a `MediaPlayer`. When the `currentTime` exceeds 0 for the first time, a transition is applied that will scale the `MediaView` from half size to full size in 3 seconds. You can see how this works by running the file `javafxmedia/Media11.fx` in the JavaFX Book GUI project.

20

Effects and Blending

In this chapter, you see how to use the classes in the `javafx.scene.effects` and `javafx.scene.effects.lighting` packages, which implement graphical effects that you can use to enhance the appearance of your application. After discussing effects in general, the first part of this chapter describes 15 different effects that you can use to create blurs, shadows, warps, and various lighting effects. The second part describes the blending effect, which provides 19 different ways to combine two inputs, such as a node and another effect, to produce an output. The same 19 blending modes can also be applied to a group (and therefore also to a container) to control how the pixels for intersecting nodes are combined. The last part of this chapter looks at the ways in which you can light a scene by using the `Lighting` effect.

Effects are a feature of the desktop profile—they do not work on mobile devices—so the example source code for this chapter can all be found in the `javafxeffects` package in the JavaFX Book Desktop project. You can use the conditional feature API described in Chapter 12, "Platform API," to determine at runtime whether effects are available to your application.

Effects Overview

An effect is a graphical filter that accepts an input (and in some cases more than one input) and modifies it in some way to produce an output. The output is either rendered as part of a scene or becomes the input for another effect. The combination of a node and one or more effects is referred to here as an *effects chain*.

Effects Chains

Figure 20-1 shows two common effects chains. An effects chain contains, at minimum, one node and one effect.

In the first chain, at the top of the figure, a single effect is applied to a node, and the result is drawn onto the scene. The second chain contains two effects. In this case, the first effect is applied to the node, which results in an output image that becomes the input for the second effect. It is the output of the second effect that will be drawn onto the scene.

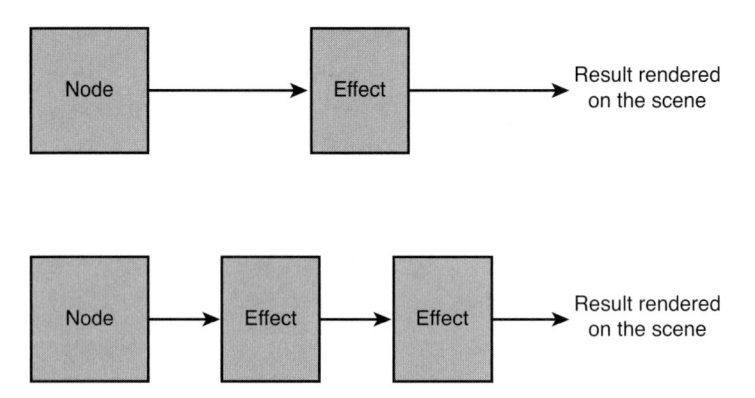

Figure 20-1   Relationship between effects and nodes

Effects and Nodes

When an effect is applied to a node, the output of the effects chain logically replaces the node itself on the screen. In general, an effect will change the bounds of a node. For example, adding a shadow to a node by using the `DropShadow` effect will typically make it wider and taller. The node's local and parent bounds are adjusted based on the result of the effects chain, but its layout bounds are not affected. When a node has both effects and transformations, the effect is applied before the transformations. This means, for example, that adding a shadow and then scaling up the node will also scale up the shadow.

An effect is linked to a node via its `effect` variable.[1] The code in Listing 20-1, which you will find in the file `javafxeffects/Effects1.fx`, shows how simple it is to add an effect to a node. In this case, a drop shadow is added by the three lines of code starting on line 19. Figure 20-2 shows the result.

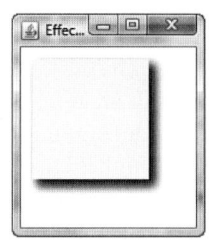

Figure 20-2   A rectangle with a drop shadow effect

---

[1] This variable does not exist in the mobile profile. If you get compilation errors when trying to run the examples for this chapter, the reason is most likely that you are trying to build for the mobile emulator.

Effects Overview

Listing 20-1   Adding an Effect to a Node

```
1    package javafxeffects;
2
3    import javafx.scene.effect.DropShadow;
4    import javafx.scene.paint.Color;
5    import javafx.scene.Scene;
6    import javafx.scene.shape.Rectangle;
7    import javafx.stage.Stage;
8
9    var rect: Rectangle;
10   Stage {
11       title: "Effects #1"
12       scene: Scene {
13           width: 150 height: 150
14           content: [
15               rect = Rectangle {
16                   x: 10 y: 10
17                   width: 100 height: 100
18                   fill: Color.YELLOW
19                   effect: DropShadow {
20                       offsetX: 5 offsetY: 5
21                   }
22               }
23           ]
24       }
25   }
26   println("Layout bounds: {rect.layoutBounds}");
27   println("Parent bounds: {rect.boundsInParent}");
```

The last two lines of Listing 20-1 print the layout bounds and parent bounds of the rectangle. Here's the result:

```
Layout bounds: BoundingBox [minX = 10.0, minY=10.0, maxX=110.0, maxY=110.0,
width=100.0, height=100.0]
Parent bounds: BoundingBox [minX = 6.0, minY=6.0, maxX=124.0,
maxY=124.0,width=118.0, height=118.0]
```

As you can see, the rectangle's layout bounds correspond to its specified width and height (because the layout bounds do not include the results of the effect), but width and height of the parent bounds have both increased from 100 to 118 because of the space occupied by the drop shadow.

Applying more than one effect is simply a matter of linking one effect to another. The following code (which you'll find in the file `javafxeffects/Effects2.fx`) adds a reflection to the drop shadow, giving the result shown in Figure 20-3:

```
Rectangle {
    x: 10
    y: 10
```

654 Chapter 20 Effects and Blending

```
        width: 100
        height: 100
        fill: Color.YELLOW
        effect: Reflection {
            input: DropShadow {
                offsetX: 5 offsetY: 5
            }
        }
    }
}
```

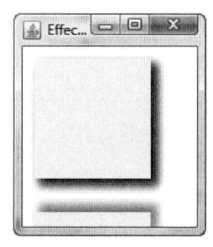

Figure 20-3 Applying two effects to the same rectangle

The linkage between the effects is made through the `input` variable of the reflection effect—the drop shadow is applied first, and the result of this becomes the input to the reflection effect. When no input is specified, the node itself is used as the input, as in the case of the drop shadow effect.

Not all effects have an `input` variable. Those that don't can only appear as the first (or only) entry in the effects chain. The `DropShadow` class is an example of this.[2] Other effects can have more than one input, such as the `Blend` effect that you'll see in the second part of this chapter.

As noted earlier, transformations are applied after any effects, so they apply to the effects, too. The following code, from the file `javafxeffects/Effects3.fx`, adds a rotation to the two effects that are applied to the `Rectangle`, as shown in Figure 20-4.

```
Rectangle {
    x: 10 y: 10
    width: 100 height: 100
    fill: Color.YELLOW
    rotate: -45
    effect: Reflection {
        input: DropShadow {
```

---

[2] The lack of an `input` variable in the `DropShadow` and other effects classes may be a temporary state of affairs. An issue has been filed at http://javafx-jira.kenai.com that may result in this being changed.

```
        offsetX: 5 offsetY: 5
    }
}
```

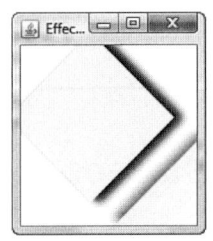

Figure 20-4   Using effects and transformations together.

Effects and Groups

A particularly powerful feature of effects is that they can be applied to a group. An effect that is applied to a group operates on the group as a whole. This is particularly useful if you want to create an effect that is uniform across the scene, such as the direction of lighting.

The following code, from the file `javafxeffects/Effects4.fx`, applies a `DropShadow` effect to a group that contains a rectangle and a circle; as you can see in Figure 20-5, this gives both of the nodes a `DropShadow` effect:

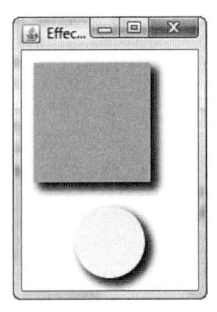

Figure 20-5   Applying an effect to a `Group`

```
Group {
    effect: DropShadow {
        offsetX: 5 offsetY: 5
    }
    content: [
        Rectangle {
            x: 10 y: 10
            width: 100 height: 100
```

```
            fill: Color.ORANGE
        }
        Circle {
            centerX: 75 centerY: 160 radius: 30
            fill: Color.YELLOW
        }
    ]
}
```

The JavaFX Effects Classes

The JavaFX SDK provides 17 different effects that can be applied to any node. This section describes and illustrates all the effects, with the exception of `Blend` and `Lighting`, which have sections of their own at the end of the chapter. Each effect has a set of variables that you can use to customize it. As we examine each effect, we'll take a look at the variables available and roughly consider what each of them does. There are too many combinations to illustrate them all in this chapter, so in most cases we limit ourselves to some typical examples. It is easy to experiment with these effects—all you need to do is modify the example source code. You can also use the Effects Playground application that you'll find among the samples at http://javafx.com.

GaussianBlur

The `GaussianBlur` effect produces a blurred version of its input. The "Gaussian" part of the name refers to the fact that the output pixels are calculated by applying a Gaussian function to the source pixel and a group of pixels surrounding it. If you are interested in the details, you'll find them at http://en.wikipedia.org/wiki/Gaussian_blur. The size of the group of adjacent pixels that are used to calculate the result is controlled by the `radius` variable (see Table 20-1). The larger the value of the `radius` variable, the greater the blur effect will be. When the value of this variable is `0`, there is no blur at all.

Table 20-1 **Variables of the `GaussianBlur` Class**

Variable	Type	Access	Default	Description
input	Effect	RW	null	The input to this effect
radius	Number	RW	10.0	The radius of the area containing the source pixels used to create each target pixel, in the range `0` to `63`, inclusive

Two example of the `GaussianBlur` effect applied to the image used in the previous two sections are shown in Figure 20-6. Here's the code used to create this effect, which you'll find in the file `javafxeffects/GaussianBlur1.fx`:

```
ImageView {
    image: Image { url: "{__DIR__}image1.jpg" }
    effect: GaussianBlur {
        radius: bind radiusSlider.value
    }
}
```

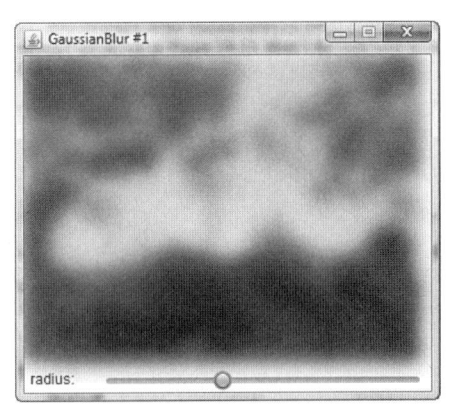

Figure 20-6   The `GaussianBlur` effect

The image on the left has a blur radius of 10, while the one on the right has radius 40.

BoxBlur

`GaussianBlur` is a high-quality effect, but it is also a relatively expensive one. The `BoxBlur` effect is a cheaper way to produce a blur, albeit one of lower quality. The variables that you can use to control the `BoxBlur` effect are listed in Table 20-2.

Table 20-2   Variables of the `BoxBlur` Class

Variable	Type	Access	Default	Description
input	Effect	RW	null	The input to this effect.
height	Number	RW	5.0	The vertical size of the box used to create the blur, in the range 0 to 255, inclusive.
width	Number	RW	5.0	The horizontal size of the box used to create the blur, in the range 0 to 255, inclusive.
iterations	Number	RW	1	The number of averaging iterations, in the range 0 to 3, inclusive. Higher values produce a smoother blur effect.

This effect works by replacing each pixel of the input by the result of averaging its value with those of its neighboring pixels. The pixels that take part in the operation are those in a rectangular area surrounding the source pixel, the dimensions of which are given by the `width` and `height` variables. You can see the effects of changing these variables by running the code in the file `javafxeffects/BoxBlur1.fx`. This example applies the `BoxBlur` effect to the same image as we used to illustrate `GaussianBlur`. The `width`, `height`, and `iterations` variables are set from three sliders that allow you to test the full ranges of values for each variable. Here's how the `BoxBlur` is applied:

```
ImageView {
    image: Image { url: "{__DIR__}image1.jpg" }
    effect: BoxBlur {
        height: bind heightSlider.value
        width: bind widthSlider.value
        iterations: bind iterationSlider.value
    }
}
```

Increasing the value of the `height` variable produces a vertical blur, as shown on the left of Figure 20-7. Similarly, the `width` variable controls the extent of the blur in the horizontal direction.

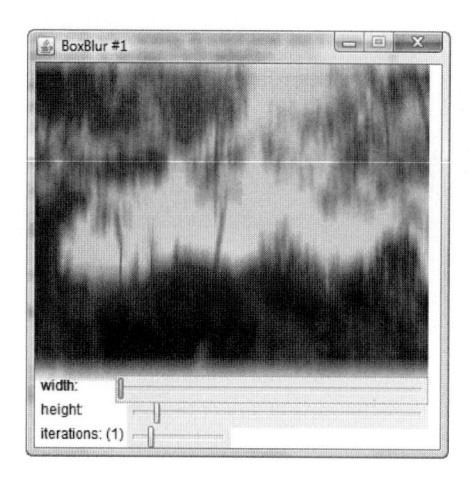

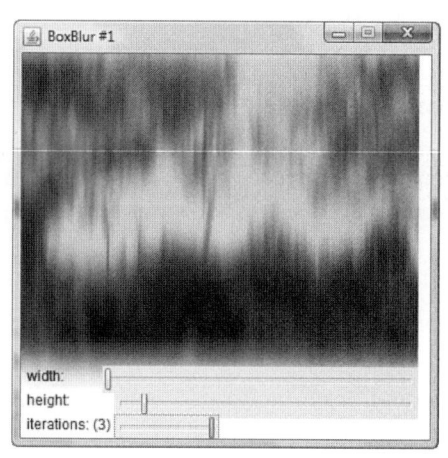

Figure 20-7   The Box Blur effect

You can use the `iterations` variable to increase the quality of the blur at the expense of greater CPU utilization. When this variable has the value 2 or 3, the averaging operation is repeated the specified number of times. On the second iteration, the averaged pixels are averaged against each other, which tends to smooth out any sharp differences that might exist near to edges in the input source. A third iteration produces an even smoother result. You can see the result of applying three iterations to a horizontal blur of the input image on the right of Figure 20-7. A `BoxBlur` with three iterations produces a result that is close to that of a `GaussianBlur`, but at a slightly lower cost.

MotionBlur

`MotionBlur` creates the effect that you would see if you look out of the window of a fast-moving vehicle. Like `GaussianBlur`, it has a `radius` variable that determines how much of a blur is to be applied. It also has an `angle` variable that lets you specify the direction of the motion. These variables are described in Table 20-3.

Table 20-3   Variables of the MotionBlur Class

Variable	Type	Access	Default	Description
input	Effect	RW	null	The input to this effect
angle	Number	RW	0	The angle of the motion blur
radius	Number	RW	10.0	The radius of the area containing the source pixels used to create each target pixel, in the range 0 to 63 inclusive

There are no restrictions on the value of the `angle` variable, but values greater than 360 are treated modulo 360, while negative values are first reduced modulo 360 and then have 180 added to them, so that −90 is the same as 270. The following extract shows how to apply a `MotionBlur` to a node.

```
image: Image { url: "{__DIR__}image1.jpg" }
effect: MotionBlur {
    angle: bind angleSlider.value
    radius: bind radiusSlider.value
}
}
```

If you run the code in the file `javafxeffects/MotionBlur1.fx`, you can experiment with the effects of different `radius` and `angle` values. Two examples with different angles are shown in Figure 20-8. The angle slider lets you vary the value of this variable from −180 when the thumb is at the far left to +180 at the far right. In the example on the left of the figure, the `angle` variable is 0, which gives a horizontal blur. In the example on the right, the `angle` variable has the value 90, and the result is a vertical blur. As is the case

660 Chapter 20 Effects and Blending

elsewhere in the JavaFX API, angles are measured with 0 at the 3 o'clock position and increase as you move in a clockwise direction.

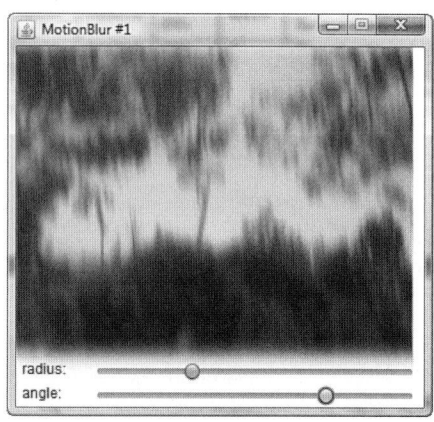

Figure 20-8 The `MotionBlur` effect

DropShadow

As you have already seen, the `DropShadow` effect draws a shadow that appears to be behind and partly obscured by the node to which it is applied. By using this effect with the appropriate variable settings, you can give the impression that the node is floating above a nearby surface or one slightly farther away. You can also change the nature of the shadow to indicate whether the light source is close to or a long way from the node. The variables that you can use to configure the `DropShadow` class are listed in Table 20-4.

Table 20-4 **Variables of the `DropShadow` Class**

Variable	Type	Access	Default	Description
blurType	Blur Type	RW	THREE_PASS_BOX	The type of blur to be used
color	Color	RW	Color.BLACK	The color to be used for the shadow
offsetX	Number	RW	0.0	The x-offset of the shadow
offsetY	Number	RW	0.0	The y-offset of the shadow
radius	Number	RW	10	The radius of the blur effect if a `GaussionBlur` is used
width	Number	RW	21	The width of the blur if `BoxBlur` is used
height	Number	RW	21	The height of the blur if `BoxBlur` is used
spread	Number	RW	0.0	The proportion of the radius (or box for `BoxBlur`) over which the shadow is fully opaque (see text)

The variables that you will most commonly set are `color`, `offsetX`, and `offsetY`. The `color` variable simply determines the color of the solid part of the shadow, which will generally be slightly darker than the background behind the node. By default, the shadow is black. The `offsetX` and `offsetY` variables control the displacement of the shadow relative to the node itself.

The `blurType` variable controls which of the supported types of blur is used at the edges of the shadow. This variable is of type `javafx.scene.effects.BlurType`, which has the following possible values:

- `BlurType.GAUSSIAN`: A `GaussianBlur`
- `BlurType.ONE_PASS_BOX`: A `BoxBlur` with one iteration
- `BlurType.TWO_PASS_BOX`: A `BoxBlur` with two iterations
- `BlurType.THREE_PASS_BOX`: A `BoxBlur` with three iteration

The code in the file `javafxeffects/DropShadow1.fx` creates a scene containing a rectangle with a `DropShadow` effect and a `GaussianBlur`. There are four sliders that let you control some of the variables listed in Table 20-5. You can use this program to experiment with various settings to see how they work. Figure 20-9 shows a typical example.

Table 20-5   Variables of the `Shadow` Class

Variable	Type	Access	Default	Description
blurType	BlurType	RW	THREE_PASS_BOX	The type of blur to be used
input	Effect	RW	null	The input to this effect
color	Color	RW	Color.BLACK	The color to be used for the shadow
radius	Number	RW	10.0	The radius of the blur effect if a `GaussianBlur` is used
width	Number	RW	21	The width of the blur if a `BoxBlur` is used
height	Number	RW	21	The height if the blur if a `BoxBlur` is used

The size of the shadow is determined by the values of the `offsetX`, `offsetX`, and `radius` variables. When the `radius` is 0, the shadow has a sharp edge as shown on the left of Figure 20-10. In this case, the `offsetX` and `offsetY` values are both 15, so the shadow is offset by 15 pixels to the right of and below the top-left corner of the node, which gives the impression of a light source that is to the left of and above the top of the node. Negative values for the `offsetX` variable would be used for a light source to the right of the node, and negative `offsetY` values for a light source that is below the node.

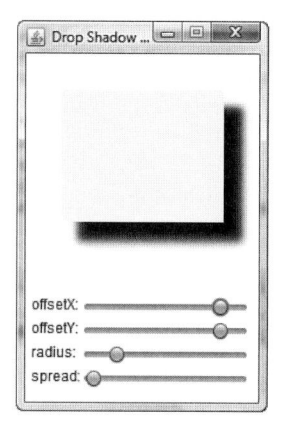

Figure 20-9   Configuring a `DropShadow` effect

Figure 20-10   Effects of the `offsetX`, `offsetY`, and radius variable of the `DropShadow` effect

When the `radius` value is non-0, the edge of the shadow is blurred by blending pixels of the shadow color with those of the background color. The `radius` determines the size of this blurred area. Increasing the `radius` value makes the blurred region, and the size of the shadow, larger, as shown on the right of Figure 20-10. As you can see, the blurring fades out with increasing distance from the original shadow area. The `radius` value can be anywhere between `0` and `63`, inclusive.

By default, the blurred area starts with the shadow color on its inside edge and progresses to the background color on its outside edge. If you want, you can arrange for a larger part of the blurred area to have the shadow color, resulting in a larger, darker shadow. You do this by setting the `spread` value, which ranges from `0.0`, the default, to `1.0`. This value represents the proportion of the blurred area into which the shadow color creeps. On the right side of Figure 20-10, the spread variable has value `0`, and you can see that the shadow gets lighter very rapidly as you move your eyes away from the edge of the rectangle. On the left side of Figure 20-11, the `spread` variable has been set to `0.5`. Now you can see that the darker region of the shadow has increased in size as it encroaches into the blurred area. On the right of Figure 20-11, the `spread` is at of `0.9`, and you can see that almost all the blurred area has been taken over by the shadow color.

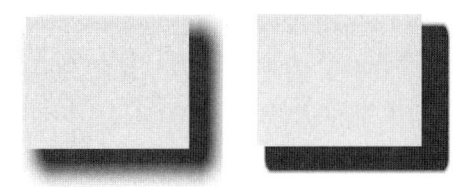

Figure 20-11 The effect of the spread variable

The idea of the `spread` variable is to allow a proper emulation of what would happen if you moved a light source quite close up to the node. A light source nearby would cause a wide shadow, corresponding to a larger blurred area, but it would also cause the darker part of the shadow to increase in size. You simulate the former effect by increasing the blur `radius` and the latter by increasing the `spread`.

InnerShadow

`InnerShadow` is very similar to `DropShadow`, the difference being that the shadow is *inside* the boundaries of the node to which it is applied, rather than outside. This gives the impression of depth within the node, because it appears to have built-up sides. The variables of this class, which are listed in Table 20-6, are almost the same as those of `DropShadow`.

You can see an example of this effect in Figure 20-12. This screenshot shows the result of running the code in the file `javafxeffects/InnerShadow1.fx`. As with the `DropShadow` examples, you can use the sliders to vary the effect parameters and see the results. The `choke` variable is equivalent to the `spread` variable of the `DropShadow` class.

Table 20-6 Variables of the `InnerShadow` Class

Variable	Type	Access	Default	Description
blurType	BlurType	RW	THREE_PASS_BOX	The type of blur to be used
color	Color	RW	Color.BLACK	The color to be used for the shadow
offsetX	Number	RW	0.0	The x-offset of the shadow
offsetY	Number	RW	0.0	The y-offset of the shadow
radius	Number	RW	10	The radius of the blur effect if a `GaussianBlur` is used
width	Number	RW	21	The width of the blur if a `BoxBlur` is used
height	Number	RW	21	The height of the blur if a `BoxBlur` is used

Table 20-6 Variables of the `InnerShadow` Class (*Continued*)

Variable	Type	Access	Default	Description
choke	Number	RW	0.0	The proportion of the radius (or box for `BoxBlur`) over which the shadow is fully opaque (see text)

Shadow

The `Shadow` effect produces a single-colored and blurred shadow from the node or input effect on which it operates. The extent of the blur depends on the value of the

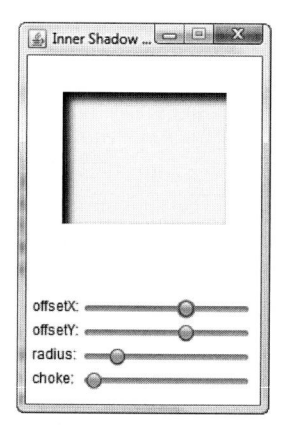

Figure 20-12 Configuring an `InnerShadow` effect

`radius`, which is one of the three variables that control this effect, all of which are listed in Table 20-5 on page 661.

You can see an example of this effect as applied to some text in Figure 20-13. You can experiment with different `radius` values by running this example, which you'll find in the file `javafxeffects/Shadow1.fx`:

```
Text {
    textOrigin: TextOrigin.TOP
    x: 30 y: 30
    content: "JavaFX Shadow Effect"
    font: Font { size: 24 }
    effect: Shadow {
        color: Color.BLUE
```

```
        radius: bind radiusSlider.value
    }
}
```

Figure 20-13   The `Shadow` effect

Unlike the other two shadow effects, this one replaces its input instead of augmenting it, so the original text node is not drawn.

Bloom

The `Bloom` effect adds a glow to those areas of its input that are made up of pixels for which the luminosity value is above a given threshold. This effect has only two controlling variable, which are listed in Table 20-7.

Table 20-7   Variables of the Bloom Class

Variable	Type	Access	Default	Description
input	Effect	RW	null	The input to this effect.
threshold	Number	RW	0.3	The luminosity above which the glow effect will be applied, from 0.0 (all pixels will glow) to 1.0. (No pixels will glow.)

The luminosity of a pixel is a measure of how bright it seems to the human eye. You can see an example of this effect in Figure 20-14, which shows the `Bloom` effect applied to an `ImageView` node[3]:

```
ImageView {
    image: Image { url: "{__DIR__}image1.jpg" }
    effect: bloom = Bloom {
```

---

[3] You'll find this code in the file `javafxeffects/Bloom1.fx`.

```
        threshold: bind (thresholdSlider.value as Number) / 10
    }
}
```

Figure 20-14   The `Bloom` effect

In the image on the left, the threshold value is `1.0`. Because no pixel has a luminosity that is greater than `1.0`, what you see here is the original image. On the right of the figure, the slider has been moved so that the threshold is now set to `0.3`. The blue regions of the image, in particular the sky, are now noticeably brighter. Notice that this effect spills over onto adjacent pixels so that the leaves on the trees near the top of the image have also been brightened.

Glow

`Glow` is very similar to `Bloom`, except that the controlling parameter works in the reverse order. The glow effect makes bright pixels appear brighter. The more of the effect that you apply, as determined by the value of the `level` variable, the brighter those pixels appear. The two variables that control this effect are listed in Table 20-8.

Table 20-8   Variables of the `Glow` Effect

Variable	Type	Access	Default	Description
input	Effect	RW	null	The input to this effect.
level	Number	RW	0.3	Controls the intensity of the glow effect. `0.0` gives no glow; `1.0` gives maximum glow.

You'll find an example that allows you to vary the `level` parameter in the file `javafxeffects/Glow1.fx`. The following extract from that file shows how the glow effect is applied to a node:

```
ImageView {
    image: Image { url: "{__DIR__}image1.jpg" }
    effect: Glow {
        level: bind (levelSlider.value as Number) / 10
    }
}
```

Figure 20-15 shows this effect applied to the same image as that used in our discussion of bloom in the previous section. In the image on the left of the figure, the level variable is 0, so no glow is applied. In the image on the right, the level is set to 0.6, and the result is almost exactly the same as the result of applying a small amount of bloom to the image, which you can see at the bottom of Figure 20-14. To apply more glow in this example, you move the slider farther to the right, whereas to apply more bloom in the example in the previous section, you moved it farther to the left.

Figure 20-15   The `Glow` effect

Identity

The `Identity` effect is a little different from the effects that you have seen so far—its sole purpose is to allow an `Image` object to be used as the input to another effect. It is always linked to a node, but that node does not appear in the scene; the result of applying one or more effects to the source image is seen instead. Table 20-9 lists the variables that control the behavior of this class.

The simplest way to explain how these variables work is by using an example. The following code, which you'll find in the file `javafxeffects/Identity1.fx`, applies a `GaussianBlur` effect to an image and places it in the `Scene`.

Table 20-9   **Variables of the `Identity` Class**

Variable	Type	Access	Default	Description
source	Image	RW	null	The source `Image`
x	Number	RW	0	The `x` coordinate of the `Image` relative to the source `Node`
y	Number	RW	0	The `y` coordinate of the `Image` relative to the source `Node`

```
1      Stage {
2          title: "Identity #1"
3          scene: Scene {
4              width: 380
5              height: 280
6              var image = Image { url: "{__DIR__}image1.jpg" }
7              content: [
8                  Circle {
9                      centerX: 100 centerY: 100
10                     effect: GaussianBlur {
11                         input: Identity {
12                             source: image
13                             x: 10 y: 10
14                         }
15                         radius: 10
16                     }
17                 }
18             ]
19         }
20     }
```

The result of running this code is shown in Figure 20-16.

Figure 20-16   The `Identity` effect

The `Identity` effect on lines 11 to 14 converts the image to an `Effect` that is then used as the input to the `GaussianBlur`, resulting in a blurred version of the image. These two effects are both linked with a circle, but because the circle is not an input to either of the effects, it does not influence the output, and the blurred image appears instead of it. The only property of the circle that *is* inherited is its coordinate system, which, in this case, is the same as the coordinate system of the scene. The x and y variables of the `Identity` effect, which are set on line 13, determine where its output would be drawn relative to the circle's coordinate system. In this case, these values cause the image to be placed a little to the right of and below the coordinate origin.

The result of an `Identity` effect, like that of the `Flood` effect that is described in the next section, is often used as one of the inputs to a `Blend` effect, which is discussed later in this chapter.

Flood

Like `Identity`, the purpose of the `Flood` effect is to create an input to another effect, in this case a rectangular area filled with a `Paint` or a solid color. The variables that determine the fill color and the bounds of the filled area are listed in Table 20-10.

Table 20-10   **Variables of the `Flood` Class**

Variable	Type	Access	Default	Description
paint	Paint	RW	Color.RED	The `Paint` used to flood the area
x	Number	RW	0	The x coordinate of the filled area relative to the source `Node`
y	Number	RW	0	The y coordinate of the filled area relative to the source `Node`
width	Number	RW	0	The width of the area to be filled
height	Number	RW	0	The height of the area to be filled

The coordinates and lengths are specified in the coordinate system of the node that this effect is linked with. As with `Identity`, the node itself is replaced in the scene by the result of the effect. The code in the file `javafxeffects/Flood1.fx` uses the `Flood` effect to fill an area with a solid blue color and then applies a `MotionBlur`, giving the result shown in Figure 20-17.

ColorAdjust

The `ColorAdjust` effect produces an output that is the result of adjusting some or all the hue, saturation, brightness, and contrast values of its input. The input may be either

670   Chapter 20 Effects and Blending

Figure 20-17   The `Flood` effect

another effect or a node of any kind, but most commonly an image in an `ImageView` object. The variables of this class are listed in Table 20-11.

You can experiment with this effect by running the example in the file `javafxeffects/ColorAdjust.fx`, which binds a slider to each of the hue, saturation, brightness, and contrast variables of a `ColorAdjust` object that is associated with an `ImageView` node. The values of the hue, saturation, and brightness sliders range from `-1.0` on the left to `1.0` on the right, while the contrast slider provides the value `0.25` in its

Table 20-11 Variables of the `ColorAdjust` Class

Variable	Type	Access	Default	Description
input	Effect	RW	null	The input to this effect.
hue	Number	RW	0.0	The amount by which the hue of each pixel should be adjusted, in the range -1.0 to 1.0. Value 0 leaves the hue unchanged.
saturation	Number	RW	0.0	The amount by which the saturation of each pixel should be adjusted, in the range -1.0 to 1.0. Value 0 leaves the saturation unchanged.
brightness	Number	RW	0.0	The amount by which the brightness of each pixel should be adjusted, in the range -1.0 to 1.0. Value 0 leaves the brightness unchanged.
contrast	Number	RW	1.0	The amount by which the contrast should be adjusted, in the range 0.25 to 4. Value 1 leaves the contrast unchanged.

minimum position and 4.0 at its maximum position. On the left of Figure 20-18, you can see the result of applying almost the maximum brightness, and on the right you see the result of applying the maximum contrast.

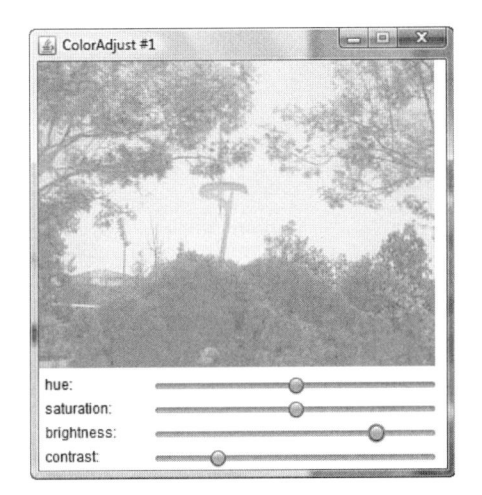

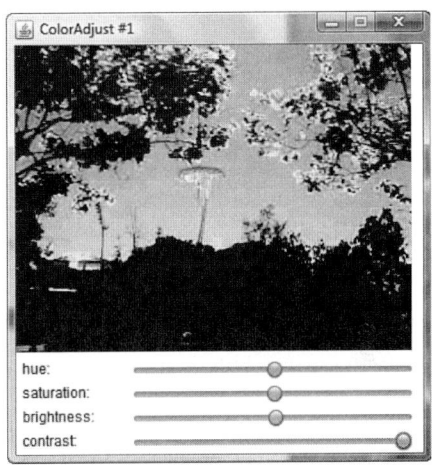

Figure 20-18 The `ColorAdjust` effect

InvertMask

The `InvertMask` effect takes another `Effect` as its input and produces a result in which all the transparent pixels from the input are opaque and all the opaque pixels are transparent. The output is typically used as one of the inputs to a `Blend` effect, which is discussed later in this chapter. The variables of the `InvertMask` class are listed in Table 20-12.

Table 20-12 The Variables of the `InvertMask` Class

Variable	Type	Access	Default	Description
input	Effect	RW	null	The input to this effect
pad	Number	RW	0	The padding to add to the sides of the resulting image

Reflection

The `Reflection` effect provides an easy way to create a reflection of a node or group of nodes. The variables that you can use to specify the required characteristics of the reflection are listed in Table 20-13.

Chapter 20 Effects and Blending

Table 20-13 The Variables of the `Reflection` Class

Variable	Type	Access	Default	Description
input	Effect	RW	null	The input to this effect
topOffset	Number	RW	0	The distance between the bottom of the input and the beginning of the reflection
fraction	Number	RW	0	The fraction of the input that is used to create the reflection
topOpacity	Number	RW	0.5	The opacity used for the topmost row of pixels in the reflection
bottomOpacity	Number	RW	0	The opacity of the bottom row of pixels in the reflection

The example code in the file `javafxeffects/Reflection1.fx` allows you to experiment with different values of these variables. A typical result, which is equivalent to the following code, is shown in Figure 20-19.

```
Text {
    content: "JavaFX Developer's Guide"
    x: 20 y: 50
    fill: Color.WHITE
    font: Font { size: 24 }
    effect: Reflection {
        topOffset:0
        fraction: 0.8
        topOpacity: 0.3
        bottomOpacity: 0.0
    }
}
```

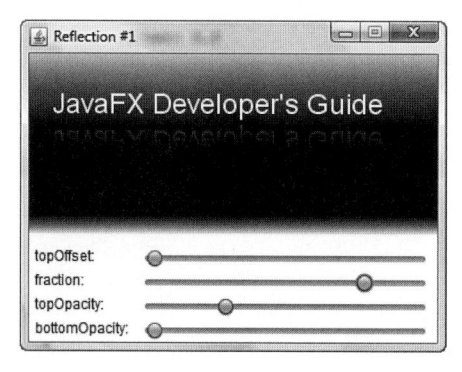

Figure 20-19 The `Reflection` effect

The `topOffset` variable lets you set the distance between the source object, here the text "JavaFX Developer's Guide" (and its reflection). Increasing this distance makes it seem that the source is further away from the reflecting surface. In Figure 20-19, the `topOffset` value is `0`, which places the reflection as close as possible to the original. In this case, the reflected text might seem to be farther away than it should be with this value—that is because of the descender on the letter *p*, which is the closest point of contact with the reflection.

The `fraction` variable determines how much of the source appears in the reflection. Typically, unless the reflecting surface is very shiny, you will not want the whole of the source object to be reflected. In Figure 20-19, the `fraction` variable has the value `0.8`, so about 80% of the source is reflected.

The `topOpacity` and `bottomOpacity` values give the opacity of the reflection at its top and bottom extents, respectively. In Figure 20-19, the `topOpacity` has been set to `0.3` and `bottomOpacity` to `0.0`.

SepiaTone

The `SepiaTone` effect is used to give images (or any group of nodes) an "Olde Worlde" look, as if they have been photographed by an old black-and-white camera, or washed out by the effects of exposure to sunlight over a long period. This effect provides only the two variables listed in Table 20-14.

Table 20-14   Variables of the `SepiaTone` Class

Variable	Type	Access	Default	Description
input	Effect	RW	null	The input to this effect
level	Number	RW	1.0	The level of this effect, from `0.0` to `1.0`

The `level` variable determines the extent to which the image is affected. The example code in the file `javafxeffects/SepiaTone1.fx` creates a `Scene` containing an image and a slider that lets you vary the value of the `level` variable and observe the result. The screenshot on the left of Figure 20-20 has `level` set to the value `0.4`, while the one on the right has `level` set to `1.0`.

PerspectiveTransform

The `PerspectiveTransform` is a useful effect that you can use to create the impression of a rotation in the direction of the z-axis—that is, into and out of the screen. It operates by deforming a node or group of nodes by moving its corners to specified locations and relocating the other pixels in such a way that straight lines drawn on the original nodes are mapped to straight lines in the result. Unlike the affine transforms that you saw in Chapter 17, "Coordinates, Transforms, and Layout," this effect does *not* guarantee that lines that are parallel in the source will be parallel in the result and, in fact, the perspective effect requires that some parallel lines be made nonparallel.

The variables that control the perspective effect are listed in Table 20-15.

Figure 20-20   The `SepiaTone` effect

Table 20-15   Variables of the `PerspectiveTransform` Class

Variable	Type	Access	Default	Description
input	Effect	RW	null	The input to this effect.
llx	Number	RW	0	The x coordinate of the location to which the lower-left corner of the input is moved
lly	Number	RW	0	The y coordinate of the location to which the lower-left corner of the input is moved
ulx	Number	RW	0	The x coordinate of the location to which the upper-left corner of the input is moved
uly	Number	RW	0	The y coordinate of the location to which the upper-left corner of the input is moved
lrx	Number	RW	0	The x coordinate of the location to which the lower-right corner of the input is moved
lry	Number	RW	0	The y coordinate of the location to which the lower-right corner of the input is moved
urx	Number	RW	0	The x coordinate of the location to which the upper-right corner of the input is moved
ury	Number	RW	0	The y coordinate of the location to which the upper-right corner of the input is moved

To see what these variables represent, refer to Figure 20-1. Here, imagine that the image is mounted vertically and can rotate about its vertical axis, as shown by the white dashed line. In the figure, the black outline represent the view of the image after it has been rotated a few degrees so that the right edge has moved closer to the viewer and the left edge farther away. This would cause the right edge to appear larger and the left edge correspondingly smaller, giving the impression of perspective.

You can use a `PerspectiveTransform` to create the rotated image from the original by moving the corners of the original to the new positions, as shown in Figure 20-21. The corner at the top left is the upper-left corner, and its position is given by the `ulx` and `uly` variables. The corner at the top right is the upper-right corner, and its position is specified by the `urx` and `ury` variables, and so on.

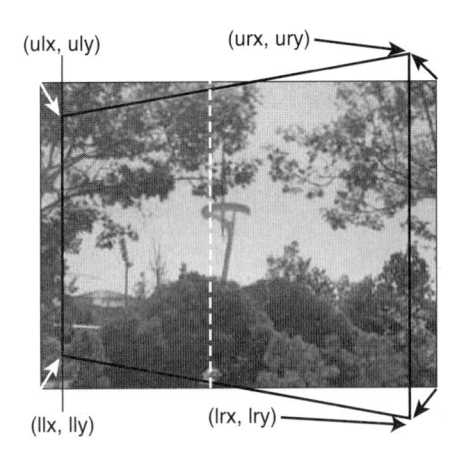

Figure 20-21   Illustrating the variables of the **PerspectiveTransform** class

It's easy to create a `PerspectiveTransform` that will rotate an image (or any other node or group) around a vertical axis that is a specified distance along its horizontal edge. It requires only a small amount of mathematics. We'll deal with the x and y coordinates separately, to make it easier to understand what is going on. The information needed to work out how to calculate the values of the x coordinates is shown in Figure 20-22.

Here, we are looking down at the image from above. The thick horizontal line, labeled APB, is the image before rotation, whereas the diagonal line, labeled A'PB', is the image after it has been rotated through an angle (shown here as `angle`) about a pivot point, marked P, that is 11 pixels from its left side and 12 pixels from its right side. In this case, the pivot point is almost equidistant from the sides of the image, but the same calculation works even if this is not the case. The x-axis is shown at the bottom of the figure.

The x coordinate of the left side of the image after rotation is given by the distance AC, while the x coordinate of the right side is given by A. The distance AC is the same as AP – CP. Because AP has the value 11, elementary trigonometry gives the following:

```
AC = AP - CP = 11 - 11 * cos(angle)
```

Similarly,

```
AD = BP + PD = 11 + 12 * cos(angle)
```

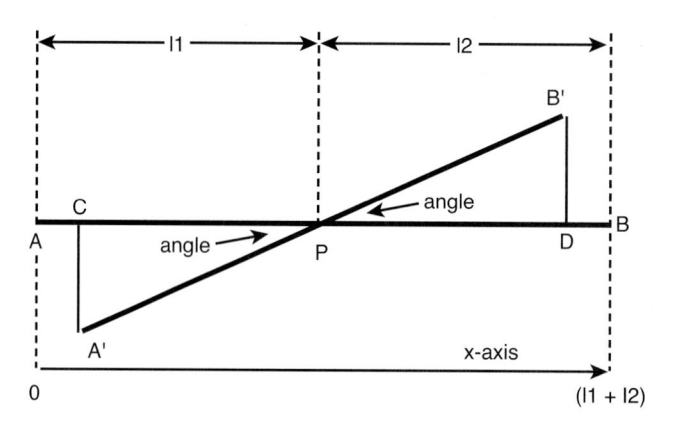

Figure 20-22   Rotating an image (top-down view)

AC is actually the value of both `ulx` and `llx`, while AD is the value that we need for `urx` and `ulx`. To make this simpler when using the `PerspectiveTransform`, we introduce two new parameters:

- `imgWidth`: The width of the image. This corresponds to the length AB and is equal to l1 + l2.
- `pivot`: The position of the pivot point along the line AB, as a ratio of `l1` to the total length AB. To place the pivot point in the center, set `pivot` to `0.5`.

Given these parameters, we so far have the following `PerspectiveTransform`:

```
PerspectiveTransform {
    ulx: l1 - l1 * Math.cos(angle)
    uly: ?? // Not yet determined
    llx: l1 - l1 * Math.cos(angle)
    lly: ?? // Not yet determined
    urx: l1 + l2 * Math.cos(angle)
    ury: ?? // Not yet determined
    lrx: l1 + l2 * Math.cos(angle)
    lry: imgHeight ?? // Not yet determined
}
```

Now let's move on to the y coordinates. This part is slightly easier. Essentially, what we need to do is make the length of the side of the image that moves toward us larger and that of the side that moves away from us smaller. We can choose by how much we want each side to grow or shrink—the closer we are to the image, the more each side would grow or shrink. We'll make this a parameter of the transform and say that we want each side to grow or shrink by `htFactor` of its actual value at each end. That means, for example, that if the image is 100 pixels tall and we choose `htFactor` to be `0.2`, the side of the image that is nearer to us after the image has rotated through 90 degree will be larger by 0.2 * 100 = 20 pixels at each end, or a total of 140 pixels tall. Similarly, the side that is farther away will shrink to 60 pixels in height.

Now refer to Figure 20-23. Here, we are looking at the image from the front again. The solid shape is the image after it has been rotated. The dashed vertical line is the axis of rotation, and the dashed extension that is outside the rectangle represents the maximum apparent height of the image when it has rotated through 90 degrees—that is, when it is edge-on to the viewer.

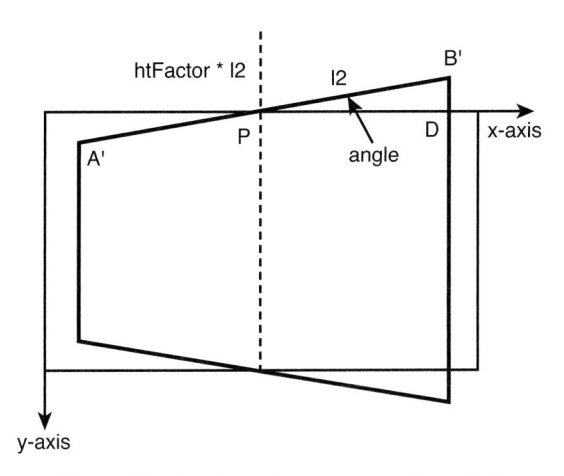

Figure 20-23   Rotating an image (front view)

In its current position, the y coordinate of the upper-right corner would be -B'D. This coordinate is negative because the y-axis runs along the top of the image, as shown. The length of B'D is `l2 * sin(angle)`, but because we are limiting the maximum vertical extension of each side by `htFactor`, we use the value `htFactor * l1 * sin(angle)` instead. Applying the same logic to each of the four corners gives us the following as the final transform, installed in an `ImageView` and with specific values assigned for the variables `pivot` and `htFactor`:

```
ImageView {
    translateX: bind (scene.width - imgWidth) / 2
    translateY: bind (scene.height - 30 - imgHeight) / 2
    image: image = Image { url: "{__DIR__}image1.jpg" }
    var angle = bind Math.toRadians(slider.value);
    var pivot = 0.5;
    var htFactor = 0.2;
    var l1 = bind pivot * imgWidth;
    var l2 = bind imgWidth - l1;
```

Chapter 20 Effects and Blending

```
    effect: bind PerspectiveTransform {
        ulx: ll - ll * Math.cos(angle)
        uly: htFactor * ll * Math.sin(angle)
        llx: ll - ll * Math.cos(angle)
        lly: imgHeight - ll * htFactor * Math.sin(angle)
        urx: ll + 12 * Math.cos(angle)
        ury: -12 * htFactor * Math.sin(angle)
        lrx: ll + 12 * Math.cos(angle)
        lry: imgHeight + 12 * htFactor * Math.sin(angle)
    }
}
```

The file `javafxeffects/PerspectiveTransform1.fx` contains an example that incorporates this transform and provides a slider that allows you to vary the value of the angle variable from −90 degrees to +90 degrees. Figure 20-24 shows a couple of screenshots taken from this example with the image rotated by two different angular amounts. You can experiment with this example by changing the value of the `pivot` variable to get a rotation about a different point. Setting `pivot` to `0` causes a rotation around the left edge, while the value `1` gives rotation about the right edge.

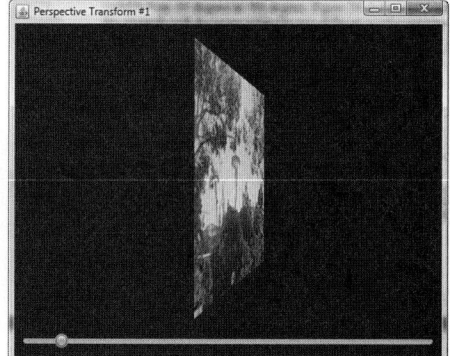

Figure 20-24   Examples of images rotated using a `PerspectiveTransform`

> **Note**
>
> You might be wondering why `PerspectiveTransform` is an effect and not one of the transforms discussed in Chapter 17. The reason is that it is not a true transform, in the sense that it does not affect the coordinate axes—it is just a visual effect. As a result of this, if you try to detect and act on mouse events from a node or group that has a `PerspectiveTransform` applied, you will not get reliable results because the coordinates in the event relate to the *untransformed* shape.

DisplacementMap

The `DisplacementMap` effect is, at first glance, the most complex of the effects that are provided by the JavaFX SDK, but it is also one of the most powerful. As its name suggests, this effect displaces pixels from their locations in the input image to different positions in the output image. Let's begin by listing the variables that you can use to parameterize the effect (see Table 20-16), and then we'll take a look at how they work.

Table 20-16 Variables of the `DisplacementMap` Class

Variable	Type	Access	Default	Description
input	Effect	RW	null	The input to this effect
mapData	FloatMap	RW	Empty map	The map that determines how input pixels are mapped to output pixels
offsetX	Number	RW	0.0	A fixed displacement along the x-axis applied to all pixel offsets
offsetY	Number	RW	0.0	A fixed displacement along the y-axis applied to all pixel offsets
scaleX	Number	RW	1.0	A scale factor applied to the map data along the x-axis
scaleY	Number	RW	1.0	A scale factor applied to the map data along the y-axis
wrap	Boolean	RW	false	Whether the displacement operation should wrap at the boundaries

How the `DisplacementMap` Effect Works

The reason for the apparent complexity of this effect is the equation that controls how the pixels are moved:

```
dst[x, y] = src[x + (offsetX + scaleX * map[x, y][0]) * srcWidth,
               y + (offsetY + scaleY * map[x, y][1]) * srcHeight]
```

At first sight, this probably looks quite daunting, but in fact it turns out to be quite simple. Basically, it says each pixel in the output (here represented by the symbol `dst`) derives from a single pixel in the input (represented by `src`). The pixel value at coordinates (x, y) in the output is obtained from a source pixel whose coordinates are displaced from those of the destination pixel by an amount that depends on a value obtained from a map, together with some scale factors and an offset. The values `srcWidth` and `srcHeight` are respectively the width and height of the input source.

Let's start by assuming that the offset values are both 0 and the scale values are both 1. In this simple case, the equation shown above is reduced to this more digestible form:

```
dst[x, y] = src[x + map[x, y][0] * srcWidth,
              y + map[x, y][1] * srcHeight]
```

The map is a two-dimensional data structure that is indexed by the x and y coordinates of the destination point, relative to the top-left corner of the output image. Each element of this structure may contain a number of floats, which is why the class that holds these values is called a `FloatMap`. The `FloatMap`s that are used with a `DisplacementMap` must have two floats in each position,[5] the first of which is used to control the displacement along the x-axis and the second the displacement along the y-axis. Suppose, for the sake of argument, that we have a `FloatMap` in which every element has the values (−0.5, −0. 5). In this case, the equation above can be written as follows:

```
dst[x, y] = src[x - 0.5 * srcWidth, y - 0.5 * srcHeight]
```

Now, you should be able to see that the pixel at any given position in the output is obtained from the source pixel that is a half of the width or height of the source away from it. If we assume that the source is 100 pixels square, we can make our final simplification:

```
dst[x, y] = src[x - 50, y - 50]
```

This says that the output pixel at any point comes from the source pixel that is 50 pixels above it and to its left. The reason for using `srcWidth` and `srcHeight` as multipliers is that the values in the map can then be encoded as fractions of the width and height of the input respectively and therefore would normally be in the range -1 to +1. A map value of −1 or +1 would move a point by the complete width or height of the input source.

A Simple Example

Let's look at how you would implement the example that you have just seen. You'll find the code in the file `javafxeffects/DisplacementMap1.fx`. Let's start by creating the map:

```
1    var image: Image = Image { url: "{__DIR__}image1.jpg" };
2    var imgWidth = image.width as Integer;
3    var imgHeight = image.height as Integer;
4    var map: FloatMap = FloatMap {
5        width: imgWidth
6        height: imgHeight
7    }
8
9    for (i in [0..<map.width]) {
10       for (j in [0..<map.height]) {
11           map.setSample(i, j, 0, -0.50);
12           map.setSample(i, j, 1, -0.50);
```

---

[5] The `FloatMap` can have more than two floats in each position, but only the first two are used.

```
13          }
14      }
```

In this example, we are going to use an image as the input source, so we create a map that has the same dimensions as the image itself. The code on lines 4 to 6 declares the `FloatMap`, setting its dimensions from the width and height of the image. The nested loops on lines 9 to 14 initialize the `FloatMap`, assigning two samples for each element. Each sample has the value `-0.5`, which is the offset that we require. Note how these samples are installed:

```
map.setSample(i, j, 0, -0.50);    // The x offset
map.setSample(i, j, 1, -0.50);    // The y offset
```

`FloatMap` has several overloaded variants of the `setSample()` function that you can use. In the variant that we use here, the first two arguments are the x and y coordinates of the element, the third argument is the band number, and the fourth argument is the offset for that band. Band 0 is used for the x-offset and band 1 for the y offset.[6]

Now, here's the code that creates and uses the `DisplacementMap` effect:

```
var scene: Scene;
Stage {
    title: "DisplacementMap #1"
    scene: scene = Scene {
            width: 500
            height: 380
            fill: Color.BLACK
            content: [
                ImageView {
                    translateX: bind (scene.width - imgWidth) / 2
                    translateY: bind (scene.height - 30 - imgHeight) / 2
                    image: image
                    effect: DisplacementMap {
                        mapData: map
                    }
                }
            ]
    }
}
```

As you can see, the effect is applied simply by creating a `DisplacementMap` based on the map data and installing it in an `ImageView` that contains the source image. We don't need to set the scale or offset values because we are using the defaults in this case. You can see the result in Figure 20-25.

---

[6] The band numbers appear in the original equations. `map[x, y]` **[0]** indicates the value in band 0 at the element in position (x, y) in the map.

Figure 20-25   A simple `DisplacementMap` effect

The original image is shown on the left of the figure and the result of applying the `DisplacementMap` on the right. As you can see, the image has been moved halfway across and halfway down the area occupied by the source. It's easy to see why this has happened if you look back at the equation that describes this effect:

```
dst[x, y] = src[x - 0.5 * srcWidth,
               y - 0.5 * srcHeight]
```

This says that the pixel at (x, y) comes from the source pixel that is half the source width to its left and half the source height above it. In other words, the image is moved down and to the right. To make this more obvious still, let's add some concrete numbers. We'll start by with the pixel at (0, 0) in the destination image. According to the equation above, the color for this pixel comes from the pixel at (0 − 0.5 * 340, 0 − 0.5 * 255) = (−170, −127). Because there is no such point, this pixel is not set, so this part of the destination is transparent. In fact, every pixel for which either of the source coordinates is negative will be transparent. The first pixel in the destination image that will not be transparent is the one at (170, 127), which gets its color from the pixel at (0, 0) in the source. By following this reasoning for any given pixel in the destination image, it is easy to see why the result of this effect is to move the source down and to the right, as shown in Figure 20-25.

The `wrap` Variable

You can achieve a slightly different effect to that shown above by setting the `wrap` variable of the `DisplacementMap` object to `true`. When you do this, the parts of the destination that would have been transparent because they correspond to points in the source image that are outside of its bounds (for example, those with negative coordinates) are populated by wrapping the coordinates modulo the size of the source. This means, for example, that the pixel at (0,0), which should come from (−170,−127) in the source, will actually come from (−170 + 340, −127 + 128), or (170, 1). You can see the overall effect of this by running the code in the file `javafxeffects/DisplacementMap2.fx`, which gives the result shown in Figure 20-26.

Figure 20-26   A `DisplacementMap` with wrap enabled

The `offset` Variables

Now that you have seen how the values in the map work in the simplest case, we'll make things a little more complex by adding back the `offsetX` and `offsetY` values. These values simply add a fixed offset to the distance between the destination pixel and the source pixel that supplies its color. Like the entries in the map, each offsets is scaled by the width or height of the source, as appropriate.

For example, let's suppose that we were to set the `offsetX` variable to `0.1` and leave `offsetY` as `0`. Then, using the same map as we did for the previous example, the equations that relate the source and destination pixel locations would now be as follows:

```
dst[x, y] = src[x + 0.1 * srcWidth- 0.5 * srcWidth,
            y - 0.5 * srcHeight]
```

If, as before, the source is 340 pixels wide, this change would produce an additional offset of 34 pixels between the source and destination pixels.

You can see how the `offsetX` value works by running the code in the file `javafxeffects/DisplacementMap3.fx`. This example uses the same `FloatMap` as the previous one, but adds a slider that allows you to vary the `offsetX` value from `0` up to `1.0`, with the initial value being `0.0`. Initially, the result looks the same as before, because the `offsetX` value is still `0`—compare the image on the left of Figure 20-27 with that on the right of Figure 20-25 to see that this is the case.

Figure 20-27 Varying the `offsetX` value of a `DisplacementMap` effect

Now if you move the offset slider to the right, you will see that the output image moves to the left. This is the offset at work. The farther you move the slider to the right, the more the result shifts to the left. The same effect would be seen along the y-axis if we had added a slider that allowed you to vary the `offsetY` value.

The `scale` Variables

The `scaleX` and `scaleY` variables are multipliers that are applied to the values from the `FloatMap`. If you use a `scaleX` value that is greater than 1, you make the offset between the source and destination pixels larger than that specified in the map. A `scaleX` value of 2 would double the offsets specified in the map. Similarly, if you use a value that is less than 1, the offset gets smaller. It is also possible to use a negative value, which would reverse the effect of the map.

The code in `javafxeffects/DisplacementMap3.fx` also includes a slider that lets you change the value of the `scaleX` variable over the range `0` to `2`, with `1` as its initial value. If you move the slider, you will find that the output image also moves to reflect the magnified or reduced offset values. In this case, because every entry in the map has the same value, the effect is very similar to that obtained by changing the `offsetX` value, but this is not always the case, as you'll see later in this section.

Using the `DisplacementMap` to Create a Warp

The example that we have been using has the same value in every element of the map. This is a rather unusual case and it doesn't produce a very interesting effect. In this section, we'll take a look at how to create a warp effect by populating the map with values that depend on their position in the map. The completed effect is shown in Figure 20-28.

As you can probably tell, the effect is produced by simulating the effect of a wave moving in the direction of the y-axis, which causes successive pixel rows to be displaced

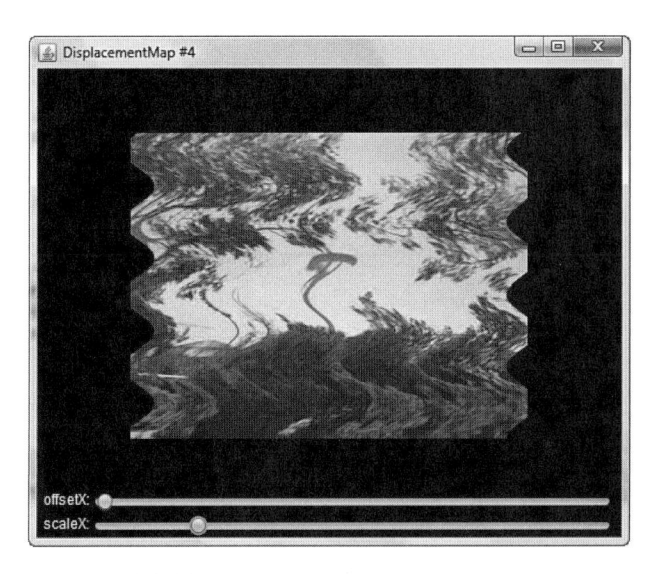

Figure 20-28 Using `DisplacementMap` to create a warped effect

to the left or right of their initial positions. As there is no movement of any kind in the y direction, you can immediately conclude that all the y values (those in the second band) in the map are 0. The wave effect is, in fact, a sine wave. Here's the code that populates the map[7]:

```
1     var image: Image = Image { url: "{__DIR__}image1.jpg" };
2     var imgWidth = image.width as Integer;
3     var imgHeight = image.height as Integer;
4     var map: FloatMap = FloatMap {
5         width: imgWidth
6         height: imgHeight
7     }
8
9     for (i in [0..<map.width]) {
10        for (j in [0..<map.height]) {
11            var value = (Math.sin(j/30.0 * Math.PI)/10;
12            map.setSample(i, j, 0, value);
13        }
14    }
```

---

[7] You'll find this code in the file `javafxeffects/DisplacementMap4.fx`.

The part that does all the interesting work is on line 11. It is obvious that this is creating a sine wave by supplying the horizontal displacement (in the first band of the map) for each row of the input source based on the value of the `Math.sin()` function. The value of this function varies from 0 at 0 radians to 1 at `PI/2` radians, back to zero at `PI` radians, to –1 at `3*PI/2` radians, and then back to zero at 2 `*PI` radians, and so on. In the inner loop, the value represents the pixel row. We divide it by 30 and multiply it by `PI` so that we get a complete wave over the space of 30 pixels. If you make this number larger, you will find that the wave spaces out more. This code would place values ranging from +1 to –1 in every element of the map. Remembering that these offsets are multiplied by the width of the source, this would mean that the image would be distorted by up to its full width. To reduce the distortion, we divide every value by 10, so we end up with values in the range –0.1 to +0.1. That's all we need to do to create a warp effect.

If you run the code in the file `javafxeffects/DisplacementMap4.fx`, you can use the offset and scale sliders to change the parameters of the `DisplacementMap`. Notice that changing the scale increases or decreases the amplitude of the sine wave, which results in more or less distortion.

Blending

Blending is the process of combining two pixels that would occupy the same space to produce a third value that is actually placed at that space. Blending can be used to determine what should be seen in a region where two nodes overlap or where two effects are applied to a node. You can use blending either as an effect or as a mode that controls the drawing of overlapping nodes in a group or container.

The `Blend` Effect

The `Blend` effect combines two inputs and produces a result that depends on the selected blend mode. The variables of the `Blend` class are listed in Table 20-17.

Here's an example that demonstrates how to construct a `Blend` effect. This code is extracted from the file `javafxeffects/BlendEffect1.fx`, which you can run to try out all the available blend modes:

```
var image1 = Image { url: "{__DIR__}image1.jpg" };
var image2 = Image { url: "{__DIR__}image2.jpg" };

ImageView {
    x: 30
    y: 30
    image: image1
    effect: Blend {
        mode: BlendMode.ADD
        topInput: Identity {
            x: 150
            y: 150
            source: image2
        }
    }
}
```

Table 20-17 **Variables of the `Blend` Class**

Variable	Type	Access	Default	Description
mode	BlendMode	RW	SRC_OVER	The mode that determines how pixels from the two inputs are combined to produce the resulting pixel.
topInput	Effect	RW	null	The top input to this effect. If this is `null`, the node to which the effect is applied is used.
bottomInput	Effect	RW	null	The bottom input to this effect. If this is `null`, the node to which the effect is applied is used.
opacity	Number	RW	1.0	The opacity applied to the top input before blending.

Here, the bottom input is the `ImageView` itself (because the `bottomInput` variable is `null`, so the node itself becomes the input), while the top input is the output of an `Identify` effect applied to an `Image`. The second image is placed 150 pixels below and to the right of the `ImageView`, giving the result shown in Figure 20-29.

As you can see, the result of this effect is the union of the two images. There is a significant area of overlap between the two images, and in this region, their pixels are combined according to the unique set of rules that apply to the selected blend mode. There are 19 different modes, all defined as constants in the `BlendMode` class. You will find the details of each mode in the documentation for the `BlendMode` class. In Figure 20-29, `BlendMode.ADD` has been used. This adds all the color and alpha components from the two pixels to produce the result pixel. For example, if the RGBA values for two pixels were $(0.6, 0.2, 0.3, 0.4)$ and $(0.5, 0.6, 0.1, 0.5)$, the value of the resulting pixel would be $(1.0, 0.8, 0.4, 0.9)$. Notice that the value of each channel is limited to `1.0`, which is why the result of combining the red channels in this example is `1.0` rather than `1.1`.

By selecting different values from the combo box at the top of the scene, you can see how each mode operates. Of particular interest are the `SRC_ATOP`, `SRC_IN`, `SRC_OUT` and `SRC_OVER` modes. In these modes, the "source" is the top input. You can see the results of applying `SRC_ATOP` mode on the left of Figure 20-30 and `SRC_IN` mode on the right.

The `SRC_ATOP` mode keeps all the bottom input plus that part of the top input that overlaps it. In the overlap area, only the top input is painted. By contrast, `SRC_IN` keeps only that part of the top input that overlaps with the bottom input, and everything else (including all the bottom input) is lost.

Figure 20-29   Using the `Blend` effect

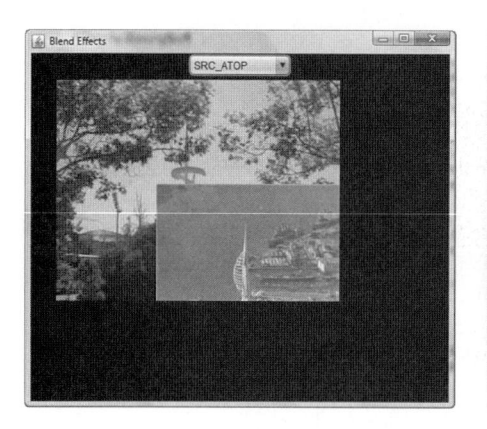

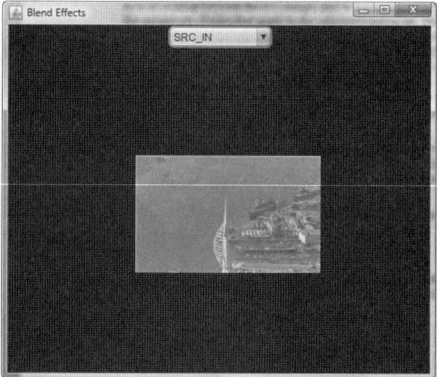

Figure 20-30   The `SRC_ATOP` and `SRC_IN` blend modes

The Group Blend Mode

A blend mode can be applied to a group (or a container, because Container is a subclass of Group) by setting its blendMode variable to one of the constants defined by the BlendMode class. The blend mode determines how the pixels in the areas in which there are overlapping nodes are constructed from those of the nodes themselves. By default, and in all the examples that you have seen so far, the blendMode variable has the value BlendMode.SRC_OVER, which causes the node in front to be drawn over those that are behind it.

Blending

The following code, from the file `javafxeffects/BlendGroup1.fx`, allows you to see how each of the possible blend modes operates when applied to the nodes of a group:

```
1     var image1 = Image { url: "{__DIR__}image1.jpg" };
2     var image2 = Image { url: "{__DIR__}image2.jpg" };
3     var scene: Scene;
4     Stage {
5         title: "Blend Group"
6         scene: scene = Scene {
7             var modeCombo: SwingComboBox;
8             var mode = bind modeCombo.selectedItem.value
9                            as BlendMode;
10            width: 500
11            height: 400
12            fill: Color.BLACK
13            content: [
14                modeCombo = SwingComboBox {
15                    translateX: bind (scene.width
16                       - modeCombo.layoutBounds.width) / 2
17                    editable: false
18                    items: [
19                        SwingComboBoxItem {
20                            value: BlendMode.ADD
21                            text: "ADD"
22                        }
23                        // Further items not shown here
24
25                    ]
26                    selectedIndex: 0
27                }
28                Circle {
29                    centerX: 100
30                    centerY: 100
31                    radius: 80
32                    fill: Color.YELLOW
33                }
34                Group {
35                    blendMode: bind if (mode != null) mode
36                                    else BlendMode.ADD
37                    content: [
38                        ImageView {
39                            x: 30
40                            y: 30
41                            image: image1
42                        }
43                        ImageView {
44                            x: 150
```

```
45                            y: 150
46                            image: image2
47                        }
48                    ]
49                }
50            ]
51        }
52    }
```

This code creates a scene containing a combo box that allows a `BlendMode` to be selected, a circle, and a group containing two overlapping two `ImageViews`. On the left of Figure 20-31, you can see the result of applying the default mode, which is `SRC_OVER`. On the right of the figure, the `MULTIPLY` mode is used.

Figure 20-31   Using blend modes in a group

As you can see, these two modes have different effects on the pixels in the area of overlap between the two images. Note, however, that the blend mode has no effect on the region in which the upper-left `ImageView` overlaps the circle, because the circle is not in the group and therefore is not subject to the blend mode.

Lighting

The final effect that we are going to look at is called `Lighting`. As its name suggests, it allows you to specify how a node or a group should be lit. Three different types of lighting can be used, all of which are represented by classes in the `javafx.scene.effect.light` package. The `Lighting` class itself, like all the other effects, is in the `javafx.scene.effect` package.

To define the lighting for a node or group, you create an instance of the `Lighting` class and install it in the `effect` variable of that node or group. Using lighting will make your scenes look more three-dimensional than they otherwise would, as you'll see in the examples in this section. The variables of the `Lighting` class are listed in Table 20-18.

Table 20-18 **Variables of the `Lighting` Class**

Variable	Type	Access	Default	Description
light	Light	RW	DistantLight	The type of light to be used.
bumpInput	Effect	RW	null	The bump map to be applied.
contentInput	Effect	RW	null	The input to this effect, which is the target node itself if this value is null.
diffuseConstant	Number	RW	1.0	Determines how much diffuse light is reflected from the surface, in the range 0 to 2, inclusive.
specularConstant	Number	RW	0.3	Determines how much specular light is reflected from the surface, in the range 0 to 2, inclusive.
specularExponent	Number	RW	20	Determines how shiny the surface appears to be in the range 0 to 40, inclusive.
surfaceScale	Number	RW	1.5	Determines the height assigned to pixels in the source, based on their opacity. Valid range is 0 to 10, inclusive.

The `light` variable determines the type of lighting required, which must be one of `DistantLight` (which is the default), `PointLight`, and `SpotLight`. The other variables set the characteristics of the surface that will be lit and will be explained in the rest of this section by reference to examples.

The `surfaceScale` Variable

To create a 3D effect when lighting a 2D surface, the opacity value of each pixel is used as a guide to how "high" that pixel should appear to be when lit. Transparent pixels appear to be the lowest, while fully opaque pixels appear to be raised up from the surface. This effect can be increased or decreased by using the `surfaceScale` variable. Values that are greater than `1` cause the effect to be increased, while values between `0` and `1` cause it to be decreased. The same effect can also be seen at the edges of shapes.

The following code, which comes from the file `javafxeffects/SurfaceScale.fx`, shines a distant light on a rectangle. The details of the lighting are not important right now, but you'll see that the `surfaceScale` variable is bound to a slider. If you run this example, you can see the effect of varying the `surfaceScale` variable over its full range:

```
Rectangle {
    x: 20
    y: 20
    width: 100
    height: 100
    fill: Color.YELLOW
    effect: Lighting {
        light: DistantLight {
            azimuth: 0
            elevation: 30
        }
        surfaceScale: bind (scaleSlider.value as Number) / 10
    }
}
```

You can see how the `surfaceScale` value is used by comparing the two screenshots shown in Figure 20-32.

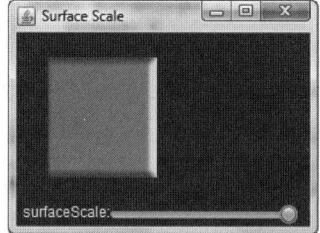

Figure 20-32　The `surfaceScale` variable of the `Lighting` effect

On the left of the figure, the `surfaceScale` value is `0`, so there is no 3D effect at all. On the right, `surfaceScale` has its maximum possible value, and now you can see that the center of the rectangle appears to be raised up above its edges. The higher the `surfaceScale` value, the higher the center will appear to be.

The Bump Map

You can add additional surface relief by creating a *bump map* and installing it in the `bumpInput` variable of the `Lighting` effect. If this variable is `null`, the node on which the effect is applied is itself used to generate a bump map, which is what causes the 3D effect at the edges that you saw in Figure 20-32.

The bump map is just an `Effect`, which supplies pixels from which the relief of the lit surface is calculated. As before, the apparent height of a pixel on the lit shape depends on the opacity of the corresponding pixel of the bump map. This effect is affected by the value of the `surfaceScale` variable, as described in the preceding section.

A common way to specify a bump map is to create an image, set the opacity to reflect the contours that you want to appear in the finished result, and then turn it into an effect by using the `Identity` class that we discussed earlier in this chapter. The code in the file `javafxeffects/BumpMap.fx` shows how to apply a bump map in the form of an image file:

```
1     var logo = Image { url: "{__DIR__}javafxlogo.gif" };
2     Stage {
3         title: "Bump Map"
4         scene: Scene {
5             width: 240
6             height: 140
7             fill: Color.BLACK
8             content: [
9                 Rectangle {
10                    x: 20
11                    y: 20
12                    width: 200
13                    height: 100
14                    fill: Color.YELLOW
15                    effect: Lighting {
16                        light: DistantLight {
17                            azimuth: 90
18                            elevation: 25
19                        }
20                        bumpInput: Identity {
21                            source: logo
22                            x: 30
23                            y: 40
24                        }
25                    }
26                }
27            ]
28        }
29    }
```

694 Chapter 20 Effects and Blending

The code on line 1 loads the bump image from a file called `logo.gif` that is in the same directory as the script file. This image is then converted to an `Effect` by the code on lines 20 to 24, and placed appropriately relative to the rectangle node to which the lighting effect is applied by using the `x` and `y` variables of the `Identity` class. The lighting itself is a `DistantLight`, to which the image is supplied as the bump map on line 20.

The image that is used as the bump map is shown on the left of Figure 20-33. The image consists of the word JavaFX in black text on a white background. The white background is actually completely transparent, while the black text is completely opaque. You can see the effect of the bump map on the right of Figure 20-33, where the lighting effect causes the word JavaFX to appear to be raised above the surface of the `Rectangle`.

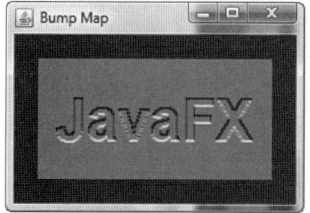

Figure 20-33   Using a bump map with a `Lighting` effect

You can apply the same effect to any node, including an `ImageView`, where you can use it to create the appearance of a watermark within the image.

`DistantLight`

The `DistantLight` class is used when you want to apply a more-or-less uniform light to a node or group. Depending on where the light source is, you may see some shadows, but you will not see reflections of the type that are a characteristic of `PointLight` and `Spotlight`, which are discussed in the sections that follow. `DistantLight`, `PointLight`, and `Spotlight` are all derived from the base class `javafx.scene.effect.light.Light`, which has a single variable called `color` (of type `Color`) that specifies the color of the light to be used, which is white by default. The other variables of the `DistantLight` class specify the position of the light source and are listed in Table 20-19.

The `azimuth` is the position of the light source on the plane of the scene. An `azimuth` angle of 0 degrees places the light source at the 3 o'clock position, one of 90 degrees moves it to 6 o'clock, and so on. Negative angles can also be used and are measured counterclockwise. For example, setting the `azimuth` variable to either `-90` or `270` places the light source at 12 o'clock.

Table 20-19 Variables of the `DistantLight` Class

Variable	Type	Access	Default	Description
azimuth	Number	RW	45	The azimuth of the light source, in degrees
elevation	Number	RW	45	The elevation of the light source, in degrees

The `elevation` gives the angle of the light source above or below the plane of the scene. When the `elevation` is 0 or 180, the light source is on the plane of the scene, when it is 90, it is overhead the scene and shining directly down on it, and when it is 270 (or -90), it is directly below the scene.

The following code, which you will find in the file `javafxeffects/DistantLight1.fx`, allows you to move a `DistantLight` source around a large yellow circle to see the effect that is created:

```
Circle {
    centerX: 200
    centerY: 180
    radius: 150
    fill: Color.YELLOW
    effect: Lighting {
        light: DistantLight {
            azimuth: bind azimuthSlider.value
            elevation: bind elevationSlider.value
        }
        surfaceScale: 5
    }
}
```

Figure 20-34 shows two different configurations of the `DistantLight` source.

On the left of the figure, the `azimuth` and `elevation` variables both have the value 45, which places the light source at approximately the 4.30 position and elevated 45 degrees above its surface. You can see that this is the case because the lower-right edge of the circle is much brighter than the rest of it. On the right, the light source has been moved to the 9 o'clock position by setting the azimuth variable to 180 and moved very close to the plane of the scene as a result of the elevation, which is very nearly 0 degrees. Because of the low elevation, most of the circle is quite dark, with the exception of the edge at around the 9 o'clock position, which is closest to the light source.

It is worth examining here the effect of the `diffuseConstant` of the `Lighting` class. This constant acts as a multiplier to the RGB values of all the pixels on the lit surface. Therefore, you can use this variable to make the surface lighter or darker. The example in

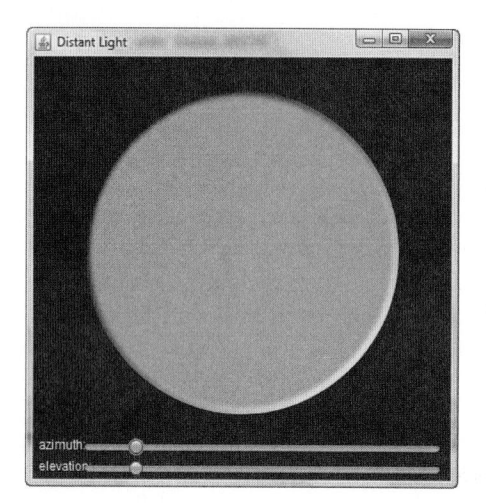

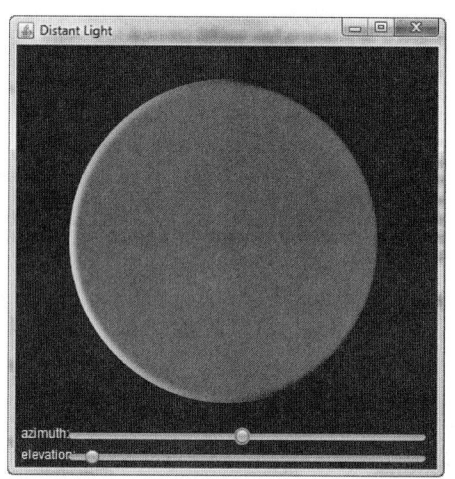

Figure 20-34   Using a `DistantLight` source

the file `javafxeffects/DistantLight2.fx` illustrates this by setting the `diffuseConstant` value of the `Lighting` effect to `1.5`, which has the result of making the circle brighter, as you can see by comparing the result shown in Figure 20-35 with Figure 20-34, where this variable had the value `1`.

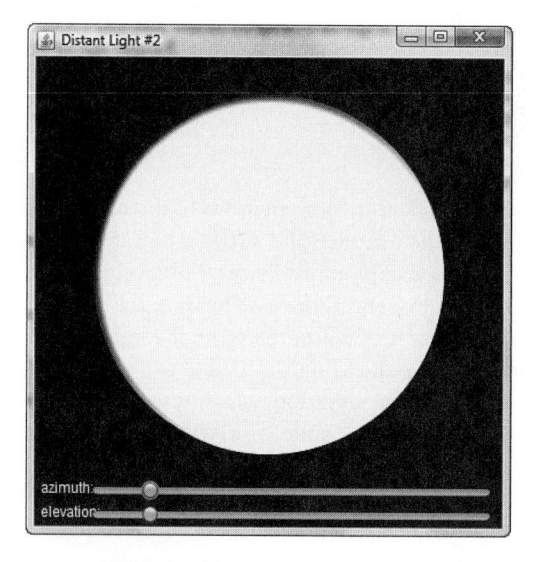

Figure 20-35   The effect of the `diffuseConstant` on a lit surface

PointLight

`PointLight` represents a single point of light that is positioned somewhere relative to the surface to be lit. The variables of the `PointLight` class, as shown in Table 20-20, allow you to specify exactly where the light source should be placed.

Table 20-20 **Variables of the `PointLight` Class**

Variable	Type	Access	Default	Description
x	Number	RW	0	The x coordinate of the light source
y	Number	RW	0	The y coordinate of the light source
z	Number	RW	0	The z coordinate of the light source

In the following code, a `PointLight` source whose position is bound to the values of three sliders is created and applied to a large yellow circle. If you run this example, which can be found in the file `javafxeffects/PointLight1.fx`, you can experiment with the effect of changing the location of the light source:

```
Circle {
    centerX: 200
    centerY: 180
    radius: 150
    fill: Color.YELLOW
    effect: Lighting {
        light: PointLight {
            x: bind xSlider.value
            y: bind ySlider.value
            z: bind zSlider.value
        }
        surfaceScale: 5
        specularConstant: bind (specCSlider.value as Number) / 10
        specularExponent: bind specESlider.value
    }
}
```

You can see two different `PointLight` configurations in Figure 20-36. On the left, the light is at (x = 45, y = 45, z = 45), which is to the top left of the circle itself. You can see that a `PointLight` source results in a more concentrated area of illumination than a `DistantLight`. On the right of the figure, the light source has been moved so that its reflection has moved more toward the center of the circle.

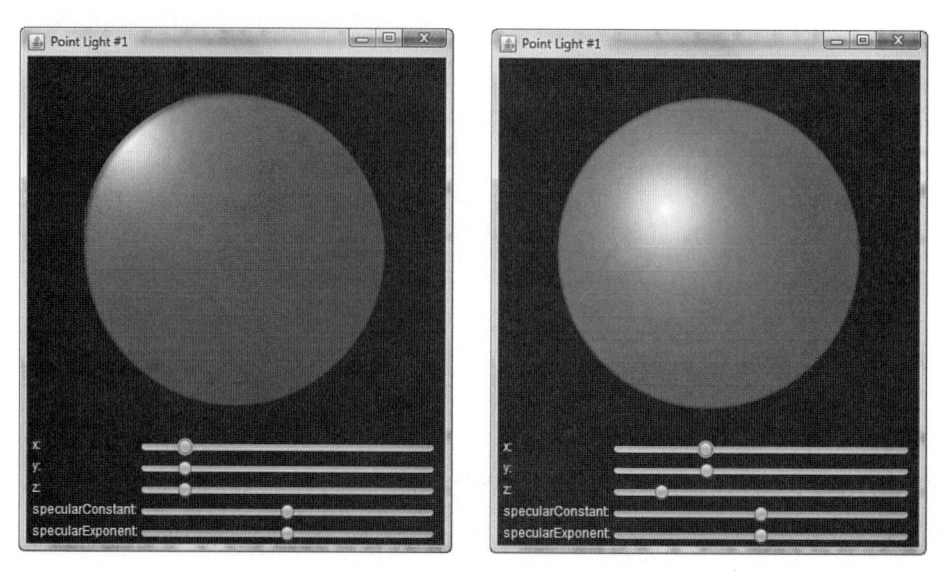

Figure 20-36   Using a `PointLight` source

The size and intensity of the reflection depends on values of the `specularConstant` and `specularExponent` variables of the `PointLight` class. Like `diffuseConstant`, `specularConstant` is a multiplier that is applied to the RGB values of the lit source, so values greater than 1 make the reflection bright, while values less than 1 make it dimmer. The `specularExponent` controls the spread of the light and therefore the radius of the reflected area. Increasing values of `specularExponent` reduce this radius and therefore make the reflection brighter. You can see examples that use different settings for these variables in Figure 20-37.

`SpotLight`

`PointLight` represents a single-point source of light that shines uniformly in every direction, much like the sun. `SpotLight` is a subclass of `PointLight` that acts like a point light source that radiates light over a more confined area. The rays of light are confined to the inside of a cone with its tip at the source. The axis of the cone points to a specified location on the surface of the object being lit. The combination of the position of the light source, the point at which it is aimed, and the width of the cone at the point at which the light reaches the lit object determines the lighting effect that you see. You can specify these values using the variables listed in Table 20-21.

The following code, which is from the file `javafxeffects/SpotLight1.fx`, applies a `SpotLight` effect to the same circle that we illuminated with a `PointLight` source in the previous example. The light source is placed 60 pixels above the center of the circle, while

Lighting   699

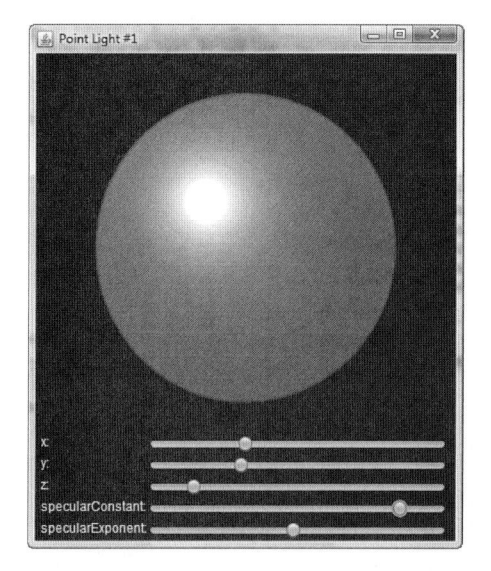

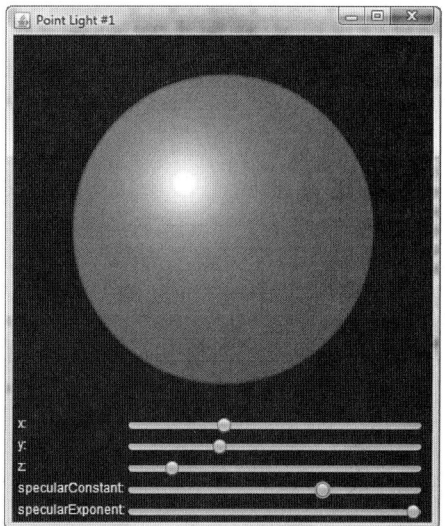

Figure 20-37   The effects of the `specularConstant` and `specularExponent` variables

Table 20-21   **The Variables of the `SpotLight` Class**

Variable	Type	Access	Default	Description
pointsAtX	Number	RW	0.0	The x coordinate of the point at which the light is aimed
pointsAtY	Number	RW	0.0	The y coordinate of the point at which the light is aimed
pointsAtZ	Number	RW	0.0	The z coordinate of the point at which the light is aimed
specular Exponent	Number	RW	1.0	Controls the width of the light cone, in the range 0 to 4, inclusive

the point at which it is aimed can be controlled by three sliders. The effect produced by the `SpotLight` with these initial variable settings is shown on the left of Figure 20-38.

```
Circle {
    centerX: 200
    centerY: 180
    radius: 150
    fill: Color.YELLOW
    effect: Lighting {
        light: SpotLight {
            pointsAtX: bind xSlider.value
            pointsAtY: bind ySlider.value
            pointsAtZ: bind zSlider.value
```

```
            x: 200
            y: 180
            z: 60
            specularExponent: bind (specESlider.value as Number)/10
        }
        surfaceScale: 5
    }
}
```

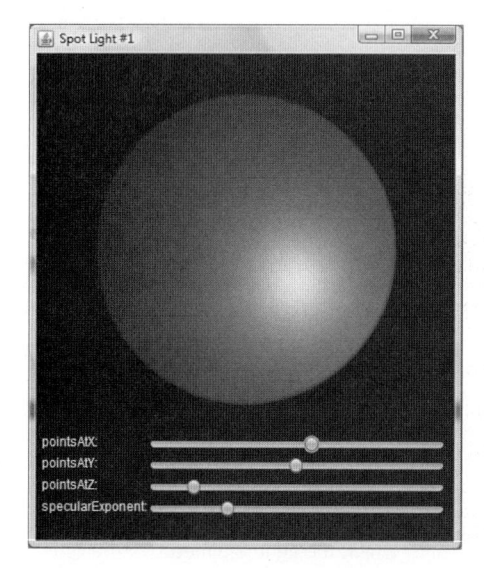

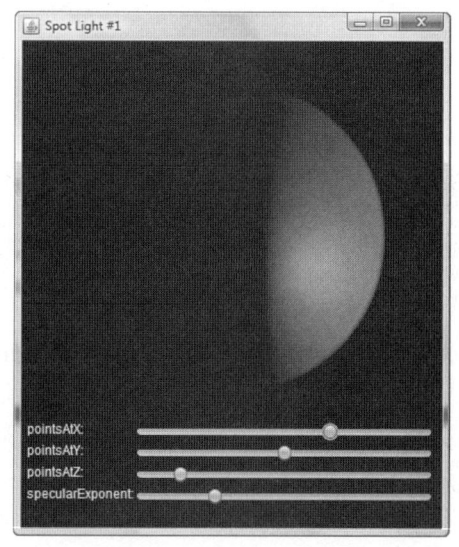

Figure 20-38   The `SpotLight` effect

Moving the aiming point changes the resultant lighting effect. When the light source is quite close to the target object, as it is in this case, even a small change in the aiming point can make a noticeable difference to the result. On the right of Figure 20-38, the aiming point has been moved only a small amount to the right and, as you can see, almost half of the circle is now in darkness.

The bottom slider in Figure 20-38 allows you to see the effect of changing the `specularExponent` value,[8] which is initially set to its default value of 1. Increasing this value makes the light cone narrower that produces a more focused beam and therefore a smaller and brighter effect on the target, as you can see in Figure 20-39, where this variable has its maximum value of 4.0. With this setting, almost all the light is confined to a small area around the aiming point.

---

[8] Do not confuse this variable with the `specularExponent` variable of the `Lighting` class.

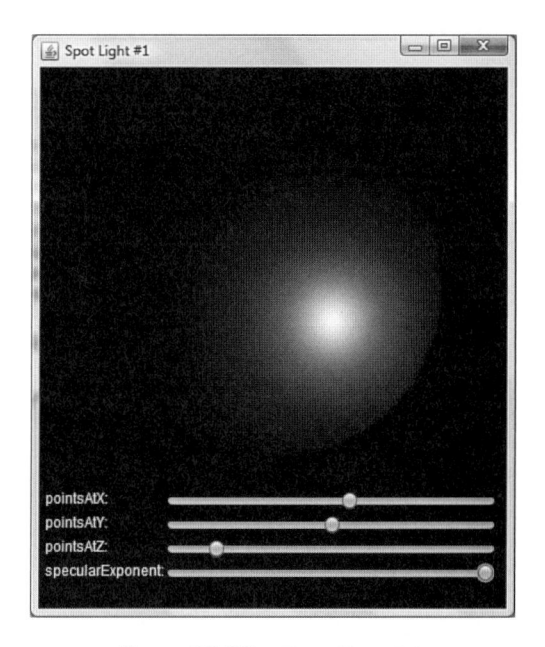

Figure 20-39   The effect of the
specularExponent variable of the
SpotLight class

21

Importing Graphics

Although you can create useable JavaFX applications by manually composing nodes and bitmap images, at some point you will probably want to bring in a graphics designer to help make your application look as slick and professional as possible. Graphics designers usually do not want to work with code and integrated development environments (IDEs). Instead, they prefer to use professional graphics programs like Adobe Illustrator or Adobe Photoshop. In this chapter, we look at the JavaFX Production Suite, which provides a suite of tools that enable you to integrate artwork created by a graphic designer into a JavaFX application. We start by taking a look at how to use the JavaFX Production Suite plug-in to export a basic piece of artwork from Adobe Illustrator to a file that can be read by a JavaFX application. Having done this, we look at how to use the runtime support for the JavaFX Production Suite that is part of the JavaFX software development kit (SDK) to create a node tree from the exported file content, which you can then include in your scene graph. You'll also see how to embed into the exported file any fonts and images that your artwork uses and how to use the Adobe tools to create an animation that can be managed by the JavaFX runtime.

The examples for this chapter can all be found in the `javafximport` package of the JavaFX Book More GUI project. To get the most from this chapter, you need to have a copy of Adobe Illustrator installed on your machine. If you don't own a copy, you can get a time-limited trial version from http://www.adobe.com. The JavaFX Production Suite supports both the CS3 and CS4 versions of Adobe Illustrator (and Photoshop, although we don't use it in this book). If you don't have access to the Internet or don't want to install Adobe Illustrator, the output files produced by the JavaFX Production Suite are included with the example source code, so you can still work with the JavaFX parts of the examples in this chapter.

The JavaFX Production Suite

The JavaFX Production Suite is made up of the following components:

- A plug-in that allows you to export artwork from Adobe Illustrator in *FXZ format*, which can be read by a JavaFX application

- A plug-in that allows you to export artwork from Adobe Photoshop in FXZ format
- A utility that converts Scalable Vector Graphics (SVG) files, produced by tools such as Inkscape, into FXZ format
- A viewer that can read and display an FXZ format file

The JavaFX Production Suite is not part of the JavaFX SDK—you need to download it separately from http://javafx.com and then install it. Installing it makes its plug-ins immediately available to Adobe Illustrator or Photoshop if you already have those applications installed, but if you install Adobe Illustrator/Photoshop *after* installing the JavaFX Production Suite, you must add an additional plug-in location to each application. Assuming that you installed the JavaFX Production Suite in the default location, which is `C:\Program Files\Sun\JavaFX Production Suite` on Microsoft Windows, do the following to activate the Illustrator Plug-in:

1. Start Illustrator.

2. Go to the menu Edit, Preferences, Plug-ins & Scratch Disks.

3. Select Additional Plug-ins Folder and click the Choose button.

4. Navigate to the folder `C:\Program Files\Sun\JavaFX Production Suite\JavaFX Plugin for Adobe Illustrator CS4\Plug-ins`, select it (or choose the directory for CS3 if you are using that version of Illustrator), and click OK.

5. Close the Preferences dialog and restart Illustrator.

The procedure for activating the Photoshop plug-in is as follows:

1. Start Photoshop.

2. Go to the menu Edit, Preferences, Plug-Ins.

3. Select Additional Plug-ins Folder and click the Choose button.

4. Navigate to the folder `C:\Program Files\Sun\JavaFX Production Suite\JavaFX Plugin for Adobe Photoshop CS4\Plug-ins`, select it (or choose the directory for CS3 if you are using that version of Photoshop), and click OK.

5. Close the Preferences dialog and restart Photoshop.

It is easy to check that the plug-ins have been activated:

- In Illustrator, open the File menu and look for an item labeled Save for JavaFX.
- In Photoshop, open the menu File, Activate, and look for an item labeled Save for JavaFX.

Note that these menu items will be grayed out until you have something to save.

If you want to try out the examples in this chapter that use the SVG converter in the JavaFX Production Suite, you need a utility that creates SVG output. I used Inkscape, an open source SVG editor, which you can download from http://www.inkscape.org. Alternatively, you can use the SVG file in the example source code for this chapter.

Using Adobe Illustrator and Photoshop Graphics

We begin our discussion of the JavaFX Production suite by demonstrating how to use it to create some simple artwork, convert it to FXZ format, and then load that artwork into a JavaFX application. In reality, unless you are artistically gifted as well as being a JavaFX developer, the first part of this process would normally be performed by a graphics designer, who would give you the FXZ file, from which you would develop the application code. After you have this workflow in place, you can iterate as many times as necessary, with the designer making changes to the artwork in Illustrator or Photoshop, resulting in a modified FXZ file.

For this simple example, we assume that you have Adobe Illustrator installed. The steps required for using graphics created in Adobe Photoshop are virtually identical.

Exporting Graphics from Adobe Illustrator

You'll find the artwork for this example in the file `Banner1.ai` in the `javafximport` package of the JavaFX Book GUI project. If you open this file with Adobe Illustrator and also open the Layers window, as shown in Figure 21-1 (use Window, Layers), you can see how the graphic that we are going to use is structured.

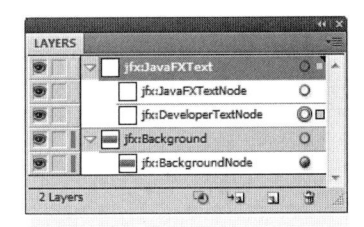

Figure 21-1   A simple graphic in Adobe Illustrator

> **Note**
>
> This chapter is not a tutorial on how to use Adobe Illustrator, so the examples all use pre-created Illustrator files. If you want to learn about creating graphics using Adobe Illustrator, there are plenty of books and web-based tutorials available. In most cases, however, you can (and should) leave the details to your graphic designer.

The graphic is just a rectangle filled with a color gradient, over which are overlaid two lines of text. Notice that the text and the rectangle are in different layers. In this case, there is no specific reason for doing this, except that it reflects the fact that the text should always appear in front of the colored background.

If you look at the Layers window, you'll see that each of the layers and all the graphics elements have been given names. These names are part of the contract between the graphics designer and the JavaFX programmer—as you'll see shortly, they are used to refer to the elements of the graphic from within the JavaFX code. In this case, all the names have the prefix `jfx:`, which, for reasons explained in a moment, is a convention that is known to the plug-ins.

The JavaFX runtime cannot read Adobe Illustrator files. Instead, you need to save the graphic in a format that is specific to JavaFX. To do this, open the File menu and select Save for JavaFX. This opens a preview screen in which you can select various options, as shown in Figure 21-2.

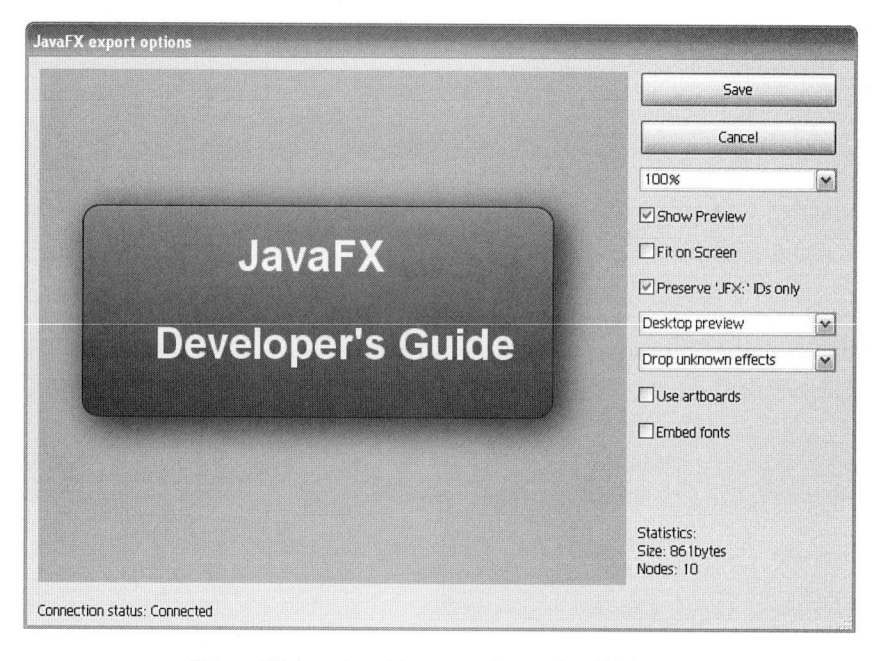

Figure 21-2   Exporting a graphic to JavaFX format

Select Show Preview to see the preview. It is useful to do this because you will sometimes find that the result is not exactly the same as the graphic as drawn in Illustrator. You'll see an example of this in the "Embedding Fonts" section, below. You can get a preview for either the desktop or mobile platforms. If you use features that are not supported on the mobile platform, they will not appear in the mobile preview. In the case of this example, there is a drop shadow behind the colored background, which will be implemented using the `DropShadow` class in the `javafx.scene.effects` package. As you saw in Chapter 20, "Effects and Blending," effects are only available in the JavaFX desktop profile, so the drop shadow would not appear in the mobile preview, unless you select Rasterize All Effects on the preview page, in which case the effect will be simulated.[1]

Notice the Preserve 'JFX:' IDs Only check box, which is selected by default. As you'll see next, these IDs are used to locate specific elements when the FXZ file is loaded into the JavaFX application. In most cases, you only need to save the IDs that the JavaFX application will use, so omitting any other IDs saves space in the output file.

To save the file, click the Save button and select a filename in the dialog that appears. For this example, the `Banner1.ai` file is in the same directory as the source code for the JavaFX application, and I also saved the output file in the same location, calling it `Banner1.fxz`. You'll see both of these files in the NetBeans project.

An FXZ file is a compressed archive (in the same format as ZIP and JAR) that, in this case, will contain a single text file called `content.fxd`. Under some circumstances, there may be other files in this archive, as you'll see later in this chapter. The `context.fxd` file is human-readable—here's an extract (reformatted to fit the page):

```
Group {
    content: [
        Group {
            id: "Background"
            content: [
                SVGPath {
                    effect: DropShadow {
                        offsetX:7.0,offsetY:7.0,
                        color:Color.rgb(0x23,0x1f,0x20), radius:40.0}
                    id: "BackgroundNode"
                    fill: LinearGradient{proportional: false startX: 225.31
                            startY:23.50 endX: 225.31 endY: 199.40 stops: [
                        Stop {offset: 0.000 color: Color.rgb(0x0,0xae,0xef)},
                        Stop {offset: 1.000 color: Color.rgb(0x21,0x40,0x9a)},
                    ]}
                    stroke: Color.rgb(0x23,0x1f,0x20)
                    strokeWidth: 1.0
                    content: "M427.12,185.72 C427.12,193.28 420.67,199.41
                            412.71,199.41 L37.91,199.41 C29.95,199.41
                            23.50,193.28 23.50,185.72 L23.50,37.19
```

---

[1] If you are going to use this option, you should create separate export files for the mobile and desktop versions of your application because you are likely to get better results on the desktop if you do not rasterize the shadow.

```
                    C23.50,29.63 29.95,23.50 37.91,23.50
                    L412.71,23.50 C420.67,23.50 427.12,29.63
                    427.12,37.19 Z "
},]
},
```

As you can see, this looks like JavaFX code. In fact, it is designed to look like JavaFX code, and you could actually compile most FXD files. However, there are some features of the FXD file format that are not directly supported by the JavaFX platform, such as the ability to programmatically embed fonts, which you'll see later in this section. As you'll see below, this file is read by the JavaFX runtime and its content is use to create an equivalent scene graph.

Previewing the JavaFX Format Files

At this point in the designer/developer workflow, the designer has created the artwork and exported it to an FXZ archive. Here's where you come in. The first thing you will probably want to do is see what the designer has created. You don't need to write any code to do that; there are a couple of easier ways to preview the graphics.

Previewing with the Graphics Viewer

The first way to preview the content of an FXZ archive is to open it with the Graphics Viewer from the JavaFX Production Suite. The simplest way to do this is to double-click the FXZ archive, which causes the Graphics Viewer to open and render whatever it finds in the archive. The FXZ file corresponding to the graphics in the Adobe Illustrator file `Banner.ai` can be found at `moregui/src/javafximport/Banner1.fxz` relative to the directory at which you installed the example source code for this book. Double-clicking this file renders its content, as shown in Figure 21-3.

Figure 21-3 Previewing an FXZ file in the Graphics Viewer

You can choose whether to see a preview for either the desktop or a mobile device. As noted earlier, these may be different if desktop-only features have been used when creating the graphic.

You can also preview an FXZ file by directly running the Graphics Viewer (which is installed by default in the folder `C:\Program Files\Sun\JavaFX Production Suite\Viewer`) and then using the File, Open command from the menu to select and open a file.

Previewing with NetBeans

The JavaFX plug-in for the NetBeans IDE contains a built-in viewer for FXZ files that works just like the Graphics Viewer. To use it, double-click an FXZ file in the Projects view, and the content will be rendered in the editor area of the IDE, as shown in Figure 21-4.

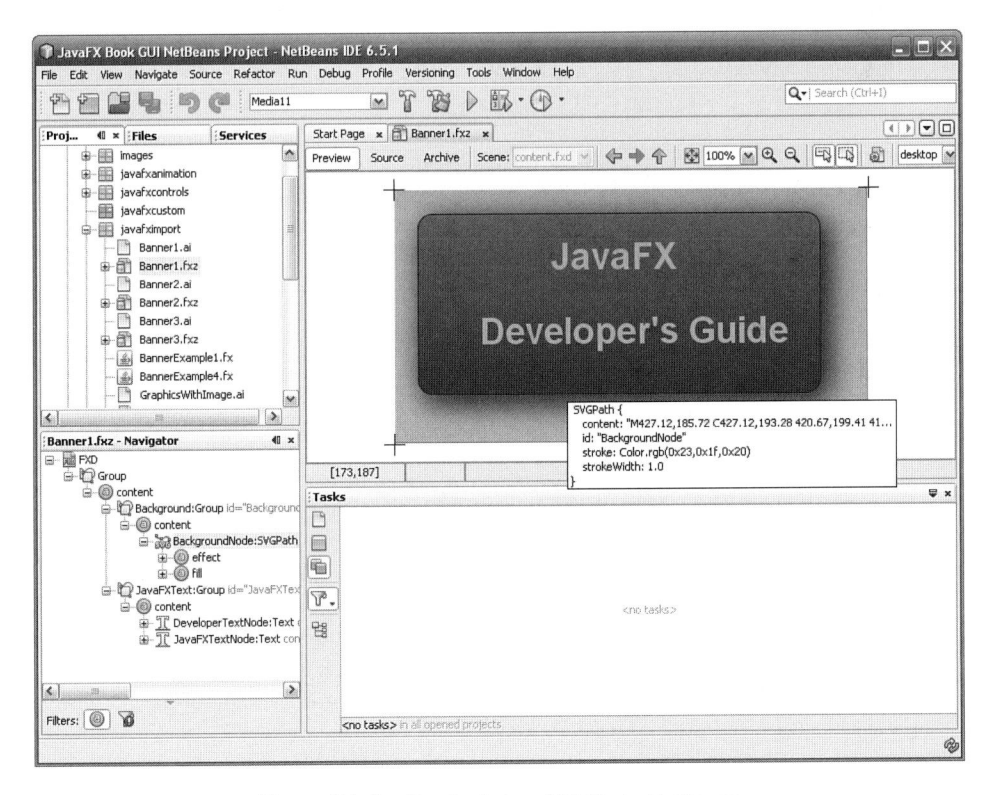

Figure 21-4   Previewing an FXZ file in NetBeans

The NetBeans previewer provides a few features that are not available in the Graphics Viewer. If you hover the mouse over part of the graphic, the part of the FXD file that creates the corresponding node in the JavaFX scene graph will be shown in a tooltip window, as shown in Figure 21-4. In addition to this, three buttons in the toolbar above the graphic let you view the graphic itself, the content of the FXD file, or a listing of all the files in the FXZ archive. Figure 21-5 shows the result of selecting the content of the FXD file.

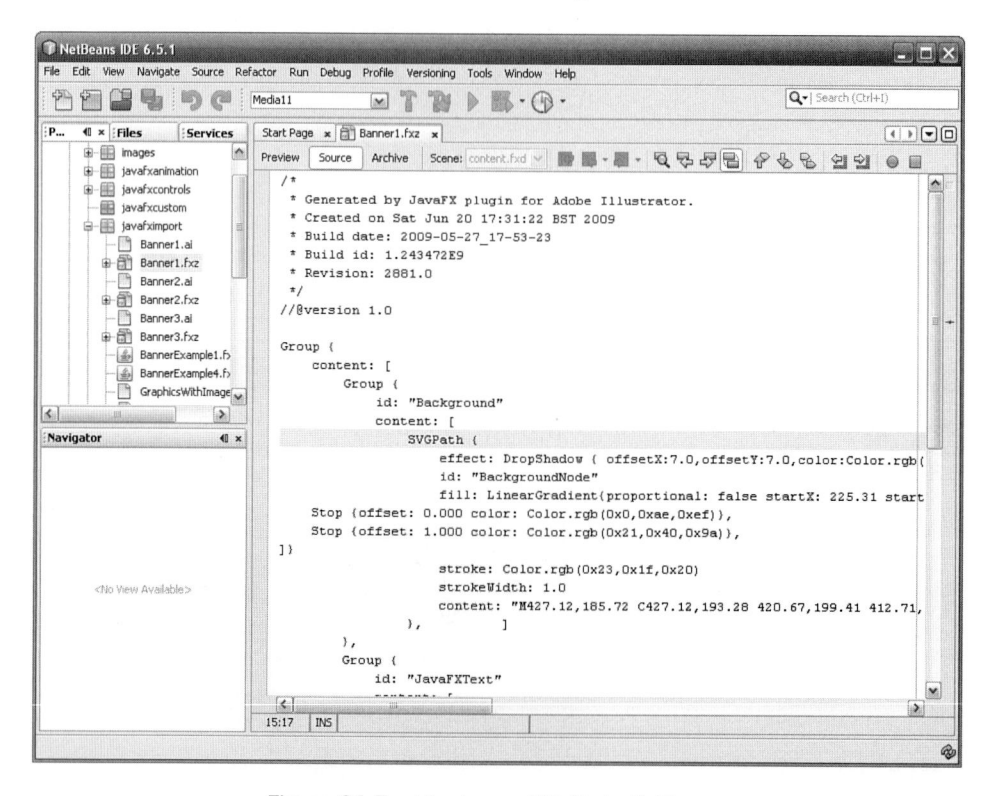

Figure 21-5   Viewing an FXD file in NetBeans

Loading Graphics into a JavaFX Application

Now that you have received and reviewed your FXZ file, the next step is to load it into your JavaFX application. As you have seen, the FXD file inside the FXZ archive contains JavaFX-like code that describes a scene graph consisting of nodes constructed from the artwork prepared by the graphic designer. Items in the artwork that were given IDs starting with `jfx:` are translated to nodes with the `id` variable set to the value of the ID with the `jfx:` prefix removed. You can use this fact to locate specific nodes after you have the content of the FXD file loaded into your application.

You can choose to load the FXD file either synchronously or asynchronously. Synchronous loading is easier to program, but is not really acceptable if the file is on a remote server, because your JavaFX application will not be responsive to the user until the file has been fully read, parsed, and converted to nodes. Asynchronous loading is slightly more complex but provides a much better user experience. We'll examine both approaches in the sections that follow.

Synchronous Loading of Content

The classes that allow you to manipulate FXZ and FXD files are all in the `javafx.fxd` package. The easiest way to load content is to use the `load()` function of the `FXDLoader` class:

```
public function load(url:String):Node
```

The `url` argument is assumed to refer to either an FXD file or to an FXZ archive containing an FXD file (and possibly other content). When this function is called, the FXD file is read, the scene graph that it describes is constructed, and the function returns its root node. The code in Listing 21-1, which you'll find in the file `javafximport/BannerExample1.fx`, illustrates how this function can be used to load the Adobe Illustrator artwork that you saw earlier in this chapter, from the file `Banner1.fxz`.

Listing 21-1   **Synchronously Loading the Content of an FXZ File**

```
1    package javafximport;
2
3    import javafx.fxd.FXDLoader;
4    import javafx.scene.Scene;
5    import javafx.stage.Stage;
6
7    var url = "{__DIR__}Banner1.fxz";
8
9    Stage {
10       title: "Banner Example #1"
11       scene: Scene {
12           content: [
13               FXDLoader.load(url)
14           ]
15       }
16   }
```

Line 7 constructs a URL that refers to the FXZ file, which is in the same directory as the script file itself. On line 13, the `FXDLoader.load()` function is used to read the file content, construct the scene graph, and get the root node, which in this case is a group object. This node becomes the content of the scene. The result of running this code is shown in Figure 21-6.

> **Note**
>
> JavaFX Mobile does not support loading content from a remote FXZ file. If your content consists only of an FXD file, you can place that file on your web server and pass its URL to the `load()` function. If the FXZ file has other elements, you can unpack them into a directory on the web server and supply the URL of the FXD file. Remote FXZ files *are* supported by the desktop profile.

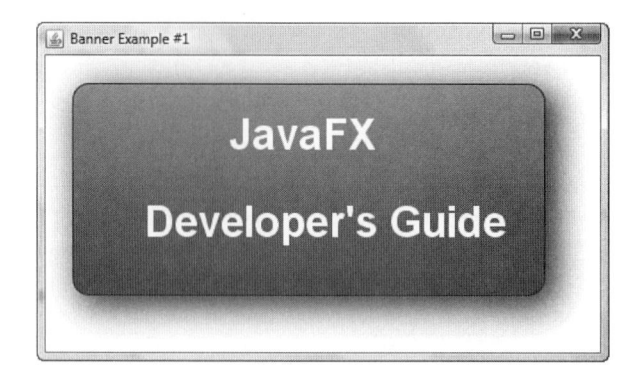

Figure 21-6   A scene created by reading an FXZ archive

The `load()` function gets the root node of the scene graph and is useful if all you want to do is display the whole scene. If you want to do more than this, you can use the `loadContent()` function instead:

```
public function loadContent(url:String):FXDContent;
```

This function returns an `FXDContent` object, from which you can get the root of the scene graph by calling the `getRoot()` function, like this:

```
var url = "{__DIR__}Banner1.fxz";
var content = FXDLoader.loadContent(url);
var rootNode = content.getRoot();
```

The real benefit of the `FXDContent` class is that it provides methods that let you find a specific node in the scene graph, given its identifier:

```
public function getGroup(id:String):Group;
public function getNode(id:String):Node;
public function getShape(id:String):Shape;
public function getObject(id:String):Object
```

To locate an element in the scene graph, you have to supply its ID, which derives from the name given to the corresponding element in the original artwork. If you refer back to Figure 21-1 and look at the Layers window, you will see the names that were assigned to each of the layers and objects in the Adobe Illustrator graphic. Taking the background rectangle, for example, the object in the illustration that corresponds to this object was assigned the name `jfx:BackgroundNode`. The JavaFX plug-in for Adobe Illustrator converts this to a `Group` object with its `id` variable set to the value `BackgroundNode`—that is, the name of the layer with the `jfx:` prefix removed. The same rule is used whenever a graphic object is converted to a scene graph element.[2] The code in Listing 21-2 uses this

---

[2] You can see how the plug-in translates any given element by looking at the FXD file in NetBeans, as shown in Figure 21-5.

Using Adobe Illustrator and Photoshop Graphics 713

information to get the node that is created for the background rectangle and changes its fill color to black before displaying in the scene.

Listing 21-2 **Using the `loadContent()` Function to Load a Scene Graph**

```
1    package javafximport;
2
3    import javafx.fxd.FXDLoader;
4    import javafx.scene.Scene;
5    import javafx.stage.Stage;
6    import javafx.scene.paint.Color;
7
8    var url = "{__DIR__}Banner1.fxz";
9    var content = FXDLoader.loadContent(url);
10   var bgShape = content.getShape("BackgroundNode");
11   bgShape.fill = Color.BLACK;
12
13   Stage {
14       title: "Banner Example #2"
15       scene: Scene {
16           content: [
17               content.getRoot()
18           ]
19       }
20   }
```

You'll find this code in the file `javafximport/BannerExample2.fx`, and the result of running it is shown in Figure 21-7.

Figure 21-7 Extracting part of the content of an FXZ file

On line 9, we load the file content into an `FXDContent` object, and then on line 10, we get the shape that represents the background by calling its `getShape()` function. On line 11, we change its fill to black and finally, on line 17, we install the loaded scene graph into the scene.

If you call one of the `getXXX()` functions with an id that does not exist, it returns the value `null`. The same happens if you supply an id that corresponds to a node of the wrong type for the function that you are calling. For example, the following invocation of the `getGroup()` would return `null` because the background node is a shape rather than a group:

```
var bgGroup = content.getGroup("BackgroundNode"); // Returns null.
```

Another way to locate nodes from an `FXDContent` object is to use its `select()` function:

```
public function select(query:String):Object
```

The query string uses a syntax similar to XQuery. To locate a node, create a path consisting of the ids of its parent nodes and the node itself, separated by forward slash (/) characters. If you open the file `Banner1.fxz` in NetBeans and look at the source, you see that it contains an `SVGPath` node called `BackgroundNode` that is located within a `Group` called `Background`. You can locate this node using the following code (which you can find in the file `javafximport/BannerExample2a`):

```
var url = "{__DIR__}Banner1.fxz";
var content = FXDLoader.loadContent(url);
var bgShape = content.select("/Background/BackgroundNode") as Shape;
```

You can access properties of a node by adding the property name to the node's path, separated by a period. The following code uses this technique to get the value of the `fill` property of the same node:

```
var fill = content.select("/Background/BackgroundNode.fill") as Paint;
```

Asynchronous Loading of Content

Synchronous loading of content is simple to incorporate into your application and convenient for code examples, but in the real world the delay caused by reading and parsing the content of an FXZ file, even if it is on the same machine as your application, may be unacceptable because the user interface may be unresponsive for a noticeable period. In real-world applications, it is better to load content asynchronously, so that the application remains responsive to the user at all times. While your content is being loaded, you could show an animation, an image, or a text message that indicates that the rest of the user interface will appear shortly.

Two script functions in the `FXDLoader` class support asynchronous loading:

```
public function loadOnBackground(url:String,
                                loader:FXDLoader):FXDLoader;
public function createLoader(url:String):FXDLoader;
```

The coding pattern used with these two functions is slightly different, as you'll see in the examples that follow. The choice between the two is largely a matter of taste. The code in Listing 21-3 uses the `loadOnBackground()` function to asynchronously load and display the content of the `Banner1.fxz` file.

Listing 21-3 **Asynchronous Loading Using the `loadOnBackground()` Function**

```
1   package javafximport;
2
3   import javafx.scene.Scene;
4   import javafx.stage.Stage;
5
6   import javafx.geometry.HPos;
7   import javafx.geometry.VPos;
8   import javafx.scene.text.Text;
9   import javafx.scene.text.Font;
10  import javafx.scene.layout.Flow;
11  import javafx.fxd.FXDLoader;
12
13  var scene:Scene;
14  var text:Text;
15  Stage {
16      title: "Banner Example #3a"
17      scene: scene = Scene {
18          width: 500
19          height: 300
20          content: [
21              Flow {
22                  width: bind scene.width
23                  height: bind scene.height
24                  hpos: HPos.CENTER
25                  vpos: VPos.CENTER
26                  content: text = Text {
27                      content: "Loading....."
28                      font: Font { size: 24 }
29                  }
30              }
31          ]
32      }
33  }
34
35  var loader:FXDLoader = FXDLoader {
36      onDone: function() {
37          if (loader.succeeded) {
38              scene.content = loader.content.getRoot();
39          } else {
40              text.content = "Load failed!";
41              println(loader.causeOfFailure);
42          }
43      }
44  }
45  FXDLoader.loadOnBackground("{__DIR__}Banner1.fxz", loader);
```

This code, which you'll find in the file `javafximport/BannerExample3a.fx`, can be separated into two parts. On lines 13 to 33, we create a scene that initially contains a text node displaying a message indicating that the real user interface is being loaded. For a short period of time after the application starts, this is what the user will see, as shown at the top of Figure 21-8. The rest of the code creates an `FXDLoader` object that is then used to asynchronously load the content of the FXZ file and, when this has been done, replaces the text node with whatever has been loaded, giving the result shown at the bottom of Figure 21-8.

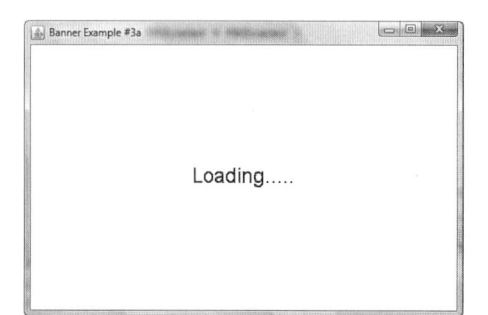

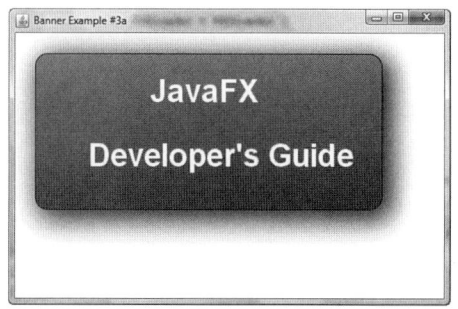

Figure 21-8 Asynchronous loading of an FXZ file

The key to asynchronous loading is the fact that the `FXDLoader` class derives from `javafx.async.Task`, which is a base class that enables you to perform operations in a background thread, while also reporting progress to code that runs in the main thread of your application. You'll read much more about this class in Chapter 26, "Charts." Here, we use the fact that the `Task` class provides callback functions and variables that are used to report significant events to the application as the background operation proceeds and when it terminates. In this case, we create an `FXDLoader` object and assign to its `onDone` variable a function that will be called when the loading process has completed, successfully or otherwise. Although we don't do so in this example, it is also possible to monitor the progress of the load operation by binding or attaching triggers to the `percentDone/progress` variables that the `FXDLoader` class inherits from `Task` and using the reported values to update a `ProgressBar` or `ProgressIndicator` (see Chapter 22, "Cross-Platform Controls") to give the user more visual feedback as the FXZ file is read.

The load operation is initiated by calling the `loadOnBackground()` function of the `FXDLoader` class, passing it the URL of the FXZ or FXD file to be read, and the `FXDLoader` instance to be used to handle it. The `onDone` function is called when the load process completes, successfully or otherwise. The `success` variable indicates whether the operation was successful and, if so, the resulting scene graph can be retrieved from the `content` variable of the `FXDLoader` object. On line 38 of Listing 21-3, if the load operation is successful, we update the scene by replacing the text object that was initially displayed with the newly loaded nodes.

On the other hand, if the load fails, the text node is left in place and its `content` variable is changed to indicate that an error has occurred. We also print the content of the `causeOfFailure` variable, which is updated to report the cause of the error. In a real application, you might use an `Alert` to display this information to the user.

The other way to asynchronously load content is to use the `createLoader()` function to create an `FXDLoader` instance, initialize its variables as required, and then call the `start()` function to initiate the load process, as shown in the following code, which is taken from the file `javafximport/BannerExample3b.fx`.

```
1      var loader = FXDLoader.createLoader("{__DIR__}Banner1.fxz");
2      loader.onDone = function() {
3          if (loader.succeeded) {
4              scene.content = loader.content.getRoot();
5          } else {
6              text.content = "Load failed!";
7              println(loader.causeOfFailure);
8          }
9      };
10     loader.start();
```

The differences between this code and Listing 21-3 are minor. Here, the `FXDLoader` is created on line 1 with the URL of the file to be loaded already set, and the function to be called when the load is complete is then assigned to its `onDone` variable. Finally, the operation is initiated by calling the `start()` function. From this point onward, everything is the same as in the previous example. As you can see, the differences between these two mechanisms are minor, and there is no strong reason to prefer one over the other.

Specifying Animation Paths with Illustrator

Now that you have seen how to create some artwork and load it into a JavaFX application, let's go a step further and add some animation. You can't actually create a JavaFX animation in Illustrator, but you *can* draw the path along which you would like a part of your graphic to move and assign that path a name so that it can be found by your JavaFX code. Having done this, you can implement the animation by adding some simple code to your application. This is, in fact, a typical division of labor between a graphic designer and an application developer—the designer specifies what needs to be done and the developer implements it, using the assets in the FXZ file that the designer creates.

In Figure 21-9, an extra layer called `jfx:TextPathLayer` has been added to our Adobe Illustrator graphic. In this layer, we have placed an arc that has been given the name `jfx:TextPath`. The idea is to animate the node created from the text "JavaFX" along this arc, starting at its bottom left and ending up at the position at which you see it in the figure.

Chapter 21 Importing Graphics

Figure 21-9 Adding an animation path in Illustrator

You'll find this artwork in the file `Banner2.ai` in the source directory for this chapter. The next step is to export it from Illustrator, to create the file `Banner2.fxz`. Having done this, we can write the code that reads the artwork and performs the animation. You'll find the code in the file `javafximport/BannerExample4.fx` and in Listing 21-4.

> **Note**
>
> In this example and the remainder of this chapter, we use synchronous loading for the sake of simplicity. Converting the example code to use asynchronous loading would be simple but would make the code less easy to read for no real gain.

Listing 21-4 **Animating Part of Some Imported Artwork**

```
1    package javafximport;
2
3    import javafx.animation.Interpolator;
4    import javafx.animation.transition.AnimationPath;
5    import javafx.animation.transition.FadeTransition;
6    import javafx.animation.transition.ParallelTransition;
7    import javafx.animation.transition.PathTransition;
8    import javafx.fxd.FXDLoader;
9    import javafx.scene.Group;
10   import javafx.scene.Scene;
11   import javafx.scene.shape.SVGPath;
12   import javafx.stage.Stage;
13
14   var url = "{__DIR__}Banner2.fxz";
15   var content = FXDLoader.loadContent(url);
16   var javafxTextNode = content.getNode("JavaFXTextNode");
17   javafxTextNode.transforms = null;
18   var javafxTextPath = content.getNode("TextPath") as SVGPath;
19   delete javafxTextPath from (javafxTextPath.parent as   Group).content;
20   var transition = ParallelTransition {
21       content: [
22           PathTransition {
23               node: javafxTextNode
```

```
24                    path: AnimationPath.createFromPath(javafxTextPath);
25                    interpolator: Interpolator.EASEOUT
26                    duration: 3s
27                }
28                FadeTransition {
29                    node: javafxTextNode
30                    fromValue: 0.0
31                    toValue: 1.0
32                    duration: 1s
33                }
34            ]
35        }
36
37        Stage {
38            title: "Banner Example #4"
39            scene: Scene {
40                content: [
41                    content.getRoot()
42                ]
43            }
44        }
45        transition.play();
```

The code on lines 14 to 19 uses functions that you have already seen to read the FXZ file, extract the nodes that represent the text "JavaFX" and the path along it will travel, and then assign references to these nodes to the variables `javafxTextNode` and `javafxTextPath`, respectively. Notice that we cast the node that represents the arc to the type `SVGPath`. How did we know that the node is of this type? The only way to work this out is to look at the FXD file that the plug-in generated, which you can do very easily if you are working in NetBeans.

The arc that represents the animation path is part of the scene graph that the `loadContent()` function created and stored in the `FXDContent` object that it returned. We need to display this scene graph, but we don't actually want the arc to appear, so on line 19 we delete the node that represents it from the scene graph. Because the arc was in a separate layer, we actually delete the group that corresponds to that layer, which we know is the parent of the node that represents the arc itself.

We are going to perform the animation by using the `PathTransition` class that you saw in Chapter 18, "Animation." We give the "JavaFX" text node as the node to be animated, and we specify the animation path by converting the `SVGPath` object that corresponds to the arc to an `AnimationPath` object by using the `createFromPath()` function on line 24. The `PathTransition` class works by setting the `translateX` and `translateY` variables of the `Text` node to the values needed to keep it moving along the path. However, this does not take into account the initial placement of the node, which is done by adding an `AffineTransform` to its `transforms` variable that places it in its initial position. If you look at the content of the FXD file, you will see that this transform is applied to the node. On line 17, we remove the transform so that the node's position is controlled entirely by the `PathTransition`.

The `PathTransition` moves the text from the start point of the arc to its ending point[3] over a time period of 3 seconds. To make this example more interesting, we use a `ParallelTransition` to simultaneously apply a `FadeTransition` to the text so that it fades in over the first second of the animation.

Finally, on lines 37 to 45 we place the scene graph (less the arc) into a scene and then start the animation. You can see three frames from this animation in Figure 21-10.

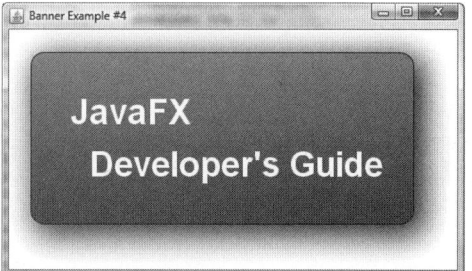

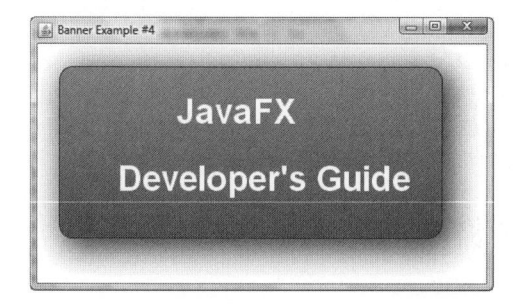

Figure 21-10   Animating part of an imported graphic

Embedding Fonts

The text in the artwork that we have used so far was created with the Arial font, which happens to exist on my laptop. Sometimes, though, this will not be the case. Although it is a pretty safe assumption that you will encounter an Arial font on most systems, this is not true of more exotic fonts.

For example, the artwork in the file `Banner3.ai` is the same as that used in the example shown in Figure 21-1, except that a font called Glass Guage has been used rather than Arial, giving the result shown in Figure 21-11.

---

[3] You may be wondering how we know which is the start point of the arc. The start point is the point from which the arc was drawn in Illustrator.

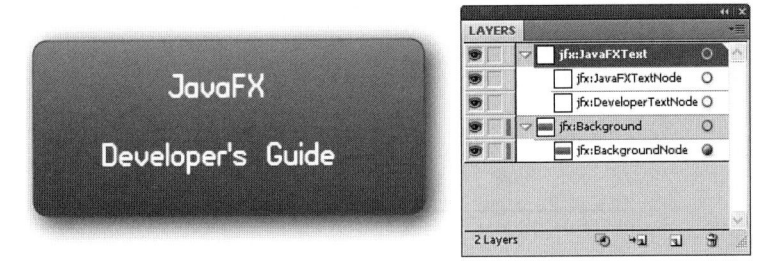

Using Adobe Illustrator and Photoshop Graphics   721

Figure 21-11   An example that uses the Glass Guage font

This font is not one of those that is installed on a typical laptop, so if these artwork were to be converted to FXZ format and imported into a JavaFX application, the text would actually be displayed in the default font for the system on which the application is run. If you are using relatively obscure fonts like this one, you can fix this by ensuring that they are available to your JavaFX application at run time by embedding them in the FXZ archive. You do this by selecting the option to embed fonts when you export your artwork, as shown in Figure 21-12.[4]

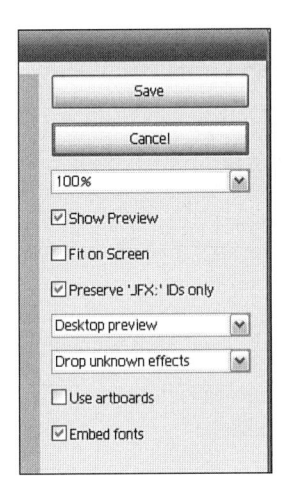

Figure 21-12   Exporting fonts to the FXZ file

When you do this, the font files that your artwork requires are copied into the FXZ archive, and a reference to them is planted in the `content.fxd` file. You can see how this looks in the NetBeans IDE in Figure 21-13.

---

[4] In fact, it will be obvious that you need to embed a font because when you attempt to export the artwork, the text in the preview will be rendered with the wrong font.

Chapter 21 Importing Graphics

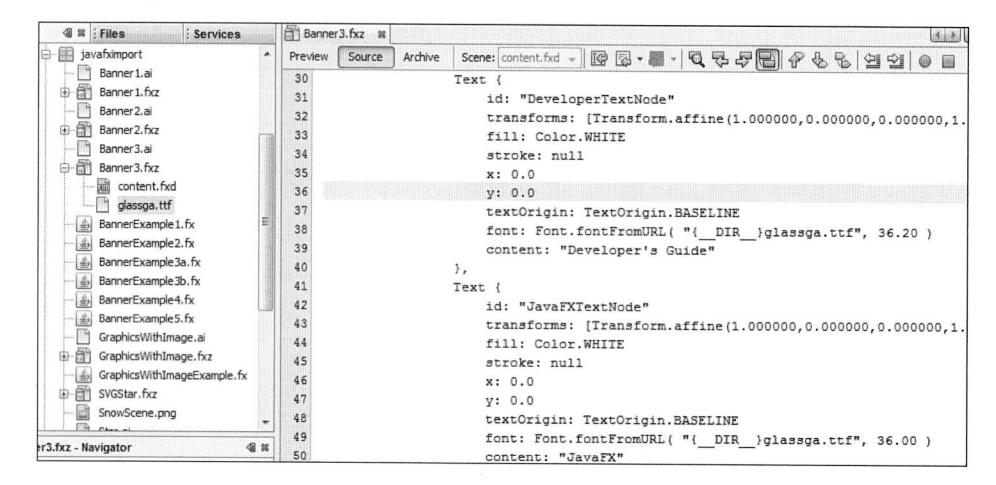

Figure 21-13   An FXZ file with an embedded font

In the Projects view on the left, you can see that the `Banner3.fxz` archive contains the usual `content.fxd` file and also a file called `glassga.ttf`, which is the embedded font file. In the FXD file itself, you can see how this font is referenced:

```
Group {
    id: "JavaFXText"
    content: [
        Text {
            id: "DeveloperTextNode"
            transforms: [Transform.affine(1.000000,0.000000,
                            0.000000,1.000000,93.384120,149.475660)]
            fill: Color.WHITE
            stroke: null
            x: 0.0
            y: 0.0
            textOrigin: TextOrigin.BASELINE
            font: Font.fontFromURL( "{__DIR__}glassga.ttf", 36.20 )
            content: "Developer's Guide"
        }
```

The font is apparently loaded by the `fontFromURL()` function of the `Font` class, which requires the location of the font file and the required font size. If you look at the API documentation for the `Font` class, you will see that no such function exists—this syntax is supported *only by the code that reads the FXD file.*

Loading artwork with embedded fonts is exactly the same as loading any other FXD file, as you can see below, or in the file `javafximport/Banner5.fx` in the example source code for this chapter.

```
var url = "{__DIR__}Banner3.fxz";
Stage {
```

```
        title: "Banner Example #5"
        scene: Scene {
            content: [
                FXDLoader.load(url)
            ]
        }
    }
}
```

Figure 21-14 shows the result of running this example on the JavaFX desktop platform.

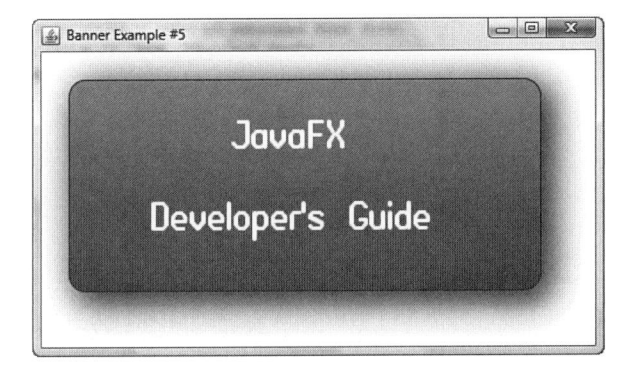

Figure 21-14   A JavaFX application with an embedded font file

However, you get a different result on the mobile platform, as shown in Figure 21-15.

Figure 21-15   An application with an embedded font on the mobile platform

As you can see, the embedded font has been ignored. The mobile platform does not support embedded fonts, because the underlying J2ME platform has no support for them.

In fact, mobile devices generally have a very limited set of fonts, so you generally should not expect your font selections to be honored on the mobile platform.

Embedding Images

If your artwork contains embedded bitmap images, those images are automatically exported into the FXZ archive and a reference to the exported image file is planted in the FXD file. The artwork file `GraphicsWithImage.ai` contains a graphics that consists of some text drawn over an image, as shown in Figure 21-16.

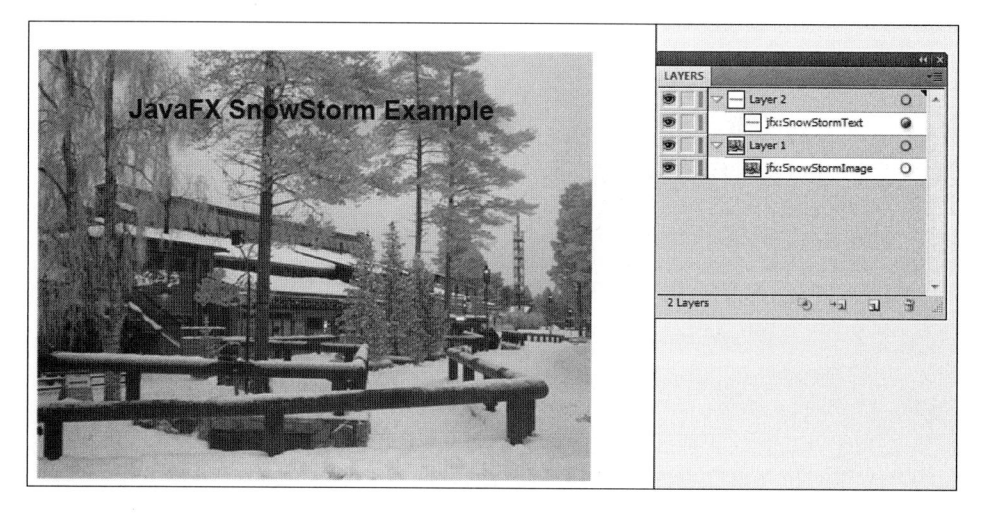

Figure 21-16   Artwork with an embedded image

When this artwork is exported, the FXZ archive contains the embedded image as well as the `content.fxd` file, as shown in Figure 21-17. As you can see, the image filename is based on the name given to the element in Adobe Illustrator, and the code in the FXD file contains an object initializer for an `ImageView` instance that refers to the embedded file.

Figure 21-17   An FXZ archive with an embedded image

Here's the (by now familiar) code required to load this artwork, which you will also find in the file `javafximport/GraphicsWithImageExample.fx`:

```
Stage {
    title: "Graphics With Image"
    scene: Scene {
        content: [
            FXDLoader.load("{__DIR__}GraphicsWithImage.fxz")
        ]
    }
}
```

Using a Stub Node

So far, we have loaded artwork from an FXZ archive by using the `FXDLoader` and `FXDContent` classes. Although this is quite simple, it can sometimes require a little more code than you would ideally want to write in what is intended to be primarily a declarative language. For example, suppose you wanted to load the artwork from the `Banner1.ai` file but change the `fill` color of the text from white to yellow. The code in Listing 21-5, which you'll find in the file `javafximport/BannerExample6.fx`, shows how this can be done.

Listing 21-5 **Changing the Fill Color of Part of an Imported Graphic**

```
1     var url = "{__DIR__}Banner1.fxz";
2     var content = FXDLoader.loadContent(url);
3     var javafxTextNode = content.getShape("JavaFXTextNode");
4     javafxTextNode.fill = Color.YELLOW;
5
6     Stage {
7         title: "Banner Example #6"
8         scene: Scene {
9             content: [
10                content._root
11            ]
12        }
13    }
```

As you can see, it takes four lines of code to retrieve the scene graph from the FXZ file and change the fill color of the first line of text. This isn't too bad, but there is another way to do this that provides a more declarative solution, which is to generate a class that transparently loads content from the FXZ file and which can be used as a node in the scene graph. When you add an instance of this node to the scene graph, it has the same effect as if you had added the root node from the `FXDContent` object in the code shown above.

Generating and Using a UI `Stub` Class

To generate the UI `Stub` class for this example, right-click the `Banner1.fxz` file in the NetBeans IDE and select Generate UI Stub. This opens a dialog that lets you choose where to put the code for the generated class. If you accept the default, it will be placed in a file called `Banner1UI.fx` in the same directory as the rest of the example code for this chapter. Listing 21-6 shows what the generated file contains.

Listing 21-6   A generated UI `Stub` Class

```
1      package javafximport;
2
3      import java.lang.*;
4      import javafx.scene.Node;
5      import javafx.fxd.FXDNode;
6
7      public class Banner1UI extends FXDNode {
8
9          override public var url = "{__DIR__}Banner1.fxz";
10
11         public-read protected var Background: Node;
12         public-read protected var BackgroundNode: Node;
13         public-read protected var DeveloperTextNode: Node;
14         public-read protected var JavaFXText: Node;
15         public-read protected var JavaFXTextNode: Node;
16
17         override protected function contentLoaded() : Void {
18             Background=getNode("Background");
19             BackgroundNode=getNode("BackgroundNode");
20             DeveloperTextNode=getNode("DeveloperTextNode");
21             JavaFXText=getNode("JavaFXText");
22             JavaFXTextNode=getNode("JavaFXTextNode");
23         }
24
25         /**
26          * Check if some element with given id exists and write
27          * a warning if the element could not be found.
28          * The whole method can be removed if such warning is not
29          * required.
30          */
31         protected override function getObject( id:String) : Object {
31             var obj = super.getObject(id);
32             if ( obj == null ) {
33                 System.err.println("WARNING: Element with id {id} not    found in {url}");
```

```
34                  }
35                  return obj;
36              }
37      }
```

The generated class extends `javafx.fxd.FXDNode`, which is itself derived from `CustomNode`. This means that it can be placed in the scene graph like any other node. What is not obvious from the preceding code is how it should be used. The answer is very simple; here's an example that uses the generated class:

```
Stage {
    title: "Banner Example #6"
    scene: Scene {
        content: [
            Banner1UI { }
        ]
    }
}
```

This code is functionally the same as that shown in Listing 21-1 and produces the same result, which you saw in Figure 21-3, but it is much simpler—all you have to do is create an instance of the `Banner1UI` class and treat it just like any other node. There is no reference to the FXZ file and no direct usage of the `FXDLoader` class, because all of that is wrapped up in the generated class. The reference to the FXZ file, for example, is held in the `url` variable of the generated class, as shown on line 9 of Listing 21-6. Code in the `FXDNode` base class uses this variable to access the FXZ file and load its content when the value of the `url` variable is set.

Subclassing a UI `Stub` Class

As you can see on lines 11 to 15 of Listing 21-6, the stub class contains a public variable of type `Node` that corresponds to each layer and graphic object in the original artwork to which an exported identifier was assigned. This makes it easy to get access to these elements from your JavaFX code. You can use these variables to change the `fill` color of the "JavaFX" text node like this:

```
var banner = Banner1UI { };
(banner.JavaFXTextNode as Shape).fill = Color.YELLOW;

Stage {
    title: "Banner Example #7"
    scene: Scene {
        content: [
            banner
        ]
    }
}
```

Chapter 21 Importing Graphics

This is simpler than the code in Listing 21-5, but it is still clumsy because it requires you to create and initialize the `Banner1UI` object outside of the declaration of the `Scene`. Ideally, you would want the stub object to have a public variable corresponding to the `fill` color of the text node. If such a variable existed, it would be possible to set the fill color from the object initializer for the `Banner1UI` object. One way to create this variable is just to add it to the `Banner1UI.fx` file, but this is a bad idea because this is a generated source file, and you would lose the changes if you had to regenerate it, perhaps because the graphics designer has to change the artwork. A better way to create this variable is to subclass `Banner1UI` and add the variable to the subclass. Listing 21-7 shows an implementation of this idea that also adds variables that correspond to the `fill` color of the second line of text and of the background object.

Listing 21-7   Subclassing a UI `Stub` Class

```
package javafximport;

import javafx.scene.paint.LinearGradient;
import javafx.scene.paint.Paint;
import javafx.scene.shape.Shape;
import javafximport.Banner1UI;

public class MyBanner1UI extends Banner1UI {
    public var javaFXTextFill: Paint on replace {
        (JavaFXTextNode as Shape).fill = javaFXTextFill;
    }

    public var developerTextFill: Paint on replace {
        (DeveloperTextNode as Shape).fill = developerTextFill;
    }

    public var backgroundGradient: LinearGradient on replace {
        (BackgroundNode as Shape).fill = backgroundGradient;
    }

    protected override function contentLoaded() {
        super.contentLoaded();
        if (isInitialized(javaFXTextFill)) {
            (JavaFXTextNode as Shape).fill = javaFXTextFill;
        }
        if (isInitialized(developerTextFill)) {
            (DeveloperTextNode as Shape).fill = developerTextFill;
        }
        if (isInitialized(backgroundGradient)) {
            (BackgroundNode as Shape).fill = backgroundGradient;
        }
    }
}
```

Using Adobe Illustrator and Photoshop Graphics

This class is simple: It declares three public variables of type `Paint` and attaches triggers to them that cause the `fill` variable of the corresponding nested node to be updated whenever their values are changed. These triggers are useful if the variables are set *after* the stub has been initialized from the FXZ file. They have no effect on the values set from an object literal because those values will be overwritten by the defaults read from the FXZ file. There is also an override of the `contentLoaded()` function of the `Stub` class, which is called as soon as the stub has been initialized from the FXZ file. The overriding function propagates the values of those variables that have been initialized, typically from an object literal, to the corresponding variable of the nested nodes, thus completing their initialization.

With this class, we can now create an instance of the original artwork and change its fill colors easily. The code in Listing 21-8, which you will find in the file `javafximport/Banner1UiStubExample1.fx`, shows how much more natural this is than the code that we started with in Listing 21-5.

Listing 21-8 Loading an Imported Graphic and Changing Its Properties

```
package javafximport;

import javafx.scene.paint.Color;
import javafx.scene.paint.LinearGradient;
import javafx.scene.paint.Stop;
import javafx.scene.Scene;
import javafx.stage.Stage;

Stage {
    title: "Banner1 UI Stub Example #1"
    scene: Scene {
        content: [
            MyBanner1UI {
                javaFXTextFill: Color.RED
                developerTextFill: Color.ORANGE
                backgroundGradient: LinearGradient {
                    startX: 0.0 startY: 0.0
                    endX: 0.0 endY: 1.0
                    stops: [
                        Stop { offset: 0.0 color: Color.WHITE }
                        Stop { offset: 1.0 color: Color.GRAY }
                    ]
                }
            }
        ]
    }
}
```

The result of running this code is shown in Figure 21-18.

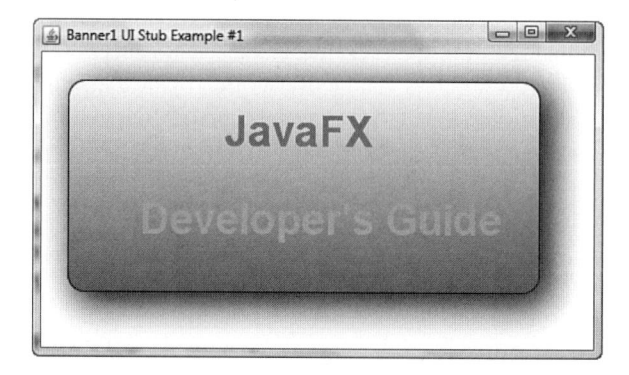

Figure 21-18 An imported graphic with modified fill colors

Background Loading and Placeholder Nodes

By default, the initialization of a UI `Stub` class is synchronous which, as you have already seen, is not desirable in real-world applications. Fortunately, `FXDNode` has support for asynchronous loading built in—all you have to do is activate it by setting the `backgroundLoading` variable of the UI `Stub` class to `true`. While the scene graph for the node is being loaded, you can display a placeholder node by setting the stub's `placeholder` variable to refer to the node or group of nodes to be shown. The placeholder is automatically removed and replaced by the content of the FXZ or FXD file when it has been loaded.

Listing 21-9 is a variant of the code in Listing 21-8 that loads the same user interface asynchronously. You'll find this code in the file `javafximport/BannerUIStubExample2.fx`.

Listing 21-9   **Asynchronous Loading of a UI `Stub` Class**

```
1     var scene:Scene;
2     Stage {
3         title: "Banner1 UI Stub Example #2"
4         scene: scene = Scene {
5             width: 470
6             height: 270
7             content: [
8                 MyBanner1UI {
9                     javaFXTextFill: Color.RED
10                    developerTextFill: Color.ORANGE
11                    backgroundGradient: LinearGradient {
12                        startX: 0.0 startY: 0.0
13                        endX: 0.0 endY: 1.0
14                        stops: [
```

```
15                        Stop { offset: 0.0 color: Color.WHITE }
16                        Stop { offset: 1.0 color: Color.GRAY }
17                    ]
18                }
19                backgroundLoading: true
20                placeholder: Flow {
21                    width: bind scene.width
22                    height: bind scene.height
23                    hpos: HPos.CENTER
24                    vpos: VPos.CENTER
25                    content: Text {
26                        content: "Loading..."
27                        font: Font { size: 24 }
28                    }
29                }
30            }
31        ]
32    }
33 }
```

The important differences between the synchronous and asynchronous cases can be seen on lines 19 to 29 of Listing 21-9. Here, we set the `backgroundLoading` variable to `true` and install as placeholder a `Stack` container that is sized to cover the whole scene containing a text node displaying a message to indicate that loading is in progress. When loading is complete, the `Stack` container is removed, and the banner shown in Figure 21-8 appears.

Creating Multiple Copies of a Graphics Element

When you read the content of an FXZ archive or an FXD file by using the `FXDLoader` class, a single copy of a scene graph based on the original artwork is created. Sometimes, this is sufficient, but in other cases, you might want to have more than a copy of the graphic. Suppose, for example, that your graphic designer has given you an FXZ archive containing the artwork for a star and you want to create a scene containing ten such stars, randomly placed. Assuming the artwork has been exported to a file called `Star.fxz`, you could try the following approach[5]:

```
1    var fxd = FXDLoader.loadContent("{__DIR__}Star.fxz");
2
3    def SIZE = 500;
4    Stage {
5        var scene: Scene;
6        title: "Star Example #1"
7        width: SIZE
```

---

[5] You'll find this code in the file `javafximport/StarExample1.fx`.

732   Chapter 21 Importing Graphics

```
8            height: SIZE
9            scene: scene = Scene {
10               fill: Color.BLACK
11               content: [
12                   for (i in [1..10]) {
13                       var node = fxd.getNode("StarNode");
14                       node.translateX = Math.random() * (SIZE - 20);
15                       node.translateY = Math.random() * (SIZE - 20);
16                       node
17                   }
18               ]
19           }
20       }
```

The FXZ file is loaded on line 1; the `for` expression on lines 12 to 17 creates a sequence containing ten nodes by getting the object with ID of StarNode, which is the star graphic, from the loaded archive. The problem with this code is that it doesn't work—it throws an exception at runtime. The reason is that the `getNode()` call on line 15 does not create a new node each time it is called; instead, it returns the same instance, so the resulting sequence actually contains ten references to the same node. That node is already in the scene graph loaded from the FXZ file, and it cannot be moved to the scene created above without first being removed from that scene graph. Even if we remove it from the original scene graph, this code will still not work because it is trying to place the same node instance in the scene ten times over!

The solution is to use the `duplicate()` function of the `javafx.fxd.Duplicator` class. This function returns a cloned copy of a given node. Given this, we can rewrite the preceding code as follows:

```
1        var fxd = FXDLoader.loadContent("{__DIR__}Star.fxz");
2        var starNode = fxd.getNode("StarNode");
3
4        def SIZE = 500;
5        Stage {
6            var scene: Scene;
7            title: "Star Example #2"
8            width: SIZE
9            height: SIZE
10           scene: scene = Scene {
11               fill: Color.BLACK
12               content: [
13                   for (i in [1..10]) {
14                       var node = Duplicator.duplicate(starNode);
15                       node.translateX = Math.random() * (SIZE - 20);
16                       node.translateY = Math.random() * (SIZE - 20);
17                       node
18                   }
19               ]
```

```
20          }
21     }
```

Here, we get the node that represents the star on line 2 and on line 14; in the body of the `for` expression, we create a duplicate of that node and position it at a random location. As a result of this change, the `content` sequence of the `Scene` now contains ten different star nodes. If you run this code, which you'll find in the file `javafximport/StarExample2.fx`, you'll get a result that looks something like Figure 21-19, although the stars will, of course, not be in the same positions.[6]

Figure 21-19   Creating duplicates of imported graphic elements

Importing SVG Graphics

If your graphics designer prefers to work with SVG graphics rather than the Adobe tools, the JavaFX Production Suite provides a mechanism for importing artwork from an SVG editor that is almost the same as the process that you have just seen. The steps required are as follows:

---

[6] Another way to do the same thing is to create a UI stub file for the star element and simply construct ten instances of it in the `for` expression. This solution is left as an exercise for the reader.

Chapter 21 Importing Graphics

1. Export the graphics from the SVG editor in XML form.
2. Import the XML into the SVG-to-JavaFX Graphics Converter, which is part of the JavaFX Production Suite.
3. Use the JavaFX Graphics Converter to create an FXZ archive.
4. Load the FXZ archive into your JavaFX application.

You have already seen how to complete step 4, so in this section we look only at the other three steps. To create the graphics for this section, I used a free SVG editor called Inkscape to create a star graphic, as shown in Figure 21-20, and exported it to a file called `star.svg` in the directory `javafximport`. As you can see from the figure, I gave the star graphic the identifier `jfx:StarNode` by settings its `id` property.

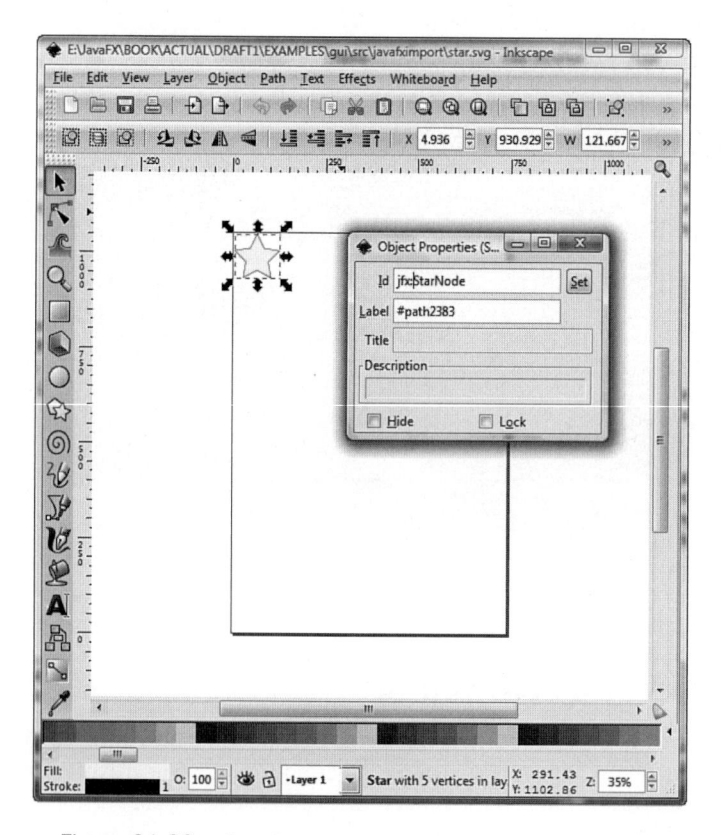

Figure 21-20 Creating a graphic in the Inkscape SVG editor

The next step is to run the SVG to JavaFX Graphics Converter, which you'll find in the directory `SVG Converter` below the installation directory of the JavaFX Production Suite. This prompts you for the location of the SVG file to convert (in this case, `star.svg`) and the name of the FXZ file to be written. I chose to name the output file `SVGStar.fxz` and put it in the same directory as the `star.svg` file (which is also the directory that contains the source code for this chapter's examples). The resulting FXZ file can be viewed in NetBeans IDE in the usual way, as shown in Figure 21-21.

Now that the artwork is in FXZ form, the JavaFX application can't tell whether it originally came from Adobe Illustrator, Photoshop, or an SVG editor—you use the same code to load it in all three cases. You'll find a modified version of the example shown in Figure 21-19 in the file `javafximport/SVGStarExample.fx`—the only change is the name of the FXZ file that is read. If you run this example, you'll see a result that is similar to that shown in Figure 21-19.

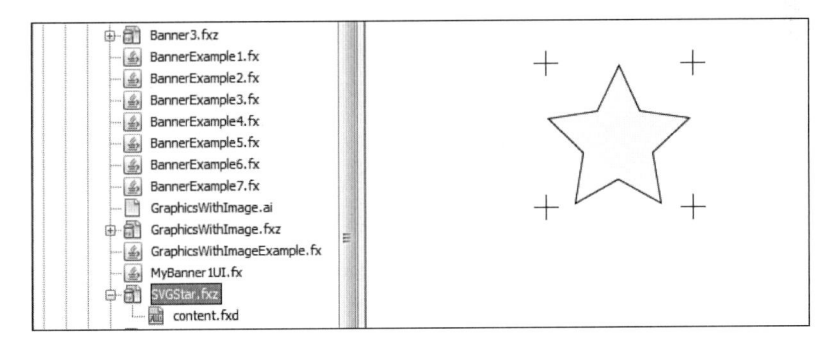

Figure 21-21   Previewing a converted SVG file in the NetBeans IDE

22

Cross-Platform Controls

The user interfaces classes you have seen so far enable you to present information to the user in the form of graphics, video, audio, or text. The only way to get user input from these classes is to handle events from the mouse or the keyboard. Although this is not difficult to do, it quickly becomes tedious. Fortunately, JavaFX has a set of *controls*, which are nodes that can display information to the user and, if appropriate, respond to input. If you are a Swing developer, you are already familiar with controls such as text fields, buttons, check boxes, sliders, and so on. In fact, you can include many of the Swing components in your JavaFX application by using the JavaFX Swing wrapper classes that we discuss in Chapter 24, "Using Swing Controls." One of the benefits of JavaFX is the relative ease with which you can write applications that can be run on different devices, but this does not extend to Swing components because they do not exist on mobile devices. For this reason, there is a set of *cross-platform controls* that rely only on features provided by the common profile and that can therefore be used anywhere that JavaFX is installed. These controls, which are similar to their Swing counterparts, are the subject of this chapter.

Except where noted, you can find the example source code for this chapter in the `javafxcontrols` package of the JavaFX Book More GUI project.

Controls Overview

JavaFX controls are classes that are derived from `javafx.scene.control.Control`. A class diagram that shows the inheritance tree for the `Control` class itself and for all the button-related controls in the `javafx.scene.control` package is shown in Figure 22-1. The most important thing to note about this diagram is that all the controls are nodes, so they can be placed in a scene graph and manipulated just like any other node—you can scale them, you can rotate them, you can shear them, you can animate them, and you can add effects to them.

The first couple of releases of JavaFX had only one control: a single-line input field called `TextBox`. In the JavaFX 1.2 and 1.3 releases, several new controls appeared and more will be added in the future. Table 22-1 lists the controls that are available in JavaFX 1.3 and shows what each control looks like. We discuss each of these controls in detail in

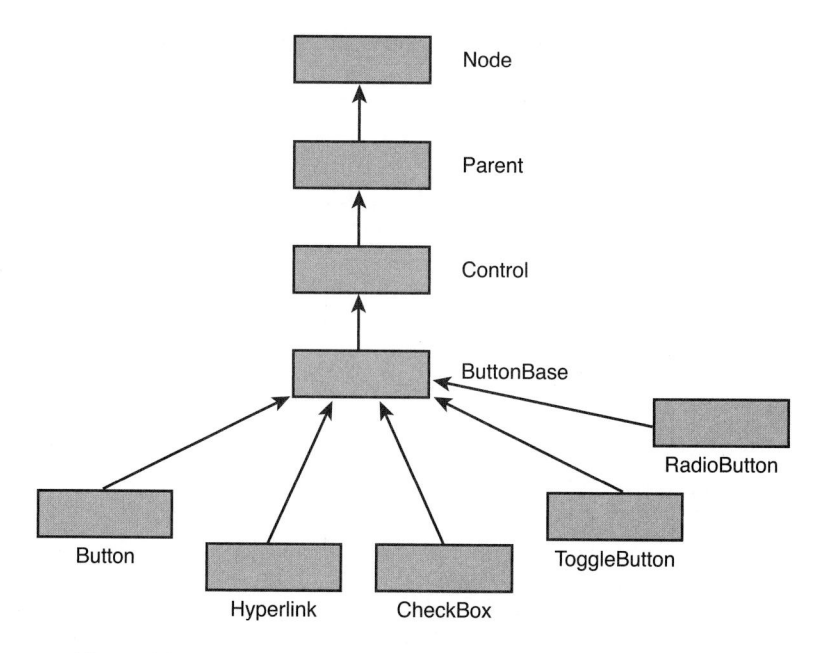

Figure 22-1   Class hierarchy for some of the JavaFX control classes

the sections that follow.[1] Some of the control classes provide variables that let you customize the control's appearance, but this is typically limited to properties such as the text font and color. To get more control over the appearance of a control, you need to use a style sheet. You'll see how to do this in the next chapter.

The Label Control

`Label` is a simple control that is typically used to attach some descriptive text to another control. You might, for example, put a label next to a `TextBox` to indicate what the user is expected to type into it. The `Label` class is similar to the `Text` node, but it has a few features that `Text` does not provide:

- Like all controls, it is `Resizable`, so its size can be changed to fit the layout policy of a container.

---

[1] JavaFX 1.3 also includes a package of additional controls that are under development. The API and appearance of these controls may change before they become officially supported. For this reason, we do not discuss them in this book, but you will find further information about them on this book's website.

Table 22-1 The Control Classes in the JavaFX 1.3 Release

Control	Typical Appearance
Button	OK Cancel
CheckBox	☑ Show tooltips at startup
ChoiceBox	
Hyperlink	http://javafx.com
Label	Label - default font
ListView	
PasswordBox	••••••••
ProgressBar	
ProgressIndicator	40%
RadioButton	⦿ Radio Button
ScrollBar	
ScrollView	
Separator	
Slider	
TextBox	Enter login name
ToggleButton	ToggleButton (selected) ToggleButton (not selected)
Tooltip	

- A label supports multiline text, placing each text run on a separate line, just like the `Text` node, but because the space allocated to a label may be too small to allow all of its content to be seen, it allows you to specify what should happen to the text that it does not have room to display.
- A label can host another node in addition to its text content. You can control the relative positions of the text and the nested node. This feature is completely general but is typically used to add an image to a label.

Label and the `Labeled` Class

Labels get most of their functionality from a mixin class called `Labeled`. This mixin is also used by the button controls, so all the functionality that we discuss in this section is also available from all the button classes and the tooltip class that you'll see later in this chapter. The variables of the `Labeled` class are listed in Table 22-2.

Table 22-2 Variables of the `Labeled` Mixin Class

Variable	Type	Access	Default	Description
text	String	RW	Empty	The text to be displayed in the label
font	Font	RW		The font to be used to render the text
graphic	Node	RW	null	An optional node to be placed within the bounds of the label
graphicTextGap	Number	RW	4	The gap between the text and the graphic
graphicHPos	HPos	RW	HPos.LEFT	The horizontal position of the graphic relative to the text
graphicVPos	VPos	RW	VPos.BASELINE	The vertical position of the graphic relative to the text
hpos	HPos	RW	HPos.LEFT	The horizontal position of the text and graphic relative to the `Label` itself
vpos	VPos	RW	VPos.BASELINE	The vertical position of the text and graphic relative to the `Label` itself
textWrap	Boolean	RW	false	Whether runs of text that are too long for the horizontal space available should be wrapped to the next line
textOverrun	OverrunStyle	RW	OverrunStyle.ELLIPSES	Determines what happens to text that is too wide to display in the space available
textAlignment	TextAlignment	RW	TextAlignment.LEFT	How lines of text should be aligned relative to each other when more than one line is required

The Label Control

The `Label` class itself adds only one variable of its own, which is described in Table 22-3.

Table 22-3 **Variable of the `Label` Class**

Variable	Type	Access	Default	Description
textFill	Paint	RW	Theme dependent	The `Paint` to be used to draw the text in the label

You'll see examples that illustrate the effect of each of these variables in the sections that follow. The default skin for the `Label` class does not add any new variables that would allow you to customize it, so the variables in these two tables are the only ones that you need be concerned with when styling a label.

Basic Labels

In the simplest case, a label contains a single line of text or some text and a graphic. As you'll see later, you can also use a label to display more than one line text, and you can control where the text appears relative to the graphic, if there is one. Some examples of labels are shown in Figure 22-2. Note that the line separators are `Line` nodes that have been added to show where the boundaries of the labels are—they are not provided by the labels themselves. You can find the code for this example in the file `javafxcontrols/Labels1.fx` in the JavaFX Book More GUI project.

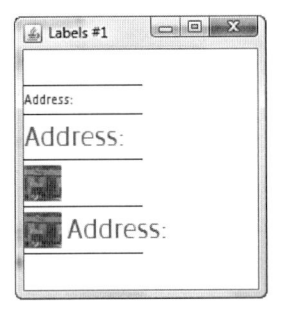

Figure 22-2   Labels with text and graphics

The `Label` at the top is the result of the following code:

```
Label {
    text: "Address:"
}
```

Here, we set only the `text` variable. The text is drawn using the platform default font (that is, the one given by the script variable `Font.DEFAULT`) and uses the default text fill for the active theme.

The second example changes the text font and the fill color by setting the `font` and `textFill` variables, respectively:

```
Label {
    text: "Address:"
    textFill: Color.GREEN
    font: Font { size: 24 }
}
```

A label is not absolutely required to display text—you can use it to display just an image, if required, as shown by the third example, which was created by the following code:

```
Label {
    graphic: ImageView {
        image: Image {
            url: "{__DIR__}houses.jpg"
        }
    }
}
```

Here, the `graphic` variable refers to an `ImageView` object that loads a small image from the same location as the class file itself. We could, if required, apply transformations to the image before it is displayed or use an arbitrary node instead of an image.

The final example has both text and an image:

```
Label {
    text: "Address:"
    textFill: Color.GREEN
    font: Font { size: 24 }
    graphic: ImageView {
        image: Image {
            url: "{__DIR__}houses.jpg"
        }
    }
}
```

By default, the graphic appears to the left of the text, but this can be changed, as you'll see in the next section.

Positioning of Text and Graphics

The `Labeled` class has four variables that let you control the positioning of the graphic relative to the text, and the overall alignment of the text and graphic relative to the boundaries of the control. The examples in the following sections show how these variables are used.

Horizontal Positioning

The horizontal position of the graphic is controlled by the `graphicHPos` variable, which is of type `HPos`. The effect of assigning various different values to this variable is shown in

Figure 22-3, which is the result of running the code in the file
`javafxcontrols/Labels2.fx`.

Figure 22-3 Horizontal positioning of the graphic relative to text in a label

In the topmost example, no explicit assignment graphic position has been specified:

```
Label {
    text: "The Eagle has landed"
    graphic: ImageView {
        image: smallEagle
    }
}
```

By default, this variable has the value `HPos.LEFT`, so the graphic appears to the left of the text. The second example sets this variable to `HPos.RIGHT` and, as you can see, the graphic is now to the right of the text:

```
Label {
    text: "The Eagle has landed"
    graphic: ImageView {
        image: smallEagle
    }
    graphicHPos: HPos.RIGHT
}
```

The values `HPos.LEADING` and `HPos.TRAILING` produce results that depend on the reading direction of the user's locale. In a locale with left-to-right reading direction (such as the United States and the United Kingdom), the `HPos.LEADING` is the same as `HPos.LEFT` and `HPos.TRAILING` is the same as `HPos.RIGHT`. The third example in Figure 22-3 shows the result of using the value `HPos.LEADING` in a left-to-right locale.

The value `HPos.CENTER` places the graphic and the text in the same horizontal location—that is, the center of the text and the center of the graphic have the same x coordinate. The bottom example in Figure 22-3, which results from the following code, illustrates this:

```
Label {
    text: "The Eagle has landed"
    graphic: ImageView {
        image: smallEagle
    }
    graphicHPos: HPos.CENTER
}
```

Vertical Positioning

You can change the vertical position of the graphic relative to the text by using the `graphicVPos` variable. The default value of this variable is `VPos.BASELINE`, which aligns the baseline of the text (i.e. the imaginary line on which the text is drawn) with the vertical centerline of the image, if there is one. This value is used in all the examples in Figure 22-3.

Some examples of the use of the other values of this variable are shown in Figure 22-4, which is the result of running the code in the file `javafxcontrols/Labels3.fx`.

Figure 22-4   Vertical positioning of the graphic relative to text in a label

Reading from top to bottom in Figure 22-4, the values used for the `graphicVPos` variable are `VPos.TOP`, `VPos.BOTTOM`, and `VPos.CENTER`. The effect of each of these should be obvious from their names. There are two other vertical position values available: `VPos.PAGE_START` and `VPos.PAGE_END`. `VPos.PAGE_START` is a locale-independent way of specifying that the graphic should be placed above or below the text depending on the vertical reading order of the user's locale. In a top-to-bottom locale, it corresponds to `VPos.TOP`, whereas the value `VPos.PAGE_END` corresponds to `VPos.BOTTOM` in a top-to-bottom locale and to `VPos.TOP` in a bottom-to-top locale.

Horizontal Alignment

When more horizontal space is available in the label than is required to draw the text/graphic, you can use the `hpos` variable to control where its content is placed relative to its left and right edges. By default, this variable has the value `HPos.LEFT`, which places the content on the left and causes any extra space to appear at the right of the control. The example code in the file `javafxcontrols/Labels4.fx` shows the effect of assigning different values to this variable, with the results shown in Figure 22-5.

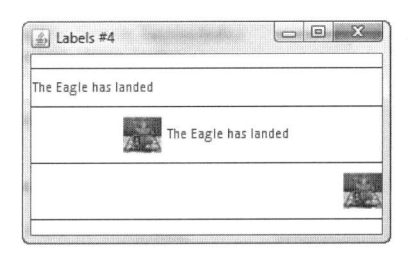

Figure 22-5   Horizontal alignment of label content

All three of these labels are made to stretch to the full width of the scene so that there is guaranteed to be some spare horizontal space. The code that creates the example at the top of the figure looks like this:

```
Label {
    text: "The Eagle has landed"
    hpos: HPos.LEADING
    layoutInfo: LayoutInfo {
        width: bind scene.width
    }
}
```

The `hpos` variable in this case has the value `HPos.LEADING`, which here has the same effect as `HPos.LEFT`—the text is left-aligned within the space assigned to the label and there is no graphic. In the second example in Figure 22-5, `hpos` has the value `HPos.CENTER`, and the label contains both text and a graphic, which are treated as a single unit, and the center of the unit is placed over the center of the label. Finally, the bottom example shows a label with only a graphic, which is aligned to the right of the space allocated to the label because the value `HPos.RIGHT` has been assigned to the `hpos` variable.

Vertical Alignment

Vertical alignment is controlled by the `vpos` variable. The code in the example source code file `javafxcontrols/Labels5.fx` shows the effect of three of the possible values of this variable. Figure 22-6 shows the result.

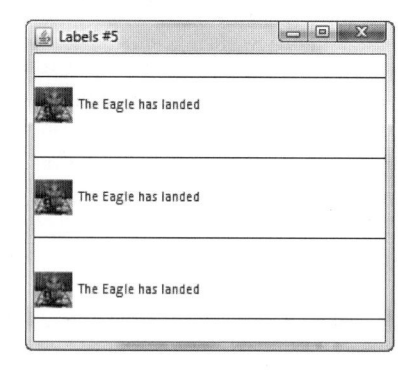

Figure 22-6   Vertical alignment of label content

The label at the top of the figure uses the value VPos.TOP, which places the graphic/text, as a unit, at the top of the available space. You can achieve the same effect by using the value VPos.PAGE_START in a top-to-bottom reading locale or VPos.PAGE_END in a bottom-to-top local. The label in the middle uses the value VPos.CENTER, while the bottom one uses VPos.BOTTOM. The remaining possible value, VTop.BASELINE (which is the default), produces the same result as VPos.CENTER.

Multiline Text

To display multiline text in a label, simply insert a newline character where a line break is required, as shown in the following extract from the file javafxcontrols/Labels6.fx:

```
Label {
    text: "The lunar module Eagle\nJuly 20, 1969."
    graphic: ImageView {
        image: smallEagle
    }
}
```

The newline character following the word *Eagle* causes the text to be split over two lines, as shown in Figure 22-7.

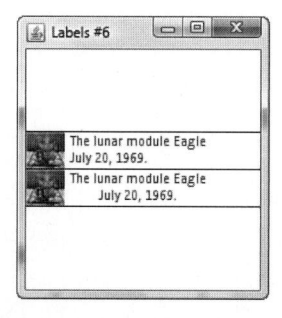

Figure 22-7   Multiline text in a **Label** control

When the text flows over multiple lines, the relative horizontal alignment of each line is controlled by the `textAlignment` variable. By default, this has value `TextAlignment.LEFT`, which causes each line to be left-aligned within the space allocated to the text, as shown at the top of Figure 22-7. Changing this to `TextAlignment.CENTER` causes each line of text to be centered, as shown at the bottom of Figure 22-7.

Text Overruns and Wrapping

When the label is not wide enough to display the label's text or the combination of text and graphic, you can choose to truncate the text or to have it wrap onto another line. The text will wrap at word boundaries if the `textWrap` variable is `true` and will be truncated if its value is `false`. Wrapping works in the same way as it does for the text node, with the wrapping limit implicitly set to the width of the label.

If you choose instead to truncate text that will not fit, you have two further options:

- You can simply drop the remaining text, with no specific indication to the user that this has happened.
- You can have the label replace part of the text with ellipses so that it is clear that some text is missing. If you choose this option, you also have some control over which part of the text is actually displayed.

Whether the text is truncated or ellipses are used depends on the value of the `textOverrun` variable, which can be assigned any of the constant values of the `OverrunStyle` class listed in Table 22-4.

Table 22-4   **Overrun Styles**

Name	Description
CLIP	Text that does not fit is truncated with no warning to the user.
ELLIPSES	Text that does not fit is truncated, and text at the end of the part that does fit is removed, one *character* at a time, until there is room to display ellipses (...). This style, and the next, causes text at the start of the string to be retained in preference to that at the end.
WORD_ELLIPSES	Text that does not fit is truncated, and text at the end of the part that does fit is removed, one *word* at a time, until there is room to display ellipses.
LEADING_ ELLIPSES	Text at the start of the content string is removed one *character* at a time until there is room to display what remains of the string, preceded by ellipses. This style, and the next, cause text at the end of the string to be retained in preference to that at the start.
LEADING_ WORD_ELLIPSES	Text at the start of the content string is removed one *word* at a time until there is room to display what remains of the string, preceded by ellipses.

Table 22-4 Overrun Styles *(Continued)*

Name	Description
CENTER_ELLIPSES	Text in the middle of the content string is removed one *character* at a time until there is room to display what remains of the string, preceded by ellipses. This style, and the next, cause text at the start and end of the string to be retained in preference to that in the center.
CENTER_WORD_ELLIPSES	Text in the middle of the content string is removed one *word* at a time until there is room to display what remains of the string, preceded by ellipses.

The example code in the file `javafxcontrols/Labels7.fx` illustrates the effects of using four of these overrun styles by creating four labels and placing them in a scene that is too narrow for all the text in the labels to be visible. You can see the result of running this code in Figure 22-8.

Figure 22-8 Using text overrun styles

The topmost label in the figure is created by the following code:

```
Label {
    text: "That's one small step for man"
    textOverrun: OverrunStyle.ELLIPSES
}
```

The widths of all the labels in this example have been set by their hosting VBox container to the width of the scene, which has been sized so that the text does not fit in the horizontal space available. In the case of the topmost label, the `textOverrun` variable has value `OverrunStyle.ELLIPSES`, so the end of the text is replaced by three dots, as you can see in Figure 22-8.

The second label uses style `OverrunStyle.WORD_ELLIPSES` and, as you can see, in this case the ellipses appear after the last complete word that will fit in the space available. The third label has `textOverrun` set to `OverrunStyle.CENTER_ELLIPSES`, with the result that the ellipses appear in the middle of the text, surrounded by the start and end of the text content. Finally, the bottom label uses the style `OverrunStyle.LEADING_ELLIPSES`, which results in the ellipses being placed before as much of the end of the text as will fit in the available space.

Button Controls

A button is a control that allows the user to initiate an action or make a selection by clicking it. As you can see from the class diagram in Figure 22-1, JavaFX supports several different types of button, all of which are discussed in the sections that follow.

The `Button` Class

The `Button` class is a simple push button that invokes an action when the user presses and then releases it. A button inherits much of its behavior from two of its base classes: `ButtonBase` and `Labeled`. You have already seen the variables provided by the `Labeled` class, which allow you to set and control the position of the text/graphic that will appear on the button's face. The variable that it inherits from the `ButtonBase` class (`armed`), together with its own variables, is described in Table 22-5.

Table 22-5 Variables of the `Button` Class

Variable	Type	Access	Default	Description
action	function():Void	RW	null	Function called when the user clicks the button.
strong	Boolean	RW	false	When `true`, makes the button visually more prominent.
armed	Boolean	R	false	Whether the button is armed. The armed state is described in the text.

Typical Buttons

You can see several examples of buttons in Figure 22-9, which shows the result of running the code in the file `javafxcontrols/Buttons1.fx`.

Chapter 22 Cross-Platform Controls

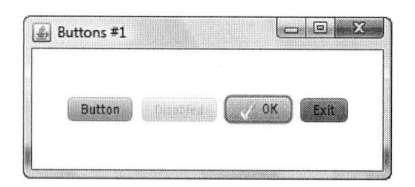

Figure 22-9   Examples of buttons

The button on the left was created by the following code:

```
Button {
    text: "Button"
    action: function() {
        println("Button pressed")
    }
}
```

The text on the face of the button is set using the `text` variable, which is inherited from the `Labeled` mixin. As you saw earlier in this chapter when we looked at the label control, you can use the variables of this mixin to change the font and the positioning of the text.

The function installed in the `action` variable is called when the button is clicked (or more precisely, when the button is *fired*—for more on this, see the section "Button States," later in this chapter). In this case, some output is written when the button is clicked.

Buttons are nodes, so you can disable a button if the application state is such that the action associated with it should not be available. The second button from the left in Figure 22-9 has its `disable` variable set to `false` and shows how a disabled button is represented:

```
Button {
    text: "Disabled"
    disable: true
    action: function() {
        println("Disabled pressed")
    }
}
```

Although this button has an action function, it will never be called because a disabled button cannot be clicked.

The third button shows that you can use a graphic in addition to (or instead of) text:

```
Button {
    text: "OK"
    graphic: ImageView {
        image: okImage
    }
```

```
    action: function() {
        println("OK pressed");
    }
}
```

By default, the graphic is placed to the left of the text, but you can use the `graphicHPos` and `graphicVPos` variables (inherited from `Labeled`) to change this, if required.

Finally, the rightmost button shows the effect of setting the `strong` variable to `true`. You can use this variable to draw the user's attention to a particular button:

```
Button {
    text: "Exit"
    strong: true
    action: function() {
        FX.exit();
    }
}
```

Button States

The `armed` variable that the `Button` class inherits from `ButtonBase` is set when the button is in a state in which it could be fired—that is, one in which an appropriate user gesture will cause its `action` function to be called. The `armed` variable can be set and cleared programmatically by calling the following functions:

```
public function arm():Void
public function disarm():Void
```

More commonly, the state of the `armed` variable is changed as a result of user actions:

- The `armed` variable is `true` if the user moves the mouse over the button and presses the primary mouse button, or the button has the focus and the user presses the Spacebar.
- The `armed` variable is set to `false` if the mouse moves outside the bounds of the button, or if the user releases the mouse while the mouse is over the button or the Spacebar when the button still has the input focus.

> **Note**
>
> The *armed* variable is not the same as the *pressed* variable that is inherited from the `Node` class. The `armed` variable is set to `false` if the user moves the mouse outside of the button even if the primary mouse button is still pressed, but the `pressed` variable is reset to `false` *only* when the mouse button is released. In addition, the `armed` variable can be manipulated programmatically and be set and cleared as a result of key presses, unlike `pressed`, which is controlled entirely by the state of the mouse.

A button's `action` function is called when the button is fired, which occurs under any of the following circumstances, assuming that the button is enabled:

- The `fire()` function inherited from `ButtonBase` is called.
- The button is armed and the primary mouse button is released.
- The button is armed and the Spacebar is released.

The color of the button is changed to reflect the following states:

- Whether the mouse has the input focus (which is actually represented by a colored border around the outside of the control)
- Whether the button is disabled
- Whether the mouse is over the button
- Whether the button is armed

Color changes are animated so that they appear to take place gradually over a short space of time. The `Button` class does not have any variables that let you change the colors that it uses to represent its various states or the color of its text. To do this, you need to use a style sheet. You'll see how to do this in the next chapter.

The `Hyperlink` Class

The `Hyperlink` control is simply a button that is styled to look like a hyperlink in a web page. Like a button, its function is to allow the user to initiate an action, which is triggered by clicking the control with the mouse or pressing and releasing the Spacebar while it has the focus. The name of this control suggests that activating it should cause a web page to be opened, but the control itself does not provide this functionality—it simply invokes its `action` function, which could choose to open a web page or do something completely different.

Like button, the `Hyperlink` class is derived from both `ButtonBase` and `Labeled`, although at the time of this writing, most of the variables inherited from the `Labeled` mixin are not actually used by the default skin, so have no effect on the appearance of the hyperlink. Table 22-6 lists the variables that the `Hyperlink` class itself defines, in addition to those inherited from `ButtonBase`.

Table 22-6 Variables of the `Hyperlink` Class

Variable	Type	Access	Default	Description
armed	Boolean	R	false	Whether the button is armed
visited	Boolean	RW	false	Indicates whether this link has already been activated
action	function():Void	RW	null	Function to be called when the hyperlink is clicked while armed

Button Controls 753

The `action` variable is the same as those of that of the `Button` class. The `visited` variable is set to `true` once the hyperlink has been clicked, which causes the text to be drawn in a different color.

Using the `Hyperlink` Control

The source file `javafxcontrols/Buttons2.fx` contains a simple application that allows you to select and view one of a small number of thumbnail images. We'll use this example to illustrate the `Hyperlink` control, along with some of the other button types that you'll see later in this chapter. The thumbnails are displayed by a custom node that incorporates a `Hyperlink` which, when clicked, opens a full-size version of the thumbnail in a separate window. Figure 22-10 shows the location of this hyperlink.

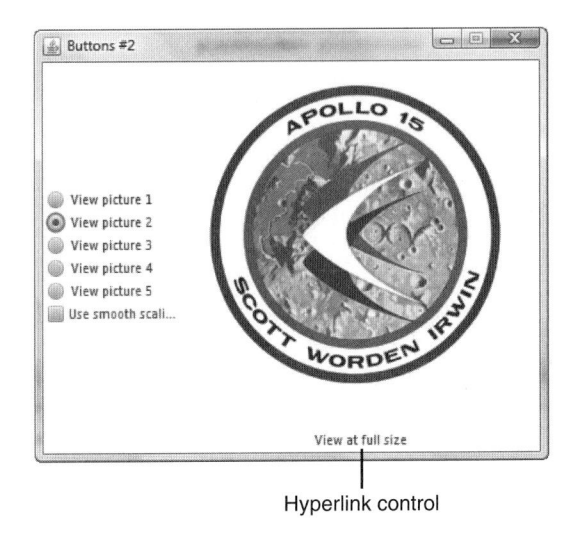

Figure 22-10   An application containing a **Hyperlink** control

If you select one of the thumbnails and then move the cursor over the hyperlink, it is armed and, as a result, two things happen:

- The cursor changes to a hand.[2]
- The hyperlink text is underlined, as shown in Figure 22-11.

---

[2] The cursor actually changes to the one installed in the `cursor` variable of the `Hyperlink` node or to the hand cursor if you don't set a more specific one.

754　Chapter 22　Cross-Platform Controls

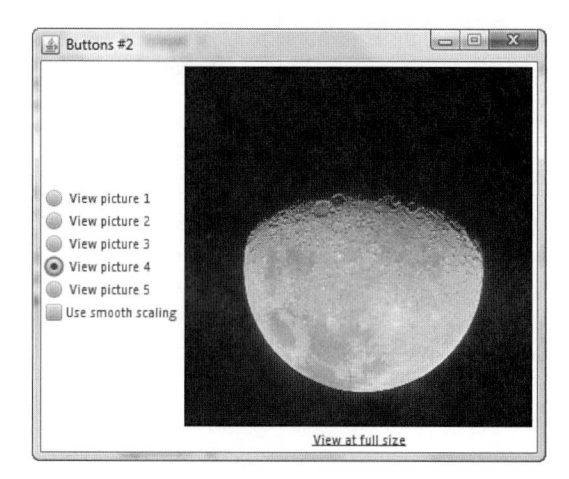

Figure 22-11　An armed **Hyperlink** control

You can see both of these effects in Figure 22-11.

The source code for the custom node that contains the image thumbnail and the hyperlink, which you can find in the file javafxcontrols/Thumbnail.fx, is shown in Listing 22-1.

Listing 22-1　**A Custom Control That Displays a Thumbnail Image and a Hyperlink**

```
1    public class Thumbnail extends CustomNode {
2        public var thumbURL:String;
3        public var thumbWidth:Number;
4        public var thumbHeight:Number;
5        public var action: function():Void;
6        public var smooth:Boolean;
7        public var placeholder:Image;
8
9        protected override var children = { 10                    [
11            var link:Hyperlink;
12            content: [
13                ImageView {
14                    fitWidth: bind thumbWidth
15                    fitHeight: bind thumbHeight
16                    preserveRatio: true
17                    smooth: bind smooth
18                    image: bind Image {
19                        url: thumbURL
20                        backgroundLoading: true
21                        placeholder: placeholder
22                    }
23                }
```

```
24                   link = Hyperlink {
25                       layoutX: bind (thumbWidth
26                                       - link.layoutBounds.width) / 2
27                       layoutY: bind thumbHeight + 2
28                       text: "View at full size"
29                       hpos: HPos.CENTER
30                       disable: bind thumbURL == ""
31                       action: bind action
32                   }
33               ]
34           }
35       }
36   }
```

The variables that the custom node provides to allow the thumbnail to be configured are declared on lines 2 to 7 of Listing 22-1, and the hyperlink itself is created on lines 24 to 31. As you can see, its `text` variable is initialized (on line 28) with a fixed string, while its `action` variable is set from the value of the `action` variable of the custom node itself. Here's how this custom control is used in the example shown in Figure 22-11.

```
1    thumbnail = Thumbnail {
2        thumbURL: bind images[selectedImage]
3        thumbWidth: 300
4        thumbHeight: 300
5        smooth: bind smooth
6        placeholder: placeholder
7        action: function():Void {
8            Stage {
9                title: "{thumbnail.thumbURL}"
10               resizable: false
11               scene: Scene {
12                   content: ImageView {
13                       image: Image {
14                           url: thumbnail.thumbURL
15                       }
16                   }
17               }
18           }
19       }
20   }
```

The `action` function that is declared on lines 7 to 19 is the one that is actually called from the hyperlink's `action` function when it is clicked. It opens a new stage to display the full-sized image corresponding to the thumbnail in the custom node.

The `ToggleButton`, `RadioButton`, and `CheckBox` Classes

The `ToggleButton`, `RadioButton`, and `CheckBox` classes provide different ways to allow the user to make an on/off or true/false selection. Toggle buttons are often used in toolbars because they can be made to be very compact if used with an icon but no text, whereas radio buttons and check boxes are usually preferred when building forms. All three of these classes incorporate the `Labeled` mixin, so you can use the variables of that class to change the text font, add an icon (although that would probably not be very useful in the case of a radio button or check box), and so on.

Toggle Buttons and Radio Buttons

`ToggleButton` and `RadioButton` (which derives from `ToggleButton`) have the same API. Both derive from `ButtonBase` and also include the `Toggle` mixin, which provides the variables listed in Table 22-7.

Table 22-7   Variables of the `ToggleButton` and `RadioButton` Classes

Variable	Type	Access	Default	Description
selected	Boolean	RW	false	`true` if the button is in the selected state
toggleGroup	ToggleGroup	RW	null	The `ToggleGroup` of which the button is a member, or `null` if it is not in a `ToggleGroup`
value	Object	RW	null	An arbitrary value that can be used to distinguish this control from others in the same `ToggleGroup`

The code in Listing 22-2, from the file `javafxcontrols/ToggleButtons1.fx`, creates two toggle buttons and reports when their states change. The result of running this code is shown in Figure 22-12.

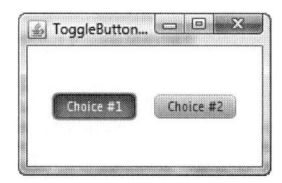

Figure 22-12   Two toggle buttons in a `ToggleGroup`

Listing 22-2 The `ToggleButton` Class

```
1    var selected1:Boolean = true on replace {
2        println("#1 selected: {selected1}")
3    }
4    var selected2:Boolean on replace {
5        println("#2 selected: {selected1}")
6    }
7
8    var scene:Scene;
9    Stage {
10       title : "ToggleButtons #1"
11       scene: scene = Scene {
12           width: 200
13           height: 100
14           content: [
15               Flow {
16                   var toggleGroup = ToggleGroup {}
17                   width: bind scene.width
18                   height: bind scene.height
19                   hpos: HPos.CENTER
20                   vpos: VPos.CENTER
21                   hgap: 16
22                   content: [
23                       ToggleButton {
24                           text: "Choice #1"
25                           toggleGroup: toggleGroup
26                           selected: bind selected1 with inverse
27                       }
28                       ToggleButton {
29                           text: "Choice #2"
30                           toggleGroup: toggleGroup
31                           selected: bind selected2 with inverse
32                       }
33                   ]
34               }
35           ]
36       }
37   }
```

The important difference between a toggle button and an ordinary button is that a toggle button stays pressed when you push and release it. Pressing and releasing it for a second time causes it to revert to its unpressed state (hence the use of the word *toggle* in the name). The toggle button on the left of Figure 22-12 is pushed in, whereas the one on the right is not. The "pushed-in" state is represented by the `selected` variable, which is `true` when the button is "in" and `false` when it is "out." The code on lines 26 and 31 of Listing 22-2 binds the state of two script variables to the `selected` variables of the two toggle buttons and uses triggers to report when each button is toggled. You can programmatically toggle the button by directly setting the value of its `selected` variable.

The toggle buttons in Listing 22-2 are linked together through a `ToggleGroup`. To place a toggle button in a toggle group, install a reference to the toggle group in its `toggleGroup` variable, as shown on lines 25 and 30 of Listing 22-2. The toggle group ensures that no more than one of its members is selected at any one time, so if you click the button on the right of Figure 22-15, you will see that the one on the left is automatically unselected. As a result, it is not possible for both toggle buttons to be selected at the same time, but it *is* possible for them to both be unselected.

Radio buttons behave and are programmed in the same way as toggle buttons, but their appearance is very different. We use radio buttons in our picture viewing application to allow the user to select which image should be displayed, as shown in Figure 22-13.

Here's the code from the file `javafxcontrols/Buttons2.fx` that creates these buttons:

```
for (i in [0..<sizeof images]) {
    RadioButton {
        toggleGroup: toggleGroup
        text: "View picture {i + 1}"
        override var selected on replace {
            if (selected) {
                selectedImage = i;
            }
        }
    }
}
```

Neither the `ToggleButton` nor the `RadioButton` class has an equivalent of the `action` variable that lets you register a function to be called when its selected state changes. Here, we detect a state change by adding a trigger directly to the `selected` variable of a radio button. In Listing 22-2, we achieved the same thing by binding a script variable to its state and triggering on a change in the value of the script variable.

Like a toggle button, a radio button can be either selected or unselected. A selected radio button is shown (by the default skin) as a depressed circle with a black dot at its center, whereas an unselected radio button does not have a black dot. When, as in this case, the radio buttons are in the same toggle group, no more than one of them can be selected at any given time. This makes radio buttons ideal when the user needs to choose exactly

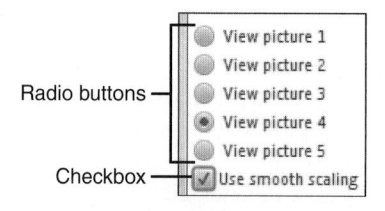

Figure 22-13   Radio buttons

one from a set of options. Unlike a toggle button, the user can only change the state of a radio button in a toggle group by pressing it when it is not selected—pressing a selected radio button that is in a toggle group does not deselect it.

Check Boxes

A check box is typically used when you want to present the user with one or more options that are independent of each other. Because there is no relationship between the selected states of different check boxes, the `CheckBox` class does not have an equivalent of the `toggleGroup` variable provided by the `ToggleButton` and `RadioButton` classes. The variables of the `CheckBox` class that are additional to those of its base class `ButtonBase` are listed in Table 22-8.

Table 22-8   Variables of the `CheckBox` Class

Variable	Type	Access	Default	Description
selected	Boolean	RW	false	`true` if the check box is in the selected state.
allowTriState	Boolean	RW	false	`true` if the check box should have three states; `false` if it should have two states.
defined	Boolean	RW	true	Used in conjunction with selected to create a third state. See text.

By default, like a toggle button and a radio button, a check box has two states: selected and unselected. A check box is represented as a square that has a tick when it is selected. You can see a check box in its selected state at the bottom of Figure 22-13.

Sometimes it is useful to have a *tri-state* check box. A tri-state check box has three states: *selected*, *unselected*, and *undefined*. A typical use for a tri-state check box is to allow the user to select or deselect all of a group of related options by clicking a single check box beneath which all the related options are placed, or to select some of those options by using their own check boxes. When some, but not all, of the group options are selected, the parent check box is usually placed in the undefined state, to indicate that it is neither selected nor unselected, mirroring the fact that the set of grouped options is neither completely selected nor completely unselected.

The `allowTriState` variable, which is `false` by default, should be set to `true` to enable tri-state mode. The code in Listing 22-3, which you will find in the file `javafxcontrols/CheckBox1.fx`, creates a tri-state check box and prints the values of the `selected` and `defined` variables as they change. You can see the result of running this example in Figure 22-14.

760   Chapter 22 Cross-Platform Controls

Figure 22-14   A tri-state check box

Listing 22-3   **A Tri-State Check Box**

```
var scene:Scene;
Stage {
    title : "CheckBox #1"
    scene: scene = Scene {
        width: 150
        height: 100
        content: [
            VBox {
                width: bind scene.width
                height: bind scene.height
                vpos: VPos.CENTER
                spacing: 8
                content: [
                    CheckBox {
                        text: "Tri-state checkbox #1"
                        allowTriState: true
                        defined: bind box1Defined with inverse
                        selected: bind box1Selected with inverse
                    }
                ]
            }
        ]
    }
}

var box1Selected = false on replace {
    println("box1Selected: {box1Selected}")
}
var box1Defined = true on replace {
    println("box1Defined: {box1Defined}")
}
```

In the screenshot on the left, the check box is in its initial, unselected state. Clicking it once changes it state to undefined, as shown in the center. Clicking it again changes it to the selected state, as shown on the right. Application code can distinguish these three states by examining the values of the `defined` and `selected` variables, as follows:

- If `defined` is `false`, the check box is in the undefined state, irrespective of the value of the `selected` variable.
- If `defined` is `true` and `selected` is `false`, the check box is in the unselected state.
- If `defined` is `true` and `selected` is `true`, the check box is in the selected state.

The `TextBox` Control

The `javafx.scene.control.TextBox` class allows you to get text input from the user. Much of the functionality of this control is provided by its base class, `TextInputControl`, which is in the same package. The variables provided by the `TextInputControl` are listed in Table 22-9 and those added by `TextBox` are shown in Table 22-10.

Table 22-9   Variables of the `TextInputControl` Class

Variable	Type	Access	Default	Description
`columns`	Number	RW	10	The expected number of characters that this control needs to display
`editable`	Boolean	RW	`true`	Whether the user is allowed to edit the content of this control
`selectOnFocus`	Boolean	RW	`true`	Whether the control's content should be selected when it gets the input focus
`font`	Font	RW		The font used to display the text
`text`	String	RW	Empty string	The committed content of the control
`rawText`	String	R	Empty string	The text that is currently displayed by the control
`promptText`	String	RW	Empty string	Text to be displayed when the control is otherwise empty

Table 22-9 Variables of the `TextInputControl` Class *(Continued)*

Variable	Type	Access	Default	Description
action	function ():Void	RW	null	Function to be called when a new value is committed to the control
adjustingSelection	Boolean	RW	false	Indicates whether the selection is in the process of being changed.
mark	Integer	R		The location of the "mark" point of the selection
dot	Integer	R		The location of the "dot" point of the selection

Table 22-10 Variables of the `TextBox` Class

Variable	Type	Access	Default	Description
multiline	Boolean	RW	false	Whether the control should display more than one line of text.
lines	Integer	RW	5	The number of lines of text that should be displayed. This value is used only if multiline is true.

The code in Listing 22-4, which you'll find in the file `javafxcontrols/TextBox1.fx`, creates three text box controls and places them in a scene, as shown in Figure 22-15. In the following sections, we discuss the variables and functions of the `TextBox` class, including those inherited from `TextInputControl`.

Figure 22-15   Illustrating the `TextBox` control

Listing 22-4   Using a `TextBox` Control

```
var scene:Scene;
Stage {
    title: "TextBox #1"
    scene: scene = Scene {
        width: 200
        content: [
            VBox {
                fillWidth: false
                height: bind scene.height
                width: bind scene.width
                spacing: 16
                padding: Insets { top: 5 left: 5
                                  bottom: 5 right: 5 }
                content: [
                    TextBox {
                        columns: 10
                        promptText: "Name"
                        layoutInfo: LayoutInfo {
                            hfill: false
                        }
                    }
                    TextBox {
                        columns: 15
                        lines: 5
                        multiline: true
                        promptText: "Address"
                        layoutInfo: LayoutInfo {
                            vgrow: Priority.NEVER
                            hfill: false
                        }
                    }
                    TextBox {
                        columns: 15
                        promptText: "Email address"
                        layoutInfo: LayoutInfo {
                            hfill: false
                        }
                    }
                ]
            }
        ]
    }
}
```

As you can see, all three text boxes initially display a string that acts as a hint as to what the user should enter into the field. This text, which is set using the `promptText` variable, is rendered using a lighter color than real content and is displayed only when the text box would otherwise be empty.

TextBox Width

The `columns` variable specifies the number of characters that the text box should display horizontally, which is ten by default. The text box takes this as a hint as to how wide it should make the control's visual representation—the exact width of the control will depend on the font in use. The top and bottom text boxes shown in Figure 22-15 have respectively 10 and 15 columns. Notice that we use the `hfill` variable of a `LayoutInfo` object to ensure that these controls are given their preferred widths, because otherwise the `VBox` container would expand all three of them to match the width of the widest, as a result of the fact that the `getHGrow()` and `getHFill()` functions of the `TextBox` class both return `true`.

The column count is *not* a limit on the number of characters that may be entered into the text box—there is no way to control that. If the user enters more characters than the control can display, the text will be scrolled so that the insertion cursor (which is called the *caret* and is represented by a vertical bar) is always visible. You can use the arrow keys on your keyboard or the mouse to move the insertion cursor, which allows you to insert new text anywhere you want to, or delete existing text by using the Delete or Backspace keys. As you'll see in the section "Selection," later in this chapter, you can also move the caret, change the cursor, and delete content programmatically.

TextBox Height

The height of the `TextBox` is set based on the font in use and, if the `multiline` variable is `true`, the value of the `lines` variable. The middle `TextBox` in Figure 22-15 is configured to show five lines of text and, as you can see, it is large enough to display all of these lines. A multiline `TextBox` allows itself to be resized vertically to absorb extra space in the container. In Listing 22-4, we prevent this behavior by setting the `vgrow` variable of its `LayoutInfo` object to `false`.

If the user were to type more than five lines of text into this control, a scrollbar would appear to allow all of the text to be viewed.

Editability

By default, the user is allowed to edit the content of a text box. This might seem to be obvious, but there are cases when you might not want this to be allowed. For example, suppose you have designed a form that shows a view of a record in a database by displaying the values from that record in text boxes. You might want to allow some users to update the record while only allowing others to read it. To do this, you need to switch the text box into a mode in which the user cannot type into it. You can do this by setting the `editable` variable to `false`, as shown on line 19 of the code in Listing 22-5, which you'll find in the file `javafxcontrols/TextBox2.fx`. You can see the result of running this code in Figure 22-16.

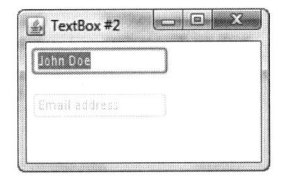

Figure 22-16   Using the editable variable of the
TextBox control

Listing 22-5   The Editable and Disable Variables of the TextBox Control

```
1    var scene:Scene;
2    Stage {
3        title: "TextBox #2"
4        scene: scene = Scene {
5            width: 200
6            height: 100
7            content: [
8                VBox {
9                    fillWidth: false
10                   height: bind scene.height
11                   width: bind scene.width
12                   spacing: 16
13                   padding: Insets { top: 5 left: 5
14                                     bottom: 5 right: 5 }
15                   content: [
16                       TextBox {
17                           columns: 15
18                           text: "John Doe"
19                           editable: false
20                       }
21                       TextBox {
22                           columns: 15
23                           promptText: "Email address"
24                           disable: true
25                       }
26                   ]
27               }
28           ]
29       }
30   }
```

If you try to type in the upper text box, you will find that you can't. You can reenable editing by setting the `editable` variable to `true`, which is its default value.

The `editable` variable should not be confused with the `disable` variable, which the text box inherits from the `Node` class. The text box at the bottom of Figure 22-16, which is created on lines 21 to 25 of Listing 22-5, has its `disable` variable set to `true`. This stops the user editing its content, but it also changes the control's appearance and prevents it getting the input focus. You would typically use the `disable` variable when the control is in a part of a form that is not available until some other condition is fulfilled, or if the whole form should be temporarily unavailable, perhaps because you are updating the database as a background activity and do not want to allow further input until the update is complete.

Setting and Getting the Content of the `TextBox`

The most useful aspect of the `TextBox` control is, of course, its capability to display and allow the user to edit a text string. If you look at the list of variables in Table 22-9, you'll see that there are two variables that appear to represent the content of a text box: `text` and `rawText`. We'll use the code in Listing 22-6, which you'll find in the file `javafxcontrols/TextBox3.fx`, to explain the difference between these variables and how you should use them.

Listing 22-6 Tracking Changes in the Content of the `TextBox` Control

```
1     var scene:Scene;
2     Stage {
3         title: "TextBox #3"
4         scene: scene = Scene {
5             width: 200
6             height: 110
7             var textBox:TextBox;
8             content: [
9                 VBox {
10                    fillWidth: false
11                    height: bind scene.height
12                    width: bind scene.width
13                    spacing: 16
14                    padding: Insets { top: 5 left: 5
15                                      bottom: 5 right: 5 }
16                    content: [
17                        textBox = TextBox {
18                            columns: 15
19                            text: "TextBox"
20                            action: function() {
21                                println("Text: {textBox.text}, "
22                                    "rawText: {textBox.rawText}");
23                            }
24                            layoutInfo: LayoutInfo {
25                                        hfill: false
26                            }
```

```
27                      }
28                      Text {
29                          content:
30                              bind "Text = "
31                      }
32                      Text {
33                          content: bind
34                              "RawText = "
35                      }
36                  ]
37              }
38          ]
39      }
40  }
```

This code creates a text box and two text objects. The content variable of the first text object is bound to the text variable of the text box and that of the second text object to its rawText variable. The text variable of the TextBox is initially set to TextBox, as shown on the left of Figure 22-17. Setting the text variable always causes the rawText variable to be given the same value, so both of the text objects show the same value at this point.

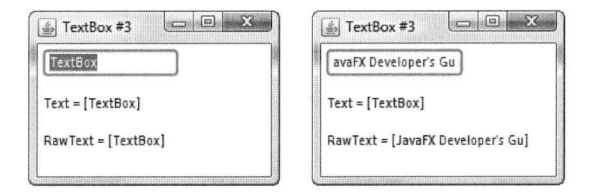

Figure 22-17 The **text** and **rawText** variables of the **TextBox** control

The rawText variable reflects the actual content of the text box and changes immediately as the user types into it. On the right of Figure 22-17, you can see that the text "JavaFX Developer's Gu" has been typed into the text box and that the value of the rawText variable reflects this. However, the text variable still contains the string Hello because the user has not yet *committed* this change of text. The change is committed when any of the following happens:

- The user presses the Enter key (or its equivalent on the device in use) in a single-line text box (but not in a multiline text box).
- The focus moves from the text box to another node or to another application.
- The commit() function of the TextBox class is called.

Committing the content causes the value of the `rawText` variable to be copied to the `text` variable. Typically, you will bind application state to the `text` variable of the text box rather than to the `rawText` variable, because usually you will only want to know about committed changes. In addition to, or as well as, using a binding to the `text` variable, you can be notified when the user commits new text by assigning a function to the `action` variable of the text box as shown on lines 21 to 23 of Listing 22-6, where the values of the `text` and `rawText` variables are printed when a change is committed. By the time the `action` function is called, these variables will always have the same value.

The `rawText` variable is typically used when you want to enable or disable a related control depending on whether the text box has valid content and you want this state to change in real time as the user types into the text box. For example, you might build a form consisting of a text box and a button and disable the button when the text box is empty or contains only white space. The code in Listing 22-7, which you will find in the file `javafxcontrols/TextBox4.fx`, shows how you can achieve this.

Listing 22-7 Disabling a Button Based on the Content of a `TextBox` Control

```
1    var scene:Scene;
2    Stage {
3        title: "TextBox #4"
4        scene: scene = Scene {
5            width: 200
6            var textBox:TextBox;
7            content: [
8                VBox {
9                    fillWidth: false
10                   height: bind scene.height
11                   width: bind scene.width
12                   spacing: 16
13                   padding: Insets { top: 5 left: 5
14                                     bottom: 5 right: 5 }
15                   content: [
16                       textBox = TextBox {
17                           columns: 10
18                           text: "TextBox"
19                           action: function() {
20                               println("Text: {textBox.text}, "
21                                       "rawText: {textBox.rawText}");
22                           }
23                       }
24                       Button {
25                           text: "OK"
26                           disable: bind textBox.rawText.trim() == ""
27                       }
28                   ]
29               }
```

```
30                   ]
31               }
32           }
```

The binding on line 26 links the state of the `disable` variable of the button to the value of the `rawText` variable of the text box. As a result of this binding, the button will be disabled if the `rawText` variable is empty or contains only whitespace characters. When this example starts, the `rawText` variable contains the values `TextBox`, so the button is enabled, as shown on the left of Figure 22-18. If the text box is cleared, as is the case on the right of Figure 22-18, the OK button is disabled. This change of state happens as the user types and does not require the text to be committed.

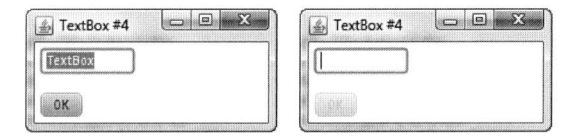

Figure 22-18   Using the rawText variable of a text box to enable or disable a button

Selection

You can select some or all the text in a text box control by dragging the mouse or moving the caret using the left- and right-arrow keys while holding down a key (typically the Shift key). The selected part of the text is highlighted, as shown in Figure 22-19.

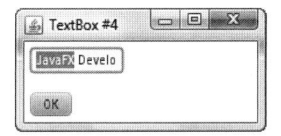

Figure 22-19   Selecting text in a text box

If you type into a text box while some of its text is selected, whatever you type replaces the text that is selected. Sometimes, you want the whole content of the text box to be automatically selected when the user gives it the input focus to make it much easier for the user to completely replace all the text. In other cases, you might not want this to happen. You can control this behavior by using the `selectOnFocus` variable. When this variable has the value `true`, as it is by default, all the text will be selected when the `TextBox` gets the focus, as is the case on the left of Figure 22-17. When it is `false`, the selection is not affected by a change in focus. (That is, the selection that was in place when the `TextBox` last had the focus is restored.)

The `TextBox` control provides two variables—`mark` and `dot`—that let you track the bounds of the selection. The `mark` variable represents the position of the caret when the user clicked to begin creating the selection. As the user drags the mouse (or uses the keyboard arrow keys) to create the selection, the value of `mark` stays the same, and the `dot` variable is updated to reflect the part of the control that is selected. The code in Listing 22-8, from the file `javafxcontrols/TextBox5.fx`, creates a text box and displays the values of the `dot` and `mark` variables as they are affected by changes in the selection.

Listing 22-8   Tracking the `mark` and `dot` Variables of a Text Box

```
var scene:Scene;
Stage {
    title: "TextBox #5"
    scene: scene = Scene {
        width: 200
        var textBox:TextBox;
        content: [
            VBox {
                fillWidth: false
                height: bind scene.height
                width: bind scene.width
                spacing: 16
                padding: Insets { top: 5 left: 5
                                  bottom: 5 right: 5 }
                content: [
                    textBox = TextBox {
                        columns: 10
                        text: "JavaFX"
                    }
                    Text {
                        content: bind "mark: "
                    }
                    Text {
                        content: bind "dot: "
                    }
                ]
            }
        ]
    }
}
```

When this application starts, the text box is given the input focus and its content is selected, because the `selectOnFocus` variable defaults to `true`, as shown on the left of Figure 22-20.

As you can see, the `mark` variable has value 0, and `dot` has the value 6. These values refer not to character positions, but to *the locations between the characters*, where 0 is the location to the left of the left most character, 1 to the location between the first and second character, and so on. If you select the characters *avaF* by clicking between the *J* and *a* characters and dragging the mouse to the right, you'll see that `mark`, which is the location

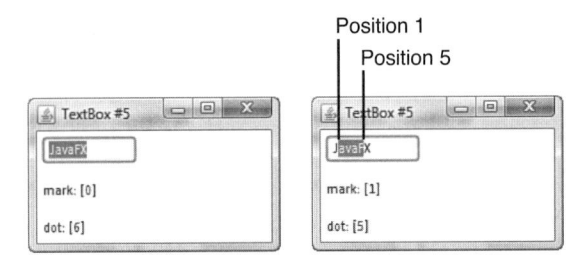

Figure 22-20   The **dot** and **mark** variables and the selection

of the initial click, becomes 1 and dot, representing the other end of the selection, changes to 5, as shown on the right of Figure 22-20. When there is no selection, the mark and dot variables have the same value, which represents the position of the input caret.

You cannot programmatically change the selection by modifying the values of the mark and dot variables because they are read-only to application code, but the TextBox class provides several functions that allow you to modify the selection, which in turn will update these variables, of which the following are examples:

```
public function selectAll():Void
public function unselect():Void
public function selectRange(dot:Integer, mark:Integer):Void
```

Copy and Paste

You can copy the currently selected content of a text box control to the system Clipboard by calling the copy() function:

```
public function copy():Void
```

The content is copied as plain text, which can be imported into virtually any other application. The text box control provides a platform-dependent key that allows the user to perform this operation—on Windows, this is Ctrl-C. The paste() function copies text from the Clipboard into the text box, replacing whatever is currently selected:

```
public function paste():Void
```

On Windows, the user can paste content by pressing Ctrl-V.

The PasswordBox Control

The PasswordBox control is a single-line-only variant of TextBox designed for the input of passwords and other information that should be hidden from casual observers. Characters entered into a PasswordBox are replaced immediately or after a short delay by a different character, called the echo character, so that they cannot be read. PasswordBox derives from TextInputControl and adds the variables listed in Table 22-11.

Table 22-11   Variables of the `PasswordBox` Class

Variable	Type	Access	Default	Description
echoChar	String	RW	*	The characters to be used to replace each character that is types
hideDelay	Integer	RW	0	The time in milliseconds for which each typed character should remain visible before being replaced by echoChar

The following code, from the file `javafxcontrols/PasswordBox1.fx`, creates a PasswordBox and configures it to replace each character typed with the two characters XY:

```
var scene:Scene;
Stage {
    title: "PasswordBox #1"
    scene: scene = Scene {
        width: 200
        content: [
            VBox {
                fillWidth: false
                height: bind scene.height
                width: bind scene.width
                spacing: 16
                padding: Insets { top: 5 left: 5
                                  bottom: 5 right: 5 }
                content: [
                    PasswordBox {
                        columns: 15
                        promptText: "Type Password"
                        echoChar: "XY"
                        hideDelay: 2000
                    }
                ]
            }
        ]
    }
}
```

By default, the user's input would be replaced immediately by the content of the echoChar variable, but the value 2000 assigned to the hideDelay variable causes a two-second delay before this replacement occurs. In Figure 22-21, three characters have been typed. The last character, an o, was typed within the last two seconds and therefore has not yet been hidden from view.

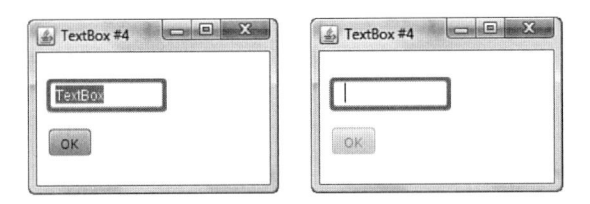

Figure 22-21   The `PasswordBox` control

The `ListView` Control

The `ListView` control displays a representation of a sequence of items. A list view contains an entry for each element of the sequence, with the order of entries matching that of the sequence elements. The elements may be displayed either horizontally and vertically. In either case, if the space required to display all the elements is larger than that available, a scrollbar is automatically added.

The user (or application code) can select an item from the list, and application code can react to changes in the selection by monitoring the values of the corresponding `ListView` variables.

Creating a `ListView`

The variables of the `ListView` class are listed in Table 22-12.

Table 22-12   **Variables of the `ListView` Class**

Variable	Type	Access	Default	Description
items	Object[]	RW	Empty	The items to be displayed.
vertical	Boolean	RW	true	Whether the list should be vertical or horizontal.
pannable	Boolean	RW	true	Whether the user can scroll the list content by holding the mouse down over a cell and dragging.

Table 22-12 **Variables of the `ListView` Class** *(Continued)*

Variable	Type	Access	Default	Description
selectedIndex	Integer	R	-1	The index of the lead selected item, or -1 if there is no selection.
selectedItem	Object	R	null	The lead selected item, or `null` if there is no selection.
focusedIndex	Integer	R		The index of the focused item in the list..
focusedItem	Object	R		The focused item in the list, or `null` if the list is empty.
cellFactory	function():ListCell	RW		A function that creates list cells on demand. If this is not provided, a default factory is used.

A functioning list view control can be created with only a few lines of code, as shown in Listing 22-9.

Listing 22-9 **Creating `ListView` Controls**

```
Stage {
    title : "ListView #1"
    var scene:Scene;
    scene: scene = Scene {
        content: [
            VBox {
                width: bind scene.width
                height: bind scene.height
                padding: Insets { top: 4 left: 4
                                  bottom: 4 right: 4 }
                spacing: 8
                nodeHPos: HPos.CENTER
                content: [
                    ListView {
                        items: for (i in [0..99]) {
                            "Element #{i}"
                        }
```

```
                    layoutInfo: LayoutInfo {
                        hgrow: Priority.NEVER
                        hfill: false
                    }
                }
                ListView {
                    items: for (i in [0..99]) {
                        "Element #{i}"
                    }
                    vertical: false
                    layoutInfo: LayoutInfo {
                        vgrow: Priority.NEVER
                        height: 40
                    }
                }
            ]
        }
    ]
}
```

This code, which you'll find in the file `javafxcontrols/ListView1.fx`, creates two list views, one vertical and one horizontal, each containing 100 elements, as shown in Figure 22-22.

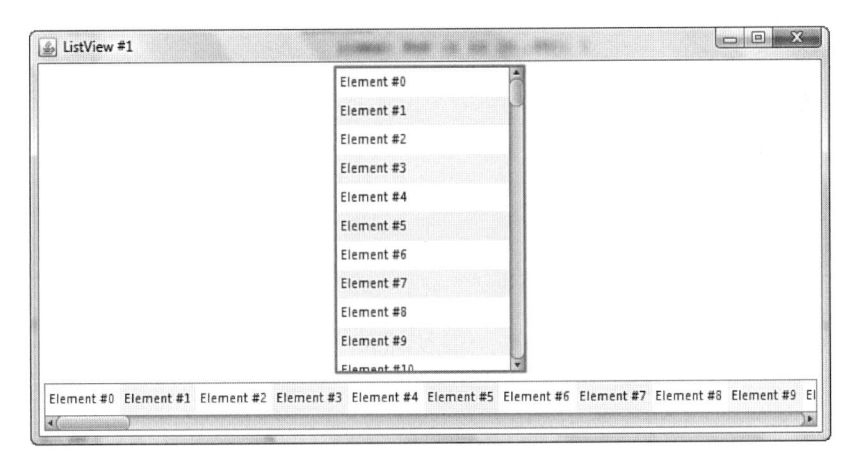

Figure 22-22 Two **ListView** controls, each with 100 elements

As you can see, the vertical list view has a fixed default preferred height that makes it take up enough vertical space to show about ten rows At the time of this writing, the same applies when it is in a horizontal configuration, which is typically not a good idea (and is probably a bug). In this example, the `height` variable of a `LayoutInfo` object is used to set a more reasonable preferred height for the horizontal `ListView`. As you can see, scrollbars have been added automatically to allow the user to scroll the control so that the other items can be brought into view. Because the `pannable` variable is `true` by default, it is also possible to scroll the set of visible items by dragging them vertically or horizontally.

Dynamic List Content

The list view is designed to efficiently display lists of data that could be very large in a relatively small area of screen. The data may be hard-coded, as it is in the examples that you have seen so far in this section, or it may be obtained from a database or a web server. JavaFX makes it easy to retrieve and present data from remote systems, as you'll see in Chapter 26, "Charts." However the data is obtained, all you have to do to make it accessible to the user is convert it to a sequence of objects and install that sequence in the `items` variable of the list view. The sequence does not have to be static—the list view updates itself automatically if you add, remove, or replace elements of the sequence. The code in Listing 22-10, which you will find in the file `javafxcontrols/ListView2.fx`, creates a list view control and a text box control and allows you to add new entries to the list view by typing them into the text box. You can see the result of running this code on the left of Figure 22-23.

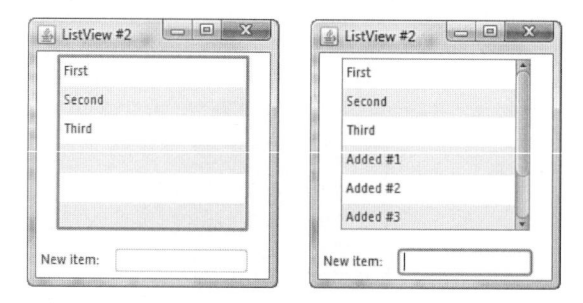

Figure 22-23 A `ListView` with content that is updated by application code

Listing 22-10 A `ListView` with Dynamic Content

```
1    var elements = [
2        "First", "Second", "Third"
3    ];
4
5    var scene:Scene;
6    Stage {
7        title : "ListView #2"
8        scene: scene = Scene {
9            width: 200
```

```
10              content: [
11                  VBox {
12                      width: bind scene.width
13                      height: bind scene.height
14                      nodeHPos: HPos.CENTER
15                      padding: Insets { top: 4 left: 4
16                                        bottom: 4 right: 4 }
17                      spacing: 16
18                      content: [
19                          ListView {
20                              layoutInfo: LayoutInfo {
21                                  hgrow: Priority.NEVER
22                                  hfill: false
23                              }
24                              items: bind elements
25                          }
26                          Flow {
27                              var textBox:TextBox;
28                              hgap: 8
29                              content: [
30                                  Label {
31                                      text: "New item: "
32                                  }
33                                  textBox = TextBox {
34                                      columns: 15
35                                      action: function() {
36                                          insert textBox.text.trim()
37                                              into elements;
38                                          textBox.text = ""
39                                      }
40                                  }
41                              ]
42                          }
43                      ]
44                  }
45              ]
46          }
47      }
```

The list view is initially populated with a sequence containing three items that is created on lines 1 to 3 of Listing 22-10. Notice that when the list view is created on lines 19 to 25, its items variable is bound to the content of this sequence. As a result of this binding, changes in the content of the sequence will be notified to the control to allow it to update itself. The action function of the text box control created on lines 32 to 39 strips leading and trailing whitespace from whatever you type into it and adds it to the elements sequence. As you can see on the right of Figure 22-23, the binding between this sequence and the `items` variable of the list view causes new entries to appear in the control.

`ListView` Selection

The usual reason for displaying a set of items in a list view control is to allow the user to select one or more of them so that the application can perform an operation based on the element or elements that have been selected. An entry can be selected by clicking it with the mouse or, if the control has the focus, using the up- and down-arrow keys to navigate the list until the required entry is found. The selected entry is highlighted differently so that it can be easily seen.

The code in Listing 22-11 is a version of the image display application shown in Figure 22-10 that uses a list view control rather than a set of radio buttons to present the set of images that the user can choose to view. You can see the result of running this example, which you'll find in the file `javafxcontrols/ListView3.fx`, in Figure 22-24.

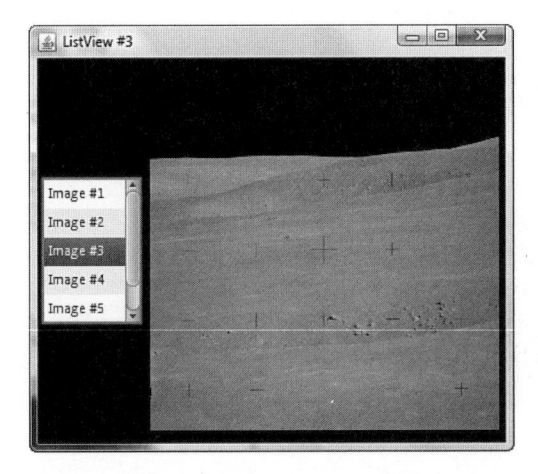

Figure 22-24   Using a list view control to select an image to be viewed

Listing 22-11   Using the `ListView` Selection

```
1    class Photo {
2        var title:String;
3        var image:Image;
4        public override function toString() {
5            title
6        }
7    }
8
9    def placeholder = Image {
10           url: http://spaceflight.nasa.gov/gallery/images"
```

The ListView Control

```
11              "/apollo/apollo15/lores/s71-30463.jpg"
12          width: 300
13          preserveRatio: true
14          smooth: true
15      }
16
17      def baseURL =
18              "http://www.hq.nasa.gov/office/pao/History/alsj/";
19      def imageURLs = [
20          "{baseURL}a15/ap15-KSC-71PC-605.jpg",
21          "{baseURL}a15/AS15-87-11720.jpg",
22          "{baseURL}a15/AS15-84-11324.jpg",
23          "{baseURL}a15/AS15-88-12013.jpg",
24          "{baseURL}a15/ap15-S71-42217.jpg",
25      ];
26
27      def photos = for (url in imageURLs) {
28          Photo {
29              title: "Image #{indexof url + 1}"
30              image: Image {
31                  url: url
32                  backgroundLoading: true
33                  placeholder: placeholder
34              }
35          }
36      }
37
38      var listView:ListView;
39      var selectedPhoto:Photo =
40                  bind listView.selectedItem as Photo;
41
42      var scene:Scene;
43      Stage {
44          title: "ListView #3"
45          scene: scene = Scene {
46              width: 400
47              height: 320
48              fill: Color.BLACK
49              content: [
50                  HBox {
51                      height: bind scene.height
52                      width: bind scene.width
53                      padding: Insets { top: 4 left: 4
54                                        bottom: 4 right: 4 }
55                      spacing: 8
56                      nodeVPos: VPos.CENTER
57                      content: [
```

```
58                         listView = ListView {
59                             items: photos
60                             layoutInfo: LayoutInfo {
61                                 vfill: false
62                                 width: 120
63                                 height: 120
64                             }
65                         }
66                         ImageView {
67                             fitWidth: 300
68                             fitHeight: 300
69                             smooth: true
70                             preserveRatio: true
71                             image:
72                                 bind if (selectedPhoto == null)
73                                     then placeholder
74                                     else selectedPhoto.image
75                         }
76                     ]
77                 }
78             ]
79         }
80     }
```

There appears to be a lot of code here, but it is really quite simple. The user interface consists of a list view control and an image view control, which are created on lines 58 to 65 and 66 to 75, respectively. Simply put, the list view control displays the values in the `photos` sequence, whereas the image view displays the selected image, or a placeholder if there is no selected image. Now let's look at the details.

In our earlier examples, the `items` sequence was populated with strings, and those strings were the values that appeared in the list view control itself. Here, things are a little more complicated (and realistic)—the sequence is populated not with strings, but with objects of type `Photo`, which is a class declared on lines 1 to 6 of Listing 22-11. Each `Photo` object encapsulates a string that describes the image and an `Image` object that contains the actual image. The sequence is constructed by the `for` expression on lines 27 to 36. Each iteration of this loop creates a single `Photo` object in which the title is of the form Image #1 and so on, and the image itself is constructed from a URL obtained from the `imageURLs` sequence declared on lines 19 to 25.

The value that the list view control displays by default for each element is obtained by calling that element's `toString()` function. In this case, the elements are of type `Photo` and we want the title of each image to be the value displayed in the list, so the `toString()` method of the `Photo` class is implemented to return the value of its `title` variable, as shown on lines 4 to 6. You'll see a more flexible way to determine what it displayed for an element in a `ListView` in the "`ListView` Cell Rendering" section, later in this chapter.

The point of this example is to demonstrate how to arrange for the `ImageView` to display the photo that the user selects. This is a two-part problem. First, we create a variable that refers to the selected `Photo` object. This is done on lines 39 and 40:

```
var selectedPhoto:Photo = bind listView.selectedItem as Photo;
```

When you make a selection in a list view control, two things happen:

- The index of the selected element in the `items` sequence is stored in the `selectedIndex` variable.
- The element that has actually been selected is stored in the `selectedItem` variable.

For example, if the user were to select the first item in the list, the `selectedIndex` variable of the list view would be set to 0, and the `selectedItem` variable would be set to `items[0]`, which in this case would be `photos[0]`—that is, the first `Photo` object in the list. As a result of this and the binding in the declaration of the `selectedPhoto` variable, its value will always be the selected `Photo` object.

The second step in arranging for the image view control to display the selected photo is to bind its `image` variable to the `image` in the selected `Photo` object. Given that the selected `Photo` object is always accessible from the `selectedPhoto` variable, we can achieve that as follows:

```
image: bind if (selectedPhoto == null)
            then placeholder
            else selectedPhoto.image
```

Notice that this is a conditional bind that checks whether `selectedPhoto` is `null` and uses a placeholder image if it is. If there is nothing selected in the list view control, its `selectedItem` variable (and hence `selectedPhoto`, which is bound to it) will be `null`, and `selectedIndex` will be -1, hence the `null` check. This happens when the application starts up, so the placeholder will be the first image that you see.

You can use this example to observe a few things about the list view control's handling of selection:

- You can only select one item at a time. In future versions, it may be possible to select more than one item.
- Once an item is selected, there is no way to return to a state in which nothing is selected. Again, this may change in a future release.
- If you select an item and then use the up and down arrow keys on your keyboard to move the selection, you will see that each image that you select is shown. This is normal behavior for a list view control.

In addition to the selected cell, the `ListView` control tracks the focused cell through its `focusedIndex` and `focusedItem` variables. When you click a cell, it becomes both selected and focused, but you can separate the focused cell from the selected cell by holding down the Ctrl key and using the up/down-arrow keys on your keyboard. When you do this, you will see that the focused cell is highlighted using its border, as shown in Figure 22-25, where the cell for image #1 is selected while the cell for image #5 is focused.

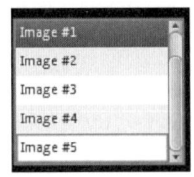

Figure 22-25   The focused and selected cells

`ListView` Cell Rendering

The items that a `ListView` contains can be of any type. By default, these items are rendered by calling the `toString()` function of each element of the `items` sequence. In Listing 22-11, we made use of this by arranging for the name of the image to be displayed in the `ListView` control by overriding the `toString()` function of the `Photo` class to return the image name. Changing the implementation of the class that provides the content of the list in this way is not always an option that is open to you, however. Fortunately, there is a more flexible way to control what is displayed in the list: by installing a function that creates `ListCell`s in the `cellFactory` variable of the `ListView`.

When the `cellFactory` variable is set, the `ListView` calls it each time it needs a `ListCell` to display an element of the list. It is important to note that the control does not need to create a `ListCell` object for each element in the `items` variable—it requires a `ListCell` only for those items that are actually visible. This is significant if the list contains many thousands of elements, only ten of which are visible at any one time, because it means that only ten `ListCell` objects need be created rather than several thousand. If the user scrolls the list, the set of visible items may change, but it does not follow that new `ListCell` objects will be created, because the `ListView` control can reuse the `ListCell` objects that were created for items that have scrolled out of view to display those that are being scrolled into view.

Using a `ListCell` Object

We can demonstrate the use of a cell factory by modifying the code shown in Listing 22-11 so that it uses a `ListCell` to determine what is shown to represent a `Photo` object in the list. To do this, we replace the code on lines 58 to 65 with the code shown in Listing 22-12, where the actual changes are shown in bold:

Listing 22-12   **Using a Cell Factory**

```
1    ListView {
2        items: photos
3        cellFactory: function():ListCell {
```

```
4              var cell:ListCell;
5              cell = ListCell {
6                  node: Text {
7                      text: bind
9                          "{cell.index}: {(cell.item as Photo).title}"
10                 }
11             }
12         }
13         layoutInfo: LayoutInfo {
14             vfill: false
15             width: 120
16             height: 120
17         }
18     }
```

You can find this code in the file `javafxcontrols/ListView4.fx`. As you can see, each time the function assigned to the `cellFactory` variable is called, it creates and returns an object of type `ListCell`. This class is derived from a class called `IndexedCell`, which itself derives from a base class called `Cell`. The `Cell` class is the basis for all cell factories—`Cell`s are also used in the `TreeView` component that is part of the component preview package that is part of JavaFX 1.3, and will be used in the table control that will appear in a future release.

The variables of the `ListCell` class, including those inherited from `IndexedCell` and `Cell`, are shown in Table 22-13.

Table 22-13   Variables of the **ListCell**, **IndexedCell**, and **Cell** Classes

Variable	Type	Access	Default	Description
listView	ListView	R		The `ListView` in which the `ListCell` will be displayed
selected	Boolean	R		Whether the cell in the `ListView` is selected
index	Integer	R		The index of the item in the source list to be drawn by this `IndexedCell`
item	Object	R		The actual item to be rendered
empty	Boolean	R		True if this cell is no longer associated with any data
node	Node	RW		The node to be used to represent this item in the control

Table 22-13 Variables of the `ListCell`, `IndexedCell`, and `Cell` Classes *(Continued)*

Variable	Type	Access	Default	Description
onUpdate	function ():Void	RW		An optional function that is called when the state of the cell has been changed

Of these variables, `listView` and `selected` belong to `ListCell`, `index` to `IndexedCell`, and the others to the `Cell` class.

A `ListCell` implementation typically creates a `Node` to represent a list item, installs it in the `node` variable, and initializes it by binding its variables to appropriate values from the `ListCell` object. Binding is required because a single `ListCell` object can be associated over time with more than one item from the list. On lines 5 to 11 of Listing 22-12, we create a `ListCell` object that uses a `Label` to represent an item from the list. The text in the label derives from the item index, which is obtained from the `index` variable of the `ListCell`, and the name of the image. The image name is obtained from the `Photo` object, a reference to which is installed in the `item` variable of the `ListCell`. You can see the result in Figure 22-26.

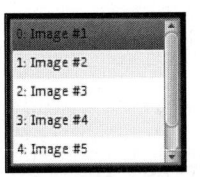

Figure 22-26 Using a `ListCell` object

Note that the object that is installed in the node variable of the `ListCell` can be any node; it does not need to be a `Control`. Note also that this node becomes part of the scene graph while it is visible and users can interact with it. It is possible, for example, to detect mouse clicks on the node and change its appearance if required. It would also be possible to capture keystrokes and use the node as an editor to modify the object being rendered, or for the node's appearance to be changed dynamically, perhaps using an animation.

A `ListView` with Variable Height Rows

In all the examples you have seen so far, all the rows of the `ListView` have been the same height, but this doesn't need to be the case. To demonstrate this, we'll modify the code in Listing 22-12 to use an `ImageView` to represent a `Photo` object rather than the image name:

```
listView = ListView {
    items: photos
```

```
    cellFactory: function():ListCell {
        var cell:ListCell;
        cell = ListCell {
            node: ImageView {
                fitWidth: 100
                preserveRatio: true
                image: bind (cell.item as Photo).image
            }
        }
    }
    layoutInfo: LayoutInfo {
        vfill: true
        width: 140
    }
}
```

   This code, which you'll find in the file `javafxcontrols/ListView5.fx`, uses a `ListCell` object in which the `node` variable refers to an `ImageView` that displays the image value from the `Photo` object in the `ListView` item that it is displaying. The important thing to note about this code is that the `fitWidth` variable of the `ImageView` is fixed at 100 pixels and the `preserveRatio` variable is `true`. This means that all the images will be scaled to the same width but their heights will differ. The `ListView` allocates each cell the space that it needs, with the result that the rows will be of various different heights to match those of the images. You can see the result of running this example in Figure 22-27.

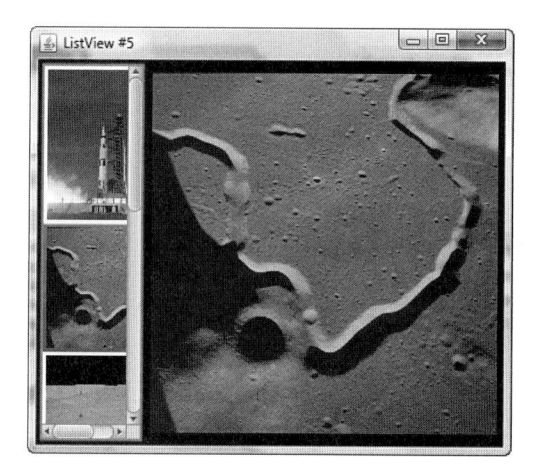

Figure 22-27   A **ListView** with variable height rows

   If you run this example, you will notice that the `ListView` automatically changes the heights of the cells as the images are loaded and their actual heights become known.

The `ChoiceBox` Control

`ChoiceBox` provides another way to present the user with a list of possible options and allowing one to be selected. Whereas `ListView` shows some or all of the available choices all the time, `ChoiceBox` shows only the selected item, except when the user is interacting with it, when it pops up a separate window containing the full list. The easiest way to demonstrate `ChoiceBox` is to use it as a replacement for the `ListView` in the example in Listing 22-11. Here's the code that we need to substitute for the declaration of the `ListView` control to do this, and which you'll find in the file `javafxcontrols/ChoiceBox1.fx`:

```
HBox {
    height: bind scene.height
    width: bind scene.width
    padding: Insets { top: 4 left: 4
                      bottom: 4 right: 4 }
    spacing: 8
    nodeVPos: VPos.CENTER
    content: [
        choiceBox = ChoiceBox {
            items: photos
        }
        ImageView {
```

As with `ListView`, the content of the `ChoiceBox` is installed in its `items` variable. The full list of variables of the `ChoiceBox` class is shown in Table 22-14.

Table 22-14 Variables of the `ChoiceBox` Class

Variable	Type	Access	Default	Description
item	Object[]	RW		The items to be displayed
selectedIndex	Integer	R		The index of the selected item, or -1 if there is no selection
selectedItem	Object	R		The selected item, or `null` if there is none
showing	Boolean	R		`true` if the full list of items is visible, `false` if not

You can see the result of running this example in Figure 22-28.

As you can see, `ChoiceBox` is more compact than `ListView`, and this is the usual reason for choosing one over the other. When the user clicks the control, a pop-up showing all of the values from the items variable appears, as shown in Figure 22-29.

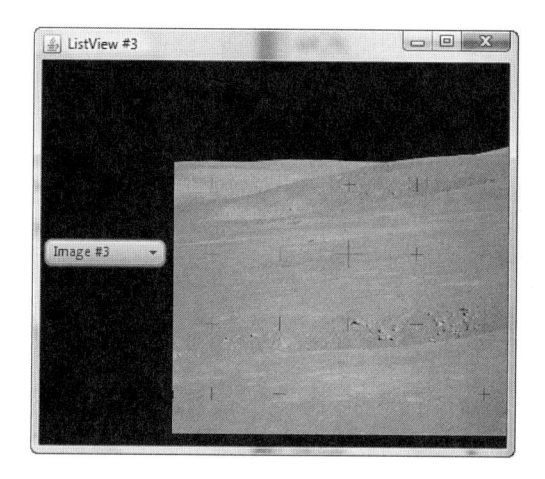

Figure 22-28   A `ChoiceBox` control

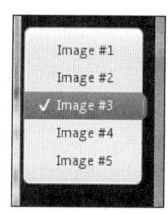

Figure 22-29   A `ChoiceBox` control with selections showing

As you can see, the item that is currently selected is indicated with a tick mark. The user can use the mouse or the arrow keys on the keyboard to move the selection highlight and either click with the mouse or press the Enter key to change the selection. Application code can track the selection by using the `selectedItem` and `selectedIndex` variables in the same way as with `ListView`.

In JavaFX 1.3, the items in the `ChoiceBox` are rendered by calling their `toString()` function. At the time of this writing, there is no cell factory and therefore no way to change the rendering.

The `ScrollBar` Control

The `ScrollBar` control allows the user to select a value from a bounded range of numbers given by its `max` and `min` variables. The current value of the scrollbar is represented by its `value` variable. Graphically, a scrollbar is typically rendered as a horizontal or vertical track with a moveable thumb. The ends of the track represent the minimum and maximum values of the scrollbar, while the position of the thumb gives the current value, as shown in Figure 22-30.

788 | Chapter 22 Cross-Platform Controls

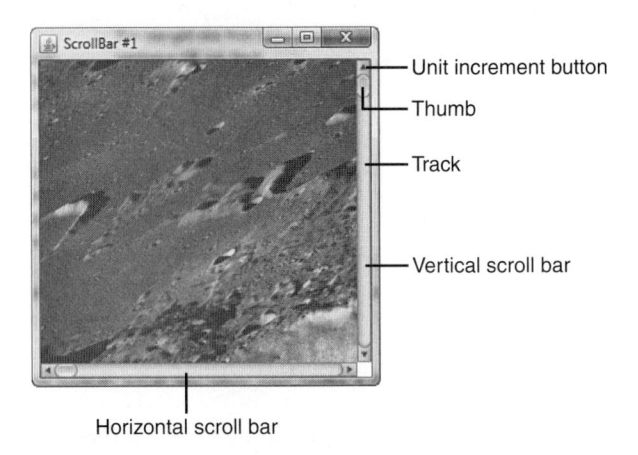

Figure 22-30 Horizontal and vertical scrollbars

A scrollbar is most commonly used when displaying a node or control that is too large to be seen all at once, such as the list of items in a list view control (as shown in Figure 22-27) or the large image shown in Figure 22-30. In this example, the user would drag the scrollbar to bring a different part of the image into view.

The `ScrollView` class, which we discuss in the next section, is a convenient control that makes internal use of two `ScrollBars` to provide just this functionality. If you don't plan to make direct use of a `ScrollBar`, you can skip the rest of this section and review the coverage of `ScrollView` that follows it.

The variables of the `ScrollBar` class are listed in Table 22-15.

Table 22-15 Variables of the `ScrollBar` Class

Variable	Type	Access	Default	Description
vertical	Boolean	RW	false	`true` for a vertical scrollbar, `false` for horizontal
min	Number	RW	0	The minimum value for the scrollbar
max	Number	RW	100	The maximum value for the scrollbar
value	Number	RW	0	The current value of the scrollbar
visibleAmount	Number	RW		The extent of the scrollbar's range that is actually visible
clickToPosition	Boolean	RW	false	Whether clicking in the track set the value that corresponds to the track position

Table 22-15 Variables of the `ScrollBar` Class *(Continued)*

Variable	Type	Access	Default	Description
unitIncrement	Number	RW	1.0	The amount by which the value changes when one of the buttons at its ends is clicked
blockIncrement	Number	RW	10.0	The amount by which the value changes when the mouse is clicked on the track if `clickToPosition` is `false`

`ScrollBar` Value and Range

When the thumb is at the far left of a horizontal scrollbar (or at the top of a vertical scrollbar), its `value` variable has the minimum value; when it is at the far right (or bottom for a vertical scrollbar) the `value` variable has the maximum value. In between, the value is proportional to the thumb bar's location. For example, for a horizontal scrollbar with a minimum value of `0` and a maximum value of `100` (which are the defaults), when the thumb is at the midpoint of the track, the `value` variable will be `50`. Moving the thumb further to right produces a value that is greater than `50`, while moving it to the left gives a value that is less than `50`.

The value of the `min` variable must always be no greater than that of the `max` variable, and the `value` variable will always have some value equal to or between these extremes. If you attempt to set any of these variables to values that would violate this constraint, the other variables are adjusted accordingly. For example, if `min` is `0`, `value` is `50`, and `max` is `100`, and you attempt to set `min` to `150`, the result will be that all three variables are set to `100`, because `min` is first clamped to the value of `max`, resulting in both having the value `100`, `value` is also set to `100` because it must be no greater than `max` and no less than `min`.

User Gestures

The user changes the scrollbar's value by moving the thumb. There are various ways to do this:

- Clicking the unit increment button (see Figure 22-30) either increases or decreases the value by the amount of the `unitIncrement` variable, which is set to `1` by default.
- Dragging the thumb causes the `value` variable to be updated to reflect the thumb's position as it moves.
- The effect of clicking in the track outside of the thumb depends on the value of the `clickToPosition` variable. When this is `false`, which is the default, the thumb moves toward the point on the track that was clicked by the amount given by the `blockIncrement` variable, which is `10` by default. If `clickToPosition` is `true`,

clicking the track moves the thumb immediately to that location and changes the `value` variable accordingly.

Using the `ScrollBar` Control

Using the `ScrollBar` control is basically a matter of linking its value to some other application state. Scrollbars are often used in conjunction with the `ClipView` control (discussed in Chapter 17, "Coordinates, Transforms, and Layout") to allow the user to view a node that is too large to be seen all at once. The movement of the node is achieved by manipulating the clip view's `clipX` and `clipY` variables to move the node relative to its viewport. It is quite straightforward to construct a custom node that provides this behavior, and you'll find an example implementation in Listing 22-13, which shows the code from the file `javafxcontrols/Scroller.fx` in the JavaFX Book More GUI project.

Listing 22-13 A Scrolling Node

```
1     public class Scroller extends CustomNode {
2         public var width:Number;
3         public var height:Number;
4         public var node:Node;
5         public var clickToPosition:Boolean;
6
7         protected override var children = {
8             var hsb:ScrollBar;
9             var vsb:ScrollBar;
10            var cv:ClipView;
11            [
12                cv = ClipView {
13                    width: bind width - vsb.width
14                    height: bind height - hsb.height
15                    node: bind node
16                    pannable: false
17                }
18                hsb = ScrollBar {
19                    clickToPosition: bind clickToPosition
20                    max: bind Math.max(0,
21                        node.layoutBounds.width -      cv.width)
22                    width: bind width - vsb.width
23                    layoutY: bind height - hsb.height
24                    blockIncrement:
25                        bind cv.layoutBounds.width - 4
26                    override var value on replace {
27                        cv.clipX = value;
28                    }
29                }
```

```
30                      vsb = ScrollBar {
31                          clickToPosition: bind clickToPosition
32                          vertical: true
33                          max: bind Math.max(0,
34                                  node.layoutBounds.height -
35                                  cv.height)
36                          height: bind height - hsb.height
37                          layoutX: bind width - vsb.width
38                          blockIncrement:
39                                  bind cv.layoutBounds.height - 4
40                          override var value on replace {
41                              cv.clipY = value;
42                          }
43                      }
44                  ];
45              }
46          }
```

This custom node is constructed from two `ScrollBars`, one horizontal and vertical, and a `ClipView`, as shown in Figure 22-31.

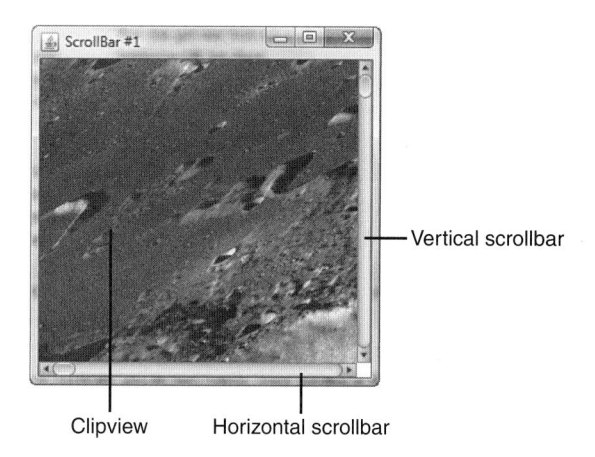

Figure 22-31   The **Scroller** custom node

The public variables of this node allow the application to control the following:

- The width and height of the area in which the node is to be placed. The `Scroller` always sizes itself so that it exactly fills this space.

- The node to be displayed in its viewport area. This can be any kind of node, such as an `ImageView` containing a large image.
- The required value for the `clickToPosition` values of the scrollbars.

The parts of the custom node that use these variables reference them through a binding, so changes made by application code are acted on automatically. This means that you can make the `Scroller` larger or smaller or change the node that it is displaying at any time.

Much of the code in Listing 22-13 is concerned with positioning the clip view and the scrollbars. This code is quite straightforward. The following extract from Listing 22-13 shows the code that positions the horizontal scrollbar, which appears at the bottom of the `Scroller` in Figure 22-31:

```
hsb = ScrollBar {
    clickToPosition: clickToPosition
    max: bind Math.max(0, node.layoutBounds.width - cv.width)
    width: bind width - vsb.width
    layoutY: bind height - hsb.height
    blockIncrement: bind cv.layoutBounds.width - 4
    override var value on replace {
        cv.clipX = value;
    }
}
```

As you can see, we set only the `width` and `layoutY` variables of the scrollbar because the defaults for `height` (its preferred height) and `layoutX` (which is 0) are the ones that we need. The scrollbar's width is the overall width of the control less the space needed by vertical scrollbar and, because we want this scrollbar to be attached to the bottom of the `Scroller`, its `layoutY` variable is bound to the `Scroller`'s height minus its own height. It should be clear from Figure 22-31 that these are the correct values to use.

This code also sets the `blockIncrement` value of the scrollbar to the width of the clip view minus 4 pixels. This means that when the user clicks on the track outside of the thumb, the view of the node will move left or right by an amount that is just smaller than the part of the node that is visible. A small overlap of 4 pixels is used so that the user can see how the new view relates to the previous one.

The most important part of the `Scroller` implementation is the way in which the scrolling is achieved. The ability to view a portion of a node is provided by the `ClipView`, which is created on lines 12 to 17 of Listing 22-13. To scroll the node horizontally, we need to change the value of the `ClipView`'s `clipX` variable, while to scroll it vertically, we change `clipY`. Here, we'll describe how the horizontal scrolling works. To scroll the node horizontally, we need to give the `clipX` variable of the `ClipView` the same value as the `value` variable of the horizontal scrollbar. The most obvious way to do this would be with a binding, like this:

```
ClipView {
    width: bind width - vsb.width
```

```
        height: bind height - hsb.height
        node: bind node
        pannable: false
        clipX: bind hsb.value
        clipY: bind vsb.value
}
```

This actually works, unless the width of the `ClipView` is changed. When this happens, the `ClipView` implementation tries to write a new value for `clipX` but fails because its value has been bound. To avoid this, we use a trigger to set `clipX` from the value variable of the horizontal scrollbar:

```
hsb = ScrollBar {
    clickToPosition: clickToPosition
    max: bind Math.max(0, node.layoutBounds.width - cv.width)
    width: bind width - vsb.width
    layoutY: bind height - hsb.height
    blockIncrement: bind cv.layoutBounds.width - 4
    override var value on replace {
        cv.clipX = value;
    }
}
```

The only part of the implementation left to be explained is how we set the `min` and `max` values of the scrollbar. When the thumb is at the far left and the scrollbar `value` is 0, we want the left side of the node to be visible at the left side of the `ClipView`, which means that `clipX` must also be 0. Because this is the smallest value of `clipX` that we will require, the `min` value of the scrollbar will always be 0, which is also the default. When the thumb of the scrollbar is at the far right, we want the right side of the node to be at the right side of the `ClipView`. The `max` value for the scrollbar will be the value of `clipX` that will achieve this positioning.

The `clipX` value is defined as the x offset into the target node of the point that appears at the left side of the `ClipView`, which in this case would be the width of the node minus the width of the `ClipView`. That means that, in terms of the variables used in Listing 22-13, we should set the `max` variable of the scrollbar like this:

```
max: bin node.layoutBounds.width - cv.width
```

Unfortunately, this is not quite correct in the case where the width of the `ClipView` is greater than that of the node being displayed, because in that case the `max` variable will be given a negative value. This can happen if the node is an image view containing an image that is being loaded in the background. In that case, the width of the image view will initially be zero, and consequently `max` will be assigned a negative value.

On its own, this is not a problem because the `max` value will be corrected when the image loads, as a result of the binding. However, setting `max` to a negative value also adjusts the min and `value` variables of the scrollbar, and these will *not* get automatically corrected when the value of `max` is recomputed. For this reason, we need to ensure that `max` is never assigned a negative value, which we can do by using the `max()` function from the `javafx.util.Math` class:

```
max: bind Math.max(0, node.layoutBounds.width - cv.width)
```

The code in Listing 22-14, which you'll find in the file `javafxcontrols/ScrollBar1.fx`, uses the `Scroller` class to display an image of the far side of the moon taken from Apollo 8 during the first circumlunar flight in December 1968. You can see the result of running this code in Figure 22-31.

Listing 22-14   Using the `Scroller` Class

```
var url = "http://www.hq.nasa.gov/office/pao/History/alsj/"
          "a410/AS8-13-2225HR.jpg";

var scene:Scene;
Stage {
    title: "ScrollBar #1"
    width: 300
    height: 300
    scene: scene = Scene {
        content: [
            Scroller {
                width: bind scene.width
                height: bind scene.height
                node: ImageView {
                    image: Image {
                        url: url
                        backgroundLoading: true
                    }
                }
            }
        ]
    }
}
```

The `ScrollView` Control

`ScrollView` is a simple control that lets you display a node that may be too large for the area in which it has been placed. The code in Listing 22-15, which you'll find in the file `javafxcontrols/ScrollView1.fx`, is the same as that in Listing 22-14 but uses the `ScrollView` class rather than the `Scroller` class that we developed in the previous section.

Listing 22-15   Using the `ScrollView` Class

```
var url = "http://www.hq.nasa.gov/office/pao/History"
          "/alsj/a410/AS8-13-2225HR.jpg";
```

The ScrollView Control

```
var scene:Scene;
Stage {
    title: "ScrollView #1"
    width: 300
    height: 300
    scene: scene = Scene {
        content: [
            ScrollView {
                width: bind scene.width
                height: bind scene.height
                node: ImageView {
                    image: Image {
                        url: url
                        backgroundLoading: true
                    }
                }
            }
        ]
    }
}
```

The result of running this code is shown in Figure 22-32. As you can see, it looks nearly identical to our custom scrolling node, shown in Figure 22-31. The principal difference is that the size of the scrollbar thumb correctly reflects the proportion of the scrolled node that is actually visible in each direction.

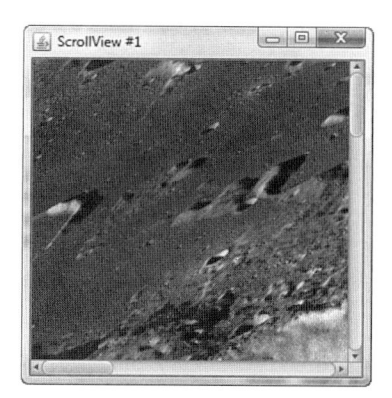

Figure 22-32   Using the `ScrollView` node

The variables of the `ScrollView` class are listed in Table 22-16.

Chapter 22 Cross-Platform Controls

Table 22-16 **Variables of the `ScrollView` Class**

Variable	Type	Access	Default	Description
`node`	Node	RW		The node to be displayed.
`fitToHeight`	Boolean	RW	`false`	Determines whether the scrolled node will always be given the same height as the viewable area of the `ScrollView`.
`fitToWidth`	Boolean	RW	`false`	Determines whether the scrolled node will always be given the same width as the viewable area of the `ScrollView`.
`pannable`	Boolean	RW	`false`	If true, the user can drag the scrolled node to change the viewed region.
`hbarPolicy`	ScrollBarPolicy	RW	`AS_NEEDED`	Determines when a horizontal scrollbar is shown.
`vbarPolicy`	ScrollBarPolicy	RW	`AS_NEEDED`	Determines when a vertical scrollbar is shown.
`hmin`	Number	RW	`0.0`	The minimum horizontal scrollbar value.
`hvalue`	Number	RW	`0.0`	The current horizontal scrollbar value.
`hmax`	Number	RW	`1.0`	The maximum horizontal scrollbar value.
`vmin`	Number	RW	`0.0`	The minimum vertical scrollbar value.
`vvalue`	Number	RW	`0.0`	The current vertical scrollbar value.
`vmax`	Number	RW	`1.0`	The maximum vertical scrollbar value.

To display a node in a `ScrollView`, all you have to do is assign it to the `node` variable and the `ScrollView` will take care of the rest. In most cases, no customization will be required.

Scrollbar Display and Values

By default, the `ScrollView` displays scrollbars only if they are needed—that is, a horizontal scrollbar will be present only if the scrolled node is wider than the width of the `ScrollView` itself (and similarly for the vertical scrollbar). You can force the `ScrollView` to change this policy by setting the `hbarPolicy`/`vbarPolicy` variables to one of the following values defined by the `ScrollBarPolicy` class.

- `AS_NEEDED`—A scrollbar is shown only if it is required (the default).
- `ALWAYS`—A scrollbar is always shown. If the scrollbar is not actually needed, the thumb will not appear.
- `NEVER`—The scrollbar is never shown. In this case, you should probably set the pannable variable to true to allow the user to view more of the scrolled node by dragging it.

As the user moves the scrolled node using either the scrollbars or by dragging it with the mouse, the value of the `hvalue`/`vvalue` variable will be changed to reflect the part of the node that is actually visible. You can also programmatically scroll the node by writing to these variables. The value of the `hvalue` variable is always constrained to lie between the values of the `hmin` and `hmax` variables, which take the values `0.0` and `1.0` by default. You can, if you want, change either or both of these values. Similar constraints apply to `vvalue`, `vmin`, and `vmax`.

Scrollable Node Size

You will normally want the scrolled node to be displayed at its normal size when placed in a `ScrollView`, but it is also possible to force it to always have the same width/height as the viewable area of the `ScrollView` by setting the `fitToWidth` or `fitToHeight` variables to `true`. Note that this works only for `Resizable` nodes, because a node that is not `Resizable` cannot have its width or height changed.

The `Slider` Control

Like `ScrollBar`, the `Slider` control is used to represent and allow the user to modify a numeric value that has defined upper and lower bounds. Whereas a scrollbar is often used to scroll a large node so that the user can see different parts of it, a slider is typically used when the user needs to actually see the value that is being set. The `Slider` and `ScrollBar` classes have many variables that have the same name and provide the same functionality, as you can see by comparing the variables of the `ScrollBar` class in Table 22-15 with those of the `Slider` in Table 22-17.

Table 22-17   Variables of the `Slider` Class

Variable	Type	Access	Default	Description
vertical	Boolean	RW	false	true for a vertical slider, false for horizontal.
min	Number	RW	0	The minimum value for the slider.
max	Number	RW	100	The maximum value for the slider.
value	Number	RW	0	The current value of the slider.
blockIncrement	Number	RW	10	The amount by which the thumb should be moved if the track is clicked and clickToPosition is false.
clickToPosition	Boolean	RW	false	If true, the thumb is moved to the mouse position when the track is clicked.
majorTickUnit	Number	RW	25	The unit distance between major ticks.
minorTickCount	Integer	RW	3	The number of minor ticks between each major tick.
showTickMarks	Boolean	RW	false	Whether tick marks should be shown.
showTickLabels	Boolean	RW	false	Whether tick labels should be shown.
labelFormatter	function (Number): String	RW	null	Optional function used to format tick labels.
snapToTicks	Boolean	RW	false	Whether the slider thumb should move to the nearest tick mark when released.

Basic Slider Operation

The code in Listing 22-16 creates a scene containing an image and a slider. The slider is configured to allow values in the range 0 to 1, inclusive, and as a result of the binding on line 22, as the slider's value changes, so does the opacity of the image. You can see the result of running this code, which you'll find in the file `javafxcontrols/Slider1.fx`, in Figure 22-33.

Figure 22-33   Using a **Slider** control to change the opacity of an image

Listing 22-16   **A Slider Control**

```
1    var slider:Slider;
2    Stage {
3        title : "Slider #1"
4        var scene:Scene;
5        scene: scene = Scene {
6            width: 540
7            height: 400
8            fill: Color.BLACK
9            content: [
10               VBox {
11                   width: bind scene.width
12                   height: bind scene.height
13                   hpos: HPos.CENTER
14                   vpos: VPos.CENTER
15                   nodeHPos: HPos.CENTER
16                   spacing: 16
17                   content: [
18                       ImageView {
19                           image: Image {
```

```
20                              url: "{__DIR__}allrollout.jpg"
21                          }
22                          opacity: bind slider.value
23                      }
24                      slider = Slider {
25                          min: 0
26                          max: 1.0
27                          value: 1.0
28                          blockIncrement: 0.2
29                      }
30                  ]
31              }
32          ]
33      }
34  }
35
36  var o = bind slider.value on replace {
37      println(o);
38  }
```

As a result of the initialization of the `value` variable on line 27, the slider thumb initially appears at the right side of the track and the image is fully opaque. As you move the slider to the left, its value reduces and so does the opacity of the image. When the thumb reaches the far left, the slider's value will be `0` (the `min` value), and the image will be completely transparent.

If you click the track to the left or right of the thumb's position, it will move by an amount equal to its `blockIncrement` value. In this case, because `blockIncrement` is `0.2`, the thumb will move one-fifth of the width of the slider on each click. If you set the `clickToPosition` variable to `true`, however, clicking in the track moves the thumb directly to the position of the click.

> **Note**
>
> If `clickToPosition` is `false` but `blockIncrement` does not have a reasonable value, the slider behaves as if `clickToPosition` were `true`. This will happen, for example, if `blockIncrement` is larger than the range of the slider.

Tick Marks

The code on lines 36 to 38 of Listing 22-16 prints the slider's value as it changes. Here is some typical output:

```
1.0
0.7669173
0.36090225
```

```
0.7218045
0.19548872
0.86466163
```

These values represent the actual location of the thumb on the track. In some case, very precise values like this are not required. You might, for example, want to allow the value to vary only by a less precise amount such a `0.1` so that you would get values like `1.0, 0.8, 0.5`, and so on. You can do this by using the tick marks feature of the slider. There are two different types of tick marks: major tick marks and minor tick marks.

Major and Minor Tick Marks

The relationship between major and minor tick marks is much the same as that between the large and small markings on a ruler or a slide rule. Major tick marks are placed at certain positions along the slider, and the minor tick marks, if required, appear between them. By default, the slider has major tick marks but no minor tick marks.

The distance between major tick marks is given by the `majorTickUnit` variable. By default, this variable has the value `25`, which is not very useful for the example in Listing 22-16 because the whole range of the slider is from `0.0` to `1.0`. To make use of the ticks feature, we make three changes to the slider's object initializer:

```
Slider {
    min: 0
    max: 1.0
    value: 1.0
    blockIncrement: 0.2
    majorTickUnit: 0.2
    minorTickCount: 0
    snapToTicks: true
}
```

These changes place a major tick at intervals of `0.2` along the slider, which means that they exist at `0.0, 0.2, 0.4, 0.6. 0.8`, and `1.0`. There are no minor ticks because the `minorTickCount` variable is `0`. Setting the `snapToTicks` variable to `true` ensures that when the user releases the thumb, it will move to the nearest tick value. If you run this code, which you'll find in the file `javafxcontrols/Slider2.fx`, and drag the thumb around and then release it, you'll see output that looks like this:

```
1.0
0.9699248
0.96240604
0.9548872
0.94736844
0.91729325
0.9097744
0.8947368
```

```
0.88721806
0.87218046
0.85714287
0.84962404
0.84210527
0.83458644
0.8270677
0.81954885
0.8120301
0.8
```

You can see that as the thumb moves, the `value` variable is still changed to reflect its position, but when it is released, it moves to the nearest major tick, in this case the one with value `0.8`. Unfortunately, there is no way to tell programmatically whether the slider has been released—it would be better if the `Slider` provided a variable that indicated this (such as the `adjustingSelection` variable of the `TextBox` control).

> **Note**
>
> The `snapToTicks` variable does not actually work in JavaFX 1.3. The text describes how it should work. This bug is being tracked at http://javafx-jira.kenai.com/browse/RT-5914.

You can place minor ticks between the major ticks by setting the `minorTickCount` variable to the number of minor ticks that should appear between each pair of major ticks. For example, setting `minorTickCount` to `1` in our ongoing example would cause minor ticks to appear at values `0.1, 0.3, 0.5, 0.7,` and `0.9`.

Tick Labels

Setting major and minor tick values does not, by default, cause any visual representation of those tick marks to appear. If you want to see the tick marks, you need to set the `showTickMarks`/`showTickLabels` variables to `true`. Here's how these variables work:

- If `showTickMarks` is `true`, the major and minor tick positions are drawn on the slider.
- If `showTickMarks` and `showTickLabels` are both `true`, tick marks and labels that indicate the associated values are drawn on the slider.

The example code in the file `javafxcontrols/Slider3.fx` has both the `showTickMarks` and `showTickLabels` variables set to `true`, giving the result shown in Figure 22-34.

As you can see, because floating-point numbers are not completely accurate, the tick values are shown with additional decimal places. This would not occur if the slider values and the major and minor tick values were all integers. In cases where the default display

Figure 22-34   Showing tick marks and tick labels

of tick values is unattractive, you can format the values yourself by installing a label formatter. The following code, from the file `javafxcontrols/Slider4.fx`, does just that:

```
1      Slider {
2          min: 0
3          max: 1.0
4          value: 1.0
5          blockIncrement: 0.2
6          majorTickUnit: 0.2
7          minorTickCount: 0
8          snapToTicks: true
9          showTickLabels: true
10          showTickMarks: true
11         var format = new DecimalFormat("0.0");
12         labelFormatter: function(value:Number) {
13              format.format(value);
14         }
15     }
```

To clean up the tick labels, we need to make sure that only one decimal place is displayed. We can do this by using the `java.text.DecimalFormat` class. On line 11, we create an instance of this class with a format string that will cause only one decimal place to be shown in formatted values. The formatting is performed by the function on lines 12 to

14, which is called with the numeric value of every tick and returns the string that should be used for that tick's label. The result of running this code is shown in Figure 22-35.

Figure 22-35   Using custom tick labels

The `ProgressIndicator` and `ProgressBar` Controls

`ProgressBar` and `ProgressIndicator` are two very similar controls that let you display the progress of an operation to the user. They share the same API but have different appearances. The variables used by both classes are listed in Table 22-18.

Table 22-18   Variables of the `ProgressIndicator` and `ProgressBar` Classes

Variable	Type	Access	Default	Description
progress	Number	RW	0.0	The progress to be displayed
indeterminate	Boolean	R		Whether the progress being displayed is determinate

Using the `ProgressBar` and `ProgressIndicator` Controls

To use either of these controls, you just set the value of the `progress` variable. Both controls can operate in either *determinate* or *indeterminate* mode. Determinate mode is used when you can accurately report the progress of an operation to the user, such as when downloading the content of a file of known size. Indeterminate mode is used when you do not have an accurate idea of progress, as would be the case if you were downloading a file of unknown size.

In determinate mode, the `progress` variable is set to a value between 0 and 1 that reflects the proportion of the total operation that has been completed, where 0 represents not started and 1 represents complete. In indeterminate mode, you can set the `progress` variable to any negative value. The `indeterminate` variable is a read-only value that indicates in which mode the control is operating. The code in Listing 22-17, which you'll find in the file `javafxcontrols/Progress1.fx`, creates one determinate and one indeterminate control of each type. The result of running this code is shown in Figure 22-36.

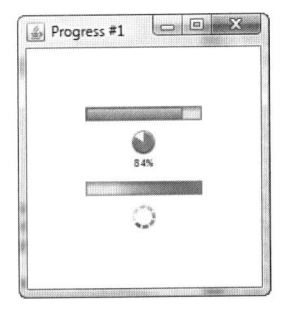

Figure 22-36 Comparing the **ProgressBar** and **ProgressIndicator** controls

Listing 22-17   **Progress Bars and Progress Indicators**

```
1    def max = 100.0;
2    var value:Number;
3
4    Stage {
5        title : "Progress #1"
6        var scene:Scene;
7        scene: scene = Scene {
8            width: 200
9            height: 200
10           content: [
11               VBox {
12                   width: bind scene.width
13                   height: bind scene.height
14                   hpos: HPos.CENTER vpos: VPos.CENTER
15                   nodeHPos: HPos.CENTER
16                   spacing: 8
17                   content: [
18                       ProgressBar {
19                           progress: bind
20    ProgressIndicator.computeProgress(max, value)
```

```
21                          }
22                          ProgressIndicator {
23                              progress: bind
24                      ProgressIndicator.computeProgress(max, value)
25                          }
26                          ProgressBar {
27                              progress: -1
28                          }
29                          ProgressIndicator {
30                              progress: -1
31                          }
32                      ]
33                  }
34              ]
35          }
36      }
37
38      var t = Timeline {
39          repeatCount: Timeline.INDEFINITE
40          keyFrames: [
41              at (10s) { value => 100 tween Interpolator.LINEAR }
42          ]
43      };
44      t.play();
```

The determinate `ProgressBar`, shown at the top of the figure, is represented by a bar that is gradually filled with color as more progress is reported, while the determinate `ProgressIndicator` is a small circle that indicates progress by the amount of the circle that is filled and with a percentage indicator underneath the circle. In this example, the operation being reported on is an animation of the `value` variable that is declared on line 2 of Listing 22-17. The timeline on lines 38 to 44 increases the value of this variable from its initial value of `0` to its maximum value of `100` over a period of ten seconds and then repeats. The value of the `progress` variable must be in the range `0` to `1`, so to report progress we could bind this variable to the `value` variable as follows:

```
progress: bind value / max
```

Alternatively, we can use the `computeProgress()` function of the `ProgressIndicator` class, which requires as arguments the maximum possible value and the value that represents the current state of the operation:

```
progress: bind ProgressIndicator.computeProgress(max, value)
```

In indeterminate mode, the `ProgressBar` contains a colored region that moves left to right across its surface and then back again, repeating forever, while the `ProgressIndicator` shows a set of rotating segments at its circumference but does not show the percentage complete indicator. You can see snapshots of these at the bottom of Figure 22-36.

In Listing 22-17, we allowed both controls to have their default sizes. You can change the width and height of the `ProgressBar` or `ProgressIndicator` by using the `layoutInfo` variable:

```
ProgressBar     {
    progress: -1
    layoutInfo: LayoutInfo {
        width: 180
        height: 50
    }
}

ProgressIndicator {
    progress: -1
    layoutInfo: LayoutInfo {
        width: 180
        height: 100
    }
}
```

Figure 22-37 shows the effect of this. As you can see, increasing the width and height makes the `ProgressBar` increase in size by the same amount. By contrast, the visual representation of the `ProgressIndicator` remains the same size, but it appears in the center of a larger area.

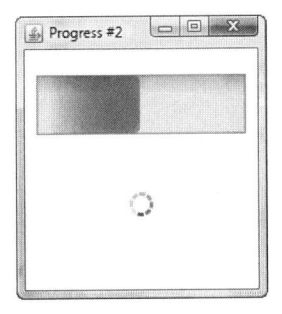

Figure 22-37 Changing the width and height of the **ProgressBar** and **ProgressIndicator** controls

The Separator Control

The `Separator` control is used to provide a horizontal or vertical divider between separate areas of a user interface. It has only three variables, which are listed in Table 22-19.

Table 22-19   Variables of the `Separator` Class

Variable	Type	Access	Default	Description
vertical	Boolean	RW	false	`true` for a vertical separator, `false` for a horizontal one.
hpos	HPos	RW	HPos.CENTER	The horizontal position of the separator within its layout area. Used only if the separator is vertical.
vpos	VPos	RW	VPos.CENTER	The vertical position of the separator within its layout area. Used only if the separator is horizontal.

To add a separator to a scene, just include a `Separator` object with the appropriate orientation. We can easily add a vertical separator to the image list example that we used in our discussion of the `ListView` and `ChoiceBox` classes by including the following line of code:

```
Separator { vertical: true }
```

You can see how this looks by writing the example in the file `javafxcontrols/Separator1.fx`, which produces the result shown in Figure 22-38.

Figure 22-38   A vertical separator

Tooltips

A tooltip is a pop-up window that appears when the user allows the mouse to hover over a control for a short period of time. You typically use a tooltip to provide the user with more information about the control—for example, in the case of an input field, the tooltip might describe the value that the user is expected to enter.

You associate a tooltip with a control by setting the value of its `tooltip` variable, which is of type `Tooltip`. The tooltip will appear a short while after the mouse enters the control, provided that it remains over it for long enough, and will disappear shortly after it leaves it. Let's demonstrate how simple it is to add a tooltip by incorporating one in the image list example from Listing 22-11. The code that we need to change to add a tooltip to the `ListView` control from this example is shown here and can be found in the file `javafxcontrols/Tooltip1.fx`:

```
1     listView = ListView {
2         items: photos
3         layoutInfo: LayoutInfo {
4             vfill: false
5             width: 120
6             height: 120
7         }
8         tooltip: Tooltip {
9             graphic: ImageView {
10                image: Image {
11                    url: "{__DIR__}apollo.png"
12                    width: 32 height: 32
13                    backgroundLoading: true
14                }
15            }
16        }
17        text: "Select an image from the\n"
18             "flight of Apollo 15"
19        }
20    }
```

The tooltip is created and installed by the code on lines 8 to 19. The `Tooltip` class incorporates the `Labeled` mixin and therefore can display both text and an arbitrary node. In this case, the tooltip will display an image and a fixed text string.

If you run this example and move the mouse over the `ListView`, at first nothing will happen, but after a short while, the tooltip will appear, as shown in Figure 22-39.

The tooltip will disappear if you move the mouse out of the control or if you leave the mouse stationary for a few seconds. The delay periods that determine when the tooltip appears (750 milliseconds), how long it takes before it disappears when the mouse moves outside of the control (400 milliseconds), and for how long it stays visible if you don't move the mouse (five seconds) are hard-coded and cannot currently be changed.

It is important to note that the `tooltip` variable is provided by the `Control` class, so only controls can have tooltips. It is not possible to give an arbitrary node a tooltip.

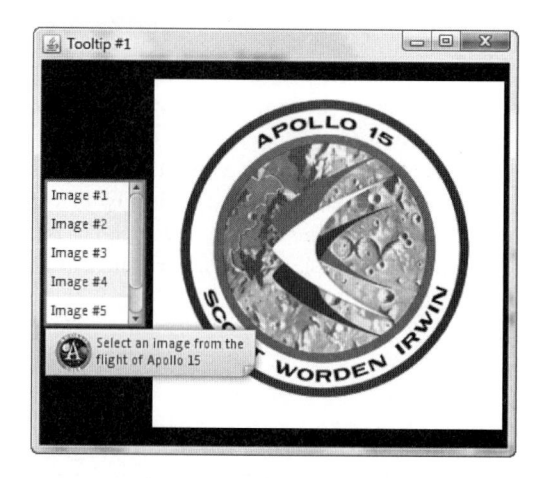

Figure 22-39   A tooltip

23

Style Sheets

Many years ago when the World Wide Web was new, I remember learning Hypertext Markup Language (HTML) and having fun creating documents with lots of colored and styled text using only a small amount of very simple markup. After a while, I realized that I was creating a maintenance problem for myself because I had lots of repeated code that was setting the same colors and fonts on multiple HTML elements. This problem was solved when Cascading Style Sheets (CSS) were introduced and supported by the mainstream web browsers. CSS made it possible to define these repeated colors and fonts as styles and to apply them to the HTML by defining rules that specify which elements should have which styles.

The same problem arises in rich client applications, whether you use Swing, JavaFX, or any other graphical user interface (GUI) toolkit to build them. There is no built-in CSS support for Swing, but the good news is that style sheets *have* been built in to the JavaFX GUI libraries. This chapter looks at the JavaFX implementation of style sheets, which, as of JavaFX 1.3, is still a work in progress. As you'll see, you can use CSS to control the appearance of almost any node, but the most comprehensive support for style sheets is provided by the control classes that were described in the preceding chapter. In the sections that follow, you'll see how you can customize these controls by using a style sheet.

The examples for this chapter are all in the `javafxstyle` package of the JavaFX Book More GUI project.

Style Sheet Basics

In HTML, style sheets allow you to apply a consistent appearance to a set of web pages by separating the rules that define the colors, fonts, and other visual properties from the tags that specify the page layout. A JavaFX style sheet enables you to do something similar, but instead of HTML tags, JavaFX has nodes, so styling in JavaFX is centered on nodes rather than tags. The function of a style sheet in JavaFX is to allow you to set the values of a node's visual properties without having to hard-code those values in an object literal. This enables you to change the appearance of your application just by switching in a different style sheet and because the style sheet can be stored on a web server, this can be done remotely without having to force the user to download the whole application again.

Using a Style Sheet

To use a style sheet, you install a reference to it in the form of a URL string in the `stylesheets` variable of a scene. It is possible to apply more than one style sheet to a scene, as you'll see later in this chapter; for now, however, we keep things simple and use just one.

The code Listing 23-1, which comes from the file `javafxstyle/Styles1.fx`, creates a scene containing two `Text` objects.

Listing 23-1   Installing a Style Sheet in a Scene

```
Stage {
    title: "Styles 1"
    scene: Scene {
        width: 200 height: 70
        stylesheets: [ "{__DIR__}Styles1.css" ]
        content: [
            VBox {
                spacing: 8
                content: [
                    Text {
                        content: "First Text"
                        styleClass: "my-style"
                    }
                    Text {
                        content: "Second Text"
                        styleClass: "my-style"
                    }
                ]
            }
        ]
    }
}
```

As you can see, in this example we do not explicitly set either colors or fonts, so you would probably expect the result to be two lines of black text in the normal font. However, this is not what happens, as you can see in Figure 23-1—the font is somewhat larger than usual, and the text is red instead of black. (Although it's not easy to see that in this black and white book!)

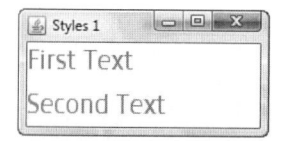

Figure 23-1   Using a style sheet to control the appearance of a JavaFX application

Style Sheet Structure

The appearance of the application in Listing 23-1 is controlled by its style sheet, which is shown in Listing 23-2.

Listing 23-2   **A Simple Style Sheet**

```
.my-style {
    -fx-fill: red;
    -fx-font-size: 32;
}
```

A style sheet consists of a list of *rules*, where each rule consists of one or more *selectors* followed by one or more *declarations* in braces:

```
selector[,selector]* {
    declaration[; declaration]*
}
```

Selection by Class

A selector identifies the elements in the scene to which the associated declarations are to be applied. There are various types of selector; the most common is a *style class* selector and an *identifier* selector. In Listing 23-2, the string .my-style is a style class selector because its name starts with a period. A style class selector is applied to any node that has the style name (without the leading period) assigned to its styleClass variable. As you can see, in Listing 23-1, the styleClass variables of both text nodes have the value my-style, so this rule is applied to both of them. You'll see examples of other selectors later in this chapter.

The declarations in a rule are of the following form:

```
name: value
```

In Listing 23-2, there are two rules: one that associates the value red with the name (-fx-fill), the other associating the value 32 with the name -fx-font-size. The names correspond to CSS properties that may or may not be recognized by the node or nodes to which the selector applies. If the name is not recognized, the declaration is ignored. In this case, the Text class recognizes the variable -fx-fill to mean the text fill color and the -fx-font-size to mean the text font size. Each node recognizes a fixed set of CSS property names, which are listed in Appendix B, "CSS Properties." The prefix -fx- is used for all the properties that are defined for JavaFX nodes. As you'll see in the section "Defining Constant Color Values," later in this chapter, it is possible to define your own CSS property names; for the sake of clarity, you should not use the -fx- prefix for your own names.

It should now be clear that the effect of this style sheet rule is to cause both Text objects to render their content in red and with a 32-point font, exactly what is shown in Figure 23-1. The syntax used for the value part depends on the type of property. Here, we used red to select a color—or rather, a Paint, because the value of a node's fill variable is `Paint`. As you'll see later, there are various different ways to define a `Paint`, which allow you to specify a solid color or a gradient.

> **Note**
>
> Style sheet filenames conventionally use the suffix `.css`. If you use the `javafxpackager` command to package your application, any files with this suffix are parsed as style sheets and converted to binary form in a file of the same name but with the suffix `.bss`. The binary style sheets can be loaded faster, so whenever your JavaFX application references a style sheet, the runtime will first look for a binary version by replacing the `.css` suffix with `.bss` and will read the original file only if the binary file is not present. This process happens automatically if you use NetBeans or Eclipse because the plug-ins for both of these integrated development environments (IDEs) use `javafxpackager` behind the scenes.

The control classes that we discussed in the preceding chapter automatically register themselves so that they can be styled by using a class name based on the control class name. For example, you can style all `TextBox` controls by using the style name `.textbox`, without setting the `styleClass` variable of the control.

Selection by ID

You use selection by class when you want to apply the same styles to a number of different nodes. An alternative to this, which is typically used to target individual nodes, is selection by ID. To apply a style sheet rule to a node with a given ID (or to multiple nodes if they all have the same ID, which would be unusual), use the ID as the rule selector, preceded by a `#`. The following style sheet contains the style class rule from the previous section plus a rule that selects any node whose ID is `third`:

```
.my-style {
    -fx-fill: red;
    -fx-font-size: 32;
}

#third {
    -fx-font-size: 48;
    -fx-font-style: italic;
}
```

To see the effect of this style sheet, we add a third text node to the code shown in Listing 23-1:

```
Text {
    content: "Third Text"
    id: "third"
}
```

If you run this example, which is in the file `javafxstyle/Styles2.fx`, you'll get the result shown in Figure 23-2.

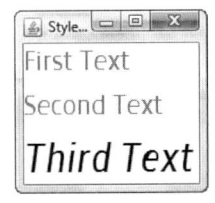

Figure 23-2   Using selection by ID to style a node

As you can see, the new style, which specifies a 48-point italic font, has been applied to the new text node, because the value of its `id` variable matches the ID selector in the style sheet.

Selection by Class and ID

If you include both a style class and an ID in your selector, the rule applies only to nodes that have both the specified style class and ID. Here's a style sheet that has such a rule:

```
.my-style {
    -fx-fill: red;
    -fx-font-size: 32;
}

#third {
    -fx-font-size: 48;
    -fx-font-style: italic;
}

#third.another-style {
    -fx-fill: lightGray;
}
```

The code in the file `javafxstyle/Styles3.fx` adds a fourth node to the previous example:

```
Text {
    content: "Fourth Text"
    id: "third"
    styleClass: "another-style"
}
```

Figure 23-3 shows the result of applying the new style sheet to this node.

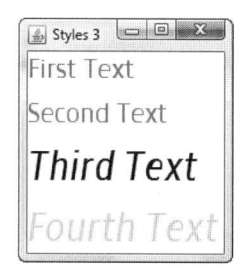

Figure 23-3   Selection by class and ID

Because the new node has both the correct style class (`another-style`) and the correct ID (`third`), the rule applies to it and, therefore, its text is drawn in light gray. It is important to note that the rule for ID `third` has been applied, as well, because this node also has the ID value needed to trigger that rule, with the result that the text is also in a 48-point italic font.

State-Dependent Styling

It often proves useful to change the appearance of a node based on some aspect of its state. Nodes in JavaFX can be styled differently based on any or all of the following states:

- `hover`: When the mouse is over the node
- `pressed`: When the mouse is over the node and a button is pressed
- `focused`: When the node has the keyboard focus
- `disabled`: When the node is disabled

To specify the styling that should apply to a given state, add the state name to a selector, separating the two with a colon, as shown by the style sheet in Listing 23-3.

Listing 23-3   **Specifying State-Dependent Styles**

```
1    .circle {
2        -fx-fill: red;
3    }
4
5    .circle:hover {
```

```
 6            -fx-fill: yellow;
 7       }
 8
 9       .circle:pressed {
10            -fx-stroke: black;
11            -fx-stroke-width: 4;
12       }
```

The code in the file `javafxstyle/Styles4.fx` applies this style sheet to a circle with style class `circle`. If you run this example, you will initially see that the circle is red, because of the rule on lines 1 to 3, as shown on the left of Figure 23-4. If you move the mouse over the circle, its `hover` variable will be set to `true` and the rule on lines 5 to 7 will come into play, causing the fill color to change to yellow. This state is shown in the middle of Figure 23-4. Finally, if you now press the mouse, the circle's `pressed` variable will be set to `true` and a black outline will appear, because of the rule on lines 9 to 12.

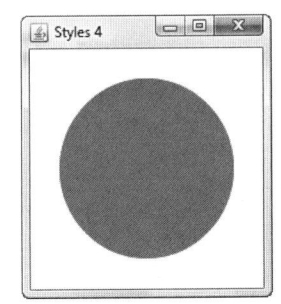

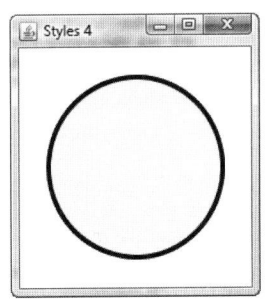

Figure 23-4 Styling by state

Notice that at this point the fill color is still yellow because the mouse is still over the circle. If you hold down the mouse button and move the mouse outside the circle, the `hover` variable will be reset to `false` and the fill color will revert to red, because the rule on lines 5 to 7 of Listing 23-3 no longer applies, but the black outline will stay until you release the mouse.

It is possible to create a rule that contains more than one state by including both in the selector. As an example, the following selector would apply when the mouse is over the circle while it has the focus (that is, both conditions must be satisfied):

`.circle:hover:focused`

Multiple Selectors

You can indicate that a rule should apply to more than one class of nodes, more than one node, or in multiple states by using multiple selectors, separated by a comma. The following rule makes the fill color of the circle change to yellow when either the mouse is over the node or the circle is disabled:

```
.circle:hover, .circle:disabled { -fx-fill: yellow; }
```

Hierarchical Selectors

The selectors that you have seen so far apply to nodes independently of their location in the scene graph. Sometimes, it is necessary to style nodes differently depending on their exact location in the hierarchy. You might, for example, want all the `Text` objects in a specific group to use a different font or have the text that they contain underlined. You can achieve this by using selectors that specify the positions in the scene graph of the nodes to be affected.

The code in Listing 23-4, which is an extract from the example in the file `javafxstyle/Styles5.fx`, contains three text nodes and two groups. The top-level group contains one of the text nodes and a nested group, and the nested group contains the other two text nodes. As you can see, all three text nodes have the style class `text`, while the top-level group has style class `group`; the nested group does not have a style class because one is not needed for this example.

Listing 23-4 **Using Hierarchical Selectors**

```
1   Group {
2       styleClass: "group"
3       content: [
4           Text {
5               content: "Top level"
6               translateY: 20
7               styleClass: "text"
8           }
9           Group {
10              translateY: 40
11              content: [
12                  Text {
13                      content: "Nested"
14                      translateY: 20
15                      styleClass: "text"
16                  }
17              ]
18          }
19      ]
20  }
```

The aim is to apply styles to the text nodes in the nested group that are different to those applied to the text node in the topmost group. Here's a style sheet that will do what we need:

```
1    .group .text {
2        -fx-fill: blue;
3        -fx-font-style: italic;
4    }
5
6    .group > .text {
7        -fx-underline: true;
8        -fx-font: 12pt "Arial Bold";
9    }
```

The result of applying this style sheet to the nodes in Listing 23-4 is shown in Figure 23-5.

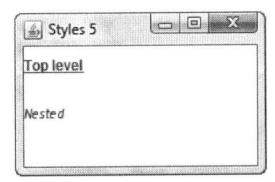

Figure 23-5 Selecting a subset of nodes using hierarchical selectors

Notice that each rule has two selectors rather than one. When you use more than one selector and you do not separate them with commas,[1] you are describing a hierarchy of objects to be located in the scene graph. The first rule, on line 1 of the style sheet, selects first the group with style class `group`, and then all objects with style class `text` that appear anywhere within that group. As a result, this rule applies to all the text nodes in Listing 23-4 because they are all nested, directly or indirectly, inside the outermost group, and they all have the correct style class. The effect of the rule is to cause the text to be rendered in blue and with an italic font.

If you look at Figure 23-5, you'll see that all the text is blue (take my word for it, or run the example to be sure!), but the text on the first line is in a larger font, is not italicized, and is underlined. This particular `Text` object is rendered differently because of the rule on lines 6 to 9 of the style sheet. Here, the two selectors are separated by a > symbol.

---

[1] The effect of separating selectors with commas is described in the section "Multiple Selectors."

820 Chapter 23 Style Sheets

This restricts the second selector to only those nodes that are *direct descendents* of the group identified by the first selector—in this case, the rule applies only to the `Text` object declared on lines 4 to 8 of Listing 23-4. This rule does not specify a fill color, so the fill is set from the first rule, which also applies to this node.

In this example, there were only two selectors in the hierarchy, but it is possible to have more if required.

Inheritance of Styles

Styles applied to a node that has descendents are sometimes inherited by children of that node, with the result that you may need to apply a style in only one place to have it take effect throughout a scene or part of a scene. The code in Listing 23-5, which is taken from the file `javafxstyles/Styles6.fx`, creates a scene containing four text nodes nested at various levels. Figure 23-6 shows the relationships between the nodes.

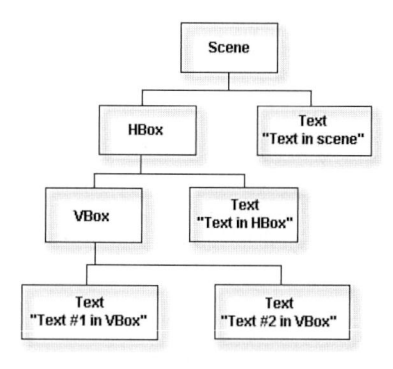

Figure 23-6   Arrangement of nodes from Listing 23-5

Listing 23-5   **Style Inheritance**

```
1      Stage {
2          title : "Styles 6"
3          var scene:Scene;
4          scene: scene = Scene {
5              stylesheets: "{__DIR__}Styles6.css"
6              content: [
7                  HBox {
8                      styleClass: "hbox"
9                      width: bind scene.width
10                     height: bind scene.height
11                     padding: Insets {
```

```
12                        top: 8 left: 8 bottom: 8 right: 8
13                    }
14                    spacing: 8
15                    content: [
16                        VBox {
17                            styleClass: "vbox"
18                            spacing: 8
19                            content: [
20                                Text {
21                                    content: "Text#1 in VBox"
22                                }
23                                Text {
24                                    content: "Text#2 in VBox"
25                                    styleClass: "text2"
26                                }
27                            ]
28                        }
29                        Text {
30                            content: "Text in HBox"
31                        }
32                    ]
33                }
34                Text {
35                    translateY: 120
36                    content: "Text in scene"
37                }
38            ]
39        }
40  }
```

Now let's apply a style sheet to this scene. Here's the style sheet that we are going to apply:

```
.scene {
    -fx-font: 18pt "Arial Bold";
    -fx-fill: lightGray;
}

.vbox {
    -fx-font: 24pt "Amble Cn";
    -fx-fill: red;
}

.text2 {
    -fx-fill: inherit;
}
```

Figure 23-7 shows the result of running this example.

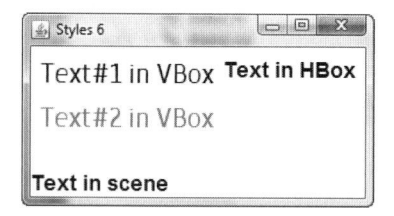

Figure 23-7   Illustrating inheritance of styles

The first thing to note about the style sheet is that it begins with a rule with a selector called .scene, which is a selector that should apply to nodes with a style class of scene. If you look at the code in Listing 23-5, you'll see that no nodes have this style. In fact, this style is applied to an invisible node that resides between the scene and the root of your scene graph, and it is typically used as a place to hold styles that you want to be applied, by inheritance, to the whole scene, or to define names that can be used elsewhere (an example of which you'll see in the next section). In this case, the .scene rule specifies an 18-point bold font and a light gray fill color. In Figure 23-7, note that the specified font has been applied to the text node that is in the scene itself and to the text node in the HBox. Fonts are automatically inherited by nodes from their ancestors, so this font actually applies to any node in the scene to which a more specific rule applies. Notice, however, the scene contains no light gray text. This is because colors are *not* inherited by ancestor nodes, at least not by default. More on this point in a moment.

Returning to Figure 23-7, you can see that the two text nodes in the VBox have a different font. This font is actually applied to the VBox by virtue of the fact that it has style class vbox, which specifies the 24-point plain Amble Cn font that you can see in Figure 23-7 and a red fill color.

As mentioned earlier, colors are not inherited from ancestor nodes, yet one of the text nodes in the VBox has inherited the red fill color from its parent VBox, whereas the other did not. This did not happen automatically—it is a result of the fact that this text node has style class text2, which is defined as follows:

```
.text2 {
    -fx-fill: inherit;
}
```

The special value inherit causes the associated value, here the value of -fx-fill, to be inherited from the parent of the node to which the style is applied. When this style is applied to the text node, it inherits the -fx-fill value of the VBox, which, as you have already seen, is red.

Defining Constant Color Values

In anything but a very simple style sheet, it is likely that you will need to use the same color in more than one rule. Instead of repeating the color declaration in each rule that needs it, you can declare it in the .scene rule and then use it anywhere else in the style sheet. This works because the .scene rule is applied to a node that is the ancestor of every other node in the scene. Here's an example:

```
.scene {
    my-color: red;
}

.text {
    fx-fill: my-color;
}
```

Here, we define a constant called my-color, which is assigned the value red, and then refer to it from the .text rule. The result of this is that the fill of any node with style class text will be red. Note that this technique works *only* for colors.

Setting the Background Color of the Scene

Despite its name, you can't use the .scene style to apply CSS rules to the Scene object. In particular, there is no way to set the background fill of a scene from a style sheet. The only way to do this is to use a Rectangle as the first element of the scene's content sequence and apply a rule to its background. The following code, from the file javafxstyles/Styles7.fx, illustrates this technique:

```
Stage {
    title : "Styles 7"
    var scene:Scene;
    scene: scene = Scene {
        stylesheets: "{__DIR__}Styles7.css"
        width: 100
        height: 100
        content: [
            Rectangle {
                width: bind scene.width
                height: bind scene.height
                styleClass: "background"
            }
        ]
    }
}
```

Applying this style sheet causes the scene to appear to have a light gray background:

```
.scene {
    bg-color: lightGray;
}

.background {
    -fx-fill: bg-color;
}
```

Note that we define the background color as part of the `.scene` rule and then use it in the definition of the style class definition used by the rectangle. This isn't necessary, but it has the advantage of keeping the definition of the background in the place where it should logically be defined.

Using Multiple Style Sheets

In all the examples so far, we have used a single style sheet, but it is also possible to spread your style sheet rules over multiple files. You might do this to group them together by function—for example, corporate styling requirements in one style sheet, differences for your specific application in another, and so on. To use more than one style sheet, you just reference them all from the `stylesheets` variable of the scene. The order in which they appear is important. In general, style sheets containing more-specific rules should appear after those with less-specific rules, so you would place your corporate style sheet before your local style sheet.

Style Sheet Property Specifications

So far in this chapter, we have looked at the overall structure of a style sheet and how the rules that it contains are applied to the nodes of a scene graph. In this section, we look more closely at how to specify fonts and colors and how to describe an effect to be applied to a node.

Fonts

A font can be specified either by using separate properties that assign values to the individual elements of the font or by a single property that includes all parts of the font definition.

Setting Individual Font Properties

You can use four properties to define a font in a style sheet rule. If you don't specify all four properties, the values that you don't specify are inherited from the parent of the node to which the style sheet rule is applied. The property names are `-fx-font-family`, `-fx-font-size`, `-fx-font-style`, and `-fx-font-weight`.

Font Family

The `-fx-font-family` property specifies the family name of the font you want to use. If the name contains spaces, it must be enclosed in quotes. Here are a couple of examples:

```
-fx-font-family: Arial;
-fx-font-family: "Arial Bold";
```

Font Size

The `-fx-font-size` property lets you specify how large the font should be. There are a number of ways to specify the size, the most being to use a numeric value followed by a measuring unit. Table 23-1 lists the recognized measuring units.

Table 23-1 Font-Size Measuring Units

Specifier	Example	Meaning
(none)	12	Size specified in pixels (same as `px`)
%	150%	Size specified as a percentage of the inherited font size
em	2.0em	Size relative to the width of the inherited font
ex	2ex	Size relative to the height of the inherited font
in	0.5in	Size specified in inches
cm	1cm	Size specified in centimeters
mm	10mm	Size specified in millimeters
pt	10pt	Size specified in points
px	12px	Size specified in pixels
pc	1pc	Size specified in picas, where 1 pica is the same as 12 points

You can also use any of the following size names to get a font that is sized relative to the inherited font:

- `xx-small` is 60% of the inherited font size.
- `x-small` is 75%.
- `small` is 80%.
- `medium` is 100%.
- `large` is 120%.
- `x-large` is 150%.
- `xx-large` is 200%.

Font Style

The `-fx-font-style` property lets you specify whether you want a plain, italic, or oblique font style. In JavaFX, oblique is the same as italic. For example:

```
-fx-font-style: plain;
-fx-font-style: italic;
```

Font Weight

You can control the boldness of the font by using the `-fx-font-weight` property. The values `normal`, `bold`, `bolder`, and `lighter` enable you to specify the boldness relative to the normal weight of the font:

```
-fx-font-weight: bold;
-fx-font-weight: lighter;
```

You can also use the values `100` through `800` to express the weight relative to normal, which has the value `400`. Not all of these values produce different visual weights.

Using the Shorthand Font Property

You can specify the properties of a font together by using the `-fx-font` property. In JavaFX 1.3, not all features of the CSS `font` property are supported. The general form of this property, as implemented in JavaFX 1.3, is as follows:

```
[font weight | font style] font-size font-family-name
```

Here are some examples:

```
-fx-font:   italic 12pt "Arial";
-fx-font:   bold 12pt "Arial";
```

Note that you can specify both a font weight and a font style, but only the last mentioned of these takes effect. Therefore, this specification gives an italic font, but the bold specifier is ignored:

```
-fx-font:   bold italic 12pt "Arial";
```

In this case, you can achieve the desired effect by changing the font family name:

```
-fx-font:   bold italic 12pt "Arial Bold";
```

Where this is not possible, you will need to specify the font properties individually, as described in the previous section.

Paints

There are various ways to specify the value of a property whose type is `Paint`, depending on whether you want a solid color, a linear gradient, or a radial gradient. These cases are all covered in the sections that follow.

Solid Colors

There are various ways to specify a solid color. The simplest way is to use a color name as declared in the `javafx.scene.paint.Color` class. When a color name is used, the case is ignored, so `YELLOW`, `yellow`, and `Yellow` are all the same:

```
-fx-fill: YELLOW;
-fx-fill: yellow;
-fx-fill: AZURE;
```

If the color that you need is not one of those defined by the `Color` class, you can give its RGB or RGBA representation in various ways:

- As six or eight hexadecimal digits preceded by `#`. For example, `#FF0000` is a fully opaque red, and `#FF000080` is a semi-opaque variant of the same color.

- Using the `rgb()` or `rgba()` functions. The red, green, and blue values passed to these functions are in the range 0 to 255, whereas the alpha component ranges from 0 for a transparent color to 1.0 for a fully opaque one. Some examples: `rgb(128, 128, 0)`, `rgba(255, 0, 0, 0.5)`.

- Using the `hsb()` and `hsba()` functions. The hue value is in the range 0 to 360, whereas the saturation and brightness are given as percentages. The alpha value is in the range 0.0 to 1.0. Examples are `hsb(180, 40%, 50%)` or `hsba(180, 80%, 80%, 0.5)`.

Another way to describe a color is to derive from another one by using the `derive()` function, which has the following form:

```
derive(color, amount%)
```

This function accepts a color value and returns another color that is brighter than it or darker than it by a given percentage, depending on whether the amount value is positive or negative. You can specify the source color in any of the ways described in this section. Here are some examples:

```
derive(red, -20%)
derive(rgb(128, 0, 128), 50%)
derive(derive(rgb(128, 0, 128), 50%), -20%)
derive(my-color, -30%)
```

In the preceding example, `my-color` is assumed to be a color property declared elsewhere in the style sheet, typically in the `.scene` rule.

Linear Gradients

You can create a linear gradient by using the keyword `linear`, followed by definitions of the start points and endpoints, the stops, and (optionally) the cycle method to be used. Here is an example:

```
linear (0%, 0%) to (100%, 0%) stops (0%, black) (25%, red) (50%, white);
```

This example produces a horizontal gradient starting with black and progressing through red one-quarter of the way along the horizontal span of the node to which it is applied and then to white at the halfway point.

The following two variants cover only half of the horizontal span of the node and specify a cycle method of `repeat` and `reflect`:

```
linear (0%, 0%) to (50%, 0%) stops (0%, black) (25%, red) (50%, white) repeat;
linear (0%, 0%) to (50%, 0%) stops (0%, black) (25%, red) (50%, white) reflect;
```

The colors used in the definition of a gradient can, of course, be specified in any of the ways described earlier in this section.

Radial Gradients

A radial gradient is specified using the `radial` keyword followed by definitions for the center of the gradient (which is optional), its radius, the optional focus point, the stops and the optional cycle method. Here's an example in which all the elements are present:

```
-fx-fill: radial (30%, 30%), 100% focus (50%, 50%) stops (0%, white)
(50%, green) (80%, yellow) reflect;
```

The value in the first parentheses is the position of the center of the gradient, the next value is its radius, the following parentheses contain the focus, and the rest of the definition lists the stops and the cycle method. Here's another example that omits all the parts that are optional:

```
-fx-fill: radial 100% stops (0%, white) (50%, green) (80%, yellow);
```

Effects

The CSS syntax currently allows you to specify one of two effects for a node via the `-fx-effect` property—an inner shadow or a drop shadow. The syntax for both of these effects is the same:

```
shadowtype(blurtype, color, radius, choke, offsetX, offsetY)
```

The shadow type is either `innershadow` or `dropshadow`, whereas the blur type is one of `gaussian`, `one-pass-box`, `two-pass-box`, or `three-pass-box`. The shadow color can be specified using any of the encodings described earlier in this section. For the meanings of the radius, choke, and offset variables, see the discussion of these shadow effects in Chapter 20, "Effects and Blending." Here's an example that produces a `dropshadow` using a three-pass box blur, where the shadow color is an almost opaque black. The shadow has radius 10 and is offset by 3 pixels horizontally and 4 pixels vertically from the node to which it is applied:

```
-fx-effect: dropshadow(three-pass-box, rgba(0, 0, 0, 0.8), 10, 0, 3, 4);
```

24

Using Swing Controls

If you are a Swing developer, you will probably be pleased to know that JavaFX enables you to continue to use Swing components, provided that you don't mind being limited to platforms that support the JavaFX desktop profile. The `javafx.ext.swing` package, which is the subject of this chapter, contains classes that are JavaFX wrappers for a subset of the Swing component set. At the time of this writing, only a small number of components are available, and it is unlikely that more will be added because the emphasis is now on creating native JavaFX controls. As you'll see at the end of this chapter, it is also possible to create your own Swing wrappers, which is useful if you need to use some of the standard components that are not supported or if you want to create a JavaFX wrapper for a custom Swing control of your own.

This chapter is not a tutorial on Swing. Basic usage of the Swing with JavaFX is covered, but if you want to make use of some of the more advanced features, you should consult a book that is more focused on Swing for further details.

The examples for this chapter can be found in the `javafxswing` package of the JavaFX Book Desktop project.

Swing Component Wrappers

In JavaFX, Swing components are used via wrapper classes in the `javafx.ext.swing` package. These classes let you create and configure a Swing component and place it in a scene graph. All the wrapper classes derive from `SwingComponent`, which itself derives from the `Node` class. The set of Swing components available is as follows:

- `SwingLabel`
- `SwingTextField`
- `SwingButton`
- `SwingCheckBox`
- `SwingRadioButton`
- `SwingToggleButton`

- `SwingList`
- `SwingScrollPane`
- `SwingComboBox`
- `SwingSlider`

The names all have the prefix `Swing` to distinguish them from the cross-platform controls in the `javafx.scene.control` package. Note that there are no container classes like `JPanel` and no layout managers—like any other nodes, Swing components must be added to a container, a group, or directly to the scene.

`SwingComponent` Variables

The variables of the `SwingComponent` class are listed in Table 24-1.

Table 24-1   Variables of the `SwingComponent` Class

Variable	Type	Access	Default	Description
name	String	RW	Empty	The component's name
font	Font	RW		The component's font
foreground	Color	RW		The component's foreground color

The `name` and `font` variables simply set the properties of the same name in the wrapped component. The `foreground` variable lets you set the foreground color of the component, but there is nothing that allows you to set the background color. To do this, you need to get access to the underlying Swing component, as described later in this section.

`SwingComponent` as a Node

Because a JavaFX Swing component is a node, anything you can do with a node you can also do with a JavaFX Swing component. This means that you can rotate, scale, translate, or shear it, set its opacity, apply a transition to it, and so on. To do those things with a real Swing component in a Java application you would have to make direct use of Java2D, which involves a nontrivial amount of work. To demonstrate how easy it is to do this in JavaFX, the code in Listing 24-1, which you'll find in the file `javafxswing/SwingNode1.fx`, places a `SwingLabel` in a scene and rotates it about its center.

Listing 24-1   Applying a `RotateTransition` to a Swing Component

```
package javafxswing;

import javafx.animation.Interpolator;
import javafx.animation.Timeline;
```

```
import javafx.animation.transition.RotateTransition;
import javafx.ext.swing.SwingLabel;
import javafx.scene.effect.DropShadow;
import javafx.scene.paint.Color;
import javafx.scene.paint.LinearGradient;
import javafx.scene.paint.Stop;
import javafx.scene.Scene;
import javafx.scene.text.Font;
import javafx.stage.Stage;

var label: SwingLabel;
Stage {
    title: "Swing Node #1"
    scene: Scene {
        width: 300
        height: 200
        fill: LinearGradient {
            startX: 0 startY: 0
            endX: 1.0 endY: 0.0
            stops: [
                Stop { offset: 0.0 color: Color.LIGHTGRAY },
                Stop { offset: 1.0 color: Color.BLACK }
            ]
        }

        content: [
            label = SwingLabel {
                text: "A SwingLabel is a Node"
                font: Font { size: 24 }
                foreground: Color.YELLOW
                translateX: 20 translateY: 80
                effect: DropShadow {
                    offsetX: 10 offsetY: 10
                }
            }
        ]
    }
}

var t = RotateTransition {
    node: label
    fromAngle: 0 byAngle: 360
    duration: 2s
    repeatCount: Timeline.INDEFINITE
    interpolator: Interpolator.LINEAR
}
t.play();
```

As you can see, there is nothing special here—you just create the `SwingLabel` as you would any other node, set its variables, and then apply a `RotateTransition`. You can see a snapshot of the result in Figure 24-1.

Figure 24-1 A wrapped Swing component as a node

Accessing the Wrapped Swing Component

Sometimes it is useful to be able to access the underlying Swing component so that you can customize it in ways not permitted by the wrapper class. The `SwingComponent` class provides the following function that lets you do this:

```
public function getJComponent():JComponent
```

You can use this function to set the background color of a component, which is not possible through an object literal because the `SwingComponent` class does not have a variable that corresponds to it. Here's how you would set the background color of the `SwingLabel` in Listing 24-1:

```
var c = label.getJComponent();
c.setOpaque(true);
c.setBackground(java.awt.Color.BLUE);
```

A Swing label is transparent by default, so you need to make it opaque to force its background to be filled. Note that the `setBackground()` method used here requires an argument of type `java.awt.Color`, not `javafx.scene.paint.Color`. The result of adding this code to the example in Listing 24-1, which you will find in the file `javafxswing/SwingNode2.fx`, is shown in Figure 24-2.

Each Swing wrapper class has an additional function that returns the wrapped component, cast to its actual type. For example, the `SwingLabel` class provides the following function:

```
public function getJLabel():JLabel
```

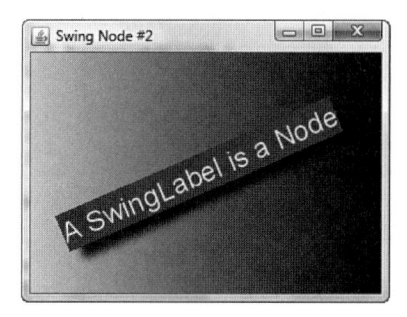

Figure 24-2   A `SwingLabel` with its background color set

Labels

The `SwingLabel` class is used to display either or both of some read-only text and an icon. As its name suggests, it is typically used to attach a label that explains the use of an adjacent control, such as an input field. The variables of this class are listed in Table 24-2 and are discussed in the sections that follow.

Table 24-2   Variables of the `SwingLabel` Class

Variable	Type	Access	Default	Description
text	String	RW	Empty	The text to be displayed in the label
icon	SwingIcon	RW	null	An image to be displayed in the label
labelFor	SwingComponent	RW	Null	The component with which this label is linked
horizontal-Alignment	SwingHorizontal-Alignment	RW	LEADING	The horizontal alignment of the label's content
vertical-Alignment	SwingVertical-Alignment	RW	CENTER	The vertical alignment of the label's content
horizontal-TextPosition	SwingHorizontal-Alignment	RW	TRAILING	The horizontal position of the text relative to the icon

834 Chapter 24 Using Swing Controls

Table 24-2   Variables of the `SwingLabel` Class (*Continued*)

Variable	Type	Access	Default	Description
vertical-TextPosition	SwingVertical-Alignment	RW	CENTER	The vertical position of the text relative to the icon
vertical-Alignment	SwingVertical-Alignment	RW	CENTER	The vertical alignment of the label's content

Text and Icon

The `text` and `icon` variables represent the visual content of the label. Most labels will have associated text, but it is possible to install just an icon or both text and an icon. Figure 24-3 shows five `SwingLabels`, each with different properties.

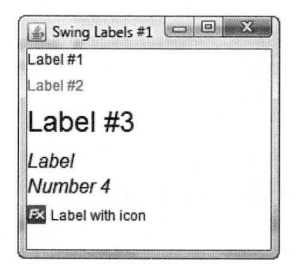

Figure 24-3   The `SwingLabel` `text` and `icon` variables

The first three labels have only the `text` variable set. The code that creates these labels is shown here:

```
SwingLabel {
    text: "Label #1"
}

SwingLabel {
    text: "Label #2"
    foreground: Color.RED
}

SwingLabel {
    text: "Label #3"
    font: Font { size: 24 }
}
```

Label #1 shows text rendered with the default font and foreground color. In the case of Label #2, the foreground color has been changed to red by setting the `foreground` variable, while Label #3 has a larger font installed in the `font` variable.

The documentation for the `text` property says that `SwingLabel` will display only a single line of text. This is not quite correct. It is certainly true that newlines in the value of the text variable will be ignored, so this does not work—the text, without the newline character, will appear on a single line:

```
SwingLabel {
    text: "Line1\nLine 2" // Does not work
}
```

If you need a multiline label, all you have to do is to wrap the text in HTML and use the `<br>` tag to force a line break, like this:

```
SwingLabel {
    text: "<html><I>Label<br>Number 4</I></html>"
    font: Font { size: 16 }
}
```

This is how Label #4 in Figure 24-3 was created. As you can see, this code forces the use of an italic font by using the HTML `<I>` element. `SwingLabel` inherits its support of HTML from the Swing `JLabel` component, which understands a reasonable subset of the HTML 4.0 standard.

The bottom label in Figure 24-3 has both the `icon` and `text` variables set:

```
SwingLabel {
    text: "Label with icon"
    icon: icon
}
```

The value used to initialize the `icon` variable is of type `SwingIcon`, which is a JavaFX implementation of the `javax.swing.Icon` interface. In Swing, you can create a class that implements this interface by drawing arbitrary content, which can then be made to appear in labels and buttons, among other places. More commonly, you would use the standard implementation in the `javax.swing.ImageIcon` class, which loads and draws an image onto the hosting component. The `SwingIcon` class is not a general implementation of the `Icon` interface—it is limited to drawing an image, supplied in the form of a `javafx.scene.image.Image` object. Here is how the icon object used by this label is created:

```
def img = Image { url: "{__DIR__}FXLogo.gif" }
def icon = SwingIcon { image: img };
```

The first line creates an `Image` object that loads the content of the specified file, which happens to contain a small JavaFX logo. The second line creates a `SwingIcon` that wraps that image so that wherever this object is used, the JavaFX logo will be drawn.

Positioning the Content of `SwingLabel`

When a label is made wider or taller than it needs to be to accommodate the text/icon that it contains, you can specify where the extra space appears relative to the content. The horizontal positioning of the text and icon is controlled by the `horizontalAlignment` variable and the vertical positioning by the `verticalAlignment` variable.

Horizontal Alignment

The `horizontalAlignment` variable is of type `SwingHorizontalAlignment`. This class defines constants that correspond to five possible ways to position the label's content, not all of which are different. The constant values are as follows:

- SwingHorizontalAlignment.LEFT
- SwingHorizontalAlignment.RIGHT
- SwingHorizontalAlignment.CENTER
- SwingHorizontalAlignment.LEADING
- SwingHorizontalAlignment.TRAILING

Figure 24-4 illustrates four of the five possible horizontal alignment values.

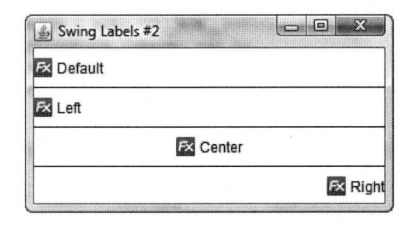

Figure 24-4 `SwingLabel`s with different horizontal alignment values

The four labels in this example have been made deliberately wider than they need to be so that you can see the effects of the different `horizontalAlignment` values. In addition, lines have been drawn between the labels so that you can see the space occupied by each of them.

The topmost label has its `horizontalAlignment` variable set to its default value, which is `SwingHorizontalAlignment.LEADING`[1]:

```
SwingLabel {
    text: "Default" icon: icon
}
```

---

[1] The code extracts in this section show only the parts of the code that are relevant to the discussion. The full source code, which you'll find in the file `javafxswing/SwingLabels2.fx`, also sets the variables that determine the size and positioning of the labels.

```
SwingLabel {
    text: "Left" icon: icon
    horizontalAlignment: SwingHorizontalAlignment.LEFT
}
```

The values `LEADING` and `TRAILING` do not correspond to fixed positions; instead, they place the label's content according to the reading direction of the user's locale. In a left-to-right locale such as en_US (English in the United States), `LEADING` is the same as `LEFT` and `TRAILING` is the same as `RIGHT`, which is why the position of the content in the top two labels in Figure 24-4 is the same. In a right-to-left locale, the content in the top label would be placed on the right side of the label instead of the left.

The values `LEFT`, `CENTER`, and `RIGHT` always place the label's content in the specified position regardless of the reading order of the user's locale, as you can see in the bottom three labels in Figure 24-4. Note that when both text and icon are present, they are treated as a single unit and are placed together. In particular, when `CENTER` is used, it is the center of the icon and text combination that is placed at the center of the label.

Vertical Alignment

Vertical alignment is simpler than horizontal alignment because it is not locale-dependent, so the `SwingVerticalAlignment` class defines only three values:

- `SwingVerticalAlignment.TOP`
- `SwingVerticalAlignment.CENTER`
- `SwingVerticalAlignment.BOTTOM`

Here's an example of a label with its vertical alignment set to `TOP`:

```
SwingLabel {
    text: "Top" icon: icon
    verticalAlignment: SwingVerticalAlignment.TOP
}
```

Examples of labels with each of the possible alignments are shown in Figure 24-5. The default vertical alignment, which is used by the label at the top of the figure, is `SwingVerticalAlignment.CENTER`.

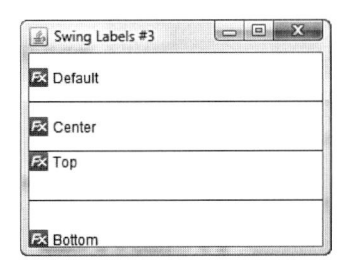

Figure 24-5 **SwingLabel**s with different vertical alignment values

Relative Positioning of Text and Icon

By default, when a label has both text and an icon, the icon appears on the leading edge of the text, as you have already seen in the example shown in Figure 24-5. You can control how the text and icon are placed relative to each other by using the `horizontalTextPosition` and `verticalTextPosition` variables. We'll look first at the `horizontalTextPosition` variable, which has type `SwingHorizontalAlignment`. You can the effect of the five different values of the variable in Figure 24-6, which is the result of running the example code in the file `javafxswing/SwingLabels4.fx`.

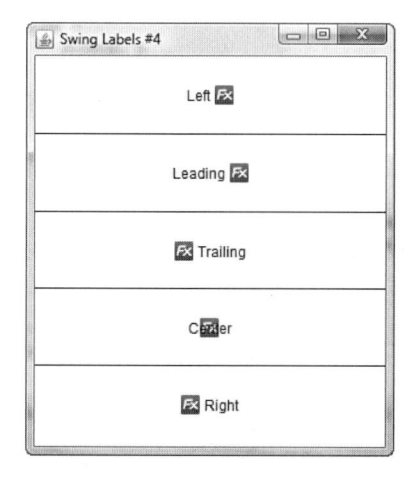

Figure 24-6 `SwingLabel`: horizontal text positions

As you can see, the value `LEFT` places the text to the left of the icon, `RIGHT` places it to its right, and `CENTER` draws the text on top of the icon, which is not especially useful, unless you change the vertical alignment, as you'll see shortly. The other two values, `LEADING` and `TRAILING`, position the text according to the reading order of the user's locale. In the case of Figure 24-6, the reading order was left to right, so `LEADING` places the text to the left of the icon and `TRAILING` to its right. In a right-to-left locale, these would be reversed.

When the `horizontalTextPosition` variable has the value `CENTER`, you can use the `verticalTextPosition` variable to specify whether the text should appear above, below, or over the icon. Figure 24-7 shows all three cases.

Note that the `verticalTextPosition` value is ignored if the `horizontalTextPosition` variable does not have the value `CENTER`.

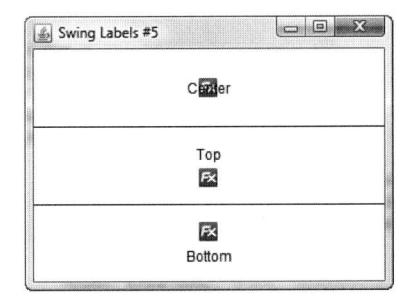

Figure 24-7 **SwingLabel**: vertical text positions

Text Input

Swing has several text input controls: `JTextField`, `JTextArea`, `JFormattedTextField`, `JTextPane`, and `JEditorPane`. JavaFX currently provides a wrapper only for the first of these. The `SwingTextField` class provides the functionality of `JTextField`, which is a single-line input field that is very similar to the cross-platform `TextBox` control discussed in Chapter 22, "Cross-Platform Controls." The variables that you can use to configure this class are listed in Table 24-3.

Table 24-3 **Variables of the `SwingTextField` Class**

Variable	Type	Access	Default	Description
`background`	`Paint`	RW	Look-and-feel dependent	The background paint to be used. This is not currently implemented.
`columns`	`Integer`	RW	0	The number of columns.
`editable`	`Boolean`	RW	`true`	Whether the user can edit the content of the
`borderless`	`Boolean`	RW	`true`	Whether a border should be drawn around the content.
`selectOnFocus`	`Boolean`	RW	`true`	Whether the whole content of the control should be selected when it gets the input focus.
`text`	`String`	RW	Empty	The content of the control.

Table 24-3 Variables of the `SwingTextField` Class (*Continued*)

Variable	Type	Access	Default	Description
horizontal-Alignment	Swing-Horizontal-Alignment	RW	LEADING	The horizontal alignment of the text in the control.
action	function(): Void	RW	null	Function to be called when the text in the control is committed.
verify	function (:String): Boolean	RW	null	Function called to check whether the content of the control is valid.

Configuring the `SwingTextField` Control

The code in the file `javafxswing/SwingTextField1.fx` creates three `SwingTextFields` that have various values for these variables. The result of running this example is shown in Figure 24-8.

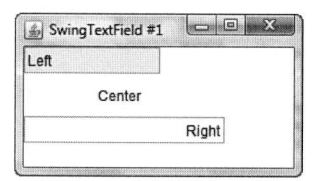

Figure 24-8 `SwingTextField`s with different variable settings

Here's the code that creates the topmost text field:

```
SwingTextField {
    columns: 10
    text: "Left"
    editable: false
    background: Color.YELLOW
    horizontalAlignment: SwingHorizontalAlignment.LEFT
}
```

As a result of the initializer for the `columns` variable, this text field is wide enough to display approximately ten characters of the installed font, which is assigned by the look-and-feel (but can be overridden by setting the `font` variable inherited from

`SwingComponent`). When you use a proportional font, the field will generally be wide enough to display more than ten characters. This limit is only a visual one; it is possible to input any number of characters into a `SwingTextField`. If the content is too wide to be displayed, it is scrolled so that the part that contains the input cursor is visible.

The `editable` variable controls whether the user can modify the content of the control. In this case, as its value is `false`, editing is not allowed, but the user can still select some or all the text and copy it to the Clipboard. Note that the background color of this `SwingTextField` is different to that of the others, because it is not editable.

The position of the text within the control is determined by the `horizontalAlignment` variable. By default, the text is placed at the leading edge of the control. Here, it is placed on the left (which is the same as the leading edge in a left-to-right locale). The other two text fields in Figure 24-8 specify center- and right-alignment. The text remains properly aligned while it is being edited, which means that the center point of the text remains over the center point of the input field when center-alignment is used.

The `background` variable specifies the `Paint` used to fill the control's background. In this case, it is the solid color yellow, but it can also be a gradient, as shown on lines 4 to 11 of Listing 24-2, which is the code that creates the bottom text field in Figure 24-8.

Listing 24-2 A `SwingTextField` Filled with a `LinearGradient`

```
1    t = SwingTextField {
2        columns: 15
3        text: "Right"
4        background: LinearGradient {
5            startX: 0 startY: 0
6            endX: 1.0 endY: 0
7            stops: [
8                Stop { offset: 0 color: Color.WHITE },
9                Stop { offset: 1 color: Color.LIGHTGRAY }
10           ]
11       }
12       selectOnFocus: false
13       horizontalAlignment: SwingHorizontalAlignment.RIGHT
14       action: function() {
15           println("Text field content is {t.text}");
16       }
17   }
```

Note, however, that as of JavaFX 1.2, the `background` variable is ignored, so you don't see a color gradient in the text field at all.

The declaration of the middle `SwingTextField` in Figure 24-8 is shown here:

```
SwingTextField {
    columns: 15
    text: "Center"
    borderless: true
    horizontalAlignment: SwingHorizontalAlignment.CENTER
}
```

This text field is 5 columns wider than the other two, has its text center-aligned, and is editable (because the default value of the `editable` variable is `true`), but it does not have a surrounding border because the `borderless` variable has been set to `false`. You can see the difference that this makes by comparing this field to the others in the same figure.

The bottom text field, created using the code shown in Listing 24-2, has its `selectsOnFocus` variable set to `false`. When this variable is `true`, which is the default, all the text will be selected when the control receives the input focus, as you can see in Figure 24-8, where the topmost text field has the focus. When this variable is `false`, the selection is not changed when the control receives the focus—it is restored to its state when it last had the focus. You can programmatically control and query the focus using the following functions provided by the `SwingTextField` class:

```
public function selectAll():Void;
public function select(start:Integer, end:Integer):Void;
public bound function getSelectionStart():Integer;
public bound function getSelectionEnd():Integer;
```

The `selectAll()` function selects all the text in the text field and places the input cursor after the last character. The `select()` function selects the part of the content from the `start` index (inclusive) to the `end` index (*exclusive*) and places the input cursor after the last selected character. For example, the following code selects the characters 0 through 3 of the text field:

```
var t = SwingTextField { columns: 10 text: "Hello, World" };
t.select(0, 4);    // Selects "Hell"
```

The `getSelectionStart()` and `getSelectionEnd()` functions return, respectively, the index of the first selected character and the index of the first character after the last selected character (which is also the position of the input cursor). When there is no selection, these functions return the position of the input cursor. Note that these are bound functions, so you can bind a variable to their return values and that variable will be continually updated as the selection changes.

Handling Input

The `action` and `verify` variables can be assigned references to functions that allow you to receive control when the user commits the content of the input field. The `action` function is called when the user presses ENTER while the field has the input focus, while the `verify` function is called when the control loses focus.

The `action` function is intended to be used when you want to react to a change in the field's content as soon as the user commits it. You can see an example of this on lines 14 to 16 of Listing 24-2, where an `action` function that prints the field's content is installed.

The `verify` function is called to perform validity checks on the content of the field when it loses the input focus. This function is called with the content of the field as its argument and returns a `Boolean` value that indicates whether or not the content is regarded as valid. The following code, which you'll find in the file `javafxswing/SwingTextField2.fx`, shows an example that uses this feature:

```
1   t = SwingTextField {
2       columns: 15
3       action: function() {
4           println("Content is ");
5       }
6       verify: function(s:String):Boolean {
7           println("Verifier called with ");
8           s.length() > 5
9       }
10  }
```

In this example, the text is considered to be valid if it is more than five characters long. If the user enters fewer than five characters and attempts to move the focus to another control, the `verify` function will return `false`. As a result of this, the input focus will remain in the text field. Once a text field with a verifier has the input focus, it is not possible to move the focus elsewhere until the `verify` function returns `true`.

It is important to note the following points:

- The `action` function is called only when the user presses Enter. It is *not* called when the control uses the input focus.
- The `verify` function is called only when the user tries to move the focus out of the control. Even if the content of the field is valid, the `action` function is *not* called in this case.

Buttons

The function of a button is to allow the user to cause the application to perform an action, or to make a choice between two or more alternatives. JavaFX has wrapper classes for all the Swing button controls. These classes all derive from `SwingAbstractButton`, which defines state that is common to all buttons. The difference in behavior between the various button types is slight, as you'll see in the sections that follow.

The `SwingAbstractButton` and `SwingButton` Classes

The `SwingButton` class is a push button that displays some text/icon. `SwingButton` has the same variables as its base class, `SwingAbstractButton`, which are listed in Table 24-4.

Table 24-4 Variables of the `SwingAbstractButton` and `SwingButton` Classes

Variable	Type	Access	Default	Description
text	String	RW	Empty	The button text.
icon	SwingIcon	RW	null	The icon used when the button is not pressed.
pressedIcon	SwingIcon	RW	null	The icon used when the button is pressed. If `null`, the unpressed icon is used.
action	function():Void	RW	null	The function to be called when the button is pressed.
horizontal-Alignment	SwingHorizontal-Alignment	RW	CENTER	The horizontal alignment of the text/icon combination.
vertical-Alignment	SwingVertical-Alignment	RW	CENTER	The vertical alignment of the text/icon combination.
horizontal-TextPosition	SwingHorizontal-Alignment	RW	TRAILING	The horizontal position of the text relative to the icon.
vertical-TextPosition	SwingVertical-Alignment	RW	CENTER	The vertical position of the text relative to the icon.

Most of these variables, and their behavior, are very similar to those of the `SwingLabel` class, so we won't spend much time discussing them here. The only new variables are `pressedIcon` and `action`.

The `pressedIcon` variable supplies the icon that will display when the button is pushed in. In the case of a `SwingButton`, the button is pushed only while the user keeps the mouse button pressed and is released when the mouse is released. If the button is activated from the keyboard (by pressing the Spacebar key while it has the focus), the button will remain pressed for a very short time before being released. This behavior differs for `SwingToggleButton`—in this case the button remains pushed in until explicitly released. If `pressedIcon` is `null` but `icon` is not `null`, the same icon displays whether or not the button is pressed. And if both variables are `null`, no icon displays at all. It is possible to supply a pressed icon without a normal icon, but this is unlikely to be useful.

The `action` variable can be set to point to a function to be called when the button is pressed. This function has no arguments and does not return a value.

If a button is disabled by setting its `disable` variable to `true`, the text and icon are drawn differently so that the user can see the difference in state, and it does nothing when pressed. The following code, from the file `javafxswing/SwingButtons1.fx`, creates two buttons with the same text and icon (one enabled, the other disabled). The result of running this code is shown in Figure 24-9.

```
SwingButton {
    text: "Enabled"
    icon: icon
    action: function():Void {
        println("Button pressed");
    }
    translateX: 70 translateY: 15
}
SwingButton {
    text: "Disabled"
    icon: icon
    disable: true
    action: function():Void {
        println("Button pressed");
    }
    translateX: 70 translateY: 60
}
```

Figure 24-9   The `SwingButton` control

The button at the top of Figure 24-9 is enabled. When it is pressed, its `action` function is called and prints a message on the standard output stream. The button at the bottom is disabled and, as you can see, both its background and the icon are grayed out, making it clear that the button is not active. Pressing the button in this state has no effect and its `action` function will not be invoked.

Toggle Buttons

The `SwingToggleButton` class represents a button that toggles between the pressed and unpressed states—pressing and releasing the mouse when over the button causes it to adopt its pressed state. It remains in this state until you click it again, at which point it reverts to the unpressed state. `SwingToggleButton` derives from `SwingAbstractButton` and therefore inherits all the variables and behavior described in Table 24-4. In addition to these variables, it has two of its own, which are listed in Table 24-5.

Table 24-5 Variables of the `SwingToggleButton` Class

Variable	Type	Access	Default	Description
selected	Boolean	RW	false	Whether the button is selected (that is, pressed)
toggle-Group	SwingToggle-Group	RW	null	The toggle group that this button is linked to

The `selected` variable reflects whether the button is in the pressed-in state. This variable toggles between `false` and `true` as the user presses the button. You can also programmatically change this variable to make the button alter its visual state.

The `toggleGroup` variable allows you to make the button a member of a toggle group, represented by the `SwingToggleGroup` class. You add a group of buttons to a toggle group if you want only one of them to be in the pressed state at any given time. The toggle group monitors the `selected` variable of each of its member buttons; if any of them transitions from not selected to selected, all the other buttons in the group are forced to be in the not selected state. There is an example of this in Listing 24-3, which you'll find in the file `javafxswing/SwingButtons2.fx`.

Listing 24-3 Using the `SwingToggleButton` and `SwingToggleGroup` Classes

```
1    package javafxswing;
2
3    import javafx.ext.swing.SwingToggleButton;
4    import javafx.ext.swing.SwingToggleGroup;
5    import javafx.scene.Scene;
6    import javafx.stage.Stage;
7
8    var toggleGroup = SwingToggleGroup {};
9    Stage {
10       title: "Swing Buttons #2"
11       scene: Scene {
12           width: 230
```

```
13              height: 155
14              content: [
15                  SwingToggleButton {
16                      text: "Price in USD"
17                      selected: true
18                      toggleGroup: toggleGroup
19                      action: function():Void {
20                          println("Price in USD changed state");
21                      }
22                      translateX: 70 translateY: 15
23                  }
24                  SwingToggleButton {
25                      text: "Price in GBP"
26                      selected: false
27                      toggleGroup: toggleGroup
28                      action: function():Void {
29                          println("Price in GBP changed state");
30                      }
31                      translateX: 70 translateY: 60
32                  }
33                  SwingToggleButton {
34                      text: "Send Email"
35                      selected: false
36                      action: function():Void {
37                          println("Send Email changed state");
38                      }
39                      translateX: 74 translateY: 105
40                  }
41              ]
42          }
43      }
```

This code creates three toggle buttons, as shown in Figure 24-10.

Figure 24-10   Three toggle buttons in two groups

848 Chapter 24 Using Swing Controls

The first two buttons represent mutually exclusive choices—display prices in pounds or dollars—so they shouldn't both be selected at the same time. To enforce this restriction, these buttons are placed in a toggle group, as shown on lines 18 and 27 of Listing 24-3. Initially, the Price in USD button is pressed, because its `selected` variable is initialized to true on line 17. If you click the Price in GBP button, the Price in USD button will be deselected automatically. The `action` function of a `SwingToggleButton` is called when it is pressed—that is, when its `selected` variable changes value. The code in this function will need to test the state of the button's `selected` variable to decide whether to take any action. Typically, it would take action only when the button is pressed in—that is, when the `selected` variable has the value `true`.

The Send Email button is not in a toggle group. Pressing it just changes the value of its `selected` variable and invokes its `action` function.

Radio Buttons and Check Boxes

Radio buttons and check boxes are simply different visual representations of toggle buttons. You typically use a set of radio buttons rather than a set of toggle buttons in a toggle group and a check box instead of a toggle button that is not in a toggle group. Radio buttons therefore represent a set of mutually exclusive choices, whereas check boxes are used to select or deselect features that are independent of each other.

Radio buttons are represented by the `SwingRadioButton` class and check boxes by the `SwingCheckBox` class. Both of these classes derive from `SwingToggleButton`, and neither of them adds any new variables or functions—only the visual representation differs. The following code extract shows how you would replace the first two toggle buttons in Listing 24-3 with radio buttons:

```
SwingRadioButton {
    text: "Price in USD"
    selected: true
    toggleGroup: toggleGroup
    action: function():Void {
        println("Price in USD changed state");
    }
    translateX: 70 translateY: 15
}
SwingRadioButton {
    text: "Price in GBP"
    selected: false
    toggleGroup: toggleGroup
    action: function():Void {
        println("Price in GBP changed state");
    }
    translateX: 70 translateY: 60
}
```

The only difference in the code is the change of classname in the object initializers. The result is a change in the visual appearance, as shown in Figure 24-11.

Figure 24-11 Comparing radio buttons and check boxes

Similarly, replacing the third toggle button in Listing 24-3 with a check box requires only a change of classname, with the result shown at the bottom of Figure 24-11:

```
SwingCheckBox {
      text: "Send Email"
      selected: false
      action: function():Void {
      println("Send Email changed state");
   }
    translateX: 70 translateY: 105
}
```

The default representation of a radio button is a circle, and a check box is represented by a square. When selected, the radio button has a dot in the center of the circle, and the check box has a tick. If you want, you can change this representation by setting the `icon` variable of the `SwingRadioButton` or `SwingCheckBox` object. If you do this, you should also create an icon that provides a different representation when the button is selected and install it in the `pressedIcon` variable.

The `SwingList` Class

The `SwingList` component displays a list of items and allows the user to select one or more of them. The items in the list are wrapped in instances of the `SwingListItem` class. The variables of the `SwingList` class are shown in Table 24-6 and those of the `SwingListItem` class in Table 24-7.

Chapter 24 Using Swing Controls

Table 24-6 Variables of the `SwingList` Class

Variable	Type	Access	Default	Description
items	SwingList-Item[]	RW	empty	The items to be displayed in the list
selected-Index	Integer	RW	-1	The index of the first selected item in the list
selected-Item	SwingList-Item	RW	null	The first selected item in the list
scrollable	Boolean	RW	true	Whether scrollbars should be shown if the list of items is too large to be seen all at once

Table 24-7 Variables of the `SwingListItem` Class

Variable	Type	Access	Default	Description
value	Object	RW	null	The value for this item
text	String	RW	Empty	The string that should appear in the list for this item
selected	Boolean	RW		Whether this item is selected

Creating a `SwingList` Control

The following code, which you can find in the file `javafxswing/SwingList1.fx`, creates and displays a list containing 100 items:

```
1     var items = for (i in [0..99]) {
2         SwingListItem {
3             value: i
4             text: "Choice #{i}"
5         }
6     }
7
8     var list:SwingList;
9     Stage {
10        title : "SwingList #1"
11        scene: Scene {
12            width: 200
13            height: 200
14            content: [
15                list = SwingList {
16                    items: items
17                    width: 150
18                    height: 190
19                }
20            ]
21        }
22    }
```

The code that creates the list is shown on lines 1 to 6. Notice that each item to be displayed is wrapped in a `SwingListItem` object. The `value` variable of this object contains the actual value of the item, while its `text` variable contains the representation of that value that should appear in the list. In this case, the value is an integer, and the visual representation is a string containing the integer value. In other cases, you might need to do something more complex, such as formatting a date in a locale-independent way. The `value` and `text` variables are provided because in most cases the `value` is what you will need to work with when an item is selected, whereas the `SwingList` control needs the `text` variable for display purposes.

> **Note**
>
> If you were using a `JList` in a Swing application, you could provide a `ListCellRenderer` to allow the list to create an appropriate string representation of each item in the list. The JavaFX solution is simpler for the developer, but less powerful. You can change the rendering mechanism of a `SwingList` by installing your own renderer in its embedded `JList` component, which you can get access to by calling its `getJList()` function. Alternatively, you can subclass `SwingList` and override its `createJComponent()` function to return a `JList` that has your custom renderer already installed.

Having created the list of items, you use it to initialize the `items` variable of the `SwingList` object, as shown on lines 15 to 19. The `SwingList` control displays the string representation of each item, in the order in which they appear in the `items` list, as shown in Figure 24-12.

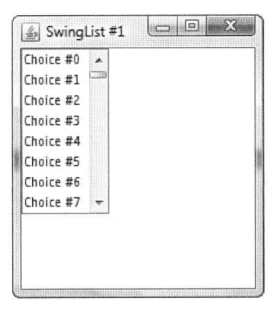

Figure 24-12   The `SwingList` control

In this (common) case, there are more items in the list than can be displayed in the space allocated to the `SwingList`. To make the other items accessible, a scrollbar is automatically added. You can disable this behavior by setting the `scrollable` variable to `false`, in which case the user has to select an item and then use the up- and down-arrow keys to cause the set of visible items to scroll. This is unlikely to be very useful.

By default, the user can select a single item by clicking it with the mouse. Once an item is selected, clicking another item, or using the up- and down-arrow keys to move the selection, will cause the new item to be selected and the old one deselected. The Swing `JList` component allows you to select more than one item, but there is no JavaFX application programming interface (API) that allows you to access this feature. If you need to be able to select more than one item, you can do so by setting the selection mode of the `JList` to one of the values defined by the `javax.swing.ListSelectionModel` class. Here's how you would configure the list to allow selection of multiple values by holding down the Ctrl or Shift keys while clicking items in the list[2]:

```
list.getJList().setSelectionMode(
            ListSelectionModel.MULTIPLE_INTERVAL_SELECTION);
```

Handling the Selection

The `selectedIndex` and `selectedItem` variables of the `SwingList` class allow you to control and respond to changes in the selected items in the control. These variables are set in response to user actions, but you can also use them to set an initial selection. The following code binds a couple of script variables to the selection-related variables of a `SwingList` and uses triggers to print the selected index and item as the user interacts with the control:

```
var selectedIndex = bind list.selectedIndex on replace {
    println("Selected index is {selectedIndex}");
}

var selectedItem = bind list.selectedItem on replace {
    println("Selected item value is {selectedItem.value}");
}
```

When the item is selected, the `selected` variable of its `SwingListItem` object is set to `true` and when it is deselected, it is set to `false`. When more than one item is selected (which is possible only if you change the selection mode of the underlying `JList` as described previously), the `selectedIndex` and `selectedItem` variables refer to the selected item with the lowest-numbered index. If you need to get all the selected items (which you almost certainly will), you can do so by traversing the `items` sequence and acting on those for which the `selected` variable is `true`.

The `SwingScrollPane` Class

`SwingScrollPane` is a wrapper around the `JScrollPane` class. It is used to allow the user to view a control that is larger than the space available for it in the scene. `SwingScrollPane` adds two variables to the `SwingComponent` class, which are listed in Table 24-8.

---

[2] You can try this out by running the example in the file `javafxswing/SwingList2.fx`.

Table 24-8 Variables of the `SwingScrollPane` Class

Variable	Type	Access	Default	Description
view	Swing-Component	RW	null	The `SwingComponent` to be placed in the scrollable area
scrollable	Boolean	RW	true	Whether scrollbars should be shown if the view component is too large to be seen all at once

The component to be viewed is assigned to the `view` variable. Initially, this component will be placed so that its top-left corner is visible in the top-left corner of the space allocated to the `SwingScrollPane`. If the `scrollable` variable has the value `true`, which is the default, a horizontal scrollbar will be shown if the component is wider than the horizontal space available, and a vertical scrollbar will appear if it is taller than the vertical space available. If this variable has the value `false`, no scrollbars are shown. This is only useful if you want to manage scrolling programmatically, which is possible if you use the `getJScrollPane()` function to get access to the embedded `JScrollPane` and then use the API that it provides to control the part of the wrapped component that is visible.

The following code, from the file `javafxswing/SwingScrollPane1.fx`, loads a large image, installs it as the icon of a `SwingLabel`, and then places the `SwingLabel` in a `SwingScrollPane` so that it can be viewed by using the scrollbar. You can see the result in Figure 24-13. As you can see, the image is much larger than the scene, so both horizontal and vertical scrollbars are provided.

Figure 24-13 The `SwingScrollPane` control

854　Chapter 24　Using Swing Controls

```
def img = Image { url: "{__DIR__}Portsmouth.JPG" }
def icon = SwingIcon { image: img };

var scene:Scene;
Stage {
    title : "Swing ScrollPane #1"
    scene: scene = Scene {
        width: 400
        height: 400
        content: [
            SwingScrollPane {
                view: SwingLabel {
                    icon: icon
                }
                width: bind scene.width
                height: bind scene.height
            }
        ]
    }
}
```

The `SwingComboBox` Class

The `SwingComboBox` class enables you to present a list of items to the user, from which one can be chosen. It is similar to `SwingList`, except that it occupies less space because the list of possible items is visible only when the user opens it to change the selection, and because it is possible to configure it so that the user can select a value that is not in the item list. The variables of the `SwingComboBox` class are listed in Table 24-9.

Table 24-9　Variables of the `SwingComboBox` Class

Variable	Type	Access	Default	Description
`items`	`SwingCombo-BoxItem[]`	RW	Empty	The items from which a selection can be made
`selected-Index`	`Integer`	RW	`-1`	The index of the selected item in the items list
`selected-Item`	`SwingCombo-BoxItem`	RW	`null`	The item selected from the items list
`editable`	`Boolean`	RW	`false`	Whether the combo box is editable, which allows an entry that is not in the items list to be entered directly into the combo box
`text`	`String`	RW		The text for the selected item

Each item in the `items` list is of type `SwingComboBoxItem`, which has the same variables as the `SwingListItem` class discussed earlier in this chapter and which are listed in Table 24-7.

The behavior of an editable `SwingComboBox` differs slightly from one that is not editable. For the sake of simplicity, we'll look first at an example of one that is not editable and then cover the changes in behavior that occur when you make the control editable.

Using a Noneditable `SwingComboBox`

Using a noneditable combo box is almost the same using a list, as the following code shows:

```
var items = for (i in [0..99]) {
    SwingComboBoxItem {
        value: i
        text: "Choice #{i}"
    }
}

var combo:SwingComboBox;
Stage {
    title : "SwingComboBox #1"
    scene: Scene {
        width: 200
        height: 200
        content: [
            combo = SwingComboBox {
                items: items
                translateX: 60
                translateY: 10
            }
        ]
    }
}
```

This code creates a noneditable combo box containing 100 selectable items, each represented by a `SwingComboBoxItem` object. If you run this code, which you'll find in the file `javafxswing/SwingComboBox1.fx` and open the list of available items by clicking the combo box arrow, you'll get the result shown in Figure 24-14.

If you select an item by clicking it with the mouse, it appears in the combo box itself and the drop-down closes. At the same time, the `selectedIndex` and `selectedItem` variables change the value to reflect, respectively, the index of the selected item in the items list and its `SwingComboBoxItem` value. In addition to this, the `text` variable is assigned the text for the selected item, as obtained from its `SwingComboBoxItem` object. When there is no selection, the visible part of the combo box is empty, and these variables have the value -1, `null`, and an empty string, respectively. Apart from its visual appearance, a noneditable `SwingComboBox` behaves in almost the same way as the `SwingList` class discussed earlier in this chapter.

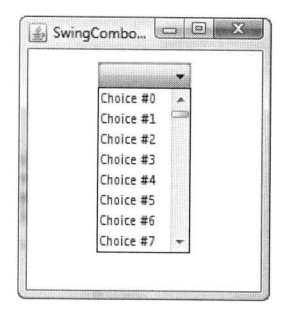

Figure 24-14 A noneditable combo box

Using an Editable `SwingComboBox`

When you set the `editable` variable of a `SwingComboBox` to `true`, the display area next to the drop-down arrow becomes an editable input field, as shown on the left of Figure 24-15. The user can either select an item from the drop-down, in which case the behavior is the same as that of a noneditable combo box, or type an arbitrary value into the input field, as shown on the right of Figure 24-15.

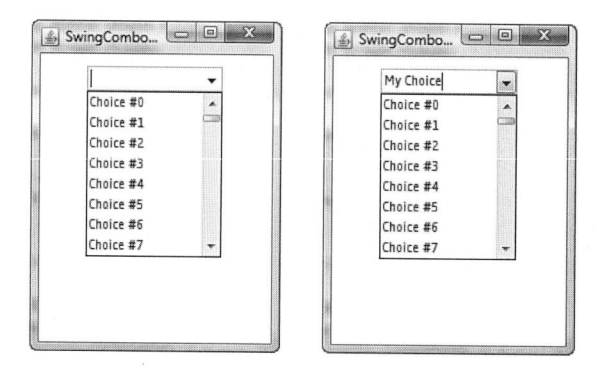

Figure 24-15 An editable combo box

If the user chooses to type a value into the editor that is not an item from the drop-down list and presses the Enter key, the `selectedIndex` and `selectedItem` variables change to `-1` and `null`, respectively, because a value has not been chosen from the `items` list in the control. You can get the value that the user entered from the text variable. The following code, which you'll find in the file `javafxswing/SwingComboBox2.fx`, monitors all three of these variables:

```
var selectedIndex = bind combo.selectedIndex on replace {
    println("Selected index is {selectedIndex}");
```

```
}

var selectedItem = bind combo.selectedItem on replace {
    println("Selected item value is {selectedItem.value}");
}

var selectedText = bind combo.text on replace {
    println("Selected text is ");
}
```

The output from this code when a value is typed into the text editor is as follows:

```
Selected index is -1
Selected item value is null
Selected text is []
Selected text is [My Choice]
```

If the user types a value that *is* the same as the text value of one of the `SwingComboBoxItem` objects in the `items` list, the effect is the same as if that item had been selected from the drop-down. Here is the output that would result from the user entering the text **Choice #4** into the input field and pressing Enter:

```
Selected item value is 4
Selected index is 4
Selected text is [Choice #4]
```

Note that the match must be exact—even adding whitespace at the beginning or end of the text will cause the value to be seen as not matching an entry in the `items` list.

The `SwingSlider` Class

The `SwingSlider` class lets the user select a numeric value from a contiguous range configured using its `maximum` and `minimum` variables. The selection is made by dragging the slider's "thumb" along its track. Table 24-10 describes the variables of this class.

Table 24-10 Variables of the `SwingSlider` Class

Variable	Type	Access	Default	Description
vertical	Boolean	RW	false	The orientation of the slider: `true` for vertical, `false` for horizontal
minimum	Integer	RW	0	The minimum value of the selectable range
maximum	Integer	RW	100	The maximum value of the selectable range
value	Integer	RW	50	The currently selected value

The following code, from the file `javafxswing/SwingSlider1.fx`, creates a slider that allows the user to select any integer value in the range `100` to `200`, inclusive:

```
var value = 125 on replace {
    println("Value is {value}");
}
Stage {
    title : "SwingSlider #1"
    var scene:Scene;
    scene: scene = Scene {
        width: 200
        height: 50
        content: [
            SwingSlider {
                minimum: 100
                maximum: 200
                value: bind value with inverse;
                translateY: 10
                translateX: 10
                width: bind scene.width - 20
            }
        ]
    }
}
```

The value variable of the `SwingSlider` is bidirectionally bound to a script variable called value that is initially set to `125`, so when the slider first appears, the thumb is placed at the position that represents the value `125`, as shown in Figure 24-16.

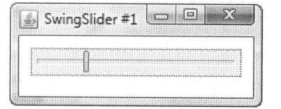

Figure 24-16 Illustrating the `SwingSlider` control

As the thumb is moved along the slider's track, its value variable is updated to reflect its position. Because of the binding, this will also cause the script variable to be set to the same value, and the trigger results in value being written to the console. In a real application, the slider's value would be bound to some more useful application state.

The slider that is created by the `SwingSlider` class is a little bare. It is not obvious what the possible range of values might be or what the selected value is. You can improve the user experience by using some of the features of the `JSlider` class that are not directly available through the `SwingSlider` wrapper. The `getJSlider()` function allows you to get access to the wrapped `JSlider` instance. The following code configures the slider to show small tick marks at the positions that represent 100, 110, 120, and so on and larger tick marks at 100, 150, and 200. The values at these latter positions are also drawn underneath the tick marks. You can see the result of running this code, which you'll find in the file `javafxswing/SwingSlider2.fx`, in Figure 24-17.

```
var value = 125 on replace {
    println("Value is {value}");
}
var slider:SwingSlider;
Stage {
    title : "SwingSlider #2"
    var scene:Scene;
    scene: scene = Scene {
        width: 200
        height: 70
        content: [
            slider = SwingSlider {
                minimum: 100 maximum: 200
                value: bind value with inverse;
                translateY: 10 translateX: 10
                width: bind scene.width - 20
                height: 40
            }
        ]
    }
}

var jslider = slider.getJSlider();
jslider.setMinorTickSpacing(10);
jslider.setMajorTickSpacing(50);
jslider.setPaintTicks(true);
jslider.setPaintLabels(true);
```

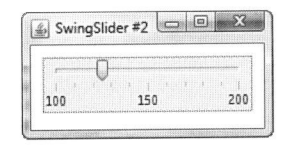

Figure 24-17   A customized `SwingSlider`

Using Other Swing Components

As you have seen, the `javafx.ext.swing` package does not provide a wrapper for all the Swing controls, so what do you do if you want to incorporate one of those that does not have a wrapper into your application? There are two ways to do this: You can either encapsulate an instance of the component that you need to use in a generic JavaFX wrapper, or you can create a specific JavaFX wrapper for the component. In this section, we use both of these approaches to include a Swing progress bar in a JavaFX application.

Using a Generic JavaFX Wrapper

By far the simplest way to convert a Swing component into a `Node` that you can add to your scene graph is to use the following class function of the `SwingComponent` class:

```
public function wrap(comp:JComponent):SwingComponent
```

This works for any Swing component, so you can use it for something as simple as a progress bar or for the more complex controls like `JTable` and `JTree`. It also works for custom controls that you have written yourself or obtained from a third party. The disadvantage of this solution is that the resulting object is a generic wrapper—you can't use an object initializer to configure the wrapped component. Instead, you typically create the Swing component, wrap it, and then place it into the scene graph. Listing 24-4 shows how you would use this technique to wrap a `JProgressBar`.

Listing 24-4 Wrapping a `JProgressBar` Control

```
1     package javafxswing;
2
3     import javafx.animation.Timeline;
4     import javafx.ext.swing.SwingComponent;
5     import javafx.scene.Scene;
6     import javafx.stage.Stage;
7     import javafxswing.WrappedProgressBar;
8     import javax.swing.JProgressBar;
9
10    var progressBar = new JProgressBar();
11    progressBar.setMinimum(0);
12    progressBar.setMaximum(100);
13    progressBar.setIndeterminate(false);
14    progressBar.setStringPainted(true);
15    progressBar.setValue(0);
16
17    Stage {
18        title: "Progress Bar Example #1"
19        scene: Scene {
20            width: 200
21            height: 40
```

```
22              var pb: WrappedProgressBar;
23              content: [
24                  SwingComponent.wrap(progressBar)
25              ]
26          }
27      }
28
29      var value:Integer on replace {
30          progressBar.setValue(value);
31          progressBar.setString("{value}% complete");
32      }
33
34      var t = Timeline {
35          repeatCount: Timeline.INDEFINITE
36          autoReverse: true
37          keyFrames: [
38              at (10s) { value => 100 }
39          ]
40      };
41      t.play();
```

The code on lines 10 through 15 creates and configures the `JProgressBar` that will appear in the scene graph. The control is configured to show values in the range `0` through `100`, and its initial value is set to `0`. The `JProgressBar` is converted to a `SwingComponent` and included in the `Scene` by the code on line 24.

The rest of this example makes use of the progress bar. The `Timeline` on lines 34 through 40 animates the value of a variable called `value` from `0` through to `100` over a period of 10 seconds, and then counts backward to `0`. This process repeats indefinitely. The trigger associated with the `value` variable, shown on lines 29 to 32, reflects its current value in the `value` property of the wrapped `JProgressBar`, which causes the onscreen representation to update, as shown in Figure 24-18.

Figure 24-18 Wrapping a `JProgressBar` for inclusion in a scene graph

Although this technique works, you can see that it looks more like Java code than JavaFX code. You are forced to work directly with the `JProgressBar`, and you can't bind the `value` property of the wrapped component to the `value` variable, which would be the most natural thing to do—instead, it is necessary to use a trigger to keep the progress bar's state updated. None of these problems exist when you create a dedicated wrapper class.

Creating a JavaFX Wrapper Class

Although more work is required to create a specific JavaFX wrapper class, the results are usually better than you can get with the `SwingComponent wrap()` function because you can use an object initializer to create and initialize the control, and you can bind variables of the wrapper class to application state instead of using a trigger to keep everything synchronized.

The general technique is to decide which properties of the Swing component you need access to, create a JavaFX class that has a variable corresponding to each of those properties, and link the variable values to those of the Swing component by using triggers. Using triggers inside the class is preferable to requiring them in application code because the complication is kept hidden from the users of the wrapper class.

Listing 24-5 shows an implementation of a JavaFX wrapper for the Swing `JProgressBar` component.

Listing 24-5 A JavaFX Wrapper for the Swing `JProgressBar` Component

```
1    package javafxswing;
2
3    import javafx.ext.swing.SwingComponent;
4    import javax.swing.JProgressBar;
5
6    public class WrappedProgressBar extends SwingComponent {
7        var pb: JProgressBar;
8        public var minimum: Integer = pb.getMinimum() on replace {
9            pb.setMinimum(minimum);
10       }
11
12       public var maximum: Integer = pb.getMaximum() on replace {
13           pb.setMaximum(maximum);
14       }
15
16       public var orientation: Integer = pb.getOrientation()
17         on replace {
18           pb.setOrientation(orientation);
19       }
20
21       public var indeterminate: Boolean = pb.isIndeterminate()
22         on replace {
23           pb.setIndeterminate(indeterminate);
24       }
25
26       public var string: String = pb.getString() on replace {
```

```
27                  pb.setString(string);
28                  pb.setStringPainted(string != "");
29              }
30
31          public var value: Integer = pb.getValue() on replace {
32              pb.setValue(value);
33          }
34
35          protected override function createJComponent() {
36              pb = new JProgressBar(orientation);
37          }
38      }
```

The core of this class is the variable `pb`, which refers to the wrapped `JProgressBar` instance. When a `WrappedProgressBar` object is created, its overridden `createJComponent()` function (see lines 35 to 37) is called. This happens during initialization of the `SwingComponent` base class, and the value returned is taken to be the wrapped Swing component. The function is called *before* any of the variables of the `WrappedProgressBar` class are initialized, so it is safe to assume that a value has been assigned to `pb` before the variable initializers are called.

As you can see, this class declares a public variable for each property of the `JProgressBar` that is to be exposed to application code. Each variable is initially set to the value of the corresponding property of the `JProgressBar`; the effect of this is that the default values of the variables are the same as the default values of the progress bar's properties. Each variable also has a trigger that fires when application code changes its value. The trigger simply updates the corresponding property of the `JProgressBar` object with the new value, this giving effect to the change. That's all that is needed to create a simple wrapper class.

> **Note**
>
> As an added extra, you could add a `PropertyChangeListener` to the `JProgressBar` to listen for changes in its bound properties. This would allow you to keep the values of the `WrappedProgressBar` class in step with those of the `JProgressBar`, which would prove useful if you want to allow application code to directly access the wrapped control and change its properties without going through the wrapper variables. In practice, this might be necessary in some cases, particularly if your wrapper is part of a library to be sold to or used by others, but it is probably overkill in other circumstances.

Once you have a wrapper object, you can use it just like any of the officially supported classes. Listing 24-6 is a rewrite of the code in Listing 24-5 that uses the `WrappedProgressBar` class rather than the `SwingComponent.wrap()` function. This code, which you'll find in the file `javafxswing/ProgressBarExample2.fx`, is much easier to understand than the original version, and it is much more in the declarative spirit of JavaFX.

Listing 24-6 **Using a `JProgressBar` Wrapper Class**

```
package javafxswing;

import javafx.animation.Timeline;
import javafx.scene.Scene;
import javafx.stage.Stage;
import javafxswing.WrappedProgressBar;

var value: Integer;
Stage {
    title: "Progress Bar Example #2"
    scene: Scene {
        width: 200
        height: 40
        var pb: WrappedProgressBar;
        content: [
            pb = WrappedProgressBar {
                minimum: 0
                maximum: 100
                indeterminate: false
                string: bind "{pb.value}% complete"
                value: bind value
                translateX: 20
                translateY: 10
            }
        ]
    }
}

var t = Timeline {
    repeatCount: Timeline.INDEFINITE
    autoReverse: true
    keyFrames: [
        at (10s) { value => 100 }
    ]
};
t.play();
```

25

Building Custom Controls

In this chapter, you see how to build new user interface components. In the first part of this chapter, we create a simple component by extending the `CustomNode` class. The advantage of this approach is that it is easy to create a working component but, on the downside, its visual appearance is more or less fixed—although you can change its colors, fonts, and so on, you can't radically change the way that it looks. Later in this chapter, you see how to build a more flexible component, at the cost of a little more effort, by subclassing the `Control` class. Unlike a custom node, a control does not have a fixed visual representation—instead, it has a *skin*, which can be replaced to give the control a different appearance and a *behavior*, which determines how it responds to user input.

This chapter also shows you how to create custom containers, which is useful if the standard containers described in Chapter 17, "Coordinates, Transforms, and Layout," do not meet your needs. We illustrate the general technique for building custom containers and the support functions provided by the JavaFX runtime by implementing a container that works like the AWT `BorderLayout` class.

The example source code for this chapter is in the `javafxcustom` package of the JavaFX Book More GUI project, unless otherwise noted.

Custom Nodes

As you saw in Chapter 16, "Shapes, Text, and Images," `CustomNode` is an abstract subclass of `Group` that you can use to create a custom component. The key to this class is the `children` variable, which you override to provide the node or, more commonly, the set of nodes, that appear wherever the custom node is included in a scene graph. In this section, you learn how to create a custom node by implementing the coordinate grid used to illustrate the effects of transformations in Chapter 17.

The `CoordinateGrid` Node

It is often useful to see the effects that a transformation has on the coordinate system of the node or nodes to which it is applied. The `CoordinateGrid` class is a custom node, shown in Figure 25-1, that you can use to show the coordinate system of either the scene or a group within your scene graph.

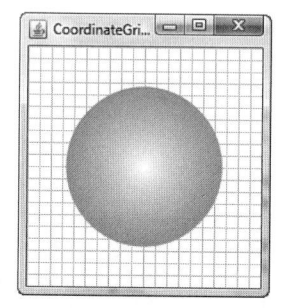

Figure 25-1 Using the `CoordinateGrid` class

The public variables of the `CoordinateGrid` class, which you can use to customize it, are listed in Table 25-1.

Table 25-1 Variables of the `CoordinateGrid` Class

Variable	Type	Access	Default	Description
gridLineColor	Paint	RW	Color.LIGHTGRAY	The color used to draw the grid lines
gridDistance	Number	RW	10	The distance between grid lines
width	Number	RW	0	The width of the area to be covered by the grid
height	Number	RW	0	The height of the area to be covered by the grid

The color of the grid lines is determined by the `gridLineColor` variable, whereas the horizontal and vertical distance between them is controlled by the `gridDistance` variable. The `width` and `height` variables specify the bounds of the area on which grid lines are to be drawn, with the origin being at the top-left corner of the grid. Typically, these values would be bound to the width and height of the enclosing scene or group. All these variables have reasonable defaults and can be set either when a `CoordinateGrid` instance is created or at any subsequent time.

The implementation of the `CoordinateGrid` class is shown in Listing 25-1.

Listing 25-1 **The `CoordinateGrid` Class**

```
1   public class CoordinateGrid extends CustomNode {
2       public var gridLineColor:Color = Color.LIGHTGRAY;
3       public var gridDistance = 10;
4       public var width:Number;
5       public var height:Number;
6
7       protected override var children = bind [
8           createHorizontalLines(),
9           createVerticalLines()
10      ];
11
12      bound function createVerticalLines() : Node[] {
13          for (column in [0..width / gridDistance]) {
14              Line {
15                  startX: column * gridDistance
16                  startY: 0
17                  endX: column * gridDistance
18                  endY: height - 1
19                  stroke: gridLineColor
20                  fill: gridLineColor
21              }
22          }
23      }
24
25      bound function createHorizontalLines() : Node[] {
26          for (row in [0..height / gridDistance]) {
27              Line {
28                  startX: 0
29                  startY: row * gridDistance
30                  endX: width - 1
31                  endY: row * gridDistance
32                  stroke: gridLineColor
33              }
34          }
35      }
36  }
```

The `CoordinateGrid` class extends `CustomNode`. A custom node is obliged to override the `children` variable to return a sequence of nodes that provide its visual representation. The `children` variable of the `CoordinateGrid` class is initialized with the following:

- A set of vertical lines created in the `createVerticalLines()` function on lines 12 to 23 by a `for` expression that places one line at the origin and subsequent lines a distance `gridDistance` apart along the horizontal axis.
- A set of horizontal lines created in the `createHorizontalLines()` function on lines 25 to 35 by another `for` expression. The first line passes through the origin, and the others are `gridDistance` units apart along the vertical axis.

As you can see on line 7, the `children` variable is bound to this set of nodes. This means that if any of the variables on which it depends were to be changed, the set of horizontal and vertical lines would be reconstructed and the appearance of the `CoordinateGrid` would change accordingly. For example, if the values of the `width` or `height` variables were to be changed, grid lines would automatically be added or removed to match the new size of the area allocated to the grid.

The following code, which you'll find in the file `javafxcustom/CoordGridExample1.fx`, creates a scene containing a circle and a `CoordinateGrid` that shows how the circle has been positioned. The result of running this code was shown in Figure 25-1 at the beginning of this section:

```
var scene:Scene;
Stage {
    title : "CoordinateGrid #1"
    scene: scene = Scene {
        width: 200
        height: 200
        content: [
            CoordinateGrid {
                width: bind scene.width
                height: bind scene.height
            }
            Circle {
                centerX: bind scene.width / 2
                centerY: bind scene.height /2
                radius: bind scene.width / 3
                fill: RadialGradient {
                    centerX: 0.5 centerY: 0.5
                    radius: 1.0 proportional: true
                    stops: [
                        Stop { offset: 0 color: Color.WHITE }
                        Stop { offset: 1 color: Color.GREEN }
                    ]
                }
            }
        }
```

            ]
        }
    }

Notice that the `width` and `height` variables of the `CoordinateGrid` class are bound to the width and height of the scene, so the grid will grow or shrink to match any change in the size of the scene and, because of the binding, the number of grid lines that are drawn will change accordingly. Similarly, the center and radius of the circle depend on the scene's width and height. You can see the effect of changing the size of the scene in Figure 25-2.

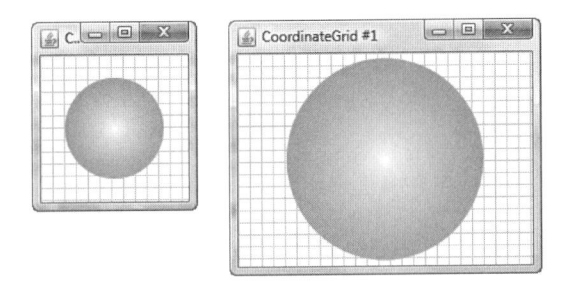

Figure 25-2   The effect of changing the width and height variables of the `CoordinateGrid`

Custom Containers

The containers in the `javafx.scene.layout` package implement some of the most commonly used layout policies, and future releases of the JavaFX runtime will undoubtedly add more. If you can't find what you're looking for among the standard containers, you can either use a third-party solution, if there is one, or create your own. In this section, we show you two ways to take the latter approach by building a custom container. We start by implementing a JavaFX version of the AWT `BorderLayout` class and, in so doing, show you what you need to do to create a container from scratch. In the second part of this section, we introduce the `Panel` class. `Panel` is a container that lets you implement layout behavior by supplying callback functions that are called at well-defined points in the container's lifecycle.

A Border Container

If you are a Swing developer, you will be familiar with the `BorderLayout` class. It is one of the most useful layout managers and also one of the simplest to use—its layout policy is easy both to understand and to implement, which makes it ideal as an illustrative example. In this section, we create a JavaFX equivalent of `BorderLayout` in the form of a class called `FXBorder`. An example of the layout policy of the `FXBorder` container is shown in Figure 25-3.

Figure 25-3 The **FXBorder** container

Nodes that are managed by the `FXBorder` container can be placed in one of five positions. In Figure 25-3, all five of these positions are occupied, but it is possible (and common) to use only a subset, in which case space is not allocated for those that are not used. Gaps can be left between the layout positions, if required. Figure 25-4 shows the space allocated to all five positions and the positioning of the gaps.

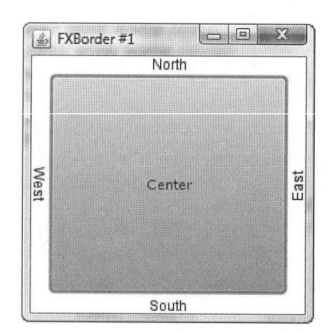

Figure 25-4 The five different layout positions provided by the **FXBorder** container

When adding a component to a panel managed by a Swing `BorderLayout`, you specify the location for that component by using one of the location constants defined by the `BorderLayout` class, like this:

```
JPanel panel = new BorderLayout();
JLabel n = new JLabel("North");
JButton c = new JButton("Center");
JLabel s = new JLabel("South");
panel.add(n, BorderLayout.NORTH);
```

```
panel.add(c, BorderLayout.CENTER);
panel.add(s, BorderLayout.SOUTH);
```

In JavaFX, nodes are added to a container simply by inserting them into its `content` sequence, so we need to find another way to specify the position for each node. In the case of the `FXBorder` container, we do this by using the node's `layoutInfo` variable. As you saw in Chapter 17, many containers enable you to specify node constraints by assigning a value of type `LayoutInfo` to this variable. The `LayoutInfo` class itself cannot express the layout position information that we need, so we create a subclass that can. Here is the definition of that class:

```
public class FXBorderLayoutInfo extends LayoutInfo {
    // The position for the associated node.
    public-init var position = FXPosition.CENTER;
}
```

`FXBorderLayoutInfo` extends `LayoutInfo` so that it can still be used to override a node's preferred size and so on. It also adds a variable of type `FXPosition` that you can use to specify the required layout position. The `FXPosition` class looks like this:

```
public class FXPosition {
    public-read var name:String;
    public override function toString() { name }
}

public def NORTH = FXPosition { name: "NORTH" };
public def SOUTH = FXPosition { name: "SOUTH" };
public def EAST = FXPosition { name: "EAST" };
public def WEST = FXPosition { name: "WEST" };
public def CENTER = FXPosition { name: "CENTER" };
```

As you can see, this class defines one constant instance for each of the possible layout positions. These are analogous to the constants defined by the `BorderLayout` class. With these definitions, it is easy to create a layout that uses the `FXBorder` container. Listing 25-2 contains the code used to create the layout shown in Figure 25-3 and can be found in the file `javafxcustom/FXBorderExample1.fx`.

Listing 25-2 Using the `FXBorder` Class

```
1     Stage {
2         title: "FXBorder #1"
3         width: 250 height: 250
4         var scene:Scene;
5         scene: scene = Scene {
6             content: [
7                 FXBorder {
8                     width: bind scene.width
9                     height: bind scene.height
10                    hgap: 4 vgap: 4
11                    content: [
```

```
12                      Text {
13                          content: "North"
14                          layoutInfo: FXBorderLayoutInfo {
15                              position: FXPosition.NORTH
16                          }
17                      }
18                      Button {
19                          text: "Center"
20                      }
21                      Text {
22                          content: "South"
23                          layoutInfo: FXBorderLayoutInfo {
24                              position: FXPosition.SOUTH
25                          }
26                      }
27                      Text {
28                          content: "East" rotate: -90
29                          layoutInfo: FXBorderLayoutInfo {
30                              position: FXPosition.EAST
31                          }
32                      }
33                      Text {
34                          content: "West" rotate: 90
35                          layoutInfo: FXBorderLayoutInfo {
36                              position: FXPosition.WEST
37                          }
38                      }
39                  ]
40              }
41          ]
42      }
43  }
```

Each node that is added to the content sequence of the FXBorder object is positioned by assigning an appropriate FXBorderLayoutInfo object to its layoutInfo variable, where the position variable is set to the corresponding FXPosition value. The only exception to this is the Button declared on lines 18 to 20. If no position is specified in a node's layoutInfo variable (or if this variable is not set or its value is not of type FXBorderLayoutInfo), the container assumes that the required position is FXPosition.CENTER.

The Swing BorderLayout always expands components to fit their layout area, but the FXBorder container does not. You can see an example of this in Figure 25-4, in the case of the Button in the center position, which is placed in the middle of its layout area but keeps its preferred size. Application code can change this by using the vfill and hfill variables of the FXBorderLayoutInfo object (inherited from LayoutInfo), which are honored by the container implementation.

In addition to the variables inherited from the `Container` class (which include `content`, `width`, and `height`), the `FXBorder` class has a small number of variables of its own that you can use to customize its behavior. These variables are listed in Table 25-2.

Table 25-2   Variables of the **FXBorder** Class

Variable	Type	Access	Default	Description
`hgap`	`Number`	RW	0	The horizontal space between nodes
`vgap`	`Number`	RW	0	The vertical space between nodes
`nodeHPos`	`HPos`	RW	`HPos.CENTER`	The default horizontal positioning for a node within its layout area
`nodeVPos`	`VPos`	RW	`VPos.CENTER`	The default vertical positioning for a node within its layout area

The `hgap` and `vgap` variables determine the sizes of the gaps between the nodes in the layout. You can see the effect of these variables in Figure 25-4. The `nodeHPos` and `nodeVPos` variables control where each node is placed within its specified layout area if it does not completely fill that area. You'll see exactly how these variables are used later in this section.

> **Note**
>
> The implementation of `FXBorder` that you see in this chapter does not include a `padding` variable that would allow application code to leave empty border space in the container. It is left as an exercise for you to add this feature.

Here is the how the `FXBorder` class and its variables are declared. The complete implementation can be found in the file `javafxcustom/FXBorder.fx`:

```
public class FXBorder extends Container {
    public var hgap:Number = 0 on replace {
        requestLayout();
    }

    public var vgap:Number = 0 on replace {
        requestLayout();
    }

    public var nodeHPos = HPos.CENTER on replace {
        requestLayout();
```

```
    }

    public var nodeVPos = VPos.CENTER on replace {
        requestLayout();
    }

    // Code not shown
}
```

As you can see, when the value of any of these variables is changed, the `requestLayout()` function is called. As mentioned in Chapter 17, this function, which is inherited from the `Parent` class, causes the container to lay out its content again at some point after it has been called. You'll see the implementation of this function in "Performing Node Layout" section, later in this chapter.

Now that you have seen the application programming interface (API), it is time to look at the details of the implementation.

A container has two main duties. First, it needs to calculate and return maximum, minimum, and preferred values for its height and width so that it can be given an appropriate size by whichever parent container it is placed into. Second, and more obviously, it needs to size and position its child nodes. We discuss these two aspects of container implementation in the context of the `FXBorder` class separately.

Calculating Sizes

The requirement for a container to calculate its preferred, minimum, and maximum sizes arises because the `Container` class incorporates the `Resizable` mixin, which requires implementations of the following functions:

```
public function getMaxWidth():Number;
public function getMaxHeight():Number;
public function getMinWidth():Number;
public function getMinHeight():Number;
public function getPrefWidth(height:Number):Number;
public function getPrefHeight(width:Number):Number;
```

In general, the values returned from these functions depend both on the container's layout policy and on the maximum, minimum, and preferred sizes of the nodes in its `content` sequence. The `Resizable` class provides default implementations for all these functions. In the case of `FXBorder`, we use the default implementations of the `getMaxWidth()` and `getMaxHeight()` functions, which both return `Integer.MAX_VALUE`, because this is consistent with the behavior of `BorderLayout`. `FXBorder` has its own implementations of the other four functions, which are all quite similar, so we look here only at the `getPrefHeight()` function.

Before explaining how this function works, we first need to describe the layout policy of the container because it determines how the preferred size is calculated:

- The layout areas for the north and south nodes are both given the preferred heights of their respective nodes and are made to stretch the whole width of the container.[1]
- The west, center, and east nodes are placed in a row between the north and south nodes. The layout areas for the east and west nodes are given the preferred widths of their nodes, and any additional horizontal space is given to the layout area of the center node.
- The layout areas of the west, east, and center nodes are all given the same height.

Obviously, if any of these layout positions is not occupied, it is not allocated any space, and it does not contribute to the width or height calculations. Using this information in conjunction with Figure 25-4, you can see that the preferred height is made up of the following components:

- The preferred height of the north node, or 0 if there is no north node
- The preferred height of the south node, or 0 if there is no south node
- The largest preferred height of the west, center, and east nodes, or 0 if none of these positions is occupied
- The gaps between the north node and the center area and between the center area and the south node

To calculate the preferred height, we need to easily access the node for each layout position. All the nodes are in the `content` sequence, so to locate the node at a given position, we would have to traverse this sequence, checking the `layoutInfo` variable of each node. This would be an expensive process, but we can speed it up by building a map from layout position (in the form of an `FXPosition` value) to the node at that position. Once we have this map, we can easily get the node at any given location by using the corresponding `FXPosition` value as the key to the map. The code that creates this map is shown in Listing 25-3.

Listing 25-3 Creating a Map of Layout Position to Node for the `FXBorder` Class

```
1    // Map from FXBorderPosition to node at that position.
2    var mapValid = false;
3    var positionMap = HashMap {};
4    var hgaps = 0;
5    var vgaps = 0;
6
```

---

[1] If you take on the challenge of implementing a `padding` variable for this container, ensure that the left and right insets are taken into account when computing the preferred width and the top and bottom insets in the case of the preferred height.

876　Chapter 25　Building Custom Controls

```
 7    // Builds the map from FXBorderPosition to node. Only one node is
 8    // allowed at each position.
 9    function buildPositionMap():Void {
10        if (not mapValid) {
11            var verticalCount = 0;
12            var horizontalCount = 0;
13            positionMap.clear();
14            for (node in getManaged(content)) {
15                var position = null;
16                var l = node.layoutInfo;
17                if (l instanceof FXBorderLayoutInfo) {
18                    position = (l as FXBorderLayoutInfo).position;
19                }
20                if (position == null) {
21                    position = FXPosition.CENTER;
22                }
23                if (positionMap.containsKey(position)) {
24                    throw new IllegalStateException(
25                  "More than one node with position {position}");
26                }
27                positionMap.put(position, node);
28
29                if (isHorizontal(position)) {
30                    horizontalCount++;
31                }
32                if (isVertical(position)) {
33                    verticalCount++;
34                }
35            }
36            vgaps = Math.max(0, horizontalCount - 1);
37            hgaps = Math.max(0, verticalCount - 1);
38            mapValid = true;
39        }
40    }
41
42    // Returns whether a border position is horizontal.
43    function isHorizontal(position:FXPosition):Boolean {
44        position == FXPosition.NORTH
45        or position == FXPosition.CENTER
46        or position == FXPosition.SOUTH
47    }
48
49    // Returns whether a border position is vertical.
50    function isVertical(position:FXPosition):Boolean {
51        position == FXPosition.EAST
52        or position == FXPosition.CENTER
53        or position == FXPosition.WEST
54    }
```

The map itself, together with a variable that indicates whether it is valid, is declared on lines 2 and 3. As you'll see later, we will call the `buildPositionMap()` function frequently, but on most occasions its content will still be valid. We use the `mapValid` variable to keep track of this. When we need to rebuild the map, we just set `mapValid` to `false`, and it will be rebuilt next time this function is called. This happens when something is added to, removed from, or changed in the `content` sequence, which we detect by adding a trigger:

```
override var content on replace {
    mapValid = false;
}
```

The variables on lines 4 and 5 keep track of how many horizontal and vertical gaps appear in the layout. If the layout contains a north, center, and south node, we need to account for two vertical gaps, whereas if it contains only a center and south node, there is just one. If there were only a south node, there would be no gaps at all. It is convenient to set the values of these variables as we create the position map.

The position map is created in the `buildPositionMap()` function. The majority of this function, on lines 14 to 35, is a loop that inspects all the *managed* nodes in the `content` sequence. As you saw in Chapter 17, by convention containers only size and position nodes that are managed, leaving application code to handle those that are not. The `Container` class provides a script function that returns only the managed nodes from a given sequence:

```
public function getManaged(content:Node[]):Node[];
```

We use this function on line 14 to get the set of nodes that will appear in the position map. Once we have a node, we need to get its `FXPosition` value and make an entry for it in the map. To get the `FXPosition` value, we need to get the value of the node's `layoutInfo` variable and, if this is of type `FXBorderLayoutInfo`, we can get the `FXPosition` value from its `position` variable. The code that does this is shown on lines 16 to 22. If the node does not have a `layoutInfo` value or it is not of type `FXBorderLayoutInfo`, we default its position to `FXPosition.CENTER`. As a result, the following is valid and places the `Text` object in the center position:

```
FXBorder {
    content: [ Text { content: "No layoutInfo - CENTER" } ]
}
```

We allow just one node to appear at each position, so before adding the node to the position map, we check that there is not already an entry with the same position as the key (lines 23 to 26). If there is not, we create the map entry (line 27).

The code on lines 29 to 34 counts how many nodes that are in "horizontal" locations and in "vertical" locations. The horizontal locations are north, center, and south; and the vertical locations are west, center, and east. (Note that center appears in both categories.) We maintain these counts so that we can set the number of horizontal and vertical gaps that will appear in the layout. After we have processed all the managed nodes, we set the number of horizontal and vertical gaps on lines 36 and 37. Refer to our discussion of gaps earlier in this section if you have any difficulty understanding how these values are set. Finally, on line 38, we record that the position map is now valid.

Now that we have the map constructed, we can easily get the node at any given position using the `getNodeAt()` function, shown here:

```
function getNodeAt(position:FXPosition):Node {
    positionMap.get(position) as Node;
}
```

At this point, we have everything that we need to implement the `getPrefHeight()` function. All we need to do is convert the steps that we described earlier into the corresponding code, as follows:

```
public override function getPrefHeight(width:Number) {
    buildPositionMap();
    var eastHeight = getNodePrefHeight(getNodeAt(FXPosition.EAST));
    var westHeight = getNodePrefHeight(getNodeAt(FXPosition.WEST));
    var centerHeight = getNodePrefHeight(getNodeAt(FXPosition.CENTER));
    var northHeight = getNodePrefHeight(getNodeAt(FXPosition.NORTH));
    var southHeight = getNodePrefHeight(getNodeAt(FXPosition.SOUTH));
    return northHeight + southHeight
        + Math.max(eastHeight, Math.max(centerHeight, westHeight))
        + vgaps * vgap;
}
```

The first thing to notice about this function is that it is passed a width value. The idea is that it should compute the ideal height for the container if it had the given width. In most cases, including this one, the width value is ignored, but for some nodes, such as those that render text, it can be useful because the desired height of the node will depend on its width due to the wrapping of text at the control boundaries. If the width argument is -1, the node is expected to compute its preferred height without assuming a specific width.

The expression associated with the return statement gives the preferred height which, as we said earlier is the sum of the preferred heights of the north node and the south node, the maximum of the preferred heights of the east, west, and center nodes, and the necessary gaps. The interesting part of this function is how we obtain these preferred heights. Here's how we get the preferred height of the east node:

```
var eastHeight = getNodePrefHeight(getNodeAt(FXPosition.EAST));
```

The `getNodeAt()` function gets us the node that is in the east position. It is safe to use this function at this point, because we have called the `buildPositionMap()` function to ensure that the position to node map is valid. Given the node, we can then use the `getNodePrefHeight()` function to get its preferred height. This is a script function provided by the `Container` class, which gets the preferred height of a given node using the algorithm that we described in Chapter 17, as follows:

- If the node is `Resizable` and the value of its `layoutInfo` variable is of type `LayoutInfo` and the `height` variable of that object is greater than or equal to zero, it is used as the preferred height.

- Else, if the node is `Resizable`, the value returned by its `getPrefHeight()` function is used.

- Else, the node is not `Resizable`, so its actual height, obtained from its `layoutBounds`, is used as its preferred height.

Similar functions can be used to get a node's preferred width and its maximum and minimum height and width. Here are the definitions of these `Container` functions:

```
public function getNodePrefHeight(node:Node, width:Number):Number;
public function getNodePrefHeight(node:Node):Number;
public function getNodePrefWidth(node:Node, height:Number):Number;
public function getNodePrefWidth(node:Node):Number;
public function getNodeMaxWidth(node:Node):Number;
public function getNodeMaxHeight(node:Node):Number;
public function getNodeMinWidth(node:Node):Number;
public function getNodeMinHeight(node:Node):Number;
```

What happens if there isn't a node in the east position? In that case, `getNodeAt()` returns `null` and the `getNodePrefHeight()` function and when called with a `null` argument, returns 0. This is the correct result because the preferred height calculation should not reserve any space for that node.

Performing Node Layout

The code that positions and sizes a container's child nodes is contained in its `doLayout()` function, which is called from the JavaFX runtime at an appropriate time, usually as a result of the `requestLayout()` function of the container, or one of its nested containers, being called.[2] When this function is called, the container's actual size has been determined and can be read from its `width` and `height` variables. When calculating the container's preferred size, you were determining the container's ideal width and height, but in the `doLayout()` function, there is no guarantee that the actual width and height are what were requested—you just have to work with what you get. The process of laying out the child nodes is usually quite simple. The code that performs the layout operation for the `FXBorder` class is shown in Listing 25-4.[3]

Listing 25-4 The `doLayout()` Function of the `FXBorder` Class

```
1    protected override function doLayout():Void {
2        buildPositionMap();
3    
4        // Place the north node.
5        var topSpace = 0.0;
6        var node = getNodeAt(FXPosition.NORTH);
7        if (node != null) {
```

---

[2] If you call the `requestLayout()` function of a container or a group, not only will it arrange for its own layout to be recalculated, but it will also call the `requestLayout()` function of its parent. This will propagate all the way up to the owning scene.

[3] This code can be found in the file `javafxnodes/RadialGradient2.fx`.

```
 8              topSpace = Math.min(height, getNodePrefHeight(node));
 9              layoutNode(node, 0, 0, width, topSpace, nodeHPos, nodeVPos);
10              topSpace += vgap;
11          }
12
13          // Place the south node.
14          var bottomSpace = 0.0;
15          node = getNodeAt(FXPosition.SOUTH);
16          if (node != null) {
17              bottomSpace = Math.min(height, getNodePrefHeight(node));
18              layoutNode(node,
19                      0, Math.max(0, height - bottomSpace),
20                      width, bottomSpace, nodeHPos, nodeVPos);
21              bottomSpace += vgap;
22          }
23
24          // Place the west and east nodes.
25          var centerHeight = height - topSpace - bottomSpace;
26
27          var westSpace = 0.0;
28          node = getNodeAt(FXPosition.WEST);
29          if (node != null) {
30              westSpace = Math.min(width, getNodePrefWidth(node));
31              layoutNode(node, 0, topSpace, westSpace, centerHeight,
32                      nodeHPos, nodeVPos);
33              westSpace += hgap;
34          }
35
36          var eastSpace = 0.0;
37          node = getNodeAt(FXPosition.EAST);
38          if (node != null) {
39              eastSpace = Math.min(width, getNodePrefWidth(node));
40              layoutNode(node,
41                      Math.max(0, width - eastSpace), topSpace,
42                      eastSpace, centerHeight, nodeHPos, nodeVPos);
43              eastSpace += hgap;
44          }
45
46          // Place the center node
47          node = getNodeAt(FXPosition.CENTER);
48          if (node != null) {
49              layoutNode(node, westSpace, topSpace,
50                      Math.max(0, width - eastSpace - westSpace),
51                      Math.max(0, height - topSpace - bottomSpace),
52                      nodeHPos, nodeVPos);
53          }
54      }
```

This code consists of five similar blocks, one for each layout position. Because the code in each block is similar, we'll look only at how the node in the north position is managed. The diagram in Figure 25-5 shows how the nodes will be placed, assuming that all the layout positions are used.

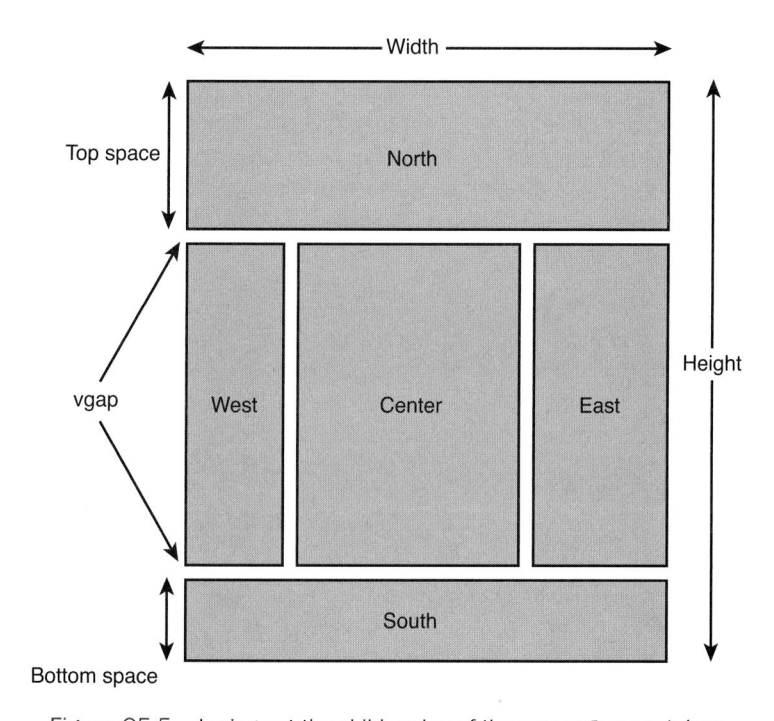

Figure 25-5   Laying out the child nodes of the **FXBorder** container

The code that handles the node in the north position is shown on lines 5 to 11 of Listing 25-4. The variable topSpace is used to hold the assigned height of this node, which is the smaller of the node's preferred height and the height of the container itself. Its width is always the full width of the container. The actual positioning and sizing of the node is performed by the code on lines 8 to 10, which uses the layoutNode() function. This is one of several script functions provided by the Container class that you can use to set the location/size of a node, some of which are listed here:

```
public function positionNode(node:Node, x:Number, y:Number);
public function positionNode(node:Node, x:Number, y:Number,
                             width:Number, height:Number);
public function setNodeHeight(node:Node, height:Number):Boolean;
public function setNodeWidth(node:Node, width:Number):Boolean;
```

```
public function resizeNode(node:Node, width:Number,
                           height:Number):Boolean;
public function layoutNode(node:Node, x:Number, y:Number,
                           width:Number, height:Number):Boolean;
public function layoutNode(node:Node, areaX:Number, areaY:Number,
                           areaW:Number, area:Number, hpos:HPos,
                           vpos:VPos):Boolean;
```

The `positionNode()` functions move a node to a given location without changing its size, the `setNodeHeight()` and `setNodeWidth()` functions changes the size of a node without moving it, while the `layoutNode()` functions both move and resize the node. Here, we discuss only the last of these functions, both because it is the most general and because it is the one that is used in the implementation of the `FXBorder` class. Here's how we use this function to place the node in the north position of the container:

```
layoutNode(node, 0, 0, width, topSpace, nodeHPos, nodeVPos);
```

The first five arguments specify the node and the bounds of the area in which it is to placed, relative to its parent container. Here, the area is anchored at the origin of the `FXBorder` container, it has the same width as the container, and its height is given by the value of the `topSpace` variable, as computed earlier. The remaining two arguments control the positioning of the node within this area. We need to tell the `layoutNode()` function how to position the node because it may not be possible to resize it so that it fills all the available space, or the node might not want to be resized. Any node that is not `Resizable`, such as the text nodes used in Listing 25-2, will always have a fixed size, which may be smaller than the space available, whereas it may be possible to set the width and height of a `Resizable` object, such as a `Button`, so that it occupies all the allocated area. However, if a `Resizable` has a maximum height/width that is smaller than the height and width of the area in which it has been placed, it will not be resized beyond its maximum sizes.[4] Whether a node is expanded to fill the layout area depends on the following factors:

- The value returned by its `getVFill()` for vertical fill and `getHFill()` functions
- The values of the `vfill` and `hfill` variables of the node's `layoutInfo` object, if it has one, which take precedence over the values returned by the node functions

The `layoutNode()` function takes these values into account, so you don't need to code this logic into your container implementation.

---

[4] Recall from Chapter 17 that the maximum width of a resizable node can be set either by overriding its `getMaxWidth()` function or by setting the `maxWidth` variable of a `LayoutInfo` object and installing in the node's `layoutInfo` variable.

Take a look back at Figure 25-4. You can see in that figure that the `Button` in the center position of the `FXBorder` container has not been expanded to fill all the otherwise unused space. It is not so easy to see that the `Text` objects in the other four positions have their original sizes but are centered in the north, south, east, and west locations. In the case of the `Button`, which is resizable, this is because its `getVFill()` and `getHFill()` functions both return `false` and there is no `layoutInfo` object to override these values. In the case of the `Text` objects, it is because they are not resizable.

The default horizontal and vertical positions of the nodes within their layout areas are obtained from the `nodeHPos` and `nodeVPos` variables of the `FXBorder` object and passed to the `layoutNode()` function. These default to `HPos.CENTER` and `VPos.CENTER`, respectively, which is why the text nodes appear in the center of their respective areas. Changing the value of either of these variables will affect the positioning of the north, south, east, and west nodes. The `layoutNode()` function allows a node to override the `hpos` and `vpos` arguments by using its `layoutInfo` variable. This is illustrated in Listing 25-5, which you will find in the file `javafxcustom/FXBorderExample2.fx`.

Listing 25-5 Controlling the Horizontal Positioning of Nodes in an `FXBorder` Object

```
1    Stage {
2        title: "FXBorder #2"
3        width: 250 height: 100
4        var scene:Scene;
5        scene: scene = Scene {
6            content: [
7                FXBorder {
8                    width: bind scene.width
9                    height: bind scene.height
10                   hgap: 4 vgap: 4
11                   nodeHPos: HPos.LEFT
12                   content: [
13                       Text {
14                           content: "North"
15                           layoutInfo: FXBorderLayoutInfo {
16                               position: FXPosition.NORTH
17                           }
18                       }
19                       Text {
20                           content: "South"
21                           layoutInfo: FXBorderLayoutInfo {
22                               position: FXPosition.SOUTH
23                               hpos: HPos.RIGHT
24                           }
25                       }
26                   ]
```

```
27                     }
28                ]
29           }
30      }
```

The overall horizontal positioning for nodes in the `FXBorder` container is set to `HPos.LEFT` by the assignment to the `nodeHPos` variable on line 11. The container has text nodes in the north and south positions. The node in the north position, created on lines 13 to 18, does not override the default horizontal positioning, whereas the one in the south position does, by setting the `hpos` variable of its `FXBorderLayoutInfo` object to `HPos.RIGHT` on line 23. The result of this is that the node in the north position is left-aligned, whereas the one in the south position is right-aligned, as shown in Figure 25-6.

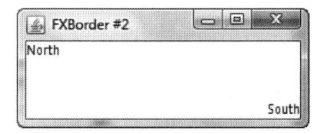

Figure 25-6   Changing node positioning in an **FXBorder** container

Using the `Panel` Class

In most cases, you would build a custom container with the intent of using it more than once. Sometimes, though, you might find that your layout needs are so specific to the problem at hand that it is unlikely that you will ever need the same code again. In cases such as this, it is not worth creating a new class to encapsulate the layout code. Instead, you can use the `Panel` class to implement the logic of the layout in functions that are linked to the panel when it is initialized. The panel calls these functions when it needs to get its preferred width, preferred height, lay out its child nodes, and so on. Table 25-3 lists the variables that the `Panel` class provides that let you hook into its lifecycle.

Table 25-3   Variables of the **Panel** Class

Variable	Type	Access	Description
`maxHeight`	`function():Number`	RW	Calculates the maximum height of the container
`maxWidth`	`function():Number`	RW	Calculates the maximum width of the container
`minHeight`	`function():Number`	RW	Calculates the minimum height of the container

Table 25-3 **Variables of the `Panel` Class** *(Continued)*

Variable	Type	Access	Description
minWidth	function():Number	RW	Calculates the minimum width of the container
prefHeight	function(width: Number):Number	RW	Calculates the preferred height of the container
prefHeight	function(height: Number):Number	RW	Calculates the preferred width of the container
onLayout	function():Void	RW	Lays out the container's child nodes

Each of these variables corresponds to one of the functions of the `Container` class that you would override if you were implementing a custom container by subclassing. The `Panel` class overrides the `Container` method to call the function installed in the corresponding variable so that, for example, the `Panel`'s implementation of `getPrefHeight()` simply calls the function pointed at by its `prefHeight` variable. Every variable initially points to a default function, so you don't need to supply a function for each of these variables.

The function in the `onLayout` variable implements a default layout policy that gives every child node its preferred size but does not change its position. The code in Listing 25-6 uses the `Panel` class to create a one-off container that places all of its child nodes such that their centers are over the center of the `Panel` itself.

Listing 25-6   **An Example of the Use of the `Panel` Class**

```
1    Stage {
2        title: "Panel #1"
3        width: 400
4        height: 400
5        var scene:Scene;
6        scene: scene = Scene {
7            var p:Panel;
8            content: [
9                p = Panel {
10                   width: bind scene.width
11                   height: bind scene.height
12                   content: [
13                       ImageView {
14                           image: Image {
15                               url: "{__DIR__}allrollout.jpg"
16                           }
17                       }
18                       Text {
```

```
19                      content: "Apollo 11 roll out"
20                      font: Font { size: 28 }
21                      fill: Color.YELLOW
22                      opacity: 0.7
23                  }
24              ]
25              onLayout: function() {
26                  p.resizeContent();
                for (node in Container.getManaged(p.content))    {
28                      Container.positionNode(node, 0, 0,      p.width,
29                                      p.height,
30                                      HPos.CENTER,
31                                      VPos.CENTER);
32                  }
33              }
34              prefHeight: function(width:Number) {
35                  var result = 0.0;
36                  for (node in Container.getManaged(p.content))    {
37                      result = Math.max(result,
38                              Container.getNodePrefHeight(node));
39                  }
40                  result;
41              }
42              prefWidth: function(height:Number) {
43                  var result = 0.0;
                for (node in Container.getManaged(p.content))    {
45                      result = Math.max(result,
46                              Container.getNodePrefWidth(node));
47                  }
48                  result;
49              }
50          }
51      ]
52  }
53 }
```

The code on lines 25 to 33 implements the layout policy. The `resizeContent()` function that is used on line 26 gives every child node its preferred size, and then the loop on lines 27 to 32 uses the `positionNode()` function of the `Container` class to center all of those nodes in the panel. You can see that we don't have to write any complicated code to compute the locations of each node because the `positionNode()` function does it all for us. To arrange for it to center everything, we specify the whole panel as the area within which the node is to be placed and request horizontal and vertical centering. You can see the result of running this code, which you'll find in the file `javafxcustom/PanelExample1.fx`, in Figure 25-7.

Figure 25-7 Centering nodes using
the **Panel** class

As you can see, the text is centered over the image, which itself is centered in the scene. If you resize the stage, you will see that the relative positions of the text and image nodes remain the same at all times.

Custom Controls

Creating a custom control requires a little bit more work than building a custom node because you need to partition the control's functionality into three separate classes: the control itself, the skin, and the behavior. In this section, we first look at what these three classes are, and then you'll learn how they work by building a custom control.

Custom Control Architecture

A control is logically composed of three parts:

- A part that implements the control's functionality, which is provided by the `Control` subclass itself.
- A part that provides the control's visual representation, called the control's *skin*.
- A part that handles user interaction with the control, called the *behavior*.

If you are familiar with the Model-View-Controller (MVC) pattern commonly used both to build GUI applications and UI toolkits (such as Swing), you will probably recognize that each of the three parts of a control corresponds to one of the roles in the MVC pattern:

- The control itself plays the role of the *model*. Variables in the control class let you specify what the control should do and represent the data that it displays/allows the user to modify. The control itself also provides the hooks to which application code can attach callback functions that are called when the control changes state. A control is, of course, also a node, and so all the public variables of the `Node` class are also available to you. Among the variables that you are particularly likely to use are `layoutX` and `layoutY` for positioning and `disable`, which you can use to determine whether the user should be allowed to interact with the control.

- The skin is the part that provides the nodes that determine the control's visual appearance. It is, therefore, the *view* in the MVC pattern. You can change the appearance of a control by installing a different skin, but each skin uses the same model state in the control class to decide what to display and how to display it. It is the skin that determines, among other things, the colors used to draw the control and its default size.

- The behavior is responsible for capturing user interaction with the control via the mouse/keyboard and translating these actions into state changes in the model/view. The behavior is the *controller* in the MVC model.

To allow the behavior class to respond to mouse events directed to the control, the skin needs to install mouse-handling functions in the actual nodes that make up the control's visual representation. When mouse events are delivered, the handlers invoke appropriate functions in the behavior class that will take whatever action is necessary. The skin class therefore needs to be written with knowledge of the behavior class and, in fact, each skin implementation is typically paired with a behavior class that is used whenever that skin is installed. As you'll learn later in this chapter, the skin is responsible for creating the behavior object when it is bound to a control. Key events are passed directly from the control to the behavior object without involving the skin.

To make this discussion more concrete, let's look at the roles that these three classes play in the implementation of the `Button` control. A `Button` is a control that a user presses to perform some action. There are various ways to represent a button, but all buttons display either some text or an icon that conveys to the user the action associated with it, or possibly both.

The JavaFX `Button` class, playing the role of the MVC model, has variables that allow the application to specify what it should display, some hints as to how it should display it, and a function to be called when the button is pressed. Here is a subset of the parameters that an application can use to configure a `Button` object:

- The text that should be displayed by the button (for example, OK)
- The font to be used to draw the text
- An image (or other node) to be displayed together with the text (or on its own)
- The relative position of the text and image

It is the application's job to supply this information, but it does not need to concern itself with how the button uses these values to create its visual representation; this will be taken care of by the button's skin class.

The skin creates nodes that provide the button's appearance. When a control is instantiated, it creates its skin, which will determine how the control is represented on the screen. Figure 25-8 shows a possible way to skin a `Button` control.

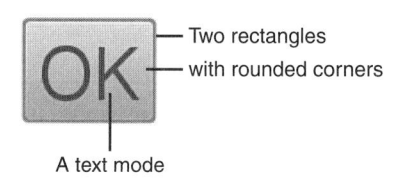

Figure 25-8   A possible way to skin a **Button** control

Here, the skin has created three nodes: two rectangles with rounded corners that represent, respectively, the focus border and the body of the button and a text node that displays its text. This is a greatly simplified representation of what the default skin for this control actually does.

To activate a button, the user can either click it with the mouse or give it the focus and then click a platform-dependent key, which on Windows is the spacebar. The skin and behavior classes are responsible for implementing this functionality as follows:

- When it is created, the skin listens for mouse events on the `Button` control.

- When the mouse is pressed over the `Button`, an event is delivered to the skin and delegated to a function in the behavior, which moves the keyboard focus to the `Button` (so that key presses are delivered to it) and *arms* it, which causes the skin to redraw it so that it looks pressed.

- When the mouse is released, another event is delivered to the skin and delegated to the behavior. If the mouse is still over the `Button`, the behavior calls the `Button`'s `fire()` function, which causes the function referenced by its `action` variable to be invoked. This is how application code that is tied to the `Button` is called.

- If the user presses or releases a key while the `Button` has the focus, it is delivered to the control and then passed to the behavior. If the user presses the spacebar, the `Button` is armed (just as it is in response to a mouse press). If the user releases the spacebar when the `Button` is armed, it calls the `Button`'s `fire()` function, just as if the mouse had been pressed and then released.

You don't need to remember all these details unless you are going to write your own control—the point is that the events that are significant to a control and what happens when those events occur depend on the implementation details of the skin and the behavior.

Control Appearance and Styling

In some cases, a control's (model) class provides variables that let you influence some aspects of the control's appearance. For example, you can use the `font` variable to specify the font used to draw the text on a button. The default buttons have rounded corners and are filled with color gradients, but because neither of these is a mandatory feature of a button, the model class does not have any variables that let you read or set the values that control them. Instead, these variables belong to the skin class.

A control's skin is created by the control itself. Each control has a dedicated skin, derived from the `javafx.scene.control.Skin` class. Skins are usually grouped together into *themes*—the idea is that you would implement a theme that provides a consistent look and feel across all the controls. At the time of this writing, the theming mechanism, although present, is not part of the public API, so it is not really possible to write your own theme. The controls currently all get their skins from a default theme and provide a set of properties that you can use to customize their appearance by using a CSS style sheet, as you saw in Chapter 23, "Style Sheets." Unfortunately, the mechanism used to apply style sheet rules to skin properties, like the theming mechanism, is not part of the public API in JavaFX version 1.3. As a result, it is not possible to use CSS to style a custom control without becoming dependent on undocumented interfaces. For that reason, you won't read any more about it in this book.

A Skeleton Custom Control

The easiest way to explain the division of functionality between the control, the skin, and the behavior is to show a very basic example of a custom control. This example is simple enough that you can use it as a starting point for any control that you want to write, because it creates the linkage between the parts of the control and implements the basic set of functions that all controls are required to have. The relationships between these three classes are shown in diagrammatic form in Figure 25-9.

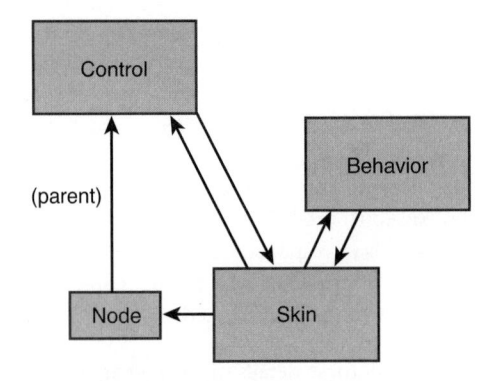

Figure 25-9   The relationships between a control and its skin and behavior classes

The `Control` Class

We'll start with the control. For the sake of simplicity, the control just displays some text. It has variables that let you configure the text, the font used to draw the text, and the text color. The implementation of the control class, which is called `MyControl` and which you'll find in the file `javafxcustom/MyControl.fx`, is shown in Listing 25-7.

Listing 25-7 **A Basic Custom Control**

```
public class MyControl extends Control {
   public var textFill:Color = Color.BLACK;
   public var font = Font.DEFAULT;
   public var text:String;
   override var skin = MySkin {};
}
```

A custom control is a subclass of `javafx.scene.control.Control`, which is derived from the `Parent` class and the `Resizable` mixin. Our simple control declares the three variables that let you customize its appearance and overrides the `skin` variable, inherited from `Control`, to assign an instance of the our custom skin class that provides the control's visual representation. The `skin` variable and the `tooltip` variable, which we discussed in Chapter 22, "Cross-Platform Controls," are the only public variables that the `Control` class adds to those of its base classes. These variables are described in Table 25-4.

Table 25-4 **Variables of the `Control` Class**

Variable	Type	Access	Default	Description
skin	Skin	RW		The class that is responsible for the visual representation of the control
tooltip	Tooltip	RW		The tooltip for this control

It is worth noting that application code can override the default skin by installing a different one when the control is created, like this:

```
MyControl {
   text: "Control with custom skin"
   skin: MyOtherSkin {}
}
```

The `Skin` Class

A control's skin is derived from the `javafx.scene.skin.Skin` class, which has the three public variables listed in Table 25-5.

Chapter 25 Building Custom Controls

Table 25-5 Variables of the `Skin` Class

Variable	Type	Access	Default	Description
control	Control	R		The `Control` with which the skin is associated
behavior	Behavior	R		The behavior class for this skin
node	Node	R		The root of the node tree that provides the control's visual appearance

Of these, the `behavior` and `node` variables are initialized by the skin class itself, whereas the `control` variable is set by the `Control` class when the skin is installed. Listing 25-8 shows an implementation of the skin class for our simple custom control.

Listing 25-8 A Simple Skin Implementation

```
1    public class MySkin extends Skin {
2        var c = bind control as MyControl;
3        override var behavior = MyBehavior {};
4        override var node = Group {
5            content: [
6                Text {
7                    content: bind c.text
8                    fill: bind c.textFill;
9                    font: bind c.font
10                   textOrigin: TextOrigin.TOP
11               }
12           ]
13           onMousePressed: function(evt) {
14               (behavior as MyBehavior).mousePress(evt);
15           }
16       };
17
18       override function getMinWidth():Number { 0 }
19       override function getMinHeight():Number { 0 }
20       override function getMaxWidth():Number { Number.MAX_VALUE }
21       override function getMaxHeight():Number { Number.MAX_VALUE }
22       override function getPrefWidth(height:Number):Number {
23           Container.getNodePrefWidth(node, height)
24       }
25       override function getPrefHeight(width:Number):Number {
26           Container.getNodePrefHeight(node, width)
27       }
28
29       override function contains(x:Number, y:Number) {
30           node.contains(x, y);
```

```
31          }
32          override function intersects(x:Number, y:Number,
33                                       width:Number, height:Number) {
34              node.intersects(x, y, width, height);
35          }
36      }
```

The main function of this class is to create the node tree that provides the node's visual representation, which is done by overriding the node variable on lines 4 to 16. In this case, the control is simply a wrapper for a text object, so the node is just a group containing a text node.[5] Notice that the variables of the text object are initialized from the values of the variables of the control itself. Access to these variables is through the variable c, which is declared on line 2 and which is bound to the value of the control variable, cast to the actual type of the custom control. There are two reasons for using a binding here:

- Binding causes changes to the control variables to be reflected automatically in the related variables of the skin, so the visual appearance of the control will change accordingly.
- When this code is executed, the control variable will actually be null. It is only after the control variable has been set from the Control object that the correct values for the text node's font and color will be available.

As part of the initialization of the node tree, on lines 13 to 15 we install a mouse handler in the group node. You'll learn why this is done in our discussion of the behavior class later in this section.

The functions on lines 18 to 27 are overrides that return the minimum, maximum, and preferred sizes of the control. These functions are actually called from the functions of the same name that the Control class inherits from Resizable. They have to be implemented by the skin because the correct answers depend on how the skin represents the control—if, for example, we created a skin that added a colored circle to the text node, these sizes would be different than if we just had the text node. The implementations shown here are about as basic as they could be—the minimum and maximum sizes are fixed, whereas the preferred height and width are obtained from the text node itself. In a real skin with a more complex geometry, you might want to provide more sophisticated versions.

Finally, the two functions on lines 29 to 35 are required to exist in some form because they are abstract functions of the Skin class. The contains() function returns whether a given point lies inside the visual representation of the control, whereas the interects() function returns whether the control lies at least partly inside a specified area. For this very basic skin, we can simply delegate both functions to the group node. For a more complicated skin, you might need additional logic here, especially if it consists of multiple regions

---

[5] It is common to use a group because you can attach mouse handlers to a group that will catch mouse events for all of its nested controls. See the discussion of the behavior class for more details.

with areas inside the bounds of the control that are not actually part of the control (that is, transparent regions).

The `Behavior` Class

The function of the behavior class is to respond to user input to the control, represented by mouse and key events. In this case, the control is so basic that it does not actually need to respond to user interaction, so the behavior class simply reports when certain events are detected.

All behavior classes derive from `javafx.scene.control.Behavior`, which has one public variable, described in Table 25-6.

Table 25-6 Variable of the `Behavior` Class

Variable	Type	Access	Default	Description
skin	Skin	R		The skin that is providing the control's visual representation

The behavior class is created by the skin; typically the skin and behavior implementations are tightly coupled, in the sense that each needs to know details of the other. The behavior class for our simple control is created on line 3 of the skin class in Listing 25-8. The `skin` variable of this class is set automatically from a trigger by the skin class when the behavior object is assigned to its `behavior` variable.

The implementation of the behavior class for our simple control is shown in Listing 25-9.

Listing 25-9 A Simple Behavior Implementation

```
1    class MyBehavior extends Behavior {
2        function mousePress(evt:MouseEvent) {
3            println("Mouse press on control");
4            skin.control.requestFocus();
5        }
6
7        override function callActionForEvent(evt) {
8            println("Key event: {evt}");
9        }
10   }
```

As you can see, the behavior responds both to a mouse press and to any key events that are delivered to the control.

As you know, mouse events are delivered to nodes. The nodes that make up the control belong to the skin, so it is the job of the skin to ensure that any mouse events that the behavior needs to respond to are delivered to it. The skin must, therefore, install mouse handlers in any node that it creates, and those handlers must notify the behavior when any events are received. For our simple control, a mouse handler for mouse presses was installed in the group object created by the skin on lines 13 to 15 of Listing 25-8. This mouse handler calls the `mousePress()` function of the behavior when an event is received. This is an example of the coupling between the skin and the behavior—the skin needs to know which events are of interest to the behavior and which function of the behavior should be called when they are received. In this case, the `mousePress()` function, shown on lines 2 to 5 of Listing 25-9, simply records the fact that an event was received and moves the input focus to the control.

Key events are delivered to the `callActionForEvent()` function of the behavior automatically by code in the `Control` class. Our simple behavior does nothing other than record that the event was received.

> **Note**
>
> For all key events to be delivered by the control class, it is important that the focus is always passed to the control class itself, as shown on line 4 of Listing 25-9. If you move the focus to one of the nodes created by the skin, key events will be delivered to that node and will not be seen by the behavior class.

A Media Player Control Bar

As you have seen, it is quite simple to create a basic custom control. In this section, you'll see how to build something slightly more complex, namely a component that enables you to control video playback from a `MediaView`. You can see what this control looks like in Figure 25-10.

Figure 25-10   A custom media player control bar

Chapter 25 Building Custom Controls

The default skin for this control is made up of five parts, each of which is identified in the figure:

- A Stop button, which is activated only while playback is in progress.
- A Play button, which is visible only when playback is paused or stopped.
- A Pause button, which is visible while playback is in progress. The Pause button is never available at the same time as the Play button, so they actually occupy the same space. In Figure 25-10, only the Pause button is visible.
- A control that looks a little like a slider and which is used to represent and control the playback position. The slider thumb can be dragged right or left to move the current playback position forward or backward, respectively. An additional feature of this custom slider, which is not available from the `javafx.scene.control.Slider` class, is the solid fill shown in Figure 25-10, which indicates how much of the video has been buffered so far and which updates as video content is received.
- A text control that shows the current playback position and the total playback time.

An example that uses this control is shown in Listing 25-10, which you can find in the file `javafxcustom/MediaPlayerBarExample.fx`. If you run this code, you'll get the result shown in Figure 25-10.

Listing 25-10 A Media Player with a Custom Control Bar

```
1   var mediaURL = "http://sun.edgeboss.net/download/sun/media/"
2              "1460825906/1460825906_2956241001_big-buck-bunny-      640x360.flv";
3
4   def player = MediaPlayer {
5       autoPlay: false
6       media: Media { source: mediaURL }
7   };
8
9   Stage {
10      title : "MediaPlayerBar Example"
11      var scene:Scene;
12      scene: scene = Scene {
13          width: 700
14          height: 500
15          fill: Color.BLACK
16          content: [
17              FXBorder {
18                  width: bind scene.width
19                  height: bind scene.height
20                  vgap: 8
21                  content: [
22                      ScalingMediaView {
23                          stretch: true
24                          mediaPlayer: player
25                          layoutInfo: FXBorderLayoutInfo {
```

```
26                              position: FXPosition.CENTER
27                              hfill: true
28                              vfill: true
29                          }
30                      }
31                      MediaPlayerBar {
32                          player: player
33                          normalFill: Color.LIGHTGRAY
34                          activeFill: Color.YELLOW
35                          layoutInfo: FXBorderLayoutInfo {
36                              position: FXPosition.SOUTH
37                              hfill: true
38                          }
39                      }
40                  ]
41              }
42          ]
43      }
44  }
```

The layout is managed by the `FXBorder` container that we created earlier in this chapter and the video itself is shown by an instance of the `ScalingMediaView` class that we built in Chapter 19, "Video and Audio." We use this class rather than `javafx.scene.media.MediaView` because it adapts itself automatically to the space that is given to it and scales the video accordingly, while preserving its aspect ratio. Because we want as much space as possible to be used for video playback, we assign the media viewer to the center position of the `FXBorder` container and use a `LayoutInfo` object with both `hfill` and `vfill` set to `true`. Our new custom control, implemented in the `MediaPlayerBar` class, is placed in the south position of the layout, and because its `LayoutInfo` object has its `hfill` variable set to `true` and `vfill` defaulted to `false`, it will be stretched right across the bottom of the scene and will be given its preferred height.

In the sections that follow, you'll see the implementation of the `MediaPlayerBar` control, its skin, and its associated behavior class.

The `MediaPlayerBar` Control Class

The `MediaPlayerBar` class is the control itself and is, therefore, derived from `Control`. Listing 25-11 shows the code for this.

Listing 25-11   The Implementation of the `MediaPlayerBar` Class

```
1   public class MediaPlayerBar extends Control {
2       public var player:MediaPlayer;
3       public var normalFill:Paint = Color.LIGHTGRAY;
4       public var activeFill:Paint = Color.WHITE;
5
6       public-read def playing =
7                   bind player.status == MediaPlayer.PLAYING;
```

```
 8          public-read def paused = bind player.paused;
 9          public-read def totalTime:Duration =
10                              bind player.media.duration;
11        public-read def currentTime:Duration =
12                              bind player.currentTime;
13          public-read def bufferedTime:Duration =
14                  bind player.bufferProgressTime on replace    {
15              if (bufferedTime > currentTime and not paused) {
16                  player.play();
17              }
18          }
19          public-read def fractionPlayed = bind if (totalTime == 0s) 0
20                                  else currentTime.div(totalTime);
21          public-read def fractionBuffered =
22              bind if (totalTime == 0s) 0
23                  else bufferedTime.div(totalTime);
24
25          override var skin = MediaPlayerBarSkin {};
26
27          public function play() {
28              player.play();
29          }
30
31          public function pause() {
32              player.pause();
33          }
34
35          public function stop() {
36              player.stop();
37          }
38
39          public function setPlayPosition(position:Number) {
40              player.currentTime = player.media.duration * position;
41          }
42
43          public function adjustPlayPosition(amount:Duration) {
44              player.currentTime += amount;
45          }
46      }
```

This is a relatively simple class. It is parameterized by three variables, declared with default initial values on lines 2 to 4. The `player` variable refers to the `MediaPlayer` object that contains the video (or audio) to be played. In Listing 25-10, this variable is set in the object initializer for the `MediaPlayerBar` object, but everything in the implementation (specifically, in the skin class) that depends on it is linked to it via a binding, so it is possible to change it any time. The `normalFill` color is used to draw most of the control, including the buttons, the slider outline, the fill that represents how much of the video has been buffered, and the text at the right of the control. The `activeFill` color is used when the mouse is moved over one of the buttons while they are in the active state—for example, if the mouse is placed over the Pause button while playback is in progress, its color will change from `normalFill` to `activeFill`.

The rest of the class consists mainly of variables that application code can read and functions that can be called to control the underlying `MediaPlayer`. When designing the public API of the control class, keep the following points in mind:

- The internals of the control should be invisible to application code. That is, application code should not need to be aware of the fact that the control is partly implemented by a skin class and a behavior class, both of which can be changed. In particular, you should not provide application programming interface (API) that makes sense only if the control is represented in a specific way. For example, the default skin for this control represents the thumb on the playback slider with a rectangle, but it would not be a good idea to add variables to the control class that would allow application code to read or change the width and height the thumb, because these would be meaningless if a skin that drew the thumb differently (for example, as a circle) were installed.

- The users of the control API are the application itself, the skin, and the behavior. In Listing 25-11, the variables declared on lines 2 to 23 are all provided for the benefit of the skin, which uses their values to keep the control's visual representation synchronized with its state. Similarly, the functions declared on lines 27 to 45 are used by the behavior to change the control's state. You will typically find that the variables and functions used internally by the control are also useful to application code.

The `MediaPlayerBar` Skin Class

The skin is typically the most complex part of a control. In the case of the media player, the skin consists of the `MediaPlayerBarSkin` class itself and four custom nodes—three simple ones for Play, Pause, and Stop buttons, and a more complex one for the time slider. In fact, the time slider could have been written as a custom control, complete with its own skin and behavior class but, for the sake of simplicity, in the implementation shown here it is a custom node. The code for the skin class itself is shown in Listing 25-12. You'll find all the code relating to the skin in the file `javafxcustom/MediaPlayerBarSkin.fx`.

Listing 25-12   The `MediaPlayerBar`'s Default Skin Class

```
1     public class MediaPlayerBarSkin extends Skin {
2         public var dragThumbColor = Color.RED;
3         public var thumbColor = Color.GREEN;
4
5         def bar = bind control as MediaPlayerBar;
6         def barBehavior = bind behavior as MediaPlayerBarBehavior;
7         var timeSlider:TimeSlider;
8         def controlSize = 12;
9         def hpad = 4;
10        def vpad = 2;
```

900 Chapter 25 Building Custom Controls

```
11          def defSliderWidth = 100;
12          def textWidth = 72;
13          def beforeSlider = hpad + controlSize + hpad
14                              + controlSize + hpad;
15          def afterSlider = hpad + textWidth + hpad;
16          def fractionPlayed= bind bar.fractionPlayed on replace {
17              timeSlider.setThumbPositionFromMedia(fractionPlayed);
18          }
19
20          override var behavior = MediaPlayerBarBehavior {};
21          init {
22              node = Group {
23                  var stop:Node;
24                  var play:Node;
25                  var pause:Node;
26                  var slider:Node;
27                  content: [
28                      stop = StopButton {
29                          layoutX: hpad
30                          layoutY: vpad
31                          onMousePressed: function(evt) {
32                              barBehavior.stopPressed();
33                          }
34                      }
35                      play = PlayButton { // Play button
36                          layoutX: bind stop.boundsInParent.maxX + hpad
37                          layoutY: bind stop.boundsInParent.minY
38                          visible: bind not bar.playing
39                          onMousePressed: function(evt) {
40                              barBehavior.playPressed();
50                          }
51                      }
52                      pause = PauseButton {
52                          layoutX: bind play.layoutX
54                          layoutY: bind stop.boundsInParent.minY
55                          visible: bind bar.playing
56                          onMousePressed: function(evt) {
57                              barBehavior.pausePressed();
58                          }
59                      }
60                      timeSlider = TimeSlider {
61                          layoutX: bind play.boundsInParent.maxX + hpad
62                          layoutY: bind play.boundsInParent.minY
63                          height: controlSize
64                          width: bind bar.width - beforeSlider
65                                      - afterSlider
66                          thumbColor: bind thumbColor
```

```
67                    dragThumbColor: bind dragThumbColor
68                    fill: bind bar.normalFill
69                    fractionBuffered: bind bar.fractionBuffered
70                    onMoved: function(position) {
71                        barBehavior.playPositionChanged(position);
72                    }
73                }
74                Text {
75                    textOrigin: TextOrigin.TOP
76                    layoutX: bind bar.width - hpad - textWidth
77                    layoutY: bind stop.boundsInParent.minY + 1
78                    content:
79                      bind "{formatTime(bar.currentTime)}"
80                            "/{formatTime(bar.totalTime)}";
81                    fill: bind bar.normalFill
82                }
83            ]
84            effect: Lighting {
85                light: DistantLight {
86                    azimuth: 45
87                    elevation: 45
88                }
89            }
90            onMouseWheelMoved: function(evt) {
91                barBehavior.mouseWheelMoved(evt.wheelRotation);
92            }
93        }
94    }
95
96    protected override function getPrefWidth(height:Number) {
97        beforeSlider + defSliderWidth + afterSlider;
98    }
99
100   protected override function getPrefHeight(width:Number) {
101       controlSize + 2 * vpad;
102   }
103
104   override function contains(x:Number, y:Number) {
105       node.contains(x, y);
106   }
107
108   override function intersects(x:Number, y:Number,
109                                width:Number, height:Number) {
110       node.intersects(x, y, width, height);
111   }
112
113   function formatTime(time:Duration):String {
```

```
114                var minutes = time.toMinutes() as Integer;
115                var seconds = (time.toSeconds() mod 60) as Integer;
116                "{%02d minutes}:{%02d seconds}"
117            }
118        }
```

The first part of the class declares variables and constants that are used elsewhere. The `dragThumbColor` and `thumbColor` variables are the default colors for the slider thumb when it is being dragged and not being dragged, respectively. Because these are public variables of the skin, they can be set from a style sheet applied to the owning control, as you'll see later.

You will see code like that shown on lines 5 and 6 in almost every skin implementation. Here, we define variables that the skin can use to refer to the control and behavior classes. As you already know, the skin has variables called `control` and `behavior` that you can use to reference these objects, but it is more convenient to have variables like `bar` and `barBehavior` that are declared to be of the actual type of the control and behavior classes. Without these variables, many (if not most) references to the control and behavior classes would require a cast.

The `getPrefWidth()` and `getPrefHeight()` functions on lines 96 to 102 are implemented to return the preferred sizes of the skin. The preferred width is the sum of the widths of the buttons, set to 12 pixels on line 8; the preferred width of the time slider, which is arbitrarily set at 100 pixels on line 11; the space allocated to the text for the playback times (72 pixels, see line 12); and some padding that appears at the start of the row of controls and between each individual control. The preferred height is the sum of the control height (given by the `controlSize` variable on line 8) and some vertical padding that will appear above and below the controls. Note that there are variables called `beforeSlider` and `afterSlider` (see lines 13–15) that contain the horizontal space that is required by everything that appears to the left of the slider and everything that appears its right. These values are used later when determining the actual amount of space available for the time slider once the whole control has been given its actual width when the user interface is laid out. The bulk of the code is the implementation of the `init` block on lines 21 to 94. This code constructs the node tree for the control, which is a group with nodes for the Stop button, the Play button, the Pause button, the time slider, and the text. The nodes are manually positioned by setting their `layoutX` and `layoutY` variables so that they appear along a line with the Stop button on the left and the text on the right. The horizontal position of each node is based on that of the neighbor to the left. For example, here is how the Play button is positioned:

```
1    play = PlayButton { // Play button
2        layoutX: bind stop.boundsInParent.maxX + hpad
3        layoutY: bind stop.boundsInParent.minY
4        visible: bind not bar.playing
5        onMousePressed: function(evt) {
6            barBehavior.playPressed();
7        }
8    }
```

The `layoutX` variable of the Play button is calculated by taking the x coordinate of the right side of the node to its left, in this case the Stop button, and adding some horizontal padding. The `layoutY` variable of the button is the same as that of its neighbor. Because the Stop and Play buttons (and the Pause button) have the same height, this ensures that they are correctly positioned relative to each other.

Lines 4 to 7 of this code illustrate how a skin typically interacts with the control and the behavior. The Play button is supposed to be visible only when the video is not already playing. To give effect to this rule, its `visible` variable is bound to the playing variable of the control. If you look back to the control implementation in Listing 25-11, you'll see that this variable is bound to the `status` variable of the `MediaPlayer`. As a result of the binding, the visibility of the Play button will change automatically when the media starts playing or stops playing. There is similar code in the implementation of the Pause button on lines 52 to 59 of Listing 25-12.

The code on lines 5 to 7 captures mouse presses on the Play button. When the button is pressed, video playback should begin. To give effect to this, the mouse handler calls the `playPressed()` function of the behavior. By decoupling the action from the mouse handler in this way, you make it possible to change what the behavior does in response to a button press without having to change the skin class. The other buttons also handle mouse presses by calling functions in the behavior class.

The `StopButton`, `PlayButton`, and `PauseButton` classes are custom nodes that provide a basic representation of a button. We don't use the standard `Button` class here because we don't need anything that complex. For the sake of completeness, here's how the `StopButton` class is implemented:

```
class StopButton extends CustomNode {
    override var children =
        Rectangle {
            width: controlSize
            height: controlSize
            fill: bind if (hover and bar.playing) bar.activeFill
                  else bar.normalFill
        }
}
```

As you can see, the only interesting feature of this class is the value assigned to its `fill` variable. The intent is that the color of the button should change from `normalFill` to `activeFill` if the user moves the mouse over it when playback is in progress. The condition that the mouse should be over the button is tested by using its `hover` variable, whereas the fact that playback is in progress is obtained from the playing variable of the `MediaPlayerBar` control.

It is worth noting that the state that this class is using is held in private variables of the skin class, so you might be wondering how it can access those variables. The reason is that the `StopButton` class is actually an inner class of `MediaPlayerBarSkin`, because `MediaPlayerBarSkin` is the class for which the source file is named and the `StopButton` class is in the same source file and, as in Java, inner classes have access to all the state of the class within which they are contained. (For more on this, see the section "Classes and Script Files" in Chapter 11, "JavaFX Script Classes.")

The code on lines 84 to 89 applies a lighting effect that makes the whole control look three-dimensional. Because it is applied at the group level, it applies to each node equally. Similarly, the handler on lines 90 to 92 also applies to every node in the group. It is called when the user moves the mouse wheel while the mouse is anywhere over the control and calls a function in the behavior. As you'll see later, this allows the user to rewind or fast forward playback by using the mouse wheel.

The largest part of the skin is the time slider, implemented by the `TimeSlider` class. Here's how this class is used by the skin:

```
1    timeSlider = TimeSlider {
2        layoutX: bind play.boundsInParent.maxX + hpad
3        layoutY: bind play.boundsInParent.minY
4        height: controlSize
5        width: bind bar.width - beforeSlider - afterSlider
6        thumbColor: bind thumbColor
7        dragThumbColor: bind dragThumbColor
8        fill: bind bar.normalFill
9        fractionBuffered: bind bar.fractionBuffered
10       onMoved: function(position) {
11           barBehavior.playPositionChanged(position);
12       }
```

Like all the other controls, the slider is positioned relative to the control to its left (in this case, the Play button). Unlike the other controls, however, it does not have a fixed width. Instead, it occupies any space that is not otherwise used. The actual width is calculated on line 5 by subtracting the space allocated to the controls to the left and right of the slider from the total width of the `MediaPlayerBar`.

The `fractionBuffered` variable controls how much of the slider's body is filled to indicate the proportion of the video content that has been loaded, in the range 0.0 to 1.0. Its value is bound to the `fractionBuffered` variable of the control class which, as shown on lines 17 to 18 of Listing 25-11 is itself bound to the result of dividing the buffered time by the total playback time. As more of the video is loaded, the value of `fractionBuffered` will increase and this will be reflected in the slider.

The implementation of the `TimeSlider` class is shown in Listing 25-13.

Listing 25-13   The `TimeSlider` Class

```
1    class TimeSlider extends CustomNode {
2        public var thumbColor:Paint = Color.GREEN;
3        public var dragThumbColor:Paint = Color.RED;
4        public var fill:Paint = Color.LIGHTGRAY;
5        public var width:Number;
6        public var height:Number;
7        public var onMoved: function(position:Number);
```

Custom Controls

```
8          public var fractionBuffered:Number;
9
10         def thumbWidth = 4;
11         def outlineWidth = 2;
12
13         var thumbPosition = 0.0;
14         var thumbMoving = false;
15
16         override var children =
17             Group {
18                 content: [
19                     Rectangle { // The fill
20                         x: 0 y: bind outlineWidth
21                         height: bind height - 2 * outlineWidth
22                         width: bind width * fractionBuffered
23                         fill: bind fill
24                     }
25                     Rectangle { // The outline
26                         x: 0 y: bind outlineWidth
27                         width: bind width
28                         height: bind height - 2 * outlineWidth
29                         stroke: bind fill
30                         strokeWidth: bind outlineWidth
31                         fill: Color.TRANSPARENT
32                     }
33                     Rectangle { // The thumb
34                         x: bind thumbPosition * width - thumbWidth / 2
35                         y: 0
36                         width: bind thumbWidth height: bind height
37                         fill: Color.TRANSPARENT
38                         stroke: bind if (thumbMoving) dragThumbColor
39                                      else thumbColor
40                         strokeWidth: bind outlineWidth
41                     }
42                 ]
43
44                 onMousePressed: function(evt) {
45                     thumbMoving = true;
46                     setThumbPositionFromMouse(evt.x);
47                 }
48                 onMouseDragged: function(evt) {
49                     thumbMoving = true;
50                     setThumbPositionFromMouse(evt.x);
51                 }
52                 onMouseReleased: function(evt) {
53                     if (onMoved != null) {
54                         onMoved(thumbPosition);
55                     }
```

```
56                          thumbMoving = false;
57                      }
58                  }
59              }
60
61              public function setThumbPositionFromMedia(pos:Number) {
62                  if (not thumbMoving) {
63                      thumbPosition = Math.max(0, Math.min(1.0, pos));
64                  }
65              }
66
67              function setThumbPositionFromMouse(x:Number) {
68                  var pos = x - outlineWidth;
69                  thumbPosition = Math.max(0, Math.min(pos, width)) / width;
70              }
71          }
```

Most of this code is straightforward, so we'll confine ourselves to discussing only the more interesting aspects. The slider is composed of three nodes—a rectangle that draws its outline (lines 25 to 32), a rectangle that represents the moving thumb (lines 33 to 41), and a filled rectangle that shows how much of the video content has been buffered (lines 19 to 24). As you have already seen, the `fractionBuffered` variable of the `TimeSlider` class is bound indirectly to the ratio of the buffered time and the total time of the media being played. On line 22 of Listing 25-13, we bind the width of the filled `Rectangle` to the product of `fractionBuffered` variable and the width of the `TimeSlider`. As a result of this, the filled part of the slider will appear to grow as more media content is buffered.

The thumb moves along the slider as the video is played. This is achieved on line 34 by binding its x coordinate to the product of the value of the `thumbPosition` variable and the width of the `TimeSlider` (with a small correction applied for the width of the thumb itself). The `thumbPosition` variable is initially 0 and can be changed in one of two ways. Firstly, and most obviously, the thumb can move as a result of media playback. The skin class defines a variable called `fractionPlayed` that is bound to the `fractionPlayed` variable of the control, which is itself bound to the ratio of the current media playback time and the total playback time:

```
def fractionPlayed= bind bar.fractionPlayed on replace {
    timeSlider.setThumbPositionFromMedia(fractionPlayed);
}
```

When the current playback time changes (that is, as the media plays or application explicitly changes it), the values of both `fractionPlayed` variables will change and the trigger shown above will fire, causing the `setThumbPositionFromMedia()` function of the skin to be called. This function, shown on lines 61 to 65 of Listing 25-13, updates the `thumbPosition` variable of the `TimeSlider` to which the thumb's position is bound. Here's the actual code that is used:

```
public function setThumbPositionFromMedia(pos:Number) {
    if (not thumbMoving) {
        thumbPosition = Math.max(0, Math.min(1.0, pos));
    }
}
```

The `pos` argument is expected to be in the range `0.0` to `1.0`, but as you can see, the `Math.max()` and `Math.min()` functions are used to ensure that an out-of-range value is clamped to the valid range. Notice that the thumb position is *not* changed if the variable `thumbMoving` is `true`, which is the case when the user is dragging the thumb with the mouse. While the thumb is being dragged, we don't want media playback to affect its position because the user would then find it difficult to move the thumb to a new location.

The code that handles the user dragging the mouse can be found on lines 44 to 57 of Listing 25-13 and is reproduced here for ease of reference:

```
onMousePressed: function(evt) {
    thumbMoving = true;
    setThumbPositionFromMouse(evt.x);
}
onMouseDragged: function(evt) {
    thumbMoving = true;
    setThumbPositionFromMouse(evt.x);
}
onMouseReleased: function(evt) {
    if (onMoved != null) {
        onMoved(thumbPosition);
    }
    thumbMoving = false;
}
```

When the mouse is pressed, the `thumbMoving` variable is set to true to inhibit updates from media playback and the `setThumbPositionFromMouse()` function is called, with the mouse's current x coordinate as its argument. The same thing happens each time a mouse drag event is received. The `setThumbPositionFromMouse()` function is implemented as follows:

```
function setThumbPositionFromMouse(x:Number) {
    var pos = x - outlineWidth;
    thumbPosition = Math.max(0, Math.min(pos, width)) / width;
}
```

The effect of this code is to update the `thumbPosition` variable to reflect the relative position of the mouse along the slider's track. Because the x coordinate of the thumb rectangle is bound to this value, the result will be that the thumb will follow the movement of the mouse. This operation is handled entirely within the skin classes (without involving the behavior) because all that is happening is that the thumb is being moved along the slider—the current playback time is not changed, and the video continues to play as normal until the mouse is released.

When the mouse *is* finally released, the function referred to by the `onMoved` variable of the `TimeSlider` is called and then the `thumbMoving` variable is reset to `false` to allow media playback updates. The skin class initializes the `onMoved` variable of the `TimeSlider` with the following function, which, as you have just seen, is called when the user releases the mouse:

```
onMoved: function(position) {
    barBehavior.playPositionChanged(position);
}
```

This allows the behavior class to act upon the user's request to change the playback position, bringing us very conveniently to the point at which we need to discuss the implementation of the behavior class.

The `MediaPlayerBar` Behavior Class

The job of the behavior class is to respond to user input received from the mouse or the keyboard. As you have seen, mouse events are received indirectly from the skin. Key events are intercepted by the control class and passed to the `callActionForEvent()` function, which is inherited from the `Behavior` class. Listing 25-14 shows the implementation of the behavior for the `MediaPlayerBar` class.

Listing 25-14   The Implementation of the `MediaPlayerBar`'s Behavior Class

```
1     package class MediaPlayerBarBehavior extends Behavior {
2         def control = bind skin.control as MediaPlayerBar;
3
4         package function playPressed() {
5             control.play();
6         }
7
8         package function pausePressed() {
9             control.pause();
10        }
11
12        package function stopPressed() {
13            control.stop();
14        }
15
16        package function playPositionChanged(position:Number) {
17            control.setPlayPosition(position);
18        }
19
20        package function mouseWheelMoved(amount:Number) {
21            control.adjustPlayPosition(amount * 1s);
22        }
23
24        public override function callActionForEvent(e:KeyEvent) {
```

```
25              if (e.code == KeyCode.VK_HOME) {
26                  control.setPlayPosition(0.0);
27              } else if (e.code == KeyCode.VK_RIGHT) {
28                  control.adjustPlayPosition(1s);
29              } else if (e.code == KeyCode.VK_LEFT) {
30                  control.adjustPlayPosition(-1s);
31              }
32          }
33      }
```

The declaration of the control variable on line 2 is something that you will see in almost all behavior classes—it makes available a reference to the control class that is properly typed to allow any of its public functions and variables to be accessed without the need for a cast. As you can see, most of the functions simply delegate to the control class itself. With the exception of the `callActionForEvent()` function, everything in this class, including the class itself, has package-level access. This is to emphasize that this class is intended to be used only by the skin that in this case, and probably in most cases, is in the same package as the behavior class.

The `callActionForEvent()` function has to be public because it is declared to be so by the `Behavior` class from which it is inherited. Any key event delivered to the control is passed to this function. As a result of the implementation shown here, the `MediaPlayerBar` responds to the keyboard as follows:

- If the Home key is pressed, the video or audio is reset to play from the start. This is achieved by calling the `setPlayPosition()` function of the control class.
- If the Right key is pressed, the current playback time is advanced by one second by calling the `adjustPlayPosition()` function of the control. Holding this key down will cause repeated calls to this function, so the playback position will continue to advance until the key is released.
- Similarly, if the Left key is pressed, the playback time is decreased by 1 second.

26
Charts

A chart is a two-dimensional or three-dimensional representation of data. The JavaFX platform provides six different types of chart, two of which also have three-dimensional variants. The chart classes are all nodes, so you can incorporate them anywhere within a scene graph and, of course, you can apply transformations to them and even animate them, if you need to.

In the first part of this chapter, we discuss the six basic chart types in some detail. Two things should immediately strike you as you look at the examples in this chapter. First, it is extremely easy to create a chart: All you have to do is create the data model, create the chart object, and then install the data in the chart; everything else is automatic. Second, even without customization, these charts have a very professional appearance, but if the defaults do not meet your requirements, they all have various customization options, which we cover as we discuss each type of chart.

The second part of this chapter concentrates on ways to customize elements that are common to all (or at least most) of the charts. Possible customizations include changing the color of almost anything in the chart, changing the font of text items, and moving or relabeling axes.

> **Note**
> In previous chapters, we listed the most useful variables for each class in tabular form. Some of the charting classes have so many variables that listing them all here would take up too much space. Instead, we describe the most important variables for each class in the text. For further information, refer to the application programming interface (API) documentation.

The example source code for this chapter can be found in the JavaFX Book More GUI project.

Chart Basics

A class hierarchy diagram for the chart classes, which can all be found in the `javafx.scene.chart` package, is shown in Figure 26-1. The chart classes derive from `javafx.scene.chart.Chart`, which provides variables that control properties that are common to all charts. There are two different types of chart: pie charts, which represent the relative magnitudes of a set of data points using slices of a circle; and XY charts, which plot data in graphical form along two axes. These two types are reflected in the class hierarchy—pie charts are derived directly from the Chart class, while the various graphical charts derive from a different subclass of Chart called XYChart.

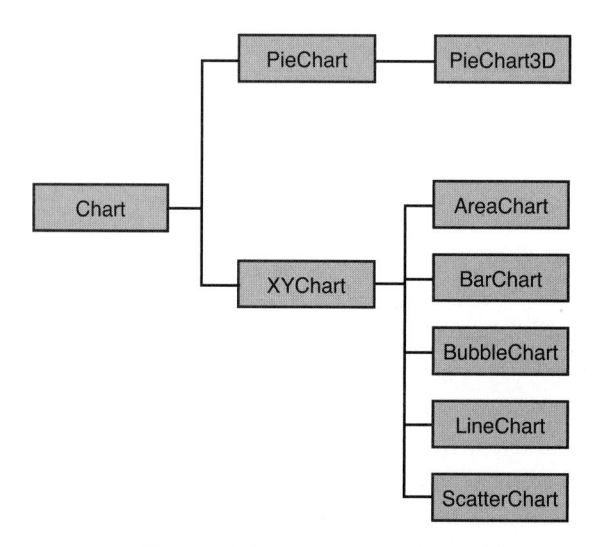

Figure 26-1   The chart classes

Chart Components

Regardless of type, all charts have the same basic components. These are shown in the bar chart in Figure 26-2, which shows four different categories of information relating to four of the six Apollo lunar landings.

The *chart title*, which is placed by default at the top of the chart, is simply a basic description of the chart. As you'll see in the "Common Customizations" section, later in this chapter, you can change the location of the title or use a different font or a different color for the text.

The *chart legend* collects together the names of the *series* of data that are shown in the chart. The legend shows the mapping between the series name and the colors used to graph its data. There are various ways to customize the legend, which we'll cover later in this chapter. It is also possible to hide the legend if it is not required.

A series is a collection of related data points. In Figure 26-2, there are four series, each containing three data points for a specific lunar landing. In this example, the data points are also arranged into three *categories* (the total flight time, the total moonwalk time, and the weight of samples returned). Categories are specific to the bar chart. As you can see in Figure 26-2, the bars for all the data in a single category are grouped together, thus allowing us to compare the values for that category across all the different series. For example, it

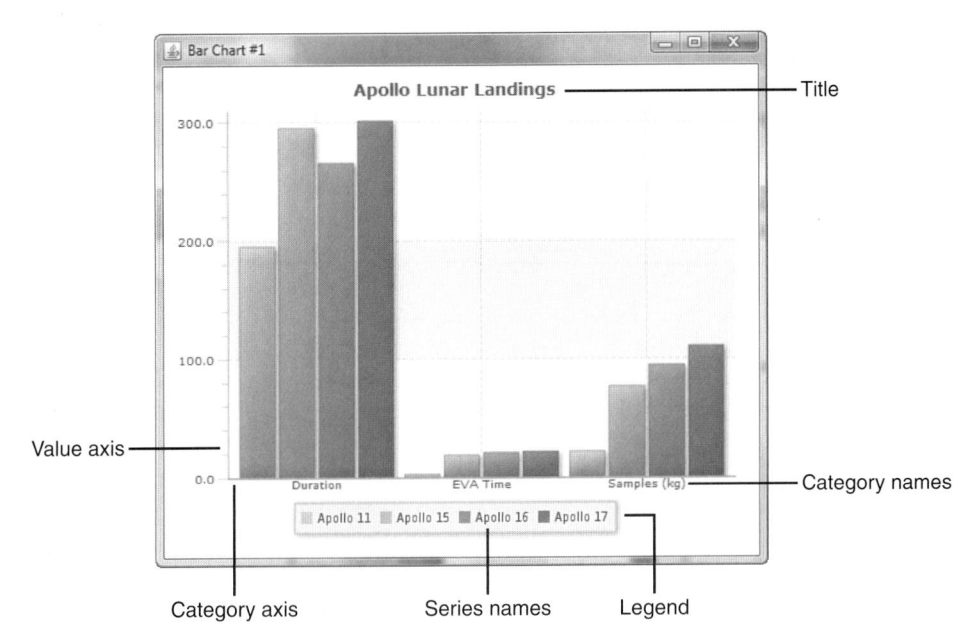

Figure 26-2 A typical bar chart

is evident from this chart that the total duration of Apollo 16 was noticeably shorter than that of the flight before and after it, but the EVA time and weight of samples returned on that flight were in line with the rising trend for both.[1]

JavaFX provides five different types of XY chart: a bar chart, a line chart, an area chart, a scatter chart, and a bubble chart, all of which will be covered in this chapter. They all have two *axes*—one horizontal (the *x*-axis) and one vertical (the *y*-axis). The axes themselves are represented by a class called `javafx.scene.chart.part.Axis`, which has variables that allow its appearance to be customized. There are two different types of axis—`ValueAxis` (and its subclass `NumberAxis`), which is used when the values plotted along the axis are numbers (which is the most common case), and `CategoryAxis`, which is used only by the bar chart and which is shown at the bottom of Figure 26-2. By default, the axes appear to the left of and below the chart itself, but it is possible to move them.

At the time of this writing, no axis type directly supports plotting data over time, but it is possible to customize a number axis to achieve the same effect. Axis customization is discussed in the "Common Customizations" section, later in this chapter.

---

[1] The shorter duration of the Apollo 16 mission was due to a problem with the spacecraft's main engine, which nearly aborted the lunar landing, and which caused mission controllers to reduce the amount of time spent in lunar orbit after the lunar module had returned to the command module.

Chart Data

The classes `Data` and `Series` in the `javafx.scene.chart.data` package represent a data point and a data series, respectively. Each chart type has its own subclass of `Data` and `Series`, which must be used in conjunction with that chart. For example, to create a `BarChart`, you need to construct your data model using `BarChart.Data` and `BarChart.Series` objects. These subclasses generally provide information that is specific to the associated chart type; for example, the subclasses for `BarChart` include variables that let you set the color of the bar used to represent an individual data point or a whole series. The exception to this rule is `PieChart`, which uses `PieChart.Data` objects that are not derived from the `Data` class.

Charts are not static objects—if the data that they are drawn from changes, the chart updates itself accordingly. It is, therefore, possible to use a chart to provide a real-time representation of data such as a stock price or the current temperature in New York City.

Chart Interaction

Charts do not have to be an entirely passive representation of data—it is possible for the application to take specific action when the user clicks on a visual element that represents a particular data value by associating a callback function with that data. When the user moves the mouse over the representation of the data in the chart, it is highlighted to show that interaction is possible and the callback function is called if the user clicks the mouse. You'll see an example of this later in the chapter.

Pie Charts

A pie chart represents a single set of data points by using slices of a circle. The larger the data point value, the larger the slice that will be used to represent it. JavaFX provides support for both two-dimensional and three-dimensional pie charts.

Creating a Pie Chart

Creating a pie chart is simplicity itself: Just convert your data into a sequence of `PieChart.Data` objects and install it in the `data` variable of a `PieChart`, as shown in Listing 26-1. You will find the code for this example in the file `javafxcharts/PieChart1.fx`.

Listing 26-1   **A Typical Pie Chart**

```
1       var data = [
2           PieChart.Data { label: "Apollo 11" value: 22 }
3           PieChart.Data { label: "Apollo 12" value: 34.4 }
4           PieChart.Data { label: "Apollo 13" value: 0 }
5           PieChart.Data { label: "Apollo 14" value: 43.0 }
6           PieChart.Data { label: "Apollo 15" value: 76.8 }
7           PieChart.Data { label: "Apollo 16" value: 94.7 }
8           PieChart.Data { label: "Apollo 17" value: 110.5 }
```

```
 9          ];
10
11      Stage {
12          title: "Pie Chart #1"
13          scene: Scene {
14              content: [
15                  PieChart {
16                      title: "Weight of Lunar Samples by Flight (kg)"
17                      data: data
18                  }
19              ]
20          }
21      }
```

For each data point, we specify the value and the label to be used when displaying it. The result of running this example is shown in Figure 26-3.

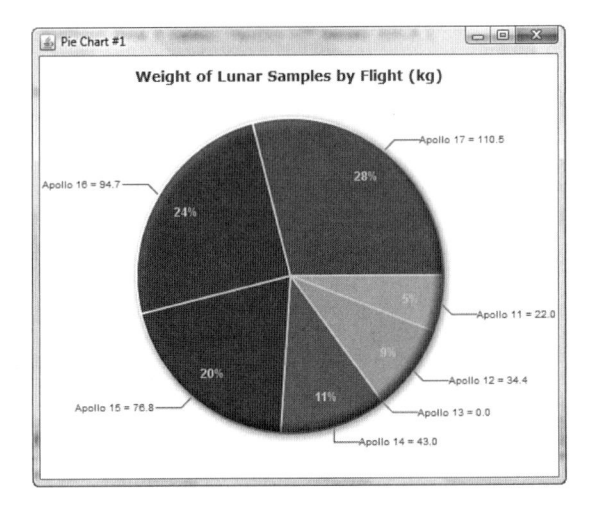

Figure 26-3   A pie chart

As you can see, each data point is represented by a proportionately sized slice of the whole pie. The name and the value supplied in the PieChart.Data object are used to construct a label that appears outside the circle and is connected to it by two straight-line segments, while the corresponding percentage value is shown in the arc itself. The fill color for each slice is taken from a default palette of eight colors; if there are more than eight slices, the colors repeat. Changing the color for a slice is one of the many customizations that the PieChart class allows and which we cover in the next section.

Because pie charts do not display multiple series of data, there is no need for a legend, and none is shown.

The radius of the pie is set automatically from the width of the area allocated to the chart. If, in this example, you were to bind its width to that of the scene and then resize the scene, you would see that the pie chart would increase and decrease in size accordingly.

A 3D Pie Chart

The `PieChart` class produces a flat representation of its data. If you'd like a more three-dimensional chart, you can use the `PieChart3D` class instead. `PieChart3D` is a subclass of `PieChart` that uses the same data objects and adds an additional variable that lets you configure the thickness of the pie. To convert a flat pie into a three-dimensional pie, just change the class name and assign a value to the `pieThickness` variable, as shown in the following code from the file `javafxcharts/PieChart2.fx`, which gives the result shown in Figure 26-4.

```
Stage {
    title: "Pie Chart #2"
    scene: Scene {
        content: [
            PieChart3D {
                title: "Weight of Lunar Samples by Flight (kg)"
                data: data
                pieThickness: 32
            }
        ]
    }
}
```

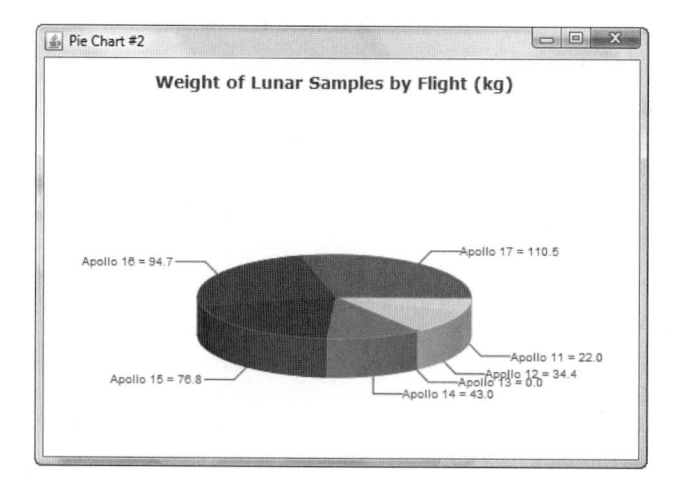

Figure 26-4   A 3D pie chart

Customizing a Pie Chart

There are many ways to change the appearance of a pie chart. Some of the available customizations apply to the whole chart and are controlled by variables in the `PieChart` class, while others are specific to a slice and are specified in the `PieChart.Data` object for that slice. An example of a customized pie chart is shown in Figure 26-5, and the code that created it, which you'll find in the file `javafxcharts/PieChart3.fx`, is shown in Listing 26-2.

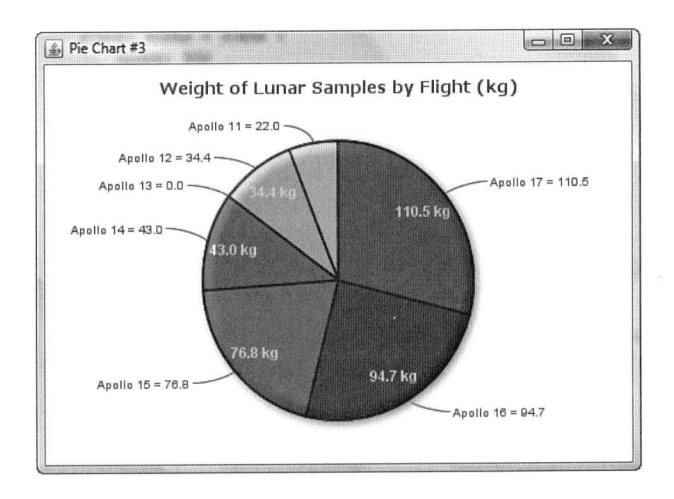

Figure 26-5   A customized pie chart

Listing 26-2   **A Pie Chart with Customizations Applied**

```
1    var data = [
2        PieChart.Data { label: "Apollo 11" value: 22 }
3        PieChart.Data { label: "Apollo 12" value: 34.4 }
4        PieChart.Data { label: "Apollo 13" value: 0 }
5        PieChart.Data { label: "Apollo 14" value: 43.0 }
6        PieChart.Data { label: "Apollo 15" value: 76.8
7                        fill: Color.CHOCOLATE }
8        PieChart.Data { label: "Apollo 16" value: 94.7 }
9        PieChart.Data { label: "Apollo 17" value: 110.5 }
10   ];
11
12   Stage {
13       title: "Pie Chart #3"
14       var scene:Scene;
15       scene: scene = Scene {
```

```
16                  width: 500
17                  height: 400
18                  content: [
19                      PieChart {
20                          width: bind scene.width
21                          height: bind scene.height
22                          title: "Weight of Lunar Samples by Flight (kg)"
23                          data: data
24                          pieToLabelLineCurved: true
25                          startAngle: 90
26                          clockwise: false
27                          pieStroke: Color.BLACK
28                          pieValueLabelFormater: function(value:Number,
29                              percent:Number):String {
30                              "{value} kg"
31                          }
32                      }
33                  ]
34              }
35          }
```

This example applies one customization to a particular slice and five customizations to the chart itself.

The slice customization changes the fill color of the slice with label Apollo 15 to Color.CHOCOLATE by setting the fill variable of its PieChart.Data value on lines 6 and 7. Other variables in this class can be used to change the stroke color, which is used to draw the outline of the slice and the stroke width. You can also set the explodeFactor variable to make the slice appear larger than its neighbors.[2]

On lines 25 and 26, we set the values of the startAngle and clockwise variables of the PieChart class to 90 and false, respectively. If you compare Figure 26-5 with Figure 26-3, you see that the slice that represents the first data item, which has the label Apollo 11, has moved from the 3 o'clock position to the 12 o'clock position, as a result of the change in the value of the startAngle variable. You can also see that the order in which the slices are drawn has been reversed, because the clockwise variable has been changed from its default value of true to false.

Setting the value of the pieStroke variable on line 27 changes the color used to draw the outlines of the pie slices from white to black. This variable applies to all the slices, but can be overridden by the stroke variable in the PieChart.Data object for any given slice. There is also a variable called pieStrokeWidth that sets the width of the slice outline.

By default, the graphic that connects a pie slice to the label that appears outside of the chart (which is referred to as the *pie label*) consists of two straight lines. There are several variables in the PieChart class that let you control the appearance of this graphic. On

---

[2] Note that some of these customizations do not actually work in JavaFX 1.2.

line 24 of Listing 26-2, we set the `pieToLabelLineCurved` variable to `true`, which switches from two lines to a curve. It is also possible to completely remove the pie labels and the associated graphic by setting the `pieLabelVisible` variable to `false`.

The label that appears inside each slice is called the *pie value label*. You can customize this label by changing its font or color, and you can also remove it by setting the `pieValueVisible` variable to `false`. By default, the label shows the percentage value for the slice followed by a percent sign, as you can see in Figure 26-3. By replacing the function assigned to the `pieValueLabelFormater` variable (note the spelling), you can change what is displayed here. This function is called with two arguments—the value from the `PieChart.Data` object for a slice and the percentage of the total value that this represents. The function that is installed on lines 28 to 31 of Listing 26-2 uses the data value instead of the percentage. You can see the effect of this in Figure 26-5, where the value label for Apollo 15 has changed from `20%` to `76.8 kg`.

> **Note**
>
> The label values are only displayed if there is room in the slice, so if your function returns a string that is too long, the label will not appear. You can see how the size of the pie chart affects this by making the scene larger and smaller. The width of the chart in this example is bound to that of the scene, so if you make the scene narrower, the radius of the chart will reduce proportionately and so will the size of each slice.

Bar Charts

A bar chart is an XY chart in which one axis is a `CategoryAxis` and the other is a `ValueAxis`. The data in a bar chart is represented by solid bars. The bar for a data point extends from its base, which is placed on the category axis, to the position along the value axis that corresponds to the value of that data point. A bar chart may be used to show one or more categories of data and within each category, the data is organized by series.

Creating a Bar Chart

Unlike pie charts, which simply display raw data, the data in a bar chart must be organized into one or more series and one or more categories. The code in Listing 26-3 creates a chart that presents data relating to four lunar landing missions. You can see the result of running this code, which you can find in the file `javafxcharts/BarChart1.fx`, in Figure 26-2.

Listing 26-3   A Bar Chart

```
1     var categories = [ "Duration", "EVA Time", "Samples (kg)" ];
2     var seriesData = [
3         BarChart.Series {
4             name: "Apollo 11"
5             data: [
6                 BarChart.Data { category: "Duration" value: 195.5 }
7                 BarChart.Data { category: "EVA Time" value: 2.5 }
8                 BarChart.Data { category: "Samples (kg)" value: 22 }
9             ]
```

```
10          }
11          BarChart.Series {
12              name: "Apollo 15"
13              data: [
14                  BarChart.Data { category: "Duration" value: 295.2 }
15                  BarChart.Data { category: "EVA Time" value: 19.2 }
16                  BarChart.Data { category: "Samples (kg)" value: 76.8 }
17              ]
18          }
19          BarChart.Series {
20              name: "Apollo 16"
21              data: [
22                  BarChart.Data { category: "Duration" value: 265.9 }
23                  BarChart.Data { category: "EVA Time" value: 20.3 }
24                  BarChart.Data { category: "Samples (kg)" value: 94.7 }
25              ]
26          }
27          BarChart.Series {
28              name: "Apollo 17"
29              data: [
30                  BarChart.Data { category: "Duration" value: 301.8 }
31                  BarChart.Data { category: "EVA Time" value: 22.1 }
32                  BarChart.Data { category: "Samples (kg)" value: 110.5    }
33              ]
34          }
35      ];
36
37      Stage {
38          title: "Bar Chart #1"
39          scene: Scene {
40              content: [
41                  BarChart {
42                      title: "Apollo Lunar Landings"
43                      data: seriesData
44                      categoryAxis: CategoryAxis {
45                          categories: categories
46                      }
47                      valueAxis: NumberAxis {
48                          upperBound: 310
49                          tickUnit: 100
50                      }
51                  }
52              ]
53          }
54      }
```

There are three categories of data in this example: the duration of each mission, the amount of time spent outside the spacecraft on the lunar surface, and the total weight of the samples brought back. The `categories` variable on line 1 contains the names assigned to these categories, which appear along the category axis of the chart.

The chart shows data for four flights—Apollo 11, Apollo 15, Apollo 16, and Apollo 17. The data for each individual flight is grouped together in its own series which, in the case of the bar chart, is represented by an instance of the `BarChart.Series` class. On lines 3 to 10, we construct the series data for Apollo 11. As you can see, the name variable of the `BarChart.Series` object is set to the name of the series, which will appear in the chart's legend. The data variable contains one `BarChart.Data` object for each category of data, which contains the value of the data point as a number and the name of the category to which it belongs. In Listing 26-3, we explicitly retyped the category names, but you could also reference the names in the categories variable, like this:

```
BarChart.Data { category: categories[0] value: 195.5 }   // Duration
```

To display the data, you construct a `BarChart` object, as shown on lines 41 to 51. The data is installed by assigning the reference to the `BarChart.Series` object in the `data` variable. This is not enough on its own to cause anything to be displayed, because the bar chart needs to be given axes along which to plot the data.[3]

The data categories are plotted along the category axis and the data point values along the value axis. By default, the category axis is placed below the chart and the value axis on its left, although as you'll see in the section "Axis Customization" later in this chapter, they can be moved. The category axis is an instance of the `CategoryAxis` class with its `categories` variable set to refer to the names of the categories of data that should appear in the chart. If you remove a category name from the `categories` sequence, the data points for that category will be ignored. The order of names in this sequence determines the order in which the categories are drawn on the chart.

The value axis must be an instance of the `NumberAxis` class. The range of values displayed on this axis is determined by the values of its `lowerBound` and `upperBound` variables. On lines 47 to 50 of Listing 26-3, we set the `upperBound` variable to a value that is larger than any of the data point values in any of the data series for this chart and default the `lowerBound` variable to `0`. If you don't set an upper bound, you won't see any data because the `upperBound` variable also defaults to `0`.

The `tickUnit` variable, which is set in this example to `100`, specifies the distance between the major ticks on the value axis. The value is given in terms of the units of the data point values—in this case, the value axis displays values from `0` to `310` with a tick

---

[3] `BarChart` is unique in this regard—the other XY chart types will automatically install a pair of `NumberAxis` objects if you don't supply them when constructing the chart. If you do not initialize a `BarChart` with two axes, nothing will display.

unit of 100, so there will be major ticks at 0, 100, 200, and 300. The major ticks are represented by a horizontal line and a label that displays the associated value. As you can see in Figure 26-2, intermediate (or minor) tick marks are also provided. By default, there are five minor ticks to each major tick, which means that you will actually see four minor tick marks on the screen. The number and size of the minor tick marks can be changed, as you'll see in the "Axis Customization" section, later in this chapter.

A 3D Bar Chart

You can create a 3D bar chart by using the `BarChart3D` class rather than `BarChart`. The `BarChart3D` class uses the same data model as `BarChart`, so all you need to do to convert one to the other is to change the class name, as shown by the following code extract, which comes from the file `javafxcharts/BarChart2.fx`:

```
Stage {
    title: "Bar Chart #2"
    scene: Scene {
        content: [
            BarChart3D {
                title: "Apollo Lunar Landings"
                data: seriesData
                categoryAxis: CategoryAxis {
                    categories: categories
                }
                valueAxis: NumberAxis {
                    upperBound: 310
                    tickUnit: 100
                }
            }
        ]
    }
}
```

The result of running this code is shown in Figure 26-6. The colors used for the shelf areas along the axes and the depth of the shelf are controlled by variables of the `BarChart3D` class that you can set to customize the effect.

Bar Chart Customization

There are several ways to customize the appearance of the bars that appear in a bar chart. Support for customization is provided in the `BarChart.Data`, `BarChart.Series`, and `BarChart` classes. In general, customizations in the `BarChart.Data` object take precedence over those in the `BarChart.Series` class, which in turn take precedence over those in the `BarChart` class.

Fill and Stroke Customizations

The following code changes the `fill` and `stroke` colors for the data in the Apollo 11 series to chocolate and black, respectively. The exception is the data point in the Samples

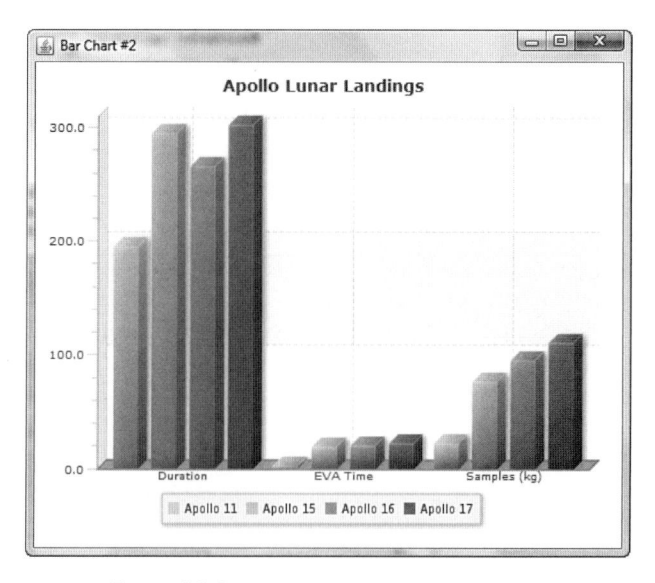

Figure 26-6   An example of a 3D bar chart

category, which will be filled in red because customizations in the `Data` object take precedence over those in the `Series`.[4]

```
BarChart.Series {
    name: "Apollo 11"
    fill: Color.CHOCOLATE
    stroke: Color.BLACK
    data: [
        BarChart.Data { category: "Duration" value: 195.5 }
        BarChart.Data { category: "EVA Time" value: 2.5 }
        BarChart.Data { category: "Samples (kg)" value: 22
                    fill: Color.RED}
    ]
}
```

You can change the gap between bars by setting the `barGap` variable in the `BarChart` object:

```
BarChart {
    title: "Apollo Lunar Landings"
    barFill: Color.ORANGERED
    barGap: 8
    data: seriesData
    categoryAxis: CategoryAxis {
```

---

[4] You'll find the code for this example in the file `javafxchart/BarChart3.fx`.

```
            categories: categories
        }
        valueAxis: NumberAxis {
            upperBound: 310
            tickUnit: 100
        }
    }
}
```

In the preceding code, the gap between bars will be 8 pixels instead of the default of 4. This code also sets the `barFill` variable. The effect of this is that every bar that does not have a fill specified in its `BarChart.Data` or `BarChart.Series` object will be filled in orange red. In this example, this setting will affect all the bars apart from those that are created from the Apollo 11 series. The `barStroke` has the same effect for the stroke applied to each bar.

Gradient Customization

If the fill `Paint` that is associated with a bar is a solid color, as it is in the examples shown in this section, the `BarChart` class creates a gradient that gives the bar a more pleasing effect. You can change the way that the gradient is created by assigning a function to the `gradientCreator` variable of either a `BarChart.Series` object to affect only the bars for that series or to the `gradientCreator` variable of the `BarChart`, which will be applied to all bars apart from those that have a `gradientCreator` for their associated series.

Listing 26-4, which is an extract from the code in the file `javafxcharts/BarChart4.fx`, installs a custom gradient creator in a bar chart by setting its `gradientCreator` variable. The algorithm implemented by this function will be applied to all the bars in the chart because none of the `BarChart.Series` objects have their own gradient creator.

Listing 26-4   Applying a Custom Gradient to the Bars in a `BarChart`

```
1     Stage {
2         title: "Bar Chart #4"
3         scene: Scene {
4             content: [
5                 BarChart {
6                     title: "Apollo Lunar Landings"
7                     data: seriesData
8                     gradientCreator: gradientCreator
9                     categoryAxis: CategoryAxis {
10                        categories: categories
11                    }
12                    valueAxis: NumberAxis {
13                        upperBound: 310
14                        tickUnit: 100
15                    }
16                }
```

```
17                ]
18            }
19      }
20
21      function gradientCreator(series:BarChart.Series,
22                              index:Integer, data:BarChart.Data,
23                              paint:Paint):Paint {
24          if (paint instanceof Color) {
25              var startColor = paint as Color;
26              var endColor = startColor.color(startColor.red * 0.4,
27                                              startColor.green * 0.4,
28                                              startColor.blue * 0.4,
29                                              startColor.opacity);
30              return LinearGradient {
31                  startX: 0 endX: 1.0 startY: 0.0 endY: 0.0
32                  stops: [
33                      Stop { offset: 0.0 color: startColor }
34                      Stop { offset: 1.0 color: endColor }
35                  ]
36              }
37          }
38          return paint;
39      }
```

The gradient creation function is shown on lines 21 to 36. As you can see, it is passed the `BarChart.Series` and `BarChart.Data` objects for the data point for the bar that is being drawn, the index of the data point within the series, and the fill that applies to the bar. If the fill is not a solid color, it is returned unchanged. Otherwise, this particular function creates a horizontal `LinearGradient` that starts with the original fill color on the left and progresses to a darker variant of that color on the right. You can see the result of running this code in Figure 26-7, which you should compare with Figure 26-2.

Bar Node Customization

If you don't like the default rectangular bars used to chart your data, you can replace them with something else. There are two ways to do this.

You can specify the node to use for a specific data point by setting the `node` variable of its `BarChart.Data` object. This allows you to replace the representation of an individual bar but would involve a lot of work if you want to do this for every data point in your model.

Create a function that returns the node for a given `BarChart.Data` object and install it in either the `barCreator` variable of a `BarChart.Series` object or in the `barCreator` variable of the `BarChart` itself.

The signature of the `barCreator` function is as follows:

```
public function barCreator(series:Series, index:Integer, data:Data):Node
```

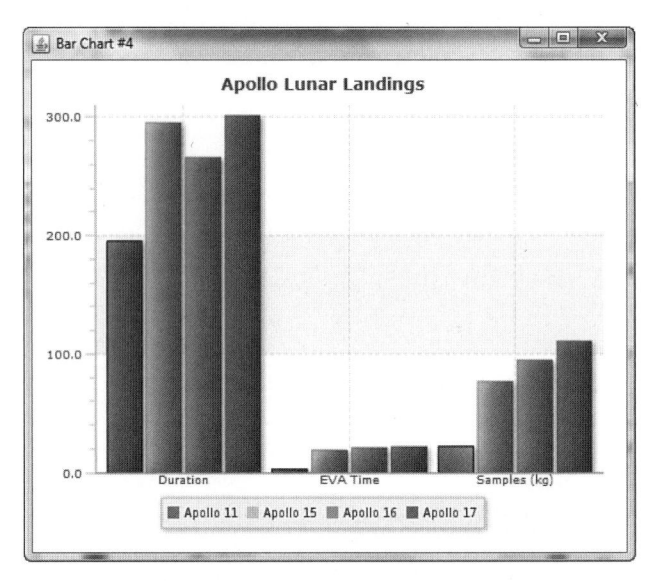

Figure 26-7   A bar chart with a customized gradient
applied to its bars

The `index` argument is the index of the `BarChart.Data` object in its owning `BarChart.Series`, which is passed as the third and first arguments, respectively. The return value is node to be used to represent the bar.

Bars are created by first checking the `node` variable of the `BarChart.Data` object. If this is `null`, the bar creator associated with the owning `BarChart.Series` is checked. If this is `null`, the bar creator in the `BarChart` is checked and, if this is also `null`, the built-in bar creator is used

Line Charts

A line chart is more commonly referred to as a graph. The `LineChart` class can plot one or more series of data. Each series consists of a set of data points that are interpreted as the (x, y) coordinates of points on the graph, and adjacent points within a series are linked by straight lines to form the graph.

Creating a Line Chart

The code in Listing 26-5, which you'll find in the file `javafxchart/LineChart1.fx`, creates a `LineChart` displaying two straight-line graphs, one for each of its data series. The result of running this example is shown at the top of Figure 26-8.

Listing 26-5 **A LineChart**

```
1      var lineSeries1 = LineChart.Series {
2          name: "Line 1"
3          data: for (x in [-50..50 step 10]) {
4              LineChart.Data { xValue: x yValue: 2 * x }
5          }
6      };
7      var lineSeries2 = LineChart.Series {
8          name: "Line 2"
9          data: for (x in [-50..50 step 10]) {
10             LineChart.Data { xValue: x yValue: 30 }
11         }
12     };
13
14     Stage {
15         title: "Line Chart #1"
16         scene: Scene {
17             content: [
18                 LineChart {
19                     data: [ lineSeries1, lineSeries2 ]
20                     xAxis: NumberAxis {
21                         upperBound: 50
22                         lowerBound: -50
23                         tickUnit: 10
24                     }
25                     yAxis: NumberAxis {
26                         upperBound: 100
27                         lowerBound: -100
28                         tickUnit: 10
29                     }
30                 }
31             ]
32         }
33     }
```

The data for the diagonal line is created on lines 1 to 6 of Listing 26-5. Each point along the line is represented by a `LineChart.Data` object, which specifies the *x* and *y* coordinates of the point by using the `xValue` and `yValue` variables, respectively. The data points are collected in the data variable of a `LineChart.Series object`, which also assigns the series name. As with the `BarChart`, a color is assigned automatically to each sequence, and the mapping from color to sequence name is shown in the legend. You can change the color used for a series by setting the `fill` variable in its `LineChart.Series` object. There is an example of this in Listing 26-6 later in this chapter.

928   Chapter 26   Charts

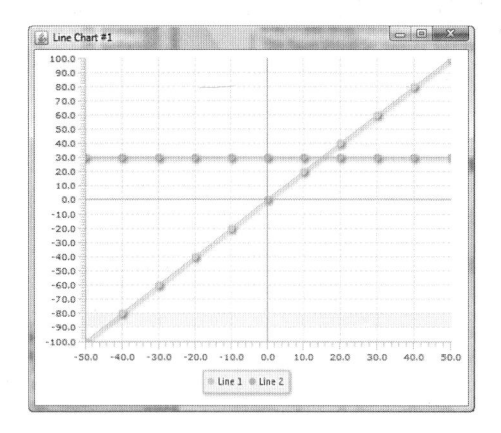

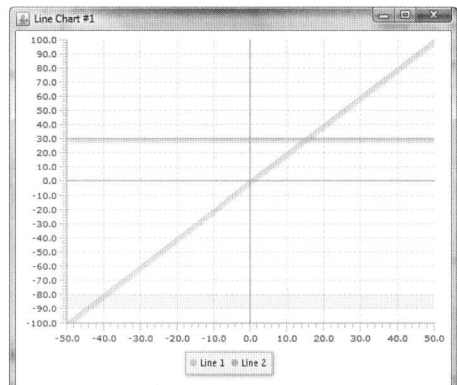

Figure 26-8   A `LineChart` with two data series

A `LineChart` requires two axes of type `ValueAxis`. Here, we create two `NumberAxis` objects and assign them to the `xAxis` and `yAxis` variables, setting the `upperBound` and `lowerBound` variables of each so that both positive and negative *x* and *y* coordinates are visible in the graph. We also set the `tickUnit` variable so that we get tick marks every 10 units along both axes.

As you can see at the top of Figure 26-8, each data point on the graph is indicated by a small circle. As you'll see later in the next section, you can change the symbols that are used to represent data points. You can also remove them completely by setting the `showSymbols` variable to `false`, which gives the result shown at the bottom of Figure 26-8.

Line Chart Customization

You can change the opacity of the symbols and plot lines by setting the `dataOpacity` variable of the `LineChart` class. This is not particularly useful, unless your data points are very tightly bunched and you are also graphing more than one series of data where there is some overlap between the series and you want to be able to see both sets of points in the regions of overlap.

By default, each series uses the same plot symbol—a small colored circle. If you want each series or even each individual data point to use a different symbol, you can do so by providing a *symbol creator* function. You can assign a symbol creator to a series or to the whole `LineChart`. If the `LineChart` has a symbol creator, it is used only for those series that do not have their own symbol creator installed. In Listing 26-6, a symbol creator has been assigned to one of the data series (see line 13) and another to the whole chart (line 23). The chart symbol creator will be used to return the plot symbols for the series that does not have its own creator—that is, the diagonal line. The result of running this code, which you'll find in the file `javafxchart/LineChart2.fx`, is shown in Figure 26-9.

Listing 26-6   Using a Symbol Creator with a `LineChart`

```
1     var lineSeries1 = LineChart.Series {
2         name: "Line 1"
3         data: for (x in [-50..50 step 5]) {
4             LineChart.Data { xValue: x yValue: 2 * x }
5         }
6     };
7     var lineSeries2 = LineChart.Series {
8         name: "Line 2"
9         fill: Color.BLUE
10        data: for (x in [-50..50 step 5]) {
11            LineChart.Data { xValue: x yValue: 30 }
12        }
13        symbolCreator: seriesSymbolCreator
14    };
15
16    Stage {
17        title: "Line Chart #2"
18        scene: Scene {
19            content: [
20                LineChart {
21                    data: [ lineSeries1, lineSeries2 ]
22                    showSymbols: true
23                    symbolCreator: chartSymbolCreator
24                    xAxis: NumberAxis {
25                        upperBound: 50
26                        lowerBound: -50
27                        tickUnit: 10
28                    }
29                    yAxis: NumberAxis {
30                        upperBound: 100
31                        lowerBound: -100
32                        tickUnit: 10
33                    }
34                }
35            ]
36        }
37    }
38
39    function seriesSymbolCreator(series:LineChart.Series,
40                                 seriesIndex:Integer,
41                                 data:LineChart.Data,
42                                 dataIndex:Integer,
43                                 paint:Paint):Node {
44        var node = PlotSymbol.HollowDiamond {
45            size: 12
```

```
46                fill: paint
47            }
48       }
49
50       function chartSymbolCreator(series:LineChart.Series,
51                                  seriesIndex:Integer,
52                                  data:LineChart.Data,
53                                  dataIndex:Integer,
54                                  paint:Paint):Node {
55            PlotSymbol.HollowTriangle {
56                size: 12
57                fill: paint
58            }
59       }
```

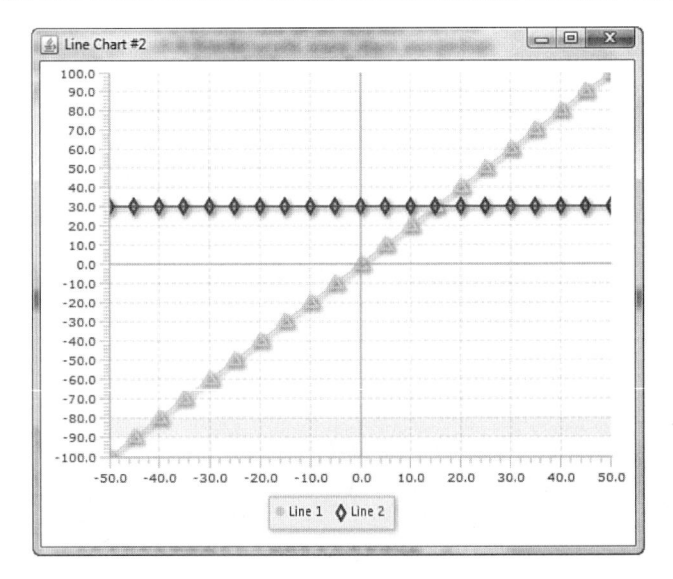

Figure 26-9   Using symbol creators with a `LineChart`

As you can see, different symbols are now used for each line. Points on the diagonal line are marked with small triangles, whereas those on the straight line are indicated by diamonds. Both of the symbol creator functions, which are shown on lines 39 to 59 of Listing 26-6, use standard plot symbols from the `javafx.scene.chart.part` package, but you could create and use your own plot symbol if necessary.

Area Charts

An area chart is a variant of the line chart in which the area between the graphed line and the horizontal axis is filled with color. The data for an area chart is provided by one

Area Charts

or more `AreaChart.Series` populated with `AreaChart.Data` objects. Listing 26-7 shows an area chart with the same data as that shown in the line charts in the previous section. The result of running this code, which is in the file `javafxchart/AreaChart1.fx`, is shown in Figure 26-10.

Listing 26-7   **An `AreaChart`**

```
1     var lineSeries1 = AreaChart.Series {
2         name: "Line 1"
3         data: for (x in [-50..50 step 10]) {
4             AreaChart.Data { xValue: x yValue: 2 * x }
5         }
6     };
7     var lineSeries2 = AreaChart.Series {
8         name: "Line 2"
9         data: for (x in [-50..50 step 10]) {
10            AreaChart.Data { xValue: x yValue: 30 }
11        }
12    };
13
14    Stage {
15        title: "Area Chart #1"
16        scene: Scene {
17            content: [
18                AreaChart {
19                    data: [ lineSeries1, lineSeries2 ]
20                    xAxis: NumberAxis {
21                        upperBound: 50
22                        lowerBound: -50
23                        tickUnit: 10
24                    }
25                    yAxis: NumberAxis {
26                        upperBound: 100
27                        lowerBound: -100
28                        tickUnit: 10
29                    }
30                }
31            ]
32        }
33    }
```

The colors used to fill each chart area, which is obtained from the fill variable of its `AreaChart.Series` object, are partly opaque so that you can see both areas in the region where they overlap. By default, the colors are drawn with an opacity of `0.5`, but this can be changed by changing the value of the `dataOpacity` variable of the `AreaChart` object.

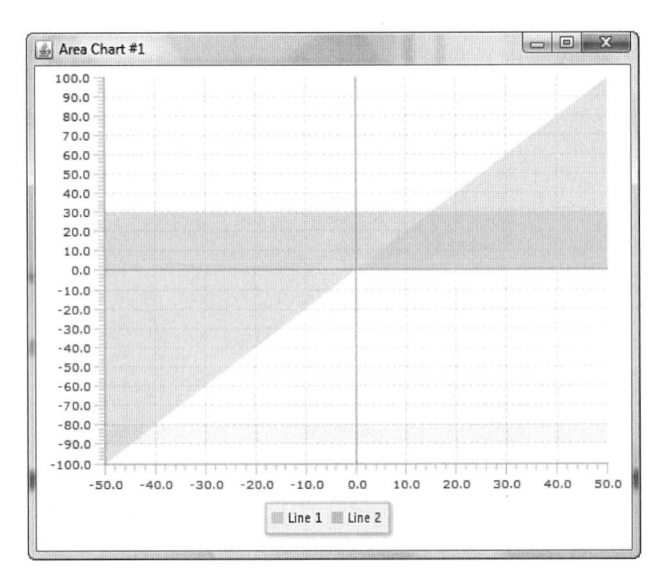

Figure 26-10 An `AreaChart` with two filled areas

Scatter Charts

Scatter charts are used to show correlation (or lack of correlation) between data points by plotting just the points themselves. Closely related data points should be easy to see because they will appear to be close together in the chart. The data model for a scatter chart is the same as that for a line chart, except that the class names are `ScatterChart.Data` and `ScatterChart.Series`.

The code in Listing 26-8 creates two series of data, each of which contains 20 points that are randomly distributed around a particular center point. Proximity of the points in each series is guaranteed by the expressions used to set the `xValue` and `yValue` variables, both of which add a random offset in the range −10 to +10 (exclusive) to the coordinates of the center point. If you run this example, which you'll find in the file `javafxcharts/ScatterChart1.fx`, you'll get the result shown in Figure 26-11.

Listing 26-8 A `ScatterChart`

```
1     var series1 = ScatterChart.Series {
2         name: "Series 1"
3         data: for (x in [1..20]) {
4             ScatterChart.Data { xValue: 20 + 10 * (Math.random() -     0.5)
5                                yValue: 20 + 10 * (Math.random() -     0.5) }
6         }
7     };
8     var series2 = ScatterChart.Series {
9         name: "Series 2"
10        data: for (x in [1..20]) {
11            ScatterChart.Data { xValue: 40 + 10 * (Math.random() -     0.5)
```

```
12                         yValue: 40 + 10 * (Math.random() -      0.5) }
13        }
14    };
15
16    Stage {
17        title: "Scatter Chart #1"
18        scene: Scene {
19            content: [
20                ScatterChart {
21                    data: [ series1, series2 ]
22                    xAxis: NumberAxis {
23                        upperBound: 60
24                        tickUnit: 10
25                    }
26                    yAxis: NumberAxis {
27                        upperBound: 60
28                        tickUnit: 10
29                    }
30                }
31            ]
32        }
33    }
```

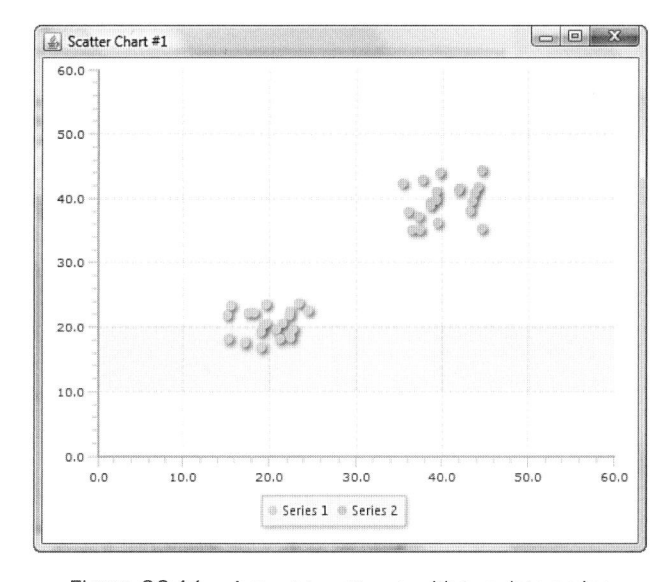

Figure 26-11   A **ScatterChart** with two data series

You can see clearly that the data points in each series are closely related to each other and unrelated to those in the other series, because their symbols for each series are tightly bunched together.

You can change the color of the symbols for a series by setting the `fill` variable of the `ScatterChart.Series` object, and you can use different symbols by installing a symbol creator function for a series or for the whole chart. You can also set the plot symbol for an individual data point by setting the `symbol` variable of its `ScatterChart.Data` object. The code extract below, from the file `javafxcharts/ScatterChart2.fx`, changes the fill color of the first data series to blue and uses a smaller circle to represent its data point. Figure 26-12 shows the result.

```
var series1 = ScatterChart.Series {
    name: "Series 1"
    data: for (x in [1..20]) {
        ScatterChart.Data { xValue: 20 + 10 * (Math.random() - 0.5)
                            yValue: 20 + 10 * (Math.random() - 0.5) }
    }
    fill: Color.BLUE
    symbolCreator: function(series:ScatterChart.Series,
                            seriesIndex:Integer,
                            data:ScatterChart.Data,
                            dataIndex:Integer,
                            fill:Paint) {
        PlotSymbol.Circle { size: 4 fill: fill };
    }
};
```

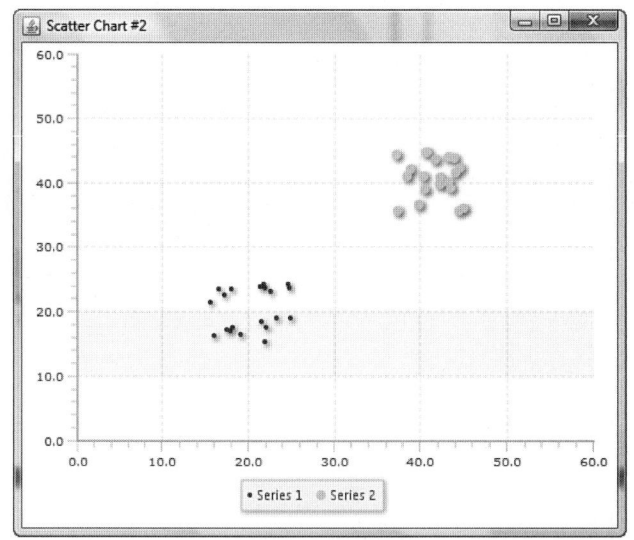

Figure 26-12   A `ScatterChart` with customized symbols

Bubble Charts

Like a `ScatterChart`, a `BubbleChart` is intended to show the correlation between data points in a series. The data points in a `BubbleChart` have an additional variable that lets you specify the radius of the plot symbol that represents it. You can use this feature to apply some kind of visual weighting to the data point. The code in Listing 26-9 creates two `BubbleChart.Series` in which the data points are randomly placed as they were in the `ScatterChart` example; each data point has a radius that is randomly chosen to be in the range 1 to 7.

Listing 26-9 A BubbleChart

```
1        var series1 = BubbleChart.Series {
2            name: "Series 1"
3            data: for (x in [1..20]) {
4                BubbleChart.Data { xValue: 20 + 20 * (Math.random() - 0.5)
5                                   yValue: 20 + 20 * (Math.random() - 0.5)
6                                   radius: 1 + 5 * Math.random() }
7            }
8        };
9        var series2 = BubbleChart.Series {
10           name: "Series 2"
11           data: for (x in [1..20]) {
12               BubbleChart.Data { xValue: 40 + 20 * (Math.random() - 0.5)
13                                  yValue: 40 + 20 * (Math.random() - 0.5)
14                                  radius: 1 + 5 * Math.random() }
15           }
16       };
17
18       Stage {
19           title: "Bubble Chart #1"
20           scene: Scene {
21               content: [
22                   BubbleChart {
23                       data: [ series1, series2 ]
24                       xAxis: NumberAxis {
25                           upperBound: 60
26                           tickUnit: 10
27                       }
28                       yAxis: NumberAxis {
29                           upperBound: 60
30                           tickUnit: 10
31                       }
32                   }
33               ]
34           }
35       }
```

If you run this code, which you'll find in the file `javafxcharts/BubbleChart1.fx`, you'll get a result that looks something like Figure 26-13.

You can use the same mechanisms that you saw used with `ScatterChart` and `LineChart` to customize the plot symbol for any data point, for a series, or for the whole graph.

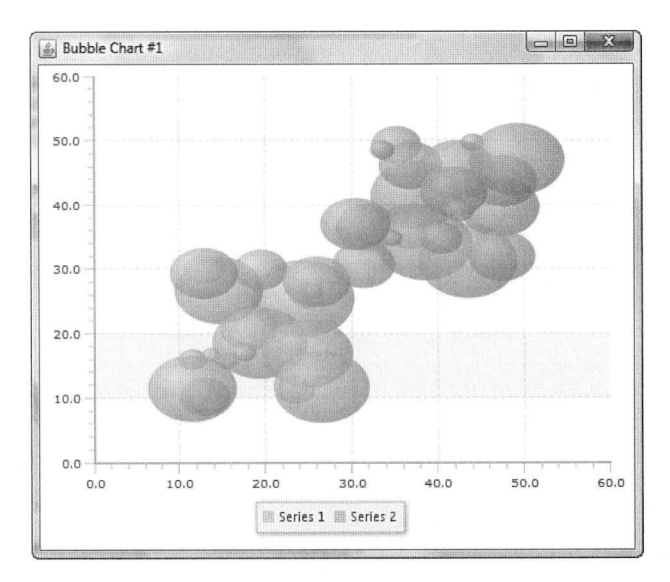

Figure 26-13   An example of a `BubbleChart`

Chart Interaction

You can allow the user to interact with your chart by installing a function in the `action` variable of any `Data` object. This function will be called whenever the user clicks on the part of the chart that corresponds to that object. The following code adds an action function to the data point for the Duration category of the Apollo 11 series of data for the bar chart that we used as an example earlier in this chapter:

```
BarChart.Series {
    name: "Apollo 11"
    data: [
        BarChart.Data { category: "Duration" value: 195.5
                        action: function() { println("Clicked") } }
        BarChart.Data { category: "EVA Time" value: 2.5 }
        BarChart.Data { category: "Samples (kg)" value: 22 }
    ]
}
```

If you run this example, which you'll find in the file `javafxcharts/BarChart5.fx`, and move the mouse over one of the bars in the duration part of the chart, you'll notice that a black outline appears around the bar. This outline appears when the mouse hovers over a part of any chart that is created from a `Data` object that has an action function. Its color and width are determined by the `hoverStroke` and `hoverStrokeWidth` variables inherited from the `Chart` class:

```
BarChart {
    title: "Apollo Lunar Landings"
```

```
    data: seriesData
    hoverStroke: Color.BLACK
    hoverStrokeWidth: 2
    categoryAxis: CategoryAxis {
        categories: categories
    }
    valueAxis: NumberAxis {
        upperBound: 310
        tickUnit: 100
    }
}
```

If you now click the bar, the action function will be called, and the text `Clicked` will appear on the console.

Note that the action function is called with no arguments, so the only way for it to obtain a reference to the data item that has been clicked is by using a reference that is in scope when the function is executed, like this:

```
BarChart.Series {
    name: "Apollo 11"
    var item:BarChart.Data;
    data: [
        item = BarChart.Data { category: "Duration" value: 195.5
                action: function() { println("Clicked on {item}") } }
        BarChart.Data { category: "EVA Time" value: 2.5 }
        BarChart.Data { category: "Samples (kg)" value: 22 }
    ]
}
```

Although this works, it is not convenient to have to create variables for this purpose, and it would clearly be very difficult to do this if there were a large number of data points that need to have associated functions. Hopefully, the API will improve in a future release.

Common Customizations

You have already seen various ways in which you can change the appearance of a chart. Those mechanisms have all been specific to a particular chart type, but there are several ways in which you can customize charts that use features that are common to all or at least to most of the chart classes. This section looks at some of the options that are available to you.

Chart Customization

You can use variables in the `Chart` class to change the appearance and position of the title and the legend, to change the background fill and stroke of the chart and to increase or decrease the empty space around the outside of the chart. Some of these customizations are used in the code in Listing 26-10, which you'll find in the file

Chapter 26 Charts

`javafxcharts/Customize1.fx`. If you run this example, you'll get the result shown in Figure 26-14.

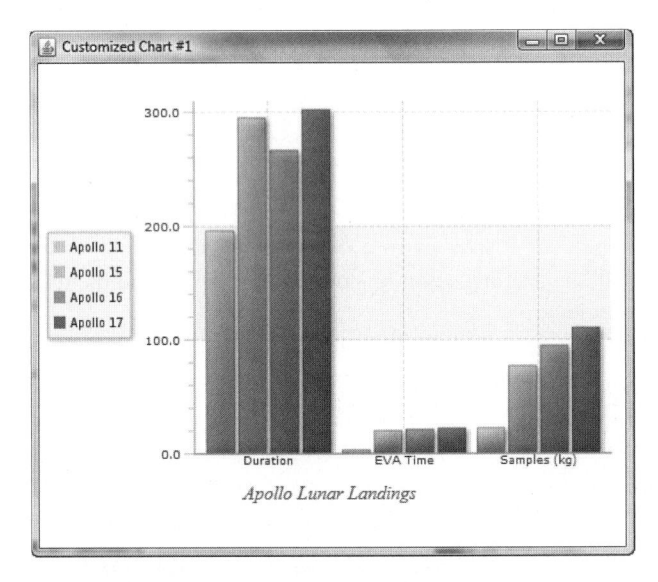

Figure 26-14 A chart with customizations

Listing 26-10 **Examples of Chart Customizations**

```
1    var chart:BarChart;
2    Stage {
3        title: "Customized Chart #1"
4        scene: Scene {
5            content: [
6                chart = BarChart {
7                    title: "Apollo Lunar Landings"
8                    titleSide: Side.BOTTOM
9                    titleFill: Color.GREEN
10                   titleFont: Font.font("Serif", FontWeight.REGULAR,
11                                        FontPosture.ITALIC, 16);
12                   chartBackgroundFill: LinearGradient {
13                       startX: 0 endX: 0 startY: 0 endY: 1
14                       stops: [
15                           Stop { offset: 0 color: Color.GREY }
16                           Stop { offset: 1 color: Color.LIGHTGRAY }
17                       ]
18                   }
19                   chartBackgroundStroke: Color.BLACK
20                   chartBackgroundStrokeWidth: 4
21                   insets: Insets { bottom: 32 left: 8
```

```
22                         top: 32 right: 8}
23                     legendSide: Side.LEFT
24                     data: seriesData
25                     categoryAxis: CategoryAxis {
26                         categories: categories
27                     }
28                     valueAxis: NumberAxis {
29                         upperBound: 310
30                         tickUnit: 100
31                     }
32                 }
33             ]
34         }
35     }
36
37     chart.legend.vertical = true;
38     chart.legend.fill = Color.YELLOW;
```

The code on lines 8 to 11 customizes the chart title. The `titleFill` and `titleFont` variables change the color and font of the title text, and the `titleSide` variable changes its position relative to the chart's content. Here, we use the value `Side.BOTTOM`, which places the title below the chart. It is also possible to move the title to the left or right of the chart and to change the gap between the title and the rest of the chart by setting the `titleGap` variable.

On lines 12 to 20, we change the chart's background fill and stroke, which produces a line border around the edge of the chart, the thickness of which is controlled by the `chartBackgroundStrokeWidth` variable. The background fill may be a solid color or, as in this example, a gradient.[5]

The code on line 23 uses the `legendSide` variable to move the legend from the bottom of the chart to the left. In this position, it would take up too much horizontal space if it were drawn in its default (horizontal) orientation, so on line 37 we arrange for its content to be organized vertically instead by setting the `vertical` variable of the `Legend` class to `true`. On line 38, we change the legend's background fill to yellow. It is also possible to change the font and color of the legend's text. Refer to the API documentation for the details.

XY Chart Customization

XY charts offer some additional possibilities for customization that we discuss in this section. There are some further customizations available that relate to the axes of the chart; we'll discuss those, along with the other axis-related features, in the next section.

---

[5] As you can see in Figure 26-14, the background fill and stroke do not work as expected in JavaFX 1.3.

Background Node

It is possible to place a custom node into an XY chart by assigning a reference to it to the `customBackgroundContent` variable. The node appears in front of the chart's background fill but behind all the charts content and is, by default, placed with its origin at the top-left corner of the area bounded by the axes. You can, of course, place the node elsewhere by setting its `layoutX` and `layoutY` variables.

The code on lines 17 to 26 of Listing 26-11 loads an image and places it in the background of a `ScatterChart`, giving the result shown in Figure 26-15. You'll find this code in the file `javafxcharts/Customize2.fx`.

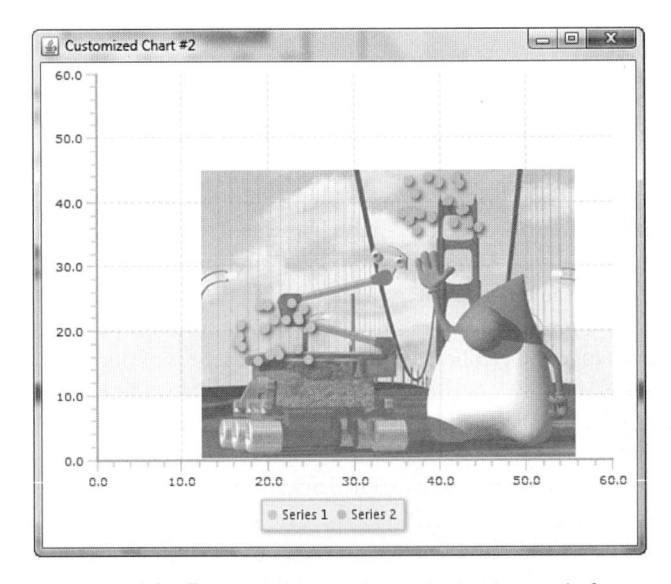

Figure 26-15 Placing an image in the background of a `ScatterChart`

Listing 26-11 Placing a Custom Node in a Chart

```
1     var chart:ScatterChart;
2     var image:Image;
3     Stage {
4         title: "Customized Chart #2"
5         scene: Scene {
6             content: [
7                 chart = ScatterChart {
8                     data: [ series1, series2 ]
9                     xAxis: NumberAxis {
10                        upperBound: 60
11                        tickUnit: 10
```

```
12                  }
13                  yAxis: NumberAxis {
14                      upperBound: 60
15                      tickUnit: 10
16                  }
17                  customBackgroundContent: ImageView {
18                      image: image = Image {
19                          url: "https://duke.dev.java.net/images/"
20                              "rover/OnBridge11small.jpg"
21                          preserveRatio: true
22                      }
23                      opacity: 0.5
24                      layoutX: bind (chart.width - image.width)/2
25                      layoutY: bind (chart.height - image.height)/2
26                  }
27              }
28          ]
29      }
30  }
```

Fills and Grid Lines

The rectangular area of an XY chart that is bounded by the axes is referred to as the *plot*. You can fill the background of the plot by setting the `plotBackgroundFill` variable, and you can draw a line border around it by setting the `plotBackgroundStroke` and `plotBackgroundStrokeWidth` variables.

XY charts provide horizontal and vertical grid lines. The visibility of these lines is controlled by the `horizontalGridLineVisible`/`verticalGridLineVisible` variables that are both true by default. However, a bug in JavaFX 1.2 causes the grid lines to not be drawn. The color, width, and dash pattern can be set independently for the horizontal and vertical grid lines. It is also possible to specify a fill the background space between horizontal or vertical grid lines by setting the `horizontalAlternateRowFill` and `verticalAlternateRowFill` variables. As the names suggest, the fill is applied to every alternate row or column.

Axis Customization

The appearance of the axes of a chart can be customized in various ways. Some customizations apply to all axis types; others apply only to the `ValueAxis` and `NumberAxis` classes.

Axis Position

By default, the *x-axis* is placed at the bottom of the chart and the *y-axis* to its left, but you can change this by setting the side variable of the Axis object. The code on lines 2 and 10 of Listing 26-12, which is taken from the file `javafxcharts/CustomizeChart3.fx`, moves the x-axis to the top and y-axis to right of the chart, as shown in Figure 26-16.

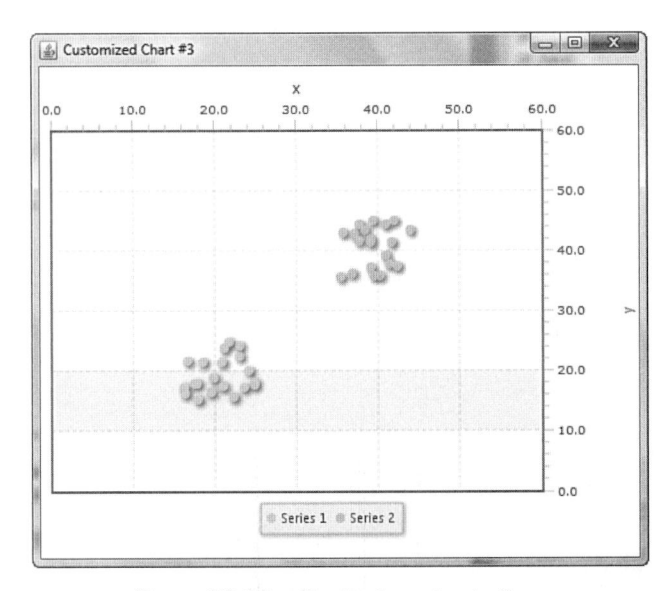

Figure 26-16   Chart axis customizations

Listing 26-12   Changing the Positions of the Axes of a Chart

```
1     xAxis: NumberAxis {
2         side: Side.TOP
3         axisStroke: Color.GREEN
4         axisStrokeWidth: 2
5         label: "x"
6         upperBound: 60
7         tickUnit: 10
8     }
9     yAxis: NumberAxis {
10        side: Side.RIGHT
11        axisStroke: Color.RED
12        axisStrokeWidth: 2
13        label: "y"
14        labelFill: Color.RED
15        upperBound: 60
16        tickUnit: 10
17    }
```

Axis Name and Color

By default, an axis does not have a label, but you can give it one by setting its `label` variable. The font and color of the label are determined by the values of the `labelFont` and `labelFill` variables. In lines 5, 13, and 14 of Listing 26-12, the axes are given the labels "x" and "y," and the color of the y-axis label is changed to red. As you can see in Figure 26-16, the label text is drawn so that it is parallel to its axis. You can vary the distance between the label and the tick marks on the axis by setting the `labelTickGap` variable.

The axis color and thickness can be changed by setting the `axisStroke` and `axisStrokeWidth` variables. In Listing 26-12, both axes are 2 pixels wide, the x-axis is green, and the y-axis is red. You can see the result in Figure 26-16.

Ticks and Tick Labels

You can change the appearance of both the ticks and the tick labels of any type of axis. Some of the possible customizations are shown in Listing 26-13, which is an extract from the code in the file `javafxcharts/Customize4.fx`.

Listing 26-13   **Tick and Tick Label Customizations**

```
1    xAxis: NumberAxis {
2        tickLabelsVisible: false
3        tickMarkVisible: false
4        upperBound: 60
5        tickUnit: 10
6    }
7    yAxis: NumberAxis {
8        upperBound: 60
9        tickUnit: 10
10       tickLabelFill: Color.RED
11       tickLabelFont: Font.font("Serif", FontWeight.BOLD,
12                               FontPosture.ITALIC, 16);
13       tickLabelTickGap: 0
14       tickMarkLength: 12
15       tickMarkStroke: Color.GREEN
16       tickMarkStrokeWidth: 2
17   }
```

You can independently remove the tick marks (that is, the short dashes that indicate the tick locations) and the tick labels (which show the tick value) by setting the `tickMarkVisible`/`tickLabelsVisible` variables to `false`. On lines 2 and 3 of Listing 26-13, both of these variables are set to `false` for the x-axis, with the result that neither tick marks nor labels appear, as you can see at the bottom of Figure 26-17. Note that both the major and minor tick marks disappear. You'll see how to remove just the minor tick marks in the next section.

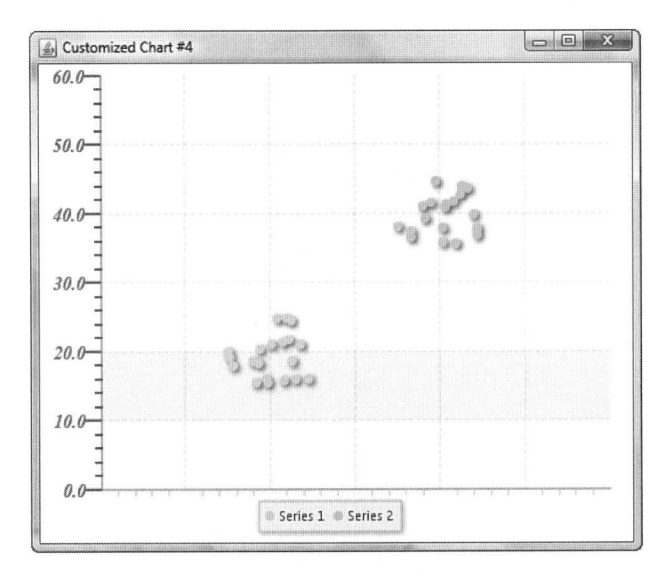

Figure 26-17   Examples of tick and tick label customizations

The `tickLabelFill` and `tickLabelFont` variables change the color and font of the tick labels, while the `tickLabelTickGap` variable controls the space between the labels and the ticks themselves. On lines 10 to 13 of Listing 26-13, we change the color of the tick labels to red, select a 16-point, bold and italic font, and reduce the gap between the labels and the tick marks to zero.

You can change the appearance of the tick marks themselves by using the `tickMarkLength`, `tickMarkStroke` and `tickMarkStrokeWidth` variables, as illustrated on lines 14 to 16 of Listing 26-13. The effect of these changes on the y-axis can be seen on the left of Figure 26-17.

Minor Ticks

On a `ValueAxis`, minor tick marks can be placed at regular intervals between the major tick marks. As you have already seen, the number of minor tick marks that appear for each major tick mark is determined by the value of the `minorTickCount` variable, which is 5 by default.

Two other variables in the `ValueAxis` class relate to minor ticks: `minorTickVisible` and `minorTickLength`. Both of these variables are used in the code in Listing 26-14, which you'll find in the file `javafxcharts/Customize5.fx`. The `minorTickVisible` variable, when set to `false`, removes minor ticks from an axis while still displaying major ticks, and the `minorTickLength` variable determines the length of a minor tick. Figure 26-18 shows the result of running this code.

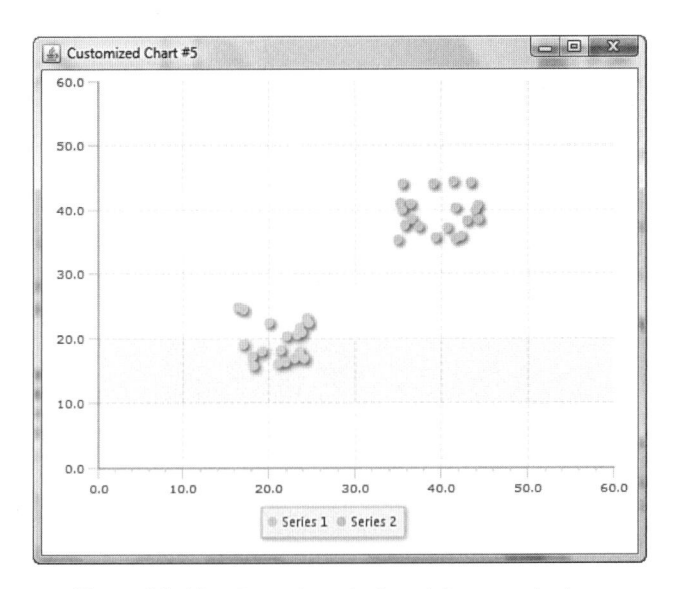

Figure 26-18   Examples of minor tick customizations

Listing 26-14   **Minor Tick Customizations**

```
1    xAxis: NumberAxis {
2        upperBound: 60
3        tickUnit: 10
4        minorTickLength: 3
5    }
6    yAxis: NumberAxis {
7        upperBound: 60
8        tickUnit: 10
9        minorTickVisible: false
10   }
```

Custom Tick Formatting

The strings that appear in tick labels are simply the result of calling the toString() function of the value associated with that tick. You can override this default behavior for an axis by installing a custom formatter in its ValueAxis object. The definition of this function, which should be assigned to the formatTickLabel function, is as follows:

public function formatTickLabel(value:Number):String;

The xValue and yValue variables of the ScatterData.Data class are both of type Number, and the tick labels on the axes of the chart are numbers that include a decimal point, even if the values themselves are actually integers, as you can in Figure 26-18. If you know that the tick values are all integers, you can remove the decimal point by installing a replacement formatter, like the one shown in the following code extract, from the file `javafxcharts/Customize6.fx`. When this code is run, the tick labels on the x-axis no longer show any decimal places, as you can see in Figure 26-19:

```
xAxis: NumberAxis {
    upperBound: 60
    tickUnit: 10
    formatTickLabel: function(value:Number):String {
        "{value as Integer}"
    }
}
```

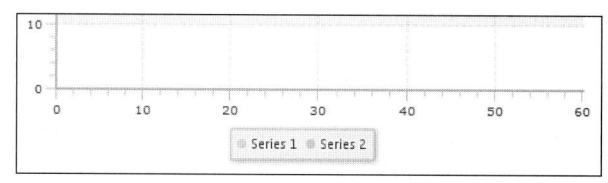

Figure 26-19   Customizing tick labels

IV

Miscellaneous

27

Using External Data Sources

The essence of a rich Internet application is its ability to display and manipulate data from the Internet, a corporate network, or even on your home network. This chapter looks at the facilities in the JavaFX platform that enable you to access external data sources. We start with the `HttpRequest` class, which provides a simple way to read data from and write data to a web server. External data access is inherently slow, so it is essential to ensure that it does not block the application thread that is responsible for updating the user interface. The `HttpRequest` class takes care of this for you by transparently doing its job in the background, while delivering its results in the user interface thread.

The second part of this chapter introduces the `PullParser` class, which allows you to parse a data stream encoded either in XML (Extensible Markup Language) or in JSON (JavaScript Object Notation). XML and JSON are commonly used to encode information returned by RESTful web services, and you see several examples that demonstrate how easy it is to use the `HttpRequest` class together with the `PullParser` to retrieve data from a web service, specifically an XML-based web service provided by Twitter and a weather service that uses the JSON format. At a slightly higher level of abstraction, the JavaFX platform can fetch or subscribe to the content of either an RSS or an Atom feed and parse it into JavaFX objects that are easier for an application to use than raw XML or JSON. In the third part of this chapter, we use the feed application programming interfaces (APIs) to create an application that displays information from the Yahoo! weather service and another that lets you search postings on the Twitter website.

This chapter closes with a discussion of the classes in the `javafx.async` package, which allow you to safely delegate to a background thread tasks that would otherwise block the user interface for an unacceptable period of time. We illustrate the general technique by showing you how to write an application that reads records from a database and uses the results to populate a `ListView` control.

The classes used in this chapter are all part of the common profile, but some of the example code in this chapter uses APIs that are available only in the desktop profile, so you will find all the example source code in the `javafxdata` package of the JavaFX Book Desktop project.

The `HttpRequest` Class

In this section, we look at the classes in the `javafx.io.http` package that let you send a request to a web server using the HTTP (or HTTPS) protocol and receive the data that is returned. The principal class in this package, `HttpRequest`, is quite complex, but in return for the complexity you get a lot of functionality. In this section, you see how to use the `HttpRequest` class to connect to a web server and receive notification as data is read from it or written to it. In the sections that follow, we go a step further by using the `HttpRequest` class along with the XML parsing classes in the `javafx.data.pull` package to invoke a web service and interpret the results.

It is worth noting that, despite its name, `HttpRequest` is not limited to the HTTP protocol. As you'll see later in this chapter, it can, in fact, retrieve data from any URL that is supported by the Java platform on which it is running.

Basic Use of the `HttpRequest` Class

The simplest possible thing you can do with the `HttpRequest` class is connect to a web server and read some data. Listing 27-1 shows how this is done.

Listing 27-1 **Example Use of the `HttpRequest` Class**

```
1       package javafxdata;
2
3       import javafx.io.http.HttpRequest;
4       import javafx.scene.image.Image;
5       import javafx.scene.image.ImageView;
6       import javafx.scene.Scene;
7       import javafx.stage.Stage;
8       import javax.imageio.ImageIO;
9       import javafx.ext.swing.SwingUtils;
10
11      var image:Image;
12      var r:HttpRequest = HttpRequest {
13          location:
14                  "https://duke.dev.java.net/images/rover/OnBridge1small.jpg"
15          sink: new ByteArrayOutputStream()
16          onDoneRead: function() {
17              var os = r.sink as ByteArrayOutputStream;
18              var is = new ByteArrayInputStream(os.toByteArray());
19              var bimg = ImageIO.read(is);
20              is.close();
21              os.close();
22              image = SwingUtils.toFXImage(bimg);
23          }
24      };
25      r.start();
26
27      Stage {
```

```
28              var scene:Scene;
29              title : "HttpRequest Example #1"
30              scene: scene = Scene {
31                  width: 350
32                  height: 280
33                  content: [
34                      ImageView {
35                          image: bind image
36                          x: bind (scene.width - image.width)/2
37                          y: bind (scene.height - image.height)/2
38                      }
39                  ]
40              }
41      }
```

The code on lines 12 to 25 creates an instance of the `HttpRequest` class and then calls its `start()` function, which assigns an integer identifier to the request, installs it in the `id` variable of the `HttpRequest`[1] object and initiates the operation in a background thread.

This simple example reads a stream of data that represents an image by installing its URL in the `location` variable of the `HttpRequest` and making an HTTP GET request, which is the default. The details of connecting to the web server, making the request, reading the response, and buffering the returned data are all encapsulated in the `HttpRequest` class and are carried out asynchronously. Under normal circumstances, a request will run to completion, but you can interrupt it by invoking the `stop()` function.[2]

As you'll see, the `HttpRequest` class provides a large number of variables and callbacks that you can use to monitor the progress of an operation, but here we just want to process the data once it is available. To do so, we create a `ByteArrayOutputStream` and install it in the `sink` variable. As data is received, it will be written to this stream, and the `onDoneRead` function will be called (in the main thread of the JavaFX application) when the whole response has been read.

In Listing 27-1, the `onDoneRead` function creates a `ByteArrayInputStream` from the data in the `ByteArrayOutputStream`. In this case, the data is an image, so we use the Java `ImageIO` class to convert the content of the `ByteArrayInputStream` into a `BufferedImage`, which is then converted to a JavaFX `Image` object by the `SwingUtils.toFXImage()` function on line 22.[3] Finally, the image is displayed in an `ImageView`, giving the result shown in Figure 27-1.

---

[1] An `HttpRequest` object can only be used to make one request. If you invoke the `start()` function for a second time, an `IllegalStateException` will be thrown.

[2] The `start()` and `stop()` functions are inherited by `HttpRequest` from the `javafx.async.Task` class, which we'll discuss later in this chapter.

[3] `BufferedImage` is part of the desktop profile, so this code will not run on a mobile device.

952　Chapter 27　Using External Data Sources

Figure 27-1　An image retrieved from a web
server using the `HttpRequest` class

Lifecycle of an HTTP Request

To initiate a connection to an HTTP server, you need to set the `location` variable to the URL of the resource that you want to operate on and the `method` variable to the HTTP operation to be performed. The `HttpRequest` class has constant definitions for each of the valid HTTP operations. In Listing 27-1, the method variable was defaulted to `HttpRequest.GET`. Later in this chapter, you'll see examples of `POST`, `PUT`, and `DELETE` operations.

If you need to write data as part of the request (which would be the case for a `POST` or `PUT` operation), you would wrap the data in an `InputStream` and install it in the `source` variable. Similarly, if you expect to receive data, you create an `OutputStream` into which the data can be written and assign it to the `sink` variable, as we did in Listing 27-1. You'll see examples of both reading and writing data in the following sections.

The overall lifecycle of an HTTP `GET` request is as follows:

1. The `location` and `method` variables of the `HttpRequest` object are set.

2. The operation is started by calling the `start()` function of the `HttpRequest` object.

3. The operation is initiated in a background thread.

4. A connection to the server is attempted.

5. The connection either succeeds and the operation continues, or an error is reported.

6. The request is sent to the web server, along with any HTTP headers in the `headers` variable of the `HttpRequest` object.

7. The response is read, starting with the HTTP headers.

8. The response code and response message are extracted from the HTTP headers.

9. If the server rejected the request, an error is notified.
10. The headers are fully processed.
11. The body of the response is read and made available to the application.
12. Completion of the request is notified.

The `HttpRequest` class has a number of variables and a corresponding set of function variables that you can use to be notified of state changes as an operation proceeds through its lifecycle. The variables that are relevant to an HTTP GET operation are listed in Table 27-1. Note that there are additional variables and functions that are used in the course of a POST or PUT operation, which we cover later in this section. In almost all cases, each status variable is paired with a callback function that is called after the variable's value has been set. This means that you can usually handle a change in state either by attaching a trigger or a binding to a state variable or by assigning a function to one of the callback function variables.[4]

The `exception` variable is set (and the `onException` function called) if an exception occurs at any point and the rest of the operation is aborted. For example, if the value of the `location` variable is not a valid URL or if the connection attempt fails, an exception will be reported. By contrast, if the connection succeeds but the server cannot return the requested data, the response code and response message are set to a value that gives the reason for the error and, in some cases, some additional information may be available through the `error` variable.

Table 27-1   Variables and Callback Functions That Track the Status of an HTTP GET Request

Variable	Variable Type	Function	Function Argument Type	Set/Function Called
started	Boolean	onStarted	None	When the operation is initiated.
exception	Exception	onException	Exception	Whenever an exception occurs.
connecting	Boolean	onConnecting	None	When the connection to the server is initiated.
doneConnect	Boolean	onDoneConnect	None	When the connection to the server has been made.

---

[4] You can also monitor progress by using variables that the `HttpRequest` class inherits from `javafx.async.Task`, which we'll discuss in "Tasks and Progress Monitoring" section, later in this chapter.

Table 27-1 Variables and Callback Functions That Track the Status of an HTTP `GET` Request (*Continued*)

Variable	Variable Type	Function	Function Argument Type	Set/Function Called
`reading-Headers`	Boolean	`onReading-Headers`	None	When the HTTP headers sent by the server are being read. The headers that are defined by the HTTP 1.1 protocol specification are all represented by constants declared by the `HttpHeaders` class.
`response-Code`	Integer	`onResponse-Code`	Integer	When the server's response code has been received. The possible values are defined as constants in the `HttpStatus` class.
`response-Message`	String	`onResponse-Message`	String	When the server's response message has been received. The response message is a textual representation of the response code.
`error`	Input Stream	`onError`	Input Stream	The value of an error response from the server, if there is one.
N/A	N/A	`onResponse-Headers`	String[]	When the response headers are available to be read.
`doneHeaders`	Boolean	`onDoneHeaders`	None	When all the HTTP headers have been processed.
`reading`	Boolean	`onReading`	None	When the body of the response is being read.
`toRead`	Long	`onToRead`	Long	When the total number of bytes of response data is known.

Table 27-1 Variables and Callback Functions That Track the Status of an HTTP `GET` Request (*Continued*)

Variable	Variable Type	Function	Function Argument Type	Set/Function Called
`read`	`Boolean`	`onRead`	`Long`	As bytes of data are received from the server.
`input`	`Input-Stream`	`onInput`	`Input-Stream`	When the response body is available to be read. This variable and its associated callback function are used only when the `sink` variable is not set. See the section "A `GET` Request to a Valid HTTP URL" for details.
`doneRead`	`Boolean`	`onDoneRead`	None	When all the body has been read.
`done`	`Boolean`	`onDone`	None	When the operation is complete, successfully or otherwise.

On completion of the operation, whether or not it is successful, the `done` variable is set to `true` and the `onDone` function is called. This is always the final step in the lifecycle.

It is important to note that, like all JavaFX objects, an `HttpRequest` must be created and used exclusively in the main thread of the JavaFX application. The process of connecting to the web server and reading/writing data are actually performed in a background thread, but the variables and callback functions in the `HttpRequest` object are always set and called in the main thread of the application. This means that application code and triggers are always called in the main thread, which is necessary because JavaFX does not support access to data from more than one thread.

If you refer back to Listing 27-1, the process of reading the image data is initiated by the invocation of the `start()` function on line 25, but it will not be complete when this function returns—receipt of data will be notified to the `onDoneRead` function at some future point and completion of the operation to the `onDone` function, which is not used in this example.

`GET` Requests

The code in the file `javafxdata/HttpRequestExample2.fx` creates a user interface with an input field into which you can type a URL, a button that can be pressed to perform a

GET request to that URL, and a textbox in which the results of the operation are displayed. The `doRequest()` function builds the `HttpRequest`, attaches triggers to the variables, and installs callbacks in all the function variables listed in Table 27-1. The triggers and callback functions all write tracking information to the textbox so that the order in which these events occur can be seen. Here is an extract from this function that shows a typical callback function and trigger:

```
function doRequest(url:String) {
    r = HttpRequest {
        location: url
        sink: new ByteArrayOutputStream()

        // Callback functions
        onConnecting: function() { addText("onConnecting\n"); }

        //
        // Code omitted
        //
        // State variables

        var connecting = bind r.connecting on replace {
                        addText("connecting -> {connecting}\n")
        //
        // Code omitted
        //
    }
    r.start();
}
```

When a callback function is invoked, its name and relevant information derived from its argument, if it has one, are recorded in the textbox. When the value of a state variable changes, its name and value are shown, separated by an arrow. In the sections that follow, we use this code to examine the results of several different GET requests. Figure 27-2 shows some typical output.

A GET Request to an Invalid URL

For our first example, we enter the URL **http://no.such.url** into the text field and click the Go button. This causes the following to be written to the textbox[5]:

```
started -> true
onStarted
connecting -> true
```

---

[5] Here and in the examples that follow, we do not show output that results from initialization of the `HttpRequest` object.

```
onConnecting
exception -> java.net.UnknownHostException: no.such.url
onException: java.net.UnknownHostException: no.such.url
done -> true
onDone
```

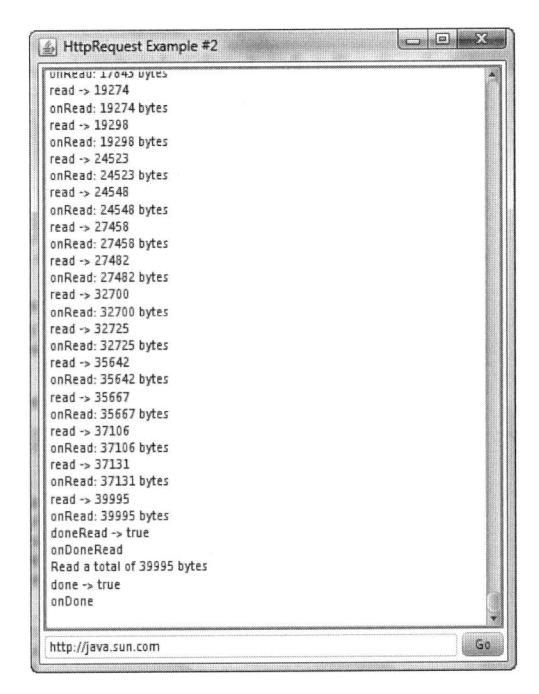

Figure 27-2   Output from an `HttpRequest`

As you can see, the request begins by notifying that it has started and is attempting to make a connection to the server. Because the URL is invalid, the attempt fails, and this results in an `UnknownHostException` being written to the `exception` variable of the `HttpRequest`, and the `onException` callback function is then called. As this terminates processing of the request, the `done` variable is set to `true`, and the `onDone` callback is called.

A `GET` Request to a URL with an Unknown Protocol

Using an unknown protocol results in an event shorter interaction than the one you have just seen. Here's the result of attempting to connect to the URL xyzzy://no.such.url:

```
started -> true
onStarted
exception -> java.net.MalformedURLException: unknown protocol: xyzzy
onException: java.net.MalformedURLException: unknown protocol: xyzzy
done -> true
onDone
```

958 Chapter 27 Using External Data Sources

Because the protocol part of the URL is not recognized, no connection handler class is found, so this request doesn't even get as far as attempting a connection. Instead, an exception is reported.

A `GET` Request to a Valid HTTP URL

For our next example, we type the URL **http://java.sun.com** into the input field and click the Go button. Because this is a valid URL, the resulting output shows the complete lifecycle for an HTTP `GET` request:

```
1     started -> true
2     onStarted
3     connecting -> true
4     onConnecting
5     doneConnect -> true
6     onDoneConnect
7     readingHeaders -> true
8     onReadingHeaders
9     responseCode -> 200
10    onResponseCode: 200
11    responseMessage -> OK
12    onResponseMessage: OK
13    onResponseHeaders    : HTTP/1.1 200 OK
14       server: Sun-Java-System-Web-Server/7.0
15       date: Sun, 26 Apr 2009 14:03:31 GMT
16       content-type: text/html;charset=ISO-8859-1
17       set-cookie: JSESSIONID=B6E70BFD3EA616ADA7C7BDB4E2F129E5;
      Path=/
18       connection: close
19    doneHeaders -> true
20    onDoneHeaders
22    reading -> true
23    onReading
24    toread -> -1
25    onToRead, length = -1
26    read -> 4156
27    onRead: 4156 bytes
28    read -> 5616
29    onRead: 5616 bytes
30    read -> 7076
31    onRead: 7076 bytes
32    read -> 10828
33    onRead: 10828 bytes
34    read -> 14580
35    onRead: 14580 bytes
36    read -> 18332
37    onRead: 18332 bytes
38    read -> 22084
```

```
39      onRead: 22084 bytes
40      read -> 25836
41      onRead: 25836 bytes
42      read -> 29588
43      onRead: 29588 bytes
44      read -> 33340
45      onRead: 33340 bytes
46      read -> 37092
47      onRead: 37092 bytes
48      read -> 40844
49      onRead: 40844 bytes
50      read -> 45236
51      onRead: 45236 bytes
52      doneRead -> true
53      onDoneRead
54      Read a total of 45236 bytes
55      done -> true
56      onDone
```

The first six lines show the process of successfully connecting to the web server at java.sun.com. At this point, the HTTP GET request is transmitted and then the HttpRequest implementation starts reading the server's response. On lines 7 to 20, the server's response and the HTTP headers are received and processed. As you can see, the start and end of this part of the exchange are clearly delineated by the onReadingHeaders call on line 8 and the onDoneHeaders call on line 20.

Strictly speaking, the response code is not part of the HTTP header block, but in the HttpRequest lifecycle it is reported at the start of header processing. The server's response code is stored in the responseCode variable, and a text string that describes the response is stored in the responseMessage variable. The possible response codes and their meanings are listed in the HTTP 1.1 protocol specification, which you can find at http://www.w3.org/Protocols/rfc2616/rfc2616.html.

The HttpStatus class defines constants that correspond to these response codes. In this case, the request was successful to the response code is 200 (which is also the value of the constant HttpStatus.OK), and the response message is simply "OK." In some cases, you might want to check the value of the response code and take specific action, but here this is not necessary.

The headers themselves each have a name and an associated string value. These are collected into a map, which is held by the HttpRequest object, and the header names are held in a sequence that is passed as an argument to the onResponseHeaders callback. Here's the code in this function that prints the header names and values:

```
onResponseHeaders: function(headers) {
    addText("onResponseHeaders");
    showHeaders(headers, r)
}
```

The `showHeaders()` function (which is part of the example code) looks like this:

```
function showHeaders(headers:String[], r:HttpRequest) {
    for (header in headers) {
        addText("    {header}: ");
        addText("{r.getResponseHeaderValue(header)}\n");
    }
}
```

The name of each header in the response is obtained from the sequence that is passed to the `onResponseHeaders` callback. The corresponding header value is obtained by calling the `getResponseHeaderValue()` function of the `HttpRequest` class, which requires a header name as its argument and returns the value of that header, or an empty string if there was no header with the given name in the server's response. This function is one of two that can be used to get response header-related information from an `HttpRequest` object:

```
public function getResponseHeaderNames():String[];
public function getResponseHeaderValue(name:String):String;
```

These functions can be called at any time, but return meaningful values only after the headers have been decoded.

> **Note**
>
> The response headers are *not* stored in the `headers` variable of the `HttpRequest` object. This variable is used only to set the outgoing *request* headers, as you'll see later in this chapter.

The response data, if any, follows the headers. In this case, the response is the HTML for the home page at java.sun.com. The sequence starts with notification that reading has begun and ends with a callback that marks the end of the processing of the data. On lines 24 and 25, the total number of bytes that will be read is stored in the `toread` variable and also passed to the `onToRead` callback function. In this case, the number of bytes is -1, which indicates that the size of the data is not known in advance. The data length is actually taken from the `content-length` header of the server's response, if it was present. In this example, this header was not present because the server is using "chunked" encoding, which is typically used to stream data from the server over a long period of time, or to return a document or other data that is constructed dynamically and for which the size will not be known until it has been generated.

As the data is being read, the total length so far received is stored in the `read` variable and reported to the `onRead` callback. It is also written to the `OutputStream` (in this case a `ByteArrayOutputStream`) assigned to the `sink` variable. In this example, the data is 45,236 bytes long and is delivered in 13 chunks. The updates to the `read` variable and the `onRead` callback are provided to allow you to display progress in the user interface. Typically, you defer handling the input until it has all been read, which is signaled by the onDoneRead callback function. Here is the code that is assigned to this callback function for this example:

```
onDoneRead: function() {
   addText("onDoneRead\n");
    var os = r.sink as ByteArrayOutputStream;
    var is = new ByteArrayInputStream(os.toByteArray());
   countStream(is);
    os.close();
}
```

The data is made accessible by creating a `ByteArrayInputStream` wrapping the content of the `ByteArrayOutputStream` that was assigned to the `sink` variable, which is then passed to the `countStream()` function, which simply counts the actual bytes that were received:

```
function countStream(is:InputStream) {
    var count = 0;
    try {
        while (is.read() != -1) {
            count++
        }
    } finally {
        is.close();
    }

    addText("Read a total of {count} bytes\n");
}
```

At this point, the request is completed, so the `done` variable is set to `true`, and the `onDone` function is called to signal the end of the request lifecycle.

An alternative mechanism is available for reading the response data that does not require you to create an `OutputStream` for the `sink` variable. If the `sink` variable is `null`, the runtime creates its own buffer in which the response data is held until it has all been received. At this point, it is wrapped in an `InputStream` that is then stored in the `input` variable and also passed to the `onInput` callback. This mechanism is used by the code in the file `javafxdata/HttpRequestExample3.fx`. Here's a snapshot of the output from this example, reading the same data from the java.sun.com website:

```
22      reading -> true
23      onReading
24      toread -> -1
25      onToRead, length = -1
26      read -> 26
27      onRead: 26 bytes
28      read -> 4141
29      onRead: 4141 bytes
30      read -> 5601
```

Chapter 27 Using External Data Sources

```
31    onRead: 5601 bytes
32    read -> 7061
33    onRead: 7061 bytes
34    read -> 8192
35    onRead: 8192 bytes
36    read -> 8216
37    onRead: 8216 bytes
38    read -> 10805
39    onRead: 10805 bytes
40    read -> 14557
41    onRead: 14557 bytes
42    read -> 16384
43    onRead: 16384 bytes
44    read -> 16408
45    onRead: 16408 bytes
46    read -> 18301
47    onRead: 18301 bytes
48    read -> 22053
49    onRead: 22053 bytes
50    read -> 24576
51    onRead: 24576 bytes
52    read -> 24600
53    onRead: 24600 bytes
54    read -> 25797
55    onRead: 25797 bytes
56    read -> 29549
57    onRead: 29549 bytes
58    read -> 32768
59    onRead: 32768 bytes
60    read -> 32792
61    onRead: 32792 bytes
62    read -> 33293
63    onRead: 33293 bytes
64    read -> 37045
65    onRead: 37045 bytes
66    read -> 40797
67    onRead: 40797 bytes
68    read -> 40960
69    onRead: 40960 bytes
70    read -> 40984
71    onRead: 40984 bytes
72    read -> 45145
73    onRead: 45145 bytes
74    read -> 45171
75    onRead: 45171 bytes
76    read -> 45226
77    onRead: 45226 bytes
78    read -> 45236
```

```
79      onRead: 45236 bytes
80      input -> com.sun.javafx.io.http.impl.WaitingInputStream@7bb290
81      onInput: 45236 bytes
82      doneRead -> true
83      onDoneRead
```

The important difference between this and our earlier example can be seen on lines 80 and 81. In this case, because the `sink` variable in the `HttpRequest` object was `null`, the runtime creates an `InputStream` to contain the response data, stores it in the `input` variable, and passes it to the `onInput` callback. The data must either be processed immediately or copied elsewhere to be used later. It is not possible to access the data later from the `onDoneRead` callback, as was done in our previous example because it will have been discarded by that time that callback is invoked. In this example, the `InputStream` is simply passed to the `countStream()` function that you saw earlier:

```
onInput: function(is) { addText("onInput: "); countStream(is)}
```

> **Warning**
>
> When using this mechanism, if the response from the web server includes any data, it will *always* be buffered, and an `InputStream` will be created and assigned to the `input` variable. *No further progress with the request will be reported until this `InputStream` is closed*. This is the case even if you do not register an `onInput` callback function. Therefore, if you do not initialize the `sink` variable and you make a request that is expected to return data, you *must* provide an `onInput` callback that will at least close the `InputStream`, In our example, the `InputStream` is closed in the `countStream()` function.

A GET Request to a URL That Does Not Exist

If you attempt to connect to a resource that does not exist on a web server that *does* exist, you will get back a response code (`HttpStatus.NOT_FOUND`, which has the value 404) reporting that the requested resource is not found. In addition, an `InputStream` that contains some supplementary information provided by the server may be stored in the `error` variable of the `HttpRequest`. Here's what happens if you try to access the URL http://java.sun.com/nosuchpage:

```
1       started -> true
2       onStarted
3       connecting -> true
4       onConnecting
5       doneConnect -> true
6       onDoneConnect
7       readingHeaders -> true
8       onReadingHeaders
9       responseCode -> 404
10      onResponseCode: 404
11      responseMessage -> Not found
12      onResponseMessage: Not found
13      error ->
        sun.net.www.protocol.http.HttpURLConnection$HttpInputStream@1e5579 4
```

```
14      onError: Error:
15
16      <!DOCTYPE HTML PUBLIC "-//W3C//DTD HTML 4.01 Transitional//EN">
17      <html>
18      <head>
19      <title>Sun Microsystems</title>
20
21      (Further content not shown)
22
23      </html>
24
25      onResponseHeaders    :
26          server: Sun-Java-System-Web-Server/7.0
27          date: Wed, 15 Apr 2009 19:51:00 GMT
28          transfer-encoding: chunked
29      doneHeaders -> true
30      onDoneHeaders
31      exception -> java.io.FileNotFoundException:
        http://java.sun.com/nosuchpage
32      onException: java.io.FileNotFoundException:
        http://java.sun.com/nosuchpage
33      done -> true
34      onDone
```

As in our previous example, the lifecycle begins with a successful connection to the web server (lines 1 to 6) and then the headers are returned. The response code, received on lines 9 and 10, and the response message, seen on lines 11 and 12, indicate that the resource does not exist. In addition to this, the `error` variable is set to point to an `InputStream` subclasses that contains additional data supplied by the web server (see line 13), and this `InputStream` is also passed as an argument to the `onError` callback on line 14. In our example code, the function assigned to this callback reads the content of that stream and writes it to the text component in the user interface (see lines 15 to 24). In this case, the content is some HTML that is intended to be displayed to the user, which is not reproduced here because it is too large. The error is also automatically converted to a `FileNotFoundException` that is stored in the `exception` variable and delivered to the `onException` callback on lines 31 and 32.

> **Note**
>
> Unlike the `InputStream` assigned to the `input` variable, you are not *required* to read the content of the `InputStream` in the `error` variable. If you don't read it, it will be discarded and the stream will be closed.

Retrieving Data from an FTP Server

Despite its name, the `HttpRequest` class can be used to read data from *any* source that has a URL with a protocol that is supported by the underlying Java platform. This includes local files (using the `file:` protocol) and FTP servers (using the `ftp:` protocol). Here's the result of reading the document /etc/motd from the FTP server at ftp.gimp.org, using the URL ftp://ftp.gimp.org/etc/motd:

```
1       started -> true
2       onStarted
3       connecting -> true
4       onConnecting
5       doneConnect -> true
6       onDoneConnect
7       readingHeaders -> true
8       onReadingHeaders
9       onResponseHeaders    content-length: 433
10      doneHeaders -> true
11      onDoneHeaders
12      reading -> true
13      onReading
14      toread -> 433
15      onToRead, length = 433
16      read -> 433
17      onRead: 433 bytes
18      input -> com.sun.javafx.io.http.impl.WaitingInputStream@1162212
19      onInput: 433 bytes
20      doneRead -> true
21      onDoneRead
22      done -> true
23      onDone
```

If you compare this with the successful requests to an HTTP server shown in the "A GET Request to a Valid HTTP URL" section, earlier in this chapter, you see that the lifecycle is broadly the same—the connection is made on lines 1 to 6, the receipt of data is reported on lines 12 to 17, the data is made available to be read via an InputStream on lines 18 and 19, and the lifecycle concludes with the done variable being set to true on lines 22 and 23. However, because this example uses the FTP protocol rather than HTTP, there is no response code, no response message, and only a single header that reports the size of the document being retrieved. Even this header is not real—it is constructed based on information returned by the FTP server. The data can be read (and in fact *must* be read, for the same reason as data returned from an HTTP server must be read) from the InputStream stored in the input variable and passed to the onInput callback, in the same way as any other HttpRequest.

PUT Requests

An HTTP PUT request is typically used to upload new data to a web server. The data is supplied in the body of the request, following the headers. The HttpRequest class provides a small number of variables and callback functions, in addition to those listed in Table 27-1 that are used when uploading data. These variables and callbacks are listed in Table 27-2.

Table 27-2 Variables and Callback Functions That Track the Status of an HTTP `PUT` or HTTP `POST` Request

Variable	Variable Type	Function	Function Argument Type	Set/Function Called
`writing`	`Boolean`	`onWriting`	None	Just before the request data is written.
`output`	`Output-Stream`	`onOutput`	`Output Stream`	When the request data is required. Not set or called when the `source` variable is not `null`. See the text for details.
`toWrite`	`Long`	`onToWrite`	`Long`	When the data to be written has been supplied and is about to be written.
`written`	`Long`	`onWritten`	`Long`	As bytes of request data are written. May be set/called multiple times.
`doneWrite`	`Boolean`	`onDoneWrite`	None	When all the request data has been written.

When uploading data, you need to set the HTTP headers that indicate the type of the data, its encoding, and its length. The `headers` variable of the `HttpRequest` object is provided for this purpose. The data itself can be supplied in either of two ways—you can wrap it in an `InputStream` and reference it from the `source` variable, or you can allow the `HttpRequest` class to create an `OutputStream` that you write to when the data is required. We'll show both possibilities in this section.

The example code in the file `javafxdata/HttpRequestExample4.fx` performs a `PUT` request and supplies its data via the `source` variable. Like the rest of the examples in this section, it uses a servlet that you need to compile and deploy. In the Preface to this book, you will find instructions for installing the integrated development environment (IDE) plug-ins required to run the servlet. To start the servlet, right click the ExternalData project in the IDE and click Run. Here, we assume that the servlet is running in a web container that is listing on port 8080 of the same computer as the one on which the examples are being run. When you run the example, you will see a familiar user interface that allows you to enter a URL, initiate the request, and then view the results, as shown in Figure 27-3.

The URL used is http://localhost:8080/ExternalData/HttpRequestServlet/a/b/c/d. The first part of this URL (up to and including `HttpRequestServlet`) refers to the servlet itself. The balance of the URL is the name of a file into which the uploaded data is to be stored. In fact, the servlet does not actually store the data—it just returns a response

The HttpRequest Class   967

```
HttpRequest Example #4
onConnecting
doneConnect -> true
onDoneConnect
writing -> true
onWriting
towrite -> 23
onToWrite, length = 23
written -> 23
onWritten, length = 23
doneWrite -> true
onDoneWrite
readingHeaders -> true
onReadingHeaders
responseCode -> 200
onResponseCode: 200
responseMessage -> Got 23 bytes, type text/plain
onResponseMessage: Got 23 bytes, type text/plain
onResponseHeaders   : HTTP/1.1 200 Got 23 bytes, type text/plain
    x-powered-by: Servlet/2.5
    server: Sun GlassFish Enterprise Server v2.1
    content-type: text/html; charset=iso-8859-1
    content-length: 0
    date: Sat, 29 May 2010 19:03:00 GMT
doneHeaders -> true
onDoneHeaders
reading -> true
onReading
onToRead, length = 0
doneRead -> true
onDoneRead
done -> true
onDone

http://localhost:8080/ExternalData/HttpRequestServlet/a/b/c/d    PUT
```

Figure 27-3   Output from an HTTP **PUT** request

message that indicates the content type of the data and how many bytes were received, both of which come from the HTTP headers set in the headers variable of the HttpRequest.

Here is the code that creates the HttpRequest for this example. As before, for the sake of brevity, we omit the lines that set triggers on the state variables and install callback functions:

```
1    function doRequest(url:String) {
2        var data = "The data to be written\n";
3        var bytes = data.getBytes("UTF-8");
4        r = HttpRequest {
5            location: url
6            method: HttpRequest.PUT
7            source: new ByteArrayInputStream(bytes);
8            headers: [
9                HttpHeader {
10                   name: HttpHeader.CONTENT_TYPE
11                   value: "text/plain"
12               },
13               HttpHeader {
14                   name: HttpHeader.CONTENT_LENGTH
15                   value: "{bytes.length}"
16               },
```

```
17                    HttpHeader {
18                        name: HttpHeader.CONTENT_ENCODING
19                        value: "UTF-8"
20                    },
21                ]
22
23                // Code omitted
24            }
25            r.start();
26       }
```

Lines 2 and 3 convert the data to be sent from a `String` to an array of bytes in the UTF-8 encoding. The `location` variable of the `HttpRequest` is set to the URL of the servlet plus the name of the imaginary file to be written, while the `method` variable is set to indicate a `PUT` operation. The `source` variable is set to a `ByteArrayInputStream` wrapping the data bytes to be uploaded and three HTTP headers, each an instance of the `HttpHeader` class, are installed in the `headers` variable. Each header has a name, as defined by the `HttpHeader` class, and a corresponding value.

The output from this request is shown here:

```
1    started -> true
2    onStarted
3    connecting -> true
4    onConnecting
5    doneConnect -> true
6    onDoneConnect
7    writing -> true
8    onWriting
9    towrite -> -1
10   onToWrite, length = -1
11   written -> 23
12   onWritten, length = 23
13   doneWrite -> true
14   onDoneWrite
15   readingHeaders -> true
16   onReadingHeaders
17   responseCode -> 200
18   onResponseCode: 200
19   responseMessage -> Got 23 bytes, type text/plain
20   onResponseMessage: Got 23 bytes, type text/plain
21   onResponseHeaders    : HTTP/1.1 200 Got 23 bytes, type text/plain
22       x-powered-by: Servlet/2.5
23       server: Sun Java System Application Server 9.1_02
24       content-type: text/html; charset=iso-8859-1
25       content-length: 0
26       date: Sun, 26 Apr 2009 15:45:33 GMT
27   doneHeaders -> true
28   onDoneHeaders
```

```
29        reading -> true
30        onReading
31        onToRead, length = 0
32        doneRead -> true
33        onDoneRead
34        done -> true
35        onDone
```

Lines 7 to 14 show the process of writing the data to be uploaded, starting with the `writing` variable being set to `true` on line 7. As you can see, the `onToWrite` variable has the value `-1`. This is always the case when you supply the data to be uploaded through the `source` variable. Lines 11 to 14 indicate that 23 bytes of data were actually written, which is the correct length for the data that is supplied in this case.

An alternative means of supplying the upload data is used in the example that you'll find in the file `javafxdata/HttpRequestExample5.fx`. Here, the data is not prepared in advance. Instead, the `source` variable has it default value (which is `null`). This causes the `HttpRequest` class to call the `onOutput` callback function when it is ready to send the data to the server. This function is passed an `OutputStream` to which the data must be written. Here is the code from this example that creates and initiates the `HttpRequest`:

```
1     function doRequest(url:String) {
2         r = HttpRequest {
3             location: url
4             method: HttpRequest.PUT
5             headers: [
6                 HttpHeader {
7                     name: HttpHeader.CONTENT_TYPE
8                     value: "text/plain"
9                 },
10                HttpHeader {
11                    name: HttpHeader.CONTENT_LENGTH
12                    value: "{data.length()}"
13                },
14                HttpHeader {
15                    name: HttpHeader.CONTENT_ENCODING
16                    value: "UTF-8"
17                },
18            ]
19
20            // Code omitted
21
22            onOutput: function(os) {
23                textArea.append("onOutput called\n");
24                var bytes = data.getBytes("UTF-8");
25                os.write(bytes);
26                os.close();
27            }
28
```

Chapter 27 Using External Data Sources

```
29                // Code omitted
30            }
31            r.start();
32        }
```

As you can see, the `source` variable is not set. Instead, the `onOutput` callback function is implemented. When it is called, the data to be written is converted to bytes in the UTF-8 encoding and written to the `OutputStream` that is passed to it, following which the stream is closed.

> **Warning**
>
> If the stream is not closed, no further progress will be made with the request. The `close()` call on line 26 is, therefore, essential.

Here is some typical output from this example:

```
1     started -> true
2     onStarted
3     connecting -> true
4     onConnecting
5     doneConnect -> true
6     onDoneConnect
7     writing -> true
8     onWriting
9     output ->
10    onOutput called
11    towrite -> 23
12    onToWrite, length = 23
13    written -> 23
14    onWritten, length = 23
15    doneWrite -> true
16    onDoneWrite
17    readingHeaders -> true
18    onReadingHeaders
19    responseCode -> 200
20    onResponseCode: 200
21    responseMessage -> Got 23 bytes, type text/plain
22    onResponseMessage: Got 23 bytes, type text/plain
23    onResponseHeaders    : HTTP/1.1 200 Got 23 bytes, type text/plain
24        x-powered-by: Servlet/2.5
25        server: Sun Java System Application Server 9.1_02
26        content-type: text/html; charset=iso-8859-1
27        content-length: 0
28        date: Sun, 26 Apr 2009 16:43:02 GMT
29    doneHeaders -> true
30    onDoneHeaders
31    reading -> true
32    onReading
33    onToRead, length = 0
```

```
34    doneRead -> true
35    onDoneRead
36    done -> true
37    onDone
```

As you can see, this is identical to the previous case apart from lines 9 and 10, which report the setting of the `output` variable and the invocation of the `onOutput` function. This is the point at which the preceding code is executed to write the request data to the `OutputStream` supplied by the `HttpRequest` class.

POST Requests

In terms of its mechanics, a `POST` request is pretty much the same as a `PUT`—you set the method, location, headers that indicate the content type, length and encoding, supply the data to be sent in the `source` variable, start the request, and eventually you handle the response. `POST` requests are often used to submit a query (typically derived from an input form) to a web server. Because this is such a common operation, we'll take a look at how to submit the content of a form using the `HttpRequest` class.

Browsers model a form as a set of parameter/value pairs, where each parameter is typically represented by an input field on the form and the value is taken from the content of that input field. When a form is submitted, the set of parameter/value pairs is encoded and sent to the web server in the body of a `POST` request.[6] Let's suppose that the form has fields called `param1` and `param2` and that these fields contain the values `value #1` and `value #2`, respectively. The data that is sent in the request body for this form would look like this:

`param1=value+%231&param2=value+%232`

As you can see, the name/value pairs are separated by an ampersand. If there were three fields on the form, there would be three such pairings and therefore two ampersands. The values themselves have been encoded according to rules defined by the HTML specification. In essence, these rules require that all spaces in a form value be replaced by a `+` character and all nonalphanumeric values be replaced by their numeric equivalent, preceded by a `%` character. Here, the `#` characters have been encoded as `%23`, because 0x23 is the ASCII representation of `#`. This set of encoding rules is referred to as *URL encoding* because it allows you to include form data in the URL of a `GET` request as well as in the body of a `POST` request.

Performing this conversion is tedious, but fortunately there is a class called `URLConverter` in the `javafx.io.http` package that will handle the details for you. This class has several functions that you can use to work with data that is or needs to be URL encoded. The particular function that we are going to use for this example is declared as follows:

`public function encodeParameters(parameters:Pair[]):String`

---

[6] Forms can also be submitted using a `GET` operation. We cover this at the end of this section.

Each name/value pair is represented as an instance of the `javafx.data.Pair` class, which holds both the name and the associated value. The result of the function call is the previous encoded string.

The code that creates and submits the POST request can be found in the file `javafxdata/HttpRequestExample6.fx`—here's an extract that shows the important details. As before, when creating the `HttpRequest` object, we install triggers and callback functions that report the progress of the request as it is executed, but we do not show those details here:

```
1    function doRequest(url:String) {
2        var params = [
3            Pair { name: "param1" value: "value #1" },
4            Pair { name: "param2" value: "value #2" },
5        ];
6        var converter = URLConverter {};
7        var postData = converter.encodeParameters(params);
8        addText("Encoded data: ");
9        var bytes = postData.getBytes("UTF-8");
10       r = HttpRequest {
11           location: url
12           method: HttpRequest.POST
13           source: new ByteArrayInputStream(bytes);
14           headers: [
15               HttpHeader {
16                   name: HttpHeader.CONTENT_TYPE
17                   value: "application/x-www-form-urlencoded"
18               },
19               HttpHeader {
20                   name: HttpHeader.CONTENT_LENGTH
21                   value: "{bytes.length}"
22               },
23               HttpHeader {
24                   name: HttpHeader.CONTENT_ENCODING
25                   value: "UTF-8"
26               },
27           ]
28           // Code omitted
29       }
30       r.start();
31   }
```

The code on lines 2 to 5 creates the name/value pairs for the form by using `Pair` objects. On lines 6 and 7, we create a `URLConverter` instance and invoke its `encodeParameters()` function to apply the URL encoding to the form parameters to produce the representation required for the request body. On line 9, we convert the parameter string to bytes in the UTF-8 encoding.

The `HttpRequest` is almost identical to the one in the PUT example shown earlier in this chapter. The only differences are the `method`, which is `HttpRequest.POST` in this case, and the content type header, which is `application/x-www-form-urlencoded`. This special value indicates that the URL encoding rules described above have been used to encode the data in the body of the request. That data is passed to the `HttpRequest` in form of a `ByteArrayInputStream` assigned to the `source` variable.

If you run this code and use the same URL as the one in the PUT example in the previous section, you will see the result of the operation in the usual place in the user interface. When it receives a POST request, the servlet reads the parameter/value pairs and values from the body and returns them as part of the response code, separated by vertical bars, to demonstrate that they have been correctly encoded. Here's an extract from the output that shows the servlet's response:

```
responseCode -> 200
onResponseCode: 200
responseMessage -> param1=value #1|param2=value #2|
onResponseMessage: param1=value #1|param2=value #2|
```

Form data can also be submitted by using a GET request. In this case, the request body would be empty and the URL encoded form data is appended to the rest of the URL and separated from it by a ? character, like this:

```
http://host/servletpath?param1=value+%231&param2=value+%232
```

DELETE Requests

As it name suggests, the HTTP DELETE operation is used to request the removal of the resource identified by the target URL. In terms of the `HttpRequest` class, the resource to be removed is specified by the `location` variable, and the method variable is set to `HttpRequest.DELETE`. The following code extract, from the file `javafxdata/HttpRequestExample7.fx`, shows how to create and perform a DELETE request:

```
function doRequest(url:String) {
    r = HttpRequest {
        location: url
        method: HttpRequest.DELETE
        // Code to add triggers and callback functions omitted
    }
    r.start();
}
```

Running this example and entering the same URL as that used in the PUT and POST examples earlier causes the servlet to respond with a message that indicates that the DELETE request was understood (although the example servlet does not actually delete anything):

```
onStarted
onConnecting
onDoneConnect
onReadingHeaders
```

```
onResponseCode: 200
```
onResponseMessage: Deleted file /a/b/c/d
```
onResponseHeaders    : HTTP/1.1 200 Deleted file /a/b/c/d
    x-powered-by: Servlet/2.5
    server: Sun Java System Application Server 9.1_02
    content-type: text/html; charset=iso-8859-1
    content-length: 0
    date: Mon, 27 Apr 2009 20:40:15 GMT
onDoneHeaders
onDone
```

Using RESTful Web Services

Two different styles of web service are in use today: SOAP-based web services and RESTful web services.

To access a SOAP-based web service, you create an XML payload, wrap it in HTTP, and POST it to a web server on which the service is running. The XML payload is constructed from a set of rules contained in a WSDL (Web Service Definition Language) file, which specifies the operations that the service provides, the parameters that you need to supply to those operations, and the value or values that will be returned. The process of constructing the payload is sufficiently nontrivial that nobody ever writes code to do it—instead, there are tools that convert a WSDL file to a Java class that has a method for each of the available operations. To invoke one of the web service's operations, you just call the corresponding method in the generated Java class, which takes care of converting the request and its parameters to XML, opening an HTTP connection to the web server, retrieving the response, and converting it back to Java objects. This whole process is synchronous to the method caller, so the calling thread will be blocked until the results of the call have been received. Because of the synchronous nature of the generated class, to access a SOAP-based web service from JavaFX, you need to invoke its methods in a background thread and then display the results in the main thread of your application. We'll look at the support that JavaFX provides for asynchronous operations of this type in the context of database access in the "Asynchronous Operations and Database Access" section, later in this chapter.

If using a SOAP-based web services sounds like a lot of work, you will probably be pleased to hear that it is much easier to use a RESTful web service. RESTful web services are usually not formally defined in an XML file, and there is no need to use a code generator to create the access methods. To use a RESTful web service, you simply identify the object to be operated on by its URL, set the HTTP method to indicate the operation to be performed, and use the `HttpRequest` class to initiate the operation. As you have seen, `HttpRequest` does its job in a background thread and notifies completion in the application's main thread, which means that your application's user interface will not freeze while the operation is in progress. The result of a RESTful web service operation is usually XML, although some services encode their response in JSON (JavaScript Object Notation—see http://www.json.org). To interpret the reply, you need either an XML or a

JSON parser. JavaFX has both, wrapped up in a single class called
`javafx.data.pull.PullParser`.

In this section, we take a look at how to access a RESTful web service from JavaFX. We start by looking at how you can use the `PullParser` class to parse XML, and we'll implement a simple JavaFX client that retrieves and displays information from the Twitter social networking website. Later, you'll see how to use the `PullParser` class to interpret the results of a web service that returns its results in the JSON encoding.

Parsing XML

There are three different styles of XML parsing:

- DOM-style parsing: This converts an XML document into an in-memory tree in which each XML element is represented by a tree node. The nesting of XML elements is mirrored exactly by the nesting of nodes in the DOM (Document Object Model) tree. This style of parsing is very convenient if you want to convert XML into Java objects, but modeling a large XML document requires a correspondingly large commitment of memory. For this reason, DOM parsing is not usually supported on small-footprint devices like cell phones.

- Stream parsing (or SAX parsing): In this style, the parser reads through the document, possibly as it is being received from its source, and notifies events to an application-supplied event handler. Examples of events are at the start of the document, start of an element, text, comments, processing instructions, end of an element, and end of the document. Stream parsing can be very efficient because it does not require the whole document to be in memory at the same time.

- Pull parsing: Whereas a stream parser invokes application code as it reads through the XML document, a pull parser does nothing unless it is told to. An application using a pull parser processes a document by "pulling" elements that it is interested in when it needs them.

The `PullParser` class in the `javafx.data.pull` package supports stream and pull parsing for both XML and JSON documents. Which of these modes you choose to use is largely a matter of taste, although as you'll see, pull parsing requires greater knowledge of the structure of an XML document than stream parsing. The variables of the `PullParser` class, which we will describe in detail in this section, are listed in Table 27-3.

Table 27-3   Variables of the `PullParser` Class

Variable	Type	Access	Default	Description
documentType	String	RW	XML	The type of document to be parsed—either `PullParser.XML` or `PullParser.JSON`

Table 27-3   Variables of the `PullParser` Class (*Continued*)

Variable	Type	Access	Default	Description
`input`	`InputStream`	RW	`null`	The source of the XML or JSON to be parsed
`encoding`	`String`	RW	"UTF-8"	The encoding used for the input document
`ignoreWhiteSpace`	`Boolean`	RW	`false`	If true, causes text elements that are entirely whitespace to be ignored
`onEvent`	`function(:Event):Void`	RW	`null`	Callback function to which parsing events are delivered
`event`	`Event`	R		The current parsing event
`characterEncoding`	`String`	R		The encoding of the input document as detected by the parser
`line`	`Integer`	R		The line number of the element currently being parsed
`column`	`Integer`	R		The column number of the element currently being parsed

Stream Parsing

To use the `PullParser` class in streaming mode, you initialize it with an input source, set the `documentType` variable to either `PullParser.XML` or `PullParser.JSON`, install a function that will handle callbacks as the input is parsed, and then call the `parse()` function. Parsing is synchronous and will be completed before this call returns. The code in Listing 27-2, which you'll find in the file `javafxdata/XMLParsing1.fx`, parses XML held in a string and reports the events delivered to its callback function on the console.

Listing 27-2 **Stream Parsing with the `PullParser` Class**

```
1    var xml =
2    '<?xml version="1.0" encoding="UTF-8"?>'
3    '<!--- Membership list -->'
4    '<members>'
5    '    <member>'
6    '        <id>'
7    '            <name>John Doe</name>'
8    '            <address type="home">Here</address>'
9    '            <address type="business">There</address>'
10   '        </id>'
11   '        <membership-type>Full</membership-type>'
12   '    </member>'
13   '</members>';
14
15   var parser = PullParser {
16       documentType: PullParser.XML
17       input: new ByteArrayInputStream(xml.getBytes("UTF-8"))
18       onEvent: function(evt) {
19           println(evt);
20       }
21   }
22   parser.parse();
```

The `PullParser` object is created on lines 15 to 21 and initialized to parse XML (line 16) from the string assigned to the `xml` variable. A `PullParser` requires an `InputStream` as its source, so we first convert the string to an array of bytes encoded in UTF-8[7] and then create a `ByteArrayInputStream` from the result. As the XML is parsed, events are reported to the function installed in the `onEvent` variable on lines 18 to 20. The argument passed to this function is of type `javafx.data.pull.Event`. The `Event` class is used when parsing both XML and JSON and has some variables that are set only when processing XML and others that are meaningful only when processing JSON. The variables that are relevant to XML processing are listed in Table 27-4.

Table 27-4 **Variables of the `Event` Class That Are Relevant to XML Parsing**

Variable	Type	Access	Description
type	Integer	R	The event type, such as `PullParser.START_ELEMENT`

---

[7] We chose UTF-8 because this is the encoding that the parser expects by default. You can use a different encoding if you want, provided that you set the `encoding` variable of the `PullParser` to reflect your chosen encoding.

Table 27-4 Variables of the `Event` Class That Are Relevant to XML Parsing (*Continued*)

Variable	Type	Access	Description
typeName	String	R	The event type in human-readable form
qname	QName	R	The fully-qualified name of the current element
level	Integer	R	The nesting level of the current element, where the root element has level 0
text	String	R	The text associated with a `TEXT` element

Each event has a type, given by the `type` variable, which indicates which event is being reported; the `typeName` variable contains a human-readable representation of the event type which is useful for debugging purposes. The `level` variable specifies the nesting level of the XML element to which the event relates and the `qname` variable is its fully qualified name. XML element names are made up of two parts—a simple name and an optional prefix that indicates the namespace that defines the name. The `qname` variable is of type `javafx.data.xml.QName`, which is a class that encapsulates the element name, its namespace prefix, and the URI of the namespace itself. Simple XML documents, such as the one in this example (and those returned by some commonly used web services), do not use namespaces at all, which makes the document easier to read and your code easier to write because you only need to check the simple name of an element to identify it. The `text` variable is set to report a run of text in the document.

We'll use the output from the code in Listing 27-2 to illustrate how the parser works. Later in this chapter, you'll see real-world examples that actually act on upon the results of an XML parsing operation:

```
1     type:7 typeName:START_DOCUMENT level:0 qname:null text:''
2     namespaces:null attributes:null
3     type:1 typeName:START_ELEMENT level:0 qname:members text:''
4     namespaces:{} attributes:{}
5     type:4 typeName:TEXT level:0 qname:members text:'       '
6     namespaces:null attributes:null
7     type:1 typeName:START_ELEMENT level:1 qname:member text:''
8     namespaces:{} attributes:{}
9     type:4 typeName:TEXT level:1 qname:member text:'         '
10    namespaces:null attributes:null
11    type:1 typeName:START_ELEMENT level:2 qname:id text:''
12    namespaces:{} attributes:{}
13    type:4 typeName:TEXT level:2 qname:id text:'            '
14    namespaces:null attributes:null
15    type:1 typeName:START_ELEMENT level:3 qname:name text:''
16    namespaces:{} attributes:{}
17    type:4 typeName:TEXT level:3 qname:name text:'John Doe'
18    namespaces:null attributes:null
19    type:2 typeName:END_ELEMENT level:3 qname:name text:'John Doe'
20    namespaces:{} attributes:null
```

```
21      type:4 typeName:TEXT level:0 qname:id text:'         '
22      namespaces:null attributes:null
23      type:1 typeName:START_ELEMENT level:3 qname:address text:''
24      namespaces:{} attributes:{type=home}
25      type:4 typeName:TEXT level:3 qname:address text:'Here'
26      namespaces:null attributes:null
27      type:2 typeName:END_ELEMENT level:3 qname:address text:'Here'
28      namespaces:{} attributes:null
29      type:4 typeName:TEXT level:0 qname:id text:'         '
30      namespaces:null attributes:null
31      type:1 typeName:START_ELEMENT level:3 qname:address text:''
32      namespaces:{} attributes:{type=business}
33      type:4 typeName:TEXT level:3 qname:address text:'There'
34      namespaces:null attributes:null
35      type:2 typeName:END_ELEMENT level:3 qname:address text:'There'
36      namespaces:{} attributes:null
37      type:4 typeName:TEXT level:0 qname:id text:'         '
38      namespaces:null attributes:null
39      type:2 typeName:END_ELEMENT level:2 qname:id text:'         '
40      namespaces:{} attributes:null
41      type:4 typeName:TEXT level:0 qname:member text:'      '
42      namespaces:null attributes:null
43      type:1 typeName:START_ELEMENT level:2 qname:membership-type
44      text:'' namespaces:{} attributes:{}
45      type:4 typeName:TEXT level:2 qname:membership-type text:'Full'
46      namespaces:null attributes:null
47      type:2 typeName:END_ELEMENT level:2 qname:membership-type
48      text:'Full' namespaces:{} attributes:null
49      type:4 typeName:TEXT level:0 qname:member text:'    '
50      namespaces:null attributes:null
51      type:2 typeName:END_ELEMENT level:1 qname:member text:'    '
52      namespaces:{} attributes:null
53      type:2 typeName:END_ELEMENT level:0 qname:members text:''
54      namespaces:{} attributes:null
55      type:8 typeName:END_DOCUMENT level:0 qname:null text:''
56      name    spaces:null attributes:null
```

The first and last events, which have the types PullParser.START_DOCUMENT and PullParser.END_DOCUMENT, respectively, report the beginning and end of the XML document. These events always occur outside of any XML element and so always have a level of zero, an empty element name and empty text.

The events on lines 3 to 8 report the <members> and <member> elements that appear on lines 4 and 5 of Listing 27-2 and the whitespace text between them. When an opening element, such as <members>, is encountered, a START_ELEMENT event that reports the element name and its indentation level is generated. The <members> element is the root element of the document, so its level variable is set to 0, while the <member> element that is nested within it has indentation level 1. The whitespace that appears between these two elements is reported by a TEXT event. In most cases, you don't want to process text that is entirely whitespace, so events like this are not useful, and you can suppress them by setting the ignoreWhiteSpace variable to true. In the rest of this discussion, we ignore events that report whitespace text.

The events on lines 15 to 20, repeated here for convenience, report the <name> element on line 7 of Listing 27-2:

```
type:1 typeName:START_ELEMENT level:3 qname:name text:''
namespaces:{} attributes:{}
type:4 typeName:TEXT level:3 qname:name text:'John Doe'
namespaces:null attributes:null
type:2 typeName:END_ELEMENT level:3 qname:name text:'John Doe'
namespaces:{} attributes:null
```

The first event is generated when the <name> element is encountered, the second when the text content of the element is read, and the third when the closing </name> element is reached. Notice that the nested text is available from both the TEXT and END_ELEMENT events, which means that you can choose to process it on receipt of either event.[8]

On lines 8 and 9 of Listing 27-2, there are two <address> elements, each with a different value for the type attribute. The events that correspond to the first of these elements, which appear on lines 23 to 28 of the output, are shown here:

```
type:1 typeName:START_ELEMENT level:3 qname:address text:''
namespaces:{} attributes:{type=home}
type:4 typeName:TEXT level:3 qname:address text:'Here'
namespaces:null attributes:null
type:2 typeName:END_ELEMENT level:3 qname:address text:'Here'
namespaces:{} attributes:null
```

As you can see, the name and value of an attribute is reported as part of a START_ELEMENT event. The attributes are not exposed as a variable of the Event class but can be obtained from the following functions:

```
public function getAttributeNames():Object[];
public function getAttributeValue(name:Object):String;
```

The getAttributeNames() function returns a sequence containing the names of the attributes that appear in the element. Of course, if you know the name of the attribute whose value you require, which is the normal case, you don't need to call this function. Given the name of an attribute, you can get its value by calling the getAttributeValue() function, which returns an empty string if the named attribute does not appear in the element:

```
// The following code returns "home" or "business"
String value = evt.getAttributeValue("type");
```

---

[8] The text is not reported by the START_ELEMENT event because it won't have been read when this event is generated.

The rest of the output follows the same pattern and should be easily understood. Note that the parser does *not* report the presence of XML processing instructions, like that shown on line 2 of Listing 27-2, or comments like the one on line 3.

> **Warning**
>
> If you try to parse XML that is not valid, events will be reported until the parser detects an error, at which point an exception will be thrown. Because JavaFX script does not have a syntax that allows a function to declare that it could throw an exception, it is not obvious from the declaration of the `parse()` function that this might happen. If you are parsing XML that might not be well formed, you may need to catch the exception and recover gracefully.

Pull Parsing

To use the pull parsing API, you create a `PullParser` in the same way as when using the streaming API, but you don't call the `parse()` function. Instead, you navigate the document structure by using the following functions:

```
public function seek(element:Object):PullParser;
public function seek(element:Object, level:Integer):PullParser;
public function forward():PullParser;
public function forward(count:Integer):PullParser;
```

The `seek()` functions work forward through the document from the current position until a given element is found. The single-argument variant looks for the element anywhere between the current position and the end of the document, while the second variant returns the element only if it occurs at the specified level of indentation.

The `element` argument to both of these functions can be either a `String` or a `QName`. If it is a `String`, any element with the specified name will match, regardless of its namespace. To match on both a namespace and a name, use a `QName` instead.

The `forward()` function skips forward by one event, while the `forward(count)` function skips forward by the specified number of events.

The code in Listing 27-3, which is taken from the file `javafxdata/XMLParsing2.fx`, uses the pull parsing API to extract the name and home address values from the same XML string as the one we used in the streaming example in Listing 27-2.

Listing 27-3   **Pull Parsing with the `PullParser` Class**

```
1    var xml =
2    '<?xml version="1.0" encoding="UTF-8"?>'
3    '<!--- Membership list -->'
4    '<members>'
5       '<member>'
6          '<id>'
7             '<name>John Doe</name>'
8             '<address type="home">Here</address>'
9             '<address type="business">There</address>'
10         '</id>'
```

```
11              <membership-type>Full</membership-type>'
12          </member>'
13      </members>';
14
15      var parser = PullParser {
16          documentType: PullParser.XML
17          input: new ByteArrayInputStream(xml.getBytes("UTF-8"))
18          ignoreWhiteSpace: true
19      }
20
21      parser.seek("name", 3);
22      parser.forward();
23      println("Name is '{parser.event.text}'");
24
25      parser.seek("address").forward();
26      println("Address is '{parser.event.text}'");
```

The `PullParser` object is created as before, except that in this case we don't install an event-handling function. Notice that we also set `ignoreWhiteSpace` to `true`—this is usually a good idea when using the pull API, especially if you are going to skip events by using the `forward(count)` function, because it is easier to count the number of events to skip if you don't have to take into account whitespace in the document.

The `seek()` call on line 21 skips forward until it finds a `<name>` element (in any namespace) at indentation level 3, which will locate the element on line 7 in Listing 27-3. When this element is reached, a `START_ELEMENT` event is written to the `event` variable of the `PullParser` and the function returns.[9] The `forward()` call on line 22 skips this event and causes the next one, which is the `TEXT` event for the `<name>` element, to be written to the `event` variable, from where is it is accessed by the `println()` function on line 23. This prints the following:

```
Name is 'John Doe'
```

The code on line 25 locates the text for the first of the two `<address>` elements. It does this by searching for the element itself, which positions it at the `START_ELEMENT` event, moves forward one event to get the text. Notice that these operations are chained together, which makes the code more compact—this is possible because the `seek()` and `forward()` functions all have the `PullParser` object as their return value.

Code written using the pull API can be much easier to understand than code that uses the streaming API, because it is linear, and you can easily see the order in which events

---

[9] If you were to install an event handler while using the pull API, you would find that all the events that are generated as the parser works through the document are delivered to it.

will be processed. However, the pull API works well *only* if you can rely on the ordering of elements in the document that you are parsing. In this case, the code assumes that the `<name>` element appears before the `<address>` element, but suppose that the ordering of these elements were to be reversed:

```
<id>
    <address type="home">Here</address>
    <address type="business">There</address>
    <name>John Doe</name>
</id>
```

The `seek()` call on line 21 of Listing 27-3 will still find the `<name>` element, but the call on line 25 will not locate the `<address>` element because it has already been read and discarded. The second `seek()` call will actually read through the remainder of the document and will return when it reaches the end, leaving and END_DOCUMENT event in the parser's event variable.

A Twitter Web Service Client

You have seen how to make HTTP requests and how to parse XML, so now it is time to put the two together and show you how to get some information from a web service and convert it into a form in which it can be displayed in a JavaFX application. The web service that we use provides a timeline that contains the 20 most recent public posts of a user of the Twitter social networking site. For this example, we will retrieve the timeline for the userInformIT. I chose to use this timeline for this example because, unlike some web services, it does not require you to register and get a key before you can use it and does not require authentication when you make a request. In addition, it can provide results in several different formats, including XML, which is the format we will use here.

To get the current content of this timeline, you just make an HTTP GET request to the URL http://api.twitter.com/1/statuses/user_timeline/informit.xml. In keeping with the spirit of RESTful web services, the GET method indicates that this is a read operation and the URL indicates the information that we want to read. The `.xml` suffix of the URL causes the results to be returned in XML format. You can find the official documentation for this service at http://apiwiki.twitter.com/Twitter-REST-API-Method%3A-statuses_timeline.

Having read the timeline, we will convert it into a sequence of objects that contains the parts of each message that we want to display. Here's the definition of the JavaFX class that represents each message, which you'll find in the file `javafxdata/TwitterEntry.fx`:

```
public class TwitterEntry {
    public-init var user:String;
    public-init var imageURL:String;
    public-init var time:String;
    public-init var content:String;
}
```

Each message will be displayed by a custom node called `InformationNode`, which we won't discuss in any detail in this chapter. If you are interested in how it works, you'll find the source code in the file `javafxdata/InformationNode.fx`.

When this application is started, it shows only a title; once the web service call has completed, it parses the returned XML to create a sequence of `TwitterEntry` objects. The user interface converts each `TwitterEntry` object into an `InformationNode` and arranges them all in a `VBox`, which is itself wrapped in a `ClipView` and linked to a `ScrollBar`. Here's the code that actually displays the messages, from the file `javafxdata/TwitterInformtITTimeline.fx`, which you should run if you want to try out this application:

```
clipView = ClipView {
    node: VBox {
        nodeHPos: HPos.CENTER
        content: bind for (entry in entries) {
            InformationNode {
                name: entry.user
                imageURL: entry.imageURL
                message: "{entry.time}\n{entry.content}"
            }
        }
    }
}
```

Invoking the Twitter Web Service

The code that gets the content of the timeline can be found in the file `javafxdata/TwitterClient.fx`. The function that is used to call the web service is shown in Listing 27-4.

Listing 27-4 Requesting the InformIT Timeline from the Twitter Web Service

```
1    public function getInformITTimeline(
2                        onDone:function(TwitterEntry[])) {
3        var entries:TwitterEntry[] = null;
4        var os = new ByteArrayOutputStream();
5        var req:HttpRequest = HttpRequest {
6            location:
7    "http://api.twitter.com/1/statuses/user_timeline/"
8                "informit.xml"
9            sink: os
10           onDone: function() {
11               if (req.responseCode == HttpStatus.OK) {
12                   insert timelineResponse(os) into entries;
13               } else {
14                   insert TwitterEntry {
15                       content: "Failed to get content\n"
16                                "{req.responseMessage}"
17                   } into entries;
```

```
18                    }
19                    onDone(entries);
20                }
21            };
22            req.start();
23        }
```

As you can see, this is a straightforward application of the `HttpRequest` class that we discussed in the first part of this chapter. The XML response is written to a `ByteArrayOutputStream`, and the `onDone` function on lines 10 to 20 is called when the whole response has been received. The conversion from XML to `TwitterEntry` objects is handled by the `timelineResponse()` function, which we'll discuss shortly, and then the callback function that is passed to to `getInformITTimeline()` is called. This function is part of the application itself and can be found in the file `javafxdata/TwitterInformITTimeline.fx`.

It is important to note that the `InformITgetTimeline()` function is called from the user interface in the main thread of the application and returns after initiating the HTTP request to the web service. At this point, of course, no data will have been received. The function that is passed to `InformITgetTimeline()` is called later, again in the main thread of the application, after the web service's response has been received and parsed.

Parsing the Web Service Response

We use the stream parsing API of the `PullParser` class to parse the XML that we get back from the Twitter web service. Here is a snapshot of a typical response, showing only the parts that we are interested in and with some data removed for the sake of clarity:

```
 1      <statuses type="array">
 2        <status>
 3          <created_at>Fri May 28 17:24:08 +0000 2010</created_at>
 4          <id>14920648241</id>
 5          <text>[Text not shown]</text>
 6          <user>
 7            <id>14347035</id>
 8            <name>InformIT</name>
 9            <screen_name>InformIT</screen_name>
10            <location>Indianapolis, IN</location>
11            <profile_image_url>
12              http://a3.twimg.com/profile_images/256118809/
13                   images_normal.jpg
14            </profile_image_url>
15            <created_at>Thu Apr 10 00:29:24 +0000 2008</created_at>
16            <favourites_count>2</favourites_count>
17            <utc_offset>-18000</utc_offset>
18            <time_zone>Indiana (East)</time_zone>
19          </user>
20        </status>
```

The response consists of a set of `<status>` blocks, one for each Twitter message. Each of these blocks will be converted to a `TwitterEntry` object by extracting the values of the following elements:

- The `<created_at>` element shown on line 3, which will become the `time` value of the `TwitterEntry`
- The `<text>` element on line 5, which will become the `content` value
- The `<screen_name>` element within the nested `<user>` block on line 9, which will be used to set the `user` value
- The `<profile_image_url>` element, which will become the `imageURL` value

The code in the `TwitterClient` class that processes the response is shown in Listing 27-5.

Listing 27-5 **Processing the InformIT Timeline from the Twitter Web Service**

```
1    function timelineResponse
         (os:ByteArrayOutputStream):TwitterEntry[] {
2        var entries:TwitterEntry[];
3        var is = new ByteArrayInputStream(os.toByteArray());
4        var parser = PullParser {
5            input: is
6            documentType: PullParser.XML
7            onEvent: function(evt) {
8                var name = evt.qname.name;
9                if (evt.type == PullParser.START_ELEMENT
10                   and name == "status") {
11                   user = imageURL = time = content = "";
12               } else if (evt.type == PullParser.TEXT) {
13                   if (name == "screen_name") {
14                       user = evt.text;
15                   } else if (name == "profile_image_url") {
16                       imageURL = evt.text;
17                   } else if (name == "created_at"
18                           and evt.level == 2) {
19                       time = evt.text;
20                   } else if (name == "text") {
21                       content = evt.text;
22                   }
23               } else if (evt.type == PullParser.END_ELEMENT) {
24                   if (name == "status") {
25                       insert TwitterEntry {
26                           user: user
27                           imageURL: imageURL
28                           content: content
29                           time: time
30                       } into entries;
31                   }
```

```
32                      }
33                  }
34                  var user;
35                  var imageURL;
36                  var content;
37                  var time;
38              }
39          parser.parse();
40          is.close();
41
42          entries
43      }
```

This function is called with the data retrieved by the `HttpRequest` class, in the form of a `ByteArrayOutputStream`. The first thing we need to do, on line 3, is to convert this to a `ByteArrayInputStream`, because the `PullParser` class only accepts input in the form of an `InputStream`. We then create the `PullParser` object, tell it to expect XML input, and pass it the `ByteArrayInputStream` containing the data to be parsed.

The parsing is handled by the function on lines 7 to 33, which makes use of the `user`, `imageURL`, `content`, and `time` variables, declared on lines 34 to 37, to hold information that is obtained from the current `<status>` block.

The first event of interest is the `START_ELEMENT` event for a `<status>` block, which occurs each time that element is found in the response message. This event, which is handled on lines 9 to 11, resets the `user`, `imageURL`, `content`, and `time` variables to empty strings. This is not strictly necessary when the first `<status>` block is seen, but it will be for the remaining blocks. Once we have started processing a `<status>` block, we need to capture the elements that we listed earlier and save the associated text.

On lines 12 to 22, we intercept `TEXT` events. If the event corresponds to one of the elements of interest, we capture the text and save it in the appropriate variable. Notice that on lines 17 to 18, where we handle the `<created_at>` element, we explicitly check that the indentation level is 2. This is necessary because, as you can see from the XML sample shown above, there are two different `<created_at>` elements in each `<status>` block— one that is directly inside the block that gives the time at which the Twitter message was posted (see line 4 of the XML snapshot) and one in the nested `<user>` element that holds the time at which the user's identity was created (see line 13). For this example, we need the first of these two, and we can distinguish it based on its indentation level.

Finally, on lines 23 to 32, when the `END_ELEMENT` event for a `<status>` block is received, we create a new `TwitterEntry` object, populating it with the values that we saved while processing the block, and add it to the sequence of `TwitterEntry` objects that will be delivered to the user interface once all the response has been processed.

This completes the implementation of our XML-based Twitter application. As you can see, the facilities provided by the JavaFX platform make it easy to invoke a web service and parse the response into JavaFX objects that can then be displayed to the user. As you'll see in the next section, it is equally easy to interface to a web service that returns a response encoded in JSON.

A JSON Web Service Client

JSON (JavaScript Object Notation) is a simple and increasing popular way to encode the results of a web service call. There are several web services that return results either exclusively in JSON format or as an alternative to XML. This section briefly introduces JSON syntax, describes how the `PullParser` class handles JSON input, and then shows you how to write a JavaFX application that queries a JSON web service.

JSON Syntax and Parsing

Listing 27-6 shows an example of JSON syntax.

Listing 27-6   **A JSON Object Definition**

```
1    {
2        "name": "Fred",
3        "address": "10 NoStreet, NoPlace",
4        "age": 21,
5        "male": true,
6        "hobbies": ["golf", "reading ", "music"]
7    }
```

The braces on lines 1 and 7 mark the beginning and end of a JSON object definition, which is composed of name/value pairs. As you can see, a JSON object definition looks very much like a JavaFX object literal, except that the comma separators between pairs are mandatory in JSON, and the names must appear in quotes. Values may be strings (indicated by quotes), integers (see line 4), numbers, booleans (line 5), null, or an array, an example of which is shown on line 6. Objects can be nested and arrays can be of mixed type, so it is legal to create an array that contains both strings and integers.

The `PullParser` class can parse JSON a document in either pull mode or streaming mode when its `documentType` variable is set to `PullParser.JSON`. The events that are reported in JSON mode are different from those used when parsing XML; the event types that are used, all of which are defined by the `PullParser` class, are listed in Table 27-5.

Table 27-5   **JSON Parser Event Types**

Event	Meaning
START_DOCUMENT	Marks the beginning of the JSON document.
START_ELEMENT	The start of a JSON object, corresponding to an opening brace.
START_VALUE	The "name" part of a name/value pair. The `name` variable of this event contains the actual name. The value itself follows and will itself be followed by an END_VALUE event.
TEXT	Indicates that a string value was encountered.
INTEGER	Indicates that an integer values was found.
NUMBER	Indicates that a floating-point number value was found.

Using RESTful Web Services 989

Table 27-5 **JSON Parser Event Types** (*Contiuned*)

Event	Meaning
TRUE	The boolean value `true`.
FALSE	The boolean value `false`.
NULL	The literal text "null" was given as the value of a name/value pair.
START_ARRAY	The beginning of a JSON array, which occurs when a [is found.
START_ARRAY_ELEMENT	The start of an element in an array.
END_ARRAY_ELEMENT	The end of an element in an array.
END_ARRAY	The end of a JSON array, indicated by a] character.
END_VALUE	Marks the end of processing of a name/value pair. As with the START_VALUE event, the `name` variable holds the actual name.
END_ELEMENT	The end of a JSON object, corresponding to a closing brace.
END_DOCUMENT	Marks the end of the JSON document.

Here are the events that the parser generates as a result of parsing the JSON document in Listing 27-6:

```
1     type:7 typeName:START_DOCUMENT level:0 arrayLevel:0 arrayIndex:0
2     name: text:'' boolean:false integer:0 number:0.0
3     type:1 typeName:START_ELEMENT level:0 arrayLevel:0 arrayIndex:0
4     name: text:'' boolean:false integer:0 number:0.0
5     type:25 typeName:START_VALUE level:0 arrayLevel:0 arrayIndex:0
6     name:name text:'' boolean:false integer:0 number:0.0
7     type:4 typeName:TEXT level:0 arrayLevel:0 arrayIndex:0 name:name
8     text:'Fred' boolean:false integer:0 number:0.0
9     type:26 typeName:END_VALUE level:0 arrayLevel:0 arrayIndex:0
10    name:name text:'Fred' boolean:false integer:0 number:0.0
11    type:25 typeName:START_VALUE level:0 arrayLevel:0 arrayIndex:0
12    name:address text:'' boolean:false integer:0 number:0.0
13    type:4 typeName:TEXT level:0 arrayLevel:0 arrayIndex:0
14    name:address text:'10 NoStreet, NoPlace' boolean:false integer:0
15    number:0.0
16    type:26 typeName:END_VALUE level:0 arrayLevel:0 arrayIndex:0
17    name:address text:'10 NoStreet, NoPlace' boolean:false integer:0
18    number:0.0
19    type:25 typeName:START_VALUE level:0 arrayLevel:0 arrayIndex:0
20    name:age text:'' boolean:false integer:0 number:0.0
21    type:21 typeName:INTEGER level:0 arrayLevel:0 arrayIndex:0
22    name:age text:'' boolean:false integer:21 number:0.0
```

```
23    type:26 typeName:END_VALUE level:0 arrayLevel:0 arrayIndex:0
24    name:age text:'' boolean:false integer:21 number:0.0
25    type:25 typeName:START_VALUE level:0 arrayLevel:0 arrayIndex:0
26    name:male text:'' boolean:false integer:0 number:0.0
27    type:22 typeName:TRUE level:0 arrayLevel:0 arrayIndex:0 name:male
28    text:'' boolean:true integer:0 number:0.0
29    type:26 typeName:END_VALUE level:0 arrayLevel:0 arrayIndex:0
30    name:male text:'' boolean:true integer:0 number:0.0
31    type:25 typeName:START_VALUE level:0 arrayLevel:0 arrayIndex:0
32    name:hobbies text:'' boolean:false integer:0 number:0.0
33    type:16 typeName:START_ARRAY level:0 arrayLevel:0 arrayIndex:0
34    name:hobbies text:'' boolean:false integer:0 number:0.0
35    type:17 typeName:START_ARRAY_ELEMENT level:0 arrayLevel:0
36    arrayIndex:0 name:hobbies text:'' boolean:false integer:0
37    number:0.0
38    type:4 typeName:TEXT level:0 arrayLevel:0 arrayIndex:0
39    name:hobbies text:'golf' boolean:false integer:0 number:0.0
40    type:18 typeName:END_ARRAY_ELEMENT level:0 arrayLevel:0
41    arrayIndex:0 name:hobbies text:'golf' boolean:false integer:0
42    number:0.0
43    type:17 typeName:START_ARRAY_ELEMENT level:0 arrayLevel:0
44    arrayIndex:1 name:hobbies text:'' boolean:false integer:0
45    number:0.0
46    type:4 typeName:TEXT level:0 arrayLevel:0 arrayIndex:0
47    name:hobbies text:'reading ' boolean:false integer:0 number:0.0
48    type:18 typeName:END_ARRAY_ELEMENT level:0 arrayLevel:0
49    arrayIndex:1 name:hobbies text:'reading ' boolean:false integer:0
50    number:0.0
51    type:17 typeName:START_ARRAY_ELEMENT level:0 arrayLevel:0
52    arrayIndex:2 name:hobbies text:'' boolean:false integer:0
53    number:0.0
54    type:4 typeName:TEXT level:0 arrayLevel:0 arrayIndex:0
55    name:hobbies text:'music' boolean:false integer:0 number:0.0
56    type:18 typeName:END_ARRAY_ELEMENT level:0 arrayLevel:0
57    arrayIndex:2 name:hobbies text:'music' boolean:false integer:0
58    number:0.0
59    type:19 typeName:END_ARRAY level:0 arrayLevel:0 arrayIndex:0
60    name:hobbies text:'' boolean:false integer:0 number:0.0
61    type:26 typeName:END_VALUE level:0 arrayLevel:0 arrayIndex:0
62    name:hobbies text:'' boolean:false integer:0 number:0.0
63    type:2 typeName:END_ELEMENT level:0 arrayLevel:0 arrayIndex:0
64    name: text:'' boolean:false integer:0 number:0.0
65    type:8 typeName:END_DOCUMENT level:0 arrayLevel:0 arrayIndex:0
66    name: text:'' boolean:false integer:0 number:0.0
```

As you can see, parsing begins with a START_DOCUMENT event and ends with an END_DOCUMENT event. The START_ELEMENT and END_ELEMENT events on lines 3 and 64 correspond to the beginning and end of the object definition on lines 1 and 7 of Listing 27-6, respectively. Between these two events are the events that report the name/value pairs that make up the object definition.

For a simple name/value pair, the parser generates a START_VALUE event that gives the name, an event that reports the actual value, and an END_VALUE event. For example, the name/value pair on line 2 of Listing 27-6 results in the following events:

```
type:25 typeName:START_VALUE level:0 arrayLevel:0 arrayIndex:0 name:name
text:'' boolean:false integer:0 number:0.0
type:4 typeName:TEXT level:0 arrayLevel:0 arrayIndex:0 name:name
text:'Fred' boolean:false integer:0 number:0.0
type:26 typeName:END_VALUE level:0 arrayLevel:0 arrayIndex:0 name:name
text:'Fred' boolean:false integer:0 number:0.0
```

In this case, the value was a string, so it generates a TEXT event, whereas the value on line 21 of Listing 27-6, which is an integer, generates an INTEGER event:

```
type:25 typeName:START_VALUE level:0 arrayLevel:0 arrayIndex:0 name:age
text:'' boolean:false integer:0 number:0.0
type:21 typeName:INTEGER level:0 arrayLevel:0 arrayIndex:0 name:age
text:'' boolean:false integer:21 number:0.0
type:26 typeName:END_VALUE level:0 arrayLevel:0 arrayIndex:0 name:age
text:'' boolean:false integer:21 number:0.0
```

Notice that an integer value is held in the integer variable of the Event class, while text is stored in the text variable. The Event class has several variables specific to JSON processing. These variables, together with the ones shared with the XML parser, are listed in Table 27-6.

Table 27-6 Variables of the `Event` Class That Are Relevant to JSON Parsing

Variable	Type	Access	Description
type	Integer	R	The event type, such as PullParser.START_ELEMENT
typeName	String	R	The event type in human-readable form
level	Integer	R	The nesting level of the current element, starting from 0
name	String	R	The name of the current element
text	String	R	The value of a TEXT element
booleanValue	Boolean	R	The value of a TRUE or FALSE element
integerValue	Integer	R	The value of an INTEGER element
numberValue	Number	R	The value of a NUMBER element
arrayIndex	Integer	R	Index of the current element in a JSON array
arrayLevel	Integer	R	Nesting depth of the current element in a JSON array

When an array is encountered, events are generated for the start and end of the value, the start and end of the array, the start and end of each element in the array, and for each individual array element. Refer to lines 31 to 62 of the parsing output above for the events generated for the array on line 6 of Listing 27-6.

The JSON Weather Service

Having seen how the parser handles JSON input, let's look at a real-world example—the airport weather web service provided at *geonames.org*, a description of which you can find at http://www.geonames.org/export/JSON-webservices.html. As with the Twitter user timeline service that we used in our earlier example, this service is free and does not require you to register for an API key to make use of it. To get the weather report for an airport, all you have to do is make a request to the URL http://ws.geonames.org/weatherIcaoJSON, supplying the ICAO code of an airport as a parameter. The ICAO (Internal Civil Aviation Organization) code is a unique four-character abbreviation used by pilots and air traffic controllers, among others. It is *not* the same as the name that appears on your baggage tag, which is an IATA (International Air Transport Association) code, which, unlike the ICAO code, is usually closely related to the actual name of the airport concerned.

The ICAO codes for all registered airports can be found in a PDF document on the ICAO website at http://www.icao.int/anb/aig/taxonomy/r4cdlocationindicatorsbystate.pdf. Some commonly used examples are KJFK (New York's Kennedy Airport), KLAX (Los Angeles International), KDCA (Washington Reagan), EGLL (London Heathrow), and EGKK (London Gatwick).

Here's a typical response from this web service, reporting the weather at KDCA:

```
{
    "weatherObservation": {
        "clouds":"few clouds",
        "weatherCondition":"n/a",
        "observation":"KDCA 081652Z 16007KT 10SM FEW055 BKN070 BKN250 29/17 A3020 RMK AO2 SLP225 T02890167",
        "windDirection":160,
        "ICAO":"KDCA",
        "seaLevelPressure":1022.5,
        "elevation":18,
        "countryCode":"US",
        "lng":-77.0333333333333,
        "temperature":"28.9",
        "dewPoint":"16.7",
        "windSpeed":"07",
        "humidity":47,
        "stationName":"Washington DC, Reagan National Airport",
        "datetime":"2009-08-08 16:52:00",
        "lat":38.85
    }
}
```

This JSON object contains a single weather report for KDCA, with fields that describe the cloud condition, temperature, wind speed and direction, and so on. In the rest of this section, you'll see how to invoke the web service from JavaFX code and parse the result into a form that can be displayed to the user. The application that we're going to create is shown in Figure 27-4.

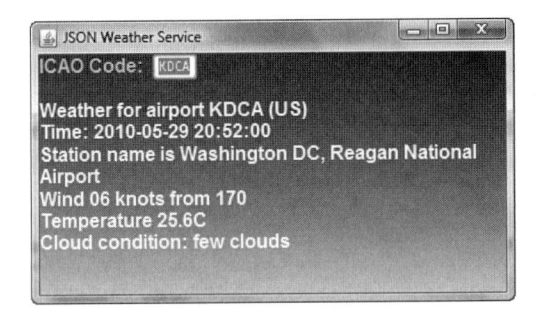

Figure 27-4   Displaying airport weather reports

You'll find the code that creates the simple user interface for this application in the file `javafxdata/JSONWeather.fx`. We're not going to discuss this code in any detail. Instead, we'll concentrate on the details of the interaction with the web service itself, which you'll find in the file `javafxdata/JSONWeatherClient.fx`.

Invoking the JSON Weather Service

The code to invoke the weather web service is shown in Listing 27-7.

Listing 27-7   Getting Information from the JSON Weather Service

```
1      public function getWeather(place:String, onDone:function(String)){
2          var os = new ByteArrayOutputStream();
3          var req = HttpRequest {
4              location:
5                  "http://ws.geonames.org/weatherIcaoJSON?ICAO={place}"
6              sink: os
7              onDone: function() {
8                  onDone(processJSONResponse(place, os));
9              }
10         }
11         req.start();
12     }
```

The parameters to the `getWeather()` function are the ICAO code of an airport and a function to be called when the web service response has been received and parsed. Unlike the Twitter client example that you saw earlier in this chapter, we don't convert the response into a JavaFX object with variables for the various parts of the response that the caller might be interested in. Instead, for the sake of simplicity and to illustrate a different response, we simply create a summary of the weather that will be displayed as is in the user interface.

To initiate the request for the weather, we create an `HttpRequest` object and initialize its location variable with a URL that the web service interprets as a request for a weather report. Notice that the URL, constructed on line 5, includes a parameter whose value is the ICAO code of the airport. Here's the URL that would used to get the weather for Washington Reagan airport:

```
http://ws.geonames.org/weatherIcaoJSON?ICAO=KDCA
```

The result is written to a `ByteArrayOutputStream` and, on completion, the parsing code in the function `processJSONResponse()` will be called. Apart from the URL, this code is almost identical to that used to get the XML-based Twitter user timeline, shown in Listing 27-4. The major difference between these two examples is, of course, in the parsing code.

Parsing the Weather Service Response

To parse the response from the weather service, we create a `PullParser`, set its `documentType` variable to `PullParser.JSON`, install an event handler, and call the `parse()` function. Listing 27-8 shows the details.

Listing 27-8   **Parsing the Response from the JSON Weather Service**

```
1       function processJSONResponse(place:String,
2                                    os:ByteArrayOutputStream):String {
3           var is = new ByteArrayInputStream(os.toByteArray());
4           var country = "(Unreported)";
5           var clouds = "(Unreported)";
6           var windDir = "(Unreported)";
7           var windSpeed = "(Unreported)";
8           var temp = "(Unreported)";
9           var stationName = "(Unreported)";
10          var time = "(Unreported)";
11          var parser = PullParser {
12              input: is
13              documentType: PullParser.JSON
14              onEvent: function(evt) {
15                  var type = evt.type;
16                  var name = evt.name;
17                  if (type == PullParser.TEXT) {
18                      if (name == "countryCode") {
19                          country = evt.text;
20                      } else if (name == "clouds") {
21                          clouds = evt.text;
22                      } else if (name == "windSpeed") {
23                          windSpeed = evt.text;
```

```
24                  } else if (name == "temperature") {
25                      temp = evt.text;
26                  } else if (name == "stationName") {
27                      stationName = evt.text;
28                  } else if (name == "datetime") {
29                      time = evt.text;
30                  }
31              } else if (type == PullParser.INTEGER) {
32                  if (name == "windDirection") {
33                      windDir = "{evt.integerValue}";
34                  }
35              }
36          }
37      }
38      parser.parse();
39      is.close();
40
41      "Weather for airport {place} ({country})\n"
42      "Time: {time}\n"
43      "Station name is {stationName}\n"
44      "Wind {windSpeed} knots from {windDir}\n"
45      "Temperature {temp}C\n"
46      "Cloud condition: {clouds}\n"
47  }
```

The variables on lines 4 to 10 will hold the values that are extracted from the response. Because values are sometimes omitted, the variables are all initialized with the string `"(Unreported)"` so that it is clear to the user that information was not provided.

The event handling function on lines 15 to 36 handles both TEXT and INTEGER events. This is necessary because some of the weather details are returned in string form and others in integer form.[10] The code simply checks the name associated with each event and stores the value in the appropriate variable. Finally, when the document has been completely parsed, the information that has been received is used to create the message that will appear in the user interface.

RSS and Atom Feeds

A large and increasing number of information sources now provide their content via a *feed* to which a user can subscribe, in addition to more traditional publication methods such as a website or an email distribution list. JavaFX has support for the two most popular feed protocols—RSS (Really Simple Syndication) and Atom. You can find documentation for

---

[10] In JSON terms, a value enclosed in quotes is reported as TEXT even if it looks like a number, so `"23"` is text, but 23 is an integer and is reported with an INTEGER event.

the RSS protocol at http://www.rssboard.org/rss-specification and for Atom at http://www.ietf.org/rfc/rfc4287.txt.

Both Atom and RSS are XML-based protocols. Access to feeds is usually provided over HTTP, so it is possible to read or subscribe to the content of a feed from a web browser or from a stand-alone application that may display either a single feed or a combination of feeds. In this section, we'll show you how to write readers for both RSS and Atom feeds in JavaFX.

Because feed data is encoded in XML, it is possible to use the `HttpRequest` class to get the content of a feed and the `PullParser` class to parse it, but this is not necessary because the classes in the `javafx.data.feed.rss` and `javafx.data.feed.atom` packages take care of the details for you. All you have to do is supply the URL of the feed source, and the data will be retrieved, parsed, converted to JavaFX objects, and delivered to your application.

Feeds Overview

You get an RSS feed by using the `RssTask` class and an Atom feed from the `AtomTask` class. Both of these classes are derived from the class `javafx.data.feed.FeedTask`, which provides the common variables and behavior for both feed implementations. The variables of the `FeedTask` class are listed in Table 27-7.

Table 27-7 **Variables of the FeedTask Class**

Variable	Type	Access	Default	Description
location	String	RI		The URL of the feed source
interval	Duration	RI		The time between successive polls for content updates
headers	HttpHeader[]	RI	null	The HTTP headers to be sent when requesting the feed
onException	function (:Exception) :Void	RW	null	Function to be called if an exception occurs while fetching the feed content
onForeignEvent	function (:Event):Void	RW	null	Function to be called when foreign elements are encountered in the feed content

The `location` variable gives the URL from which the feed is to be obtained. Most feed sources extract all the information that they need from the URL, but in some cases it is possible to configure the feed source by supplying further information in the form of HTTP headers. For example, the Twitter search API allows more requests per hour to a client that supplies the User-Agent header than to one that does not. You can specify the headers to be send by setting the `headers` variable.

The `FeedTask` class allows you to make a one-off request for the content of a feed or to subscribe and have the content automatically updated periodically. You choose the mode of operation that you want by using one of the following functions to fetch the feed content:

- The `update()` function fetches and parses the whole feed.
- The `poll()` function fetches and parses only those items in the feed that have changed because the last time the feed was read.
- The `start()` function performs an `update()` immediately and then repeats the operation with the frequency given by the `interval` variable of the `FeedTask` object, until the `stop()` function is called. Use this function if you want automatic, periodic updates to be delivered to your application (that is, a subscription).

The RSS and Atom feed protocols consist of a set of standard XML elements that the `RssTask` and `AtomTask` classes parse and convert into equivalent JavaFX objects. The XML elements and the JavaFX objects to which they are converted are feed-dependent and are discussed in the sections that follow. For example, an RSS feed is converted to a `Channel` object, which contains information about the feed itself, and a set of `Entry` objects, one for each entry in the feed.

Some feeds use additional XML elements that are not part of the protocol definition. This is often done to make it easier for the receiver of the feed to decode and use its content. You'll see an example of this when we create a JavaFX client for the Yahoo! Weather service in the next section. These additional XML elements are referred to as "foreign elements" and are delivered to the `onForeignEvent` function of the `FeedTask`. Because the meaning of these elements is unknown to the RSS and Atom parsers, they are simply delivered as a stream of raw XML events.

RSS Feeds

To access an RSS feed, you need to initialize an instance of the `RssTask` class and invoke its `start()`, `update()`, or `poll()` function, depending on whether you want to create a subscription or obtain a single snapshot of the feed's content. The `RssTask` class adds three variables, which are listed in Table 27-8, to those of the `FeedTask` class.

The easiest way to explain how an RSS feed works is to look at an example. This section shows you how to create an application that displays information from the Yahoo! Weather feed. Figure 27-5 shows the user interface for this application.

Table 27-8   **Variables of the `RssTask` Class**

Variable	Type	Access	Default	Description
`onChannel`	`function (:Channel): Void`	RW	`null`	Function to which the feed's `Channel` object is delivered
`onItem`	`function (:Item): Void`	RW	`null`	Function to which `Item` objects that hold the feed's content are delivered
`factory`	`Factory`	R		Class used to convert the XML content of the feed to the corresponding JavaFX objects

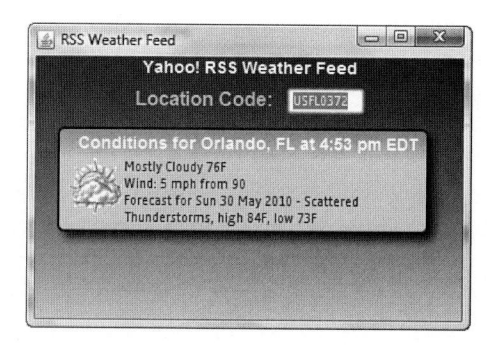

Figure 27-5   The Yahoo! RSS Weather feed

The Yahoo! RSS Weather Feed

This Yahoo! Weather feed provides the current weather conditions and a weather forecast for many thousands of locations worldwide. To get the weather for a particular place, you make a request to the following URL:

`http://weather.yahooapis.com/forecastrss?p=place`

The `place` value in the URL is not a real place name, but an identifier that you can obtain for any given location by looking it up on the Yahoo! Weather page at http://weather.yahoo.com. If you visit this page and ask for the weather for Orlando, Florida, you will be redirected to a page with URL http://weather.yahoo.com/forecast/USFL0372.html. This tells us that the location identifier for Orlando is `USFL0372`, so the URL for the Orlando weather feed is
http://weather.yahooapis.com/forecastrss?p=USFL0372.

If you make an HTTP request to this URL, you'll get back a response like that shown in Listing 27-9 (where some of the content has been omitted for the sake of clarity).

Listing 27-9   Data from the Yahoo! RSS Weather Feed

```
1   <?xml version="1.0" encoding="UTF-8" standalone="yes" ?>
2   <rss version="2.0"
3     xmlns:yweather="http://xml.weather.yahoo.com/ns/rss/1.0"
4     xmlns:geo="http://www.w3.org/2003/01/geo/wgs84_pos#">
5   <channel>
6   <title>Yahoo! Weather - Orlando, FL</title>
7   <link>http://us.rd.yahoo.com/dailynews/rss/weather/Orlando__FL/*ht
8   tp://weather.yahoo.com/forecast/USFL0372_f.html</link>
9   <description>Yahoo! Weather for Orlando, FL</description>
10  <language>en-us</language>
11  <lastBuildDate>Sun, 26 Jul 2009 5:53 am EDT</lastBuildDate>
12  <ttl>60</ttl>
13  <yweather:location city="Orlando" region="FL"   country="US"/>
14  <yweather:units temperature="F" distance="mi" pressure="in"
15  speed="mph"/>
16  <yweather:wind chill="76"   direction="0"  speed="0" />
17  <yweather:atmosphere humidity="87"  visibility="10"
18  pressure="30.07" rising="0" />
19  <yweather:astronomy sunrise="6:43 am"   sunset="8:19 pm"/>
20  <item>
21  <title>Conditions for Orlando, FL at 5:53 am EDT</title>
22  <geo:lat>28.55</geo:lat>
23  <geo:long>-81.38</geo:long>
24  <link>
25  http://us.rd.yahoo.com/dailynews/rss/weather/Orlando__FL/*http://
26  weather.yahoo.com/forecast/USFL0372_f.html</link>
27  <pubDate>Sun, 26 Jul 2009 5:53 am EDT</pubDate>
28  <yweather:condition  text="Fair"  code="33"  temp="76"
29  date="Sun, 26 Jul 2009 5:53 am EDT" />
30  <description><![CDATA[
31  <img src="http://l.yimg.com/a/i/us/we/52/33.gif"/><br />
32  <b>Current Conditions:</b><br />
33  Fair, 76 F<BR />
34  <BR /><b>Forecast:</b><BR />
35  Sun - Scattered Thunderstorms. High: 88 Low: 76<br />
36  Mon - Scattered Thunderstorms. High: 87 Low: 76<br />
37  <br/>
38  <a href=
39  "http://us.rd.yahoo.com/dailynews/rss/weather/Orlando__FL/*http://
40  weather.yahoo.com/forecast/USFL0372_f.html">Full Forecast at
41  Yahoo! Weather</a><BR/><BR/>
42  (provided by <a href="http://www.weather.com" >The Weather Chan
43  nel</a>)<br/>]]></description>
44  <yweather:forecast day="Sun" date="26 Jul 2009" low="76" high="88"
45  text="Scattered Thunderstorms" code="38" />
46  <yweather:forecast day="Mon" date="27 Jul 2009" low="76" high="87"
```

```
47          text="Scattered Thunderstorms" code="38" />
48          <guid isPermaLink="false">USFL0372_2009_07_26_5_53_EDT</guid>
49      </item>
50    </channel>
51 </rss>
```

An RSS feed contains one `<channel>` element that describes the feed itself and one or more `<item>` elements that contain the feed data. In this example, the `<channel>` element starting on line 5 will be converted to a `Channel` object that will be delivered to the feed's `onChannel` function, and the content of the single `<item>` element on lines 20 to 49, which contains the weather report for Orlando, will be delivered as an `Item` element to its `onItem` function.

The feed elements in Listing 27-9 that do not have a namespace prefix are defined by the RSS specification, and their content will appear in either the `Channel` or the `Item` object. For example, the content of the `<title>` element on line 6 will be made available in the `title` variable of the `Channel` object, while the value of the `<guid>` element on line 48 will be stored in the `guid` variable of the `Item` object.

Elements that have a namespace prefix, like the `<yweather:forecast>` element on line 44, are not part of the RSS specification—they are extensions used by the Yahoo! Weather service to provide additional information or to make it easier for nonbrowser clients to extract information from the feed. The content of these foreign elements is not available from either the `Channel` or `Item` objects; instead, their XML representation is parsed and passed to the `onForeignEvent` function of the `Channel` object.

When an RSS feed is read by a browser, it uses certain elements to construct a page—the `<title>` element of the channel is typically used to get the page title, and the `<description>` element of each item is the useful information that the user will see. For this reason, feed sources often encode the content of the `<description>` element in HTML so that it can be directly displayed by the browser. The Yahoo! Weather service uses this technique to provide a summary of the weather, complete with a small image that represents the associated weather conditions (sunny, cloudy, raining) and so on, as you can see on lines 30 to 43 of Listing 27-9. Although this is convenient for browser clients, it is not very useful to an application that does not handle HTML markup, such as our example feed client.

The foreign elements in the weather feed are there for the benefit of applications such as our JavaFX weather feed client. If you scan through the foreign elements in Listing 27-9, you'll find that most of the information that is shown in our application's user interface (refer back to) can be obtained from these foreign elements. Here's a list of the information that we need and the elements in which it be found:

- The name of the location to which the report applies and the time of the report. This is contained in the item's `<title>` element on line 21 of Listing 27-9.
- An image that represents the current weather. Unfortunately, this is only available from the `<description>` element of the feed item. To get it, we need to locate the HTML `<img>` tag shown on line 31 and extract the image URL from it.

- A summary of the current weather conditions. This is supplied by the `text` attribute of the `<yweather:condition>` element on line 28 of Listing 27-9. Like the remaining elements in this list, this is a foreign element.
- The temperature, which comes from the temp attribute of the `<yweather:condition>` element.
- The wind speed and direction. This is provided by the speed and direction attributes of the `<yweather:wind>` element on line 16.
- The forecast for the next day's weather, which we get from the `<yweather:forecast>` element on line 46. Notice that there are actually two such elements, and we need the one that describes tomorrow's weather. In practice, for the sake of simplicity, we accept whichever of these elements appears last in the feed.

From this information, we create an `RSSWeather` object, which is shown here and defined in the file `javafxdata/RSSWeatherFeedClient.fx`:

```
public class RSSWeather {
    public-read var title:String;
    public-read var conditions:String;
    public-read var temp:String;
    public-read var wind:String;
    public-read var forecast:String;
    public-read var imageURL:String;
}
```

Fetching and Decoding the Feed

As with the previous feed-related examples in this chapter, the source code for the user interface is separate from the code that deals with the feed itself. In fact, we are not going to discuss the user interface code at all, except to say that it uses an instance of the `InformationNode` class that you saw in the Twitter user timeline example to display the content of an `RSSWeather` object created from the feed data. As you can see if you look back at Figure 27-5, there is also a `TextBox` that allows you to enter the location code of the place for which you want to see the weather. If you want to run this example or look at the source code for the user interface, you'll find it in the file `javafxdata/RSSWeatherFeed.fx`.

The code that fetches and handles the feed data can be found in a function called `getRSSWeather()` in the file `javafxdata/RSSWeatherFeedClient.fx`, which is shown in Listing 27-10.

Listing 27-10   Handling the Yahoo! RSS Weather Feed

```
1    var task:RssTask;
2    public function getRSSWeather(place:String,
3                                  onDone:function(RSSWeather)) {
4        var weather = RSSWeather {};
5        var params = Pair {
```

```
6              name: "p" value: "{place}"
7          };
8          var converter = URLConverter {};
9          var urlParams = converter.encodeParameters(params);
10
11         if (task != null) {
12             task.stop();
13         }
14
15         task = RssTask {
16             location:
17          "http://weather.yahooapis.com/forecastrss?{urlParams}"
18             interval: 60s
19             onItem: function(item) {
20                 weather.title = item.title;
21                 var description = item.description;
22                 var index = description.indexOf("img src=");
23                 if (index != -1) {
24                     var startIndex = index + 9;
25                     var endIndex = description.indexOf('"',
26                                                       startIndex);
27                     weather.imageURL =
28                         description.substring(startIndex, endIndex);
29                 }
30             }
31             onForeignEvent: function(evt) {
32                 if (evt.type == PullParser.START_ELEMENT) {
33                     var name = evt.qname.name;
34                     if (name == "wind") {
35                         var speed = evt.getAttributeValue("speed");
36                         var direction =
37                                 evt.getAttributeValue("direction");
38                         weather.wind =
39                             "Wind: {speed} mph from {direction}";
40                     } else if (name == "condition") {
41                         var condition = evt.getAttributeValue("text");
42                         var temp = evt.getAttributeValue("temp");
43                         weather.conditions = condition;
44                         weather.temp = "{temp}F";
45                     } else if (name == "forecast") {
46                         var day = evt.getAttributeValue("day");
47                         var date = evt.getAttributeValue("date");
48                         var high = evt.getAttributeValue("high");
49                         var low = evt.getAttributeValue("low");
50                         var text = evt.getAttributeValue("text");
52                         weather.forecast = "Forecast for {day} "
52                                 "{date} - {text}, high {high}F, "
53                                 "low {low}F";
```

```
54                    }
55                }
56            }
57            onDone: function() {
58                onDone(weather);
59            }
60        }
61        task.start();
62    }
```

Following the same pattern as our earlier examples, this function requires the location code and a callback function that is used to deliver the `RSSWeather` object that is created from the feed content. This object is created on line 5, and its variables are populated as the corresponding events are received from the `RssTask`.

The `RssTask` itself is created on line 15 and a reference to it is held in a script variable. This is necessary, because we subscribe to the feed by setting its `interval` variable to request that the feed be polled for updates every 60 seconds, until such time as its `stop()` function is called. If the user changes the location in the user interface, this function will be called again, and we need to remove the previous subscription. We do this by calling the `stop()` function on lines 11 to 13.

As you saw in our discussion of the feed itself, we need to extract some of the information that we need from the `<item>` element and the rest from three foreign elements. We therefore assign functions to the `onItem` and `onForeignEvent` variables so that we are notified when these elements are received. Notice that, unlike our previous examples, we don't use an `HttpRequest` to fetch the data and a `PullParser` to process it—all of this is taken care of by the `RssTask` object. Like `HttpRequest`, `RssTask` is (indirectly) derived from `javafx.async.Task`, so it does most of its work in the background and runs its callback functions in the main thread.

The code in the `onItem` function is straightforward. It receives an argument of type `Item` that contains the result of parsing the content of the `<item>` element of the feed and extracts values from the `title` and `description` variables. The code that handles the `description` value, on lines 19 to 30 of Listing 27-10, is nontrivial because it needs to extract the URL of the weather image from the embedded HTML `<img>` tag.

The code in the `onForeignEvent` function is different from that in `onItem` because it receives events from the XML parser that the `RssTask` uses to process the feed data, instead of JavaFX objects created from the parser output. Because the values that we are interested in are carried in attributes of the `<wind>`, `<condition>`, and `<forecast>` elements, we intercept the `START_ELEMENT` event for each of the elements and use its `getAttributeValue()` function to get the required values, and then store them in the corresponding variables of the `RSSWeather` object.

Finally, when the feed data has been processed, the `RssTask` object calls the `onDone` function, which in turn delivers the `RSSWeather` object to the callback passed to `getRSSWeather()` function. This whole process will be repeated automatically every 60 seconds because we set the `interval` variable of the `RssTask` object and subscribed to the

1004 Chapter 27 Using External Data Sources

feed by calling its `start()` function. If you want a one-time capture of the feed, you should use the `update()` function instead.

Atom Feeds

The Atom feed protocol is newer and more complex than RSS, but for the JavaFX developer, it is just as easy to write an application that works with an Atom feed as it is to handle an RSS feed. You connect to an Atom feed by using the `javafx.data.feed.atom.AtomTask` class, which, like `RssTask`, derives from `FeedTask`. Whereas an RSS feed consists of one or more `<item>` elements nested inside a `<channel>` element, in Atom the feed itself is represented by a `<feed>` element, which is converted to a `Feed` object, and the individual items in the feed are contained in `<entry>` elements, which become `Entry` objects. The `AtomTask` class has two callback variables, listed in Table 27-9, that are used to deliver `Feed` and `Entry` objects to application code.

Table 27-9 **Variables of the `AtomTask` Class**

Variable	Type	Access	Default	Description
onFeed	function (:Feed):Void	RW	null	Function to which the feed's `Feed` object is delivered
onEntry	function (:Entry):Void	RW	null	Function to which `Entry` objects that hold the feed's content are delivered
factory	Factory	R		Class used to convert the XML content of the feed to the corresponding JavaFX objects

The Twitter Search Feed

Twitter has a search API that returns its results in either JSON or Atom format. It is convenient to use this API for an example of an Atom feed because the information that it contains is similar to that in the user timeline, which means we can reuse the `TwitterEntry` class that we used to encapsulate the timeline data earlier in this chapter, and we can also reuse the user interface code with only a minor change, namely the addition of a `TextBox` that allows you to enter a search term.

We are not going to discuss the user interface code in this section because our focus is on how to work with the feed, but if you'd like to look at it or run the example, you'll find it in the file `javafxdata/TwitterAtomSearch.fx`.

To perform a Twitter search based on a keyword or keywords, you make a request to a URL that looks like this:

```
http://search.twitter.com/search.atom?q=javafx&rpp=50
```

The `q=` parameter specifies the keyword or keywords for the search, and the `rpp=` parameter is the maximum number of results to return (that is, results per page). You can see part of a typical response to this query in Listing 27-11, which shows the `<feed>` element and the first of the 50 `<entry>` elements from the reply, with some of the data anonymized.

Listing 27-11   The Twitter Search Atom Feed

```
1    <feed xmlns:google="http://base.google.com/ns/1.0"
2    xml:lang="en-US" xmlns:openSearch="http://a9.com/-
3    /spec/opensearch/1.1/" xmlns=http://www.w3.org/2005/Atom
4    xmlns:twitter="http://api.twitter.com/">
5       <id>tag:search.twitter.com,2005:search/javafx</id>
6       <link type="text/html" rel="alternate"
7    href="http://search.twitter.com/search?q=javafx"/>
8       <link type="application/atom+xml" rel="self"
9    href="http://search.twitter.com/search.atom?q=javafx&rpp=10"/>
10      <title>javafx - Twitter Search</title>
11      <link type="application/opensearchdescription+xml" rel="search"
12   href="http://search.twitter.com/opensearch.xml"/>
13      <link type="application/atom+xml" rel="refresh"
14   href="http://search.twitter.com/search.atom?q=javafx&rpp=10
15   &since_id=3250464807"/>
16      <twitter:warning>since_id removed for pagination.
17      </twitter:warning>
18      <updated>2009-08-11T19:24:26Z</updated>
19      <openSearch:itemsPerPage>10</openSearch:itemsPerPage>
20      <link type="application/atom+xml" rel="next"
21   href="http://search.twitter.com/search.atom?max_id=3250464807&
22   page=2&q=javafx&rpp=10"/>
23      <entry>
24         <id>tag:search.twitter.com,2005:3250464807</id>
25         <published>2009-08-11T19:24:26Z</published>
26         <link type="text/html" rel="alternate"
27   href="http://twitter.com/tiainen/statuses/3250464807"/>
28         <title>Installing #netbeans 6.7.1 so i can continue my #javafx
29   adventures.</title>
30         <content type="html">Installing &lt;a
31   href="http://search.twitter.com/search?q=%23netbeans"&gt;#netbeans
32   &lt;/a&gt; 6.7.1 so i can continue my &lt;a
33   href="http://search.twitter.com/search?q=%23javafx"&gt;#&lt;b&gt;j
34   avafx&lt;/b&gt;&lt;/a&gt; adventures.</content>
35         <updated>2009-08-11T19:24:26Z</updated>
36         <link type="image/png" rel="image"
37   href="http://s3.amazonaws.com/twitter_production/profile_images/46
38   626732/2_normal.gif"/>
39         <twitter:source>&lt;a href=
40          data removed/a&gt;</twitter:source>
```

```
41            <twitter:lang>en</twitter:lang>
42            <author>
43              <name>removed</name>
44              <uri>removed</uri>
45            </author>
46          </entry>
```

As you can see, there is a mixture of elements with and without namespace prefixes. As with the RSS feed, the elements without a namespace prefix are defined by the Atom specification, while those with namespace prefixes are foreign elements meant to be interpreted by a nonbrowser client specifically written to handle this feed. You can see how each of the standard elements is mapped to variables of the `Feed` and `Entry` classes by consulting their API documentation.

For our example application, we need to extract from each Atom `Entry` the information necessary to construct a `TwitterEntry` object. The values that we need are all available from elements that are defined by the Atom specification itself, so unlike the RSS example in the previous section, we don't need to provide code to extract information from foreign elements. The values that we need are as follows:

- The name of the entry's author, which will be used to set the `user` variable of the `TwitterEntry` object. This value is contained in the `<author>` element, which you'll find on lines 42 to 45 of Listing 27-11. An Atom entry can have more than one author, so the `authors` variable in the `Entry` object is actually a sequence. As you'll see later, we use the first element in the sequence as the user value.

- The entry content, which is taken from the `<title>` element on lines 28 and 29 of Listing 27-11. We use the `<title>` value rather than the content of the more obvious `<content>` variable on line 30 because the latter contains the same text, but also has HTML markup, which we do not want the user of our application to see. The `<title>` value is used to set the `content` variable of the `TwitterEntry` object.

- The publication time of the entry, which we will use to set the `time` variable of the `TwitterEntry` object. We get this from the `<published>` element shown on line 25 of Listing 27-11, which becomes the value of the `published` variable of the feed's `Entry` object.

- The URL of the user's image, which you'll find in the `<link>` element on line 36. There is more than one `<link>` element in this feed entry—you'll find another one on line 26. All the `<link>` elements are gathered into a sequence of `Link` objects and stored in the `links` variable of the feed's `Entry` object. As you'll see later, we need to search this sequence to locate the link that refers to the image,

Fetching and Decoding the Feed

The code that gets the feed content and converts it to `TwitterEntry` objects is shown in Listing 27-12 and can be found in the file `javafxdata/TwitterAtomSearchClient.fx`.

Listing 27-12 **Handling the Twitter Search Feed**

```
1     public function doTwitterAtomSearch(query:String, count:Integer,
2                          onDone:function(TwitterEntry[]):Void) {
3         var params = [
4             Pair { name: "q" value: query },
5             Pair { name: "rpp" value: "{count}" }
6         ];
7         var converter = URLConverter {};
8         var urlParams = converter.encodeParameters(params);
9
10        var task = AtomTask {
11         location: "http://search.twitter.com/search.atom?{urlParams}"
12            var entries:TwitterEntry[];
13            onEntry: function(entry) {
14                var user = entry.authors[0].name;
15                var content = entry.title.text;
16                var time = new
17                    Date(entry.published.datetime.instant).toString();
18                var imageURL = "";
19                for (link in entry.links) {
20                    if (link.rel == "image") {
21                        imageURL = link.href;
22                        break;
23                    }
24                }
25                insert TwitterEntry {
26                    user: user
27                    content: content
28                    time: time
29                    imageURL: imageURL
30                } into entries;
31            }
32            onDone: function() {
33                onDone(entries);
34            }
35        }
36        task.update();
37    }
```

The `doTwitterAtomSearch()` function requires a query string, the number of results to be returned, and the function to be called when the results are available. The structure of this function should, by now, be familiar. On lines 3 to 8, we use the `Pair` and `URLConverter` classes that were discussed earlier in this chapter to create and encode the parameter string, which will contain the query and the number of results per page. For the query string "Cessna 172" and a maximum of 50 results, the query string would look like this:

```
q=Cessna+172&rpp=50
```

Lines 10 to 35 create the `AtomTask` object that will connect to the feed, parse the response, and deliver the resulting `Entry` objects to the `onEntry` function defined on lines 13 to 31. We do not supply an `onFeed` function because we have no use for the feed information in this example. If you compare this code with the RSS feed code in Listing 27-10, you'll notice that we do not assign a value to the `interval` variable, and we use the `update()` function (on line 36) to access the feed instead of the `start()` function. This is because you typically don't want the results of a search to update automatically, so instead of a subscription, we make a one-time request for a snapshot.

The feed data is handled on lines 13 to 31. As you can see, because all the information we need is contained in the `Entry` object, we can simply extract it and use it to create a `TwitterEntry` object. Most of the code is straightforward, but two points are worth noting:

- The publication date is obtained from the `publication` variable, which is of type `javafx.date.DateTime`. This class holds a single value (in a variable called `instant`) that represents the date and time as a number of milliseconds since 00:00 on Jan 1, 1970. In the desktop profile, you could use the `java.text.DateFormat` class to convert this to a date and time string, but this class is not available on MIDP-based devices, so for the sake of portability, we use the time value to create a `java.util.Date` object and then use its `toString()` method to get a string representation of the date and time.

- As mentioned earlier, an `<entry>` element may contain any number of `<link>` elements that refer to related data of different types. In Listing 27-11, there are two `<link>` elements, one that refers to an HTML page and the other to the user's image, which is the information that we need. The `AtomTask` class converts the `<link>` elements to a sequence of `javafx.data.feed.atom.Link` objects. To find the URL of the user's image, we search through this sequence until we find a `Link` object for which the `rel` variable has value `image`. The code that does this is shown on lines 18 to 24. If there is no such link, the space allocated for the user's image in the user interface will be blank.

Tasks and Progress Monitoring

Three of the classes that you have seen in this chapter—`HttpRequest`, `RssTask`, and `AtomTask`—perform asynchronous operations in a background thread while reporting their status and delivering results in the main application thread. These classes all derive from `javafx.async.Task`, which is intended to be the basis for all asynchronous operations on the JavaFX platform. As you'll see in the next section, this class can be used to implement your own background operations. In this section, we look at the features of the `Task` class that allow you to monitor and control the state of an asynchronous operation.

Task State Variables

The common state of an asynchronous operation is held in the variables of the `Task` class, which are listed in Table 27-10. Subclasses may add additional state, as appropriate. For example, the `HttpRequest` class adds variables that indicate whether data is currently being read or written.

Table 27-10   Variables of the `Task` Class

Variable	Type	Access	Default	Description
onStarted	function() :Void	RW	null	Function called when the task is about to start.
onDone	function() :Void	RW	null	Function called when the task has completed (successfully or otherwise).
started	Boolean	R		Indicates whether the task has been started.
stopped	Boolean	R		`true` when the task has been stopped by calling the `stop()` function.
succeeded	Boolean	R		Indicates that the task ran to a successful completion.
failed	Boolean	R		`true` if the task failed to complete normally.
done	Boolean	R		Indicates that the task is no longer running.
causeOf-Failure	Object	R	null	A value that indicates the reason why the task failed, if this is known. This will typically be a `Throwable`.
progress	Number	R	-1	The progress made by the task so far, or `-1` if the task is not yet started or the progress made is not known.
progress-Max	Number	R	-1	The value of progress that would indicate that the task is complete, or `-1` if the task is not yet started or the progress made is not known.

Table 27-10 Variables of the `Task` Class *(Continued)*

Variable	Type	Access	Default	Description
percent-Done	Number	R	-1	The progress made so far as a proportion of the maximum. The value will be in the range 0 to 1, or -1 if the operation is not started or if the progress made or maximum progress value is not known.

The variables `started`, `stopped`, `succeeded`, `failed`, and `done` describe the current state of the operation. Initially, all these variables are false. When the `start()` function is called, the `started` variables is set to `true` and remains in that state, *even when the operation has completed.* You cannot, therefore use the `started` variable on its own to determine whether the operation is in progress. When the operation ends, the `done` variable is always set to `true`, so the correct test for whether the operation is in progress is as follows:

(started and not done).

An operation can terminate for any of three reasons:

- The `stop()` function has been called. In this case, the `stopped`, `failed`, and `done` variables are all set to `true`.
- The operation fails. In this case, a message giving the reason for the failure may be stored in the `causeOfFailure` variable, and the `failed` and `done` variables will be set to `true`.
- The operation succeeds, in which case both the `succeeded` and `done` variables will be set to `true`.

Note that because of the way these variables are managed, it is possible for an operation to be simultaneously started and stopped or started and done.

The values of these variables are typically used to enable or disable user interface controls whose state should depend on that of the operation with which they are connected. You'll see an example of this in Listing 27-13 later in this section. Some state changes are also reported by a callback function—the `onStarted` function is called just before the operation is initiated, and the `onDone` function is invoked just after it terminates. You have already seen examples in this chapter that use the `onDone` function to do things such as trigger parsing of XML that has been read by an `HttpRequest`.

Progress Monitoring

The `progress` and `progressMax` variables allow a task to periodically report how much of an operation has been performed. If a task chooses to report progress, the `Task` class will maintain a third variable—`percentDone`—that represents the proportion of the operation that has been completed. In the case of an operation that has just begun and not yet made any progress, the `percentDone` variable would be 0, while for one that has succeeded it would have the value 1. It is important to note the following if you plan to use these variables:

- Task implementations are not required to report progress at all. In this case, all three variables will have the value -1, which is conventionally interpreted to mean that the amount of progress made is unknown.
- A task that reports progress must set both the `progress` and `progressMax` variables before the value of the `percentDone` variable will be set. If either of these variables is subsequently changed (which is very likely in the case of `progress` but less likely for `progressMax`), the value of `percentDone` will be recalculated accordingly.

A State Monitoring Example

The `HttpRequest` class correctly maintains the state variables that it inherits from the `Task` class and also reports progress as it reads or writes data. The code in Listing 27-13 creates an `HttpRequest` to read a PDF version of the Java Language Specification from Sun Microsystems' website and a simple user interface that monitors that lets you see the progress that is reported. It also reports the state of the `started`, `stopped`, `succeeded`, `failed`, and `done` variables on the console. You'll find this code in the file `javafxdata/TaskExample1.fx`.

Listing 27-13   Displaying the State of an `HttpRequest` Operation

```
1      var r:HttpRequest = HttpRequest {
2          location: "http://java.sun.com/docs/books/jls/download/"
3                    "langspec-3.0.pdf";
4          sink: new ByteArrayOutputStream()
5      };
6
7      Stage {
8          var scene:Scene;
9          title : "Task Example #1"
10         scene: scene = Scene {
11             width: 350
12             height: 200
13             content: [
14                 VBox {
15                     width: bind scene.width
16                     height: bind scene.height
17                     spacing: 16 vpos: VPos.CENTER
18                     hpos: HPos.CENTER nodeHPos: HPos.CENTER
19                     content: [
20                         Text {
21                             content: bind
22                                 "Read {r.progress} of {r.maxProgress} "
```

```
23                            "({100 * r.percentDone}%)"
24                        }
25                        ProgressBar {
26                            progress: bind if (r.percentDone == -1) -0
27                                              else r.percentDone;
28                        }
29                        Text {
30                            wrappingWidth: bind scene.width
31                            content: bind
32                             if (r.stopped) "Stopped"
33                             else if (r.succeeded) "Complete"
34                             else r.causeOfFailure.toString()
35                        }
36                        Button {
37                            text: "Press to start..."
38                            disable: bind r.started
39                            action: function() {
40                                r.start();
41                            }
42                        }
43                        Button {
44                            text: "Press to stop..."
45                            disable:
46                            bind not r.started or r.done
47                            action: function() {
48                                r.stop();
49                            }
50                        }
51                    ]
52                }
53            ]
54        }
55    }
56
57    var started = bind r.started on replace {
58                     println("started: {started}") };
59    var stopped = bind r.stopped on replace {
60                     println("stopped: {stopped}") };
61    var succeeded = bind r.succeeded on replace {
62                     println("succeeded: {succeeded}") };
63    var failed = bind r.failed on replace {
64                     println("failed: {failed}") };
65    var done = bind r.done on replace { println("done: {done}") };
66    var causeOfFailure = bind r.causeOfFailure on replace {
67                     println("causeOfFailure: {causeOfFailure}");       };
```

The result of running this code is shown in Figure 27-6.

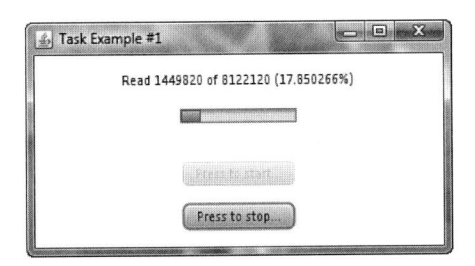

Figure 27-6 Tracking the progress of a task

The values of the `progress`, `progressMax`, and `percentDone` variables are shown in the `Text` node created on lines 20 to 24 of Listing 27-13. You can see that the value of `progressMax` has been set to the total length of the PDF file, while the `progress` variable is being updated to reflect how much has been read so far. The `percentDone` value is automatically recalculated as the value of the `progress` variable changes. When the application starts, these variables all have the value `-1`.

The value of the `percentDone` variable is also reflected in the progress bar, which gives a visual representation of how much of the document remains to be read.

The two buttons that appear below the progress bar enable you to start and stop the operation by calling respectively the `start()` and `stop()` functions of the `HttpRequest`. The start buttons is enabled only when the operation has not yet been started, while the stop button is enabled only while it is in progress. This is done by linking the disable variable of each button with the state variables of the `HttpRequest`. Here's the expression that is used to determine the value for the `disable` variable of the start button is controlled:

```
disable: bind r.started
```

This makes sense, because the button should be enabled only when the operation has not yet been started. Turning this the other way up, it should be disabled when the operation *has* been started. The expression required to assign the correct state to the stop button is slightly more complex:

```
disable: bind not r.started or r.done
```

The easiest way to understand this is to work out when the button should be enabled and then invert the condition—it should be possible to stop an operation if it has been started *and* it is not yet done. Inverting this, we get the condition shown above for disabling the button.

The triggers on lines 57 to 67 of Listing 27-13 let you see the changes to the `started`, `stopped`, `failed`, `succeeded`, `done`, and `causeOfFailure` variables as they occur. Here's the output that results from the normal completion of the `HttpRequest`:

```
started: true
done: true
succeeded: true
```

If the operation failed because the document you are trying to fetch does not exist, you would see the following:

```
started: true
failed: true
causeOfFailure: java.io.FileNotFoundException: (file name not shown)
done: true
```

Asynchronous Operations and Database Access

Most nontrivial applications are likely to need to perform an operation that would take long enough to complete that it could not be allowed to execute in the application's main thread, because to do so would block user interaction and make the application appear to be unresponsive. The classes that you have seen so far in this chapter let you access resources on the Internet without blocking the user interface, but there is (at least at the time of this writing) no prepackaged solution for asynchronous access to other information sources that are not capable of delivering data immediately, such as databases.

In this section, you'll see how to create a JavaFX application that populates a `ListView` control from the values in a database table. The focus will be on the data access part of the application, which we will perform in a background thread, rather than on how we display the results to the user. If you want to look at the code that creates the user interface, you'll find it in the file `javafxdata/TaskExample2.fx`. The result of running this code is shown on the left of Figure 27-7.

As you can see, the `ListView` control is initially empty. If you click the Fetch Customers button, there will be a small delay, and then the `ListView` will be populated with a set of customer names obtained from a database table. The reported progress will also change from 0 to 100, as shown on the right of Figure 27-7.

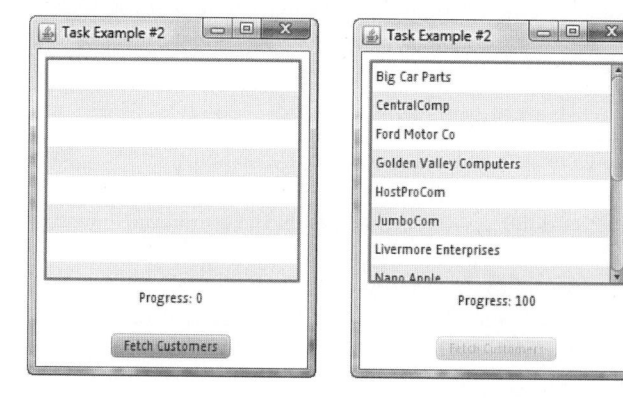

Figure 27-7   A JavaFX database application

To run this example, you need to be running a database server that has a table containing the customer data to be displayed in the `ListView`. The easiest way to achieve this is to install the GlassFish application server, the JavaDB database, and the NetBeans IDE plug-ins needed to access them, as described in the Preface. As part of this installation, a sample database containing the data used by this example will be added to the JavaDB database server. To start the server from with NetBeans, display the Services tab in the IDE and open the Databases node. You should see an entry for a JavaDB database server on your machine, as shown in Figure 27-8. To start the database server, right-click its node, and select Connect from the context menu. After a few seconds, the database will be running and, if you now expand the database node, you'll find the CUSTOMERS table, which will be the source of the data for the example application.

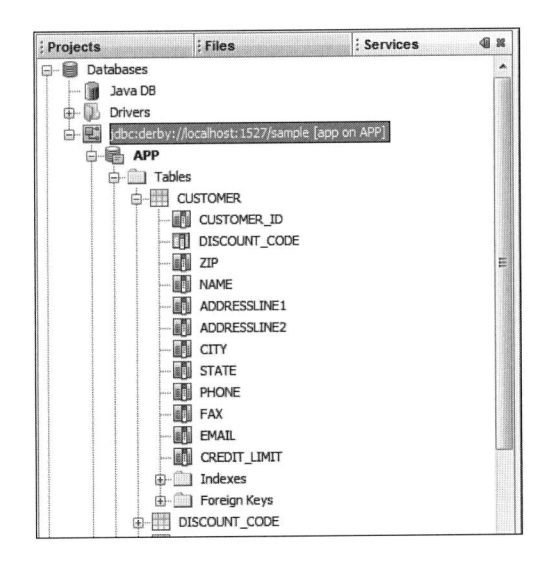

Figure 27-8   Viewing the sample database in the NetBeans IDE

A Database Access Task

To access the database, we need to create a class that can be configured with the information needed to locate and connect to a database server, will read the content of the CUSTOMERS table in a background thread, and will finally deliver the data that we need to a callback function in the application's main thread. Here's a sketch of what this class might look like[11]:

---

[11] The final result will look very much like this, although it is not identical.

```
public class FetchCustomersTask extends Task {
    public-init var dbURL:String;
    public-init var params:Pair[];
    public-read var customers:JavaFXCustomer[];
    public var onCustomers:function(JavaFXCustomer[]):Void;
}
```

As you saw in the preceding section, asynchronous operations in JavaFX are based around the `Task` class, so we use it as the base for this class. In so doing, we inherit functions that can be used to start and stop the task and variables for status reporting (`started`, `stopped`, and so forth). The `dbURL` and `params` variables are intended to be used to specify the location of the database and the user name and password needed to log in.

Having created an instance of the `FetchCustomersTask` class with these two variables initialized, the application would then call its `start()` function and let it get on with its job in the background. On completion, the records read from the database would be converted to instances of the `JavaFXCustomer` class, installed in the `customers` variable, and then the `onCustomers` function would be called to notify the application that the results are available.

Here is the definition of the `JavaFXCustomer` class:

```
public class JavaFXCustomer {
    public-init var customerId:Integer;
    public-init var name:String;
}
```

Because we are only creating an example, this class is pretty minimal and does not include most of the information from the database table—in fact, the example application uses only the value of the `name` column. The class is called `JavaFXCustomer` rather than simply `Customer` to emphasize that it is a JavaFX class; you'll see shortly why this is a good idea.

Having seen the outline of what we are going to implement, let's look at how it will be used. The code in Listing 27-14 shows how the example application uses the `FetchCustomersTask` to read the `CUSTOMERS` table—this is the actual code from the finished application.

Listing 27-14   Asynchronous Database Access

```
1     var customers:JavaFXCustomer[];
2     var task:FetchCustomersTask;
3
4     function getCustomers() {
5         task = FetchCustomersTask {
6             dbURL: "jdbc:derby://localhost:1527/sample"
7             params: [
8                 Pair { name: "user" value: "app" },
9                 Pair { name: "password" value: "app" }
10            ]
```

```
11              onCustomers: function(result):Void {
12                  customers = result;
13              }
14          }
15          task.start();
16      }
```

The `getCustomers()` function creates an instance of the `FetchCustomersTask` object; initializes it with the database URL, username, and password required to log in; and a function, to be called when the customer records have been located, calls the `start()` function to initiate the operation. The data in the CUSTOMERS table will be read in the background, converted to `JavaFXCustomer` objects, and installed in the `customers` variable of the `FetchCustomersTask` object, and finally the `onCustomers` function will then be called. This function copies the returned records into a sequence variable called `customers`, to which the `ListView` control is bound, as shown here:

```
ListView {
    items: bind for (c in customers) {
        c.name
    }
}
```

Here's a breakdown of the steps involved in reading from the database and returning the results to the application:

1. A background thread must be created.
2. A connection must be made to the database.
3. The CUSTOMER_ID and NAME columns of each row of the CUSTOMERS table must be read and a `JavaFXCustomer` object created for each row.
4. The resources used to access the database must be released.
5. The `JavaFXCustomer` objects must be stored in the `customers` variable of the `FetchCustomersTask` object.
6. The `onCustomers` function of the `FetchCustomersTask` object must be called.

Step 1 is performed in the application's main thread and steps 2 to 4 in the background thread. Step 5 requires the background thread to update the state of the `FetchCustomersTask` object and finally, step 6 must be executed in the application's main thread.

At first glance, you may think that implementing this task is going to be fairly straightforward—it looks like all you need to do is start a background thread, perform steps 2 to 4 in that thread, write the results to the `FetchCustomersTask` object, and finally call the `onCustomers` function back in the main thread. However, JavaFX is a single-threaded language, and the compiler and runtime make the following assumptions:

- That access to JavaFX variables is made only from the application's main thread. If this were not the case, there would either need to be language-level support for synchronization, or the compiler and runtime would have to cooperate somehow to transparently guarantee thread safety (which they do not).
- That JavaFX code is executed only in the application's main thread.

The consequence of the first assumption is that the variable updates required in step 5 cannot be made directly from the background thread, and the result of the second assumption is that the code that runs in the background thread has to be written in Java instead of JavaFX.

Writing the code that runs in the background thread in Java causes another problem, arising from the fact that in step 3, we have to create a `JavaFXCustomer` object for each row of the CUSTOMERS table. The problem is that creating a JavaFX object in a background thread is not allowed. We can solve this problem by creating a Java class that is equivalent to the `JavaFXCustomer` class, which will have the same variables and which will be called `JavaCustomer` to make clear that it is a Java class. As you'll see later, the `JavaCustomer` objects will be converted to `JavaFXCustomer` objects at step 5 of the process.

It follows that we need at least four classes to implement the `FetchCustomersTask`:

- The `FetchCustomersTask` class itself, which is a JavaFX class
- The JavaFXCustomer class, which is another JavaFX class
- The class that contains the code that will run in the background thread, which must be a Java class
- The `JavaCustomer` class, which is also a Java class

In fact, as you'll shortly see, we also need to create a Java interface that will allow Java code to update the state of the `FetchCustomersTask` object.

Implementing the Database Access Task

The `JavaTaskBase` class in the `javafx.async` package is intended to be used as the base class for all asynchronous operations. It derives from `Task` and adds one additional function, which must be implemented by subclasses:

```
protected abstract function create():RunnableFuture;
```

This function is required to return the object that contains the code that will be run in the background thread. As we have already seen, this class must be written in Java, and the signature of the `create()` function requires it to implement the `javafx.async.RunnableFuture` interface, which consists of a single method:

```
public abstract void run() throws Exception;
```

If this function returns a JavaFX object, an exception will be thrown. It is, therefore, not possible to implement the background task in JavaFX.

The `JavaTaskBase` class arranges for the `create()` function to be called and the code in the `run()` method of the returned Java object to be executed in a background thread. If this method completes normally, it is assumed that the operation succeeded and the `succeeded` and `done` variables of the task will be set to `true`. If it throws an exception, that exception will be stored in the `causeOfFailure` variable of the task, and the `failed` and `done` variables will be set to `true`.

The implementation of the `FetchCustomersTask` class is shown in Listing 27-15.

Listing 27-15 **The `FetchCustomersTask` Class**

```
1      public class FetchCustomersTask extends JavaTaskBase, TaskUpdater   {
2          public-init var dbURL:String;
3          public-init var params:Pair[];
4          public-read var customers:JavaFXCustomer[];
5          public var onCustomers:function(JavaFXCustomer[]):Void;
6
7          protected override function create():RunnableFuture {
8              var props = new Properties();
9              for (param in params) {
10                 props.put(param.name, param.value);
11             }
12             new JavaCustomerFetcher(dbURL, props, this);
13         }
14
15         // Implementation of TaskUpdater interface
16         public override function setReturnValue(value:Object) {
17             var javaCustomers = value as nativearray of JavaCustomer;
18             for (javaCustomer in javaCustomers) {
19                 insert JavaFXCustomer {
20                     customerId: javaCustomer.customerId;
21                     name: javaCustomer.name;
22                 } into customers;
23             }
24             if (onCustomers != null) {
25                 onCustomers(customers);
26             }
27         }
28
29         public override function setProgress(progress:Long,
30                                              maxProgress:Long) {
31             this.progress = progress;
32              this.maxProgress = maxProgress;
33         }
34     }
```

Chapter 27 Using External Data Sources

As you can see, this class derives from `JavaTaskBase`. The implementation of the `create()` function on lines 7 to 13 converts the name/value pairs in the `params` sequence variable into a `Properties` object and then creates and returns an instance of the `JavaCustomerFetcher` class, passing it the URL of the database, the `Properties` object, and a reference to the task object itself. This reference is needed to allow the background task to indirectly update the `customers` variable and to update the progress-related variables of the task. The `JavaCustomerFetcher` class, which you'll see shortly, is the class that contains the code that will run in the background thread. It is required to implement the `RunnableFuture` interface.

The remaining two functions in this class are required by the `TaskUpdater` interface, which is the third Java class in our implementation of this task. These functions are provided to allow the code in the `JavaCustomerFetcher` class to do the following:

- Return the objects constructed from the content of the CUSTOMERS table by calling the `setReturnValue()` function.
- Set the `progress` and `maxProgress` variables (which are inherited from `Task`) by calling the `setProgress()` function.

The `setReturnValue()` function (lines 16 to 27) is called with argument that is actually a Java array of `JavaCustomer` objects.[12] The content of this array is converted to a sequence of `JavaFXCustomer` objects that is stored in the `customers` variable and then delivered to the `onCustomers` callback function, if one has been installed. This function and the `setProgress()` function on lines 29 to 33 are called from the code running on the background thread, but execute in the main thread of the application, to satisfy the constraint that all JavaFX code must run on this thread. You'll see how this is done when we look at the implementation of the `JavaCustomerFetcher` class, which is shown in Listing 27-16.

Listing 27-16 The `JavaCustomerFetcher` Class

```
1    class JavaCustomerFetcher implements RunnableFuture {
2        private final String dbURL;
3        private final Properties params;
4        private final TaskUpdater task;
5
6        JavaCustomerFetcher(String dbURL, Properties params,
7                            TaskUpdater task) {
8            this.dbURL = dbURL;
9            this.params = params;
10           this.task = task;
```

---

[12] The argument to this function is defined to be of type object to allow the `TaskUpdater` interface to be used in the implementation of other tasks that need to return a value from the code that runs in the background.

```
11          }
12
13          @Override public void run() throws Exception {
14              updateProgress(0, 100);
15
16              Class.forName("org.apache.derby.jdbc.ClientDriver");
17              Connection conn = null;
18              Statement stmt = null;
19              List customers = new ArrayList();
20              try {
21                  conn = DriverManager.getConnection(dbURL, params);
22                  stmt = conn.createStatement();
23                  ResultSet rs = stmt.executeQuery(
24               "SELECT CUSTOMER_ID, NAME from CUSTOMER ORDER BY NAME");
25                  while (rs.next()) {
26                      int id = rs.getInt("CUSTOMER_ID");
27                      String name = rs.getString("NAME");
28                      customers.add(new JavaCustomer(id, name));
29                  }
30                  JavaCustomer[] results =
31                                  new JavaCustomer[customers.size()];
32                  setCustomers(
33                          (JavaCustomer[])customers.toArray(results));
34                  rs.close();
35              } finally {
36                  if (stmt != null) {
37                      stmt.close();
38                  }
39                  if (conn != null) {
40                      conn.close();
41                  }
42              }
43
44              updateProgress(100, 100);
45          }
46
47          private void updateProgress(final long progress,
48                                      final long progressMax) {
49              FX.deferAction(new Function0() {
50                  @Override public Void invoke() {
51                      task.setProgress(progress, progressMax);
52                      return null;
53                  }
54              });
55          }
56
57          private void setCustomers(final JavaCustomer[] results) {
```

```
58                FX.deferAction(new Function0() {
59                    @Override public Void invoke() {
60                        task.setReturnValue(results);
61                        return null;
62                    }
63                });
64            }
65        }
```

The principal task of the `JavaCustomerFetcher` class, which is a Java class, is to read the content of the CUSTOMERS table and convert each row to a `JavaCustomer` object. The code that handles this task can be found on lines 16 to 44, most of which is standard JDBC code that we won't discuss it in detail. The rest of the code is concerned with returning results to the `FetchCustomersTask` class, which must be done in the main thread of the application. There are three points at which this code needs to do this:

- On lines 14, it reports progress by calling the `updateProgress()` function.
- Progress is again reported on line 44.
- On line 32, it calls the `setCustomers()` function to pass the `JavaCustomer` objects created from the CUSTOMERS table to the `FetchCustomersTask` class.

In all three cases, the desired action is simply to write a value to a variable in the JavaFX class. However, this is not possible for two reasons:

- JavaFX variables can be read and written only from the main thread, and this code is not running in the main thread.
- There is no officially supported way for Java code to directly access a JavaFX variable. This is because the way in which JavaFX variables are represented in compiled class files is currently a detail known only to the compiler and the runtime. The only way to read or write JavaFX variables from Java is by calling a getter or setter function in the JavaFX class that can do the job for you. This is why the `setReturnValue()` and `setProgress()` functions were included in the `FetchCustomersTask` class.

To update the state of the `FetchCustomersTask` class, the `updateProgress()` function must call the `setProgress()` function of the `FetchCustomersTask` class, but it cannot do so directly because the call must occur in the application's main thread. To do this, it uses the `deferAction()` function of the `javafx.lang.FX` class. This is the same function that was introduced in Chapter 12, "Platform APIs," and which is used to execute a JavaFX function at some future point on the main application thread. Here, we are calling it from a *Java* class on a *different* thread. Because Java does not have the concept of function pointers, we cannot directly pass a reference to the `setProgress()` function. Instead, we have to use the following construct:

```
FX.deferAction(new Function0() {
    @Override public Void invoke() {
        task.setProgress(progress, progressMax);
        return null;
    }
});
```

`Function0` is a class that allows a function with no arguments to be called. The code that does must be placed in the `invoke()` method, which is overridden in this example to call the `setProgress()` function of the `FetchCustomersTask` object.

It might at first seem that implementing an asynchronous task is quite a complex undertaking, but in reality it is simpler than it looks. Much of the discussion in this section has been around how and why the work should be divided between the task itself and the class that contains the code that is to be run in the background, and we have spent a lot of time looking at the details. In practice, if you need to create your own asynchronous task, you can do so by taking the example in this section as a template, removing all the code that is specific to database access, and replacing it with your own code. In future releases of JavaFX, it is likely that support will be added to make it easier for the Java code that runs in the background thread to communicate with the JavaFX class, which would make it possible to simplify or remove much of the code that appears in this example.

28

Packaging and Deployment

This chapter deals with packaging your JavaFX application and deploying it so that users can download and run it on their desktops, laptops, cell phones, and, in the future, TVs and other devices. If you have been building the example source code for this book in either the NetBeans or Eclipse integrated development environments (IDEs), you have already been packaging JavaFX code, because both IDEs use the `javafxpackager` tool that comes with the JavaFX software development kit (SDK) to compile the source code before running it. Given this fact, you might be wondering why there needs to be a chapter dedicated to packaging and deployment in this book. There are several reasons for this chapter to exist:

- To show you how to use `javafxpackager` as a command-line utility. This is useful for a couple of reasons. First, although it is convenient (and usually faster) to develop using an IDE, production builds are typically done from a batch script, which means using `javafxpackager`. Second, there are some very useful things that you can do with `javafxpackager` that the JavaFX NetBeans and Eclipse plug-ins don't currently let you do from within the IDE.
- Although `javafxpackager` creates the files that you need to place your packaged application or applet on a web server, those files may need to be tailored to suit your deployment environment. We'll take a look at all the files that `javafxpackager` creates and show you how they can be customized.
- When you run your JavaFX code as a stand-alone application from within the IDE, it is run with all available privileges and so has full access to your system and to the network. However, when your application is deployed, this might not be the case. In the course of this chapter, you'll see some of the restrictions that apply by default and how you can arrange for your application to be given the additional privileges that it needs to do its job.

Because this chapter is based around a command-line tool, there are no IDE projects for the example source code. Instead, you will find the source code that you need in several subdirectories below the `deployment` directory of the book's example source.

Instructions for compiling and packaging each example are given in the relevant section of this chapter.

> **Warning**
> All the deployment mechanisms listed in this chapter involve installation of a JavaFX application over a network. This is the only mechanism that is currently supported. Although it would be technically possible to distribute an application by bundling your code with a copy of the JavaFX runtime and distributing it to users on a DVD (or similar), this would breach the terms of the licensing agreement that you accepted when you downloaded JavaFX. *You are not permitted to redistribute the JavaFX runtime—the only legal way for a customer to acquire the JavaFX runtime is directly from Sun Microsystems.* The deployment mechanisms described in this chapter automatically download the JavaFX runtime (and, if necessary, a compatible JRE) onto the target computer and require the end user to accept the relevant licensing terms before running any JavaFX code.

Packaging and Deployment for the Desktop

The `javafxpackager` command can package your code for the desktop, for a mobile device, or for a device supporting Java TV, depending on the profile that you specify with its `--p` argument. In this section, we take a look at how to package a couple of simple JavaFX applications for the desktop environment. In the section that follows, you'll see how to package one of those applications for deployment on a mobile device.

Creating a Packaged Application and Applet with `javafxpackager`

The application that we use in this section consists of a single JavaFX source file and an image of Duke relaxing in a chair. The source code is shown in Listing 28-1.

Listing 28-1   **Source Code for the Duke Sitting Example**

```
package deployment;
import javafx.stage.Stage;
import javafx.scene.Scene;
import javafx.scene.layout.VBox;
import javafx.geometry.HPos;
import javafx.geometry.VPos;
import javafx.scene.text.Text;
import javafx.scene.image.Image;
import javafx.scene.image.ImageView;

Stage {
    title : "Duke Relaxing"
    var scene:Scene;
    scene: scene = Scene {
        width: 220
        height: 200
```

```
            content: [
                VBox {
                    width: bind scene.width
                    height: bind scene.height
                    hpos: HPos.CENTER
                    vpos: VPos.CENTER
                    nodeHPos: HPos.CENTER
                    spacing: 8
                    content: [
                        ImageView {
                            image: Image {
                                url: "{__DIR__}img.jpg"
                            }
                        }
                        Text {
                            content: "Duke Relaxes"
                        }
                    ]
                }
            ]
        }
}
```

You'll find this code in a file called `DukeSitting.fx`, which is in the directory `deployment/example1/src/deployment` relative to the installation directory of the example code for this book, as shown in Figure 28-1. The image file, which is called `img.jpg`, is located in the directory `deployment/example1/resources/deployment`.

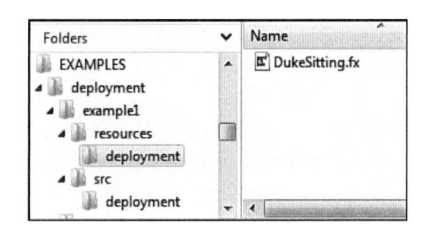

Figure 28-1　Directory layout for the Duke Sitting example

To build and package this example, open a command window, make `deployment/example1` your working directory, and type the following command, all on one line:

```
javafxpackager -p desktop -src src -res resources -draggable
        -appClass deployment.DukeSitting
        -appName "DukeSitting" -appVendor "JavaFX Productions Inc"
```

```
-appVersion 1.0 -appWidth 220 -appHeight 200
-appCodebase http://JavaFXProductions.com
```

The `-p desktop` argument causes the `javafxpackager` command to compile the application using the class libraries for the desktop profile (which is the default, so this argument can actually be omitted.) The `-src` (or `-sourcepath`) argument points to a directory or directories that contain the source code to be compiled. In this simple example, there is only one source file and therefore only a single source root. To specify more than one source root, separate the directory names with the appropriate path separator character for your platform, which would be ; on Windows and : on UNIX-based systems (that is, Solaris, Linux, or Mac OS), for example:

```
javafxpackager -sourcepath src1;src2 ....    // Windows
javafxpackager -src src1:src2 ....           // Solaris/Mac OS/Linux
```

The result is the same whether you use `-src` or `-sourcepath` as the argument name. If this argument appears more than once, only the source root directories associated with the last occurrence are used; this is a general rule for all `javafxpackager` arguments. The source files within a source root must be organized in subdirectories that correspond to their package names, as usual.

The `javafxpackager` command creates a working directory for its outputs (which, by default, is in the location in which the host platform creates temporary files but which can be overridden with the `-workDir` argument) and then compiles all the Java and JavaFX source files in the source root directories, writing the class files to the working directory.

Any files in the source directories that are not Java or JavaFX source files are copied directly to the output location, which means that you can mix resource files with your source code and have them bundled automatically into the generated Java Archive (JAR) files. Alternatively, if you want to keep your resources in a separate location, you can use the `-res` (or `-resourcepath`) argument to specify one or more resource directories. The image file that is used in the example application can be found in the directory `resources/deployment`, so we use the argument `-res resources` to have `javafxpackager` copy it to a directory called `deployment` in the working area, along with the class file created from the `DukeSitting.fx` file. If you would like to see which files `javafxpackager` is compiling and where it is looking to find source files and resources, you can do so by using the `-verbose` argument.

> **Note**
>
> When it is compiling, `javafxpackager` uses a built-in copy of the Java 5 Runtime Environment to resolve references to system classes, even if you have a later version of the JRE or JDK installed on your computer. This means that your JavaFX application cannot use Java 6 application programming interfaces (APIs) and, at the time of writing, there is no supported way to change this. At runtime, however, your application can be run with a more recent version of the JRE, if the user has one installed. This is important, because some features, such as stage transparency, only work with Java 6 or higher.

The remaining arguments in the `javafxpackager` command line are used when creating the supporting files that are written to the output directory, which we look at in the following paragraphs. By default, the output is written to a directory called `dist` in the current directory, but you can change this by using the `-d` option. If the output directory already exists when `javafxpackager` is run, it will be used but its content will not be deleted automatically.

The content of the output directory after running `javafxpackager` is shown in Figure 28-2.

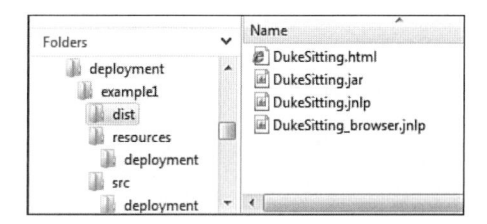

Figure 28-2   Files created for the Duke Sitting example in desktop mode

Here's a brief description of these files, which we discuss in greater detail below:

- `DukeSitting.jar` contains the compiled class files and the accompanying resources.
- `DukeSitting.jnlp` is a JNLP file that you can use to deploy the example as a desktop application to be installed and run using Java Web Start.
- `DukeSitting.html` is a skeleton HTML page that contains the tags required to run the example as an applet.
- `DukeSitting_browser.jnlp` is a Java Network Launcher Protocol (JNLP) file that is used when the example is deployed as an applet.

You can use these files to deploy the example so that it can be run as either an application or an applet. As a quick test that the example has been built correctly, you can run it from the command line by using the following command:

```
javafx -jar dist\DukeSitting.jar
```

Application Deployment

To deploy the example, you need to have a web server installed and running. In the rest of this chapter, we will assume that you have installed and started the GlassFish application server, as described in the Preface. If your installation is correct and you open a web browser and point it at the URL http://myhost:8080, where myhost is the name of your computer, you should see the GlassFish welcome page.[1] If you do not, return to the Preface and review the installation instructions.

To deploy the example code so that it can be run as an application, you need to copy the `DukeSitting.jar` and `DukeSitting.jnlp` files to an appropriate location within the part of the file system managed by your web server and then edit the JNLP file so that it reflects that location. Here's the simplest way to deploy this application:

1. Go to the GlassFish installation directory and locate the folder called `docroot`.
2. Create a subdirectory of `docroot` called `example1`.
3. Copy the files `DukeSitting.jar` and `DukeSitting.jnlp` to the `example1` directory, as shown in Figure 28-3.

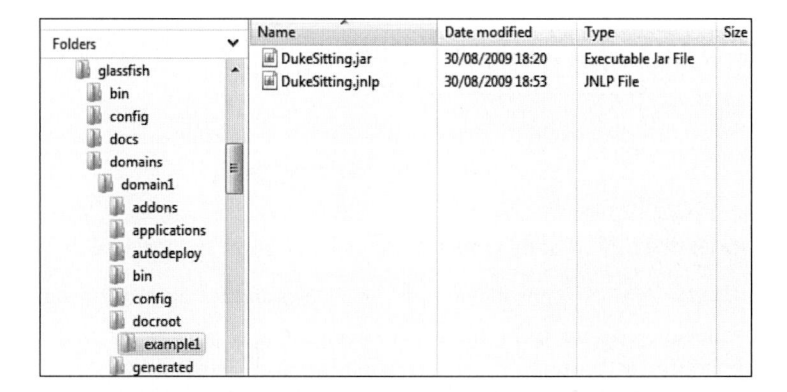

Figure 28-3   Deploying a JavaFX application with GlassFish

If you now enter the URL **http://myhost:8080/example1** into a web browser, you should see a directory listing showing the JAR file and the JNLP file. At this point, if you click the JNLP file, the browser downloads it and runs Java Web Start, but the application will not start because the JNLP file needs to be customized to match its location in the web server's file store. Listing 28-2 shows the content of JNLP file created by `javafxpackager`:

Listing 28-2   **The JNLP File for the Duke Sitting Example**

```
1      <?xml version="1.0" encoding="UTF-8"?>
2      <jnlp spec="1.0+" codebase=http://JavaFXProductions.com/
```

---

[1] Here and throughout this chapter, you should replace myhost when it appears in a URL with the hostname of your computer as it appears on your TCP/IP network.

```
3              href="DukeSitting.jnlp">
4          <information>
5              <title>DukeSitting</title>
6              <vendor>JavaFX Productions Inc</vendor>
7              <homepage href="http://JavaFXProductions.com/"/>
8              <description>DukeSitting</description>
9              <offline-allowed/>
10             <shortcut>
11                 <desktop/>
12             </shortcut>
13         </information>
14         <resources>
15             <j2se version="1.5+"/>
16             <extension name="JavaFX Runtime"
17                 href="http://dl.javafx.com/1.2/javafx-rt.jnlp"/>
18             <jar href="DukeSitting.jar" main="true"/>
19         </resources>
20         <application-desc
21                 main-class="com.sun.javafx.runtime.main.Main">
22             <argument>
23                 MainJavaFXScript=deployment.DukeSitting</argument>
22         </application-desc>
23         <update check="background">
24     </jnlp>
```

> **Note**
>
> A complete description of this JNLP file is outside the scope of this book. If you want to find out more about Java Web Start and JNLP files, a good place to start is the JDK documentation for Java Web Start. For Java 6, you can find this at http://java.sun.com/javase/6/docs/technotes/guides/javaws/index.html.

The reason that the application does not start is that the value of the `codebase` attribute on line 2 of Listing 28-2 is not correct—you need to replace it with the URL of the directory containing the JNLP file *as seen by your browser*, which in this case would be http://myhost:8080/example1. After this change, the first three lines of the JNLP file should look like this:

```
1      <?xml version="1.0" encoding="UTF-8"?>
2      <jnlp spec="1.0+" codebase="http://myhost:8080/example1"
3            href="DukeSitting.jnlp">
```

You should also change the `homepage` element on line 7 to point to the same location, although this is not critical to the correct operation of the JNLP file.

If you now enter the URL **http://myhost:8080/example1/DukeSitting.jnlp** into your browser, you will be asked whether to create desktop shortcuts for the application. Click the OK button to allow a desktop shortcut to be created, and the example code will be downloaded and run under the control of Java Web Start, with the result shown in Figure 28-4.

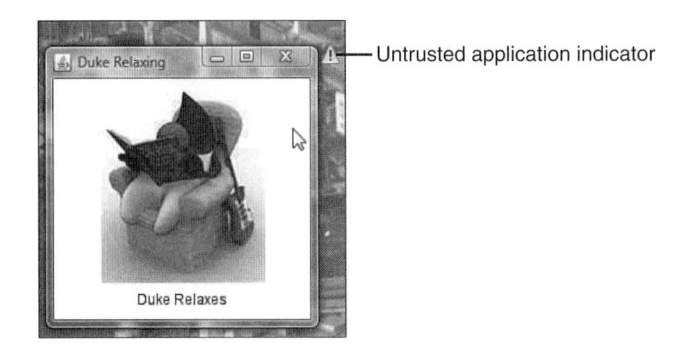

Figure 28-4   The Duke Sitting example as an application

Notice that there is a small triangular indicator next to the application window. This indicator is present because Java Web Start applications are, by default, not trusted.[2] To remove it, you must sign your application so that the user can decide whether to trust it. You'll see how to sign an application later in this chapter.

After the application has been downloaded, it is installed into a local cache that is managed by Java Web Start. Running the same application again, either by entering the JNLP URL into the browser or by using the desktop shortcut created by Java Web Start, will cause the application to be run using the cached JAR file, unless there is a more recent copy on the web server, in which case the newer version is downloaded automatically and replaces the one in the cache.

Some of the content of the JNLP file in Listing 28-1 was set from the command-line arguments passed to the `javafxpackager` command:

- The `codebase` value on line 2 and the `href` value on line 7 were set from the value of the `appCodebase` argument.
- The name of the JNLP file, which appears as the value of the `href` attribute on line 3, was set from the `appName` argument. This argument also determines the content of the `title` and `description` elements on lines 5 and 8 and the name of the JAR file itself, which is referenced on line 18. Note that because the application name is used to generate filenames, it is not a good idea to use a name that includes whitespace.

---

[2] No warning indicator appears when you run an application directly from an IDE or from the command line because an application run in this way is implicitly trusted.

- The vendor name on line 6 is obtained from the `appVendor` argument.
- The name of the main application class, which appears on line 21 of Listing 28-1, is set from the value of the `appClass` argument.

As you'll see in the following sections, some of the other arguments that we used when packaging the example (`appWidth`, `appHeight`, and `draggable`) are used only when it is deployed as an applet, and the value of the `appVersion` argument is used when packaging the example for deployment on a mobile device.

The only part of the JNLP file that you had to change to match your deployment environment was the `codebase` attribute on line 2 of Listing 28-1. Given that this attribute is set from the value of the `appCodebase` argument, you can avoid having to modify the JNLP file at all by using the correct value for this argument when running `javafxpackager`, like this:

```
javafxpackager -p desktop -src src -res resources -draggable
          -appClass deployment.DukeSitting
          -appName "DukeSitting" -appVendor "JavaFX Productions Inc"
          -appVersion 1.0 -appWidth 220 -appHeight 200
          -appCodebase http://myhost:8080/example1
```

Applet Deployment

To deploy the example to run as an applet, you need to first copy the files `DukeSitting.jar`, `DukeSitting.html`, and `DukeSitting_browser.jnlp` to your web server's file store. As before, we use the directory `docroot/example1` to host the applet, so copy the files to this location. Next, you need to change the `codebase` and `homepage` values in the file `DukeSitting_browser.jnlp` in the same way as you did when deploying the example as an application. Listing 28-2 shows the content of this file after this change has been made. As you can see, it is similar to the application JNLP file shown in Listing 28-1.[3]

> **Note**
>
> You may be surprised to see that a JNLP file is used as part of the applet deployment. This is a feature that was introduced as part of a new Java Applet plug-in in Java 6 update 10. Using a JNLP file to describe an applet allows greater control over the environment in which the applet is run. For example, it is possible to specify the minimum version of the Java platform on which it can run (which is Java 5 for all JavaFX applets). If the applet is loaded in an environment that does not have the new plug-in, it will still work, provided that the browser is configured to use Java 5 or later, but the JNLP file will be ignored. For more information on this, refer to the documentation at http://java.sun.com/developer/technicalArticles/javase/newapplets and https://jdk6.dev.java.net/plugin2.

---

[3] As with the application JNLP, you can avoid having to make these modifications if you use the correct value for the `appCodebase` argument when running the `javafxpackager` command.

Listing 28-2 The Browser JNLP File for the Duke Sitting Applet

```
1   <?xml version="1.0" encoding="UTF-8"?>
2   <jnlp spec="1.0+" codebase="http://myhost:8080/example1/"
3          href="DukeSitting_browser.jnlp">
4      <information>
5          <title>DukeSitting</title>
6          <vendor>JavaFX Productions Inc</vendor>
7          <homepage href="http://myhost:8080/example1/"/>
8          <description>DukeSitting</description>
9          <offline-allowed/>
10         <shortcut>
11             <desktop/>
12         </shortcut>
13     </information>
14     <resources>
15         <j2se version="1.5+"/>
16         <extension name="JavaFX Runtime"
17             href="http://dl.javafx.com/1.2/javafx-rt.jnlp"/>
18         <jar href="DukeSitting.jar" main="true"/>
19     </resources>
20     <applet-desc name="DukeSitting"
21               main-    class="com.sun.javafx.runtime.adapter.Applet"
22               width="220" height="200">
23         <param name="MainJavaFXScript"
24             value="deployment.DukeSitting">
25     </applet-desc>
26     <update check="background">
27  </jnlp>
```

To run the deployed applet, open the `DukeSitting.html` page by entering the URL **http://myhost:8080/example1/DukeSitting.html** in your browser. The applet will be loaded and run, as shown in Figure 28-5.

As you can see, the applet is shown in an otherwise empty page, because the HTML that is generated is a fragment that you are expected to incorporate into a more complete page. The content of this file is shown in Listing 28-3.

Listing 28-3 The Skeleton HTML Page for the Duke Sitting Example

```
1   <html>
2   <head>
3   <meta http-equiv="Content-Type" content="text/html; charset=utf-    8">
4   <title>DukeSitting</title>
5   </head>
6   <body>
7   <h1>DukeSitting</h1>
8   <script src="http://dl.javafx.com/1.2/dtfx.js"></script>
```

```
 9      <script>
10          javafx(
11              {
12                      archive: "DukeSitting.jar",
13                      draggable: true,
14                      width: 220,
15                      height: 200,
16                      code: "deployment.DukeSitting",
17                      name: "DukeSitting"
18              }
19          );
20      </script>
21      </body>
22      </html>
```

Figure 28-5   The Duke Sitting example as an applet

You may have expected to see an `<APPLET>` or `<OBJECT>` tag in this page, but there isn't one—instead, there is simply a call to a JavaScript function called javafx() with a list of parameters that are derived from the arguments to the javafxpackager command. You can see that there are parameters that specify the location of the JAR file containing the code and resources (line 12), the width and height of the applet (lines 14 and 15, derived from the values of the `appWidth` and `appHeight` arguments to `javafxpackager`), the name of the main class (on line 16), and the name of the applet itself (on line 17). The javafx() function causes some additional HTML to be written to the document once it is loaded in the browser. One way to work out what is written is to download the script file whose location is shown on line 8 and examine it, but it is easier to set the value `displayhtml` to `true` by adding the following highlighted line to the HTML page instead:

```
javafx(
    {
```

```
        displayhtml: true,
        archive: "DukeSitting.jar",
        draggable: true,
        width: 220,
        height: 200,
        code: "deployment.DukeSitting",
        name: "DukeSitting"
    }
);
```

If you now reload the page in your browser, you see the HTML that is generated instead of the applet itself, as shown in Listing 28-4.

Listing 28-4   HTML Generated for the Duke Sitting Applet

```
1     <div id="deployJavaApplet1Overlay"
2       style="width:220;height:200;position:absolute;background:white">
3     <table width=220 height=200 border=0 padding=0 margin=0>
4     <tr><td align="center" valign="middle">
5     <img src="http://dl.javafx.com/javafx-loading-100x100.gif"
6         width=100 height=100>
7     </td></tr></table>
8     </div>
8     <div id="deployJavaApplet1" style="position:relative;left:-  10000px">
9     <APPLET MAYSCRIPT
9           code="org.jdesktop.applet.util.JNLPAppletLauncher"
10          archive="DukeSitting.jar,http://dl.javafx.com/applet-
11    launcher__V1.2.0_b233.jar,http://dl.javafx.com/javafx-rt-windows-
12    i586__V1.2.0_b233.jar,http://dl.javafx.com/emptyJarFile-
13    1251724532108__V1.2.0_b233.jar"
14          width=220
15          height=200
16    >
17      <param name="codebase_lookup" value="false">
18      <param name="subapplet.classname"
19            value="com.sun.javafx.runtime.adapter.Applet">
20      <param name="progressbar" value="false">
21      <param name="classloader_cache" value="false">
22      <param name="draggable" value="true">
23      <param name="MainJavaFXScript" value="deployment.DukeSitting">
24      <param name="subapplet.displayname" value="DukeSitting">
25      <param name="jnlpNumExtensions" value="1">
26      <param name="jnlpExtension1"
27            value="http://dl.javafx.com/javafx-  rt__V1.2.0_b233.jnlp">
28      <param name="jnlp_href" value="DukeSitting_browser.jnlp">
29      <param name="deployJavaAppletID" value="deployJavaApplet1">
30    </APPLET>
31    </div>
```

You can see the generated <APPLET> element on lines 9 to 30 of Listing 28-4. This element is constructed so that it works with either the new applet plug-in or the old one. For example, the archive attribute shown on lines 10 to 13 specifies the location of the JAR file containing the example code and the JAR files that contain the JavaFX runtime, but this attribute is used only by the *old* plug-in. If the browser is using the *new* plug-in (that is, Java version 6 update 10 or later is installed and activated), it uses the browser JNLP file referenced on line 28 (and which you saw in Listing 28-2) to locate the code archive and the JavaFX runtime.

Setting and Reading Parameters

As you saw in Chapter 12, "Platform APIs," a JavaFX application can read the values of command-line arguments by using the getArgument() function of the javafx.lang.FX class. The same function can also be used to read parameters supplied to applets and, on mobile devices, MIDlets. You can supply parameters to a JavaFX application at packaging time by using the -paramFile argument of the javafxpackager utility. The code in Listing 28-5 is a variant of the Duke Sitting example that gets the text strings for its title from its parameters. You can find the code for this example in the directory deployment/example2 relative to the installation location of the source code for this book.

Listing 28-5 **Parameterizing a JavaFX Application, Applet, or MIDlet**

```
1     package deployment;
2
3     import javafx.stage.Stage;
4     import javafx.scene.Scene;
5     import javafx.scene.layout.VBox;
6     import javafx.geometry.HPos;
7     import javafx.geometry.VPos;
8     import javafx.scene.text.Text;
9     import javafx.scene.image.Image;
10    import javafx.scene.image.ImageView;
11
12    Stage {
13        title : FX.getArgument("Title") as String
14        var scene:Scene;
15        scene: scene = Scene {
16            width: 220
17            height: 200
18            content: [
19                VBox {
20                    width: bind scene.width
21                    height: bind scene.height
22                    hpos: HPos.CENTER
23                    vpos: VPos.CENTER
24                    nodeHPos: HPos.CENTER
25                    spacing: 8
```

```
26                        content: [
27                            ImageView {
28                                image: Image {
29                                    url: "{__DIR__}img.jpg"
30                                }
31                            }
32                            Text {
33                                content: FX.getArgument("Text") as String
34                            }
35                        ]
36                    }
37                ]
38            }
39        }
```

To compile and package this example, make `deployment/example2` your working directory and enter the following command. Note that to avoid editing the generated files, you should use the correct value for the `appCodebase` argument, which in this case will be `http://myhost:8080/example2`:

```
javafxpackager -p desktop -src src -res resources -draggable
        -appClass deployment.DukeSitting
        -appName "DukeSitting" -appVendor "JavaFX Productions Inc"
        -appVersion 1.0 -appWidth 220 -appHeight 200
        -appCodebase http://myhost:8080/example2
        -paramFile props.txt
```

To deploy the example, create a directory called `example2` in the `docroot` directory of your GlassFish application server and copy all the files from `deployment/example2/dist` into it. You can then run the example as an application by pointing your web browser at the URL http://myhost:8080/example2/DukeSitting.jnlp or as an applet by opening the page at the URL http://myhost:8080/example2/DukeSitting.html. In both cases, you should see that the caption below the image of Duke has changed to "Duke in his armchair," while the application title is now "Duke Relaxes." These values come from the parameters set in the file `props.txt`, which you can find in the directory `deployment/example2` and the content of which is shown here:

```
Title = Duke Relaxes
Text = Duke in his armchair
```

This file is not copied to the output directory. Instead, the parameter values are included in the generated JNLP files and the applet's HTML page. Here's an extract from the `DukeSitting.jnlp` file, which is used when the example is run as an application:

```
<application-desc main-class="com.sun.javafx.runtime.main.Main">
    <argument>MainJavaFXScript=deployment.DukeSitting</argument>
    <argument>Title=Duke Relaxes</argument>
    <argument>Text=Duke in his armchair</argument>
</application-desc>
```

As you can see, in this case the parameters are passed to the application as command-line arguments. In the applet case, the parameters appear in two places (the HTML page and the browser JNLP file). Here's the relevant part of the HTML page:

```
var appParams = new Array();
appParams["Title"] = "Duke Relaxes";
appParams["Text"] = "Duke in his armchair";
javafx(
    {
        archive: "DukeSitting.jar",
        draggable: true,
        width: 220,
        height: 200,
        code: "deployment.DukeSitting",
        name: "DukeSitting"
    }
    , appParams
);
```

The parameters set here become `<param>` elements nested in the `<applet>` element that is generated by the `javafx()` function; you can verify this by looking at the resulting HTML by setting `displayhtml` to true. The nested `<param>` elements are used only when the old plug-in is active. For the new plug-in, the parameters are obtained from the browser JNLP file, part of which is shown here:

```
<applet-desc name="DukeSitting"
             main-class="com.sun.javafx.runtime.adapter.Applet"
             width="220" height="200">
    <param name="MainJavaFXScript" value="deployment.DukeSitting">
    <param name="Title" value="Duke Relaxes"/>
    <param name="Text" value="Duke in his armchair"/>
</applet-desc>
```

Even though the parameters are passed in different ways in these three cases, the same JavaFX code can be used to read their values. As you'll see later in this chapter, the same code also works when the example is deployed to a mobile device.

> **Note**
>
> At the time of writing, there is no way to set parameters when running JavaFX code from within the NetBeans or Eclipse IDEs.

Incorporating Libraries

Whereas some JavaFX applications require only the libraries in the underlying JavaFX and Java platforms, more sophisticated ones need to use additional libraries. In Chapter 27, "Using External Data Sources," you saw an example that made use of the JavaDB database and which required one of the JAR files from the JavaDB distribution to be made available at runtime. If you plan to work exclusively in an IDE, you can incorporate these libraries by using the appropriate IDE feature (as we did in Chapter 27), but if you are packaging your application with `javafxpackager`, you need to be able to tell it where to find the additional libraries that your application requires so that they can be included at compile time and can be deployed with the application itself.

The directory `deployment/example3/src` contains a copy of the source code for the database example shown in Chapter 27. There is also an empty directory at `deployment/example3/lib`, in which we will place the additional library that this example requires. To compile and package this example, do the following:

1. Make `deployment/example3` your working directory.

2. Copy the file `derbyclient.jar` from the `lib` directory of the JavaDB distribution to the directory `deployment/example3/lib`. On Windows, this library will be found, by default, in `C:\Program Files\Sun\JavaDB\lib`.

3. Run `javafxpackager` using the command line shown here:

```
javafxpackager -src src -draggable -appClass deployment.DBExample
               -appName "DBExample" -appVendor "JavaFX Productions Inc"
               -appVersion 1.0 -appWidth 220 -appHeight 200
               -appCodebase http://myhost:8080/example3
               -cp lib/derbyclient.jar
```

Notice the two significant differences between this and earlier examples. First, the `appCodebase` value has been changed to reflect the fact that this is a new example. Second, we have used the `-cp` argument of `javafxpackager` to add the JavaDB library that we need to the classpath.[4] This has the effect of making the classes in this library available at compile time (which is not actually necessary in this case) and also copies the JAR file to a directory call `lib` within the output directory, as shown in Figure 28-6.

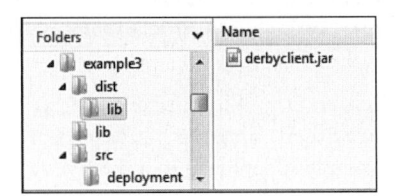

Figure 28-6   Including an additional library in a packaged JavaFX application

To deploy this application, create a directory called `example3` in the `docroot` directory of the GlassFish application server and copy everything in the output directory, including `lib` and its contents, to that directory, being careful to preserve the directory structure. Appropriate references to the additional library have been included in the generated JNLP

---

[4] There are two other option names that you can use rather than `-cp`, namely `-classpath` and `-librarypath`. It doesn't matter which one you choose.

Packaging and Deployment for the Desktop   1041

and HTML files so that it will be located correctly when you run the example as an application or as an applet. Here, for example, is the application JNLP file for this example:

```
1   <?xml version="1.0" encoding="UTF-8"?>
2   <jnlp spec="1.0+" codebase="http://myhost:8080/example3/"
3         href="DBExample.jnlp">
4       <information>
5           <title>DBExample</title>
6           <vendor>JavaFX Productions Inc</vendor>
7           <homepage href="http://myhost:8080/example3/"/>
8           <description>DBExample</description>
9           <offline-allowed/>
10          <shortcut>
11              <desktop/>
12          </shortcut>
13      </information>
14      <resources>
15          <j2se version="1.5+"/>
16          <extension name="JavaFX Runtime"
17                  href="http://dl.javafx.com/1.2/javafx-     rt.jnlp"/>
18          <jar href="DBExample.jar" main="true"/>
19          <jar href="lib/derbyclient.jar"/>
20      </resources>
21      <application-desc main- class="com.sun.javafx.runtime.main.Main">
22          <argument>MainJavaFXScript=deployment.DBExample</argument>
23      </application-desc>
24      <update check="background">
25  </jnlp>
```

As you can see, the JavaDB library is referenced on line 19. To run this example as an application, use the URL `http://myhost:8080/example3/DBExample.jnlp`, or to run it as an applet use `http://myhost:8080/example3/DBExample.html`. Running the example as an application gives the result shown on the left of Figure 28-7.

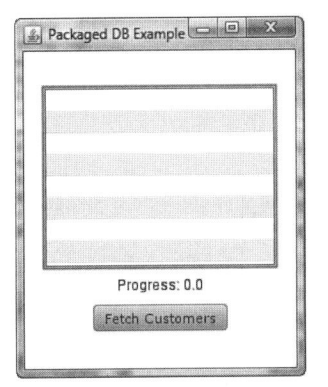

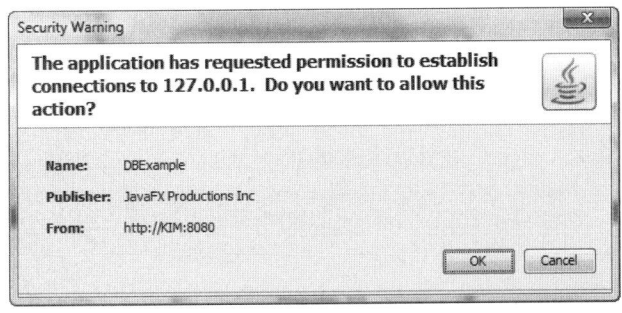

Figure 28-7   Running a database access example as an unsigned application

Chapter 28 Packaging and Deployment

If you click the Fetch Customers button, the application attempts to read the content of the CUSTOMERS table in the JavaDB database, but it doesn't immediately succeed. Instead, you see a dialog requested permission to make a network connection to the database, as shown on the right in Figure 28-7. If you click the OK button, the connection will be permitted and a list of customer names appear.[5] The dialog appears because the application is not trusted, so the user is given the opportunity to allow or disallow access to the database. The same dialog would also appear if you were to run the example as an applet. This dialog would not appear if the application were signed, as you'll see later in this chapter.

If your application needs more than one additional library, you should copy them all to the `lib` directory of your project and include each library in the `-cp` argument of the `javafxpackager` command, using the correct path separator (that is, `:` or `;`) for your host platform, as follows:

```
javafxpackager -cp lib/lib1.jar;lib/lib2.jar ....// Windows
javafxpackager -cp lib/lib1.jar:lib/lib2.jar ....// Mac OS/Solaris/Linux
```

> **Note**
> At the time of writing, it is possible to supply just the name of the directory containing the additional libraries as a command line argument, like this:
>
> ```
> javafxpackager -cp lib ....
> ```
>
> The command appears to complete normally, but the resulting output is not usable—it fails at runtime because the classes in the included libraries cannot be found.

Compressing the JAR Files

It is possible to apply additional compression to JAR files that will speed up the download of your JavaFX application. To get the benefits of this, you need to do two things:

- Request pack200 compression when you use `javafxpackager`.
- Copy the pack200-compressed JAR files along with the standard archives when you deploy your application.

> **Note**
> Pack200 compression was introduced in Java 5. To make use of it, suitably compressed archives must be made available on the web server and a version of Java Web Start that supports it must be used on the client computer. If the client's version of Java Web Start does not support pack200 compression, the standard JAR files will be automatically downloaded

---

[5] In this case, the user is prompted to authorize behavior that might constitute a security breach, but this does not always happen—if your untrusted application were to attempt to access the system clipboard, for example, an exception would be thrown instead.

instead. It is, therefore, always safe to use pack200 compression, provided that you always deploy all the JAR files that are generated by the packaging process. For further information, refer to http://java.sun.com/j2se/1.5.0/docs/guide/deployment/deployment-guide/pack200.html.

You request pack200 compression by using the `-pack200` argument. The following command line will generate pack200-compressed archives for the example used in the previous section, in addition to the standard ones:

```
javafxpackager -src src -draggable -appClass deployment.DBExample
            -appName "DBExample" -appVendor "JavaFX Productions Inc"
            -appVersion 1.0 -appWidth 220 -appHeight 200
            -appCodebase http://myhost:8080/example3
            -cp lib/derbyclient.jar
            -pack200
```

The files that are generated by this command are shown in Figure 28-8.

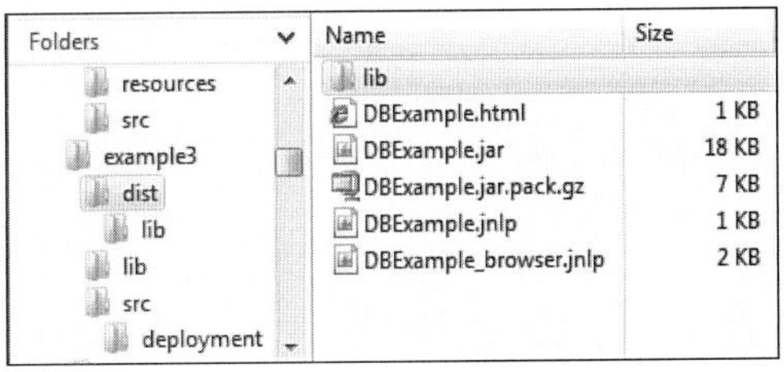

Name	Size
lib	
DBExample.html	1 KB
DBExample.jar	18 KB
DBExample.jar.pack.gz	7 KB
DBExample.jnlp	1 KB
DBExample_browser.jnlp	2 KB

Figure 28-8 The result of requesting pack200 compression

As you can see, there are now two JAR files: `DBExample.jar` is the normal archive with standard compression; and `DBExample.jar.pack.gz` is the pack200 version, which is substantially smaller. There are also two copies of the `derbyclient.jar` file in the `lib` subdirectory. If you copy all these files to `docroot/example3`, you can then use your browser to run this version of the example either as an application or as an applet. Given the small size of these files, it will be difficult to detect any improvement in performance due to the pack200 compression, but for larger files the difference will be noticeable, especially if the network over which they are being downloaded is slow.

Signing Applications and Applets

Applets and applications run under Java Web Start are subject to security restrictions that prevent them from doing certain things, such as accessing the user's file system (other than via the Storage API), making network connections to a location other than the host from which they were downloaded, and so on. As you saw earlier in this chapter, in some cases the system will prompt the user for authorization and will permit the operation if the user agrees. If you don't want these prompts to appear, you can convert your untrusted application or applet to a trusted one by signing it. When the user runs a trusted application or applet, a single prompt appears at startup, asking the user whether the application or applet should be trusted. If the user agrees, all the security restrictions are removed.

To sign an application or applet, you need a digital certificate. For real-world deployment, you need to obtain a certificate from a trusted certificate issuing authority such as Verisign. To obtain such a certificate, you need to create a certificate signing request (CSR) and follow a procedure specified by the issuer that includes some form of verification of your identity. This takes time, so in the meanwhile, for development purposes, you can use a self-signed certificate. A self-signed certificate can be generated on your own computer and works the same way as a real certificate, except that the user will be told that the certificate was not issued by a trusted issuer and will, therefore, probably not want to allow your application to run with unrestricted privileges.[6]

Using a Self-Signed Certificate

To sign an application using a self-signed certificate, you just need to add the `-sign` argument to the `javafxpackager` command line. Here's how you would sign the database example in `deployment/example3` for development purposes:

```
javafxpackager -src src -draggable -appClass deployment.DBExample
               -appName "DBExample" -appVendor "JavaFX Productions Inc"
               -appVersion 1.0 -appWidth 220 -appHeight 200
               -appCodebase http://myhost:8080/example3
               -cp lib/derbyclient.jar
               -sign
```

This command creates a self-signed certificate and uses it to sign both the application and the library JAR file. If you copy the content of the directory `deployment/example3/dist` to `docroot/example3` and then run the application from your web browser, you will be prompted to allow it to run with privileges, as shown in Figure 28-9.

Notice that the dialog box indicates that the digital signature of the application cannot be verified. This because a self-signed certificate is, effectively, vouching for its own identity and therefore should not be trusted. By contrast, when you obtain a real certificate, the issuer signs it to vouch for your identity. As long as the issuer is trusted, the whole certificate chain can be trusted.

If you allow the application to run, you find that you are not prompted to permit it to access the database.

---

[6] When you use the option to sign your application or applet in the NetBeans or Eclipse IDE, a self-signed certificate is used. At the time of this writing, the only way to sign a JavaFX application or applet with a real certificate is to use `javafxpackager`, as described in this section.

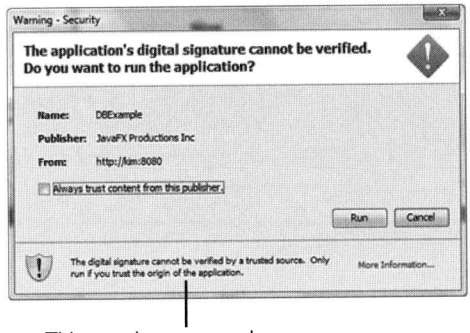

Figure 28-9 Running an application with a self-signed certificate

Using a Real Certificate

A production application or applet must be signed with a real certificate obtained from a bona fide certificate issuer. The process that you need to follow to get a real certificate and import it into a Java keystore can be found at http://java.sun.com/docs/books/tutorial/security/sigcert/index.html. For the purposes of this section, we assume that you have acquired a certificate and have imported it, along with its associated private key, with alias myalias into a keystore called `keystore.jks`, with keystore password storepass and with key password keypass.

To sign an application with this certificate, you use the `-sign`, `-keyalias`, `-keystore`, `-keystorePassword`, and `-keyaliasPassword` command-line arguments of `javafxpackager`:

```
javafxpackager -src src -draggable -appClass deployment.DBExample
               -appName "DBExample" -appVendor "JavaFX Productions Inc"
               -appVersion 1.0 -appWidth 220 -appHeight 200
               -appCodebase http://myhost:8080/example3
               -cp lib/derbyclient.jar
               -sign -keyalias myalias -keystore keystore.jks
               -keystorePassword storepass -keyaliasPassword keypass
```

If you now deploy the application in the usual way and run it, you see a similar prompt to that shown in Figure 28-9, except that it indicates that the application's digital signature has been verified.

Packaging and Deployment for Mobile Devices

Packaging an application for a mobile device is almost identical to packaging for the desktop. In this section, you see how to package a simple JavaFX application and how to deploy it onto the cell phone emulator that is provided as part of the JavaFX SDK.

Creating a Packaged Mobile Application

To demonstrate packaging and deployment for a mobile device, we use the Duke Sitting example that we used earlier in this chapter. You'll find the source code for this example (which is exactly the same as the desktop version) in the directory `deployment/example4`. To compile and package this example, make `deployment/example4` your working directory and use the following command:

```
javafxpackager -p mobile -src src -res resources
        -appClass deployment.DukeSitting
        -appName "DukeSitting" -appVendor "JavaFX Productions Inc"
        -appVersion 1.0 -paramFile props.txt
```

The most obvious difference between this command line and the ones that have been used earlier in this chapter is the argument `-p mobile`, which specifies packaging for the mobile environment. This causes the code to be compiled with a JRE that contains the system classes that are available on cell phones (MIDP 2.1, CLDC 1.1) together with a set of additional APIs that all mobile devices that support JavaFX are required to provide. This results in just two files in the output directory, as shown in Figure 28-10.

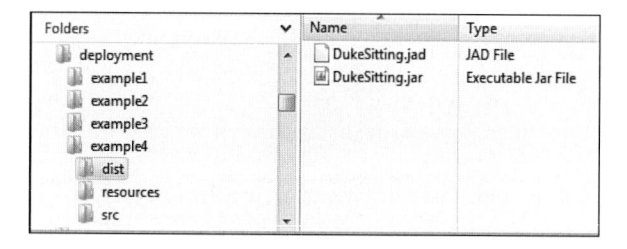

Figure 28-10 Files created by `javafxpackager` for deployment to a mobile device

The code and resources are packaged into a JAR file, in the same way as they are when deploying an application or an applet. The file `DukeSitting.jad` is a *Java Application Descriptor*, which provides information about the application that is used when it is loaded into the target device. The content of this file is shown in Listing 28-6.

Listing 28-6 The Java Application Descriptor for the Duke Sitting Example

```
1    MIDlet-Name: DukeSitting
2    MIDlet-Version: 1.0
3    MIDlet-Vendor: JavaFX Productions Inc
4    MicroEdition-Profile: JAVAFX-1.2
5    MicroEdition-Configuration: CLDC-1.1
6    MIDlet-1: DukeSitting,,deployment.DukeSitting_MIDlet
7    MIDlet-Jar-URL: DukeSitting.jar
8    MIDlet-Jar-Size: 9320
```

```
9       Title: Duke Relaxes
10      Text: Duke in his armchair
```

As you can see, the information in this file includes a reference to the application code JAR (on line 7), the minimum version of Java ME that is required to run the application (on lines 4 and 5), and the parameters obtained from the `props.txt` file (on lines 9 to 10), which the JavaFX application will read by using the `FX.getArgument()` function, as shown in Listing 28-5.

Deployment

If you want to make this application available for user download to a real device, you may need to process it further using a tool provided by the device vendor and then upload it to a site from which the user can access it. One such location is the Java AppStore at store.java.com, where users can buy Java and JavaFX applications and download them onto their mobile devices. It is also possible, for development purposes, to directly load a JavaFX application onto a device through a local connection, such as a USB cable. For information on this, refer to the documentation for the device itself. At the time of this writing, Sun Microsystems provides a version of JavaFX that runs on Windows Mobile devices that enables you to install applications over a USB connection either from the IDE or using the `emulator` command-line utility. For information on this, go to http://javafx.com/downloads.

The easiest way to test your JavaFX application is to run it on the mobile device emulator that ships with the JavaFX SDK. This is the same emulator that the NetBeans and Eclipse IDEs use when you run JavaFX code in mobile mode. You can deploy and run your packaged application from the command line by using the `emulator` command.[7]

> **Warning**
> If you have both the JavaFX SDK and the Java ME SDK installed, make sure that you run the version of the `emulator` command that is supplied by the JavaFX SDK. To do this, either make sure that it appears in your `PATH` variable before the one in the Java ME SDK, or use an explicit path to reference it.

Before deploying your application, you need to get the list of available devices. To do this, enter the following command:

```
emulator -Xquery
```

This command produces a lot of output, but you are only interested in the device names, which appear near the top and look something like this:

```
device.list: DefaultFxPhone1,DefaultFxTouchPhone1,QwertyFxPhone1
```

---

[7] At the time of this writing, the `emulator` command is supported only on the Windows platform.

You can choose any of these device names as the deployment target for your application. To run the Duke Sitting example on the emulated device `DefaultFxPhone1`, make `deployment/example4/dist` your working directory, and type the following command:

```
emulator -Xdescriptor:DukeSitting.jad -Xdevice:DefaultFxPhone1
```

After a few moments, the emulator starts, the packaged application is read, and an image of Duke relaxing in his chair should appear.

A

Using JavaFX Command-Line Tools

In Chapter 3, "JavaFX Script Development," you saw how to compile and run a JavaFX application in an integrated development environment (IDE). In most development projects, you will, at some point, need to introduce a more formal build process, which could be anything from a shell script to a continuous build tool such as CruiseControl or Hudson. In this appendix, you see the command-line tools that are provided with the JavaFX software development kit (SDK) and how to create an Ant build script that will compile and run your application.

Development Using Command-Line Tools

Although it is convenient to use an IDE for development, sometimes it is necessary to use command-line tools, typically because you want to automate your build process through a batch file. The JavaFX SDK includes commands that enable you to compile and execute applications and extract documentation from your source files. This section shows you how to do the first two of these; extracting documentation is covered in the section "Generating Documentation from JavaFX Source Files," later in this chapter. In the rest of this appendix, we make the following assumptions:

- You have downloaded and installed the example source code for this book in a folder that we refer to using the symbolic name EXAMPLESDIR. If you have not yet done this, refer to the Preface for download and installation instructions.
- You have installed the JavaFX SDK in a folder that we refer to using the symbolic name SDKDIR.
- If you are going to use an Ant build script, you have installed Ant version 1.7.0 or later.

Compiling a JavaFX Application

Let's assume you want to compile and run the animation example that you saw in Chapter 3. To do this, open a command window and make EXAMPLESDIR\intro\src your working directory and type the following commands, replacing SDKDIR with the full path of the folder in which the JavaFX SDK has been installed and \ with / if you use a UNIX-based platform such as Linux, Solaris, or Mac OS:

```
mkdir ..\..\classes
SDKDIR\bin\javafxc -d ..\..\classes javafxbasics\*.fx
```

The `javafxc` command runs the JavaFX compiler on the set of source files given as its last argument and writes the class files that it creates to the directory given by the `-d` option, as shown in Figure A-1. Notice that a subfolder has been created in the `classes` folder for the `javafxbasics` package and that, in this case, our single JavaFX source file has produced more than one Java class file.[1]

The `javafxc` command accepts the same arguments as the Java compiler launcher (`javac`), the documentation for which can be found at http://java.sun.com/javase/6/docs/technotes/tools/index.html#basic. There is also a manual page for `javafxc` in the documentation that is delivered with the JavaFX SDK. The basic forms are as follows:

```
javafxc -help
javafxc [options] [source files]
```

The first form prints help information, and the second runs the JavaFX compiler on the specified source files with the given options, if any. For quick reference, some of the most useful compiler options are listed here:

- `-profile` *name*: Specifies whether the compiler should compile for the desktop or the mobile platform. To compile for the desktop, use `-profile desktop` or omit this argument, because desktop is the default. To compile for a mobile platform, use `-profile mobile`. Note that the mobile platform has a smaller set of Java application programming interfaces (APIs) than the desktop platform, and you may find that some of the Java classes and methods that you frequently use are not present.

- `-classpath` *path* or `-cp` *path*: Defines the path of folders, JAR files, or ZIP files that `javafxc` uses to look up compiled classes that are referenced from the files being compiled. The classes in the JavaFX runtime library for the selected profile (desktop or mobile) are automatically available and do not need to appear in the path. Elements of the path should be separated by semicolons on Windows and colons on UNIX. If the compiler does not find a referenced class but does find a correspon-

---

[1] Not all JavaFX source files compile to more than one class file. You should treat the mapping between JavaFX source files and class files as an implementation detail that may change over time. The only thing you need to assume is that a JavaFX file called `package/file.fx` will always produce a class file called `package/file.class` that you can run by using the `javafx` or `javafxw` command described later in this chapter.

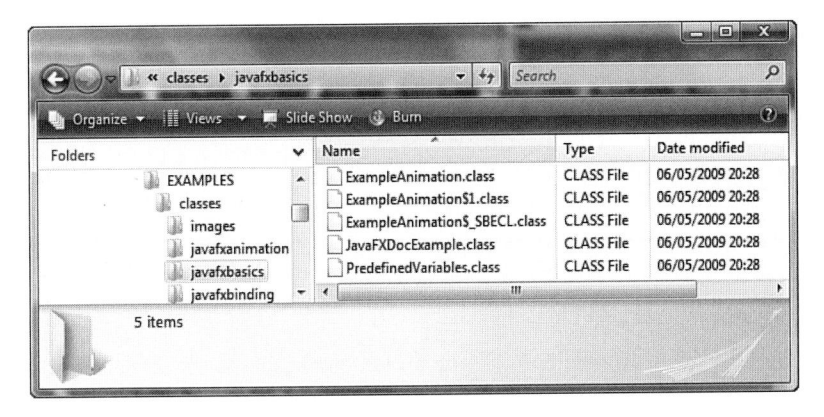

Figure A-1 The result of running the `javafxc` command on the source file
ExampleAnimation.fx

ding source file, it will compile it automatically. However, if the -sourcepath
option is used (see below), the compiler ignores source files that it finds in class
path directories.

- -d *classdirectory*: Specifies the folder into which compiled class files are written,
  organized into subfolders named according to the package names in the JavaFX
  source files. If this option is not used, the class files are written to the same directory as the corresponding source files.
- -sourcepath *path*: Lists the directories from which the source for JavaFX classes
  referred to in the files being compiled can be found. The path separator is as
  described under the entry for the -classpath option above. If the class files for a
  referenced JavaFX class cannot be located among the set of files being compiled, a
  search is performed among the directories in this path and, if successful, the referenced files are compiled.
- -verbose: Prints information on what the compiler is doing. You can use this to
  find out which files are being compiled.

Running a JavaFX Application

Having compiled the application, you can run it using the javafx command from the
JavaFX SDK,[2] which has the same arguments as the java command:

SDKDIR\bin\javafx -cp ..\..\classes javafxbasics.ExampleAnimation

---

[2] JavaFX source is compiled to Java class files, but those class files do not contain a main()
method, so you can't run them directly using the java command. The javafx command uses a
launcher class that knows how to run a compiled JavaFX script. This class is part of the JavaFX runtime; its name and the interface that it uses to execute the script class file are implementation
details that may change in the future. (In fact, this did change between JavaFX versions 1.1 and 1.2.)

To get help on the syntax of the `javafx` command, use the following:

```
javafx -help
```

To execute a JavaFX application from its class files with given options and arguments, use this:

```
javafx [options] class [args...]
```

Finally, to execute an application packaged in a JAR file, with the entry point class specified by the `Main-Class` entry in the manifest file, use this:

```
javafx [options] -jar jarfile [args...]
```

You can find full documentation for the options applicable to the `javafx` command in the documentation that accompanies the JavaFX SDK. Note that there is a related command called `javafxw` that is the same as `javafx` but which runs the target class in the background and does not block until it has completed execution.

Development Using an Ant Script

The JavaFX SDK includes a task that lets you compile JavaFX code from an Ant build script. To illustrate how this works, we'll examine the build script used for the example source code for this book, which you'll find in the file `EXAMPLESDIR/build.xml`. The first few statements set the scene, as shown in Listing A-1.

Listing A-1 An Ant Build Script for JavaFX Code: Setup

```
1    <!-- Builds the desktop examples -->
2    <project name="javafxbook" basedir="." default="build">
3        <property file="${basedir}/build.properties"/>
4        <property name="lib.dir" value="${javafxsdk.dir}/lib"/>
5        <property name="bin.dir" value="${javafxsdk.dir}/bin"/>
6        <property name="intro-src.dir" value="${basedir}/intro/src"/>
7        <property name="language-src.dir"
8                  value="${basedir}/language/src"/>
9        <property name="gui-src.dir" value="${basedir}/gui/src"/>
10   <property name="desktop-src.dir" value="${basedir}/desktop/src"/>
11       <property name="classes.dir" value="${basedir}/classes"/>
12       <condition property="libdir.set">
13           <available file="${lib.dir}/shared/javafxc.jar"/>
14       </condition>
15       <fail message=
16           "Please set the javafxsdk.dir property"
17           unless="libdir.set"/>
18
19       <!-- JavaFX compiler and runtime -->
20       <path id="build.classpath">
```

```
21          <fileset dir="${lib.dir}"
22                   includes="shared/*.jar, desktop/*.jar"/>
23      </path>
24      <path id="compiler.classpath">
25          <fileset dir="${lib.dir}"
26                   includes="shared/*.jar"/>
27      </path>
28
29      <!-- Get the JavaFX compiler task -->
30      <taskdef resource="javafxc-ant-task.properties"
31              classpathref="compiler.classpath"/>
```

Lines 1 to 11 define properties that refer to the locations of the example source code (there are several folders because the example source is split into several IDE projects), the folder that contains the JARs for the JavaFX compiler and its runtime, and the folder beneath which the class files will be written. Here, we assume that you have set the value of the property `javafxsdk.dir` in the file `build.properties` as described in the installation instructions for the example source code in the Preface. If this property is not correctly set, the build will be aborted by the error check on lines 12 to 17.

The `path` element on lines 20 to 23 creates a `classpath` called `build.classpath` that includes the JARs that contain the runtime libraries for JavaFX on the desktop. Lines 24 to 27 similarly define a `classpath` called `compiler.classpath` that contains the classes for the compiler and a minimal runtime that the compiler requires. Finally, the `taskdef` statement on lines 28 and 29 causes the definition of the JavaFX compiler's Ant task (`javafxc`) to be loaded from the JARs in `compiler.classpath`.

Compilation

The next part of the file, shown in Listing A-2, contains the target that compiles all the Java and JavaFX source files into the `classes` folder and also copies any resource files (images and so on) to the same location:

Listing A-2   **An Ant Build Script for JavaFX Code: Compilation**

```
1   <target name="build" description="Compiles all source files"
2           depends="init">
3       <javac destdir="${classes.dir}"
4              classpathref="build.classpath" debug="true">
5           <src path="${intro-src.dir}"/>
6           <src path="${language-src.dir}"/>
7           <src path="${gui-src.dir}"/>
8           <src path="${desktop-src.dir}"/>
9       </javac>
10      <mkdir dir="${basedir}/javadump"/>
```

```xml
11      <javafxc destdir="${classes.dir}"
12              classpathref="build.classpath"
13              compilerclasspathref="compiler.classpath"
14              debug="true">
15          <src path="${intro-src.dir}"/>
16          <src path="${language-src.dir}"/>
17          <src path="${gui-src.dir}"/>
18          <src path="${desktop-src.dir}"/>
19          <compilerarg value="-XDdumpjava=${basedir}/javadump"/>
20      </javafxc>
21
22      <!-- Copy resources -->
23      <copy todir="${classes.dir}">
24          <fileset dir="${intro-src.dir}"
25                  excludes="**/*.fx, **/*.java"/>
26          <fileset dir="${language-src.dir}"
27                  excludes="**/*.fx, **/*.java"/>
28          <fileset dir="${gui-src.dir}"
29                  excludes="**/*.fx, **/*.java"/>
30          <fileset dir="${desktop-src.dir}"
31                  excludes="**/*.fx, **/*.java"/>
32      </copy>
33  </target>
```

Here, on lines 11 to 20, you can see the `javafxc` task in action. This task is similar in form to the `javac` task, which is described in the Ant documentation. It adds two new attributes—`compilerclasspath` and `compilerclasspathref`—either of which can be used to indicate where the compiler and its runtime classes can be found, as shown on line 13. In this case, we use the `compilerclasspathref` attribute to cause the compiler to be loaded from the JARs in `compiler.classpath`. By contrast, the `classpathref` attribute used on line 12 refers to the classes that can be imported or otherwise referenced by the JavaFX files being compiled. In this case, the source code to be compiled refers only to classes in the JavaFX and desktop runtime libraries. If the source code referred to classes in other libraries, we would add those libraries to the set referred to by `classpathref`, but leave `compilerclasspathref` unchanged.

The build script compiles all the Java and JavaFX source files in the five source folders. The `javafxc` task internally filters the set of files in this folder and all of its subfolders so that only those whose names end in `.fx` are actually compiled. Here, we use nested `<src>` elements to specify the source folders. Alternatively, you can use a file set to define the files to be compiled. Refer to the documentation in the Ant distribution for further details.

Note

The `-XDdumpjava` option passed to the compiler on line 19 is an unofficial option that causes an *approximate* representation of the Java generated for each JavaFX source file to be written to the folder specified. This option is not documented or supported and may be withdrawn at any time. It is *not* intended to produce code that can be compiled.

Execution

No Ant task corresponds to the `javafx` command, so to run the examples it is necessary to use the Ant `exec` task to run the `javafx` command, as shown in Listing A-3.

Listing A-3   **An Ant Build Script for JavaFX Code: Execution**

```
1       <!-- Runs an example given by the property "example.class" -->
2       <target name="run">
3           <condition property="example.specified">
4               <isset property="example.class"/>
5           </condition>
6           <fail
7       message="Use -Dexample.class=pkg.name to name the class to run"
8               unless="example.specified"/>
9           <exec executable="${bin.dir}/javafx">
10              <arg line="-classpath ${classes.dir}"/>
11              <arg value="${example.class}"/>
12          </exec>
13      </target>
```

Lines 3 to 7 check that the class to be run has been given using the `example.class` property, and then lines 9 to 12 use the `exec` task to run the `javafx` launcher. The `run` target executes the class given by the system property `example.class` and is used like this:

`ant -Dexample.class=javafxbasics.ExampleAnimation build run`

If you want to delete all the class files before compiling and running an example, you may do so by using the `clean` target:

`ant -Dexample.class=javafxbasics.ExampleAnimation clean build run`

Generating Documentation from JavaFX Source

Documentation comments can be extracted from a JavaFX file by using the command-line tool `javafxdoc`, which is part of the JavaFX SDK. As you saw in Chapter 3, you can also view JavaFX documentation in NetBeans and Eclipse.

Like `javafxc` and `javafx`, `javafxdoc` supports all the command-line arguments of its Java language counterpart `javadoc`. For that reason, we are not going to discuss javafxdoc in any depth here. Instead, you'll see a simple example of its use. Listing A-4 shows some JavaFX source code, which you'll find in the file EXAMPLESDIR/intro/src/javafxbasics/JavaFXDocExample.fx, that contains some documentation comments. As you can see, this file defines a JavaFX class with a public function called createScene() that creates and optionally displays a Scene object[3] containing some text. Comments have been attached to the class itself, to the instance variable that holds the text to be displayed, and to the createScene() function. This is the same code that we used to show you can view JavaFX documentation in an IDE in Chapter 3.

Listing A-4   *Illustrating the Command-Line Tool* `javafxdoc`

```
package javafxbasics;

import javafx.scene.paint.Color;
import javafx.scene.Scene;
import javafx.scene.text.Text;
import javafx.stage.Stage;

/**
 * A JavaFX class that illustrates JavaFX documentation.
 * @author Kim Topley
 */
public class JavaFXDocExample {
    /**
     * The text that will be displayed in the scene.
     */
    var text:String;

    /**
     * Creates a Scene containing some text.
     * @see javafx.scene.Scene
     * @see javafx.scene.text.Text
     * @param color the color to be used for the text.
     * @return a scene displaying the given text.
     */
    public function createScene(color:Color):Scene {
        Scene {
            content: [
                Text {
                    x: 10
                    y: 20
                    content: text
```

---

[3] Scene is a class that acts as a container for a user interface, in this case for a Text object that displays a string.

```
                fill: color
            }
        ]
    }
}

function run() {
    // Show the Scene.
    var e = JavaFXDocExample {
            text: "JavaFX Documentation Example"
        };
    Stage {
        title: "JavaFX Documentation Example"
        visible: true

        scene: e.createScene(Color.RED);
    }
}
```

To extract the documentation from this file in HTML form, make `EXAMPLESDIR` your working directory and type the following commands, substituting the appropriate folder name for `SDKDIR`:

```
mkdir javadoc
SDKDIR\bin\javafxdoc -d javadoc -sourcepath intro\src javafxbasics
```

The `-d` option specifies the folder in which the documentation will be written. The `-sourcepath` option gives the location of the source files from which documentation is to be extracted, which, in this case, is the `intro\src` directory of the example source code for this book. You can specify multiple source locations, which should be separated by `:` characters on UNIX and `;` characters on Windows. The final argument specifies that only the script files in the `javafxbasics` package should be read and processed. It is possible to specify multiple packages by listing them all, separated by spaces.

As an alternative, you can specify the names of individual files for which you want to extract the documentation instead of package names, like this:

```
SDKDIR\bin\javafxdoc -d javadoc intro\src\javafxbasics\JavaFXDocExample.fx
```

The file list can contain wildcards that select a group of files to be documented. The following extracts the documentation for all the JavaFX files in the `intro\src\javafxbasics` folder:

```
SDKDIR\bin\javafxdoc -d javadoc intro\src\javafxbasics\*.fx
```

Figure A-2 shows the files created in the output directory.

1058   Appendix A Using JavaFX Command-Line Tools

Name	Type	Size	Date modified
images	File Folder		12/12/2008 19:58
javafxbasics	File Folder		12/12/2008 19:58
empty.html	HTML Document	1 KB	12/12/2008 19:58
general.css	Cascading Style S...	1 KB	12/12/2008 19:58
index.html	HTML Document	2 KB	12/12/2008 19:58
master-index.html	HTML Document	2 KB	12/12/2008 19:58
mootools-1.2.1-yui.js	JScript Script File	74 KB	12/12/2008 19:58
sdk.css	Cascading Style S...	8 KB	12/12/2008 19:58
sdk.js	JScript Script File	5 KB	12/12/2008 19:58
sessvars.js	JScript Script File	7 KB	12/12/2008 19:58

Figure A-2   `javafxdoc` output files

Opening the file `index.html` in a web browser shows that an entry has been created on the left of the page for the `javafxbasics` package. Clicking this entry opens it to show entries for each of the three classes in this package, as shown in Figure A-3.[4]

Selecting the entry for the `JavaFXDocExample` class causes the documentation for that class to be displayed, as shown in Figure A-4. You can see that the comments for both the class itself and the `createScene()` function have been extracted and included, but those for the instance variable `text` have not. That is because the instance variable is accessible only within the script and, by default, `javafxdoc` only includes documentation for those elements that are public or protected. You can change this by using the `-public`, `-protected`, `-package`, or `-private` options on the command line to set the threshold visibility for the elements that should be documented.

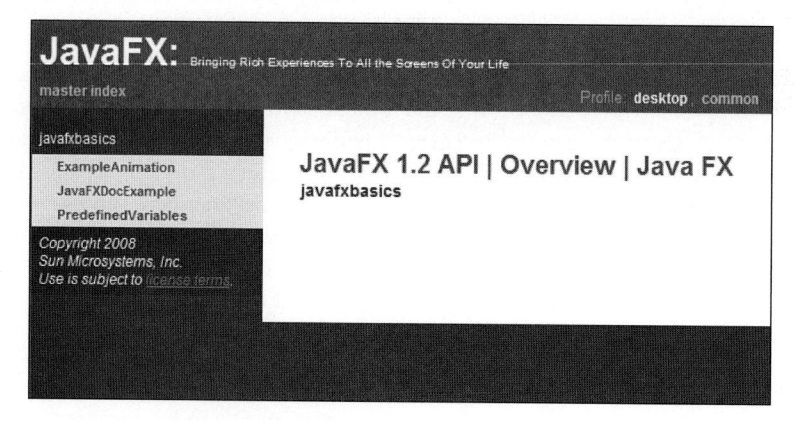

Figure A-3   `javafxdoc` summary information

---

[4] The documentation includes an entry for the `ExampleAnimation` class even though the source for that example does not contain an explicit definition of a class. That is because the compiler always creates a class named after the source file, even if one is not explicitly requested.

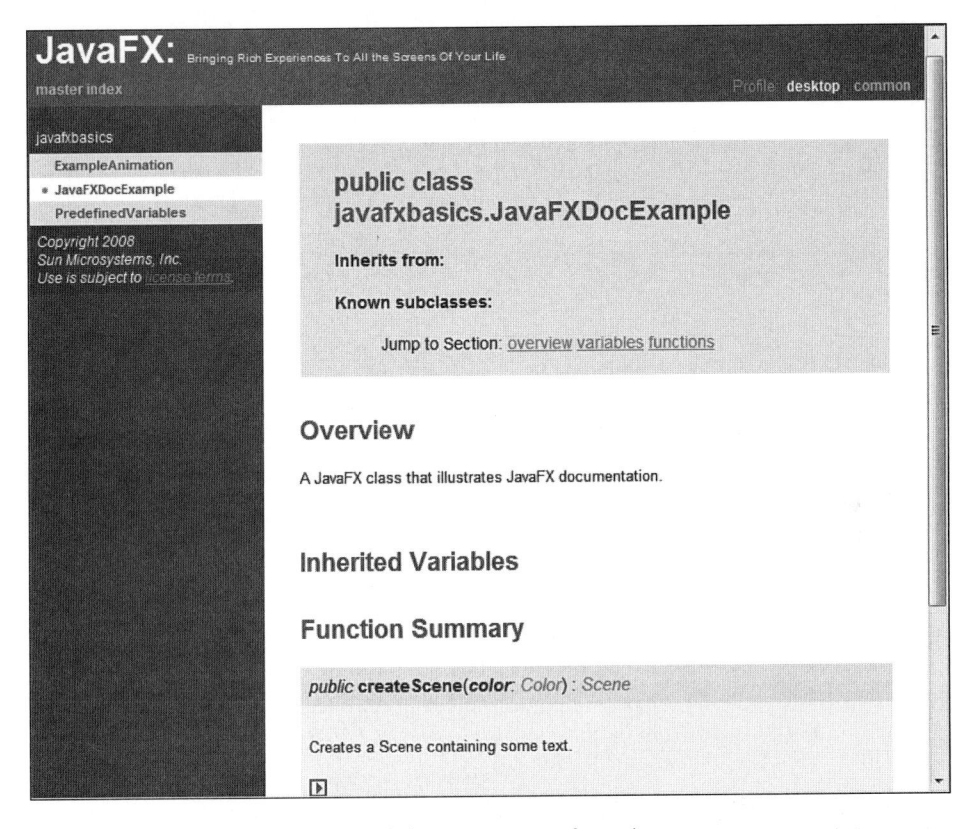

Figure A-4 `javafxdoc` for a class

B

CSS Properties

As you saw in Chapter 23, "Style Sheets," JavaFX supports the styling of all nodes, including controls, using Cascading Style Sheets (CSS). This appendix lists the CSS properties that are supported in the JavaFX 1.3 release. For each property, this appendix lists its name, its type, and the name of the node variable to which it corresponds.

Properties Applicable to Nodes

A small set of properties can be used with all nodes. These properties are listed in Table B-1. The rest of this appendix lists the properties that apply to more specific node subclasses, such as `Shape`, `Control`, and so on.

Table B-1   Properties That Can Be Applied to All Nodes

Property Name	Type	Comment
-fx-cursor	Cursor	Cursor name as defined by the Cursor class, such as HAND.
-fx-effect	Effect	An effect specification as described in Chapter 23.
-fx-focus-traversable	Boolean	true or false.
-fx-opacity	Number	Value range is 0.0 to 1.0 inclusive.
-fx-rotate	Number	Rotation angle in degrees. Positive value for a clockwise rotation.
-fx-scale-x	Number	
-fx-scale-y	Number	
-fx-scale-z	Number	
-fx-translate-x	Number	

Table B-1 Properties That Can Be Applied to All Nodes *(Continued)*

Property Name	Type	Comment
`-fx-translate-y`	`Number`	
`-fx-translate-z`	`Number`	Negative values move the node closer to the viewer; positive values, farther away.

Group Properties

The `Group` node has a single property that specifies the blend mode to be used, as described in Table B-2.

Table B-2 Properties That Can Be Applied to a `Group`

Property Name	Type	Comment
`-fx-blend-mode`	`BlendMode`	The name of a blend mode, such as `SRC_OVER`

ImageView Properties

The `ImageView` class lets you specify the image to be loaded from the style sheet. See Table B-3.

Table B-3 Properties That Can Be Applied to an `ImageView`

Property Name	Type	Comment
`-fx-image`	`URL`	The URL of an image in string form, such as "http://history.nasa.gov/ap11ann/kippsphotos/logo.jpg". Note that the quotes are required.

Text Properties

The additional CSS properties that can be applied to a `Text` node are listed in Table B-4.

Table B-4 Properties That Can Be Applied to a `Text` Node

Property Name	Type	Comment
`-fx-font`	`Font`	A font definition (see Chapter 23)
`-fx-strikethrough`	`Boolean`	`true` or `false`
`-fx-text-alignment`	`TextAlignment`	`CENTER`, `JUSTIFY`, `LEFT`, or `RIGHT`
`-fx-text-origin`	`TextOrigin`	`BASELINE`, `BOTTOM`, or `TOP`
`-fx-underline`	`Boolean`	`true` or `false`

Properties Applicable to Shapes

Some properties can be applied to all Shape subclasses. These properties are listed in Table B-5.

Table B-5   Properties That Can Be Applied to Shapes

Property Name	Type	Comment
-fx-fill	Paint	A paint specification (see Chapter 23)
-fx-smooth	Boolean	true or false
-fx-stroke	Paint	A paint specification (see Chapter 23)
-fx-stroke-dash-array	Number[]	See text below
-fx-stroke-dash-offset	Number	
-fx-stroke-line-cap	StrokeLineCap	ROUND, SQUARE, or BUTT
-fx-stroke-line-join	StrokeLineJoin	ROUND, BEVEL, or MITER
-fx-stroke-miter-limit	Number	
-fx-stroke-width	Number	

The value of the -fx-stroke-dash-array property is a sequence of numbers separated by spaces, representing the lengths of the gaps and dashes in the stroke, as described in the "Outline Dashing" section in Chapter 16, "Shapes, Text, and Images." As an example, the following style sheet rule, when applied to a Rectangle, gives the result shown in Figure B-1.

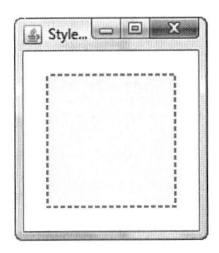

Figure B-1   The **-fx-stroke-dash-array** property

```
.rectangle {
    -fx-fill: yellow;
    -fx-stroke: red;
    -fx-stroke-width: 2;
```

```
    -fx-stroke-dash-offset: 8;
    -fx-stroke-dash-array: 2 4;
}
```

ClipView Properties

The `ClipView` class lets you control its `pannable` variable from a style sheet. Table B-6 shows the details.

Table B-6   Properties That Can Be Applied to a `ClipView`

Property Name	Type	Comment
`-fx-pannable`	Boolean	true or false

Rectangle Properties

You can set the width and height of the arc of the rounded corners of a `Rectangle` from a style sheet using the properties listed in Table B-7.

Table B-7   Properties That Can Be Applied to a `Rectangle`

Property Name	Type	Comment
`-fx-arc-height`	Number	The height of the rounded corner arc, or 0 for a squared corner
`-fx-arc-width`	Number	The width of the rounded corner arc, or 0 for a squared corner

Properties Applicable to Containers

A single property, listed in Table B-8, can be applied to all containers. In addition, some container subclasses have properties of their own (as covered in the following sections).

Table B-8   Properties That Can Be Applied to all Containers

Property Name	Type	Comment
`-fx-snap-to-pixel`	Boolean	true or false

Flow Properties

Table B-9 lists the additional CSS properties for the `Flow` container.

Table B-9 **Properties That Can Be Applied to a `Flow` Container**

Property Name	Type	Comment
-fx-hgap	Number	
-fx-hpos	HPos	A valid HPos value, such as CENTER
-fx-node-hpos	HPos	A valid HPos value, such as CENTER
-fx-node-vpos	VPos	A valid VPos value, such as CENTER
-fx-vertical	Boolean	true or false
-fx-vgap	Number	
-fx-vpos	VPos	A valid VPos value, such as CENTER

HBox Properties

The `HBox` container provides the CSS properties listed in Table B-10.

Table B-10 **Properties That Can Be Applied to a `Flow` Container**

Property Name	Type	Comment
-fx-hpos	HPos	A valid HPos value, such as CENTER
-fx-node-vpos	VPos	A valid VPos value, such as CENTER
-fx-spacing	Number	
-fx-vpos	VPos	A valid VPos value, such as CENTER

Stack Properties

Table B-11 lists the CSS properties for the `Stack` container.

Table B-11 **Properties That Can Be Applied to a `Stack` Container**

Property Name	Type	Comment
-fx-node-hpos	HPos	A valid HPos value, such as CENTER
-fx-node-vpos	VPos	A valid VPos value, such as CENTER

Table B-11 Properties That Can Be Applied to a `Stack` Container *(Continued)*

Property Name	Type	Comment
`-fx-padding`	Number	

Tile Properties

The CSS properties for the `Tile` container are listed in Table B-12.

Table B-12 Properties That Can Be Applied to a `Tile` Container

Property Name	Type	Comment
`-fx-columns`	Number	
`-fx-hgap`	Number	
`-fx-hpos`	HPos	A valid `HPos` value, such as `CENTER`
`-fx-node-hpos`	HPos	A valid `HPos` value, such as `CENTER`
`-fx-node-vpos`	VPos	A valid `VPos` value, such as `CENTER`
`-fx-rows`	Number	
`-fx-tile-height`	Number	
`-fx-tile-width`	Number	
`-fx-vertical`	Boolean	`true` or `false`
`-fx-vgap`	Number	
`-fx-vpos`	VPos	A valid `VPos` value, such as `CENTER`

VBox Properties

The `VBox` container provides the CSS properties listed in Table B-13. You can see that this property set is almost identical to that of the related `HBox` container.

Table B-13 Properties That Can Be Applied to a `VBox` Container

Property Name	Type	Comment
`-fx-hpos`	HPos	A valid `HPos` value, such as `CENTER`
`-fx-node-hpos`	HPos	A valid `HPos` value, such as `CENTER`
`-fx-spacing`	Number	
`-fx-vpos`	VPos	A valid `VPos` value, such as `CENTER`

Properties Applicable to Controls

Many of the JavaFX control classes provide CSS properties that you can use to configure their appearance (in addition to those inherited from the Node class listed in Table B-1). The following sections list the properties that are defined by the control classes themselves. In addition to the CSS properties described here, there are others that belong to the skins that render these controls. Because these properties are defined entirely by the skin in use, they are not described here. If you would like to see which properties are available when the controls are skinned by the default Caspian theme, you can find a file called `caspian.css` in the file `javafx-ui-controls.jar`, which is part of the JavaFX SDK, which defines all the properties that are used.

Some of the properties that are used by the Caspian theme and which are applied to many of the controls are listed in Table B-14.

Table B-14   Common Properties That Are Used by the Caspian Theme

Property Name	Type	Comment
`-fx-background`	Paint	A paint specification (see Chapter 23)
`-fx-text-fill`	Paint	A paint specification (see Chapter 23)

Properties Applicable to Labeled Nodes

The set of properties listed in Table B-15 apply to all controls that incorporate the `Labeled` mixin, such as `Label`, `Button`, and `Tooltip`.

Table B-15   Properties That Can Be Applied to `Labeled` Nodes

Property Name	Type	Comment
`-fx-font`	Font	A font definition (see Chapter 23).
`-fx-graphic`	URL	The URL of an image in string form, such as "http://history.nasa.gov/ap11ann/kippsphotos/logo.jpg". Note that the quotes are required.
`-fx-graphic-hpos`	HPos	A valid `HPos` value, such as `CENTER`.
`-fx-graphic-vpos`	VPos	A valid `VPos` value, such as `CENTER`.
`-fx-graphic-text-gap`	A valid `VPos` value, such as `CENTER`.	A number.
`-fx-hpos`	HPos	A valid `HPos` value, such as `CENTER`.

Table B-15 Properties That Can Be Applied to `Labeled` Nodes *(Continued)*

Property Name	Type	Comment
`-fx-text`	`String`	
`-fx-text-alignment`	`TextAlignment`	`CENTER`, `JUSTIFY`, `LEFT` or `RIGHT`.
`-fx-text-overrun`	`OverrunStyle`	`CENTER_ELLIPSES`, `CENTER_WORD_ELLIPSES`, `CLIP`, `ELLIPSES`, `LEADING_ELLIPSES`, `LEADING_WORD_ELLIPSES`, or `WORD_ELLIPSES`.
`-fx-text-wrap`	`Boolean`	`true` or `false`.
`-fx-vpos`	`VPos`	A valid `VPos` value, such as `CENTER`.

The value of the `-fx-graphic` property is the URL of an image to be loaded. If this is not an absolute URL, it is taken to be relative to the location of the style sheet. In the following example, the image file must be in the same directory as the style sheet itself:

```
-fx-graphic: "image.jpg";
```

At the time of this writing, the `-fx-graphic` property works only if an `ImageView` object has been installed in the `graphic` variable of the `Labeled` object, like this:

```
Label {
    text: "A label with a graphic"
    graphic: ImageView {}
}
```

ListView Properties

The `ListView` class provides the two additional CSS properties described in Table B-16.

Table B-16 Properties Supported by the `ListView` Control

Property Name	Type	Comment
`-fx-pannable`	`Boolean`	`true` or `false`
`-fx-vertical`	`Boolean`	`true` or `false`

ScrollBar Properties

Table B-17 lists the four CSS properties that are specific to the `ScrollBar` class.

Table B-17 Properties Supported by the `ScrollBar` Control

Property Name	Type	Comment
-fx-block-increment	Number	
-fx-click-to-position	Boolean	true or false
-fx-unit-increment	Number	
-fx-vertical	Boolean	true or false

ScrollView Properties

The `ScrollView` control has five properties that you can use to configure its behavior, as listed in Table B-18.

Table B-18 Properties Supported by the `ScrollView` Control

Property Name	Type	Comment
-fx-fit-to-height	Boolean	true or false
-fx-fit-to-width	Boolean	true or false
-fx-hbar-policy	ScrollBarPolicy	ALWAYS, AS_NEEDED, or NEVER
-fx-pannable	Boolean	true or false
-fx-vbar-policy	ScrollBarPolicy	ALWAYS, AS_NEEDED, or NEVER

Separator Properties

The `Separator` class provides two CSS properties, listed in Table B-19, that let you position it within its layout area.

Table B-19 Properties Supported by the `Separator` Control

Property Name	Type	Comment
-fx-hpos	HPos	A valid HPos value, such as CENTER
-fx-vpos	VPos	A valid VPos value, such as CENTER

Slider Properties

The behavior and appearance of the `Slider` control can be customized by the properties listed in Table B-20.

Table B-20 **Properties Supported by the `Slider` Control**

Property Name	Type	Comment
`-fx-block-increment`	Number	
`-fx-click-to-position`	Boolean	true or false
`-fx-major-tick-unit`	Number	
`-fx-minor-tick-unit`	Number	
`-fx-show-tick-labels`	Boolean	true or false
`-fx-show-tick-marks`	Boolean	true or false
`-fx-snap-to-ticks`	Boolean	true or false
`-fx-vertical`	Boolean	true or false

TextBox and PasswordBox Properties

The `TextBox` and `PasswordBox` controls share the CSS properties that are listed in Table B-21, and each of them has an additional property that is specific to the functionality that it provides. These additional properties are listed in Table B-22 and Table B-23.

Table B-21 **Properties Supported by the `TextBox` and `PasswordBox` Controls**

Property Name	Type	Comment
`-fx-columns`	Number	
`-fx-editable`	Boolean	true or false
`-fx-font`	Font	A font specification (see Chapter 23)
`-fx-select-on-focus`	Boolean	true or false

Table B-22 **Properties Supported by the `TextBox` Control**

Property Name	Type	Comment
`-fx-lines`	Number	The number of lines of text

Table B-23 **Properties Supported by the `PasswordBox` Control**

Property Name	Type	Comment
`-fx-echo-char`	String	The echo character or characters

Index

Symbols and Numerics

+= (add and assign) operator, 122
+ (addition) operator, 122
= (assignment) operator, 122
/= (divide and assign) operator, 122
/ (division) operator, 122
== (equality) operator, 8, 122, 133, 157
\" escape sequence, 103
\' escape sequence, 103
\\ escape sequence, 103
\b escape sequence, 103
\f escape sequence, 103
> (greater than) operator, 122
>= (greater than or equal) to operator, 122
!= (inequality) operator, 122, 133-134
< (less than operator), 122
<= (less than or equal to operator), 122
* (multiplication) operator, 122
*= (multiply and assign) operator, 122
\n escape sequence, 103
{ object literal } operator, 122
. (period) operator, 131
++ (postfix) operator, 122
— (postfix) operator, 122
++ (prefix) operator, 122
— (prefix) operator, 122
\r escape sequence, 103
-= (subtract and assign) operator, 122
- (subtraction) operator, 122
\t escape sequence, 103
- (unary minus) operator, 122
\012 escape sequence, 103
3D features, 372-374

A

Absolute resource names, 306-307
Abstract base class, 249-251
abstract keyword, 26
Access control, 306
Accessing
    arrays, 176
    databases, 1015, 1023
    external data sources, 949
    instance variables, 96-97
    wrapped Swing component, 832
action variable
    Button class, 749
    Hyperlink class, 752
    MediaTimer class, 638
    SwingButton component, 844
    SwingTextField class, 840
    TextInputControl class, 762
    Transition class, 614
Adobe Illustrator, 14, 703-704
Adobe Photoshop, 14, 704
after keyword, 26
Alerts
    confirm alert, 370-371
    defined, 342
    information alert, 369-370
    question alert, 371
Alignment of text, 468-469
altDown variable
    KeyEvent class, 431
    MouseEvent class, 414
and keyword, 26
and operator, 122
angle variable (MotionBlur class), 659
Animation
    automatically reversing, 607-608
    changing speed and direction, 609-610
    defined, 591
    Duration class, 595-596
    javafxanimation package, 591
    length, 613
    media players, 633

    pausing, 608
    repeating, 605-607
    restarting, 609
    starting timeline from the end, 610-611
    stopping, 608-609
    support, 10-12
    Timeline class, 12, 594
    timelines, 591-594, 611-613
    transitions, 591, 613-614
Animation paths, 717-720
Anonymous functions, 145-147
Ant build script, 33, 1049, 1052-1055
Ant task, 13
Ant version 1.7.0 or later, 1049
APIs (Application Programming Interfaces). See also Platform API
    audio, 627
    common profile, 4-5
    desktop profile, 4-5
    documentation, 5
    Java Scripting API, 9
    JavaFX Desktop, 9
    JavaFX Mobile, 9
    JavaFX platform, 3-4
    JavaFX runtime, 9
    JavaFX Script language, 6-7
    networking APIs, 12-13
    profiles, 4-5
    Reflection, 309
    video, 627
Appearance of controls, 738
Applets
    converting into desktop applications, 70
    converting to installed applications, 15
    deploying, 14, 1033-1037
    Java plug-in, 15
    Java VM settings, 15
    loading, 15
    signing, 1043-1045
    writing, 4
AppletStageExtension class, 307
Application launcher, 13

Application Programming Interfaces (APIs).
See also **Platform API**
  audio, 627
  common profile, 4-5
  desktop profile, 4-5
  documentation, 5
  Java Scripting API, 9
  JavaFX Desktop, 9
  JavaFX Mobile, 9
  JavaFX platform, 3-4
  JavaFX runtime, 9
  JavaFX Script language, 6-7
  networking APIs, 12-13
  profiles, 4-5
  Reflection, 309
  video, 627
Applications
  compiling, with command-line tools, 1049-1051
  compiling, with NetBeans, 39
  converting applets to an installed application, 15
  deploying, applets, 14
  deploying, desktop applications, 14
  deploying, in multiple environments, 4
  deploying, mobile applications, 14
  deploying, TV applications, 14
  deployment options, 14
  executing, 1049-1052
  Graphical User Interface (GUI), 5
  packaging options, 14
  running, with command-line tools, 1049, 1051-1052
  running, with Eclipse, 42
  running, with NetBeans, 39
  shutdown, 292-294
  signing, 1043-1045
Arc class, 442-444
Architecture of JavaFX platform, 3
ArcTo class, 453-455
Area charts, 930-931
args argument, 28

Arguments
  args, 28
  getting, 287-288
  named arguments, 288-290
Arithmetic operations, 123-125
Arrays
  accessing, 176
  declaring, 174-175
  initializing, 175-176
  iterating over an array, 193
  modifying, 176
  scope, 174
  similarity to sequences, 24
  size of, 177
  support for, 153
Artwork
  exporting, 14
  importing, 14
as keyword, 26
as operator, 122, 131-132
assert keyword, 26
Assigning values, 23
associate() function, 297-298
at keyword, 26
Atom feeds, 949, 1004, 1008
Attaching triggers, 221, 229
attribute keyword, 26
Attributes
  classpathref, 1054
  compilerclasspath, 1054
  compilerclasspathref, 1054
Audio
  Application Programming Interfaces (APIs), 627
  controlling media playback, 630-631
  FLV, 630
  FXM, 630
  media players, 627
  MP3 files, 629
  pausing, 632
  playing, 10, 627-628
  repeating playback, 632-633
  restricting playback, 632-633

speeding up playback, 632
stopping playback, 632
support, 10
volume control, 633
autoKern variable (Font class), 478
Automating build process, 1049
autoPlay variable (MediaPlayer class), 631-632
autoReverse variable (Timeline class), 594
Axes (charts), 913

B

background variable (SwingTextField class), 839
backgroundLoading variable (Image class), 488
balance variable (MediaPlayer class), 634
Bar charts, 919-926
Batch files for automating build process, 1049
before keyword, 26
Behavior class, 894-895
Bidirectional binding, 24-25, 203-206
bind keyword, 8, 26
Binding
    bidirectional, 24-25, 203-206
    conditional expressions, 202-203
    creating, 194
    def statement, 201
    eager, 206-207
    explained, 8, 194
    expressions, 24-26, 199-200
    functions, 25-26, 207-211, 217
    instance variables, 201-202
    javafxbinding package, 194
    lazy, 206-207
    object literals, 196-199
    script variables, 194-196
    sequences, 217
    triggers, 223-224
    unidirectional binding, 24-25, 206
Blend class, 686-690
Blending
    defined, 686
    groups, 651, 688-690

Bloom class, 665-666
blurType variable
    DropShadow class, 660
    InnerShadow class, 663
    Shadow class, 661
Boolean data type, 92, 102-103
Boolean operations, 129-130
Border container, 869-884
borderless variable (SwingTextField class), 839
bottlenecks, 46
bottomInput variable (Blend class), 687
bottomOpacity variable (Reflection class), 672
Bound functions, 134, 208-211, 217, 258-259
bound keyword, 26
Bounds class, 528-529
Bounds of nodes, 527-538
BoxBlur class, 657-659
break keyword, 26
break statement, 182-183
Breakpoints
    deleting, 76-77
    disabling, 76-77
    removing, 76-77
    setting, 72-73
brightness variable (ColorAdjust class), 670
Bubble charts, 934-935
bufferProgressTime variable (MediaPlayer class), 635
Build process, automating, 1049
Building SnowStorm application, 46
Built-in functions, 285
Bump map, 693-694
bumpInput variable (Lighting class), 691
Button control
    appearance, 739
    Button class, 749
    CSS properties, 1067-1068
    examples, 749-751
    features and functionality, 749
    states, 751-752
button variable (MouseEvent class), 410
Byte data type, 91

C

Call Stack view, 73
Cameras, 372-374
Cascading Style Sheets (CSS). *See* CSS (Cascading Style Sheets)
Caspian theme, 1067
catch keyword, 26
causeOfFailure variable (Task class), 1009
Centering nodes, 577-579
centerX variable, 393
centerY variable, 393
Certificates, 1044-1045
Changing variable values, 74
char variable (KeyEvent class), 429
Character data type, 92, 101-102
characterEncoding variable (PullParser class), 976
Charts
    area charts, 930-931
    axes, 913
    bar charts, 919-926
    bubble charts, 934-935
    components, 912
    creating, 911
    customizing, 911, 937-946
    data, 914
    defined, 911
    hierarchy of classes, 912
    legend, 912
    line charts, 926-928
    pie charts, 914-919
    scatter charts, 932-934
    series, 913
    title, 912
    user interaction, 914, 936-937
CheckBox control
    appearance, 739
    CheckBox class, 759
    tri-state checkboxes, 759-761
ChoiceBox control, 739, 786-787
choke variable (InnerShadow class), 664
chooseBestCursor() method, 378
Circle class, 433, 438-439

Class files
    deleting, 1055
    JavaFX Script language, 8-9
    package/file.class, 1050
    source files, 1050
Class instances, creating, 328, 336-337
class keyword, 26
Class mapping, 297-298
Classes
    abstract base class, 249-251
    AppletStageExtension, 307
    Arc, 442-444
    ArcTo, 453, 455
    Blend, 686-690
    Bloom, 665-666
    Behavior, 894-895
    Bounds, 528-529
    BoxBlur, 657-659
    Button, 749
    Circle, 433, 438-439
    ClipView, 574-577, 1064
    ColorAdjust, 669-671
    composite pattern, 267
    Container, 501
    Control, 735, 891
    CoordinateGrid, 866-869
    CubicCurve, 448-449
    CubicCurveTo, 453
    declaring, 240
    defining, 26
    DelegateShape, 434
    direct class references, 23
    DisplacementMap, 679-686
    DistantLight, 694-696
    documentation, 1058
    DropShadow, 651, 660
    Duration, 595-596
    Ellipses, 439-440
    example class, 241-242
    extending a base class, 251-253
    FadeTransition, 618-619
    FeedTask, 997

Classes

Flood, 669
Flow, 547-548
Font, 477-479
FXContext, 309
GaussianBlur, 656-657
Glow, 666-667
Group, 482
HBox, 560-562
HttpRequest, 949-952
HttpStatus, 959
Identity, 667, 669
Image, 377, 433, 487-488
ImageCursor, 377
ImageView, 433, 497-501, 1062
importing, automatic imports, 22-23
importing, by name, 20
importing, static imports, 20-22
importing, wildcard imports, 20
initializing, 261-265
InnerShadow, 664
instance functions, 246, 248
instance variables, 243-246
InvertMask, 671
Java classes, 97, 239-240
JavaFX classes versus Java classes, 239-240
JavaFX Script language, 6
javafxclasses package, 240
javafx.scene.Cursor, 375
javafx.scene.paint.LinearGradient, 384
javafx.scene.paint.RadialGradient, 393
javafx.scene.text.Font, 7
javafx.scene.text.Text, 7
javafx.util.Math, 7
java.lang.Math, 7
java.lang.System, 6
java.util.Random, 6-7
KeyFrame, 596-600
LayoutInfo, 542
Lighting, 651, 690-694
Line, 434-436
ListView, 773-776
Media, 628-630

MediaPlayer, 628, 630
MediaPlayerBehavior, 908-909
MediaTimer, 638-639
MediaView, 10, 628, 639-640
mixins, 266-267
MotionBlur, 659-660
MouseEvent, 403-404
nesting, 266
Observable, 267
Panel, 884-887
ParallelTransition, 622-625
PasswordBox, 771-773
Path, 451
PathElement, 452-453
PathTransition, 619-622
PauseTransition, 622
PerspectiveTransform, 673-678
PointLight, 697-698
Polygon, 440-442
Polyline, 440-442
PullParser, 949, 975
QuadCurve, 444-448
QuadCurveTo, 453
Rectangle, 433, 436-438, 1064
Reflection, 671-673
reserved words, 26
Resource, 302-303
RotateTransition, 616-617
ScaleTransition, 617-618
Scene, 358-360
Screen, 585-590
script files, 265-266
ScrollBar, 788-789
Scroller, 794
ScrollView, 794-797
SepiaTone, 673
SequentialTransition, 622-625
Shadow, 664-665
Shape, 433
ShapeIntersect, 449-451
ShapeSubtract, 449-451
Skin, 891-894

Slider, 797-804
Spotlight, 698-700
Stack, 556-557
Stage, 342, 358
states, 239
Storage, 301-302
subclassing, 249
SVGPath, 456
SwingComponent, 830
Text, 433, 466-472
TextOrigin, 467-468
Tile, 564
Timeline, 12, 594, 605
TimeSlider, 904-908
Transition, 614
TranslateTransition, 614, 616
user interface classes, 9-10
VBox, 563
visibility, 242-243
-classpath path compiler option, 1051
classpathref attribute, 1054
clean target, 1055
clear() function, 303
clickCount variable (MouseEvent class), 410
Clipping nodes, 523-526
ClipView class
   -fx-pannable property, 1064
   variables, 574-577
Code, example source, 1049
code variable (KeyEvent class), 429
color variable
   DropShadow class, 660
   InnerShadow class, 663
   Shadow class, 661
ColorAdjust class, 669, 671
Colors
   CSS (Cascading Style Sheets), 822-828
   cycle methods, 388-390
   linear gradients, 383-392
   nodes, 367, 378
   radial gradients, 392-401

   solid colors, 379-381
   Stop objects, 385-388
   Swing JColorChooser component, 382-383
column variable (PullParser class), 976
columns variable (SwingTextField class), 839
Combining transforms, 517
Command-line compiler, 13
Command-line tools
   development, 33, 1049
   javafxdoc, 13, 1055-1058
   javafxpackager, 13-14, 46, 1025-1026
Commands
   exec, 1055
   java, 1051
   javac, 1054
   javafx, 1050-1052
   javafxc, 1050, 1054
   javafxw, 1052
Comments
   documentation comments, 18
   extracting from documentation, 1055-1056
   multiline comments, 18
   single-line comments, 18
   source files, 18
Common profile (APIs), 4, 5
Comparing
   objects, 286-287
   sequences, 167-168
Comparing objects, 133-134
Comparison operators, 127-128
Compiler options
   -classpath path, 1051
   -cp path, 1051
   -d classdirectory, 1051
   -profile name, 1051
   -sourcepath path, 1051
   -verbose, 1051
   -XDdumpjava, 1055
compilerclasspath attribute, 1054
compilerclasspathref attribute, 1054

Compiling applications
  with command-line tools, 1049-1051
  with Eclipse, 42
  with NetBeans, 39
compositable variable (MediaView class), 648
Composite pattern, 267
Compressing JAR files, 1042-1043
Concatenation of strings, 104-105
Conditional expressions, binding, 202-203
Conditional features, 307
Confirm alert, 370-371
connecting variable (GET operation), 953
Constraints for triggers, 224-225
Consumer JRE, 15
Container class, 501
Containers
  Border container, 869-884
  CSS properties, 1064-1066
  customizing, 869-887
  fill color, 572-574
  Flow container, 547-555, 1065
  HBox container, 560-562, 1065
  layout of notes, 540-542
  Panel container, 572-574
  Stack container, 555-559, 1065-1066
  Tile container, 563-572, 1066
  VBox container, 562-563, 1066
containsFocus variable (Stage class), 342
content variable (Scene class), 359
contentInput variable (Lighting class), 691
continue keyword, 26
continue statement, 184
contrast variable (ColorAdjust class), 670
controlDown variable
  KeyEvent class, 431
  MouseEvent class, 414
Controlling media playback, 630-631
Controls. See also Swing controls
  appearance, 738
  available controls, 738
  Button control, 739, 749-752
  CheckBox control, 739, 759-761
  ChoiceBox control, 739, 786-787
  Controls class, 735
  CSS properties, 1067-1070
  customizing, 864, 887-909
  features and functionality, 735
  Hyperlink control, 739, 752-755
  javafxcontrols package, 735
  Label control, 738-749
  ListView control, 739, 773-785, 1068
  PasswordBox control, 739, 771-773, 1070
  ProgressBar control, 739, 804-807
  ProgressIndicator control, 739, 804-807
  RadioButton control, 739, 756-759
  ScrollBar control, 739, 787-794, 1068-1069
  ScrollView control, 739, 794-797, 1069
  Separator control, 739, 807-808, 1069
  Slider controls, 739, 797-804, 1069-1070
  TextBox control, 739, 761-771, 1070
  ToggleButton control, 739, 756-759
  Tooltip control, 739, 808-809
Control class, 735, 891
Converting
  applets, into desktop applications, 70
  applets, into installed applications, 15
  media files into FXM file format, 630
  numeric values, 99-101
  SVG-to-JavaFX Graphics Converter, 734
CoordinateGrid class, 866-869
Coordinates
  nodes, 501
  screens, 585-590
Copying sequences, 158
-cp path compiler option, 1051
CPU profiling, 78-80
createScene() function, 1056
Creating
  binding, 194
  charts, 911
  class instances, 328-337
  mappings, 297-298

CSS properties

multiple copies of graphics, 731-733
objects, 95, 131
packages, in Eclipse, 41
packages, in NetBeans, 38
projects, in Eclipse, 40
projects, in NetBeans, 34
script files, 41
sequences, 153-155
SnowStorm application, 46-47
triggers, 221

CROSSHAIR cursor, 376
Cross-platform controls. *See* **Controls**
CSS (Cascading Style Sheets)
colors, 822-828
effects, 828
features and functionality, 809
fonts, 824-826
hierarchical selectors, 818-820
inheritance, 820-822
installing a style sheet, 812
JavaFX support, 809, 1061
multiple selectors, 818
multiple style sheets, 824
paints, 826-828
selection by class, 813-814
selection by class and ID, 815-816
selection by ID, 814-815
state-dependent style, 816-818
structure, 813
Swing, 809

CSS properties
-fx-arc-height, 1064
-fx-arc-width, 1064
-fx-background, 1067
-fx-blend-mode, 1062
-fx-block-increment, 1069-1070
-fx-click-to-position, 1069-1070
-fx-columns, 1066, 1070
-fx-cursor, 1061
-fx-echo-char, 1070
-fx-editable, 1070
-fx-effect, 828, 1061
-fx-fill, 826, 1063
-fx-fit-to-height, 1069
-fx-fit-to-width, 1069
-fx-focus-traversable, 1061
-fx-font, 826, 1062, 1067, 1070
-fx-font-family, 824
-fx-font-size, 824
-fx-font-style, 825
-fx-font-weight, 825-826
-fx-graphic, 1067-1068
-fx-graphic-hpos, 1067
-fx-graphic-text-gap, 1067
-fx-graphic-vpos, 1067
-fx-hbar-policy, 1069
-fx-hgap, 1065-1066
-fx-hpos, 1065-1069
-fx-image, 1062
-fx-lines property, 1070
-fx-major-tick-unit, 1070
-fx-minor-tick-unit, 1070
-fx-node-hpos, 1065-1066
-fx-node-vpos, 1065-1066
-fx-opacity, 1061
-fx-padding, 1066
-fx-pannable, 1064, 1068-1069
-fx-rotate, 1061
-fx-rows, 1066
-fx-scale-x, 1061
-fx-scale-y, 1061
-fx-scale-z, 1061
-fx-select-on-focus, 1070
-fx-show-tick-labels, 1070
-fx-show-tick-marks, 1070
-fx-smooth, 1063
-fx-snap-to-pixel, 1064
-fx-snap-to-ticks, 1070
-fx-spacing, 1065-1066
-fx-strikethrough, 1062
-fx-stroke, 1063
-fx-stroke-dash-array, 1063
-fx-stroke-dash-offset, 1063
-fx-stroke-line-cap, 1063

-fx-stroke-line-join, 1063
-fx-stroke-miter-limit, 1063
-fx-stroke-width, 1063
-fx-text, 1068
-fx-text-alignment, 1062, 1068
-fx-text-fill, 1067
-fx-text-origin, 1062
-fx-text-overrun, 1068
-fx-text-wrap, 1068
-fx-tile-height, 1066
-fx-tile-width, 1066
-fx-translate-x, 1061
-fx-translate-y, 1062
-fx-translate-z, 1062
-fx-underline, 1062
-fx-unit-increment, 1069
-fx-vbar-policy, 1069
-fx-vertical, 1065-1070
-fx-vgap, 1065-1066
-fx-vpos, 1065-1069

CubicCurve class, 448-449

CubicCurveTo class, 453

currentCount variable (MediaPlayer class), 631

currentRate variable (Timeline class), 594

currentTime variable (MediaPlayer class), 635

cursor variable

    cursor shapes, 375

    Scene class, 358

Cursors

    CROSSHAIR, 376

    cursor variable, 375

    customizing, 377-378

    DEFAULT, 376

    E_RESIZE, 376

    HAND, 376

    H_RESIZE, 376

    javafx.scene.Cursor class, 375

    Microsoft Windows Platform, 376

    MOVE, 376

    NE_RESIZE, 376

    nodes, 375

    N_RESIZE, 376

    NW_RESIZE, 376

    SE_RESIZE, 376

    setting, 375-378

    shape of, 375

    S_RESIZE, 376

    SW_RESIZE, 376

    TEXT, 376

    V_RESIZE, 376

    WAIT, 376

    W_RESIZE, 376

Customizing

    charts, 911, 937-946

    containers, 869-887

    controls, 864, 887-909

    cursors, 377-378

    nodes, 482-485, 864

Cycle methods

    linear gradients, 388-390

    radial gradients, 398-399

cycleDuration variable (Timeline class), 594

cycleMethod variable

    linear gradients, 384

    radial gradients, 393

D

-d classdirectory compiler option, 1051

Data

    reading, 299, 301

    removing, 303-305

    writing, 299, 301

Data sources, accessing, 949

Data types

    Boolean, 92, 102-103

    Byte, 91

    Character, 92, 101-102

    defined, 89

    Double, 91

    Duration, 92-97

    Float, 91

    Integer, 91, 97-99

    Long, 91

    Number, 91, 99

    numeric, 97-98

    Short, 91

String, 92, 103-108
variables, 6
Databases, accessing, 1015-1023
data-manipulation statements, 24
Debug toolbar, 75
Debugging
   breakpoints, disabling, 76-77
   breakpoints, removing, 76-77
   breakpoints, setting, 46-73
   Call Stack view, 73
   Local Variables view, 73-74
   SnowStorm application, 46-76
   stepping through code, 75-76
Declaring
   arrays, 174-175
   classes, 240
   functions, 134-137
   triggers, 221-222
   variables, 6, 23, 89-95
def keyword, 6, 26
def statement, 92, 201
DEFAULT cursor, 376
deferAction() function, 294
Deferring operations, 294-295
Defining
   classes, 26
   functions, 25
DelegateShape class, 434
delete keyword, 26
DELETE requests, 973-974
Deleting
   breakpoints, 76-77
   class files, 1055
Deletion operations with sequence variables, 230-232
Deploying applications
   applets, 14, 1033-1037
   default restrictions, 1025
   desktop applications, 14, 1029-1033
   mobile applications, 14, 1047-1048
   in multiple environments, 4
   options, 14

support for deployment mechanisms, 1026
TV applications, 14
Desktop applications
   converting applets into desktop applications, 70
   deploying, 14, 1029-1033
   packaging, 1026-1029
   SnowStorm application, 70
Desktop environments, 4
Desktop profile (APIs), 4-5
Development
   Ant build script, 33, 1049, 1052-1055
   command-line tools, 1049
   Eclipse, 3, 33, 39-42
   Integrated Development Environment (IDE), 33
   NetBeans, 3, 33, 34-39
   options, 33
diffuseInput variable (Lighting class), 691
__DIR__ variable, 31
Direct class references, 23
disable variable (Node class), 426
disabled state, 816
disabled variable (Node class), 426
Disabling breakpoints, 76-77
disassociate() function, 298
DisplacementMap class, 679, 686
Displaying
   images, 486, 497, 501
   text, 467
DistantLight class, 694, 696
Division
   of a nonzero value by zero, 127
   of zero by zero, 127
Documentation
   APIs (Application Programming Interfaces), 5
   classes, 1058
   comments, 1055-1056
   Eclipse, 44
   extracting, 13, 1049, 1055-1058
   generating, 1055-1058

NetBeans, 43-44
source code, 43
source files, 1057
viewing, 1055-1056
Documentation comments, 18
documentType variable (PullParser class), 975
done variable (GET operation), 955
done variable (Task class), 1009
doneConnect variable (GET operation), 953
doneHeaders variable (GET operation), 954
doneRead variable (GET operation), 955
doRequest() function, 956
Double data type, 91
Downloading
    example source code, 33, 1049
    JavaFX, 4
    JavaFX Production Suite, 704
    Production Suite, 14
dragAnchorX variable (MouseEvent class), 416
dragAnchorY variable (MouseEvent class), 416
dragX variable (MouseEvent class), 416
dragY variable (MouseEvent class), 416
Drawing
    arcs, 443-444
    ellipses, 439-440
    lines, 435
    polygons, 440-441
    rectangles, 437
DropShadow class, 651, 660
Duplicating graphics, 731-733
Duration class, 595-596
Duration data type, 92-97
duration variable (Media class), 628

E

Eager binding, 206-207
Eclipse
    development, 3, 33, 39-42
    documentation, 44
    Installing, 33
    Java Web Start, 67

mobile emulator, 71
support, 3, 13
TV emulator, 72
viewing documentation, 1055
editable variable
    SwingComboBox component, 854
    SwingTextField class, 839
Effects
    blend, 686, 690
    bloom, 665-666
    box blur, 657-659
    bump map, 693-694
    chains, 651
    color adjust, 669-671
    CSS (Cascading Style Sheets), 828
    defined, 651
    displacement map, 679-686
    drop shadow, 651, 660
    experimenting with, 656
    flood, 669
    Gaussian blur, 656-657
    glow, 666-667
    groups, 655
    identity, 667-669
    inner shadow, 663
    invert mask, 671
    javafxeffects package, 651
    javafx.scene.effects package, 651
    javafx.scene.effects.lighting package, 651
    lighting, 651, 690-700
    motion blur, 659-660
    nodes, 368-369, 654
    perspective transform, 673-678
    reflection, 671-673
    sepia tone, 673
    shadow, 664-665
    transformations, 654
    video, 646
    warp, 684-686
Effects Playground application, 656
Ellipses class, 439-440
else keyword, 26

Embedded expressions, 105-106
Embedding
    fonts, 720-724
    images, 724-725
embolden variable (Font class), 478
encoding variable (PullParser class), 976
endX variable, 384
endY variable, 384
Equality of sequences, 157
equals() function, 8
E_RESIZE cursor, 376
error variable (GET operation), 954
error variable (Image class), 488
Escape sequences, 103-104
Escape sequences for string literals, 103
Evaluation order of operators, 121-123
event variable (PullParser class), 976
Events
    keyboard events, 425-432
    mouse events, 402
    nodes, 367, 401-402
Example source code
    downloading, 33, 1049
    installing, 33, 1049
example.class property, 1055
Exception handling, 193-194
exception variable (GET operation), 953
exclusive keyword, 26
exec command, 1055
Executing
    applications, 1049-1052
    triggers, 221-222
exit() function, 293
Experimenting with effects, 656
Exporting graphics, 14, 705-708
Expressions
    binding, 24-26, 199-200
    defined, 121
    embedded, 105-106
    formatting, 106-108
    for statement, 186-187
extends keyword, 26

Extensible Markup Language (XML)
    HttpRequest class, 949
    PullParser class, 949
extensions variable (Stage class), 357
External data sources, accessing, 949
Extracting documentation, 13, 1049, 1055-1058

F

fader variable (MediaPlayer class), 634
FadeTransition class, 618-619
failed variable (Task class), 1009
false keyword, 26
family variable (Font class), 478
FeedTask class, 997
__FILE__ variable, 31
Files
    class files, 1050
    package/file.class, 1050
    source files, 15-18, 20, 1050
fill variable (Scene class), 358
Fills
    shapes, 434, 463-466
    text, 470-471
Filtered searches, 326-327
finally keyword, 26
findClass() method, 310
first keyword, 26
fitHeight variable
    ImageView class, 498
    MediaView class, 640
fitWidth variable
    ImageView class, 498
    MediaView class, 640
Float data type, 91
Flood class, 669
Flow class, 548
Flow container
    CSS properties, 1065
    Flow class, 547-548
    -fx-hgap property, 1065
    -fx-hpos property, 1065

-fx-node-hpos property, 1065
-fx-node-vpos property, 1065
-fx-snap-to-pixel property, 1064
-fx-vertical property, 1065
-fx-vgap property, 1065
-fx-vpos property, 1065
layout, 547
Flow-of-control statements
   break statement, 182-183
   continue statement, 184
   defined, 26
   if statement, 179-181
   if/else statement, 26
   Java versus JavaFX, 179
   return statement, 26
   for statement, 26, 184, 193
   throw statement, 26
   try/catch/finally statements, 26, 194
   while statement, 26, 181-182
FLV media files, 630
focused state, 816
focused variable (Node class), 426
focusTraversable variable (Node class), 426
focusX variable, 393
focusY variable, 393
Font class, 477-479
font variable
   SwingComponent class, 830
   Text class, 472
Fonts
   characteristics, 473
   CSS (Cascading Style Sheets), 824-826
   embedding, 720-724
   font family name, 473-474
   font name, 473-474
   font variable, 472
   font weight, 474
   listing fonts and font families, 479
   logical fonts, 477
   object literals, 480-481
   physical fonts, 476-477
   position, 475-476
   posture, 474

   searching, 481-482
   selecting, 479-482
   size, 476
for keyword, 26
for statement, 26, 184-193
foreground variable (SwingComponent class), 830
Formatting expressions, 106-108
fraction variable (Reflection class), 672
framerate variable (Timeline class), 594
from keyword, 26
fullScreen variable (Stage class), 348
function keyword, 26
Function overloading, 253-254
Function overriding, 254-257
function() operator, 122
Functions
   anonymous functions, 145-147
   associate(), 297-298
   binding, 25-26, 207-211, 217
   bound functions, 134, 208-211, 217, 258-259
   built-in, 285
   clear(), 303
   createScene(), 1056
   declaring, 134-137
   deferAction(), 294
   defined, 121, 134
   defining, 25
   disassociate(), 298
   doRequest(), 956
   equals(), 8
   exit(), 293
   within functions, 138
   getArguments(), 287-288
   getFontNames(), 479
   getMembers(), 327-328
   getProperty(), 290
   getting, 324-326
   invoking, 95-96, 131, 138
   isReadOnly(), 206
   isSameObject(), 286-287
   logic, 134

object literals, 150-151
onConnecting, 953
onDoneConnect, 953
onException, 953
onReadingHeaders, 954
onResponseCode, 954
onStarted, 953
passing a function to another function, 142-144
print(), 286
println(), 9, 285-286
random(), 7
reserved words, 26
run(), 28-29, 287
script functions, 137-138
selecting by classname, 258
start(), 951, 955
stop(), 951
substring(), 108
toString(), 155
trim(), 8
unbound functions, 207-208
updateViewport(), 501
uses, 25
variables, 137-142
visibility, 147, 255-256
.fx naming suffix, 15
-fx-arc-height property, 1064
-fx-arc-width property, 1064
-fx-background property, 1067
-fx-blend-mode property, 1062
-fx-block-increment property, 1069-1070
FXClassType class, 315-316, 324
-fx-click-to-position property, 1069-1070
-fx-columns property, 1066, 1070
FXContext class, 309
-fx-cursor property, 1061
-fx-echo-char property, 1070
-fx-effect property, 828, 1061
-fx-fill property, 826, 1063
-fx-fit-to-height property, 1069
-fx-fit-to-width property, 1069

-fx-focus-traversable property, 1061
-fx-font property, 826, 1062, 1067
-fx-font-family property, 824
-fx-font-size property, 824
-fx-font-style property, 825
-fx-font-weight property, 825-826
FXFunctionType class, 316-317
FXFunctionValue class, 320
-fx-graphic property, 1067-1068
-fx-graphic-hpos property, 1067
-fx-graphic-text-gap property, 1067
-fx-graphic-vpos property, 1067
-fx-hbar-policy property, 1069
-fx-hgap property
   Flow container, 1065
   Tile container, 1066
-fx-hpos property
   Flow container, 1065
   HBox container, 1065
   Labeled nodes, 1067
   Separator control, 1069
   Tile container, 1066
   VBox container, 1066
-fx-image property, 1062
FXJavaArrayType class, 316
-fx-lines property, 1070
FXM media files, 630
-fx-major-tick-unit property, 1070
FXMember class, 320, 322
FXMemberFilter class, 326
-fx-minor-tick-unit property, 1070
-fx-node-hpos property
   Flow container, 1065
   Stack container, 1065
   Tile container, 1066
   VBox container, 1066
-fx-node-vpos property
   Flow container, 1065
   HBox container, 1065
   Stack container, 1065
   Tile container, 1066
FXObjectValue class, 319
-fx-opacity property, 1061

-fx-padding property, 1066
-fx-pannable property
    ClipView class, 1064
    ScrollView control, 1069
FXPrimitiveType class, 315
FXPrimitiveValue class, 318-319
-fx-rotate property, 1061
-fx-rows property, 1066
-fx-scale-x property, 1061
-fx-scale-y property, 1061
-fx-scale-z property, 1061
FXSequenceType, 316
FXSequenceValue class, 320
-fx-show-tick-labels property, 1070
-fx-show-tick-marks property, 1070
-fx-smooth property, 1063
-fx-snap-to-pixel property, 1064
-fx-snap-to-ticks property, 1070
-fx-spacing property, 1065-1066
-fx-strikethrough property, 1062
-fx-stroke property, 1063
-fx-stroke-dash-array property, 1063
-fx-stroke-dash-offset property, 1063
-fx-stroke-line-cap property, 1063
-fx-stroke-line-join property, 1063
-fx-stroke-miter-limit property, 1063
-fx-stroke-width property, 1063
-fx-text property, 1068
-fx-text-alignment property, 1062, 1068
-fx-text-fill property, 1067
-fx-text-origin property, 1062
-fx-text-overrun property, 1068
-fx-text-wrap property, 1068
-fx-tile-height property, 1066
-fx-tile-width property, 1066
-fx-translate-x property, 1061
-fx-translate-y property, 1062
-fx-translate-z property, 1062
FXType class, 314-315
-fx-underline property, 1062
-fx-unit-increment property, 1069
FXValue class, 318
FXVarMember class, 322

-fx-vbar-policy property, 1069
-fx-vertical property
    Flow container, 1065
    ListView control, 1068
    ScrollBar control, 1069
    Slider control, 1070
    Tile container, 1066
-fx-vgap property, 1065-1066
-fx-vpos property
    Flow container, 1065
    HBox container, 1065
    Labeled nodes, 1068
    Separator control, 1069
    Tile container, 1066
    VBox container, 1066
FXZ file, 705

G

garbage collection, 81-82
GaussianBlur class, 656-657
Generating documentation, 1055-1058
GET requests
    callback functions, 953
    connecting variable, 953
    doneConnect variable, 953
    exception variable, 953
    lifecycle, 952-955
    onConnecting function, 953
    onDoneConnect function, 953
    onException function, 953
    onReadingHeaders function, 954
    onResponseCode function, 954
    onStarted function, 953
    readingHeaders variable, 954
    responseCode variable, 954
    started variable, 953
    variables, 953
getArguments() function, 287-288
getBestSize() method, 377
getFontNames() function, 479
getMembers() function, 327-328
getName() method, 310
getProperty() function, 290

getSuperClasses() method, 310-313
Getting
    arguments, 287-288
    class information, 313
    functions, 324-326
    previous value of variables, 223
    system properties, 290
getValue() method, 316
GlassFish application server, 1015
Glow class, 666-667
Graphical User Interface (GUI) applications and JavaFX Script langauge, 5
Graphics
    animation paths, 717-720
    creating multiple copies, 731-733
    duplicating, 731-733
    embedding fonts, 720-723
    embedding images, 724-725
    exporting, 14, 705-708
    FXZ file, 705
    importing, 14, 703, 733-735
    loading, 710-717
    previewing, 708-710
    Scalable Vector Graphics (SVG), 704-705, 733-735
    UI Stub class, 725-731
Graphics effects. *See* Effects
greater than (>) operator, 122
greater than or equal (>=) to operator, 122
Group class, 482
Grouping import statements, 20
Groups
    blending, 651, 688-690
    effects, 655
    nesting, 364
    nodes, 9, 482-485
    shapes, 482
GUI (Graphical User Interface) applications and JavaFX Script langauge, 5

H

HAND cursor, 376
HBox class, 560-562

HBox container
    CSS properties, 1065
    -fx-hpos property, 1065
    -fx-node-vpos property, 1065
    -fx-snap-to-pixel property, 1064
    -fx-spacing property, 1065
    -fx-vpos property, 1065
    HBox class, 560-562
headers variable (FeedTask class), 996
height variable
    BoxBlur class, 657
    DropShadow class, 660
    Flood class, 669
    Image class, 488
    InnerShadow class, 663
    Media class, 628
    Scene class, 358
    Shadow class, 661
    Stage class, 348
Hello, World example
    Java, 5-6
    JavaFX Script language, 5-6
high identifier, 230
horizontalAlignment variable
    SwingButton component, 844
    SwingLabel class, 833, 836-837
    SwingTextField class, 840
horizontalTextPosition variable
    SwingButton component, 844
    SwingLabel class, 833, 838
hotspotX variable (CursorImage object), 377
hotspotY variable (CursorImage object), 377
hover state, 816
hover variable (Node class), 424-425
H_RESIZE cursor, 376
HTTP request
    DELETE requests, 973-974
    doRequest() function, 956
    GET requests, 952-964
    InputStream, 952
    lifecycle, 952-955
    OutputStream, 952

HTTP request

POST requests, 971-973
PUT requests, 965-971
HttpRequest class
   doRequest() function, 956
   example use, 950-951
   functionality, 949-950
   HTTP operations, 952
   HTTP protocol, 950
   main thread, 955
   retrieving data from an FTP server, 964-965
   start() function, 951, 955
   stop() function, 951
   streams, 951
HttpStatus class, 959
hue variable (ColorAdjust class), 670
Hyperlink control, 739, 752-755

I

icon variable
   SwingButton component, 844
   SwingLabel class, 833, 834-835
iconified variable (Stage class), 348
icons variable (Stage class), 342-344
ID3 format metadata, 629
IDE (Integrated Development Environment), 3, 33
identifiers
   high, 230
   low, 230
   newVals, 230
   oldVals, 229
Identity class, 667-669
if keyword, 26
if statement, 179-181
if/else statement, 26
ignoreWhiteSpace variable (PullParser class), 976
IllegalArgumentException, 225
Illustrator (Adobe), 14, 703-704
Image class, 377, 433, 487-488
image variable (ImageView class), 498

ImageCursor class, 377
Images
   displaying, 486, 497, 501
   embedding, 724-725
   fetching image data, 490-493
   loading, 486-487
   resizing images, 493-497
   specifying location of, 488-489
ImageView class, 433, 497-501, 1062
Immutable sequences, 154
import keyword, 26
import statements
   grouping, 20
   source files, 15, 20
Importing
   classes, automatic imports, 22-23
   classes, by name, 20
   classes, static imports, 20-22
   classes, wildcard imports, 20
   graphics, 14, 703, 733-735
in keyword, 26
indexof keyword, 26
indexof operator, 122
Infinity, 128-129
Information alert, 342-370
Inheritance
   CSS (Cascading Style Sheets), 820-822
   mixins, 273-280
init block, 263-265
init keyword, 26
Initializing
   arrays, 175-176
   classes, 261-265
   mixins, 281-283
   objects, 148-149
Inkscape, 14, 705, 734
InnerShadow class, 663
input variable
   Bloom class, 665
   BoxBlur class, 657
   ColorAdjust class, 670
   DisplacementMap class, 679
   GaussianBlur class, 656

Glow class, 666
InvertMask class, 671
MotionBlur class, 659
PerspectiveTransform class, 674
PullParser class, 976
Reflection class, 672
SepiaTone class, 673
Shadow class, 661
input variable (GET operation), 955
InputStream, 952
insert keyword, 26
Insertation operations with sequence variables, 230, 233-234
Inserting elements into sequences, 163-165
Inspecting variables, 73
Installing
Ant version 1.7.0 or later, 1049
Eclipse, 33
example source code, 33, 1049
Java, 14
NetBeans, 33
Software Development Kit (SDK), 1049
style sheets, 812
Instance functions, 246, 248
Instance methods, 24
Instance variables
accessing, 96-97
binding, 201-202
classes, 243-246
object creation, 95
triggers, 236-237
instanceof keyword, 26
instanceof operator, 122, 132-133
Integer data type, 91, 97-99
Integer overflow, 125-126
Integrated Development Environment (IDE), 3, 33
Internationalization, 109-117, 295, 298
Internet access, 12-13
interpolate variable (Timeline class), 594
Interpolation, 600-603
interpolator variable (Transition class), 614

interval variable (FeedTask class), 996
into keyword, 26
invalidate keyword, 26
inverse keyword, 26
InvertMask class, 671
invokeLater() method, 294
Invoking
functions, 95-96, 131, 138
methods, 24, 138-139
isAssignableFrom() method, 313-314
isJfxType() method, 313
isMixin() method, 313
isReadOnly() function, 206
isSameObject() function, 286-287
isSupported() method, 307
items variable (SwingComboBox component), 854
Iterating
over a list, 190-191
over a map, 191-192
over a sequence, 184-186
over an array, 193
over an iterable, 190
over multiple sequences, 188-190
iterations variable (BoxBlur class), 657

J

JAR files, compressing, 1042-1043
Java
Hello, World example, 5-6
installing, 14
platform dependencies, 14-15
Java classes, 97, 239-240
java command, 1051
Java ME, 4
Java methods, invoking, 138-139
Java plug-in, 15
Java Runtime Environment (JRE), 14-15
Java Scripting API, 9
Java SE, 4
Java TV, 4
Java VM settings for applets, 15

Java Web Start
   Eclipse, 67
   features, 46-66
   NetBeans, 66-67
javac command, 1054
JavaFX
   CSS support, 809, 1061
   downloading, 4
   overview, 3
javafx command, 1050-1052
JavaFX Desktop and APIs, 9
javafx launcher, 1055
JavaFX Mobile and APIs, 9
JavaFX platform
   APIs (Application Programming Interfaces), 3-4
   architecture, 3
   security, 3
JavaFX Production Suite, 703-705
JavaFX runtime
   APIs (Application Programming Interfaces), 9
   Desktop environments, 4
   Java TV, 4
   mobile devices, 4
   profile-dependence, 9
   profile-independence, 9
   versions, 4
JavaFX Script language
   APIs (Application Programming Interfaces), 6-7
   class files, 8
   classes, 6
   defined, 3
   Graphical User Interface (GUI) applications, 5
   Hello, World example, 5-6
   Java Scripting API, 9
   overview, 5
   scripts, 8-9
   syntax, 3
   Type inference, 6
JavaFX TV emulator, 72, 371

javafxanimation package, 591
javafx.applet.codebase property, 291
javafx.application.codebase property, 291
javafx.async package, 949
javafxbinding package, 194
javafxc command, 1050, 1054
javafxclasses package, 240
javafxcontrols package, 735
javafxdata package, 949
javafx.data.pull package, 950
javafxdoc command-line tool
   classes, 1058
   command-line arguments, 1056
   -d option, 1057
   illustration of, 1056-1057
   output files, 1057-1058
   source files, 1057
   -sourcepath option, 1057
   summary information, 1058
   uses, 13, 1055-1056
javafxeffects package, 651
javafx.encoding property, 291
javafx.file.separator property, 291
javafximport package, 703
javafx.io.http package, 950
javafx.java.ext.dirs property, 291
javafx.java.io.tmpdir property, 291
javafx.java.vendor property, 291
javafx.java.vendor.url property, 291
javafx.java.version property, 291
javafx.language property, 291
javafx.line.separator property, 291
javafxmedia package, 628
javafxnodes package, 375
javafx.os.arch property, 291
javafx.os.name property, 291
javafx.os.version property, 291
javafxpackager command-line tool, 13-14, 46, 1025-1026
javafx.path.separator property, 291
javafx.reflect package, 309
javafxreflection package, 309
javafx.region property, 291

javafx.runtime.version property, 291
javafx.scene.Cursor class, 375
javafx.scene.effects package, 651
javafx.scene.effects.lighting package, 651
javafx.scene.paint.LinearGradient class, 384
javafx.scene.paint.RadialGradient class, 393
javafx.scene.text.Font class, 7
javafx.scene.text.Text class, 7
javafx.scene.transform.Transform class, 505
javafx/SequenceTriggers.fx file, 230
javafxshapes package, 433
javafxstyle package, 809
javafxswing package, 829
javafx.timezone property, 291
javafxtriggers package, 221
javafx.user.dir property, 291
javafx.user.home property, 291
javafx.util.Math class, 7
javafx.version property, 291
javafxw command, 1052
java.lang.Math class, 7
java.lang.reflect package, 309
java.lang.System class, 6
java.scene.input.MouseEvent argument, 402-403
JavaScript Object Notation (JSON), 949
java.util.Random class, 6-7
Joins, 459-460
JRE (Java Runtime Environment), 14-15
JSON (JavaScript Object Notation), 949
JSON weather service, 992-995
JSON web service client, 988, 992
jvisualvm profiler, 46

K

Keyboard events
   defined, 425-426
   input focus, 426-429
   modifier keys, 431
   noncharacter keys, 432
   receiving key events, 429-430
   repeated keys, 432
   types of key events, 430-431

KeyEvent class
   altDown variable, 431
   char variable, 429
   code variable, 429
   controlDown variable, 431
   metaDown variable, 431
   shiftDown variable, 431
   text variable, 429
KeyFrame class, 596-600
keyFrames variable (Timeline class), 594
Keywords
and, 26
as, 26
at, 26
before, 26
for, 26
from, 26
in, 26
into, 26
on, 26
with, 26
abstract, 26
after, 26
assert, 26
attribute, 26
bind, 8, 26
bound, 26
break, 26
catch, 26
class, 26
context, 26
continue, 26
def, 6, 26
delete, 26
else, 26
exclusive, 26
extends, 26
false, 26
finally, 26
first, 26
function, 26
if, 26
import, 26

indexof, 26
init, 26
insert, 26
instanceof, 26
invalidate, 26
inverse, 26
last, 26
lazy, 26
mixin, 26
mod, 26
nativearray, 26
new, 7, 26
not, 26
null, 26
or, 26
override, 26
package, 26
postinit, 26
private, 26
protected, 26
public, 26
public-init, 26
public-read, 26
replace, 26
reserved words, 26
return, 26
reverse, 26
sizeof, 26
static, 26
step, 26
super, 26
then, 26
this, 26
throw, 26
trigger, 26
true, 26
try, 26
tween, 26
typeof, 26
types of, 26
var, 6, 26
where, 26
while, 26

L

Label control
   appearance, 739
   basic labels, 741-742
   CSS properties, 1067-1068
   features and functionality, 738-739
   icons, 834-835
   Label class, 741
   Labeled class, 739-741
   multiline text, 746-747
   positioning content, 836-838
   positioning text and graphics, 742-746
   text, 834-835
   text overruns and wrapping, 747-749
   variables, 833-834
labelFor variable (SwingLabel class), 833
last keyword, 26
LayoutInfo class, 542
Layouts of nodes, 501, 538-579
layoutX variable, 504
layoutY variable, 504
Lazy binding, 206-207
lazy keyword, 26, 206
length variable (Resource class), 302
less than operator (<), 122
less than or equal to operator (<=), 122
letterSpacing variable (Font class), 478
level variable
   Glow class, 666
   SepiaTone class, 673
Libraries, 1039-1042
Lifecycle of HTTP request, 952-955
ligatures variable (Font class), 478
light variable (Lighting class), 691
Lighting class, 651, 690-694
Line charts, 926-928
Line class, 434-436
line variable (PullParser class), 976
Linear gradients
   cycle methods, 388-390
   defined, 383

direction of, 386
example, 384-385
javafx.scene.paint.LinearGradient class, 384
multicolor linear gradients, 387
nonproportional gradients, 390-391
resizing areas filled linear gradients, 386
Stop object, 385-388
stops, 384
strokes, 391-392
support for, 383
variables, 384

Listing fonts and font families, 479

ListView control
appearance, 739
cell rendering, 782-785
CSS properties, 1068
dynamic list content, 776
features and functionality, 773
-fx-pannable property, 1068
-fx-vertical property, 1068
ListView class, 773-776
selection of list items, 778-782

llx variable (PerspectiveTransform class), 674
lly variable (PerspectiveTransform class), 674

Loading
applets, 15
graphics, 710-717
images, 486-487

Local storage, 298-299
Local Variables view, 73-74
Localization, 108-116
location variable (FeedTask class), 996
Logging, 267-271
Logic of functions, 134
Logical fonts, 477
Long data type, 98
Loops and bound functions, 216-217
low identifier, 230
lrx variable (PerspectiveTransform class), 674
lry variable (PerspectiveTransform class), 674

M

main() method, 28
mapData variable (DisplacementMap class), 679
Mapping between source files and class files, 8-9, 1050

Mappings
class mapping, 297-298
creating, 297-298
package mapping, 297
removing, 298

maximum variable (SwingSlider component), 857
maxLength variable (Resource class), 302
Media class, 628-630

Media players
animation, 633
control bar, 895-909
functionality, 627
monitoring playback, 634-635
synchronizing external events with playback, 637-638
triggers, 635-636
Volume control, 633

media variable (MediaPlayer class), 631
MediaPlayer class, 628, 630
mediaPlayer variable (MediaView class), 639
MediaPlayerBehavior class, 908-909
MediaTimer class, 638-639
MediaView class, 10, 628, 639-640
Memory leaks, 46, 80-82
Memory profiling, 80-82
metadata variable (Media class), 628

metaDown variable
KeyEvent class, 431
MouseEvent class, 414

Methods
chooseBestCursor(), 378
cycle methods, 388-390, 398-399
findClass(), 310
getBestSize(), 377
getName(), 310
getSuperClasses(), 310-313

Methods

getValue(), 316
instance, 24
invokeLater(), 294
invoking, 24
isAssignableFrom(), 313-314
isJfxType(), 313
isMixin(), 313
isSupported(), 307
main(), 28
references, 24
static, 24

Microsoft Windows Platform and cursors, 376
middleButtonDown variable (MouseEvent class), 410
MIDlets, 4
MIDP (Mobile Information Device Profile)-based cell phones, 7
minimum variable (SwingSlider component), 857
mixin keyword, 26
Mixins

characteristics, 272-273
defined, 266-267
inheritance, 273-280
initializing, 281-283
logging, 267-271
triggers, 280-281
uses for, 267

Mobile applications

deploying, 14, 1047-1048
packaging, 1045-1047
system properties, 292

Mobile devices

JavaFX runtime, 4
Mobile Information Device Profile (MIDP)-based cell phones, 7
Stage class, 350-351, 354

Mobile emulator, 70-72
Mobile Information Device Profile (MIDP)-based cell phones, 7
mod keyword, 26
mod operator, 122, 124
mode variable (Blend class), 687

Modifying

arrays, 176
sequences, 162

Monitoring playback, 634-635
MotionBlur class, 659-660
Mouse cursors

CROSSHAIR, 376
cursor variable, 375
customizing, 377
DEFAULT, 376
E_RESIZE, 376
HAND, 376
H_RESIZE, 376
javafx.scene.Cursor class, 375
Microsoft Windows Platform, 376
MOVE, 376
NE_RESIZE, 376
nodes, 375
N_RESIZE, 376
NW_RESIZE, 376
SE_RESIZE, 376
setting, 375-377
shape of, 375
S_RESIZE, 376
SW_RESIZE, 376
TEXT, 376
V_RESIZE, 376
WAIT, 376
W_RESIZE, 376

Mouse events

delivery of, 419-424
dragging, 415-418
hover variable, 424-425
modifier keys, 414-415
mouse buttons, 410-414
mouse wheel, 418-419
mouse-related node state, 424
pickOnBounds variable, 424
propagation, 406-410
reporting of, 402-403

MouseEvent class

altDown variable, 414
button variable, 410

clickCount variable, 410
controlDown variable, 414
defined, 403
dragAnchorX variable, 416
dragAnchorY variable, 416
dragX variable, 416
dragY variable, 416
metaDown variable, 414
middleButtonDown variable, 410
node variable, 403
popupTrigger variable, 411
primaryButtonDown variable, 411
sceneX variable, 404
sceneY variable, 404
screenX variable, 404
screenY variable, 404
secondaryButtonDown variable, 411
shiftDown variable, 414
source variable, 403
variables, 403-404
wheelRotation variable, 419
x variable, 404
y variable, 404
MOVE cursor, 376
Moving nodes, 9
MP3 files, 629
Multicolor linear gradients, 387
Multiline comments, 18
mute variable (MediaPlayer class), 634

N

N/A variable (GET operation), 954
name variable
Font class, 478
Resource class, 302
SwingComponent class, 830
Naming
projects, in Eclipse, 40
projects, in NetBeans, 34
NaN, 128-129
nativearray keyword, 26
NE_RESIZE cursor, 376

Nesting
classes, 266
groups, 364
object literals, 7, 149
sequences, 154
NetBeans
development, 3, 33-39
documentation, 43-44
installing, 33
Java Web Start, 66-67
mobile emulator, 70-71
profiler, 46-82
support, 3, 13
viewing documentation, 1055
Network access, 12-13
Networking APIs, 12-13
new keyword, 7, 26
new operator, 122, 131
newVals identifier, 230
unnnn escape sequence, 103
Node class
disable variable, 426
disabled variable, 426
focused variable, 426
focusTraversable variable, 426
hover variable, 424-425
node variable
MouseEvent class, 403
Transition class, 614
Nodes
bounds, 527-538
centering, 577-579
clipping, 523-526
colors, 367, 378
coordinate systems, 501
coordinates, 362-364
CSS properties, 1061-1062
cursors, 375
customizing, 482-485, 864
defined, 9, 342-361, 375
effects, 368-369, 654
events, 367, 401-402

example, 9-10
groups, 9, 482-485
identification, 361
javafxnodes package, 375
layouts, 153-501, 538-579
MediaView node, 10, 628
moving, 9
organization, 361
placement of, 9
rotating, 9
rotation, 508-511
scaling, 9, 511-514
shearing, 9, 515, 517
Swing components, 830-832
transforms, 501-504
translation, 506-508
types of, 341
user interaction, 401
user interfaces, 341
visibility, 364-365
z-axis, 372-374
Z-order, 365-366
Nonproportional gradients, 390-391
not keyword, 26
not operator, 122
N_RESIZE cursor, 376
null keyword, 26
Null value for numeric data types, 102
Number data type, 91, 99
Number overflow, 126
Number underflow, 126-127
Numeric data types
converting numeric values, 99-101
Integer, 91, 97-99
null value, 102
Number, 91, 99
value ranges, 98
Numeric operations, 123
NW_RESIZE cursor, 376

O

Object comparison, 133-134
Object literals
binding, 196-199
defined, 7, 121
fonts, 480-481
functions, 150-151
nesting, 149
syntax, 147
uses, 148-149
variables, 149-150
Objects
comparing, 286-287
creating, 95, 131
initializing, 148-149
instance variables, 95
oblique variable (Font class), 478
Observable class, 267
offsetX variable
DisplacementMap class, 679, 683-684
DropShadow class, 660
InnerShadow class, 663
offsetY variable
DisplacementMap class, 679
DropShadow class, 660
InnerShadow class, 663
oldVals identifier, 229
On keyword, 26
On2 Technologies utility, 630
onBuffering variable (MediaPlayer class), 635
onConnecting function, 953
onDone variable (Task class), 1009
onDoneConnect function, 953
onEndOfMedia variable (MediaPlayer class), 635
onError variable
Media class, 628
MediaPlayer class, 635
MediaView class, 639
onEvent variable (PullParser class), 976
onException function, 953
onException variable (FeedTask class), 996

onForeignEvent variable (FeedTask class), 996
onMouseClicked variable, 402
onMouseDragged variable, 402
onMouseEntered variable, 402
onMouseExited variable, 402
onMouseMoved variable, 402
onMousePressed variable, 402
onMouseReleased variable, 402
onMouseWheelMoved variable, 402
onReadingHeaders function, 954
onRepeat variable (MediaPlayer class), 635
onResponseCode function, 954
onStalled variable (MediaPlayer class), 635
onStarted function, 953
onStarted variable (Task class), 1009
opacity variable
   Blend class, 687
   Stage class, 354
Operators
   and, 122
   as, 122, 131-132
   += (add and assign), 122
   + (addition), 122
   = (assignment), 122
   /= (divide and assign), 122
   / (division), 122
   == (equality), 122, 133-134, 157
   . (function invocation), 131
   != (inequality), 122, 133-134
   * (multiplication), 122
   *= (multiply and assign), 122
   { object literal }, 122
   ++ (postfix), 122
   — (postfix), 122
   ++ (prefix), 122
   — (prefix), 122
   -= (subtract and assign), 122
   - (subtraction), 122
   - (unary minus), 122
   == operator, 8
   arithmetic operations, 123-125
   Boolean operations, 129-130

comparison operators, 127-128
division of a nonzero value by zero, 127
division of zero by zero, 127
evaluation order, 121-123
function(), 122
greater than (>), 122
greater than or equal to (>=), 122
indexof, 122
infinity, 128-129
instanceof, 122, 132-133
integer overflow, 125-126
less than (<), 122
less than or equal to (<=), 122
mod, 122, 124
NaN, 128-129
new, 122, 131
not, 122
number overflow, 126
number underflow, 126-127
numeric operations, 123
object comparison, 133-134
or, 122
() parentheses, 122-123
priority values, 121
range errors, 125
reverse, 122, 154-155
sizeof, 122
supported, 121
Or keyword, 26
or operator, 122
Outline dashing, 460-462
OutputStream, 952
override keyword, 26
Overriding variables, 259-261

P

Pack200 compression, 1043
package keyword, 26
Package mapping, 297
package modifier, 120
package statement in source files, 15, 20
package/file.class file, 1050

1098 Packages

Packages
    creating, in Eclipse, 41
    creating, in NetBeans, 38
    javafxanimation, 591
    javafx.async, 949
    javafxbinding, 194
    javafxclasses, 240
    javafxcontrols, 735
    javafxdata, 949
    javafx.data.pull, 950
    javafxeffects, 651
    javafximport, 703
    javafx.io.http, 950
    javafxmedia, 628
    javafxnodes, 375
    javafx.reflect, 309
    javafxreflection, 309
    javafx.scene.effects, 651
    javafx.scene.effects.lighting, 651
    javafxshapes, 433
    javafxstyle, 809
    javafxswing, 829
    java.lang.reflect, 309
    platformapi, 285
Packaging
    desktop applications, 1026-1029
    javafxpackager command-line tool, 1025
    mobile applications, 1045-1047
    options, 14
    SnowStorm application, 46
pad variable (InvertMask class), 671
paint variable (Flood class), 669
Panel class, 884-887
Panel container, 572-574
ParallelCamera, 373-374
ParallelTransition class, 622-625
Parameters, setting, 1037-1039
() parentheses in operators, 122-123
Parsing XML
    DOM-style parsing, 975
    pull parsing, 975-981
    stream parsing, 975-981

Passing a function to another function, 142-144
PasswordBox class, 739, 771-773
PasswordBox controls
    appearance, 739
    CSS properties, 1070
    features and functionality, 771
    -fx-columns property, 1070
    -fx-echo-char property, 1070
    -fx-editable property, 1070
    -fx-font property, 1070
    -fx-select-on-focus property, 1070
    operation of, 772-773
    PasswordBox class, 739, 771-773
Path class, 451
PathElement class, 434-453
PathTransition class, 619-622
paused variable
    MediaPlayer class, 635
    Timeline class, 594
PauseTransition class, 622
Pausing animation, 608
Pausing audio/video, 632
percentDone variable (Task class), 1010
PerspectiveCamera, 372-374
PerspectiveTransform class, 673-678
Photoshop (Adobe), 14, 704
Physical fonts, 476-477
pickOnBouonds variable, 424
Pie charts, 914, 919
placeholder variable (Image class), 488
Platform API
    platformapi package, 285
    security, 285
Platform dependencies, 14-15
platformapi package, 285
Playing audio/video, 10, 627-628
PointLight class, 697-698
Polygon class, 440-442
Polyline class, 440-442
popupTrigger variable (MouseEvent class), 411

Position
   fonts, 475-476
   label content, 836-838
   text, 466-468
position variable (Font class), 478
POST requests, 971, 973
postinit block, 265
postinit keyword, 26
Postponing actions, 294-295
Predefined variables, 31
preserveRatio variable
   Image class, 488
   ImageView class, 498
   MediaView class, 640
pressed state, 816
pressedIcon variable (SwingButton component), 844
Previewing graphics, 708-710
primaryButtonDown variable (MouseEvent class), 411
print() function, 286
println() function, 9, 285-286
Priority values of operators, 121
Prism toolkit, 372-374
private keyword, 26
Production Suite
   downloading, 14
   features, 14
-profile name compiler option, 1050
__PROFILE__ variable, 31
Profilers
   jvisualvm, 46
   NetBeans, 46-82
Profiles and APIs, 4-5
Profiling
   CPU profiling, 78-80
   memory profiling, 80-82
   SnowStorm application, 46-82
Progress monitoring, 1010-1014
progress variable
   Image class, 488
   Task class, 1009
ProgressBar controls, 739, 804-807

ProgressIndicator controls, 739, 804-807
progressMax variable (Task class), 1009
Projects
   creating, in Eclipse, 40
   creating, in NetBeans, 34
   naming, in Eclipse, 40
   naming, in NetBeans, 34
   source files, in Eclipse, 41
   source files, in NetBeans, 34-36
proportional variable
   linear gradients, 384
   radial gradients, 393
protected keyword, 26
protected modifier, 120
public keyword, 26
public modifier, 120
public-init keyword, 26
public-read keyword, 26
public-read modifier, 120
public-read package modifier, 120
public-read protected modifier, 120
PullParser class, 949, 975
PUT requests, 965, 971

Q

QuadCurve class, 444-448
QuadCurveTo class, 453
Querying sequences, 158-161
Question alert, 371

R

Radial gradients
   changing the bounds of a filled shape, 395-397
   cycle methods, 398-399
   defined, 392-393
   example, 393-395
   focus, 399-401
   javafx.scene.paint.RadialGradient class, 393
   moving the center, 397-398
   variables, 393

RadioButton controls, 756-759
radius variable
  DropShadow class, 660
  GaussianBlur class, 656
  InnerShadow class, 663
  MotionBlur class, 659
  RadialGradient class, 393
  Shadow class, 661
random() function, 7
Range errors, 125
Range notation, 156-157
rate variable
  MediaPlayer class, 631
  Timeline class, 594
read variable (GET operation), 955
readable variable (Resource class), 302
Reading data, 299, 301
reading variable (GET operation), 954
readingHeaders variable (GET operation), 954
Rectangle class, 433, 436, 438
  -fx-arc-height property, 1064
  -fx-arc-width property, 1064
  height and width of rounded corners, 1064
References
  to classes, 23
  to methods, 24
Reflection
  access to classes, 310-314
  Application Programming Interfaces (APIs), 309
  FXContext class, 309
  javafx.reflect package, 309
  javafxreflection package, 309
  java.lang.reflect package, 309
  reflection context, 309-310
Reflection class, 671, 673
Rejecting an invalid value, 225-227
Removal operation with sequence variables, 230-232
Removing
  breakpoints, 76-77
  data, 303-305

  elements from sequences, 165-166
  mappings, 298
repeatCount variable
  MediaPlayer class, 631
  Timeline class, 594
Repeating
  animation, 605-607
  audio/video playback, 632-633
replace clause, 229-230
replace keyword, 26
Replacement operations with sequence variables, 230-231
Replacing
  elements of sequences, 162-163
  a range of elements in a sequence, 166-167
Reserved words, 26
resizable variable (Stage class), 348
Resource class, 302-303
Resource names, 305-306
responseCode variable (GET operation), 954
responseMessage variable (GET operation), 954
Restarting animation, 609
RESTful web services, 13, 974-975
Restricting audio/video playback, 632-633
return keyword, 26
return statement, 26
reverse keyword, 26
reverse operator, 122, 154-155
Reverting to the previous value, 227-229
rotatable variable (MediaView class), 648
rotate variable, 504
RotateTransition class, 616-617
Rotating nodes, 9
Rotation of nodes, 508-511
rotationAxis variable, 504
RSS feeds, 949-950, 1004
run target, 1055
run() function, 28-29, 287
Running
  applications, with command-line tools, 1049-1052
  applications, with Eclipse, 42

applications, with NetBeans, 39
SnowStorm application, as an applet, 67-70
SnowStorm application, from JavaFX TV emulator, 72
SnowStorm application, from Java Web Start, 46-67
SnowStorm application, on a mobile emulator, 70-72
running variable (Timeline class), 595
Runtime libraries
   animation, 10-12
   audio, 10
   features, 3, 9
   network access, 12-13
   user interface classes, 9-10
   video, 10

S

saturation variable (ColorAdjust class), 670
Scalable Vector Graphics (SVG), 704-705, 733-735
Scalable Vector Graphics (SVG) editor, 14
ScaleTransition class, 617-618
scaleX variable, 504, 679, 684
scaleY variable, 504, 679, 684
scaleZ variable, 504
Scaling nodes, 9, 511-514
Scatter charts, 932-934
Scene class, 342-360
sceneX variable (MouseEvent class), 404
sceneY variable (MouseEvent class), 404
Scope of variables, 93
Screen class, 585-590
screenX variable (MouseEvent class), 404
screenY variable (MouseEvent class), 404
Script files
   classes, 265-266
   creating, 41
Script functions, 137-138
Script variables, binding, 194
Scripting mode, 31

Scripts
   Ant build script, 33, 1049, 1052-1055
   JavaFX Script language, 8-9
   run() function, 28-29
ScrollBar class, 788-789
ScrollBar controls
   appearance, 739
   CSS properties, 1068-1069
   features and functionality, 787-788
   -fx-block-increment property, 1069
   -fx-click-to-position property, 1069
   -fx-unit-increment property, 1069
   -fx-vertical property, 1069
   operation of, 790-794
   ScrollBar class, 788-789
Scroller class, 794
ScrollView controls
   appearance, 739
   CSS properties, 1069
   display and values, 797
   features and functionality, 794
   -fx-fit-to-height property, 1069
   -fx-fit-to-width property, 1069
   -fx-hbar-policy property, 1069
   -fx-pannable property, 1069
   -fx-vbar-policy property, 1069
   scrollable node size, 797
   ScrollView class, 794-797
SDK (Software Development Kit)
   Ant task, 13
   API documentation, 5
   application launcher, 13
   command-line compiler, 13
   command-line tools, 1049
   contents of, 13
   extracting documentation, 1049
   installing, 1049
   javafxdoc command-line tool, 1055-1058
   javafxpackager command-line tool, 13
Searching
   fonts, 481-482
   sequences, 172-173

Searching sequences for elements, 168-169
secondaryButtonDown variable (MouseEvent class), 411
Security, 3, 285
select() function, 712
selectedIndex variable (SwingComboBox component), 854
selectedItem variable (SwingComboBox component), 854
Selecting
  fonts, 479-482
  functions by classname, 258
selectOnFocus variable (SwingTextField class), 839
Self-signed certificate, 1044
Separator control
  appearance, 739
  CSS properties, 1069
  -fx-hpos property, 1069
  -fx-vpos property, 1069
Separator controls
  adding, 808
  features and functionality, 807
  Separator class, 807-808
SepiaTone class, 673
Sequences
  binding, 217
  comparing, 167-168
  copying, 158
  creating, 153-155
  defined, 153
  equality, 157
  finding largest and smallest elements, 169-171
  immutable, 154
  inserting elements, 163-165
  iterating over, 184-190
  modifying, 162
  nesting, 154
  obtaining an element of, 159
  obtaining part of, 160
  obtaining size of, 158
  querying, 158-161
  range notation, 156-157
  removing elements, 165-166
  replacing a range of elements, 166-167
  replacing elements of, 162-163
  searching, 172-173
  searching for elements, 168-169
  shuffling, 174
  size of, 154
  sorting, 171-172
  string form, 155
  syntax, 153
  triggers, deletion operations, 230-232
  triggers, example of, 234-236
  triggers, insertion operations, 230, 233-234
  triggers, replacement operations, 230-231
  triggers, syntax of, 229-230
SequentialTransition class, 622-625
SE_RESIZE cursor, 376
Setting
  breakpoints, 46-73
  cursors, 375
  parameters, 1037-1039
Shadow class, 664-665
Shape class, 433
shape of cursors, 375
ShapeIntersect class, 449-451
Shapes
  Arc class, 442-444
  ArcTo class, 453, 455
  Circle class, 433, 438-439
  CSS properties, 1063-1064
  CubicCurve class, 448-449
  CubicCurveTo class, 453
  defined, 433
  DelegateShape class, 434
  Ellipses class, 439-440
  fills, 434, 463-466
  groups, 482
  Line class, 434-436
  morphing, 603, 605
  outline dashing, 460-462

Path class, 451
PathElement class, 452-453
Polygon class, 440-442
Polyline class, 440-442
QuadCurve class, 444-448
QuadCurveTo class, 453
Rectangle class, 433, 436-438
Shape class, 433
ShapeIntersect class, 449-451
ShapeSubtract class, 449-451
strokes, 456, 458
SVGPath class, 456
ShapeSubtract class, 449-451
Shearing nodes, 9, 515, 517
shiftDown variable
    KeyEvent class, 431
    MouseEvent class, 414
Short data type, 91
Shuffling sequences, 174
Shutdown, 292-294
Signing applications and applets, 1043-1045
Simple variables and triggers, 221
Single-line comments, 18
size variable (Font class), 478
sizeof keyword, 26
sizeof operator, 122
Skin class, 891-894
Slicing strings, 108
Slider controls
    appearance, 739
    CSS properties, 1069-1070
    features and functionality, 797
    -fx-block-increment property, 1070
    -fx-click-to-position property, 1070
    -fx-major-tick-unit property, 1070
    -fx-minor-tick-unit property, 1070
    -fx-show-tick-labels property, 1070
    -fx-show-tick-marks property, 1070
    -fx-snap-to-ticks property, 1070
    -fx-vertical property, 1070
    operation of, 798-800
    Slider class, 797-798

tick labels, 802-804
tick marks, 800-802
smooth variable
    Image class, 488
    ImageView class, 498
    MediaView class, 640
SnowStorm application
    animation, 58
    background image, 49-52, 581-582
    building, 46
    creating, 46-47
    debugging, 46-76
    desktop application, 70
    dynamic part, 47
    functionality, 45
    packaging, 46
    performance problems, 46
    previewing, 52-53
    profiling, 46-82
    running, as an applet, 67-70
    running, on a mobile emulator, 70-72
    running, with JavaFX TV emulator, 72
    running, with Java Web Start, 46-67
    screen display, 579-581
    snowflakes, adding, 58-62, 582-585
    snowflakes, animating, 62-64, 582-585
    snowflakes, counting, 64-65
    source code, 46-85
    stage and scene, 48-49
    static part, 47
    text, 53-58
    user interface, 47
SOAP-based web services, 950
Software Development Kit (SDK)
    Ant task, 13
    API documentation, 5
    application launcher, 13
    command-line compiler, 13
    command-line tools, 1049
    contents of, 13
    extracting documentation, 1049
    installing, 1049

Software Development Kit (SDK)

javafxdoc command-line tool, 1055-1058
javafxpackager command-line tool, 13
Sorting sequences, 171-172
Source code
    documentation, 43
    example source code, 33, 1049
    SnowStorm application, 46-85
Source files
    class files, 1050
    comments, 18
    documentation, 1057
    .fx naming suffix, 15
    import statement, 15, 20
    package statement, 15, 20
    structure, 15
source variable
    Identity class, 668
    Media class, 628
    MouseEvent class, 403
__SOURCE_FILE__ variable, 31
-sourcepath path compiler option, 1051
specularConstant variable (Lighting class), 691
specularExponent variable (Lighting class), 691
Speeding up audio/video playback, 632
Spotlight class, 698, 700
spread variable (DropShadow class), 660
S_RESIZE cursor, 376
Stack class, 555-559
Stack container
    CSS properties, 1065-1066
    -fx-node-hpos property, 1065
    -fx-node-vpos property, 1065
    -fx-padding property, 1066
    -fx-snap-to-pixel property, 1064
    Stack class, 555-559
Stage class
    appearance, 342-343
    bounds, 348-350
    closing the stage, 347-348
    extensions, 357-358
    features, 342
    focus, 344-345
    icons, 343-344
    mobile devices, 350-351, 354
    opacity, 354-357, 367
    stage position and size, 348
    states, 342-343
    style, 354, 357
    variables, 342
    visibility, 344
    Z-order control, 345-347
stage variable (Scene class), 358
started variable (GET operation), 953
started variable (Task class), 1009
start() function, 951, 955
startTime variable (MediaPlayer class), 631
startX variable, 384
startY variable, 384
States
    Button controls, 751-752
    of classes, 239
    disabled state, 816
    focused state, 816
    hover state, 816
    pressed state, 816
    Stage class, 342-343
    state-dependent CSS styling, 816-817
static keyword, 26
Static methods, 24
status variable (MediaPlayer class), 634-635
step keyword, 26
Stepping through code, 75-76
stop() function, 951
stopped variable (Task class), 1009
Stopping animation, 608-609
Stopping audio/video playback, 632
stops variable
    linear gradients, 384
    radial gradients, 393
stopTime variable (MediaPlayer class), 631
Storage class
    available and used space, 302
    listing resources, 301-302
Streams in HttpRequest class, 951
Strikethrough text, 471

String data type, 92, 103
String form of sequences, 155
String literals
   concatenation, 104-105
   defined, 103
   escape sequences, 103
   internationalization, 109-110
   localization, 108-109
   slicing, 108
Strokes
   linear gradients, 391-392
   shapes, 456, 458
   text, 470-471
Structuring source files, 15
Style sheets. *See* CSS (Cascading Style Sheets)
style variable
   Font class, 478
   Stage class, 354
stylesheets variable (Scene class), 358
Subclassing, 249
substring() function, 108
succeeded variable (Task class), 1009
super keyword, 26
supportsMultiViews variable (MediaPlayer class), 640
surfaceScale variable (Lighting class), 691-692
SVG (Scalable Vector Graphics), 704-705, 733-735
SVG (Scalable Vector Graphics) editor, 14
SVGPath class, 456
SVG-to-JavaFX Graphics Converter, 734
Swing controls
   accessing the wrapped Swing control, 832
   CSS (Cascading Style Sheets), 809
   javafxswing package, 829
   nodes, 830-832
   support for, 829
   wrappers, 829-830, 860-864
Swing JColorChooser component, 382-383
SwingButton component
   defined, 829, 843
   variables, 843-846

SwingCheckBox component, 829, 848-849
SwingComboBox component, 830, 854, 857
SwingComponent class, 830
SwingLabel component, 829, 833-834
SwingList component, 830, 849-850, 852
SwingRadioButton component, 829, 848-849
SwingScrollPane component, 830, 852-853
SwingSlider component, 830, 857, 859
SwingTextField component
   configuring, 840-842
   defined, 829
   handling input, 842-843
   variables, 838-839
SwingToggleButton component, 829, 846-848
SW_RESIZE cursor, 376
Synchronizing external events with playback, 637-638
Syntax
   class declarations, 240
   def statement, 92
   if statement, 179
   JavaFX Script, 3
   object literals, 147
   sequences, 153
   triggers, 221, 229
   var statement, 89
   while statement, 181-182
System properties
   example.class, 1055
   getting, 290
   javafx.applet.codebase, 291
   javafx.application.codebase, 291
   javafx.encoding, 291
   javafx.file.separator, 291
   javafx.java.ext.dirs, 291
   javafx.java.io.tmpdir, 291
   javafx.java.vendor, 291
   javafx.java.vendor.url, 291
   javafx.java.version, 291
   javafx.language, 291
   javafx.line.separator, 291
   javafx.os.arch, 291
   javafx.os.name, 291

System properties

javafx.os.version, 291
javafx.path.separator, 291
javafx.region, 291
javafx.runtime.version, 291
javafx.timezone, 291
javafx.user.dir, 291
javafx.user.home, 291
javafx.version, 291
mobile, 292

T

Targets
   clean, 1055
   run, 1055
Task class,
Tasks, 13, 1009-1010
Text
   alignment, 468-469
   decoration, 471-472
   displaying, 467
   fills, 470-471
   fonts, 472
   -fx-font property, 1062
   -fx-strikethrough property, 1062
   -fx-text-alignment property, 1062
   -fx-text-origin property, 1062
   -fx-underline property, 1062
   multiline, 468-469
   overline, 471
   positioning, 466-468
   strikethrough, 471
   strokes, 470-471
   underline, 471
   wrapping, 468-469
Text class, 433, 466, 472
TEXT cursor, 376
Text node, 424
text variable
   KeyEvent class, 429
   SwingButton component, 844
   SwingComboBox component, 854

   SwingLabel class, 833-835
   SwingTextField class, 839
TextBox control
   appearance, 739
   content, setting and getting, 766-769
   copy and paste, 771
   CSS properties, 1070
   editability, 764
   -fx-columns property, 1070
   -fx-editable property, 1070
   -fx-font property, 1070
   -fx-lines property, 1070
   -fx-select-on-focus property, 1070
   height, 764
   selection, 769-771
   TextBox class, 762-764
   TextInputControl class, 761-762
   width, 764
TextOrigin class, 467-468
then keyword, 26
this keyword, 26
threshold variable (Bloom class), 665
throw keyword, 26
throw statement, 26
tick labels (Slider controls), 802-804
tick marks (Slider controls), 800-802
Tile class, 563-572
Tile container
   CSS properties, 1066
   -fx-snap-to-pixel property, 1064
   Tile class, 563-572
Time literals, 595-596
time variable
   MediaTimer class, 638
   Timeline class, 594
Timeline class, 12, 594, 605
Timelines
   Duration class, 596
   example, 592-594
   functionality, 591
   KeyFrame class, 600
   keyframes, 596

time literals, 595-596
timer, 611-613
variables, 594-595
TimeSlider class, 904-908
title variable (Stage class), 342
ToggleButton controls, 739, 756-758
Tooltip controls
  appearance, 739
  CSS properties, 1067-1068
  features and functionality, 808-809
topInput variable (Blend class), 687
topOffset variable (Reflection class), 672
topOpacity variable (Reflection class), 672
toRead variable (GET operation), 954
toString() function, 155
totalDuration variable (Timeline class), 594
Tracking mouse motion, 404-406
tracks variable (Media class), 628
transformable variable (MediaView class), 648
Transformations, 654
Transforms
  combining, 517, 523
  defined, 501
  functionality, 501
  javafx.scene.transform.Transform class, 505
  layoutX variable, 504
  layoutY variable, 504
  order of multiple transfer effects, 517-520
  rotate variable, 504
  rotationAxis variable, 504
  scaleX variable, 504
  scaleY variable, 504
  scaleZ variable, 504
  transforms variable, 504
  translateX variable, 504
  translateY variable, 504
  translateZ variable, 504
  variables, 501-505
transforms variable, 504
Transition class, 614

Transitions
  animation, 591, 613-614
  video, 646-649
TranslateTransition class, 614, 616
translateX variable, 504
  Timeline class, 12
translateY variable, 504
translateZ variable, 371, 504
Translation of nodes, 506-508
trigger keyword, 26
Triggers
  attaching, 221, 229
  binding, 223-224
  constraints, 224-225
  creating, 221
  declaring, 221-222
  defined, 26
  deletion operations, 230-232
  executing, 221-222
  getting the previous value of variables, 223
  insertion operations, 230, 233-234
  javafx/SequenceTriggers.fx file, 230
  javafxtriggers package, 221
  media players, 635-636
  mixins, 280-281
  rejecting an invalid value, 225-227
  replacement operations, 230-231
  reverting to the previous value, 227-229
  syntax, 221, 229
  uses, 221
  variables, instance, 236-237
  variables, sequence, 229-230, 234-236
  variables, simple, 221
trim() function, 8
true keyword, 26
try keyword, 26
try/catch/finally statements, 26, 194
TV applications, deploying, 14
TV emulator, 72, 371
tween keyword, 26
Twitter search feed, 1004, 1008

Twitter web service client, 983-985, 987
Type inference, 6, 117-119
typeof keyword, 26
Types
    FXClassType, 315-316
    FXFunctionType, 316-317
    FXJavaArrayType, 316
    FXPrimitiveType, 315
    FXSequenceType, 316
    FXType, 314-315
    representation of, 314

U

ulx variable (PerspectiveTransform class), 674
uly variable (PerspectiveTransform class), 674
Unbound functions, 207-209, 214
Underline text, 471
Unicode
    Character data type, 101
    escape sequences, 103-104
    String data type, 103
Unidirectional binding, 24-25, 206
updateViewport() function, 501
url variable (Image class), 488
urx variable (PerspectiveTransform class), 674
ury variable (PerspectiveTransform class), 674
user gestures, 789-790
User interaction
    charts, 914, 936-937
    nodes, 401
User interface classes, 9-10
User interfaces
    nodes, 341
    SnowStorm application, 47

V

value variable (SwingSlider component), 857
Values
    assigning, 23
    FXFunctionValue class, 320
    FXObjectValue class, 319
    FXPrimitiveValue class, 318-319
    FXSequenceValue class, 320
    FXValue class, 318
    getValue() method, 316
    representation of, 316
var keyword, 6, 26
var statement, 89
Variables
    binding, 194-196
    changing values, 74
    data types, 6, 89
    declaring, 6, 23, 89-95
    __DIR__, 31
    __FILE__, 31
    functions, 137-142
    FXVarMember class, 322
    getting all variables of a class, 323
    getting previous value of variables, 223
    inspecting, 73
    instance variables, 95
    linear gradients, 384
    named variables, 322-323
    object literals, 149-150
    overriding, 259-261
    predefined, 31
    __PROFILE__, 31
    radial gradients, 393
    reserved words, 26
    scope, 93
    __SOURCE_FILE__, 31
    triggers, instance variables, 236-237
    triggers, sequence variables, 229-230, 234-236
    triggers, simple variables, 221
    Type inference, 6
    type inference, 6, 117-119
    visibility, 119-120
VBox class, 562-563
VBox container
    CSS properties, 1066
    -fx-hpos property, 1066
    -fx-node-hpos property, 1066
    -fx-snap-to-pixel property, 1064

-fx-spacing property, 1066
-fx-vpos property, 1066
VBox class, 562-563
-verbose compiler option, 1051
verify variable (SwingTextField class), 840
Versions of JavaFX runtime, 4
vertical variable (SwingSlider component), 857
verticalAlignment variable
    SwingButton component, 844
    SwingLabel class, 833-834, 837
verticalTextPosition variable
    SwingButton component, 844
    SwingLabel class, 834
Video
    Application Programming Interfaces (APIs), 627
    controlling media playback, 630-631
    effects, 646
    FLV, 630
    FXM, 630
    media players, 627
    MP3 files, 629
    pausing, 632
    playing, 10, 627-628
    repeating playback, 632-633
    restricting playback, 632-633
    size and position of video frame, 640-644
    speeding up playback, 632
    stopping playback, 632
    support, 10
    transitions, 646-649
    viewport, 644-646
    volume control, 633
Viewing documentation, 1055-1056
viewport variable
    ImageView class, 498
    MediaView class, 640
Visibility
    of classes, 242-243
    of functions, 147, 255-256

of nodes, 364-365
Stage class, 344
of variables, 119-120
visible variable (Stage class), 342
VM settings for applets, 15
Volume control (media players), 633
volume variable (MediaPlayer class), 634
V_RESIZE cursor, 376

W

WAIT cursor, 376
warp effect, 684-686
Web services
    RESTful, 13, 949-975
    SOAP-based, 950
weight variable (Image class), 488
wheelRotation variable (MouseEvent class), 419
where keyword, 26
while keyword, 26
while statement, 26, 181-182
width variable
    BoxBlur class, 657
    DropShadow class, 660
    Flood class, 669
    InnerShadow class, 663
    Media class, 628
    Scene class, 358
    Shadow class, 661
    Stage class, 348
with keyword, 28
wrap variable (DisplacementMap class), 679, 682-683
Wrapping text, 468-469
W_RESIZE cursor, 376
writable variable (Resource class), 302
Writing
    applets, 4
    data, 298-301
    MIDlets, 4
    to the system output stream, 286

X

x-axis, 372
x variable
   Flood class, 669
   Identity class, 668
   ImageView class, 498
   MediaView class, 639
   MouseEvent class, 404
   Scene class, 358
   Stage class, 348
-XDdumpjava compiler option, 1055
XML (Extensible Markup Language)
   HttpRequest class, 949
   PullParser class, 949
XML parsing
   DOM-style parsing, 975
   pull parsing, 975, 981
   stream parsing, 975-976, 981

Y

y-axis, 372
y variable
   Flood class, 669
   Identity class, 668
   ImageView class, 498
   MediaView class, 639
   MouseEvent class, 404
   Scene class, 358
   Stage class, 348
Yahoo! RSS Weather Feed, 998, 1004

Z

z-axis, 372-374
Zero
   division of a nonzero value by zero, 127
   division of zero by zero, 127
Z-order
   nodes, 365-366
   Stage class, 345-347

informIT.com
THE TRUSTED TECHNOLOGY LEARNING SOURCE

PEARSON

InformIT is a brand of Pearson and the online presence for the world's leading technology publishers. It's your source for reliable and qualified content and knowledge, providing access to the top brands, authors, and contributors from the tech community.

Addison-Wesley | Cisco Press | EXAM/CRAM | IBM Press | QUE | PRENTICE HALL | SAMS | Safari

LearnIT at InformIT

Looking for a book, eBook, or training video on a new technology? Seeking timely and relevant information and tutorials? Looking for expert opinions, advice, and tips? **InformIT has the solution.**

- Learn about new releases and special promotions by subscribing to a wide variety of newsletters. Visit **informit.com/newsletters**.

- Access FREE podcasts from experts at **informit.com/podcasts**.

- Read the latest author articles and sample chapters at **informit.com/articles**.

- Access thousands of books and videos in the Safari Books Online digital library at **safari.informit.com**.

- Get tips from expert blogs at **informit.com/blogs**.

Visit **informit.com/learn** to discover all the ways you can access the hottest technology content.

Are You Part of the IT Crowd?

Connect with Pearson authors and editors via RSS feeds, Facebook, Twitter, YouTube, and more! Visit **informit.com/socialconnect**.

informIT.com
THE TRUSTED TECHNOLOGY LEARNING SOURCE

PEARSON

Addison-Wesley | Cisco Press | EXAM/CRAM | IBM Press | QUE | PRENTICE HALL | SAMS | Safari

FREE Online Edition

Your purchase of **JavaFX™ Developer's Guide** includes access to a free online edition for 45 days through the Safari Books Online subscription service. Nearly every Addison-Wesley Professional book is available online through Safari Books Online, along with more than 5,000 other technical books and videos from publishers such as Cisco Press, Exam Cram, IBM Press, O'Reilly, Prentice Hall, Que, and Sams.

SAFARI BOOKS ONLINE allows you to search for a specific answer, cut and paste code, download chapters, and stay current with emerging technologies.

Activate your FREE Online Edition at www.informit.com/safarifree

> **STEP 1:** Enter the coupon code: SEBJPXA.

> **STEP 2:** New Safari users, complete the brief registration form. Safari subscribers, just log in.

If you have difficulty registering on Safari or accessing the online edition, please e-mail customer-service@safaribooksonline.com